Europe Since 1945
An Encyclopedia

Europe Since 1945
An Encyclopedia

Volume I
A–J

Bernard A. Cook
Loyola University New Orleans
Editor

Garland Publishing, Inc.
New York & London
2001

Published in 2001 by
Garland Publishing, Inc.
29 West 35th Street
New York, NY 10001

Garland is an imprint of the Taylor & Francis Group

Production Editors:	Jeanne Shu, Andrew Bailis
Copyeditor:	Edward Cone
Project Management/Composition:	Impressions Book and Journal Services, Madison, Wisconsin
Editorial Assistant:	Dan Yacavone
Director of Development:	Richard Steins
Publishing Director, Reference:	Sylvia K. Miller

10 9 8 7 6 5 4 3 2 1

ISBN: 0-8153-4057-5 (vol. I)
ISBN: 0-8153-4058-3 (vol. II)
ISBN: 0-8153-1336-5 (set)

Library of Congress Cataloging in Publication Data

Cataloging in Publication data available at the Library of Congress

Printed on acid-free, 250-year-life paper
Manufactured in the United States of America

Contents

Volume I

Introduction   vii

Subject Guide   ix

Chronology of Major Political Events Since 1945   xxiii

Contributors   xxxv

A–J Entries   1

Volume II

K–Z Entries   703

Index   1405

Introduction

The collapse of Communism in Eastern Europe in 1989 seemed a logical conclusion to a historical epoch launched by World War II (1914–18), but more specifically to the Europe that was produced by the changes of World War II (1939–45). The latter conflict completed the exhaustion of France and Great Britain that was so evident in World War I. Germany in 1945 was prostrate and under military occupation. The Soviet Union, though it had experienced horrific devastation during the war, moved into the vacuum in the east created by the defeat of Nazi Germany. The last half of the twentieth century saw the rise of the Cold War as the United States assumed a leadership role in the dual effort to contain the Soviet Union and to assist in the reconstruction of Western Europe.

The period after 1945 also witnessed the reconstitution of the western part of Germany as a democratic state and vibrant economic power in an increasingly integrated Western Europe. The evident inability of the Soviet Union to develop into a more open and democratic society and its repression of the reform movement in Czechoslovakia in 1968 destroyed hope among still-idealistic socialists that "socialism with a human face" was possible within the Soviet sphere. But when Communism collapsed in Eastern Europe and then in the Soviet Union, it had the paradoxical result of inspiring the effort to construct open societies on the one hand and the unleashing of a wave a nationalism and extremism on the other.

The end of the century was filled with images of hope and with others that seemed to return full circle to the century's beginning. There is perhaps no more visible symbol of the change from national hostility to one of amity in Western Europe than the presence today on the World War I battlefield of Verdun, France, of three flags flying side by side: the tricolor of France, the circle of stars in the blue field of the European Union, and the red, black, and gold of Germany. Other potent images of change in Europe also come to mind: The celebrations atop the Berlin Wall when it finally was breached on the evening of November 9, 1989, and the defiant Russian president Boris Yeltsin as he faced down Communist hard-liners on August 20, 1991, are just two moments that revealed how dramatically Europe had changed since 1945. But beneath the surface of positive change were also disturbingly familiar tendencies. For those who had hoped that the Nazi Holocaust against the Jews, which was one of wartime Europe's most indelible horrors, would usher in an era of tolerance, the end of the Cold War saw the rise of brutal local conflicts, ethnic cleansing, and even genocide.

Although the images and realities of Europe today are mixed, the present does offer hopeful prospects. Its motivation and overall success are often debated, but the North Atlantic Treaty Organization (NATO) intervened in Kosovo to stop ethnic cleansing and forced relocation of the population. Skinheads, a particularly violent phenomenon of post–Cold War Europe, are not finding societal toleration or wide support for their xenophobic outbursts. A special international tribunal has been set up to try accused perpetrators of war crimes in the former Yugoslavia. In Croatia, Franjo Tudjman and his nationalist Croatian Democratic Union were replaced by the Social Democrats and a new president who expressed conciliation toward the Serbs driven from Croatia in 1995. In Northern Ireland, hope was raised for era of peace and reconciliation after a series of agreements reached in the late 1990s. The Council of Europe, feeble though its action was, put Russia on notice that it had gone far beyond the acceptable in its efforts to crush a nationalist uprising in Chechnya. Despite Russian concern over the expansion of NATO, the Cold War has not re-ignited, and despite rampant corruption and cronyism, formal democracy is still operating in Russia.

The period between 1945 and 2000 is packed with dramatic and complicated developments that are important for an understanding of the present situation in Europe. This encyclopedia has been created to provide a wide variety of useful information and assessments for scholars, students, and general readers interested in postwar Europe. Although the book's main focus is largely political, readers will also find ample coverage of social and economic trends and of the arts and popular culture. Indeed, the context of political developments in Europe cannot be understood without considering the immense social, economic, and cultural changes that occurred as Europe was propelled from postwar devastation to the age of the Internet. No single encyclopedia can contain entries on everyone and everything, but the book's many comprehensive survey entries and the extensive index at the end volume II will reveal the depth and broad scope of coverage. From Scandinavia in the north to Italy in the south, and from Iceland in the west to Russia in the east, the encyclopedia offers a fascinating insight into one of the most turbulent and defining eras in European history.

Acknowledgments

I have been gratified by the response of the 286 scholars from 30 countries who participated in the project. I wish to express my thanks to all my collaborators. The quality of the work was greatly enhanced by the efforts and assistance of my editors at Garland Publishing. Richard Steins, Director of Development, and Dan Yacavone, Editorial Assistant, offered much assistance, encouragement, and support in bringing this long project to fruition.

I would also like to thank my advisory editors for their assistance. Thanks are due to Vilho Harle for entries on Finland, to Henry Frendo for his assistance on the Malta entries, to Daniele Conversi for his entries and the collaborators he recruited at the Central University in Budapest, and to Andrej Alimov of St. Petersburg State University, who contributed entries and translated others from Russian. Special thanks are due to Eugenio Guccione of the University of Palermo and Maria Nawojczyk of Nicolaus Copernicus University in Torun, Poland, for their assistance on the topic list for Italy and Poland and for their recruiting of numerous contributors from their countries. Dr. Nawojczyk's efforts also included providing translators and referees for the article on Poland supported by a grant from Nicolaus Copernicus University. For that I am deeply indebted. Günter Bishof of the University of New Orleans wrote entries and recruited many contributors in a number of countries, and his advice and encouragement were invaluable.

Special thanks is also owed to Spencer Tucker of Virginia Military Institute, who was generous with his time, advice, and encouragement, and to Hermann Hiery of the University of Bayreuth, who offered advice and refereed entries written by his graduate students. My colleague Nancy Fix Anderson of Loyola University New Orleans read several of my entries and offered her sage advice and welcome encouragement. My secretary, Vicki Horrobin, is due special thanks for her always cheerful support and extraordinary effort. I have been very fortunate to have had the aid of several helpful student assistants from Loyola's Department of History: Catherine Horan, Christine Smith, and especially Heather Mack, whose talent, effort, and resourcefulness were deeply appreciated. My greatest gratitude and thanks are to Rosemary, my wife, who tolerated this long project and the moods it engendered in me. She not only offered her support and encouragement but spent many hours proofreading and offering wise suggestions.

Bernard A. Cook

Subject Guide

Alliances
North Atlantic Treaty Organization
Warsaw Pact

Art
Abakanowicz, Magdalena
Art
Beksinski, Zdzislaw
Duda-Gracz, Jerzy

Business
Agnelli Family
Bosch, Robert
Cuccia, Enrico
Dassault, Marcel
Gardini, Raul
Mattei, Enrico
Rohwedder, Detlev
Sindona, Michele
Tourism
Trade Fairs

Cinema
Antonioni, Michelangelo
Bergman, Ingmar
Bunuel, Luis
De Sica, Vittorio
Czech Cinema
Godard, Jean Luc
Fassbinder, Rainer Werner
Fellini, Federico
German Cinema
Greek Cinema
Herzog, Werner
Hungarian Cinema
Italian Cinema

Kiesłowski, Krzysztof
Malle, Louis
Mercouri, Melina
Polish Cinema
Reitz, Edgar
Russian Cinema
Schlöndorf, Volker
Spanish Cinema
Truffault, François
von Trotte, Margarethe
Wajda, Andrzej
Winders, Wim
Yugoslavian Cinema
Zanussi, Krzysztof

Cold War
Clay, Lucius D.
Cold War
Cominform
Congress for Cultural Freedom
Détente
Gladio
Korean War and Europe
Kennan, George
Literary Institute (Institut Literacki)
Marshall Plan
McCloy, John J.
Peace and Liberty
Peaceful Coexistences
Proletarian Internationalism
Truman Doctrine
Wartime Conferences

Crime
Buscetta, Tommaso
Camorra

Mafia
Liggio, Luciano
Ndrangheta
Sindona, Michele

Culture
Art
Music
Theater

Decolonization
Algerian War
Beligum's Decolonization
France and Indochina
Netherlands' Decolonization
Portugal's Decolonization

Dissidents
Arbnori, Pjeter
Bahro, Rudolf
Brodsky, Joseph
Cohn-Bendit, Dany
Djilas, Milovan
Dutschke, Rudi
Havel, Vaclav
Kuron, Jacek
Michnik, Adam
Sakharov, Andrei
Sinyavsky, Andrei
Solzhenitsyn, Alexander
Walesa, Lech

Economics
Austria
Balcerowicz, Leszek
Barre Plan
Belarus
Belgium
Beveridge, Sir William
Bulgaria
Cyprus
Czechoslovakia
Denmark
European Bank for reconstruction and Development
France
Germany
Haavelmo, Trygve
Hagan, Karl
Hungary
Iceland
International Monetary Fund

Ireland: Economic Programs
Italy: Economic Miracle
Kornai, Jainos
Liberman, Evsei
Macedonia
Marshall Plan
Monnet Plan
Netherlands
Norway
Poland
Romania
Russia
Schuman Plan
Serbia
Sik, Ota
Spain
Sweden
Switzerland
Ukraine
United Kingdom: Economy
United Kingdom: Nationalization
United Kingdom: Taxation

Education
Belgium
Denmark
France
Germany
Italy
Netherlands
Norway
Portugal
Spain
Sweden
United Kingdom

Environment
Chernobyl
Danube Dam
Environmental Degradation in Eastern Europe
Environmental Degradation in Western Europe
Nuclear Power

European Integration
Baltic Assembly
Conference for Security and Cooperation in Europe
Council of Europe
European Bank for Reconstruction and Development (EBRD)
European Coal and Steel Community
European Commission

European Free Trade Association (EFTA)
European Defense Community
European Monetary Institute
European Parliament
European Union
North Atlantic Cooperation Council
Organization for European Economic Cooperation
Organization for European Economic Cooperation and
  Development
Spaak, Paul-Henri
Turkey and the EU
Western European Union (WEU)

Extremists of the Right
Beliguim: Flemish Extreme-Right
Hungary: Extreme Right
Le Pen, Jean-Marie
Miceli, Vito
Neo-Fascism in Western Europe
Neo-Nazism
Rauti, Pino
Romǎnia mǎre
Secret Army Organization
Zhirinovsky, Vladimir Volfovich

Geography
Abkhazia
Ajaria (Adzharia)
Åland Islands
Albania
Andorra
Armenia
Austria
Azerbaijan
Basque Country
Belarus
Belgium
Berlin
Bosnia-Hercegovina
Bukovina
Bulgaria
Catalonia
Channel Islands
Chechnya
Crimea
Croatia
Cyprus
Denmark
Dobruja
Estonia
Faroe Islands

Finland
France
Friuli-Venezia Giulia
Galicia
Germany, Democratic Republic
Germany, Federal Republic
Gibraltar
Greenland
Hebrides
Hungary
Iceland
Ireland, Northern
Isle of Man
Jan Mayen
Kalingrad Oblast
Karelia
Kazakhstan
Kosovo
Kyrgyzstan
Latvia
Liechtenstein
Lithuania
Luxembourg
Macedonia
Malta
Moldava
Monaco
Montenegro
Nagorno-Karabakh
Poland
Portugal
Norway
Orkney Islands
Porkkla
Republika Srpska (Serbian Republic)
Romania
San Marino
Sarajevo
Scotland
Serbia
Shetland Islands
Slovakia
Slovenia
South Ossetia
South Tyrol
Spain
Svalbard
Sweden
Switzerland
Tajikistan
Timisoara

Transcarpathia
Transnistrian Moldovan Republic
Transylvania
Turkey
Turkmenistan
Ukraine
United Kingdom
Uzbekistan
Valle d'Aosta
Vatican City
Vojvodina
Wales

Human Rights
Charter 77
Conference for Security and Cooperation in Europe
Corrigan, Mairead
Displaced Persons
Dolci, Danielo
Germany, Democratic Republic: Human Rights Groups
Gulag
Human Rights
Human Rights: The European Convention on Human
  Rights and the European Social Charter
Hume, John
Kurón, Jacek
La Pira, Giorgio
Michnik, Adam
Pannella, Marco
Pire, Dominique Georges
Williams, Betty

Immigrants and Refugees
Bosnia: War Refugees
Displaced Persons
Expellees-Refugees
France: Pieds niors
Netherlands: Immigrants
Norway: Immigrants
Portugal: Retornados

Intellectuals
Berlin, Isaiah
Braudel, Fernand
Dahrendorf, Ralf
Geremek, Bronislaw
Miglio, Gianfranco
Myrdal, Karl
Negri, Toni
Sturzo, Luigi
Zuckerman, Solly

International Agreements
Anglo-Irish Agreement
Arms Control Treaties and Agreements
Austrian State Treaty
Commonwealth of Independent States
Comprehensive Test Ban Treaty
Conference for Security and Cooperation in Europe
Dayton Accords
General Agreement on Tariffs and Trade
Intermediate-Range Nuclear Forces (INF) Treaty
Mutual and Balanced Dorce Reductions (MBFR)
Nuclear Non-Proliferation Treaty
Osimo, Treaty of
Strategic Arms Limitation Talks I (SALT I)
Strategic Arms Limitation Talks II (SALT II)
Strategic Arms Reduction Treaty (START I)
Threshold Test Ban Treaty (TTBT)
Two plus Four Treaty
Wartime Conferences

International Crises
Berlin Blockade
Berlin Wall
Cuban Missile Crisis
Suez Crisis

International Disputes
Cod War

International Incidents
Corfu Channel Incident
KAL 007

Intervention
Afghanistan
Brezhnev Doctrine
Congo Intervention
Hungarian Revolution
Prague Spring

Labor Unions
Austrian Trade Union Federation (ATUF)
Danish Confederation of Trade Unions
France: Labor Movement
Germany: Labor Movement
Ingrao, Pietro
Italy: Labor Unions
Jouhaux, Léon
Lama, Luciano
Netherlands: Foundation of Labor
Netherlands: Labor Movement

Norway: Labor Movement
Portugal: Trade Union Confederations
Scargill, Arthur
Spain: Labor Movements
Sweden: Labor Movements
United Kingdom: Trade Union Congress

Literature
Akhmatova, Anna
Banville, John
Baranczak, Stanislaw
Beehan, Brendan
Bolger, Dermot
Böll, Heinrich
Bowen, Elizabeth
Brodsky, Joseph
Calvino, Italo
Cannetti, Elias
Camus, Albert
Claus, Hugo
Csoori, Sandor
De Beauvoir, Simone
Demirkan, Renan
Doyle, Roddy
Eco, Umberto
Esterhazy, Peter
Grass, Günter
Golding, William
Gombrowicz, Witold
Herbert, Zbigniew
Herling-Grudzinski, Gustaw
Hochhuth, Rolf
Hrabal, Bohumil
Kazantzakis, Nikos
Keane, John Brendan
Koestler, Arthur
Kundera, Milan
Lampedusa, Giuseppe Tomasi di
Lem, Stanisław
Levi, Carlo
Laxness, Halldór
Illyeis, Gyula
Iwaszkiewicz, Jarosław (Eleuter)
Konrad, Gyorgy
Konwicki, Tadeusz
Magritte, René
Mauriac; François
McGahern, John
Milosz, Czeslaw
Montale, Eugenio
Moravia, Alberto

O'Brien, Connor Cruise
O'Brien, Flann
O'Casey, Sean
O'Faolain, Sean
Pasternak, Boris
Quasimodo, Salvatore
Seifert, Jaroslav
Silone, Ignazio
Simenon, Georges
Sinyavsky, Andrey
Wolf, Christa
Yevtushenko, Yevgeni

Military
Force de Frappe
Franco-German Brigade/Corps
Kessler, Heinz
Pershing II Missile
Strategic Defense Initiative
Supreme Allied Commander Europe
Supreme Headquarters Allied Powers in Europe
United States Armed Forces Europe
USCINCEUR
USSR: Nuclear Weapons
Wörner, Manfred
Zhukov, Georgi

Military Alliances
European Defense Community
North Atlantic Treaty Organization
Warsaw Pact

Minorities
Åland Islands: Swedish Speaking Minority of Finland
Alsatian Identity
Arberesh (Arvenites)
Bubis, Ignatz
Bulgaria: Turkish Minority
Cossacks
Gaguaz
Hungarian Minority in Slovakia
Latvia: Citizenship Issue
Lithuania: Citizenship Issue
Macedonia: Albanian Minority
Jews
Jews in Eastern Europe
Muslims in Europe
Poland: Ethnic Groups
Roma
Saami
Turks in Germany

Music
Karajan, Herbert von
Lutosławski, Witold
Masur, Kurt
Music
Oi Music
Penderecki, Krzysztof
Theodorakis, Mikis
Rock Music in the United Kingdom

Paramilitary Groups
Irish Republican Army
Mkherrioni
Seselj, Vojislav
Ulster Defense Association/Ulster Freedom Fighters
Ulster Volunteer Force
Raznatovic, Zeljko ("Arkan")

Philosophy
Adorno, Theodor
Althusser, Louis
Barthes, Roland
Baudrillard, Jean
Bloch, Ernst
Bourdieu, Pierre
Camus, Albert
Canetti, Elias
Castoriadis, Cornelius
Deleuze, Gilles
Del Noce, Augusto
Derrida, Jacques
Eco, Umberto
Foucault, Michel
Frankfurt School
Gilson, Etienne
Habermas, Jurgen
Heidegger, Martin
Horkheimer, Max
Kolakowski, Leszek
Kristeva, Julia
Lacan, Jacques
Levinas, Emmanuel
Levi-Strauss, Claude
Lukács, Georg
Lyotard, Jean François
Maritain, Jacques
Merleau-Ponty, Maurice
Monod, Jacques (Lucien)
Nouveaux Philosophes
Philosophy
Pollock, Friedrich

Ricour, Paul
Russell, Bertrand
Sartre, John-Paul
Tischner, Jozef

Political Figures
Albania
Alia, Ramiz
Arbnori, Pjeter
Berisha, Sali
Bufi, Ylli
Ceka, Neritan
Hoxha, Enver
Hoxha, Nexhmije
Nano, Fatos
Ramiz, Alia
Shehu, Mehemet
Xoxe, Koci
Austria
Busek, Erhard
Gruber, Karl
Fiegl, Leopold
Haider, Jöorg
Klestil, Thomas
Kreisky, Bruno
Mock, Alois
Raab, Julius
Renner, Karl
Schärf, Adolf
Sinowatz, Fred
Vranitsky, Franz
Waldheim, Kurt
Belarus
Kebich, Vyacheslav
Lukashenko, Alyaksandr
Shushkevich, Stanislav
Belgium
Albert, King
Baudouin, King
Claes, Willy
Cools, André
Eyskens, Gaston
Dehaene, Jean-Luc
Leopold III and the "Royal Question"
Martens, Wilfried
Spaak, Paul-Henri
Tindemans, Leo
Bosnia-Hercegovina
Abdič, Fikret
Boban, Mate
Izetbegovič, Alija

Karadzik, Radovan
Mladic, Ratko
Sacirbey, Muhammed
Silajdzič, Haris
Bulgaria
Dimitrov, Filip
Dimitrov, Georgi
Filipov, Grisha
Georgiev, Kimon
Lilov, Alexander
Lulchev, Kosta
Mladenov, Petar
Muraviev, Constantine
Popov, Dimitar
Todorov, Stanko
Videnov, Zhan
Zhelev, Zhelyu
Zhivkov, Todor
Chechnya
Basayev, Shamil
Dudayev, Dzhokhar
Maskhadov, Aslan
Croatia
Mesić, Stipe
Tudjman, Franjo
Cyprus
Clerides, Galfcos
Denktash, Rauf
Makarios, Archbishop
Vassiliou, George
Czechoslovakia
Beneš, Eduard
Calfa, Marian
Carnogursky, Jan
Cernk, Oldrich
Dienstbier, Jirí
Dubcek, Alexander
Fierlinger, Zdenek
Gottwald, Klement
Havel, Vaclav
Husák, Gustav
Jakes, Milos
Klaus, Vaclav
Kovak, Michal
Masaryk, Jan
Meciar, Vladimir
Novotny, Antonin
Seifert, Jaroslav
Sladek, Miroslav
Strougal, Lubomir
Svoboda, Ludvik

Urbanek, Karel
Weiss, Peter
Zapotocky, Antonin
Czech Republic
Dienstbier, Jirí
Havel, Vaclav
Klaus, Vaclav
Denmark
Auken, Svend
Buhl, Vihelm
Eriksen, Erik
Glistrup, Mogens
Hansen, Preben Moeller
Hedtoft, Hans
Jorgensen, Anker
Krag, Jens Otto
Kristensen, Knud
Nielsen, Holger K.
Rasmussen, Poul Nyrup
Schlüter, Poul
Estonia
Meri, Lennart
Ruutel, Arnold
Savisaar, Edgar
Toome, Indrek
Finland
Aho, Esko
Ahtisaari, Martii
Kekkonen, Uhro
Koivisto, Mauno
Lipponen, Paavo
Mannerheim, Karl Gustav
Paasikivi, Juho
France
Auriol, Vincent
Balladur, Edouard
Barre, Raymond
Bérégovoy, Pierre
Bidault, Georges
Bonnet, Henri
Blum, Leon
Cassin, René
Chirac, Jacuqes
Cohn-Bendit, Daniel
Coty, René
Cresson, Edith
Debré, Michel
Debrey, Régis
De Gaulle, Charles
Delors, Jacques
De Murville, Maurice Couve

De Villiers, Philippe
Duclos, Jacques
Fabius, Laurent
Giscard, d'Estaing, Valery
Gouin, Pierre
Jouhaux, Léon
Le Pen, Jean-Marie
Malraux, Andre
Marchais, Georges
Massu, Jacques
Mauroy, Pierre
Mendes-France, Pierre
Mitterrand, Francois
Mollet, Guy
Monnet, Jean
Pfimlin, Pierre
Pleven, Rene
Pompidou, Georges
Ramadier, Paul
Rocard, Michel
Schumann, Robert
Soustelle, Jacques
Thorez, Maurice
Georgia
  Chanturia, Georgi
  Gamsakhurdia, Zviad
  Patsatsia, Otar
  Shevardnadze, Eduard
  Sigua, Tengiz
German, Democratic Republic
  de Maizière, Lothar
  Grotewohl, Otto
  Gysi, Gregor
  Honecker, Erich
  Kessler, Heinz
  Krenz, Egon
  Modrow, Hans
  Pieck, Wilhelm
  Stoph, Willi
  Ulbricht, Walter
  Wolf, Markus
Germany, Federal Republic
  Adenauer, Konrad
  Augustein, Rudolf
  Bahr, Egon
  Barschel, Uwe
  Brandt, Willy
  Brenner, Otto
  Brentano, Heinrich
  Carstens, Karl
  Dehler, Thomas

Engholm, Björn
Erhard, Ludwig
Fischer, Joshka
Genscher, Hans Dietrich
Hallstein, Walter
Heuss, Theodor
Heinemann, Gustav
Heitman, Steffan
Herzog, Roman
Kelly, Petra
Kiesinger, Kurt Georg
Kinkel, Klaus
Klarsfeld, Beate
Kohl, Helmut
Lafontaine, Oskar
Lambsdorff, Otto von
Lübke, Heinrich
Merkel, Angela
Ollenhauer, Eric
Rau, Johannes
Reuter, Ernst
Scheel, Walter
Scharping, Rudolf
Schiller, Karl
Schmidt, Carlo
Schmidt, Helmut
Schroeder, Gerhard
Schumacher, Kurt
Späth, Lothar
Stolpe, Manfied
Strauss, Franz-Josef
Vogel, Hans-Jochen
Waigel, Theo
Wehner, Herbert
Weizsäcker, Richard von
Wörner, Manfred
Greece
  Constantine
  Damanaki, Maria
  George II
  Gizikis, Phaidon
  Grivas, George
  Ioannides, Demetrios
  Karamanlis, Konstantinos
  Lambrakis, Gregory
  Mercouri, Melina
  Mitsotakis, Constantine
  Papadoupoulos, Georgios
  Papandreou, Andreas
  Papandreou, Georgios
  Paul

Sartzetakis, Christos
Hungary
  Antall, Joszef
  Bekesi, Laszlo
  Flock, Jero
  Gero, Erno
  Goncz, Arpad
  Grosz, Karoly
  Hegedus, Andras
  Horn, Gyula
  Kadar, Janos
  Kovacs, Bela
  Kuncze, Gabor
  Lazar, Gyorgy
  Marothy, Laszlo
  Miklos, Bela
  Mindszenty, Cardinal Joseph
  Nagy, Ferenc
  Nagy, Imre
  Nemeth, Miklos
  Poszgay, Imre
  Rajk, Laszlo
  Rakosi, Mathias
  Tildy, Zoltan
Iceland
  Finnbogdóttir, Vigdis
  Hallgrimsson, Gier
  Jóhannesson, Olafur
  Oddsson, David
  Hermannson, Steingrimur
  Palsson, Thorsteinn
  Thoroddsen, Gunnar
Ireland
  Aiken, Frank
  Barry, Peter
  Bruton, John
  Childers, Erskine
  Costello, John
  Daly, Cahal
  de Rossa, Prionsias
  DeValera, Eamon
  Dillon, James
  Duffy, Joseph
  Dukes, Alan
  FitzGerald, Garret
  Flynn, Padraig
  Harney, Mary
  Haughey, Charles
  Hillery, Patrick
  Keane, John
  Lemass, Sean

  Lynch, John "Jack"
  McAleese, Mary
  McBride, Sean
  O'Ceallaigh, Sean
  O'Dalaigh, Cearbhall
  O'Malley, Desmond
  Reynolds, Albert
  Robinson, Mary
  Spring, Dick
Italy
  Amato, Giuliano
  Andreotti, Giulio
  Berlinguer, Enrico
  Berlinguer, Luigi
  Berluscone, Silvio
  Bonomi, Ivanoe
  Borsellino, Paolo
  Bossi, Umberto
  Cossiga, Francesco
  Craxi, Bettino
  Curcio, Renato
  Dalla Chiesa, Alberto
  D'Alema, Massimo
  D'Amato, Carlo
  De Gasperi, Alcide
  De Mitta, Ciriaco
  De Nicola, Enrico
  Di Pietro, Antonio
  Einaudi, Luigi
  Falcone, Giovanni
  Fanfani, Amintore
  Fini, Gianfranco
  Forlani, Arnaldo
  Goria, Giovanni
  Gronchi, Giovanni
  Ingrao, Pietro
  Lama, Luciano
  La Malfa, Ugo
  La Torre, Pio
  Leone, Giovanni
  Miceli, Vito
  Moro, Aldo
  Mussolini, Alessandra
  Natta, Allessandro
  Nenni, Peitro
  Occhetto, Achile
  Orlando, Leoluca
  Pannella, Marco
  Parri, Ferruccio
  Pertini, Alessandro
  Rauti, Pino

Rumor, Mariano
Salvadori, Bruno
Saragat, Giuseppe
Scalfaro, Oscar Luigi
Segni, Antonio
Sindona, Michele
Spadolini, Giovani
Staller, Ilona
Sturzo, Luigi
Tambroni, Fernando
Togliatti, Palmiro
Latvia
  Gorbunovs, Anatoly
  Godmanis, Ivars
Lithuania
  Brazauskas, Algirdas
  Landsbergis, Vytaulas
Luxembourg
  Santer, Jacques
Kosovo
  Rugova, Ibrahim
  Surroi, Venton
Macedonia
  Gligorov, Kiro
Malta
  Adami, Eddie Fenech
  Mifsud-Bonnici, Carmelo
  Mintoff, Dom
  Tabone, Censu
Moldava
  Grossu, Semion
  Lebed, Aleksander
  Smirnov, Igor
  Snegur, Mircea
Netherlands
  Beatrix
  Bernhard
  Juliana
  Kok, Wim
  Lubbers, Ruud
  Luns, Joseph
Norway
  Borten, Per
  Brundtland, Gro Harlem
  Five, Kaci Kullmann
  Gerhardsen, Einar
  Hagen, Karl
  Haavelmo, Trygve
  Hoist, Johan
  Lahnstein, Anne Inger
  Lie, Trygve

  Nordli, Odvar
  Stoltenberg, Thorvald
Northern Ireland
  Adams, Gerry
  Alderdice, John
  Corrigan, Mairead
  Devlin, Bernadette
  Hume, John
  Mayhew, Patrick
  Mowlam, Mo
  Molyneau, James
  Napier, Oliver
  O'Neill, Terrence
  Paisley, Ian
  Trimble, David
  Williams, Betty
Poland
  Balcerowicz, Leszek
  Bielecki, Jan Krzysztof
  Cyrankiewicz, Jozef
  Geremek, Bronisław
  Gierek, Edward
  Glemp, Jósef
  Gomułka, Wladysław
  Jaruzelski, Wojciech
  Kania, Stanisław
  Kuron, Jacek
  Kwasniewski, Aleksander
  Mazowiecki, Tadeusz
  Michnik, Adam
  Mikołajczyk, Stanisław
  Ochab, Edward
  Olszewski, Jan
  Pawlak, Waldemar
  Piasecki, Bolesław
  Popieluszko, Jerzy
  Sikorski, Wladysław
  Suchocka, Hanna
  Wałesa, Lech
  Wyszynski, Stefan
Portugal
  Caetano, Marcelo
  Carvalho, Maj. Otelo Sraiva de
  Cavaco e Silva, Anibal
  Cunhal, Alvaro
  Eanes, António Ramalho
  Gomes, Gen. Francisco Costa de
  Gonçalves, Vasco
  Salazar, Antonio de Oliveira
  Sampaio, Jorge
  Soares, Mario

Spinola, Gen. António de
Romania
  Antonescu, Ion
  Bodnaras, Emil
  Bratianu, Gheorghe
  Brucan, Sylviu
  Ceausescu, Nicolae
  Constantinescu, Emil
  Coposu, Corneliu
  Draghici, Alexandru
  Gheorghiu-Dej, Gheorghe
  Groza, Petru
  Iliescu, Ion
  Luca, Vasile
  Maniu, Iuliu
  Maurer, Ion Gheorghe
  Michael
  Patrascanu, Lucretiu
  Pauker, Ana
  Roman, Petre
  Stolojan, Theodore
  Tudor, Corneliu Vadim
  Vacaroiu, Nicolae
Russia
  Burulis, Gennady
  Chernomyrdin, Viktor
  Chubais, Anatoly
  Dudayev, Dzhokhar
  Gaidar, Yegor T.
  Grachev, Pavel
  Khasbulatov, Rusland I.
  Korzhakov, Aleksandr
  Kozyrev, Andrei
  Ligachev, Yegor
  Nemtsov, Boris
  Putin, Vladimir
  Rutskoi, Aleksandr V.
  Rybkin, Ivan P.
  Stepashin, Sergei
  Travkin, Nikolai
  Yakovlev, Aleksandr
  Yeltsin, Boris
  Zhirinovski, Vladimir
  Zyuganov, Gennady Andreyevich
Serbia
  Adzić, Blagoje
  Cošić, Dobrica
  Draskovic, Vuk
  Marković, Ante
  Marković, Mihajlo
  Marković, Mirjana

  Milošević, Slobodan
  Panic, Milan
  Raznjatović, Zelyko
  Rugova, Ibrahim
  Seselj, Vojislav
  Simović, Milos
  Surroi, Venton
  Varady, Tibor
Slovakia
  Kovac, Michael
  Meciar, Vladimir
Slovenia
  Drnovsek, Janez
  Kucan, Milan
  Peterle, Lojze
Spain
  Anguita, Julio
  Arias Navarro, Carlos
  Aznar, José Maria
  Blanco, Carrero
  Carrillo, Santiago
  González, Felipe
  Iribarne, Manuel Fraga
  Juan Carlos
  Franco, Francisco
  Piñar, Blas
  Suárez Gonzalez, Adolfo
Sweden
  Bildt, Carl
  Carlsson, Ingvar
  Erlander, Tage
  Falldin, Thorbjorn
  Hammarskjöld, Dag
  Hansson, Per
  Ohlin, Bertil
  Palme, Olof
  Ullsten, Ola
Ukraine
  Chornovil, Vyacheslav
  Kravchuck, Leonid
  Kuchma, Leonid
Union of Soviet Socialist Republics
  Allilueva, Svetlana
  Andropov, Yuri
  Beria, Lavrenty
  Bessmertnykh, Alexandr
  Brezhnev, Leonid
  Bulganin, Nikolay
  Cherninko, Konstantin
  Dobrynin, Anatoli
  Gorbachev, Mikhail

Gromyko, Andrei
Khrushchev, Nikita
Kosygin, Alexei
Kryuchkov, Vladimir
Liberman, Yevsei
Ligachëv, Yegor
Malenkov, Georgi
Mikoyan, Anastas
Molotov, Vyacheslav
Pavlov, Valentin
Popv, Gavriil
Pugo, Boris
Rasputin, Valentin
Rybakov, Anatoly
Ryzhkov, Nikolai
Sakharov, Andrei
Sinyavsky, Andrei
Sobchak, Anatoly
Starodubtsev, Vasilii
Stalin, Josef
Yakovlev, Aleksandr
Yanayev, Gannadi
Yavinsky, Grigori
Zhdanov, Andrei A.
Zhukov, Georgi
United Kingdom
Ashdown, Paddy
Archer, Jeffrey
Atlee, Clement
Benn, Tony
Bevan, Aneurin (Nye)
Bevin, Ernest
Blair, Tony
Brittan, Leon
Callaghan, James
Churchill, Winston
Crosland, Anthony
Douglas-Home, Alec
Eden, Anthony
Foot, Michael
Gaitskell, Hugh
Heath, Edward
Heseltine, Michael
Howe, Goeffrey
Hurd, Douglas
Jenkins, Roy
Kinnock, Neil
Lawson, Nigel
Macmillan, Harold
Major, John
Meade, James

Noel-Baker, Philip
Owen, David
Orr, John Boyd
Scargill, Arthur
Smith, John
Stone, Richard
Thatcher, Margaret
Williams, Shirley
Williams, Raymond
Wilson, Harold
Zilliacus, Konni
Yugoslavia
Broz-Tito, Josep
Cosić, Dobrica
Djilas, Milovan
Marković, Ante
Mesić, Stipe
Mihailovich, Draja
Peter
Rugova, Ibrahim
Stepinać, Alois

Political Parties
Austria
Belarus
Belgium
Bosnia-Hercegovina
Bulgaria
Czech Republic
Denmark
Estonia
Finland
France
Germany
Greece
Hungary
Iceland
Ireland
Ireland, Northern
Italy
Latvia
Lithuania
Macedonia
Netherlands
Norway
Poland
Portugal
Romania
Russia
Serbia
Slovakia

Spain
Sweden
Switzerland
United Kingdom

Press
Augustein, Rudolf
Austria
Denmark
France
Germany
Iceland
Italy
Poland
Spain
Springer, Axel
Springer Publishing Group
Sweden
United Kingdom

Regionalism
Basque Nationalism
Bossi, Umberto
Catalan Nationalism
Corsican Nationalism
Friuli-Venezia Giulia
Italy: Regionalism
Miglio, Gianfranco
Nationalism and Regionalism
Pujol, Jordi
Regionalism
Salvadori, Bruno
Sardinian Autonomy
Sicilian Autonomy
Scotland: Scottish Nationalism and
  the Scottish National Party
Spain: Regionalism
Val d'Aosta
Welsh Nationalism

Religion
Albania: Official Atheism
Albania: Religion
Barth, Karl
Belgium: Catholicism
Daly, Cahal Brendan
Glemp, Jósef
Jews in Eastern Europe
Jews in Western Europe
John XXIII
John Paul I
John Paul II

Mindszenty, Joseph
Muslims
Netherlands: Catholic Church
Opus Dei
Paul VI
Poland: Catholic Church
Pius XII
Religion
Stepinac, Alois
Teilhard de Chardin, Pierre
Tomasek, Frantisek
Vatican Council
Willebrands, Johannes
Wyszynski, Stefan

Right-wing Conspiracies
Borgese Coup
Compass Rose Plot
De Lorenzo Coup
Gladio P2
Piazza Fontana Massacre

Secret Police
Albania: Secret Police
KGB
Stasi
Wolf, Markus

Social Policy
Austria: Parity Commission
Belgium: Social Policy
Denmark: Social Services
France: Social Welfare Policy
Germany: Social Market Economy
Iceland: Welfare and Taxation
Ireland: Abortion and Divorce Referenda
Ireland: Mother and Child Scheme
Ireland: Unemployment
Netherlands: Euthanasia
Netherlands: Social Security
Norway: Social Welfare
Poland: Abortion Issue
Sweden: Welfare System
Switzerland: Social Services
United Kingdom: Social Services
Welfare State in Europe

Sport
Olympics
Soccer (Football) Hooliganism
Sport

Terrorism
Curcio, Renato
Grenzschützgruppe 9 (GSG-9)
Irish Republican Army
Red Army Faction
Red Brigades
Terrorism, Right-wing

Theater
Banville, John
Beckett, Samuel
Brecht, Bertold
Grotowski, Jerzy Maria
Kantor, Tadeusz
Keane, John Brendan
Mrozek, Slawomir
Swinarski, Konrad
Theater
Tomaszewski, Henryk

War
Afghanistan, War in
Algerian War
Bosnian War
Chechen War

Croatian independence and War
Falklands War
Korean War and Europe
Kosovo: Ethnic Cleansing and War

War Crimes
Ethnic Cleansing in Croatia and Bosnia
Germany: Trials against War Criminals
Katyn Forest Massacre
Nuremberg Tribunal
War Crimes in Bosnia
War Crimes Trials for the Former Yugoslavia

Women's Issues
Ireland: Abortion and Divorce Referenda
Ireland: Mother and Child Scheme
Italy: Radical Party and Civil Rights
Poland: Abortion Issue
Switzerland: Female Suffrage

Women's Movement
De Beauvoir, Simone
Netherlands: Women's Movement
Women's Movements in Europe
Sweden: Women's Rights

Chronology of Major Political Events Since 1945

1945

January 1	Soviet Union recognizes the Lublin Committee as the provisional government of Poland
January 20	Hungary signs armistice with Soviet Union
February 4–11	Yalta Conference
March 3	Groza of the Plowman's Front becomes prime minister in Romania with the support of the Communists, followed by a purge of Peasant Party (Maniu) and Liberals (Bratianu)
April 3	President Beneš of Czechoslovakia appoints a National Front government under Social Democrat Fierlinger
May 8–9	Germany surrenders to the Allies
July 17	Potsdam Conference begins
July 5	British Labour Party victorious in parliamentary election; Attlee replaces Churchill as prime minister
August 8	Soviet Union declares war on Japan
October 18	Nuremberg trials of top Nazi leaders begin
October 24	United Nations charter officially approved
November 3	Tildy becomes president and Nagy prime minister of Hungary
November 18	Fatherland Front victorious in Bulgarian elections
November 30	De Gasperi forms an Italian government supported by all parties Women receive the right to vote in France

1946

January	De Gaulle resigns as provisional president of France to campaign against the proposed constitution
March 5	Churchill's Iron Curtain Speech
March 31	Georgiev forms a Communist-dominated government in Bulgaria
May 26	Communists largest party in Czech elections; Beneš appoints Gottwald prime minister
October	French voters approve the constitution of the Fourth French Republic
November	British Labour Party passes the National Insurance Act and the National Health Service Act
November 21	Dimitrov becomes premier in Bulgaria
June 2	End of the Italian monarchy and the establishment of the Constituent Assembly for the Italian Republic

1947

January 1	British and Americans unify their zones of occupation in Germany
January 19	Polish election victory claimed by Communists
January	Monnet Plan enacted
May	Communists forced out of the French government; the end of Tripartism
March 12	Truman Doctrine announced
May 31	De Gasperi forms new Italian government without the Communists
June 5	Marshall Plan announced
September	Cominform founded
December	King Michael forced to leave Romania

1948

February 25	Communist consolidation of power in Czechoslovakia
March 27	Split between Tito of Yugoslavia and Stalin
April 18	First Italian elections under new constitution give victory to Christian Democrats

June 1	British, French, and American occupation zones of Germany are united
June 24	Soviet blockade of Berlin begins; start of Berlin Airlift
1949	
January	Council of Mutual Economic Assistance founded
April	North Atlantic Treaty Organization formed
May 5	Berlin blockade ends
May 5	Council of Europe formed
May 8	West German Constitutional Assembly approves the Basic Law (constitution) of the Federal Republic of Germany
September 15	Konrad Adenauer becomes first chancellor of the Federal Republic of Germany
October 9	USSR recognizes the German Democratic Republic (East Germany)
October 15	Benelux Treaty signed
1950	
June 26	Korean War begins
August 29	Soviet Union tests its first atomic bomb
November 4	European Charter of Human Rights
1951	
October	Churchill and the British Conservative Party return to power
1952	
February 6	Elizabeth II of Great Britain succeeds her father, George VI
May	European Defense Community formed
June 2	Gheorghiu-Dej becomes prime minister of Romania
July 25	European Coal and Steel Community formed
1953	
March 5	Stalin dies; Malenkov becomes Chairman of the Soviet Council of Ministers
June 17	Uprisings in East Berlin and other East German cities
June 26	Arrest of Beria
September	Khrushchev becomes first secretary of the Communist Party of the Soviet Union

1954

| | Khrushchev transfers the Crimea from Russia to Ukraine |
| July 21 | Geneva Conference ends France's involvement in Indochina, but the Algerian War begins |

1955

February 8	Bulganin replaces Malenkov as chairman of the Soviet Council of Ministers
May 5	West Germany joins NATO and regains full sovereignty
May 14	Warsaw Pact formed
May 15	Austrian State Treaty signed
September	Visit by Adenauer to Moscow

1956

February 14–25	Twentieth Party Congress of the Communist Party of the Soviet Union; Khrushchev launches de-Stalinization program
June	Demonstrations by workers in Poznán, Poland
October	Gomułka heads the Communist Party in Poland and the Soviets acquiesce to degree of Polish autonomy
October 23	Violence in Hungary in response to demands for change
October 25	Imre Nagy recalled as Hungarian prime minister to lead program of reform
October 28	Soviets began withdrawing troops from Hungary
October 29	Israel invades Egypt beginning the Suez Crisis
October 30	Britain and France bomb Egypt; Khrushchev approves independence of Hungary but Nagy establishes a multiparty system and coalition government
October 31	Nagy declares neutrality; repudiates the Warsaw Pact; Soviet Presidium reverses position on Hungary
November 1	Nagy appeals to UN for support
November 4	Soviet forces begin crushing the Hungarian Revolution

1957

| March | Ghana first British colony in Africa to gain independence |

March 25	Treaty of Rome signed to form the European Economic Community
June 17–29	Unsuccessful attempt by the Soviet Presidium to remove Khrushchev
October 4	Soviet Union launches Sputnik

1958

January 18	Treaty of Rome goes into effect
March 27	Khrushchev replaces Bulganin as chairman of the Council of Ministers
June 1	De Gaulle returns to power and forms the Fifth French Republic
October 28	Angelo Roncalli elected pope, taking name of John XXIII

1959

January 1	Fidel Castro comes to power in Cuba
September	European Free Trade Association formed
October 15	Bad Godesberg reform of the German Social Democratic Party

1960

May 1	U.S. U-2 spy plane shot down over the USSR
June 30	Belgium leaves Congo French colonies fully independent

1961

April	Bay of Pigs invasion in Cuba
August 13	Berlin Wall erected

1962

July 1	France recognizes independence of Algeria
October	Second Vatican Council begins
October	*Spiegel* Affair in West Germany
October 22–28	Cuban Missile Crisis

1963

June 21	Giovanni Battista Montini elected pope, taking name of Paul VI
August 5	Nuclear Test Ban Treaty signed

October 15	Adenauer resigns
October 16	Ludwig Erhard becomes West German chancellor
December 5	Socialists join the Christian Democrat Aldo Moro's cabinet in Italy's "Opening to the Left"

1964

October 14	Khrushchev ousted and replaced by Brezhnev

1965

March	Nicolae Ceausescu becomes general secretary of the Romanian Communist Party

1966

December 1	Grand Coalition of Christian Democrats and Social Democrats in the Federal Republic of Germany

1967

	Troubles begin in Northern Ireland as Civil Rights Association demonstrators are attacked by Unionists
April 21	Military regime comes to power in coup in Greece

1968

January–August	Prague Spring period of liberalization in Czechoslovakia
May	Student unrest in Paris
August 20–21	Warsaw Pact invasion of Czechoslovakia

1969

April	De Gaulle resigns
September	Social Democrat Willy Brandt becomes chancellor the Federal Republic of Germany

1970

August 12	Russian-German Treaty
December 6	German-Polish Treaty

1971

September 3	Berlin Agreement

1972

January 30	Bloody Sunday in Derry as British paratroopers kill Catholics
March	Constitution of Northern Ireland suspended and Britain assumes direct rule of province
May 22–30	SALT I
December 21	Basic Treaty between the Federal Republic of Germany and the German Democratic Republic

1973

	United Kingdom, Ireland, and Denmark enter the European Community
May 3	Walter Ulbricht replaced as East German leader by Erich Honecker

1974

April 25	Carnation Revolution in Portugal
May	Brandt resigns as West German chancellor and is replaced by Helmut Schmidt
July	Attempt to oust President Makarios of Cyprus and unite island with Greece fails; Turkey seizes northern part of the island and the military regime collapses in Greece

1975

August 1	Helsinki Accord establishes the Organization for Security and Cooperation in Europe
November 20	Franco of Spain dies

1978

March 16	Aldo Moro kidnapped and murdered by the Red Brigades
October 16	Karol Woytła of Poland elected pope, taking name of John Paul II

1979

	Greece enters the European Community
May	Margaret Thatcher becomes prime minister of Great Britain
December	Soviet intervention in Afghanistan

1980

May 5	Tito dies

| August | Solidarity, the independent trade union, established in Poland under the leadership of Lech Wałesa |

1981

| May 10 | Socialist François Mitterrand elected president of France |
| December 13 | Martial law imposed in Poland |

1982

April 2	Falklands War between Great Britain and Argentina begins. Spain joins NATO
October 1	Helmut Kohl, leading a coalition of Christian Democrats and Free Democrats, replaces Helmut Schmidt as chancellor of the Federal Republic of Germany
November 10	Brezhnev dies and Andropov succeeds as head of the Communist Party in the Soviet Union

1983

| September 1 | KAL 007, Korean passenger jet, shot down by Soviets over Sea of Japan |

1984

| February 9 | Andropov dies and is succeeded by Chernenko as head of Soviet Communist Party. |

1985

	Spain and Portugal admitted to the European Community
March 10	Gorbachev succeeds Chernenko as head of Soviet Communist Party.
November	Anglo-Irish Accord signed

1986

February 28	Olaf Palme, Swedish prime minister, assassinated
April 26	Chernobyl nuclear reactor disaster in Ukraine
June	Kurt Waldheim elected president of Austria

1987

| | Boris Yeltsin ousted from Central Committee and the Communist Party of the USSR |

1988

| | Nagorno-Karabakh crisis |

1989

April	Solidarity legalized in Poland
May 8	Slobodan Milosevic becomes president of Serbia
June 4	Solidarity sweeps Polish election
August 24	Mazowiecki, a non-Communist, appointed prime minister in Poland
October 18	Erich Honecker removed as East German leader
November 9	Berlin Wall falls
November	Velvet Revolution in Czechoslovakia
December	Ouster and execution of Romania's Ceausescu and wife

1990

March 18	Christian Democrats victorious in East German election
March 29	New Congress of People's Deputies elected in the USSR
May	Gorbachev elected president of the USSR by the Congress of People's Deputies
August 2	Iraq invades Kuwait and precipitates crisis leading to Persian Gulf War
October 3	Reunification of East and West Germany
November 28	Thatcher resigns and is replaced by John Major as British prime minister
December 20	Shevardnadze resigns as Soviet foreign minister

1991

January 13	Attack by Soviet troops on Lithuanian supporters of independence
June 12	Yeltsin elected Russian president
June 25	Slovenia and Croatia declare independence from Yugoslavia
July 1	Warsaw Pact dissolved
August 18–25	Attempted coup by hard-line Communists in USSR
December 7–8	Minsk agreement between Yeltsin, Leonid Kravchuk of Ukraine, and Stanislav Shushevich of Belarus to replace the USSR with a Commonwealth of Independent States (CIS)
December 21	Eleven former Soviet republics join the Commonwealth of Independent States

December 25	Gorbachev resigns as president of USSR
December 30	Commonwealth of Independent States leaders abolish all institutions of the Soviet Union
December	Treaty of Maastricht signed

1992

April 6	Bosnian independence recognized by the European Union and the United States; Bosnian war begins

1993

January 1	Separation of Czech Republic and Slovakia
October 3–4	Attack by Yeltsin on opposition in parliament December 12. Zhirinovsky's Liberal Democrats emerge as largest party in Russian parliamentary election
November 1	European Union established

1994

January 1	European Monetary Institute established
December 11	First Russo-Chechen War launched by Russian invasion

1995

January 1	Austria, Finland, and Sweden enter the European Union
May 17	Jacques Chirac becomes president of France
July 11	Srebrenica "safe-haven" in Bosnia falls to Bosnian Serbs; thousands of Muslim males massacred
August 4–5	Croatia conquers Serb stronghold of Krajina; Serbs expelled
August 28	NATO bombing campaign against Bosnian Serbs begins
November 21	Dayton Accords signed ending war in Bosnia
December 17	Communists largest party in Russian parliamentary election

1996

April 21	Dzhokar Dudayev killed
June–July	Yeltsin wins Russian presidential election against Communist Gennady Zyuganov
August 30–31	Aleksandr Lebed negotiates peace with Chechnya

1997

April 2	Russia and Belarus sign treaty of union
May	Labour Party sweeps election in Great Britain; Tony Blair replaces John Major as prime minister

1998

April	Good Friday Accord in Northern Ireland
September	Social Democrats win election in Germany; Gerhard Schröder replaces Helmut Kohl as chancellor

1999

March	Czech Republic, Hungary, and Poland join NATO
March 24	NATO air attacks against Serbia to halt Serb ethnic cleansing in Kosovo begin
August	Chechen militants invade Dagestan
October	Russia invades Chechnya, launching second Chechen War
December 31	Yeltsin resigns and hands Russian presidency over to Vladimir Putin

2000

March	Putin elected president of Russia

Contributors

Aili Aarelaid-Tart
University of Tallinn

Andrej Alimov
St. Petersburg State University, Russia

John B. Allcock
University of Bradford, UK

Myrdene Anderson
Purdue University

Anthony Amato
Southwest State University, Minnesota

Nicola Antonietti
University of Parma

Gisle Aschim
Research Council of Norway, Oslo

Roman Bäker
Nicolaus Copernicus University, Torun, Poland

Anni Baker
Wheaton College

Shannon Baker
Texas Christian University

Jeffrey M. Bale
Columbia University

Svelta Baloutzova
Central European University, Budapest

Csilla Ban
Central European University, Budapest

Michael A. Baum
University of Massachusetts–Dartmouth

Mark Beasley
Texas Christian University

Karel C. Berkhoff
University of Toronto

Peter J. Bernardi, S.J.
Loyola University New Orleans

Florian Bieber
Central European University, Budapest

Annette Biener
University of Bayreuth

Günter Bishof
University of New Orleans

Benita Blessing
University of Wisconsin, Madison

Daniel K. Blewett
Loyola University, Chicago

Peter Botticelli
Harvard University

Patrick L. Bourgeois
Loyola University New Orleans

James M. Boyden
Tulane University

Paul Brasil
University of California, Santa Barbara

Hugo Brems
Catholic University of Leuven, Belgium

Ted R. Bromund
Yale University

Brian D. Bunk
University of Wisconsin

Robert J. Bunker
California State University San Bernadino

Anjana Buckow
Martin Luther University, Halle-Wittenberg

Matti Bunzl
University of Chicago

Scott Burris
University of Missouri

Mauro Buscemi
University of Palermo

Erik Buyst
Catholic University of Leuven

Dario Caroniti
University of Messina

Murat Cemrek
Bilkent University, Ankara, Turkey

Dariusz Chmielewsli
Institute of Conservation and Renovation of Cultural
Property, Nicolaus Copernicus University, Torun

Mark Choate
Yale University

Fereriga Maria Bndi Calussi
European University Institute, Florence

Lisa Forman Cody
Claremont Graduate University

Daniele Conversi
Central European University, Budapest

Bernard A. Cook
Loyola University New Orleans

Bernard J. Cook
Georgetown University

Rosemary Cook
Jefferson Parish Public School System, Louisiana

Irina D. Costache
Loyola University New Orleans

Ted Cotton
Loyola University New Orleans

Ronald Creagh
Université Paul Valéry, Montpellier

Don M. Cregier
University of Prince Edward Island

Walter E. Crivellin
University of Turin

Stephen M. Cullen
Eton College, Eton, Windsor

Carlos A. Cunha
Dowling College

Mary Daly
Queens University, Belfast

Martin V. Dangerfield
University of Wolverhampton, UK

Joel Dark
Tennessee State University

David R. Davila Villers
Universidad de las Américas, Puebla, Mexico

Camille Dean
Texas Christian University

Edward G. Declair
Duke University

Paul Delbouille
University of Liège

Herman Deleeck
University of Antwerp

Pascal Delwit
University of Brussels

Scott Denham
Davidson College

Mike Dennis
University of Wolverhampton

Guillaume De Syon
Albright College, Pennsylvania

Robert Dewell
Loyola University New Orleans

Lyudmila Iordanova Dicheva
University of Rosse, Bulgaria

Ruud Van Dijk
University of Pittsburg

Conrad L. Donakowski
Michigan State University

Timothy Dowling
Tulane University

Henk Driessen
University of Nijmegen, Netherlands

Peter Duignan
Hoover Institute, Stanford University

William Duvall
Willamette University, Salem, Oregon

Marta Dyczok
University of Western Ontario

Henrik Eberle
Martin Luther University Halle-Wittenberg

Alagisa Effacace
University of Palermo

Gundy Björk Eydal
University of Iceland

Norbert P. Feldinger
University of Salzburg

John Fink
New York

Robert Forrest
McNeese State University, Lake Charles, Louisiana

Christopher Forth
Australian National University

Page S. Foshee
Texas Christian University

Ronald E. Foust
Loyola University New Orleans

Maritheresa Frain
Universidade Lusíada, Portugal

Claudia Franceschini
Istituto Sturzo, Rome

Henry Frendo
University of Malta

Tom Gallagher
University of Bradford, UK

Jena M. Ganes
University of Western Michigan

Reinhold Gärtner
Martin Luther University Halle-Wittenberg

Michael Gehler
University of Innsbruck

Jay Howard Geller
Yale University

Jill Gillespie
Cornell University

Mark P. Gingerich
Ohio Wesleyan University

Todd Alan Good
Bowling Green State University, Kentucky

Eric Gorham
Loyola University New Orleans

Ronald J. Granieri
University of Chicago

Eugenio Guccione
University of Palermo

David Guillet
Catholic University of America

Gudmundur Halfdanarson
University of Iceland

William M. Hammel
Loyola University New Orleans

Gerd Hardach
University of Marburg, Germany

Vilho Harle
University of Hameenlinna, Finland

Richard A. Hawkins
University of Wolverhampton, UK

Rebecca Hayes
Florida State University

Alisa Henderson
University of Edinburgh

Hermann Hiery
University of Bayreuth, Germany

William I. Hitchcock
Yale University

Peter C. Holloran
Mount Ida College, Massachusetts

Memory Holloway
University of Massachusetts

Andrew Horton
Oklahoma State University

Julian Thomas Hottinger
University of Fribourg, Switzerland

Krzysztof Janiszewski
Nicolaus Copernicus University

Marek Jezinski
Nicolaus Copernicus University

Mary Troy Johnston
Loyola University New Orleans

Jouko Jokisalo
University of Oulu, Finland

Pawel Kacprzak
Nicolaus Copernicus University

Christopher Kaczor
Loyola Marymount University, Los Angeles

Wolfram Kaiser
Institute for History, University of Vienna

Maria Kalinowska
Nicolaus Copernicus University

Ferdinand Karlhoffer
University of Innsbruck

James C. Kennedy
Valparaiso University, Indiana

Michael J. Kennedy
Queen's University, Belfast

Kenneth Keulmann
Loyola University New Orleans

Barbara Keys
Harvard University

Charles King
Georgetown University

Anthony Kinik
University of British Columbia

René Knüsel
University of Fribourg, Switzerland

Daniel Kowalsky
University of Wisconsin, Madison

Oleg N. Kozhin
Russian State Hydrometeorological University,
St. Petersburg

Gudrun Kruip
University of Tübingen

Janusz Kryszak
Collegium Maius, Torun, Poland

Arkadiusz Kubalewski
Nicolaus Copernicus University

Thomas Lane
University of Bradford, UK

Russel Lemmons
Jacksonville State University, Alabama

Agnieszka Lenska
Nicolaus Copernicus University

Valerie Leonard
University of Wolverhampton, UK

Bernd Leupold
University of Bayreuth

Thomas T. Lewis
Mount Senario College, Ladysmith, Wisconsin

David Lilly
University of London

Richard Lofthouse
Oxford University

David Longfellow
Baylor University, Texas

S.A. Longstaff
York University, Canada

Catherine Lutard
Institut du Monde Soviétique et de l'Europe Centrale
et Orientale

Eileen Groth Lyon
Florida State University

Andre Mach
University of Lausanne

Jerzey Z. Maciejewski
Institute of Polish Philology, Torun, Poland

Paul Robert Magocsi
University of Toronto

Tamas Magyarics
Eötvös Lor ánd University, Budapest

Michal Maliszewski
Nicolaus Copernicus University

Martin Manning
US Information Agency, Washington

Paul Christopher Manuel
Saint Anselm College, New Hampshire

Tomasz Marciniak
Nicolaus Copernicus University

Marta Markova
University of Innsbruck

Fabio Marino
University of Palermo

Giuseppe Carlo Marino
University of Palermo

Rosanna Marsala
University of Palermo

Ellen Mastenbroek
University of Nijmegen

Franz Mathis
University of Innsbruck

Thomas W. Maulucci, Jr.
Yale University

Alexander Maxwell
University of Wisconsin

Stefan Mayer
University of Salzburg

Stefania Mazzone
University of Catania

Mary A. McCay
Loyola University New Orleans

Robert D. McJimsey
Colorado College

Guglielmo Meardi
European University Institute, Florence

David A. Meier
Dickinson State University, North Dakota

Regina Mezei
Mercer County Community College, New Jersey

Marko Milivojevic
University of Bradford, UK

Ken Millen-Penn
Fairmont State College, West Virginia

Glenn Wright Miller
Denison University, Ohio

Dimiter Minchev
Bulgarian Association of Military History

Giuseppe Carlo Marino
University of Palermo

William J. Miller
Saint Louis University

Zofia Mocarska-Tyc
Nicolaus Copernicus University

David Moore
Loyola University New Orleans

Lilja Mosesdottir
University of Manchester

Francis J. Murphy
Boston College

Maria Nawojczyk
Nicolaus Copernicus University

Kinga Nemere-Czachowska
Nicolaus Copernicus University

James L. Newsome
Texas Christian University

Michael R. Nicols
Texas Christian University

Aldo Nicosia
University of Catania

Jørn Boye Nielsen
International People's College, Helingør, Denmark

Norma C. Noonan
Augsburg College, Minnesota

Heino Nyyssönen
University of Jyväskylä, Finland

Krzysztof Olechnicki
Nicolaus Copernicus University

Mark Orsag
Michigan State University

Maria Gabriella Pasqualini
University of Palermo

Paolo Pastori
University of Lecce, Italy

Patrick Pasture
Catholic University of Leuven

Maria Pia Paterno
University of Rome

Denis G. Paz
University of North Texas

Anton Pelinka
University of Innsbruck

Sofia A. Perez
Boston University

Barbara Bennett Peterson
University of Hawaii

Jonathan Petropoulos
Loyola College of Maryland

Daniele Petrosino
University of Bari

Roumyana Petrova
University of Rousse, Bulgaria

Peggy Phillips
University of Miami

Aleksandr J. Pidzhakov
St. Petersburg State University, Russia

Wendy A. Pojmann
Boston College

Adrian Pop
Institute for Defence Political Studies and Military
History, Budapest

Gabriella Portalone
University of Palermo

Christoph Priller
University of Bayreuth

Slawomir Przybulek
Nicolaus Copernicus University

Stanisao G. Puliese
Hofstra University

Conrad Raabe
Loyola University New Orleans

Bob Reinalda
University of Nijmegen

Michael Richards
Sweet Briar College, Virginia

Sybille Reinke De Buitrago
American University, Washington, DC

John Riley
London, U.K.

Jeff Roberts
Tennessee Technical University

William Roberts
Fairleigh Dickinson University, New Jersey

Peter S. Rogers, S.J.
Loyola University New Orleans

Steven D. Roper
Eastern Illinois University

Mark Edward Ruff
Brown University

Eric C. Rust
Baylor University, Texas

Nickolai Sannikov
Russian State Hydrometeorological University,
St. Petersburg

Ricki Schoen
Centre for European Economic and Public Affairs,
University College Dublin

Daniel L. Schlafly, Jr.
Saint Louis University

Agnieszka Schramke
Nicolaus Copernicus University

Frank Schumacher
University of Bonn

Carl Schuster
SHAPE INTEL/CCIRM

Thomas Alan Schwartz
Vanderbilt University

Quinn Sebesta
Texas Christian University

Paul Sendziuk
Monash University, Australia

Daniel E. Shannon
Depauw University, Illinois

Janusz Skuczynski
Institute of Polish Philology, Torun

Piotr Skuz
Nicolaus Copernicus University

David Simonelli
Tulane University

Thomas A. Smith
Loyola University New Orleans

Andreas Sobisch
John Carroll University, Cleveland

Valery V. Sokolov
Russian State Hydrometeorological University,
St. Petersburg

Bruce Olav Solheim
Green River Community College, Auburn, Washington

Ragnhild Sollund
Research Council of Norway

Thomas C. Sosnowski
Kent State University Stark Campus, Ohio

Sheldon Spear
Luzerne County Community College, Nanticoke,
Pennsylvania

Jerzy Speina
Institute of Polish Philology, Torun, Poland

Marc Spruyt
University of Antwerp

Rod Stackelberg
Gonzaga University, Spokane, Washington

Tomasz Stapf
Nicolaus Copernicus University

Tamas Stark
Hungarian Academy of Science

Yelena V. Stetsko
Russian State Hydrometeorological University,
St. Petersburg

Andrzej Stoff
Nicolaus Copernicus University

Nathan Stoltzfus
Florida State University

David Stone
Yale University

Hillie J. Van De Streek
University of Utrecht

Jürgen Streller
University of Bayreuth

Jackie Stroud
Texas Christian University

Ryszard Sudzinski
Nicolaus Copernicus University

Janusz Skuczynski
Nicolaus Copernicus University

Miroslaw Supruniuk
Nicolaus Copernicus University

Michael Thompson
Miyazaki International College, Japan

Erika Thurner
University of Innsbruck

André Tihon
Facultés Universitaires Saint-Louis, Brussels

Jaroslaw Tomaszewski
Nicolaus Copernicus University

Pablo Toral
Florida International University

Ester Trassel
Bayreuth University

David Travis
Syracuse University, Florence

Fabio Tricoli
University of Palermo

Spencer C. Tucker
Texas Christian University

Roger Tuller
Texas Christian University

Karina Urbach
University of Bayreuth

Jeffrey William Vanke
Harvard Center for European Studies

Erik Vogt
Loyola University New Orleans

W.G.C. Voigt
University of the Americas, Puebla, Mexico

Paul R. Waibel
Belhaven College, Jackson, Mississippi

Georg Wagner
Martin Luther University, Halle-Wittenberg

William T. Walker
Chestnut Hill College, Philadelphia, Pennsylvania

Kirk West
Cognac, France

Lee C. Whitfield
Brandeis University

Willy Wielemans
Catholic University of Leuven, Belgium

Grzegorz Wilczewski
Nicolaus Copernicus University

Adam Willma
Nicolaus Copernicus University

Lode Wils
Catholic University of Leuven

Philip E. Wynn
Norfolk, UK

Antonia Young
Bradford University

David T. Zabecki
U.S. Army, Freiburg, Germany

Stelios Zachariou
Archives of the Ministry of Foreign Affairs, Athens

Pawel Zalecki
Nicolaus Copernicus University

Tom Zaniello
Northern Kentucky University

Adam Zdunek
Nicolaus Copernicus University

Peteris Zilgalvis
World Bank, Riga, Latvia

Andrzej Zybertowicz
Nicolaus Copernicus University

A

Abakanowicz, Magdalena (1930–)

Polish artist. Magdalena Abakanowicz, born on June 20, 1930, lives in Warsaw. Abakanowicz studied at the Warsaw Academy of Fine Arts from 1950 to 1954 and subsequently taught there. In the 1960s she created the "abakans," monumental spatial tapestries successfully displayed at the Biannual Contemporary Art Exhibit in Lausanne, Switzerland, in 1967. In the 1970s she created the "Alterations," a series of figurative and abstract sculptures made of hardened sackcloth. In 1981, the year martial law was imposed by the authorities in Poland, Abakanowicz created the "Cage," according to some critics symbolizing imprisonment; in 1989, impressed by mass strikes and protests, she created the "Crowd." Abakanowicz, however, claims that her art is not politically inspired.

From the 1980s she erected spatial compositions in the open air in Italy, Israel, Korea, the United States, and Germany. She began utilizing new materials such as bronze, stone, and wood. In 1990 Abakanowicz won a competition for designing changes to the extension of the Paris axis, beyond the business district of La Défense. Abakanowicz's proposal addressed ecological and social problems of big cities. She created a fantastic project of "arboreal architecture" where buildings had the shapes of trees, completely covered in plants, and were energy self-sufficient. Their crowns housed recreational areas and their "roots" contained garages, underground stations, and shopping centers.

In 1993 Abakanowicz was the first non-American to receive the award of the New York Sculpture Center.

Tomasz Marciniak

Abbott, Diane (Julie) (1953–)

First black woman to be elected to the British House of Commons. Diane Abbott was born in London on September 27, 1953. She studied at Newnham College, Cambridge, and was an administrative trainee with the Home Office before being employed successively as a race relations officer for the National Council for Civil Liberties, a television researcher and reporter, a public relations officer for the Greater London Council, and the principal press officer for the Lambeth Borough Council. Abbott, who became a member of the Labour Party in 1971, was elected to the Westminster City Council in 1982. In 1987 she was elected as a Labour MP from Hackney North and Stoke Newington.

Bernard Cook

Abdić, Fikret (1940–)

Breakaway Muslim leader in Bosnia who turned the Bihac area into an independent enclave between 1993 and 1995. A leading Bosnian Communist in the 1980s, he brought prosperity to Bihac with his dynamic and, some would allege, corrupt management of Agrokomerc, Yugoslavia's biggest state food company. In 1987, he was sentenced to two years in prison for allegedly issuing one billion dollars in unsecured promissory notes. In 1990, he won more votes than any other Muslim politician in Bosnia's first post-Communist election, but failed to obtain the state presidency. Accusing his rival, President Izetbegović, of unnecessary intransigence, this consummate intriguer and tycoon declared the Bihac region self-governing on September 27, 1993, and formed his own Muslim Democratic Party. He sold arms, food, and fuel to the rebel Bosnian Serbs and his militia even fought together with them in 1994–95 before his power base was overrun in August 1995. The Abdić phenomenon illustrated the complexity of the war in Bosnia and suggested that it could not be reduced to a religious conflict alone.

Tom Gallagher

Abkhazia

Autonomous region of the former Georgian Soviet Socialist Republic of the USSR, 3,343 square miles (8,660 sq km) with an estimated population of 516,600 in 1993. The region in northwestern Georgia along the Black Sea coast, as a result of military victory over the Georgian government in 1993, achieved defacto sovereignty.

From the sixteenth to the seventeenth centuries, as Georgia fell under the influence of Turkey and Persia, Islam began to spread along the Abkhazian coast, though it never entirely replaced Orthodox Christianity. Most Abkhazians today are, to the extent that they practice any religion, nominal Christians. In 1810 Russia persuaded a member of the Abkhazian ruling family to ask for Russian protection and progressively asserted its control over the region, annexing it in 1864. In 1989 ethnic Abkhazians constituted only 18 percent of the population of their home region, while Mingrelians and Georgians proper constituted 46 percent. Contrary to the assertions of Georgian nationalists, 90 percent of the "Georgians" of Abkhazia were Mingrelians, Svans, and Georgians proper who, in contrast, to many Mingrelians in Georgia proper, spoke Mingrelian as their first language. The Abkhazians assert that the losses suffered during their resistance to the Russians and the subsequent forced displacement of many Abkhazians to Turkey is the source of their demographic weakness. At the beginning of the nineteenth century there were approximately 321,000 Abkhazians, but by 1897, after losses suffered at the hands of the Russians, there were only 58,697.

After the Russian Revolution of 1917, Nestor Lakoba led Abkhaz peasants and their self-defense militias, *kiaraz,* in an effort to prevent annexation of Abkhazia by General Mazniashvili (Mazniev), acting for the Georgian Social Democratic regime. Though the Georgians, led by Noe Zhordania, granted Abkhazia autonomy, Georgian nationalists claim that the Abkhaz nationality is a Bolshevist construct designed to weaken Georgia. When the Bolsheviks defeated Georgia in March 1921, they recognized Abkhazia, under Lakoba, as a Soviet republic equal in status to Georgia within the Transcaucasian Federation. In December 1921 Abkhazia became part of the Georgian Soviet Socialist Republic, but its ambiguous status was reflected in its 1925 constitution, and it nominally retained its status as a union republic until April 1930. It was then demoted to the status of autonomous republic.

Stalin furthered Abkhaz numerical weakness by ordering the settlement there of various peoples but predominantly from Mingrelia. Numbers increasingly became a key to Abkhaz concerns. While in 1886 there had been only an estimated 3,474 Mingrelians and 515 other Geor-

gian speakers in Abkhazia, by 1979, of the population of 486,082, only 83,097 were Abkhaz, but Georgian speakers numbered 213,322. In 1945–46, as part of the Georgianization drive of Stalin, Beria, and Chark'viani, the use of Abkhaz in schools was replaced by Georgian and there were no further publications in the Abkhaz language. The Abkhaz saw their eclipse in their home territory as a threat to their economic and political future: their ability to control land and gain access to public jobs.

When the Georgian government, responding to pressure from Georgian nationalists led by Zviad Gamsakhurdia, made Georgian the official language throughout Georgia, Abkhazians launched a campaign to secede from Georgia and join the Russian SSR. They also demanded that their language become the official language of Abkhazia. Many Abkhazians, like other Caucasian peoples, had flourished by taking advantage of the "real economy" of the late Soviet era. They did not want their businesses to be threatened by Georgian independence and animosity toward the Soviet Union (later, Russia). They also saw their amalgamation into an independent Georgia as a threat to the upward mobility of their community. The second language of most Abkhazians is Russian rather than Georgian. If Georgian were to become the official language of all Georgia, the Abkhaz and their children would suffer a disadvantage in education, their quest for government posts, and business.

In 1978, 130 Abkhaz intellectuals wrote to Soviet President Brezhnev asking for permission for Abkhazia to secede from Georgia and join Russia. Moscow refused but did offer Abkhazia cultural and economic concessions. The pedagogical institute in Sukhumi (the Abkhaz prefer "Sukhum," without the Georgian nominative case ending; but in Abkhaz the city is AqW'a), the chief Abkhaz city, was transformed into a full university. Television and additional print media in Abkhaz were established. Ethnic Abkhaz were promised 40 percent of government and judicial posts.

Georgians were outraged by these concessions. Reacting in July 1989, Georgians attempted to transform their branch of the Abkhaz State University into a section of the Tbilisi State University. This led to two weeks of ethnic violence in Sukhumi and twenty-two deaths.

In August 1990 the Georgians altered their election laws to exclude from the forthcoming Georgian Supreme Soviet elections purely regional parties, and therefore the Abkhazian Popular Front, *Aydgylara.* The Abkhaz delegates to the Abkhaz Supreme Soviet responded by declaring Abkhazia a completely sovereign republic. The Abkhazians refused to submit to the new Georgian nationalist leader, Zviad Gamsakhurdia, and in December

1990 elected Abkhaz intellectual Vladislav Ardzinba chairman of their Supreme Soviet. Ardzinba asserted the Abkhaz desire to remain in the Soviet Union as a union republic. Far from being the tool of the Kremlin, as claimed by some Georgian nationalists, Ardzinba and the other Abkhazians saw association with a restructured Soviet Union as the best protection from the chauvinistic nationalism rampant in Tiblisi. Abkhazia, despite a Georgian boycott, participated in the March 1991 referendum on preserving the Soviet Union. Of the 52.4 percent of the electorate actually voting in Abkhazia 98.4 percent expressed their support for the continuation of the Soviet Union, undoubtedly as a counter to the pretensions of a nationalist Georgia.

In spring 1991 the Abkhaz and Georgians had worked out a compromise electoral law for the region that would guarantee the Abkhaz twenty-eight delegates, the Georgians twenty-six, and other groups a total of eleven. The agreement with its ethnic quotas was actually suggested by Levan Alexidze, later an adviser to Eduard Shevardnadze, and pushed by Gamsakhurdia as a means to forestall changes to the status of Abkhazia. The agreement stipulated a two-thirds vote for important legislation. However, when the new Abkhaz parliament met in early 1992, the Georgians viewed it as a body intent on secession. Georgians in Abkhazia launched a campaign of noncompliance. The ouster of Gamsakhurdia in January 1992 did not improve the situation. The tension intensified after July 23, when the Abkhaz Supreme Soviet voted thirty-five to thirty to restore the constitution of 1925, which specified that Abkhazia was a separate union republic rather than a mere component of Georgia.

The Georgian State Council immediately declared the Abkhaz move null and dispatched three thousand Georgian National Guard troops to Abkhazia. Despite the claim that they had been sent to counter the "Zviadists," who had taken Georgian officials hostage, Georgian Defense Minister Tengiz Kitovani led an attack on the Abkhaz parliament on August 18. In fact the hostages had been seized in Mingrelia and were being held there, not in Abkhazia. In the face of the Georgian attack, Ardzinba and Abkhaz deputies withdrew to the majority-Abkhaz town of Gutauta in the north and called for armed resistance.

By October 1992, however, Abkhaz forces mounted an offensive and seized control of the north. On October 23 Georgian forces in Sukhumi burned down the state archive and the archives of the Institute of Abkhazian Language, History, and Literature. Fighting intensified between Georgians and Abkhazians in early 1993. The Georgians held Sukhumi, but they had to attempt to deal simultaneously with Zviadists rebels in western Georgia. The Georgians also claim that Russians had been assisting the Abkhaz to pressure Georgia to accommodate itself to Russian interests. The Abkhaz for their part charged that Russian President Boris Yeltsin had given his approval in advance to the Georgian invasion and that toward the end of the war Russian aircraft had bombed Abkhaz installations.

In mid-September 1993 the Abkhazians launched a new offensive. Shevardnadze flew to Sukhumi personally to lead the defense, but within eleven days Abkhaz forces were victorious. Georgian troops were expelled not only from Sukhumi but from all of Abkhazia. Up to two hundred thousand Georgian civilians fled the advance of the victorious Abkhaz. Despite U.N.-sponsored peace talks in 1993 and 1994 and the signing by Georgian and Abkhazian representatives of a 1994 April Quadripartite Agreement in the presence of U.N. and Western observers in Moscow, there were continued clashes. So far at least seven thousand people have died in the conflict. While Georgians claimed that the Abkhazians were unwilling to allow Georgian civilians who had fled to return, Abkhazians argued that though they were willing to abide by the document, the Georgians attempted unilaterally to rewrite it.

A chastened Georgia signed a treaty of friendship with Russia in February 1994 and agreed to join the Commonwealth of Independent States (CIS), which it had previously spurned. In return for its acquiescence to Russian interests, the Georgians were to be provided with badly needed military hardware. In June 1994 Yeltsin deployed a CIS peacekeeping force of 2,500 troops, principally Russians, along the Ingur River to separate Georgian and Abkhaz forces. There is heated disagreement concerning the issue of refugees. According to the Abkhazian government, not nearly as many Georgian speakers fled as the Georgian government asserted, and the Abkhazians claim that sixty thousand Georgians had returned by the end of 1996. They also assert that by the end of 1996 the number of Georgian speakers in Abkhazia numbered one hundred thousand.

On September 19, 1994, Russia closed its border with Abkhazia and on October 30, 1995, imposed a sea blockade. In November 1994 the Abkhaz parliament approved a constitution that declared the Republic of Abkhazia a sovereign state, and Ardzinba was elected president. In response to Abkhazia's declaration of sovereignty, the CIS in January 1996 imposed economic sanctions, supplementing the Russian land and sea blockade, until the Abkhaz rejoin Georgia.

At a February 15, 1996, meeting in Moscow, Ardzinba said that the Abkhaz were willing to accept a mix between federation and confederation, a "federative union" rather than a "federative state." The two equal units would have their own constitutions, but a common federative administration would have authority over foreign policy, border controls, energy, communications, and human rights. A settlement, however, still has not been reached. Talks between Georgians and Abkhazians on the status of Abkhazia remain deadlocked.

BIBLIOGRAPHY

Fuller, Liz. "The Vagaries of Russia's Abkhaz Policy." *OMRI Analytical Brief* 1, no. 51 (March 29, 1996).

"Georgia." *The Europa World Year Book 1996.* London: Europa Publications, 1996, Vol. 1, 1331–32.

Goldenberg, Suzanne. *Pride of Small Nations: The Caucasus and Post-Soviet Disorder.* London: Zed Books, 1994.

Hewitt, B. G. "Abkhazia: A Problem of Identity and Ownership." *Central Asian Survey* (December 3, 1993).

———, ed. *Abkhazians: A Handbook.* New York: St. Martin's Press, 1998.

Bernard Cook

SEE ALSO Georgia

Adamec, Ladislav (1926–)

Czechoslovakian prime minister at the beginning of the Velvet Revolution. Ladislav Ademic, the son of peasants, was born in Frenstat pod Radhostem on September 10, 1926. In 1942 he began work as an unskilled laborer in his hometown. He joined the Czechoslovak Communist Party in 1946 and developed a reputation as a capable administrator and able economist. In January 1969, shortly after the crushing of the Czechoslovak reform movement known as the Prague Spring, he became first deputy prime minister, then prime minister of the Czech regional government.

When Ľubomír Strougal was forced to relinquish the post of prime minister on October 10, 1988, Adamec, regarded a trustworthy technocrat, assumed it. Following the November 17 use of security forces against student demonstrators and the subsequent snowballing of pro-democracy demonstrations, Adamec initiated a dialogue with the opposition Civic Forum. He resigned as prime minister on December 10, however, when his proposal for a reshuffled cabinet that would contain sixteen Communists out of a total of twenty-one members was rejected

by Civic Forum and sparked mass protests. His successor, Marian Calfa, though a Communist Party functionary, agreed to a cabinet half of whose members would consist of political independents. The new cabinet, constituted the same day, contained a majority of non-Communists. Jiři Dienstbier, a founder of Charter 77, was appointed foreign minister and Václav Klaus, a market economist, became finance minister.

On December 20, 1989, the Communist Party in an emergency session expelled its former general secretary, Milos Jakes, and the head of the party in Prague, Miroslav Stepan. It then elected Adamec as its chairman, and Vasil Mohorita, a thirty-seven-year-old member of the Politburo and youth organizer, was elected first secretary. Following Adamec's resignation as prime minister, Mohorita had served as the party's chief negotiator with Civic Forum. Adamec replaced Karel Urbánek, who had replaced the hard-liner Jakes fewer than four weeks previously. Adamec, regarded as a pragmatist rather than a convinced reformer, was opposed by the reform-minded Democratic Forum of Communists. The party, nevertheless, used the occasion to apologize "to the working people, artists, intelligentsia and young people for its past policies," and Adamec said that he would attempt to work with the reform Communist group.

BIBLIOGRAPHY

Tagliabue, John. "Unheaval in the East: Czechoslovak Communists Replace Chairman of the Party," *New York Times,* December 21, 1989.

Bernard Cook

Adams, Gerry (1949–)

President of Sinn Fein, MP for West Belfast, 1983–92 and 1997–. Assembly member for West Belfast, 1982–. Vice president of Provisional Sinn Fein (PSF), 1978–83. President of PSF, 1983–.

Gerry Adams was born in Belfast in 1949. He worked as a barman in Belfast when he became involved in what Republicans describe as "defence work during the pogroms," and he was believed by security forces to be head of the Provisional IRA (PIRA) in the Ballymurphy area of West Belfast when he was interned in 1971. In 1972 he was released to take part in secret London talks between PIRA and British Secretary of State William Whitelaw, which gave rise to a brief cease-fire. In the resumed campaign, he was believed by British intelligence sources to be the Belfast brigade commander of PIRA, and in 1973 one of a three-man group running PIRA after the arrest of Sean MacStiofain, chief of staff. After

Gerry Adams, the leader of Sinn Fein and one of the key figures in the peace talks in Northern Ireland.
Illustration courtesy of Bernard Cook.

being arrested with other leading Republicans in Belfast in 1973, Adams tried to escape from the Maze prison. For this, he was sentenced to eighteen months imprisonment and released in 1976. Both as an internee and a convicted prisoner, he was in the PIRA compound at the Maze, but he has repeatedly denied that he has been a member of PIRA. In February 1978 he was charged with membership in PIRA, but after being remanded in custody for seven months, he was freed after the lord chief justice, Lord Lowry, ruled that there was not sufficient evidence for a conviction. He has on several occasions stressed the need for increased political action by Republicans. In June 1979 he told a Wolfe Tone commemoration ceremony at Bodenstown, County Kildare, that the aims of the movement could not be achieved simply by military means, and their failure to develop an alternative to constitutional politics had to be continually analyzed. At the 1980 Provisional Sinn Fein (PSF) *ard fheis* (annual conference), he said that the British now realized that there could not be a military victory, and it was time that Republicans realized it, too. He had a leading role in de-

ciding policy on the 1981 H-Block hunger strike, and when he topped the poll in West Belfast in the 1982 assembly election, he became the dominant Northern Ireland personality in his party. Tim Pat Coogan, a leading authority on the IRA, called him a "Shogun-like figure" in Northern Republicanism. He is among those who have campaigned for a more socialist approach by PSF, and when the party dropped federalism from its policy in 1982, it was a further triumph for Adams and his supporters and put him at odds with some leading Southern PSF figures such as Daithi 'Conaill. In December 1982 Adams was banned by Home Secretary William Whitelaw, under the Prevention of Terrorism Act, from entering Britain to speak to Labour MPs and councilors at the invitation of Greater London Council leader Ken Livingstone. But the ban was lifted by the Home Office in June 1983, when he took West Belfast in the general election with a majority of more than five thousand, unseating veteran MP Gerry Fitt. In 1984 loyalist gunmen shot and wounded Adams when they opened fire on his car. He began having regular contact with John Hume, the leader of the predominantly Catholic Social Democratic Labour Party, in the late 1980s, but the meetings really came to the fore in September 1993, when the two nationalist political leaders relaunched the Irish Peace Initiative. After the IRA called its cease-fire in 1994, PSF was finally admitted to the multiparty talks that eventually culminated in the 1998 Good Friday Agreement.

Ricki Schoen

Adenauer, Konrad (1876–1967)

Christian Democratic chancellor of the Federal Republic of Germany, 1949–63. After a prestigious career as lord mayor of Cologne, 1917–33 and his enforced retirement during the Nazi era, Adenauer helped establish the Federal Republic in 1949 and was the central actor in its politics until 1963.

Son of a minor official in the Cologne civil service, Adenauer pursued legal studies in Freiburg, Munich, and Bonn. In 1897 he entered the Prussian justice administration, then worked briefly as a private attorney. In 1906 the Catholic Center Party delegation in the Cologne legislature sponsored his election to the City Council. Three years later he was deputy lord mayor. He oversaw the municipal food supply during the First World War until a March 1917 automobile accident hospitalized him. This mishap left him what some later observers called an "Asiatic" facial appearance.

Konrad Adenauer, first postwar leader of West Germany and the architect of the country's remarkable recovery from the ruins of Word War II. *Illustration courtesy of the German Information Center.*

Lord mayor since September 18, 1917, Adenauer was instrumental in keeping order in Cologne during the revolutionary upheavals of 1918–19. Both then and around the time of the "Ruhr Struggle" in 1923, he advocated a separate Rhenish state within a new, federal German Reich. He believed this would promote stability in the Rhineland and also banish any threat of French annexations in western Germany. During the Weimar Republic (1918–33) Cologne prospered under Adenauer's leadership. New areas were incorporated into the city, a university was founded, and his favorite project realized, a "green girdle" of parks around the city. This era of foreign investment and full municipal coffers ended with the onset of the Great Depression and the Reich's deflationary financial policies. Nationally, Adenauer served in 1921–33 as president of the Prussian State Council and in both 1921 and 1926 was considered a possible candidate for chancellor.

Like many German bourgeois politicians, Adenauer apparently believed that the other parties could control National Socialism should it come to power. In March 1933 the Nazis removed him from office. Among the charges against him were separatism, "mismanagement" of municipal and personal finances, and a certain philo-Semitism. They arrested him for three days after the Röhm Putsch in 1934 and then again in both August and September 1944, although Adenauer had displayed great reluctance about active contact with resistance circles.

After his dismissal as caretaker mayor of Cologne by British authorities in September 1945, the sixty-nine-year-old helped create the Christian Democratic Union (CDU). Although not well known until 1949, Adenauer quickly became the party's leader throughout West Germany, owing not least to a combination of political experience and personal authority unmatched by any of his potential rivals. Between 1945 and 1949 he established several themes fundamental to his subsequent political work. His vision for German civil society, inimical to both liberalism and socialism, gave high priority to individual rights while emphasizing that the individual was firmly bound to the family and, as was the state, subject to the Christian laws of morality. In foreign policy Adenauer recognized as early as 1945 that the division of Europe would last indefinitely. Therefore, creating a free and secure West German state took priority over reunification for the foreseeable future. Adenauer thought Western integration (*Westbindung*), or close political and institutional ties with Western countries and especially the United States, was crucial for ensuring German security. Once the Soviet Union saw it could not win the Cold War against a united West without unacceptable risk, reunification and improved East-West relations would follow (the "Policy of Strength"). Relatedly, Western European integration, if possible with British participation, would help reverse the continent's decline since 1914 and prevent future wars. Domestically, he saw the Social Democratic Party (SPD) as the CDU's main political opponent and rejected any formal alliance with it. Although he had enjoyed close ties to industry since the First World War and generally favored management over labor, Adenauer also advocated progressive social policies that would alleviate class tensions. Impressed with the 1948 currency reform, he strengthened ties with the head of the Frankfurt Economics Administration, Ludwig Erhard, eventually bringing him into the CDU. As president of the Parliamentary Council in 1948–49, Adenauer created a working relationship with leading Western occupation officials. After the CDU/Christian Social Union (CSU) won the close August 1949 federal elections on a platform emphasizing Erhard's "social market economy,"

Adenauer became chancellor in September by a single vote and established a center-right coalition.

His chancellorship can be divided into three phases. From 1949 to 1953 Adenauer's priority lay in establishing a close relationship with the Western powers and transforming the Occupation Statute into a contractual relationship. These goals were initially complicated by issues such as the dismantling of German heavy industry and the French occupation of the Saar. Adenauer calculated that the Occupation Powers would reward German cooperation in the Cold War by loosening controls and used the outbreak of hostilities in Korea in June 1950 to offer German participation in Western defense. In 1951 the start of negotiations on the European Defense Community (EDC) and the Occupation Statute proved him right. By 1953 the Western Powers were treating the Federal Republic like a sovereign state, although the Occupation Statute technically remained in effect. They also recognized the Federal Republic of Germany's (FRG) claim to be sole representative of the German nation after the German Democratic Republic (GDR) was created in 1949 and, strongly encouraged by Adenauer, rejected Joseph Stalin's 1952 proposal for a neutral, united Germany. While none of the West German parties in the 1950s dwelt on the Nazi past, since this might alienate potential voters, Adenauer negotiated the 1953 Restitution Agreement with Israel and pushed it through parliament despite opposition from within his own CDU/CSU about its potential cost. Domestically, the Bundestag (lower house of parliament) passed the most important legislation concerning immediate postwar reconstruction, such as the 1950 Dwellings Construction Law (*Wohnungsbaugesetz*) and the 1952 Equalization of Burdens Law (*Lastenausgleich*), which benefited refugees. The "economic miracle," which started fully unfolding around 1952, played an important role in solidifying Adenauer's political fortunes. This first phase of his chancellorship ended with German ratification of the Contractual Agreements and the EDC Treaty in January 1953 and the CDU/CSU's electoral victory the following August, which gave it 45.3 percent of the vote.

From 1953 to 1958 Adenauer was at the height of his reputation and power, as demonstrated domestically by the 1957 federal elections. Using the slogan No Experiments, the CDU/CSU captured an absolute majority of the popular vote. In foreign policy two apparent mishaps proved fortunate. On August 30, 1954, the French National Assembly rejected the EDC Treaty, thereby clearing the way for a German national army within NATO—Adenauer's preferred goal—and more favorable contractual agreements in 1955. Also in 1955 the Saar's population, against Adenauer's better judgment, voted for incorporation into the Federal Republic; "reunification in the West" ensued in 1957. The Saar vote did not produce a crisis with France primarily because between 1955 and 1957 the European Economic Community (EEC) and Euratom had taken center stage internationally. As with the European Coal and Steel Community in 1950, Adenauer prioritized the political benefits of European integration. He overruled the objections of German free traders like Erhard to the EEC.

Decreasing Cold War tensions after 1953 provided an opportunity to establish diplomatic relations with the USSR in September 1955 and secure the release of remaining German prisoners of war there. However, the thaw also increased Adenauer's fears that the four occupying powers might reach agreement on Germany over the FRG's head (his "Potsdam complex") and that the European status quo, including the GDR, would solidify. His government met the first danger by continually professing unshakable loyalty to the West and pursing a very cautious Eastern policy and the second largely by threatening to break relations with any state that recognized East Germany (the so-called Hallstein Doctrine). At home in January 1957 the Bundestag passed legislation dear to Adenauer that linked pensions to the cost of living, a welcome innovation in a society with a vivid memory of past inflations. Yet his greatest domestic accomplishments had more to do with the overall shape of the Federal Republic's political system. Most crucially, his CDU/CSU integrated wide segments of the German center-right, including potentially troublesome groups like old-school Protestant nationalists and refugees. By 1958 the trend toward a stable three-party system—CDU/CSU, SPD, and the liberal Free Democratic Party—was unmistakable.

Contemporary observers coined the term "Chancellor Democracy" to describe Adenauer's dominant personal role in government during the 1950s. Prone to micromanage at times, he depended on a small group of advisers and kept a tight reign over his ministers, especially in the vital area of foreign policy. Adenauer also skillfully manipulated the various groups within the coalition and especially within the CDU/CSU. His own values were typical of the nineteenth-century German middle class: discipline, industry, respect for authority, frugality, love of nature, and great piety. Normally he represented his office with quiet, reassuring dignity. But he possessed a strong, combative streak and could play hardball, especially during electoral campaigns. Moreover, at heart he was a pessimist. He harbored recurrent doubts, sometimes when overreacting to individual incidents, about the ability of party colleagues to continue his policies, the steadfastness of foreign allies, and, on occasion, the political sense of the entire German people.

During the difficult last phase of his chancellorship, from 1958 to 1963, the weaknesses of Adenauer's method of governing became increasingly apparent. Adenauer's characteristic pessimism expressed itself in sharp disputes with party colleagues over questions like Eastern policy and relations with the SPD. Long-standing tensions between Adenauer and Erhard came into the open during the complicated process of selecting a new federal president in 1959. The aging chancellor remained reluctant to leave his post as long as Erhard, whose political skills he highly mistrusted, seemed likely to replace him. In 1959–60 the SPD made a serious bid for long-term electoral success by abandoning its Marxist platform and embracing Adenauer's own policy of Western integration. Discontent with Adenauer's authoritarian tendencies also grew, culminating in the public fallout from the 1962 Spiegel affair. The Second Berlin Crisis of 1958–62, and especially the erection of the Berlin Wall in August 1961, symbolized for many West Germans the bankruptcy of the "Policy of Strength." Moreover, it intensified Adenauer's doubts about Western and particularly Anglo-American resolve to support the Federal Republic's positions on the German Question and military—i.e., nuclear—equality within NATO. His alternative, closer cooperation with France, proved unsatisfactory despite the historic January 1963 Franco-German Treaty of Friendship and Cooperation. French President Charles de Gaulle's confrontation course with the United States on NATO and opposition to EEC membership for Britain conflicted with basic German interests. Though Adenauer led the CDU/CSU to a fourth electoral victory in 1961, his days as chancellor were numbered, and he resigned in October 1963.

Adenauer remained active politically and continued to serve as national chairman of the CDU until 1966. His memoirs, whose first volume appeared in 1965, provided a central source for German contemporary history. Adenauer died at his home in Rhöndorf near Bonn on April 19, 1967, at the age of ninety-one. Twenty-five heads of state and over one hundred ambassadors attended his state funeral in Cologne, a glowing tribute to his political accomplishments. His two most important legacies are the Federal Republic's continued pro-Western orientation, even after reunification, and the unprecedented creation of a German federal, nondenominational center-right party, the CDU/CSU, that has dominated the FRG's conservative politics since 1945.

BIBLIOGRAPHY

Adenauer, Konrad. *Memoirs 1945–1953.* Tr. by Beate Ruhm von Oppen. London: Weidenfeld and Nicholson, 1966.

———. *Erinnerungen.* Stuttgart: DVA, 1965, 1966, 1967, 1968. Vol. 1: 1945–1953; Vol. 2: 1953–1955; Vol. 3: 1955–1959; Vol. 4: 1959–1963. *Fragmente.*

———. *Briefe.* Berlin: Siedler, 1983, 1984, 1985, 1987, 1995 (Rhöndorfer Ausgabe). Ed. by Hans-Peter Mensing. Vol. 1: 1945–1947; Vol. 2: 1947–1949; Vol. 3: 1949–1951; Vol. 4: 1951–1953; Vol. 5: 1953–1955.

———. *Reden 1917–1967. Eine Auswahl.* Ed. by Hans-Peter Schwarz. Stuttgart: DVA 1975.

———. *Teegespraeche.* Berlin: Siedler, 1984, 1986, 1988, 1992 (Rhöndorfer Ausgabe). Ed. by Hanns Juergen Kuesters: Vol. 1: 1949–1954; Vol. 2: 1955–1958; Vol. 3: 1959–1961. Ed. by Hans Peter Mensing: Vol. 4: 1961–1963.

Koehler, Henning. *Adenauer. Eine politische Biographie.* Berlin: Ullstein, 1994.

Schwarz, Hans-Peter. *Konrad Adenauer: German Politician and Statesman in an Era of War, Revolution and Reconstruction.* Vol. 1: *From the German Empire to the Federal Republic, 1876–1952.* Tr. by Louise Willmot. Providence, R.I.: Berghahn Books, 1995 (1986). Vol. 2: *The Statesman, 1952–1967.* Tr. by Geoffrey Penny. Providence, R.I.: Berghahn Books, 1997 (1991).

Adenauer's personal papers are located at the Stiftung-Bundeskanzler-Adenauer-Haus, Rhöndorf, Germany.

Thomas W. Maulucci Jr.

SEE ALSO Erhard, Ludwig; European Defense Community; Germany, Federal Republic of; *Spiegel Affair*

Adorno, Theodor Wiesengrund (1903–)

German philosopher. Theodor Wiesengrund Adorno was born in Frankfurt in 1903, the son of an assimilated Jewish wine merchant, Oskar Wiesengrund, and his Catholic wife, Maria Calvelli-Adorno, a Corsican by descent and an accomplished singer.

In 1918 Adorno began reading Kant under the direction of Siegfried Kracauer. In 1921 he began to study at the University of Frankfurt and met Leo Löwenthal. He also became acquainted with Max Horkheimer in 1922. Adorno received a doctorate under Cornelius with a dissertation on Husserl.

Adorno, whose interest was not limited to philosophy but extended equally to music, attended a performance of Alban Berg's *Wozzeck* and was so fascinated by it that he went to Vienna in 1925 to study under Berg. There he established contact with the Schoenberg circle. He returned to Frankfurt in 1927 and worked on Kant, Marx, and Freud.

From the end of the 1920s Adorno was associated with the circle surrounding the *Zeitschrift für Sozialforschung* and with scholars and artists like Ernst Bloch, Bertolt Brecht, Walter Benjamin, and Kurt Weil. Though they all lived in Berlin, Adorno maintained his contacts in Vienna as well.

In 1931 Adorno completed his habilitation with a work on Kierkegaard and gave his inaugural lecture in philosophy at the University of Frankfurt. From 1932 he regularly published in the *Zeitschrift für Sozialforschung*. Between 1934 and 1938 he did postdoctoral work at Merton College, Oxford. There he elaborated the foundations of his work *Against Epistemology.* In 1938 Adorno became an official member of the Institute for Social Research in New York City and accepted a part-time job in the Radion Research Project, directed by Paul Lazarsfeld at Princeton University. Adorno followed Horkheimer to Southern California and worked there on the *Dialectic of Enlightenment.* In 1949 he returned to Frankfurt but spent a year in the United States in 1952 following an invitation by the Hacker Foundation. From 1958 he was in charge of the Institut für Sozialforschung. He died of heart failure in 1969.

Adorno's most important publications after his return to Germany are collections of essays such as *Prisms* (1955) and *Notes to Literature* (four volumes, 1958–74), as well as collections of aphorisms *Minima Moralia* (1951), *The Philosophy of Modern Music* (1949), *Negative Dialectics* (1966), and *Ascetic Theory* (unfinished and published posthumously in 1970).

Adorno's negative dialectics attempts to answer some of the questions formulated in the *Dialectic of Enlightenment:* How could one conceive a nondominant relation between man and the world? What would be the form of acts of thought that no longer subsume the object under them and identify it? This is to be understood as an explicatory attempt at nonidentifying dialectical thought the fundamental methodical feature of which is determinate negation. The goal of this kind of thinking "against itself" is to transform philosophy's conceptuality toward the nonidentical. The goal of reason is the reconciliation of spirit and nature, however, only in the form of a phantasm.

Owing to the limitations of thought, negative dialectics needs to be supplemented by a form of appropriating the world that presents an already accomplished reconciliation. This reconciliation, however, is not a mere copy reproducing and mimicking, thereby affirming the antag-

onistic state of late capitalistic society. It is rather already the other. Negative dialectics, therefore, needs art. Yet since art is without judgment, it needs aesthetic theory to give it voice. This basis of Adorno's extensive aesthetic studies represents perhaps the definitive aesthetics of modernity.

Erik Vogt

SEE ALSO Frankfurt School

Adzic, Blagoje (1933–)

Chief of staff of the Yugoslav army since 1989 and close collaborator of Slobodan Milošević. The Serbian general was the leader of the hard-liners in army who strenuously opposed the secession of any republics from the Yugoslav federation. He was responsible for the intervention of the army in Slovenia in July 1991 and has never concealed his pro-Serbian nationalist sentiments.

Catherine Lutard
(Tr. by Bernard Cook)

Afghanistan, War in

Afghanistan, sandwiched between the USSR and British India, prudently remained neutral throughout World War II. Given few other possibilities, the Afghan government became largely dependent on British economic and military assistance. Fearful of Soviet aggression, the postwar Afghan government remained resolved on accommoda-

Afghanistan. *Illustration courtesy of Bernard Cook.*

tion with Britain. Despite their misunderstandings of the previous century, Britain and Afghanistan seemed headed toward an extensive partnership. For example, Britain had assumed a dominant influence in training and supplying the Afghan military through the so-called Lancaster Plan.

The triumph of the Indian nationalist movement, however, led to the demise of British hegemony in South Asia. Despite efforts by the British to retain some element of control over subcontinent defense, or ensure the maintenance of previous strategic policies, the plethora of differences that made inevitable the partition of the subcontinent into India and Pakistan likewise precluded continuation of the strategic status quo. Once Britain lost access to Indian manpower and facilities, India was no longer paramount in imperial defense. Since the strategic importance of Afghanistan had always remained adjunct to the defense of the subcontinent, once India and Pakistan achieved independence, Afghanistan became of minimal value to the British. Thus Britain, weakened from World War II and soon divested of both political and military responsibility for the subcontinent, was neither capable nor particularly interested in assisting Afghanistan.

The successor states, meanwhile, emerged from the partition weak and poised against each other. Disputes over Kashmir, the Punjab, and Bengal, the division of military and industrial assets, and communal atrocities aggravated existing grievances and left Pakistan and India more inclined to battle each other than forge common policy. The economic and political disruption that accompanied partition also ensured that neither Pakistan nor India would have much to spare for Afghanistan, even in the absence of political hindrances. India, technically responsible for the continuation of the Lancaster Plan, showed little desire to assist the Muslim Afghans. Continual border controversy, the Pushtunistan dispute, precluded close relations between Afghanistan and Pakistan.

Throughout the ensuing period Afghanistan, searching for a replacement for the departed British, courted the United States. Though the Afghan government repeatedly expressed a desire for partnership with Washington, the Truman and Eisenhower administrations proved largely disinterested. The Truman administration did offer limited support to an agricultural development program in the Helmand Valley, embassy officials briefly tried to mediate the Pushtunistan controversy, and at one time Pentagon officials even approved Afghan purchases of U.S. military hardware. The Helmand Valley Project, however, would prove a dismal failure, and the stipulations of the military aid agreement rendered purchase impractical.

Meanwhile, Pushtunistan negotiations were aborted in the face of Pakistani protests.

In time the United States moved to support Pakistan and Iran, deeming both assets to the worldwide Soviet containment effort. But the Americans proved disinterested in Afghanistan since it possessed no strong conventional military forces, valuable strategic facilities, vital resources, or substantial economic worth, yet was dangerously exposed to Soviet encroachment. Though the Afghans detested both the Soviets and communism, showed no objection to ideas of collective security, and might well have joined a Western-sponsored alliance of Islamic states given suitable preconditions, the Eisenhower administration thought it best to leave Afghanistan outside the American area of responsibility.

By late 1955 persistent American rejection of Afghan requests for economic, military, and political support had alienated the Kabul regime. Aid programs to Pakistan and Iran undermined American excuses that global commitments, strained finances, or requisite congressional approval precluded similar assistance to Afghanistan. That the United States was sufficiently concerned with the security of Afghanistan's neighbors to risk Soviet retaliation, but did not extend its concern to Kabul, seems to have irritated the Afghans most of all.

Denied access to the Western alliances and their accompanying economic assistance, Prime Minister Muhammad Daoud's nation faced a choice between a continuum in an economic, political, and military vacuum or a rapprochement with the USSR. Daoud, tired of Afghanistan's economic weakness and convinced that Pakistan would always retain a greater priority with the United States, signed a comprehensive aid agreement in December 1955 that effectively mortgaged much of Afghanistan's economy to the USSR. The following August Daoud consigned the armed forces to Soviet tutelage in an agreement that promised wholesale renovation of the Afghan military establishment.

In the late 1950s Daoud's bargain seemed born of genius. The aid package included credits for the construction of hydroelectric plants, industrial complexes, storage facilities, three major irrigation projects, two modern airports near Kabul, and a north-south highway from Kabul through the Hindu Kush to the Oxus. Furthermore, the acceptance of the Soviet offer prompted the heretofore uninterested United States to implement a sizable assistance program of its own. Hoping to limit Soviet influence and preserve Afghan independence, the Eisenhower administration financed several economic plans, some of which it had rejected earlier. Through the next decade, Soviet and American engineers built a variety of civic, industrial, mining, agricultural, health, education, and communications facilities across Afghanistan, to the delight of Daoud's regime. Throughout the late 1950s and 1960s, Afghanistan remained the only country in the world where the United States and the USSR cooperated, at times even collaborated, in development programs.

The modernization of his military supplied Daoud with the force needed to guarantee stability in the wake of social and economic reforms. Daoud used the army to enforce government policy, and on more than one occasion it responded successfully to domestic protests. The possession of Soviet military hardware, however, brought with it a dependency on the USSR for training, ammunition, spare parts, and replacement items that effectively limited Afghan political options, even in the absence of formal treaty arrangements. Soviet instructors also assumed responsibility for training Afghan officers, creating opportunities for subversion within the government's most important enforcing instrument. The United States could find no substantial way to offset Soviet domination of the Afghan military.

Daoud implemented extensive precautionary measures to avoid possible infiltration of the military. He discharged officers who expressed hostile opinions and prohibited all members of the armed forces from seeking public office. He increased the size of the West German–trained national police force and had them monitor the activities of Soviet officers and technicians as well as domestic organizations with progressive or leftist leanings. Daoud rotated Soviet technicians frequently and rarely renewed their contracts upon termination of designated projects.

In October 1964, King Zahir Shah dismissed Daoud and approved a new constitution. It contained elements typical of Western democracies, including separation of powers, secret ballot, right to trial, and freedom of the press. Within the more open atmosphere that followed, radical groups found the armed forces a fertile field in which to recruit. As a result of contacts with Soviet instructors, some officers and enlisted men came to support radical groups demanding sweeping changes to Afghanistan's existing socioeconomic structure.

Throughout the constitutional period (1964–73) the government routinely called on the army to keep order among political factions, which it did effectively while its loyalty remained with the royal family. Frustrations with the status quo, however, would undermine loyalty to the king.

By 1973 perhaps as many as six hundred Afghan officers supported the Communist People's Democratic Party of Afghanistan (PDPA). By that time many such

officers had reached ranks of major or colonel in command of key army and air force units and installations. These officers played critical roles in both the 1973 coup that overthrew the monarchy and the 1978 revolt that brought the PDPA to power. Thereafter, several ill-advised reform programs, implemented amid severe repression, alienated the vast majority of the Afghan population and prompted civil war. With the PDPA government on the verge of collapse, the USSR sent in troops in December 1979, who remained in Afghanistan for over nine years.

The Soviet decision to invade likely stemmed most from fears of Islamic revival along its southern border, heightened not only by Afghan resistance but also by the advent of the Khomeini regime in Iran. Successful precedents of proxy activity in Ethiopia, Angola, and South Yemen further encouraged invasion. Certain Soviet officials may have dreamed of future offensives toward the Persian Gulf. Most clearly discounted any unfavorable world reaction, and like many powers before them, the Soviets underestimated the Afghans' guerrilla potential.

While Afghanistan eventually came to resemble a "Soviet Vietnam," initially most strategists thought that the Afghan mujahideen would fade away in the face of a Soviet onslaught. Such pessimism remained prominent even as the war progressed. Continued stalemate seemed palatable to the USSR. The Soviet government, apparently immune to public opinion, seemed prepared and capable of waging a sustained battle of attrition against the Afghans, as they had done before in Central Asia and the Caucasus. With no perceived threat of popular protests and no upcoming elections, the Soviet hierarchy could even resort to forms of warfare not palatable to a Western democracy. The Soviet Union repeatedly violated Geneva protocols in the first years of the war, employing in several instances chemical and biological weapons. Soviet and Afghan government forces, supported by aircraft and helicopter gunships, directed their attacks against civilians, agricultural areas, water facilities, and livestock, as well as the mujahideen.

Despite their overwhelming technological superiority and the ability to wage a veritable war of extermination, the USSR proved unable to suppress the mujahideen or discourage the vast majority of Afghans from supporting the resistance. The Afghan combination of ballistic familiarity, tactical know-how, rugged endurance, and unyielding refusal to tolerate any sort of foreign rule, which has made Afghanistan a graveyard of armies throughout the years, again proved insurmountable. Increased amounts of Western aid supplied in the mid-1980s, most notably American-built Stinger missiles, proved of great help to the Afghans, but Soviet casualties never became truly excessive. Above all else the Soviets simply could not break the will of the Afghan people to resist.

Historians continue to debate the effect of the Afghan war on the collapse of the Soviet Union. Though direct expenditures were not extravagant, when combined with the loss of access to Western grain, technology, and other items, the war imposed a steady drain on the already failing Soviet economy. Furthermore, as long as Soviet troops remained in Afghanistan, the USSR suffered severe foreign policy repercussions. The vast majority of Third World nations, especially Islamic-majority states, resented the naked aggression and routinely demonstrated their feelings through condemning resolutions at the United Nations. The USSR evoked hostility on its southern border that gave impetus to Islamic independence movements in Azerbaijan and Georgia, throughout the Central Asian republics, and within the Russian Republic in Chechnya. Perhaps most important, psychological frustration passed from veterans through the Soviet general population, overwhelmed government propaganda, and added to other venues of discontent. Faced with an increasingly dissatisfied and increasingly vocal population, and left with no hope for victory beyond the mass extermination of the Afghan people, General Secretary Mikhail Gorbachev ultimately determined that the price of retreat would entail less economic and political damage than continuation of the war.

While one could argue that the war ultimately proved beneficial to Western policy in speeding the collapse of Soviet communism, it would be callous to overlook that these repercussions came at a terrible cost for the Afghan people. Between one and two million Afghans perished, while over half the population was made homeless. Sadly, in the aftermath of war, Afghanistan has been unable to sustain lasting peace but has instead become a battleground for warring factions.

BIBLIOGRAPHY

Bradcher, Henry S. *Afghanistan and the Soviet Union.* Durham, North Carolina: Duke University Press, 1983.

Dupree, Louis. *Afghanistan.* Princeton, N.J.: Princeton University Press, 1973.

Hammond, Thomas T. *Red Flag over Afghanistan: The Communist Coup, the Soviet Invasion, and the Consequences.* Boulder, Colo.: Westview Press, 1984.

Hauner, Milan, and Robert L. Canfield, eds. *Afghanistan and the Soviet Union: Collision and Transformation.* Boulder, Colo.: Westview Press, 1989.

Klass, Rosanne, ed. *Afghanistan: The Great Game Revisited.* New York: Freedom House, 1987.

Saikal, Amin, and William Maley, eds. *The Soviet Withdrawal from Afghanistan.* Cambridge: Cambridge University Press, 1989.

Jeff Roberts

Agnelli Family

Piedmontese family that has had a prominent role in the economic, political, and social life of Italy since Giovanni Agnelli founded the Fabbrica Italiana di Automobili Torino, FIAT, in 1899. A shrewd industrialist, Giovanni developed important alliances with Italian leaders and made FIAT the leading producer of automobiles and an important force in the national economy. His son, Gianni, took over FIAT in 1966 and expanded its involvement into many industries, including banking, publishing, sports, and the media. Giovanni's daughter, Susanna, became a senator and leader of the Republican Party. Since the mid-1980s politicians, industrialists, and the general public have criticized the Agnelli group, claiming it has become a monopoly with too much power in too many aspects of Italian life. Yet the Agnellis maintain widespread popular support and have a public position somewhat analogous to that of the Kennedy family in the United States. During World War I the FIAT company, under Giovanni Agnelli's leadership, secured its future by becoming a primary manufacturer of automobiles, trucks, airplane engines, and other machinery for the war effort. Giovanni also established a beneficial, though allegedly apolitical, relationship with dictator Benito Mussolini following the Great War and guaranteed FIAT a role in World War II. FIAT quickly became Italy's number one automobile manufacturer, a position it has maintained through a veritable monopoly of the auto trade. When Giovanni died in December 1945, his family's fortune was estimated to be worth a billion dollars.

Vittorio Valetta assumed control at FIAT following Giovanni's death. Gianni is rumored to have enjoyed a jet-set lifestyle during Valetta's tenure as FIAT chairman. When Gianni took over FIAT in 1966, he was confronted with a turbulent period of worker unrest but was able to keep FIAT at the top of the Italian economy. Through a series of business dealings, Gianni guaranteed FIAT a role in most of Italy's leading industries, including Gemina, Mediobanca, and Pirelli. The Agnellis acquired media influence when they bought control of two of Italy's leading daily newspapers, *Corriere della Sera* and *La Stampa* and took over an Italian-language television station based in

Montecarlo. They also bought the popular Italian soccer team Juventus.

To criticisms that the Agnellis had too much power, the family responded that what was good for FIAT was good for Italy and that they needed to increase their holdings to guarantee FIAT a place in the world market. Despite challenges from a new group of politicians and industrialists, the Agnelli family has proved its ability to remain strong in Italy as well as in the international marketplace. This could change, however. In poor health, Gianni turned FIAT over to long-time colleague Cesare Romiti in February 1995. Since then, there have been rumors of other possible changes in FIAT and its subsidiaries. With several leading FIAT executives, as well as those of its important partners, reaching retirement age, there is speculation that Gianni's son, Giovanni, may become the new Agnelli leader.

BIBLIOGRAPHY

Castronovo, Valerio. *Giovanni Agnelli: La Fiat dal 1899 al 1945.* Turin: Einuadi, 1977.

Friedman, Alan. *Agnelli and the Network of Italian Power.* London: Harrap Limited, 1988.

Pietra, Italo. *I tre Agnelli.* Milan: Garzanti, 1985.

Rossant, John. "Italian Industry—Twilight of the Gods: A Scandal Touching Italy's Big Three Signals the End of an Era." *Business Week* (international edition), August 19, 1996.

Wendy A. Pojmann

Ahern, Bertie (1951–)

Irish politician. Bertie Ahern, a former accountant, was elected to the Dail as a Fianna Fail representative in 1977. He served as minister for state at the Departments of the Taoiseach (prime minister) and Defense in 1982; minister for labor, 1987–91; and minister for finance, 1991–94. He was director of elections for Brian Lenihan in the 1990 presidential campaign. Ahern supported Charles Haughey in the 1992 leadership battle. Despite being seen as a prospective candidate to replace Haughey, he did not run for office. However, Ahern did replace Albert Reynolds as leader of Fianna Fail in 1994. Following the success of Fianna Fail in the 1997 election, Ahern became taoiseach.

Michael J. Kennedy

SEE ALSO Haughey, Charles; Reynolds, Albert

Aho, Esko (1954–)

Prime minister of Finland from 1991 to 1995. Esko Aho, who was born on May 20, 1954, became prime minister

in 1991 when the Finnish Center Party (CP), under his chairmanship, succeeded in winning thirteen seats in the parliamentary elections. When the Social Democrats refused to participate in the government, Aho formed a nonsocialist majority coalition. The CP had eight ministers, the Conservatives six, and the Swedish National Party two. In addition, the Finnish Christian Union had one. In June 1994, however, the Finnish Christian Union withdrew from the government because it opposed the agreement to join the European Union (EU).

Aho became chairman of the CP in 1990 when he defeated his rivals in an exciting contest during the party congress. The post was vacated by Paavo Väyrynen, chairman from 1980 to 1990, who announced that he would not continue in the post. Aho's victory came as a surprise to most outside the party. While Aho was just thirty-six years old in 1990, he had been active in the CP for almost two decades. He was chairman of the party's youth organization from 1974 to 1980 and political secretary to Foreign Minister Väyrynen from 1979 to 1980. From 1980 to 1983 Aho worked as an official in a small municipality, where he was responsible for the development of industries. This job was intended to provide him with the popular support necessary for a political career. Aho was elected to the Eduskunta (parliament) in 1983; in 1991 he was elected to a third term. In parliament he worked behind the scenes, while carefully preparing for more challenging tasks.

As prime minister Aho was one of a long line of prominent political leaders produced by the Agrarian Union/ Center Party. He surprisingly turned out to be independent of his predecessor, Väyrynen, whom he was expected to support in the 1994 presidential elections. The fight between the two became open in early summer 1994. While Väyrynen led the intraparty opposition against Finland's membership in the EU, Aho obtained a vote of confidence in the Eduskunta, forcing the party congress to approve EU membership within a single dramatic week in June.

While Aho's popularity decreased after the 1991 parliamentary elections, he became one of the strongest politicians in Finland in 1994 because of his party's decisive role in the EU issue.

BIBLIOGRAPHY

Häikiö, Martti. *A Brief History of Modern Finland.* Helsinki: University of Helsinki, Lahti Research and Training Centre, 1992.

Vilho Harle

SEE ALSO Ahtisaari, Martti; Finland; Lipponen, Paavo

Ahtisaari, Martti (1937–)

President of Finland, March 1, 1994. Martti Oiva Kalevi Ahtisaari was born on June 23, 1937, in Viipuri (Vyborg) on the Karelian isthmus. Ahtisaari did not have any experience in Finnish politics; his international career had kept him away from Finland for more than two decades. He worked as a teacher at the Swedish Pakistani Institute of Technology in Karachi from 1960 to 1963, and as managing director for the Helsinki International Student Club and Students' Association for Development Aid in 1964–65. Ahtisaari joined the Ministry for Foreign Affairs of Finland in 1965, holding various posts in the Bureau for Technical Co-operation, finally serving as assistant director in 1971–72. In 1972 he became deputy director of the Department for International Development Cooperation. Ahtisaari served as the Finnish ambassador to Tanzania from 1973 to 1976, and was also accredited to Zambia, Somalia, and Mozambique (1975–76).

Ahtisaari was U.N. commissioner for Namibia between 1977 and 1981. In 1978 he was appointed special representative in Namibia of the U.N. secretary-general. Between 1984 and 1986 he served as undersecretary of state in charge of international development cooperation in the Finnish Ministry for Foreign Affairs, and from 1987 to 1991 as U.N. undersecretary general for administration and management. As special representative of the U.N. secretary-general for Namibia, Ahtisaari led the U.N. operation (UNTAG) in Namibia in 1989–90.

On July 1, 1991, Ahtisaari became secretary of state in the Finnish Ministry for Foreign Affairs. From September 1992 until April 1993 he was chairman of the Bosnia-Herzegovina Working Group of the International Conference on the former Yugoslavia. Despite being the Social Democratic (SDP) presidential candidate for the 1994 elections, Ahtisaari spent four months as special adviser to the International Conference on Former Yugoslavia. He returned to Finland only about two months before the first election day.

Ahtisaari's international reputation was an asset in the competition for the post of Finland's president. When he was introduced to opinion polls as a potential candidate, he immediately obtained 55–60 percent support against less than 10 percent for any other candidate.

While Kalevi Sorsa, a former secretary-general and chairman of the SDP, as well as prime minister and foreign minister for several years in the 1970s and 1980s, was expected to become the SDP's presidential candidate after Mauno Koivisto, widespread antipolitical feelings prompted a demand for an alternative. Furthermore, the new electoral system demanded a candidate who, in a direct vote, would win a sufficient number of votes in the first round to be one of two leading candidates and then win a majority during the second round. In the new situation all the parties selected their candidates in primary elections. The SDP decided to open voting in its primary to nonmembers, negatively influencing Sorsa's chances since it was certain that nonmembers would prefer Ahtisaari. However, Ahtisaari won a narrow majority among members as well, receiving altogether 61.2 percent of the vote against Sorsa's 34.4 percent.

While Ahtisaari's original support in opinion polls decreased dramatically to about 20 percent during the campaign, he won the first round with 25.9 percent. Elisabeth Rehn (Swedish People's Party, SFP) received 22 percent, Paavo Väyrynen (The Finnish Center, KESK) 19.5 percent, and Raimo Ilaskivi (National Coalition Party, the conservatives) 15.2 percent. Keijo Korhonen and Eeva Kuuskoski (both KESK members) together received 8.4 percent; each of the other candidates received from 0.2 to 3.8 percent. According to opinion polls Elisabeth Rehn was more popular (with 55 percent) than Ahtisaari at the beginning of the campaign for the second round. However, Ahtisaari conducted a better campaign, achieving 53.9 percent of the vote in the second-round general election.

In his presidential campaign Ahtisaari deviated from Koivisto's efforts to decrease the president's power in relation to the Eduskunta (parliament) and especially in relation to the Council of State, not only in foreign policy but in domestic politics as well. His campaign was balanced between popular antipolitical feelings and similarly popular socialist alternatives in welfare politics, with promises to reduce unemployment and to save the welfare state through strong political determination. After taking office Ahtisaari broke the traditional distance between the president and the nation by personally visiting and meeting with common people and frequently speaking to the nation through the mass media. President Ahtisaari boldly declared that no party had been able to achieve the same level of popular support as he did, with 54 percent of the vote, so he alone was elected by and represented the people.

BIBLIOGRAPHY

Pesonen, Pertti. "The First Direct Election of Finland's President." *Scandinavian Political Studies* 17, no. 3 (1994):259–72.

Vilho Harle

SEE ALSO Aho, Esko; Finland; Lipponen, Paavo

Aiken, Frank (1898–1983)

Irish politician, minister for finance, 1945–48; minister for external affairs, 1951–54, 1957–68; deputy prime minister, or tanaiste 1965–69. Frank Aiken played a central role in the operation and development of Ireland's post–1945 foreign policy. On his return to office in 1957, Aiken promoted an independent Irish policy at the United Nations. Disregarding Cold War polarizations, Ireland spoke out in favor of decolonization in the developing world and, against American wishes, in support of the admission of Communist China. The prominent stance adopted by Aiken at the United Nations is often seen as a golden age of Irish foreign policy. Aiken's ministry saw the first deployments of Irish peacekeeping forces in Sinai in 1958 and in the Congo from 1961 to 1964. Aiken's interest in disarmament led in 1958 to resolution 1665 [XVI], which led to the Nuclear Non-Proliferation Treaty of 1968. Aiken's role was acknowledged by the fact that his signature headed those on the Moscow copy of the treaty. Yet Aiken paid little attention to European policy and showed little interest in the European Community.

Michael J. Kennedy

SEE ALSO Nuclear Non-Proliferation Treaty

Ajaria (Adzharia)

Autonomous republic of the former Georgian Socialist Soviet Republic of the USSR. Ajaria, whose population consists principally of Islamized Georgians, is located in southwestern Georgia along the Black Sea coast, and its principal city is the strategic port Batumi.

Ajaria's autonomous status within Georgia was rooted in geopolitical considerations following World War I and the Russian Civil War. Batumi was coveted by Azerbaijan, Armenia, and Georgia. The Bolsheviks arrived in March 1921 just before the Turks. The Georgian Mensheviks, who had occupied the city, preferred even Bolshevik Russians to the Turks. Moscow, however, anxious to appease Kemal Atatürk, granted autonomy to the Muslims of Ajaria in the Treaty of Kars.

That Ajarians' identity was primarily religious rather than linguistic or cultural made their territory vulnerable to attacks by the Communist establishment. The linguistic complexity of the area contributed to the success of a Georgian literacy campaign. Georgian became the lingua franca and assimilation progressed rapidly. After the Second World War, 80 percent of the region's population identified as Georgians.

As a result of the uncertainty and turmoil that accompanied the collapse of the USSR, however, Ajaria seceded from Georgia in 1991 and became virtually independent. Secession was largely the work of Aslan Abshidze, a former apparatchik who had profited from the "real economy" of the Caucasus during the late Soviet era. In 1990 Georgian ultranationalist Zviad Gamsakhurdia attempted to abolish the autonomy of Ajaria. This directly endangered the economic and political position of the local Soviet elites. To maintain the economic advantages enjoyed by the area and their own system of patronage, they, under the leadership of Ajaria, recruited sufficient popular support against Gamsakhurdia to challenge Tbilisi successfully and to organize a separate regime for all practical purposes.

Bernard Cook

Akhmatova, Anna Andreevna (Gorenko) (1889–1966)

Russian poet. Well known for her love poems of the 1920s, Anna Akhmatova emerged during the Second World War as a patriotic and moral voice. In 1946, however, her work was banned by the Soviet government, and she was expelled from the Writers Union. Rehabilitated after 1956, she received the Etna-Taormina prize in 1964 and an honorary degree from Oxford University the following year.

Her most famous later works, *Requiem* (published in 1958) and *Poem Without a Hero* (1963), are noted for the distinctive mirror-writing style Akhmatova employed. Today, Anna Akhmatova is recognized as "the conscience of Russia" and its greatest female poet.

BIBLIOGRAPHY

Akhmatova, Anna. "Korotkoye o sebye" in *Poemi: Requiem, Severnii Elegi.* Leningrad: Sovietskii Pisatel, Leningradski Otdel, 1989.

Haight, Amanda. *Anna Akhmatova: A Poetic Pilgrimmage.* New York: Oxford University Press, 1990.

Reeder, Roberta, ed. *The Complete Poems of Anna Akhmatova* (2 vols., bilingual edition). Sommerville, Mass.: Zephyr Press, 1990.

Timothy C. Dowling

Åland Islands and the Swedish-Speaking Population of Finland

Finnish islands at the entrance to the Gulf of Bothnia, the inhabitants of which are largely Swedish. When Finland became independent in 1917 the Åland Islands became a bone of contention between Finland and Sweden. The population of the Ålands identified themselves as Swedish and wished the Ålands to join Sweden. Sweden supported the idea, but the League of Nations decided, on June 27, 1921, that the Åland Islands had been and were to be an inseparable part of Finland. However, an exceptional autonomous status was granted to the Ålands by the Finnish parliament. The Ålands received a local parliament to determine local laws, which could not conflict with national ones. After the international decision, the Ålands were demilitarized, and males were excused from military service. In August 1922, an additional law included international guarantees to the Ålands' autonomy. The law on Åland autonomy has been revised three times (1951, 1991, and 1993), but only for practical and technical reasons.

The Åland question reflected a more serious issue concerning the two languages spoken in Finland. During Sweden's rule the Finns were forced to adopt Swedish as the official language of politics and administration. When, under Russian rule, Finnish became the official language of the grand duchy in the 1860s, a battle between the two languages began. To resolve the issue, both Finnish and Swedish were made official languages by law in 1920. But the Åland population identified as Swedish and maintained that they had therefore no duty to use or understand Finnish. This has continued until the present. Swedish is the only official language in the Ålands, and a Finn must live for five years on the islands to become a citizen there. While all this has been accepted in Finland without debate, Finns including the Swedish-speaking population on the mainland have occasionally been annoyed by the privileges enjoyed in the Åland Islands.

On the mainland, municipalities may adopt either Finnish or Swedish as the official language of local administration and instruction, or they may choose to be bilingual. In 1990 Finnish was the official language in 395 municipalities, Swedish in 24, and 41 municipalities were bilingual, with Finnish constituting the linguistic majority in 21, Swedish in 20. Everyone has the right to use Finnish or Swedish when dealing with the state and in the courts. In the universities, students can use either language. University education is given in Swedish in three cities—Turku, Helsinki, and Vaasa—and some universities in Helsinki have professorships allocated to Swedish speakers. Swedish literature and theater have achieved a prominent role in Finnish cultural life. The Swedish-speaking population has a central role in the political, and even more so in the economic, life of Finland.

The number of Swedish speakers, however, is decreasing. In 1950, 348,286 persons, 8.6 percent of the Finnish population, belonged to the Swedish minority; in 1970, the number was 303,406, or 6.6 percent; and in 1993, it was 9,000 fewer, or 5.9 percent. The Swedish People's Party (SFP) had twenty-one to twenty-six seats in the Eduskunta (parliament) between 1907 and 1917; in the 1970s the SFP held only ten. However, since 1945 the SFP has participated in all majority governments. The party had as many as four ministers in Mauno Koivisto's second government (1979–82), and has had two since then. The SFP in recent presidential elections has attempted to unite the nonsocialists, who were otherwise divided among contending parties. In the 1994 presidential elections, Elisabeth Rehn, a candidate from the Swedish-speaking minority, lost the general election to Martti Ahtisaari by just 240,000 votes.

BIBLIOGRAPHY
Barros, James. *The Åland Islands Question.* New Haven: Yale University Press, 1968.
Haikio, Martti. *A Brief History of Modern Finland.* Helsinki: University of Helsinki, Lahti Research and Training Centre, 1992.

Vilho Harle

Albania

The Republic of Albania (Republika E Shqipërisë) is bordered by the two remaining republics of Yugoslavia, Mon-

Albania. *Illustration courtesy of Bernard Cook.*

tenegro and the Kosovo area of Serbia, and by Macedonia and Greece. To the west lie the Adriatic and Ionian Seas. Albania is separated from southern Italy by the Strait of Otranto, which is 48 miles (77 km) wide. Albania covers 11,000 square miles (28,750 sq km). The capital, Tirana, has a population of almost half a million. Once malarial swamps, the coastal plain is now reclaimed and has come into full agricultural use since World War II. Some 77 percent of the country is mountainous, rising to over 8,862 feet (2,700 meters). Albania is rich in mineral resources, with thirty known types, the major ones being chromium (third-largest deposits in the world), copper, ferro-nickel, lignite, iron ore, natural gas, bitumen, coal, timber, and oil.

The 3.4 million inhabitants of Albania, 40 percent of whom are under the age of twenty-five, are approximately 91 percent Albanian, 7 percent Greek, and 2 percent Vlach, Macedonian, Serb, Rom, Bulgarian, and Montenegrin. A small Jewish community avoided the ravages of the Holocaust but virtually disappeared when three hundred Albanian Jews were airlifted to Israel in 1991. Since World War II Albania has had the highest population growth rate in Europe, about 2 percent per year until 1990; now, however, it is declining at 1.16 percent per year. Life expectancy at birth has increased from 38 in 1938 to 70.83 for males and 77.02 for females.

The Albanian language, a unique Indo-European language evolved from Thraco-Illyrian, is now spoken by the inhabitants of Albania and two million more Albanians in the adjacent regions of former Yugoslavia, including pockets of Albanian speakers living in Greece (Chams and Arvenites) and Italy (Arbëresh). Within Albania there are two dialects: Geg, spoken in the north, and Tosk, in the south. The present Latin alphabet was adopted in 1908. Greek is spoken by the Greek minority. Nearly a million others of Albanian descent live outside the Balkans, mostly in the United States (the first recorded Albanian immigrant arrived in the 1880s), several hundred thousand Arvenites live in Greece and Arbëresh in southern Italy, and others in communities in almost every European country, as well as in Argentina, Australia, Canada, Egypt, and Turkey.

The prewar literacy rate was below 10 percent. There was no national university until Tirana University opened in 1957; prior to World War II there were only 380 university graduates in Albania; by 1985 there were 744,000. There are now seven universities in Albania.

Albania's strategic position in Europe has long attracted the interest of other countries. Durrës, Albania's main port, brought travelers along the ancient Via Egnatia from Asia into contact with Rome and the later Venetian cities. More recently Serbia, Italy, and the USSR sought to gain this Adriatic port. Albania gained its independence following the First Balkan War of 1912. However, it was occupied during World War I and overrun by Fascist Italy in April 1939.

In support of the struggle to overcome the German forces that following the surrender of Italy, invaded and occupied Albania in September 1943, Britain supplied weapons to the Communist partisans, the National Liberation Front. The British saw the Communists as the force in Albania with the strongest motivation to fight the Germans effectively. The partisans gained control of southern Albania in January 1944 and central and northern Albania by July. On May 24–28, 1944, Albania's first National Liberation Congress, with about two hundred delegates, met in Përmet and proclaimed a new democratic Albania. Enver Hoxha became chairman of the executive committee and supreme commander of the Army of National Liberation.

In December 1944 the state took control of production and, under the Agrarian Reform Law of August 1945, ownership of land, including that of over two thousand religious institutions. All German- and Italian-owned assets, the National Bank, and 111 joint stock companies were nationalized. The same year, Kosovo, which Hitler in 1941 had joined to Italy's puppet, Albania, was returned to Yugoslavia. In the December 1945 elections for the People's Assembly, the only ballot choices were Democratic Front candidates. Meanwhile, the National Liberation Front carried out a program of political and social revolution. It took control of the police, the courts, and the economy and eliminated its political opponents—several hundred former politicians and civil servants—through a series of show trials conducted by judges without legal training. In 1946 Albania was declared a people's republic and its constitution was ratified. In November Albania broke diplomatic relations with the United States and in July 1947 refused to participate in the Marshall Plan. Albania's close links with Yugoslavia lasted only until the latter's rift with the USSR in 1948. The rift enabled Hoxha to rebuff Yugoslav economic and political pressure. Koci Xoxe, the pro-Yugoslav minister of interior, was purged and executed, and the Albanian Communist Party was renamed the Party of Labor of Albania (PLA).

With the devastation of the war and lack of scientifically and technologically trained personnel, dependence on the USSR became almost total. During the 1950s Albania was a member of the international communist movement, playing a full part in its assemblies and deliberations. Albania became a founding member of the Warsaw Pact in 1955, but relations with the USSR deteriorated over the latter's relaxed relationship with Yugoslavia after Stalin's death in 1953, and Albania formally withdrew from the pact in 1968.

Albania's First Five-Year Plan was proclaimed in 1951. Considerable increase in production in all fields was achieved by 1960; such overall increase was never again achieved as a result of the split with the Soviet Union in 1961 and its withdrawal of material and technological aid. Full collectivization was achieved in 1967. A new constitution introduced in 1978 allowed the monopolization of power by the leader of the PLA. Hoxha took increasing control of all decisions within the party and concentrated effort and expense on certain major economic projects: the iron and steel combine at Elbasan, hydroelectric works in the northern mountains, increasing kilowatt-hours from 3 million in 1938 to 900 million in 1970, and the electrification of villages program, declared completed in 1970. However, since 1988 Albania has become a net importer of energy.

Hoxha's increasing obsession with power led him to distrust his long-standing comrade in arms, Mehmet Shehu, who allegedly committed suicide in December 1981. It is suspected that he was assassinated. Hoxha used ruthless means of controlling Albania's population, punishing not only those committing such "crimes" as attempting to leave the country but also their families. Such political "criminals" were imprisoned or sent to work camps or into exile in remote areas of the country, sometimes for decades, and their children were deprived of any education beyond the primary level. The Helsinki Committee estimates that at least twenty six thousand people lived out such sentences. Another form of Hoxha's paranoia toward the outside world remains littered all over the country in the form of seven hundred thousand concrete bunkers whose function was to protect the country's defenders against attack by foreign powers.

On Hoxha's death in April 1985, Ramiz Alia, his chosen successor, assumed responsibility for Albania's administration. Alia slightly relaxed the tight isolationist dictatorial hold. He established diplomatic relations with 113 countries, including links with some Western states. Discussions were resumed with Britain, in secret, to resolve the Corfu Incident of four decades earlier. In August 1987 Alia officially ended the state of war with Greece, which had been in effect since World War II, though this was not officially reciprocated by Greece. In the same year, formal diplomatic relations were instituted with West Germany. Economic and cultural links were made with other Western European states and Turkey. In 1988 Albania participated in the six-member Balkan States' Con-

ference in Belgrade, hosting the organization the following year in Tirana. With this new access to the world beyond Albania's borders, especially with the ability to view foreign television stations, discontent grew within the country. Several demonstrations were brutally suppressed and many people were imprisoned for participating. Prior to U.N. Secretary-General Javier Pérez de Cuellar's visit in May 1990, extensive reforms were approved by the People's Assembly, including the reestablishment of the Ministry of Justice, which allowed defendants a right to their own lawyers, and the reduction in the number of capital offenses from thirty-four to eleven; the right to worship was permitted and passports could be obtained. On December 12, 1990, the Democratic Party (DP), the first Albanian opposition party permitted since World War II, was created. On December 21 the last of Stalin's statues was removed from Albania, and on December 31 a new draft constitution sanctioned a multiparty political system and extensive civil liberties. Formal agreement to restore diplomatic relations with the USSR was made. Further government restrictions were removed, permitting contact with foreigners and press freedom.

Student protests begun late in 1990 gathered momentum until February 1991, when the thirty-foot-high statue of Hoxha in Tirana's main square was toppled. At this time economist Fatos Nano was appointed chairman of the provisional Council of Ministers. The first mass exodus of about six thousand people, mostly young men who ultimately traveled to the Federal Republic of Germany, followed the occupation of certain foreign embassies. Before the first free elections planned to take place in February 1991, about twenty thousand fled the country to Italy and Greece. Many more left after the elections, taking residence in those countries both legally and illegally.

The 1991 elections, postponed until March, were won by the PLA with a two-thirds majority provided by support from the rural peasantry. Nano retained the prime ministership. These elections were widely believed to have been distorted by electoral malpractice. During protests in Shkodër over the vote tally, four people died. In April the country was renamed Republic of Albania and Ramiz Alia was elected to the new post of president of the republic and commander of the armed forces, which consisted of an army of 31,500, a navy of 2,000, an air force of 7,200, 10,000 frontier guards, and 30,000 *sigurimi* (secret police), later replaced by the National Information Service (SHIK). The new government restored diplomatic relations with the United States. Albania was granted observer status at the Conference on Security and Cooperation in Europe (CSCE) summit in Paris and full membership in June 1991, and diplomatic relations were established with the EC.

In May 1991 a miners' hunger strike drew tens of thousands of protesters to demonstrate in Tirana. A general strike continued into June, forcing the government of Nano to resign after fewer than two months in office. There was mass anger directed at government property and destruction of schools, party headquarters, agricultural cooperatives, and factories. Thousands of political prisoners were released, some greeted with heroes' welcomes. Pjeter Arbnori, free after nearly thirty years in prison, was made speaker of parliament. The last political exiles were freed by July 1991, though many had nowhere to go once freed.

By October there were demands for Alia's resignation, and in December the government collapsed, owing to the withdrawal of DP support. Shortly afterward widespread food riots resulted in thirty-eight deaths in Fushë Arrez. A draft law on public order was introduced in January 1992, and a new electoral law approved in February 1992, using both majority vote and proportional representation. Omonia, the party of the Greek minority, which had five deputies elected to parliament in the 1991 election, was outlawed in July of that year and effectively banned from participation in the 1992 general election, provoking extensive protest and exacerbating the deteriorating relations with Greece. Omonia was subsequently permitted to re-form as the Union of Human Rights Party, which won two seats. Eleven political parties participated in the election. The DP, Socialist, Social Democratic, Union of Human Rights, Republican, and Agrarian parties all ran complete lists.

As a result of the March 1992 election, in which 90 percent of the electorate participated, the DP came to power under the leadership of Sali Berisha, a cardiac surgeon from the Tropoje region of northern Albania who had been a PLA member for twelve years. One of Berisha's main aims was to introduce a market economy, and he was intolerant of opposition. In July both communist and fascist parties were outlawed. The following year, the government imprisoned the leaders of two opposition parties. Nano, of the former PLA now transformed into the Socialist Party, was jailed in July 1993 on charges of embezzlement. Idejet Beqiri, of the right-wing Party of National Unity, was charged with slander. A number of newspaper editors and reporters critical of the new government were also imprisoned; and the government took control of all TV broadcasting. By September, Alia, Nexhmijë Hoxha, Enver Hoxha's widow, and nineteen former Communist officials were arrested on various charges connected with abuse of power. They were later given jail sentences of up to twelve years each, though most sentences were later considerably reduced, and by 1997 they were freed.

Petrit Kalakula, expelled from the DP, and Abdil Baleta became leaders of the new Democratic Party of the Right and formed a coalition with the Republican Party, the monarchist Legaliteti, and the anti-communist nationalist Balli Kombetar. A further group of DP members, many of whom had been the party rounders, were expelled from that party in August 1992 for their criticism of Berisha. The following month they formed the Democratic Alliance, led by Neritan Ceka, Shahin Kadare, and others.

In December 1992 Albania joined the Organization of the Islamic Conference. Yet Albania was the first post-Communist country in Eastern Europe to apply for associate membership in NATO, which was granted in February 1994. Following this there were numerous Albanian-American joint maneuvers. Albania as a member of NATO's Partnership for Peace granted the United States military bases in the northern part of the country and allowed reconnaissance flights to Bosnia.

Conditions of membership in the Council of Europe demanded the drawing up of a new constitution. Berisha's draft constitution gave him more much authority in appointing ministers, judges, ambassadors, and other top officials. However, the constitutional referendum held on November 6, 1994, was rejected by 54 percent of those voting, thus producing the first majority vote of no confidence in Berisha's leadership. Berisha interpreted this as a statement condemning widespread corruption in the government, especially concerning arms sales and shipments to Bosnia. He then deposed nine of nineteen cabinet ministers.

From that time human rights abuses increased. In September 1995 the chief justice of the Court of Cassation, Zef Brozi, was unconstitutionally relieved from his duties by parliament following his preparation to hear the appeal of jailed Fatos Nano. There were also a number of recorded cases of police brutality and deaths in custody. Further electoral restrictions were imposed in the form of the "genocide law" of September 22, 1995, preventing any former high-ranking Communist official or secret police "collaborator" from standing for public office before the year 2001, thus disqualifying several key opposition candidates. State-controlled television reflected the ruling party's line, especially in the run-up to the 1996 election when opposition views were allowed only minimal exposure; there was also legal action against and even imprisonment of journalists expressing views critical of the government. Berisha's invitation to the White House following his handling of the Kosovo question in September 1995 was seen as U.S. endorsement of his policies.

Following the elections of May 1996, supposedly won overwhelmingly by the DP, there was international condemnation of its execution as having been rife with all kinds of irregularities. The Council of Europe suggested that the election results be annulled and new elections held within a period of eighteen months. The major opposition parties boycotted the new parliament. From this time Western support of Berisha's increasingly autocratic government declined. The economy was ravaged by fraudulent "pyramid" investment schemes seen to have been supported by the government, whose members were suspected of being beneficiaries of the schemes. Their collapse, causing considerable financial losses for up to three-quarters of the population, and Berisha's refusal to resign as president, led to widespread violence and anarchy in early 1997. The opening up of armories all over the country provided the population with an estimated one million Kalashnikovs, grenades, and other lethal weapons. Over 1,500 people were killed in the first six months of the year. International concern led to the demand for a general election as a precondition to the provision of foreign aid. International mediators assisted in setting up an interim coalition government of reconciliation headed by Bashkim Fino, a young Socialist. Italy, once again recipient of mass migrations of destitute refugees, headed a seven thousand-man Multinational Protection Force (MPF) of troops from Austria, Denmark, France, Greece, Romania, Spain, and Turkey to oversee preparations for and the election itself on June 29.

The Socialist Party won 100 of the 155 seats with Fatos Nano, only just released from four years of his twelve-year prison sentence under Berisha, as prime minister and Rexhep Mejdani, president. Their priority to end violence began taking effect despite the setback of the shooting of a DP member by an SP member inside the parliament building in September and continued attacks by members of the DP against non-DP political figures. Several armed gangs were arrested.

With the possible exception of present-day Bosnia, Albania is the only European country to have a Muslim majority, approximately 70 percent of the population. Shkodër, in northern Albania, is the country's center of Roman Catholicism, approximately 10 percent of the population, and home to the largest Catholic cathedral in the Balkans, now restored from being a sports hall during the era of official atheism. The constitution of 1951 severed all relations with the Vatican. This was the area of greatest religious persecution during the dictatorship of Hoxha, especially from 1967 to 1990 during the state ban on any form of public religious observance. From 1967, 2,169 churches, mosques, and monasteries were closed and at least a third of these completely destroyed. Almost 20 percent of the population was Orthodox Christians prior to World War II; when the state ban on religion was lifted, the proportion, prior to mass emigration to Greece, was thought to be about the same, with most Orthodox residing in the south of Albania.

Greece and Albania maintained a tense relationship until 1997, each demanding rights for its own minorities within the other country. Turkey, historically at loggerheads with Greece but with its own sizable Albanian minority, is a close ally of Albania. In July 1993 Albanian authorities expelled a Greek Orthodox priest: Greece responded by expelling thirty thousand Albanians from Greece. In April 1994 a Greek extremist group killed three Albanian soldiers inside Albania; ten days later five Omonia leaders were arrested. Their trial in September exhibited many violations of both Albanian and international law. All were imprisoned. Greece expelled a further seventy thousand Albanians, and, as chair of the European Union, was able to veto $43 million accorded to Albania. The dispute over the Greek minority in Albania was partially resolved, and the funds finally reached Albania. Before the visit of Greek Foreign Minister Carolis Papoulias to Tirana in March 1995, negotiations for the release of the imprisoned Omonia leaders were made; relations between Greece and Albania improved and the releases were completed. Under Nano's leadership there have been renewed negotiations concerning the countries' respective nationals, and substantial loans and investment by Greece as well as Italy and other countries, were promised to Albania.

Economically the poorest country in Europe, Albania lacks infrastructure. Its first standard-gauge railroads were built in 1947 and still cover only just over 720 kilometers. Before 1990 there were no private cars on the roads. Between 1991 and 1994 an estimated total of 150,000 used cars were imported from neighboring countries, but little improvement was made to the roads. Banking and tax laws are still in the making and the legal system is being developed.

On reversing its policy of economic self-sufficiency in 1991, Albania became a member of the World Bank, the International Monetary Fund (IMF) and the newly formed European Bank for Reconstruction and Development (EBRD). Remittances from Albanians abroad, $330 million in 1993, exceeded the foreign aid of that year, $300 million. These remittances represented 16 percent of Albania's GNP. However, Albania received the highest foreign aid per capita between 1991 and 1997 of all the former Communist East European countries. Albania's GDP growth of 11 percent in 1993 was the highest of any post-Communist Eastern European country; its growth in 1994 was 7.4 percent. Investment was attracted by the tourist industry with the incentive of a five-year, 50 percent profits tax exemption. Italian companies accounted for 53 percent of foreign capital and Greek for 20 percent in 1996. In that year Albania's first stock exchange was opened and inflation was apparently down to 19 percent annually and the state budget deficit was 9 percent of GDP. These statistics appear to be offset by the fact that they were contrasted to figures in 1991, when the Albanian economy was at its lowest ebb in decades. Furthermore the economy was artificially boosted by foreign aid and remittances from relatives abroad as well as by the growth of so-called investment companies.

In October 1996 Britain agreed to return the Albanian gold, taken by the Germans during World War II and stored in vaults of the Bank of England since 1947. However, $2 million of the $19 million was to be paid as compensation for the Corfu Incident, when two British warships hit mines off the Albanian coast in 1946, killing forty-four sailors.

Unemployment is variously estimated at between 40 and 60 percent of the working population. Benefits are minimal following the 1992 abolition of unemployment compensation of 80 percent of previous salary. The cost of living is increasing rapidly, while average incomes are around $40 per month (about $20 for pensioners). Besides emigration, there has been major migration to urban centers. Yet 65 percent of Albania's population still lives in rural areas, now recovering from local destruction following the fall of communism. Land has been unevenly distributed. It is estimated that 65 percent of agricultural land has been parceled according to the law, the remainder according to pre-1945 boundaries, though the ownership of many properties both rural and urban is still in dispute. Agricultural production has increased yearly since its nadir in 1992 and accounts for over half of GNP.

BIBLIOGRAPHY
Abrahams, Fred. *Human Rights in Post-Communist Albania.* New York: Human Rights Watch, 1996.
"Albania." *The Europa World Year Book 1997.* London: Europa Publications, 1997.
Hall, Derek. *Albania and the Albanians.* London: Pinter, 1994.
Hibbert, Sir Reginald. *Albania's National Liberation Struggle: The Bitter Victory.* London: Pinter, 1991.
Pettifer, James, and Miranda Vickers. *From Anarchy to a Balkan Identity.* London: Hurst; New York: New York University Press, 1997.
Young, Antonia. *Albania.* Santa Barbara, Calif./Oxford: CLIO Press (World Bibliographical Series no. 94 [revised]), 1997.
Zickel, Raymond, and Walter Iwaskiw, eds. *Albania: A Country Study.* Washington, D.C.: Area Handbook Series, 1994.

Antonia Young

Skanderbeg in Albanian Memory

In the final volume of his monumental *History of the Decline and Fall of the Roman Empire,* eighteenth-century English historian Edward Gibbon introduces his reader to one George Kastriota, called Skanderbeg, thus: "John Castriot, the father of Scanderbeg, was the hereditary prince a small district of Epirus, or Albania, between the mountains and the Adriatic Sea. Unable to contend with the sultan's power, Castriot submitted to the hard conditions of peace and tribute: he delivered his four sons as the pledges of his fidelity: and the Christian youths, after receiving the mark of circumcision, were instructed in the Mohammedan religion and trained in the arms and arts of Turkish policy."

Gibbon goes on to describe Skanderbeg's military prowess in the service of the Ottomans (the Turkish appellation "Skanderbeg," or "Iskander beg," translates into English as Lord Alexander), his eventual revolt against his Turkish overlords and abjuring of Islam, his return to Christianity and his ancestral lands centered on Krujë, and the manner in which he managed to successfully lead his Albanian followers for almost a quarter-century against the repeated onslaughts of the Ottoman armies despatched by successive sultans against his Albanian mountain stronghold.

Gibbon's two-hundred-year-old account of the fifteenth-century Albanian hero's exploits is, in essence, historically accurate and goes a long way to explain the supreme importance of Skanderbeg in Albanian historical memory, for it was under his leadership that Albanians first banded together to oppose the numerically overwhelmingly superior forces of an external enemy. As leader of the small Communist partisan movement in 1941 pitted against the might of the Axis war machine, Enver Hoxha could be forgiven if he saw certain parallels between his own position and that of his illustrious forbear, the Albanian David again battling against the invading foreign Goliath.

The figure of Skanderbeg provided the postwar Communist regime with possibly the most potent symbol of Albanian nationalism available, and questions of the medieval warrior's religion and "class" were conveniently forgotten by a ruling elite concerned with harnessing nationalist fervor in the service of the socialist Albanian state. The central square in the capital, Tirana, was renamed Skanderbeg Square and provided with a suitably imposing statue of the man on horseback. The hillside village of Krujë, focal point of the Skanderbeg epic, was accorded the accolade of "hero city" in the 1960s, while in the early 1980s a massive museum constructed in the style of a medieval castle, and incidentally designed by Hoxha's daughter Pranvera, was built on the supposed site of the hero's medieval fortress. A major academic conference was convened in Tirana in 1968 on the five-hundredth anniversary of Skanderbeg's death. His name was even used on the labeling of the superior Albanian cognac! Albanians, especially the postwar generation, could not but be aware of Skanderbeg and his exploits, for the Communist regime invested considerable time and effort in underlining that their current leader, Enver Hoxha, was in the Skanderbeg mold. Both had led the nation against a foreign enemy in wartime; both had been accorded power in recognition of their military prowess; both had "gone it alone" when the outside world left Albania and its people in the lurch. That this party-sponsored ideology was little more than myth is of less importance than the fact that the ruling elite understood the significance of such parallelism in their quest to mold a new Albanian national identity that regarded the contemporary Albanian socialist state and its leader as the natural culmination of the nation's history.

This conscious molding of the past to fit present politics can be discerned in the 1967 *George Kastriot-Scanderbeg and the Albanian-Turkish War of the 15th Century*, published by the State University of Tirana: "For 25 years on end, the Albanian popular masses, anonymous heroes, fought under the leadership of Skanderbeg to defend their soil, their freedom and independence, building the solid foundations of the edifice which the future generations were to complete: the union of the Albanian people in a national state." It was also apparent in the 1982 *Portrait of Albania,* published in Tirana, which said: "The common war under a single leadership, in the first place bound the popular masses of Albania to a common destiny. The continuation of this war for a long period strengthened the union of the Albanians of various regions and reinforced the feelings of national unity. As a war for independence, it became a precious heritage for the generations to come."

A similar form of language was continually used in official publications dating from the Hoxha years to describe the "epic struggle" of the partisan-led National Liberation War of 1941–45. The figure of Skanderbeg, the Albanian national hero, was unashamedly used by the regime as a component in the creation of the personality cult surrounding the party leader, in an attempt to invest the Albanian dictator with historical legitimacy in the popular perception. As subsequent events were to show, the propagandists were unsuccessful. According to Nathalie Clayer, since the collapse of communism Skanderbeg has been adopted as the particular champion of each of the three principal Albanian religious communities. For Orthodox and Roman Catholics Skanderbeg has become the champion of Christianity, while for Muslims he has become the champion of Albanianism.

Philip E. Wynn

Kanun of Lekë Dukagjini

The traditional law of north Albania, codified in the fifteenth century by Lekë Dukagjini, a contemporary of the national hero Skanderbeg, and firmly adhered to through subsequent centuries, was little affected by Ottoman rule. In spite of the Communist ban on all mention of the Kanun, its laws are now once again overtly implemented.

Dukagjini, a wealthy chieftain who visited the pope in 1466, standardized the already existing oral Illyrian laws. These applied equally to Catholics and Muslims. Albanian Franciscan Shtjefen Gjeçov published the first written form of the Kanun in 1913 by installments in an Albanian periodical, *Hylli i Drites*. Incomplete at the time of his 1926 murder, his work was continued by monks and first published in toto in 1933. In 1941 an Italian version appeared. In 1989 a dual-language (Albanian-English) edition was published, followed by an Albanian paperback edition in 1993.

The 1,262 articles of the code cover all aspects of mountain life: regulation of economic and family organization, hospitality, brotherhood, clan, boundaries, work, marriage, land, livestock, and the like. They also clarify the manner and rights of retaliatory killing—the *gjakmarre* (blood feud)—to restore honor to the offended when the laws are disobeyed. *Besa* (honor), the cornerstone of personal and social conduct, is of prime importance throughout the code.

Margaret Hasluck asserted that "the self-government of the Albanian mountaineers went far towards being true democracy in the Anglo-American sense. . . . In its primitive way it was really government of the People, by the People, for the People . . . the legal system worked well on the whole, was often speedier and always cheaper than any European counterpart, and left few crimes unsolved."

Parts of the Kanun have been considered an appropriate basis for Albania's new legal code.

BIBLIOGRAPHY
Gjeçov, Shtjefen. *Kanuni i Lekë Dukagjinit: The Code of Leke Dukagjini.* Tr. and intro. Leonard Fox. New York: Gjonlekaj, 1989.
———. *Kanuni i Lekë Dukagjinit.* Tirana: Albniform, 1993.
Hasluck, Margaret. *The Unwritten Law in Albania.* Cambridge: Cambridge University Press, 1954.
Kadare, Ismail. *Broken April.* London: Harper-Collins, 1991.

Antonia Young

Foreign Policy under Hoxha

The foreign policy of Albania under Enver Hoxha was characterized by a xenophobic nationalism. Four years of guerrilla fighting against the occupying Axis powers during World War II and the effective destruction of any concerted resistance to the Communist partisans had delivered Albania to the Communists by January 1945. Stalin's Red Army had not set foot in the country, but the influence of Tito's Yugoslavia on its tiny southern neighbor was considerable. During the 1945–48 period when Koci Xoxe, minister of the interior and organizational secretary of the Albanian Communist Party, seemingly eclipsed Hoxha, Albania was politically and economically a Yugoslav colony. Diplomatic relations with the United States and Britain were nonexistent, since these two nations were considered the most dangerous "enemies of socialism." With civil war raging in neighboring Greece along Cold War lines, Albanian foreign policy was confined to the nations of the "fraternal socialist" bloc.

The Cominform resolution expelling Tito's Yugoslavia from the international Communist movement was first made public in Czechoslovakia on June 28, 1948. Hoxha lost no time in violently condemning Tito. Within weeks all ties between Albania and Yugoslavia were severed. A Soviet military delegation headed by Colonel General G. I. Mihonovitch attended Albanian Army Day on July 9, and the number of Soviet advisers in Albania rose rapidly, replacing the expelled Yugoslavs. By year's end Albania was firmly in the Soviet fold. That the Tito-Stalin break permitted Hoxha to liquidate the ambitious Xoxe, sentenced to be shot for "Titoism" on June 8, 1949, indicates the inextricable link between "policy" and personal survival tactics on Hoxha's part.

Hoxha's attitude to the West in 1949 is summarized in his memoir *With Stalin.* According to Hoxha's "official" version of his March-April conversations held with the Soviet leader in Moscow, the Albanian leader denounced the United States for making diplomatic relations conditional on Albania's acceptance of the agree-ments made between the United States and the "anti-popular government" of King Zog, Albania's interwar ruler. He denounced the United Kingdom for demanding naval bases on the Albanian coast as a precondition for diplomatic relations.

Hoxha's assessment of Anglo-American hostility was accurate. The Anglo-American stance was summarized in a Department of State memorandum of conversation with British Foreign Secretary Ernest Bevin dated September 14, 1949. Bevin admitted that "the British had followed a policy of unrelenting hostility to the Hoxha government." When Bevin asked "whether we would basically agree that we try to bring down the Hoxha government when the occasion arises?" the U.S. response was affirmative.

Hoxha and his number two, Mehmet Shehu, dutifully toed the Kremlin line in foreign policy until Premier Nikita Khrushchev's rapprochement with Tito in 1955, the latter reportedly demanding the removal of Hoxha, Bulgaria's Chervenkov, and Hungary's Rákosi as the price for realignment with Moscow. Khrushchev's repudiation of Stalin at the Twentieth Congress of the Communist Party of the Soviet Union in 1956 signaled to Hoxha that he was in mortal danger should the Soviets succeed in enticing members of the Albanian Party to launch a coup against him.

As in 1948, dissension within the socialist bloc came to Hoxha's aid. The Hungarian Revolution of October 1956 set alarm bells ringing in Peking, where Tito's unorthodox brand of communism was blamed for the Budapest events. Notwithstanding the savage Soviet repression of the Hungarian uprising in November 1956, Mao Tse-tung grew increasingly concerned over the Soviet-Yugoslav rapprochement and eventually decided to challenge Moscow's leadership of the bloc. At first the Chinese challenge was covert, but by 1960 it had become public.

Hoxha had found an unlikely savior in the leader of the world's most populous nation. This international realignment helped to save the Albanian dictator and provided the Chinese with a strategic and ideological toehold in Europe. During the seventeen years of Sino-Albanian "fraternal alliance," some $5 billion in Chinese aid at 1981 prices flowed into Hoxha's Balkan outpost, and a visitor to the country in the early 1970s would have seen countless Chinese "advisers" assisting with such grand projects as the extension of the railroad line from Elbasan to the nickel mines of Prrenjas. Thus, for a time, Hoxha's foreign policy succeeded in gaining investment from a friendly power. But that power was geographically distant enough to pose little threat of undermining Albanian freedom of action either internally or externally, yet powerful enough to dissuade the Kremlin from entertaining any ideas of launching an invasion of its ideological opponent.

President Nixon's visit to Peking in February 1972 and the subsequent thawing of Sino-American relations was mirrored by a cooling in relations between Tirana and Peking, culminating in the *Zeri i Popullit* ideological diatribe of July 8, 1977, the penultimate paragraph of which read: "The present-day anti-Leninist theories of the 'three worlds,' 'nonalignment,' and so on, are also aimed at undermining the revolution, extinguishing the struggle against imperialism, especially against U.S. imperialism, splitting the Marxist-Leninist movement, the unity of the proletariat advocated by Marx and Lenin, creating all kinds of groupings of anti-Marxist elements to fight the true Marxist-Leninist parties which stand loyal to Marxism-Leninism, the revolution." This outburst marked the decisive parting of the ways between Tirana and Peking.

Though Albanian propaganda trumpeted the nation's diplomatic relations with ninety-five states in 1981, foreign policy initiative played a secondary role to doctrinal purity in Hoxha's final years. Albania took no part in the European Helsinki process, the "state of war" with Greece officially ended only two years after Hoxha's death, and there were no diplomatic ties with the United States, the USSR, or the United Kingdom.

Ideological dogmatism, extreme nationalism, and an overwhelming concern for personal survival were the three constants in Hoxha's foreign policy during the four decades of his control over Albania's contacts with the outside world.

Philip E. Wynn

SEE ALSO Corfu Channel Incident

Secret Police (Sigurimi)

From the Albanian, *sigurim* (security, insurance), the Sigurimi was the name of the Albanian secret police established by the postwar Communist regime. The Sigurimi, organized and overseen by the Ministry of the Interior, was charged with eliminating all opposition to the ruling party and government. Individual Sigurimi departments dealt with prisons and labor camps, counterintelligence, political affairs, and censorship. In addition to uniformed men, Sigurimi agents and informers were in position throughout the country from the 1950s, giving rise to Western calculations that eventually more than a quarter of the population was in some way associated with Sigurimi internal surveillance.

Mehmet Shehu, during his tenure at the Ministry of the Interior between 1948 and 1954, was the principal architect of the Albanian secret police structures. Even after his departure to become premier, he always maintained a close interest in the organization through his brother-in-law, Kadri Hasbiu, interior minister from 1954 to 1978, and his nephew, Feçor Shehu, interior minister from 1978 to 1982.

Although forced labor had been introduced in Albania in the summer of 1947, in 1952 a new version of the Albanian penal code made large-scale forced labor central to government plans for the "building of socialism." Under fulfillment of work quotas, absenteeism and production of low-quality goods rendered the individual liable to a term of up to four years in Sigurimi-run labor camps, while regime opponents were often incarcerated for decades in dreadful conditions. It is alleged that the Sigurimi even recruited agents among camp and prison populations, mainly from among real criminals, to spy on fellow prisoners and report any disaffection. Only with the collapse of communism in Albania did the true extent of the Sigurimi-controlled internal GULAG become widely known outside the country through the testimony of survivors.

The regiments of frontier guards whose job was to prevent Albanians from escaping from their "socialist" homeland rather than to prevent foreign incursion, even though organized along military lines, possessed closer ties with the Sigurimi than with the regular army. Both groups were controlled by the Ministry of the Interior with Sigurimi personnel acting as policy coordinators in matters of internal security with these units as well as with the civilian people's police and auxiliary police forces. Members of the Sigurimi also patrolled the embassy area in Tirana, from which the population at large was barred.

The tentacles of the Sigurimi reached into every aspect of the individual's life. Following Stalin's practice, children were encouraged by their schoolteachers to spy on their parents. There was a widespread belief, as yet unproved, that a Sigurimi biography existed of every Albanian, one copy being at the central Sigurimi archives in Tirana and two further copies being stored in underground vaults in Berat and Korçë. Such a widely held belief among the population is evidence of the fear and dread with which the Sigurimi was regarded. It is claimed that Sigurimi agents were often individuals with, in Communist terms, bad biographies, parents who had opposed the regime or relatives who had served the pre-Communist governments. In a society in which the state was the sole employer of many individuals, Sigurimi employment would have been the only alternative to destitution.

With the establishment of a new security agency, SHIK, in 1992 by President Sali Berisha, the Sigurimi officially ceased to exist. Many observers at the time, however, were of the opinion that the old secret police structures were merely repopulated with Berisha supporters, many from his home region of Tropoja in the far north. While in power Berisha was further accused of using material from old Sigurimi files to blacken the reputations of political opponents. According to Ismail Kadare, inconvenient "compromising clues" were also expunged. Should this be the case, a complete history of the Sigurimi will never be written. What is certain is that the legacy of organized terror perpetrated by the Sigurimi over almost half a century will continue to haunt Albanian society well into the new millennium.

BIBLIOGRAPHY

Kadare, Ismail. *Albanian Spring: The Anatomy of Tyranny.* London: Saqi Books, 1995.

Philip E. Wynn

Religion

When Enver Hoxha's avowedly atheistic Communist partisans seized power in Albania in the aftermath of World War II, the new rulers inherited a complex religious legacy. From the time of the Roman Empire's administrative division, Albanians had inhabited the borderland where Western Roman Catholic and Eastern Orthodox Christian religious traditions overlapped. With the Ottoman conquest of the Albanian lands in the fifteenth century, a third religious force, Islam, vied for Albanians' allegiance. During the centuries of Ottoman Turkish control, which ended only in 1912, Islam gained at least the nominal adherence of approximately 70 percent of the Albanian population, often for reasons more to do with social and economic advancement than with matters of spirituality or faith. This multiplicity of religious traditions constituted a divisive element in the welding together of the Albanian nation in the nineteenth century, and from the outset, Hoxha's post-1945 regime was implacably hostile to all religious sects and their priesthoods, seeing in them a competitor for the hearts and minds of the people and a hindrance to the establishment of a united, secular nation-state where Communists were to hold a monopoly of power.

The heartland of the Roman Catholic influence in the Albanian lands lay in the Geg north, with the city of Shkodër at its center. Albanian communism was largely a creation of southern Tosks, and the more traditionalist clan-based society of the northern mountains was always regarded with suspicion by the new elite in Tirana. The

north has provided the leadership of the non-Communist anti-Fascist groupings, and even before the end of World War II, a civil war had erupted between these groupings and the partisans. To buttress its dominance of the north, the postwar Albanian regime arrested, imprisoned, tortured, and shot hundreds of Catholic priests. The Roman Catholic Church was vilified in the Communist-controlled media as a haven of reaction and anti-Albanian machinations, while Catholic priests were demonized as foreign agents, spies, and counterrevolutionaries. The scale of persecution of Catholics during 1945–90 was fully revealed only following the collapse of communism and the release of the few surviving priests from incarceration.

The banning of organized religion by Hoxha's government as part of the "cultural revolution" of 1967 and the proclamation of Albania as "the world's first atheist state" was the culmination of two decades of antireligious crusading that particularly singled out the Catholic Church and its adherents. Catholic orders were obliterated by a state system that brooked no opposition, yet belief systems are notoriously difficult to eradicate overnight. The survival of Catholicism privately in the family circle is evidenced by the reemergence of the rites associated with the church following Ramiz Alia's decree permitting public religious observance in 1990.

In an interview published in 1996, Rrok Mirdita, archbishop of Tirana and Durrës, claimed that the Catholic Church in Albania represented some 13 percent of believers of all faiths in the country.

It is often asserted that 70 percent of Albania's population is Muslim or of Muslim religious background. This simple formula does not take account of the division between Sunni Muslims, some 55 percent of Islamic believers, and the followers of Bektashism and other Sufic orders, some 15 percent of the Islamic community. This important subdivision into followers of orthodox Sunni Islam and the almost pantheistic dervish fraternities is a peculiarly Albanian phenomenon and has had a profound influence on the historical development of Albanian Islam since the Ottoman conquest. Bektashism in particular tends toward a liberal interpretation of traditional Islamic canons; for example, there is no interdict on alcohol consumption, and it shows tolerance toward and respect for alternative religious beliefs. Indeed, Christians and Muslims in the Albanian lands have traditionally shared the same holy places, for example, Mt. Tomor, near the central Albanian city of Berat; any inter-Albanian conflicts over the centuries have derived more from clan-based rivalries than from differences in religious affinities.

Many nineteenth-century Albanian nationalist writers and publicists, including the Frashëri brothers Abdul, Naim, and Sami, were Bektashi by religion, but to such men to be Albanian was of greater importance than their religious creed. Following Kemal Atatürk's dissolution of the dervish orders in Turkey in the 1920s, Albania became the world center of Bektashism, and many a Bektashi "baba" swelled the ranks of the partisan forces during World War II.

The postwar Hoxha regime did not immediately pursue the Muslim priesthood with the same ferocity that it attacked the northern Catholics, but the antireligious zeal of the extremist Hoxha/Shehu duumvirate was, in 1967, finally directed against the mosque and the tekke, and Islamic observance was banned throughout the country. The Muslim priesthood was decimated by execution and imprisonment, mosques and tekkes were destroyed or put to purely secular use such as warehouses or sports centers.

Following almost half a century of state-inspired hostility, it is unsurprising that when freedom of religious expression was restored in 1990, only a small proportion of the population, predominantly from the older generation, had any real understanding of Islamic tenets and ritual. The opening up of the country in the 1990s witnessed an upsurge in mosque building in all major centers and many villages, financed in the main by Middle Eastern Islamic countries. By the mid-1990s ten Islamic theological schools had been opened to create a new generation of Muslim clerics, again financed by states of the Muslim world. When in power in the 1990s, President Sali Berisha gained membership in the Organization of the Islamic Conference for his nation, thereby giving official recognition to the traditional majority role of Muslims in Albanian society.

The depth of the Islamic revival in Albania is impossible to gauge. In a country where the average age is about twenty-five, it is unlikely that the new generation will show much religious fervor because of the history of state-sponsored antireligious indoctrination. It may well be that Albanian youth will share with the youth of the West little regard for matters of religious faith, and secularism will triumph among the descendants of Albania's Muslim community.

The Orthodox Church has a long tradition in the Albanian lands dating back to the time when much of southern Albania formed part of the Byzantine Empire. The Byzantine Orthodox churches preserved in the medieval city of Berat testify to this centuries-long association. The Onufri Museum in the same city contains icons and other religious artifacts that reveal the considerable influence of Byzantine-Orthodox canons on the evolution of at least a part of the Albanian artistic and cultural heritage.

In 1945 four hundred Orthodox priests were estimated to be ministering in the country, but it is claimed that only eleven of these survived to see the collapse of the Communist regime. Not a single Orthodox monk survived communism, and thus no resident of Albania met the canonic rules of the church in relation to holding high ecclesiastical office. During the Communist years some 1,600 Orthodox churches and monasteries were destroyed or given over to other purposes approved by the state. Despite this wholesale destruction of the Orthodox material heritage, it is generally assumed that some 20 percent of the Albanian population judge themselves to be followers of the Orthodox cultural and historical tradition, even if they do not claim membership in the Orthodox religious community. Geographically the Orthodox heartland is in the south, centered on such cities as Korcë and Gjirokastër, close to the border with Greece where the Greek ethnic minority resident in Albania is concentrated.

All the religious communities traditionally found in Albania, having witnessed the same persecution under communism, have, since 1990, experienced similar problems in their attempts to reconstitute themselves: a dearth of trained functionaries, confiscation of land and buildings that traditionally sustained those communities, and relative indifference on the part of the younger generation to embrace organized religion. A further problem peculiar to the Orthodox Church is that some Albanian nationalists have accused it of acting as fifth column for Greek irredentism, and in the post-Communist decade relations have often been severely strained between Albania and its southern neighbor as a result of Greek appointments to the hierarchy of the Albanian Orthodox Church. Religion has always played a divisive role in Albanian history, and although Albania has been a traditionally tolerant society in matters spiritual, the legacy of competing religious sects will long be felt.

Philip E. Wynn

Official Atheism

In 1967 the regime of Enver Hoxha proclaimed Albania, where 73 percent of the population was Muslim, 17 percent Orthodox Christian, and 10 percent Roman Catholic, "the first atheist state in the world."

In February 1967, as part of a wider government campaign of social upheaval inspired by China's "Cultural Revolution," Hoxha urged the nation's youth to close the mosques and churches. In April the property of all religious organizations was nationalized without compensation. In September all 2,169 religious buildings were closed, and on November 13, Decree 4337 deprived all religious communities of their legal status and forbade the clergy from exercising their functions.

A hurricane of persecution followed. Mosques and churches were destroyed or turned into warehouses or meeting halls. Wearing beards was forbidden, and Orthodox priests had their beards publicly shaved off. Muslim or Christian forenames were forbidden and parents had to choose the names of their newborn from an ideologically acceptable list. Muslim and Christian clergy who refused to renounce their ministries and take up other employment were charged with "agitation and propaganda hostile to the state" and imprisoned. Roman Catholic priest Shtjefen Kurti was executed in February 1972 for secretly baptizing a child; Jesuit priest Ndoc Luli was executed in the early 1980s for the same "crime."

The previous tolerance among religious communities had grown out of the need for national unity during four centuries of Ottoman rule. The Bektashi Muslim Sufi sect, which embraces aspects of Christianity, was centered in Albania. In the north of the country Muslim men often had Christian wives. However, Catholicism in the north offered the only serious intellectual and organizational challenge to the Hoxha regime. In 1953 Hoxha cited with exasperation a "candidate for party membership in Shkodra who crossed himself whenever he heard the church bell ring . . . and who preferred to be expelled from the party than part from the cross."

While the 1946 constitution guaranteed freedom of worship, education was secularized, church lands confiscated, and all spoken and written utterances subject to censorship. Having executed certain religious leaders for alleged collaboration during the war, the regime gradually restricted the rights of Muslims and replaced troublesome Orthodox bishops with more pliable individuals. Although claiming that religion in 1967 had been outlawed by the "will of the people," the official press regularly denounced the continuation of religious customs and practices: Muslims still avoided eating pork, factory canteens were largely empty during Ramadan, secret baptisms continued, and grandmothers retold the gospel in the guise of bedtime stories.

In February 1991, with the regime crumbling, the right to worship was restored and the surviving clergy were freed. In March Mother Teresa, an Albanian from Macedonia, opened a convent in Tirana, an event described as "God's Sweet Revenge."

BIBLIOGRAPHY

Hoxha, Enver. *Selected Works.* Vol. 2. Tirana: Nentori, 1982.

Logoreci, Anton, ed. *The Albanians: Europe's Forgotten Survivors.* London: Gollancz, 1977.

Kirk West

Albert II (1934–)

King of the Belgians from 1993, upon the death of his older brother, Baudouin. Born June 6, 1934, in Brussels, Albert Félix Humbert Théodore Christian Eugène Marie, Prince of Belgium and Prince of Liège, was the second son of Leopold III and Astrid of Sweden. His mother was killed in a car accident when he was four, the first of many tragic events that were to affect his life. He was educated at the Royal Castle of Ciergnon and at the Château de Stuyvenberg, but his education was interrupted in June 1944 when the Belgian royal family was deported to Germany and detained first at Hirschstein and later in Strobl, Austria. When the royal family was liberated by the Seventh United States Army in May 1945, Albert continued his education in Geneva and completed his studies in Brussels. Like his brother, he was deeply distressed by the bitter feelings many Belgians felt toward King Leopold for surrendering to the Germans and for remarrying a commoner whose family was accused of being Nazi German sympathizers. A referendum brought Leopold III and his family back to Brussels on July 22, 1950, but the country was quickly torn by civil unrest. Leopold agreed to transfer his royal powers to Baudouin and to the latter's accession on his twenty-first birthday. Albert and Baudouin always maintained warm relations with their stepmother.

Albert followed royal tradition and entered the Belgian military in 1953. He served with the Belgian naval forces in the Mediterranean and in the Middle East and participated in NATO maneuvers aboard a mine sweeper. As heir to the throne and as regulated by the Belgian constitution, the prince was a member of the Belgian Senate. He was also president of the Belgian Red Cross and a member of the International Olympic and Interfederal Committee. During his brother's reign Albert supported environmental issues and efforts to protect Belgium's architectural and historical heritage; he maintained an active interest in urban issues and housing, and presided over the Belgian Committee of the European Year of Urban Renewal (1981). As honorary chairman of the Belgian Office of Foreign Trade, a position he held from 1962 to his accession to the throne, Albert developed expertise on transportation issues, especially shipping, and led over ninety top-level economic missions to five continents. In 1984 the Prince Albert Fund was created to train foreign trade specialists. This was a scholarship established by the King Baudouin Foundation and the Federation of Belgian Enterprises to honor Prince Albert's success in attracting foreign investors to Belgium; the fund allows young Belgian graduates or executives to intern in subsidiaries of Belgian companies outside Western Europe.

Albert married Donna Paola Ruffo di Calabria on July 2, 1959; they have three children. He became heir apparent to his brother when the latter's marriage proved childless. Baudouin died suddenly on July 31, 1993, while on vacation in Motril, Spain, only weeks after a constitutional revision turned the nation into a federal state of Dutch-speaking Flanders, Francophone Wallonia, and bilingual Brussels. Albert II took the constitutional oath on August 9, 1993, becoming the sixth king of the Belgians.

Albert II is a hereditary constitutional monarch. The king rules without governing, although his role is of vital importance. According to the constitution, the person of the king has immunity; his ministers are liable for him. Not a single deed by the king can have any consequence without being countersigned by a minister. But the king is the guardian of the country's unity and independence.

BIBLIOGRAPHY

Aronson, Theo. *Defiant Dynasty: The Coburgs of Belgium.* Indianapolis: Bobbs-Merrill, 1968.

Boulay, Laure, and Francoise Jaudel. *There are Still Kings.* New York: Clarkson N. Potter, 1981.

Martin J. Manning

SEE ALSO Baudouin; Leopold III

Alderdice, John (1955–)

Leader of the Alliance Party in Northern Ireland. John Alderdice (Lord Alderdice of Knock) was born in Ballymena in 1955. A consultant psychiatrist, he also turned to politics by the late 1970s. In 1987 he defeated Seamus Close to become the new leader of the Alliance Party. Two years later he unsuccessfully stood in the elections to the European Parliament. He has stood in several general elections but has never been elected as an MP. In August 1996 he was given a peerage, which finally gave him his seat in Westminster. Throughout his political career he has argued that only with compromise can a way forward be found that is acceptable to a majority in both the Catholic and Protestant communities. He was also one of the first nonnationalist politicians to agree to speak directly to members of Sinn Fein after the Irish Republican Army (IRA) called its cease-fire in 1994. In Britain he has established strong links with the Liberal Democratic Party, and in Ireland he has close ties with the Progressive Democrats.

Ricki Schoen

Algerian War

Decolonization struggle from November 1954 to July 1962 over the North African territory, which had been directly incorporated into the French state and constituted the chief French overseas settlement. Eight years of French efforts to repress the Algerian fight for independence ended in the French military victory and political surrender to the Armée de Libération Nationale (ALN), with the proclamation on July 1, 1962, of the Democratic and Popular Republic of Algeria. Governance of the new state fell to the leadership of the military generals of the Front de Libération Nationale (FLN), who continue to hold it.

In reconstructing France and its relations with its empire in 1945, the French did not prepare their overseas possessions for the transfer of power, much less for peaceful withdrawal of the French presence. Nationalists in Algeria nonetheless demanded emancipation from France in June 1945, well aware that their claim had merit within the logic of postwar decolonization. Their aspiration to statehood fit well within the pattern of nation-state formation inspired by the Europeans themselves. The United Nations Charter in 1945 promulgated this process for colonized populations, endorsing the principle that "all peoples shall have the right of self-determination."

From 1952 the Algerian nationalist cause gained support abroad from Egyptian leader Gamal Abdel Nasser, his Arab colleagues, and other newly independent nations. Noting France's defeat at Dien Bien Phu by the Viet Minh and (attacks to its sovereignty in next-door Tunisia and Morocco), the Algerian rebels ignited their own national insurrection in November 1954.

Eight years of fighting in Algeria chronicled a remarkable change in French popular attitudes toward the French-Algerian relationship. When the rebellion broke out, the vast majority of metropolitan French citizens virtually ignored the conflict, content to relegate it to the political and military experts. Most believed that France was obligated to protect the civilian population, and they backed the limited measures against the rebels, carried out by professional troops. Alongside their sentimental attachment to the remnants of France's colonial empire, many French shared their leaders' sense that France's economic partnership with Algeria was vital to the renewal of the mother country after World War II. The desire for economic recovery and the transition to modernization consumed their attention. Yet in the early phase, such goals did not undermine support for *Algérie française* (a French Algeria).

The experience of Indochina nevertheless left the French public adamantly opposed to any future entanglement in colonial warfare. The electorate evidenced this in January 1956, when a majority chose candidates who favored negotiations over force to resolve Algeria. Astonishment marked popular reactions when, two months later, the new Socialist-led government plunged France into full-scale war and imposed a civilian draft. Consequent to this shift in policy, the public grew more concerned about the conflict and impatient for a solution.

The first six months of 1956 marked an escalation in the war: terrorism intensified, the geography of the rebellion enlarged, rural engagement in the revolt deepened, and the rebel cause steadily gained support from the masses. At home, France at war entered into a state of slow deterioration in the economy, at the Treasury, and in domestic politics. By the summer some began to reconsider the importance of Algeria as three months of intensified operations had not reversed the rebels' advantage over the French army. The choice between guns or butter, not yet rivals, made inroads into popular thinking, for many understood that the drain of labor for the draft, inflation, and the imbalances in national finance undermined economic recovery. The war did not yet appear in absolute opposition to recovery at home, but some began to blame their setbacks on Algeria. Community and business leaders engaged in regional development began to question the war policy. Nevertheless, no French constituency in July 1956 backed Algeria's right to independence. To do so at that phase of the war would have been regarded as unpatriotic and defeatist. For the time being opposition to the war was not shrill. But this was not a popular war and support steadily declined.

This explains why the French leadership viewed opportunistically Nasser's nationalization of the Suez Canal in July 1956. Evaluating his "act of international brigandage" in terms of its correlation with Algeria, the French devised a strategy to destroy Nasser. Their primary motive was to cut off the Egyptian lifeline to the FLN, thereby gaining a quick victory in Algeria. The ensuing propaganda campaign that cast Nasser as the Arab Hitler rallied the public, and the Suez policy briefly buoyed popular confidence in the leadership. But it created false expectations for a quick end to the war, and the French failure at Suez brought bitter disappointment. The letdown diminished popular resolve to fight for Algeria.

The material reasons for popular discouragement over the war also grew exponentially after Suez. The Arab oil embargo was at the origin of the turmoil that followed, economic at first, political thereafter. The hardships borne of the fuel crisis served as a daily reminder of French reversals, and the high-cost oil replacements were inextricably linked to the slowdown in growth and a sharp rise in inflation. The consequences of Suez led to a breach between the people and their leaders. Some even suspected that France might be on the brink of financial ruin. In this light, the popular idea began to form that ending the war in Algeria was the only way to recover.

Over the final months of the Fourth Republic the systematic economic crises and spectacles of political instability that bedeviled various cabinets continued to torpedo war morale. The virtual absence of antiwar demonstrations did not represent a sign of popular satisfaction, because protests were legally banned as was media criticism of the war policy. Neither were political loyalties significant in shaping opinion, for the public no longer felt certain about party positions as the war fractured alliances within and between political parties. As to the issue of torture, despite individuals being disturbed over the violation of human rights and the discrediting of French values, there was no mass repudiation of French army conduct. Various criteria were at work in determining popular attitudes, but the fundamental preoccupation was economic, a factor that rarely stood in isolation to others. At the same time that enthusiasm for *Algérie française* diminished, concerns about regional revival intensified and ambitious locals grew frustrated with the distraction of the war as they sought state cooperation to develop their economies. They denounced the fight for Algeria as a burden antagonistic to renewal and, more generally, ordinary citizens felt considerable anxiety over the economic-military-political disorder. By early 1958 the sense of impending catastrophe enlarged and deepened.

Paradoxically, the fight for Algeria lost backing just when the French had militarily gained the upper hand. In Algeria, the character of the war changed to that of an urban-centered conflict, in Algiers in particular. During the Battle of Algiers the FLN attracted more international media attention to the liberation cause. After twelve months of a perpetual cycle of killing, General Jacques Massu and his paratroopers emerged victorious, having cut through the ALN network of terrorism. But their methods in Operation Casbah—sweeping operations throughout the Muslim quarters and systematic interrogation by torture—gained worldwide attention; domestic and world opinion denounced the French action. The criticism raised the question of the legitimacy of the defense of French sovereignty and held out the promise of a political victory for the FLN.

In the field the war also turned in favor of the French. Finally, strategies better adapted to guerrilla war enabled the army to recapture much of the territory from the rebels. Two electrified barriers sealed off the borders between Algeria and Morocco and Tunisia, cutting off the enemy's lifeline of reinforcements and weapons. Search-and-destroy operations combed the villages locating many of the rebels and their protectors. The army gained physical control over the masses through a variety of methods that included systematic identity checks, summary execution of suspects, interrogation by torture, and displacing whole villages into detention camps. Together they severely reduced the sources of ALN revitalization. But the tactics poisoned the Muslims and Berbers' psychological attachment to France.

By May 1958 four years of French efforts to repress the Algerian nationalists' struggle for independence precipitated the collapse of the Fourth Republic, divided the country, depressed its morale, and imposed financial constraints that brought the nation's decade-long economic expansion to a halt. With the military coup on May 13 in Algiers, France summoned Charles de Gaulle back to power to solve the Algerian burden, but, almost everywhere, the will to fight for French Algeria had lost its strength.

The return of de Gaulle led to a changing course in Algeria that reflected the desire of the majority. Popular support made possible his disengagement of France from the war as he drew on it to finesse the military command, the intransigeant *Pieds-Noirs* (long-term French settlers in Algeria), and the last few enemies of the republic. The general returned intent on revolutionizing France, a task that left no energy and resources to continue the colonial effort.

The theme of French modernization and renewal cloaked in patriotic colors formed the heart of Gaullist domestic diplomacy. De Gaulle took this message in person to his fellow citizens, explaining that only if France built a competitive economy, technologically prepared military, and independent foreign policy could it redeem its place among world leaders. The time had come to end the imperial era, to set France on a new course.

To lead France and to solve Algeria, de Gaulle obtained durable power through the constitution of the Fifth Republic. Had this authority been in place sooner, a costly war in Algeria might have been averted. Two reasons largely explain popular cooperation with de Gaulle as he worked to end the conflict. First, the economic and political changes the Gaullist republic delivered restored confidence in both the personal and the public realms. Second, de Gaulle's domestic diplomacy fostered a relationship between him and the people that rendered the French activists in Algeria impotent against his authority.

The task of ending the war proved disappointingly slow and various obstacles constrained and even determined de Gaulle's choices. The challenges tested every aspect of his political acumen, courage, determination, and relations with the French, but de Gaulle never lost their confidence with regard to Algeria. In the ensuing moments of crisis to his authority during the week of the barricades in January 1960 and during the renegade colonels' insurrection in April 1961, the masses mobilized in support of de Gaulle and the republic. Above all, the vast majority wanted him to end the war. Despair over the eventual loss of rights to Saharan oil and the fate of the Europeans in Algeria was evident, but the public overwhelmingly favored the negotiations that ended in the Evian peace accords in March 1962. Nevertheless, it was the Organisation Armée Secrète (OAS) that got the last vindictive hurrah. The OAS set off on a rampage of devastation, wrecking any hopes of eventual cooperation between the two communities in Algeria and abolishing much of France's impressive accomplishments of 130 years.

His critics called de Gaulle's Algerian policy ruthless, in disregard of the *Pieds-Noirs* and the strategic interests of France. Such complaints remain surprisingly vitriolic even today. The vast majority of his contemporaries were grateful for his accomplishments, and historians can argue convincingly that Algeria was among the general's finest hours. Under de Gaulle the French regained confidence in themselves and in France's time-honored traditions and prestige. His efforts restored popular respect for the state. Out of political chaos, emerged order. Out of despair came assurance as the experience of French life. For better or worse, the war changed French citizens' perceptions of their country. It made them realize the inevitability of relinquishing the empire, the essentiality of strong government, the fragility of democratic authority, and the necessity of economic strength linked to open trade borders with Europe. With de Gaulle the people came to accept a different France, one no less grand without Algeria.

BIBLIOGRAPHY

Clayton, Anthony. *The Wars of French Decolonization.* New York: Longman, 1994.

Horne, Alistair. *The Savage War of Peace: Algeria 1954–1962.* London: Penguin, 1977.

Lacouture, Jean. *De Gaulle.* Vol. 2, *The Ruler, 1945–1970.* New York: Norton, 1991.

Rioux, Jean-Pierre, ed. *La Guerre d'Algérie et les Français.* Paris: Fayard, 1990.

Schalk, David. *War and the Ivory Tower: Algeria and Vietnam.* New York: Oxford, 1991.

Talbott, John. *The War Without a Name: France in Algeria, 1954–1962.* New York: Knopf, 1980.

Vaïsse, Maurice, "France and the Suez Crisis," in *Suez 1956: The Crisis and Its Consequences.* Wm. Roger Louis and Roger Owen, eds. Oxford: Oxford, 1989.

Lee C. Whitfield

SEE ALSO De Gaulle, Charles; France; Suez Crisis

Alia, Ramiz (1925–)

Second, and last, Communist leader of Albania. Ramiz Alia was born in the northern city of Shkodër to Muslim parents from Kosovo, the region of Yugoslavia where the majority population was ethnically Albanian. He joined the Communist Party of Albania in 1943 and in 1944 served as political commissar with the Albanian forces that aided Tito's Partisans in the liberation of Kosovo from Axis control. In 1948 Alia was elected to the party's Central Committee. He was in overall charge of the Communist Youth Organization from 1949 until 1955, when he was appointed minister of education under Prime Minister Mehmet Shehu, a post he retained for three years. A candidate (nonvoting) member of the ruling Politburo by 1956, and a full member of that all-powerful institution by 1961, Alia had a spectacular rise to prominence, especially considering that postwar Albanian communism was led by Tosks from the south of the country (Enver Hoxha, Mehmet Shehu, and Hysni Kapo), while Alia was a Geg from the north. In fact, communism in Albania was always a largely Tosk-dominated philosophy, the northern region of the country being the center of anticommunist resistance both during the later stages of World War II and into the first decade of postwar peace.

Throughout his career Alia remained utterly loyal to Enver Hoxha and the party leader's brand of dogmatic Stalinist communism. He is said to have enjoyed the confidence and patronage of Hoxha's wife, Nexhmije, a valuable asset for any aspirant to high party office during the 1950s and 1960s. During the latter decade Alia played a prominent role in the Albanian Cultural Revolution from its inception. A major component of the Cultural Revolution was the attack on organized religion that led to the wanton destruction of innumerable churches and mosques while those that were not destroyed were converted to warehouses, sports halls, or small-scale factories. The antireligious campaign resulted in Albania's becoming the world's only self-proclaimed atheist state. A Museum of Atheism was established in Shkodër, Alia's hometown and a traditional center of Albanian Catholicism.

During the final years of Enver Hoxha's life, especially following Mehmet Shehu's alleged suicide in December 1981, it became clear to observers that Alia was the aging dictator's personal choice as successor. Albanian publications from the period increasingly featured photographs of the two men, sometimes deep in conversation, sometimes together at mass events, pointed indications of the person in line to lead Albania in the post-Hoxha era.

On April 15, 1985, Alia, in his funeral oration for Hoxha, described the late dictator as "the greatest man that Albanian soil has ever brought forward." Alia made a public commitment to upholding the tenets of his predecessor, but on assuming power he initiated a mildly reformist trend toward decentralization of the economy and greater material incentives for Albanian workers. However, the systematic problems that Hoxha bequeathed to his political heir were of a nature and on a scale that necessitated drastic and immediate attention, and Alia's 1985–89 tentative attempts to overhaul the system were insufficient to stave off disaster.

In the period of "Self-Reliance," from 1978 to 1985, when Albania had no major foreign source of aid, the economy stagnated to an alarming degree. Industrial machinery, largely of Soviet or Chinese manufacture and technologically obsolete, was prone to continual breakdown mainly because of age and unavailability of spare parts. The agricultural sector, forcibly collectivized in the 1950s and only imperfectly equipped with modern farming machinery, could not feed the population, which had tripled since 1945, and increased grain imports were needed to supplement home-produced corn and wheat. The secret police, the Sigurimi, continued to exercise arbitrary control over every Albanian's life including place of abode, permission for internal travel, type of education, and eventual employment. Alia had to contend with entrenched attitudes and vested interests inimical to change. As a lifelong bureaucrat with few if any original ideas as to how to solve the myriad problems that confronted his government, he was not the man to effect profound and meaningful changes in a system that he himself had done so much to create.

The revolutions of 1989 that swept the whole of Communist Eastern Europe seemed to have little immediate effect on the Albanian regime. But the anti-Communist ferment, especially news of the execution of Nicolae and Elena Ceauşescu in Romania, soon penetrated the last bastion of Stalinism in Europe, and Alia was able only to react to events over the next two years, never to fashion them. Calls for political pluralism began to be heard in Tirana among students and the intelligentsia. This culminated in the pulling down of the gilded statue of Enver Hoxha in Skanderbeg Square in February 1991, an event that appears to have convinced Alia of the necessity of jettisoning the concept of the one-party state. Although the first multiparty elections of March 1991 resulted in a majority for the ruling Albanian Party of Labor, the general strike and the mass exodus of Albanians to Italy and Greece later that year resulted in the creation of a "national stability" government containing some members of the newly formed Democratic Party in ministerial positions. New elections in March 1992 resulted in a landslide in favor of the Democratic Party. President Alia even lost his seat. He resigned soon after to make way for President Sali Berisha, the Democratic Party nominee for head of state. Alia was later arrested for alleged corruption while in office. He was released from jail in July 1995, no longer of any political importance.

Philip E. Wynn

Allensbach Institute

German public opinion polling institute. The Allensbach Institute for Public Opinion Polling (Institut für Demoskopie Allensbach) was founded in 1947 by Elisabeth Noelle-Neumann (1916–), professor of communication research at the University of Mainz, and Erich Peter Neumann (1912–73), member of the Bundestag and adviser to Konrad Adenauer, after the model of the Viennese Wirtschaftspsychologische Forschungsstelle (Research Institute for Business Psychology) and the U.S. Gallup poll. The Allensbach Institute performs market research as well as media and social research and political opinion polling.

The institute has striven to develop new and better methods by using new findings in psychology and by addressing sections of the population who until then were not considered likely interviewees, and it has never hesitated to ask delicate questions. Every month since 1949 the Allensbach Institute has questioned a two-thousand-respondent representative cross section of the German population on several issues. In 1950 the federal government entered into a contract with the institute for monthly polls to research prevailing opinion. This contract has never been discontinued. Also since 1949, the institute has taken part in or conducted international opinion research projects, a field of ever-growing importance. All in all, every year the institute conducts around

one hundred polls with altogether seventy thousand to eighty thousand interviews. The institute has extensive archives where it stores all the records of its polls.

In May 1996 Noelle-Neumann transferred all shares in the Allensbach Institute, of which she was previously the sole shareholder, to the Stiftung Demoskopie Allensbach (Allenbach Foundation for Public Opinion Research).

BIBLIOGRAPHY

Allensbach reports (*Allensbacher Berichte*) are published three times per month, and the *Frankfurter Allgemeine Zeitung* regularly publishes results of Allensbach opinion polls.

Noelle-Neumann, E. and E. P. Neumann, eds. *The Germans: Public Opinion Polls 1947–1966.* Westport, Conn.: Greenwood Press, 1981.

———. *The Germans. Public Opinion Polls 1967–1980.* Westport, Conn.: Greenwood Press, 1981.

Noelle-Neumann, E. *The Spiral of Silence. Public Opinion—Our Social Skin.* Chicago: University of Chicago Press, 1993.

Anjana Buckow

Alsatian Identity

Alsatians have become more culturally "French" since World War II than they had been at any time before. Some Alsatian writers claim that a distinct Alsatian identity is disappearing. Others claim that it is evolving. Others claim that it exists but cannot adequately be described to outsiders. Germain Muller, perhaps the most influential of postwar Alsatian playwrights, is well known for the line, "Enfin, redde m'r nimmer devon," which in the Alsatian dialect means "Let's not talk about it anymore." To a great extent this sentence summarizes the feelings of postwar Alsatians about their regional identity.

The first language of most Alsatians was a German dialect. Autonomist and regionalist organizations during the 1920s and 1930s attracted a cross section of popular support by championing the rights of Alsatians to speak their German dialect, to maintain their tradition of self-administration, and to keep their state-subsidized religious schools. After 1933 a small but vocal separatist minority joined forces with National Socialists across the Rhine and openly demanded the attachment, or *Anschluss,* of Alsace to the German Reich.

During World War II the collaboration of Alsatian politicians and private citizens with the occupiers was by many accounts higher than anywhere else in France. According to Chanoine Eugène Muller, a longtime advocate of Alsatian cultural particularism, the immediate postwar era marked a time "in which Alsatians no longer liked themselves." Alsatians found themselves questioning their own choices and those of their relatives and neighbors. They also had to deal with the suspicions of people from other parts of France who assumed that they had made their peace with the enemy.

After 1945 Alsatians were expected to relinquish traditions and customs that were reminiscent of their German heritage. Alsatians for their part were compelled to turn away from using German and the German dialect. From 1944 until 1952 the French Fourth Republic banned the use of German in the classrooms of the region. The press law of September 1945 stipulated that newspapers and magazines had to have at least one-fourth of their material in French, including the banner, headlines, sports section, and articles geared to youth. Knowledge of German as the first language declined significantly among the young. Parents, teachers, and clergy accepted the active promotion of French, which Catholic leaders had traditionally vilified as the language of godlessness and revolution. The memories of the Second World War and Alsatian participation in the occupation regime compelled the people of the region to demonstrate their loyalty to France by making a concerted effort to ensure that French would be the first language of their children.

These language policies affected the working classes in the towns and in rural areas more than they did the middle and upper classes, who already spoke French as their first language. The Alsatian public, however, did not at first resist these initiatives to remove the German language. The only dissension came from regional poets, playwrights, and novelists whose preferred language was German. These artists feared not only the loss of their audience but the loss of an integral part of the Alsatian particularism, or cultural personality. They viewed the limitations on the teaching and use of German as the first step toward eradication of the Alsatian identity. Regional intellectuals and writers tried after 1945 to resuscitate dialect literature and theater but found that dialect carried a political and cultural message their audience now found unpalatable.

Other defenders of the *Muttersprache*, as Alsatians call their dialect, included older politicians, many of whom had belonged to the regionalist and autonomist movements of the interwar period. Regionalism and autonomism had become anathema in postwar Alsace because of their association with extremist elements. The fact that some of these former *Heimatrechtler* (fighters for the rights of the homeland) had been active in the Resistance did little to rehabilitate them in the minds of people who considered them less than genuine French patriots.

Joining in their efforts were older members of the Catholic clergy, who hoped to revive the influence of the church in the political and social life of the region. The Catholic Church in particular had provided Alsatians with a sense of identity and community at times when Alsatians could find neither under French or German rule. Yet after 1945 the church in Alsace was an institution in decline. It seems that this decline reflected less a loss of faith than a generational change among the population.

The rising generation of clergy of the 1940s and 1950s was also more national in its political views, and encouraged the faithful to join mainstream parties instead of adhering to the tradition of regional Catholic political organizations. These younger priests were less resistant to the idea of delivering sermons and religious instruction in French. For the first time, Alsatian identity, Catholic faith, and the German language were ceasing to be synonymous in the public pronouncements of religious leaders.

In the late 1960s Alsatian writers, alarmed and perhaps feeling some slight guilt over what they feared was the impending demise of dialect, began anew to call for a revival of interest in local language and culture. As part of a regional literary revival, Alsatian writers and students demanded the preservation of a dialect theater and literature. One result of this movement was the formation of the Council of Alsatian Writers in 1971.

The Alsatian Cultural Front, established in 1974, promoted what it termed "cultural self-management," a program oddly reminiscent of the interwar autonomist programs. The front championed a continuing role for German in public life, inclusion of regional history in school curricula, and regional radio and television programming. The goal of the front was to limit the incursion of outside cultures (presumably Parisian and American) by giving as much exposure as possible to the Alsatian heritage. Neither the Council of Alsatian Writers nor the Alsatian Cultural Front, however, found a wide reception beyond intellectual circles.

The official reconciliation of France and Germany, cemented by economic partnership, allowed assertions of Alsace's German heritage to be depoliticized. With the seat of the European Parliament in Strasbourg, and with Alsace serving as a base of the new Franco-German Corps, references made to Alsace's European vocation and the peculiarity of Alsace can be viewed in a more positive fashion.

BIBLIOGRAPHY

Phllipps, Eugène. *L'Alsace face à son destin: la crise d'identité.* Strasbourg: Société d'édition de la Basse-Alsace, n.d.

Jena M. Ganes

Althusser, Louis (1918–90)

French political philosopher. Louis Althusser's works appeared at a time when Marxist thought was at the center of French intellectual life. In that period of the Cold War influential intellectuals, such as Henri Lefebvre and Jean-Paul Sartre, defended Marx's works as the royal road to an understanding of the contemporary world; prestigious journals such as *Tel Quel* or *Nouvelle Critique* as well as staunch opponents like Raymond Aron had to seriously consider it. Althusser considered the French working class to be sorely in need of an authentic theoretical culture, and he proposed literally to "think within Marx." His investigation of Marx's philosophical thought suggested a new reading that contrasted strongly with other Western interpretations.

Born in Birmandreis, Algeria, Althusser studied in Lyon under the direction of Jean Guitton and Jean Lacroix, two Catholic philosophers who led him to the prestigious École Normale Supérieure in Paris. But he was inducted into the military in September 1939 and, with the French defeat, was taken prisoner by the Germans. After the Liberation, Althusser resumed studies in the section of philosophy of the École Normale Supérieure from 1945 to 1946 under Gaston Bachelard and passed the *agrégation.* In 1948 he began teaching philosophy in that institution and later was appointed maître de conférences.

He became more and more divided between his faith and his social inclinations. When the Vatican condemned priest-workers in 1948, he abandoned the Catholic Church, in which he had till then been an activist in the Jeunesse de l'Église, a Catholic youth group. In quest of universal concepts, he became a member of the French Communist Party. Ironically, he will later describe these universal views as belonging to bourgeois ideology.

During the 1960s Althusser's influence was at a peak. His students and collaborators included Michel Foucault, Pierre Bourdieu, Michel Serres, Jacques Derrida, Alain Badiou, Jacques Bouveresse, and André Compte-Sponville, who rallied more around his structuralist approach than his Marxist analyses. They questioned the concept of a "subject," and Althusser engaged in epistemological research in an attempt to reconstruct a new Marxist orthodoxy. Rejecting the historiographical debate about Marx's early writings, *Reading Capital* and *For Marx*

introduce a philosophical reading of Marx's theoretical evolution and defined an epistemological break that Althusser claimed Marx himself failed to notice, which led the author of *Capital* to go beyond ideology and establish the proper foundations of science. Rejecting humanism, Althusser elaborated the frame of a new version of dialectical materialism. This sophisticated approach, defined as a theory of theoretical praxis, redefined old notions such as "superstructure" or elaborated new ones such as the concepts of thought-concretes, overdetermination, and the ideological state apparatuses.

In the period after 1967 Althusser, after a flirtation with the Maoist opposition to the Communist Party, made a desperate attempt to defend Marxism-Leninism. Althusser attacked New Left currents, disparaged the student revolt of May 1968, remained silent during the Soviet-led Warsaw Pact invasion of Czechoslovakia that same year, and generally adopted orthodox Communist views.

The end of the 1970s saw his growing dissatisfaction with the political impotence of his own work. He modified some of his former positions and also focused on the crises of Marxism and of the Communist movement. He published a strong indictment of the Communist Party, which, in turn, pilloried him. While his articles in the *New Left Review* received a wide audience, his strong declaration, "The Crisis of Marxism," which appeared in *Marxism Today* in 1978, was not published in French until 1991.

Althusser's life ended as a tragedy. The drama reached a climax on November 16, 1980, when the philosopher became an assassin: he murdered his wife in a fit of madness (in fact, he was receiving treatment for manic depression). This act marked the beginning of the decline of his influence, but overall the tragic distress of Althusser, who no longer published, except for a pathetic explanation of his action. The crisis of the Soviet Union and the decline of communism also led to the increasing unpopularity of Marxism in French universities, and his influence remained strong only in South America.

BIBLIOGRAPHY

Althusser, Louis. *Essays in Self-criticism.* Tr. by Grahame Lock. London: New Left Books/Atlantic Highlands, N.J.: Humanities Press, 1976.

———. *Philosophy and the Spontaneous Philosophy of the Scientists & Other Essays.* London: Verso, 1990.

Elliott, Gregory. *Althusser: The Detour of Theory.* London: Verso, 1987.

Moulier Boutang, Y. *Louis Althusser: une biographie: La Formation du mythe (1918–1956).* Paris: Grasset, 1992.

Resch, Robert Paul. *Althusser and the Renewal of Marxist Social Theory.* Berkeley: University of California Press, 1992.

Ronald Creagh

Amato, Giuliano (1938–)

Italian professor of law and prime minister. Born in 1938, Giuliano Amato studied law at the University of Pisa, where he graduated in 1960; in 1962 he received a master's degree in comparative law at the School of Law of Columbia University in New York City. A full professor of comparative constitutional law at the University of Rome's School of Political Science since 1975, Amato had been a professor at the universities of Modena, Perugia, and Florence. From 1979 to 1981 he was head of IRES, the research institute of the General Confederation of Italian Labor (CGIL). From 1981, he was a member of the leadership of the Socialist Party (PSI) and later became the party's vice secretary. Member of parliament from 1983 to 1994, he was undersecretary to the prime minister's office from 1983 to 1987, minister of the treasury from 1987 to 1989, and deputy prime minister from 1987 to 1988. He was prime minister from June 1992 to April 1993. His government was composed mostly of new political figures and sought to cut spending and to reform the system of welfare. In July 1992 he promoted trilateral agreements among the government, unions, and employers—a pact aimed at containing inflation through salaries containment, thus starting a new course in labor relations that still influences the Italian wage bargaining system.

From 1994 to the end of 1997 Amato was chairman of the Italian Antitrust Authority. His present area of teaching and research is law aimed at promoting competition in Europe.

BIBLIOGRAPHY

Amato, G. *Antitrust and the Bounds of Power.* Oxford: Hart, 1997.

———. *Economia, politica e istituzioni in Italia.* Bologna: Il Mulino, 1976.

———. *Il governo dell'industria in Italia.* Bologna: F. Angeli, 1972.

———. "The impact of Europe on National Policies: Italian Anti-Trust Policy," in *Adjusting to Europe: The Impact of the European Union on National Institutions and Policies.* London: Routledge, 1996.

———. *Una repubblica da riformare: il dibattito sulle istituzioni in Italia dal 1975 a oggi.* Bologna: Il Mulino, 1980.

Stefania Mazzone

Andorra

Principality of 188 square miles (487 sq km) in the Pyrenees bordered by France and Spain. Catalan is the official language, but French and Spanish are widely spoken. Under a system established in 1278, Andorra had been governed jointly by two "princes," the ruler of France and the Bishop of Urgel in Spain, in whom were vested complete executive, legislative, and judicial powers. A "Plan of Reform" in 1866 set up a General Council of twenty eight members with four members elected for four-year terms from each of Andorra's six parishes. This council did not possess formal legislative power but served as the administrative body. It elected a manager (sindic), a sub-sindic, and a president of the government, who appointed an Executive Council.

On March 14, 1993, the 75.7 percent of the 9,123 eligible voters of Andorra participated in a referendum, and 74.2 percent approved a new constitution. Under the new constitution, Andorra became a parliamentary co-principality with clearly differentiated legislative, executive, and judiciary branches of government. The modernization was spearheaded after 1990 by Oscar Ribas Reig, who was elected to the presidency for a second time, and Josep Maria Beal Benedico, the mayor of Les Escaldesa, who was elected syndic. The new constitution reduced the power of the princes, but they still retain the right to veto security measures and are represented on the constitutional tribunal.

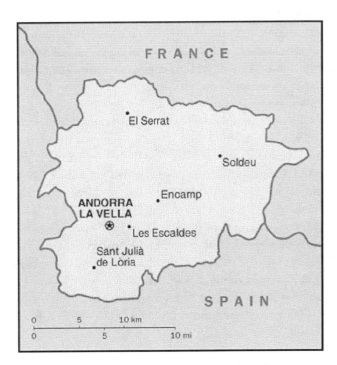

Andorra. *Illustration courtesy of Bernard Cook.*

Forné Molne became head of the government in December 1994. In the General Council election of February 16, 1997, Molné's Liberal Union won an absolute majority with eighteen of the twenty-eight seats.

Following the March 1993 referendum Andorra applied for membership in the Council of Europe. In June 1993 the government of Andorra signed a treaty with France and Spain in which those states formally recognized its sovereignty, and in July Andorra became the 184th member state of the United Nations.

Until 1970 only third-generation Andorran males over twenty-five were allowed to vote. That year the franchise was extended to second-generation Andorrans, male or female, over the age of twenty-one. The voting age for second-generation Andorrans was reduced to eighteen in 1985. In 1977 the vote was extended to first-generation Andorrans twenty-eight or older. Immigration is limited to French and Spanish citizens who desire to work in Andorra. They are permitted entry on the basis of a quota system. In 1991 only 15,616 of Andorra's 54, 507 inhabitants were citizens.

In April 1988 Andorra accepted the U.N.'s Universal Declaration of Human Rights. In June French and Spanish unions, which had advocated freedom of expression and association and the right to strike for the twenty thousand guest workers in Andorra, organized a union in the principality. In July, however, the General Council reiterated its ban on unions and threatened to expel any foreign workers who joined the union. In July 1989 the Council of Europe's Commission for Political Affairs called for a referendum in Andorra on a written constitution that would embody citizens' rights, including the right of association and easier access to citizenship. The 1993 constitution permits residents of Andorra to join unions and to organize political parties.

There is competition between the capital, Andorra la Vella, which contains 20,437 of the country's inhabitants, and the rural parishes. The country has no armed force, and its foreign affairs were handled by France until 1993. Residents pay no income tax, and Andorra's secretive banking laws have attracted large deposits to its Credit Agricol i Commercial d'Andorra. In 1996 foreign nationals were allowed to become nominal residents of Andorra for tax purposes if they paid a fee of one million pesetas and deposited funds in Andorran banks. In 1997 restrictions were removed on foreign investments in Andorra.

Duty free, Andorra would like to enter the European Union or at least negotiate a comprehensive free-trade agreement with it. In 1993 it was treated as a member of the EU for industrial goods only.

BIBLIOGRAPHY

"Andorra." *Europa World Year Book 1996*. London: Europa Publications, 1996, vol. 2, 352–53.

Jack, Andrew. "Andorra Liberal Union Party Re-elected," *Financial Times* (London), February 18, 1997.

Lluelles Larrosa, Maria Jesus. *La transformacio economica d'Andorra*. Barcelona: L'Avenc, 1991.

Morgan, Bryan. *Andorra, the Country in Between*. Nottingham, England: Palmer, 1964.

Palau, Montserrat. *Andorra: historia, institucions, costums*. Lleida: Virgili & Pages, 1987.

Vinas Farre, Ramon. *La nacionalitat andorrana*. Barcelona: Institut d'Estudis Andorrans, 1980.

Bernard Cook

Andreotti, Giulio (1919–)

Italian politician; prime minister in 1972, 1976, 1978, 1979, 1989–91, and 1991–92. Giulio Andreotti was born in Rome on January 14, 1919. He studied law and in 1942 became president of the Italian Catholic University Federation. Andreotti thought Catholic students should work to establish a future society inspired by the principles of Christianity.

During the years he spent at university, Andreotti met Alcide De Gasperi and they laid the foundations for the Christian Democratic Party (DC). After the fall of fascism, De Gasperi and Andreotti worked for political renewal with a democratically minded group, which included Giuseppe Spataro, Guido Gonella, Mario Scelba, Giovanni Gronchi, Pietro Campilli, and Sergio Paronetto.

At the Interregional Congress in Naples on July 29 and 30, 1944, Andreotti was elected national delegate of the youth groups to the DC, an office he held until June 1947. During this period, he tried to combine the needs of De Gasperi's leadership with the more lively expectations of the young Christian Democrats.

In September 1945, he was asked to be a DC representative to the Constituent Assembly. He remained a delegate, first to the Constituent Assembly then to parliament, until 1991, when he was appointed a life member of the Senate by President Francesco Cossiga.

When the fourth government led by De Gasperi was formed, in May 1947, Andreotti started his long and important career as a member of the executive. He was appointed undersecretary of the presidency of ministers and held that office until January 1954. This experience strengthened Andreotti's loyalty to De Gasperi. On the occasion of what is known as "Operation Sturzo," in 1952, Andreotti played an important role and supported De Gasperi's political view; that is, when the Vatican sug-

gested the idea that a civic list should be formed to oppose the left-wing ones in Roman administrative elections, De Gasperi balked. He was afraid that such a maneuver, creating an alliance between the right wing and the Christian Democrats, would endanger the solidarity of the centrist parties, which were allies of the DC in the government. Andreotti wrote a letter to Pius XII in which he explained the dangers of the proposal: the DC would not be supported by the church and it would no longer be the expression of an antifascist perspective. Its image as a church-supported antifascist party had allowed the DC to win support from workers and farmers. Furthermore, he reassured the pope about the Roman elections and reminded him of the anticommunist ideas of De Gasperi. As a result, Operation Sturzo was stillborn.

In opposition to a possible approach to the Socialist Party, even if only on an administrative level, Andreotti strongly defended the centrist formula, which he publicly supported at the Congress of Trentino in October 1956. According to Andreotti, there was an obvious contrast between socialism, on the one hand, and religious principles and freedom, on the other. According to him, it was necessary to create a society in which the middle class should play a key role in social life, while a center–left wing political strategy ran the risk of collapsing the already difficult democratic balance in Italy. He did not agree with Aldo Moro's position at the Congress of Naples in 1962, which marked the last stage of the long path toward the center-left movement. At that point, however, it was obvious that the process would go forward, and it was, in Andreotti's opinion, necessary not to break the unity of the party.

After De Gasperi's retirement and death, Andreotti's political ascendancy continued. He was secretary of state for the interior (1954), for finance (1955–58), for the treasury (1958–59), for defense (1959–66), for industry (1966–68), for the budget (1974–76), and for foreign affairs (1983–88). He was president of the council of ministers (prime minister) in seven governments (1972, 1976, 1978, 1979, 1989–91, and 1991–92). Between 1976 and 1979 Andreotti led three governments known as "governments of national solidarity," because they marked a new stage of cooperation among all parties, including the Communist Party, although it was not part of the formal government. However, the difficult domestic situation, dominated by the spread of terrorism and increasing tension among the parties, soon ended this political experiment.

Andreotti's foreign policies were directed toward increasing an atmosphere of détente between East and West and at supporting European integration. He was elected a member of the European Parliament at Strasbourg in 1984 and 1989.

On March 27, 1993, judges at Palermo asked authorization to start legal proceedings against Andreotti, who was suspected of criminal and Mafia associations. This was based on statements made by individuals who cooperated with the judges. Andreotti asserted that he was ready to explain everything he did and that he was at the disposal of the committee of inquiry.

In September 1999 Andreotti was acquitted of the charge that he had conspired to have a journalist killed in 1979, and in October 1999 a trial in Palermo, which had lasted for six years and was billed the Italian "trial of the century," also ended with an acquittal of Andreotti, who had been charged with protecting the Sicilian Mafia while he was a dominant force in Italian politics. The prosecutors in both cases had largely relied on Mafia "*pentiti*," apprehended Mafiosi who were accused by the defense of trading manufactured testimony in return for grants of immunity.

BIBLIOGRAPHY

Franco, Massimo. *Andreotti visto da vicino.* Milan: Mondadori, 1989.

Malgeri, Francesco. "Giulio Andreotti," in *Il Parlamento Italiano. Storia parlamentare e politica dell'Italia 1861–1988.* Vol. 24. Milan: Nuova CEI, 1989.

Orfei, Ruggero. *Andreotti.* Milan: Feltrinelli, 1975.

Pallotta, Gino. *Giulio Andreotti: il Richelieu della politica italiana.* Rome: Newton Compton, 1988.

Claudia Franceschini

SEE ALSO Gladio; Italy, Historic Compromise and Red Brigades; Mafia; Moro, Aldo

Andropov, Yuri Vladimirovich (1914–84)

General secretary of the Communist Party of the Soviet Union (CPSU), 1982–84. Yuri Andropov, who came to power as an advocate of peace and internal reform, rose to leadership of the USSR via the state security services. Born in the Stavropol region, he became a protégé of Finnish Communist leader Otto Kusinnen and joined the CPSU in 1939. Technically attached to the Communist Youth Organization (Komsomol) in Karelia, Andropov purportedly managed forced-labor projects in the region for the NKVD (precursor of the KGB). He was rewarded with rapid promotion, becoming second party secret in Yaroslavl in 1937 and first secretary of the Kom there in 1938. During the Second World War A supervised partisan activity in Karelia; in 1947

secretary of the Central Committee of the Autonomous Karelian Republic. By 1950 Andropov was a deputy of the Supreme Soviet.

With the death of Joseph Stalin in 1953, however, Andropov's career suffered a setback. That year he was sent to Hungary as a counselor to the Soviet Embassy, and the following year he failed to gain reelection to the Supreme Soviet. Though he became ambassador in 1954, Andropov was still in Hungary in 1956. He played a central, if shadowy, role in suppressing the Hungarian rebellion. His reward was a return to Moscow and a revived career.

In 1961, after a term as head of the Central Committee's foreign department, Andropov became a full member of the CPSU Central Committee. Three years later he was selected by Premier Nikita Khrushchev to give the keynote speech on Lenin Day, a privilege usually reserved for senior party leaders, and in 1967, Andropov was appointed head of the Committee for State Security (KGB).

Andropov quickly made his mark on the KGB, carrying out an internal campaign against corruption and curtailing most of the heavy-handed methods inherited from Stalin's NKVD. He created a markedly more sophisticated and professional service that was no less effective and perhaps even more efficient. Under his leadership the KGB began to use psychiatric hospitals and drug treatments to deal with dissidents.

Using the KGB as his power base, Andropov rose within the CPSU. He became a full member of the Politburo in 1973 and an army general in 1976. He played a key role in pushing forward the Soviet invasion of Afghanistan in 1979 and was, speculatively, linked with both the takeover of the U.S. Embassy in Tehran in 1979 and the attempted assassination of Pope John Paul II in 1981. Elected as a full member of the CPSU Secretariat in 1982, Andropov succeeded General Secretary Leonid Brezhnev in November of that year. At sixty-eight Andropov was the oldest person ever to become general secretary of the party. In early 1983 he launched a campaign against work absenteeism in the USSR and followed it up with campaigns against sloth, alcoholism, and corruption. He became head of the Defense Council in the spring of 1983 and chairman of the Presidium of the USSR Supreme Soviet in June. From that position of strength he launched a "peace offensive" designed to counter Western initiatives for disarmament and inhibit the placement of more missiles in Western Europe. This maneuver was at least temporarily derailed by the shooting down of KAL flight 007 over Soviet territory in September, but Andropov pushed on, publicly corresponding with American schoolgirl Samantha Smith regarding the need for peace and disarmament.

Though Miss Smith visited Moscow in 198 never met the Soviet leader. Andropov, who had undergoing dialysis treatments for nearly a year, w and out of the public eye. He died in February 1984 a fewer than two years at the head of the USSR.

Andropov is often remembered as a Westernizer and reformer, though his policies altered little of Brezhnev's neo-Stalinist regime. His reformist campaigns proved ineffective and unpopular internally, and he had little impact on foreign affairs. Andropov's true significance lay in his role as the sponsor of a new generation of Soviet leaders, including Mikhail Gorbachev, who said of his political patron in 1987: "We owe everything to him."

BIBLIOGRAPHY

Ebon, Martin. *The Andropov File: The Life and Ideas of Yuri V. Andropov, General Secretary of the Communist Party of the Soviet Union.* New York: McGraw-Hill, 1983.

Medvedev, Zhores. *Andropov.* Oxford: Basil Blackwell, 1983.

Steele, Jonathan, and Eric Abraham. *Andropov in Power: From Komsomol to Kremlin.* Oxford: Martin Robertson, 1983.

Timothy C. Dowling

SEE ALSO Afganistan, war in; Hungary; KAL 007 Incident

Anguita, Julio (1941–)

Mayor of Cordova (1979–87), secretary general of the Spanish Communist Party, and general coordinator of the United Left.

Julio Anguita leads the United Left, currently the third-largest party in Spanish national politics. A popular figure, he helped engineer the revival of left-wing politics in Spain. Under his leadership the Communist Party, through participation in the United Left, has regained some measure of political prominence.

Anguita is the son of an army sergeant who fought under Francisco Franco during the Spanish Civil War. He graduated from the University of Barcelona with a degree in history and soon began a sixteen-year career as teacher. He became politically active during the final ye of the Franco regime, joining the Spanish Commu Party in the early 1970s.

In 1979 he was elected mayor of Cordova, wh governed as head of a coalition but was returne post in 1983 with an absolute majority. His came at a time when the Communist Party was following a disastrous showing in the 1982 g

tion. These results and the dramatic loss of membership that followed produced serious infighting and a reexamination of tactics within the movement. Anguita remained largely above the fray but generally supported those calling for renovation of the party and its leadership.

The campaign resisting Spain's entry into NATO in 1986 revived the party's sagging fortunes. Although the referendum to join NATO was eventually successful, the amount of dissent revealed the potential strength of left-wing voters. In 1986 the Communist Party joined with other organizations in forming an electoral coalition called the United Left. Results for municipal voting in 1986 made the newly formed party the third largest, and the coalition won seven seats in the national legislature.

In 1988 Anguita was elected secretary-general of the Communist Party, and he immediately led the party into deeper involvement with the United Left. At the first national assembly of the United Left, held in 1989, the group declared itself a political and social movement aimed at promoting a leftist socialist agenda. Since then the popularity of the United Left has continued to grow. In the national elections of 1989 they won seventeen seats, and by 1996 that number had increased to twenty-one.

Often considered controversial and polemical, Anguita remains one of the most popular left-wing politicians in Spain. He has helped restore the political standing of the Communist Party and as head of the United Left represents a significant number of progressive voters dissatisfied with mainstream politics.

BIBLIOGRAPHY

Haywood, Paul. *The Government and Politics of Spain.* New York: St. Martin's Press, 1995.

Jáuregui, Fernando. *Julio Anguita.* Madrid: Grupo Libro, 1992.

Brian D. Bunk

SEE ALSO Spain

Antall, József (1932–93)

Hungarian politician, historian, and prime minister of Hungary (1990–93). József Antall graduated from Eötvös Loránd University in Budapest and worked at the National Archives and at the Pedagogical Institute in the mid-1950s before he started teaching at a high school. He participated in the reorganization of the Independent Smallholders Party in October 1956. After the suppression of the Hungarian Revolution he was arrested and dismissed from his job. He worked at different places as a teacher and a librarian between 1957 and 1964. He became an associate of the Semmelweis Medical History Museum in 1964 and worked there in various capacities and was its director general from 1984 to 1990.

Antall was one of the founding members of the Hungarian Democratic Forum (MDF) in 1988 and was elected president of the party in 1989. When the MDF emerged as the largest party in the general elections in spring 1990, Antall was elected prime minister of the coalition government of Hungary. However, he was soon incapacitated by illness and was hospitalized during 1993. He died in office in December 1993.

Antall was the embodiment of the "gentleman politician" who was also a scholar. He wrote several books and some three hundred articles on political science, cultural history, and medical history. His scope of activities while he was in office was limited by the fact that he headed a weak, heterogeneous coalition, while the opposition, mostly reform Communists, called "socialists," and members of the Alliance of the Free Democrats (SZDSZ), possessed the key positions in the economic life of Hungary and those in the media. He was also hamstrung by the structural problems of the transition from communism, the problems of privatization, and the reorientation of Hungarian foreign trade.

Tamàs Magyarics

Antonescu, Ion (1882–1946)

Authoritarian leader of Romania during the Second World War, tried and executed by the Romanian Communist government in 1946. Ion Antonescu was a forbidden subject of historical research during the Communist period. But after the anti-Communist revolution of December 1989 Antonescu's role in Romanian history, including the nature of his regime, his alliance with Nazi Germany, and the treatment of Romanian Jews and other minorities during the war, was reevaluated. Controversy surrounded his legacy, with some researchers stressing his position as defender of Romania's territorial integrity against the Soviets and others stressing his culpability for the Romanian Holocaust.

Born in Pitesti in south-central Romania in 1882, Antonescu began his military career in 1904 as a second lieutenant. From 1907 he participated in several important military operations, including the quashing of the great Romanian peasant revolt in 1907, the Bulgarian campaign in 1913, the Transylvanian campaign in 1916, and the battles of Marasti and Marasesti in 1917. In the 1920s he served in various diplomatic posts, including one as the military attaché at the Romanian Embassies in

Paris and London, and was elevated to the rank of general in 1931. In 1937 and 1938 Antonescu served as minister of defense in two successive governments. But his opposition to the royal dictatorship declared by King Carol II in February 1938, as well as Antonescu's links with the ultraright Legion of the Archangel Michael (Iron Guard) movement, alienated him from the political mainstream.

After vehemently protesting the cession of Bessarabia and northern Bukovina to the Soviet Union, Antonescu was arrested and imprisoned in July and August 1940. However, with Romania sliding toward war the popular general was called by Carol II to become prime minister in early September 1940. A day after his appointment Antonescu forced Carol's abdication in favor of the king's young son, Prince Michael (Mihai). Romania was declared a "national Legionary state," with Antonescu taking the title of conducator (supreme leader). Antonescu made overtures to the Iron Guard, inviting the group's leader, Horia Sima, to share power. But the Iron Guard instead launched a rebellion against the Antonescu regime in January 1941, which was put down by the Romanian army; the Iron Guard was banned and its leaders jailed or exiled.

To retake the territories seized by the Soviets in 1940, Antonescu ordered an attack on the Soviet Union in June 1941 in cooperation with Nazi Germany. Although the territories ceded to the USSR had been retaken by the end of 1941, Antonescu pressed on into the Soviet heartland. The Romanian army, along with the Germans, was defeated at the battle of Stalingrad in late 1942. With the army in retreat toward Romania and the Soviet army on its heels, on August 23, 1944, King Michael staged a coup against Antonescu, handed the general over to Romanian Communists, and switched Romania's allegiance from Germany to the Allies in the hope of avoiding the country's destruction by the approaching Red Army. With the growing Communist influence in Romania after the war, Antonescu became a major target of Communist propaganda. Held in jail in the Soviet Union for nearly two years, he was finally tried in Bucharest and executed in Jilava prison on June 1, 1946.

BIBLIOGRAPHY

Antonescu, Ion. *Românii: originea, trecutul, sacrificiile si drepturile lor.* Iasi, Romania: Editura Moldova, 1991.

Fisher, Julius S. *Transnistria: The Forgotten Cemetery.* New Brunswick, N.J.: T. Yoseloff, 1969.

Hillgruber, Andreas. *Hitler, König Carol und Marschall Antonescu.* Wiesbaden, 1954.

Jagendorf, Siegfried. *Jagendorf's Foundry: Memoir of the Romanian Holocaust, 1941–1944.* New York: HarperCollins, 1991.

Shachan, Avigdor. *Burning Ice: The Ghettos of Transnistria.* Boulder, Colo.: East European Monographs, 1996.

Watts, Larry L. *Romanian Cassandra: Ion Antonescu and the Struggle for Reform, 1916–1941.* Boulder, Colo.: East European Monographs, 1993.

Charles King

Antonioni, Michelangelo (1912–)

Critically acclaimed Italian film director. Michelangelo Antonioni is most noted for his probing films of alienation, lack of communication, ennui, and emptiness of modern life, especially upper-middle-class life. His mastery of expressive visual technique is widely acknowledged.

L'avventura (1960) established Antonioni as master of the modern malaise and modern cinema. A sailing party of the beautiful and the bored lands on a deserted island, and one of the characters is lost—a suicide, a planned disappearance? Two friends, a man and a woman, search, become sexually involved, then abandon the quest. In this film Monica Vitti established herself as quintessential Antonioni heroine. In a 1982 poll of leading film critics by influential film journal *Sight and Sound, L'avventura* was in the top ten films of all time.

La notte (1961) and *L'eclisse* (*Eclipse*, 1962) formed the second and third parts of a trilogy that extended the topics of ennui among the upper middle class and the difficulties of relationships begun in *L'Avventura.*

The *Il deserto rosso* (Red Desert, 1964) was Antonioni's first color film, and it remains a masterpiece of expressive color cinematography. Set in the industrial north of Italy, the film chronicles the degradation of the physical and human environment through the eyes of a neurotic woman (Vitti again) whose relationship with her engineer husband and little son are strained.

Blow-Up (1966), Antonioni's first film in English and probably his most famous in the United States, is set in the swinging London of the 1960s. The film takes the structure of a puzzle as a trendy fashion photographer (David Hemmings) shoots some film that apparently chronicles a murder. Antonioni leaves us hanging as we question the very nature of perception. In a classic final scene, the photographer joins a group of mimes playing an imaginary tennis game, and we begin to hear the sounds of the tennis ball.

Zabriskie Point (1970) is named for the lowest point in the United States, and many critics feel the film is Antonioni's artistic low point. His love song to 1960s alienated, radical American youth is nonetheless visually memorable, and its attack on American materialism fascinating. The film ends with the explosion of a spectacular desert house.

The Passenger (1975), also in English, stars Jack Nicholson as a burned-out journalist who changes identity with a dead man and begins a doomed trek through Africa, Spain, Germany, and England. Once again the film is visually stunning, especially the desert sequences.

The Marxist critique of society and his slow-paced investigations of the modern malaise and the difficulty of relationships are Antonioni's favorite themes, while the visual beauty of his images forms a rich reinforcement in the work of this challenging, intellectual director.

BIBLIOGRAPHY

Arrowsmith, William. *Antonioni: The Poet of Images.* New York: Oxford University Press, 1995.

Chatman, Seymour Benjamin. *Antonioni, Or, The Surface of the World.* Berkeley: University of California Press, 1985.

Rohdie, Sam. *Antonioni.* Bloomington: Indiana University Press, 1990.

William M. Hammel

SEE ALSO Italy

Arbëresh (Arvenites)

Albanian minorities living in southern Italy, Sicily, and northern Greece. The Arbëresh are descended from refugees who fled from Albania at times of religious persecution from 1448 onward and from Epirus around 1480 following Ottoman colonization of Albania. They take their name from Arberia, an earlier name for Albania. They now live predominantly in over four hundred communes in the mountainous regions surrounding Cosenza and Calabria and in the vicinity of Palermo in Sicily. They are estimated to number between one hundred thousand and two hundred thousand. Some emigrated again, especially to the United States. The Arbëresh language is close to Albanian, but many words of Latin origin have also been introduced. The Arvenites are a minority living in over six hundred villages in sixteen regions of Greece; their language, Arvanítika is further removed from Albanian than is Arbëresh. The populations in these Albanian-inhabited areas became depleted after 1950 with migration to towns and attempts by the governments of Italy and Greece to integrate their Albanian minorities.

BIBLIOGRAPHY

Bellusci, Antonio. *Ricerche e studi tra gli arberori dell'Ellade: da radici arbereshe in Italia e matrici arberore in Grecia testi e documenti.* Cosenza, Italy: Centro Ricerche Socio-Culturali Giorgio Castriota Skanderbeg, 1994.

Hutchings, Raymond. *Historical Dictionary of Albania.* Lanham, Md.: Scarecrow Press, 1996.

Nasse, George Nicholas. *The Italo-Albanian Villages of Southern Italy.* Washington, D.C.: National Academy of Sciences—National Research Council, 1964.

Young, Antonia. *Albania.* World Bibliographical Series no. 94 [revised]. Santa Barbara, Calif.: Clio Press, 1997.

Antonia Young

Arbnori, Pjeter (1934–)

Albanian dissident and political figure. Born in 1934 into a deeply committed Catholic family in Durrës, Pjeter Arbnori was already labeled as a danger to Enver Hoxha's Communist state by the time he was fourteen. His anti-Communist stance was strongly influenced by the death of his father, an Albanian police officer who died fighting the Communist partisans during the Italian occupation of Albania. Arbnori's political record barred him from secondary and further education despite an outstanding academic record. After national service he worked as an agricultural laborer; by this time his sister Antoinette was sentenced to ten years' imprisonment for her anti-Communist activities. Using false documents Arbnori registered at Tirana University and received qualification to teach literature in a school in Kavaja, but within a year he was arrested and sentenced to death for his part in organizing a group of intellectuals to form a social democratic movement based on the principles of pluralism in Western countries. This was in 1960 at the time of Albania's break from Soviet influence. Some of the severe tortures that Arbnori suffered in the ensuing twenty-eight years have been documented, and it is claimed that he spent longer in the notorious Burrel prison than any other person. During that time he maintained hope for a better life, wrote more than one book, smuggled from prison, and was finally freed in 1989 under Ramiz Alia. He joined the Democratic Party (DP) prior to the 1991 election, married a family friend, and was given the post of parliamentary speaker when the DP won the 1992 election. Following Sali Berisha's fall from power in the June 1997 election, Arbnori stood as candidate for the DP leadership but lost the vote to Berisha by 115 to 791. Later in 1997 Arbnori led demonstrations and hunger strikes protesting alleged unfairness in the allocation of radio and television time allotted the DP under the new Socialist government.

BIBLIOGRAPHY
Hamilton, Bill. "Who cares? The exclusive inside story," *New World,* November 3, 1997.

Antonia Young

Archer, Jeffrey (1940–)

British novelist and politician. Jeffrey Archer (Lord Archer of Weston-Super-Mare) was a member of the Greater London Council from 1966 to 1970, a Conservative member of Parliament from 1970 to 1974, and deputy chairman of the Conservative Party from 1985 to 1986. He became a life peer in 1992.

Archer, after early success in public relations and fundraising, became the youngest member of the Greater London Council, and in 1970 the youngest sitting member of Parliament. His parliamentary career was shortened by bankruptcy, but within two years he recovered financial solvency by writing a best-selling novel loosely based on his experiences. Archer went on to publish many other novels, and in the 1980s became Great Britain's best-known popular writer.

After attracting Margaret Thatcher's attention as a Conservative speaker, Archer was appointed to the deputy party chairmanship. His extreme right-wing views drew undesirable press coverage. In 1986 he was accused by the London *Star* of having sex with a prostitute and paying her to keep quiet. Archer won huge damages from the tabloid but had to resign his party post.

BIBLIOGRAPHY
Mantle, Jonathan. *In for a Penny: The Unauthorized Biography of Jeffrey Archer.* London: Hamish Hamilton, 1988.

Don M. Cregier

Architecture

See under individual country articles.

Arias Navarro, Carlos (1908–89)

Provincial governor, mayor of Madrid, 1965–73, and president of Spain, 1974–76.

Carlos Arias Navarro was a career politician during the dictatorship of Francisco Franco. His most successful appointment was as mayor of Madrid. Arias presided over the final national government appointed by Franco, and his resignation signaled the conclusive end of the dictatorship.

Born in Madrid in 1908, Arias studied law and held judiciary posts in military and civilian courts during and immediately after the Spanish Civil War (1936–39). Throughout the 1940s and 1950s he was civil governor in a succession of locales including León, Santa Cruz de Tenerife, the Canary Islands, and finally Navarre. In these posts he earned a reputation as a champion of law and order. In 1957 he was appointed national deputy director for security.

Arias's most successful and extended post was as mayor of Madrid. Under his leadership the capital enjoyed a dramatic increase in construction during which the city was almost completely modernized.

His first cabinet post came in 1973, when he served as minister of the interior during the brief presidency of Admiral Luis Carrero Blanco. After the assassination of Carrero, Franco shocked his ministers my naming Arias president of the government. As president, Arias faced several challenges including increased terrorist activity, growing politicization of the populace, as well as an economic recession brought on by the oil crisis. In addition, the failing health of Franco and the death of Carrero heightened uncertainty over the future of the regime. A weak president, Arias had little say in the appointment of his ministers. Therefore, he led an unruly cabinet plagued by disunity and disloyalty. Things collapsed following the death of Franco in 1975. Arias was trapped between potential reformers led by King Juan Carlos I and hard-line conservatives bent on retaining the structure of the Franco regime. In these difficult times Arias had neither the ability nor the political clout to implement a clear program of reform or retrenchment. He was finally asked by the king to resign and did so on July 1, 1976.

The most significant accomplishment of the Arias government was to reveal the untenability of the old regime. Mounting political and economic crisis combined with a strong reformist movement made it clear even to conservative politicians that change was inevitable. In the end the pace and scope of reforms left little political room for a career Francoist diplomat such as Arias, and he was asked to resign.

BIBLIOGRAPHY
Coverdale, J. F. *The Political Transformation of Spain after Franco.* New York: Praeger, 1979.
Payne, Stanley G. *The Franco Regime, 1936–1975.* Madison: University of Wisconsin Press, 1987.
Preston, Paul. *The Triumph of Democracy in Spain.* New York: Methuen, 1986.

Brian D. Bunk

Armenia

Independent successor state to the Armenian Soviet Socialist Republic of the former USSR, the smallest of the USSR's former republics. The republic of Armenia (Hayastani Hanrapetut'yun) consists of 11,500 square miles (29,800 sq km) of landlocked territory in the lesser Caucasus Mountains of southern Transcauscasia. It is surrounded by Georgia, Azerbaijan, Iran, and Turkey. Nakhichevan (Naxçivan), a noncontiguous segment of Azerbaijan, borders Armenia on the southwest. The predominantly Armenian enclave of Nagorno-Karabakh (Karabagh) lies to the east. The population of Armenia is approximately 3.7 million.

The country consists of a high plateau and mountains, the highest of which, Mt. Aragats, is an extinct 13,419-foot volcano northwest of the capital, Yerevan (Erevan). The area is a volcanic region with much seismic activity. The last major earthquake, which occurred in 1988, was devastating. The climate is cold and dry. Its principal water source is Lake Sevan, situated 6,234 feet above sea level. It is the source of the Razdan River, which cascades down to the Aras (Araks, Araxes), the country's longest river and its border with Turkey, Nakhichevan, and Iran. Agriculture and forestry provided 56.7 percent of the country's net material product in 1993 and employed 32.2 percent of the country's workers. Vegetables and fruit, especially grapes, are grown in the Yerevan basin watered by the Razdan and in the valley of the Aras.

Armenia. *Illustration courtesy of Bernard Cook.*

Though its mountain streams produce hydroelectric power, Armenia possesses no petroleum, gas, or coal.

The unfortunate history of the Armenians in the nineteenth and twentieth centuries has convinced many of the necessity of holding on to what they have to preserve themselves from destruction. In the 1820s Armenia was divided between the Russians and the Turks. The frontier between the empires ran through the lands of the Armenians, with approximately two-thirds of Armenian territory within the Ottoman Empire. The Armenians on the Russian side of the frontier were more fortunate. Misrule, massacre, and genocide were the fate of those within Turkey. In 1895–96 Armenians in Turkey were subjected to organized massacre and despoliation. In 1908 Armenians in the southern town of Adana were slaughtered. This was followed by the genocidal slaughter of Armenians within Turkey in 1915 during which approximately 1.5 million Armenians died.

The short-lived Armenian Republic, established in Russian Armenia following the collapse of the Russian Empire, succumbed to the double assault of the Kemalist Turks and the Bolsheviks. When the Bolsheviks reorganized the Transcaucasus, they assigned Nakhichevan and Nagorno-Karabakh to Azerbaijan. Nakhichevan, though not contiguous to the rest of Azerbaijan, was assigned to Azerbaijan in deference to the Kemalists. In 1921 Nagorno-Karabakh was handed over to the Azeris, though its population was 92 percent Armenian. It has been argued that this move was also out of deference to Turkey, but Stalin would often deliberately mix peoples to dilute national cohesiveness and enable Moscow to pit group against group.

In March 1922 Armenia was fused with Georgia and Azerbaijan to form the Transcaucasian Soviet Federated Socialist Republic (TSFSR), which became a constituent republic of the Soviet Union on December 30, 1922. In 1936 the TSFSR was dissolved and Armenia, Georgia, and Azerbaijan became separate union republics of the USSR.

The Armenian church was a significant unifying force for the Armenian people under foreign domination and in the Armenian diaspora. St. Gregory the Illuminator converted king Tridates III, and in A.D. 301 Armenia became the first state to adopt the Christian religion. The Armenian church, like the Georgian, is an independent church not organizationally affiliated with other Christian churches. The seat of its head, the Catholicos, is Echmiadzin, twelve miles west of Yerevan and about twelve miles from the Turkish border. The Armenian alphabet was designed in the fifth century by St. Mesrop, and church music, art, and architecture are deeply associated with Armenian cultural identity.

Under communism the Armenian church was persecuted. Churches were closed and the Ejmiatsin monestary was expropriated in 1928. Thousands of Armenians were deported for opposing collectivization and thousands perished during Stalin's great purge of the 1930s. However, there were advances in infrastructure and education for Armenia that had been neglected during the tsarist era. Armenia escaped damage during the Second World War and saw significant development after its conclusion. The war also resulted in some temporary relaxations on the Armenian church and expressions of Armenian national consciousness, both of which were utilized to rally support for the war effort. Armenia also figured for a while in Soviet postwar propaganda as a refuge for dispersed Armenians, and as many as 150,000 Armenians were encouraged to return from the diaspora. During the postwar period, though the agricultural sector continued to employ almost half the population, industrial development was stressed over agriculture. Much of the industry, however, was highly polluting, and, though Leninakan (Gyumri) became a textile center, 60 percent of Armenia's industry was concentrated around Yerevan.

Grigor Arutiunov, a Georgian-speaking associate of Larenty Beria, who had become first secretary of the Armenian Communist Party (CPA) in 1936, was arrested in 1953 following the purge of Beria. Arutiunov was succeeded by Suren Tovmasian (1953–58), Iakov Zarobian (1958–66), Anton Kochinian (1966–74), and Karen Demirchian (1974–88). Under Tovmasian some of those purged for nationalism in the 1920s and 1930s were rehabilitated, and controls were loosened over literature and thought. Under these conditions there was a resurgence of religion and national sentiment. According to Stephen and Sandra L. Batalden, "Soviet officials were reluctant to crack down on a republic that they touted as an Armenian homeland made possible only under benevolent Russian tutelage." They also point out that Armenian autonomy was related to the success of its industry, "which met and exceeded almost all production quotas." The Soviets were disinclined after Stalin to risk disrupting one of the few efficient areas of their domain.

The first impact of Mikhail Gorbachev's glasnost (openness) and perestroika (restructuring) were campaigns against corruption in the Communist Party, but popular attention quickly centered on the ecological degradation of Armenia and defense of conationals in Nagorno-Karabakh. When Armenians there took advantage of the growing disintegration of the USSR to vote in February 1988 for a transfer of their region to Armenia,

the Azeri government responded with a pogrom in Sumgait. A spontaneous defensive reaction in Armenia became the great catalyst for political change and independence. As many as a million people turned out for demonstrations in Yerevan organized by the Karabakh Committee. When the Azeris responded by killing Armenians in Sumgait and the Presidium of the Supreme Soviet refused to transfer Nagorno-Karabakh to Armenia, Armenian dissatisfaction became intense. Unable to control the situation First Secretary Demirchian was replaced by a Gorbachev lieutenant, Suren Arutunyan, who, however, was no more successful in taming the nationalists than his predecessor. The December 1988 earthquake that devastated Leninakan, destroyed Spitak, and killed twenty-five thousand was used by Gorbachev as an opportunity to arrest the Karabakh Committee ostensibly for interfering with the relief that they in fact were directing. The arrested became national heroes and were released without trial six months later in May 1989. The committee reorganized as a political party, the Pan-Armenian National Movement (Hayots Hamazgayin Sharzhum, HHS).

Gorbachev had attempted in January 1989 to defuse the Nagorno-Karabakh issue by replacing Azerbaijan's control of the autonomous republic with direct control from Moscow. But he surrendered to Azeri opposition, including a rail, road, and pipeline blockade of Armenia, and returned it to Azeri control in November. The Armenian Supreme Soviet responded by declaring the area part of a "unified Armenian republic." When the Supreme Soviet in Moscow declared the Armenian move unconstitutional, the Armenian Supreme Soviet asserted the right to veto legislation from Moscow.

In the May–June 1990 elections the HHS emerged as the largest party, with 35 percent of the seats. Its leader, Levon Ter-Petrossian, defeated Vladimir Movsissian, the Communist first secretary, in the election for chairman of the Supreme Soviet, and Vazgen Manukian from the HHS was appointed prime minister. On August 23 the Supreme Soviet declared the sovereignty of the "Republic of Armenia." Before Armenia attained full independence, the new government began to dismantle Armenia's Soviet-era collective farms through a privatization program. By the end of 1993, 90 percent of arable land, employing 32.2 percent of the working population, had been transferred to private owners.

Armenia refused to participate in the March 1991 referendum on the preservation of the USSR. Instead, it scheduled a referendum on secession for September 1991. Tensions over Nagorno-Karabakh increased with Azeri accusations of Armenian involvement in the fighting that had erupted between Armenians of the region and Azeri government forces. The Armenians for their part accused the Soviet government of assisting the Azeris, who had voted to preserve the USSR.

The HHS government's effort to establish good relations with Turkey as a prelude to independence was attacked by the extreme nationalist Union for National Self-Determination (UNS), the CPA, and the Armenian Revolutionary Federation (Dashnaktsutyun, AFR), which had governed Armenia from 1918 to 1920. The CPA opposed secession, the UNS desired immediate secession, and the AFR wanted gradual secession in accord with the five-year process stipulated by the law on secession passed by the Union Supreme Soviet in April 1991. The failed coup against Gorbachev in Moscow, however, settled the issue. In the aftermath the CPA dissolved itself, while 99.3 percent of the 94.4 percent of the electorate who participated in the September 21 referendum voted for independence. On September 23 the Armenian Supreme Soviet declared Armenia independent. On October 16, 1991, Ter-Petrossian, running against five opponents, was elected president with 87 percent of the vote.

On December 21 Armenia joined the Commonwealth of Independent States, and early in 1992 it was admitted to the United Nations and the Conference on Security and Cooperation in Europe (CSCE). However, as Armenia organized its independent status, its economic situation worsened. The Azeri blockade was joined by Turkey, and fighting in Georgia disrupted that path of entry. The new country and particularly Yerevan were flooded with refugees from the intensified fighting in Nagorno-Karabakh. Increasing calls were raised for the resignation of Ter-Petrossian. In February 1993 he dismissed Arutyunian and appointed economic reformer Hrant Bagratyan prime minister. Nevertheless, giant rallies protested the lack of energy and called for the resignation of the president.

Armenia is extremely dependent on imported energy. Other than hydroelectrical production, which supplied 68 percent of Armenia's electricity in 1993, the country is lacking in resources. It has a nuclear power plant that was taken off line because of earthquake damage in 1988; in desperation, one unit was put back on line in late 1995. Before the Azeri blockade almost 90 percent of Armenia's Russian oil and Turkmeni natural gas had come through controlled Azeri pipelines. In January 1993 the sole pipeline bringing gas to Armenia was blown up in Georgia. Though some gas began flowing through a temporary line in February, the lack of energy caused the closure of most factories. During 1993–94 Armenia suffered its third winter with only intermittent heat and lighting, and thousands of Armenians emigrated. Nevertheless, Bagratyan presided over a gradual economic improvement that led to growth in 1994 after four years of decline. Exports increased and progress was made in stabilizing the currency while inflation decreased.

In July 1994 opposition parties organized a series of large anti–Ter-Petrossian rallies. The Union of Civic Accord (UCA), an opposition umbrella group, was formed to maintain the pressure with demonstrations in Yerevan and oppose HHS proposals in the legislature, now called the Supreme Council, for a new constitution that would strengthen presidential power at the expense of the legislature.

Following the assassination of Ambartsum Galstian, former mayor of Yerevan, the leading opposition party ARF was suppressed and a number of its leading members tried. In May the government was accused of attempting to murder Paruir Hairikian, leader of the UNS. The ARF and eight other parties were barred from the July legislative elections, and the Republican Bloc of six parties led by the HHS won a decisive majority with 119 seats. The next-largest group, the Shamiram Women's Party, won eight. The reorganized CPA won seven and UNS three. A simultaneous referendum approved the presidential constitution with a 68 percent vote from the 56 percent of the electorate who participated.

The year 1996 was dominated by preparations for the presidential election, held on September 22. Three of the seven candidates withdrew in September, throwing their support to Vazgen Manukyan, the leading challenger to Ter-Petrossian. International monitors cited irregularities and questioned the official tally, which gave Ter-Petrossian 51.75 percent to Manukyan's 41.29 percent. There were massive demonstrations and an attack on the parliament on September 25. Government troops, however, restored order. On November 4 Bagratyan, who had attempted to step down in January, resigned. He was replaced on November 6 by Armen Sarkisyan; Vano Siradeghyan, who left the Interior Ministry, became mayor of Yerevan.

Political tension continued. Robert Kocharian, a native of Nagorno-Karabakh who had been elected president of that region on December 22, 1994, became prime minister in 1997. On February 3, 1998, Ter-Petrossian was forced from office by a number of factors, including the economy, his increasingly authoritarian style, and his willingness to compromise with the Azeri on the issue of Nagorno-Karabakh. Ter-Petrossian was willing to recognize formal Azeri sovereignty over the Armenian enclave if the Azeris respected the de facto independence of the area. Ter-Petrossian was replaced by Kocharian. In the subsequent presidential election Kocharian won 37 percent of the vote in the first round on March 16.

BIBLIOGRAPHY

"Armenia." *Europe World Year Book.* London: Europa Publications, 1996, Vol. 2, 406–10.

Batalden, Stephen K., and Sandra L. Batalden. *The Newly Independent States of Eurasia: Handbook of Former Soviet Republics.* Phoenix, Ariz.: Oryx, 1993.

Chorbajian, Levon, Patrick Donabedian, and Claude Mutafian. *The Caucasian Knot: The History and Geo-Politics of Nagorno-Karabagh.* London: ZED, 1994.

Goldenberg, Suzanne. *Pride of Small Nations: The Caucasus and Post-Soviet Disorder.* London: Zed Books, 1994.

Hovannisian, Richard G., ed. *The Armenian People from Ancient to Modern Times.* Vol. 2. New York: St. Martin's Press, 1997.

Malkasian, Mark. *"Gha-ra-bagh!" The Emergence of the National Democratic Movement in Armenia.* Detroit: Wayne State University, 1996.

Bernard Cook

SEE ALSO Nagorno-Karabakh

Arms Control Treaties and Agreements

1963 Partial Test Ban Treaty (PTBT): Banned the testing of nuclear weapons in the atmosphere, in outer space, and under water. The signatories agreed to conduct nuclear weapons tests, or any other nuclear explosions, only underground. Signed August 5, 1963, it entered into force October 10, 1963.

1967 Outer Space Treaty: Established principles governing the activities of states in the exploration of outer space, including the moon and other celestial bodies. It prohibited the placing in orbit around the earth, installing on the moon or any other celestial body, or stationing in outer space of nuclear or other weapons of mass destruction. Signed January 27, 1967, it entered into force October 10, 1967.

1968 Non-Proliferation Treaty (NPT): Designed to prevent the spread of nuclear weapons, while promoting the peaceful uses of nuclear energy. Signed July 1, 1968, it entered into force March 5, 1970. It was scheduled to expire in 1995 but was extended at the 1995 NPT conference.

1971 Seabed Treaty: Prohibited emplacement of nuclear weapons and other weapons of mass destruction on the seabed and the ocean floor and in the subsoil thereof. Signed February 11, 1971, it entered into force May 19, 1972.

1972 Biological Weapons Convention (BWC): Prohibited development, production, and stockpiling of bacteriological, biological, and toxic weapons, and provided for the destruction of existing weapons of these types. Parties to the convention agreed not to develop, produce, stockpile, or acquire biological agents or toxins "of types and in quantities that have no justification for prophylactic, protective, and other peaceful purposes," as well as related weapons and means of delivery. Signed April 10, 1972, it entered into force March 26, 1975.

1972 SALT I Interim Agreement: Agreement between the United States and the USSR on certain measures with respect to the limitation of strategic offensive arms. It froze existing aggregate levels of American and Soviet strategic nuclear missile launchers and submarines until an agreement on more comprehensive measures could be reached. Signed May 26, 1972, it entered into force March 26, 1975.

1972 ABM Treaty: Limited the deployment of U.S. and Soviet antiballistic missile systems. Signed May 26, 1972, it entered into force October 3, 1972. A protocol on the limitation of antiballistic missile systems, further limiting each party to a single ABM system deployment area, was signed on July 3, 1974, and entered into force May 24, 1976.

1974 Threshold Test Ban Treaty (TTBT): Treaty between the United States and the USSR prohibiting underground nuclear weapons tests of more than 150 kilotons. Signed July 3, 1974, it entered into force December 11, 1990.

1975 Helsinki Final Act: Concluding document of the Conference on Security and Cooperation in Europe (CSCE). Signed by thirty-five nations, it provided for notification of major military maneuvers involving more than 25,000 troops and other confidence-building measures. It was signed and entered into force August 1, 1975.

1976 Peaceful Nuclear Explosions Treaty (PNET): Treaty between the United States and the USSR limiting any individual underground nuclear explosion carried out by the parties outside U.S. and Soviet weapons test sites to 150 kilotons. Signed May 28, 1976, it entered into force December 11, 1990.

1977 ENMOD Convention: Prohibited military or any other hostile use of environmental modification techniques with widespread, long-lasting, and severe effects. Signed May 18, 1977, it entered into force October 5, 1978.

1979 SALT II Treaty: Treaty between the United States and the USSR on the limitation of strategic offensive arms, replacing the SALT I Interim Agreement. Signed June 18, 1979, the treaty never entered into force and was superseded by Start I in 1991.

1981 Inhumane Weapons Convention: Prohibited or restricted the use of certain conventional weapons deemed to be excessively injurious or to have indiscriminate effects. Signed by thirty-five states April 10, 1981, it entered into force December 2, 1983.

1986 Stockholm Document: Document of the Stockholm conference on confidence and security-building measures (CSBMs) and disarmament in Europe. It contained a set of six concrete and mutually complementary CSBMs, including mandatory ground or aerial inspection of military activities, which improved upon those contained in the Helsinki Final Act. Adopted September 19, 1986, it entered into force January 1, 1987.

1987 INF Treaty: This treaty between the United States and the USSR eliminated and banned all U.S. and Soviet ground-launched ballistic and cruise missiles (intermediate-range and shorter-range missiles) with a range capability of between 300 and 3,400 miles (500 and 5,500 km). Signed December 8, 1987, it entered into force June 1, 1988, and was fully implemented June 1, 1991.

1990 Vienna Document: Document of CSCE Negotiations on CSBMs. It incorporated the Stockholm document of 1986 but added measures related to military forces and activities, and improved communications, contacts, and verification. Adopted November 17, 1990, it entered into force January 1, 1991.

1990 CFE Treaty: Treaty on Conventional Armed Forces in Europe. It reduced and set ceilings from the Atlantic to the Urals on key armaments essential to surprise attack and the initiating of large-scale offensive operations. Signed by the twenty-two NATO and Warsaw Pact states on November 19, 1990, and applied provisionally July 17, 1992, it entered into force November 9, 1992. It was to be implemented within forty months of entry into force.

1991 START I: Treaty between the United States and the USSR on the reduction and limitation of strategic offensive arms. It established significantly reduced limits for intercontinental ballistic missiles and their associated launchers and warheads; submarine-launched ballistic missile launchers and warheads; and heavy bombers and their armaments, including long-range nuclear air-launched cruise missiles. It was signed July 31, 1991. The protocol to the treaty between the United States and the USSR on the reduction and limitation of strategic offensive arms (Lisbon START Protocol) enabled implementation of the START I Treaty. The protocol constituted an amendment to and is an integral part of the START Treaty, and provided for Russia, Belarus, Ukraine, and Kazakhstan to succeed to the Soviet Union's obligations

under the treaty. Also, Belarus, Kazakhstan, and Ukraine committed themselves to accede to the Nuclear Non-Proliferation Treaty (NPT) as nonnuclear weapons states in the shortest possible time. In accompanying letters they committed themselves to eliminate all nuclear weapons from their territory within seven years. It was signed May 23, 1992. All signatory states have ratified, with Belarus and Kazakhstan acceding to the NPT. It entered into force on December 5, 1994.

1991 UN Register of Conventional Arms Transfers: Encouraged greater openness and simplified monitoring of excessive arms buildup in any one country. The register requests all participating states to record their imports and exports of certain major weapons systems, and to submit this information by April 30 of the following year. Created by a resolution of the U.N. General Assembly on December 10, 1991, it called on members to submit their information beginning April 30, 1993. More than sixty countries provided information within the first year.

1992 Vienna Document: Document of the negotiations on CSBMs convened in accordance with the relevant provisions of the concluding document on the Vienna Meeting of the CSCE. It incorporated the Vienna Document 1990 and added further measures related to transparency regarding military forces and activities, and to constraints on military activities. It expanded the zone of application for CSBMs to include the territory of USSR successor states beyond the traditional zone in Europe (i.e., all of Kazakhstan, Kyrgyzstan, Tajikistan, Turkmenistan, and Uzbekistan). Adopted March 4, 1992, it entered into force May 1, 1992.

1992 Treaty on Open Skies: Committed member nations in Eurasia and North America to open their airspace, on a reciprocal basis, permitting the overflight of their territory by unarmed observation aircraft to strengthen confidence through the openness of military activities. Signed and applied provisionally March 24, 1992, it entered into force in 1993 after twenty states had deposited instruments of ratification.

June 1992 Oslo Final Document: Final Document of the Extraordinary Conference of the states party to the CFE Treaty. It enabled implementation of the CFE treaty in the new international situation following the dissolution of the Warsaw Pact and the Soviet Union. This agreement noted the May 15, 1992, agreement in Tashkent among the successor states of the USSR, which possessed territory within the area of application of the CFE Treaty, and apportioned among them the obligations and rights of the USSR, thus making them parties to the CFE Treaty. It was signed and entered into force June 5, 1992.

1992 CFE 1A: Concluding act of the Negotiations on Personnel Strength of Conventional Armed Forces in Europe. It set declared national limits on the personnel strength of conventional armed forces in the area from the Atlantic to the Urals. Signed July 10, 1992, it entered into force July 17, 1992, with the provision that it was to be implemented within forty months of entry into force.

1993 Chemical Weapons Convention (CWC): Agreement drafted by the thirty-nine nations of the Conference of Disarmament to Ban Chemical Weapons Worldwide. It prohibits the development, production, stockpiling, and use of chemical weapons, and provides for their destruction. Opened for signature in Paris on January 13, 1993, it was scheduled to enter into force 180 days after deposit of the sixty-fifth instrument of ratification, but no earlier than January 13, 1995. By April 1994 it had been signed by more than 150 nations.

1993 START II: Further reduced U.S. and Russian strategic offensive arms by eliminating all MIRVed (Multiple Independently targetable Reentry Vehicles) ICBMs (including all "heavy" Inter Continental Ballistic Missiles) and by reducing the overall total of warheads for each side to between 3,000 and 3,500. Signed January 3, 1993, it will enter into force following ratification by the United States and Russia and after entry into force of the START I Treaty of 1991. Start I entered into force on December 5, 1994. Start II was ratified by the U.S. Senate on January 26, 1996. It awaits ratification by the Russian Duma.

1994 Trilateral Nuclear Agreement: Statement by the presidents of the United States, Russia, and Ukraine detailing the procedures to be followed once START I enters into force and Ukraine becomes a nonnuclear weapons state party to the Nuclear Non-proliferation treaty (NPT), in the transfer of SS-19 and SS-24 warheads from Ukraine to Russia for dismantling and the associated compensation to Ukraine in the form of fuel assemblies for nuclear power stations, as well as security assurances to Ukraine. It was signed in Moscow on January 14, 1994.

BIBLIOGRAPHY
NATO Factsheet No. 7. gopher://gopher.nato.int:70/1 and
   http://www.nato.int/

Bernard Cook

SEE ALSO Comprehensive Test Ban Treaty; Conference for Security and Cooperation in Europe; Intermediate-Range Nuclear Forces Treaty; Mutual and Balanced Force Reductions; Nuclear Non-Proliferation Treaty; Partial Test Ban Treaty; Strategic Arms Reduction Treaty; Threshold Test Ban Treaty

Aron, Raymond (1905–83)

French sociologist, political scientist, philosopher, professor, and journalist. Raymond Aron analyzed historical developments from a liberal, skeptical perspective in more than forty books, six hundred articles, and four thousand newspaper and magazine editorials.

Raised in an assimilated Jewish family in Paris, Aron was an outstanding student at the École Normale Supérieure, and his 1935 book on German sociology, *La Sociologie Allemande Contemporaine,* established his reputation. During World War II he edited *La France libre,* the journal of the Free French Movement, in London, and in 1955 he became professor of sociology at the Sorbonne. Sympathetic to socialism in his youth, with the beginning of the Cold War he became an outspoken opponent of Marxism and the Soviet Union. His long-lasting dispute with Jean-Paul Sartre and his criticism of the student rebellion in France in 1968 attracted much attention. Although to the right of most French intellectuals, he often took independent positions, including his support for Algerian independence and his criticism of Charles de Gaulle's position on NATO.

BIBLIOGRAPHY
Aron, Raymond. *Memoirs of Raymond Aron: Fifty Years of Political Reflection.* Tr. by George Heloch. New York: Holmes & Meier, 1994.
Colquhoun, Robert. *Raymond Aron.* 2 Vols. Beverly Hills, Calif.: Sage, 1986.
Mahoney, Daniel. *The Liberal Political Science of Raymond Aron: A Critical Introduction.* Lanham, Md.: Rowman & Littlefield, 1991.

Thomas T. Lewis

Art

The political division of Europe after World War II was immediately visible in culture. The dictatorial regimes of Eastern Europe embraced the arts as propaganda and a convenient politicized platform for Iron Curtain policies and way of life. In contrast, the visual arts in Western European countries celebrated individual freedom and creative expression. While literature and film were concerned with bringing cultural closure to the complex experiences of the war, painting and sculpture have, with only sporadic exceptions, distanced themselves from descriptive representation of this event. Prophetic of things to come in culture, the films of the postwar era demonstrated that their narrative power could displace the role previously held by other visual forms of expression.

After the war Europe had to confront its recent historic and artistic legacy. Modern art and the innovative visual and theoretical explorations of the avant-garde had been ridiculed and discredited by the dictatorial regimes of the prewar era. Hitler's Degenerate Art Exhibition of 1937 demonstrated how political oppression can curtail artistic freedom. Institutions and large international exhibitions continued, however, to play an important role in the development of European art. The Salon de la Libération held in Paris only a few weeks after the war celebrated past achievements but also marked the starting point of a new artistic era. In Italy the Venice Biennale, which in 1995 celebrated its centennial, reasserted the European continent as an important showcase for the arts. Other forums, such as the international exhibition Documenta, and the London-based Institute for Contemporary Arts, also aimed to reestablish and validate the leading position of European art within an international arena. In the decades to come they were at the forefront of many artistic developments.

The "cry of rebellion" of the early European avant-garde so vociferously expressed in its art and behavior was replaced in the immediate postwar era with a subdued attitude and search for healing through aesthetic novelty. The restoration of faith in art, and Western humanism, was coupled with an existentialist inquiry about individual identity that propelled the artistic quests into thoughtful investigations of visual and conceptual meanings. The fact that many artists started their careers before the war established a complex, often even uneasy dialogue between past and present. In this context the continuing activity of well-known artists such as Pablo Picasso (1881–1973) and Henri Matisse (1869–1954), who was earlier called the "dean of Degenerate art," provided a model for the reconciliation and rejuvenation of the arts. Picasso's art remained rooted in reality. In addition to still life, such as *Pitcher, Candle and Enamel Saucepan* (1945), landscapes from the south of France, *Mediterranean Landscape* (1952), portraits, and nudes, Picasso pursued his experiments with ceramics and sculpture based on found objects as visible in *Woman with Baby Carriage* (1950), in which he used a real carriage. Matisse adopted a highly colorful, almost abstract approach. This direction, developed partly because of his illness, became a statement of defiance toward his disability and a celebration of life. After a 1941 operation for an intestinal disorder, Matisse was largely bedridden. In the 1950s he also was afflicted by asthma and heart problems. At times he was forced to paint with the aid of a pole and crayon while lying in bed. *The Snail* (1953), a work in which the artist used gouache on cut and pasted paper, perfectly illustrates the rhythm and simplicity of forms and color that can be read both as abstraction and stylized reality. It is precisely this delicate balance between nonrepresentation and reality that was an essential part of post–World War II European art.

The need for visual expression and the desire to surpass the narrative while exploring self-identity led European artists to develop a style that paralleled the American abstract expressionism movement. Labeled *art informel* (literally, formless art) and using existentialist philosophy as its conceptual platform, this painterly style explored creativity while allowing artists to symbolically venture into the past. In France Georges Mathieu (1921–) in *Capetians Everywhere* (1954) and Portuguese-French artist Maria Elena Vieira da Silva (1908–) in *The Invisible Stroller* (1951) expressed in their canvases a powerful and dynamic calligraphy with lyrical and even historical connotations. Similar concerns with a gestural painterly approach are visible in *Painting 51–12* (1952) by the German artist Hans Hartung (1904–89) and in the work of his fellow countrymen Frans Wols (1913–51). In Italy Emilio Vedova (1919–99) and Afro Basaldella (1912–76) created nonrepresentational images in which the brush strokes and the palette are the focal tools of expression.

Several artists furthered nonfigurative research and became preoccupied with the materiality of surfaces. This development was named *tachism* (from the French word *tache,* meaning "stain"). Among the artists in this group are Italians Alberto Burri (1915–95) and Lucio Fontana (1899–68), whose paintings and sculptures use fabric not as a concealed support but rather as the purpose of their visual investigation. In France Nicholas De Stael (1914–55), in paintings such as *Composition of Roof Tops* (1952), used heavy impasto and transformed the subtleties of the painted surface into a textural relief. Abstraction was also adopted by the northern European group CoBrA (the name stood for the cities Copenhagen, Brussels and Amsterdam, where the artists came from). In works such as *Exploded Head* (1958), Dutch artist Karel Appel (1921–), one of the main figures of the group, evokes through a dialogue between expressiveness and abstraction the extremes of the human condition.

Postwar figurative art in Europe is defined by a search for reflection on the modern individual. A certain level of anxiety fueled by philosophical ideas replaced the classical notion of "man as a measure of all things." Alberto Giacometti's (1901–66) disquieting sculptures of elongated figures as in *City Square* (1948) and his monochromatic paintings reveal a nostalgic narrative and a need to examine the relationship between the individual and the world. Similar concerns are found in *La Semaine des quatres jeudis* (1949) by Balthus (1908–) who, here as in other paintings, created scenes of intense tension and desire. More painterly but equally dramatic and filled with anxiety and even violence are the works of British artist Francis Bacon (1909–).

European sculpture of the postwar era was influenced in the first decades by earlier twentieth-century art, in particular the work of Brancusi and cubist and surrealist assemblages. British artists Henry Moore (1898–1986) and Barbara Hepworth (1903–75) acknowledged their connection with Brancusi's aesthetics and produced works in which biomorphic exploration of form was paralleled by a deep concern for the specificity of the materials used. Other sculptors, however, wanted to detach themselves from past models and investigate ways to establish links with contemporary developments in painting. For example, Jean Dubuffet (1901–85), a painter and sculptor concerned with rendering an archaic sense of nature and the solitude of the human figure, translated textures and intricate forms from the two-dimensional surface into sculptures. The fantasy, playfulness, even childlike qualities of his works contrasted with an inner anguish that would later develop into monumental sculptures such as the 1971 *Group of Four Trees.* Other artists of the period—Italian Arnaldo Pomodoro (1926–) and Spaniard Eduardo Chillida (1924–)—were interested in establishing a sculptural version of tachism and *art informel.* Their works explored new possibilities of free forms and the effects of juxtaposing different materials and textures.

If mimesis was rejected in Western Europe in the years following the war, social realism would find its place at the center of Eastern European art. The lack of ambiguity and possibilities of direct messages made realism the norm in all these countries. Innovative approaches and individual creativity were strongly discouraged. An abundance of official portraits and scenes depicting work, in factories or in the fields, flooded the art scene. The war was also a popular subject scene and together with historical subjects served as political metaphors for the present. Massive monuments of leaders and various symbols of the political system were erected everywhere. The extent of these projects became known outside the Eastern bloc in the 1990s, after the fall of the Iron Curtain.

The 1960s marked a decisive shift from the introspect postwar inquiries to an interest in the dialogue between mass media and everyday life. The major movement of the decade was pop art, and its impact was felt throughout the world. It started in the late 1950s in Great Britain at the ICA. Richard Hamilton's famous 1956 collage *Just*

what is it that makes today's homes so different, so appealing? eloquently illustrates the direction of pop art. Other artists in this group include Eduardo Paolozzi (1924–), David Hockney (1937–), and R. B. Kitaj (1932–). Their works dealt with mundane subject matter that combined a pictorial approach with the directness of advertising techniques.

In continental Europe pop art tendencies are known mostly under the name *le nouveau réalisme* (new realism). French artist Yves Klein (1928–62), a central figure of the movement, established in his paintings and performances the human figure as an essential link between abstraction and representation. Like American pop art, new realism is heterogeneous and includes artists whose directions crossed over into minimalism, assemblage, performance, as well as conceptual, environmental, and process art. The eclectic styles and ideas within the movement reinforce the late stage of these modernist traits and foreshadow postmodern practices. New realism included artists with very different concerns and modes of expression. For example, Italian Michelangelo Pistelotto (1933–) used mirrors to create an immediate connection with the viewer while nostalgically referring to mimesis and the Renaissance tradition. Also in Italy Mimmo Rotella (1918–) created images, such as the 1962 *The Assault,* using layers of torn posters and constructing through this unexpected texture a sentimental view of mass media culture. Valerio Adami (1935–) was interested in another aspect of pop culture: the directness offered by cartoons, which he linked in his imagery to the surrealist tradition. French sculptor César (César Baldaccini, 1921–) was initially interested in the human form and gender identity in works such as *Thumb* (1967), and later, in his assemblages, became preoccupied with abstracted forms deriving from compressing automobiles. Gender, often perceived as a response to César, was also an issue in the sculptures and assemblages of Nikki de Saint Phalle (1930–), as articulated in her *Nana* (1965) and *Black Venus* (1967).

European artists explored other possibilities that would take them outside traditional art forms and space. For example, Christo's (Christo Juvacheff, 1935–) projects of wrapping in fabric and plastic large urban structures transformed assemblage, performance, and installation into monumental yet temporary works. American happenings played a significant role in heightening European artists' interest in performance and inspired them to revisit examples offered by the futurists, dadaist and other avant-garde movements. In Britain, happenings were also connected to the dynamic and popular rock scene.

Parallel to pop art, two different movements, op art and kinetic art, developed during the same decade. They operated on a different level of visual perception. In contrast to pop art's playful immediacy and commentary on mass media and contemporary life, op art and kinetic art explored visual illusionism. Using experiments of the early European abstraction from constructivism and the Bauhaus school, artists such as Victor Vasarely (1908–), the best known of the op art group, created images that linked pure abstraction with scientific approaches. His *Orion Noir* (1963–70) clearly demonstrates the optical effects created by the rigor of the palette and the orderly dynamism of geometric forms. British artist Brigdet Riley's (1931–) almost monochromatic works are even more mesmerizing, owing to the powerful illusionism deriving from the precise linear pattern. This group also included artists such as Italian Enrico Castellani (1930–), who translated in his works, such as *Silver Surface* (1969), his understanding of surfaces and materials into an abstract sensibility.

Expanding the op art ideas, kinetic artists revived early modernist ideas and developed structures that combined visual effects with mechanical attributes and even computer technology as in the case of Nicolas Schöffer (1912–). These developments overtly acknowledged a significant change in the attitude toward the object and the creative process.

A discontent with the tangibility of art and a greater concern with the process of making art that emerged parallel to the development of conceptual art in the United States would become the essential inquiry for many European artists in the seventies. Rejecting defined categories and traditional materials and means of expression, these artists were more diverse in style and theoretical approaches than the previous decade. Installations and performances, assemblages and photomontages and text and video contributed to redefine the entire discourse of visual representation. One of the most influential figures of this period was German artist Joseph Beuys (1921–86). Briefly connected with the group Fluxus, Beuys, using avant-grade strategies, was able paradoxically to establish some of the essential postmodern directions in European art. Combining sculpture with performance and critical theory with feelings, he was an inspiration for revitalizing the arts by displacing the modernist rejection of the past. His legacy, which includes the powerful performances *How to Explain Pictures to a Dead Hare* (1965) and the installation *The Pack* (1969), influenced generations of artists. During the same period, Belgian artist Marcel Broodthaers (1924–76) created assemblages that he labeled "museums," aimed at challenging the display and organization of exhibitions.

In Italy conceptual art is represented by the group Arte Povera, (literally, poor art), a reference to its celebration of everyday, ordinary materials. The main precursor of this movement was Piero Manzoni (1933–63), whose interest in recording presences was articulated in sculptures, drawings, paintings, and performances with an eclectic selection of materials (cotton, fiber, oil paint, bread, fur, stone, charcoal, chrome, etc.). Arte Povera artists included Giovanni Anselmo, Luciano Fabro, Jannis Kounellis, Mario Merz, and others. Their works juxtaposed everyday, often perishable materials to durable metals and even to live animals or plants to create startling metaphors. Rejecting the traditional notion of art, they infused in their works, however, subtle connotations to the European artistic heritage, more specifically references to the classical ideals so prevalent in Italian culture. Merz's (1925–) installation *Double Igloo: Alligator with Fibonacci Numbers to 377* (1979) is a visual and conceptual contrast between primordial and high-tech forms and meanings. Similarly, in his installation *Cavalli* (1969), in which he used real horses, Kounellis (1936–) not only reflects on the relationship between nature and built environment but also brings, in an unexpected way, the classical tradition within the modern artistic space. Anselmo (1936–) was also interested in juxtaposing opposites as visible in his 1968 sculpture *Untitled (Sculpture That Eats)*, in which the apparent banality is a clever symbolism that examines the complexity of life and death.

In France Daniel Buren (1938–) explored ways to separate art from the European tradition of illusionism and further exposed possibilities of merging art and its surrounding. In his *140 Stations du métro parisien* (1970), he not only abandoned traditional gallery spaces but also, by inserting his abstracted forms into the billboards of the subway, created a paradoxical link between the traditional picture format and the new visual means of modern culture. His later work *Deux plateaux* (1985–86), a site-specific installation, reveals his continued concern with the relationship between art and the environment. German conceptual artist Hans Haacke (1936–) critically investigated in his installations the role institutions play in the art world. His 1975 *On Social Ground* exposes his critique of corporate art patronage.

Many conceptual artists looked at language and text as essential factors in constructing meanings. The group Art-Language included many British artists such as Terry Atkinson, David Bainbridge, Michael Baldwin, Ian Burn, and Charles Harrison, who were dissatisfied with the modernist concept of art and inserted linguistics theories into the process of visual representation. Another group of artists in England simply known as Gilbert (1943–)

and George (1942–) brought a new dimension to the meaning of art. Considering themselves living sculptures, the two artists, dressed in suits and sometimes with their heads and hands painted in gold, copper, or red, performed live, moving in a mechanical manner. Their claim that their daily activities were continuously producing art created an ambiguous relationship between art and life. Among their well-known performances are *The Singing Sculpture,* first performed in London in 1969 and later in New York, and *The Red Sculpture,* from 1976. Some of their performances were documented in photographs, books, and drawings.

Earthworks and environmental projects of European artists were often more conceptual than site-specific. The work of Dutch artist Jan Dibbets, *Sea-Horizon, 0–135 Degrees,* from the early 1970s representing various photographic angles of the landscape juxtaposed to create a conceptual redefinition of the environment is a perfect example of this approach. British artist Richard Long (1945–) explored a more direct relationship with nature. His concern for site-specific works like *A Line in Ireland* (1974) was coupled with an interest in inserting nature into the exhibition space, as witnessed by his *Red Slate Ring* and *Avon Mud Circle* (1986).

Realism continued to be explored by European artists in the seventies regardless of the latest trend. In England Lucian Freud (1922–) painted in a style reminiscent of the Renaissance tradition but also with connotations to modernist movements. The central role of the human figure either bluntly present or implied is charged in his paintings with a sense of desire, sensuality, and voyeurism. In contrast to Freud's descriptive realism Frank Auerbach's (1931–) style is more painterly and expressive.

While Western European artists were exploring new modes of expression and means of visual display, Eastern European artists were developing their art in a completely different context. The arts continued to be part of a carefully orchestrated and controlled propaganda. State sponsorship was the only form of funding, and the visual arts and artists were totally dependent on it. As in previous decades there was an abundance of official portraits, sometimes with historical connotations. As political changes occurred and various figures fell into disgrace, some portraits and monuments disappeared as new ones were made. Politicized representations of historical events and contemporary subjects were the overwhelming choice. Landscapes, still lifes, and portraits were also painted but they were never the center of attention of the official taste; mimetic reproductions and social realism prevailed. Creativity, talent, and idiosyncratic poetics were dismissed in favor of political agenda. However, the ten-

dency to incorporate new ideas slowly appeared in art. Experiments were permitted mostly in graphic design and other art forms such as ceramics, printmaking, and textiles, considered marginal and thus not threatening to the particular regime. Polish artist Magdalena Abakanowicz (1930–), whose art was well received in Western Europe, used materials and dramatic representations of the human form and spirit as in her *Backs* (1976–80) to reveal the intense but quiet drama of repression. Similarly, Czech artist Magdalena Jetelová's abstract wood sculpture *Table* (1988) juxtaposes opposites (enclosures and openings, finished and raw materials) to signify lack of freedom. The disparity between the developments in Eastern Europe and the West were best revealed at the Venice Biennale, where many European countries continue to exhibit. In the 1990s, after the fall of the Iron Curtain, a greater connection between European artists has been reestablished, and in the 1990s the Venice Biennale demonstrated the reemergence of a wider European artistic dialogue.

The 1980s brought a plurality of styles and ideas that carried, in Europe, a certain level of nostalgia. "Neo" was a favorite term of the decade: neoexpressionism, neoabstraction, neoconceptual. By the beginning of the 1980s German artists brought to the forefront a painterly style. Georg Baselitz (1935–) and Anselm Kiefer (1945–) revived expressionism and revisited Germany's recent past, more precisely World War II. With strong, complementary color schemes and formal contortions reminiscent of Nolde and Kirchner, Baselitz's emotions explode on the canvas. Keifer, on the other hand, employed a somber palette, heavy impasto, and a concise yet poignant narrative that immediately directs the viewer into an inquiry about war, the Holocaust, and human oppression. His works include *Margarethe* (1981), and *Nurnberg-Festspeil-Weise* (1991).

The past, but a more distant one, often even classicism, was also a source for Italian neoexpressionism. Francesco Clemente (1952–), Sandro Chia (1946–), Mimmo Paladino (1948–), and Enzo Cucchi (1949–), also known as the Italian transavangarde, explored their national artistic heritage in terms of subject matter, techniques, representations, styles, and appropriating and redefining tradition. Clemente's use of the fresco technique in *Fraternità* (1988) and Chia's references to the Renaissance and the baroque in *The Scandalous Face* (1981) clearly represent the directions of these artists. Similar to the Italian artists, the French artist team Anne and Patrick Poirier made nostalgic references to antiquity as articulated in their 1989 work *Fall of the Giants.*

The artistic energy and eclecticism of the 1990s opened up new possibilities and venues of artistic inquiry. Looking at international developments, in particular those from the United States, but also building on their on traditions, experiences, contexts, and histories, European artists of the second half of this century produced a vibrant and meaningful art that explored with audacity and novelty the boundaries of visual expression.

BIBLIOGRAPHY

Arnason H. *Modern Art.* Englewood Cliffs, N.J.: Prentice-Hall, 1991.

Celant, Germano, exhibition organizer. *The Italian Metamorphosis.* Exhibition catalogue. New York: Guggenheim Museum, 1994.

Hunter, Sam, and Jacobus John. *Modern Art.* Englewood Cliffs, N. J.: Prentice-Hall, 1994.

Lucie-Smith, Edward. *Movement in Art Since 1945: Issues and Concepts.* New York: Thames and Hudson, 1995.

Stokvis, Willemijn. *CoBrA: An International Movement in Art after the Second World War.* New York: Rizzoli, 1988.

Varnedoe, Kirk, and Adam Gopnik. *High and Low, Modern Art and Popular Culture.* Exhibition catalogue, New York Museum of Modern Art. New York: Harry N. Abrams, 1991.

Wheeler, Daniel. *Art Since Mid-Century, 1945 to the Present.* Englewood Cliffs, N.J.: Prentice-Hall, 1991.

Irina D. Costache

Asgeirsson, Asgeir (1894–1972)

Second president of Iceland. Asgeir Asgeirsson studied theology at the University of Iceland from 1912 to 1915, and theology and philosophy at the Universities of Copenhagen and Uppsala in 1916 and 1917. He taught at the Teachers College in Reykjavík from 1918 to 1927, and served as superintendent for Icelandic schools from 1927 to 1931 and from 1934 to 1938. In 1938 he became director of the Fisheries Bank of Iceland, a position he held until he was elected president. Asgeirsson was first elected to parliament for the Progressive Party (the center party) in 1923, holding a seat continuously until 1952. He served as minister of finance in 1931–32 and prime minister from 1932 to 1934. In 1937, he joined the Social Democratic Party.

After a fierce campaign, Asgeirsson won a narrow victory in the presidential elections of 1952 and was re-elected president without opposition in 1956, 1960, and 1964 but stepped down at the end of his fourth term in 1968. He was generally highly regarded as president.

Gudmundur Halfdanarson

Ashdown, Paddy (1941–)

British politician. Paddy Ashdown has been the member of parliament for Yeovil since 1983. In 1988 he was elected leader of the Liberal Democrats.

Following careers in the military, diplomatic service, and industrial management, Ashdown turned his attention to politics. In 1983 he entered parliament as a Liberal for the constituency of Yeovil in southwest England and soon became one of his party's most promising parliamentarians. He initially supported unilateral nuclear disarmament and won great favor among radical Liberals, though he later switched his position to the multilateral policy propounded by David Steel and others in the Social Democrat Party (SDP).

He was the Liberal spokesman on trade and industry affairs (1983–86), a position that gave him an opportunity to gain wider recognition as the Westland Affair had created a deep rift between Margaret Thatcher and Michael Heseltine, the minister of defense. Heseltine had favored the sale of Westland Helicopters to a European consortium rather than to an American corporation, the option favored by Thatcher. Ashdown's military background and the location of the Westland factory within his constituency gave him scope for impressive performances during the ensuing debates in the Commons. During the 1987 general election campaign he became the Liberal/Social Democratic Party Alliance spokesman on education and science.

After the election Ashdown set his sights on becoming leader of the newly merged party (Social and Liberal Democrats). He defeated Alan Beith by a considerable margin to become leader but was to face a difficult start to his leadership. A minority of the SDP continued as a separate party under the leadership of David Owen, the agenda of the SLD was somewhat in flux, and there was even controversy over the name of the new party. Ashdown consolidated his position through an impressive performance at the party conference in September 1989. By late 1990 the Liberal Democrats seemed to have recovered and were polling well; they made large gains in the 1997 general election, which resulted in the largest group of Liberal Democrats in Commons since the founding of the party.

BIBLIOGRAPHY

Ashdown, Paddy. *Citizen's Britain: A Radical Agenda for the 1990's.* London: Fourth Estate, 1989.

———. *Beyond Westminster: Finding Hope in Britain.* New York: Simon & Schuster, 1994.

Eileen Groth Lyon

SEE ALSO Heseltine, Michael; Owen, David

Atkins, Humphrey Edwards (1922–)

Secretary of state for Northern Ireland, May 1979–September 1981. Humphrey Atkins (Lord Colnbrook) was born in 1922. After service in the Royal Navy between 1940 and 1948, he developed an interest in politics and became Conservative MP for Merton and Morden (1955–70) and Spelthorne (1970–87). He was parliamentary private secretary to civil lord of the Admiralty, 1959–62, and honorary secretary of the Conservative Defense Committee, 1965–67. From 1967 to 1979 he served either as an opposition or government whip, and was government whip, 1973–74. His appointment as Northern Ireland secretary of state was one of the few surprises in Margaret Thatcher's first cabinet. It became necessary because of the assassination of the party's spokesman, Airey Neave. Like Neave, Atkins was a close ally of the new prime minister. The upsurge of Provisional IRA violence in August 1979 led to his increasing the Royal Ulster Constabulary's strength by one thousand. His most severe test came with the Republican hunger strikes in 1980–81. He reflected Thatcher's uncompromising opposition to the protest, which was still under way when he left office. He tried two unsuccessful political initiatives. The first was a Constitutional Conference at Stormont, January–March 1980, attended by the Democratic Unionist Party, the Social Democratic Labor Party, and the Alliance Party. The Official Unionists boycotted it. And in 1981 Atkins proposed a fifty-member Advisory Council that would consist of nominated members. On leaving Northern Ireland he became deputy foreign secretary, but he resigned along with the foreign secretary at the start of the Falklands crisis with Argentina in 1982. He was knighted in 1983.

Ricki Schoen

Attlee, Clement Richard (1883–1967)

Labour Party leader and prime minister of the United Kingdom from 1945 to 1951. Clement Attlee (Earl Attlee) was born on January 3, 1883, in London's conservative Putney district. He attended Halleybury School and studied law at Oxford. Legal practice proved disenchanting and, as his interest in the law declined, Attlee's concern for the poor increased. In 1907 he became a social worker in London's East End, where he had witnessed substantial poverty. Despite his background, Attlee became a socialist, joining first the Fabian Society and in 1908 the Labour Party. In 1914 Attlee volunteered for service in World War I and rose to the rank of major.

He was elected mayor of Stepney in 1918, and in 1922 was elected to the House of Commons from the Limehouse division. Attlee served as parliamentary private secretary to Ramsay MacDonald's first Labour government in 1924. When Labour was returned to power in 1930, MacDonald appointed Attlee chancellor of the Duchy of Lancaster and in 1931 postmaster general. Later that year Attlee and the Labour Party broke with MacDonald when he betrayed his party and established a national government.

In October 1935 Attlee spoke for a growing number of members when he called for collective security against Mussolini and Hitler. Subsequently, Attlee assumed party leadership when pacifist George Lansbury resigned the post. Attlee joined Churchill's coalition government in 1940 as deputy prime minister.

Attlee directed the government during Churchill's frequent wartime absences. After Germany's surrender in May 1945, Churchill called for July elections. Attlee wanted to wait until the Japanese had been defeated, but Churchill was adamant. The English people were ready for change and, in a stunning verdict, returned a Labour majority. Attlee became prime minister.

Attlee's socialist perspective dictated his government's approach. It initiated steps to nationalize heavy industry and introduced national health insurance. England's postwar economy suffered from the severe winter of 1947 and government mismanagement. Bread and gasoline rationing were continued and taxes on luxury goods increased.

In foreign affairs, the Attlee government granted independence to India, Pakistan, and Burma in 1947, and to Ceylon (Sri Lanka) in 1948. Attlee also directed the Royal Air Force to participate in the Berlin Airlift.

In the 1950 elections, the Labour Party kept its majority by the slimmest of margins and Attlee nationalized the steel industry. The following year three cabinet members resigned because Attlee's Cold War policies gave military spending priority over social expenditures. In 1951 the Conservatives won control of the House of Commons, and Attlee resigned as prime minister. He retained his parliament seat and, in October 1952, regained the party leadership.

Attlee left government service in 1955 and received an earldom on December 7, 1955. He lived with his wife in the country until her death in June 1964. He then moved into London, where he resided until his death on October 8, 1967.

BIBLIOGRAPHY

Attlee, Clement, and Francis Williams. *Twilight of Empire: Memoirs of Prime Minister Clement Attlee.* New York: Barnes, 1962.

Burridge, Trevor. *Clement Attlee: A Political Biography.* London: Jonathan Cape, 1985.

Page S. Foshee

SEE ALSO United Kingdom

Augstein, Rudolf (1923–)

Editor of the West German newsmagazine *Der Spiegel.* As a journalist Rudolf Augstein closely observed and criticized political, economic, and social developments in the Federal Republic of Germany. His generally skeptical outlook also played a major role in the style of *Der Spiegel,* which became influential in West Germany because of its investigate journalism and its early uncovering of domestic scandals, usually backed by extensive research.

Augstein was born in Hanover on November 5, 1923. Even in his youth he demonstrated a skeptical evaluation of official announcements. As early as 1940 he wrote an essay in school on why it was impossible for Germany to win the war. At the same time, however, he developed a national outlook that he retained. Never having been involved with the Nazi regime, he was allowed to work as a journalist immediately after the war. *Diese Wocrie,* the magazine for which he wrote was modeled on Anglo-Saxon counterparts and took seriously the new democratic values of the press as a neutral corrective to authorities. Augstein even criticized the British occupation government. Instead of dismissing him, however, the British gave him his own license. The magazine was renamed *Der Spiegel* but continued the same critical journalistic style, and thereby established investigative journalism in Germany.

This journalistic style led to several arguments between Augstein's *Spiegel* and the authorities of the federal republic, the best known of which was the Spiegel affair. In the course of the affair Augstein was jailed for several weeks together with Conrad Ahlers, the author of an October 10, 1962, cover story on a recent NATO exercise in which the West German army was rated in the lowest category of readiness. Strauss asserted that there had been a breach of security that amounted to treason. Augstein and *Der Spiegel* became famous for their clear political stand against Konrad Adenauer and his policy of German integration with the West, as well as for the journalistic support of Chancellor Willy Brandt's *Ostpolitik.* Since German reunification, the political profile of *Der Spiegel* has become less clear. Augstein's critical journalism has often been attacked as mere carping without suggesting how to improve matters. However, Augstein's success must be seen as keeping alive a critical awareness of domestic and international affairs and developments among the magazine's readership.

BIBLIOGRAPHY

Brawand, Leo. *Rudolf Augstein.* Düsseldorf: Econ-Verlag, 1995.

Greiwe, Ulrich. *Augstein—Ein gewisses Doppelleben.* Berlin: Brandenburgisches Verlagshaus, 1994.

Gudrun Kruip

SEE ALSO *Spiegel* Affair

Auken, Svend (1943–)

Danish Social Democratic politician. Svend Auken, who was born in 1943, studied political science in Aarhus, the United States, and Paris, and received a master's in social sciences from the University of Aarhus in 1969. The same year he was employed as lecturer at Aarhus University's Institute of Political Science, and from 1973 to 1989 he was an associate professor. He was elected to the Folketing (parliament) in 1971. His special interest was labor market affairs. From 1975 to 1977 he served as chairman of the parliamentary labor market committee, and from 1977 to 1982 he was minister of labor. He was the political spokesman for the Social Democratic Party in 1977 and again from 1983 to 1992. In 1985 he was chosen vice chairman of the party, and from 1987 to 1992 Auken served as chairman. In 1993 he was appointed minister for the environment, and in 1994 the ministry of energy was added to his responsibilities.

Auken's outlook placed him in the left wing of the Social Democratic Party, and he worked closely with the trade union movement. He had strong popular support and was sent to parliament with some of the strongest majorities on the Danish political scene. However, he was replaced as party chairman in 1992 by Poul Nyrup Rasmussen at an extraordinary congress of the party. The Social Democrats had been in the opposition since 1982, and it was thought that Rasmussen would have a better chance to gain middle-class votes and again win control of the government. In fact, the Social Democrats under Rasmussen did return to power in 1993. As minister of the environment in the new government, Auken gained a reputation internationally as a strong and radical advocate for the environment and won popularity among the green movement.

Jørn Boye Nielsen

SEE ALSO Rasmussen, Poul Nyrup

Auriol, Vincent (1884–1966)

French Socialist who was the first president of the Fourth Republic, 1947–54. As president, Vincent Auriol had to deal with economic depression, unstable coalitions, twelve ministerial crises, and the war in Indochina. His cautious policies included colonial reform within the French Union and support for the North Atlantic Treaty Organization.

While practicing law in Toulouse, Auriol joined the Socialist Party in 1905 and was a member of the Chamber of Deputies from 1914 to 1940. A close associate of Léon Blum, the Socialist premier of France, Auriol served as finance minister in Blum's popular front government of 1936. A prisoner of the Vichy regime from 1940 to 1943, he escaped to become a prominent member of Charles de Gaulle's Free French forces. As a moderate and conciliatory Socialist, he was minister of state in de Gaulle's cabinet in 1945, and was elected president of the constituent assemblies of 1945 and 1946. Although unable to achieve most of his goals as president, Auriol is remembered as a capable elder statesman of high ideals. Early in the Fifth Republic, he served on the Constitutional Council but resigned in 1960 because of concern about de Gaulle's expansion of presidential powers.

BIBLIOGRAPHY

Auriol, Vincent. *Mon Septennat, 1947–1954.* P. Nora and J. Ozous, eds. Paris: Gallimard, 1970.

Dansette, Adrien. *Histoire des présidents de la république.* Paris: Ameot-Dumont, 1960.

Guilleminault, Robert. *La France de Vincent Auriol, 1947–1953.* Paris: Denoel, 1968.

Thomas T. Lewis

SEE ALSO Blum, Léon

Austria

Mountainous central European country. Austria (Republik Österreich), which is 185 miles (300 km) long from east to west, has an area of 32,378 square miles (83,858 sq km), approximately twice the size of Switzerland. Despite its idyllic countryside, Austria is predominantly ur-

ban. Half its people live in cities or towns of more than 10,000 residents, with approximately a fifth of the country's 7,623,600 (1989) inhabitants residing in its capital, Vienna (Wien), a city of 1.6 million. Austria is bordered by eight countries: Switzerland, Liechtenstein, Germany, the Czech Republic, Slovakia, Hungary, Slovenia, and Italy. Over 98 percent of the Austrian population is German-speaking but there are small minorities of Hungarians and Croats in the Burgenland and Slovenes in Carinthia (Kärnten). In the 1990s Roman Catholics constituted approximately 84 percent of the population and Protestants 6 percent. Jews, who were such an important component of pre-Nazi Vienna, number only ten thousand nationwide.

Austria, the Germanic core of the former multinational Austro-Hungarian Empire, became an independent republic in 1918. After a period of political and social strife and the establishment of a conservative authoritarian government, it was absorbed by Hitler's Third Reich in the March 1938 *Anschluss.* At an October 1943 meeting of the foreign ministers of the United Kingdom, the Soviet Union, and the United States, the *Anschluss* was declared void. Though British Prime Minister Winston Churchill continued to ruminate about the establishment of some sort of Danubian confederation, the stage was set for the postwar resumption of a separate existence for Austria.

Following the liberation of Vienna by Soviet troops on April 13, 1945, Austrians were allowed to reorganize their political parties. The Soviets chose Karl Renner, an old socialist who had been the first chancellor of the first Austrian Republic, to form and head a provisional government. The Soviets apparently thought that they could control Renner; however, the wily politico surprised them. On April 27, 1945, Renner established a provisional government composed of the Socialist Party (Sozialistische Partei Österreichs, SPÖ), the Christian Socialists, now calling themselves the Austrian People's Party (Österreichische Volkspartei, ÖVP), and the Communists. The Communists were delighted to receive the ministries of the interior, education, and public information and worship. But Renner stymied any advantage that they might have drawn from this by organizing all ministries under a minister and two vice ministers, one of whom would be drawn from each of the three parties. Since a vice minister could veto any decision, gridlock resulted and all important decisions were thrown back to the full cabinet. There Renner facilitated compromise with the reward of a meal (in hungry Vienna) at the conclusion of cabinet meetings.

Suspicion of Soviet intentions and distrust of the Renner government delayed the approval by the Western powers of four zones of Allied occupation in Austria until July 1945. Then segments of Austria were assigned to France, the United Kingdom, the USSR, and the United States; Vienna, like Berlin, was subjected to four-power occupation, and administrative and political power was placed in the hands of the commanders of the four occupying powers. In September the jurisdiction of the Renner government was extended to all Austria and elections were organized for November. The ÖVP won 49.8 percent of the vote and eighty-five seats and the SPÖ 44.6 percent and seventy-six seats. The Communists won only 5.42 percent and four seats. This election ended the hope of the Communists to gain control. The ÖVP and the SPÖ formed a grand coalition under the chancellorship of Leopold Figl, leader of the ÖVP. Renner became the first president of the second Austrian Republic, a post he held until his death in December 1950. The coalition between the ÖVP and the SPÖ lasted until 1966. They agreed on a proportional system (*Proporzsystem*) that divided cabinet posts, administrative positions, and even jobs in the large state sector between members of the two principal parties according to their relative strength in national elections. This enabled the two parties to work together, rather than seek the support of minor extremist groups, and it enabled them to present a united front in advancing the interests of Austria vis-à-vis the powers and eventually regain sovereignty.

The coalition agreed to resurrect the constitution of 1920 as amended in 1929 rather than draw up a new instrument. On June 28, 1946, the Allied Control Council (ACC) agreed that decisions on the Austrian government submitted to the ACC could not be vetoed by one power but would become law if not rejected by a majority of the ACC commanders. The Soviets were also prevented from making reparation demands against Austria by an agreement to that effect at Potsdam. The Soviets attempted to circumvent this by seizing the economic assets in Austria that had been controlled by the Nazi state. To forestall a Soviet rape of Austrian assets and resources, the Austrian government embarked on a massive program of nationalization. But continued economic and political interference by the Soviets in their zone of occupation prompted a migration of capital and industry from Vienna and Lower Austria to the western part of the country occupied by the Western powers. In the dire economic conditions following the war, the physical survival of Austrians was facilitated by U.N. Relief and Rehabilitation Agency (UNRRA) aid and from July 1948 by the U.S.-sponsored Marshall Plan. When Julius Raab of the ÖVP succeeded Socialist Figl in 1953, he appointed Reinhard Kamitz minister of finance. The Raab-Kamitz course with its modified free-market policies is credited with stimulating Austrian recovery and growth.

Austria was occupied until 1955. The Cold War long blocked an agreement. However, following the death of Soviet dictator Stalin in 1953, the Soviets agreed that they would henceforth pay the occupation costs of their forces in Austria. Faced with the rearmament of West Germany, the USSR extended an invitation to the Austrian government to come to Moscow for bilateral talks. In April 1955 the USSR agreed to the restoration of Austrian sovereignty if Austria pledged itself to permanent neutrality. The USSR agreed to withdraw its troops by the end of the year and agreed to hand over all its economic holdings in Austria to the Austrian government in return for $152 million and a million tons of oil a year for ten years. The treaty restoring Austrian sovereignty, the State Treaty, was signed in Vienna on May 15, 1955, by representatives of the four occupying powers. It went into effect on July 27, 1955, and by October 25 all occupation forces were withdrawn. The treaty forbade *Anschluss* between Austria and Germany and restoration of the Habsburgs. It also contained guarantees for the Slovene and Croatian minorities in Carinthia, Styria, and the Burgenland. Austria was admitted to the United Nations in 1955 and to the Council of Europe in 1956. It joined the European Free Trade Association (EFTA) in 1958 but was long prevented by its delicate status between East and West from more than associate status with the European Economic Community (EEC).

The coalition of the ÖVP and the SPÖ endured until 1966. While the ÖVP provided the chancellors for the coalition cabinets after 1953, Theodor Körner, Socialist mayor of Vienna, was elected president following the death of Renner on December 31, 1950. He was succeeded in 1957 by Adolf Schärf, leader of the SPÖ. And in 1965 Franz Jonas, former Socialist mayor of Vienna, was elected president. The grand coalition was undermined by economic difficulties and disagreements over the budget. The government resigned in 1965 and in the subsequent election on March 6, 1966, the ÖVP won an outright majority. Josef Klaus, who had been chancellor since April 1964, then formed a cabinet exclusively composed of his ÖVP. Fears of political instability did not materialize, and when the SPÖ rebounded and gained an eighty-one–seat plurality in the March 1970 election, Bruno Kreisky formed the first all-Socialist cabinet. In April 1971 the SPÖ's Jonas was reelected president in a contest with the ÖVP's Kurt Waldheim. An early election, called by Kreisky in October 1971, gave the Socialists a clear majority with ninety-three seats. When Jonas died in April 1974, he was succeeded by another Socialist, Rudolf Kirchschläger, a former minister of foreign affairs. While the SPÖ was profiting from a remarkable period of prosperity, low unemployment, and popular satisfaction with an elaborate system of social welfare, the ÖVP was weakened by leadership struggles. The SPÖ again repeated its electoral success in the October 1975 parliamentary elections.

Though Kreisky's project to commission Austria's first nuclear power plant was torpedoed by a national referendum in November 1978, he survived and the SPÖ's position was even strengthened in the May 1979 election. However "Green" sentiment cost the SPÖ its majority in the April 1983 election, when 3 percent of the vote went to two small Green parties. Kreisky, unwilling to head a coalition cabinet, resigned. He was succeeded by the SPÖ's Fred Sinowatz, who formed a coalition with the small right-wing Freedom Party (Freiheitliche Partei Österreichs).

Kreisky and the SPÖ had also been hurt by allegations of financial scandal connected with Hannes Andrich, who had served as Kreisky's minister of finance and was his heir apparent. Further scandals in the 1980s associated with the SPÖ obscured the success of Kreisky's governments in the areas of reform and modernization. In addition, the growth of prosperity and social mobility in Austria fostered a new "individualism" and undermined the old system of "social partnership" in which social and economic decisions were mediated through the interaction of competing economic groups.

Sinowatz's chancellorship and eventually his coalition foundered as a result of the presidential victory of Waldheim in June 1986. When Waldheim, despite allegations concerning his conduct as a member of the German army in World War II, defeated SPÖ candidate Kurt Steyrer, Sinowatz relinquished the chancellorship. He was succeeded by Franz Vranitzky, SPÖ minister of finance. When the ultra right-wing Jörg Haider became head of the Freedom Party in September, the coalition was no longer tenable. In the November 1986 election the SPÖ with eighty seats won a plurality but fell short of a majority. The ÖVP won seventy-seven seats, the Freedom Party eighteen, and an electoral alliance of Green parties eight. In January 1987 a new SPÖ-ÖVP grand coalition was formed. Steps were taken toward fiscal reform and privatization of the nationalized sector of the economy. However, despite prosperity the coalition was troubled by scandal, and the ÖVP was debilitated by continuing leadership struggles.

The results of the October 1990 election were troubling. Though the SPÖ with 43 percent gained an additional seat, the ÖVP with only 32 percent lost seventeen

seats. The Freedom Party, on the other hand, profited from growing hostility toward immigrants and asylum seekers, to increase, with its 17 percent of the vote, its number of seats by fifteen. A new SPÖ-ÖVP coalition was formed and Vranitzky was reelected chairman of his party, now renamed the Social Democratic Party of Austria (Sozialdemokratische Partei Österreichs, SPÖ). Haider was removed as governor of Carinthia after praising Nazi economic policies. In response to neo-Nazi activity and sentiment, the parliament, hoping to foster more successful prosecution, reduced the prison sentence for Nazi activity to one year and made denial of the Holocaust a criminal offense.

The Waldheim affair was moved off center stage when he declined to run for reelection. In April 1992 Thomas Klestil of the ÖVP defeated the SPÖ's Rudolf Steicher in the presidential campaign. However, the right continued to plague Austria. In June the Freedom Party organized a national petition to force the parliament to consider banning all immigration to Austria. Though the legislation foundered, 7 percent of the Austrian electorate signed the petition. Though five Freedom Party parliamentary delegates led by Heide Schmidt, the party's vice president, left the party in February 1993 and formed the Liberal Forum, the sentiments that the extreme right had successfully tapped into remained. In December 1993 letter bombs were sent to supporters of immigrant rights, including the mayor of Vienna who was wounded by one. In February four Gypsies were killed by an explosive device in the Burgenland.

The Freedom Party also opposed Austrian entry into the European Union (EU), which had been made possible by the end of the Cold War. In June 1994, 66.4 percent of Austria's voters approved entry and it became a member on January 1, 1995. Austria also became a member of NATO's Partnership for Peace and was granted observer status in the Western European Union (WEU). In the October 1994 parliamentary election the Freedom Party's opposition to these moves was rewarded with an increase of 6 percent of the vote. With 23 percent it received forty-two seats, despite the secession of the Liberal Forum, which won ten seats. The SPÖ and the ÖVP reconstituted their coalition, but it was plagued by disagreement over fiscal policies and collapsed in late 1995. In the December elections the SPÖ increased its percentage from 35 to 38.1 and a grand coalition was once again formed, but only after difficult negotiations centering on economic policies.

In January 1997 Vranitzky relinquished the chancellorship, offering as his reasons his age and the length of his tenure. Viktor Klima, the minister of finance, assumed both the chancellorship and the chairmanship of the SPÖ. But the SPÖ had suffered reversals in 1996. The public reacted against the austerity measures necessitated to meet the requirements for Austria's entry into the European Monetary Union. The Freedom Party, since January 1995 renamed the Freiheitlichen, capitalized on this and won 27.6 percent of the national vote in elections for the European Parliament in October 1996. The SPÖ suffered its worst electoral result with only 29.1 percent, while the ÖVP won 29.6 percent. In the Vienna city elections that took place at the same time, the SPÖ lost the absolute majority that it had held since 1945.

BIBLIOGRAPHY

"Austria," *Europa World Yearbook 1998.* London: Europa Publications, 1998, 480–81.

Bischof, Gunter, and Anton Pelinka, eds. *Austria in the new Europe.* New Brunswick: Transaction Publishers, 1993.

———. *Austria in the Nineteen Fifties.* New Brunswick, N.J.: Transaction Publishers, 1995.

———. *The Kreisky Era in Austria.* New Brunswick, N.J.: Transaction Publishers, 1994.

Pelinka, Anton. *Austria: Out of the Shadow of the Past.* Boulder, Colo.: Westview Press, 1998.

Sully, Melanie A. *A Contemporary History of Austria.* New York: Routledge, 1990.

Wagnleitner, Reinhold, "Austria, history of," *Encyclopædia Britannica Online.* ⟨http://search.eb.com/bol/topic?eu=117984&sctn=2⟩ [Accessed May 20, 1999].

Bernard Cook

Austrian State Treaty

Treaty that restored Austrian sovereignty after World War II. The Austrian treaty negotiations (1946–55) represent a rare success story in the diplomatic arena of the early Cold War. In spite of frequent delays owing to the ups and downs of East-West tensions, the treaty was signed on May 15, 1955, as a result of changes in the Kremlin leadership in the wake of Stalin's death (1953). The quadripartite Austrian occupation finally came to an end. The Austrian government insisted on calling it a "state treaty" (not a peace treaty), because Austria had been annexed and occupied by Nazi Germany before World War II and thus had not been a belligerent power like Hitler's satellites Finland or Hungary. Most of the hard work of drafting a "peace treaty" with Austria after the war was accomplished by specialists in the various foreign offices. The special deputies of the American, British, French, and Soviet foreign ministers conducted the interminable nego-

tiations on the details in the course of 260 meetings between 1947 and 1953. At the postwar Council of Foreign Ministers (CFM) sessions, Austrian treaty negotiations frequently languished in the shadow of Great Power disagreement over the German peace treaty.

The U.S. State Department had a first "Draft Outline of Treaty Recognizing an Independent and Democratic Austria" ready by February 6, 1946. The Soviets refused to put the Austrian draft treaty on the agenda of the Paris CFM in the summer of 1946 before the peace treaties with Germany's satellites Italy, Hungary, Romania, Bulgaria, and Finland. But it quickly became clear in preliminary talks in Paris that the disentanglement of Austria from Germany would become the major issue. High-level Soviet diplomats would hold Austria responsible for "cleaning out all remnants of Nazism."

The foreign ministers' special deputies on the Austrian treaty began their work in their first meeting in London in January/February 1947 and, in the midst of the growing escalation of Cold War tensions owing to U.S. President Truman's containment speech in Congress, the foreign ministers met for another meeting on the German and Austrian treaties in Moscow in March/April 1947. In these sessions the Austrian reparations issue—the question of "German external assets" in Austria—already emerged as the principal stumbling block.

The Soviets insisted on milking to the maximum the German assets, i.e., the massive German industrial network built in Austria during World War II, insisting that the Austrians pay reparations for their participation on Nazi Germany's side in World War II. This would allow Moscow to establish a permanent foothold in the country to add to Stalin's "revolutionist-imperial" foreign policy paradigm of securing maximum borders and security for the postwar Soviet empire. During the Moscow CFM the Soviets also supported extensive Yugoslav reparations and territorial claims against Austria.

As the negotiations dragged on over these economic issues, the Soviet occupation power annually extracted some $50 million of reparations out of the current production of seized German assets in their zone. The foreign ministers appointed a special Vienna Treaty Commission in the summer of 1947 to reach an agreement on the intractable German assets issues.

French Deputy General Paul Cherriere presented an American-inspired compromise proposal in the spring of 1948 allowing the Austrians to pay a "lump sum" of $150 million to the Soviet Union for the German assets. Moscow accepted in the spring 1948 negotiating round and in 1949 even desisted from supporting Yugoslav demands against Austria as a result of the Tito-Stalin split. In the fall of 1949 international observers widely expected the signing of the Austrian treaty, but the Soviets introduced new demands by insisting on Austrian repayment of loans and linking the Austrian question to Great Power disagreements over Trieste. This hardening of the Kremlin's position was related to the escalation of Cold War tensions following the initiation of the Marshall Plan.

To the American military establishment renewed Soviet intransigence on the Austrian treaty was welcome news. After the Czech coup of 1948, American military strategists anticipated that Austria might be next on the list of Communist takeovers. Now the Pentagon lost interest in concluding an Austrian treaty in spite of the Soviet concessions in the 1948–49 deputies' negotiations. To U.S. military planners Austrian rearmament became more important to protect the country against domestic subversion than giving the country back its independence with the signing of a treaty. With the coming of the Korean War and the Communist general strike ("putsch" attempt) in Austria in the fall of 1950, the Pentagon embarked on its secret rearmament program of western Austria. The goal was to establish the nucleus of a future Austrian army before a treaty was signed. The Cold War experienced its ice age because of the Korean conflict, with the superpowers engaging in psychological warfare instead of serious diplomacy. As a result of these superpower tensions, Austrian treaty negotiations languished. A U.S. proposal of March 1952, designed to ratify the drastically shortened version of an Austrian treaty, did not end the diplomatic impasse, because the Kremlin did not take it seriously.

Stalin's unexpected death on March 6, 1953, stirred new expectations for easing Cold War tensions. Stalin's successors in the Kremlin unleashed a new program of "peaceful coexistence." After Western capitals dismissed it as propaganda, the new Raab government in Vienna started behind-the-scenes bilateral negotiations with Moscow, introducing Austrian neutrality as a new option. In the January–February 1954 Berlin CFM, Stalinist hardliner Vyacheslav Molotov dismissed Austrian neutrality as a means to end the occupation and continued to link the Austrian with the German question. But Molotov's traditional hard-line foreign policy ended in diplomatic disaster for the Soviets in the October 1954 Paris Agreements, which remilitarized West Germany and incorporated it into the Western defense system.

In February 1955, the Kremlin responded with the dismantling of Molotov's overbearing influence and the consolidation of the Nikita Khrushchev and his more conciliatory policy. Now Austria's patient bilateral diplomacy came to fruition. The Kremlin invited Chancellor Julius Raab and a high-level Austrian delegation to Moscow in mid-April. Moscow made economic concessions and agreed that Austria could pay the lump sum for the German assets with payments in kind out of current production rather than cash. Austria accepted a Swiss-style neutrality. The isolated Western powers were surprised and shocked about this diplomatic breakthrough. The Moscow agreements were reluctantly accepted by the West because of Soviet economic concessions and the "armed" Austrian neutrality that would allow the nucleus of an Austrian army. The Great Powers' ambassadors met with an Austrian delegation in Vienna to nail down the final details in the Austrian treaty draft that had almost been completed in 1949. On May 15, 1955, the foreign ministers met in Vienna to sign the treaty. By the end of October, the last occupation soldiers left Austria. The country that had been "liberated" in 1945 was free again and declared its permanent neutrality.

As a neutral nation in a strategically sensitive position in Central Europe, Austria resumed its traditional role as bridge builder between East and West and as a bridgehead of détente.

BIBLIOGRAPHY

Allard, Sven. *Russia and the Austrian Treaty: A Case Study of Soviet Policy in Europe.* University Park: Pennsylvania State University Press, 1970.

Bischof, Günter. "Between Responsibility and Rehabilitation: Austria in International Politics, 1940–1950." Ph.D. diss., Harvard University, 1989.

Cronin, Audrey Kurth. *Great Power Politics and the Struggle over Austria, 1945–1955.* Ithaca, New York: Cornell University Press, 1986.

Richter, James G. *Khrushchev's Double Bind: International Pressures and Domestic Politics.* Baltimore: Johns Hopkins University Press, 1994.

Steiner, Kurt. "Negotiations for an Austrian Treaty," in Alexander George, Philip J. Farley, and Alexander Dallin, eds. *U.S.-Soviet Security Cooperation: Achievements—Failures—Lessons.* New York: Oxford University Press, 1988.

Stourzh, Gerald. *Geschichte des österreichischen Staatsvertrages 1945–1955: Österreichs Weg zur Neutralität,* 4th. ed. Graz: Styria, 1997.

Zubok, Vladislav, and Constantine Pleshakov. *Inside the Kremlin's Cold War: From Stalin to Khrushchev.* Cambridge, Mass.: Harvard University Press, 1996.

Günter Bischof

SEE ALSO Kreisky, Bruno; Raab, Julius; Renner, Karl

European Integration

The case of Austria is of particular interest because of its high degree of economic dependence on the European Community (EC) and its larger neighbor, the Federal Republic of Germany, its precarious security position, and its neutrality status. Austria's participation in the Marshall Plan (1948–52), membership in the Council of Europe (1956) and the European Free Trade Association (1960), and the bilateral free-trade agreements with the European Economic Community (EEC) and the European Coal and Steel Community (ECSC) of 1972–73 finally led to full EU membership in 1995.

The key dilemma for Austrian European policymakers before 1955 was the need to take account of Austria's dependence on U.S. financial aid and of its fast-growing economic interdependence with Western Europe without, however, antagonizing the Soviet Union. In 1947 the Austrian government decided to accept the invitation to the Paris conference that was to decide the institutional and policy framework for the administration of the Marshall Plan. In 1948 Austria joined the Organization for European Economic Cooperation (OEEC) despite the refusal by the Soviet Union and its Eastern European satellites to participate. During 1948–52 Austria received $1.962 billion from the Marshall Plan, or 13.5 percent of all Marshall Plan funds. Austria was initially an associate member and then a full member of the European Payments Union (EPU) from 1953 onward. The greater long-term significance of the Marshall Plan was its impact on the liberalization and accelerated redirection of trade. By 1948 more than 15 percent of Austrian exports still went to the Soviet Union and its satellites. However, OEEC and EPU membership in conjunction with American restrictions on the export of modern technology to the Soviet bloc, which Austria had to accept, led to a decline of the share of Austrian trade with Eastern Europe. By 1955 Austrian exports to Eastern Europe had declined to 8 percent, compared with 28 percent in 1937. Exports to OEEC countries rose from 53 percent to 71 percent. Austrian economic dependence on West Germany increased again. By 1960, 27 percent of Austrian exports went to the Federal Republic and 40 percent of Austrian imports came from there.

In addition to the OEEC and the EPU, Austria also became a member of other Western economic organizations: the International Monetary Fund (IMF) and the International Bank for Reconstruction and Development (IBRD) in 1948, and the General Agreement on Tariffs and Trade (GATT) in 1951. Within the OEEC Austria occupied a special status during 1948–53, before an improved balance-of-payments position allowed it to follow OEEC rules and participate fully in trade liberalization. But Austria was particularly careful to avoid association with Western defense organizations like the Brussels Pact (1948), NATO (1949), or the Western European Union (WEU, 1954).

Austria had little freedom to maneuver in matters of European integration. Ultimately, neutrality was the price Austria paid in 1955 in exchange for the Soviet Union's approval of the State Treaty, the withdrawal of Soviet troops from eastern Austria, and the regaining of national sovereignty. The Soviet Union accepted Austria's accession to the United Nations in December 1955 and had to accept Austrian membership in the Council of Europe in April 1956. It was unclear what degree of economic integration Austria would consider compatible with its new neutrality policy. The Soviet safeguard here was article 4 of the State Treaty, which prohibited economic or political union with Germany, a provision that from the very beginning was wide open to conflicting interpretations.

In 1955 the exact shape of Austria's future neutrality policy and how it would limit the country's choice in matters of European integration still had to be defined. Nonparticipation in the ECSC temporarily appeared likely to undermine Austria's economic recovery because of its dependence on German coal and its need for markets for Austrian steel. Austria could not hope to compensate fully for any possible export losses in the European Economic Community (EEC, 1958) market with greater exports to other OEEC countries.

Despite the potentially adverse economic effects of nonmembership, the Austrian government never seriously considered during 1955–57 joining the EEC as a full member, particularly after it was reminded of Austria's precarious security position on the Iron Curtain when the Soviet Union brutally suppressed the Hungarian Revolution of 1956. Austria therefore welcomed the British initiative to create a wider, industrial free-trade area (FTA), which would not involve the harmonization of tariffs and would be organized entirely along intergovernmental lines. It would thus ideally safeguard the country's trade interests without provoking Soviet opposition and diplomatic pressure. But French objections caused the FTA's failure in 1958. So the Austrian government decided unanimously in the summer of 1959, albeit without great enthusiasm, to participate in setting up a small free-trade zone of the so-called outer seven (European Free Trade Association, EFTA), including Great Britain, Sweden, Norway, Denmark, Switzerland, and Portugal.

Austria initially hoped, as did the British, that the creation of EFTA would provide enough counterpressure on the six members of the EEC to induce them to agree to renewed negotiations about multilateral association within a wider FTA. Austria hoped that EFTA would provide a bridge to the EEC and a wider economic solution acceptable to all sides. Austrian Trade Minister Fritz Bock, with support from Austrian industry, got this common aim enshrined in the preamble of the EFTA Treaty.

The main reason for initial Austrian support for EFTA membership was the hope that the country could thus continue to enjoy the advantages of economic interdependence and of political independence at the same time, minimizing any legal obligations and avoiding a commitment to long-term political integration. Neutrality and EFTA membership would facilitate the ongoing Austrian nation-building process in conscious demarcation from Germany. For Foreign Minister Bruno Kreisky, Austrian EEC membership was undesirable on political grounds and would be in contradiction to the State Treaty's prohibition of *Anschluss* with the Federal Republic of Germany.

With the British government's decision in the summer of 1961 to apply for EEC membership, which finally put an end to the search for a multilateral solution to the trade conflict between the EEC and EFTA, Austria decided in December of that year to apply for economic association according to article 238 of the EEC Treaty alongside the two other neutrals within EFTA, Sweden and Switzerland. Bock pressed for a more active association policy, if necessary on a bilateral basis, and without close rapport with the other EFTA members. De Gaulle's veto against British EEC membership made it clear that there would be no wider solution between the EEC and all EFTA countries for the foreseeable future. The renewed grand coalition now decided against the advice of Kreisky but, with his reluctant cooperation, to pursue the association option independently in bilateral talks with the EEC, and on February 26, 1963, renewed its association request.

Negotiations between the community and Austria finally failed in 1967, ostensibly because of Italy's veto in the wake of a crisis in bilateral relationship with Austria over a series of bomb attacks in South Tyrol. Within the EEC only West Germany, not least because of its own export interests in the Austrian market, had vigorously supported the Austrian application for association, which would have been in the form of a de facto customs union, probably with special arrangements for agriculture. Neither were the Benelux governments happy about the Austrian policy of going it alone—the so-called *Alleingang nach Brüssel*—even though for different reasons. The community would not treat the Austrian case as a political

priority. After the breakdown of Austria's efforts to reach a separate agreement with the EEC, de Gaulle's retirement from French politics in 1969 finally permitted the wider solution. In 1973 Britain, Denmark, and Ireland joined the community. The other EFTA members, including Austria, signed free-trade agreements with the EEC and the ECSC, which had been amalgamated to become the EC in 1967. In Austria's case, the successful conclusion of bilateral negotiations with Italy concerning South Tyrol in 1969 had previously removed the most difficult diplomatic obstacle. According to the free-trade agreement, all tariffs on industrial goods between Austria and the EEC were to be abolished by 1977. The 1972 free-trade agreement safeguarded Austria's core economic interests in the EC market.

After a period of political stagnation within the community in the 1970s, the EC Commission suggested in 1985 to abolish these nontariff barriers and to create an internal market in goods, capital, services, and people by 1992. This initiative started a dynamic phase in European integration that lasted until the signing of the Maastricht Treaty in 1992. Soviet leader Mikhail Gorbachev's accession in 1985 changed fundamentally the external political context for Austrian European policy. It sharply reduced the political eroticism of neutrality and excluded completely the possibility of serious political sanctions in case of Austrian EC membership.

It now seemed that only by joining as a full member could Austria prevent a severe competitive disadvantage with regard to the enlarged EC. Moreover, by the mid-1980s the corporatist economic system within Austria was seen to be in need of structural reform, and EC membership was to provide the necessary external pressure to cushion politically the economic and social effects of deregulation. Against this changing economic background, EC membership was first demanded by the Federation of Austrian Industrialists in May 1987. In 1988 the smaller of the two coalition parties, the People's Party (ÖVP) followed. Finally the Social Democratic Party (SPÖ) favored applying for EC membership in April 1989, and the application was made on July 17, 1989. EC Commission President Jacques Delors had proposed the participation of EFTA countries in the internal market program without actual EC membership, an initiative designed to delay enlargement of the community until after its institutional deepening in the Maastricht process. The resulting European Economic Area (EEA) Treaty was signed on May 2, 1992. Austria did not regard the EEA solution as a suitable substitute for full membership in the community. Throughout the negotiations the Austrian government emphasized the importance of including agriculture as well as full participation in EC decision making.

Austria's entry negotiations began on February 1, 1993, and concluded on March 1, 1994. In Austria a referendum on membership in the EU (name changed from EC on November 1, 1993) was obligatory under the constitution and was called by the government for June 12, 1994. On voting day turnout was 82.4 percent; 66.6 percent voted in favor of EU membership, and only 33.4 percent voted against it. After the parliamentary ratification process was concluded, Austria joined the EU on January 1, 1995.

Austrian governments from the postwar period onward had only a limited choice in matters of European integration. Austrian European policy oscillated between the poles of neutrality and full integration. During the Kreisky era, Austria was presented as arbiter between East and West and in the North-South conflict. Essentially, nonparticipation in the EEC was a pragmatic policy choice, and the neutrality-EFTA strategy was increasingly instrumental in advancing domestic interests and enhancing Austria's international role.

EU accession represents most of all a shift toward a different political strategy of a small European state in order to assert its economic interests and enhance its political influence in an ever more interdependent Europe, with considerable domestic repercussions.

BIBLIOGRAPHY

Albrich, Thomas, et al. *Österreich in den Fünfzigern.* Innsbruck-Vienna: Studienverlag, 1995.

Bischof, Günter, and Josef Leidenfrost, eds. *Die bevormundete Nation: Österreich und die Alliierten 1945–1949.* Innsbruck: Haymon, 1988.

Bischof, Günter, and Anton Pelinka, eds. *Austria in the New Europe.* (Contemporary Austrian Studies 1). New Brunswick, N.J.: Transaction Publishers, 1993.

———, eds. *Austria in the Nineteen Fifties.* (Contemporary Austrian Studies 3). New Brunswick, N.J.: Transaction Publishers, 1994.

———, eds. *The Kreisky Era in Austria.* (Contemporary Austrian Studies 2). New Brunswick, N.J.: Transaction Publishers, 1994.

Breuss, Fritz. *Österreichs Außenwirtschaft 1945–1982.* Vienna: Signum Verlag, 1983.

Gehler, Michael, and Wolfram Kaiser. "A Study in Ambivalence: Austria and European Integration 1945–95." *Contemporary European History,* Vol. 6. Oxford: Cambridge University Press, 1997, 75–99.

Gehler, Michael, ed. *Karl Gruber: Reden und Dokumente 1945–1953: Eine Auswahl.* Vienna: Böhlau, 1994.

Gehler, Michael, and Rolf Steininger, eds. *Österreich und die europäische Integration 1945–1993: Aspekte einer wechselvollen Entwicklung.* Vienna: Böhlau, 1993.

Gerlich, Peter, and Heinrich Neisser, eds. *Europa als Herausforderung: Wandlungsimpulse für das politische System Österreichs.* Vienna: Signum Verlag, 1994.

Hummer, Waldemar, ed. *Österreichs Integration in Europa 1948–1989: Von der OEEC zur EG.* Vienna: Orac, 1990.

Kaiser, Wolfram, et al. "Die EU-Volksabstimmungen in Österreich, Finnland, Schweden und Norwegen: Folgen für die Europäische Union." *Integration* 18 (1995): 76–87.

Kaiser, Wolfram. "Austria in the European Union." *Journal of Common Market Studies* 33 (1995): 411–25.

———. "The Silent Revolution: Austria's Accession to the European Union," in Günter Bischof and Anton Pelinka, eds., *Austrian Historical Memory and National Identity,* (Contemporary Austrian Studies 5). New Brunswick, N.J.: Transaction Publishers, 1996, 135–62.

Luif, Paul. *On the Road to Brussels: The Political Dimensions of Austria's, Finland's and Sweden's Accession to the European Union.* Vienna: Braumüller, 1995.

Pelinka, Anton, ed. *EU-Referendum: Zur Praxis direkter Demokratie in Österreich.* Vienna: Signum Verlag, 1994.

Michael Gehler

Political Parties

The founding parties of Austria's Second Republic in 1945 were the Austrian People's Party (Österreichische Volkspartei, ÖVP), the Socialist Party of Austria (Sozialistische Partei Österreichs, SPÖ), the name of which would be changed in 1991 to Social Democratic Party of Austria (Sozialdemokratische Partei Österreichs), and the Communist Party of Austria (Kommunistische Partei Österreichs, KPÖ). The influence of the KPÖ soon vanished. It received only 5.4 percent of the vote in the 1945 elections, 3 percent in 1962, and 0.3 percent in 1994. Until 1983 the ÖVP and SPÖ gained some 90 percent of the vote cast in general elections (ÖVP: 49.8 percent in 1945, 43.2 percent in 1983; SPÖ: 44.6 percent in 1945, 47.7 percent in 1983). The third political party represented in parliament for more than forty years is the Austrian Freedom Party, (Freiheitliche Partei Österreichs, FPÖ). The party, currently known as die Freiheitlichen, was originally the Independent Party (Wahlpartei der Unabhängigen).

Owing to the experiences of Austro-Fascism (1933–38) and civil war (1934), the ÖVP and the SPÖ informally agreed in 1945 to a democracy of consensus or concordance. Until the 1980s Austria's party system was a relatively stable one of $2\frac{1}{2}$ parties, with grand coalitions (ÖVP-SPÖ) from 1947 to 1966, a single-party ÖVP cabinet from 1966 to 1970, a SPÖ minority government in 1970–71, a single-party SPÖ cabinet from 1971 to 1983, a small coalition of the SPÖ and the FPÖ from 1983 to 1986, and again a grand coalition of the SPÖ and the ÖVP from 1986.

Since the mideighties some remarkable changes have taken place. First, new political parties, the Greens (Grünen) and the Liberal Forum (Liberales Forum, LF) entered parliament in 1986 and 1994, respectively. Second, support for the SPÖ and the ÖVP has been decreasing, down to some 62 percent of votes cast and some 50 percent of those entitled to vote, respectively, in 1994. Third, within eight years the FPÖ, a radical right-wing populist party, has increased its share from 5 percent in 1986 to more than 22 percent in 1994. In the December 1995 election, however, its vote declined slightly. The Greens fell below the 5 percent mark in the same election, as a number of Green and LF voters cast their vote for the SPÖ to block the rise of the FPÖ's Jörg Haider. But by the late 1990s, the party had regained its loses. In Carinthia, it received a majority of the votes, and Haider became governor of the province. In February 2000, the conservative People's Party invited Haider's party to join the government on the national level. Although Austrian president Thomas Klestil was uneasy about the inclusion of the Freedom Party in the federal government, he felt he had no choice but to approve the new government, which had a comfortable parliamentary majority. Before entering the government, however, Haider was required by President Klestil to publicly sign a document denouncing Nazi atrocities and pledging his support of democratic values. The fourteen-member European Union, however, was not appeased, and it imposed sanctions on Austria and froze bilateral ties.

The foundation of the LF in 1993 was a response of former FPÖ members of parliament, led by Heide Schmidt, to the FPÖ's increasing antiforeigner policy. While the FPÖ was seen as a party representing both liberalism and nationalism, the LF claimed to be the real representative of the liberal element in Austria's politics. During the 1970s and up to 1986, the FPÖ under Norbert Steger tried to strengthen its liberal elements, but the national element gained more and more influence with the ascendancy of Haider as party chairman. In the mid-1990s the FPÖ became increasingly a catchall party, owing to Haider's ambition to become chancellor.

The decrease in support for the SPÖ and the ÖVP, on the one hand, shows the "normalization" of Austria's party system and, on the other hand, the growing independence of voters. Until the mid-1990s some 1.2 million Austrians were party members (compared with some 1.9 million at that time in the Federal Republic of Germany). For years political parties were seen as parents taking care of their children. This can be explained by the system of party patronage (*Parteienproporz*), through which the allocation of posts and public employment was dispensed on a party basis. After the mid-1990s the number of party members decreased, and the percentage of voters changing their choice of party from election to election rose. Growing political disaffection has been demonstrated in an unwillingness to vote. Especially in local elections the percentage of voters has decreased steadily; even in general elections the number of eligible voters actually voting declined from 92.6 percent in 1983 to 81.9 percent in 1994.

With five parties represented in parliament, the options for coalitions have increased. While in recent years (1986–94) both the SPÖ and the ÖVP refused to form coalitions with the FPÖ, with the only alternative being a grand coalition, in the future there might be more options for coalition formation.

BIBLIOGRAPHY

Dachs, Herbert, et al., eds. *Handbuch des politischen Systems Österreichs.* Vienna: Manz, 1992.

Müller, Wolfgang C., Fritz Plasser, and Peter A. Ulram, eds. *Wählerverhalten und Parteienwettbewerb: Analysen zur Nationalratswahl 1994.* Vienna: Signum Verlag, 1995.

Nick, Rainer, and Anton Pelinka. *Österreichs politische Landschaft.* Innsbruck: Haymon Verlag, 1993.

Pelinka, Anton. "Die Entaustrifizierung Österreichs: Zum Wandel des politischen Systems 1945–1995." *Österreichische Zeitschrift für Politikwissenschaft* 1 (1995): 516.

Pelinka, Anton, and Fritz Plasser, eds. *The Austrian Party System.* Boulder, Colo.: Westview Press, 1989.

Plasser, Fritz, and Peter A. Ulram. "Überdehnung, Erosion und rechtspopulistische Reaktion: Wandlungsfaktoren des österreichischen Parteiensystems im Vergleich." *Österreichische Zeitschrift für Politikwissenschaft* 2 (1992): 147–64.

Reinhold Gärtner

The Kreisky Era

The Kreisky era was the high point of Bruno Kreisky's political career during which the Socialist Party of Austria (SPÖ) was the most successful party not only in the Socialist International but also among all industrially developed nations with multiparty systems. No other party in a pluralistic system anywhere in Europe succeeded in attaining an absolute majority of the vote in three successive elections. This era, in which over 50 percent of all ballots were cast for the Socialists and voter turnout was approximately 93 percent, lasted until the elections of April 1983.

The transformation of the SPÖ into a modern party capable of forming a majority began with Kreisky's assumption of the position of chairman in 1967. The party clearly distanced itself from the Communists, opened its ranks to the middle class, strove toward more harmonious relations with the Catholic Church, and sought out politically independent experts in developing the party's platform. The SPÖ's programs and political efforts aimed at implementing a wide-ranging democratization and liberalization for broad segments of society combined with traditional Social Democratic initiatives in the areas of economic and social policy. The party proved to be not only socially conscious but liberal as well. Kreisky broke down the camp mentality (*Lagermentalität*) whereby Austria's political landscape was divided into mutually hostile camps. Rather, he appealed to voters from other milieux and other parties "to go a part of the way together with him and the SPÖ" in a Socialist-liberal Kreisky-voter coalition.

Even as early as the Socialist minority government (1970–71), a reform package was carried through with the support of the Freedom Party (FPÖ). Along with electoral reforms benefiting the smaller parties, this included changes in the tax system, family law, and the penal code. With the successful enactment of the popular campaign promise "six months are enough" through the amendment to the military conscription law in 1971, younger voters were won over to the SPÖ.

With an absolute majority Kreisky attempted to bring into existence "a welfare state for all." Using Sweden as a model, he expanded or implemented the system of state aid to provide, for example, assistance for young married couples, infant care stipends, and family aid. Economic policy was characterized by structural changes, modernization, and strengthening Austria's ability to compete internationally. Parallel to this, especially during the years after 1973, when the business boom had tapered off as a result of the oil crisis, full-employment policies (Austro-Keynesianism) determined the political course. Kreisky's full-employment policies were wildly successful. With 2 percent unemployment, Austria consistently figured at the low end of averages for the Organization for European Cooperation and Development (OECD).

Additional measures to further equality of opportunity and equity of distribution were taken through reforms of the educational system: various educational institutions were opened, admission to them was made free, and the educational system was democratized. The reforms carried out with respect to Austrian marriage and family law, as well as the legal regulation of abortion, constituted a step toward dismantling gender hierarchies. The so-called *Fristenlösung* (grace period), the legality of abortion during the first three months of pregnancy, was the most highly disputed legislation during the entire Kreisky era. In this matter Kreisky yielded to pressure exerted by various women's groups and movements, both within the SPÖ and from outside the party. The establishment of four secretaries of state and the creation of a Secretary of State for Women's Affairs in 1979 can also be understood in this context.

While the reforms of penal and labor laws constituted problem areas of a highly controversial nature, Kreisky and the SPÖ generally took great pains to avoid conflict. The majority of the laws enacted were written and passed with the cooperation of the opposition and represented the consensus of the social partners (with the approval of the Federation of Unions representing labor and the Chamber of Commerce representing management).

The elections of April 1983 ended the Kreisky era. As early as the late 1970s new lines of social cleavage had begun to emerge. Ecological, antinuclear power, and other social movements led to a breakup of the Kreisky-voter coalition. Moreover, the governing party along with its parliamentary representatives and internal functionaries came under increasing pressure in a changed media landscape, while the economic crisis, including budget problems associated with the financing of the welfare state, made them targets of a strengthened opposition. The SPÖ's share of the vote sank to 47.6 percent, necessitating a coalition and causing Kreisky to resign. His successors as chancellor were SPÖ politicians Fred Sinowatz and Franz Vranitzky.

BIBLIOGRAPHY

Amerongen, Martin van. *Kreisky und seine unbewaltigte Gegenwart.* Graz/Vienna/Cologne: Verlag Styria, 1977.

Erika Thurner

SEE ALSO Kreisky, Bruno

Economy

All figures and dates relevant to the ranking of national economies show that Austria in the 1990s is clearly one of the most highly developed countries of the world. Its per capita income places it among the top twenty countries in the world and among the top five among the countries of the European Union. Within about a century and a half, but mainly within the last fifty years, Austria has been transformed from a predominantly agrarian country with little division of labor, low overall productivity, and a population of which only small sections were working for a market into a highly productive country with an almost complete division of labor. Its economy is characterized by nonagrarian structures, in which agriculture accounts for less than 10 percent of overall employment and a subsistence economy virtually no longer exists. A mostly rural way of living mainly geared to the daily production and reproduction of a minimum level of existence and characterized by high mortality and nativity rates has been replaced by urban life patterns with small households and many fewer deaths, in which no longer a small minority but the large majority of Austria's more than eight million people can enjoy a high and still rising standard of living. Whereas in 1950, to give one example, there were only fifty one thousand cars in all of Austria, their number had risen to over three million by 1991.

The economic structures of modern Austria are the result of both the legacy of former centuries dating back to the Middle Ages and the revolutionary transformations of the nineteenth and twentieth centuries. As a consequence of this, modern economic development has been characterized by strong regional differences. At least four different patterns may be observed:

1. Development in and around Vienna was determined by the mass demand of a large city with relatively high purchasing power. Because of its position as the capital of the Habsburg monarchy, Vienna's population rose from about 175,000 around the middle of the eighteenth century to over two million on the eve of World War I. The city not only provided a huge market for industrially manufactured goods but also enough merchants, artisans, and skilled and unskilled labor to establish small, medium-sized, and large-scale factories, making Vienna and its surrounding areas one of the most important centers of Austrian industrialization. In 1913, of the eighty mining and manufacturing enterprises employing more than one thousand people in the area that would constitute the Republic of Austria, no fewer than thirty-two were located in Vienna and another twenty-four in the province of Lower Austria, most of them around and especially south of the capital. Although, later on, as other regions engaged

in industrialization, the Vienna area maintained its position as the country's most important industrial region.

2. Another region with a long tradition of nonagrarian economic activities was Upper Styria. These nonagrarian pursuits were based on the mining, smelting, and manufacturing of the Erzberg's rich deposits of iron ore. During the second half of the nineteenth century the region modernized production of iron and steel, creating an industrial link between the Vienna area in the northeast and Austria's second-largest city, Graz, in the south, which, though on a smaller scale than Vienna, has also attracted a relatively large number of industrial enterprises.

3. In the extreme west the small province of Vorarlberg was among the first regions of Europe to develop—at about the same time as Switzerland and only a few decades after Britain—a strong cotton industry. This textile activity, rooted in the labor supply provided by relative overpopulation, began in the early 1800s and thrived until well into the period after World War II, before it finally gave way to the general crisis of the textile industries in developed countries. Since the 1970s and the 1980s, however, it has been replaced by modern metallurgical and especially electrotechnical industries.

4. In all other parts of today's Austria it took much longer to change from primarily agrarian to mainly nonagrarian economic structures. Despite some earlier beginnings, in general they did not begin to be transformed into modern, highly developed societies before the middle of the twentieth century. Some of them, such as the central region of Upper Austria, where large manufacturing plants were founded during World War II, or the better-situated main valleys of Carinthia, Salzburg, and Tyrol, followed the traditional path of modernizing through industrialization. In others, however, owing to the mountainous regions of the last three provinces, modernization resulted from mass tourism, which expanded above all between the 1950s and the 1980s. Although those three provinces account for less than 20 percent of Austria's population, more than 60 percent of all nights spent annually in Austria's hotels have been registered there. Because of tourism, in Carinthia, Salzburg, and Tyrol the relative share of people employed in agriculture had fallen to less than 10 percent by 1981, even lower than in the provinces of Lower Austria, Upper Austria, Styria, and Burgenland, where because of large areas of fertile land the respective shares ranged between 10 and 15 percent.

All in all, between the end of the nineteenth and the end of the twentieth centuries, Austria was transformed from a relatively little developed and highly agrarian country into a modern, highly productive, mainly non-agrarian society in which more people than ever before live in urban surroundings and draw their incomes from jobs in the services sector accounting for about two-thirds of overall employment. The dominance of that sector is due to the relative stagnation of manufacturing, which from about the 1960s onward could no longer offer employment to as many people from the agricultural sector as before. This was, as in other countries, the result of partial saturation in demand for manufactured goods on the one hand and the continuing rise in industrial productivity on the other. At the same time, personal income and purchasing power also continued to grow, thus raising the demand for services.

With regard to regional differences, the formerly backward western regions have caught up in almost every respect, creating a less lopsided and much better balanced economy than existed one hundred and even fifty years ago. For most of the twentieth century in the western provinces of Vorarlberg, Tyrol, and Salzburg the population has grown far above the national average, whereas in the eastern provinces of Lower Austria, Burgenland, and, above all Vienna, population has been reduced, with the remaining provinces of Upper Austria, Styria, and Carinthia showing a relatively moderate rise. While at the turn of the century, outside Vienna more than half the population still lived in villages with fewer than two thousand inhabitants, by the end of the century this percentage had fallen to less than 30 percent. Whereas in 1900 outside Vienna the share of active population employed in agriculture varied between 41 percent in Vorarlberg and 67.5 percent in Burgenland, this margin had clearly been reduced by 1981, ranging from only 3 to 14 percent in the two provinces, respectively. Modernization, for a long time limited to only a few parts of the country, has now come to almost all, leaving only a few areas still relatively backward.

BIBLIOGRAPHY

Bruckmüller, Ernst. *Sozialgeschichte Österreichs.* Vienna: Herold, 1985.

Butschek, Felix. *Die österreichische Wirtschaft im 20. Jahrhundert.* Vienna/Stuttgart: G. Fischer/Osterreichisches Institut für Wirtschaftsforschung, 1985.

Mathis, Franz. *Big Business in Österreich: Österreichische Grozunternehmen in Kurzdarstellungen.* Munich: R. Oldenbourg, 1987.

Sandgruber, Roman. *Ökonomie und Politik: Österreichische Wirtschaftsgeschichte vom Mittelalter bis zur Gegenwart.* Vienna: Ueberreuter, 1995.

Franz Mathis

Parity Commission of Wages and Prices

The Parity Commission (Paritätische Kommission für Lohn- und Preisfragen) was established in Austria in 1957 to control the wage-price spiral by coordinating action with regard to the economy. Special attention is given to the issues of growth, consumer prices, and unemployment. Each of the four largest associations—the Austrian Trade Union Federation and the Chamber of Labor on labor's side, and the Chamber of Business and the Chamber of Agriculture on the employers' side—sends an equal number of delegates to the assembly, whose decision-making process is through unanimous vote. The Parity Commission has four subcommittees: Subcommittee for Wages (set up in 1957), which controls the "timing" of sectoral collective bargaining; Subcommittee for Prices (set up in 1957), setting prices for certain products and services; Advisory Board for Economic and Social Questions (set up in 1963), providing the commission with expertise and advice; Subcommittee for International Issues (set up in 1992), called into being with regard to Austria's entry into the European Union on the one hand and the opening of the Eastern market on the other.

Since the late 1980s a certain loss of influence of the Parity Commission has been observed. In particular the Subcommittee for Prices has lost its former function as an instrument for price control. Two major changes explain this decline. Against the background of internationalization and increasing economic flexibility, macro-economic steering by controlling the wage-price spiral has, in a sense, become anachronistic. Also, the chambers involved, mainly the Chamber of Business, are suffering from a serious crisis of legitimacy because of the obligatory membership for entrepreneurs. This has a strong negative impact on continuity with the Parity Commission. As a result, observers have predicted that its days are numbered.

Ferdinand Karlhoffer

Austrian Trade Union Federation (ATUF)

The Austrian Trade Union Federation (ATUF) (Österreichischer Gewerkschaftsbund) was established in April 1945 as a result of an interparty agreement among the Socialists, the People's Party, and the Communists. It represents the interests of Austria's workers in a highly organized and centralized fashion. Its affiliates, which numbered sixteen in 1945, were reduced to fifteen in 1978 and to fourteen in 1991.

The ATUF was decisively involved in the foundation of the Parity Commission of Wages and Prices, the core of the Austrian social partnership. Having strongly contributed to economic recovery after 1945 by deliberate wage moderation, the ATUF also became an influential and highly regarded authority in the political arena. The proportion of organized workers, peaking at about 70 percent in the early 1950s, gradually declined to 42 percent in 1993. The strength of unions in Austria, however, continues to be significant.

Ferdinand Karlhoffer

Press

The Austria newspaper market is characterized by a high concentration of ownership and prominent involvement by German media groups. In 1994, four of the sixteen principal papers, *Neue Kronen Zeitung, täglich alles, Kurier,* and *Kleine Zeitung,* constituted three-quarters of the total daily circulation of three million. The market leader, *Neue Kronen Zeitung,* founded in 1959, with a daily circulation of 1.1 million in 1994, was unique in its numerical circulation and geographical reach.

In 1945, with the collapse of the Nazi regime, all independent publications were prohibited by the Allied occupation forces and replaced by communiqués and papers in the German language issued by the Allies. The Allies allowed Austrian edited papers only when they were judged to be politically reliable and then they had to operate under censorship. The daily *Vienna Kurier,* set up by the Americans in 1945, successfully gained a sizable readership. Transferred to Austrian editorship in 1954, it continued to be one of the major Austrian newspapers into the 1990s.

The dailies *Oberösterreichische Nachrichten, Salzburger Nachrichten, Tiroler Tageszeitung,* and *Vorarlberger Nachrichten,* all created as independent newspapers in 1945 by U.S. and French occupation forces, are still leaders in their regional markets. The Soviet Union and Great Britain favored newspapers edited by political parties. In the long run, because of mismanagement and heavy dependence on party lines, these proved unsuccessful. The most important of these were the leading dailies of the Left, the Socialist *Arbeiter-Zeitung* (1945–91) and the Communist *Österreichische Volksstimme* (1945–91), and the conservative People's Party's *Das kleine Volksblatt* (1945–70). Independent papers in the Soviet and British zones developed only later. Of these the southern Austrian daily *Kleine Zeitung* (1948–) was the most prominent.

The mid 1950s to the early 1970s were characterized by a contraction in the number of papers and a concentration in ownership. The papers of the political parties continuously became less influential, declining from twenty-seven in the early 1950s to three papers of minor importance in the 1990s. Independent papers also suffered from attrition, but the yellow press emerged and flourished. The small-sized independent daily *Neue Kronen Zeitung,* established in 1959 by Austrian media tycoons Hans Dichand and Kurt Falk, thoroughly penetrated the Austrian newspaper market within a few years.

To prevent a monopolized newspaper market with financially weak papers constantly being driven out of business, a system of press subsidy was introduced in 1975. Primarily planned to provide assistance to financially strapped party papers, the subsidies failed.

No cartel regulations in Austria oppose press concentration, and an efficient, long-term media policy has never been adapted. Amendments in 1984 to the 1975 press law, stressing the importance of a diversified market, led in fact to further consolidation. The constant danger of press monopolism became evident when, in 1988, the German media giant *Westdeutsche Allgemeine Zeitung (WAZ)* acquired at little less then 50 percent interest in two of the most widely circulated Austrian dailies, the *Neue Kronen Zeitung* and *Kurier.*

From the 1970s, the Austrian press market experienced a thorough expansion with new titles and types of newspapers. *Trend,* an economic magazine, and the newsmagazine *profil* were created in 1969–70 by Oscar Bronner. Bronner, in 1988, with a 50 percent investment by German publishing house Springer, established the quality daily *Der Standard.* Lifestyle magazines like *Wiener* and *Basta,* the latter launched by Wolfgang and Helmuth Fellner, flooded Austria in the early 1980s. In 1992 the Fellners created the magazine *News.* In 1985 the yellow press weekly *Die ganze Woche,* established by Kurt Falk after he left the *Neue Kronen Zeitung* in discord, proved to be his first step to establish market dominance. In 1992, with money raised from the selling of his interests in the *Neue Kronen Zeitung,* Falk introduced a small-sized, low-priced yellow press daily in color, *täglich alles.* The *Neue Kronen Zeitung* has, nevertheless, so far maintained its dominance.

BIBLIOGRAPHY

Massenmedien in Österreich: Medienbericht 1–4. Vienna: Internationale Publikationengesellschaft, 1977–93.
Pressehandbuch: Medien und Werbung in Österreich. Vienna: VOZ, 1953–.
Purer, Heinz. *Presse in Österreich.* Vienna: VOZ, 1990.

Norbert P. Feldinger

Azerbaijan

Independent successor state to the Azerbaijan Soviet Socialist Republic of the former USSR. The Republic of Azerbaijan consists of 33,430 square miles (86,000 sq km) of noncontiguous territory located south of the Caucasus Mountains on the western shore of the Caspian Sea. In addition to the Caspian Sea its main section is surrounded by Russia, Georgia, Armenia, and Iran. Its discontiguous segment, Nakhichevan (Naxçivan) is separated from the rest of Azerbaijan by a strip of Armenian territory twenty-five to thirty miles wide. Nakhichevan, which is approximately 3,420 square miles in area, is bordered, in addition to Armenia, by Turkey and Iran. The population of Azerbaijan is 7,500,000. Its capital, Baku, has 1,800,000 inhabitants.

The variegated topography of Azerbaijan, which includes the Caspian coast and the basins of the Kura and Aras Rivers as well as mountains that rise to fifteen thousand feet in the north and to twelve thousand feet in the west, produces different climatic regions. Various parts of the country are suited for different crops from cotton to grapes, wheat, tea, and mulberries. Azerbaijan has a number of resources but the most important by far is oil.

Oil, a source of economic hope for contemporary Azerbaijan, has created serious ecological problems. Contamination from its extraction, processing, and the petrochemical industry has polluted the air and the Caspian Sea. The dumping of petroleum waste and raw sewage into the Caspian was scheduled to end in 1985, but that

year it is estimated that 104,000 tons of oil and sediment were discharged into the sea. Caspian pollution is accentuated by the diversion of water from the Aras and Kura Rivers for irrigation. The country's crops too have been contaminated by pesticides and other chemicals.

The official language of Azerbaijan, Azerbaijani, is a south Turkic language. The Cyrillic alphabet, imposed in 1939, was replaced by the Turkish version of the Latin alphabet in 1992. In 1989 Azerbaijanis constituted 78 percent of the population. Part of the Oguz Seljuk migration, they settled in the area in the eleventh century and fused with the Iranian inhabitants. The approximately 10,300,000 Azerbaijanis who live in the Iranian Azerbaijan province of neighboring Iran have been recently augmented by approximately 2,500,000 Azerbaijani refugees from the Nagorno-Karabakh conflict with Armenia. Russians, most of whom reside in Baku and the industrial city Sumgait (Sumqayit), constituted 8 percent of the population of Azerbaijan in 1989. Armenians constituted 7.9 percent. In 1995, as a result of emigration—the flight of Azerbaijanis into Azerbaijan from Georgia, Armenia, and Nagorno-Karabakh; the flight of Armenians from Azerbaijani territory; and the de facto secession of predominantly Armenian Nagorno-Karabakh—the population ratios changed. In 1995 Azerbaijanis constituted 90 percent, while Russians constituted only 2.5 percent, and Armenians 2.3 percent. The country is predominantly Islamic. The dominant form of Islam is Jafarite Shia, but approximately 30 percent of the country's Muslims are Sunnis.

After the arrival of the Turkic people in the area, it was dominated successively by the Mongols and the Turkmen. An "Azeri" state was established under the Shirvan-Shahs. Late in the fifteenth century the area became the base of the Shia Safavid dynasty. The area of present-day Azerbaijan became a battleground between the Sunni Ottomans and the Shia Safavids. After the assasination of Persian ruler Nadir Shah in 1747, his kingdom including present-day Azerbaijan disintegrated into combative Turkic Muslim khanates. This provided Russia the opportunity to dominate Transcaucasia. In 1783 Catherine the Great seized western Transcaucasia and established Russia as the protector of Georgia. In 1801 Alexander I absorbed Georgia and the Azeribaijani areas of Kazakh and Shamshadil. Two Russo-Persian Wars in 1804–13 and 1826–28, followed by the Treaties of Gulistan and Turkmanchai, gave Russia control of "Azerbaijan" to the ARAS (Araks) River. Many Azerbaijani Shiites fought on the side of the Russians against the Sunni resistance in the Caucasus. Sectarian differences played a role, but for

Azerbaijan. *Illustration courtesy of Bernard Cook.*

many Azerbaijanis Russian rule was viewed as preferable to that of Persia.

Though the Russians gradually supplanted the rule of the local khanates and replaced Islamic law, the Sharia, with Russian laws and courts, life for the Azerbaijanis changed little until the discovery of oil. With the development of the Baku oil fields in the late nineteenth century, Baku became the fastest-growing Russian city. The Revolution of 1905 ushered in a period of political ferment and ethnic conflict. There was resentment among the Azerbaijanis against the Armenians who had been favored by the tsarist government and who harbored ambitions to establish a Greater Armenia at least partially with territory regarded by the Azerbaijanis as theirs. Among Azerbaijanis the Musavat (Equality) Party gained increasing support for its nationalist program. Musavat at first supported the Bolsheviks, but the Baku Communist Party was dominated by Russians and Armenians who had no sympathy for the desire of Azerbaijani socialists to govern themselves. In March 1918 Bolsheviks and Armenian nationalists fought the Azerbaijanis and slaughtered over three thousand of them after they had surrendered. Though the Bolsheviks were victorious in Baku, where they established a Bolshevik Baku Soviet, an anti-Bolshevik Azerbaijan National Council, temporarily dominant elsewhere, proclaimed the Azerbaijan Democratic Republic. Azerbaijan, heretofore, had been a rarely used geographical term. It now was utilized to signify a state and a people previously referred to as Caucasian or Transcaucasian Turks, Tartars, or Muslims. Azerbaijan was occupied by the Turks and then the British until August 1919. The republic lasted, however, until April 28, 1920, when it was overrun by the Bolsheviks.

In December 1922 Azerbaijan was linked with Georgia and Armenia in the Trancaucasian Socialist Federated Soviet Republic (TSFSR). This became a constituent part of the Soviet Union on December 30. In 1936 the TSFSR was divided into its constituent parts and Azerbaijan became the Azerbaijan Soviet Socialist Republic (ASSR).

The Soviet period can be credited with greatly expanded literacy, but resistance to collectivization of agriculture led to uprisings that were brutally repressed. Stalin's great purge eliminated leading literary figures Javid, Salman Mumtaz, Taqi Shahbazi, Ali Nazim, and Mikail Mushfiq. The purges, directed by Mir Jafar Baghirov, commissar for internal affairs from 1921 to 1933 and first secretary of the Azerbaijan Communist Party (ACP) from 1933 to 1953, were replete with deportations and widespread murder. Between 1921 and 1940 an estimated 120,000 Azerbaijanis were killed. The purges reached into the ranks of the ACP. The purges aimed at completely crushing religious and national sentiment and were accompanied by a vigorous program of Russification. Azerbaijanis did not constitute a majority in the party or administration in Azerbaijan again until the 1970s.

During the Second World War the Germans never penetrated the Caucasus Mountains. Though hundreds of thousands of Azerbaijanis fought for the Soviet Union, 35,000 Azerbaijani prisoners joined the Germans. From 1941 until 1946 the USSR occupied Iranian Azerbaijan. The Soviets promoted a campaign of Azerification and sponsored the establishment of an autonomous "Azerbaijan People's Government" in Iranian Azerbaijan in November 1945. In the developing Cold War the Soviets were thwarted in their effort to amalgamate the area with the ASSR, and as a result of U.S. pressure they were forced to withdraw.

Following the death of Stalin in 1953, his client, Baghirov, was not only removed from office but arrested and three years later executed. His successor was Imam Dashdemiroglu Mustafaev, a scientist. As the production of oil developed in new areas of the USSR, the Soviet government decreased its investments in Azerbaijan, whose fields were aging. Mustafaev had attempted to gain some autonomy for the republic, reinvigorate its oil industry, and make Azerbaijani the official language. But he was replaced for his nationalism in 1959 and the oil industry continued to languish. In the 1960s Azerbaijan had the highest rate of population growth among the republics of the USSR but the lowest rate of growth in economic output. The growing economic crisis fueled tensions between Azerbaijan's Azerbaijani and Armenian inhabitants, particularly in the cities.

Mustafaev's successor, Veli Akhundov, was eventually blamed for the economic crisis, accused of corruption, and removed in 1969. Akhundov's replacement was Heydar Aliyev (Aliev, 1923–), who had climbed through the ranks of the KGB in Nakhichevan. Aliyev promoted growth of nonpetroleum-related industry but also consolidated Azerbaijani control of dominant positions in the political and economic administration. Though appointed to root out corruption, he replaced Akhundov's corruption with his own patronage system. In 1982 Aliyev became the first Azerbaijani appointed to the Politburo, but he was ousted from that post in 1987 because of his toleration of corruption and opposition to Mikhail Gorbachev's reforms. Under Kiamran Baghirov, Aliyev's successor, corruption thrived while the economy languished. Economic dissatisfaction was fueled because despite Azerbaijan's trade surplus with the rest of the USSR, its per capita income was lower than that of any other republics except those in Central Asia.

The increasing discrimination in Azerbaijan against non-Azerbaijani speakers helped to increase tensions in Nagorno-Karabakh, the autonomous region of Azerbaijan predominantly inhabited by Armenians. The Armenians of Nagorno-Karabakh requested in February 1988 to join Armenia. In reaction riots, which broke out in Sumgait, led to the murder of twenty-six Armenians. Gorbachev's subsequent moves only exacerbated the situation. When he removed the first secretaries of both republics' Communist parties, there was a nationalist reaction among Azerbaijanis against the party. Gorbachev in January 1989 removed the administration of Nagorno-Karabakh from Azerbaijan. Though Moscow temporarily assumed direct control, under Azerbaijani pressure Gorbachev restored control to Azerbaijan. This indecisive, and ultimately pointless, shuffling settled nothing and only enraged both sides.

In the summer of 1989 the Azerbaijan Popular Front (APF) was established to protect the republic's national interests. In August it staged mass demonstrations and strikes. In September the APF blockaded road and railroad routes into Armenia on which that republic's economy depended. On September 13 Abdul Vezirov, the new first secretary of the ACP, gave way to APF pressure and agreed to call a special meeting of the Supreme Soviet (AzSS) to enact a declaration of sovereignty. This was done on September 23. In face of the blockade and a massive demonstration in Baku, Gorbachev retreated. In November hundreds of thousands of Azerbaijani demonstrators filled Lenin Square in Baku to protest the situation in Nagorno-Karabakh. However, other issues emerged. The demonstrators expressed concern over Azerbaijani self-determination, environmental problems, and the stifling of expressions of Azerbaijani culture. Although Azerbaijani Turkish had been the republic's official language since the 1950s, official business was nonetheless conducted in Russian. Before 1958 students had been required to pass an examination in Azerbaijani, but after 1958 they could demonstrate proficiency merely in Russian. Russian became the dominant language in higher education, and many educated Azerbaijanis were not truly fluent in their own language.

In response to popular pressure in Baku, the Supreme Soviet of the USSR canceled Moscow's direct administration of Nagorno-Karabakh on November 28 yet agitation continued. The Birlik (Unity) Society, formed at first largely by Azerbaijani immigrants from Iran and by this time the second-largest popular organization in the country, fused with the APF. A central goal of Birlik was unification of Soviet and Iranian Azerbaijan into a single Azerbaijani state. A number of nascent political parties formed within the APF and demanded a referendum on secession. In January 1990 APF members seized control of Länkäran, a city in the southeast of the country, on the Caspian Sea. They then destroyed border markers and frontier control posts along the Azerbaijani-Iranian frontier. Violence against Armenians in Baku the same month was utilized by Gorbachev as an excuse to remove Vezirov, dispatch Soviet troops to restore order, and prevent a coup by the APF. Many APF leaders were jailed, and Prime Minister, Ayaz Niyaz Mutalibov was made head of the ACP.

The Azerbaijanis were not cowed. Almost a third of ACP members tore up their party cards. Elmira Kafarova, chair of the AzSS, decried the intervention as a "gross violation of Azerbaijani sovereignty." More than a million mourners attended the funeral of the 131 Azeris killed by Soviet troops. Nevertheless, Azerbaijan agreed to sign the new union treaty and, although the official tally was questioned, a majority of its voters seemed to support the March 1991 referendum on the preservation of the USSR. After the attempted coup in August 1991, Mutalibov, whose apparent support of the coup led to large protest demonstrations, resigned from the party, declared Azerbaijan independent on August 30, and asked the AzSS to establish a directly elected presidency. In an uncontested election in September, Mutalibov was elected president, and on October 18 the AzSS formally ratified the Azerbaijani declaration of independence. In December 99 percent of the 54 percent of Azerbaijani voters who participated in a referendum affirmed their support for the decision for independence. The same month Azerbaijan signed the Alma Ata accord formally establishing the Commonwealth of Independent States (CIS).

At the beginning of November Mutalibov cut the pipeline that carried natural gas to Armenia. After the downing of an Azerbaijani helicopter over Nagorno-Karabakh, he cut all rail lines to Armenia and ordered the minister of defense to restore order in the region with the new 25,000-person Azerbaijani army. Owing to Azerbaijan's failure to subdue Nagorno-Karabakh, Mutalibov was pressed by the APF to resign, and he gave way on March 6, 1992. The presidency was temporarily conferred on Yagub Mamedov, chairman of the Milli Majlis (National Assembly), the successor to the AzSS. In May Mutalibov attempted to reclaim the presidency and cancel the impending election. Though he was supported by parliament, the APF with the aid of the army thwarted his effort. The presidential election was held on June 7 amid increasingly dismal news from the battlefront. Abulfez Elchibey (Elchibay) (1938–), head of the APF and a former dissident and political prisoner, won 60 percent of the vote.

Elchibey opposed continued membership in the CIS and sought closer relations with Turkey and Azerbaijanis in Iran. He favored free-market reform, but the country was too preoccupied with the struggle over Nagorno-Karabakh to consider new economic initiatives. There were shortages of food and fuel and Azerbaijan had to deal with a massive number of refugees. Its gross domestic product declined by 11.7 percent in 1990, .7 percent in 1991, 22.4 percent in 1992, approximately 13 percent in 1993, and approximately 21.9 percent in 1994.

Elchibey's position was undermined by Armenian successes in Nagorno-Karabakh. Despite Azerbaijani successes in the second half of 1992, in early 1993 Azerbaijani forces were routed. The enclave and a land bridge to Armenia proper were now in Armenian hands, and 250,000 to 300,000 new Azerbaijani refugees were created.

When Elchibey attempted to discipline one of his critics, the former military commander in Nagorno-Karabakh, Colonel Surat Husseynov (1958–), Husseynov launched a military rebellion against Elchibey in June 1993. Elchibey sought the support of Aliyev, who was at the time chairman of the Nakhichevan legislature. When Aliyev reached Baku, the former head of the KGB in Azerbaijan and the leader of its Communist Party during the Brezhnev years was elected chairman of the parliament. Elchibey sought refuge in Nakhichevan but refused to resign. The parliament then recognized Aliyev as acting head of state. Aliyev settled the rebellion by naming Husseynov prime minister. Over 90 percent of the voters in an August 29 referendum repudiated Elchibey, and Aliyev was elected president by 98.8 percent of those voting on October 3. Under Aliyev the Nagorno-Karabakh issue remains unsettled but Azerbaijan did rejoin the CIS in September 1993 and has sought Russian mediation in its conflict with Armenia.

Stephen and Sandra Batalden have pointed out the striking parallel between the former Communist Party leader Aliyev's reincarnation as a nationalist and the transformation of Leonid Kravchuk in Ukraine, Eduard Shevardnadze in Georgia, Islam Karimov in Uzbekistan, and Slobodan Milošević in Serbia into nationalist leaders. They all adopted a new ideology but were able to exploit their contacts with the former bureaucratic nomenklatura.

The year 1994 was marked by growth in crime and political violence. In two bombings of the Baku metro, nineteen were killed. Political opponents of Aliyev and his party, the New Azerbaijan Party (NAP) were harassed, and access of the APF to the media was restricted and many members arrested. Large demonstrations, however, were organized by the APF to protest the May cease-fire in Nagorno-Karabakh. The deputy chairman of the legislature and Aliyev's security chief were both assassinated on September 29. Three members of the special militia (OPON) of the Ministry of Internal Affairs were arrested. This was followed in October by seizure of the office of the procurator general by Rovshan Javadov, deputy minister of internal affairs, and one hundred OPON troops. After they secured the release of their comrades, they withdrew.

Mutinies multiplied. One in Gyanja (Gāncā) was reputedly staged by relatives of Surat Huseynov. Although Huseynov protested his loyalty, he was replaced by Aliyev, who appointed Fuad Guliyev, the first deputy prime minister, as acting prime minister. Aliyev, however, assumed direct control of the government. As parliament moved to lift Huseynov's immunity, he fled the country. Some blame the turmoil on Russian intrigues, asserting that Russia wanted to prevent the Majlis from approving an agreement with a consortium of U.S. and European companies to exploit Azeri oil reserves. The agreement was approved, nevertheless, on September 20, 1994.

In March 1995 new trouble erupted with the OPON. After the government ordered the disbanding of the militia, OPON units attacked a police station in Baku and government and police headquarters in the northwest. Many died in the fighting. Javadov demanded that Aliyev step aside and a new coalition government be formed with himself as minister of internal affairs. But government troops seized OPON headquarters in Baku. Javadov and many of his followers were killed and 160 were arrested. Aliyev claimed that Elchibey and Huseynov were involved in the attempted coup. Aliyev imposed a state of emergency and banned the APF.

The first post-Soviet legislative election took place on November 12, 1995, preceded by much unrest. Aliyev claimed that a coup was being plotted, and excluded a number of parties and six hundred independent candidates from the election. When a disastrous fire in the Baku metro took three hundred lives in October, it was at first erroneously thought that this had been an act of terrorism intended to disrupt the election. When the election was held, only eight of the thirty-one registered parties were allowed to participate. Of these only the APF, which had again been legalized, and the National Independence Party (NIP) were opposition parties. Twenty-six proportional representation and one hundred direct-constituency seats were contested. Voters from Nagorno-Karabakh and other areas under Armenian control elected district representatives from their places of refuge. Aliyev's NAP won nineteen of the twenty-five seats assigned by proportional representation. The APF and NIP each won three. NAP candidates and independents who supported Aliyev won an overwhelming victory in the single-seat constituencies. On the same day as the Milli Majlis election, the new constitution was ratified, according to the government count, by 91.9 percent of those voting. The constitution established a secular state in which the president had extensive executive powers. But international observers reported serious electoral improprieties, and the Round Table bloc, which represented twenty-one parties, labeled the election illegal.

Political repression continued in 1996 and 1997. Supporters of Huseynov and Elchibey were sentenced to long prison terms, and Imranov Nariman and Alikram Gumbatov, former members of the government, were tried for treason and were executed. Despite charges of electoral fraud, Aliyev was reelected president on October 12, 1998. However, in April 1999 he was hospitalized for open-heart surgery.

Despite Azerbaijan's political difficulties and war over Nagorno-Karabakh, the country's mineral wealth constitutes an asset for the future. Azerbaijan's known reserves of petroleum amount to approximately a billion metric tons. There are also large reserves of natural gas. In Azerbaijan's 1994 agreement with the U.S.-European consortium, the companies agreed to a thirty-year project to develop three Caspian Sea fields containing an estimated 511 million metric tons of petroleum and 55 billion cubic meters of natural gas.

BIBLIOGRAPHY

"Azerbaijan." *The Europa World Yearbook 1996.* London: Europa Publications, 1997, Vol. 1, 468–72.

"Azerbaijan Leader Claims Victory Amid Alleged Violations," *Los Angeles Times,* October 13, 1998.

Batalden, Stephen K., and Sandra L. Batalden. *The Newly Independent States of Eurasia: Handbook of Former Soviet Republics.* Phoenix, Ariz.: Oryx, 1993.

Shoemaker, M. Wesley. *Russia, Eurasian States, and Eastern Europe 1997.* Harpers Ferry, West Virginia: Stryker-Post, 1997.

Zinin, Yuri N., and Alexei V. Maleshenko. "Azerbaijan," in Mohiaddin Mesbahi, ed. *Central Asia and the Caucasus after the Soviet Union.* Gainesville: University Press of Florida, 1994.

Bernard Cook

SEE ALSO Armenia; Nagorno-Karabakh

Aznar Lopez, José María (1953–)

Member of the Spanish legislature from 1982 to 1986, president of the province of Castile and León from 1987 to 1989, and president of Spain.

The election of conservative José María Aznar Lopez as president in 1996 ended fourteen years of control over government by the Spanish Socialist Workers Party. While in office Anzar has instituted a series of reforms that have improved the economy and enabled Spain to enter the first stage of the European Economic and Monetary Union that began in 1999.

The son of a diplomat in the regime of Francisco Franco, Aznar was born in Madrid and studied law at the city's Complutense University. Aznar's first governmental position came in 1976, when he was appointed inspector of finances. In 1978 he joined a conservative political party, the Popular Alliance, and shortly afterward was named party secretary for the region of La Rioja. Aznar rose quickly within the party hierarchy and was twice elected to the national legislature. While in office he became the party spokesman on economic issues and was a member of the legislature's constitutional committee.

In 1987 Aznar was elected president of the province of Castile and León. During the same year he became director of the Popular Alliance, now renamed the Popular Party. Under his leadership the party moved further away from its personal and ideological connections to the Franco dictatorship. Aznar strove to give the organization a mainstream Christian Democratic identity more in line with other large European conservative parties. These changes, combined with general dissatisfaction with the Socialist government, increased acceptance of the Popular Party. After a narrow defeat in 1993, Aznar was elected president of the government (prime minister) on March 3, 1996, heading a coalition government supported by several large minority parties.

Fiscally conservative, Aznar embarked on a plan to reduce public spending, increase productivity, and lower domestic prices. These programs cut the public deficit and inflation levels by more than 50 percent in fewer than two years. Despite such accomplishments Aznar has been unable to eliminate unemployment and the high production costs that have plagued Spain in recent years.

The election of Aznar as prime minister represented a milestone in the country's history and can be viewed as the symbolic completion of the transition to democracy. He is the first freely elected conservative to head the government since the death of Franco. His first two years in office witnessed significant economic improvement, but he still faces substantial challenges such as high unemployment and escalating terrorism by the Basque separatist organization ETA.

BIBLIOGRAPHY

Aznar, José María, *España: la segunda transicion.* Madrid: Espasa Calpe, 1994.

Aznar, José María. *Retratos intimos de José María Aznar: un hombre, un proyecto.* Barcelona: Plaza & Janes, 1996.

Haywood, Paul. *The Government and Politics of Spain.* New York: St. Martin's Press, 1995.

Brian D. Bunk

Baburin, Sergei (1959–)

Russian politician. Sergey Baburin was born on January 31, 1959, in the city of Semipalatinsk in the Kazakh Soviet Socialist Republic. After graduating from the faculty of law of Omsk State University, Baburin served in the Soviet army (1981–83) and took part in military actions in Afghanistan. Following his military service, he earned a Ph.D. in law in 1986 at Leningrad (St. Petersburg) State University. He was a member of Communist Party of the Soviet Union (CPSU) from 1987 to 1991. Baburin then taught at the Faculty of Law at Omsk State University, where he became the dean in 1988.

In 1988–89 he began his political career taking part in democratic movements during the period of President Mikhail Gorbachev's policies of *glasnost* (openness) and *perestroika* (restructuring). He failed in his first political campaign for the Congress of People's Deputies of the Soviet Union in 1989 but a year later was elected a deputy of the Supreme Soviet of the Russian Soviet Federated Socialist Republic. As a deputy he entered the opposition against the democratic majority led by Russian President Boris Yeltsin and became the leader of the "Russia" faction, a group of nationalistic-oriented former members of the CPSU.

In December 1991 he was one of the six deputies of the Supreme Soviet of the Russian Federation who voted against ratification of the Minsk (Belovezhskoya) Declaration of December 8, 1991, which abolished the Soviet Union. The same month he organized and became the leader of a party called "The Union of All Russian People," which sharply opposed the Yeltsin administration. In 1993, Baburin headed the Committee of the Supreme Soviet of Russian Federation for Legal Reforms and took part in the activities of the Constitutional Committee.

During the armed clash of September 21 to October 4, 1993, between Yeltsin's supporters and his opponents in the parliament, Baburin was one of the most active defenders of the Supreme Soviet building. After the defeat of Yeltsin's parliamentary opponents and the dissolution of the Supreme Soviet by Yeltsin, Baburin successfully took part in the election for the new lower house and became a deputy of the state Duma. There he headed a faction that actively opposed the expansion of the North Atlantic Treaty Organization (NATO) to the east to include former members of the Soviet-dominated Warsaw Pact.

As a deputy of the first and second Duma, Baburin was one of the sharpest critics of Yeltsin and the government. He voted no confidence against the government, voted against the state budget, supported impeachment procedures against Yeltsin, and voted for the war against the breakaway republic of Chechnya.

During presidential elections in June 26, 1996, Baburin supported Gennady Zuganov, the candidate of the Communist Party, but he subsequently refused to join Zuganov's People's Patriotic Union because, in his opinion, it was too supportive of Yeltsin and the government. In December 1999 Baburin failed to be elected to the third Duma, but his Russian All Peoples Union continues to be popular in the southern parts of Russia, especially in those areas located close to the North Caucasus, in some regions of Siberia, and in his Omsk District.

Nickolaj Sannikov
Andrey Alimov

Bahr, Egon Karl-Heinz (1922–)

German politician and journalist. Egon Bahr was born on March 18, 1922, in Thuringia, the only child of a teacher. In 1940 he earned the Abitur. Rather than being allowed to study music as he desired, he received business training at the industrial firm Rheinmetall-Borsig. From 1942 to 1944 he served in the German army then returned to

Borsig. In May 1945 he went to work for the Soviet-sponsored *Berliner Zeitung,* but he soon changed to the American *Allgemeine Zeitung.* From 1950 to 1960 he was RIAS commentator at Bonn and from 1953 until 1954 at the same time chief editor of RIAS. In 1956 he became a member of the Social Democratic Party (SPD) and a long and friendly relationship with Willy Brandt began. From 1960 to 1966 Bahr worked for Brandt as director of the Public Relations and Information Office of Berlin. In 1966 Bahr followed Brandt to Bonn, where in November 1967 he became the head of the planning staff at the Foreign Office. From 1969 until 1972 he was state secretary (Staatssekretär, or deputy chancellor) at the office of Federal Chancellor Brandt, whose adviser he was through all those years. In 1972 Bahr was elected a member of the Bundestag. From 1974 to 1976 he was minister of economic cooperation and development under Chancellor Helmut Schmidt.

From 1976 to 1981 Bahr held the office of secretary of the SPD, and until 1991 he was a member of the SPD collective leadership. An expert in foreign relations and disarmament, he was chairman of the subcommittee for disarmament and arms control of the German federal parliament from 1980 until 1990, and since 1984 director of the Institute for Peace Studies and Security Policy (Institut für Friedensforschung und Sicherheitspolitik) at the University of Hamburg.

Bahr developed the concept of *Ostpolitik* and presented it to the public in a 1963 speech in Tutzing: "Change through Rapprochement" (*Wandel durch Annäherung*). After the static German foreign policy up to the early 1960s, this new approach was more positive and constructive, emphasizing the well-being of the people on both sides of the Berlin Wall, but especially of the East Germans. During the crucial years of the implementation of *Ostpolitik* (negotiations began in early 1970), Bahr was one of the leading figures on the West German side. In later years his concerns shifted to worldwide peace policy, including north-south relations and disarmament, especially of nuclear arms. He opposed NATO's double-track policy and spoke up in favor of more concessions to the East. He summarized his view with the words "peace is not everything, but without peace everything is nothing."

BIBLIOGRAPHY

Bahr, Egon. *Sicherheit für und vor Deutschland: vom Wandel durch Annäherung zur Europäischen Sicherheitsgemeinschaft.* Munich: Hanser, 1991.

Lutz, Dieter S., ed. *Das undenkbare Denken: Festschrift für Egon Bahr zum 70. Geburtstag.* Baden-Baden: Nomos, 1992.

Heinlein, Stefan A. *Gemeinsame Sicherheit: Egon Bahrs sicherheitspolitische Konzeption und die Kontinuität sozialdemokratischer Entspannungsvorstellungen.* Münster, New York: Waxmann, 1993.

Staffa, Rangmar. *Egon Bahr: der geheime Diener.* Landshut, Germany: Verlag Politisches Archiv, 1974.

Anjana Buckow

SEE ALSO Brandt, Willy

Bahro, Rudolf (1935–97)

German intellectual and dissident. Rudolf Bahro studied philosophy at Humboldt University in East Berlin between 1954 and 1959, joined the Socialist Unity Party (SED) in 1954, and worked as a deputy editor of the Free Democratic Youth (FDJ) magazine *Forum.* From 1967 to 1977 he was head of an office for labor efficiency at a factory in East Berlin. Convinced by the Prague Spring (1968) of the ideological bankruptcy of "real existing socialism" in the Soviet bloc, Bahro argued in his comprehensive analysis, *The Alternative in Eastern Europe* (1977), that the burgeoning crisis of the system could be overcome only by a fundamental redivision of labor and by the harnessing of popular imagination ("the massive surplus consciousness in society") by a League of German Communists. Although his book could not be published in the German Democratic Republic (GDR), excerpts appeared in the West. Bahro was arrested in 1977 and eventually sentenced in 1978 to eight years' imprisonment on trumped-up charges of betraying state secrets. In 1979 an international campaign secured his release and permission for him to go to the Federal Republic of Germany.

Bahro became involved in the West German Green movement, but his radical solutions to the spiritual, ecological, social, and economic problems of Western civilization and to its "logic of self-extinction" led to his marginalization and eventual break with the Green Party in 1988. He returned to the GDR after the collapse of SED rule and secured a chair in social ecology at Humboldt University.

At Humboldt Bahro headed the Institute of Social Ecology. There he attempted to elaborate a fusion of socialism and the Green movement. The suicide of his second wife, Beatrice, in 1993 burdened his final years. Bahro died of leukemia on December 5, 1997.

BIBLIOGRAPHY

Bahro, Rudolf. *From Red to Green.* London: Verso, 1984.

Staunton, Denis. "Obituary: Rudolf Bahro: Perestroika's Prophet." *Guardian,* December 10, 1997.

Mike Dennis

Balcerowicz, Leszek (1947–)

Economist, professor of the Main School of Economics in Warsaw, politician, chairman of Freedom Union (UW), and Polish minister of finance from 1989 to 1991 and from 1997. In 1970 Leszek Balcerowicz graduated from the Main School of Economics and started his academic career there, becoming professor in 1992.

In the first non-communist cabinet of Tadeusz Mazowiecki (1989–90) and the second of Jan Krzysztóf Bielecki (1990–91) Balcerowicz held the positions of vice prime minister and minister of finance. He authored the program of stabilization and transformation of the Polish economy called the "Balcerowicz Plan," or "shock therapy." Ten bills passed by the Seim (parliament) in 1989 contained the basic tools for implementation of two main goals: the struggle against hyperinflation and the introduction of the institutional infrastructure of a market economy. From the economic point of view the program succeeded in the stabilizing the economy, liberalizing the domestic market, and opening the economy to foreign markets. However, the social costs of economic transformation were high. In public opinion Balcerowicz became a symbol of pauperization of society and has been used since as such by many left-wing and right-wing politicians.

With time, two views on the Balcerowicz Plan crystallized. According to the first, thanks to this plan, Poland has been able to overcome economic crisis relatively quickly and a stable basis was laid for a 6 percent increase in GNP yearly (since 1995). According to the second opinion, if the plan had not been introduced, it would have been possible to avoid the deep decrease in standard of living and in the economic parameters.

In 1995 Balcerowicz became a member and chairman (replacing Mazowiecki) of the Freedom Union. He is considered a pragmatic, centrist politician. After the parliamentary election in 1997, the Freedom Union formed a coalition with the Solidarity Electoral Action (AWS). Balcerowicz again became vice prime minister and minister of finance.

Maria Nawojczyk

Balladur, Édouard (1929–)

French politician and premier from March 29, 1993, to May 1995. Balladur's family returned to France shortly after his birth on May 2, 1929, at Smyrna, Turkey. He was educated at the law faculty at Aix-en-Provence, the Institut d'Études Politiques, and the École Nationale d'Administration. After a stint at Radio-Télévision de France, he became an adviser to Prime Minister, later

President, Georges Pompidou. After the latter's death in 1974 he worked for a time in the private sector. Increasingly the leader of the neo-Gaullist Rally for the Republic (RPR), Balladur was frequently sought out for advice by Jacques Chirac. In March 1986 Balladur was elected to the National Assembly from Paris on the RPR list. That same month he became finance minister and served in the post until May 1986.

Following the rightist sweep in the March 1993 national parliamentary elections, President François Mitterrand bowed to the inevitable and appointed Balladur premier. Chirac evidently hoped that the mild-mannered Balladur would prepare the way for him to run for the presidency in 1995, but Balladur developed presidential ambitions of his own.

As premier Balladur headed a coalition including the Rally for the Republic and the center-right Coalition for French Democracy. Balladur's first action was a popular measure to tighten immigration controls, but he was soon under fire on many fronts. He announced that his top priority would be restoring the French economy. To address a budgetary imbalance he proposed an austerity program with new taxes on liquor and gasoline, as well as social security. He hoped the need for economic belt-tightening might be blamed on the former Socialist government of Pierre Bérégovoy, which Balladur charged had produced France's greatest economic crisis since the Second World War.

Balladur's pro-Europe policies provoked protests by farmers against a European Community agreement to reduce farm subsidies. Students and workers objected to a new and lower minimum wage for those younger than twenty-five, and Air France employees objected to a cut in jobs. Soon Balladur was in retreat. He gave in to fishermen's demands for limits on fish imports and he caved in on a government plan to aid private schools. He was also hurt by problems in the economy, principally an unemployment rate of over 12 percent, government scandals, and a split within the conservative government between those loyal to him and those who favored Jacques Chirac for the presidency.

In the April 1995 presidential elections Balladur, who had been the front-runner in February, was damaged by charges of corruption and phone tapping. He secured only 19 percent of the vote, third behind Chirac with 21 percent and Socialist Lionel Jospin with 23 percent, and thus did not make the runoff. He asked his supporters to vote for Chirac, and after Chirac's victory in May, Balladur resigned as premier.

Spencer C. Tucker

SEE ALSO Chirac, Jacques; Jospin, Lionel; Mitterrand, François; Pompidou, George

Baltic Assembly

Consultative and coordinating body to foster cooperation among Estonia, Lithuania, and Latvia. The Baltic Assembly consisting, of twenty representatives from the parliaments of each country, was launched on November 8, 1991, in Tallinn, the Estonian capital. It enables representatives of the three Baltic republics to consult with one another on matters of mutual interest. The assembly, which is financed by all three countries, meets twice a year and its site rotates. Each delegate participates in one of the six committees dealing with legal issues, social and economic affairs, the environment and energy, communications, education, science and culture, and security and foreign affairs. The Presidium of the assembly, consisting of two members from each delegation, assisted by a secretariat, which is located in Riga, Latvia, coordinates the assembly's work between sessions and carries out preparatory work for the two annual sessions. The work of each national delegation is organized by a national secretariat. The assembly's president rotates every six months and is chosen by the appropriate national delegation, depending on the rotation.

The first two sessions in 1992 were principally concerned with the removal of Russian troops from the newly independent countries. In 1994 the fourth and fifth sessions dealt with the establishment of the Baltic Council of Ministers, which together with the Baltic Assembly forms the Baltic Council.

The Baltic Assembly and Council have entered into formal relations with similar organizations. In 1992 a formal agreement of cooperation was signed with the Nordic Council. The two councils held a joint meeting in April 1996 in Vilnius, Lithuania. In November 1994 the assembly signed an agreement with the Benelux Interparliamentary Consultative Council.

The assembly and council have helped moderate disputes among the three Baltic republics. In 1995 and early 1996 there were clashes between Latvian fishing boats and Estonian border guards in disputed waters in the Gulf of Riga. A border agreement, however, was drawn up and ratified by the countries' two parliaments in August 1996. There was an additional agreement on fishing rights in early 1997.

Another contention, which has been more difficult to resolve, has concerned the sea border between Latvia and Lithuania. The settlement of this dispute was complicated by an October 1996 agreement between Latvia and two petroleum countries to exploit oil in the area under dispute. But Latvia insisted that the agreement was merely preliminary to a final settlement.

BIBLIOGRAPHY
"Latvia." *Europe World Year Book.* London: Europa Publications, 1997, p. 1986.

Bernard Cook

Banville, John (1945–)

Irish novelist and dramatist. John Banville, born in Wexford in 1945, was one of the major and most acclaimed Irish novelists to appear in the 1970s. He was subeditor of the Irish Press to 1984, and became literary editor of *Irish Times* in 1988.

His first novel, *Long Lankin* (1970), related folk themes to Irish life. *Nightspawn* (1971) found the narrator alone on an island and won wide acclaim for its use of language. Banville's next novel, *Birchwood* (1973), is a Gothic novel set in nineteenth-century Ireland taking the form of a first-person narrative. This was followed by *Doctor Copernicus* (1976), a psychological historical novel about the Polish astronomer priest. Then followed *Kepler* (1981) and *The Newton Letter* (1982), which was adapted to film as *Reflections* (1984). *Mefisto* (1986) is also in the Gothic genre. The *Book of Evidence* (1989) was shortlisted for the 1989 Booker Prize.

BIBLIOGRAPHY
Imhof, Rudiger. *John Banville—A Critical Introduction.* Dublin: Wolfhound Press, 1989.
McMinn, J. *John Banville: A Critical Study.* Dublin: Gill and Macmillan, 1990.

Michael J. Kennedy

Barańczak, Stanisław (1946–)

Polish poet, translator, critic, and historian of literature. Stanisław Barańczak is one of the leading personalities in Polish literature after 1968. In his works he observed the principle that language should be consistent with the reality it depicts, and he promoted an antiauthoritarian ethics of independent thinking.

Barańczak had unquestionable influence on Polish poetry between 1968 and 1989, both in axiological and in aesthetic categories. He belongs to those early intellectuals who, having gotten over the fear of punishment, protested openly against the system and signed "The Letter of 59" (List 59) or went on hunger strike in St. Martin's Church. He is an artist for whom honesty in writing equals honesty in life.

He received a Ph.D. in Polish literature at Poznan University in 1976. As a result of his opposition activity, however, he was not only dismissed from his academic post but was forbidden to publish as well. Not discouraged, Barańczak involved himself in founding the Committee for the Defense of Workers and the organization of underground press system and its organs *Zapis* and *Krytyka.* Then in 1983 he co-edited *Zeszyty Literackie* in Paris, in which many central European writers were published.

Barańczak has lived in the United States since 1981 and lectures at the Slavonic Studies Department of Harvard University. Barańczak was editor in chief of the *Polish Review* in New York from 1987 to 1990.

Barańczak has published over seventy works, including collections of poems, critical essays, anthologies, and translations of English, Russian, and other poets. His *Korekta twarzy* (*The Face Correction,* 1968) showed his great originality and won the poet the prestigious Tadeusz Peiper award. Both as a poet with his *Jednym tchem* (*In One Gasp,* 1970) and *Sztuczne oddychanie* (*Rescue Breathing,* 1974) and as a critic with *Nieufni i zadufani* (*Distrustful and Pompous,* 1971), Barańczak determined the moral and aesthetic attitudes of the "Generation 1968" poets, called in Poland the New Wave. He compared distrust in language and the word games of poets-linguists to the function of language in the socialist system, in which poetry had to be a "denouncer of lies in the language of ideology and propaganda" and had to reveal the dehumanization of man's existence under the Communist system. His protest against totalitarianism stemmed from his respect for subjectivity and the integrity of the individual and existence in general. Barańczak's poetry has never been purely political but possesses a metaphysical content that let him create an axiological space for discrediting the political system. His poetry of complex reflection and mood combines rationalistic passion, lyricism, and a sense of humor. Deep reflection and sublime existential and metaphysical problems take the form of sophisticated metaphors and rich-sounding poetic techniques.

In the 1970s Barańczak's essays and criticism (*Zmieniony glos Settembriniego* [The Changed Voice of Settenbrini]) launched a discussion of the status of writers and literature under a totalitarian system. According to Barańczak, poetry should meet the high moral requirements of testifying to the truth through a veracious and trustful language that, in itself, is able to rescue humanity, culture, and the world. Only if it is true can poetry reveal transcendental references and axiological categories, said Barańczak in *Etyka i poetyka* (*Ethics and Poetics,* 1979) and *Tablica z Macondo* (*The Board of Macondo,* 1990). His scoffing and derisive literary essays sought to bring discredit on the trumpery of the so-called court literature of the Polish People's Republic (*Książki najgorsze* [*The Worst Books,* 1981]), and to show the effects of cultural policy of the party and censorship in *Czytelnik ubezwlasnowolniony* (*The Incapacitated Reader,* 1983).

Barańczak also wrote remarkable works devoted to modern poets and his masters, Miron Białoszewski and Zbigniew Herbert, the artists who present two entirely different patterns of resistance to the political system through the mastery of poetical art.

BIBLIOGRAPHY
Barańczak, Stanisław. *The Weight of the Body: Selected Poems.* Evanston, Ill: TriQuarterly Books Northwestern University, 1989.
———. *Breathing under Water and Other East European Essays.* Cambridge, Mass: Harvard University Press, 1990.

Zofia Mocarska-Tyc

SEE ALSO Poland

Barbie, Klaus (1913–91)

Nazi German war criminal. Klaus Barbie was born in Bad Godesberg, Germany, on October 25, 1913, the son of an office worker who had become a teacher. In 1935 he joined the notorious SS Schutzstaffel. In 1942 he was made head of the Gestapo (Nazi secret police) in Lyon, France, during World War II. Thousands of people were killed or deported under his orders. He personally tortured prisoners and commanded the operation that netted French Resistance leader Jean Moulin. He denied that he himself killed or personally ordered the execution of Moulin. He was also responsible for the deportation of forty-four Jewish children and their teachers from the French village of Izieu to the death camp at Auschwitz, Poland. His crimes earned for him the notorious appellation Butcher of Lyon.

After the war Barbie was recruited by U.S. army counterintelligence (CIC) to provide information on Communists in East Germany, Eastern Europe, and France. He was paid $1,700 a month for his weekly reports. The United States protected him against the French and enabled him to escape with his family to Bolivia in 1951. He lived in Bolivia and Peru under the name Klaus Altmann. Nazi hunter Beate Klarsfeld discovered him in 1972, but the Bolivian government did not agree to his extradition to France until 1983. He had been twice sentenced in absentia to death but was tried again in Lyon for crimes against humanity. The unrepentant Barbie was found guilty and sentenced to life imprisonment in 1987. He died on September 25, 1991.

BIBLIOGRAPHY
Saxon, Wolfgang. "Klaus Barbie, 77, Lyons Gestapo Chief," *New York Times,* September 26, 1991, D22.

Bernard Cook

SEE ALSO Klarsfeld, Beate

Barbu, Eugen (1924–93)

Romanian anti-Semitic writer and nationalist politician. Eugen Barbu enjoyed official approval during the national Stalinist dictatorship of Nicolae Ceauşescu, articulating nationalist themes and harassing liberal intellectuals. His influence, which had waned, revived following Ceauşescu's overthrow in 1989 as the late dictator's successors attempted to use nativist themes to manage change with their own minimalist agenda, and to prevent any large-scale challenge to a Communist elite modifying itself to benefit from post-Communist times. Along with his protégé, Corneliu Vadim Tudor, Barbu launched the successful *România mâre* (*Greater Romania*) newspaper in June 1990 and a political party of the same name in 1991. He was elected to parliament in 1992 and, until his death, did not hesitate to defend pro-Communist and anti-Semitic views.

Tom Gallagher

SEE ALSO Romania

Barre Plan

Set of economic measures advanced in 1976 by French Prime Minister Raymond Barre with the unfulfilled goal of revitalizing the national economy in response to the recession of the late 1970s.

President Valéry Giscard d'Estaing gave Barre full responsibility to initiate a new economic policy that would stifle inflation, stimulate foreign trade, and solidify France's position in the "leading group of middle-sized countries in the world." In September 1976, Barre promulgated his plan, based on neoliberal economic principles. Its provisions included a temporary freeze on prices, reduction of the value-added tax (VAT), incentives to encourage investments, and restraints on wages and salaries. Organized labor protested against these measures in a series of one-day strikes. The electorate, in reaction to the continuing economic difficulties facing France, shifted leftward in the 1977 municipal elections. In response Barre revised his economic policy, in what is often termed the Second Barre Plan (1977), so as to stimulate employment, increase family allowances, and raise pensions. The

electorate, however, repudiated the administration's policies in the legislative elections of 1978 and the presidential elections of 1981.

In retrospect it is clear that the Barre Plan did not achieve its desired results. Yet France did experience less dislocation than Great Britain and Italy in the wake of the oil crisis of 1973 and the resulting global recession. In an ever more tightly integrated international economy, the Barre Plan enhanced French industrial competitiveness but simultaneously revealed the limitations of national policy in the global economy.

BIBLIOGRAPHY
Balassa, Bela. "The French Economy under the Fifth Republic, 1958–1978," in William Andrews and Stanley Hoffmann, eds., *The Impact of the Fifth Republic on France.* Albany: SUNY Press, 1981, 117–38.
Frears, J. R. *France in the Giscard Presidency.* London: George Allen & Unwin, 1981.
Mouriaux, René. "Trade Unions, Unemployment, and Regulation: 1962–1989," in James Hollifield and George Ross, eds., *Searching for the New France.* New York: Routledge, 1991, 173–92.

Francis J. Murphy

SEE ALSO Barre, Raymond; France; Giscard d'Estaing, Valéry

Barre, Raymond (1924–)

Economist, politician, prime minister of France, and mayor of Lyon. Raymond Barre was born on April 2, 1924, on the French island La Réunion in the Indian Ocean, where he grew up in a bourgeois Catholic family and received his early education.

In 1946 Barre came to study in Paris, where he was awarded degrees in law and economics at the Institut d'Études Politiques. His subsequent professional life can be divided into three distinct periods. During the years 1950–59 Barre established himself as one of the leading academic economists in France. He taught first at the University of Caen and subsequently on the most prestigious faculties in Paris. During this period he wrote his acclaimed textbook, *Économie politique* (1955). Barre relished the academic life but soon was drawn into government service.

The second period (1959–81) of Barre's career began with his appointment to the staff of Jean-Marcel Jeanneney, minister of industry in the new Gaullist administration. After a brief return to academic life, he assumed a series of progressively more important government po-

Barth, Karl   81

sitions, including appointments as French representative for economic affairs at the European Economic Commission in Brussels (1967–72) and as minister for foreign trade and commerce (1976). Eight months later, because of his expertise in economics, his grasp of European affairs, and his personal integrity, Barre was appointed prime minister (1976–81) by President Valéry Giscard d'Estaing. In that capacity, he attempted to revitalize the French economy in the wake of the recession following the 1973 oil crisis. His economic austerity program, called the Barre Plan, failed to raise the standard of living and to reduce unemployment. The inability of the Giscard government to solve the economic problems facing France in the years of Barre's premiership is generally considered to have been a major factor in the triumph of François Mitterrand and the Socialist Party in the 1981 presidential elections.

In the third stage of his career, after 1981, Barre occupied a prominent, varied place in French national life as an academic, economic consultant, author, and deputy. With the passage of time and the continuing economic problems of France in the 1980s, Barre's appeal grew and led to his unsuccessful campaign for the presidency in 1988. Nonetheless, he remained a widely respected figure in French national politics and has four times been elected to the National Assembly for the Lyon district. In the municipal elections of June 1995, Barre was elected mayor of Lyon, the second-largest city in France.

Throughout his career Barre has remained an independent figure, eschewing party affiliation. Because of his intellectual and personal qualities, even his opponents recognize him as a person of principle. He once described himself politically as having "the head of a Gaullist and the heart of a Christian Democrat." His political philosophy draws on his Catholic social background, his neo-liberal economic principles, and his commitment to European union. He continues to be one of the most highly regarded figures in French national life.

BIBLIOGRAPHY
Amouroux, Henri. *Monsieur Barre.* Paris: Robert Laffont, 1986.
Barre, Raymond. *Un Politique pour l'avenir.* Paris: Plon, 1981.
———. *Questions de confiance.* Paris: Flammarion, 1988.
Rizzuto, Franco. "Anti-Political Politics: The Barre Phenomenon." *Government and Opposition* 22 (1987): 145–62.

Francis J. Murphy

SEE ALSO Barre Plan; Giscard d'Estaing, Valéry; Mitterrand, François

Barry, Peter (1928–)

Irish politician. Peter Barry, chairman of Cork-based Barry's Tea, was elected as Fine Gael deputy for Cork South Central in 1969. Barry served as deputy leader of Fine Gael from 1979 to 1990. He was minister for transport and power, 1973–76; education, 1973–77; environment, 1981–82; and foreign affairs, 1982–87. In the ministry of foreign affairs his main achievement was the 1985 Anglo-Irish Agreement concerning Northern Ireland.

Michael J. Kennedy

Barschel, Uwe (1944–87)

Minister-president of Schleswig-Holstein from 1982 to 1987. Barschel's quick rise into the ranks of West Germany's political elite paralleled his devotion to athletic training, especially boxing, and academic studies. Born in Gleinicke bei Berlin in 1944, Uwe Barschel studied law, economics, and political science at Kiel. From 1969 to 1970 he taught at the Pädagogische Hochschule in Kiel. In the early 1970s Barschel practiced law and entered politics. Elected to the state parliament in 1971, he chaired the Christian Democratic parliamentary group from May 1973 until January 1979. Barschel served Schleswig-Holstein as minister of finance and subsequently as minister of the interior. In 1982 he succeeded Gerhard Stoltenberg as Schleswig-Holstein's minister-president. Implicated in a preelection scandal in 1987 known as "Waterkantgate," Barschel resigned on September 25. On October 11, 1987, he was found dead in a Geneva hotel.

BIBLIOGRAPHY
Barschel, Uwe. *Die Staatsqualität der deutschen Länder.* Heidelberg: R. V. Decker, 1982.
———. *Der Kieler Untersuchungsausschuss.* Kiel: Verlag Schmidt & Klaunig, 1988.
Barschel, Uwe, et al. *Was wir wunschen: junge Bundesbürger über die Zukunft ihres Staates.* Cologne: Verlag Wissenschaft und Politik, 1974.
Kalinka, Werner. *Opfer Barschel.* Berlin: Ullstein, 1993.

David A. Meier

Barth, Karl (1886–1968)

Swiss theologian and central figure in the development of neo-orthodox theology. Born in Basel, the son of a Reformed pastor, Karl Barth pursued theological studies in Berne, Berlin, Tübingen, and Marburg; his teachers included Adolph von Harnack, Adolph Schlatter, and preeminently Wilhelm Herrmann. He deeply imbibed the thought of Friedrich Schleiermacher (1768–1834), the fountainhead of nineteenth-century liberal theology. Ordained in 1908, he was pastor in the village of Safenwil in the Aargau from 1911 to 1921, a decisive formative period during which he initially embraced the Christian Socialism of Leonhard Ragaz, Hermann Kutter, and Christoph Blumhardt.

Barth became disillusioned when in 1914 ninety-three German intellectuals, among them some of his revered theological teachers, issued a manifesto aligning themselves with the war policy of Kaiser Wilhelm II and Chancellor Bethmann-Hollweg. Barth diagnosed this ethical shortcoming as stemming from a radical theological failure, and found his own convictions profoundly shaken. He moved away from both Christian Socialism and theological liberalism, convinced that each in its way made the Gospel message prey to projects of human self-improvement and political causes. The new direction in Barth's thinking found its initial public expression in the 1919 first edition of his commentary on St. Paul's Epistle to the Romans (*Römerbrief*). This work signaled a sudden departure from the dominant trends of liberal theology: in place of a familiar God who valorized noble human enterprises, Barth presented a God who is *totaliter aliter,* wholly other, whose kingdom stands in contradistinction from any and all human attempts at religiosity.

Though he rejected theological liberalism, Barth could not simply return to the confessional, biblicist, baroque Protestant orthodoxy of the seventeenth and eighteenth centuries. Yet in important respects Barth's work represented a reassertion of classical doctrines of orthodoxy. For this reason, his theology has been termed "neo-orthodox." Its denial of an anthropological "point of contact" with God, and its emphasis on the dialectical character of the encounter between God and humanity, have also earned it the sobriquet "dialectical theology." Barth's thought developed and changed over the years, finding its fullest expression in his massive *Church Dogmatics,* published in several volumes between 1932 and 1967.

From the vantage point of a professorship in Bonn, Barth witnessed the rise of National Socialism in Germany. His refusal to give the Hitler salute and numerous dissenting remarks led to his dismissal from Bonn in 1935, whereupon he received an appointment at the University of Basel. Barth continued to follow events in Germany, supporting the efforts of the Confessing Church and criticizing as heretics the "German Christians" who cooperated with the Nazi regime. He was the main author of the 1934 Barmen Declaration, which became the theological manifesto of the Confessing Church. With the outbreak of World War II, Barth, despite Swiss neutrality, supported a policy of resistance; he was a friend of martyred theologian Dietrich Bonhoeffer.

After the war Barth's fame and following increased. He lectured and traveled widely, maintaining a remarkable level of productivity until his death in Basel in 1968.

Thomas A. Smith

Barthes, Roland (Gérard) (1915–80)

Writer, journalist, lecturer at the École Pratique des Hautes Études, and member of the Collège de France. Roland Barthes was one of the foremost intellectuals and literary theorists in Europe after World War II. His influence extended primarily to the fields of semiology, literary criticism, anthropology, and art criticism but also to history, sociology, and philosophy.

In his various works, Barthes explored language and writing (*Writing Degree Zero,* 1953; *Elements of Semiology,* 1964; *The Pleasure of the Text,* 1973), culture (*Mythologies,* 1957; *The Fashion System,* 1967; *The Empire of Signs,* 1970), and art (*Camera Lucida,* 1980), among other subjects.

The intellectual influences on Barthes included Ferdinand de Saussure, Bertolt Brecht, André Gide, Algirdas Greimas, Louis Hjelmslev, Roman Jakobson, and Maurice Nadeau. Barthes's work is considered to be representative of poststructuralism. He taught literary and film theorists such as Julia Kristeva and Christian Metz.

His writing is at once playful, systematic, ironic, and creative, and readers have found his ideas complex and his style, especially his neologisms, difficult. Intellectually adventurous, Barthes challenged himself and his readers to discover structures and patterns in discourse, and he sought to subvert both commonplace and academic understandings of literature and speech. A self-declared Marxist, Barthes eschewed politics, though Marxist politics influenced essays such as those collected in *Mythologies,* and in some of his earlier articles and commentaries.

BIBLIOGRAPHY

Barthes, Roland. *Roland Barthes by Roland Barthes.* Tr. by Richard Howard. London: Macmillan, 1977.

Calvet, Louis-Jean. *Roland Barthes: A Biography.* Tr. by Sarah Wykes. Bloomington: Indiana University Press, 1994.

Freedman, Sanford, and Carole Anne Taylor. *Roland Barthes: A Bibliographical Reader's Guide.* New York: Garland, 1983.

Kristeva, Julia. *Desire in Language: A Semiotic Approach to Literature and Art.* Tr. by Thomas Gora, Alice Jardine, and Leon S. Roudiez. New York: Columbia University Press, 1980.

Lavers, Annette. *Roland Barthes: Structuralism and After.* Cambridge, Mass.: Harvard University Press, 1982.

Eric Gorham

Basayev, Shamil (1965–)

Commander of the military of the breakaway Russian province of Chechnya. Shamil Basayev was born in Vedeno, Chechnya, in 1965. He studied at the Institute of Land-Tenure Regulations Engineers in Moscow and participated in the defense of the "White House" (parliament building) in Moscow during the attempted coup of August 1991. He then returned to Chechnya and joined the Confederation of the People of the Caucasus (KHK). As a KHK commander he fought on behalf of the Abkhazians in 1992 during their war with Georgia. For several months in 1994 he trained under the mujahideen in Afghanistan. He returned to Chechnya and fought on behalf of Dzhokhar Dudayev against Russian-inspired efforts to topple his regime. He was a Chechen officer during the struggle against the Russian invasion. In June 1995 he led a Chechen raid against Budyonnovsk, deep in Russian territory. In April 1996 he became commander of the Chechen military but stepped down in December to campaign for the presidency. In the January 27, 1997, election he received 23.7 percent of the vote and was second to the victor, Aslan Maskhadov.

Basayev opposed Maskhadóv's moderation as president, and he resigned after six months as Chechen prime minister in 1998. He then formed the Congress of the Peoples of Chechnya and Dagestan to struggle for their union. On August 7, 1999, he led a Chechen incursion into Dagestan, joined in this venture by a fundamentalist from Jordan known as Khattab. Although Khattab is a proponent of fundamentalist Wahhabism, which opposes the presence of "infidels" in an Islamic country, Basayev has spoken against enforcing fundamentalism in Chechnya.

BIBLIOGRAPHY

"Chechen Says He Leads Revolt in Nearby Area," *Reuters,* August 12, 1999.

Gall, Carlotta. "Dagestan Skirmish Is Big Russian Risk," *New York Times,* August 13, 1999.

Bernard Cook

SEE ALSO Chechnya

Basque Country (Euskadi)

Name coined by Sabino de Arana (1865–1903), founder of the Basque Nationalist Party, to define the seven Basque provinces: in Spain there are Alva (*Araba*), Vizcaya (*Bizkaia*), Guipúzcoa (*Gipuzkoa*), which form the Autonomous Community of Euskadi; and Navarre (*Nafarroa*), which forms a separate autonomous community (*Comunidad Foral de Navarra*); the remaining three provinces are in France: Labourd (*Lapurdi*), Soule (*Zuberoa*), and Basse Navarre (*Baxanabarral Benaparre,* or Low Navarre). Basque nationalists call the former area Euskadi Sur (*Hegoaldea*) and the latter Euskadi Norte (*Iparralde*). Euskadi Sur includes 85 percent of the Basque land mass, more than half of which lies in Navarre. The more traditional term *Euskal-Herria* is also used to refer to the lands where Basque is spoken. More recently, the term *Euskal-Herria* has also been used by radical nationalists to identify all the seven provinces to distinguish them from the Autonomous Community of Euskadi. The population of the Basque Country in the 1986 census was 2,176,790.

Daniele Conversi

Basque Language (Euskara)

Language spoken in the Basque provinces of Spain and France. Since Basque was fragmented into at least seven dialects, a considerable effort was made to unify its orthography, syntax, and lexicon during the twentieth century. The majority of Basques are today monolingual Spanish-speakers and the language is spoken only in an area of approximately 3,900 square miles (10,000 sq km). The first book printed in Basque dates back to 1545, but

Shamil Basayev, leader of the Chechen rebels.
Illustration courtesy of Bernard Cook.

only recently has the language begun to produce a more robust literary tradition. A standard version (*batua*) was proposed by the Basque Language Academy and accepted by all mainstream cultural institutions in 1983. After being banned in Spain under Franco, in 1980 Basque, or Euskara, became, with Spanish, a co-official language of the Autonomous Communities of Euskadi and Navarre. Laws of linguistic normalization were passed in these regions in the early 1980s to regulate public use of Basque. The origins of Euskara are still an enigma and it is probably the most ancient language in Europe, the remnant of a pre–Indo-European aboriginal stratum spoken in Southwestern Europe before Romanization.

Daniele Conversi

Basque Nationalism

Nationalist movement founded by Sabino de Arana y Goiri (1865–1903) in the late 1880s as a reaction to the increased centralization of Spain. Arana saw race and religion as the pillars of Basque identity, although the Basque language was also important. Following the Spanish Civil War (1936–39), in which Basque nationalists sided with the Spanish Republic against Francisco Franco, a strong repression ensued. In 1959 a group of youth disaffected with the inactivity and moderation of mainstream nationalists (Basque Nationalist Party, PNV), founded Euskadi 'Ta Askatasuna (ETA, Basque Country and Freedom). The latter's increasingly violent actions gave a militant cast to the entire nationalist movement, but nonviolent and cultural activities also boomed. In 1963 the first *ikastolas* (Basque schools) were set up, inaugurating a highly efficient network where the entire curriculum was taught in Basque.

The Autonomous Community of Euskadi with its capital at Vitoria/Gasteiz was established by the Spanish government in 1979. This was made up of three provinces, Alava, Vizcaya, and Guipúzcoa. Navarre, which the nationalists consider to be an integral part of Euskadi, became a separate community. Terrorism slowly waned, as popular political participation increased, while the new Basque government increased its powers through negotiations with Madrid.

BIBLIOGRAPHY

Conversi, Daniele. *The Basques, the Catalans and Spain: Alternative Routes to Nationalist Mobilization.* London: C. Hurst, 1996.

Daniele Conversi

Basque Nationalism: Euskadi 'Ta Askatasuna (Basque Country and Freedom, ETA)

Underground political organization formally founded in 1959 by young Basque nationalists, in opposition to the moderate Basque Nationalist Party (PNV). ETA was influenced by Franz Fanon's (1925–61) theory of violence as a regenerating force against colonialism and by the experience of Third World liberation movements, especially the Algerian revolution (1959–63). In the earliest stage ETA activity consisted of low-key operations, such as wall daubings and occasional robberies. In 1968 they escalated by perpetrating the first political murder against police commissioner Melitón Manzanas. After this a spiral of violence ensued with attacks by ETA and counterattacks by state security forces. The peak of terrorist activity was reached after the end of the Franco dictatorship in 1977–78, when hundreds of people were killed yearly in ETA-related violence. The advent of democracy provided the first condition for a possible political normalization. In 1976 a leading sector of ETA left the armed struggle, joining the Communist and other pro-democracy activists to form the electoral alliance *Euskadiko Ezkerra* (Basque Left), which became an important national party. However, violence increased until an autonomy statute was granted to the Autonomous Community of Euskadi in 1979.

Each transfer of power to the Basque government from Madrid detracted legitimacy from the partisans of armed struggle, but violence had a self-perpetuating quality that made it extremely difficult for it to subside. ETA continued to pursue its violent strategy aimed at total independence from Spain. Popular support for ETA remained relatively high until the late 1980s, as its political front, the coalition Herri Batasuna (Popular Unity), gained around 15 percent of the vote at each election.

ETA was tormented by internecine ideological conflict: Maoists, Trotskyists, and other trends within ETA ended up forming their own cells and splinter organizations. After a Marxist phase, the control of the prestigious "trademark" ETA returned to the hands of committed nationalists. Perhaps the most important split occurred in 1974 between the radical ETA-m (military) and the more moderate ETA-pm (political military). Once the Spanish constitution (1978) and a statute of autonomy for the Basque Country (1979) had been approved, the latter slowly abandoned armed struggle.

Daniele Conversi

Bassanini, Franco (1940–)

Italian politician. Franco Bassanini was born in Milan on May 9, 1940. He is a professor of constitutional law at the University of Rome. From 1973 to 1975 he worked at the Ministry of Regional Affairs and served on the Giannini Commission studying the transfer of power to the regions of Italy. In the 1980s he headed the interministerial commission considering a change in the relationship between the central government of Italy and its regions.

He had joined the Socialist Party but resigned in 1981, remaining a political independent until the formation of the Party of the Democratic Left (PDS). With the establishment of the PDS, Bassani became a member of its secretariat.

Elected to parliament in 1979, Bassanini was named to the bicameral commission for institutional reform and the constitutional affairs commission. In 1993 he drafted legislation to reform the Italian government. In 1996, a candidate of the Olive Tree alliance, he was elected to the Senate from the province of Sienna and was appointed minister of regional affairs in the government of Romano Prodi.

Bernard Cook

Baudouin (1930–93)

King of the Belgians from 1951 to 1993. He restored confidence and stability to the Belgian monarchy after the stormy reign of Leopold III.

Baudouin was the eldest son of Leopold III and Astrid of Sweden. He was born on September 7, 1930, at Château de Stuyvenberg, near Brussels. His mother was killed in a car accident when he was four, the first of many tragic events that were to affect his life. His private education was interrupted by the German invasion of 1940. Baudouin was deeply distressed by the bitter feelings many Belgians felt toward his father for surrendering to the Germans without a fight and for remarrying a commoner whose family was accused of sympathizing with the Nazis. During World War II Baudouin shared his father's internment by the Germans and his postwar exile in Switzerland. Baudouin continued his education while Leopold, who was exiled for his alleged pro-Nazi sympathies during the war, remained abroad. The king's brother, Charles, acted as regent while the politicians argued the future of the monarchy. In March 1950, a referendum ended the king's exile and he returned to Brussels on July 22, 1950. The country, however, was torn by civil unrest. Leopold had to agree to transfer his royal powers to Baudouin and to the latter's accession on his twenty-first birthday. By special parliamentary action, Baudouin became prince royal and lieutenant general of the kingdom on August 11, 1950, with the constitutional powers of king. On July 16, 1951, Leopold abdicated, and Baudouin formally acceded to the throne the next day when he took the oath to uphold the constitution.

Like his grandfather, Albert I, Baudouin, despite his introspective character and initial timidity, restored respectability to the monarchy. He was a stabilizing influence in the bitter infighting between the Flemish-speaking north and the French-speaking Walloon south. The king played a significant role in smoothing the transition to a federal state. In April 1990, he sparked a controversy when he refused, because of his Roman Catholic principles, to sign an act legalizing abortion. At Baudouin's request the monarchy was temporarily suspended and Belgium had no king for forty-four hours, until he was reinstated by parliamentary vote.

The king married a Spanish noblewoman, Fabiola de Mora y Aragon, on December 15, 1960, but they had no children. Baudouin died suddenly on July 30, 1993, while on vacation in Motril, Spain. He was succeeded by his brother, Albert, prince of Liège.

BIBLIOGRAPHY
Aronson, Theo. *Defiant Dynasty: The Coburgs of Belgium.* Indianapolis: Bobbs-Merrill, 1968.

Martin J. Manning

SEE ALSO Leopold III

Baudrillard, Jean (1929–)

French sociologist and critic. Jean Baudrillard, one of the leaders of French postmodernism, is noted for his controversial work in sociology and political philosophy. Among his major publications are *Simulation and Simulacra, For the Critique of Political Economy of the Sign,* and *Seduction.* Baudrillard is principally concerned with social images, especially those that shape behavior or show manipulation of power. He has concentrated on erotic images as found in movies, advertisements, and novels. He contends that such images are simulacrums produced by capitalism for commercial purposes to displace erotic desires with phantom longings. These creations are manipulated by economic forces so that consumers are willing to spend money and energy on trying to attain satisfaction of desires that can never be satisfied. His principal influence has been on media studies and contemporary literary theory.

BIBLIOGRAPHY
Gane, Mike. *Baudrillard: Critical and Fatal Theory.* New York: Routlege, 1991.

Kellner, Douglas. *Jean Baudrillard: From Postmodernism and Beyond.* Stanford, Calif.: Stanford University Press, 1989.

Nordquist, Jean. *Jean Baudrillard: A Bibliography.* Santa Cruz, Calif.: Reference and Research Services, 1991.

Pefanis, Julian. *Heterology and the Postmodern: Bataille, Baudrillard, and Lyotard.* Durham, N.C.: Duke University Press, 1991.

Stearns, William, ed. *Jean Baudrillard: The Disappearance of Art and Politics.* New York: St. Martin's Press, 1992.

Daniel E. Shannon

Beatrix (1938–)

Queen of the Netherlands, crowned in 1980. Beatrix of Orange-Nassau has received much praise for her performance as sovereign, despite initial public suspicion of her and a disruptive coronation.

Born to Crown Princess Juliana and Bernhard zu Lippe-Biesterfeld in 1938, Beatrix was the oldest of four girls. She studied at Leyden University, receiving a law degree in 1961. In 1965 Beatrix became engaged to West German diplomat Claus-Georg von Amsberg, a choice that elicited much public hostility. Amsberg's past in the Hitler Youth and the Wehrmacht provoked violent protests in the streets of Amsterdam when the couple married there in 1966. The birth of their first son in 1967, Willem-Alexander, did much to restore enthusiasm for the royal house, and Claus soon found acceptance.

In 1980 Juliana abdicated the throne to her daughter. Beatrix's coronation, held in Amsterdam, precipitated serious riots, led by squatters angry at the housing shortage. Beatrix's somewhat austere personality, differing markedly from her mother, Juliana, did not at first endear her to her subjects, but she gained a favorable reputation as "the smiling Queen" and as a "professional" monarch who performed her duties well.

BIBLIOGRAPHY

Hoffman, Betty. *Born to Be Queen.* Oranjestad, Netherlands: Lago, 1955.

Lammers, Fred J. *12 1/2 jaar majesteit.* Kampen, Netherlands: La Rivière & Voorhoeve, 1992.

J. C. Kennedy

Beckett, Samuel Barclay (1906–89)

Irish playwright and novelist who wrote both in French and in English and changed the course of twentieth-century theater. Samuel Beckett challenged not only the forms of modern literature but the tenants of twentieth-

century philosophy. His work strips human experience to its barest common denominators not to denigrate humans but to understand what it is about experience, or people's response to it, that makes them human.

Born of middle-class, Protestant parents in a suburb of Dublin, Beckett experienced a comfortable childhood, attending an Anglo-Irish boarding school as a teenager, and Trinity College, where he took a degree in comparative literature with highest honors in 1927. When he began teaching in Paris he met James Joyce, a significant influence on his writing. An unhappy year of teaching at Trinity College (1930–31) led him to abandon academe forever, despite his success in the classroom.

A trip to Germany in 1936–37 opened his eyes to the real threat of Nazism. His response: "I say that expressions 'historical necessity' and 'Germanic destiny' start the vomit moving upwards." Throughout his tours of Germany, he was also trying to publish his novel, *Murphy,* with little success. The complaints from publishers in Paris, England, and the United States were that the book was too obscure, to which Beckett replied: "take every 500th word, punctuate carefully and publish a poem in prose in the *Paris Daily Mail.*"

The Second World War focused Beckett's activities on the French Resistance. He could have left the country but preferred to stay and translate documents for a small Parisian Resistance group, Gloria. When the group was betrayed, he and his companion, Suzanne Deschevaux-Dumesni, escaped from Paris and farmed in the countryside until the Liberation.

On returning to Paris, Beckett moved beyond Joyce's literary influence, which had heretofore caused several publishers to reject him. He began to work feverishly in his own vein, and that new approach was signaled by his writing directly in French. His novel trilogy in French, *Molloy, Malone meurt,* and *L'Innommable,* was written between 1947 and 1950. These novels and *En attendant Godot* (*Waiting for Godot*) all reveal the impact of the war on Beckett's style and on his sense of himself as a writer. He brought to all his postwar work what he called "the cold eye," a technique that combined memory with a sense of waiting, a sense of silence and quietism in the face of adversity.

Waiting for Godot, perhaps the most famous twentieth-century theater experience, was followed by *Endgame* and *Krapp's Last Tape.* In the latter, Krapp, an old man, listens to tapes of himself as a young man, and the actual experiences of the young man are so transformed by time that only the feelings of loss or nostalgia remain. All the plays of this period marked Beckett as one of the leading writers of the theatre of the absurd, but Beckett was not chronicling what was ridiculous in human existence; rather, he was trying to understand what it meant to be truly human.

In 1961 he secretly married Suzanne, who had been his companion for more than twenty years, to secure the rights to his works for her, but he did not change his lifestyle. He continued to have liaisons with other women, continued to travel to direct his plays in England, Germany, Italy, and Eastern Europe, and essentially lived a monkish existence in the country outside Paris while writing.

His political involvement also continued. He refused to allow his plays to be produced in South Africa in segregated theaters; he continued to support dissidents in Eastern Europe, and he supported student protestors in France. While he always remained politically engaged, his work moved toward disengagement to find a point from which to study humanity. In 1969, he won the Nobel Prize in literature for "a body of work that transmuted the destitution of modern man into his exaltation."

His last work, *Quoi où* (*What Where*), is Beckett's epitaph: "Time passes. / That is all. / Make sense who may. / I switch off." He died on December 22, 1989, leaving a legacy that still challenges conceptions of humanity in the postmodern world.

BIBLIOGRAPHY
Bair, Deidre. *Samuel Beckett: A Biography.* New York: Harcourt Brace Jovanovich, 1978.
Cronin, Anthony. *Samuel Beckett: The Last Modernist.* New York: HarperCollins, 1997.
Knowlson, James. *Damned to Fame: The Life of Samuel Beckett.* New York: Simon & Schuster, 1996.
Mary A. McCay

Behan, Brendan (1923–64)

Irish dramatist and novelist. Brendan Behan was born into a Dublin republican-nationalist background. It was to be his major influence and provide the themes for his work. Behan is best known for his autobiographical novel, *Borstal Boy* (1958), based on his experiences in a juvenile reformatory to which he was sent from 1939 to 1941 for his Irish Republican Army activities in Britain. His play *The Quare Fellow* (1954), based on his imprisonment in Ireland from 1941 to 1945, is well known, as is *The Hostage* (1959). By the late 1940s Behan had established himself as a successful writer and as a Dublin "character." His nonfiction includes *Brendan Behan's Island* (1962) and the posthumous *Brendan Behan's New York* (1964). Behan wrote short plays for radio, such as *Moving Out* and

A Garden Party, and short stories that were serialized in the daily press. Among the best known are *The Confirmation Suit* and *After the Wake.* In the late 1940s he wrote verse in Irish of uneven quality, and by the early 1950s Behan gave up writing Irish poetry.

Behan will be popularly remembered as boisterous, drunk, and scandalous. However, his drama and latterly his prose works will ensure that his literary reputation lives on.

BIBLIOGRAPHY
Behan, Brendan. *The Complete Plays of Brendan Behan.* London: Methuen, 1978.
———. *Interviews and Recollections.* Ed. by E. H. Mikhail. London: Macmillan, 1992.
Michael J. Kennedy

Bekesi, László (1942–)

Socialist member of parliament in Hungary. As finance minister of the last Communist government in 1989–90 and of the Socialist-Free Democratic coalition in 1994–95, László Bekesi helped terminate the command economy and introduce free-market forces in Hungary.

Bekesi earned a Ph.D. in economics from the University of Economic Sciences in Budapest in 1979 and has been a titular full professor at that university since 1981. After graduating Bekesi entered the civil service and held various lower-ranking positions until he joined the cabinet as undersecretary of finance in 1985, and became head of the department in 1989. After the elections of 1990 his Socialist Party went into opposition. Bekesi served as deputy chair of the parliamentary Committee on Budget, Taxes, and Finances. At the same time, in 1990 he became president of the Girozentrale Investment Corp. and a member of the board of directors of an American-Hungarian joint venture, FOTEX Corp. He became finance minister again in 1994 when the Socialist Party won the parliamentary elections, but was forced to resign when Prime Minister Gyula Horn opposed his economic plans in early 1995.

Bekesi belonged to the so-called reform Communists in the 1980s who saw that the socialist economic system was doomed. Bekesi, like the majority of Communist Party members in the 1980s, was not ideologically committed to Marxism-Leninism; instead he may be characterized as a technocrat or a pragmatic politician who preferred professional to ideological debates. Though he embraced a large portion of the teachings of neoconservative economists, he also wished to maintain a relatively strong safety net for the losers in the economic transformation of Hungary. It was on this issue that he clashed with the prime minister and the leaders of the Alliance of the Free Democrats, who pushed for a more radical program, a sort of "shock therapy."

BIBLIOGRAPHY
Keri, László. *Bekesi Laszlo.* Budapest: Szazadveg, 1994.

Tamás Magyarics

Beksiński, Zdzisław (1929–)

Polish artist. Zdzisław Beksiński was born in Sanok and graduated from the department of architecture of Kraków Technical University. At the beginning of his career Beksiński was interested in a type of photography in which the world was not repeatable and was transformed to the maximum by the personality of the artist. He showed his displeasure with the natural and naturalism and fascination with the artificial. Beksiński left photography for drawing in the late 1950s.

His drawing leaned toward popular expression. He also experimented with various forms and techniques, abstract plastic and metal reliefs, as well as drawing. Beksiński became well known thanks to his erotic drawings, often considered scandalous because of their almost biological style of portrayal.

He started painting in oil in the mid-1960s and since 1974 has painted only in that medium. His calls his art "photographing the vision" and wishes to paint "beautifully" (in the nineteenth-century sense of the word). His visions are rather sleepy, surreal, often shocking, cruel, and frightening. His motifs are often muscles, skin, decay, destruction, and apocalyptic death. He works several hours a day listening to nineteenth-century music. Beksiński did not move to Warsaw until 1978, and shuns artistic circles, claiming that it does not matter to him what meanings the critics assign to his works.

His biggest collections are in the Regional Art Gallery in Sanok and in Piotr Dmochowski's Gallery in Paris. Dmochowski, fascinated with Beksiński's art, organized several exhibits in Paris devoted to his work.

Tomasz Marciniak

Belarus

Republic bordering Poland, Lithuania, Latvia, Russia, and Ukraine. Formerly the Byelorussian Soviet Socialist Republic (BSSR, 1921–91), this founding member of the United Nations is also known as Belorussia, Byelorussia, White Russia, and (since its independence) Belarus. In the 1989 census the population was 10.2 million, of

Belarus. *Illustration courtesy of Bernard Cook.*

which 78 percent were East Slavic Belarusans (Belarusy). Many if not most citizens consider themselves to be both Belarusan and Russian.

The first years after World War II were marked by large-scale purges in the Byelorussian Communist Party. Meanwhile in western Belarus, which had been part of Poland from 1921 to 1939, peasants were forced into collective farms. Since the late 1940s the political and cultural climate in Byelorussia was more conservative than in most other Soviet republics, partly because of the country's relatively successful economic development. By the 1970s Byelorussia was not only an important agricultural producer but also an industrial region known especially for its tractors and trucks. Its labor productivity and standard of living were above the Soviet average. Industrial development, however, severely damaged the environment.

The conservative climate was probably also reinforced by the continuing spread of the Russian language and culture. In the Khrushchev years some criticism of this mostly forced Russification was possible, but its impact was negligible. Of the 3,430 titles of books and pamphlets published in Byelorussia in 1985, only 380 were in Belarusan. As there was no dissident movement in Byelorussia the authorities went no further than condemning or taking administrative reprisals against intellectuals it considered to be liberal or nationalist. Meanwhile the republican media praised the performance of Belarusan athletes in international competitions as evidence of the republic's achievements.

The awakening of Belarus started with the Chernobyl nuclear reactor disaster in nearby Ukraine on April 26, 1986, which contaminated two-fifths of its territory. Also important was the revelation in June 1988 that more than five hundred mass graves of victims of the Stalinist terror of 1937–41 had been found in the Kurapaty Forest near Minsk. In December 1986, twenty-eight intellectuals sent a letter to Soviet leader Mikhail Gorbachev asking him to intervene to save the Belarusan language. Some three years later, on January 26, 1990, Belarusan became the official language of the republic.

In March 1990 the first real elections to the Supreme Soviet of the BSSR took place. Although dominated by the Byelorussian Communist Party, the legislative body—taking the example of other Soviet republics—on July 27, 1990, declared Belarus to be sovereign. The attempted putsch in Moscow against Gorbachev led to the declaration of independence on August 8, 1991. Stanislau Shushkevich became acting head of state. Minsk became the headquarters of the newly formed Commonwealth of Independence States (CIS). By ratifying the START I Treaty on February 4, 1993, Belarus became the first state in history to give up all its nuclear missiles. In 1994 the first presidential elections were won by Alyaksandr Lukashenka, and a new constitution was adopted.

BIBLIOGRAPHY

Urban, Michael, and Jan Zaprudnik. "Belarus: A Long Road to Nationhood," in Ian Bremmer and Ray Taras, eds., *Nation and Politics in the Soviet Successor States.* Cambridge: Cambridge University Press, 1993, 99–120.

Zaprudnik, Jan. *Belarus: At a Crossroads in History.* Boulder, Colo.: Westview Press, 1993.

Karel C. Berkhoff

SEE ALSO Lukashenka, Alyaksandr; Shushkevich, Stanislau

Culture

From 1945 to 1991 music and, especially, literature were practically the only cultural spheres in Byelorussia where a national identity could be sustained. In the immediate postwar years Soviet Belarusan patriotism, which had developed during the war, was still allowed, but in the late 1940s Stalinist orthodoxy with its socialist realism was restored. A second period of liberalization lasted from 1956 to 1965, and Gorbachev's policy of glasnost in the late 1980s ushered in the most liberal period.

Like other literatures in the Soviet Union, Belarusan literature suffered severely from ideological constraints. Unlike the prewar period, however, writers were not exiled or executed. One author, Vasil Bykau (1924–, also known as Bykov), the only prominent Belarusan writer never to join the Communist Party, became well known in other Soviet republics as well. Because of the values he expressed in word and deed, such as his opposition at the 1966 Congress of Belarusan Writers to neo-Stalinism, Bykau has been called the conscience of Belarus. His best stories and novels, which appeared in the 1960s, deal with the struggle against the Germans during World War II. His best-known work is *The Dead Feel No Pain* (1965), a novel about frontline combat and contemporary Stalinism that was immediately condemned by *Pravda*, the official newspaper of the Communist Party of the Soviet Union, and was never reprinted. Bykau's *Sotnikov* (*The Ordeal*, 1970) deals with the choice of two captured Soviet partisans between execution or collaboration with the Germans. The Russian partisan chooses a heroic death, but the Belarusan partisan chooses to collaborate in order to live. Some critics regard this response as representative of the Belarusan people under Nazi German rule. Stalinist dogma about heroism is again subverted in *The Obelisk* (1971), a testimony to the oppressive climate in Belarus in the 1970s that Bykau was among those who felt compelled to sign a petition denouncing Andrei Sakharov, a distinguished Soviet physicist and dissident of the time.

Among the best works published since 1945 by other authors is *The People of the Marsh* (1960) by Ivan Melezh (1921–76), set in the 1920s and depicting traditional peasant life. For years, Uladzimir Karatkevich (1930–) has been the only Belarusan author of prose about nineteenth-century Belarus.

There are more Belarusan poets than prose writers. Their poetry addresses universal human problems and Belarusan patriotism, but, in the Soviet period, exhibited mandatory praise for the Communist Party. Among the prominent poets are Ryhor Baradulin (1935–) and Nil Hilevich (1931–). Drama is the weakest branch of postwar Belarusan literature. The leading playwright is Andrei Makayonak (1920–). Literature by women is little developed, but of note is Volha Ipatava (1945–).

Most of Belarusan composers worked in the genre of "mass songs," as individualistic experimentation was not allowed. Among the most important postwar Belarusan composers of classical music is Dzmitry Lukas (1911–), most of whose oeuvre is vocal music. Some of his best-known works are the opera *Kastus Kalinouski* (1947), about the peasant uprising of 1863–64, and the song "The Partisan's Daughter" (1969). Ryhor Pukst (1900–

60) composed the first Belarusan opera for children, *Marynka* (1955), and six symphonies. Among his best-known works are also the choir songs "Become More Beautiful," "Belarus," and "Partisan Trenches." Another prominent composer is Anatol Bahatyrov (Anatoli Bogatyrev, 1913–), author of the historical opera *Durau's Hope* (1946). Rock music in Belarus is performed in the Russian language.

BIBLIOGRAPHY

McMillin, Arnold B. *Die Literatur der Weissrussen: A History of Byelorussian Literature, From its Origins to the Present Day.* Giessen, Germany: Wilhelm Schmitz Verlag, 1977.

Stankevich, Stanislau. "Belorussian Literature," in George S. N. Luckyj, ed., *Discordant Voices: The Non-Russian Soviet Literatures, 1953–1973.* Oakville, Ontario: Mosaic Press, 1974, 29–45.

Karel C. Berkhoff

Economy

In 1945 Belarus was the Byelorussian Soviet Socialist Republic (BSSR), one of the constituent republics of the then USSR. The republic was run by an administration controlled by the Belarusan Communist Party, with a centrally planned economy primarily run from Moscow by the All-Union planning ministries. The economy to a large degree was not under the control of the republic itself. This resulted in some anomalies. The BSSR had been developed during the Stalinist industrialization drive into one of the USSR's major centers of heavy industry, specializing particularly in tractors, agricultural machinery, trucks, machine building, and mineral fertilizers. However, the raw materials for such production came from other republics of the USSR, and the energy to drive production was imported primarily from Russia. The legacy of this interlinkage of the economies of the republics of the USSR continues to this day. Belarus still has to import energy from Russia and steel for its industries. The BSSR was one of the major exporting republics of the USSR, exporting industrial goods not only to other Union republics but also abroad for hard currency. Because all extra-USSR exports had to be processed via the All-Union agency, the BSSR largely did not receive and benefit from the hard currency thus earned. The BSSR was also a major agricultural producer for the USSR, specializing in animal husbandry, meat, butter, and potatoes, much of it exported to other republics of the USSR.

The economy of the BSSR was completely devastated during World War II. Occupation by the invading German army destroyed much of the transport and economic infrastructure, as well as many towns and villages. Many thousands of people were deported or killed during the war, and the population declined dramatically. In 1945 the productive capacity of the economy was considerably lower than prewar levels. Rebuilding the economy was a long, difficult process achieved with limited aid from the other republics of the USSR. Prewar industrial production levels were not achieved for some years. The postwar reconstruction program concentrated on rebuilding the heavy industrial capacity. However, the destruction of machinery, technology, and plant and its postwar replacement with more modern technology meant that postwar labor productivity in the BSSR was higher than the average for the USSR.

By the early 1980s the economy of the USSR had reached terminal sclerosis. USSR President Mikhail Gorbachev launched his perestroika program in 1985, designed to restructure and reform the ailing economy by introducing elements of the market. This reform program was less than enthusiastically received by the somewhat conservative administration of Byelorussia.

On April 26, 1986, a major nuclear accident took place at the Chernobyl reactor in Ukraine. Because of the prevailing wind, 70 percent of the radioactive fallout from this accident fell on the BSSR. Media coverage of the disaster within the BSSR was controlled by the Moscow administration, and the full extent of the devastation caused to the BSSR was not initially admitted. This accident had a devastating effect on the economy of Byelorussia and on the health of its citizens. Much of the country is now severely contaminated, the worst affected areas being in the southeast. Thousands of people still live and work in these heavily contaminated areas. There is particularly heavy contamination in the Mogilev and Gomel oblasts. It has been estimated that the direct economic costs of the disaster to Byelorussia (and then Belarus) have been equal to ten annual state budgets. Little financial help was forthcoming from the rest of the USSR, including the USSR Atomic Energy Ministry, which was responsible for the reactor at Chernobyl. The underfunded and underresourced medical facilities have been forced to cope with a sharp increase in cancers and with other radiation-induced illnesses.

In August 1991 the country declared independence and changed its name to Republic of Belarus. The All-Union ministries were transformed into Belarusan republic ministries. In December 1991 the presidents of the BSSR, the Ukrainian SSR, and the Russian SSR met on Belarusan territory to set up the Commonwealth of Independent States (CIS), thus precipitating the collapse of the old USSR.

The government of Belarus since the collapse of the USSR has been conservative in implementing market reforms, attempting instead to develop a viable mixed economy with a private sector growing alongside a reinvigorated state sector. Privatization and other market reforms of a limited nature have been extremely slow. By 1994, 80 percent of the productive capacity of the economy was still in state ownership.

In 1993 the government, in negotiations with multilateral institutions (IMF, World Bank) for financial support, was obliged to agree to a more reformist approach. A number of joint ventures got underway, as did some internationally financed projects for the reconstruction of industries. Closer contacts with European Union countries were fostered. In 1992, 38.9 percent of Belarusan exports went to Western Europe, and 42.4 percent of Belarusan imports came from there. But the economy was still very dependent on Russia, with which it experienced a balance-of-payments deficit, partly because of the increased price of energy imported from Russia.

By September 1996 the economy was collapsing, and President Lukashenka effectively halted the process of economic reform. The economy contracted by 22 percent in 1994 and another 10 percent in 1995 as the collapse continued. The IMF and the World Bank suspended aid, and Lukashenka sought closer union with Russia in an effort to secure aid. At the end of the 1990s the situation for Belarus, then one of Europe's poorest countries, was bleak.

BIBLIOGRAPHY

Lubachko, Ivan S. *Belarussia Under Soviet Rule, 1917–1957.* Lexington: University of Kentucky Press, 1972.

Zaprudnik, Jan. *Belarus at a Crossroads in History.* Boulder, Colo.: Westview Press, 1993.

Valerie Leonard

Political Parties

From 1945 to 1990 the only political party in Belarus was the republic branch of the Communist Party. By the mid-1990s Belarus had a multiparty system but in name only. All but the Communist parties were small and uninfluential, partly because of censorship of the media.

In the first postwar years purges within the Byelorussian (pre-independence spelling) Communist Party (CPB) replaced most Belarusan leaders with Russians. Ultimately, however, the CPB became dominated by a network of former Soviet Belarusan partisans. By 1988 the party had 692,000 members, of which 493,000 were ethnic Belarusans. The first Belarusan after 1945 to become first secretary was Kiryl Mazurau (Mazurov), who held

office from 1956 to 1965. He gained a seat in the Politburo of the Communist Party of the Soviet Union (CPSU) as a reward for supporting the removal of Premier Nikita Khrushchev in 1964 and took members of the Belarusan network with him. His successor for most of the Brezhnev period (1965–80) was Pyotr Masherau (Masherov). Although Masherau denounced nationalism, he was the first postwar Belarusan leader to address his compatriots on solemn occasions in Belarusan instead of Russian. His death in 1980 occurred under mysterious circumstances. During the attempted putsch against Soviet president Gorbachev in 1991, the leader of the CPB, Anatol Malafeyeu (Malofeyev), supported the conspirators. On August 29, 1991, the CPB was banned.

In post-Soviet Belarus the CPB, relegalized in February 1993, has been the most influential political force. It has a rival that was created in June 1992, the Party of Communists of Belarus, but the two are divided only over personalities, not issues. In 1992 these and other pro-Russian political parties formally united into an umbrella Popular Movement of Belarus (PMB). Other PMB members are the Communist Movement for Democracy, Social Progress, and Justice, founded in 1993, and various nonparty organizations, such as the Slavic Assembly Belaya Rus and the Union of Officers of Belarus.

The other side of the political spectrum has been dominated by the Belarusan Popular Front (BFP), created in October 1988 by archaeologist Zyanon Paznyak (Zenon Poznyak) and transformed into a political party in May 1993. Although it is nationalist in ideology, it denounced the Belarusan government's claim to the region around Vilnius, when Lithuania declared independence in 1990. After the breakup of the Soviet Union in 1991, the BPF was the main organization upholding Belarusan statehood vis-à-vis Russia. Because of this the BPF was supported by parties established in 1990 and 1991: the Belarusan Christian Democratic Union, the Belarusan Peasants Party, the Belarusan Social Democratic Party/Hramada, the right-wing National Democratic Party, and the United Democratic Party of Belarus, as well as by the Belarusan Association of Servicemen.

There are also parties not associated with either the PMB or the BPF: the Labor Party, the Liberal Democratic Party (allied to Russia's Vladimir Zhirinovsky), and two parties which focus on economic reform, the Party of Popular Accord and the Republican Party.

BIBLIOGRAPHY

Markus, Ustina. "Belarus," in Bogdan Szajkowski, *Political Parties of Eastern Europe, Russia and the Successor*

States. Harlow, Essex, England: Longman Information and Reference, 1994, 67–78.

Karel C. Berkhoff

Belgium

Constitutional monarchy that gained its independence from its neighbor the Netherlands in the Revolution of 1830. Belgium has always been deeply divided politically and culturally. Several linguistic-ethnic regions or communities exist together: Dutch-speaking Flanders in the north with 5.7 million inhabitants; French-speaking Wallonia in the south with 3.1 million inhabitants; a small region of 66,000 German speakers in the east; and bilingual but predominantly French-speaking Brussels with 1 million inhabitants. Until the 1960s, the economic, political, and cultural center was situated in Wallonia and Brussels. The cultural and economic elites spoke French, even in Flanders. In the post–World War II era the Flemish movement, which since the nineteenth century reacted against this situation, strove mainly for the complete Dutchification and political autonomy of Flanders. Equally, if not more important, was the political cleavage between Roman Catholics and non-Catholics, or anticlericals. Industrialization also led to class opposition between labor and capital.

These three cleavages partly tend to converge, since Wallonia was industrialized much earlier than Flanders,

Belgium. *Illustration courtesy of Bernard Cook.*

and consequently a strong anticlerical working-class consciousness developed in its coal mines and heavy-metal industries. Despite the existence of coal mines in the Campine area and the growing industry around its ports, Flanders remained until the 1960s a poor, mainly rural region, where the church still stood at the heart of society. However, Belgium has managed to overcome its internal divisions by developing an extensive but politically segregated civil society, mainly based on organizationally integrated networks of alliances among Catholics, socialists, and, to a lesser extent, liberals. Through this "compartmentalization" (*verzuiling,* often translated as "pillarization," refers to the social organizations and subcultures of the various political groupings) of society, conflicts were successfully mitigated and social and political life was stabilized. Yet this was accomplished at the price of political paternalism of the "compartment" ("pillar") elites and a lack of democratic candor.

Political developments after the May 28, 1940, armistice were influenced by what had happened during the German occupation. Leopold III refused to follow the government into exile and remained in Belgium. At the time this made him very popular among the population but it caused an institutional problem. Equally important was that the Flemish Nationalist Party (VNV), which in the late 1930s was quite popular, in particular among Flemish Catholics, had collaborated with the Germans.

In 1945 attempts were made to overcome prewar political immobility by new class-based formations. These largely failed, however, as demonstrated by the disastrous results in the 1946 parliamentary elections of the newly formed party, the Belgian Democratic Union (Union Démocratique Belge, UDB). As a consequence of the persecution of collaborators and owing to the attitude toward the return to the throne of Leopold III, who had been taken to Austria by the Germans in June 1944, deep rifts appeared in public opinion. From 1946 these rifts converged with prewar political cleavages. As it turned out, non-Catholics demanded prosecution of collaborators and argued against the return of Leopold III. Most Catholics on the other hand, particularly in Flanders, favored the return of the sovereign. Moreover, many Flemish Catholics felt that many so-called collaborators were punished solely because of their Flemish sympathies.

In March 1950, 58 percent of the population voted in favor of Leopold III, while the royalist Christian Democratic party won the subsequent elections. But the country was deeply divided: the king received overwhelming confidence in Flanders with 72 percent of the vote but did not obtain a majority in Wallonia and Brussels, with only 42 and 48 percent, respectively, in favor of his return.

A massive protest forced Leopold to abdicate in favor of his son Baudouin (Boudewijn). This, however, was considered by Christian Democrats as capitulation to street violence and humiliation at the hands of Walloons and non-Catholics.

In the 1950s divergent policies between Catholics and socialists concerning the role of the state gave way to tensions regarding state subsidization of private education, mainly organized by Catholics, as well as the organization and finance of social security. These tensions culminated in the 1954–58 School War pitting Catholics against socialist-liberal Van Acker Government. The political tug-of-war ended with the so-called School Pact in 1958 followed by similar political agreements concerning social security in 1963.

The importance of the political conflicts in the 1950s can hardly be overestimated. They confirmed the gap between Catholics and socialists at a time when secularization and socioeconomic changes undermined the original logic of "compartmentalization." The Liberal Party, on the other hand, was transformed from an anticlerical formation into a popular conservative party. Even more important, the School Pact was the expression of a basic compromise in which both public and private (mainly Catholic) institutions would coexist, the latter subsidized and backed up by the state. The School Pact put this principle into practice with regard to education, but it would also be adopted, in slightly different terms, with regard to social security, housing, and cultural facilities. This basic compromise not only reinforced compartmentalization, it also increased the far-reaching mutual penetration between the state and the political and social organizations characteristic of Belgian society.

Notwithstanding the political conflicts of the postwar years, the labor movement, ideologically divided into a socialist, Catholic, and much smaller liberal movement, made important progress. First, obligatory social security was extended to all employees. It provided health care and unemployment relief for the first time, and also old age pensions, insurance against industrial accidents and disability, child allowances, and annual vacations. Existing social organizations remained deeply involved in the management of social security and the payment of benefits, while the social security system was mainly financed by social contributions of employers, employees, and, through a separate program, the self-employed.

Moreover, trade unions and employers worked out a joint consultative and collective bargaining system, recognizing the trade unions as representatives of the workers at national, sectoral, and company level. However, with unfavorable economic conditions and reluctant employ-

ers, the implementation of these principles turned out to be particularly difficult. Only in the late 1950s did social bargaining develop into a neocorporatist system of social programming at the sectoral and national levels, while the "social partners" gained influence in regional and national economic planning via tripartite bodies representing employers, labor, and the public.

After the conciliation of the conflicts between Catholics and non-Catholics, the ethnic-cultural division came to the fore. This was accompanied, and partly caused, by important shifts in the industrial pattern. Foreign investments, particularly important for the small and open Belgian economy, were oriented toward the ports of Flanders, while the obsolete heavy industries of Wallonia declined. After the 1961 general strike organized by the socialist labor movement against the so-called Unity Law for economic recovery, the militant left-wing Walloon socialists formed the Popular Walloon Movement (Mouvement Populaire Wallon, MPW), hoping through the MPW to combat the decline of their region by setting up a regional socialist self-government. The success of this MPW did not outlast the sudden death of its charismatic leader, André Renard, in 1962, but its objective was taken over by the French-speaking socialist labor movement.

In spite of the decline of Walloon industry, Belgium experienced a period of increased economic welfare in the 1960s, which produced a particularly affluent consumer society, with television as window to the world as well as the main source of entertainment. In Flanders, the position of the church waned, which was, among other things, expressed in rapidly declining church attendance as well as falling birth rates. The "compartment" organizations, however, managed to hold tight by widening their activities.

In the 1960s the Flemish movement, which had recovered from its setback after the war, again strove for the Dutchification of Flanders. In 1963 linguistic borders were fixed by law, but in a few border communities so-called facilities were granted to the minorities, which caused much dissatisfaction among the Flemish because they undermined their desired unilingualism. Moreover, the position of a few communities remained disputed, in particular that of Voeren (Fourons), which became part of the Flemish province of Limburg. After massive student protest, in 1968 the French section of the Catholic University of Louvain (Leuven) in Flanders was transferred to Wallonia. This transfer caused a deep rift between the two communities and resulted in the split of the Christian Democratic and later the Liberal and Socialist Parties. In this heightened climate nationalist parties gained electoral success in Flanders, as well as in Brussels and Wallonia, and they were often included in government coalitions.

Student protest was an expression of a general spirit in the late 1960s and early 1970s. In the early 1970s workers went on wildcat strikes. In general compartmentalization was severely criticized as being wasteful and democratically deficient. Contrary to the situation in the Netherlands, however, political segregation was reinforced and even institutionalized in the cultural field by the Culture Pact of 1973. But the compartments fundamentally changed in nature, the loss of ideological identity being the price for successful modernization. Mutual competition for members and for state support of their activities is mainly what keeps the compartments apart until today.

The economic crises of 1974 and 1989 hit the country severely and led, rather than to a decrease in incomes, to increasing unemployment and deteriorating working conditions. The gravity of the situation, at first not fully recognized, was countered by a Keynesian policy of public spending. The situation was further aggravated by communal tensions caused by the unequal economic development of the regions. Only after the constitutional reform of 1980 did the newly formed Christian Democratic/Liberal coalition put aside communal dissent to pursue a policy of wage restraint and reconstruction of public finances. The national system of collective bargaining collapsed and collective bargaining was decentralized to the sectoral and company level. With economic recovery and the political comeback of the Social Democrats in a coalition with the Christian Democrats in 1986, interprofessional collective bargaining was restored to a certain extent, but with the government as "general supervisor." Since the public debt in the 1970s and early 1980s had risen drastically, the government in the 1990s was required to pursue a thorough austerity policy in order to meet the criteria for entering the new European monetary system as designed in the Maastricht Treaty.

Economic developments served as the breeding ground for the consecutive state reforms and constitutional revisions since 1970, which gradually transformed Belgium into a federal state in which three socioeconomic regions were recognized: Flanders, Wallonia, and Brussels, along with three "communities" responsible for cultural and personal matters. The constitutional revisions of 1991 and 1994 explicitly recognized the federal character of Belgium, including the regions' limited right to levy taxes and to conclude international agreements. The federal bicameral system was altered too, among other things by transforming the upper house into a chamber for political "reflection." Parallel to the divergent economic developments of the respective regions and the institutional fed-

eralization, a cultural curtain developed between Flanders and Wallonia. The Flemish developed an assertive sense of their own identity, orienting themselves economically and culturally toward the Anglo-Saxon world, while French-speaking Belgians, in particular in Brussels, increasingly felt part of the Francophone world. A Walloon identity is also emerging that exhibits at the political level the still mainly hidden tensions between French-speaking Brussels and Wallonia.

The 1980s witnessed important changes in values and culture. The ecological and pacifist movements gained much support in public opinion, in particular in Flanders. But since 1989, the extreme-right parties, taking advantage of a widespread feeling of political and social malaise, have also made themselves heard. Some attempts, in particular by the strongly breathe neoliberal Flemish Liberal Party, were made to modernize and breathe new life into the Belgian political scene, but a real transformation of the political landscape failed to occur. The malaise, however, was accompanied by an outburst of cultural renewal and the international success of Belgian artists and art managers, in particular in modern dance, music, and multimedia arts.

Neither internal tensions nor its small size kept the country from playing its role on the international scene. Until 1961 Belgium maintained colonial control over the Democratic Republic of the Congo (formerly Zaire) and ruled Rwanda and Burundi. It remained involved in central Africa after independence, even if its relations with Congo/Zaire were at times very difficult. Belgium had formed an economic union with Luxembourg in 1922, and in 1948 a customs union was formed between Belgium, Luxembourg, and the Netherlands. On February 3, 1959, the three countries signed the Benelux Treaty. When it went into effect in 1960 it provided for the free movement of labor, capital, and services between the three countries. Belgium was also one of the driving forces behind the broader economic integration of Europe through the European Coal and Steel Community of 1952 and the European Economic Union of 1958.

BIBLIOGRAPHY

Boudart, Marina, Michel Boudart, and René Bryssinck, eds. *Modern Belgium.* Palo Alto, Calif.: Society for the Promotion of Science and Scholarship, 1990.

Fitzmaurice, John. *The Politics of Belgium: A Unique Federalism.* London: Hurst & Company, 1996.

Lijphart, Arendt. *Conflict and Coexistence in Belgium: The Dynamics of a Culturally Divided Society.* Berkeley: University of California Press, 1981.

Luykx, Theo, and Mark Platel. *Politieke geschiedenis van België van 1789 tot 1985,* Vol. 2. Antwerp: Kluwer, 1985.

Luyten, Guy. *Sociaal-economisch overleg in België sedert 1918.* Brussels: VUB press, 1995.

Mommen, André. *The Belgian Economy in the Twentieth Century.* London: Routledge, 1994.

Vanthemsche, Guy. *De beginjaren van de sociale zekerheid, 1945–1963.* Brussels: VUB Press, 1994.

Vos, Louis. "Nationalism, Democracy and the Belgian State", in Richard Caplan and John Feffer, eds. *Europe's New Nationalism: States and Minorities in Conflict.* Oxford: Oxford University Press, 1996.

Patrick Pasture

Decolonization

After the Second World War, Belgium's central African colonies, the Congo and Ruanda-Urundi, seemed immune to the strife and nationalist violence plaguing Britain's and France's colonial empires. Despite this calm, Belgian decolonization was among the quickest and most violent once it began in December 1959. By mid-1960 Belgium had abandoned the Congo but found itself involved in a civil war there. Two years later Belgium withdrew from Ruanda-Urundi.

Before 1959 the Belgian government made little preparation for colonial self-rule or independence. Belgian colonial rule was marked by paternalism and a basic welfare system, including medical care and strong primary schools. However, secular higher education was closed to Africans. The Catholic Church controlled virtually all colonial education and emphasized vocational and practical training, discouraging the development of an indigenous professional class. Belgian colonials did not mix with the small but loyal indigenous middle class in urban areas.

A Socialist-Liberal coalition government elected in 1954 made some attempts at liberalization. Secular schools were founded, and the first local elections were held in 1957. Virtually no native political party had a mass following, but African mayors were elected in the major cities.

External events influenced and quickly overwhelmed the Congo. In 1958 the world price of copper dropped, devastating the Congolese economy. That same year the Socialist-Liberal government in Brussels fell from power. Meanwhile, French President Charles de Gaulle began the process of independence for neighboring French Congo. In December 1959 Patrice Lumumba, a former postal clerk, represented the Congo at a pan-African conference in Accra, Ghana. On his return, he announced his desire to press for independence. Soon thereafter, riots broke out in the capital, Leopoldville (Kinshasa). In response, on January 13, 1960, Belgian King Baudouin announced his intention to end colonial rule. In negotiations, Belgium accepted the Africans' maximal demands, transferring power on June 30, 1960. The Belgians did not want to repeat the French experience in Vietnam or Algeria. At independence Joseph Kasavubu's Bakongo tribal party, ABAKO; Lumumba's Mouvement National Congolais; and Moïse Tshombe's federalist Conakat Party dominated. Kasavubu served as president, Lumumba as prime minister, and Joseph Désiré Mobutu (later Mobutu Sese Seko) as defense minister.

Immediately after independence, civil war broke out across the country. In their haste to withdraw from Africa, the Belgians endorsed a flawed plan. While African politicians took control of the government, the civil service and military remained temporarily staffed by white Belgian officers. Congolese soldiers, wary of losing the leading role in society to the political class, mutinied against their white officers. The withdrawal agreement also failed to indicate whether the new state would be unitary or federal; and soon mineral-rich Katanga province seceded under Tshombe. Tshombe had the support of many white settlers and Belgian mining concerns, which feared losing access to Katanga's natural wealth.

Ultimately outside forces intervened to end the conflict. Belgium sent troops to protect its interests in the former colony. With U.S. help, Mobutu ousted Lumumba, who fled the capital and established a rival government with Soviet help. Later government troops captured Lumumba and allowed Katangan forces to execute him in January 1961. The Congolese government requested help from the United Nations. U.N. General Secretary Dag Hammarskjöld attempted to mediate an end to the conflict but died in a plane crash in the Congo. In 1963 Tshombe abandoned the cause of Katangan independence in favor of a place in the national government, effectively ending the war. In 1965 Mobutu replaced Tshombe as head of state. He ruled the Congo (later Zaire) for over thirty years.

In July 1962 the United Nations voted to end Belgium's trusteeship over Ruanda-Urundi, in effect since World War I. The independent states of Rwanda and Burundi then came into being.

The violence of Belgian decolonization had a long-lasting effect on the region, shattering the nation that decolonization could be a gradual, managed process. The white minorities of southern Africa feared quick decolonization by the metropolitan powers and civil war under black majority rule. This impression influenced Rhodesia's declaration of independence in 1965 and led to increased brutality by the Portuguese colonial army in Angola.

BIBLIOGRAPHY

Ansprenger, Franz. *The Dissolution of the Colonial Empires.* London: Routledge, 1989.

Grimal, Henri. *Decolonization: The British, French, Dutch and Belgian Empires 1919–1963.* London: Routledge and Kegan Paul, 1965.

Holland, R. F. *European Decolonization 1918–1981: An Introductory Survey.* London: Macmillan, 1985.

Jay Howard Geller

SEE ALSO Congo Intervention

Political Parties

As they did in the interwar years, the Catholic, Socialist, and Liberal parties have dominated postwar Belgian politics between 1944 and 1998. In the 1960s and 1970s each of these parties divided respectively into independent Flemish and francophone halves, and they collectively lost some ground to new language-based parties. Belgium has seen frequent cabinet reshuffling and recourse to early elections, but with more stability in the 1990s.

The Belgian Chamber of Representatives is elected by proportional representation. Enough of the Senate is directly elected so that its composition largely mirrors the Chamber's; the Senate usually follows the Chamber's legislative lead.

The leading party has been the Christian People's Party (CVP, Flemish name) or Christian Social Party (PSC, francophone name), Belgium's Christian Democrats. The CVP/PSC started the postwar era as the most conservative of the large parties, and its support is especially strong among practicing Catholics. Belgium's small Protestant community has often opposed CVP/PSC policies. The CVP/PSC ranks first in the more populous and religious Flanders, and second in francophone Wallonia. Its performance in Brussels, as that of other parties, has varied significantly. As the largest party it is almost always in the government.

Most popular in Wallonia and second in Flanders is the Socialist Party (PS or SP). Its electorate includes especially the non-Catholic working classes, which explains its relative strength in historically more industrialized Wallonia.

Third in both larger regions, but often more successful in Brussels, the liberals especially enjoy middle-class support. In the early postwar years, the Liberal Party mixed economic liberalism with anticlericalism.

The first two postwar governments included all main parties as well as the Communists (PCB/KPB), who outperformed the liberals in the 1946 national elections despite low support in Flanders. The Communists left the government in 1947 (as in France and Italy), and their electoral fortunes then plunged quickly and permanently (unlike the French and Italian experiences). The small, progressive Belgian Democratic Union (UDB) quickly disappeared after 1946.

Although the three main parties generally agreed on NATO membership and European integration, the CVP/PSC differed from the others on two important questions. The CVP/PSC was the only mainstream party to support the return to Belgium of King Leopold III. Strengthened after the 1949 introduction of female suffrage since women vote in greater proportions for the Catholics, the CVP/PSC facilitated the king's return in July 1950. Ensuing riots, however, prompted his abdication. The "Royal Question" divided Belgian society and, combined with the question of collaboration amnesties, intensified the divide between the somewhat more royalist Flemish and their francophone compatriots.

In sole control of the government from 1950 to 1954, the CVP/PSC increased state subsidies to Catholic schools as well as the Catholic share in directing state schools. Debated since the 1880s the schools question now brought Socialists and Liberals together into a governing coalition, 1954–58, which more than reversed the CVP/PSC's changes. The schools question dominated the 1958 elections, and after Catholic gains, the three party presidents met and reached a compromise, the famous Schools Pact.

Soon thereafter the liberals dropped their anticlericalism and focused on economic policy (and later on Belgian unity), and openly welcomed Catholic members. These changes were institutionalized in 1961 when the Liberal Party became the Party of Freedom and Progress (PLP/PVV), with reduced francophone dominance.

In 1960 the Catholic-liberal government proposed a *loi unique,* including reduced social expenditures. With their coal industry in crisis since 1958, Walloons reacted with widespread strikes and the creation of new Walloon movements. The Popular Walloon Movement (MPW) and others went through several mergers and changes before becoming the Walloon Union (Rassemblement Wallon, RW) in 1968. Separately, the Democratic Front of Francophones (FDF) was created in Brussels in 1965 to defend francophone interests there. Since 1976 the RW has been markedly center-left, while the FDF has maintained a somewhat broader ideological appeal.

Following Flemish movements of the late nineteenth century and political parties in the interwar period, the first postwar Flemish party, the People's Union (VU), was founded in 1954 to represent cultural and economic claims. It fared poorly for the next decade before peaking in the 1970s at close to 19 percent of the Flemish vote.

These regional, or linguistic "community," parties began their substantial electoral progress in the later 1960s. The RW was the first to enter a government, in 1974, and both the VU and the FDF participated in subsequent governments.

During the same period, as Belgium moved from a unitary to a federal state, its political parties divided on the linguistic problems that have racked the country since the 1960s. Although the new pairs' party platforms varied little on traditional issues, they diverged completely on the now dominant questions of nationalities politics. The six parties (three pairs) saw their combined parliamentary representation fall from 95 percent or higher to between 75 and 85 percent.

Already partially divided, the CVP/PSC split completely in 1968 over the question of the traditionally francophone Catholic University of Louvain, which became Flemish. The liberals divided next in 1972. Flemish liberals retained the 1961 name (PVV) until their 1992 change to Flemish Liberals and Democrats (VLD). The francophone liberals went through several changes while absorbing some centrist RW members, before settling into the Liberal Reform Party (PRL) in 1979. Both liberal parties continued the shift rightward toward neoliberalism. After the Socialist Party divided in 1978, its two offspring quickly showed some significant policy differences, most notably on the question of the U.S. desire to deploy Pershing and cruise missiles in Europe in the late 1970s and early 1980s. The Flemish SP opposed the missiles more directly, although it tended generally to be more pragmatic than the francophone PS.

Ecological parties appeared in national balloting in 1978 and entered parliament in 1981, the first ecologists in any national parliament. The two main Green parties are Ecolo (Walloon) and AGALEV (Flemish).

More marginal parties have been somewhat aided by Belgium's century-old requirement to vote. The LRT/RAT Trotskyites renamed themselves the Labor Party in 1979. Also on the extreme left is AMADA/TPO (All Power to the Workers). The UDRT/RAD (founded 1978–79) opposes established parties and extra-EEC immigration, and promotes the liberation of business from government controls and from employers' and employees' associations. The racist extreme-right Flemish Bloc

(*Vlaams Blok*) has its origins in the 1970s; it received over 10 percent of Flemish votes in the 1990s.

The CVP has constantly supplied the Flemish prime minister since 1974. While coalition governments in Belgium continue to pivot around the CVP/PSC, the profusion of parties has complicated Belgian politics.

BIBLIOGRAPHY

Craeybeckx, Jan, et al. *La Belgique: Politique de 1830 à nos jours.* Brussels: Éditions Labor, 1987.

Delwit, Pascal, et al. *Les partis politiques en Belgique.* Brussels: Éditions de l'Université, 1996.

Desama, Claude, ed. *1985/1985: Du Partie Ouvrier Belge au Parti Socialiste.* Brussels: Éditions Labor, 1985.

Dewachter, Wilfried, et al., eds. *Un Parti dans l'histoire, 1945–1995: 50 ans d'action du Parti Social Chrétien.* Louvain-la-Neuve: Duculot, 1996.

Fitzmaurice, John. *The Politics of Belgium.* London: Westview. 1983; 2d ed., London: Hurst & Company, 1996.

Kitschelt, Herbert, ed. *Beyond the European Left: Ideology and Political Action in the Belgian Ecology Parties.* Durham, N.C.: Duke University Press, 1990.

Vandeputte, Robert. *De Christelijke Volkspartij, 1944–1988.* Brussels: CEPESS, 1991.

Verhulst, Adriaan, et al., eds. *Le libéralisme en Belgique: deux cents ans d'histoire.* Brussels: Centre Paul Hymans, 1989.

Jeffrey William Vanke

SEE ALSO Leopold III; Pershing II Missile

Nationalities Politics

Since 1970 the unitary Belgian nation has been reshaping itself into a federal state with complex bipartite and tripartite structures. It is not yet certain that this peaceful revolution will bring stability.

The unification of the Belgian nation as a francophone kingdom in 1830 led to the awakening of a Flemish national feeling among the Dutch-speaking majority of the population, in particular within the clerical Catholic party. As a reaction to this, after 1884 a Walloon consciousness emerged among French speakers, especially free-thinking liberals and socialists. In the 1930s legislation recognized Flanders, the northern half of the country, as Dutch-speaking, the capital city of Brussels as bilingual, and Wallonia as francophone.

During both world wars the German occupier tried to destabilize the country by favoring the Flemish over the Walloons. This led in 1940–44 to a collaborationist right-wing Flemish Nationalist Party. The Flemish movement was, consequently, severely affected by the people's hatred of collaboration. In the 1947 census many tens of thousands no longer wished to be counted as Flemish.

The Walloon movement emerged from the war victorious, though there was an acute awareness of Wallonia's industrial and demographic decline. The Walloon population declined from 40.3 percent of the total Belgian population in 1900 to 32.9 in 1962. In 1962 the Flemish districts constituted 51.3 percent and the ever more francophone capital 15.7 percent. The Walloon movement asked for institutional safeguards for the predominantly socialist Walloon minority against the predominantly Christian Democratic Flemish majority.

The Walloon movement propagated the federalist idea, especially at times when the socialists were in opposition. There was, nevertheless, much Flemish discontent as well, both about the bilingual economic, social, and cultural life in the larger Flemish towns and about the strong predominance of French in the capital. Since the interwar period young people in Flanders had been educated in Dutch rather than in French. Within this generation liberal or socialist sympathies no longer excluded Flemish sympathies. In 1960, Flemish opposition prevented the decennial census from being used again as a language referendum, as it had been in 1947.

In December 1960, the socialist trade unions called a general strike against the government's austerity policy. When the action began to crumble for lack of support from Flemish workers Walloon trade union leaders turned the action into a Flemish-Walloon confrontation, denouncing the transfer of the Walloon metal industry from the exhausted coal mining region to the Flemish seaports. The Popular Walloon Movement (Mouvement Populaire Wallon), separated from the Belgian Socialist Party and gave impetus to the formation of a series of Walloon nationalist parties.

A new Flemish Nationalist Party achieved a breakthrough during elections in March 1961. In response to growing national sentiments, a government of mainly Flemish Christian Democrats and Walloon Socialists prepared a new constitutional arrangement safeguarding the Walloon minority, while eliminating the linguistic grievances of the Flemish. In 1962 the language boundary was fixed by law to remove it from the controversial arena of the decennial population census. In 1963, language legislation concerning education, the civil service, and the judiciary was reviewed, strengthening the monolingual status of the regions and the bilingual provisions in the Brussels urban area. Private companies were also made subject to this legislation.

The two-thirds majority in parliament required for a new constitutional arrangement was impossible to achieve, given the increasing polarization. French-speaking inhabitants of Brussels created their own party, the Front des Francophones, to oppose the new legislation in alliance with the Mouvement Populaire Wallon, and to demand a tripartite federal state, with Brussels as a full third region that would swallow a large surrounding district as well. The Flemish rejected this and demanded autonomy for the country's two linguistic communities.

In 1968, a new height in polarization brought about the transfer of the French-language section of the Catholic University of Leuven to Wallonia. This crisis caused the Christian Democratic Party to break up along language lines. The same was to happen soon within the Liberal Party and, in 1978, within the Socialist Party. All six new parties evolved toward a federalist position; this would permit the Socialist Party (Parti Socialiste) to swallow up the Walloon nationalist parties.

In 1970–71, a partial revision of the constitution was effected. French speakers gained parity in the cabinet "with the possible exception of the Prime Minister," the Flemish gained the establishment of two linguistic community councils, each having exclusive competence to issue decrees concerning cultural policy with the exception of education.

In 1980, three administrative regions were created: Flanders, Wallonia, and Brussels, with power over town and country planning, housing, the environment, and supervision of local government. The institutions for the Brussels region were not set up at the time. French speakers demanded a larger territory for this region than was allocated in 1962–63. The reform resulted in asymmetrical structures. The new Flemish regional council and executive merged with the Flemish community institutions, which had existed since 1971, with jurisdiction also in Brussels, to form a single Flemish Council and Executive. On the French-speaking side, apprehension that Brussels would undo the socialist domination in the Walloon Regional Council resulted in a side-by-side coexistence of regional institutions and community institutions.

A Consultative Committee was set up between the government and the various federalized executives, as well as a Court of Arbitration in 1985 composed equally of francophones and Dutch speakers. During the economic crisis of the 1980s the distribution of government money was the main bone of contention among the regions. The reluctance on the French-speaking side to accept the finality of the language boundary as fixed in 1962 also continued to cause irritation.

In 1988, a two-thirds majority was found for comprehensive reforms. Education was transferred to the two communities; economic policy, transport, and public works to the three regions. The Brussels region was instituted. Within its executive two out of five ministerial posts were guaranteed for Dutch speakers, even though they constituted less than 20 percent of the Brussels electorate. In 1993, further steps were taken, in accord with the 1988 agreement, to complete federalization. The regions and communities saw their powers once more extended, even to foreign policy with regard to matters for which they were responsible internally. The French Community received the right to assign some of its responsibilities to the Walloon Region and to the French Linguistic Group of the Council of the Brussels Capital Region. The whole written constitution was adapted to the devolution that had taken place since 1970. Signed by Albert II on February 17, 1994, it acquired full force of law after the elections of May 21, 1995.

In the federal house and senate proportional representation has been maintained, while in sensitive matters a two-thirds majority vote is required with a majority in each linguistic group in each body. The Council of the French Community is composed of the 75 members of the Walloon Regional Council and the 19 representatives of the French Linguistic Group of the Council of the Brussels Capital Region. The Flemish Council is composed of 6 representatives of the Dutch Linguistic Group of the Brussels Council and 118 members elected in the Flemish Region.

Since 1984, cultural autonomy has been granted to the German-speaking Community comprising nine municipalities with sixty-nine thousand inhabitants. Its administrative offices are located in Eupen. In addition, the Walloon Region has assigned some of its responsibilities to this community.

BIBLIOGRAPHY

Alen, André, and Rusen Ergec. *Federal Belgium after the Fourth State Reform of 1993.* Brussels: Ministry of Foreign Affairs, 1994.

Hermans, Theo, Louis Vos, and Lode Wils. *The Flemish Movement: A Documentary History 1780–1990.* Atlantic Highlands, N.J.: The Athlone Press, 1992.

Vos, Louis. "Nationalism, Democracy and the Belgian State", in Richard Caplan and John Feffer, eds. *Europe's New Nationalism: States and Minorities in Conflict.* Oxford: Oxford University Press, 1996.

Lode Wils

SEE ALSO Leopold III

The Flemish Extreme Right

After the Second World War the extreme right in Belgium, which had collaborated massively with the German occupier, went into temporary eclipse. However, as early as December 1944, three months after the Germans had been driven from Belgium, youth movements were set up for the children of former collaborators by Flemish nationalists, who felt that they were being victimized by the victors. The Flemings who fought on the eastern front with the SS organized several Nazi-nostalgic societies after the war.

The extreme right sought a political party as mouthpiece for its political demands such as amnesty for prosecuted collaborators and Flemish autonomy. After some abortive attempts the Popular Union (Volksunie, VU) was founded in 1954. Although not an extreme-right but a democratic Flemish national party, the VU contained right-wing militants.

The VU could depend on the support of the Order of Flemish Militants (Vlaamse Militanten Orde, VMO), a paramilitary organization modeled on prewar private militias, which paraded in uniform but without arms. The VMO was founded in 1949 to defend meetings of Flemish nationalists but became an offensive gang of toughs who attacked demonstrations of left-wing and national opponents. In 1971 the original VMO was disbanded, but extreme-right militants reorganized it in short order. While the VU became a democratic and pluralistic party, the VMO became more and more radical. In 1981 it was condemned as a private militia and outlawed.

In the meantime, the intellectual extreme right also staged a comeback. In 1962 the think tank Protect Yourself (Were Di) was founded. Its monthly magazine *Dietsland-Europa* (*Germany-Europe*) advanced a modern, antiegalitarian, and corporatist ideology, as a third way between capitalism and communism, and advocated the unification of Flanders and the Netherlands. In general the extreme right focused on nonparliamentary activities and bided its time.

In 1977 for the first time the VU joined a Belgian government on the basis of a platform to transform the Belgian unitary state into a federal state. The extreme right reacted furiously. The Belgian state, in its opinion, must not be reformed but liquidated. Any collaboration with Belgium meant a betrayal of Flanders. On October 2, 1977, the extreme right founded its own party, the Flemish Bloc (Vlaams Blok, VB). Besides former members of the VU, the VB attracted militants from right-wing groupings like Were Di, the VMO, the direct-action group Outpost (Voorpost), and the Nationalist

Students' Association (Nationalistische Studentenvereniging, NSV).

The VB, which believes in a fundamental, natural inequality, strives for a conservative revolution to liquidate the Belgian state and proclaim an independent Republic of Flanders, including all places that were ever Flemish. That Flanders must be mono-ethnic (one people, one nation, one culture) and thus ethnically cleansed, a white Flemish Flanders without foreigners (monoracial and monocultural). Other VB positions are the diminution of political party and trade union influence, amnesty for former collaborators, a corporate relationship between employers and employees, demolition of the welfare state, European economic protectionism, neocolonialism, a European military alliance independent of NATO, ejection of the European Union from Brussels, traditional values, and promotion of law and order.

In the general elections of December 1978, the VB won one seat with 76,000 votes, or 2.2 percent. In election after election the VB kept advancing. After fifteen years it has became the fourth-largest party in Flanders with 475,000 votes, or 12 percent (1995). In Antwerp, the most important city in Flanders, it is the biggest political party, with 28 percent of the vote. Only a coalition of all other parties, could prevent VB control of the municipality. In 1995 the VB counted 150 branches, a secretariat in the 15 most important towns, 60 employees, two European Parliament delegates, 32 members of the national parliament, 204 town councilors in 86 municipalities and around 10,000 members.

BIBLIOGRAPHY

Mudde, Cas. "One against All, All against One: A Portrait of the Vlaams Blok." *Patterns of Prejudice* 29, no. 1 (1995): 5–28.

Spruyt, Marc. *Grove borstels: Stel dat het Vlaams Blok morgen zijn programma realiseert, hoe zou Vlaanderen er dan uitzien?* Leuven: Van Halewyck, 1995.

Verhoeyen, Etienne. "L'Extrême-droite au sein du nationalisme flamand," *Courrier Hebdomadaire du CRISP,* 1975, 675–76.

Verlinden, Peter. "Morfologie van de uiterst-rechtse groeperingen in België." *Res Publica* 2–3 (1981): 373–407.

Marc Spruyt

Economy

The Belgian economy suffered relatively little damage during the Second World War, so production resumed rapidly once shortages of coal and other raw materials eased. Moreover, during the reconstruction period Belgium's specialization in the manufacturing of steel, non-ferrous metals, glass, and cement coincided almost exactly with the European demand structure. Strong domestic and foreign demand soon caused labor shortages, which resulted in substantial wage increases. A considerable extension of the social security system added to the upward pressure on wage costs.

By 1948 the so-called Belgian miracle came to an end. As other European economies were getting back on their feet, the time of "easy exports" faded. In addition, Belgium decided in 1949 to devalue its currency by only 12.3 percent vis-à-vis the U.S. dollar instead of by 30.5 percent, as did most of its European competitors, for example, Britain and the Netherlands. This de facto revaluation of the Belgian franc against most European currencies magnified Belgium's labor cost handicap. As a result, many enterprises faced a profit squeeze that undermined private investment. Moreover, the structure of corporate capital formation changed as firms favored rationalization investment over extension investment in an effort to increase efficiency. As extension investment crumbled, employment growth slowed considerably. Consequently, Belgium suffered from relatively high unemployment rates in the 1950s.

During the 1950s Belgium's competitive position gradually recovered as continuously high unemployment rates put downward pressure on wage demands. From the late 1950s the start of European integration gave an additional stimulus to Belgian economic growth. The accelerated dismantling of protectionist measures in neighboring countries aided Belgian exports. Even more important was that many multinational enterprises looking for a stronghold in the European Economic Community (EEC, Common Market) were attracted by the availability of Belgium's trained labor reserve. Together with the country's central location in the EEC and its flexible monetary and financial arrangements, such as the easy repatriation of profits, it triggered a wave of foreign direct investment in Belgium in the 1960s and early 1970s.

The activities of multinational firms contributed to a substantial modernization of Belgium's manufacturing structure: the share of chemicals, petrochemicals, and car production in total value added rose considerably in the 1960–73 period. In addition, these multinationals introduced new technologies and new forms of organization that spilled over to domestic firms and thus improved their efficiency. Especially the northern part of the country benefited from foreign investment, so that Flanders by the mid-1960s surpassed Wallonia in per capita income.

In the 1960s accelerated employment not only absorbed the unemployed but soon created severe labor shortages. Wages rose quickly, giving a strong impetus to private consumption. Unit labor costs, however, remained in check because of a rapid increase in productivity. Despite this brilliant record the Belgian economy continued to suffer from important structural weaknesses. Public finances, for example, became more subject than ever to the demands of special interest groups. So the state increasingly subsidized the loss-making coal mines and the ever-expanding social security system. In addition, mounting tensions between the Dutch and the French speakers were bought off by expensive compromises. As a result, public finances showed considerable deficits even in periods of economic upswing.

The first oil shock in late 1973 pushed up inflation to double-digit figures. In combination with the system of automatic wage indexing and large real wage increases, it triggered a wage-price spiral. Consequently, Belgian unit labor costs rose much faster than those of its main competitors. Loss of market shares abroad and increased penetration of foreign products on the domestic market were the obvious results. In addition, higher oil prices caused Belgium's terms of trade to worsen considerably. In these circumstances Belgium's current account showed ever-increasing deficits. Corporate profitability took a hard blow, which provoked the restructuring of many industries. Serious job losses in the private sector combined with a quick rise in the labor force brought on a spectacular increase in unemployment.

Despite a substantial rise in fiscal pressure the government's borrowing requirement soared in the second half of the 1970s. Public spending skyrocketed as unemployment benefits exploded and numerous new civil servants were hired to put the brakes on unemployment growth. The second oil shock of 1979–80 and its aftermath pushed the Belgian economy further out of balance. Not surprisingly, confidence in the Belgian franc faded and it fell victim to speculative attacks. Gradually it became clear that only a dramatic change in economic policy could stop the vicious circle of decline. In February 1982 the Belgian franc was devalued by 8.5 percent. Accompanying measures included strict wage restraint to prevent the inflation, a normal outcome of devaluation in a small, open economy, from being reflected in labor costs. Otherwise, the competitive edge resulting from the devaluation would quickly have been lost. Consequently, Belgian exports could take full advantage of the revival of the world economy in the 1980s. At the same time income restraint curbed private consumption, so that imports stagnated. As a result, Belgium's current account soon regained equi-

librium. Once corporate competitiveness was restored, the focus of economic policy shifted to budgetary reform. Spending cuts and tax increases dominated the picture, but the measures taken remained insufficient to restore budgetary equilibrium. By 1988 the public debt had reached 130 percent of GDP.

From the mid-1980s the spectacular plunge in oil prices gave the European economies extra momentum. Belgium participated fully in the expansion, so that employment growth resumed. By 1990 shortages appeared in certain segments of the labor market, thereby causing wage increases to accelerate. At the same time, the Belgian franc appreciated vis-à-vis such currencies as the British pound and the Italian lira. Belgium's loss of competitiveness undoubtedly worsened the impact of the 1993 recession. Again the government had to intervene to impose wage restraint. In addition, painful budgetary measures had to be taken to reduce the government's general borrowing requirement below the 3 percent target agreed to in the Maastricht Treaty. On the one hand, the austerity policy delayed economic recovery, but, on the other hand, it allowed the country to join the European Monetary Union (EMU) in 1999.

Erik Buyst

Social Policy

After the Second World War Belgium developed into a typical Western European welfare state, though with its own particular characteristics. Between 1950 and 1985 Belgium's GNP almost tripled in real value; public social expenditure increased from 10 to 40 percent of GNP; and social security expenditure, including social assistance, doubled between 1970 and 1975.

The welfare system developed gradually during the postwar period and was supported by a steadily growing economy. This process peaked at the beginning of the 1970s. After 1975 economic growth decreased and unemployment increased. Social expenditure, despite the decrease in economic growth, declined only moderately during the 1980s.

In general, the growth of social expenditure in Belgium represents a trend visible in other Western European countries. Participation in the labor force has grown steadily (82 percent in 1994), with a parallel increase in social insurance benefits (unemployment, disability, retirement). Following an extension of the years of schooling, expenses for education and family allowances increased. The aging of the population and the increase in early retirement raised spending for benefits to the elderly. An aging population, higher standard of living, together with great advances in medical technology increased health insurance expenditures dramatically. Public policy also aimed at constant improvement of social protection by extension of the population covered and by heightening the benefit standards. All these factors caused an almost uncontrollable growth of the welfare state, creating problems with respect to the budget and social security.

Except for the period of sharp political and ideological conflict immediately after the Second World War, the politics of social policy in Belgium has been characterized by compromise. Belgian politics almost always functioned through coalition governments (Christian Democrats together with Social Democrats or Liberals). Moreover, Christian Democracy itself may be considered as a sort of coalition, because it contains, in addition to the political party, several social organizations that take action, partly autonomously, partly by means of the party. With respect to social policy these social organizations, because of their role within Belgium's compartmentalized ("pillarized") institutional system and their involvement in the social security administration, play a more important role than do political parties. In such a complex situation the necessity of consensus is obvious, and the role of Belgian governments, except during periods of economic crisis, has been more that of follower than leader.

Within the context of the transformation of Belgium from a unitary toward a federal state in the 1980s, social security and labor relations remained a federal competence; competencies with respect to education, social housing, and social work were transferred to the respective Flemish and to the French communities.

Belgium has an extensive system of councils for advice and coordination at the national, sectoral, and local levels. In the advisory enterprise councils, employee representatives are elected every four years on lists selected by the trade unions. The rate of trade union membership is approximately 70 percent. Coordination between the employers' organization and trade unions has resulted since 1960, with an interruption in the period of economic crisis between 1977 and 1986, in national agreements. There is a very extensive system of labor legislation.

Belgium has a compulsory social security system based on the principles of social insurance (the so-called Bismarckian model). This means that there is proportionality among employment, contributions paid, and benefits received. There are three separate professional systems (for private-sector employees, self-employed workers, and civil servants) and a residual system of social assistance benefits. Replacement incomes (for labor income lost because of sickness, unemployment, or old age) equal a certain percentage of earnings and thus guarantee maintenance of existing standards of living within specified limits. The

pension system is based on pay-as-you-go financing. Compensatory benefits are flat-rate payments compensating for medical care and parenthood expenses. A fixed allowance per child is provided. Medical care expenses are largely reimbursed. In Belgium medical care is free and relations among physicians, hospitals, and health insurance agencies are regulated by conventions.

For employees there are seven different social security schemes: pensions, health-care allowances, sickness and disability benefits, unemployment benefits, child allowances, compensation for employment-related accidents, and compensation for occupational diseases. Only four schemes exist for the self-employed: pensions, health-care allowances, disability benefits, and child allowances. Permanently appointed civil servants are covered for old age and disability pensions and for child allowances. Their health-care coverage is equivalent to that of wage earners in general.

The social insurance schemes are financed through contributions by employers, employees, and self-employed individuals. In addition there are state subsidies, in 1993 amounting to 18 percent. The management of the social security institutions is in the hands of the organizations of employees and employers (the so-called social partners) and the self-employed. They also participate in decision making. Depending on the case, social security payments are made by powerful autonomous social organizations such as trade unions (unemployment benefits) and health insurance agencies (health-care and disability benefits). Social assistance benefits, which provide only a safety net and are means-tested, are financed entirely by the state. There are four different types: guaranteed income for the elderly who have a pension below the guaranteed income or no pension at all; for the handicapped; for other persons; and the guaranteed child allowance.

The actual social security system for employees has been established by the decree-law of December 28, 1944. It was based on the so-called Pact of Social Solidarity, developed clandestinely during the Second World War by a small number of employers and employees' representatives. This pact did not follow the Beveridge model, a comprehensive system of social insurance administered by the state, but elaborated the system of voluntary insurance developed before the war. The main features of this social security decree-law were as follows: all elements of social security coverage were compulsory; one single agency, the National Office for Social Security, collected the contributions of employers and employees; and existing private organizations (trade unions, mutual insurance funds, family allowance funds) were maintained and coordinated through a national office. These national offices were self-governed by an equal representation of employers and employees. The spirit of this social pact dominated the social security system during the whole period of growth of the welfare system up to 1975. The main power for social matters was placed in the hands of the social partners, making the trade unions and the health insurance agencies the most important and powerful actors in the administration of social policies. An extensive socialization of national income went hand in hand with the maintenance of free enterprise and free choice by citizens. Thus, the Belgian welfare system is an optimal combination of freedom and solidarity.

Since 1944 the structure of the system has been maintained, although with a gradual extension of coverage and a permanent growth of the amounts (and of the replacement ratios) of benefits, especially during the golden sixties. Social security was extended to the self-employed in 1967. In the mid-1970s the means-tested guaranteed income schemes were created as ultimate safety nets.

Belgian social security policy has undergone significant evolution. In the period of social security expansion, a forward consensus resulted in an enormous quantitative growth without fundamental structural changes. This consensus flourished in a climate of economic growth, and policy was determined mainly by the social organizations, consecutive governments restricting their roles to enforcement. From 1975 on, however, the signs of the forthcoming crisis were becoming obvious. Social security became caught between decreasing revenues and increasing expenditure. In the public debate in Belgium as well as in other Western European countries, expenditure restraint was the central issue. Furthermore, financing social security by means of wage-related contributions, which stimulated labor-saving investments and consequently was responsible for high unemployment, was criticized. In the absence of consensus among the social partners, a government policy of moderation was made possible by means of special powers authorized by parliament in 1982, 1983, and 1986. Although the basic principles of the system remained intact, social security was significantly eventually reformed. On the revenue side the state subsidy was decreased. Expenditure was constrained by weakening the (automatic) linkage between benefits and prices, by increasing selectivity by means of adapting benefits to household composition. Another kind of selectivity was that benefit cuts were not applied to low-income categories.

In contrast to other countries, Belgian social security continued to provide subsistence security. Research of the European Centre for Social Welfare Policy and Research, a U.N.-affiliated research center based in Vienna, has demonstrated that the number of poor in Belgium has not increased; this is also the outcome of statistical analyses of Eurostat, the statistical office of the European Union. This can be attributed to the quality of the Belgian welfare state and to the crisis management of Belgian governments at the time.

The government announced the need for a fundamental readjustment of the social security system in 1996. At the time of writing, no consensus (either among political parties or among social partners) had been reached about this future reform.

In Belgium education is provided by public authorities or, most of all, by mainly Catholic private organizations. The relationship between the different "school networks" has been a major political issue in Belgian history. The so-called school war (1954–58) was brought to an end in 1958 by the School Pact, an agreement among the three main political parties (Christian Democrats, Socialists, and Liberals). It introduced an equitable distribution of state grants for education among all kinds of approved schools. Parents are free to choose between state and private schools for their children; in 1989–90, 74 percent of Flemish and 53 percent of French-speaking students on secondary level attended Catholic schools.

The Belgian educational system is of high quality but expensive for the state. The level of schooling is the highest of the European Community. In 1984, 13 percent of eighteen-year-olds attended universities and 40 percent attended nonuniversity schools of higher education. The democratization of the educational system has gone very far; everyone who wants to study can do so without financial barriers. However, because of sociocultural differences in aspirations, there are still large social differences in participation in these educational opportunities.

In Belgium, housing policy is oriented toward private ownership of middle-sized dwellings, especially for moderate- and low-income households. The 1948 De Taeye Act introduced three kinds of subsidies for promoting home ownership: building premiums for persons building their own home, purchase premiums for private individuals buying a dwelling built by a social housing society, and credit facilities such as low-interest mortgages and fiscal advantages. These three provisions are available only to those under certain income ceilings, depending on type of dwelling and maximum taxable income. Psychologically, ownership of a family home is important for the great majority of Belgians. Since World War II half of all new buildings have been directly subsidized.

A particular characteristic of this policy was that the initiative to build or to buy houses was not taken by government but by individuals or local societies for social housing construction. The latter often were connected with municipalities or social organizations; they also build rental houses. This is a particular difference between Belgian housing policy and the housing policies of neighboring countries. The difference is fourfold: first, initiative does not lie with government but with families and local societies; second, home ownership is the primary policy goal; third, attention is given almost exclusively to new building; fourth, there is an absence of housing benefits for tenants. The consequences of this policy have been far-reaching: a high rate of home ownership (which leads to a considerable spread of property, but also to financial security at old age); a modest housing shortage in the postwar period (contrasting with the situation in neighboring countries); and housing of high quality. Individual home ownership has, to a considerable extent, determined the outlook of the Belgian landscape: connected houses, one-street villages, the dispersion of buildings outside of towns, and loss of open space. The stimulation of home ownership has resulted in a strong increase of the share of people who own their home from about 50 percent in 1961 to more than 65 percent in 1991. This is by far the largest proportion of owner-occupied dwellings in the whole of Europe. Of the total stock of rental houses, approximately 15 percent, or 5.2 percent of all houses, are let by public societies. In comparison with other Western European countries, the intervention of government in the housing market is limited; in most countries the common share of private and social rental housing is considerably higher, and the social housing sector makes up from half to three-quarters of rented houses.

This traditional policy diminished at the end of the seventies and almost ceased in the eighties because of the decreased dynamism of local housing societies, owing to decreased credits and financial pressure as a result of debts from the past; increased costs of building, building grounds, and mortgages; and increasing preference for rented housing among the younger generation. The new policy emphasizes renovation, rented housing, and renewal of inner cities, especially of deprived neighborhoods.

BIBLIOGRAPHY

Berghman, J., and B. Cantillon. *The European Face of Social Security: Essays in Honour of Herman Deleeck.* Aldershot: Avebury, 1993.

Boudart, M., ed. *Modern Belgium.* Palo Alto, Calif.: 1990.

Deleeck, H. "The Adequacy of Social Security in Belgium, 1976–1985." *Journal of Social Policy* (1989): 91–117.

Dewachter, W., and E. Clijsters. "Belgium: Political Stability Despite Coalition Crisis," in E. Browne and J. Dreijmanis, eds. *Government Coalitions in Western Democracies.* New York: Longman, 1982.

Fitzmaurice, J. *The Politics of Belgium: Crisis and Compromise in a Plural Society.* London: Hurst, 1983.

Lorwin, V. "Labor Unions and Political Parties in Belgium." *Industrial and Labor Relations Review* 2 (1975): 243–63.

Pieters, D. *Introduction into the Social Security Law of the Member States of the European Community.* Antwerp, Belgium: Maklu, 1993.

Van den Brande, A. "Neo-corporatism and Functional-Integral Power in Belgium," in I. Scholten, ed. *Political Stability and Neo-corporatism: Corporatist Integration and Social Ceavages in Western Europe.* London: Sage, 1987.

Herman Deleeck

Catholicism

The constitution of Belgium guarantees religious freedom and the independence of churches and religious groups. The state pays the salaries of the parish clergy and those ministers whom it recognizes. The Social Christian Party, although a nonconfessional party of Christian inspiration, defends the perspective and interests of Roman Catholics. It won 45 percent of the vote in 1946. In 1995, however, only 24.9 percent voted for the two parties spawned by the old Belgian-wide party. The Flemish branch, the Christian Peoples Party (Christelijk Volkspartij), received 17.2 percent and the Waloon, Christian Social Party (Parti social chrétien), 7.7 percent.

Catholicism is much more vigorous in Flanders than in the capital, Brussels, which is largely francophone and has been for some time dominated by the Liberal Party, and in Wallonia, which was transformed by nineteenth-century industrialization, and where the Socialist Party dominates. In 1947, when Belgium had a population of 8,512,195, there were 9,895 secular priests, 12,725 members of male religious orders, and 49,624 nuns. After the 1960s these numbers diminished rapidly. In 1994, with 10,130,574 inhabitants, of whom approximately 80 percent were of Roman Catholic background, there were only 5,848 diocesan priests, 5,166 male religious, and 19,800 nuns. The average age in all these categories had risen considerably. Since the Second Vatican Council in the 1960s, approximately 450 permanent deacons have been ordained to fulfill various religious functions.

Catholic education, with 5,196 institutions in 1991, is thoroughly developed, extending from elementary schools to universities. There are also religion courses in public schools. The struggle between Catholics, promoters of free religious schools, and anticlericals, defenders of education organized by public authorities, has been intense since the nineteenth century. After World War II the struggle centered on financing secondary education. It ended with a compromise between the principal parties. Complementing other laws, the Pacte scolaire (Educational Compact) of 1958 provides basic financing by the state of all educational institutions, public or private. This development permitted an opening of the Liberal Party to Catholics, contrary to the Socialist Party, where anticlericalism remained dominant. Tensions shifted toward linguistic and community problems between Flemish and francophones. These led in 1968 to the expulsion of the francophone section of the Catholic University of Louvain and in 1993 to the federalization of the country. To avoid the control of one single ideological group over the cultural life of a region, a Cultural Pact, on the model of the Educational Compact, was signed by the parties in 1972.

Christian social charitable institutions, such as hospitals and homes for the aged, flourish with 1,057 in 1994. The system of social security established in 1944 sustains them. The cleavage among Catholics, secularists, and socialists is also perpetuated in social organizations, unions, and benevolent associations.

If the great movements of Catholic Action formed before 1940 had lost their vitality, the postwar period witnessed a religious renewal: A renaissance in theological studies; a growth in Bible reading inspired among other things by the new French translation of the Bible published by the Abbey of Maredsous at Denée, Belgium; liturgical innovations; updating of the catechism, in which the international Institute Lumen Vitae played an important role; and ecumenical overtures symbolized by the influence of the monastery of Chevetogne. Missionary endeavors flourished into the 1960s with 8,411 male and female missionaries taking their vows in 1964. In 1953 a Latin American College was created at Louvain to prepare priests, religious, and laypeople to work in South and Central America.

Social change, the shock of the Vatican Council, and the alienation and radicalization of students provoked deep confusion. Sunday Mass attendance, stood at 50 percent of the population in 1950 (60 percent in Flanders and 40 percent in Wallonia) fell to 21 percent in 1987 (27 percent in Flanders, 17 percent in Wallonia, and 10 percent in Brussels). At the same time church funerals remained high, at 87 percent of funerals in 1987. Church marriages were lower, at 67 percent of marriages, partly because of divorce and remarriage. Baptisms were also lower: 77 percent of infants, in part because of the birth of numerous infants to Muslim immigrants.

Still strong, the various Christian institutions, schools, and hospitals, in which the majority of the personnel was composed of priests and religious, have undergone an internal secularization. Since *Humanae vitae*, Pope Paul VI's 1968 encyclical that condemned artificial contraception, the majority of Catholics have distanced themselves from the moral directives of the hierarchy. Many Catholics have become more confused with regard to official doctrine. By contrast, a sizable number of laypeople have taken a more active part in the life of the church. After years of progressive social-political engagement on the part of an active minority, there has been a growth of the charismatic movement and a renewed interest in traditional Catholicism.

BIBLIOGRAPHY
Aubert, Roger. *150 ans de vie des Eglises, 1830–1980.* Brussels: P. Legrain, 1980.
Jadoulle, J. L. "Les Visages de l'Église en Belgique a la veille du Concile Vatican II," in *Vatican II et les Belges,* Ed. by Cl. Soetens. Louvain-la-Neuve: ARCA, 1996.
André Tihon
(Tr. B. Cook)

Civil Society and Pressure Groups

Pressure groups ("pillars") are an essential part of civil society in Belgium. Especially in Flanders, pressure groups constitute the basis of compartmentalization ("pillarization") and of the neocorporatist socioeconomic order. "Pillarization," or *verzuiling,* refers to the social organizations and subcultures of the various political minorities. The pressure groups are active in the political, socioeconomic, as well as cultural field and exercise their activities in a multitude of ways. Not only do they meet government officials in advisory bodies, but sometimes they also manage semipublic funds. Hundreds of those bodies exist. Some are extremely important and even overshadow the parliament. The most powerful pressure groups also have a direct impact on government policy. Since 1968 collective agreements concluded in the National Labor Council between employers' organizations and trade unions may be made compulsory by decree law. However, evaluation of the political impact of the pressure groups is subject to debate. Some consider them detrimental to parliamentary democracy; others see them as democratic representatives defending the real interests of specific constituencies.

Trade unions and employer organizations are the best-known social and professional pressure groups. Belgium has one of the highest unionization rates of the world, exceded only by the Scandinavian countries. Since the 1950s ACV/CSC the General Christian Trade Union Confederation (Algemeen Christelijk Vakverbond van België/Confédération des Syndicats Chrétiens de Belgique-ACV/CSC) outnumbers its socialist competitor the General Federation of Belgian Workers (Algemeen Belgisch Vakverbon/Fédération Générale du Travail de Belgique-ABVV/FGTB) ABVV/FGTB. There is also a smaller liberal trade union, an organization for middle management, and minor specialized unions. Belgian trade unions owe their strength mainly to the extensive services they provide. They pay out unemployment benefits and are omnipresent at all levels of the economy, where they are empowered to perform important social functions, even within the companies themselves.

The most representative employers' organization is the Federation of Belgian Enterprises (VBO/FEB), which resulted from the fusion in 1973 of the former Federation of Belgian Industry, founded in 1946, and the Belgian Federation of Non-Industrial Companies, constituted in 1953. There are also regional employers' associations in Flanders, Wallonia, and Brussels, of which the Flemish Economic Federation (VEV), founded in 1926, is not only the oldest but by far the most important. However, only the VBO/FEB is authorized to conclude collective agreements.

Among other representative social organizations, only the Farmers League (Boerenbond) holds a position of power comparable to that of the social partners. In fact, the Boerenbond is a conglomerate providing extensive services, including banking and insurance. In Flanders, it holds a virtual monopoly as representative of farming and the agricultural industry.

The trade unions are also part of larger entities. In particular the Christian labor movement, to which the ACV/CSC belongs, has developed considerable cooperatives in banking, insurance, social housing, and other services. The socialist movement in the postwar era has been less successful in this respect. The organization and representation of the middle class and small companies has remained limited and is divided between Catholics and nonsectarian organizations.

Health insurance funds, which organize the health insurance scheme, are important pressure groups. There are five: the Christian and the Socialist health insurance funds together represent approximately 80 percent of all obligatorily insured employees; the nonsectarian, professional, and Flemish funds represent the remaining 20 percent. Together with the two medical doctors' professional associations and the organizations of care institutions, of which an overwhelming majority belongs to the Catholic

interest group or pillar, the health insurance funds largely determine social policy.

Even in the educational and cultural fields, free associations play an important role as pressure groups. Since 1970 the Culture Pact Act (1973) has guaranteed representation to and state support of all social and ideological currents, in particular the Catholic "minority" in Wallonia and non-Catholics in Flanders, where Catholic sociocultural organizations dominate. By 1995 seven umbrella organizations were legally recognized for that purpose. Apart from public education there is also a free, subsidized educational scheme, mainly organized by Catholics, the National Secretariat of Catholic Education, which is one of the country's major pressure groups.

BIBLIOGRAPHY

Dewachter, Wilfried. *Besluitvorming in politiek België,* 2d ed. Leuven-Amersfoort: Acco, 1995.

Van den Brande, August. "Neo-Corporatism and Functional-Integral Power in Belgium," in Ilya Scholte, ed. *Political Stability and Neo-Corporatism: Corporatist Integration and Societal Cleavages in Western Europe.* London: Sage, 1987, 95–119.

Patrick Pasture

Education

As a result of the third revision of the Belgian constitution in 1988, authority in educational matters, with a few exceptions, was transferred on January 1, 1989, to the Dutch-, French-, and German-speaking communities. In article 17 of the first Belgian constitution (1831), freedom of education was already defined. Consequently, schools can be established without permission of the authorities. Nevertheless, if schools want to present officially acknowledged certificates and diplomas be granted by the community, they must observe legal stipulations and rules. Parents also have freedom of choice regarding the type of education or the school they select for their children.

Educational facilities organized by the public authorities (state, provincial, and local) are known as "official schools." They are obliged to provide a "neutral" education, which must respect parents' philosophical or religious opinions. Educational facilities organized by private individuals or by associations are known as "free schools." These are state-aided; most are based on religion, with Roman Catholic schools being by far the most numerous.

Compulsory school attendance from ages six to fourteen was first introduced in 1914 and was extended to twelve years, from the age of six to eighteen, in 1983. Compulsory schooling is full-time until the age of fifteen or sixteen and includes six years of primary education and at least the first two years of secondary education. This is followed by compulsory part-time attendance, or by training that fulfills compulsory attendance requirements. Children may also be taught at home if the teaching satisfies the requirements set by the state.

Traditionally, there are three levels of education: elementary, secondary, and higher. There is also special education for mentally or physically handicapped children, from the age of two and a half, and for adolescents until twenty-one years of age who require special care, as well as adult education, which serves approximately 15 percent of the working population. In the field of vocational guidance and counseling, an important part is played by psycho-medical-social centers.

Elementary education consists of nursery school and primary school. Though these levels are not linked structurally, an attempt is made to achieve a smooth transition between them. Nursery school is provided for children from the age of two and a half years to six. This education is not compulsory but it is free. Most Belgian children attend nursery school. Primary education takes six years, attended by children of the six-to-twelve age group. After completing the sixth year, the pupil is granted a primary education certificate. There is mostly a year-class system, in which a teacher or class tutor leads the activities. A strongly individual approach is opted for here to fully develop the child's personality.

Secondary education is provided for youngsters aged twelve to eighteen, consisting of six years. Belgian secondary education has gone through many stages during the last twenty years. After the Second World War, some fairly symbolic changes were introduced to meet new social, industrial, and scientific requirements. But the 1960s were even more creative and effective, especially in producing a thorough reform of secondary education in both state and private schools. In 1971, Belgium passed a law concerning a more integrated, comprehensive system. The traditional division of secondary education into general academic, technical, artistic, and vocational (more practical and employment-oriented) schools, each leading to different career possibilities, was abolished in the "official" system. Justification for this was provided by new educational, social, and psychological theories unanimously supporting the three main objectives of comprehensive education: a broad, general, common basic education; postponement of the crucial choice of studies to a later age; and elimination of sociocultural discrimination.

Because of Belgium's federal structure, there are considerable differences both in the organization and in the form of secondary schooling, between the autonomous communities as well as between the networks of the "free," or subsidized schools and the "official" education system. In the big network of Catholic schools, a traditional type of secondary education has always functioned side by side with the new comprehensive type, which still continues in Wallonia and lasted in Flanders until 1989. In the well-organized Flemish free schools, the two competing systems have reached a compromise. Since 1989 a new and unified structure for secondary education has been implemented in the official schools as well as in the subsidized system.

Higher education consists of university education (a minimum of four years of study) and short-term (three years of study) and long-term (four or five years of study) "higher nonuniversity education." To gain access to higher education, a student must possess a higher secondary education diploma, received upon completion of full secondary education or of a seventh year in vocational education. A numerus clausus, or excluding quota, to limit the numbers of students allowed to major in a particular discipline, does not exist. Only for engineering science is there a special entrance examination.

Since the early 1990s, the educational policy of the autonomous communities has been characterized by three fundamental principles: realizing more equal financing of the different educational networks, enhancing and consolidating the local autonomy of schools, and introducing the "quality control" concept and improving educational achievement.

The new federal structure, one of the consequences of the cultural and language problems typical of the country, has brought about different education systems, making Belgium an interesting field of comparative educational research.

BIBLIOGRAPHY

Education in Belgium: The Diverging Paths. OECD: Review of National Policies for Education. Brussels: The Ministry of Education, 1992.

OCDE. *Examens des politiques nationales d'éducation: Belgique.* Paris: OCDE, 1993.

Wielemans, Willy. *Het onderwijs in België.* Leuven/Apeldoorn: Garant/Open Universiteit Heerlen, 1994.

Willy Wielemans

Benediktsson, Bjarni (1908–70)

Icelandic politician and legal scholar. Bjarni Benediktsson studied law in Reykjavík and Berlin from 1926 to 1932, and taught law at the University of Iceland from 1932 to 1940. He sat in the city council of Reykjavík from 1934 to 1942, serving as mayor of the capital from 1940 to 1947. Benediktsson represented the city of Reykjavík in parliament for the Independence Party (center-conservative party) from 1942 to 1946, and from 1949 until his death in 1970. Selected to his first ministerial post in 1947, Benediktsson served as minister of foreign affairs and of justice from 1947 to 1949 and again from 1950 to 1953, as minister of foreign affairs and of education from 1949 to 1950 and from 1953 to 1956, as minister of justice, ecclesiastical affairs, industry, and health from 1959 to 1963, and finally, as prime minister from 1963 to 1970. At the time of his death in 1970, he had led the so-called Reconstruction Government of the Independence Party and the Social Democratic Party continuously for almost seven years, a record in Iceland.

Benediktsson was one of the most influential politicians in Iceland in the post–World War II era, especially in foreign affairs. Thus, in addition to leading the largest political party in Iceland for a number of years, he was instrumental in deciding that Iceland would be a founding member of NATO, forming a close cooperation with the United States and its Western allies during the Cold War. His economic and social views were in accordance with the traditions of the Independence Party, with strong emphasis on laissez-faire economics in theory but supporting an extensive system of welfare programs and widespread state intervention in the economy in practice.

Gudmundur Halfdanarson

Beneš, Edvard (1884–1948)

Founder of the Czechoslovak state, president of Czechoslovakia from 1935 to 1938, founder of the Czechoslovak National Committee in 1939, and president again to 1948. Edvard Beneš was born in Kožlany, Bohemia, on May 28, 1884. He studied at Prague, Paris, and Dijon. After earning a doctorate in law in 1908, he taught at the Czech University in Prague. He was influenced by the nationalism of his mentor, Tomáš Masaryk. Beneš joined Masaryk and Slovak Milan Štefánik in the establishment of a Czechoslovak provisional government in Paris on October 14, 1918. He served as foreign minister of the new Czechoslovak state from 1918 to 1935, representing it at the Paris Peace Conference in 1919. Beneš bolstered the Little Entente treaty linking Czechoslovakia to Romania, Yugoslavia, and, eventually, France by negotiating a mutual assistance pact with the USSR in 1935.

Following the resignation of Masaryk in 1935, Beneš was elected president of Czechoslovakia. Following the September 1938 occupation of the Sudetenland by Germany and the loss of Teschen to Poland, Beneš resigned

on October 5, 1938, and went into exile. When war erupted in September 1939 Beneš organized the Czechoslovak National Committee in Paris. From London after 1940 he attempted to guarantee the postwar independence of Czechoslovakia. Beneš became convinced, however, that Czechoslovakia had no alternative but to establish friendly relations with the USSR. In December 1943 he traveled to Moscow to confer with Stalin and sign a twenty-year treaty of friendship. In March 1945 he again conferred with Stalin in Moscow. With the blessing of the Soviets a provisional government was set up on Czechoslovak soil at Kosice on April 3. Beneš was president and Zdenek Fierlinger, the pro-Soviet head of the Social Democrats, became prime minister. Beneš returned to Prague on May 16, five days after the city had been liberated by Soviet Marshal Ivan Konev.

Following the success of the Communists in the 1946 election, Beneš appointed the leader of the Czechoslovak Communist Party, Klement Gottwald, to head a coalition government. When twelve democratic ministers withdrew from the government in February 1948 in an effort to thwart the Communists, Gottwald pressured Beneš, who had been enfeebled by two strokes in 1947, to accept their resignations and to allow him to reconstitute the government. Beneš was pressed by Communist-dominated groups, and the Communist-led militia began arming sympathetic factory workers. Feeling powerless in the face of support for the Communists, their willingness to use force, and their external support, Beneš acquiesced on February 25. He appointed Gottwald to head a new government of Communists and left-wing Social Democrats led by fellow traveler Fierlinger. The success of the Communists and the death of his friend Jan Masaryk, the foreign minister, two weeks later, coupled with his deteriorating health, led Beneš, who was unwilling to assent to the new Communist-authored constitution, to resign on June 7, 1948. He died on September 3, 1948.

Bernard Cook

SEE ALSO Czechoslovakia; Fierlinger, Zdeněk; Gottwald, Klement; Masaryk, Jan

Benn, Tony (1925–)

Labour Party member of Parliament and cabinet minister of Great Britain from 1964 to 1970 and from 1974 to 1979. After the 1979 general election defeat, Tony Benn became a focus of left-wing agitation within the Labour Party, unsuccessfully running as candidate for the leadership and deputy leadership. Subsequently, he was a backbench critic of the reformist, "modernizing" movement within the party.

Benn's initial attempts to enter the House of Commons were thwarted by his inherited peerage. He was eventually permitted to disclaim the title of Vincount Stansgate, and went on to represent Bristol South-East, and from 1984, Chesterfield. A long-standing member of the Labour Party's National Executive Committee, Benn also reached high office in government. He was postmaster general from 1964 to 1966, minister of technology from 1966 to 1970, also acting as minister of power. He was largely responsible for undertaking negotiations with international oil companies over Britain's newfound oil, the outcome sometimes being unfavorably compared with the greater success of Norway in similar negotiations. In the Labour Party's 1974–79 period in power, Benn again held cabinet office as secretary of state for industry, post, telecommunications, and energy.

In opposition in the 1980s, the party endured a prolonged period of internal strife. Benn was the focus of much left-wing activity in this period, arguing for a radical, socialist platform. However, this tendency was eventually defeated by the modernizers. As a result, Benn became increasingly marginalized within the parliamentary party.

Benn represents a particular strain in the labour movement, basing his approach on a mix of native ideas inherited from seventeenth-century radicals and nineteenth-century Chartists, along with Marxist elements. His diaries provide useful insight into British politics since 1945 and Benn's own contribution to the period.

BIBLIOGRAPHY

Adams, Jad. *Tony Benn: A Biography.* London: Macmillan, 1992.

Benn, Tony. *Diaries.* 5 Vols. London: Hutchinson, 1987–92.

Benn, Tony, and Ruth Winstone. *Years of Hope: Diaries, Letters and Papers, 1940–1962.* London: Hutchinson, 1994.

Stephen M. Cullen

Beran, Josef (1888–1969)

Archbishop of Prague. In 1946 Josef Beran was consecrated the Roman Catholic archbishop of Prague, the fifty-eighth successor to St. Adalbert (Vojtech), the first Czech bishop of Prague. After the Communists came to power in 1948, they banned public church ceremonies. In 1949 Beran left St. Vitus Cathedral in Prague when his Mass was forcibly halted. He was interned by the Czechoslovak Communist authorities from 1949 to 1963, named a cardinal in 1965, and allowed to travel to Rome to accept his appointment. But once in Rome, Beran was forbidden by the Czech government to return to Czechoslovakia and his diocese. To replace the exiled Beran, František Tomášek, auxiliary bishop of Olomouc, who was allowed to attend the Second Vatican Council, was appointed apostolic administrator of the Prague diocese. In December 1977 the pope publicly gave Tomášek the full title of resident archbishop.

Bernard Cook

SEE ALSO Czechoslovakia; Tomášek, František

Bérégovoy, Pierre (1925–93)

Prime minister of France from April 1992 to March 1993. Pierre Bérégovoy was born into a leftist working-class family on December 23, 1925, in Déville-les-Rouen, seventy miles northwest of Paris. His father, a factory worker, had emigrated to France from the Ukraine after the Russian Revolution of 1917. In 1941 Bérégovoy was forced to leave school to help support his family. He worked first as a machinist in a textile factory and then for the railroad as a ticket seller in Rouen. During World War II he was associated with the Resistance. Following the war he was employed by the French national gas company as a sales representative. During his thirty-one years with Gaz de France, he rose through the ranks to become the executive director for economic and commercial affairs. During this period he attended the Labor Institute at the law school of the University of Strasbourg and received a diploma in scientific management.

Following World War II Bérégovoy joined the Socialist Party (Section Française de l'International Ouvrière, SFIO), and Pierre Mendès-France became his mentor. In 1958, in opposition to the Algerian War, Bérégovoy left the SFIO and founded with others the Autonomous Socialist Party (PSA). In 1960 the PSA merged with another socialist group to form the Unified Socialist Party (PSU). Bérégovoy was its secretary from 1963 to 1967, abandoning the PSU in 1967 to form the Modern Socialism Club, one of the groups attempting to build a reinvigorated, non-Communist left. He joined the reorganized Socialist Party in 1969 and became a member of its executive committee. He was the party's national secretary for social affairs from 1973 to 1975, and from 1975 to 1981 directed its external affairs, including its difficult relations with the Communist Party. After François Mitterrand's election in 1981, Bérégovoy was appointed secretary-general of the presidential staff and, in June 1982, minister of social affairs. The appointment of Bérégovoy, who immediately implemented such measures as higher social security taxes and copayments for recipients of services to cut costs and balance the budget, signaled a rightward turn for Mitterrand's administration. In 1983 Bérégovoy, with the support of Mitterrand, achieved his first electoral success when he was elected mayor of Nevers, a post he held until his death in 1993. In July 1984 Bérégovoy was appointed minister of finance, virtually the only top-level official in Mitterrand's administration with a working-class background; rather than the product of an elite institute, he was largely self-educated. Despite the misgivings of some, Bérégovoy restored the confidence of the business community in the Socialist administration. He implemented a rather conservative economic policy of cutbacks in government spending and a restrained monetary policy to promote a strong franc. He modernized the Bourse (stock exchange), established the Matif, a futures exchange, and initiated banking deregulation.

The Socialist government was replaced as a result of the 1986 election, but Bérégovoy was elected to parliament from Nevers and became a member of the Socialist Party's national secretariat. In 1988 he directed Mitterrand's successful campaign for reelection, and after the Socialist victory Bérégovoy resumed his post as minister of finance.

In April 2, 1992, Bérégovoy replaced prime minister Édith Cresson, whose brief ministry eroded the popularity of the Socialists. Yet the replacement did not restore their popularity. Bérégovoy and the party were hurt by an economic downturn and rising unemployment. There were also charges of corruption against leading Socialists including Bérégovoy. While minister of finance, Bérégovoy had accepted an interest-free loan from businessman Roger-Patrice Pelat, and was subsequently accused of insider trading. French voters overwhelmingly repudiated the Socialists in the March 21 and 28, 1993, election. On March 29 Mitterrand appointed a conservative ministry under Édouard Balladur. Bérégovoy distraught by the scandal, the electoral defeat, and the failure of Mitterrand to come to his support, shot himself near Nevers on May 1, 1993.

BIBLIOGRAPHY

"Bérégovoy, Pierre." *1993 Current Biography Yearbook.* New York: H. W. Wilson, 1994. 53–56.

Bernard Cook

Bergman, Ernst Ingmar (1918–)

Swedish film, stage, and television director, Ernst Ingmar Bergman is considered one of his country's greatest artists.

He was born on July 14, 1918, in Uppsala, Sweden, son of Erik Bergman, a Lutheran pastor, and Karin Akerblom Bergman, a trained nurse. In 1937 he entered the University of Stockholm, where he ran a youth club theater. In the early 1940s he was appointed assistant director at the Swedish Royal Opera House. In the following years he directed productions at municipal theaters in Hälsingborg, Göteborg, and Malmö. In 1959 he became the youngest director ever appointed to Stockholm's Royal Dramatic Theater, which he headed from 1963 to 1966. While pursuing a career as a stage director Bergman became internationally famous as the producer/director of haunting and searching motion pictures. His film career began in 1944 with the Swedish production of his film script *Torment,* which won the Grand Prix du Cinéma at the Cannes Film Festival in 1946. Between 1947 and 1952 he directed the films *Crisis, Seaport, Three Strange Loves,* and *Monica.* He wrote and directed his first comedy, *Waiting Women,* in 1952. After this he wrote and directed almost all his motion pictures. He also created a troupe of actors with whom he has worked for many years.

In 1950 Bergman produced *Summer Interlude,* which he considered one of his favorite films. However, one of his most popular films and one that helped establish his reputation, was his 1955 *Smiles of a Summer Night,* a rare comedy for him and the basis for the 1973 Stephen Sondheim musical, *A Little Night Music.* Bergman's themes are metaphysical, agonizing examinations of his own inner world or the human predicament, as well as studies in human psychology with the interior life of women a dominant concern. Among his most important works are *The Seventh Seal* (1956), his existential medieval fable; *Wild Strawberries* (1957); *The Silence* (1963); *Persona* (1966); *Cries and Whispers* (1972); and the autobiographical *Fanny and Alexander* (1982), which won four Academy Awards, including one for Bergman's screenplay. In April 1971 he was awarded the prestigious Irving Thalbert Memorial Award.

Bergman's other films include *The Magician* (1956); *The Virgin Spring* (1959); *Through a Glass Darkly* (1961); Mozart's *The Magic Flute* (1975), a tribute to Mozart and his only film musical; *Face to Face* (1976), his masterwork on suicide and on depression; *Autumn Sonata,* his only film with the other famous Swedish import to Hollywood, Ingrid Bergman; *Scenes From a Marriage* (1973), the full-length version of his treatise on matrimony; and *The Faro Document* (1979), Bergman's return to the island of Faro that he first profiled in 1970. Like that of his contemporary Federico Fellini, Bergman's style made each of his films a personal statement.

In 1951 Bergman wrote and directed nine commercials for AB Sunlight for the soap Bris, Sweden's first deodorant soap. He has also directed a number of theatrical productions for television, including Hjalmar Bergman's *Mr. Sleeman's Coming* (1957); *The Venetian* and Olle Hedberg's *Rabies* (both 1958); two by August Strindberg: *Storm Weather* and *First Warning* (both 1960); *A Dream Play* (1963); and Molière's *School for Wives* (1983). Celebrated films such as *Scenes from a Marriage* (1973), *The Magic Flute* (1975), *Face to Face* (1976) and *After the Festival* (1983) were first aired on television.

Bergman's reputation has declined since its peaks in the later 1950s and mid-1960s, partly because he has made only a handful of films. He angrily left Sweden in 1976 after being arrested on tax charges; these were later dropped and the director has gone back to his native land. In recent years Bergman has directed only plays and operas, including *Nora,* his adaptation of Henrik Ibsen's *A Doll's House.* In his theatrical career, he directed about 140 stage productions, including *Cat on a Hot Tin Roof* and *Per Gynt.*

BIBLIOGRAPHY

Bergman, Ingmar. *Bergman on Bergman.* New York: Simon and Schuster, 1975.

———. *Images: My Life in Film.* New York: Arcade, 1990.

———. *The Magic Lantern.* New York: Viking, 1988.

Cohen, Hubert I. *Ingmar Bergman: The Art of Confession.* New York: Twayne, 1994.

Cowie, Peter. *Ingmar Bergman: A Critical Biography.* New York: Scribner, 1982.

Gado, Frank. *The Passion of Ingmar Bergman.* Durham, N.C.: Duke University Press, 1986.

Kaminsky, Stuart M., ed. *Ingmar Bergman: Essays in Criticism.* London: Oxford University Press, 1975.

Steene, Birgitta. *Ingmar Bergman: A Guide to Reference and Resources.* Boston, Mass.: G.K. Hall, 1987.

Martin J. Manning

Beria, Lavrenty (1899–1953)

One of Joseph Stalin's top deputies. Lavrenty Beria, who played a central role in the Stalinist terror as chief of the People's Commissariat of Internal Affairs (NKVD), also achieved full membership in the Politburo and became the deputy chairman of the Council of Ministers. After Stalin's death in 1953, Beria was arrested and shot.

Born in the Georgian village of Merkheuli in March 1899 to a poor peasant family of Georgia's Mingrelian ethnic minority, Beria eventually rose to become one of the most powerful figures in the Stalin-era USSR. Having received his early education in the town of Sukhumi, Beria enrolled in the Baku Polytechnical School for Mechanical Construction in 1915 and graduated in 1919. Beria married Nina Gegechkori in 1921. The couple had one son, Sergo, in 1924.

Beria's political career began in 1915, when students in Baku formed an illegal Marxist study and agitation organization. Beria became a Bolshevik in March 1917. His conscription into the Russian army provided additional avenues for revolutionary activity. On his return to Baku in 1918, he received an appointment to the secretariat of the Bolshevik-controlled Baku Soviet. The chaos of civil war brought with it further opportunities for Beria. His assignments as a Bolshevik mole within the rival nationalist (Musavat) government of Azerbaijhan and as an underground agitator in Menshevik-controlled Georgia were important stepping-stones into the world of police and intelligence work.

After the Bolshevik victory and the incorporation of Transcaucasia into the USSR, Beria served in both the Azerbaijhani and Georgian Chekas (secret police). Between 1922 and 1934 he ascended through the ranks of the Soviet secret police in Transcaucasia, obtaining the top post within the Transcaucasian State Political Administration (successor to the Cheka) in 1931. Using his powers as a top Chekist to attack potential political rivals, Beria also rose rapidly within the Communist Party. Becoming a powerful regional figure, he gained the top post in the Georgian Soviet Socialist Republic in 1934.

Beria's rise to national prominence began with contributions to the growing cult of personality of surrounding Soviet leader Stalin. Beria ordered the lavish restoration of Stalin's birthplace in the Georgian town of Gori and produced a false version of the history of Georgian Bolshevism, *On the History of the Bolshevik Organizations in Transcaucasia* (1935), that enlarged Stalin's role in revolutionary activities.

The great purges of the 1930s provided another opportunity for advancement. Beria moved to Moscow in 1938 and assumed the number two position in the hierarchy of the all-Union NKVD. Promotion to the top post at the NKVD followed later that year when Beria purged his superior, Nikolay Yezhov on Stalin's orders. Quickly employing his new power to become one of the most feared men in the USSR, Beria played a particularly brutal role in the purging of the Soviet military and of the NKVD itself. Nikita Khrushchev would later allege that Beria also used his position to rape and otherwise molest hundreds of young women and girls.

By the end of 1941 Beria had achieved membership in both the Council of People's Commissars and the Politburo. During World War II he served on the State Defense Council, his primary area of responsibility being counterintelligence. In the aftermath of the war, Beria played a leading role in running the USSR's vast labor camp system, as well as the Soviet atomic bomb project; he also helped supervise a massive transfer of technology from defeated Germany that enhanced the capabilities of the USSR's military-industrial complex. Having proved himself to be a highly capable if brutal administrator, Beria used his ever-increasing influence to instigate the elimination of a potential rival, famed wartime economic planner Nikolay Voznesensky, in the 1948 purge known as the Leningrad Affair.

Before Stalin's death in 1953, somewhat inconclusive signs of tension between Stalin and his top deputy have prompted certain scholars to conclude that Beria might have somehow plotted to speed the ailing dictator's end. Firm evidence for such a conclusion is still lacking, and Beria's behavior at Stalin's deathbed seems to indicate fear and uncertainty as opposed to foreknowledge. In any case, Beria did not long outlive Stalin. Hated by the top military leadership and seen by Stalin's other surviving political deputies as a mortal threat, Beria attempted but failed to redefine himself through innovative and "liberal" foreign and domestic policy proposals. Personifying the worst aspects of Stalinism, Beria's arrest, secret trial, and execution in 1953 can be seen as having marked the true end of the Stalin era in the USSR.

BIBLIOGRAPHY

Avtorkhanov, Abdurakhman. *Zagadka smerti Stalina zagovor Beriia.* Frankfurt: Posev, 1976.
Holloway, David. *Stalin and the Bomb: The Soviet Union and Atomic Energy, 1939–1956.* New Haven: Yale University Press, 1994.
Knight, Amy. *Beria: Stalin's First Lieutenant.* Princeton: Princeton University Press, 1993.
Khrushchev, Nikita. *Khrushchev Remembers.* Vol. 1. Tr. and ed. by Strobe Talbott. Boston: Little, Brown, 1970; Vol. 2. *The Last Testament.* Tr. and ed. by Strobe Talbott. Boston: Little, Brown, 1974.
Stickle, D. M., ed. *The Beria Affair: The Secret Transcripts of the Meetings Signaling the End of Stalinism.* Tr. by Jeanne Farrow. Comack, N.Y.: Nova Science, 1992.
Mark Orsag

Berisha, Sali (1944–)

Post-Communist political leader in Albania. Sali Berisha was born into a Muslim family in Tropoja in the northeast region of Albania. He completed his university education as a cardiologist in Tirana in 1967. In 1978 he pursued postgraduate studies in Paris on a UNESCO scholarship. By 1981 he was a member of the National Commission for Medical Research attached to the World Health Organization and a member of the European Commission for Science-Medical Research; he published several original studies on cardiology. Berisha had been a member of the Party of Labor of Albania (Communist Party) for twelve years when he resigned in 1990. He became politically active in the movements for change and participated in the December 1990 student demonstrations. As one of the founding members of the Democratic Party (DP), Berisha took a leading role from the day that opposition parties were legalized. In the first free elections in 1991 he won the electorate of Kavaja with about 98 percent of the district vote, although the DP was defeated in the rural areas. Following political turmoil during 1991, new elections were held in March 1992, bringing the DP overwhelming victory and Berisha the presidency. However, in the view of many his promises of democracy and regard for human rights were not honored. His authoritarian actions, especially toward those who opposed his government, resulted in a negative vote in the referendum for his proposed new constitution in November 1994. Manipulation of the subsequent elections in 1996 by Berisha's officials was widely condemned. His apparent victory in the election was recognized by few internationally. A crisis point was reached by early 1997 with the failure of the "pyramid investment" schemes in which his government was allegedly implicated. Refusing to resign from the presidential office, Berisha was voted out as president in the June 29, 1997, elections, and left office only within minutes of the formation of the new parliament. But he retained a seat in that new socialist-dominated parliament.

BIBLIOGRAPHY

Hutchinson, Raymond. *Historical Dictionary of Albania.* Lanham, Md.: Scarecrow Press, 1996.
Young, Antonia. *Albania.* (World Bibliographical Series no. 94 [revised]). Santa Barbara, Calif./Oxford: CLIO Press, 1997.
Zanga, Louis. "Albanien," in Klaus-Detlev Grothusen, ed. *Südosteuropa-Handbuch Band,* Vol. 7. Göttingen: Vandenhoeck & Ruprecht, 1993.
Antonia Young

Berlin

German capital city divided into four zones of occupation as a result of Allied agreements made during World War

Berliners crowded atop the Berlin Wall in 1989 as they celebrate the end to the division of the city. East German authorities had just allowed their citizens unrestricted access to West Berlin, an action that in effect brought the Wall down. *Illustration courtesy of the German Information Center.*

II. The presence of the Western Allies in the city, deep within the Soviet zone of occupation (later the German Democratic Republic) became one of the most important controversies of the Cold War. A series of crises regarding the status of the city during the 1940s, 1950s, and 1960s threatened to provoke armed conflict between East and West. A wall, which was erected by the communist East German government, divided the city between 1961 and 1989 but was opened on November 9, 1989. Germany was re-unified on October 3, 1990 after the collapse of communism in East Germany. A year later, the German government decided to move the capital of the country from Bonn back to Berlin. The German parliament moved to Berlin in July 1999, and its first official session in the city was held on September 7. On August 25, Chancellor Gerhard Schroeder moved into his new offices, thus reestablishing the city as the seat of the German government after a hiatus of 54 years.

In 1944, the European Advisory Commission (EAC) drew up plans for the occupation of Germany following the Allied victory. The EAC decided that Germany and its capital, Berlin, would each be divided into three zones of occupation. The United States and Great Britain would occupy the western portions of the former Third Reich, while the Soviet Union would control the eastern part of the country. Berlin, which lay far inside the Soviet zone, would be divided in similar fashion. At the Yalta Conference in February 1945, the three powers agreed to a French role in the occupation of Germany, but it was

not until May 1945 that the Soviets agreed to a French presence in Berlin. The French zone was carved out of the American and British sectors. On June 5, 1945, with a meeting of the U.S., British, French, and Soviet commanders, the four-power occupation of Berlin began. In July 1945, the "inter-Allied governing authority," or Kommandatura, went into operation. Its role was to coordinate the occupation policies of the four powers.

As relations between the Western Allies and the Soviet Union began to deteriorate, friction developed regarding the Western presence in Berlin. Hoping to drive out the Western powers, the Soviets began to harass train and automobile passengers seeking access to West Berlin. The situation came to a head on June 25, 1948, when the Soviets began the Berlin Blockade, cutting off all surface access to West Berlin. The Soviets also withdrew from the Kommandatura. On July 14, 1948, the Soviet Union justified its actions in a statement declaring that West Berlin was legitimately a part of the Soviet Zone. The Western response was the airlifting of food, coal, and other supplies to the people of Berlin. This solution proved effective, and on May 12, 1949, the Soviets lifted the blockade. Both sides agreed to return to the status quo of March 1, 1948. The struggle over the status of Berlin continued, however, and intensified after the creation of the Federal Republic of Germany (FRG) on May 23, 1949, and the German Democratic Republic (GDR) on October 7, 1949.

Although the FRG's constitution applied to West Berlin, the Western powers refused to permit their occupation zones to be officially incorporated into the new country. Most West German laws would apply there, although the occupying powers reserved the right to stop the application of West German law in West Berlin. The Western sectors of the city would also have nonvoting representatives in the Bundestag and Bundesrat, the lower and upper houses, respectively, of the FRG's parliament. East Berlin, in violation of agreements made during the war, became the capital of the GDR.

West Berlin posed serious problems for the new Communist regime. First, the existence of a successful capitalist enclave deep inside its territory was an embarrassment to the GDR. Even more important, each year thousands of East Germans emigrated to the FRG by crossing the interzonal border in Berlin. During the period 1958–61, Soviet leader Nikita Khrushchev issued a series of ultimatums to the Western powers, demanding that they leave West Berlin, which the Soviets now considered East German territory. This series of crises over Berlin's status culminated in the construction of a wall, beginning August 13, 1961, through the center of the city. While the erection of the Berlin Wall led to a temporary increase in Cold War pressures, in the long run it eased tensions within the city.

The signing of the Four Power, or Quadripartite, Pact on September 3, 1971, further stabilized the situation. In this agreement, signed by the occupying countries, the Soviets recognized the right of the Western powers, which had continued to exercise their right to patrol the Soviet zone, to be in Berlin. The pact also permitted West Berliners to travel relatively freely in the GDR and guaranteed the right of citizens of France, Great Britain, West Germany, and the United States to visit East Berlin. Most important, both sides renounced the use of force to solve the Berlin dilemma.

The status of Berlin remained unchanged until the 1989 East German revolution. On November 9, 1989, the GDR's ruling Socialist Unity Party announced that travel restrictions on East German citizens would be eased. East Berliners interpreted this as an announcement that the wall was open. They convinced the border guards to open the gates, and the people moved through into West Berlin. Berlin was no longer a divided city. With the reunification of Germany on October 3, 1990, it was decided that Berlin would once again become the capital of Germany.

BIBLIOGRAPHY

Clay, Lucius D. *Decision in Germany.* Garden City, N.Y.: Doubleday, 1950.

Great Britain, Foreign Office. *Selected Documents on Germany and the Question of Berlin, 1944–1961.* London: Her Majesty's Stationery Office, 1961.

Hillenbrand, Martin J. "The Legal Background of the Berlin Situation," in Martin J. Hillenbrand, ed. *The Future of Berlin.* Montclair, N.J.: Allanheld, Osmun & Co., 1980, 41–80.

Nelson, Daniel J. *Wartime Origins of the Berlin Dilemma.* University: University of Alabama Press, 1978.

Schick, Jack M. *The Berlin Crisis, 1958–1962.* Philadelphia: University of Pennsylvania Press, 1971.

Stanger, Roland J., ed. *West Berlin: The Legal Context.* Columbus: Ohio State University Press, 1966.

Sutterlin, James S., and David Klein. *Berlin: From Symbol of Confrontation to Keystone of Stability.* New York: Praeger, 1989.

Russel Lemmons

SEE ALSO Brandt, Willy; Berlin Blockade; Berlin Wall; Reuter, Ernst; Wartime Conferences

Berlin, Isaiah (1909–1997)

Latvian-born British historian and philosopher renowned for his writings in political philosophy. After his family immigrated to England in 1920, Isaiah Berlin attained academic distinction at Oxford University, where he later joined the faculty in 1932 at New College. Eventually, Berlin served as president of Wolfson College, Oxford, and since 1975 was a professor at All Soul's, Oxford. Berlin directed his scholarly interests to the issues of freedom and individuality in a modern society affected by the antidemocratic threats from the Right and the Left and to the impact of depersonalization on free will. Berlin was a prolific author; his most enduring works include *Karl Marx* (1939; revised 1963); *Historical Inevitability* (1955); *The Age of Enlightenment* (1956); *Four Essays on Liberty* (1969); *Against the Current* (1979); and *The Crooked Timber of Humanity: Chapters in the History of Ideas* (1990). He died on November 5, 1997.

BIBLIOGRAPHY

Berlin, Isaiah, and Ramin Jahanbegloo. *Conversations with Isaiah Berlin.* New York: Scribner, 1991.

Galipeau, Claude J. *Isaiah Berlin's Liberalism.* New York: Clarendon, 1994.

Gray, John. *Isaiah Berlin.* London: Harper Collins, 1995.

Margalit, Edna, and Avishai, eds. *Isaiah Berlin: A Celebration.* Chicago: University of Chicago Press, 1991.

William T. Walker

Berlin Blockade

First dramatic confrontation (1948–49) of the Cold War. By the summer of 1946 there was a collision of interests over Germany between the former wartime allies. A conference of foreign ministers in Moscow in March 1947 failed to resolve differences. The Western powers had berated the Soviets for failing to carry out the Potsdam agreement to ship food to the Western zones of occupation in return for reparations. Because of the failure of a cooperative approach toward Germany, Britain and the United States on May 29, 1947, merged their two zones into Bizonia. Meanwhile an intensified Cold War produced the Truman Doctrine and the Marshall Plan. Bizonia, Russian tactics, and the prospect of Marshall Plan aid led France to cooperate with Britain and the United States.

To stabilize the economies of their zones, the United States, Britain, and France discussed the introduction of a new currency to replace the grossly inflated occupation mark, which was also utilized by the Soviets. The Soviets also felt threatened by talks in London among the West-

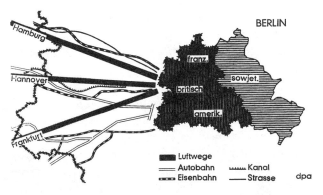

A German map showing the access routes to West Berlin, which was surrounded by the communist German Democractic Republic (East Germany). The maps shows air corridors (*Luftwege*); highways (*Autobahn*); railroads (*Eisenbahn*); canals (*Kanal*); and streets (*Strasse*). The main air corridors originated in the West German cities of Hamburg, Hannover, and Frankfurt. The map also shows the main sector of West Berlin, which was divided into the French (*franz.*), British (*british*), and American (*amerik.*) zones of occupation. East Berlin was occupied by Soviet (*sowjet.*) forces and eventually became the capital of East Germany. *Illustration*

ern powers concerning the establishment of a German government for their combined zones.

In these circumstances the USSR applied pressure to Berlin. Soviet seizure of the Western zones of the city, deep within the Soviet zone of Germany, might dishearten Germans and intimidate the West. However, West Berliners had demonstrated their rejection of communism. In 1947 Social Democrat Ernst Reuter had been elected mayor of the entire city by a wide margin.

On April 1, 1948, the Soviets began to reduce surface access to Berlin. The Elbe road bridge was closed, ostensibly for repairs. The Western powers, focusing on currency reform, were slow to react. Their announcement on April 7 of the introduction of a new currency in their three zones caused the Soviets to expand the blockade. By June 24, the Soviets had cut all rail traffic in and out of the Western zones of Berlin. Soon they also blocked highways and canals. By August 4, the blockade was complete.

General Lucius Clay, U.S. military commander in Germany, informed Washington that if West Berlin were abandoned the Soviet Union might then be emboldened to try to seize the rest of Germany. He said, "If we withdraw, our position in Europe is threatened, and Communism will run rampant." Clay presented three options: Allied withdrawal from West Berlin; an effort to push an armored column up the Autobahn to Berlin; or an airlift to supply the city from the air. President Harry Truman's response was, "We shall stay, period."

Many favored the second choice, including Berlin Mayor Ernst Reuter, because they felt that it would be impossible to supply the needs of over two million Berliners by air. Washington rejected that option for fear it might lead to war with the Soviet Union.

In the euphoria at the end of the world war, nothing had been done to guarantee Western air access to Berlin. Later Clay blamed himself for not having secured this. In place was a low-level agreement concerning air corridors to supply British, French, and U.S. garrisons in the city. In the end this was enough.

In mid-June Clay informed Reuter of Washington's decision for the airlift. Planners initially thought in terms of an operation that might last five or six weeks and reach 500 to 700 tons a day. But what the Germans called the "Air Bridge" and the Americans "Operation Vittles" continued for 320 days and transported 1,736,000 tons of supplies in 212,000 flights. The first twin-engined C-47 (DC-3) arrived in Berlin on the morning of June 25. Each C-47 could carry about 2.5 tons of cargo. Soon the four-engined C-54 (DC-6), capable of carrying ten-ton loads, was in service, and other aircraft participated later. The planes were flown not only by American pilots but also by British, French, and Germans. The aircraft landed principally on three Berlin airfields, Tempelhof, Gatow, and Tegel. By December they were bringing in a daily average of 4,500 tons of cargo, including food and fuel. Eventually the airlift reached the remarkable total of 8,000 tons a day, the amount formerly reaching the city by land. Planes landed or took off every thirty seconds. Moscow had expected the West to capitulate over Berlin, but the Soviets never did challenge the West's right to supply the city by air. Still, the airlift was dangerous; seventy-nine pilots lost their lives: thirty-nine British, thirty-one Americans, and nine Germans.

The blockade was a difficult time for Berliners. Food was strictly rationed and there was little variety. Fuel and electricity were also strictly rationed, their use being rotated so that the burden would be borne equally. Public services ran only from 6:00 A.M. to 6:00 P.M., and unemployment soared to one-third of the working-age population.

Despite the hardships, West Berliners were unified behind the airlift. Reuter coined a phrase, "It's cold in Berlin, but colder in Siberia." Berliners staged large political rallies, and the December 1948 elections saw more than 86 percent of those eligible to vote turn out in a referendum on Western democracy. The Western powers also confirmed Reuter in his position as mayor. In the Soviet sector a second city government took power.

Numerous diplomatic meetings tried to resolve the

blockade. In the course of one of these, in Moscow in August 1948, Soviet Foreign Minister Vyacheslav Molotov held out for Soviet terms. The Soviets maintained that the blockade had been imposed to prevent the Western currency reform from adversely affecting the economy of East Berlin and the Soviet zone of Germany. With the failure of the Moscow talks, the Western powers brought the issue of the blockade to the U.N. Security Council, which was powerless, however, in the face of a confrontation between the two super powers.

By early 1949 the Soviets were forced to concede that the blockade was a failure. The Western powers had imposed their own counterblockade on the Soviet zone and deprived it of vital coking coal and steel. Jacob Malik, Soviet representative to the United Nations, finally suggested to his American counterpart, Philip Jessup, that the USSR was prepared to end the blockade. On May 12, 1949, land traffic to Berlin resumed.

The blockade was an important event in European history. It solidified the integration of the Western zones of Germany with the West, helped promote Western unity leading to the North Atlantic Treaty Organization (NATO), and was a clear defeat for the Soviets in the first direct confrontation of the Cold War.

BIBLIOGRAPHY

Clay, Lucius. *Decision in Germany.* Garden City, N.Y.: Doubleday, 1950.

Davison, Walter P. *Berlin Blockade: A Study in Cold War Politics.* Princeton, N.J.: Princeton University Press, 1958.

LaFeber, Walter. *America, Russia, and the Cold War, 1945–1992,* 7th ed. New York: McGraw-Hill, 1993.

Maier, Charles S., ed. *The Origins of the Cold War and Contemporary Europe.* New York: New Viewpoints, 1975.

Spencer C. Tucker

SEE ALSO Berlin; Clay, Lucius D.

Berlinguer, Enrico (1922–83)

Leader of the Italian Communist Party (PCI), 1972–83. Enrico Berlinguer was born in Sassari, Sardinia, on May 25, 1922, an antifascist family. His father was a deputy who had opposed Mussolini. Berlinguer attended law school at the University of Sassari. In 1937 he contacted Sardinian antifascist groups and in 1943 joined the Italian Communist party, soon becoming secretary of its youth section in Sassari.

In January 1944 he was arrested for protesting against the high cost of living, but after a few months he was acquitted and released from prison. In June of the same year he met Palmiro Togliatti, the general secretary of the PCI, and a few months later moved to Rome, working there for the national secretary of the Communist youth movement. In 1945 he was transferred to Milan and in 1948 became a member of the directing board of the youth movement. In 1949 he was elected general secretary of party's Youth Federation, a position he held until 1956. From 1950 to 1957 he held several posts: president of the World Federation's Democratic Youth, manager of PCI's Central School, and regional vice secretary for the PCI in Sardinia. In 1958 he joined the Party Secretariat. In 1968 he was elected to parliament from Rome and became a member of the Foreign Affairs Committee in the Chamber of Deputies.

At the twelfth PCI congress in 1969, Berlinguer became the party's general vice secretary. In June 1969 he led the Italian delegation at the International Conference of Communist and Labor Parties at Moscow. On this occasion he announced the refusal of the PCI to sign the final document of the congress. In 1972, at the thirteenth congress of PCI, he was elected general secretary. His leadership was confirmed at congresses in 1975, 1979, and 1983. In the general election in May 1972, he was reelected to parliament from Rome. In 1973, while he was recovering from an accident, he wrote three famous articles for the party's weekly, *Rinascita.* With these articles Berlinguer promoted the strategy of "historic compromise" drawn on reflections on the tragic experience of Salvador Allende in Chile. Berlinguer advocated joint management of political power with the Christian Democrats (CD).

In 1976, at the twenty-fifth congress of Soviet Communist Party in Moscow, Berlinguer confirmed the PCI's autonomy. While returning to Italy, he stated, during an interview, that he felt more secure "under NATO's umbrella." In 1977 at Madrid he announced another component of his political platform: Eurocommunism, meaning a socialism independent of Moscow and a common policy with the three other most important Communist parties of Western Europe: Portugal, Spain, and France. In the same year he gave a public speech on this subject that was censured by the Soviet Communist Party organ *Pravda.* On October 13, 1977, *L'unità* and *Rinascita* published correspondence between Berlinguer and a Catholic bishop, Antonio Bettazzi, about the relation between Communists and Catholics. In the next years Berlinguer concentrated his attention on disarmament.

During the kidnapping of Aldo Moro, a leading CD politician who advocated bringing the PCI into the government, the PCI under Berlinguer unhesitatingly denounced terrorism. Elected deputy for the third time in 1979, he was again a member of the Foreign Committee in the Chamber of Deputies. Berlinguer harshly condemned the Soviet invasion of Afghanistan and decided not to participate in Paris at the Conference of Communist parties. At the end of the same year the policy of "historic compromise" was terminated. Berlinguer proposed that the democratic alternative did not mean an exclusively "left" government but a government without the Christian Democratic Party, open to various other democratic parties. In January 1982 the Central Committee officially decreed the party's definitive separation from Moscow. At the general election of 1983, Berlinguer was elected deputy for the fourth time.

In the last months of his life he was involved in the opposition to a revision of the *scala mobile* (gearing of wages to inflation) proposed by Bettino Craxi's government. The PCI shared Berlinguer's concern on this issue and in May, by means of a parliamentary boycott, unsuccessfully tried to block the approval of the decree. On June 7, 1983, in Padua during a campaign meeting for the forthcoming election of members to the European parliament. Berlinguer suffered a cerebral hemorrhage, which caused his death on June 11.

Among Berlinguer's writings are *Per un governo di svolta democratica* (1972); *Democrazia e sicurezza in Europe* (1973), written in collaboration with Georges Marchais, secretary of the French Communist Party; *Il compromesso storico* (1975); *La questione comunista* (2 vol., 1975); *Unita del popolo per salvare l'Italia* (1975); *La politica internazionale dei comunisti italiani* (1976); *Austerità: occasione per trasformare l'Italia* (1977); and *Partito di massa negli anni Ottanta* (1981).

BIBLIOGRAPHY

Gorresio, V. *Berlinguer.* Milan: Feltrinelli, 1976.
Fiori, G. *Vita di Enrico Berlinguer.* Rome: Laterza, 1989.
Valentini, C. *Berlinguer.* Milan: Mondadori, 1989.

Claudia Giurintano

SEE ALSO Eurocommunism; Italy; Moro, Aldo

Berlinguer, Luigi (1932–)

Italian educator and politician. Luigi Berlinguer, a cousin of Enrico Berlinguer, the former leader of the Italian Communist Party, was born in Sassari on July 25, 1932. He received a doctorate in law from the University of Sassari in 1955 and taught law there. In 1968 he began teaching the history of Italian law in the Law Faculty of

the University of Siena. He became a professor of law there in 1970. He served as the rector of the University of Siena from 1985 to 1994 and was chosen secretary-general of the conference of Italian university rectors.

Berlinguer joined the Communist Party and became a member of its control commission, its national directorate. He was elected a provincial councilor for Sassari in 1950 and served as mayor of Sassari from 1962 to 1966. Following his move to Siena he became a regional councilor in Tuscany. Berlinguer was elected to parliament for the first time in 1963 from the constituency of Cagliari. He was a founding member of the Party of the Democratic Left and a member of its national directorate. He served as a cabinet member first in the government of Carlo Azeglio Ciampi in 1993, but his tenure as minister of universities and scientific research was extremely brief. Berlinguer resigned after only forty-eight hours in protest over the parliament's politically motivated refusal to authorize legal proceedings against Bettino Craxi, the former premier from the Socialist Party who had been accused of political corruption. He left his post as rector at Siena to run successfully for parliament in 1994. In 1996 he was again elected to parliament as part of the Olive Tree alliance for the constituency of central Florence. He was appointed minister of education and scientific research in the government of Romano Prodi.

Bernard Cook

Berlin Wall

Wall was erected beginning on August 13, 1961 (and fortified in the coming years), to end the flow of East Ger-

The Berlin Wall at the Brandenburg Gate in the early 1960s. The barrier between East and West Berlin first consisted of barbed wire, followed by a concrete wall. To prevent escape attempts from East Berlin, the East German authorities later built a mined no-man's land around the Wall. *Illustration courtesy of the German Information Center.*

mans to the Federal Republic (FRG) through West Berlin and to affirm the permanence of the Communist German Democratic Republic (GDR).

Concerned by the entry of a rearmed FRG into NATO, the Soviets attempted to use Berlin as a pawn to gain recognition by the West of the status quo in Germany. On November 10, 1958, Premier Nikita Khrushchev announced that the USSR was reconsidering the status of Berlin and contemplating the transfer of control over East Berlin to the GDR. In May and July 1959 at Geneva meetings of foreign ministers of the city's four occupying powers, the USSR demanded that the occupation of West Berlin be ended and that the city be transformed into a "free city." Rebuffed by the West, the GDR supported by the USSR began in August to harass transportation between West Berlin and the FRG in order to convince the West that its position in the city was insupportable. Willy Brandt, the mayor of West Berlin, responded that the city, far from being a Western untenable enclave within East Germany, was an indispensable symbol of freedom.

Following the collapse of the Paris summit (May 1960) between the United States and the USSR, Khrushchev chose Berlin as a point to press the West and simultaneously to bolster the USSR's client regime, the GDR. In August 1960 the USSR temporarily closed the Soviet sector of the city to West Germans. On September 8, the GDR imposed a new condition that West Germans before being allowed to enter East Berlin had to obtain visitor permits. On September 13 GDR authorities stated that they no longer would recognize FRG passports as legal documentation for West Berliners and on January 1, 1961, suspended its trade agreement with the FRG.

When Khrushchev met President John F. Kennedy in Vienna in June 1961, he demanded Western recognition of the GDR and an independent status for West Berlin. Barring that, he threatened to sign a separate peace treaty with the GDR and give it control over communications with West Berlin. On June 15 GDR leader Walter Ulbricht demanded that West Berlin stop accepting fleeing East Germans and cease directing undermining propaganda to the residents of the GDR. On July 25, Kennedy reaffirmed his support of West Berlin but, by neglecting to mention East Berlin, convinced the Soviets that he would not assert Western rights in East Berlin or challenge the USSR there.

The GDR leadership believed that drastic action was necessary to preserve their regime. Before the Wall was built, city residents could circulate fairly freely through both parts of Berlin. Almost 60,000 East Berliners commuted daily to work in West Berlin and others crossed

daily to visit, shop, or seek entertainment. The porous frontier, however, created an enormous problem for the GDR. By 1960 its annual birthrate exceeded deaths only by 8,000, and 250,000 East Germans were leaving for the West annually. Those leaving were often young, highly educated, or skilled, and their loss was a blow to the East German economy and a challenge to the legitimacy of the GDR. In the seven years before the Wall was erected, 5,000 doctors, 17,000 teachers, and 20,000 engineers and technicians had chosen to move to the West. In the summer of 1961 the flow turned into a torrent. Some 19,000 left in June, and 30,444 in July. In the first eleven days of August, 16,000 East Germans crossed into West Berlin; on August 12, 2,400 crossed, the largest number recorded for a single day. Ulbricht had asked Khrushchev for permission to seal off West Berlin in March. Khrushchev, who had withheld permission then, now granted it.

Right after midnight on August 13, the East Germans began sealing off West Berlin with a barbed wire barrier. At one A.M. it was announced that the border had been closed. Thirty Soviet and East German divisions were on alert to counter any attempt by the West to interfere. Brandt, who demanded an immediate forceful diplomatic protest by the West against this violation of the Four Power agreement on Berlin, was dismayed by the slow and weak response of the West. Konrad Adenauer, the chancellor of West Germany, who was in the midst of a parliamentary campaign against Brandt, had never expressed overwhelming interest in Berlin. He reacted slowly and ineffectually. The United States did dispatch General Lucius Clay and 1,500 reinforcements, but the GDR continued to strengthen the barrier.

The Wall, was eventually fortified into a one-hundred-mile concrete barrier that included mine fields encircling West Berlin. It was complemented by 238 watch towers, 132 gun emplacements, a cleared "death strip," and 20,000 guards. There were few crossing points. The most famous one, Checkpoint Charlie, was outfitted with a fifty-yard slalomlike barrier to impede efforts to run the gauntlet. Between August 13, 1961, and November 9, 1989, 77 people were killed trying to cross the Berlin Wall. An additional 114 were killed elsewhere attempting to cross the deadly fortified frontier separating the two Germanies. In 1974, Erich Honecker, Ulbricht's successor, in order to bolster the deterrent to flight, issued a shoot-to-kill order to guards along the Wall. Deadly force, however, predated 1974. In August 1962, for example, a young man, Peter Fechter, was shot by East German guards as he tried to get across the Wall and was allowed to bleed to death in full view of West Berliners.

In the short term the Wall seemed to be a success. The

West did not prevent its erection and it stopped the massive flight of East Germans. It also played a significant role in the formulation of Brandt's policy of *Ostpolitik.* The Wall convinced Brandt that reunification was improbable and that, without some sort of an understanding, the Germans of the two German states would with time be transformed into two separate peoples. As chancellor he attempted to bring the people of the two Germanies closer together. He also wished to end the separation of families divided by the Wall. The Basic Treaty between the FRG and the GDR, signed on December 21, 1972, and ratified on June 1973, granted permission to West Germans to travel to the GDR and enter East Berlin. The Basic Treaty, however, did not eradicate the self-conscious defensiveness of the East German regime. In 1980, to discourage contact between its subjects and West Germans, the GDR increased the visa fee and daily exchange requirements for foreign visitors.

In the long run, the Wall was a failure, a physical manifestation of the failure of the GDR. With the advent of Mikhail Gorbachev as president of the USSR, the real support of the regime, the armed might of the Soviet Union, was ultimately withdrawn. Deserted by the Soviets and rejected by the East German people, Honecker was forced from office on October 18. When his successor, Egon Krenz, announced on November 9, 1989, that the Wall would be opened, it was mobbed and breached. The event was a vivid repudiation of the GDR and a prelude to German reunification.

BIBLIOGRAPHY

Merritt, Richard L., and Anna J. Merritt, eds. *Living with the Wall: West Berlin, 1961–1985.* Durham, N.C.: Duke University Press, 1985.

Prittie, Terence. *Willy Brandt: Portrait of a Statesman.* New York: Schocken Books, 1974.

Waldenburg, Hermann. *The Berlin Wall Book.* London: Thames and Hudson, 1990.

Whetten, Lawrence L. *Germany East and West: Conflicts, Collaboration, and Confrontation.* New York: New York University Press, 1980.

Wyden, Peter. *Wall: The Inside Story of a Divided Berlin.* New York: Simon and Schuster, 1989.

Bernard Cook

SEE ALSO Berlin; Brandt, Willy; Germany, Federal Republic of

Berlusconi, Silvio (1936–)

Italian entrepreneur and politician. Silvio Berlusconi was born in Milan on September 29, 1936. He received a law degree from the University of Milan. As a developer he made a fortune in the residential real estate market. At the end of the 1970s, as a result of success with the local television station, Telemilano, Berlusconi built a media empire. In 1980 he founded Canale 5, his first national television network and the country's first commercial network. In 1982 he acquired the television network Italia 1 and in 1982 Retequattro (Network 4), both of which he developed into national television networks. He founded Publitalia '80, an agency for television advertising, and in 1984 he acquired the weekly *Sorrisi e Canzoni TV* (*TV Smiles and Songs*), the most widely read periodical in Italy. With this entrée he consolidated his position in the world of newspapers and periodicals, which he had already asserted at the end of the 1970s with his control of *Il Giornale,* the daily edited by Indro Montanelli. His position in publishing, which was developed at the end of the 1980s, was affirmed in 1991 with the acquisition of the premier publishing house, Mondadori. The success of commercial television enabled him to pursue a number of initiatives that were lumped together in his holding company, Fininvest, which he founded in 1978. In television he created the French network "5" (La Cinq), which began operations in 1986, the German network Telefünf in 1987, and the Spanish network Telecinco in 1990. Fininvest developed a strong position in insurance and the sale of financial securities through Mediolanum and Programma Italia, and entered into distribution with the acquisition of the Standa company. At the beginning of the 1990s, Fininvest became the second-largest Italian private corporation, with over forty-thousand employees. In 1986 Berlusconi became the president of the soccer team Milan. In 1992, because of the law regulating television, he gave up ownership of *Il Giornale,* handing it over to his brother Paolo along with his interests in the construction area.

At the beginning of 1994 Berlusconi resigned direct management of Fininvest. Concerned that the Democratic Party of the Left would emerge as the dominant political force after the collapse of the Christian Democratic and Socialist Parties, Berlusconi founded and became president of the new political movement Forza Italia. It espoused a program of private enterprise and the end of government regulation of business. He allied his party in an electoral coalition with the Northern League and the National Alliance. In the March 28, 1994, election Forza Italia emerged as the largest party and his coalition, the Freedom Alliance, won a majority of seats in the Chamber of Deputies. On May 11, Berlusconi became prime minister. His advent to power was touted as a revolution that would transform the Italian political scene. However, Berlusconi's coalition partner, federalist Umberto Bossi of the Northern League, became disenchanted with Berlusconi and the National Alliance. And the pervasive politicoeconomic scandal known as "Mani pulite" (clean hands) or "Tagentopoli" (bibe city), which involved a decades long system of financial and political corruption, and which had done in the Christian Democrats and the Socialists, began to draw close to Berlusconi. In December magistrates questioned Berlusconi about his business practices. Facing a vote of no confidence, he resigned on December 22, 1995. Berlusconi was succeeded by a government of technocrats headed by Lamberto Dini, an economist, who had been the minister of treasury in the Berlusconi government.

Following his resignation, charges of corruption continued to plague Berlusconi, his business interests, and his brother.

On December 3, 1997, Berlusconi was convicted of helping to compile false accounts concerning the purchase of the Medusa film company by his Fininvest group. He was sentenced to sixteen months imprisonment. However, because of his parliamentary immunity, his right to two appeals, and the nature of the Italian judicial system, it is doubtful that he will ever spend time in jail. On July 7, 1998, Berlusconi was convicted of bribing tax officials, and on July 13, 1998, he was sentenced to two years and four months in jail and a $5.6 million fine for paying a bribe of £6 million to the Socialist Party in 1991. Despite his legal difficulties, in October 1998 he was able to call out a million supporters in Rome for a mass rally in support of himself and in opposition to the government of new Italian prime minister, Massimo D'Alema. In March 1999 he was acquitted of tax fraud.

BIBLIOGRAPHY

"Berlusconi is Convicted," *Financial Times* (London), December 4, 1997.

Johnston, Bruce, "Berlusconi Convicted," *The Daily Telegraph,* July 14, 1998.

———. "Berlusconi Jailed," *The Daily Telegraph,* July 8, 1998.

Bernard Cook

SEE ALSO Bossi, Umberto; Dini, Lamberto; Fini, Gianfranco; Italy

Bernhard zu Lippe-Biesterfeld (1911–)

Prince consort of the Netherlands between 1948 and 1980. Bernhard zu Lippe-Biesterfeld acquired a reputation as Holland's most effective goodwill ambassador dur-

ing the postwar period before a scandal forced him from public life.

Bernhard, a German noble, was born in 1911. In 1937, after receiving a degree in law, he married Juliana of Orange, the Dutch crown princess. During the Second World War, the ex-German Bernhard proved his firm commitment to the Allied cause, a service that propelled him into the highest ranks of the Dutch armed forces. The prince consort, upon his wife's ascension to the throne in 1948, effectively used his position to cultivate a wide variety of military, political, and business contacts throughout the world. Bernhard's jet-setting provided important connections, lucrative contracts, and high visibility for his adopted country, although his lavish lifestyle among the world's rich and famous did nothing to help his strained marriage with Juliana.

In 1976 Lockheed Aircraft officials revealed that Prince Bernhard had accepted a $1 million payment to promote the sale of Starfighters in the Netherlands, and a Dutch government investigation soon exposed other irregularities. As prince consort, Bernhard was never prosecuted for criminal wrongdoing, but the government did force his resignation from all his public positions. Since then, he has lived in quiet at Juliana's residence of Soestdijk. In 1994 Bernhard narrowly escaped death from pneumonia.

BIBLIOGRAPHY

Hatch, Alden. *Bernhard, Prince of the Netherlands.* Garden City, N.Y.: Doubleday, 1962.

Klinkenberg, Wim. *Prins Bernhard: Een politieke biografie, 1911–1979.* Amsterdam: Onze Tijd, 1986.

J. C. Kennedy

SEE ALSO Juliana

Bessarabia

Territory in southeastern Europe bounded by the Prut Dniester Rivers and the Black Sea, and the subject of diplomatic controversy in the nineteenth and twentieth centuries. The historic territory of Bessarabia (Romanian, Basarabia; Russian, Bessarabiia), now lying in Ukraine and the Republic of Moldova, covers roughly 17,143 square miles (44,400 sq km). The name comes from the Basarab dynasty, which ruled much of the Romanian principality of Wallachia in the fourteenth and fifteenth centuries. The name originally applied only to those lands located along the Black Sea, but by the nineteenth century it became the geographic designation for the entire Prut-Dniester interfluvial zone.

Until 1812 Bessarabia formed the eastern portion of the Principality of Moldavia, a vassal state of the Ottoman Empire. Bessarabia's annexation by the Russian Empire in that year was denounced by local Moldavian nobles, who protested that they had not been consulted on the annexation. From 1812 to 1918 Bessarabia remained a province of the Russian Empire. At the end of the First World War a local assembly in the region voted for union with Romania, which the western portion of the Moldavian principality had joined in 1859. However, the region's status was never secured by international treaty, and it remained a source of controversy between Romania and the Soviet Union throughout the interwar years. In June 1940 the Soviet Union forcibly annexed Bessarabia and transformed it into the Moldovan Soviet Socialist Republic (MSSR), one of the constituent republics of the Soviet Union. Although Romania and the Soviet Union became allies after the war, the status of Bessarabia remained a veiled source of controversy between the two Communist states.

With the collapse of the Soviet Union in 1991 the MSSR declared itself an independent state, the Republic of Moldova. Although Romania was the first state to recognize the independence of Moldova, some political groups in both Moldova and Romania argued that the former Soviet republic, which contained the Bessarabia region, should move toward eventual reunion with Romania.

BIBLIOGRAPHY

Cioranesco, George. *Bessarabia: Disputed Land Between East and West.* Munich: Editura Ion Dumitru, 1985.

Clark, Charles Upson. *Bessarabia: Russia and Roumania on the Black Sea.* New York: Dodd, Mead, 1927.

Dobrinescu, Valeriu Florin. *The Diplomatic Struggle over Bessarabia.* Iasi, Romania: Center for Romanian Studies, 1996.

Jewsbury, George F. *The Russian Annexation of Bessarabia: 1774–1828.* Boulder, Colo.: East European Quarterly, 1976.

Nistor, Ion. *Istoria Basarabiei.* Bucharest: Humanitas, 1991.

Popovici, Andrei. *The Political Status of Bessarabia.* Washington, D.C.: Ransdell, 1931.

Van Meurs, Wim P. *The Bessarabian Question in Communist Historiography.* Boulder, Colo.: East European Monographs, 1995.

Charles King

SEE ALSO Bukovina; Moldova

Bessmertnykh, Aleksandr A. (1933–)

Russian foreign minister, 1991. Aleksandr Bessmertnykh, son of a civil servant, was born in Biysk in south-central Siberia on November 10, 1933. He graduated in law and political science from Moscow State Institute of International Relations. He became an assistant in the press department of the Ministry of Foreign Affairs in 1957. In 1960 he was posted abroad for the first time as a member of the U.N. Secretariat. During his six-year stint in New York City he joined the Communist Party. After his return to Moscow he eventually became first secretary to Foreign Minister Andrey Gromyko. In 1970 he became first secretary to the Soviet ambassador to the United States, Anatoly Dobrynin. In 1977 he became Dobrynin's second as minister-counselor, participating in the negotiations for the Strategic Arms Limitation Treaty (SALT II).

In 1983 he was posted to Moscow as the head of the U.S. department of the Ministry of Foreign Affairs. After 1985 he supported Mikhail Gorbachev's effort to establish better relations with the United States through negotiated disarmament. In June 1986 as deputy foreign minister he publicly denounced President Ronald Reagan's decision not to continue to observe the conditions of SALT II, which had not been ratified by the U.S. Senate. Following the Gorbachev-Reagan summit in Reykjavík, Iceland, Bessmertnykh gained notoriety by contradicting the official U.S. account of Reagan's reaction to Gorbachev's proposal to abolish all nuclear weapons within a decade. According to Bessmertnykh the president had actually endorsed Gorbachev's proposal as worthy of pursuing.

As rapprochement progressed between the two superpowers, Gorbachev, signaling the need for a new approach at the Soviet Embassy in Washington, appointed Bessmertnykh Soviet ambassador to the United States in May 1990. However, when Eduard Shevardnadze, the Soviet foreign minister, resigned in December warning of an inexorable drift toward dictatorship in the USSR, Gorbachev turned to Bessmertnykh to reassure the West. Though the new foreign minister affirmed Soviet support for the use of force to liberate Kuwait, which had been invaded by Iraq in August, Soviet support wavered once the U.S.-led bombing of its erstwhile client began. The situation was complicated by U.S. condemnations of Soviet actions against nationalists in Latvia and Lithuania seeking independence from the USSR. The United States then apparently muted its complaints against Soviet action in the Baltics in exchange for continued Soviet support in the Gulf War. Bessmertnykh also apparently gained agreement from the United States to exercise some flexibility with regard to Iraq and to link a settlement there to progress in addressing Palestinian complaints against Israel.

Bessmertnykh, though pleased that rapprochement with the United States survived the Gulf War, did not long survive as Soviet foreign minister. At the time of the conservative coup against Gorbachev in August 1991, Bessmertnykh decided to await the outcome. His failure to denounce the coup led Gorbachev, once out of the grasp of his opponents, to dismiss Bessmertnykh on August 23.

BIBLIOGRAPHY
Current Biography Yearbook 1991, New York: H. W. Wilson, 1992, 60–65.

Bernard Cook

Bevan, Aneurin (1897–1960)

British Labour minister of health, 1945–51, and minister of labor in 1951. Aneurin Bevan, son of a miner, was born on November 15, 1897, at Tredegar, Monmouthshire. He went to work in the coal mines at thirteen but had to quit work there after a few years because of an eye disease. Bevan overcame a severe stammer to become a first-rate public speaker. He was elected chairman of his local lodge of the South Wales Miners' Federation and was also elected a local councilor.

Bevan attended the Central Labour College in London and was elected to the House of Commons from Ebbw Vale in 1929, holding that seat until his death in 1960. As editor of the independent left-wing *Tribune* from 1940 to 1945, he was critical not only of Winston Churchill's Conservative government but of his own Labour Party.

With the victory of Labour in 1945, Bevan was appointed minister of health and oversaw the implementation of the United Kingdom's National Health Service. In January 1951 he was appointed minister of labor, but he resigned that post and his place in the government in April when the government introduced charges under the National Health Service for false teeth and eyeglasses. Bevan was at odds with Clement Atlee over Britain's involvement in the Cold War and its consequent program of rearmament, believing that the military buildup would damage the development of an ample social welfare program. Bevan, henceforth, led the maverick left wing of Labour, dubbed the Bevanites. He ran for party chairman in 1955 but was defeated by Hugh Gaitkill. Bevan died on July 6, 1960.

Bevan's wife, Jenny Lee, later Baroness Lee, was a Labour MP and served as minister for the arts.

BIBLIOGRAPHY
Bevan, Aneurin. *In Place of Fear.* Wakefield, UK: EP Publishing, 1976.
Campbell, John. *Aneurin Bevan and the Mirage of British Socialism.* New York: Norton, 1987.
Jenkins, Mark. *Bevanism, Labour's High Tide: The Cold War and the Democratic Mass Movement.* Nottingham, UK: Spokesman, 1979.
Lee, Jennie. *My Life with Nye.* London: Cape, 1980.
Smith, Dai. *Aneurin Bevan and the World of South Wales.* Cardiff: University of Wales Press, 1993.

Bernard Cook

SEE ALSO Gaitskell, Hugh

Beveridge, William (1879–1963)

Economist whose 1942 report, *Social Insurance and Allied Services,* or the Beveridge Report, served as the foundation for the United Kingdom's post–World War II welfare state. William Beveridge, son of a judge in the Indian Civil Service, was born in Rangpur, India, on March 5, 1879. He was educated at Balliol College of Oxford University.

In 1903 Beveridge was appointed subwarden of the London settlement house, Toynbee House. From 1909 to 1916 as director of Labour Exchanges, he organized a national system of labor exchanges and played a key role in the development of a compulsory unemployment insurance scheme.

From 1919 to 1937 he was director of the London School of Economics, and under his leadership it developed an international reputation. From 1937 to 1944 he was master of University College, Oxford, and from 1941 to 1944 president of the Royal Statistical Society. In 1941 he was appointed to the Committee on Social Insurance and Allied Services. Under his leadership this committee produced the Beveridge Report, which proposed a comprehensive scheme of social insurance without any means test. Beveridge served as a Member of Parliament from Berwick upon Tweed in 1944–45. He was made a baron in 1946. He died at Oxford on March 16, 1963.

His books include *Unemployment: A Problem of Industry* (1906), *Insurance for All* (1924), *Planning under Socialism* (1936), *Full Employment in a Free Society* (1944), *Pillars of Security* (1948), and *A Defense of Free Learning* (1959).

BIBLIOGRAPHY
Cutler, Tony. *Keynes, Beveridge, and Beyond.* London: Routledge & Kegan Paul, 1986.

Harris, Jose. *William Beveridge: A Biography,* 2d ed. Oxford: Clarendon Press, 1997.

Bernard Cook

Bevin, Ernest (1881–1951)

British foreign secretary in the 1945–51 Labour government. Before World War II Ernest Bevin was a trade union organizer and official, best known for creating the Transport and General Workers' Union in 1921 and leading it from 1922 to 1940. From 1940 to 1945, Bevin was minister of labor and national service in Winston Churchill's coalition government, and a member of the War Cabinet.

As a trade union leader between the world wars, Bevin was sympathetic to the Soviet Union but critical of Soviet manipulation of international communism. After 1945 he believed that the Soviet regime intended to spread its influence over both Eastern and Western Europe and adjacent regions, and that British foreign policy must address this threat. As the war had weakened British power, Bevin assumed that the United States would lead anti-Soviet resistance. Close and willing cooperation with the Americans therefore became the cornerstone of Bevin's foreign policy.

Realizing that postwar European economic chaos provided an opening for the advance of communism, Bevin strongly supported U.S. Marshall Plan aid and the creation of the Organization for European Economic Cooperation (OEEC) in 1948. He also persuaded the United States to adopt the 1947 Truman Doctrine of economic and military aid to countries, particularly Turkey and Greece, believed to be threatened by Soviet aggression. Bevin was mainly responsible for the 1948 Brussels Treaty of mutual assistance among Western European states, which in 1949 was enlarged into the American-dominated North Atlantic Treaty Organization (NATO). Bevin staunchly upheld the Americans against the Soviets in the Berlin Blockade and the Korean War. He was determined, however, that Britain should develop and control its own nuclear weapons as proof of its Great Power status.

Bevin's advocacy of Western European economic and military cooperation did not extend to support for Anglo-European integration. He was an old-fashioned British patriot and arguably something of an imperialist. Bevin was resolved to preserve British hegemony in the Middle East and maintain a military presence there, particularly in Egypt and Palestine, in the face of the region's rising nationalism. His undisguised sympathy for Arabs over Zionists during the movement for Israeli independence

was unpopular in Britain, Western Europe, and, especially, the United States. Paradoxically, Bevin's anti-Zionism was attacked by many of the same domestic critics, mostly in his own Labour Party, who condemned his pro-Americanism. In 1947, Bevin reluctantly agreed to hand over Britain's Palestine Mandate to the United Nations.

One of Bevin's last, but also most important, accomplishments was his sponsorship of the Colombo Plan (1950–51) for financial and technical assistance to southeast Asian Commonwealth countries, and economic cooperation among them, based on the Marshall Plan and the OEEC. Bevin resigned as foreign secretary because of illness and died soon afterward. Contemporaries, including Conservative opponents, appraised him as decisive, capable, and trustworthy, estimates that historians generally have confirmed.

BIBLIOGRAPHY

Barclay, Sir Roderick. *Ernest Bevin and the Foreign Office.* London: Latimer, 1975.

Bullock, Alan. *Ernest Bevin: Foreign Secretary, 1945–1951.* London: Heinemann, 1983.

Stephens, Mark. *Ernest Bevin: Unskilled Labourer and World Statesman.* London: Stevenage, 1981.

Williams, Francis. *Ernest Bevin.* London: Hutchinson, 1952.

Don M. Cregier

Bidault, Georges (1899–1983)

French Resistance leader and politician. A prewar Catholic liberal, Georges Bidault played a prominent role in the Resistance and as foreign minister and premier in postwar governments. He was an architect of the Marshall Plan, NATO, and the Organization for European Economic Cooperation (OEEC), a forerunner of the European Economic Community (EEC).

A distinguished prewar history teacher and editor of the Catholic daily, *L'Aube,* Bidault was an active opponent of fascism and appeasement. He joined the French Resistance in 1942, co-founding the Combat organization and taking a seat on Jean Moulin's Conseil Nationale de la Résistance (CNR). As CNR head after Moulin's death, Bidault drew up the Resistance Charter of March 1944, which called for a postwar planned economy, nationalization of banks and insurance companies, extended social services, and a clear break with both Vichy and the legacy of the Third Republic. Bidault welcomed de Gaulle to a liberated Paris in August 1944 and shared his triumphal promenade down the Champs-Élysées.

As minister of foreign affairs in the Provisional Government and Fourth Republic, Bidault favored harsh treatment of a defeated Germany. He helped found France's first Christian Democratic political party, the Popular Republican Movement (Mouvement Républicain Populaire, MRP) in November 1944, rallying conservative and Catholic voters uncomfortable with both traditional republicanism and communism. Though he had worked with the French Communist Party (PCF) in the CNR and in the postwar PCF/MRP/Socialist "tripartite" government, Bidault supported the expulsion of the PCF from the coalition after the collapse of the Moscow foreign ministers conference in March–April 1947.

Muting his criticism of German reconstruction and collaborating with British Foreign Secretary Ernest Bevin, Bidault set up the sixteen-member Organization for European Economic Cooperation to supervise the distribution of Marshall Plan aid. Bidault was determined to commit the United States to the defense of Europe, partly as a counterweight to a rearmed Germany. He signed the Brussels Treaty in March 1948, a British/French/Benelux military pact that foreshadowed the NATO agreement. Though Bidault left the foreign ministry in 1948, he was succeeded by his MRP colleague Robert Schuman. Together the two provided nearly a decade of continuity in the formulation of French foreign policy.

As foreign minister from 1944 to 1948 and premier in 1946 and from 1949 to 1950, Bidault worked for European integration and domestic reform, but his return to the Quai d'Orsay in 1953–54 focused on colonial conflict. An ardent imperialist, Bidault repressed nationalist movements in French North Africa and sought U.S. backing for France's Indochina war. Having hoped de Gaulle's 1958 return to power would keep Algeria French, Bidault bitterly condemned the general's negotiated settlement of that war. He was the last head of the subversive Secret Army Organization (OAS) in 1961. Five years of exile in Brazil ended with a 1968 amnesty, and he spent the remainder of his life defending his career.

BIBLIOGRAPHY

Bidault, Georges. *Resistance.* New York: Praeger, 1967.
Bosworth, W. *Catholicism and Crisis in Modern France.* Princeton, N.J.: Princeton University Press, 1962.
Callot, E.-F. Le M. R. P., *Origine, structure, doctrine, programme, et action politique.* Paris: M. Rivière, 1978.

David Longfellow

SEE ALSO Algerian War; De Gaulle, Charles; European Defense Community; France; Marshall Plan; Schuman, Robert

Biedenkopf, Kurt Hans (1930–)

Minister president of Saxony. Kurt Hans Biedenkopf was born on January 28, 1930, in Ludwigshafen, Germany. While applying for a press license for a school newspaper from the American occupation authorities in the U.S. zone of occupied Germany, a U.S. officer suggested that Biedenkopf apply for a scholarship in the United States. Biedenkopf studied political science at Davidson College, North Carolina, but left after one year. He subsequently studied law and economics at Frankfurt and Munich, and received a doctorate in 1958. He then received a master of law at Georgetown University in 1962. In 1964 Biedenkopf became a professor at the newly founded university of Bochum. When the president of the university had to step down because of ill health in 1967, Biedenkopf became the youngest university president in Germany.

Biedenkopf joined the Christian Democratic Union (CDU) in 1965, and in 1969 gained political recognition as head of the Federal Joint Management Commission (Biedenkopfkommission). In 1970 Biedenkopf moved from academia to industry, joining the board of the Henkel chemical corporation in Düsseldorf as head of human resources. Chancellor Helmut Kohl appointed Biedenkopf general secretary of the CDU in 1973, and together they transformed the stagnant CDU into a party with wide general appeal, thanks to its social policies. Biedenkopf reorganized the structures and finances of the party. During his term the membership of the CDU rose by 46 percent, to over 650,000.

In 1977 Biedenkopf switched to regional politics in the German state of Westphalia. The defeat of the CDU in the 1980 election undermined Biedenkopf's position within the party. In 1987 he was voted out of office as chairman. By 1989 Biedenkopf's political career appeared to be over. Immediately after the fall of the Berlin Wall Biedenkopf involved himself in East Germany, becoming a professor at the University of Leipzig and an executive of the East German companies Buna and Baukema. In 1990, when the CDU was unable to find a suitable candidate for the elections in the newly established state of Saxony, a CDU consultant proposed Biedenkopf. State elections were held on October 14, 1990, and the CDU gained 53.8 percent of the vote. Biedenkopf rapidly rose to be the spokesman for East German causes. In 1992 he said, "Today, I am an East German." As a result of the massive problems besetting the former East Germany, Biedenkopf shifted from his liberal economic position to one of interventionism. For unified Germany Biedenkopf proposed a complete reconstruction of social policies, reform of tax law, and reorganization of the federal system.

The Saxon state (Landtag) elections in 1994 resulted in a significant majority for the CDU, with 58.1 percent of the vote. To the people of Saxony Biedenkopf is the undisputed father figure and is jokingly referred to by the press as King Kurt.

BIBLIOGRAPHY

Biedenkopf, Kurt H. *Einheit und Erneuerung: Deutschland nach dem Umbruch in Europa.* Stuttgart: Deutsche Velrags-Anstalt, 1994.

———. *Fortschritt in Freiheit.* Munich: R. Piper, 1974.

———. *Zeichen der Zeit.* Munster: Verlag Regensberg, 1990.

———. *Zeitsignale: Parteienlandschaft im Umbruch.* Munich: Bertelsmann, 1989.

Schneider, Horst. *"Landesvater" Biedenkopf: wohin treibt Sachsen?: über seine Ansichten, Absichten und Politik: ein Gesprachsangebot.* Schkeuditz: GNN-Verlag, 1993.

Wendt, Alexander. *Kurt Biedenkopf: ein politisches Portrat.* Berlin: Schwarzkopf, 1994.

Henrik Eberle

Bielecki, Jan Krzysztóf (1951–)

Polish prime minister, 1991. Jan Krzysztóf Bielecki was born in 1951 in Bydgoszcz. He received a degree in economics from the College of Economics in Sopot. He was a member of the Solidarity trade union movement, but helped to form the Liberal Democratic Congress as the old movement splintered. He succeeded Tadeusz Mazowiecki as prime minister in January 1991. His appointment by Lech Wałęsa was seen as an indication of the president's commitment to rapid privatization. Following the October 1991 election, in which the Democratic Left Alliance won 12.1 percent of the vote and its ally, the Peasant Party, won 8.9 percent, Bielecki was replaced in December 1991 by former Communist Jan Olszewski. Bielecki served as minister for European integration in the government of Hanna Suchocka from July to November 1992. He was then appointed Polish representative to the European Bank for Reconstruction and Development, and subsequently became its director.

Bernard Cook

SEE ALSO Olszewski, Jan; Suchocka, Hanna

Biermann, Wolf (1936–)

East German songwriter and dissident. Wolf Biermann was born in Hamburg on November 15, 1936. His Jewish father, Dagobert Biermann, a shipyard worker, and his mother, Emma, were both members of the German Resistance against the Third Reich. Because of these activities his father was arrested by the National Socialists in 1936 and killed in Auschwitz in 1942. These experiences strongly influenced young Biermann. He joined the Young Pioneers, a Communist youth organization, participated in the World Youth Meeting in East Berlin in 1950 and in 1953, and finally moved to the German Democratic Republic (GDR). In 1957 he suspended his studies at Humboldt University for two years to work as assistant director in the Berlin Ensemble, the theater established by Bertolt Brecht in 1950. In 1959 he took up his studies again and in 1963 passed the state examination in philosophy and mathematics.

In 1960 he began writing and composing songs, though his first works, because of their critical content, had to be published in West Berlin. In 1961–62, after the construction of the Berlin Wall, he founded the Berlin Theater for Workers and Students in East Berlin, which was supposed to have his play *Berliner Brautgang* (*Berlin Walk of a Bride*) as its inaugural production. The play was forbidden by the authorities, however, shortly before the premiere, and in 1963 the theater was closed. In 1962 Biermann published his first poems, and on December 11, 1962, he made his debut at a lyric evening of the Academy of Arts. With his texts, written in the tradition of Heinrich Heine and Bertolt Brecht, Biermann, although an ardent Communist, continued his criticism of the state. In 1962 his unerring invective and criticism of the Communist Party led to a ban on his lectures and publications in the German Democratic Republic. One year later the United Socialist Party of Germany (SED) expelled him. His public appearances in West Germany, on the other hand, from 1964 had been very successful. In 1965 the plenum of the Central Committee of the SED accused him of anarchist behavior, arrogance, skepticism, and cynicism. The authorities classified him as an "officially recognized public enemy."

As a result of Biermann's activities, the "Lex Biermann" was enacted in 1966. This law stated that all authors of the GDR first had to offer their works to East German publishers. In 1973 the Ministry for State Security began working for the expatriation of this troublesome artist. In November 1976 he was given an exit permit and accepted an invitation of the industrial trade union IG-Metall for a concert tour to the West. His first public appearance in Cologne, which could also be received via Western television in East Germany, caused the Eastern authorities to withdraw the national status of the songwriter according to article 13 of the Nationality Law of the GDR. He was found guilty of having severely neglected his civic duties because of his hostile behavior toward the GDR. In spite of this measure he still declared the GDR to be "the better German State."

Biermann took up residence in Hamburg and France and went on concert tours in many Western countries. He continued writing songs and poetry and was praised by leading literary critics, but audiences took less notice of him. Nevertheless, he was considered to be one of the most outstanding German songwriters and won numerous prizes. In 1983 he accepted a visiting professorship at Ohio State University and gave concerts in the United States. In 1989 Biermann, a supporter of the German peace movement of the eighties, returned to the GDR in December 1989 to give public performances there. From 1993 to 1995 he was a guest professor at the University of Düsseldorf.

BIBLIOGRAPHY

Biermann, Wolf. *Wolf Biermann: Poems and Ballads.* London: Pluto Press, 1977.

Roos, Peter, ed. *Exil. Die Ausburgerung Wolf Biermanns aus der DDR. Eine Dokumentation.* Cologne: Kiepenheuer & Witsch, 1977.

Rosellini, Jay. *Wolf Biermann.* Munich: C. H. Beck, 1992.

Shreve, John. *Nur wer sich andert, bleibt sich treu: Wolf Biermann im Westen.* Frankfurt am Main: P. Lang, 1989.

Esther Trassel

Bierut, Bolesław (1892–1956)

Leading Communist political figure, chairman of the National Home Council (1944–47) and president of Poland (1947–52).

After Władysław Gomułka's removal from power in 1948, Bolesław Bierut (pseud. Iwaniuk, Tomasz) became a leader of the Polish Workers Party (PWP), and later that year of its successor, the Polish United Workers Party, (PUWP). As a professional Comintern activist and a puppet of Stalin and Comintern chief Georgy Dimitrov, he played a key role in the transmission of Stalinism to Poland. Not all the details of his life are yet clear.

Bierut, a typesetter, was associated with the Communist Party from its very beginnings in 1918. In the interwar period he underwent in-depth party training in the USSR, first as a student in a party school near Moscow (1925–26) then as a student in the international Leninist School (1928–30). In 1931 he worked for the Comintern and carried out for it unspecified activities in Austria, Czechoslovakia, and Bulgaria. He enjoyed Stalin's and Dimitrov's trust and this advanced his career.

On his return to Poland in 1933, Bierut became secretary of the International Support Organization for Revolutionaries. In 1935, owing to his Communist activities, he was sentenced to seven years' imprisonment. This probably saved his life during the Stalinist purges.

Bierut was in the USSR during World War II. Initially, he worked for Soviet intelligence in German-occupied Minsk. In 1943 he was sent to Poland to clarify the situation in the PWP, which was torn by internal conflicts and weakened by Gestapo arrests of its members. He became a member of the Central Committee and later (1944–48) of the Political Committee of the PWP. These positions were kept secret because in 1943 he also became chairman and later (1944–47) president of the National Council of the Homeland, set up as a broad democratic or popular front organization, ostensibly non-Communist but through which the Communists could co-opt other political movements.

Assured by the presence of the Red Army in Poland and enjoying the trust of Stalin and Dimitrov, Bierut opposed widening the base of the Communist Party. He also supported a hard line toward political opponents. He fell into sharp conflict with Gomułka, who was more sensitive to national matters and wanted to build socialism in Poland in an evolutionary manner, though with support from the USSR.

After Gomułka's removal from the position of general secretary of the Central Committee of the PWP in mid-1948, Bierut introduced dictatorship. He personally held the party leadership, presidency, and premiership. Holding these multiple positions, he forced on Poland the Stalinist state model (the monoparty system, enormous power to the security apparatus, opposition to independent thought and the church, collectivization of agriculture, building heavy industry). Bierut shared power with officials previously accepted by Stalin, especially J. Berman, H. Minc, S. Radkiewicz, and A. Zawadzki. Bierut was directly responsible for the abuse of authority and the repression of the Stalinist system (1949–56). After Stalin's death (1953), Bierut, a fanatic disciple of Communist doctrine, did not change his political line. On the contrary, he carried it out with even greater determination until his death in 1956.

BIBLIOGRAPHY

De Weydenthal, Jan B. *The Communists of Poland.* Stanford, Calif.: Hoover Institution Press, 1978.

Hiscocks, Richard. *Poland: Bridge for the Abyss? An Interpretation of Post-war Poland.* London: Oxford University Press, 1963.

Ryszard Sudziński

Bilak, Vasil (1917?–)

Czechoslovak Communist politician. Vasil Bilak was born into a Ukrainian peasant family that had become assimilated into Slovak culture. He was a member of the Presidium of the Czechoslovak Communist Party and the party's ideological chief at the time of the Warsaw Pact invasion in August 1968. Bilak, an opponent of the Prague Spring, with four of his hard-line party colleagues—Drahomir Kolder, Alois Indra, Oldrich Svestka, and Antonín Kapek—signed a letter delivered to Soviet leader Leonid Brezhnev on August 3, 1968, at the Bratislava Conference asking for assistance from the Soviet Union against the "counterrevolutionary threat" in Czechoslovakia. Brezhnev referred to the letter when he met with other East bloc leaders in Moscow on August 18, the day after the Soviet Politburo decided to intervene.

Bilak, who denied that he had invited the Soviet Union and other Warsaw Pact members to intervene, was an important figure in the Czechoslovak Communist Party until the Velvet Revolution of 1989. He was a member of the hard-line minority of the Presidium that rallied to the Soviets, and as secretary of the Central Committee he rose to a position in the party second only to Gustav Husák. On December 21, 1989, the party membership of Bilak and 31 others was suspended by the Communist Party as it attempted to reconstruct itself to stave off complete disaster. Bilak, however, later became active in the Slovak Democratic Party of the Left.

In July 1992 Russian President Boris Yeltsin delivered copies of the August 1968 letter to the Czechoslovak government. Bilak, the only signatory still alive, was indicted for treason. In October 1997, however, the Czech high court lifted the indictment, judging that what Bilak had done was not a criminal act.

BIBLIOGRAPHY

"La Cour suprême lève définitivement l'inculpation d'ex-dirigeants comunistes." Agence France Presse, October 3, 1997.

"Czech Hardliners' 'Request' for Soviet Intervention, August 1968." Agence France Presse, Tr. and intro. by Mark Kramer. ⟨http://www.seas.gwu.edu/nsarchive/CWIHP/BULLETINS/b2a2.htm⟩

"Czechoslovakia Indicts Communist in Fraud." *New York Times,* February 7, 1992.

Kramer, Mark. "New Sources on the 1968 Soviet Invasion of Czechoslovakia." ⟨http://www.seas.gwu.edu/nsarchive/CWIHP/BULLETINS/b2a4.htm⟩

Tagliabue, John. "Upheaval in the East: Party in Prague Is Suspending 32." *New York Times,* December 22, 1989.

Bernard Cook

Bildt, Carl (1949–)

Swedish Moderate prime minister, 1991–94. Carl Bildt, born on July 15, 1949, was educated at the University of Stockholm. He was chairman of the Conference of Liberal and Conservative Students in 1972–73 and the European Democrat Students from 1974 to 1976. He served on the Stockholm County Council from 1974 to 1977. In the early 1970s Bildt was an assistant to Gösta Bohman, leader of the Moderate Party. Bildt served as an undersecretary of state for policy coordination in the non-Socialist governments of 1976–78 and 1979–81, first as an adviser on policy coordination at the Ministry of Economic Affairs, then as undersecretary of state for coordination and planning at the cabinet office. He entered parliament in 1979 as a representative from Stockholm and was appointed a member of the parliamentary standing committee on foreign affairs from 1982 to 1986. Bildt became a member of the executive committee of the Moderate Party in 1981 and was elected party leader of the Moderates in 1986.

Bildt became prime minister in 1991. In his inaugural address to the Swedish parliament, he declared that "the age of collectivism is over." A dedicated European, Bildt made Sweden's into the European Union (EU) a prime objective of his government. Although his government fell in 1994 as a result of its rejection by voters opposed to cuts in Sweden's welfare system, Sweden did enter the EU in 1995.

Bildt is a member of the International Institute for Strategic Studies in London and, since 1992, chair of the International Democrat Union. From 1995 to 1997, he was the high representative of the United Nations and the EU in Bosnia.

Bernard Cook

Bindi, Rosy (1951–)

Italian politician. Rosaria (Rosy) Bindi was born in Sinalunga in the province of Sienna on February 12, 1951. She studied administrative law in the Faculty of Political Science of the University of Rome, "La Sapienza." She taught there serving as a research assistant to Vittorio Bachelet, who was later killed by the radical terrorist Red Brigades. Bindi, a Catholic activist, became the national vice president of the Azione Cattòlica movement. She joined the Christian Democrats (DC), but in the 1980s she headed a left-wing faction within the party that vociferously opposed the national DC leadership. She was particularly critical of what she called the "appetite for power" of the Christian Democratic prime minister, Ciriaco De Mita. In 1989 she was elected to the European Parliament on the DC list. She was secretary of the DC in the Veneto region at the time of the DC's demise. She was a founding member of the Popular Party and served as its regional coordinator in Veneto, responsible for publicity and information.

In 1994 she was elected to parliament on the Popular Party's proportional list. On April 21, 1996, she was reelected to parliament, this time as part of the Olive Tree alliance of Popular Democrats. In the Cortona district of Tuscany she won 60,443 of the 92,923 votes cast, or 65 percent. In Romano Prodi's government, formed in May 1996, Bindi was the minister of health.

Bernard Cook

Bitburg Controversy

Controversy surrounding the visit of U.S. President Ronald Reagan and West German Chancellor Helmut Kohl to the military cemetery at the West German town of Bitburg on May 5, 1985. The wreath-laying ceremony was intended as a symbolic act of reconciliation between the United States and the Federal Republic of Germany on the fortieth anniversary of the ending of World War II. Reagan's visit took place despite widespread criticism from legislators and Jewish, Christian, and veterans groups in the United States when it was revealed that the Bitburg cemetery was the burial site not only of Wehrmacht (German army) soldiers but of at least forty-seven members of the Waffen SS (a military unit of the SS) as well. No American soldiers were buried at Bitburg.

Cancellation, ostensibly at the request of the West German government, of earlier plans to hold the official ceremony at Dachau concentration camp added to the furor that developed when the existence of SS graves at Bitburg became known. Growing protests in the United States led to the belated inclusion of Bergen-Belsen concentration camp on the president's itinerary. On April 27, 1985, eighty-two U.S. senators appealed to President Reagan to drop the intended visit to Bitburg, and 257 members of the U.S. House of Representatives signed a letter to Chancellor Kohl urging him to withdraw his invitation. Political considerations such as the need for West German support for his Strategic Defense Initiative and the wish to solidify German commitment to NATO were crucial in Reagan's decision not to forgo the visit to Bitburg. But

Reagan defended his projected visit by asserting that the young, conscripted members of the Waffen SS buried there were as much victims of Nazism as the inmates of the concentration camps. Reagan's suggestion that fallen German soldiers and exterminated Jews were equally victims of Hitler seemed to deny the exceptionality of the Holocaust.

Although the controversy abated after completion of the official visit, Bitburg remained a symbol of the tendency or willingness to forget or revise the history of Nazi German atrocities. The controversy anticipated the bitter dispute (*Historikerstreit*) that broke out in 1986 among West German historians about the historiography of the Holocaust.

BIBLIOGRAPHY
Hartman, Geoffrey H., ed. *Bitburg in Moral and Political Perspective.* Bloomington: Indiana University Press, 1986.
Levkov, Ilya, ed. *Bitburg and Beyond: Encounters in American, German and Jewish History.* New York: Shapolsky, 1987.

Rod Stackelberg

Bjerregaard, Ritt (1941–)

Danish Social Democratic politician and EU commissioner for the environment. Born in 1941, Ritt Bjerregaard taught school from 1964 to 1970 then was an instructor at a teachers' training college from 1970 to 1982. She was a member of the Danish parliament from 1971 to 1995, serving as minister for education in 1973 and from 1975 to 1978, minister for social welfare from 1979 to 1981, and auditor of public accounts from 1982 to 1994. She was chairperson of the Social Democratic parliamentary group from 1981 to 1982 and 1987 to 1991.

In her 1979 book, *Strid (Strife)*, Bjerregaard argued that social change cannot be attained without conflict and controversy. In her own political career she often annoyed the Social Democratic leadership by publicly raising controversial issues. Nevertheless, in the 1994 general election she received the third-highest number of votes in Denmark.

Bjerregaard was vice president of the Parliamentary Assembly of the Organization of Security and Cooperation in Europe from 1992 to 1995, and in 1995 became commissioner for environment of the European Commission.

BIBLIOGRAPHY
Frastein, Susi. *Ritt, portraet af en politiker.* Copenhagen: Tiderne skifter, 1986.

Jørn Boye Nielsen

Björnsson, Sveinn (1881–1952)

First president of Iceland. Sveinn Björnsson received a law degree from the University of Copenhagen in 1907. He sat in Reykjavík's City Council from 1912 to 1920 and in the Icelandic parliament from 1914 to 1916, then again from 1919 to 1920. Isolated from Denmark during World War I, Iceland was granted full independence by Denmark in December 1918. Iceland, however, agreed to recognize the king of Denmark as its sovereign. Björnsson served as Iceland's first ambassador to Denmark from 1920 to 1924 and from 1926 to 1940, but returned to Iceland when Germany occupied Denmark in 1940. In 1941 he was elected the first and only governor of Iceland (*rikisstjori*), replacing the Danish king as the highest official in Iceland because of the communications interrupted in wartime between Copenhagen and Iceland. At the founding of the Republic of Iceland on June 17, 1944, Björnsson was elected its first president, and he was re-elected without opposition in 1948. Björnsson died in 1952 as his second term was coming to an end. For the most part, he played an inactive role in Icelandic politics as president, in the same way as the Danish king had done before him. Thus, although the president of Iceland has extensive formal power, he serves primarily as a symbolic figurehead.

Gudmundur Halfdanarson

Tony Blair, Labour prime minister of Great Britain and successor to John Major. *Illustration courtesy of the British Information Service.*

Blair, Anthony Charles Lynton (Tony) (1953–)

Labour prime minister of the United Kingdom since 1997. Tony Blair, elected leader of the Labour Party in July 1994, reformed the party and led it to victory in the 1997 election.

Blair was born May 6, 1953, in Edinburgh. From 1972 to 1975 he attended St. John's College, Oxford, where he showed more interest in rock music than politics. Nevertheless, motivated by a Christian belief in social community, he joined Labour in 1975. He was called to the bar in 1976, and married fellow barrister Cherie Booth in 1980. In the late 1970s, unhappy with both the remote Labour leadership and what he considered irresponsible local Labour activists, he entered politics. He was elected for Sedgefield in the 1983 election and in 1984 joined the front bench as spokesman on treasury and economic affairs, where he demonstrated his determination, quick intelligence, speaking ability, and mastery of detail. After the 1987 election he was promoted to opposition spokesman on trade and industry. In 1988 he was elected to the shadow cabinet as energy secretary, rising to the shadow posts of employment secretary (1989–92) and home sec-

retary (1992–94). In 1993 he gained notice by asserting that Labour would be "tough on crime, tough on the causes of crime," a claim that retained Labour's concern for the welfare of the less fortunate while seeking to deprive the Conservatives of their traditional law-and-order appeal. He thus aligned himself with the "modernizers" who believed Labour needed a new identity as a party of democratic socialism, not piecemeal reform, if it was to gain power.

In May 1994, John Smith, Labour's leader, died suddenly. Blair, who believed Smith had not understood the implications of Labour's defeat in 1992, decided to stand for the leadership. In the early 1990s Blair's friend Gordon Brown looked likely to succeed Smith, but Brown's visibility as heir apparent had alienated some of his colleagues. He withdrew from the leadership contest, and Blair was elected. Initially derided as "Bambi" for his wide eyes and youth, Blair proved determined to continue party reform. In April 1995, overcoming an obstacle that had defeated past Labour leaders, he persuaded the party to revise clause four of its constitution, which had committed it to public ownership of the means of production. Before the 1997 election he presided over a rapid increase in the party's membership, revitalized its media center, and supported Brown, now shadow chancellor, in his efforts to eradicate the party's tax-and-spend image. The election went smoothly and "New Labour" won a majority of 179. Blair then began to carry out Labour's manifesto, including its promise of devolution for Scotland and Wales. In opposition and government Blair sought to present Labour as a pragmatic socialist party that welcomed the aspirations of ordinary voters. His youth and vigor appealed to a nation hungry for the sense of change and purpose he seemed to embody, but, apart from his personal qualities, his greatest asset was that he came to Labour too late to be tainted by public commitments to its vote-losing causes of the early 1980s.

BIBLIOGRAPHY

Blair, Tony. *New Britain: My Vision of a Young Country.* London: Fourth Estate, 1996.

Butler, David, and Dennis Kavanagh. *The British General Election of 1997.* London: Macmillan, 1997.

Draper, Derek. *Blair's Hundred Days.* London: Faber and Faber, 1997.

Mandelson, Peter, and Roger Liddle. *The Blair Revolution: Can New Labour Deliver?* London: Faber and Faber, 1996.

Sopel, Jon. *Tony Blair: The Moderniser.* London: Michael Joseph, 1995.

Ted R. Bromund

SEE ALSO Kinnock, Neil; Smith, John; United Kingdom

Blaney, Neil T. (1922–96)

Irish politician. Neil Blaney was born in Rossnakill, County Donegal. In 1948 he ran as a candidate of the republican Fianna Fail party to the Irish parliament and won the seat previously held by his father. He served as minister for posts and telegraphs from March to December 1957, then as minister for local government until November 1966. In the first government of Jack Lynch, Blaney became minister for agriculture and fisheries. In May 1970 he was dismissed by Lynch and expelled from the party in November 1971 because of his opposition to Lynch's more moderate policy toward the Northern Iceland problem. As the sole member of the Independent Fianna Fail (until joined by Patrick Keaveney from June 1976 to June 1977), Blaney maintained constant criticism of Fianna Fail and the National Coalition governments for their policies on Northern Ireland and the republican movement. Blaney's control of the Fianna Fail organization in Donegal has been the subject of a study, *The Don-*

egal Mafia (1977). He headed the poll in the Connaught-Ulster constituency in the direct election to the European Parliament in June 1979.

Michael J. Kennedy

SEE ALSO Lynch, John

Bloch, Ernst (1885–1977)

German philosopher and social critic. Ernst Bloch was a prolific writer whose chief contributions were in the areas of social philosophy and criticism, philosophy of religion, and music theory. In philosophy he argued that both religious sentiment and left-wing social programs aspired to a perpetual renewal of the human spirit in a utopian world. This led him eventually to his major philosophical opus, *The Principle of Hope.* In essence this work deals with a dilemma in the human condition: the human desire for an ideal future; the historically demonstrated fact that humans act on this desire; and the struggle with the material condition of social reality, which alienates and subverts this hope. Bloch's response to the problem was to emphasize the possibilities inherent in the material condition. It is not the reality of materialism that must be overcome, but material existence should itself be considered as an active potential for change and renewal. Bloch's sentiment may best be expressed in a sentence from *Social Utopia:* "the world is not true, but it shall reach its homecoming through humanity." The actuality of the world is not what matters but human action, which transforms the alienated world into a hospitable dwelling.

Bloch in his interviews and essays was an outspoken critic of the German Nazis during the 1930s and 1940s. He was an opponent of Stalinism as well, and spoke in favor of socialism with a human face during the Prague Spring of the late 1960s. Bloch's influence has been strong in religious studies, social theory, and aesthetics.

BIBLIOGRAPHY

Hudson, Wayne. *The Marxist Philosophy of Ernst Bloch.* New York: St. Martin's Press, 1982.

Neher, André. *They Made Their Souls Anew.* Albany: State University of New York, 1990.

Nordquist, Joan. *Ernst Bloch: A Bibliography.* Santa Cruz, Calif.: Reference and Research Service, 1990.

Daniel E. Shannon

Blum, Léon (1872–1950)

French Socialist and premier. Léon Blum succeeded Jean Jaurès as leader of France's Socialist Party (Section Française de l'Internationale ouvrière, SFIO), and became France's first Socialist premier in 1936. Blum advocated a humane and democratic socialism for France while opposing both fascism and communism.

Born into a commercial Alsatian-Jewish family in Paris, Blum abandoned his studies at the École Normale Supérieure after a year to pursue a law degree. As a junior counsel with the administrative Conseil d'État he also earned a reputation as a literary and drama critic for the *Revue blanche.* A nonpracticing Jew and political liberal, Blum was drawn to socialism by the Dreyfus affair and an introduction to Jean Jaurès, then head of the Parti Socialiste Français, which he joined in 1902. The murder of Jaurès in 1914 and wartime experience in Socialist minister Marcel Sembat's Ministry of Public Works deepened Blum's commitment to social justice through government action. By 1919 he was formulating SFIO policy and had a seat in the Chamber of Deputies.

At the landmark Tours party congress in 1920, a three-to-one majority voted to organize the French Communist Party (PCF). Blum led the opposition, attacking the dictatorial tendencies in Leninism and defending liberal democracy as a necessary precondition for the peaceful electoral achievement of socialism. Through the 1920s Blum worked successfully to rebuild the SFIO, shaping its policies through daily editorials in the party paper, *Le Populaire.* Despite Radical victories in 1924 and 1932, Blum declined to formally participate in any government where the SFIO was not the senior partner.

After the February 6, 1934, Paris riots by French fascists, Blum gradually negotiated a Popular Front electoral alliance with the Radicals and Communists, a policy that led to victory in the June 1936 election and made Blum premier. Though his government lasted barely a year, he negotiated raises, union rights, collective bargaining, paid vacations, and a forty-hour week for French workers. Less successful in foreign policy, Blum reluctantly adopted Britain's nonintervention policy in the Spanish Civil War. Capital flight, which undermined economic recovery, and Senate opposition to his program brought his resignation in 1937.

Blum long hoped the League of Nations and disarmament would prevent a general war. After France's defeat Blum voted against granting Marshall Philippe Pétain full powers in July 1940. Blaming the Third Republic's leaders for France's collapse, the Vichy regime put Blum on trial at Riom in 1941, but Blum's aggressive defense forced the court to recess without a verdict. Imprisoned at Buchenwald concentration camp in Germany from 1943 to 1945, Blum returned to France as a national hero. In his last years he removed lingering Marxist ele-

ments in SFIO ideology and participated in international conferences that founded UNESCO and liquidated French war debts with the United States.

BIBLIOGRAPHY
Blum, Léon. *L'Oeuvre de Léon Blum.* 7 Vols. Paris: Albin Michel, 1954–65.
Colton, Joel. *Léon Blum: Humanist in Politics.* New York: Knopf, 1966.
Jackson, Julian. *The Popular Front in France.* Cambridge: Cambridge University Press, 1988.
Lacouture, Jean. *Léon Blum.* New York: Holmes & Meier, 1982.

David Longfellow

SEE ALSO France, Gouin, Félix

Blüm, Norbert (1935–)

Christian Democratic (CDU) minister of labor and social affairs of the Federal Republic of Germany, 1982–98. Norbert Blüm was born in Rüsselsheim on July 21, 1935. He attended a technical school, learned tool making, and worked for Opel in his hometown from 1949 to 1957. He also worked as a construction worker and a truck driver. He studied at night school and entered the University of Cologne, where he studied philosophy and history. He earned a Ph.D. at Bonn in 1967.

Blüm joined the CDU in 1950 and edited the party's journal *Soziale Ordnung* (Social Order) from 1966 to 1968. From 1968 to 1975 he was chief manager of the Social Committee of the Christian Democratic Employees' Association. He became a member of the CDU's Federal Executive and was elected to the Bundestag in 1969. He became deputy chair of the CDU in 1981. In 1982 he was appointed minister of labor and social affairs by Helmut Kohl. He was the longest-serving of Kohl's ministers.

He has consistently defended the social system and the social market economy of the Federal Republic. He touted the dual system for creating a unique degree of social peace, arguing that one of the positive outcomes of Germany's system has been the partnership between labor and management. He cautioned against endangering Germany's social welfare state by an expansion that would be financially insupportable or by reductions that would break commitments and endanger social tranquillity. He advocated a balance between individual responsibility and the obligations of social solidarity. As a solution to unemployment and the financial burden of early retirements, he advocated a flexible system of part-time work.

BIBLIOGRAPHY
"An Interview with Norbert Blüm," *Deutschland* 5 (October 1996): 8–11.

Bernard Cook

Boal, Desmond (1929–)

Ulster Unionist MP for Shankill, 1960–71; Democratic Unionist Party MP, 1971–72. Desmond Boal was born in Derry City in 1929. He became one of Northern Ireland's leading barristers and also one of its most intriguing political figures. As a Unionist MP he was frequently at odds with the party leadership. Deprived of the position of party whip for criticism of Lord Brookeborough as prime minister, he was prominent in the backbench revolt against Terence O'Neill largely because of O'Neill's decision to invite Sean Lemass, taoiseach (Irish prime minister), to Stormont for unannounced talks. And he was highly critical of the law-and-order policies of the Chichester-Clark and Faulkner governments. In 1966 Boal lost his post as counsel to the attorney general after he had defended the right of Presbyterians to protest at the General Assembly of Irish Presbyterian Church. In 1971 he resigned from the Unionist Party after describing the tripartite talks among Brian Faulkner, Jack Lynch, and Edward Heath as adding a new dimension of dishonesty to Unionist politics. Soon afterward he joined the Reverend Ian Paisley in launching the Democratic Unionist Party (DUP), of which he became the first chairman. He resigned his Shankill seat immediately following the introduction of direct rule in March 1972 in protest against Westminster's move. In 1974, after he had given up the chairmanship of the DUP, he announced support for a federal scheme in Ireland. He wanted an Irish federal parliament holding the powers reserved to Westminster under the 1920 Government of Ireland Act and the restoration of the Stormont parliament with its old powers. The idea attracted some interest in Dublin but was generally rejected by Unionists. Paisley joined in the denunciation. In 1977 Boal was involved with Sean MacBride in a chain of contacts between the Provisional IRA and loyalist paramilitaries aimed at securing a cease-fire.

Ricki Schoen

Boban, Mate (1939–97)

Bosnian Croat politician and leader of the secessionist state of Herceg-Bosna in 1993–94. Mate Boban is a Croat nationalist from western Herzegovina who seized control of the Croatian Democratic Union (HDZ) of Bosnia in March 1992, which until then had been in alliance with Bosnia's Muslim Party. With the Bosnian state soon reeling from the outbreak of internal warfare, speculation became rife that Croatia and Serbia were ready to partition Bosnia between them. In Croatia the powerful Herzegovina lobby, composed in large part of wealthy émigrés from this part of Yugoslavia, urged this course on president Franjo Tudjman, who was keen to acquire more territory and defensible borders for his vulnerable state.

Boban, a former clothing store manager, put the land grab into effect after July 7, 1992, when a Croatian Republic of Herzeg-Bosna was set up on Bosnian territory. The city of Mostar, hitherto shared between Muslims and Croats, was declared its capital. Croat-Muslim fighting erupted in earnest in January 1993, much of it centered around Mostar, whose Muslim population was subjected to a relentless siege. Militarily Boban's forces made little headway, and their actions caused mounting dissension within Croatia, the Catholic Church being at the forefront of the criticism.

Boban was always a vassal of Tudjman, and when the Croatian president was informed by Germany and the United States that support for Croatia would be withdrawn and international sanctions imposed unless the Croatian attacks on Bosnia were halted, he was banished to obscurity in January 1994. He remained officially the leader of the HDZ in Bosnia but virtually nothing was heard of him following the U.S.-brokered peace settlement of March 1, 1994, which led to a federation of Croat and Bosnian government—held parts of Bosnia on March 31, 1994.

Tom Gallagher

Bodnaras, Emil (1904–76)

Professional soldier who held important posts in the Romanian Communist Party and government, the most important of which was minister of national defense, 1947–57. From a proletarian family in Bukovina, Emil Bodnaras graduated from military school in 1928 but fled to the USSR in 1932, where he probably became associated with the NKVD (Soviet secret police). The Romania police arrested him when he returned home around 1933, and he remained imprisoned with other Romanian Communists until 1944. When released he worked closely with the invading Red Army. Bodnaras and Lucretiu Patrascanu were the Communist representatives in the group that successfully plotted the overthrow of Ion Antonescu.

Bodnaras's ties with Moscow made him one of the most feared men in Romania. Essentially an opportunist, he transformed this fear into power by making himself useful to Moscow and Romanian leader Gheorghiu-Gheorghe Dej. He helped Soviet Premier Nikita Khrushchev's attempt to reconcile with Tito and supported de-Stalinization. This upset Stalinist Gheorghiu-Dej, who worried that Khrushchev wanted to remove him. Bodnaras's significance, however, stems from being instrumental in convincing Khrushchev to withdraw Soviet occupation troops from Romania in 1958. He faded from power in the 1960s, probably owing mainly to an unwillingness to support fully the party's increasing desire from around 1958 to lessen Soviet control of Romania.

Robert F. Forrest

SEE ALSO Gheorghiu-Dej, Gheorghe

Böhme, Ibrahim (1944–)

Chairman of the Social Democrats in the German Democratic Republic (GDR) in 1989–90. Manfred Böhme was born on November 18, 1944, near Leipzig. It is possible that his parents, or at least his father, were Jewish. His parents died some years after his birth and he grew up with other families. Later he became a mason. During his education he became acquainted with the books and critical thinking of Robert Havemann (1910–82), a scientist and dissident murdered by the Stasi, the East German secret police.

In 1967 Böhme joined the Socialist Unity Party (SED) and became a member of the county directorate of the Kulturbund (cultural organization) for Greiz, now in the state of Thuringia. There he had his first contacts with individuals and groups associated with the opposition and his first contact with the Ministry for State Security (Ministerium für Staatssicherheit, MfS). Böhme was first given the cover name "August Drempker," and later "Paul Bongartz," and he collected information about the opposition scene, including writer Reiner Kunze.

In 1975 Böhme married and his daughter was born. After the songwriter Wolf Biermann was stripped of his East German citizenship, Böhme left the SED and lost his job. Because of a protest action in Magdeburg, he was arrested and detained three months (fifteen months according to his version). After this the MfS sent him to Neubrandenburg in the northern GDR to observe dissidents in the Protestant Church, among them Markus Meckel, later foreign minister of the GDR. Böhme's new cover name was "Dr. Rudolf." Böhme worked at the theater but was discharged after a meeting with opposition poets. Next he was a waiter, librarian, forester, and translator of Russian.

In 1986 Böhme received a new order from the MfS. He moved to East Berlin and changed his first name to Ibrahim, allegedly to manifest his Jewish origin. Under the new cover name Maximilian, he observed additional opposition groups but also cooperated with them. In autumn 1989 Böhme cofounded the Social Democrat Party of the GDR (Sozialdemokratische Partei der DDR, SDP) and later served as party chairman. He participated in the consultations of the opposition round table (Runder Tisch), a forum of the noncommunist parties organized in December 1989 to push for the democratization of East Germany. Before the parliamentary elections of March 18, 1990, Böhme was the leading candidate of the Social Democrats. However, he lost the election, and his MfS membership became known. Böhme denied the allegations and ran for the federal committee of the Social Democrats (Bundesvorstand der SPD). But the files' indication of his role was clear, and he resigned from all party duties. Until December 1990 he worked as commissioner for the police in the East Berlin administration. In 1991 Böhme became severely depressed. In June 1992 he was expelled from the Social Democratic Party and lived afterward as a private person in Berlin.

BIBLIOGRAPHY
Lahann, Birgit. *Genosse Judas: Die zwei Leben des Ibrahim Böhme.* Berlin: Rowohlt 1992.

Jürgen Streller

Boland, Frederick H. (1904–85)

Irish civil servant and diplomat. Frederick Boland joined the Department of External Affairs in 1929. From 1930 to 1931 he was a junior administrative officer. He then served as first secretary in the Paris legation (1932–34) and head of the League of Nations section (1934–36). From 1936 to 1938 he moved departments to become principal officer at the Department of Industry and Commerce, in charge of the overseas trade section. He returned to External Affairs as assistant secretary from 1938 to 1946. During World War II Boland was responsible for defending Irish neutrality, though with an Anglophile stance.

Boland was secretary to the Department of External Affairs from 1946 to 1950. During his tenure Ireland greatly expanded its foreign diplomatic representation and the concerns of its foreign policy. In 1949 Boland was in part responsible for Ireland's Long-Term Recovery Programme, which enabled the state to get loans from the Marshall Plan. From 1950 to 1955 Boland held the senior

Irish diplomatic posting of ambassador to the Court of St. James in London.

On December 15, 1955, Ireland was admitted to the United Nations. Boland was appointed permanent U.N. representative in 1956, holding the post until 1964. On September 20, 1960, Boland was elected president for the 1960–61 session of the U.N. General Assembly. He received a strong endorsement from the United States and a positive vote from the USSR.

Boland's presidency coincided with one of the most eventful General Assemblies of the Cold War. His most famous moment was when he called Soviet Premier Nikita Khrushchev to order for calling Spanish leader Francisco Franco "the hangman of Spain whom the Americans support." During debate on the seating of mainland China, he asked Khrushchev "to be good enough to cooperate with the Chair." Though Khrushchev hit the speaker's rostrum with his shoe in anger and Boland broke the president's gavel trying to restore order, the two men were seen laughing and chatting about the incident some days later. Khrushchev later sent Boland a case of wine as an apology. The death of Secretary-General Dag Hammarskjöld in a plane crash occurred during Boland's presidency, and he turned down the post of acting secretary-general. He served on the Security Council during Ireland's half-term, from 1962–63. As one of independent Ireland's first career diplomats, he provided part of the intellectual basis for Frank Aiken's foreign policy.

Following his retirement from the diplomatic service, Boland served as chancellor of Trinity College Dublin from 1964 to 1982.

Michael J. Kennedy

SEE ALSO Ireland

Bolger, Dermot (1959–)

Irish poet and novelist. Dermot Bolger, born in Dublin, was employed as a factory worker and library assistant before managing the Raven Arts Press. His first novels were a trilogy about Dublin life: *Night Shift* (1985), *The Woman's Daughter* (1987), *The Journey Home* (1990). These were followed by *Emily's Shoes* (1992). Bolger has also written plays, including, *The Lament for Arthur Cleary* (1989) and *Blinded by the Light* (1990). His poems include *Never a Dull Moment* (1978), *The Habit of Flesh* (1980), *No waiting America* (1982), and *Internal Exiles* (1986). Bolger is a Member of the Arts Council of Ireland.

BIBLIOGRAPHY
Bolger, Dermot, ed. *The Bright Wave—An Tonn Gheal: Poetry in Irish Now.* Dublin: Raven Arts Press, 1986.
———. *The Picador Book of Contemporary Irish Fiction.* London: Picador, 1993.
———. *Ireland in Exile, Irish Writers Abroad.* Dublin: New Island Books, 1993.

Michael J. Kennedy

Böll, Heinrich (1917–85)

West Germany's best-known and best-selling postwar author. Böll, who won the Nobel Prize in literature in 1972 after publication of his best-known novel, the 1971 *Group Portrait with a Lady* (*Gruppenbild mit Dame*). Heinrich Böll is, perhaps more than any other German author, representative of the German postwar experience. He engaged German history and West German society critically and with wide public acclaim for nearly four decades in his many literary and essayistic works. His writings tend to center on three main themes: the hopelessness and nihilism of war, the hypocrisy of a society that represses its own history, and contemporary social, religious, and political issues.

Böll's formative experiences came from his liberal-minded and nonconformist Rhineland-Catholic parents and from the war. He was drafted early and fought as an infantryman in several theaters, spent some time as a POW of the Americans and British, and was released from the army in December 1945. His first creative writings, short stories very much in the American tradition of Ernest Hemingway (Böll also cotranslated O. Henry and J. D. Salinger), deal almost exclusively with the grinding senselessness of war as seen from the perspective of the common soldier. *Der Zug war punktlich* (1949; *The Train Was on Time,* 1956) and *Wanderer, kommst du nach Spa . . .* (1950; *Traveller, If You Come to Spa . . .*, 1956) gained immediate popularity; stories in these collections, along with other war stories written through the early 1960s, have been read by nearly every German schoolchild born after the war. His main characters, nearly always the common man, the little person, the misfit, or the outsider, provide an ironic and sometimes satirical point of view of the machinations of the dominant military culture of conformism. Almost every reader could identify with Böll's uncomplicated first-person narrators. The hero of his first and most famous war novel, *Wo warst du, Adam?* (1951; *Adam, Where Art Thou?* 1955), is a victim of the absurdity of war when he returns home from the front at the end of the war only to be killed with his parents by a German shell fired at his own house shortly before the capitulation.

The crass materialism of the postwar "economic miracle" is Böll's theme and target of criticism in his works from the middle period: *Billard um halbzehn: Roman* (1959; *Billards at Half-past Nine,* 1961), *Ansichten eines Clowns* (1963; *The Clown,* 1963), and *Gruppenbild mit Dame* all get at the heart of the conflict between middle-class materialism and religious, moral, and ethical values. Leni Pfeiffer, famous heroine of *Gruppenbild,* has been called a "secular beatification" (Theodore Ziolkowski) because of the way she takes on "the whole weight of [German] history" (Böll), yet she is also a revolutionary figure in her complete rejection of the work ethic, itself a kind of German national religion during the immediate postwar decades.

Böll, a vital public intellectual for the young German republic, became very active politically in the 1970s through his defense of the principle of due process for the Baader-Meinhof terrorists, his merciless critique of the popular yellow press in *Die verlorene Ehre der Katharina Blum* (1974; *The Lost Honor of Katharina Blum,* 1975), and in his many essays and speeches on German politics and history. His late works include travel essays, previously unpublished war stories from the early period, and less acclaimed novels. He remained a prominent public intellectual and moral compass for West German society until the end of his life.

BIBLIOGRAPHY

Butler, Michael. *The Narrative Fiction of Heinrich Böll: Social Conscience and Literary Achievement.* Cambridge: Cambridge University Press, 1995.

Conrad, Robert C. *Understanding Heinrich Böll.* Columbia: University of South Carolina Press, 1992.

Linder, Christian. *Heinrich Böll: Leben & Schreiben, 1917–1985.* Cologne: Kiepenheuer & Witsch, 1986.

Reid, James H. *Heinrich Böll: A German for His Time.* Oxford: Berg, 1988.

Schröter, Klaus. *Heinrich Böll.* Reinbek bei Hamburg: Rowohlt, 1995.

Sowinsky, Bernhard. *Heinrich Böll.* Stuttgart: Metzler, 1993.

Scott Denham

Bondevik, Kjell Magne (1947–)

Norwegian prime minister since 1997. Kjell Magne Bondevik was born on September 3, 1947, in Molde. Married, with three children, Bondevik studied theology and was ordained a Lutheran priest in 1979. He became a deputy member of the Storting (Norwegian parliament) for Møre og Romsdal county in 1969. He served as a member of the Nesodden Municipal Council and Board of Education in 1972–73. In 1973 he was elected to the Storting. In 1972–73 he was state secretary at the office of the prime minister. From 1983 to 1986 he served as minister of church and education, and in 1989–90 as minister of foreign affairs. In 1997 he formed a minority government composed of his Christian Democratic Party, the Liberals, and the Center Party.

Bondevik became deputy chairman of the Norwegian Young Christian Democrats in 1968 and their chairman in 1970. In 1975 he became the political vice chairman of the Christian Democratic Party and in 1983 its chairman. He held that post until 1985. He served as the chairman of the Christian Democratic Party parliamentary group in 1981–83, 1986–89, and 1993–97.

BIBLIOGRAPHY

Bondevik, Kjell Magne. *Det tredje alternativ: Kristendemokratisk politikk på norsk.* Oslo: Folkets Framtid, 1995.

Bernard Cook

SEE ALSO Jagland, Thorbjørn; Lahnstein, Anne Enger

Bonner, Yelena Georgievna (1923–)

Soviet human rights activist. Yelena Bonner was the wife of the physicist and human rights advocate Andrey Sakharov, who won the Nobel Peace Prize in 1975. She served as a nurse with the Soviet army in World War II and was partially blinded. She studied medicine after the war and became a doctor. She was a founder of the Helsinki Watch organization in Moscow in 1975. She and other Helsinki Watch members monitored the USSR's violations of the human rights statement to which it assented in Helsinki in 1975. As a result, she was sentenced to five years of internal exile in 1984 but was released in 1985. She continued her human rights activities after the death of Sakharov on December 14, 1989.

Bernard Cook

SEE ALSO Sakharov, Andrey

Bonnet, Henri (1888–1978)

French diplomat. Henri Bonnet was born at Château-ponsac on May 26, 1888. He graduated from the École Normale Supérieure in Paris and, after serving in the First World War, was an editor of *L'Ère nouvelle.* After the establishment of the Vichy regime during the German occupation of the Second World War, Bonnet represented the Free French government in the United States. From 1943 to 1944 he was minister of information for the Committee of National Liberation in Algiers. He served as French ambassador to the United States from 1944 to 1955. He died in Paris on October 25, 1978.

Bernard Cook

Bonomi, Ivanoe (1873–1951)

Wartime Italian anti-fascist leader and prime minister, 1944–45. Ivanoe Bonomi was born in Mantua on October 18, 1873. In 1898, he began his career as a journalist. Despite being a moderate socialist, he was in favor of Italy's occupation of Libya in 1911, and he later supported the government's involvement in World War I. Expelled from the Socialist Party in 1919, he soon became one of the founders of the Socialist Reformist Party. Secretary for public works in 1916 and in 1919, he also was minister of war in the second Nitti cabinet and in the last Giolitti cabinet. Bonomi was prime minister from June 1921 to February 1922, and his opposition to the rise of fascism in the country was at first weak and ineffective. During the Mussolini regime (1922–43) he was forced into retire.

In 1942, Bonomi joined the antifascist movement and was among those liberals who suggested to the king that Mussolini be ousted and the alliance with Germany abandoned. Mussolini was removed in July, 1943, and during the government of his successor, General Badoglio, Bonomi chaired the National Liberation Committee (CLN) composed of all antifascist parties. As a representative of the liberation committee, Bonomi became prime minister once again in 1944 because he represented those moderate forces accepted by the Allies. Bonomi resigned right after the liberation of northern Italy from German occupation. He was one of the three Italian negotiators at the 1947 international peace talks, and in 1948 he became the president of the Italian senate.

His works include: *La finanza comunale e i suoi problemi* (Palermo, 1903); *Le vie nuove del Socialismo* (Palermo, 1906); *Dieci anni di politica italiana* (Milano, 1924); *Dal socialismo al Fascismo* (Roma 1924); *Leonida Bissolati e il movimento socialista in Italia* (Milano, 1929); *La politica italiana dalla breccia di Porta Pia a Vittorio Veneto* (Torino, 1945); *Diario di un anno, 2 giugno 1943–10 giugno 1944* (Milano, 1947); and *La politica italiana dopo Vittorio Veneto* (Torino, 1953).

BIBLIOGRAPHY

Arfé, G. *Storia del socialismo italiano (1892–1926)*. Torino: G. Einaudi, 1965.

Cavazzoli, L., and G. Degli Ippoliti. *Bonomi, un protagonista del '900*. Mantova, 1993.

Stefania Mazzone

Borghese Coup

Attempted right-wing coup d'état in Italy in an attempt to forestall a draft to the left. On the night of December 7–8, 1970, Prince Junio Valerio Borghese, commander of the Decima Mas, an elite Fascist division during the Salò Republic in 1944–45, attempted to stage a coup d'état, which has been described as a "coup d'état of pensioners." The conspirators were united in Rosa dei Venti, a right-wing extremist organization whose members were drawn from the Italian armed forces, extraparliamentary groups, and ex-parachutists. The intent of this small, over-ambitious group was to abolish the parliamentary system to create a "government of colonels." The authors of the conspiracy, in addition to Borghese, were Remo Orlandini and Sandro Saccucci, a lieutenant of the parachutists.

Borghese occupied for a few hours the building that housed the Ministry of the Interior, but was then forced to surrender. Even though he was suspected of having connections with the army and the secret service, Borghese was obviously an adventurer without much support. What happened during that night came to light only in March 1971. At an early stage of inquiry the Freemasons, four hundred officers, groups of industrialists, and leaders of the Christian Democrats were suspected of being involved in the conspiracy. These accusations, however, proved groundless. Nevertheless, some groups took advantage of Rosa dei Venti to advance their own conspirational agendas. Members of the secret service knew what was going to happen before the coup. Furthermore, even though the responsible ministers were immediately informed, no measures were taken against the authors of the coup until the press exposed it. This implies the possibility that the coup was controlled by those of higher level.

In 1974, after many delays, four officers were accused of complicity in the attempted coup d'état, among them Vito Miceli, head of the secret service. During the trial, however, they were all acquitted.

BIBLIOGRAPHY

Beltrametti, Eggardo. *Il colpo di stato militare in Italia*. Rome: Giovanni Volpe, 1975.

De Lutiis, Giuseppe. *Storia dei servizi segreti in Italia*. Rome: Editori Riuniti, 1991.

Ginsborg, Paul. *A History of Contemporary Italy: Society and Politics 1943–1988.* New York: Penguin, 1990.

Claudia Franceschini

SEE ALSO Gladio; Italy; Terrorism, Right-wing

Borg Olivier, Giorgio (1911–80)

Premier of Malta. Giorgio Borg Olivier, a notary, succeeded Nerik Mizzi as leader of the Nationalist Party (PN) in 1950 and was premier from 1950 to 1955, then again from 1962 to 1971. His administration led Malta to independence from Britain in 1964 and strove to avert the worst possible consequences of the cessation of British economic support and services, gradually transforming the economy from one dependent on imperial needs and employment to one based increasingly on tourism, manufacturing, and more modern agricultural methods. Independence was accompanied by a defensive and a financial treaty with Britain, with which Borg Olivier, who was pro-Western, sought to maintain cordial relations as Malta made its debut into the international community. He died when Dom Mintoff was premier in 1980 and was given a state funeral. Borg Olivier's administrations were peaceful and progressive on the whole, liberal if not laissez-faire, overseeing a smooth transition from colonial rule to independent status. In the 1960s Borg Olivier and his party benefited from the confrontation between Mintoff and Catholic Archbishop Gonzi and the imposition of mortal sin by the church on those supporting the Socialists. However, Mintoff's authoritarian tendencies while in office, his resignation, and the riots following it in 1958, which led to the loss of self-government, would also have cost the Labour Party votes. Borg Olivier was defeated in the polls by Mintoff twice, in 1955 and in 1971, in the latter case by a very narrow margin. He was replaced as PN leader by Eddie Fenech-Adami in 1977.

Henry Frendo

SEE ALSO Fenech-Adami, Edward; Malta; Mintoff, Dom

Boross, Péter (1928–)

Prime minister of Hungary, 1993–94. Péter Boross succeeded József Antall upon the latter's death in December 1993, but his party, the Hungarian Democratic Forum, was defeated in the May 1994 parliamentary elections.

Boross graduated from the Law School of Eötvös Loránd University in Budapest in 1951 and was a civil servant until 1957. He was dismissed from his job because of his activities during the revolution in 1956 and ultimately found employment in the catering industry. He retired in 1989 but was recalled by Prime Minister Antall in 1990. Boross served on the prime minister's staff, was then appointed minister without portfolio in charge of intelligence services, and finally was appointed minister of interior in December 1990. He joined the Hungarian Democratic Forum in 1992 and was promoted to vice president and became heir-apparent to the gravely ill Antall in 1993.

Boross lacked the initiative and charisma of Antall and was unable to attract the support of larger groups of society and smooth over the differences in his own party after the electoral defeat of May 1994. He became a member of a renewed Hungarian Democratic Forum, which stressed the importance of Christian and patriotic values.

Tamás Magyarics

Borsellino, Paolo Emanuele (1940–92)

Italian magistrate killed by the Mafia on July 19, 1992. With Giovanni Falcone, Paolo Borsellino headed a new stage in the struggle against the Cosa Nostra from 1980 to 1992. After the Mafia enjoyed decades of virtual impunity, he succeeded in uncovering the rules, structures, and identities of components of the criminal organization and its connections with the political and institutional world.

Born in Palermo in the popular quarter of Kasla, son of a pharmacist, Borsellino joined the magistracy at the age of twenty-four. He became a judge at Enna in 1965 and was appointed magistrate of the lower court at Mazara del Vallo in 1967 for his "exceptional magisterial abilities." In 1970 he became magistrate of the lower court at Monreale. In 1975 he was transferred to the office of preliminary investigation, where he conducted his first inquests into Mafia dealings. Promoted to the appellate magistrate, in 1980 he became part of the first anti-Mafia "pool," created by the head of the office of investigation, Rocco Chinnici. These were the years when the most ferocious Mafia war in the history of the organization erupted. Magistrates and prominent politicians and police were frequently victims of attack. After the assassination of Chinnici in 1983, the leadership of the office of investigation passed to Antonio Caponnetto.

Caponnetto organized a new anti-Mafia pool composed of Borsellino, Falcone, Giuseppe Di Lello, and Leonardo Guarnotta. It was the historic pool that, with the testimony of the first *pentiti* (former mafiosi who provided information on their old associates)—Tommaso Buscetta, Francesco Marino Mannoia, and Salvatore Contorno—developed an inquest that for the first time brought to trial the heads of Cosa nostra. The great trial against 475 accused concluded on December 16, 1987, with nineteen life sentences and a total of 2,665 years in prison.

In 1986 Borsellino, at that time a magistrate of appeal, was promoted because of "special merit" to be district attorney at Marsala (Trapani). There he combined all the investigations against the Mafia undertaken since 1970 and developed a case against fifty-nine mafiosi. On December 11, 1991, he became the assistant district attorney for Palermo. He was among the principal supporters of a law for the protection of the *pentiti* and the creation of a new investigative structure for the apprehension of fugitives. He proposed an effort of this sort for the capture of Salvatore Riina, head of Cosa Nostra. After the assassination of Falcone on May 23, 1992, he evoked the testimony of new *pentiti,* Gaspare Mutolo and Leonardo Messina, who testified to the alleged collusion with the Mafia of magistrates and the director of the Secret Services, Bruno Contrada. The same *pentiti* also subsequently accused Prime Minister Giulio Andreotti. Borsellino investigated the murders of Salvo Lima and the magistrates Falcone, Livatino, and Saetta. After the establishment of the National Anti-Mafia Office he was mentioned by Minister of the Interior Vincenzo Scotti as the natural candidate to lead the new organization.

Borsellino was assassinated on Sunday, July 19, while he was being brought, as was his custom, to visit his elderly mother. An automobile packed with eighty kilos of TNT parked in front of the entrance to his mother's building exploded, killing the magistrate and his five-person escort. Investigations traced the ordering of the attack to members of the "Cupola" (the "Dome" of leadership circle) and the actual perpetrators to members of the Mafia led by "super" fugitive Pietro Aglieri. Other inquiries have concentrated on the possible involvement of people outside Cosa Nostra.

On February 13, 1999, Salvatore "Toto" Riina, who had been the Mafia boss of bosses at the time of his arrest in 1993, was convicted and sentenced to life imprisonment for ordering the murder of Borsellino.

BIBLIOGRAPHY

Bartocelli, Marianna, Claudia Mirto, and Anna Pomar, eds. *Magistrati in Sicilia: Interventi pubblici di Giovanni Falcone e Paolo Borsellino a Palermo.* Palermo: Ila Palma, 1992.

Lucentini, Umberto. *Paolo Borsellino: il valore di una vita.* Milan: Mondadori, 1994.

Fabio Tricoli
(Tr. by B. Cook)

Borten, Per (1913–)

Norwegian politician, member of parliament (1949–77), chairman of the Center Party (1955–66), prime minister (1965–71), in a coalition cabinet with the Conservative Party, the Liberal Party, and the Christian Democrats.

Per Borten played a crucial role in the transformation of the Agrarian Party into the Center Party in 1959, extending the political appeal of the party from its agrarian and rural base. After 1945 the four nonsocialist parties aspired to create an alternative to the Labor Party government. In the general election in 1965 the four parties gained a majority in parliament. The three center parties refused to accept a prime minister from the Conservative Party, which had received more votes than any of the three center parties. The only candidate from the center parties acceptable to the Conservatives was Borten, whose Center Party had won 10 percent of the vote.

The difference between the Borten cabinet and the previous Labor Party cabinet was more rhetorical than political. The Borten cabinet continued the development of the Norwegian welfare state, and in the most important political issues there existed a strong consensus.

The exception to this consensus was the issue of the European Community (EC), which split the coalition. In 1971, the year before the EC referendum, the coalition broke down. After showing confidential documents to the leader of the anti-EC organization, Borten was strongly criticized by several of his cabinet members and had to leave office. The coalition failed to form a new cabinet, mainly because of the Center Party's opposition to Norwegian membership in the EC. A minority cabinet led by social demmocrat Trygve Brattelie was formed.

Borten was a popular political leader, well known for his straightforward and informal personal style. Borten's most important impact as prime minister was his ability to achieve compromises in his heterogeneous cabinet.

BIBLIOGRAPHY

Allen, Hilary. *Norway and Europe in the 1970s.* Oslo: Norwegian Foreign Policy Studies, 1979.

Hoemnsnes, Ole N. *Skjebnedogn: om Borten-regjeringens fall.* Oslo: Gyldendal, 1986.

Rovde, Olav. "Borgarleg samling," in Trond Bergh and Helge Pharo, eds. *Vekst og velstand. Norsk politisk historie 1945–1965.* Oslo: Universitetsforlaget, 1989.

Unneberg, Bjorn. *Per Borten: Bonde og statsmann.* Oslo: Cappelen, 1988.

Vassbotn, Per. *Da Borten falt: gjensyn med regjeringens Lakkasje og forlis 1971.* Oslo: Cappele, 1986.

Gisle Aschim

SEE ALSO Norway

Bosch, Robert (1861–1942)

German industrialist. Robert Bosch was born on September 23, 1861, in Albeck near Ulm, where he was trained as a mechanic. He worked in several German cities then moved to the United States, where he worked with Thomas Edison. Finally, he began working in Great Britain with Siemens Brothers. After this period of training, Bosch returned to Germany, where he established an electrical machine in Stuttgart in 1886 and invented the magneto ignition for Otto engines. At the beginning of his career he was supported by his family. Because of financial concerns he constantly worried that his inventions would not make a profit. But he became more and more successful and established companies of his own abroad. The industrialist had close contact with Gottlieb Daimler, Rudolf Diesel, and politicians, yet, despite his left-wing sentiments, he never became directly involved in politics. It was not only in the field of electronics that he was an inventor and trendsetter; he also played an important role as a sponsor and patron in cultural affairs. In the social sphere Bosch introduced in 1906 the eight-hour workday that was to be embodied in the constitution of the Weimar Republic. Bosch died from an ear infection on March 12, 1942. Robert Bosch Ltd., whose headquarters are still located in Stuttgart, has continued to specialize in automobile accessories, communication techniques, and producer and consumer goods.

BIBLIOGRAPHY

Heuss, Theodor. *Robert Bosch: His Life and Achievements.* New York: Henry Holt, 1994.

Annette Biener

Bosnia-Hercegovina

Republic of 19,741 square miles (51,129 sq km) in a mountainous region in the western Balkans, triangular in shape, with only a small outlet to the Adriatic Sea.

The original province of Bosnia took shape in the tenth century, bounded by the Sava, Drina, and Una Rivers. The territory was controlled by rulers drawn from the local Slav population as well as Hungarians, Venetians, Serbs, and Byzantines. Bosnia enjoyed self-rule in the fourteenth century before its conquest by the Ottoman Turks in 1463. Much of the Slav elite converted to Islam, which thereafter was strong in the towns and among the landowning class. The Ottoman *millet* system, under which inhabitants were administered according to their religious faith, permitted the Catholic and Orthodox religions to be practiced, though under constraint, and this preserved the heterodox character of Bosnia.

Bosnia-Hercegovina. *Illustration courtesy of Bernard Cook.*

In the 1878 Treaty of Berlin, Austria-Hungary secured from Constantinople the right to administer Bosnia. The territory was annexed by the Habsburgs in 1908, and the assassination in Bosnia's capital, Sarajevo, on June 28, 1914, of the heir to the Habsburg throne, Archduke Franz Ferdinand, precipitated the First World War.

The defeat of the Habsburgs pushed to the fore the nationalist agendas of the Serbs and the Croats, the most numerous of the South Slav peoples. After 1918 Bosnia was part of the Kingdom of Serbs, Croats, and Slovenes (after 1929 renamed Kingdom of Yugoslavia). Between 1941 and 1945 Yugoslavia was occupied by the Axis powers. Bosnia was the location of bitter fighting as a result of the excesses of the Ustasha Croatian regime and the ultimately successful resistance of the Communist Partisans led by Josip Broz (Tito).

The population of Bosnia spoke the same Serbo-Croatian language and sprang from similar South Slav stock, but they were set apart by religion and contrasting historical experiences and memories. Bosnia's ethnic complexity meant that it was ill-suited for the rise of nationalism, which sought to impose the straitjacket of conformity on a region whose identity could not be reduced to a single national state tradition. For over forty years Tito's distinctive brand of nonaligned communism suited Bosnia's multicultural traditions. Tito sought to bury ethnic particularism within loyalty to wartime Yugoslavia's revolution and the subsequent federalist Communist state.

To contain Serb-Croat conflict in Bosnia, the territory was organized as one of six republics in federal Yugoslavia. By the time of the 1971 census, the Slav Muslims had been granted a distinct ethnic status as a nation of Yugoslavia. The high level of intermarriage among Bosnia's mixed population, especially in the cities and towns, and the absence of any overt Bosnian nationalism, signaled acquiescence to the Yugoslav model. Following Tito's death in 1980, unrest on economic grounds quickly emerged in Kosovo and then Slovenia, and the Yugoslav federation was plunged into crisis in the late 1980s when an attempt was made from within Serbia to centralize Yugoslavia around Belgrade.

The Yugoslav Communist Party's monopoly ended in Bosnia, as in other parts of Yugoslavia, at the end of the 1980s. Elections in Bosnia in November-December 1990 resulted in victory for ethnic parties as in other ethnically mixed parts of Yugoslavia such as Macedonia and Vojvodina. This should not necessarily be viewed as a sign of polarization, but may well have denoted a backlash against the corruption and incompetence of many federally based institutions as well as the resilience of confessional loyalties.

The 1991 census showed that Bosnian Muslims made up 43.7 percent of the total population; Serbs, 31.4 percent; and Croats, 17.3 percent. Yugoslavia disintegrated in the summer of 1991 when Slovenia and Croatia broke away from the Belgrade's control. In Bosnia, Muslim and Croat leaders were opposed to the territory's being absorbed into a rump Yugoslavia controlled by hard-line Serb nationalists, but the opposition of local Serb nationalists made any independence bid fraught with danger.

On October 15, 1991, the parliament in Sarajevo declared that the Republic of Bosnia-Hercegovina was a sovereign state within its existing borders. The Serbian Democratic Party, led by Radovan Karadžić, rejected this as a move toward secession. It was committed to the idea that all Serbs in what had been Yugoslavia should live in one state. It formed a new assembly in Pale and staged a referendum in Serb areas, which endorsed that aim. This development suggested that only with difficulty could Bosnia remain aloof from the violent Serb-Croat rivalry. Its location at the heart of the former Yugoslavia where essential lines of communication converged, not to mention where arms factories and important mineral resources were located, meant it was likely to be fought over.

The willingness of several hundred thousand Serbs to remain loyal to the Sarajevo government after the outbreak of war in 1992 suggests that Serb opinion was far

from unanimous. During the winter of 1991–92, the West's increasing involvement in the Yugoslav war suggested to the Muslim Party of Democratic Action that, after disengaging from rump Yugoslavia, it was likely to receive the necessary help to defend itself. Few measures were taken by the government to prepare Bosnia against attack from within or without. Economic sanctions had been imposed on the Belgrade regime and the independence of Slovenia and Croatia recognized by the European Union before a referendum in Bosnia. In the referendum of February 29, and March 1, 1992, 99.4 percent of the 63 percent of the electorate who participated voted in favor of full independence. The Bosnian president, Alija Izetbegović, immediately declared Bosnia independent, and the European Union and the United States formally recognized it on April 6, 1992.

A Serbian Republic of Srpska, comprising over half of Bosnia, was declared on April 7, its architects having already launched a war on Bosnian soil with the help of Serb paramilitaries and units of the Yugoslav Peoples Army (JNA), the aim being to extinguish Bosnian independence. The expulsion of hundreds of thousands of Muslims from their homes, atrocities committed against countless civilians, and the bombardment of Sarajevo and other towns, were perpetrated in the name of carving out a homogeneous Serb state linked with Serb areas in Croatia as well as Serbia proper. Although much of multicultural Bosnia soon lay in ruins, an independent state continued to function from Sarajevo, retaining the loyalty of a mixed population and its fortunes revived in 1995 following serious defeats inflicted on its Serb opponent.

Tom Gallagher

SEE ALSO Izetbegović, Alija; Karadžić, Radovan

Bosnian War

The warfare in Bosnia-Hercegovina began shortly after the declaration of independence by the parliament in Sarajevo dominated by representatives of the Muslim and Croat ethnic groups. In Sarajevo, on April 6, 1992, gunmen loyal to the rebel Serb leadership, which had declared a Bosnian Serb Republic, fired shots into a crowd of some twenty thousand peace demonstrators. By May 2 Sarajevo had been encircled by rebel Serbs who placed it under a siege that lasted until late 1995. Many thousands of inhabitants were killed by shell- and gunfire that rained down on the city.

The Serb forces consisted of units of the Yugoslav Peoples Army (JNA) and Serb irregulars. They made rapid advances in eastern Bosnia against the unprepared and scarcely armed government. Terror tactics were used, above all by Serb paramilitary leader and international outlaw Zeljko Raznatović ("Arkan"), whose "Tigers" indiscriminately killed large numbers of Muslim villagers. By May it was becoming clear that the rebel Serb aim was to forcibly expel Muslims from large areas of Bosnia. In the absence of a well-armed opponent, the war was directed mainly against civilians. Serbs who resisted the persecution of their Muslim neighbors and friends were also considered to be enemy. By the end of 1992, rebel Serbs had captured much of northern Bosnia, which placed them in control of 70 percent of the country.

On May 26, 1992, following the first of many massacres of civilians in Sarajevo, when a large number were killed by a mortar as they queued for water, the United Nations approved a plan to send 1,100 peacekeepers to secure the airport at Sarajevo in order to bring in humanitarian aid. The West, led by Britain, decided that military intervention would be unable to stop what was described as a civil war between warring factions, one of them, Bosnia, having already been recognized as a sovereign state with a seat at the United Nations. Britain was also instrumental in extending to Bosnia the arms embargo imposed on all the ex-Yugoslav states in 1991. This was widely seen as a covert form of intervention on the side of the Serbs, who were not short of weapons, as well as a contravention of the U.N. Charter, which provides member states with the right to individual and collective defense when faced with outside aggression. When, unexpectedly, the rebel Serbs failed to clinch their early gains with an outright victory, the British "minimalist" policy led to mounting dissension within NATO. European security was seen to be threatened by the triumph of aggression in Bosnia, and a serious strain was placed on Anglo-American relations.

By the end of 1994, twenty-three thousand U.N. troops from twenty-eight countries were in Bosnia as part of the U.N. Protection Force (Unprofor). These lightly armed troops found themselves at the mercy of rebel Serbs who did not hesitate to make hostages of them or shoot down NATO planes. As a result, between May 1992 and August 1995, the mandates given to Unprofor by the Security Council to defend and deliver humanitarian aid and to safeguard "safe zones" were never properly carried out. The policy of maintaining neutrality between the different sides, even though the vast majority of human rights abuses were coming from one quarter, associated in particular with U.N. officials Cedric Thornberry and Yashusi Akashi, created mounting controversy as the war intensified.

The doctrine of neutrality was encapsulated in the peace plans advanced by U.N. and European Union negotiators Lord Owen, Cyrus Vance, and Thorvald Stoltenberg in 1992–93. The plans treated the rebel Serbs as an equal party in the negotiations and proposed to award up to 50 percent of Bosnia to them, territories from which huge numbers of Muslims had been "ethnically cleansed." Plans that proposed to divide Bosnia into ethnically based provinces or cantons held out nothing for people of mixed background in a territory where, before the war, 27 percent of marriages in Bosnia's urban centers had been mixed.

These plans were a crude form of conflict management and they fell through mainly because of rebel Serb obduracy and the reluctance of the United States to provide ground troops for schemes widely felt in Washington to be both unjust and unworkable. But the first Owen-Vance plan helped spark off a war in 1993–94 between irregular Croat forces, supported by elements in the Croatian government, determined to occupy territory allocated to them under the envoys' plan, and government forces who were able to withstand them. A U.S.-brokered agreement led to a cease-fire and a confederation of Croat-held and Bosnian government territory on March 31, 1994.

Contrary to widespread predictions, the Bosnian government was not overwhelmed by its rebel adversaries in the winter of 1992–93, and thereafter it slowly began to regain territory. An army was created whose assets of manpower, mobility, and morale were offset by a lack of heavy weapons. The morale of rebel Serb forces began to wane when it was clear that victory would not be swift, and by 1994 a shortage of manpower was resulting in refugees in Serbia being kidnapped and sent home to the frontline.

The role of the international media in exposing rebel Serb atrocities complicated efforts by international actors to end the war on terms suitable to the rebel Serbs. Assistance from Islamic states also placed funds at the disposal of Bosnia and enabled its government to obtain a fairer international hearing. Turkey, for example, ensured that Bosnia was admitted to the Organization of Security and Cooperation in Europe (OSCE) and other global forums. Finally, support from well-placed U.S. politicians and State Department officials frustrated British attempts to railroad through a peace on Serb terms. The Clinton administration was often irresolute and contradictory in its approach, but whatever strong actions were taken by the international community were usually U.S.-inspired.

Between January 1993 and July 1995 the Bosnian conflict was locked in stalemate. Horrific attacks on civilians led to limited attacks on rebel Serb forces reluctantly sanctioned by U.N. civilian bureaucrats. The Contact group of powers—Britain, France, Germany, Russia, and the

United States—which replaced the earlier failed peace initiatives, pursued a twin-track policy of negotiating peace while threatening firm action whenever the rebel Serbs scandalized world opinion by their actions. But the latter repeatedly called the bluff of the West, most notably in May–June 1995 when the airlift to Sarajevo was halted, weapons exclusion zones were repeatedly violated, and hundreds of U.N. troops were regularly taken hostage.

A defining moment occurred on July 11, 1995, when the "safe haven" of Srebrenica fell to General Ratko Mladić's forces. Thousands of men and boys were executed by the rebel Serbs. France's newly elected president, Jacques Chirac, the one Western leader unconnected with the string of policy failures in the Balkans since 1991, warned that Europe's self-respect and basic security were now endangered, and made a comparison with the 1938 capitulation to Nazi tyranny at Munich. Soon after a "Rapid Reaction" force with heavy weaponry was deployed in Bosnia by NATO, and U.N. civilian bureaucrats were prevented from making any more military decisions there.

Croatia's capture of Serb-occupied Krajina and its driving out 170,000 ethnic Serbs on August 4 and 5, 1995, destroyed the myth of Serb military invincibility that had been at the root of Western policy. Following the killing of thirty-seven civilians in Sarajevo by a Serb mortar on August 28, NATO forces carried out heavy bombing raids that did considerable damage to the rebel Serb military infrastructure. Against this background Croatian and Bosnian government forces launched an offensive in September 1995 that reduced the proportion of Bosnian territory in rebel Serb hands from 70 to around 40 percent. Simultaneously, a peace proposal was advanced by U.S. envoy Richard Holbrooke, which still gave rebel Serbs control of half of Bosnia in a loose federation. In November the parties to the conflict agreed, after much resistance, to the U.S.-sponsored Dayton accords, formally signed in January in Paris. This was followed by the introduction of twenty-thousand U.S. troops, part of a sixty thousand–person force under NATO, rather than U.N., command, to attempt to enforce the tenuous peace agreement.

BIBLIOGRAPHY

Glenny, Misha. *The Fall of Yugoslavia: The Third Balkan War.* New York: Penguin, 1992.

Magas, Branka. *The Destruction of Yugoslavia: Tracking the Break-up 1980–92.* London: Verso, 1993.

Tom Gallagher

Dayton Accords

The Bosnian peace accords were agreed to at Dayton, Ohio, on November 21, 1995, and formally signed in Paris on December 14, 1995, by the presidents of Bosnia, Croatia, and Serbia. Following the advance into Bosnia by Croatian forces after they had succeeded in overrunning the Serbian Krajina Republic on Croatian territory, and the NATO air offensive against Bosnian Serbs launched in August, the Bosnian Serbs, pressed by Serbian President Slobodan Milošević, agreed to peace talks in the United States sponsored by U.S. President Bill Clinton. Milošević, who wished to appear as a peacemaker after his Greater Serbian machinations had led to disaster, represented the Bosnian Serbs, whose leaders Radovan Karadžić and General Ratko Mladić, had been indicted as war criminals by the war crimes tribunal at The Hague. U.S. Secretary of State Warren Christopher and Richard Holbrooke, assistant secretary of state, brokered the settlement.

Central to the accord was the Muslim-Croat Federation, an alliance cobbled together by U.S. pressure in 1994 after a year of fighting between Bosnian Croats and Muslims. According to the Dayton accords the federation would control 51 percent of Bosnian territory and the Bosnian Serb Republic (Republika Srpska) would control the remaining 49 percent. The accord insisted that Bosnia-Hercegovina would be a single state, divided between the two entities, and that state would have its own institutions. Sarajevo, including the suburbs held by Serbs, became a unified city under Muslim-Croat Federation control. Opposing military forces were required to be moved out of seventy zones of separation between the two entities. Sixty thousand I-FOR (Implementation Force) troops, including twenty thousand Americans, were to enforce the settlement.

By 1999, the agreement had not succeeded in constructing a viable pan-Bosnian government; most refugees had not been able to return to their homes; Karadžić and Mladić had not been apprehended; and cooperation between Croatians and Muslims was tenuous at best. I-FOR troops, who were supposed to remain for only one year, were still in place with no prospect for their removal.

BIBLIOGRAPHY

"Is Dayton Accord a Comprehensive Peace Plan?," *The Straits Times* (Singapore), December 6, 1995.

Newsom, David, "Trouble Spots in Dayton Accord," *The Christian Science Monitor,* December 27, 1995.

Bernard Cook

Refugees

By the summer of 1993, international relief agencies reckoned that more than 2.2 million people had been driven from their homes in Bosnia. A primary war aim of the civil and military leaders of the Bosnian Serb Republic (Republika Srpska) was to render any territory that they conquered ethnically pure by driving out non-Serbs. Ethnic cleansing was the name this strategy acquired, and it was at its most concentrated in northwestern Bosnia around the city of Banja Luka and to the southeast in the Drina valley, where Muslims had formed an absolute majority of the population. By mid-1994 the U.N. high commission for refugees estimated that nine out of every ten Muslims and Croats who had lived in territory occupied by the Republika Srpska had been driven out or killed. This amounted to the largest forced population movement in Europe since 1945. During the expulsions, hundreds of thousands of Muslims and Croats had to sign documents surrendering all future rights to their property. Often they would then be charged a fee for being transported to Croatia or government-held areas of Bosnia.

Controversy ensued among Western European governments about how to respond to the exodus. Britain urged that the refugees stay in adjacent countries or that safe havens be established. Germany, on the other hand, demanded that a quota system be established, with each country accepting an agreed number of refugees according to its size and ability to accommodate them. But Prime Minister John Major's government blocked this policy, even though its insistence on placing an arms embargo on the Bosnian government contributed to the toll of ethnic cleansing.

Croatia's seizure of the breakaway Krajina region in August 1995 led to a mass exodus of Serb refugees into Bosnia. Many of the 170,000 Serb refugees were settled in Serb-held areas of the country, and Muslim and Croat Bosnians were often displaced as their homes were assigned to Serbs. Following the Dayton accords, Bosnian Serb refugees fled sections of Sarajevo that were returned to the Bosnian government. The repatriation of refugees called for in the agreement has been generally resisted by local Serb populations.

Tom Gallagher
Bernard Cook

SEE ALSO Croatia

Political Parties

The Party of Democratic Action (Stranka Demokratske Akcije, SDA) was founded on May 26, 1990, as a "political alliance of Yugoslav citizens belonging to Muslim cultural and historical traditions." It emerged as the largest party in competitive elections held in November 1990. Its leader, Alija Izetbegović, became head of the Bosnian presidency and head of state when Bosnia declared itself independent in March 1992. During the fighting that ensued, the SDA tightened its hold on the territory remaining in Bosnian hands. Though the government was technically a multiethnic coalition, confessional elements in the party became increasingly prominent.

The Serbian Democratic Party (Srpska Demokratska Stranka Bosne i Hercegovine, SDS) was founded on July 12, 1990. It received approximately 30 percent of the vote in elections later that year. The SDS was led by Radovan Karadžić, flanked by hard-line Bosnian Serb academics Nikola Koljević and Biljana Plavšić, who were determined to prevent Bosnia from severing links with rump Yugoslavia controlled by Serbia. On April 7, 1992, following international recognition of Bosnian independence, the SDS proclaimed a Bosnian Serb Republic, the Republic of Srpska. It became the governing party of the secessionist republic, which quickly seized around 70 percent of Bosnian territory. Relations with Serbia have fluctuated markedly, but dissent of whatever kind is ruthlessly suppressed in the Republic of Srpska. In 1993 mutinies occurred in the army in protest over war profiteering by members of the political leadership.

The Croatian Democratic Union (Hrvatska Demokratska Zaednica, HDZ) emerged on August 18, 1990, as the Bosnian Croat branch of the ruling party in Croatia. Under Stjepan Kljujić, the HDZ was committed to defending the integrity of Bosnia. In 1992 moderates who derived their support from Croats in central Bosnia were eclipsed by hard-liners from Hercegovina who were influential in Zagreb because of their émigré connections and wealth. Under Mate Boban the HDZ declared a secessionist state, Herceg-Bosna, in mid-1992 on Bosnian territory inhabited mainly by Croats, and turned it into a one-party ethnic state. Armed conflict with the Sarajevo government occurred in 1993, but U.S. pressure on President Tudjman of Croatia resulted in the removal of Boban in January 1994 and the reemergence of moderate Stjepan Kljujić, who signed a peace treaty that paved the way in March 1994 for a Croat-Muslim federation of Bosnia and Hercegovina.

Tom Gallagher

SEE ALSO Boban, Mate; Izetbegović, Alija; Karadžić, Radovan

Republika Srpska (Serbian Republic)

Serbian political entity within Bosnia that emerged during the war from 1992–95. The Republika Srpska was created by the Serbian Democratic Party in 1992 as an attempt to break away from Bosnia and create a Greater Serbia. Its secession from Bosnia was effected by the Yugoslav-equipped and -trained Bosnian Serb army, which conquered up to 70 percent of Bosnian territory and expelled most members of the two other ethnic groups of Bosnia, the Croats and Muslims. The Republika Srpska also depended on financial and logistical support from Serbia. With the 1995 Dayton peace accords, it was recognized as one of the two entities constituting Bosnia, but was allowed to establish special ties with Yugoslavia (Serbia and Montenegro).

The first elections in Bosnia in 1990 lead to a victory of ethnic parties. The main Serb party, the Serbian Democratic Party (SDS), lead by Radovan Karadžić, insisted that Bosnia remain part of Yugoslavia.

As its sister party had done before in Croatia, the SDS established Serbian Autonomous regions in Bosnia in September 1991. These territories, Bosanska Krajina, Romanija, and Eastern Hercegovina, firmly under control of the SDS, withdrew from government control and sought military support from the Yugoslav Peoples Army (JNA).

After Croatian and Muslim deputies declared the sovereignty of Bosnia in October 1991, the Serb deputies walked out of the parliament and ended all cooperation with the government in Sarajevo. In December 1991 the SDS declared the Republika Srpska i Bosna-Hercegovina (later renamed the Republika Srpska, or Serbian Republic). After failed negotiations over the future structure of Bosnia, the Croatian and Muslim parties organized a referendum on independence that was boycotted by the SDS. This led to low participation in the vote among the Serb population, thereby undermining its validity. The time between the vote on March 1, 1992, and the declaration of independence a month later marked the beginning of the war in Bosnia. On March 27, the Republika Srpska passed its own constitution, while the Bosnian Serb army began the conquest of areas outside the autonomous areas with the support of the army and paramilitaries from Serbia and Montenegro.

The parliament, consisting mostly of members of the Serbian Democratic Party, the government, and the president of the Serb-controlled parts of Bosnia, Radovan Karadžić, took their seat in Pale, a former resort close to the capital, Sarajevo. The structures of the republic explicitly excluded other ethnic groups and sought only to protect the interests of Serbs. As it lacked even the democratic representation of Bosnian Serbs, it was until the end of the war in 1995 very much an authoritarian regime of the SDS.

The official aim of the Republika Srpska was unification with all other Serb lands, the Serb Republic of Krajna (Serb-held parts of Croatia), and rump Yugoslavia (Serbia and Montenegro). Despite close military cooperation with Serbia and close political contacts with the Serbs in Croatia, the creation of Greater Serbia never materialized, as the international community was not willing to accept the change of borders.

In August 1994 Serbian president Slobodan Milošević broke with Karadžić and the Republika Srpska. The reason for the split was not only Western pressure but also the challenge the president of the SDS posed to Milošević as a Serb leader. As a consequence Yugoslavia imposed sanctions on its previous allies in Bosnia. Despite this pressure from its only ally, the leadership of the Serb Republic of Bosnia remained defiant and continued the conquest of further territories. While the army of the Republika Srpska managed to overrun the U.N.-declared "safe havens" of Zepa and Srebrenica in the spring and summer 1995, killing several thousand of their inhabitants, the military balance had changed. The Croatian conquest of the largest Serb-held parts of Croatia (Kirajina) and the NATO air strikes after a shell killed several dozen people in Sarajevo in August led to a collapse of the front lines and a Serb withdrawal. This loss led to a cease-fire in October 1995 and the peace negotiations in Dayton under the auspices of U.S. negotiator Richard Holbrooke. The accords signed in November granted 49 percent of Bosnian territory to the Serb Republic. While its quest for independence was not recognized, it was granted the legally vague status of an entity of Bosnia. The Dayton Peace Accords provided for a weak central government and an international peace force (first the Implementation Force, IFOR, and later the Stabilization Force, SFOR) to implement the provisions of the Dayton treaty. The Serb entity was furthermore permitted to establish close ties with Yugoslavia.

In the aftermath the president of the Republika Srpska, Karadžić, had to resign from all political offices, but he remained an important political player for most of 1996. The new leadership under President Biljana Plavšić and its member of the Bosnian presidency, Momčilo Krajišnik, still aimed at unification with Yugoslavia and sought to undermine the peace treaty. As a consequence international aid was withheld and the Serbian entity suffered from high unemployment (over 50 percent), little reconstruction, and international isolation. The first elections after the war in September 1996 largely confirmed the dominant role of the SDS, not a surprising outcome as the media and all state institutions remained under firm control of the leading party. By mid-1997 President Plavsić, however, sought closer ties with the West and agreed to full implementation of the peace accords, leading to a break with the more radical wing of the SDS. This split effectively divided the Republika Srpska into the territories under control of the president, centered in the largest city of the entity, Banja Luka, and the areas under the control of Krajišnik and other radical SDS members, centered in Pale. Milošević brokered an agreement between both sides, leading to elections in the fall of 1997 in which moderate forces managed to balance the radical wing of the SDS. The subsequent government under the premiership of Socialist Milorad Dodik cooperated closely with SFOR and other international organizations and agreed to cooperate with the central institutions of Bosnia-Hercegovina. Nevertheless the influence of nationalist extremists waned only slowly. The adherence of Dodik to the peace accord led to economic support from the United States and the European Union. Still, the economic situation remained precarious. The biggest problem for the Republic Srpska remains the repatriation of refugees. The Dayton accords provide for a return of refugees that by early 1998 had happened only sporadically and was frequently met by the violent resistance of the local Serb population. While Muslims and Croats were allowed to participate in the Republika Srpska elections, they could not return. As the Serb entity hosted many Serb refugees from other parts of Bosnia and Croatia, a return of refugees, often to houses now occupied by Serbs, was difficult to attain.

The Republika Srpska is a part of Bosnia with an uncertain future. It is divided into two sections, connected only through an extremely narrow corridor at the city of Brčko, lacks access to the sea, and, with the exception of Banja Luka, any urban centers. While it is nearly exclusively populated by Serbs, many Serbs originally inhabiting its lands left for Yugoslavia or Western countries, to be replaced by Serb refugees from other parts of Bosnia and Croatia. The original aim of the republic's founders, a union with Serbia, is out of reach, and the international presence in Bosnia undermines many components of the independence of the Republika Srpska. Despite the weaknesses of the Serb entity, very few institutions and organizations overarch the interentity boundary, and cooperation is rendered very difficult because of the memories of the recent war.

BIBLIOGRAPHY

Cigar, Norman. *Genocide in Bosnia: The Policy of "Ethnic Cleansing."* College Station: Texas A & M University Press, 1995.

Hayden, Robert M. "Constitutional Nationalism and the Logic of the Wars in Yugoslavia." *Problems of Post-Communism* 43, no. 5 (September/October 1996): 25–35.

Judah, Jim. *The Serbs: History, Myth & the Destruction of Yugoslavia.* New Haven: Yale University Press, 1997.

Kesic, Obrad. "Politics, Power, and Decision Making in the Serb Republic." *Problems of Post-Communism* 43, 5 (March/April 1996): 56–64.

Malcolm, Noel. *Bosnia: A Short History.* New York: New York University Press, 1994.

Shoup, Paul. "The Bosnian Crisis in 1992," in Sabrina Petra Ramet and L. S. Adamovich, eds. *Beyond Yugoslavia: Politics, Economics, and Culture in a Shattered Community.* Boulder: Westview Press, 1995, 155–88.

Silver, Laura, and Allan Little. *The Death of Yugoslavia.* London: Penguin & BBC, 1995.

Udovicki, Jasminka, and Ejup Ctikovac. "Bosnia and Herzegovina: The Second War," in Jasminka Udovicki and James Ridgeway, eds. *Burn This House: The Making and Unmaking of Yugoslavia.* Durham, N.C.: Duke University Press, 1997, 174–214.

Woodward, Susan L. *Balkan Tragedy: Chaos and Dissolution after the Cold War.* Washington, D.C.: Brookings Institution, 1995.

Florian Bieber

Bossi, Umberto (1941–)

Italian politician, founder of the Northern League. Umberto Bossi came from a farming family. He was born on September 19, 1941, at Cassano Magnago in the province of Varese. He obtained a high school diploma when he was nearly thirty, then enrolled at the University of Pavia in the faculty of medicine but did not obtain a degree. From his youth he sympathized with the Left but was not actively involved in politics. In 1979 he met Bruno Salvadori, leader of the autonomist Valdotaine Union. Following this meeting Bossi decided to form a political group to reassert the culture, history, and language of the people of Lombardy. With this objective he started the newspaper *Lombardia autonomista* in 1982 and founded the Lega Lombarda in 1984, of which he became the secretary and undisputed leader. The movement gained immediate notoriety for its opposition to immigrants from the south of Italy and from non-EC countries, and for its unrestrained criticism of the traditional political parties.

Bossi was elected senator in the elections of June 15, 1987. From this point he redirected the movement, minimizing if not completely abandoning the assertion of

Lombardian "ethnicity." The program of the Lega was henceforth based on the actual economic interests of workers and, above all, on that of the small firms in Lombardy and northern Italy in general. The general political crisis prompted by disclosures of corruption that hit the principal Italian political parties gave Bossi the opportunity to expand his movement, notwithstanding the attacks it received from most of the mass media and intellectuals.

At the beginning of the 1990s the movement spread beyond the Lombardy region, gaining adherents all over northern Italy. In 1991 the Lega di Nord (Northern League) was created, and Bossi was elected secretary of this new league that subsumed Lega Lombarda. His political program was now directed toward changing the Italian nation into a federal state. He was strongly influenced by the theories of political theorist Gianfranco Miglio, an advocate of federalism. Bossi's tone and language was as before characterized by aggressiveness and a notable dose of vulgarity. His political speeches were often laced with threats, such as a call to arms for the people of Lombardy. His speeches, however, were received as a radical protest against the corrupt political system.

In the elections of 1992 the Northern League was remarkably successful, establishing itself as the major political party in much of northern Italy. Bossi himself was elected to the chamber of deputies by a large vote. The rise of the league was favored by the inquiries being carried out by the magistrates on illicit party financing and on political corruption, which seemed to support the colorful statements of Bossi and his movement against Italian politicians, whom he called "Roman Robbers." Bossi himself was drawn into the scandal, however, accused by the Milanese magistrates of having received two hundred million lire from an Italian businessman to finance his political movement. This coincided with a halt in electoral growth of the league, which was evident in local government elections held in autumn 1993.

With a view to the elections of 1994, Bossi formed an alliance with the forces of the center, but after just one day he denied everything. He finally drew up an agreement with the newly born Forza Italia, created by popular Milanese businessman Silvio Berlusconi. This new party had astonishing electoral success at the expense of the league itself. But the agreement with Forza Italia guaranteed the league a larger number of deputies and senators than its real electoral weight warranted.

Bossi himself was reelected as a deputy, thanks to an electoral board made up of the league and Forza Italia. Notwithstanding this fact, Bossi immediately began attacking the leaders and the program of Forza Italia. In May 1994, however, he consented to the league's entry into the government presided over by Berlusconi, where the presence of deputies from the party of the Right, the National Alliance, which Bossi had accused of being neofascist, was important. The league obtained significant economic offices and the Ministry of the Interior, as well as the office of deputy prime minister. Nevertheless, the parliamentary policy of Bossi was anything but progovernment.

Bossi continued to openly criticize the government to such an extent that he contributed decisively to political instability. Some deputies decided to abandon the league's parliamentary group because of their opposition to Bossi. Among those who broke away was Miglio.

In December 1994 Bossi, despite opposition from his parliamentary group, decided to present a motion of no confidence against Berlusconi's government. This led to the league's most serious crisis since its foundation. As a result of Bossi's responsibility for the fall of the government and his attempt to form a new government in alliance with the center and Left, a serious split developed within the movement and there was an indignant reaction among many who had voted for the league.

BIBLIOGRAPHY

Bertolini, Sergio. *Umberto Bossi: I suoi uomini, le sue donne: luci ed ombre del leghismo.* Milan: SO.G.EDI, 1992.

Bossi, Umberto, and Daniele Vimercati. *Vento dal nord: La mia lega la mia vita.* Milan: Sperling & Kupfer, 1992.

———. *La rivoluzione.* Milan: Sperling & Kupfer, 1993.

Diamanti, Ilvo. *La lega: Geografia, storia e sociologia di un nuovo soggetto politico.* Rome: Donzelli, 1993.

Iacopini, Roberto, and Stefania Bianchi. *La lega ce l'ha duro: Il linguaggio del Carroccio, nei suoi slogan, consigli, manifesti.* Milan: Mursia, 1993.

Introvigne, Massimo. *Tra leghe e nazionalismi: "Religione civile" e nuovi simboli politici.* Milan: Effedieffe, 1992.

Dario Caroniti

SEE ALSO Berlusconi, Silvio; Italy

Bourdieu, Pierre (1930–)

French sociologist. The son of a minor functionary in the village of Béarn, Pierre Bourdieu was admitted to the prestigious École Normale Supérieure in 1951. Engaged in ethnographic fieldwork as an assistant at the University of Algiers, Bourdieu experienced firsthand the Algerian crisis in 1957. In 1975 he founded the journal *Actes de la recherche en sciences sociales* as a forum for his innovative sociology. Appointed to the Collège de France in 1982, he currently heads the Paris-based École Européenne de Sociologie.

Greatly influenced during the 1960s by the structural anthropology of Claude Lévi-Strauss, Bourdieu grew dissatisfied with structuralism's tendency to reduce human agency to an effect of objective cultural structures. Unwilling to return to a traditional philosophy of subjective humanism, however, Bourdieu developed the concept of the *habitus* to mediate between objectivism and subjectivism. A set of inculcated, structured, durable, generative, and transposable dispositions, the *habitus* gives agents a "practical sense," enabling them to act in a regular fashion in a variety of changing conditions, which Bourdieu terms "fields." These concepts are developed in Bourdieu's major works, including *Distinction, Homo Academicus, The Logic of Practice,* and *The Rules of Art.*

BIBLIOGRAPHY
Bourdieu, Pierre. *Distinction: A Social Critique of the Judgment of Taste.* Cambridge, Mass.: Harvard University Press, 1984.
Robbins, Derek. *The Work of Pierre Bourdieu: Recognizing Society.* Boulder, Colo.: Westview Press, 1991.
Christopher E. Forth

Bowen, Elizabeth (1899–1973)

Irish novelist and short-story writer. Elizabeth Bowen was born in County Cork and educated at Trinity College Dublin and Oxford. Bowen spent most of her life in England. Her short stories include "Encounters" (1923). Of her ten novels, *The Last September* (1929) is the work on which her reputation rests. It deals with the 1919–21 troubles in Ireland. *The Death of the Heart* (1938) offers Bowen's standard theme of adult-child relations. *The Heat of the Day* (1949) is the story of a divorcée in wartime London. Her postwar works include *A World of Love* (1955), *The Little Girls* (1964), and *Eva Trout* (1969). *Eva Trout,* which concerns the attempts of a misfit to integrate into the modern world, was a departure from Bowen's standard theme. Bowen, one of the great names of modern Irish literature, has also written over half a dozen works of nonfiction, including numerous essays and local and family history. Bowen's novels show a definite relation to Ireland, but their themes of passion, jealousy, and loneliness are above national boundaries.

BIBLIOGRAPHY
Blodgett, Harriet. *Patterns of Reality.* Paris, Mouton, 1973.
Bowen, Elizabeth. *Collected Short Stories of Elizabeth Bowen.* London, Cape, 1980.
———. *Irish Short Stories.* Dublin: Poolbeg Press, 1978.
Michael J. Kennedy

Boyd Orr, John, First Baron (1880–1971)

Lord John Boyd Orr was a Scottish biologist dedicated to the improvement of nutrition in children. After the Second World War he was appointed the first director general of the U.N. Food and Agricultural Organization and won the Nobel Peace Prize.

John Boyd Orr was born September 23, 1880. Educated at the University of Glasgow, he became a nutritional physiologist and assumed an appointment as director of the Rowett Research Institute at the University of Aberdeen, a position he held until 1945. In the late 1920s his studies in Kenya and Scotland proved that the intake of milk was directly related to physiological growth and susceptibility to disease in children. In 1927, as a result of his studies, provision was made for state subsidies to purchase milk for all Scottish schoolchildren.

With the onset of the worldwide depression of the 1930s, Boyd Orr became a powerful advocate for the improved nutrition of British children, an effort that attracted popular attention. In 1935 he was knighted for his reports on Scottish schoolchildren. A year later, he published a controversial study, *Food, Health and Income,* which claimed that 50 percent of Britain's population was poorly fed. Boyd Orr claimed that this discrepancy was directly related to family income. His proposals for optimum standards of food availability for children were considered to be tantamount to a socialist redistribution of wealth, and his proposals were temporarily ignored.

With the outbreak of war, however, Boyd Orr was asked to provide statistics on the minimal standards of nutrition for all British subjects. This time, his targeting of per diem totals for the consumption of milk, potatoes, vegetables, oatmeal, bread, fats, and sugars was adopted wholesale by the Churchill government, and he was retained as an adviser to Lord Woolton, the minister of food, throughout the war. Boyd Orr also became an editor, along with William Beveridge, of a Pilot Press pamphlet series called *Targets for Tomorrow* that discussed postwar social planning. He contributed a pamphlet to the series, "Food and the People" (1943), which declared that Britain's agricultural policy should be linked to its nutritional needs rather than production for economic capacity or export.

With the foundation of the United Nations, Sir John Boyd Orr was appointed the first director general of the

U.N. Food and Agricultural Organization. In this position he traveled throughout the world's poorer countries, advising on food policy, and he also developed a World Food Plan, which would establish a U.N. food board to buy up food stocks, fund research and development, and finance the supplying of food to poorer nations. The plan was rejected by the United Nations, prompting Boyd Orr's resignation in 1948. Nevertheless, for his efforts, Boyd Orr was granted the Nobel Peace Prize in 1949 and was also elevated to a life peerage.

After he left the United Nations, Boyd Orr's career lapsed into retirement. He produced another controversial work, *The White Man's Dilemma: Food and the Future* (1952), in which he declared the Cold War immoral and stated that unless the governments of the world dedicated themselves to feeding all their citizens, the very foundations of Western civilization would collapse. His memoirs, *As I Recall,* were published in 1966. Boyd Orr died June 25, 1971.

David Simonelli

SEE ALSO Beveridge, William

Brandt, Willy (1913–92)

Chancellor of the Federal Republic of Germany, 1969–74. Willy Brandt was born in Lübeck on December 18, 1913, Herbert Ernst Karl Frahm, the illegitimate child of Martha Frahm, a nineteen-year-old grocery store clerk. The great influences in his early life were his socialist grandfather, a truck driver and man of principle; Eilhard Erich Pauls, the history teacher at Johanneum, a prestigious school, to which Brandt won a scholarship, who encouraged the excellent student to read and write; and Julius Leber, who encouraged Brandt's socialist political and journalistic activities. Brandt, who regarded the Social Democrats as too tame, joined the more radical Socialist Workers Party. When Hitler came to power in 1933, the young leftist, who adopted the underground name "Willy Brandt," was sent to open a headquarters in Norway to help refugees and to spread information about the Nazi dictatorship. When the Germans invaded Norway Brandt sought refuge in Sweden. After the war, Brandt, who had become a Norwegian citizen in 1940, was sent to Germany by the Norwegian government as a press attaché.

In 1948 Brandt applied for the reinstatement of his German citizenship, which the Nazis had stripped from him in 1936, and settled in Berlin to work for the German Social Democratic Party (SPD). Brandt worked closely with Ernst Reuter, the mayor of West Berlin. Brandt's experiences in Scandinavia had freed him of his

Willy Brandt, major of postwar West Berlin and first Social Democratic chancellor of West Germany (1969-74). *Illustration courtesy of the German Information Center.*

earlier dogmatism. Together with Reuter he advocated a pragmatic reorientation of the SPD. Though Reuter died in 1953, Brandt played a central role in the transformation of the party at its congress at Bad Godesberg in 1959. Brandt and Reuter also viewed the support of the West as the sole hope for freedom in West Berlin and wholeheartedly advocated the integration of West Germany into the Western world.

On October 3, 1957, Brandt became the mayor of West Berlin, and his rise within the SPD culminated in 1963 with his election as party chairman. The construction of the Berlin Wall by the East German government on August 13, 1961, greatly affected Brandt and has been seen as instrumental in the developing of his *Ostpolitik* (Eastern policy). Brandt was deeply disappointed by the acquiescence of the Western Allies and Konrad Adenauer, the West German chancellor. He believed that reunification in the short term was unattainable, and he was concerned that the walled-off German Democratic Republic would in isolation become more and more separate from the rest of Germany. To deal with this new situation, Brandt and his adviser, Egon Bahr, elaborated a new policy, "Change through Approach." They regarded the Western military alliance and continued European integration as prerequisites but believed that a better future for all the German people depended on improved relations with the Soviet Union and Eastern Europe. They also believed that détente with the Soviets could be used to pressure the East German regime to pursue a less rigid policy and that a feared estrangement of Germans in the East from those in the West could thus be thwarted. He advocated contacts with the authorities in East Germany to prevent the two parts of the German nation from growing further apart and to improve the lives of the Germans living there.

Because of the withdrawal of the Free Democrats from their coalition with the Christian Democrats in 1966, Brandt received the double opportunity to bring his party for the first time into a governing coalition in the Federal Republic and to implement his ideas on improved relations with the East. He became foreign minister and vice chancellor of a grand coalition formed with the Christian Democrats. His first step was the establishment of diplomatic relations with Romania in January 1967. This was followed by a trade agreement with Czechoslovakia and the resumption of diplomatic relations with Yugoslavia. For some Christian Democrats, however, the changes were too great and too swift.

Following the September 1969 election, Brandt, who constructed a new coalition with the liberal Free Democrats, became chancellor. As chancellor he expressed willingness to meet with East German authorities and to normalize the postwar frontiers with the Soviet Union and Poland. Simultaneously he advocated expansion and strengthening of the European Community. One of his first steps was to sign the Nuclear Non-Proliferation Treaty in November 1969. Talks were held in March and May 1970 between Brandt and Willi Stoph, the East German premier. The East Germans were at first intractable but, as Brandt had predicted, treaties with the USSR and Poland brought them around.

On August 12, 1970, the Soviet-German treaty was signed. It stipulated mutual renunciation of force and recognition of existing boundaries. The Soviet Union renounced its rights as a wartime victor over West Germany, and Brandt demanded that an agreement of the four Occupation Powers on the rights of West Berlin precede ratification of the treaty. This Berlin agreement, which recognized West Berlin's connection with and access to West Germany, was signed on September 3, 1971. The treaty with Poland was signed on December 6, 1970. When Brandt went to Warsaw for the signing, he dramatically symbolized Germany's repudiation of and contrition for the crimes of the Nazi regime by kneeling in front of the Warsaw Ghetto memorial. West Germany recognized the Oder-Neisse line as the de facto and inviolable frontier between the two countries. Despite opposition from the Christian Democrats, the West German electorate supported Brandt's initiatives, and the treaties were ratified by the West German parliament on May 17, 1972. At the time of ratification, Brandt prophetically stated that the treaties did not preclude the right of the German people to self-determination.

The West German agreements with the Soviet Union and Poland put pressure on the East Germans. Following a series of negotiations, an agreement on traffic between the two states was signed on May 26, 1972. On December 21, 1972, the Basic Treaty between the two states was signed. The Federal Republic, which ratified the treaty in June 1973, recognized the German Democratic Republic but continued to regard it as a special part of the one German nation. It also continued to regard all Germans as citizens of the Federal Republic, but both German states agreed to apply simultaneously for membership in the United Nations, which was granted in 1973. According to the treaty, access between West Germany and West Berlin was guaranteed and West Germans were allowed to visit East Germany, including East Berlin.

Brandt's policies received strong endorsement from the West German electorate in the November 1972 election. The Social Democrats received the highest percentage of the vote in their history and, with their partners, the Free Democrats, easily continued their governing coalition. Despite this victory, Brandt was discouraged by increasing economic problems, many of which were connected to the 1973 OPEC oil embargo. He was forced to shelve projected reforms in which he was deeply interested because of opposition to the tax increases needed to fund them. There were also rising recriminations over the failure of the East German regime to live up to the expectations, nurtured by many, for a more humane policy toward its people. The disclosure in April 1974 that Brandt's aide, Günther Guillaume, was an East German spy, led Brandt, over the objections of many, to resign the chancellorship on May 7. Though this scandal was an unfortunate way to end Brandt's leadership of West Germany, he reacted positively to the release from the tedium of governing.

The Guillaume Affair in no way brought an end to Brandt's political career. He continued to serve as chairman of the SPD until his retirement in 1987. The party valued his leadership and his ability to bridge its factional differences. Brandt took advantage of his greater leisure to devote himself to the problems of peace and justice on a worldwide basis. In 1976 he was chosen leader of the Socialist International, a coordinating body for labor and democratic socialist parties, and in 1977 assumed the chairmanship of the North-South Commission, also known as the Independent Commission on International Development Issues. Apart from his political duties on behalf of the SPD, he spent his time lobbying, speaking, and writing on behalf of world peace, economic development and justice, and human rights.

When the Berlin Wall came down in October 1989 and Germany was reunited on October 3, 1990, Brandt, because of his dedication to a free Berlin, to the concept of a single German nation, and to détente, was widely recognized in Germany as having contributed to these developments. Brandt's original contentions, that détente would make the West less threatening to the Soviet Union and that West Germany's increased contact with the East would undermine the Soviet Union's control over its satellites, had been borne out.

Brandt died of cancer on October 8, 1992. German President Richard von Weizsäcker in his eulogy said that Brandt had "shaped an era. . . . He changed the Germans' relationship with the world, as well as the world's to Germany."

BIBLIOGRAPHY

Binder, David. *The Other German: Willy Brandt's Life and Times.* Washington, D.C.: New Republic, 1975.

Bracher, Karl Dietrich, Wolfgang Jäger, and Werner Link. *Geschichte der Bundesrepublik Deutschland: Republik im Wandel, 1969–1974: Die Ära Brandt.* Stuttgart: Deutsche Verlags-Anstalt, 1986.

Brandt, Willy. *My Life in Politics.* London: Hamish Hamilton, 1992.

———. *People and Politics: The Years 1960–1975.* Boston: Little, Brown, 1976.

Griffith, William E. *The Ostpolitik of the Federal Republic of Germany.* Cambridge, Mass.: MIT Press, 1978.

Hofmann, Gunter. *Willy Brandt—Porträt eines Aufklärers aus Deutschland.* Hamburg: Rowohlt, 1988.

Koch, Peter. *Willy Brandt: eine politische Biographie.* Berlin: Ullstein, 1988.

Prittie, Terence. *Willy Brandt: Portrait of a Statesman.* New York: Schocken, 1974.

Bernard Cook

SEE ALSO Bahr, Egon; Berlin Wall; Détente; Reuter, Ernst; Stoph, Willi

Brâtianu, Gheorghe I. (1898–1953)

Romanian historian and politician, member of the Romanian Academy. Gheorghe I. Brâtianu was born on February 3, 1898, in Ruginoasa, Iasi county. He was the nephew of I. C. Brâtianu and the son of Ion I. C. Brâtianu, both key political figures of Romanian history. In 1916, when Romania entered the First World War to fulfill its national aspirations, Gheorghe I. Brâtianu voluntarily joined the army. In the same year, after graduating from the national lyceum in Iasi, he began to attend the law faculty courses there. A few years later, in 1921, he moved to Paris to attend the Sorbonne and the École des Chartes. In 1923 he passed his doctorate in philosophy in Cernauti and in 1928 his doctorate in history in Paris (Sorbonne).

In 1940, after sixteen years of serving as a professor of world history in Iasi, Brâtianu moved to a similar position at Bucharest University, where he also became the head of the Nicolae Iorga Institute of Universal History and of its review, *Revue historique du sud-est européen.* In 1942, he became a member of the Romanian Academy. Between 1927 and 1950, Brâtianu authored numerous works published in French and Romanian devoted to European medieval history.

Brâtianu's intellectual career was intertwined with a political one. A member of the National Liberal Party (NLP), in 1930 he entered into a conflict with its leaders because he favored the "restoration" of Carol II on June 8, 1930 (on January 4, 1926, the King had officially renounced his claim to the throne). Consequently, after being expelled from the NLP, he established his own party, the National Liberal Party–Gheorghe I. Brâtianu, which acted on its own until January 10, 1938, when it rejoined the mother party. On this occasion, Brâtianu was elected vice president of the NLP.

After the Communist takeover of Romania in 1947, Brâtianu was forced to quit his posts at Bucharest University and the Nicolae Iorga Institute. On May 6, 1950, he was arrested along with other prominent political figures and confined in the Sighetu Marmatiei prison. The cause and exact date of his death are not well documented. According to the prison's records, Brâtianu died on April 27, 1958, from circulatory problems. But according to an investigation conducted by his wife and daughter among former inmates in the jail, Brâtianu was severely beaten by guard in the prison's courtyard on April 24, 1953, and died soon afterward either because of the injuries inflicted or because he committed suicide.

Brâtianu's body was buried in a nearby former Jewish cemetery. In 1971, his family received permission for his remains to be reburied near those of his father and grandfather in Florica (Stefanesti). Yet as asserted by members of Brâtianu's family, the bones delivered to them were not his.

Adrian Pop

Braudel, Fernand (1902–85)

Influential French historian and spokesman for the *Annales* school of historiography. Fernand Braudel advocated the use of quantitative methods to investigate the material, geographical, and economic aspects of history, and criticized the traditional emphasis on events, personalities, and narration. In addition to his voluminous writings, he promoted his views as editor of the journal *Annales* (1956–68) and as president of the sixth section of the École Pratique des Hautes Études (1956–72).

While a German prisoner during World War II, Braudel wrote most of his seminal classic, *The Mediterranean and the Mediterranean World in the Age of Philip II* (1949; rev. 1955), which emphasized *la longue durée,* or long-term structures shaped by geographical forces. His second major work, the ???? volume *Capitalism and Material Life* (1967–79), was a global approach to social and economic history with little reference to individuals and their ideas. Although not a consistent determinist, Braudel referred to events as "crests of foam that the tides of history carry on their strong backs."

BIBLIOGRAPHY

Burke, Peter. *The French Historical Revolution: The "Annales" School, 1929–89.* Stanford, Calif.: Stanford University Press, 1990.

Hufton, Olwen. "Fernand Braudel." *Past and Present,* no. 112 (May 1986): 208–13.

Stoianovich, Traian. *French Historical Method: The "Annales" Paradigm.* Ithaca, N.Y.: Cornell University Press, 1976.

Thomas T. Lewis

Brazauskas, Algirdas (1932–)

First secretary of the Lithuanian Communist Party, 1988–90, and president of Lithuania, 1993. Algirdas Brazauskas was the most successful of the Soviet-era Communist leaders in the Baltic states in retaining a powerful political position after the achievement of independence from the USSR.

Denied the chairmanship of the Supreme Council in favor of Vytautas Landsbergis after the 1990 Supreme Council elections returned a Sajudis (reformist) majority, Brazauskas took the opportunity to restructure the Com-

munist Party, renaming it the Lithuanian Democratic Labor Party (LDLP). Successful in the parliamentary election of 1992, this party went on to form the government. Brazauskas himself assumed the presidency following his victory in the presidential election of 1993. He has espoused reform, particularly in the field of economic policy, and has strongly advocated European Union (EU) and NATO membership for Lithuania.

After joining the Communist Party in 1959, he briefly became a minister before serving as deputy chair of the State Planning Committee, 1966–77, and Central Committee secretary for Economic affairs, 1977–88. During the rise to prominence of Sajudis in 1988, Brazauskas was one of the few leading party officials to attend rallies and, though he was cautious on constitutional issues, to speak on behalf of economic reforms. In October 1988 he was chosen as first secretary of the Lithuanian Communist Party and, in 1989, chair of the Supreme Council. In those offices he actively pursued the role of mediator between Sajudis and the Kremlin. While making concessions to reformers on such issues as nuclear power, use of the old national flag, and return of Vilnius Cathedral to the church authorities, in deference to Moscow he opposed, with damage to his reputation among reformers, a declaration of Lithuanian sovereignty in October 1988. However, in the spring of 1989 the sovereignty declaration was passed, along with a law on economic self-management. As the tide flowed strongly in favor of reform and the membership of the Lithuanian Communist Party rapidly declined, Brazauskas engineered the independence of the party from the Soviet Communist Party in 1989. This was a crucial factor in restoring its legitimacy and assisting in its conversion to a Democratic Labor Party in 1990–91.

In the 1990 elections to the Supreme Council Sajudis gained an overwhelming majority, and Brazauskas was one of only two party members elected. Although he retained great popularity among the Lithuanian population, the Supreme Council replaced him as chair with Landsbergis. But it, appointed him deputy prime minister, partly because of his popularity and partly as a means of facilitating communications with Moscow. During the bloody confrontation between protesters and Soviet forces in Vilnius in January 1991, and during the failed coup attempt in Moscow in August 1991, Brazauskas was pessimistic, even defeatist, about the outcome. In this he was proved wrong, and Landsbergis right.

In the period of Sajudis government from 1990 to 1992, Brazauskas led the Lithuanian Democratic Labor Party in opposition. In the 1992 parliamentary election and the 1993 presidential election, he and his party promised to soften the blow of market reforms, to improve relations with Russia, and to restore formerly established trading links. He drew on his own personal popularity, refusing at the same time to launch personal attacks on his opponents. He also benefited from the support of the Lithuanian peasantry.

As president Brazauskas enjoyed a stronger constitutional base than his counterparts in Estonia and Latvia, having more powers in the formulation of foreign policy, taking legislative initiatives, and exercising the veto over legislation. He worked in close association with the ruling LDLP government, which continued the IMF-backed policy of economic reforms. The parliamentary elections of 1996 led to the return of a conservative government, with which Brazauskas was required to "cohabit." It remains to be seen whether the change of government will affect the balance of power between parliament and president.

BIBLIOGRAPHY

Hiden, John, and Patrick Salmon. *The Baltic Nations and Europe: Estonia, Latvia and Lithuania in the Twentieth Century.* Harlow U.K.: Longman, 1991.

Lieven, Anatol. *The Baltic Revolution: Estonia, Latvia and Lithuania and the Path to Independence.* New Haven: Yale University Press, 1993.

Misionas, Romoald, and Rein Taagepera. *The Baltic States: Years of Dependence, 1940–1990.* London: Hurst, 1993.

Norgaard, Ole, et al. *The Baltic States after Independence.* Cheltenham U.K.: Edward Elgar, 1996.

Senn, Alfred Erich. *Lithuania Awakening.* Berkeley: University of California Press, 1990.

Smith, Graham, ed. *The Baltic States: The National Self-Determination of Estonia, Latvia and Lithuania.* Basingstoke U.K.: Macmillan, 1994.

Thomas Lane

SEE ALSO Landsbergis, Vytautas

Brecht, Bertolt (1889–1956)

Although Bertolt Brecht has been dead for over forty years and many of his best-known works were written before the rise of the Nazis in 1933, Brecht was one of the most controversial and influential dramatists of the postwar period in both Germanies and abroad. From his beginnings in expressionist circles in Augsburg and Munich—*Baal* (1920, premiere 1923), *Trommeln in der Nacht* (*Drums in the Night,* 1919, premiere 1922), *Im Dickicht der Städte* (*In the Jungle of Cities,* 1923, premiere 1927)—to his

avant-garde collaborations (with Kurt Weill, Hans Eisler, Elisabeth Hauptmann, and Helene Weigel, to name a few) and Marxist Lehrstücke (plays for learning) of his Berlin years (1924–33)—*Mann ist Mann* (1924/55, premiere 1926), *Die Dreigroschenoper* (*The Threepenny Opera,* 1928, premiere 1928), *Aufstieg und Fall der Stadt Mahagonny* (*The Rise and Fall of the City of Mahagonny,* 1927, premiere 1930), *Die Maßnahme* (*The Measures Taken,* 1929, premiere 1930), *Die heilige Johanna der Schlachthöfe* (*Saint Joan of the Stockyards,* 1929; radio premier 1932, premier 1959)—to his exile and postwar works—*Furcht und Elend des dritten Reiches* (*Fear and Misery of the Third Reich,* 1937, premiere 1938), *Leben des Galilei* (*Life of Galileo,* 1938, premiere 1943), *Mutter Courage und ihre Kinder* (*Mother Courage and Her Children,* 1939, premiere 1941), *Der aufhaltsame Aufstieg des Arturo Ui* (*The Resistible Rise of Arturo Ui,* 1941, premiere 1958), *Der kaukasische Kreidekreis* (*The Caucasian Chalk Circle,* 1944, premiere 1948)—Brecht's dramatic work was consistent in its energies directed toward real social change, the fall of capitalism, and the advent of socialist revolution. Because of this, his plays regularly caused scandal and have been minutely analyzed in both written and produced versions by the two distinct groups of Brecht scholars on either side of the Wall. Since the fall of the Wall, Brecht's reception continues to be hotly debated with new topics of interest being his relationship to the German Democratic Republic (GDR) during his years there after the war (1949–56) and the important but rarely acknowledged roles played by his many collaborators.

The international success of *Mother Courage* gave Brecht freedom and power as director of the now legendary Berliner Ensemble after his move to the GDR, where his collective working methods and practical exercises in his famous ideas on the *Verfremdungseffekt* (alienation effect) and "Epic Theater" provided a rich environment for young East German actors, writers, and directors, though he still had to negotiate with cultural functionaries in order not to offend party sensibilities. And in the hyper-politicized world of Adenauer's West Germany, some of his work was even censored. To know Brecht in the West in the 1960s was to be a card-carrying leftist, antiwar progressive, and free-speech activist. By the 1970s he had become a modern classic and is read today by every German schoolchild. Recent literary-critical disputes, continued hotly debated productions, and a new appreciation of Brecht's lesser-known poetic works show his continued relevance.

BIBLIOGRAPHY

Brooker, Peter. *Bertolt Brecht: Dialectics, Poetry, Politics.* London: Croom Helm, 1988.

Fuegi, John. *The Life and Lies of Bertolt Brecht.* London: HarperCollins, 1994.

Kleber, Pia, and Colin Visser, eds. *Re-interpreting Brecht: His Influence on Contemporary Drama and Film.* Cambridge: Cambridge University Press, 1990.

Mews, Siegfried, ed. *Critical Essays on Bertolt Brecht.* Boston: Hall, 1989.

Whitaker, Peter. *Brecht's Poetry: A Critical Study.* Oxford: Clarendon Press, 1985.

Willett, John. *Brecht in Context: Comparative Approaches.* London: Methuen, 1984.

———. *The Theater of Bertolt Brecht: A Study in Eight Aspects.* London: Methuen, 1996.

Wright, Elizabeth. *Postmodern Brecht: A Re-presentation.* London: Routledge, 1989.

Scott Denham

Brenner, Otto (1907–72)

West German labor leader, chairman of the metal workers' union (IG Metall), 1952–72. Rising through the ranks from general laborer to electrical engineer, Otto Brenner was a central figure in the postwar German labor movement, first as cochair with Hans Bruemmer of IG Metall (1952–56), then sole chair (1956–72).

An outspoken advocate of worker interests, nicknamed "Otto the Iron Man" for both his office and his personality, Brenner began his career in labor politics in the Weimar years and was imprisoned by the Nazis. After the war his commitment to labor's cause led to fierce conflicts with national governments and even with leaders of other unions within the German Trade Union Congress (DGB). As the largest union within the DGB, IG Metall represented the vanguard of West German organized labor, and Brenner used that position to put IG Metall in the forefront of major campaigns for shorter work weeks and higher wages. Rejecting the more conciliatory courses of other DGB leaders and the calls for more cooperation between management and labor, Brenner did not shrink from the rhetoric of class conflict. He also challenged the notion that labor unions should be politically neutral. He allied IG Metall closely with the Social Democratic Party and its campaigns against West German rearmament. As an architect of the postwar German labor movement, Brenner deserves recognition as one of the founders of postwar German democracy.

BIBLIOGRAPHY

Otto Brenner's papers are located in the DGB Archive, Düsseldorf.

Hermanns, Johannes. *Otto Brenner [Persönlichkeiten der Gegenwart 4].* Freudenstadt, Germany: Eurobuch Verlag, 1967.

Oertzen, Peter von, ed. *Festschrift für Otto Brenner zum 60. Geburtstag.* Frankfurt am Main.: Europaeische Verlagsanstalt, 1967.

Schneider, Michael. *A Brief History of the German Trade Unions.* Bonn: Verlag Dietz, 1991.

Ronald J. Granieri

Brentano, Heinrich von (1904–64)

German Christian Democratic politician, foreign minister of the Federal Republic of Germany (1955–61). Heinrich von Brentano, one of the founders of the Christian Democratic Union (CDU) in the state of Hesse, quickly became one of the most prominent national leaders of the CDU during the Adenauer era. After serving on the Parliamentary Council, which drafted the West German Basic Law, Brentano was elected to the first Bundestag (lower house of parliament) in 1949, and then served as chair of the CDU/Christian Social Union Bundestag Parliamentary Caucus (1949–55). As caucus leader and foreign minister, Brentano was a leading advocate of European integration and close cooperation between the Federal Republic and the United States.

Descendant of a famous literary and diplomatic family, and as foreign minister always in the shadow of Chancellor Konrad Adenauer, Brentano suffered, according to the popular magazine *Der Spiegel,* under the double burden of "carrying a great poet's name and a great Chancellor's briefcase." In spite of his high position in both the government and the CDU party organization, contemporary accounts tended to dismiss Brentano, a shy, chain-smoking, lifelong bachelor, as a secondary character, a mouthpiece for Adenauer and his foreign policy. One editorial cartoon portrayed Brentano as a human railroad signal, with Adenauer, the conductor, controlling the switch. When, after the 1961 Bundestag election, the Free Democratic Party failed to force Adenauer to resign as chancellor, it insisted that Brentano resign as foreign minister. This symbolized the degree to which he had come to be seen as a stand-in for Adenauer. Brentano eventually resigned in protest and returned to the caucus leadership, where he served until dying of cancer in 1964.

Recent works have modified the contemporary image of Brentano as Adenauer's mouthpiece. These revisionist works cite numerous behind-the-scenes conflicts between chancellor and foreign minister on the German Question and on relations with the United States. Brentano was at pains, however, to avoid public conflict with Adenauer, in spite of their occasionally significant differences, so it is difficult to accept attempts to paint the former as a rebel. Yet the revisionists are correct in trying to refocus attention on Brentano as an important figure in the development of West German foreign policy in his own right. In both his agreement and disagreement with Adenauer over that policy, Brentano represented the variety of opinion even within the pro-Western consensus of the Adenauer governments.

BIBLIOGRAPHY

Brentano's personal papers are located in the Bundesarchiv (Federal Archives) in Koblenz, Germany, NL 239.

Baring, Arnulf. *Sehr verehrter Herr Bundeskanzler! Heinrich von Brentano im Briefwechsel mit Konrad Adenauer.* Hamburg: Hoffmann und Campe, 1974.

Brentano, Heinrich von. *Germany and Europe: Reflections on German Foreign Policy.* New York: Praeger, 1964.

Kosthorst, Daniel. *Brentano und die deutsche Einheit: Die Deutschland- und Ostpolitik des Außenministers im Kabinett Adenauer 1955–1961.* Düsseldorf: Droste, 1993.

Ronald J. Granieri

Brezhnev, Leonid (1906–82)

Leader of the Soviet Union 1964–82. Dominating the Soviet bloc for two decades, Leonid Brezhnev presided over an era of stability, stagnation, and, eventually, decline. On the domestic front, Brezhnev abandoned de-Stalinization and reversed many of Nikita Khrushchev's reforms. In foreign affairs, his reign marked the apogee of the Soviet Union's international power and prestige.

The leaders of the Politburo (then called the Presidium) deposed Premier and General Secretary Khrushchev in October 1964 and established a collective leadership. As was the case following the death of Stalin, a power struggle broke out among those vying for supremacy. The highest political positions in the country were occupied by Brezhnev, first secretary of the party; Alexi Kosygin, prime minister; and Nikolay Podgorny, who became president in December 1965.

Brezhnev's biography is that of the model apparatchik, rising steadily up the party ladder, accumulating allies and protégés but few enemies. The son of a Russian factory worker, he was born in 1906 in Kamenskoe (later renamed Dneprodzerzhinsk). After finishing vocational school, he worked for several years at agricultural agencies before changing his profession to engineering. At the age of 25 he joined the party, and in 1937 was elected deputy chairman of the Dneprodzerzhinsk city Soviet. The fol-

lowing year he was appointed deputy to Nikita Khrushchev, who was then first secretary of the Ukrainian party. Through Khrushchev's influence Brezhnev gradually rose to hold the successive posts of secretary of the Kazakhstan Central Committee, president of the Supreme Soviet of the USSR, and secretary of the Soviet Communist Party's (CPSU) Central Committee. As his own power grew Brezhnev accumulated a stable of underlings to whom he could later confer powerful positions while endeavoring to demote or isolate possible rivals. Brezhnev's rise was majestically slow. He was largely outshadowed by Kosygin from 1964 to 1968, and only in the early 1970s did he emerge as first among equals. It was not until 1977, when he became chairman of the Presidium of the Supreme Soviet, that he finally achieved primacy in both party and state.

Under Brezhnev's leadership, many of Khrushchev's unpopular reforms were reversed, including the division of the party into industrial and agricultural sectors. De-Stalinization was also halted, and along with it the relative cultural freedom that had flourished in the late 1950s. In 1965 Brezhnev won wide support among bureaucrats by instituting his policy of "stability in cadres," which translated into guarantees of comfort and job security for the medium- and upper-level party-state apparatus. Khrushchev's earlier promise of a transition to communism gave way to Brezhnev's theory of "developed socialism," which stated that the road to communism would be a long one. In the new schema, social differentiation would increase, and a new army of skilled workers would usher in an era of scientific and technical innovations that would transform the USSR. Finally, the Soviet constitution of 1977 brought few real changes from the 1936 Stalin document, though significantly, the notion of the dictatorship of the proletariat was dropped.

The industrial and agricultural reforms of Khrushchev that had promised so much had yielded little. The 1965 reforms of Prime Minister Kosygin proposed greater freedom for individual enterprises. The new program dropped Khrushchev's regional economic councils in favor of the central industrial ministries of the Stalin era. Opposition from conservatives soon halted the experiment in limited economic freedoms, and the bureaucratic market was restored. As before, the goal of every enterprise was not to make a profit but to become a monopoly producer. Planners once again submitted comprehensive centralized plans of the type first developed under Stalin. At the expense of the light consumer-goods branches, heavy and defense-related industries dominated economic output. A lack of investment capital and labor reserves made the goals of successive five-year plans impossible to meet. By the 1970s the Soviet Union could not maintain high rates of growth in the industrial sector. The only bright spots were in the defense and space industries, where the USSR made major strides and equaled or surpassed foreign rivals.

Agricultural progress lagged, and even with increased investments, growth fell below 1950s levels. From 1971 to 1975 there was negative agricultural growth of 0.6 percent annually. Frequent droughts throughout the 1970s forced the Soviet Union to import large quantities of grain from the United States. Brezhnev continued Khrushchev's policy of converting collective farms into state farms. While this successfully raised the wages of farm workers, it did not significantly increase output, and the most productive acreage continued to be backyard plots cultivated privately.

Living standards, after rising steadily through the 1960s, leveled off and then declined over the last decade of Brezhnev's reign. With industrial and agricultural stagnation, the Soviet regime could not satisfy increasing consumer demand. Though the largest cities were generally well supplied, food lines became common in many provincial towns. Corruption filtered down from the political elite and became pervasive at all levels. A growing black market flourished wherever the planned economy had ceased to function. Vodka remained cheap, and alcoholism was an important factor in both the declining life expectancy and the rising infant mortality of the later Brezhnev years. Investment in social and medical services dropped precipitously; medical care in some parts of the Soviet Union was no better than in the poorest Third World countries.

In education and science the Brezhnev era brought uneven progress. Although an increasing percentage of the population received secondary and higher degrees, access to higher education grew more restrictive. Between 1960 and 1980 the percentage of secondary-school graduates admitted to universities dropped by one-third. Meanwhile, despite earlier success in space technology, the Soviets failed in the race with the United States to put a man on the moon. However, advances in the fields of metallurgy and thermonuclear fusion compared favorably with those abroad. In computer technology, the most important emerging scientific area, the Soviets lagged far behind the West.

In art and literature Brezhnev had no toleration for experimentation, and his tastes were limited to works that praised the Soviet system. During his reign, many writers and artists were arrested, exiled, or sent to labor camps. In attempting to crush cultural dissent, the state stimulated the development of a counterculture, and private

gatherings by intellectuals and artists flourished. At such meetings, works of dissent were circulated in typescript, or samizdat. By the mid-1970s a great variety of creative works had become accessible to the Soviet public. Gradually, the state began to permit greater experimentation, and subtly critical works soon appeared.

In music, appearances by Western jazz and rock ensembles drew enormous crowds and led to the popularity of alternative Soviet musicians, such as balladeer Vladimir Vysotsky. The arrival of the inexpensive audiocassette and later the videocassette facilitated wide dissemination of underground popular culture. By the last years of Brezhnev's reign the state had lost cultural control of the population. Similarly, religious life in the Soviet Union gradually freed itself of state control. Despite official disapproval, the late 1970s witnessed a resurgence in popular devotion to the major faiths.

In foreign affairs, the first concern of Khrushchev's successors was to undermine China's influence among Communist states. The new leaders originally hoped for rapprochement, but Mao Tse-Tung's intransigence soon led to a worsening of relations between the two countries. A low ebb in Sino-Soviet relations was reached in March 1969 when clashes broke out along the disputed Ussuri River in the far east. The Chinese backed down in the face of Soviet military superiority, but a similar incident followed in August on the Soviet border with the Chinese province of Sinkiang. To check Chinese expansion, the Soviets extended military aid to India, Pakistan, and North Vietnam. Relations remained strained through the balance of Brezhnev's reign.

In Eastern Europe, Soviet and other Warsaw Pact troops intervened in Czechoslovakia in August 1968 to crush the reforms begun by the Czechoslovak Communist Party leader Alexander Dubček, who had begun liberalization and sought ties with the West. These tragic events were the result of a misunderstanding between Moscow and Prague over the rights of satellite regimes to initiate reform. In response, the Kremlin issued what came to be known as the Brezhnev Doctrine, which warned that the Soviet Union would act to defend the socialist gains of its allies and thereby maintain its hegemony in Eastern Europe.

The Brezhnev Doctrine remained in force down to 1989, effectively capping any further revolt in the Soviet bloc. Romania, already a maverick for having convinced Moscow to remove Soviet troops from its soil and then establishing trade ties with the West, desisted from further gestures of defiance. But the Brezhnev Doctrine did much to encourage the development of Eurocommunism, which freed Western European Communist parties to pursue political programs independent of Moscow.

In the developing world Brezhnev continued Khrushchev's earlier expansion of Soviet influence. New Communist regimes with close ties to Moscow emerged in Ethiopia, Nicaragua, and Southeast Asia. In the Middle East, the Soviet Union supported the Arabs in their dispute with Israel and subsidized the defeated Syrian and Egyptian armies after the June 1967 war with Israel. Moscow's influence in the Arab world was undermined after its 1979 invasion of Afghanistan, when Brezhnev sent in armed forces to support the Communist government in that country. A large part of the Afghan population resisted both the occupiers and the Marxist Afghan regime, and a protracted and bloody conflict resulted in tens of thousands of Soviet casualties, not to mention countless Afghan casualties.

Soviet relations with the West deteriorated in 1965 during the U.S. bombing of North Vietnam. After 1968 the gradual withdrawal of American forces from Southeast Asia led to negotiations between the United States and the USSR on the subject of nuclear arms. The Nuclear Non-Proliferation Treaty was signed in July 1968, and the two countries began the Strategic Arms Limitation Talks (SALT) in 1969. In the May 1972 Moscow summit Brezhnev and President Richard Nixon signed the Anti-Ballistic Missile Treaty and the Interim Agreement on the Limitation of Strategic Offensive Arms. These treaties signaled an era of relaxed tensions, or détente. The spirit of détente was best exemplified in the signing of the 1975 Helsinki Accords, which ratified the postwar status quo in Europe and bound the signatories to basic principles of human rights. But Afghanistan effectively ended détente. The United States imposed a grain embargo on the Soviet Union and boycotted the 1980 Moscow Summer Olympics. Tensions between the United States and the Soviet Union did not abate until the arrival of Mikhail Gorbachev.

In the last years of his reign, Brezhnev's health deteriorated, and he increasingly delegated authority to his long-time associate Konstantin Chernenko and later, KGB chief Yuri Andropov. Brezhnev's emerging cult of personality was hampered by his own inactivity, though he did manage to publish several ghostwritten volumes and receive a series of absurd official honors: Marshal of the Soviet Union, 1976; Order of Victory, 1978; Lenin Prize for Literature, 1979. In 1975 he suffered his first stroke and from then on was probably dependent on drugs and other medications. By early 1982 economic failures and scandals in his family had irreparably damaged Brezhnev's prestige, but he would not relinquish of-

fice. Toward the end of his life, in one of the great ironies of the Soviet period, Brezhnev's visible confusion, slurred speech, and physical breakdown perfectly symbolized the stagnation and rottenness of the system he presided over. In November 1982, following an inert public appearance marking the anniversary of the Russian Revolution, Brezhnev died.

The Brezhnev era was politically and socially the most stable period in the history of the Soviet Union. In an age that required dynamism and progressive reform, however, the price of stability was physical deterioration and a loss of power and prestige for the USSR. While Brezhnev may have contributed to the stagnation of the Soviet Union, he understood the essential nature of the system. In refusing to tinker with an inoperable patient, he prolonged its life as long as possible.

BIBLIOGRAPHY

Breslauer, George. *Khrushchev and Brezhnev as Leaders.* Boston: Allan and Unwin, 1982.

Brown, Archie, and Michael Kaser, eds. *The Soviet Union Since the Fall of Khrushchev.* 2d ed. New York: Free Press, 1978.

Kelley, Donald, ed. *Soviet Politics from Brezhnev to Gorbachev.* New York: Praeger, 1987.

Daniel Kowalsky

SEE ALSO Afghanistan, War in; Brezhnev Doctrine; Détente

Brezhnev Doctrine

Kremlin doctrine named for Soviet First Secretary Leonid Brezhnev to justify the 1968 Soviet-led Warsaw Pact invasion of Czechoslovakia and the 1979 Soviet invasion of Afghanistan. The Brezhnev Doctrine was, in effect, the high point of Soviet pretensions to control its satellites.

Discontent with the system in Czechoslovakia led in 1968 to the reform movement known as the Prague Spring. On August 21 Soviet and Warsaw Pact forces invaded Czechoslovakia and overthrew the reformers. The justification for this invasion was spelled out in a Soviet statement published in *Pravda* on August 21. Moscow claimed that "the fraternal communist parties of the socialist countries" had taken "political measures to help the Czechoslovak people to halt the anti-socialist forces' offensive in Czechoslovakia." According to *Pravda*, only after exhausting these efforts to prevent a "counter-revolution" did the Soviet Union and its allies send troops, and then only after having been invited to do so by unnamed Czechoslovak state and party leaders. Those forces, it continued, would be withdrawn from Czechoslovakia "as soon as the threat that exists to the gains of socialism in Czechoslovakia and the threat to the security of the socialist commonwealth countries is eliminated and the lawful authorities find that the further presence of these armed units is no longer necessary there."

The Kremlin claimed it had both the right and the duty to intervene in the affairs of other Communist states to protect socialist interests. The doctrine stated that "every Communist party is responsible not only to its own people but also to all the socialist countries and to the entire communist movement." The socialist commonwealth was one bloc, supported by the power of the Soviet Union and its armed forces. "The weakening of any link in the world socialist system has a direct effect on all the socialist countries."

The Brezhnev Doctrine in effect limited the sovereignty of those Communist-ruled states within the Kremlin's military reach and had a chilling effect on reform in Eastern Europe. Western governments protested the doctrine but did nothing else. This was in part because they wished to preserve détente and in part frank recognition that the Communists could do as they wished within their sphere of influence. The Brezhnev Doctrine was reminiscent of the 1947 Truman Doctrine and frequent U.S. statements regarding Latin America.

Moscow again invoked the Brezhnev Doctrine in Afghanistan. At the end of 1979 the Soviets sent troops into that country, overthrowing a government headed by homegrown Afghan Communists who had seized power in a coup in April 1976 against Moscow's advice and were in danger of being overwhelmed by their opponents. Brezhnev defended the Kremlin action in these words: "Some bourgeois leaders affect surprise over the solidarity of Soviet Communists, the Soviet people, with the struggle of other peoples for freedom and progress. . . . We make no secret of the fact that we see détente as the way to create more favorable conditions for peaceful socialist and Communist construction."

In 1988 Mikhail Gorbachev repudiated the Brezhnev Doctrine. When he declared that the Soviet Union would no longer employ force to preserve Communist regimes, it was the death sentence to the Communist regimes of Eastern Europe; within a year they had all disappeared.

BIBLIOGRAPHY

Edmonds, Robin. *Soviet Foreign Policy: The Brezhnev Years.* New York; Oxford University Press, 1983.

Hanak, Harry. *Soviet Foreign Policy since the Death of Stalin.* London: Routledge & Kegan Paul, 1972.

Staar, Richard F. *USSR Foreign Policies after Détente.* Stanford, CA.: Hoover Institution Press, 1985.

Valenta, Jiri. *Soviet Intervention in Czechoslovakia, 1968: Anatomy of a Decision.* Baltimore: Johns Hopkins University Press, 1979.

Spencer C. Tucker

SEE ALSO Brezhnev, Leonid; Afghanistan, War in

Brittan, Leon (1939–)

British Conservative politician. Leon Brittan was born September 25, 1939. After pursuing degrees from Trinity College at Oxford University and at Yale University, Brittan gained a reputation as a Conservative spokesman, by chairing the conservative Bow Group and, particularly, by publishing the polemic, *Millstones for the Sixties*. He was elected as the Conservative MP for Cleveland and Whitby in 1974. He entered Prime Minister Margaret Thatcher's first cabinet in 1979 and was appointed home secretary in her second cabinet in June 1983.

Brittan's ministry was marked both by a strong management style and by scandal. In 1984 the Home Office expertly masterminded the defeat of a terrorist takeover of the Libyan Embassy in London. Brittan also managed the effort to respond to the bombing of the Conservative Party's conference hotel in Brighton by IRA terrorists. In 1985 Brittan's ministry was attacked in the Commons and in the British press for his efforts to pursue Margaret Thatcher's Conservative agenda using allegedly undemocratic principles. The BBC went on strike for twenty-four hours to protest government interference in its news broadcasts. Brittan resigned his ministry in September 1985 to become state secretary for trade and industry.

In 1989 Brittan was appointed as one of two commissioners for competition by the European Commission. While in office, he pursued a controversial but very successful effort to open up free trade within the European Community, cutting off state subsidies to industries in decline and breaking up monopolies. Though opposed by many nations, his policies proved profitable for the EC's industrial producers. He was also a strong advocate of the European Monetary Union (EMU) and the exchange rate mechanism that was a necessary prerequisite for the Euro, which was established in 1999.

In 1995, after restructuring the European Commission, Brittan was made one of its vice presidents. He was mainly responsible for the maintenance of economic relations with the nations of Eastern Europe and the Commonwealth of Independent States.

Brittan was knighted by Queen Elizabeth in 1989. His brother, Sir Samuel Brittan, is an assistant editor and commentator for the London Financial Times.

BIBLIOGRAPHY
Brittan, Leon. *Europe: The Europe We Need.* London: Hamish Hamilton, 1994.
Thatcher, Margaret. *The Downing Street Years.* New York: HarperCollins, 1993.

David Simonelli

Brodsky, Joseph (Iosif) (1940–96)

Russian poet, winner of the Nobel Prize in literature in 1987. Joseph Brodsky was born in Leningrad on May 24, 1940. Brodsky, a Jew, received a secular and assimilated upbringing, yet he experienced anti-Semitism in school. He quit school at age fifteen. While working at various jobs, he began to write poems, some of which were mimeographed and passed among friends, but others appeared in an underground journal, *Sintaksis*.

Brodsky was a disciple of Anna Akhmatova and was influenced by John Donne and W. H. Auden. A spiritual rather than political dissident, he lamented the physical and intellectual drabness of Soviet life. His underground poems were denounced by the state in 1963 as "pornographic and anti-Soviet," and he was twice consigned to a psychiatric institution, a common Soviet treatment of dissidents. In 1964 he was charged with "parasitism," failing "to work honestly for the good of the motherland." He was sentenced to five years in an Arctic labor camp but, owing to foreign protests, his sentence was reduced to eighteen months. After having been previously denied permission to travel abroad, in 1972 he was expelled from the Soviet Union. He became a poet-in-residence at the University of Michigan. Brodsky became a U.S. citizen in 1977 and moved to New York in 1980. There he continued to teach and to write plays, essays, and criticism, as well as poetry. Though he wrote his poems in Russian and translated his work into English, he became a powerful English-language poet. Portions of his English-language poetry were published in *A Part of Speech* (1977) and *To Urania* (1988). His book of essays, *Less Than One* (1986), won the National Book Critics Circle Award. A constant theme of his playfully crafted work was exile from his country and spiritual exile. He died of a heart attack in Brooklyn Heights, New York, on January 28, 1996.

BIBLIOGRAPHY
Bethea, David M. *Joseph Brodsky and the Creation of Exile.* Princeton, N.J.: Princeton University Press, 1994.
Brodsky, Joseph. *Less Than One: Selected Essays.* New York: Farrar, Straus & Giroux, 1986.
Polukhina, Valentina. *Brodsky Through the Eyes of His Contemporaries.* New York: St. Martin's Press, 1992.
———. *Joseph Brodsky: A Poet for Our Time.* Cambridge: Cambridge University Press, 1989.

Bernard Cook

SEE ALSO Akhmatova, Anna Audreevna

Brooke, Basil (Lord Brookeborough) (1888–1973)

Ulster Unionist politician and prime minister of Northern Ireland, 1943–63. Basil Brooke was born in Fermanagh in 1888. He served on the western front from 1914 to 1918. In 1921 he helped in the foundation of the "B" Specials, the exclusively Protestant force formed to supplement the regular police force. In 1921 he became a member of the first Senate of Northern Ireland. Brooke was returned as the Ulster Unionist Party MP for Lisnaskea in 1929 and held that seat until 1968. He was initially assistant whip of the party from 1930 until 1933, when he became minister for agriculture, a post he held until 1941. As minister for commerce (1941–43), he was a leading member of the younger generation of Unionists who were critical of the older members of the party, including Prime Minister John Miller Andrews. Andrews resigned and in May 1943 Brooke replaced him as leader of the party and as prime minister, holding the position for twenty years, the longest term of any prime minister of Northern Ireland. He replaced the older members of the government with younger men and set about planning the future growth of Northern Ireland, which was enjoying a new-found prosperity during World War II. The Labour government in Britain committed itself to aiding Northern Ireland to achieve parity with the rest of the United Kingdom in the spheres of education, medicine, social welfare, and so on. These advances took place under Lord Brookeborough, which Brooke became in 1952. Being a member of the Orange Order, he had a history of anti-Catholic statements behind him and did nothing to resolve the sectarian tension that marked life in the Northern state. His government introduced internment to deal with the threat of republicanism between 1956 and 1962. When he resigned office in 1963, he was replaced by a more liberal Unionist, Captain Terence O'Neill. Brooke resigned his seat in 1968.

Ricki Schoen

SEE ALSO O'Neill, Terence

Brosio, Manlio Giovanni (1897–1980)

Secretary-general of NATO, 1964–71. Manlio Brosio was born in Turin, Italy on July 10, 1897. He served as an artillery officer of the Alpine Corps during World War I. He received a doctorate in law from the University of Turin, and was active in the Liberal Party until the consolidation of the Fascist regime. In 1943–44 he was a member of the underground National Liberation Committee in German-occupied Italy. In 1944–45 he served as general secretary of the Liberal Party. He was a member of the Bonomi government in 1944 and deputy prime minister of the Parri government in 1945. He served as minister of war in the first government of de Gasperi (1945–46). He was appointed ambassador to the USSR (1947–52), the United Kingdom (1952–55), the United States (1955–61), and France (1961–64). From 1952 until 1954 he played a key role in the negotiations that led to the recognition of Italian sovereignty in Trieste.

Brosio was chosen by the North Atlantic Council to succeed Dirk Stikker as secretary-general of NATO in 1964. He resigned in 1971 and was succeeded by Joseph Luns.

Bernard Cook

Browne, Noel (1915–)

Irish Politician. Noel Browne was born in Athlone and studied medicine at Trinity College, Dublin. Browne's parents and members of his immediate family had died from tuberculosis; after he contracted the illness, he devoted his medical career to ridding Ireland of the disease. His social-reformist outlook led him to join the new political party, Clann na Poblachta (Republican Family), and he was elected to the Dail, the lower house of the Irish parliament, for Dublin South East in 1948. At the instigation of Sean MacBride, the leader of Clann na Poblachta, he became minister for health on his first day in parliament. As minister his greatest success was the eradication of tuberculosis by devoting huge funds to building new hospitals and liberally dispensing the latest drugs. He is best remembered for the mother-and-child program of 1951 where his plans for a nonmeans-tested health-care system for children to age sixteen and their mothers incurred the wrath of the clergy and medical practitioners. The cabinet, his party leader, Sean MacBride, and Clann na Poblachta refused to back him, and he resigned from government.

Following the fall of the Inter-Party Government in 1951, Browne was returned as an independent member of the Dail from 1951 to 1953. He was a member of Fianna Fail; the economically conservative and anti-British party, from 1953 to 1957 without a Dail seat. He regained his seat as an independent in 1957 and in 1958 was cofounder of the National Progressive Democrats, and he held a Dail seat for that party to 1963. In 1963 he joined the Labour Party until he was elected to the Senate for Dublin University in 1973. He returned to the Dail in the 1970s and early 1980s as an independent.

Browne's career appears full of contradictions and inconsistencies, but the earnestness of his convictions are evident. He was one of the few Irish politicians to speak out against the Catholic Church, which exercised a dominant role in Irish Society, but it has been argued that he damaged the cause of progressive politics in Ireland. Though at times reviled and scorned, with the passage of time he gained wide respect.

BIBLIOGRAPHY
Browne, Noel. *Against the Tide.* Dublin: Gill and Macmillan, 1986.

Michael J. Kennedy

Brucan, Silviu (1918–)

Intellectual and government functionary who played a leading role in the 1989 Romanian uprising and later became an influential commentator on political affairs. A talented Jewish intellectual from Bucharest, Silviu Brucan enrolled at an early age in the Romanian Communist Party. He edited the party's newspaper, *Scînteia,* in the late 1940s as the party was consolidating its hold on power. He was ambassador to the United States from 1956 to 1959 and to the United Nations from 1959 to 1962. After serving as head of Romanian television, Brucan switched to an academic role and published books on socialism and the state that were widely translated abroad. He enjoyed freedom to travel under the increasingly repressive Ceaușescu regime. However, he began to criticize the regime openly in the late 1980s. Released from internal exile shortly after the start of the December 1989 uprising, he was a top insider in the ruling National Salvation Front (NSF), and he played an important role in the first months of the new regime. He encouraged the NSF to enter the political process and stand in elections, but he retired to the sidelines to act as a commentator and critic in post-Communist Romania.

Tom Gallagher

Brundtland, Gro Harlem (1939–)

Social Democratic prime minister of Norway (1981, 1986–89, 1990–96). Gro Harlem Brundtland was the first woman prime minister of Norway and, at forty-one, the youngest Norwegian prime minister. Having long since moved beyond the issue of gender and leadership, Brundtland firmly established her power in Norway and built an international reputation as an environmental leader.

Gro Harlem Brundtland was born in Oslo on April 20, 1939. Her father, Gudmund Harlem, was the Norwegian minister of social affairs from 1955 to 1961, and minister of defense from 1961 to 1965. Brundtland graduated from the University of Oslo in 1963 as a medical doctor and later received a degree at Harvard University. Her career began in the civil service as the assistant medical director at the Board of Health in Oslo. Having been active in the Norwegian Labor Party from an early age, she accepted her first public office as minister of environment in 1974, a position she held until 1979. Brundtland was elected to the Norwegian Storting (parliament) in 1977 and served on committees dealing with finance, foreign policy, and constitutional affairs. In February 1981 she became prime minister of Norway and leader of the Norwegian Labor Party.

In 1983 U.N. Secretary-General Javier Pérez de Cuellar asked Brundtland to chair the World Commission on Environment and Development. In 1987, her efforts culminated in the publishing of *Our Common Future,* which quickly became known as the "Brundtland Report." This report was the blueprint for the 1992 U.N. Conference on Environment and Development (UNCED), held in Rio de Janeiro, Brazil.

During her second term as prime minister in 1986. Brundtland formed what has been called the "women's government." Eight of the eighteen cabinet ministers were women. Throughout her public life Brundtland had actively promoted equal rights and the role of women in politics. Her nineteen-member cabinet in 1990 included nine women.

Norway's remarkable achievement in promoting women in politics was partially due to the passing of its Equal Status Act in 1979, which prevented discrimination in hiring and wages. An addition to this act in 1988 required a minimum of 40 percent representation of both sexes on all public boards, councils, and committees. This 40 percent goal has since been incorporated into the organizational structure of political parties as well. Norway also has a proportional representation electoral system. This system allows for more parties and, consequently, a greater number of women to participate and get elected. The result has been that Norway now has the world's highest percentage of women in parliament, nearly 40 percent.

Although it may be too early to determine what difference a higher percentage of women in politics will have on public policy around the world, in Norway there was a clear indication that more attention was being paid to issues of childcare, parental leave, and health policy. Brundtland, even though she represented a small country, was at the crest of the wave of emerging women world leaders who may indeed provide a different perspective on solving seemingly intractable common global problems.

On October 23, 1996, Brundtland resigned as prime minister and was succeeded by Thorbjørn Jagland. She said she would run for reelection to the Storting in September 1997, but that her resignation would allow her Labor Party time to prepare for the election. She resigned as leader of the party in October 1992, following the suicide of her son. Her successor was Jagland.

BIBLIOGRAPHY

Gonovese, Michael A., ed. *Women as National Leaders.* London: Sage, 1993.

Hansson, Steinar, and Ingolf Håkon Teigene. *Makt og Mannefall: Historien om Gro Harlem Brundtland.* Oslo: J.W. Cappelens Forlag, 1992.

Hirsti, Reidar, ed. *Gro: Midt i Livet.* Oslo: Tiden Norsk Forlag, 1989.

Opfell, Olga S. *Women Prime Ministers and Presidents.* Jefferson, N.C.: McFarland, 1993.

Bruce Olav Solheim

Bruton, John (1947–)

Leader of Fine Gael (Family of the Irish), the traditional Irish establishment party, and Irish prime minister (*taoiseach*), December 1994 to June 1997. John Bruton was educated at University College, Dublin and King's Inns. He possessed large farming interests in County Meath in the Irish midlands. He was elected to the Dail, the lower house of the Irish parliament, in 1969. He served as junior minister for education (1973–77) and was opposition spokesperson on finance (1981–82) and agriculture (1972–73, 1977–81). He was minister for finance in 1981 and 1982, but his budget proposals for a tax on children's shoes led to the fall of Prime Minister Garret FitzGerald's first coalition government. He served as minister for industry, commerce, and tourism from 1983 to 1986, and minister for finance from 1986 to 1987. He was deputy leader of Fine Gael from 1987 to 1990, and took over leadership of Fine Gael from Alan Dukes in 1990. In 1994 he became *taoiseach* as leader of a coalition of Fine Gael, Labour, and the Democratic Left. Fine Gael suffered a narrow defeat in the June 1997 election, and

Bruton was succeeded as prime minister by Bertie Ahern of the Fianna Fail party.

Michael J. Kennedy

Bubis, Ignatz (1927–99)

Chairman of the Central Council of Jews in Germany (Zentralrat der Juden in Deutschland), and thus the highest-ranking public figure for Jewish concerns in Germany after 1992. Bubis was born in Breslau (Wrocław, Poland), grew up in the Polish town of Dęblin, and survived the war and persecution (ghetto in Dęblin 1939–42, concentration camp Dęblin 1942–1944, Czestochowa 1944–45) to settle finally in Frankfurt am Main, Germany, in 1956 as a dealer in precious metals and gems and, after the early 1970s, a real estate investor.

Bubis became active in the Frankfurt Jewish community in the early 1960s, helping with such projects as the Jewish kindergarten and school, a nursing home, and apartments. Bubis played a leading role in demonstrations against filmmaker Rainer Werner Fassbinder's anti-Semitic play *Die Stadt, der Müll und der Tod* in Frankfurt in 1985, which was also hotly debated in the context of the *Historikerstreit* (historians dispute) at the time. After his election as chairman of the Central Council in 1992, he played a principled and highly pragmatic role in German-Jewish relations and German politics in general (he was a member of the Free Democratic Party). He spoke frankly and often on topics of broad social concern, not merely those relating specifically to concerns of Jews in Germany, or as he chose to say: "German citizens of the Jewish faith," part of the title of one of his books (which he credited to Heinz Galinsky, his immediate predecessor in office). After the *Wende* (turning point, or collapse of communism in the German Democratic Republic and the turn toward reunification), he was especially forceful in his calls for tolerance and mutual understanding among people of different faiths and ethnic backgrounds in Germany, speaking out often against xenophobia and racial violence. Bubis received many honors and awards, including the Bundesverdienstkreuz (the Service Cross of the Federal Republic) and Moses-Mendelssohn-Medaille.

Bubis died on August 13, 1999. The year before his death he had decried Martin Walser's assertion that the Holocaust should not be "exploited for present purposes" against contemporary Germany and that Auschwitz not be used as a "moral cudgel." Bubis denounced this as an example of "intellectual nationalism" tantamount to "moral arson."

BIBLIOGRAPHY
Bubis, Ignatz. *Damit bin ich noch längst nicht fertig: Die Autobiographie.* With the collaboration of Peter Sichrovsky. Frankfurt: Campus, 1996.
———. *Ich bin ein deutscher Staatsbürger jüdischen Glaubens: ein autobiographisches Gespräch.* With Edith Kohn. Cologne: Kiepenheuer & Witsch, 1993.
———. *Juden in Deutschland.* Wilhelm von Sternburg, ed. Berlin: Aufbau, 1996.
Stern, Susan, ed. *Speaking Out: Jewish Voices from United Germany.* Carol Stream, Il.: Edition Q, 1995.

Scott Denham

Bufi, Ylli (1948–)

Albanian prime minister, June to December 1991. Ylli Bufi was born on May 25, 1948, in the southern industrial city of Fier. Trained as a chemical engineer, he was appointed an alternate member of the Central Committee of the Party of Labor (PL), the Albanian Communist party. He served as minister of foodstuffs industries in 1990–91, of food and light industry from February to May 1991, and of nutrition from May to June 1991. A week after the Communist cabinet of Fatos Nano was forced to resign as a result of a general strike, the Albanian parliament on June 12, 1991, gave its approval to a non-Communist government of "national salvation" headed by Bufi. Bufi had the reputation of an honest nonideological technocrat. The new government contained twelve members from the old PL, which at this time changed its name to the Socialist Party, and twelve non-Communist members. Seven of the remaining twelve members came from the Democratic Party, the leading opposition party in parliament, and the remainder came from the Social Democratic Party, the Republican Party, and the Party of Agriculture. Gramoz Pashko, from the Democratic Party, became the deputy prime minister and minister of economics. Bufi, who was prime minister from June to December 1991, was intended to head a non-Communist caretaker government until elections in May or June 1992. Comments by Bufi about the precarious state of food reserves, however, apparently set off food riots in December that led to his resignation and replacement by Vilson Ahmet. Ahmet headed the caretaker government until elections moved up to March 22 by President Ramiz Alia. Those elections gave the Democratic Party an absolute majority with 62 percent of the vote.

BIBLIOGRAPHY
Sudetic, Chuck. "Albania Appoints a Non-Communist Cabinet," *New York Times,* June 13, 1991.

Bernard Cook

Buhl, Vilhelm (1881–1954)

Danish politician and prime minister in 1942 and 1945. Vilhelm Buhl became a member of the Social Democratic Party in his youth. After studying law, he became a member of the Lanstinget (upper house of parliament) in 1932. He was a member of the Folketinget (lower house), the main organ of parliament, from 1939 to 1953. He was finance minister from 1937 to 1942 and pursued a traditional finance policy. After the death of Prime Minister Thorvald Stauning in 1942, Buhl was appointed prime minister but was in charge only for one year when the German occupation authority during World War II demanded his removal. Throughout the national strikes in 1944 against the German occupation, Buhl acted as intermediary between Werner Best, the German plenipotentiary, and the Danish resistance movement, urging restraint on both sides. Some of the repressive German measures were repealed and work was resumed.

Buhl became the first prime minister of liberated Denmark in May 1945, holding the post only until November, when a general election paved the way for a nonsocialist prime minister. Buhl is remembered as the personality who bridged the gap between the old politicians who functioned legally during the occupation and the underground resistance movement that fought the German occupation power with acts of sabotage.

Jørn Boye Nielsen

Bukovina

Region located in present-day northeastern Romania and western Ukraine, with its historic capital in the Ukrainian city of Chernivsti (Romanian, Cernauti; Russian, Chernovtsy). The region, with a total area of around 4,000 square miles (10,360 sq kms), consists of a portion of the northeastern Carpathian Mountains and surrounding plains. Major rivers include the Dniester, Prut, Siret, Suceava, Moldova, and Bistrişa. Agriculture and forestry have been important, and the name "Bukovina" itself derives from the German *Buche* or Slavic *Buk* (beech tree). Bukovina is quintessentially central European: Ukrainians, Jews, Romanians, Poles, Germans, Russians, and others have all left their cultural and linguistic mark on the region. Paul Celan and other important figures in European intellectual life were originally from the region.

Bukovina (Ukrainian, Bukovyna; Romanian, Bucovina; German, Bukowina) was a part of the Ottoman-controlled principality of Moldavia until 1775, when it was incorporated into the Habsburg Empire. From 1786 it formed part of the Austrian province of Galicia but was made a separate crown land in 1849. After the creation of an independent Romania in 1878, politicians in Bucharest issued calls for the incorporation of Bukovina into an enlarged Greater Romania, since much of the population (especially in southern Bukovina) was ethnic Romanian. According to the 1910 census the region had a total population of 794,942, of which 38 percent were Ukrainian and 34 percent Romanian, with the rest consisting of Germans, Poles, Jews, Armenians, and Hungarians. With the collapse of the Habsburg, Russian, and Ottoman Empires as a result of the First World War, the region's major ethnic groups found themselves at odds over their future. In October 1918 Ukrainians and Romanians issued separate declarations proclaiming Bukovina's union with an independent Ukraine and an enlarged Romania. Its army's occupation of Bukovina ensured that Romania's claims were recognized by the Allied powers, and Bukovina's status within Greater Romania was enshrined in the Treaty of Saint Germain (1919).

Throughout the interwar years the Soviet Union agitated for the cession of the northern portion of Bukovina with its large Ukrainian population. On June 26, 1940, the Soviet government issued an ultimatum to Romanian demanding the immediate handover of northern Bukovina, and Soviet troops occupied the region two days later. Although Romania managed to reassert control over the area from 1941 to 1944, the postwar peace treaty (February 1947) recognized Soviet annexation of the area. The northern portion, including the city of Chernivtsi, remained within Soviet Ukraine and the southern portion within Romania.

The question of northern Bukovina became a thorny issue in relations between Ukraine and Romania after the collapse of communism. Romania contended that ethnic Romanian communities in northern Bukovina were being persecuted by the newly independent Ukrainian state, while Ukraine saw Romania's concern as veiled irredentism. However, in 1997 the two countries signed an interstate treaty renouncing all mutual territorial claims and pledged to respect the rights of ethnic communities in both parts of historic Bukovina.

BIBLIOGRAPHY

Colin, Paul. *Paul Celan: Holograms of Darkness.* Bloomington: Indiana University Press, 1991.

Himka, John-Paul. *Galicia and Bukovina: A Research Handbook about Western Ukraine.* Alberta, Canada: Alberta Culture and Multiculturalism, 1990.

Nistor, Ion. *Istoria Bucovinei.* Bucharest: Humanitas, 1991.

Turczynski, Emanuel. *Geschichte der Bukowina in der Neuzeit: zur Sozial- und Kulturgeschichte einer mitteleuropäischen geprägten Landschaft.* Wiesbaden: Harrassowitz, 1993.

Weigand, Gustav. *Die Dialekte der Bukowina und Bessarabiens.* Leipzig: Johann Ambrosius Barth, 1904.

Charles King

SEE ALSO Bessarabia

Bulganin, Nikolay Aleksandrovich (1895–1975)

Premier of the Union of Soviet Socialist Republics from 1955 to 1958. Nikolai Bulganin, the son of a factory clerk, was born in Nizhny Novgorod on June 11, 1895. He left secondary school to become first a clerk then a worker in a textile factory. After the February Revolution in 1917 he joined the Bolsheviks. Following the Bolshevik Revolution of October of that year, he became an officer in the Cheka (secret police) in 1918 and played a role in suppressing opposition during the civil war. From 1922 to 1927 he worked in the Supreme Council of the National Economy. After 1927 he gained recognition as a efficient administrator in a Moscow electrical equipment factory and was awarded the Order of Lenin. He became chairman of the Moscow Soviet in 1931 and served as premier of the Russian Republic in 1937–38. In 1938 he became deputy premier of the USSR and head of the State Bank. In 1939 Bulganin was appointed a full member of the Central Committee of the Communist Party of the Soviet Union. In 1940 he headed the Board of Metallurgical and Chemical Industries and played an important role in preparing the USSR industrially for the coming war. In 1941 he was given the rank of lieutenant general and from 1941 to 1943 served on the War Council for the Western Front. In 1944 he was promoted to full general and appointed deputy commissar for defense and a member of Stalin's State Defense Committee, the inner war cabinet. In 1947 he again assumed the deputy premiership of the Soviet Union and was appointed by Stalin to succeed the leader as minister of the armed forces. In 1948 Bulganin was promoted to marshal and became a full member of the Politburo.

Following the death of Stalin in 1953, Bulganin became deputy premier and minister of defense in the government of Georgy Malenkov. He kept the army in line during the execution of Lavrenty Beria. Bulganin supported Nikita Khrushchev in his struggle with Malenkov. On February 8, 1955, with the backing of Khrushchev, Bulganin became chairman of the Council of Ministers,

the premier of the USSR. For a while Bulganin was paired with Khrushchev, but in June 1957 he was part of the leadership that attempted to remove Khrushchev. Bulganin was kept on temporarily after Khrushchev's victory, but was removed as premier on March 27, 1958. He was ousted from the Presdium (former Politburo) on September 5, 1958. He also lost his rank as marshal and was relegated to a minor party post. In 1961 he was finally ousted from the Central Committee. He died in Moscow on February 24, 1975.

BIBLIOGRAPHY
"Bulganin, Nikolai." *Current Bibliography 1955,* (New York: H. W. Wilson, 1956), pp. 78–80.

Bernard Cook

Bulgaria

Balkan state with a history of turbulent domestic politics, terrorism, an army prone to political intervention, and a near total lack of democratic tradition. In 1945 the country seemed likely to become Communist without prodding from the USSR.

Bulgaria was drawn into World War II because of pressure from Germany and its own revisionist hopes, especially regarding Macedonia and Thrace. Following the 1941 German conquest of Yugoslavia and Greece, Bulgaria provided armies of occupation for both areas. But the German invasion of the Soviet Union in June of that

Bulgaria. *Illustration courtesy of Bernard Cook.*

chief Zhivkov, then Eastern Europe's longest-surviving Communist leader.

The Communists then rechristened their organization the Bulgarian Socialist Party (BSP). After peaceful demonstrations by the fragmented but growing opposition, the BSP initiated negotiations that led to national elections in June 1990. Some thirty-five parties competed in the elections and, to the great shock of most Bulgarians and foreign observers, the BSP won 47 percent of the vote, secured 211 seats in parliament, and formed a minority government. The Union of Democratic Forces (UDF), an umbrella organization of opposition parties, won only 144 seats. Nevertheless, President Petar Mladenov, who had threatened to use tanks against dissidents in December 1989, was forced to resign and the assembly chose as his successor former dissident Zheliu Zhelev.

Bulgaria was in the best of times a poor country, but the early 1990s were certainly not the best of times. The USSR, far and away Bulgaria's largest treading partner, halved delivery of cheap oil imports, which led to the shutdown of factories and power blackouts. Inflation ballooned and foreign debt exceeded $11 billion, an enormous burden for a country of only nine million. The lev, the nation's currency, was not convertible. Thousands of trained specialists, despairing of opportunities at home, fled abroad.

Ethnic problems also troubled the country. For a time tensions were high with Turkey over Bulgaria's Turkish minority. In 1989 more than three hundred thousand ethnic Turks fled Bulgaria for Turkey in an exodus provoked by persecution in the final years of the Zhivkov government. The regime restricted Muslim religious practices, forced ethnic Turks to adopt Bulgarian names, and forbade the use of the Turkish language on radio or television. Numbering about a million, the ethnic Turks make up about 11 percent of the population, and many ethnic Bulgars professed to see them as a fifth column intent on reconquering Bulgaria for Turkey.

In October 1991, with unemployment near 25 percent and inflation running over 30 percent, there were new national elections. Some sixty parties competed, with the UDF securing 36 percent of the vote and a narrow victory over the second-place BSP, with 32 percent. The Movement for Rights and Freedom (MRF), representing ethnic Turks, won 7 percent and held the balance of power. Zhelev called on Filip Dimitrov, leader of the UDF, to form a government of technocrats with the goal of stabilizing the economy and laying the groundwork for privatization. In January 1992 Zhelev, the UDF candidate, was elected president in Bulgaria's first direct vote for that office. The suffering caused by Dimitrov's economic mea-

sures, however, led to the collapse of his government and a period of political instability as the UDF splintered. An economist and independent, Lyuben Berov, formed a coalition composed of the UDF and the MRF, but further UDF erosion made the government dependent on support from the Socialists.

The Socialists won the December 1994 national elections, and Zhan Videnov, who became party leader in 1992, took over as premier. The Socialists were less inclined toward a market economy, popular support for which was far weaker in Bulgaria than in Hungary or Poland. The new government tried to prop up ailing large industries that had not restructured or laid off superfluous workers, and also sought closer trade relations with Russia. Bulgaria's basic problems remain and solving them will be a daunting task.

BIBLIOGRAPHY
Brown, J. F. *Bulgaria Under Communist Rule*. New York: Praeger, 1970.

Crampton, R. J. *A Short History of Modern Bulgaria*. New York: Cambridge University Press, 1987.

Lampe, John R. *The Bulgarian Economy in the Twentieth Century*. London, 1986.

Tzvetkov, Plamen. *A History of the Balkans: A Regional Overview from a Bulgarian Perspective*. San Francisco: E. Mellen Press, 1993.

Spencer C. Tucker

Political Parties and Economy

The Socialist government was ousted by a vote of no confidence in February 1977. A caretaker government appointed by the president took over until parliamentary elections were held in April. Thirty-four political parties and coalitions ran slates of candidates, of which only six received the 4 percent of the national vote necessary to place representatives in parliament. The Union of Democratic Forces (UDF), led by Ivan Kostov, won 123 of the 240 seats and regained control of the parliament and the government. The People's Union, which had formed an electoral coalition with the UDF, won 14 seats. The Bulgarian Socialist Party (BSP), headed by Georgi Purvanov, lost its 1994 majority, dropping from 125 to 58 seats. The Movement for Rights and Freedoms (MRF), led by Ahmed Dogan, joined with a number of smaller parties to form the Alliance for National Salvation and won 19 seats. The Euroleft, a social democratic party formed by disenchanted members of the BSP and led by Alexander Tomov, won 14 seats. The Bulgarian Business Bloc (BBB) won 12.

In 1947 the Communists achieved total power, and Georgy Dimitrov, leader of the Bulgarian Communist Party (BKP) and prime minister from November 1946 until his death in April 1949, adopted an economic strategy based on that of the Soviet Union: nationalization of all private property. The USSR had already nationalized most of the financial sector before the BKP achieved power. In December 1947 that part of the industrial sector not nationalized in 1945–46 was brought into the public sector. The BKP's program encountered strong resistance from the peasants, and collectivization was not completed until 1952.

To achieve Bulgaria's transition to a command economy, the BKP introduced, in 1948, a system of long-term central planning consisting normally of Five-Year Plans after the one-year experiment of 1947–48. Central planning was underpinned by Bulgaria's membership in the Council of Mutual Economic Assistance (CMEA), founded in 1949. The transition to a command economy was not completed until 1958. Rapid growth of heavy industry was achieved and the industrial labor force was enlarged by an influx of peasants. During the 1950s economic growth averaged 11 percent per annum.

A smaller rural labor force was left on the mechanized collective farms to produce the surplus needed to feed a growing, urban population. Bulgaria's Third Five-Year Plan, launched in 1958 oversaw the merger of the existing collective farms into 957 giant units, with an average size of 4,500 hectares (11,120 acres).

In 1963 industry was further concentrated by the grouping of all enterprises into combines that were used to coordinate experimental reforms toward decentralization in 1964; decentralization became part of explicit economic policy at the end of 1965. These industrial reforms may have partially reversed the decline in economic growth. Growth increased from an average annual rate of 6.7 to 8.2 percent between 1960–65 and 1965–70. However, the BKP reversed the policy of industrial decentralization in 1968, and by 1970 only 2,500 industrial enterprises remained. In addition, during the late 1960s and early 1970s, there was a further combination of collective farms into new agro-industrial complexes that sought to industrialize agricultural production, with considerable success in the case of viticulture. The growing level of debt denominated in hard currency led Bulgaria to search for new sources of export income. It developed tourism and promoted direct investment under license or through joint ventures from the mid-1960s onward. During the 1970s the average rate of economic growth declined to 7 percent per annum, although this was still relatively high compared with European economies of similar size. Yet the productivity of capital failed to keep up with that of labor.

The BKP introduced an economic reform program in 1978 and the New Economic Mechanism in 1979. The main objectives were to increase productivity, improve the quality of production, increase competitiveness of exports to markets outside the CMEA, and increase technological progress. These reforms failed to reverse the decline in the annual rate of economic growth, which fell to under 3.5 percent annually during 1980–89. The decline resulted from mismanagement, embezzlement of state funds, the unfavorable external environment, and factors outside the control of the BKP, such as successive droughts during the 1980s leading to a reduction in agricultural output. During the second half of the 1980s the BKP raised large external credits and sought to satisfy consumer demand with imports. By the end of the 1980s rigid price and exchange-rate controls, coupled with nominal wage increases and expansion of domestic credit, had led to the emergence of a huge monetary overhang and to severe shortages of basic necessities.

In November 1989 Zhivkov was removed by a regular BKP party conference. In January 1990 the BKP government of Georgi Atanassov was replaced by a caretaker government led by the "reform Communist" Andrei Lukanov (assassinated in October 1996). Led by Lukanov, the BKP, now renamed Bulgarian Socialist Party (BSP), won a small majority in the general election of June 1990. Lukanov failed to introduce radical economic reforms. A lack of consumer goods food shortages, and a huge monetary overhang led to a general strike in November 1990. This was inspired by the political opposition and resulted in the resignation of the Lukanov government.

A coalition in December 1990 between the BSP and the opposition Union of Democratic Forces (UDF) formed a new government headed by a nonpartisan lawyer, Dimitar Popov. It started to implement an IMF and World Bank–approved program of economic reform. The program removed controls on prices, tariffs, interest and exchange rates and, thereby, released suppressed inflation. Popov also began a program of land restitution and liquidating the collective farms. By the second half of the 1990s this program resulted in sharply reduced agricultural output. Many urban families benefited from the program and some, consequently, showed no interest in cultivating their land.

The UDF won the general election of June 1991 and formed a government headed by Filip Dimitrov. Once again economic reforms were not successfully implemented, and at the end of 1992 the National Assembly passed a motion of no confidence in the Dimitrov government. In December 1992 Ljuben Berov was appointed prime minister and led a government of nonparty technocrats, supported by factions from both the UDF and the BSP. Berov proved just as unsuccessful in delivering economic reform as his two immediate predecessors. He resigned in September 1994 and in the following month a caretaker government was appointed. This was led by Reneta Indjova, who attacked government corruption and oversaw the introduction of a program of mass privatization based on vouchers. The BSP won the December 1994 general election, and Zhan Videnov became prime minister in February 1995.

The political instability of the first five years of transition (1990–94) was accompanied by an average negative real economic growth of minus 6.5 percent per annum during 1990–93, followed by a modest recovery to a positive rate of 2.2 percent in 1994. The Videnov government failed both to revive the Bulgarian economy and to implement mass privatization. Economic growth declined from 2.5 percent in 1995 to minus 10.9 percent in 1996. By fall 1996, 95 percent of state industry had not yet been privatized. Indeed, most of those companies that had been privatized had been sold to managers from the Zhivkov era. The economy was crippled by illegal use of state-owned enterprises and banks as sources of cash by shadowy economic groups, which were run mostly by former nomenklatura from the Zhivkov era. In 1996 a banking crisis resulted in a short period of hyperinflation, the collapse of the external value of the Bulgarian lev, and shortages of bread and gasoline. The economic crisis resulted in strikes and mass protests against the Videnov government. Videnov was forced to resign in January 1997, and a caretaker government led by the UDF's Stefan Sofianski was followed by a general election in April 1997, won by the UDF.

The new prime minister, Ivan Kostov, began another attempt to stabilize and revive the economy. He established a currency board monetary system agreed under a $658 million IMF loan agreement. The World Bank also approved projects worth $290 million. From July 1997 the lev was pegged to the German mark. Kostov also began the privatization, to be completed by December 1998, of some of Bulgaria's biggest companies by cash sale to foreign investors.

In its 1997 survey of the Bulgarian economy the OECD suggests that, during the 1990s, Bulgarian "stabilisation has . . . been hindered by problems in the implementation of key economic laws and regulations, particularly in the areas of taxation, foreign exchange transactions and prudential regulation for banks." By 1996 the Bulgarian Academy of Science calculated that

as many as 90 percent of Bulgarians lived below the threshold of relative poverty. According to the World Bank, Bulgaria's per capita GNP was only $1,160 in 1994.

BIBLIOGRAPHY
Bristow, John A. *The Bulgarian Economy in Transition.* Cheltenham, Vt.: Edward Elgar, 1996.
Lampke, John R. *The Bulgarian Economy in the Twentieth Century.* London: Croom Helm, 1986.
The London *Financial Times* has published occasional surveys of the Bulgarian economy since 1984.
The OECD began publication of occasional surveys of the Bulgarian economy in 1997.
Richard A. Hawkins

Turkish Minority

Approximately 10 percent of Bulgaria's nearly ten million inhabitants are of Turkish descent; of these approximately eight hundred thousand are Muslim. This human residue of the former Ottoman Empire suffered a number of harassing restrictions imposed by the regime of Todor Zhivkov. The use of the Turkish language in public was banned and people were forced to change their Turkish names to Slavic ones. After the collapse of the Communist regime in 1990, the cultural rights of ethnic Turks were restored. They were allowed to reassume their former Turkish names, practice their Islamic faith, and use the Turkish language openly. In 1992 the Bulgarian government authorized half-hour programs in Turkish on the government radio. In 1998 the Bulgarian parliament permitted unrestricted broadcasts in Turkish. Since the ending of the anti-Turkish campaign, half of the three hundred thousand Bulgarian Turks who sought refuge in Turkey have returned.

Bernard Cook

Buñuel, Luis (1900–1983)

Film director and writer. Luis Buñuel was one the most successful and influential Spanish filmmakers. He was among the first to incorporate surrealist art and technique into film. Buñuel was awarded many of the top prizes in the field including Best Director in 1951 and Best Picture in 1961 at the Cannes Film Festival, as well as the Academy Award for best Foreign Film in 1973.

Buñuel was born in a rural town into an upper-middle-class family. His mother was a devout Catholic who sent him to religious schools until he attended the University of Madrid. In Madrid Buñuel became friends with fellow classmates Salvador Dalí and Federico García Lorca. In

1925 he moved to Paris and began making films. His first work as director was *An Andalusian Dog* (1928). Made in collaboration with Dalí, the film was highly innovative and is now regarded as the quintessential statement of surrealist cinema. He returned to Spain to make another influential film, *Land Without Bread* (1932) but was forced into exile following the end of the Spanish Civil War.

Buñuel's story of poor youths, *Los olvidados* (1950), earned him Best Director honors at the 1951 Cannes Film Festival. The simple, direct combination of narrative story line and surrealist elements became his trademark style. For the remainder of the 1950s he produced a series of commercial films in Mexico. He was invited back to Spain to make *Viridiana* (1960), a savage commentary on family, religion, and middle-class values—themes common to Buñuel's work. Although deemed blasphemous and banned by the Spanish government, the film was awarded Best Picture at the Cannes Film Festival in 1961.

During the 1960s Buñuel's pictures continued to explore surrealist themes such as dreams and the unconscious. Films like *The Exterminating Angel* (1962) and *Belle de jour* (1967) attempted to reveal the fundamental hypocrisy of the established social order through an examination of religion, politics, and sexuality. Another film in a similar vein, *The Discreet Charm of the Bourgeoisie* (1972), was named Best Foreign Film at the Academy Awards of 1973. Buñuel made his last picture in 1977 and published his autobiography, *My Last Sigh* (1983), shortly before his death.

Buñuel is considered one of the most innovative and original filmmakers not only for the quality of his work but also for his consistency. His childhood upbringing, religious indoctrination, and interest in surrealism provided him with themes he would explore throughout his career. Buñuel had a rare talent for making films containing social criticism and avant-garde technique that nonetheless remained entertaining and accessible.

BIBLIOGRAPHY

Aranda, J. Francisco. *Luis Buñuel: A Critical Biography.* London: Secker and Warburg, 1975.

Buñuel, Luis. *My Last Sigh.* New York: Knopf, 1983.

Edwards, Gwynne. *The Discreet Art of Luis Buñuel: A Reading of His Films.* London: M. Boyars, 1982.

Mellen, Joan, ed. *The World of Luis Buñuel: Essays in Criticism.* New York: Oxford University Press, 1978.

Williams, Linda. *Figures of Desire: A Theory and Analysis of Surrealist Film.* Urbana: University of Illinois Press, 1981.

Brian D. Bunk

Burbulis, Gennady (1945–)

Russian politician, for a time Boris Yeltsin's chief adviser. Gennady Burbulis was born on August 4, 1945, in Pervoualsk in the Sverdlovsk region. Burbulis received a degree in philosophy from the Urals State University. Before completing postgraduate work there he worked as an electrical fitter and performed his compulsory military service. From 1974 to 1983 he was a lecturer in dialectical materialism at the Urals Polytechnical Institute. From 1983 to 1989 he was deputy director of the Institute for Advanced Training of Specialists of the Ministry of Non-Ferrous Metalurgy. In 1987 he organized a political club in Sverdlovsk as he evolved from an expert on Marxism-Leninism to a Westernizer. In 1990 Burbulis was tapped by Boris Yeltsin, the president of the Russian Republic, to serve as his representative and served as deputy chairman of Yeltsin's consultative Supreme Council. From 1991 to the end of westernizes 1992 he continued to advise Yeltsin. In June 1991 he became state secretary of the Russian Federation and secretary of the State Council. In May 1992 Yeltsin appointed him first vice chairman of the Russian government, and in December as head of a group of his advisers. However, by the end of December, in an effort to appease the Congress of Peoples Deputies and save the rest of his administrative team, led by Yegos Gaidar, Yeltsin discarded the widely disliked, opinionated Burbulis.

In the December 1993 parliamentary election Burbulis was elected to the Duma as a member of the party Russia's Choice. In August 1995 he became cochairman of the organization Russian Alliance of Business People. In the December 1995 Duma election, Burbulis was elected from a district of the Sverdlovsk region.

BIBLIOGRAPHY

⟨http://www.russia.net/politics/people/BurbulisGE.html⟩

Bernard Cook

Bureau of International Expositions (BIE)

Paris-based organization that regulates the number of world's fairs and other special exhibitions throughout the world. The Bureau International des Expositions (BIE) was established in 1928 to regulate the fairs industry, including the number of fairs held at a given time and to determine the levels of participation. BIE became the primary means of reducing the diplomatic and financial embarrassment of too many host nations pressing the case for their events. In the years following the Crystal Palace exhibition of 1851 in London, the number of expositions increased dramatically. At first it was at intervals of a few years, then annually, finally several expositions per year. In a number of nations committees endeavored, on a national basis, to regulate expositions within their borders. The first was in France (1902); others quickly followed. In 1912, sixteen governments gathered at Berlin and formed a permanent alliance, the Fédération des Comités Permanents des Expositions, in Brussels in 1908, but it was apparent that without full diplomatic cooperation, control was difficult. In 1928 the French government revived the issue and forty-three nations participated in a convention in Paris. Five nations, including the United States, sent observers. This convention formulated the agreement regulating the holding of international expositions and the BIE became its executive arm. The Paris Convention of November 22, 1928, became international law on January 17, 1931. It specified the frequency at which expositions of different categories were held and set recommendations for the better control of expositions, many still valid today.

Between the wars the BIE was one of a number of international organizations that came under the authority of the League of Nations. It has not enjoyed a similar relationship with the United Nations. From its Paris headquarters the BIE utilizes the services of the French government and external relations agencies to carry out its international contacts. The small permanent staff is headed by a secretary-general. The hard-core membership, which is not expensive and which is based on population and relative prosperity, is principally from the developed nations, but there has been movement toward enrolling less-developed countries, with a larger share of BIE's operating costs coming through registration fees required from nations organizing expositions.

The 1928 convention was modified on several occasions by new protocols, significantly by those of May 10, 1948; November 16, 1966; and November 30, 1972. The United States participated in the drafting of the 1972 protocol. The new rules effectively limited universal expositions to every ten years, twenty if in the same member state, but did little to curb the smaller specialized exhibitions that can still take place every year. By limiting the frequency of expositions, the new protocol tried to reduce the financial demands on participating governments.

The United States joined the bureau in 1968 after it became apparent that it would be in the national interest to coordinate the planning of U.S. expositions with those in other countries. The United States ratified the treaty in 1973. One of the objectives of bureau membership was to give the United States a voice in modernizing the convention.

In other countries one government department is responsible for all fair participation. In the United States there are two: Commerce Department expos held in the continental United States and the U.S. Information Agency (USIA) for those fairs held overseas. The U.S. government is the only major BIE member that does not assume full responsibility for underwriting its country's participation, depending on the private sector as it did to recoup the losses of Expo 84 in New Orleans.

There are presently forty-seven BIE members. One of its rather eccentric attributes is that it does not seek to promote the medium it represents. BIE was founded out of a need to restrict international expositions and has continued to apply increasing constraints on the proliferation of these events while seeking to raise the significance and quality of the medium.

BIBLIOGRAPHY

Allan, Ted. "Bureau of International Expositions," in *Historical Dictionary of World's Fairs and Expositions, 1851–1988.* Ed. by John E. Findling and Kimberly D. Pelle. Westport, Conn.: Greenwood, 1990.

"Convention Relating to International Exhibitions." Convention between the United States of America and other governments, concluded at Paris November 22, 1928, and Protocol modifying the convention concluded at Paris May 10, 1948. Washington, D.C.: Government Printing Office, 1968.

"Protocol Amending the 1928 Convention Concerning International Expositions. Message from the President of the United States." Washington: Government Printing Office, 1973.

Martin J. Manning

SEE ALSO International Expositions

Buscetta, Tommaso (1928–)

Sicilian-born Mafioso who was arrested in Brazil in 1983 and gave the police detailed information about Mafia activities, the highest-level informant ever to do so. Tommaso Buscetta's testimony led to arrest warrants for 366 members of the Mafia. Moreover, Buscetta named the Mafiosi responsible for hundreds of murders in Sicily in the early 1980s, explained the workings of the Mafia-controlled heroin trade, and described the structure of this previously misunderstood international criminal organization. Buscetta, a native of Palermo, used his pizzeria as a front for the Badalamenti organization's illegal activities. After the dissolution of his first marriage, Buscetta moved to New York City, where he remarried and continued his

Mafia activities. He also bought a farm in Brazil through which heroin was moved. After his arrest on heroin-trafficking charges in 1972, Buscetta was sentenced to jail in Italy. He served only eight years of his sentence before escaping while at work as a glass cutter and returning to Brazil. In 1982 he returned to Sicily to assist his gang in a dispute for the control of western Sicily against the group led by Luciano Liggio. Several of Buscetta's family members were killed during the battle for dominance. Fearing for his own life Buscetta again fled Sicily for Brazil, where he was arrested in October 1983. Fearing the wrath of the Mafia and wanting revenge, Buscetta agreed to talk to the police. He outlined the contemporary history of the Mafia in his interviews with the police, which resulted in three thousand pages of transcripts. He explained the Mafia's pyramid structure and claimed the organization was becoming increasingly violent and less respectful of honored traditions. Buscetta also provided confirmation of many of the Mafia's activities that had long been suspected but not proven, such as the existence of two separate Mafia groups in the United States. Finally, he detailed the transfer of the heroin trade from Marseilles to Sicily.

BIBLIOGRAPHY

"Breaking the Mafia's Silence." *America* 151 (1984): 219.

Calvi, Fabrizio. *La vita quotidiana della mafia dal 1950 ai nostri giorni.* Milan: Biblioteca Universale Rizzoli, 1986.

"The Sicilian Connection." *Time* 124 (1984): 42–46.

Wendy A. Pojmann

SEE ALSO Liggio, Luciano; Mafia; Moro, Aldo

Busek, Erhard (1941–)

Austrian vice chancellor and head of Austria's Conservative People's Party. He has been labeled "too smart for politics," though his intellectual capacities are widely recognized. Busek's ideological foundations are rooted in Catholic youth work. At age eighteen he became central secretary of a Catholic students' union. In 1962 he served as federal secretary of the Male Catholic Youth and then as chair of the Federal Youth Association from 1966 to 1968.

Busek's political career started in the Austrian parliament, when he was asked to become club secretary of the Conservative People's Party in 1964, one year after he completed his doctoral studies in law at the University of Vienna. He became a party member and had to master his first major challenge two years later, when the grand coalition government between Socialists and Conservatives was succeeded by a majority government of the latter. The change of power brought about a change of political culture in parliament in which the Socialists played an active opposition role and broke with the tradition of depoliticized postwar Austrian politics. Busek paved the way through the parliamentary process for the Conservatives in a book titled *Criticism of Democracy: Reform of Democracy,* in which he called for democratic openness and competition and opted to lift the veil from the closed doors of politics.

His combination of Christian belief and political activity confused advocates of a strict separation of church and state. Busek moved to the Conservatives' economic association, where he started to open the interest group to a broader spectrum of members. Until then, postwar Austrian interest groups had been characterized (and in many cases still are) by strict ideological and partisan affiliation with one of the leading parties. The untimely death of Karl Schleinzer in 1975 had left the Conservatives without a leader. His successor, Josef Taus, asked Busek to become secretary-general of the party at age thirty-four. However, the subsequent federal elections brought about another success for the Socialists, headed by Bruno Kreisky, and the challengers stagnated. Busek's reforms of the party management had just started when he again switched his position and left for party chair of the city of traditionally "red" Vienna in 1976. He started to revive the declining regional party by opening the doors to idealistic, constructive individuals who did not want to identify with partisan politics.

Long before the Iron Curtain came down, Busek inconspicuously established political contact with opposition groups in Communist Eastern Europe. In addition to his function as municipal party chief, he was elected city councilor from 1978 to 1983 and was vice mayor from 1978 to 1987. The Conservatives suffered a bitter defeat in 1987 that forced Busek to leave municipal politics. He moved to the federal level again, becoming minister for science two years later. The Conservatives, who lost 10 percent in the 1990 elections, made a desperate search for a new leader after Josef Riegler resigned from office as national party chief. Against internal opposition, Busek became party chief and vice chancellor in the government of Franz Vranitzky. One of his first moves in that position was to nominate the unknown Thomas Klestil as presidential candidate of the Conservative People's Party, which led to an unexpected victory of the latter in the 1992 presidential elections. Busek paved the way for Austria's accession to the European Union in 1995 and, with that goal in mind, followed a strict grand coalition policy.

After a life in the forefront of politics, Busek focused his research and writing on globalization and integration internationalization and central and Eastern European issues. Consequently, he became chair of the Institute for the Danube Area and Central Europe in 1995 and was chosen as coordinator of the Southeastern European Cooperative Initiative (SECI), initiated by the U.S. National Security Council.

BIBLIOGRAPHY

Bretschneider, Rudolf, ed. *Mensch im Wort: Erhard Busek: Reden und Aufsätze.* Vienna: Wiener Journal, Zeitschriftenverl., 1994.

Busek, Erhard. *Heimat—Politik mit Sitz im Leben: Ein Essay.* Vienna: Braintrust, 1994.

———. *Mitteleuropa. Eine Spurensicherung.* Vienna: Kremayr & Scheriau, 1997.

———. *Sprache und Phantasie: ein Gesprach zwischen Wissenschaft und Politik.* Vienna: Verlag für Geschichte und Politik, 1984.

———. *Wissenschaft und Freiheit—Ideen zu Universität und Universalität.* Vienna: Verlag für Geschichte und Politik, 1989.

Busek, Erhard, and E. Brix. *Projekt Mitteleuropa.* Vienna: Überreuter, 1986.

Busek, Erhard, and Gerhard Wilflinger. *Demokratiekritik und Demokratiereform.* Vienna: Selbstverl. d. Arbeitsgemeinschaft f. staatsbürgerliche Erziehung u. politische Bildung, 1969.

Busek, Erhard, C. Festa, and J. Görner. *Auf dem Weg zur qualitätiven Marktwirtschaft: Versuch einer Neuorientierung.* Vienna: Verl. f. Geschichte u. Politik, 1975.

Welzig, Elisabeth, ed. *Erhard Busek: Ein Porträt.* Vienna: Böhlau, 1992.

Stefan Mayer

SEE ALSO Klestil, Thomas; Kreisky, Buno; Vranitzky, Franz

Buttiglione, Rocco (1948–)

Italian philosopher and politician. Rocco Buttiglione was born in Gallipoli (Lecce), Italy in 1948. A professor of philosophy, Buttiglione has close contact with the leadership of the Roman Catholic Church, who find his thought congenial. Buttiglione learned to speak Polish while studying philosophy under Karol Woityla, who later became Pope John Paul II. Buttiglione has also been actively involved in conservative Catholic politics. In 1993 he served as a member of the executive of the reorganized Christian Democrats (Democratico Christiano, DC). In 1994, he left the DC to form the Italian Popular Party (Partito Populare Italiano, PPI), where he served as secretary. In 1995, Buttilglione broke with the PPI to form an alliance with the right-wing coalition "Polo," thus creating the United Christian Democrats (CDU).

BIBLIOGRAPHY

Buttiglione, Rocco. *Karol Wojtyla: the Thought of the Man Who became Pope John Paul II.* Grand Rapids, Mich.: Eerdmans, 1997.

———. *Il problema politico dei cattolici: dottrina sociale e modernita.* Casale Monferrato: Piemme, 1993.

———. *L'uomo e il lavoro: riflessioni sull'enciclica "Laborem exercens".* Bologna: CSEO biblioteca, 1982.

Di Tullio, Ugo. *La crisi politica del partito cattolico: spunti per una riflessione.* Prato: Omnia minima, 1994.

Federiga Bindi Calussio

C

Caetano, Marcelo Jose das Neves (1906–80)

President of the Council of Ministers of Portugal (1968–74) and a distinguished historian, jurist, political theorist, professor and rector at the University of Lisbon. Marcelo Jose Caetano served as minister in various cabinets of dictator António Salazar and was appointed to succeed Salazar in September 1968. He was overthrown and exiled in April 1974.

Caetano initiated his public life in the early 1920s as an activist of the youth branch of the Integralismo Lusitano (Portuguese Integralism) movement. By 1929 he was a collaborator of Salazar as a lawyer for the Ministry of Finances. In 1931 he was one of the youngest members of the Executive Committee of the National Union party and played a major role in writing the 1933 constitution. During the 1930s he pursued a prestigious career at the University of Lisbon as professor of law, institutions, and administration and as a major theorist of corporativism. During the same period he was in charge of the reform of the Portuguese Administrative Code along a centralist, authoritarian line.

In 1940 he began his political career as national commissioner for Mocidade Portuguesa (Portuguese Youth), where he undertook to replace its Germanophile/militarist tendencies with an orientation more in line with Portuguese neutrality. From this position Caetano gained a reputation as a critic of Salazar and as the leader of the reformist wing of the regime while being the leading political defender and theoretician of the "New State."

Salazar realized that Caetano was a critic who must be kept tied to the regime. In 1947 Caetano became head of the Executive Committee of the União Nacional (National Union) party and in 1949 president of the Chamber of Corporations. In these posts he built a circle of friends with similar political views and at the third party conference in 1951 blocked the Conservative attempt to make Salazar both president of the republic and prime minister as a first step to restore the monarchy. Appointed in 1955 as minister of the presidency, he became an ally of President Craveiro Lopes, prompting fear among Salazar allies that Lopes would substitute Caetano for the dictator. Consequently, Salazar removed Caetano from the cabinet in the aftermath of the 1958 elections. Although considered as the replacement for Salazar by the leaders of a failed coup in 1961, Caetano never participated in it. That year he became rector of the University of Lisbon, but in April 1962 resigned in protest of the police invasion of the university to crush student protests. Thereafter, he followed the political situation from a discrete distance until his sudden appointment as Salazar's replacement in 1968.

Appointed prime minister on September 26, 1968, Caetano initiated a policy of reform and openness. In 1969 he permitted the Socialist leader Mario Soares, historian Oliveira Marques, and Bishop Antonio Fereira Gomes of Porto to return from exile. He also relaxed the institutions of repression. In the 1969 elections he permitted the nonparty opposition to gain seats in parliament, including future Prime Ministers Sá Carneiro and Pinto Balsemão.

However, distrusted by hard-line followers of Salazar and not progressive enough for the reformers, by the early 1970s Caetano had proven unable to find a political solution to Portugal's colonial wars, which had raged since 1961 and lost both the support of both conservatives and reformers. The consequence of this failure was a conservative retrenchment that prevented him from blocking the reelection of conservative President Americo Tomaz, paralyzed his reforms, and led to a resurgence of repressive elements. In the meantime under the protection of the chief and vice chief of the General Staff, Generals Costa

Gomes and Antonio de Spinola, respectively, a movement of junior officers overthrew the New State on April 25, 1974.

Arrested in the aftermath of the coup, Caetano was exiled to Madeira Island and from there left for Brazil in late May. In Brazil, he became a professor at Gama Filho University in Rio de Janeiro. Among his major works are *A Crise Nacional de 1383–1385, Constituições Portuguesas, Manual de Dereito Administrativo, Manual de Ciencia Politica e Direito Constitutional,* and *Historia do Direito Portugues.*

Caetano was not allowed to return to Portugal and died in Brazil in 1980. He had one of the most distinguished academic careers in twentieth-century Portugal and his works will remain essential for students of medieval and twentieth-century Portuguese history and politics. As a politician he worked within the system to bring about reform and more openness. His failure was the result of the colonial war he inherited and his unwillingness to break completely with the Salazarist old guard and begin a process of democratization.

Paul Brasil

SEE ALSO Portugal; Salazar, António

Calfa, Marián (1946–)

Prime minister of Czechoslovakia, 1989–92. Marián Calfa was born in Trebisov on May 27, 1946. He joined the Communist Party in 1964 and graduated in law from Charles University in Prague in 1970. From 1972 to 1987 he worked in the office of Prime Minister Lubomír Strougal.

Calfa, though previously a Communist functionary, became prime minister as a result of the Velvet Revolution. When Ladislav Adamec resigned as prime minister on December 10, 1989, Calfa agreed to a cabinet half of whose members would consist of political independents. The new cabinet, constituted the same day, contained a majority of non-Communists. Jiří Dienstbier, a founder of Charter 77, was appointed foreign minister and Václav Klaus, a market economist, became finance minister.

In January 1990 Calfa resigned from the Communist Party and ran in the June election as a member of the Slovak Public Against Violence, the ally of the Czech Civic Forum. Together the two parties won 46 percent of the vote and 169 seats in the 300-seat federal parliament. On June 12 Calfa was directed by President Václav Havel to form the first democratically elected government in Czechoslovakia since 1946.

The 1992 election accentuated the national and ideological split developing in Czechoslovakia. In the Czech Republic the free-market Civic Democratic Party led by Klaus emerged the winner, while in Slovakia the nationalist and populist Movement for a Democratic Slovakia, led by Vladimir Mečiar, was victorious. Jan Strásky replaced Calfa in an interim government that presided over the devolution of the federation into two separate countries on January 1, 1993.

Bernard Cook

Callaghan, James (1912–)

Prime minister of Great Britain, 1976–79. James Callaghan was a government clerk, trade union official, Labour MP (1945–87), and junior minister (1947–51). In Harold Wilson's two Labour governments he was successively chancellor of the exchequer (1964–67), home secretary (1967–70), and foreign and commonwealth secretary (1974–76). Callaghan led the Labour Party from 1976 to 1980. In 1987 he accepted a life peerage, becoming Lord Callaghan of Cardiff.

Following Wilson's retirement the highly experienced Callaghan easily defeated Michael Foot, the left-wing candidate, for the Labour Party leadership and automatically became prime minister. After 1977 his government lacked a House of Commons majority and depended on an informal pact with the small Liberal Party.

The galloping inflation, balance-of-payments shortfalls, monetary instability, and labor-management disputes that Callaghan inherited from Wilson eased after a very rocky start. Britain in 1976 had to apply humiliatingly to the International Monetary Fund for assistance in stabilizing its currency. The Callaghan ministry's large new income from North Sea oil enabled it to minimize budget deficits. By 1979 Britain was not only self-sufficient in oil but among the world's major producers.

Callaghan continued Wilson's policy of mediating a "social contract" between industry and labor, but most of the advantages went to organized labor. New legislation strengthened the closed union shop, forced employers to give ninety-day warnings of layoffs to unionized workers, and mandated big severance pay for redundancy. These pro-labor reforms were not popular and did not translate into Labour Party votes in by-elections.

Callaghan kept the lid on, but did not solve, Britain's chronic problems of race relations and Northern Ireland. The Race Relations Act of 1976 established special courts, with trained judges and officers, to resolve discrimination cases. This law eased strains in racially mixed neighborhoods but did not overcome the racism of many white

Britons, including police officers. The Callaghan government's policy in Northern Ireland of interning suspected terrorists without trial did Britain's international image no good, but improved security work, though involving questionable procedures, reduced the scope of violence.

Early in 1979 Callaghan decided to settle the long-standing issue of regional autonomy, or devolution. In referenda in Scotland and Wales voters were asked whether they wanted limited self-government. To the surprise of many Britons, neither nationality gave devolution the required majority. The results dealt a heavy blow to Scottish and Welsh nationalism, and in the 1979 parliamentary election the nationalist parties lost most of their MPs.

The Callaghan government and the Labour Party plummeted in voters' esteem during the "winter of discontent" (1978–79), when public-sector unions struck for higher wages, greatly inconveniencing millions of people. In March 1979 Callaghan's became the first British government in fifty-five years to be overthrown on a confidence motion. The subsequent election, won by the Conservatives, was a "no confidence" vote on the Wilson-Callaghan "social contract" and its coddling of too-powerful trade unions.

The foundation of "Sunny Jim" Callaghan's political success was his affability, but behind his smiles and back-slapping he was tough, hard, and businesslike. His government was a holding operation. Britain's many problems did not go away but were kept in check by Callaghan and his moderate, unadventurous cabinet.

BIBLIOGRAPHY
Callaghan, James. *Time and Chance.* London: Collins, 1987.
Kellner, Peter, and Christopher Hitchens. *Callaghan: The Road to Number 10.* London: Cassell, 1976.
Morgan, Kenneth O. *Labour People: Leaders and Lieutenants, Hardie to Kinnoch.* London: Oxford, 1987.
Don M. Cregier

Calvino, Italo (1923–85)

Italian writer, one of the most prominent figures in post-war European literature. Italo Calvino is best known for his remarkable talent for writing adult fables, full of imagination and fantasy. Calvino's work includes novels, short stories, collections of folktales, and critical essays on the art of writing.

Born in 1923 in Santiago, Cuba, Calvino grew up in northern Italy. He was active in the Italian Resistance

from 1943 to 1945. He then studied at the University of Turin, graduating in 1947.

Calvino started writing immediately after the war. His earliest works reflect the neorealist style of Italian literature at that time. His first novel, *Il sentiero dei nidi di ragno* (*The Path to the Nest of Spiders*), published in 1947, is an account of his partisan experience.

Over the next three decades, Calvino wrote more than twenty-five short stories and novels. His best-known works include *Cosmicomiche* (*Cosmicomics,* 1968), *Fiabe italiane* (*Italian Folktales,* 1956), *Se una notte d'inverno un viaggiatore* (*If on a Winter's Night, a Traveler,* 1979), and *Palomar* (1983). His most acclaimed novel and the book he considered his "most finished" work was *Le citta' invisibili* (*Invisible Cities,* 1972), for which he won the prestigious Feltrinelli Prize. Among many other honors, Calvino was elected to the American Academy and Institute of Arts and Sciences in 1975.

Called a "literary adventurer" by Sara Adler, Calvino has often been compared to other masters of the modern fable including Gabriel García Marquez and Jorge Luis Borges.

BIBLIOGRAPHY
Adler, Sara Maria. Calvino: *The Writer as Fablemaker.* Potomac, Md.: Ediciones Jose Porrua Turanzas, 1979.
Carter, Alex Howard. *Italo Calvino: Metamorphoses of Fantasy.* Ann Arbor, Mich.: UMI Research Press, 1987.
Hume, Kathryn. *Calvino's Fiction: Cogito and Cosmos.* Oxford: Clarendon Press, 1992.
Weiss, Beno. *Understanding Italo Calvino.* Columbia: University of South Carolina Press, 1993.
David Travis

Camus, Albert (1913–60)

French novelist, essayist, playwright, and journalist, often regarded as the conscience of his generation. Albert Camus appeared on the French intellectual scene during the Second World War as author of a short novel, *The Stranger* (1942), and as a voice for the Resistance through his editorial work at the newspaper *Combat.* Centered on the themes of absurdity and revolt, his literary and philosophical work has enjoyed an admiring international readership and has been the focus of an extensive critical scholarship. His prose is marked by formal control, constraint, and clarity, his thought by an intensely ethical search and the desire to move beyond the nihilism of this century.

Camus was born into a working-class family in Algeria, where he also received his education. He contracted tuberculosis, which cut short his early interest in athletics and prevented him from culminating his philosophy studies with the diploma necessary to become a professor. He then turned to the theater and to journalism. Appealing for social justice, he wrote about the oppressive living conditions of the Arab population in Algeria, and shortly after the French defeat by Germany (1940), he moved to France as a journalist, went to work at *Combat* (1943), and remained a central figure in Left Bank Parisian intellectual life in the years following the Liberation.

Camus's attraction to the sensual and lyrical pervades his writing. Yet his works take up the central intellectual, ethical, and political questions of the midcentury. He created in "cycles," each cycle consisting of a novel, an essay, and plays. His first cycle, on living through the absurdity and meaninglessness of life, included *The Stranger, The Myth of Sisyphus* (1942), and the plays *The Misunderstanding* (1944) and *Caligula* (1945). The second cycle, generated out of the Resistance and Liberation and replacing Sisyphus with Prometheus, took up the questions of rebellion, resistance, and revolution. It included *The Plague* (1947), *The Rebel* (1951), and the plays *State of Siege* (1948) and *The Just Assassins* (1949). He had projected further cycles, particularly one on Nemesis, or measure and limits.

A scathing critique of *The Rebel* prompted a break with philosopher Jean-Paul Sartre and opened for Camus a painful decade of writer's block, domestic crisis, and agonizing over the Algerian war. He did complete a novel, *The Fall* (1956), perhaps his richest work, and a collection of six short stories, *Exile and the Kingdom* (1957). Camus received the Nobel Prize in literature in 1957 and was once again at work, assuming the direction of an experimental theater in Paris and writing a novel to be entitled *The First Man,* when he was killed in an automobile accident in 1960.

Through all his writings Camus explored the challenges of living and creating in the face of absurdity and extreme injustice. Absurdity was for him the result of the human demand for clarity and meaning in a world indifferent to such a demand; injustice was the consequence of the modern tendency toward totality and excess. Acknowledging human suffering while refusing both metaphysical consolation and despair, rejecting abstraction while insistently focusing on the concrete, Camus opted for dialogue and solidarity, for hope without certainty, and for moderation and limits—a lucid, practical, and what Sartre called "stubborn humanism." If his writing bears witness to crucial ethical struggles for human dignity and against the arrogance of modern ideologies, Camus himself wished above all to be considered an artist.

Inspired by Nietzsche, Camus adopted multiple styles—fiction, theater, philosophy, journalism—to manifest his creative powers. He anticipated tendencies in recent continental thought with his abandonment of the grand narratives of our culture and his insistence on the close link between the aesthetic and the ethical. Despite a relatively brief writing career, Camus holds a major position in the literature of this century.

BIBLIOGRAPHY

Brée, Germaine. *Camus.* New Brunswick, N.J.: Rutgers University Press, 1964.

Lottman, Herbert R. *Albert Camus: A Biography.* Garden City N.Y.: Doubleday, 1979.

Sprintzen, David. *Camus: A Critical Examination.* Philadelphia: Temple University Press, 1988.

William E. Duvall

SEE ALSO Sartre, Jean-Paul

Canetti, Elias (1905–94)

Quintessential central European and complicated author of the canonical modernist novel, his 1935 *Die Blendung* (English translation: *Auto-da-fé,* 1946), but whose best-known work consists of his anthropological studies and autobiographical writings. Elias Canetti was born into a Sephardic Jewish merchant family in the Bulgarian town of Rustchuck (though Turkish at the time), and grew up a traveler and a polyglot, living successively in Manchester, Lausanne, Vienna, Zurich, and Frankfurt before studying chemistry in Vienna from 1925 to 1929. In Vienna and during visits to Berlin he came into contact with the vibrant literary and artistic scene of the late twenties (e.g., Karl Kraus, Hermann Broch, Robert Musil, Wieland Herzfeld, George Grosz, Isaak Babel, Bertolt Brecht). He emigrated to London in 1938 but spent the last years of his life in Switzerland.

Having witnessed worker demonstrations, experienced German hyperinflation, and seen the rise of fascism during the 1920s, he decided early on to dedicate himself to the study of the relationship between crowds and power, which provided the title of his theoretical book that appeared in 1960 as *Masse und Macht* (Crowds and Power). This work aroused interest in his earlier novel *Auto-da-fé,* which was republished to great acclaim in 1965, and brought Canetti his first broad critical success. Canetti won the Nobel Prize in literature in 1981.

Peter Kien, the unpleasant anti-hero of *Auto-da-fé,* is a world-renowned but reclusive sinologist whose sole place of power is within his enormous private library—also his apartment. This private sphere is threatened and finally taken over by his proletarian housekeeper and wife, Theresa, who in her greed ultimately drives him from his books and out into the world. He goes mad and burns himself up with his books, symbolically demonstrating the helplessness of the misguided intelligensia in the face of the power and desires of the base and common masses. Like few other literary works of the period (Kafka, Broch), *Auto-da-fé* can be read as a prophetic critique of fascism that is also powerful satire and poetically brilliant. This theme of the alienated intellectual lost in the violent world of the masses dominates Canetti's work. In an early play, *Hochzeit* (*Marriage*, 1932) the petit-bourgeois world of the characters comes literally crashing down around them as they are shown seeking marriage only to satisfy their own sordid material and sexual desires. Two other plays treat narcissism and self-centeredness in a world where mirrors are forbidden and a world in which everyone knows the date of his or her impending death: *Komödie der Eitelkeit* (*Comedy of Vanity,* 1950) and *Die Befristeten* (*People with a Time Limit,* 1956). Canetti wrote no other novels but continued to publish many essays and autobiographical writings into his last years.

BIBLIOGRAPHY

Barnouw, Dagmar. "Elias Canetti," in *Major Figures of Contemporary Austrian Literature.* Ed. by Donald G. Daviau. New York: Peter Lang, 1987, 117–41.

Canetti, Elias. *Essays in Honor of Elias Canetti.* Tr. by Michael Hulse. New York: Farrar, Straus & Giroux, 1998.

Durzak, Manfred. *Zu Elias Canetti.* Stuttgart: Klett, 1983.

Falk, Thomas. *Elias Canetti.* New York: Twayne, 1993.

Foell, Kristie A. *Blind Reflections: Gender in Elias Canetti's Die Blendung.* Riverside, Calif.: Ariadne, 1994.

Lawson, Richard H. *Understanding Canetti.* Columbia: University of South Carolina Press, 1991.

"Special Elias Canetti Issue." *Modern Austrian Literature* 16:3/4 (1983).

Stevens, Adrian, and Fred Wagner, eds. *Elias Canetti: Londoner Symposium. Stuttgarter Arbeiten zur Germanistik,* Vol. 245. Stuttgart: Heinz, 1991.

Scott Denham

Carlsson, Ingvar (1934–)

Prime minister of Sweden. Ingvar Carlsson was born in Borås, Sweden, on November 9, 1934. He studied political science and economics at the University of Lund. After graduating in 1958 he became an assistant in the office of Prime Minister Tage Erlander. He received a leave to study economics at Northwestern University in Illinois. After returning to Sweden Carlsson became the chair of the Social Democratic Youth League. He was elected to parliament in 1964 and held a number of cabinet positions in the Social Democratic governments of Erlander and Olof Palme. He was minister for the environment, of housing and physical planning, and of education and cultural affairs.

When Palme was assassinated in 1986, Carlsson, who was deputy prime minister, became prime minister and acting chairman of the Social Democratic Workers Party (SAP). In the September 1991 election, although the SAP remained the largest party, it did not have enough strength to form a government. Carl Bildt of the Moderate Party formed a non-Socialist coalition. In the September 1994 election Bildt's coalition partners did poorly, and Carlsson, with the support of the Greens and the Left Party, formed a minority government. Carlsson made securing approval of the Swedish electorate for joining the European Union (EU) a prime concern of his government. A national referendum on EU membership in November 1994 was passed by 52.2 percent of those voting and Sweden became a member on January 1, 1995. In August 1995 Carlsson announced that he would retire from politics in March 1996. After his handpicked successor, Mona Sahlin, had to stand aside because of a finding that she had improperly used her government credit card, Göran Persson, the minister of finance, succeeded him.

BIBLIOGRAPHY

Carlsson, Ingvar. *Carlsson: en samtalsbok med Ingvar Carlsson.* Stockholm: Tidens forlag, 1991.

———. *En el camino de la historia: temas de nuestro tiempo.* Mexico: Sociedad Cooperativa Publicaciones Mexicanas, 1988.

Isaksson, Christer. *Revanschen: Ingvar Carlssons vag tillbaka.* Stockholm: Ekerlid, 1995.

Kratz, Anita. *Ingvar Carlsson: Erlanders siste pojke.* Stockholm: Bonnier Alba, 1996.

Bernard Cook

Čarnogursky, Ján (1944–)

Slovak politician who briefly served as prime minister of the former Czechoslovakia in 1991–92. A law graduate of Charles University in Prague, Ján Čarnogursky worked as a company lawyer, while at the same time dealing with human rights cases, until 1987, when he became unemployed. Banned from his profession for political reasons, he was convicted of incitement against the socialist order and briefly imprisoned in 1989. Following the Velvet Revolution at the end of the same year, he served as a deputy federal premier until June 1990. A founding member of the mainly Slovak Christian Democratic Movement (CDM), which favored a looser Czechoslovak federation, he was invited to join a new coalition government in Prague, but instead became first deputy premier of the Slovak Republic in Bratislava, the city of his birth. In April 1991 he moved back to the Czech Republic to serve briefly as the federal premier, but was replaced after the new parliamentary elections in June 1992, when the CDM gained only eighteen seats in the Slovak National Council (SNC). He subsequently remained a deputy of the SNC and chairman of the CDM. With the rise to power of the former and again soon-to-be Slovak premier, Vladimir Mečiar, the CDM was in opposition, although it briefly participated in a new coalition government in 1994. Čarnogursky, on the other hand, declined to serve in this government, mainly because of his strong antipathy to some of its members. Following new parliamentary elections in September–October 1994, when Mečiar became Slovak premier for the third time, Čarnogursky's CDM was prominent in its support of the then Slovak president, Michal Kovač, in his long-standing dispute with the Slovak premier. That stance was to earn the CDM the undying enmity of Mečiar, whose government-controlled media subjected it and its leaders to all kinds of slanders in the years to come.

Marko Milivojevic

Carrero Blanco, Luis (1903–73)

Admiral and president of Spain, 1973. Luis Carrero Blanco was dictator Francisco Franco's most trusted adviser and played an important role in policy formulation and political nominations. He was instrumental in limiting the power of the Fascist Party and, through key appointments, helped break Spain's economic and political isolation after 1950. As Franco's health declined in the 1960s and 1970s, Carrero was seen as his possible successor. He was named president in 1973 but was assassinated shortly afterward by the Basque separatist group ETA.

Carrero received his first political appointment in 1941 and quickly became indispensable to Franco. In the late 1950s Franco, following Carrero's advice, appointed a cabinet of younger, less political bureaucrats, many of whom were linked with the Catholic organization Opus Dei. The new government embarked on a series of economic reforms culminating in the Stabilization Plan of 1959. This policy ended Spain's economic isolation and stimulated the economic boom that occurred in the

1960s. These new politicians helped limit the power of the Fascist Party and thereby eliminated a threat to the stability of the regime.

As Franco grew older, Carrero's role became increasingly important in part because the future structure of the regime remained undecided. Carrero led a movement designed to have Juan Carlos, the grandson of the last Spanish being, Alfonso XIII, who had gone into exile in 1932, named successor to Franco, and this was achieved in 1969. However, many in the regime still hoped Carrero would be the true authority in a post-Franco regime. In 1967 he was named vice president and became president in 1973. Carrero led a transitional cabinet that would accommodate change but still retain the structure of the old administration. He opposed political pluralism and remained committed to a conservative, Catholic state. On December 20, 1973, he was killed in Madrid by the ETA. His death, two years before Franco's, ended the last, best hope for the continuation of the regime beyond the death of the dictator.

Carrero played a key role in ending the political influence of the Fascist Party. Through the sponsorship and promotion of Opus Dei technocrats, he helped spur economic modernization. During the final years of his life he was instrumental in Franco's decision to name Juan Carlos future head of state. Carrero's death marked the symbolic, if not actual, end of the Franco regime and the beginning of the transition to democracy.

BIBLIOGRAPHY

Fernandez, Carlos. *El almirante Carrero.* Esplugues de Llobregat, Spain: Plaza & Janes, 1985.

Payne, Stanley G. *The Franco Regime, 1936–1975.* Madison: University of Wisconsin Press, 1987.

Tusell, Javier. *Carrero: la eminencia gris del regimen de Franco.* Madrid: Temas de Hoy, 1993.

Brian D. Bunk

SEE ALSO Franco, Francisco; Opus Dei

Carrillo, Santiago (1915–)

Secretary-general of the Spanish Communist Party (1960–82). Under Santiago Carrillo's leadership the party, whose political profile had deteriorated during the 1940s and 1950s, regained its position as the primary leftist opposition to the regime of Francisco Franco. This popularity enabled Carrillo to play an important role during the transition to democracy following the death of the dictator in 1975.

Carrillo began his political career at age nineteen when he was named secretary-general of the Young Socialists. In 1936 he joined the Communist Party and became part of the defense junta that controlled Madrid during the Spanish Civil War. Following the war he spent time in the Soviet Union, Czechoslovakia, France, and the Americas. In 1960 he was named secretary-general of the Spanish Communist Party. Although technically outlawed, the influence and popularity of the party within Spain grew during the 1960s and 1970s, mostly owing to its relationship with the growing trade union movement.

In 1976 Carrillo abandoned the revolutionary stance of his youth and became a proponent of Eurocommunism. The Spanish Communist Party disavowed Stalinism, distanced itself from Moscow, and dropped its call for a dictatorship of the proletariat. This change caused many of the most radical members to leave the party. Carrillo returned to Spain in December 1976 and was immediately arrested but was soon released. Shortly afterward the Communist Party was legalized and soon helped negotiate a 1977 labor agreement known as the Moncloa Pact. The party supported the 1978 constitution and participated in the 1979 elections, winning 10 percent of the vote. These results, however, were viewed as a disappointment by many within the organization. Carrillo's democratic centrism alienated party radicals, while at the same time moderate support shifted to the more mainstream Spanish Socialist Party. These trends culminated in the 1982 elections when the Socialists won an overwhelming victory, marking the end of the Communist Party as a major political force. Carrillo resigned in November 1982.

Carrillo's primary achievement was to shift the focus of the Communist Party from revolution to democracy. His support for the new constitution and the installation of democratic government insured a peaceful transition.

BIBLIOGRAPHY

Alba, Victor. *The Communist Party in Spain.* New Brunswick, N.J.: Transaction Books, 1983.
Carrillo, Santiago. *Eurocommunism and the State.* Westport, Conn.: L. Hill, 1978.
———. *Memorias.* Barcelona: Planeta, 1993.
Mujal-Leon, Eusebio. *Communism and Political Change in Spain.* Bloomington: Indiana University Press, 1983.

Brian D. Bunk

SEE ALSO Eurocommunism

Carstens, Karl (1914–92)

German diplomat and Christian Democratic (CDU) politician, president of the Federal Republic of Germany (1979–84). Karl Carstens is a unique figure in postwar German history, one of the few architects of West German foreign policy in the early years who lived to see reunification. While spending much of his early career in the background, he became an influential and prominent public representative of the new West German state. A former professor of international law, Carstens served in the Foreign Office from 1954 to 1966, rising to the rank of state secretary (a civil servant responsible for the administration of the ministry, equivalent to a British junior minister) in 1960. He went on to serve in the latter capacity in the Defense Ministry (1966–67) and the Federal Chancellery (1968–69).

In 1972 Carstens was elected to the Bundestag (lower house of parliament) for the CDU. Largely because of his expertise in foreign policy, he was chosen to be chair of the CDU caucus (*Fraktion,* 1973–76). In the 1976 Bundestag campaign, CDU chancellor candidate Helmut Kohl named Carstens his shadow foreign minister. After the CDU's narrow failure to win the 1976 elections, Kohl took over the post of *Fraktion* chair and Carstens was elected Bundestag president. Successes in state elections gave the CDU a majority in the Federal Assembly, consisting of all the Bundestag deputies and an equal number of representatives drawn from all of the state parliaments, which elected the federal president in 1979. Carstens, who had become one of the party's elder statesmen, emerged as the Christian Democratic candidate and the front-runner for the state's highest office. His election was cast in doubt by an intense controversy over his former Nazi Party membership, but the intervention of prominent politicians and journalists on his behalf, and clear evidence that he had been a member in name only, secured his victory.

BIBLIOGRAPHY

Carsten's personal papers are located in the Bundesarchiv, Koblenz, NL 1337.
Carstens, Karl. *Erinnerungen und Erfahrungen.* Ed. by Kai von Jena and Reinhard Schmoeckel [Schriften des Bundesarchivs 44] Boppard, Germany: Boldt Verlag, 1993.

Ronald J. Granieri

Carvalho, Otelo Saraiva de (1936–)

Known by his uncommon first name, Otelo, he has been called the "Che Guevara" of the Portuguese revolution.

He was a founding member of the Armed Forces Movement (MFA), commanded the successful April 25, 1974, coup against Portuguese dictator Marcelo Caetano, and was a candidate for president in the 1976 and 1980 elections. He attended the Portuguese Military Academy in Lisbon, and served under General António de Spínola in the Portuguese colony of Guinea-Bissau in 1970.

At their December 1, 1973, meeting, the MFA delegated to him the responsibility to plan and to command the coup against the Portuguese dictatorship. After the MFA Coordinating Committee decided that the regime was not open to their demand for a political settlement to end the colonial wars in Africa, they authorized Otelo to carry out a coup d'état.

This plan was executed successfully on April 25, 1974. The "go" sign was the playing of the revolutionary song "Granola, Vila Morena" on national radio in the early hours of April 25. The plan was predicated on four objectives. First, the MFA gained control of the country's radio and television broadcast centers. Second, the MFA took over the military headquarters in Lisbon and Oporto. Third, there were MFA troop movements throughout the country, designed to give the impression of a large military movement. Fourth, the MFA closed the border with Spain to ward off intervention to aid Caetano, which might have been ordered by Spanish dictator Francisco Franco. By the end of the day, in a swift and bloodless operation, Otelo became a national hero.

From 1974 to 1976 Otelo commanded the special Continental Operations Command (COPCON), assigned to keep order in the postcoup period. Throughout this time Otelo argued for the radicalization of the Portuguese revolution along the lines of the Cuban revolution. Otelo visited Fidel Castro in Cuba during the summer of 1975 and, on his return, suggested "en masse" that anyone resisting the revolution should be tried and shot in the Campo Pequeno Bullring in Lisbon. His opponents feared him, and his supporters loved him.

For the most part, Otelo's supporters were young, idealistic, and radical. His rhetoric encouraged them to resist their more moderate commanders. Indeed, when the moderates gained control of the MFA in September 1975, his supporters tried a left-wing coup against the MFA moderates on November 25, but were defeated. The coup organizers were tried and jailed. Otelo had no direct role in the coup.

He ran for president in the June 1976 election, finishing a distant second to General Ramalho Eanes, with 16.9 percent of the vote. He ran again in 1980, gaining a mere 1.49 percent. At that point moderate and conservative forces had gained control of the nation's political life, and

Otelo's revolutionary ideas no longer carried much appeal.

Yet his followers refused to accept the moderate trend of the government and organized a revolutionary group known as the FP-25 (Popular Forces–25 April). This terrorist group wanted to return the country to the goals of the April 25, 1974, revolution, engaging in terrorist attacks in the early 1980s, including bank robberies and bombings, which resulted in some deaths. Although he denied having an active role in FP-25, Otelo was found guilty in May 1987 in what some called the trial of the century in Portugal and sentenced to fifteen years in prison.

He will be most remembered for planning and commanding the successful April 25, 1974, coup, which ended the forty-eight-year *Estado Novo* (New State) dictatorship.

Paul Christopher Manuel

SEE ALSO Portugal

Cassin, René (-Samuel) (1887–1976)

French jurist and champion of universal human rights. As vice chairman of the U.N. Commission on Human Rights, René Cassin was one of the principal authors of the Universal Declaration of Human Rights. He was awarded the Nobel Peace Prize in 1968.

After practicing law in Paris, Cassin was seriously wounded while serving as an infantry officer during World War I. He then taught international law and served as French delegate to the League of Nations and to several disarmament conferences in Geneva. A key member of General Charles de Gaulle's government-in-exile during World War II, Cassin in 1944 became president of the Council of State and a member of the Constitutional Council. He helped found the United Nations Educational, Scientific and Cultural Organization (UNESCO), and following the adoption of the Human Rights declaration in 1948, he served on the Court of Arbitration at the Hague (1950–60) and was president of the European Court of Human Rights (1965–68). With his Nobel prize money, he established the International Institute for Human Rights at Strasbourg, France. Cassin was also a committed Zionist and president of the Alliance Israelite in France.

BIBLIOGRAPHY

Agi, Mark. *René Cassin: Fantassin des droits de l'homme.* Paris: Plon, 1979.

Cassin, René. *La Pensée et faction.* Bologne, Italy: F. Lalow, 1972.

Humphrey, John. *Human Rights and the United Nations: A Great Adventure.* Dobbs Ferry, N.Y.: Transnational Publications, 1984.

Thomas T. Lewis

Castle, Barbara Anne (1911–)

British politician. Barbara Castle (née Betts), daughter of a tax official, was born at Bradford, West Yorkshire, in 1911. After studying at Oxford she married in 1944 journalist Edward Cyril Castle, later Baron Castle. Her political carrier began when she served as a delegate to the Labour Party Day in 1943. In 1945 Castle was elected to Parliament as a Labour MP for Blackburn. In 1950 she joined the Labour Party's National Executive Committee, and from 1958 to 1959 she served as party chair. In 1964–65 she was minister of overseas development and in 1965–68 minister of transport. She roused controversy by introducing a speed limit of seventy miles per hour and the "breathalyzer" test for intoxicated drivers. From 1968 to 1970 Castle served as secretary of state for employment and productivity and from 1974 to 1978 as secretary of state for health and social security. In 1979 she gave up her Blackburn seat and resigned from Labour's National Executive Committee. The same year, however, she was elected to the European Parliament and from 1979 to 1985 served as vice chair of its Socialist Party group. In 1989 she retired from the European Parliament.

BIBLIOGRAPHY

"Castle, Barbara." *The Cambridge Biographical Encyclopedia.* Cambridge: Cambridge University Press, 1994.

Bernard Cook

Castoriadis, Cornelius (1922–97)

French philosopher, economist, and psychoanalyst, and a major theorist of radical left, non-Marxian socialism. Cornelius Castoriadis emerged after World War II as the leading spokesman for the "*gauchiste*" or radical leftist, movement in France and founder and editor, with Claude LeFort, of the journal *Socialisme ou Barbarie* (*Socialism or Barbarism*). His critical commentary focused not only on capitalism but on Soviet communism, asserting that both were overly bureaucratic and inhibiting of human autonomy and creativity. He became a strong advocate of workers' self-management.

Castoriadis was born in Constantinople (Istanbul) in 1922. He participated in the Communist youth movement and the Greek Communist Party as part of the resistance to German domination in World War II. He broke with Stalinist politics, joined the Trotskyists, and spent much of the war avoiding Stalinist agents as well as the Nazi Gestapo. In 1945 he went to Paris to study philosophy, broke with the Trotskyist Fourth International, and formed the Socialisme ou Barbarie group in 1949. He remained editor of the group's journal until 1966. During the same period he was a bureaucratic insider, observing international capitalism in his position as economist at the Organization for Economic Cooperation and Development (OELD). In 1974 he became a practicing psychoanalyst, and in 1979 director of studies at the École des Hautes Études en Sciences Sociales.

Much of Castoriadis's writing still awaits translation into English, and he has yet to be the focus of a significant book-length study. Among his major works are *La Société bureaucratique* (1973, 2 volumes), *L'Institution imaginaire de la société* (1975; *The Imaginary Institution of Society,* 1987), and *Les Carrefours du labyrinthe* (1978; *Crossroads in the Labyrinth,* 1984). Three further volumes have appeared in the Crossroads series: *Domaines de l'homme* (1986), *Le Monde morcelé* (1990; *The World in Fragments,* 1997), and *La Montée de l'insignifiance* (1996). In addition, he published *Capitalisme moderne et révolution* (1979, 2 volumes) and *Devant la guerre* (1980), which positioned him at the center of French debates about the Soviet Union. With Daniel Cohn-Bendit he wrote *De l'Écologie a l'autonomie,* and with Edgar Morin and Claude LeFort he analyzed the revolutionary days of 1968, for which his ideas may well be seen as a stimulus, in *Mai 68: La Brèche suivi de vingt ans après.*

Castoriadis's works exhibit a remarkable breadth of interests, but consistent themes run through them: critique of modern bureaucratic institutions; advocacy of a "praxis" philosophy and an emancipatory politics that would result in genuine socialist revolution and human autonomy; examination of the significance of ancient Greece and Rome for the postmodern world; critique of Western philosophy and rationalist ontology; reflections on the radical imagination as it springs from the psychic streams of the subjective and manifests itself in self-representations of a self-instituting collective society. Castoriadis died in December 1997. His commitment to social criticism and philosophical reflection that would lead to human self-assertion did not wave in more than forty years of writing and intellectual engagement.

BIBLIOGRAPHY

Castoriadis, Cornelius. *Philosophy, Politics, Autonomy.* Ed. by David Ames Curtis. Oxford: Oxford University Press, 1991.

————. *Political and Social Writings.* 2 Vols. Tr. and ed. by David Ames Curtis. Minneapolis: University of Minnesota Press, 1988.

Hirsh, Arthur. *The French New Left: An Intellectual History from Sartre to Gorz.* Boston: South End Press, 1981.

William E. Duvall

Catalonia (Principat)

Region of northeast Spain. Catalonia covers 12,328 square miles (31,930 sq km) and in 1991 had a population of six million. It is basically defined by a distinctive and rich cultural tradition centered on the Catalan language. Catalonia is divided into four provinces—Barcelona, Girona, Lleida, and Tarragona—with most of its population living in the capital, Barcelona. The origins of Catalan statehood date back to around 988, when the Spanish March (Marca Hispanica, with its capital at Barcelona) ruled by Count Borrell began to act independently from the Carolingian realm on which it nominally depended. From 1137 Catalonia was united to Aragon under the same ruler. In the thirteenth and fourteenth centuries the crown of Aragon expanded its Mediterranean empire eastward as far as Sardinia, Sicily, southern Italy and Athens (Neopatria).

During Spain's Civil War (1936–39), Catalan nationalists supported the republic, which granted local autonomy to Catalonia. Under the victorious Franco, however, the unitary state was reestablished. Following Franco's death in 1975 the Spanish government again accepted the principal of local self-rule. In 1979 Catalonia became one of Spain's seventeen Autonomous Communities and is the richest and most industrialized of them. Catalan nationalists consider Catalonia to be merely one of the Catalan "countries," referring occasionally to it as the Principat.

Daniele Conversi

Catalan Language

One of the main languages of Spain, belonging to the Romance family. It is spoken in Catalonia, the Balearic Islands (Mallorca, Menorca, and Ibiza, or Eivissa), the Valencian region (Alacant, Valencia, Castelló), and a southern strip of Aragon. It is also used outside Spain: in Roussillon (France), the Principality of Andorra, and the town of L'Alguer (Alghero) in Sardinia, Italy. According to the 1986 census 8,623,202 people living in the three main Catalan-speaking regions (Catalonia, Valencian Country, Balearic Islands) are able to understand Catalan. In the Balearics and Valencia the census questions concerned only "passive competence," or the ability to understand Catalan. Catalan "understanders" are distributed as follows: 5,287,200 in Catalonia (Principat), 2,775,007 in the Valencian region, and 560,995 in the Balearic Islands. No reliable data are available on the other Catalan-speaking areas.

After being repressed under the dictatorship of Francisco Franco, Catalan has experienced a powerful revival. Since 1979 it is the co-official language of Catalonia alongside Spanish. It has long been official in the Principality of Andorra and in the 1980s gained co-official status in the Valencian Country (officially defined as the Valencian language), southern Aragon, and the Balearic Islands. The two states where Catalan has not yet been officially recognized are France and Italy. Catalan does not possess equal status throughout its territory. It enjoys a high prestige in the Principat. In other regions, especially in Valencia, it is more stigmatized, even though it is increasingly associated with academic, intellectual, and artistic endeavors.

Daniele Conversi

Catalan Nationalism

Regional movement in Catalonia that has slowly developed into a fully fledged nationalism. Its ideological bases were laid between the publication of *Lo Catalanisme* (1868) by Valentí Almirall and *La nacionalitat catalana* (1906) by Enric Prat de la Riba. In contrast to Basque nationalism, postwar Catalan nationalism was thoroughly peaceful and moderate, focusing on cultural revival. State repression reached its peak in the aftermath of the Spanish Civil War (1936–39), when hundreds of Catalanists were killed, thousands were exiled, and Catalan culture was thoroughly forbidden.

A clandestine cultural revival began in the late 1950s. In 1971 all opposition forces united in the Assembly of Catalonia under the slogan "liberty, amnesty and statute of autonomy." In 1977 two years after the death of Francisco Franco, over one million people marched in the streets of Barcelona and other Catalan centers to demand autonomy on the occasion of the Catalan national holiday, Diada. The prewar regional government (Generalitat) was reinstated that year. In 1979 an autonomy statute was approved in a plebiscite by 88.1 percent of the voters (of an electoral turnout of 60.5 percent). Nationalist politics have dominated Catalan elections ever since, and no

Spanish mainstream party can hope to achieve an electoral breakthrough in Catalonia without Catalanizing at least its name and program. Since the 1984 regional election, the moderate nationalist party (Convergencia i Unió) has been firmly in control of the Catalan parliament, through its long-time leader Jordi Pujol.

BIBLIOGRAPHY

Conversi, Daniele. *The Basques, the Catalans and Spain: Alternative Routes to Nationalist Mobilization.* London: C. Hurst, 1996.

Daniele Conversi

SEE ALSO Pujol, Jordi

Cavaco Silva, Aníbal António (1939–)

Leader of the Portuguese Social Democratic Party (PSD) and prime minister from 1985 to 1995. During the Salazar-Caetano authoritarian regime, Aníbal Cavaco Silva completed his studies in economics with a Ph.D. from the University of York in England. Returning to Portugal, he began a distinguished career as professor of economics and adviser to the Bank of Portugal. Once Portugal began the transition from authoritarianism to democracy in 1974 and political parties were legalized, Cavaco Silva joined the newly founded PSD.

In January 1980 he was appointed minister of finance by the newly elected prime minister and PSD party leader, Francisco Sa Carneiro. Cavaco Silva was first elected a deputy in October 1980 on the PSD ticket. As minister, in an attempt to liberalize the Portuguese economy, he began the difficult task of undoing the nationalizations that had taken place during the leftist-dominated phase of the transition to democracy. Cavaco Silva realized early on that Portugal would have to change the illiberal features of its 1975 constitution, which posited a socialist economy. Cavaco Silva wanted to link Portugal's economic development to that of its European neighbors. After the untimely death of Prime Minister Francisco Lumbrales de Sá Carneiro and the succession of Francisco Pinto Balsemão as party leader, Cavaco Silva resigned his government position in January 1981 to return to his university position and advisory role to the Bank of Portugal. Although the PSD coalition government successfully revised the constitution in 1981, it managed only to water down many of the socialist economic features and fell far short of the liberalization envisioned by Cavaco Silva.

After a series of leadership crises within the PSD from 1981 to 1985 and the weak governing coalition with the Socialist Party, Cavaco Silva decided to challenge the dominant party leadership at the May 1985 party congress. His bold, charismatic speech calling for an end of the alliance with the Socialists and development of a clearer strategy in the upcoming presidential elections inspired party delegates to support him as the new party leader. Once the government signed Portugal's treaty of accession into the European Union (EU) in June 1985, Cavaco Silva and the PSD broke with the PS and the coalition government came to an end, provoking early elections.

The PSD won the October 1985 elections, and Cavaco Silva became prime minister of a PSD minority government. During its two-year duration Cavaco Silva was seen as a competent, efficient, strong leader. His government's enjoyment of an improved international economic situation strengthened Portugal domestically. Cavaco Silva's leadership coincided with Portugal's entry into the EU, and the new prime minister's European vocation served to link Portugal's economic development to that of its European neighbors. His government's concrete actions and pragmatism in modernizing the country through badly needed structural reforms gained the confidence of a people accustomed to government immobilism. Nevertheless, Cavaco Silva's opponents mounted a successful vote of censure, which ended his first government, and early elections were called.

Under the determined leadership of Cavaco Silva, the PSD easily won the 1987 elections with over 50 percent of the vote. For the first time in democratic Portugal, the government would be able to fulfill its four-year mandate. Cavaco Silva began to implement the significant economic reforms needed for Portugal's modernization: privatization of major industries and fiscal, housing, labor law, and trade union reforms. The prime minister emphasized competition, efficiency, and private initiative to strengthen the economy. Under his leadership the National Assembly approved a revised constitution in 1989 that finally eliminated the socialist economic features and established a neoliberal foundation for Portugal's economic development.

Cavaco Silva and his party increased their governing majority in the 1991 legislative elections by winning once again more than 50 percent of the vote, a feat few political parties in post–World War II Europe have realized. With an even stronger mandate, Cavaco Silva continued reforming the economy and linking reform with the building of a more integrated EU. Portugal was a different country after ten years of Cavaco Silva's leadership. The quality of life improved as gross domestic product per capita levels went from 53.1 percent of the EC average in

1985 to 64 percent in 1994. In anticipation of meeting the strict economic criteria of the Economic Monetary Union within the EU, Cavaco Silva endorsed a rigorous economic plan to reduce inflation, decrease public-sector deficit and not allow public debt to grow, maintain a stable escudo against the German mark, and keep inflation as low as possible. Cavaco Silva wanted Portugal to be among the first "ins" in establishing a single EU currency.

The final years of Cavaco's government were marked by a worsening domestic economic situation, charges of corruption among political appointees, and complicated relations between the prime minister and the president, Mário Soares. In late January 1995 Cavaco Silva announced his decision to abandon the party leadership. Citing personal reasons, he noted that he had sufficiently fulfilled his party's program for Portuguese development. Fernando Nogueira succeeded him as party leader, but the PSD lost the legislative elections of October 1995.

With the Socialist Party dominant in the assembly, Cavaco Silva declared his intent to run for the presidency as a check on the Socialists' performance in the government and the legislature. Had the PSD sneaked by with a plurality of the votes in the October election, perhaps Cavaco Silva would not have run. He based his campaign for the presidency on his experience and commitment to representing Portugal's interests in foreign policy, especially in the EU. The Socialist candidate, Jorge Sampaio, won the election on the first round by receiving approximately 8 percent more of the vote than Cavaco Silva. During his short candidacy, Cavaco Silva stabilized the center-right against the Socialists, winning more votes than the combined votes of the right (PSD and People's Party) in the earlier legislative elections.

After his failed bid for the presidency, Cavaco Silva returned to his university position as professor of economics and consultant to the Bank of Portugal. While still a member of the PSD, he holds no elected party position. Yet a place has been reserved for him in modern European and Portuguese history for his significant role in the liberalization and democratization of Portuguese society.

BIBLIOGRAPHY

Costa Figueira, João. *Cavaco Silva: homem de estado.* Lisbon: Livraria Popular Francisco Franco, 1987.

Maritheresa Frain

Ceauşescu, Nicolae (1918–89)

Communist leader of Romania between 1965 and his execution in December 1989, noted for his authoritari-

Nicolae Ceausescu (right), president of Romania, waving from the balcony of the Hradcany Castle in Prague on a visit to President Ludvik Svoboda (left) of Czechoslovaia, August 24, 1968. *Illustration courtesy of Archive Photos.*

anism, cult of personality, inflexibility, and mediation of the East-West and Arab-Israeli conflicts until 1980.

Nicolae Ceauşescu, the third of ten children, was born on January 26, 1918, into a poor peasant family in the village of Scorniceşti, near Bucharest. He was a short man, slight of build, and spoke with a stammer that he never entirely overcame. His major personality traits were shrewdness, paranoia, courage, and a taste for vengeance. Lacking creativity, he rose to the top on his ability to manipulate and outmaneuver others. He possessed an excellent memory and a knack for detail. In short, he was the mass society's quintessential organization man.

Little is known for certain about his youth because Romanian Communist mythographers altered his police records in the 1960s. He seems to have left school at age eleven when his father apprenticed him in Bucharest to the shoemaker husband of one of his sisters. While in Bucharest, Ceauşescu became involved with the Romanian Communist Party (RCP), for which he was imprisoned from the late 1930s until 1944. During the 1940s he was jailed together with Romania's Communist leaders and became the virtual servant of Gheorghe Gheorghiu-

Dej, Romania's future Communist dictator, who was so impressed with Ceauşescu's loyalty and commitment to communism that he became his mentor.

After his release from prison in 1944, although Ceauşescu was barely literate, Gheorghiu-Dej made him secretary of the Communist youth organization and a candidate member of the party's Central Committee. The "Moscow Stalinist" and RCP Politburo member Ana Pauker, Gheorghiu-Dej's main rival, disliked Ceauşescu and excluded him from the party leadership. Nevertheless, he still received important governmental positions in the Ministry of Agriculture and the armed forces. After purging his rivals in 1952, Gheorghiu-Dej elevated Ceauşescu to the Romanian Workers Party's Central Committee (T)he RCP was called Romanian Worker's Party [RWP] between 1948 and 1965). In 1955 Gheorghiu-Dej advanced him to the Politburo, with responsibility for organization and personnel, a powerful position that permitted Ceauşescu to build his own coterie within the RWP.

Gheorghiu-Dej died in 1965. Soviet Premier Nikita Khrushchev's de-Stalinization and scheme for a "socialist division of labor" had prompted Gheorghiu-Dej to pursue what amounted to desatellitization but not de-Stalinization. Desatellitization consisted primarily of using nationalism to distance Romania from Moscow so that the RWP could perpetuate its Stalinist centralized planning, which emphasized heavy industrialization while agriculture and consumer goods production languished. In 1964 he had also liberalized Romanian cultural life to improve the RWP's popularity. RWP leaders who favored liberalization secured Ceauşescu's election as first secretary of the RWP over fierce opposition from such Stalinists as Minister of the Interior Alexander Draghici and Gheorghe Apostol, the latter of whom Gheorghiu-Dej may have preferred as his successor.

Ceauşescu desired to control the RWP and the government totally, but between 1965 and 1969 he was only the most prominent member of a genuine collective leadership. At the Ninth Party Congress in 1965 the liberal reformers promised Romanians greater participation in public affairs (democracy) and socialist justice, which meant substituting adjudication for arbitrary imprisonment by the Interior Ministry's secret police (Securitate). Henceforth Romania's leaders would use the Securitate to frighten but not terrorize. To achieve socialist justice, the liberals seriously weakened their most powerful opponent, Draghici, by securing his resignation as interior minister. The congress also promulgated a new constitution with a provision substituting a fifteen-member Presidium for the former twelve-member Politburo. Ceau-

şescu filled the new openings with his allies. Finally, to win the allegiance of intellectuals and promote technological development, the congress decided to emphasize education and science. In 1966 the RCP placed more intellectuals and technocrats on the Central Committee to underline this commitment.

Romania's new leaders also preserved their predecessor's policies on national independence and heavy industrialization. Ceauşescu, believing that common ownership was motive and incentive enough for economic success, never lost his faith in Stalinist economics, even when Romania's economy stagnated in the 1980s. Nationalism mixed with a populism that included anti-intellectualism also held a major place in Ceauşescu's politics. To demonstrate his faith in the masses, he constantly visited towns, factories, and farms until some Jiu Valley miners complained to him about their working conditions in 1972. After that incident he met only with local officials and "representatives" of the workers under carefully controlled conditions.

By 1967 Ceauşescu had amassed sufficient power to become president of the State Council, head of the government, as well as the RCP's titular leader despite a provision in the 1965 constitution prohibiting the simultaneous holding of party and government offices. That same year Ceauşescu started requiring party officials to begin absorbing state positions at their same level to reduce the bureaucracy's size and insure that technocrats did not place modernization ahead of his desire to institutionalize the revolution.

While the government was falling under his control, Ceauşescu was also subduing the party. First, in 1968 he denounced Gheorghiu-Dej's purges and forced Draghici, who was involved in them, to quit the party. Now Ceauşescu gradually gained complete control of the Securitate by granting its members a better lifestyle than that of most Romanians and by turning it into a military organization that rivaled the army. He completed his conquest of the party in 1969 by excluding all but two of Gheorghiu-Dej's men from the Central Committee. Then, to prevent his adversaries from organizing against him, over the years he enlarged various political bodies, such as the Central Committee, to render government less effective and to dilute the elite with his own clients. Beginning in 1971, he also frequently transferred officeholders to fragment the bureaucracy.

During the 1960s Ceauşescu preserved Romania's autonomy with an astute foreign policy and used the status it earned him at home and abroad to help realize his personal ambitions. Autonomy meant involving Romania in the Soviet-dominated Warsaw Pact as little as possible, remaining cordial with both sides in the Sino-Soviet conflict, and creating more cultural and diplomatic ties with the West; consequently, in 1967 Romania became the only Warsaw Pact member to establish diplomatic relations with West Germany and to preserve diplomatic relations with Israel. Simultaneously Romania worked closely with the Arab world and sought to improve its standing in the Third World. Finally, despite real fears of a Soviet invasion, Ceauşescu refused to join the 1968 Warsaw Pact invasion of Czechoslovakia, although he did nothing to help the Czechoslovaks, whose liberalization he disliked. Nevertheless, his defiance of Soviet leader Leonid Brezhnev won him the overwhelming admiration of the nationalistic, anti-Russian Romanians and such a reputation as a "maverick Communist" among Western governments that President Nixon visited Bucharest the next year.

The slogan "on the road to a multilaterally developed socialist society," meaning not only communism's promised economic growth but, more important, the creation of a more egalitarian, altruistic, and productive summarized Ceauşescu's ideological vision for Romania's future. In 1971 he visited China and North Korea. The leaders of these Asian countries had enhanced their power and mobilized the masses with it to achieve communism through "cultural revolution." Ceauşescu concluded that their methods would also work in Romania and proceeded to drop all pretense of liberalization and democracy. In 1974 he created the office of president for himself to exercise total control over the party, the state, and the armed forces. He had also started a cult of personality to personalize his dictatorship by portraying himself as the fountainhead of all truth and the culmination of Romania's historical destiny, its "Golden Age." Romanians unable to accept the new regimentation faced police harassment, loss of employment, frequent relocations, and, as a last resort, sentences to prisons or psychiatric hospitals.

Ceauşescu felt that creating his "new socialist person" required heightened emphasis on social engineering. Architecture was an important element of this program. One of its main objective was to generate complete equality by providing everyone with the same amount of living space. To accomplish this Ceauşescu built row upon row of apartment houses, frequently by demolishing older buildings that failed to meet his ideological standards, in which the state size of an apartment varied directly with the number of persons living in it.

Throughout the 1970s Ceauşescu intensified his foreign policy initiatives partly to enhance further his standing as a world leader and partly for economic reasons. He hoped to exploit his maverick image to help realize ambitious goals for Romanian economic growth by purchasing advanced Western technology on credit and increasing Romania's world trade to pay the loans. Equating economic success with gigantic industrial enterprises, he created ever larger installations. These prestige projects often depended on imported raw materials, expensive Western technology, and large quantities of inexpensive energy.

By 1979–80 his standing as a world leader and Romania's economic outlook had diminished significantly. The Sino-American rapprochement and the end of the Vietnam War had markedly reduced his value as an intermediary between the Americans and Asian Communists. When his significance as a mediator between Israelis and Arabs also diminished after 1980, Ceauşescu turned increasingly to the Third World in the vain hope of preserving his status and Romania's international trade. Yet overdiversification and irresponsible investments especially in petrochemicals had strained to the limit Romania's labor, natural, and financial resources by 1980. When the economy failed to grow in 1981 for the first time since 1945, Ceauşescu blamed the Romanian people for the problem. Having convinced himself that the West was destroying communism with its loans, he refused offers of help from Western financial experts.

After resting his dictatorship on the absolute truth of communism, he chose withdrawal into a fantasy world rather than reform after 1981. He defended communism with slogans and relied more on nationalism to legitimize his regime. Besides distancing himself from the RCP, his extreme nationalism isolated Romanians from the world community and from each other by condemning foreigners and questioning the loyalty of Romania's ethnic minorities. Finally, Ceauşescu intensified his cult of personality by presenting himself as such a singular genius that only he could solve Romania's problems. Consequently, he ordered the pace of industrialization to increase so that Romania would become completely self-sufficient and debt-free through exporting more than it imported.

For his own glory and the victory of socialism, Ceauşescu also decreed more social engineering despite Romania's economic weaknesses. He planned to replace all the country's historic religious and secular edifices with apartment buildings or factories. He also decided to implement a 1968 plan for rural Romania called systematization, designed to eliminate all distinctions between town and country by demolishing over half of Romania's farm villages and moving the peasants into urbanlike centers composed of apartment houses. The altered environment would accelerate the emergence of the new Communist person in the countryside and increase agricultural production. Only a few of them were built near Bucharest before Ceauşescu's demise.

While Romanians suffered deprivation, the dictator lived in luxury, seemingly oblivious to their plight. His fear of revolt, not from the masses but from the military or the technocrats and plant managers, intensified as his dependence on them for order and exportable products grew. Increasingly, Ceauşescu relied on the Securitate for protection and trusted only members of his own family and a few cronies. His wife, Elena, became virtual coruler with him, and his son Nicu designated heir apparent. Ceauşescu filled as many important offices as possible with such cronies, rotated others to new positions more frequently, and centralized decision making completely within his immediate entourage. Nevertheless, a few dissidents rose to attack his regime, while numerous others sought to emigrate. Ceauşescu branded these individuals as traitors and controlled them with renewed social fragmentation. For example, he greatly restricted Romanian intellectuals' contacts with foreigners and required typewriter owners to deposit a sample of their machine's type with the police. While largely effective with minimal violence, this ever-intensifying spiral of oppression brought foreign criticism that further tarnished the dictator's greatly diminished international reputation. By December 1989 Ceauşescu had isolated Romania from the world and himself from Romanians. The economy was completing its second year of negative growth, but, although Communist regimes were disintegrating all around Romania, he had nothing to offer Romanians but more communism and nationalism. At that point the Romanian people deposed him and his family despite the opposition of the Securitate. He and his wife were captured trying to flee the country. After a brief trial by the army, the man who had once been honored as a world leader was executed along with his wife on December 25 by the very people he had sought to lead to greatness.

BIBLIOGRAPHY

Almond, Mark. *The Rise and Fall of Nicolae and Elena Ceauşescu.* London: Chapmans, 1992.

Behr, Edward. *Kiss the Hand You Cannot Bite: The Rise and Fall of the Ceauşescus.* New York: Villard Books, 1991.

Sweeney, John. *The Life and Times of Nicolae Ceauşescu.* London: Hutchinson, 1991.

Robert Forrest

SEE ALSO Gheorghiu-Dej, Gheorghe; Romania

Ceka, Neritan (1941–)

Albanian scholar and democratic politician. Neritan Ceka followed in the academic footsteps of his archaeologist father, Hasan Ceka. Before World War II, all major excavations were directed by foreign specialists, and many priceless artifacts were shipped abroad. To the postwar regime of Enver Hoxha the results of archaeological investigations held an important place in the nation-building process. They gave concrete proof of Albania's "glorious Illyrian past." Scholars like the younger Ceka were provided with the necessary funding to accomplish much useful original research. Neritan Ceka published widely, both at home and abroad, and despite a period of internal exile in the southern town of Fier, by the 1980s he had risen to the position of chairman of the Department of Antiquity, attached to the prestigious Albanian Institute of Archaeology.

The 1989 collapse of communism in Eastern Europe initially had slight impact on the Albanian regime of Ramiz Alia, but by December 1990 student protests forced Alia to consider the inevitability of political change, and Ceka as a respected figure in the Tirana intelligentsia was drawn into politics. A political moderate, he exercised a restraining influence on students following the toppling of Hoxha's statue in Skanderbeg Square on February 20, 1991, and he was a founding member of the Democratic Party (DP). Ceka was elected to the post of vice president at the first DP congress in September 1991.

The decision on December 6, 1991, by DP Chairman Sali Berisha to pull the seven DP ministers out of the coalition government led by Ylli Bufi was opposed by Ceka. Ceka argued that preservation of the coalition was in the national interest, and he resigned his party post. The March 1992 elections, which resulted in a DP landslide and the installation of Sali Berisha as Albania's first non-Communist president on April 9, 1992, also revealed major differences within DP ranks. Ceka shared the view articulated by Gramoz Pashko, who had been DP deputy premier in the 1991 coalition government, warning against dictatorial tendencies on Berisha's part. In September 1992, Ceka was instrumental in forming the centrist Democratic Alliance in a country racked by famine, civil strife, and growing presidential authoritarianism. Ceka still found time, however, to attend international academic gatherings.

Following the anarchy that erupted in early 1997 and the June 1997 general election, Ceka was appointed minister of the interior in the government of Fatos Nano. By then half of the country was outside government control, armed bands roamed freely, and safe travel to Greece was possible only by air. In a debate in parliament in July 1997, Ceka was shouted down by opposition MPs when he pledged that the country would be "calmed within weeks and disarmed within months." By December 1997, however, although complete pacification of the country remained some way off, law and order had improved considerably under Ceka's stewardship of the Interior Ministry.

In early 1998 Ceka concluded that it was appropriate to step down from his ministerial post, handing over responsibility to a fellow member of the Democratic Alliance, thus maintaining the political balance within the governing coalition led by the Socialist Party and headed by Nano. Ceka accepted the post of chairman of the parliamentary commission overseeing internal affairs, a political appointment reflecting a broad endorsement from his fellow members of parliament.

Philip E. Wynn

Cerník, Oldrich (1921–94)

Czechoslovak Communist, prime minister, April 1968 to January 1970. Oldrich Cerník, son of a miner, was born in Ostrava on October 27, 1921. He began working in an Ostrava steel mill at sixteen. He joined the Communist Party of Czechoslovakia (CPC) in 1945 and began working full-time in the party organization in 1949. In 1956 he was chosen to be a member of the Central Committee and was appointed minister of fuel in 1960. Cerník earned a degree in engineering through a correspondence school in 1964. He became convinced that decentralization was an answer to the economic difficulties that Czechoslovakia experienced in the 1960s, and he cautiously tried to advance that agenda. He was elected to the CPC Presidium in 1966 and in April 1968 was appointed prime minister by Alexander Dubček, the first secretary of the CPC.

At the time of the August 1968 invasion of Czechoslovakia by Warsaw Pact forces, Cerník was taken prisoner to Moscow. When the Soviets failed in their initial effort to set up a conservative administration, Cerník was brought back. He tried to walk a tightrope, advocating cooperation with the USSR as a prerequisite for the continuation of reform, but his effort was doomed. Though he was appointed prime minister of the reorganized Czechoslovak federation in 1969, his efforts to distance himself from the "excesses" of the Prague Spring failed to stave off the ultimate reckoning. Cerník was replaced as prime minister in January 1970 by Lubomír Strougal and ousted from the CPC later that year.

Cerník hoped to reenter politics after the Velvet Revolution of 1989 but, again, his hopes were dashed. He died in Prague on October 19, 1994.

BIBLIOGRAPHY

Michaela, Rebbeck. "Oldrich Cernik." *Guardian,* October 27, 1994.

Bernard Cook

SEE ALSO Czechoslovakia

Cerny, Ján (1959–)

Czech politician. Ján Cerny was born on April 23, 1959. In 1984 he graduated from the Veterinary University in Brno. After 1991 he worked as a private veterinary surgeon in Česky Brod in central Bohemia. In 1992 he was elected as delegate from the Civic Democratic Party (ODS) to the Czech National Council, which was the parliament for the Czech part of the Czechoslovak Federation. This was transformed into the Czech Chamber of Deputies on January 1, 1993. Cerny, who was deputy chairman of the Union of Landowners and Private Farmers, became chairman of the agricultural committee. He was reelected to the Chamber of Deputies on June 1, 1996. He was elected vice chair of the ODS on July 16, 1996, and after the resignation of the party chairman, Jiří Honajzer, was elected chair on December 16, 1997. However, he was critical of the outgoing ODS premier, Václav Klaus, who wanted ODS to go into opposition rather than participate in a new government, and held that post only until January 19, 1998. Cerny agreed to become local development minister in Josef Tosovsky's government. On January 20, 1998, he helped establish a new party, the Freedom Union, formed by ODS members opposed to Klaus. Cerny was joined by two other ODS ministers, Finance Minister Ivan Pilip and Labor and Social Affairs Minister Stanislav Volak, and thirty of the sixty-nine parliamentary representatives of ODS.

BIBLIOGRAPHY

"Cerny, Honajzer Leave ODS." CTK National News Wire, January 19, 1998.

"Cerny Thinking of Joining ODS Platform." CTK National News Wire, January 4, 1998.

"Jan Cerny: New Man at the Helm of Faction and in ODS Leadership." CTK National News Wire, December 16, 1997.

"Quick Political Rise of Jan Cerny." CTK National News Wire, December 30, 1997.

Bernard Cook

Cerny, Václav (1905–87)

Czechoslovak literary critic, professor, and human rights activist. Václav Cerny studied at Charles University in Prague, and at the universities of Dijon and Geneva, becoming a professor of comparative literature at Charles University. During World War II he was a leader of the Czechoslovak resistance against the Germans and was arrested by the Gestapo. After the Communists came to power in 1948, he was dismissed from his position at the university and forbidden to publish. He was employed in a minor position at the Czechoslovak Academy of Sciences until he was rehabilitated during the Prague Spring of 1968. After the Warsaw Pact invasion of Czechoslovakia on August 20 of that year, he was again banned from the university. He was an author of the Charter 77 document.

Bernard Cook

SEE ALSO Czechoslovakia

Chaban-Delmas, Jacques-Pierre-Michel (1915–)

French premier, 1969–72. Jacques Chaban-Delmas was born Jacques Delmas on March 7, 1915. He studied political science at the Institut d'Études Politiques in Paris and law at the Sorbonne before joining the army in 1938. He played a leading role in the Resistance while simultaneously completing a law degree. He used the nom de guerre "Chaban," which he subsequently legally added to his cognomen. He served as the principal liaison between the Resistance and the Free French government, which he joined in October 1943. He played a central role in coordinating the successful liberation of Paris. De Gaulle rewarded his effort by promoting him to general.

In 1945, after passing the civil service examination, Chaban-Delmas became an inspector of finance. In 1946 he was elected to the National Assembly from the bourgeois Radical Socialist Party, but he joined the Gaullists when their party was organized in 1947. He was elected chairman of the Gaullist Social Republicans in 1953 and served as a leader of its successor, the Union for a New Republic. In 1947 Chaban-Delmas began his long tenure as mayor of Bordeaux. He also held a number of ministerial posts in the 1950s, including minister of public works (1954–55), minister of state (1956–57), and minister of defense (1957–58). He actively supported the return of de Gaulle and the establishment of the Fifth French Republic.

He surrendered the presidency of the National Assembly, which he had held since 1958, to become premier under Georges Pompidou from June 20, 1969, to July 5, 1972. In 1973 he was appointed inspector general of finance.

Chaban-Delmas was defeated by Valéry Giscard d'Estaing in the first round of the 1974 presidential election. He resumed the presidency of the National Assembly, however, from 1978 until the Socialist victory in 1981. With the conservative victory in 1986, he was again chosen as president of the National Assembly. The choice of Chaban-Delmas was promoted by the Gaullist Prime Minister Jacques Chirac to prevent Giscard d'Estaing from gaining the post to use as a launching pad for the 1988 presidential race. Chaban-Delmas relinquished the position in January 1992 following another Socialist victory, but on November 12, 1996, after another shift in the electorate, he was made honorary president of the National Assembly. On May 19, 1995, having announced in 1993 that he would not run again for mayor of Bordeaux, Chaban-Delmas relinquished his municipal function.

BIBLIOGRAPHY

Bernstein, Richard. "French Assembly Picks Moderate Rightist as Chief." *New York Times,* April 3, 1986.

Chaban-Delmas, Jacques. *Charles de Gaulle.* Paris: Paris Match, 1980.

———. *La Libération.* Paris: Paris Match, 1984.

———. *Mémoires pour demain.* Paris: Flammarion, 1997.

Chastenet, Patrick. *Chaban.* Paris: Seuil, 1991.

Cherruau, Pierre. *Chaban de Bordeaux.* Bordeaux: Éditions Sud Ouest, 1996.

Savary, Gilles. *Chaban, maire de Bordeaux: Anatomie d'une féodalité républicaine.* Bordeaux: Éditions Auberon, 1995.

Bernard Cook

Channel Islands

Archipelago located in the English Channel at the entrance of the Gulf of Saint-Malo, eighty miles south of England and ten miles from France at the closest point, dependencies of the British crown but not part of the United Kingdom. Remnants of the Duchy of Normandy, tied to the British crown since 1066, the islands are governed by their own parliaments, the States of Deliberation on Guernsey and the Assembly of States on Jersey, and executive committees with their own local laws and customs. A lieutenant governor represents the British monarch. U.K. taxes do not apply. The total land mass is 75 square miles (194 sq km). There are four main islands, Jersey, Guernsey, Alderney, and Sark, the admin-

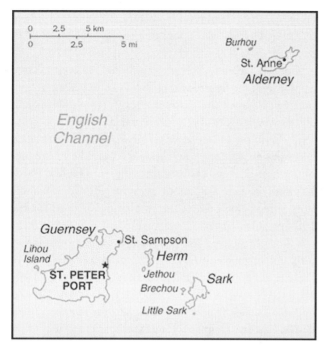

Channel Islands. *Illustration courtesy of Bernard Cook.*

istration of which is divided into two bailiwicks headquartered on Jersey and Guernsey. Guernsey has responsibility for the dependencies of Alderney, Sark, Herm, Jethou, Lihou, and Brechou. Jersey has the dependencies of Ecrehous rock and Les Minquiers, which were claimed by France until the International Court of Justice in 1953 judged in favor of the British monarchy. But the question is still broached because control of those islands affects oil rights in the area. The islands were occupied by German forces from July 1940 to May 1945.

The Channel Islands have 143,683 inhabitants. In addition to English, French and a Norman-French dialect are spoken. English is the official language on Guernsey, French on Jersey. The principal towns and bailiwick capitals are St. Peter Port on Guernsey and St. Helier on Jersey.

BIBLIOGRAPHY

King, Peter. *The Channel Islands War, 1940–1945.* London: R. Hale, 1991.

Bernard Cook

Chanturia, Georgi (1960–94)

Georgian politician and prominent younger member of the nationalist opposition to Communist rule in the late Soviet period in the Republic of Georgia. A cofounder and then the leader of the national Forum, which later became the National Democratic Party (NDP), Georgi ("Gia") Chanturia initially came to prominence as a nationalist poet and anti-Communist who was also to oppose independent Georgia's first elected leader, Zviad Gamsakhurdia. In 1990 he urged the boycott of the Supreme Soviet elections that legitimated Gamsakhurdia's power, arguing instead for the creation of a new, democratic National Congress to act as a parliament when Georgia formally declared its de facto independence from the Soviet Union in 1991. Arrested as one of the most serious opponents of the Gamsakhurdia regime in 1991, he was freed later than year by the armed rebel forces that later forcibly ousted the first Georgian president in January 1992. Then allied with the moderate democratic opposition to Gamsakhurdia, Chanturia was later strongly opposed to the semi-criminal warlords who replaced him. Under the rule of Gamsakhurdia's successor, President Eduard Shevardnadze, a former Georgian Communist Party leader and Soviet foreign minister, Chanturia's NDP briefly participated in government but fell out with the new Georgian president after his rapprochement with Russia in 1994.

Gia Chanturia was wounded on October 26, 1990, as he left a meeting with others who had joined him in a boycott of Georgian Supreme Soviet elections. He hinted that he had been shot on the orders of Gamsakurdia, whose supporters won a majority in the subsequent election and then chose him head of state. Chanturia was jailed by Gamsakhurdia in the fall of 1991.

Chanturia announced at the beginning of December 1994 that his National Democratic Party would enter an alliance in opposition to Shevardnadze. Within a week he was assassinated and the perpetrators were not discovered.

BIBLIOGRAPHY

Rosen, Roger. *Georgia: A Sovereign Country of the Caucasus.* New York: Odysses Publications, 1999.

Marko Milivojevic

SEE ALSO Gamsakhurdia, Zviad; Shevardnadze, Eduard

Charles, Prince of Wales (1948–)

Son of Elizabeth II (1926–) and heir to the throne of England. He was born on November 14, 1948, the first-born child of Princess Elizabeth, daughter and heir to King George VI and her husband Philip, Duke of Edinburgh. He attended private boarding school at Hill House, Cheam School, Gordonstoun in Scotland, and Timbertop in Australia. Charles became a Counselor of State at age eighteen and was invested as a Knight of the Garter in June of 1968. He attended Trinity College,

Cambridge, and graduating with a lower second class degree in 1970, became the first heir to the throne to secure a university degree.

In March of 1971, Charles did four-months of service with the Royal Air Force at Cranwell to qualify as a jet pilot. In 1974, he joined the Fleet Air Arm, took a helicopter conversion course, and was assigned to the 845 Naval Air Squadron as a pilot on board the commando carrier HMS *Hermes*. In 1976, Charles was given command of the coastal mine hunter HMS *Bronington*. After finishing his five-year term of service in the navy, Charles often expressed his frustration over the limitations of royal responsibilities. Charles's desire to do more led him to found the Prince's Trust in 1976. This organization provided individual grants to help young people escape from poverty and crime by setting up self-help programs. It became a multi-million pound organization and the biggest independent charity of its kind in the country. Charles also served as the president of the International Council of the United World Colleges.

In February of 1981, the prince, who was thirty-two, announced his engagement to Lady Diana Spencer, who was nineteen at the time. The wedding, which received extraordinary media coverage, took place on July 29, 1981. The nation rejoiced in a mood of universal celebration as the beautiful, shy bride married what seemed to be her "Prince Charming."

Charles and Diana celebrated the birth of their first son, Prince William, on June 21, 1982. Another son, Prince Henry ("Harry"), followed in September of 1984. As Charles and Diana made official tours around the world, her popularity grew. The media interest in her soared and the press focused less on Charles, although he continued his work with community organizations such as the Prince's Trust. In 1986, the Prince's Youth Business Trust was founded to disperse modest loans and grants to beginning entrepreneurs who were refused by banks. By 2000, the organization had helped over 40,000 people start new businesses. Charles also became president of Business In The Community (BITC) that tried to break through barriers of class and race that separated industrial executives from leaders of the black community.

By 1986, Charles's marriage had disintegrated. The following year speculation over the marriage became a preoccupation of the British and international media, and rumors abounded about Charles and Diana's behavior and alleged affairs. On December 9, 1992, Prime Minister John Major announced in the House of Commons that the royal couple was separating, but that they would not divorce. However, strained relations between the two continued and in December of 1995 the Queen wrote to Charles and Diana suggesting they resolve their differences amicably for the sake of the children. In February 1996, the two met privately to discuss the details of the divorce settlement. The royal divorce became final on August 28, 1996.

The scandal and humiliation the royal family began to endure in 1987 continued as accusations flew and "tell-all" books were published by former employees and supposed friends. Charles's popularity plummeted as opinion polls published in 1996 showed that 77 percent of the British people believed he lacked the public respect to be an efficient king. However, both Charles and Diana appeared to be moving on with their respective lives. Then tragedy struck on August 31, 1997, when Diana was killed in an automobile accident in Paris. Following her death, Charles has continued to raise his sons and work. He also has become more responsive to the media and increased his public appearances. A 1999 survey indicated that 63 percent of the British people believed he would be an effective king.

BIBLIOGRAPHY

Dimbleby, Jonathan. *The Prince of Wales: A Biography.* New York: William Morrow & Company Inc., 1994.

Rebecca Hayes

Chechnya

Area in the northeast Caucasus, bordering on Dagestan, Georgia, southern Russia, and the ethnically related area of Ingushetia. Until the dissolution of the Soviet Union in 1991, Chechnya and Ingushetia formed a united autonomous republic inside the Russian Federation. The territory of Chechen-Ingushetia was 7,450 square miles (19,300 sq km) and had a population of 1,289,700. The Chechens, the titular nationality, belong to the Nakh-Daghestani linguistic group, found exclusively in Caucasia. Their ethnolinguistic genealogy can be traced back approximately six thousand years.

After the collapse of Turkic-Mongol nomadic empires in the sixteenth century, Chechen communities began venturing from their mountainous refuges to the adjacent fertile plains. Chechen society remains dominated by free, property-owning, and usually armed males, whose behavior is strictly circumscribed by the complexes of honor and shame. Islam, adopted as late as the last century, has further cemented the institutions of this frontier warrior-peasant democracy.

In the eighteenth century Chechnya, with the rest of the Caucasus, became a crucial field in the Russo-Ottoman imperial rivalries. The Russian military even-

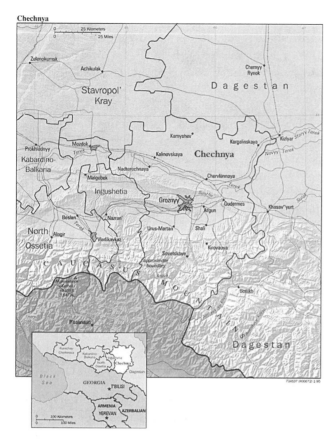

Chechnya. *Illustration courtesy of Bernard Cook.*

tually resorted to an increasingly repressive policy toward the poor and inaccessible (therefore untaxable and difficult-to-police) Caucasian mountaineers. Resistance was organized around the popular Islamic movements. In the 1830s, under the leadership of a Dagestani, Shamil, who had assumed the title of imam, short-lived uprisings and movements gave way to sustained revolution and state making. Imam Shamil sought to spread the democratic egalitarianism and militancy of early Islam into the entire northern Caucasus, from Dagestan on the Caspian Sea to Abkhazia on the Black Sea. Old princely elites were largely subdued, eliminated, and supplanted by the new Islamic organs of rule. Imam Shamil was thus able to field a formidable multiethnic army, in which Chechens fought prominently. This mountaineer army forced Russia to wage its most protracted colonial war. In 1859, after an enormously destructive campaign, the Russian army captured Shamil and annihilated Chechen and Dagestani resisters. Scores of villages were forcibly resettled into the more accessible areas, or forced into exile in the Middle East. This exodus was the source of sizable Chechen communities in Turkey, Syria, and especially Jordan.

Animosities between Chechens and Russian Cossack settlers flared during the Russian civil war of 1918–20.

After the fleeting alliance between the Chechen Islamic clan-based guerrillas and the Bolsheviks, relations with the new authorities quickly soured. Stalin's collectivization led to a series of massive and lengthy uprisings and eventually, in 1940, to the proclamation of a Chechen "People's Revolutionary Government." On February 23, 1944, Stalin initiated a forced deportation of the Chechens, accusing them of collaborating with the invading Germans. Almost one-third (more than a hundred thousand) of all Chechens perished during the deportation to Kazakhstan and Siberia. Survivors were allowed to return only in 1957 under General Secretary Nikita Krushchev.

The newly reestablished autonomous republic of Chechen-Ingushetia was the most underdeveloped in the Russian Federation, despite its oil resources. Oil was exclusively processed in Grozny, the colonial capital of Chechnya, whose name appropriately means "Fort Terrible" and where Russian settlers were a majority. The Chechens were mostly rural and relatively impoverished, but their numbers grew rapidly and, owing to their conditions, they were increasingly criminalized. Glasnost-era public debates penetrated into Chechen-Ingushetia against great obstacles erected by the local archconservative leadership. By the end of 1990, however, political mobilization finally reached the Chechen countryside, while President Mikhail Gorbachev's discourse of reform critically shifted to the historical ethnic grievances suffered under tsarist Russia and the Stalinist Soviet Union, and, in particular, the genocides of 1859 and 1944. The reactionary coup attempt in Moscow in August 1991 wiped out the Soviet loyalist leadership in Chechen-Ingushetia. In the ensuing tumultuous weeks, radical Chechen nationalists proclaimed full independence despite the objections of Chechen moderate intelligentsia and urban cadres, and the refusal of the Ingush to participate in the assertion of independence.

From 1992 to 1994 Chechnya existed as an unrecognized state whose economy seemed to have critically depended on smuggling and other illicit activities. Dzhokhar Dudayev (or, in its Chechen, spelling Johar Dudaev), former Soviet Air Force general and the vitriolic leader of the Chechen revolution, tried to consolidate his personal tyranny but ran across the well-armed clan militias. Chechnya effectively became an example of a functioning clan-based anarchy.

The Russian government, after failing to reassert its control through surrogates and Russians masquerading as Chechens, used this situation as a pretext for invasion in 1994. Bounded by strong ethnic ties and values, most Chechens were reluctant to fight a civil war against fellow

Chechens. The political ineptitude of President Boris Yeltsin's government led to a prolonged war.

BIBLIOGRAPHY

Goldenberg, Suzanne. *The Pride of Small Nations: The Caucasus and Post-Soviet Disorder.* London: Zed, 1994.
                                                    Luiba Derluguian

SEE ALSO Chechnya: Russo-Chechen War; Dudayev, Dzhokhar

Chechnya: Russo-Chechen War

After five futile attempts to overthrow Dzhozkhar Dudayev, the Chechen rebel leader, Russian President Boris Yeltsin launched a full-scale attack on the breakaway region of Chechnya on December 1994. The last dismal effort on November 26, 1994, in which the Chechens had captured Russian officers and soldiers who were operating in conjunction with opponents of Dudayev, had humiliated the Yeltsin government. Between 1991 and 1994 the Chechens built up a cache of weapons by purchasing or extorting them from Soviet and then Russian units that had been stationed in the Chechen-Ingush Autonomous Republic. The Chechens in the November 26 action, as in others, augmented their supply of weapons with those captured from their opponents.

Pavel Grachev, the Russian minister of defense, took personal control of the Russian operation in late December, deciding to attempt to take a major city street by street. Ignoring the lesson of Stalingrad, he asserted that the city would fall in two hours. On December 31, the day after Dudayev appealed for a cease-fire, Grachev executed an assault on Grozny. As the Russians claimed victory and an end to the fighting, a desperate struggle continued in the streets of the Chechen capital. The presidential palace from which Dudayev commanded the resistance did not fall until January 19. By the end of the month Dudayev and most of the surviving Chechen fighters withdrew from the city and continued resistance from the countryside. The Russians did not seal off the city until February 22, but their artillery and air power eventually dominated that local battlefield. Among widely disparate assessments of casualties, the Russian government's own human rights minister, Sergey Kovalev, stated that 25,000 civilians had died in Grozny and that the Russians suffered 1,800 to 5,000 deaths to the 8,000 dead Chechen fighters.

Shamil Basayev, on June 14, led one hundred Chechen fighters two hundred miles inside Russia, bribing Russian troops along the way, to the city of Budyonnovsk in the Stavropol district. There his men killed sixty policemen and civilians and occupied a hospital seizing two thousand hostages. Viktor Chernomyrdin, the Russian prime minister, negotiated with Basayev on live television for the release of the hostages, allowing the Chechens safe passage back to Chechnya.

The talks between Chernomyrdin and the Chechens led to a partial peace agreement. Dudayev in principle accepted a relationship with the Russian central government similar to that enjoyed by the provincial government of Tatarstan. This agreement proved illusory, generally because of Russian bad faith or the inability of the Russian civilian government to control its local forces.

The Russians seemed determined to impose their will on the Chechens by force. In December 1995 the Russians in a major action took Gudermes, the second-largest city in Chechnya. The incompetence of the Russians, however, was exceeded only by their bad faith and mendacity. On January 9, 1996, a group of Chechen fighters led by Salman Raduyev seized a hospital in the town of Kizlyar in neighboring Daghestan. After agreeing to allow the Chechens and hostages to return to Chechnya, the Russians blocked them at the border and surrounded them in the town of Pervomaiskoye. The Russians, falsely claiming that the Chechens were executing the hostages, attacked. Though a number of civilians were killed in the assault, Raduyev and many of his fighters, plus a number of hostages who felt that their chances were better with the Chechens, slipped through the Russian encirclement.

In February and March the Russian military launched major drives to conclude the campaign. In March, however, Chechen fighters launched a series of coordinated attacks against Grozny, and on April 17 ambushed an armored column fifty kilometers south of the capital. In that attack the Russians lost fifty-three men. But on the night of April 21–22, Dudayev was killed apparently in a rocket attack on the outskirts of the village of Geki Chu. Zelimkhan Yandarbiyev, a cofounder with Dudayev of the All-National Congress of the Chechen People and Chechen vice president, succeeded Dudayev.

Yandarbiyev expressed his willingness to negotiate with the Russians, but the withdrawal of all Russian troops was an absolute precondition. But Yeltsin, desiring a quick resolution to bolster his chances in the impending presidential election, held out for a peace plan he had offered on March 31. It called for a cease-fire and the gradual withdrawal of Russian troops but said that the final determination of the status of Chechnya could be settled later. On May 27 Yandarbiyev met with Yeltsin and Chernomyrdin in Moscow, and signed an agreement terminating hostilities on June 1.

While the Chechen commanders restrained their fighters in the interests of Yeltsin's reelection, the Russian military, unhappy with the agreement, violated the cease-fire. Nevertheless, at a June 10 meeting in Nazran, Ingushetia, Russian Nationalities Minister Vyacheslav Mikhailov and Chechen Chief of Staff Aslan Maskhadov signed an agreement for the withdrawal of Russian troops from Chechnya by the end of August. The Russian military, however, intensified their operations in July and there were no indications that they intended to withdraw. The Chechen leadership decided on a dramatic response.

On August 6 the Chechens under field commander Ruslan Gelayev and led by Basayev launched a concerted and determined attack on Grozny. On the first day the Russians confirmed the loss of four helicopters. The same day Chechen fighters taking advantage of the Russian disarray took the cities of Argun and Gudermes. By August 7 the Chechens controlled key positions in the capital, and by August 8 Basayev claimed full control of the city. In the midst of boastful disinformation from the Russian side, a spokesman for the Russian forces admitted on August 9 that Interior Ministry troops were blockaded in Grozny and that the situation was out of control.

Finally, after first vowing to crush the rebels, Yeltsin on August 10 appointed Aleksandr Lebed, at that time chairman of the Russian Security Council, his plenipotentiary representative in Chechnya. On August 11 Lebed went to Chechnya and conferred with Chechen Chief of Staff Maskhadov. On August 16 Lebed and the separatists agreed to postpone the question of Chechnya's future status until after the solution of the military issues. On August 30 Lt. Gen. Konstantin Pulikovsky revealingly "went on leave," and that night, August 30–31, the final peace agreement was hammered out and signed in Khasavyurt, Dagestan by Lebed and Maskhadov. The agreement called for an end to hostilities and the evacuation of Russian forces, but Chechnya's definitive status would be put in abeyance for five years until 2001. Nevertheless, Chechen fighters believed they gained what they had fought for—independence, at least de facto, from Russia.

BIBLIOGRAPHY

Celestan, Gregory J. "Wounded Bear: The Ongoing Russian Military Operation in Chechnya." ⟨http://leav-www.army.mil/fmso⟩

Colarusso, John. "Chechnya: The War without Winners." *Current History* 94 (October 1995):329–36.

Lieven, Anatol. *Chechnya: Tombstone of Russian Power.* New Haven, Conn.: Yale University Press, 1999.

Tolz, Vera. "The War in Chechnya." *Current History* 95 (October 1996):316–21.

Bernard Cook

SEE ALSO Basayev, Shamil; Dagestan; Dudayev, Dzhokhar; Maskhadov, Aslan

Chernenko, Konstantin Ustinovich (1911–85)

Leader of the Union of Soviet Socialist Republics from February 1984 to March 1985. Konstantin Chernenko was born in Bolshaya Tes, a village in the Krasnoyarsk region of Siberia, on September 24, 1911. He left school at twelve to work for a kulak (well-to-do peasant). In 1926 he joined the Komsomol (Communist Youth League). By 1929 he had become the group's leading propagandist and agitator (agitprop). In 1930 he joined the Border Guards for a three-year stint along the Sino-Soviet frontier. He joined the Communist Party in 1931 and became the secretary of a party cell at a frontier post. After his service with the guard he was appointed head of agitprop for the Novoselovo and Uyar regions, then director of the Krasnoyarsk center for party education, and, finally, deputy head of agitprop for Krasnoyarsk.

At the beginning of World War II Chernenko was secretary of the party in Krasnoyarsk. In 1943 he was sent to study at the Superior School for Party Organizers in Moscow. After graduating in 1945 he became a member of the Penza regional party committee. From 1948 to 1956 he was head of agitprop for the Moldavian SSR. There he was noticed by Leonid Brezhnev, whose patronage made Chernenko's career. Brezhnev promoted Chernenko in 1956 as head of the agitprop department of the Central Committee in Moscow. When Brezhnev became general secretary in 1964, Chernenko became his chief of staff. His ability to remember details was valued by Brezhnev, who referred to his aide and close friend as "my notebook." In 1965 Chernenko was appointed head of the General Department of the Central Committee; in 1971 he became a full member of the Central Committee; in 1976 he became a member of the Party Secretariat; and in 1978 he became a full member of the Politburo. Despite this positioning, facilitated by Brezhnev, Chernenko, after the death of his mentor on November 10, 1982, lost out in the succession struggle. The anti-Brezhnev forces, upset with the corruption, inefficiency, and stagnation that characterized the latter part of his regime, opted for KGB chief Yuri Andropov. Chernenko was ousted from the General Department, but Andropov's purge foundered because of his own deteriorating health. As Andropov weakened, Chernenko's star rose again. His reputation as an administrator and his traditionalism reassured the conservatives, who had opposed Andropov's reform measures. Chernenko's appointment as general secretary on February 13, 1984, four days after the death of Andropov, enabled the conservatives to delay the day of reckoning. Andropov's anticorruption measures and his efforts to decentralize economic planning and create monetary incentives for efficient production were all shelved. The delay was not long. Chernenko's rapidly deteriorating health made him little more than an interim figure. As a sop to the technocratic reformers who had reluctantly agreed to support Chernenko, Mikhail Gorbachev was appointed party ideologist. More quickly than the traditionalists had anticipated, Gorbachev parlayed this position into that of general secretary after the precipitous demise of Chernenko on March 10, 1985.

BIBLIOGRAPHY

Current Biography Yearbook 1984. New York: H. W. Wilson, 1985, pp. 71–75.

Bernard Cook

Chernobyl

Ukrainian city north of Kiev and site of a massive nuclear accident in April 1986. The explosion of Reactor Four at the Chernobyl nuclear power station marked a turning point for the fortunes of both atomic energy and the Soviet system. As a result of the accident, thirty-one people died outright, hundreds of thousands were exposed to high doses of radiation, and large areas of the Soviet Union were contaminated. Soviet mismanagement of the disaster damaged the USSR's reputation at home and abroad. Chernobyl heightened public perceptions of nuclear risk and led many countries to reassess their atomic energy programs.

On April 25, 1986, a test was to be carried out at Reactor Four of the Chernobyl plant during a routine maintenance shutdown. The test program, which was to assess the viability of alternative electrical power supplies in the event of the loss of main power, included numerous actions that violated established nuclear safety regulations. Errors included the disabling of key components of the emergency shutdown system and the inadvertent lowering of reactor power to an unstable level. Flaws in the scheduled test were compounded by particular design features of the reactor itself, a light water-cooled RBMK1000 graphite-moderated unit, which was one of the most dangerous types of nuclear reactors.

During the experiment, plant technicians attempted to manually control the reactor after it reached a dangerous operating state. This intervention made matters worse, and at 1:23 A.M. on April 26, the reactor experienced a surge in power of one hundred times normal operating capacity. The result was a catastrophic steam explosion that blew off the top plate of the reactor, exposing the reactor core to the air. Seconds later, a hydrogen explosion ignited a graphite-moderator fire. Gases from the fire carried melted uranium fuel into the atmosphere. Meteorological and wind conditions transported the radioactive material over much of the Northern Hemisphere.

The causes of the Chernobyl accident and the series of events that led to the destruction of Reactor Four have been the subject of intense inquiry by international committees and individual scientists. Most investigations have pointed to an insufficient level of "safety culture" in both the Chernobyl plant and the Soviet nuclear industry. The reactor's faulty design was unforgiving of operator error, while the technicians themselves betrayed a lack of respect for the potential dangers involved in deviating from established nuclear safety procedures. Moreover, the entire Soviet nuclear industry suffered from shoddy construction materials, chronic supply problems, and insufficient training of personnel. Much of the onus for Chernobyl must also rest on the Soviet Communist Party, which preferenced economic goals over responsible and safe energy production. In sum, the Chernobyl disaster was the product of the myriad curses of the Soviet system in its final stage of decay.

The magnitude of the accident was without precedent, and Soviet officials had no emergency plan in place to cope with such a disaster. Aggressive countermeasures at the plant were generally successful and reduced the threat of additional damage. To contain the graphite fires, helicopters dropped wet sand, boron carbide, lead, and dolomite on the burning reactor. Official Soviet reaction was characterized by delays in notification and underestimation of the scale of the danger. The evacuation of the nearby town of Pripyat and a thirty-kilometer zone around the reactor was delayed nearly thirty-six hours. For two weeks the Kremlin released only limited information about the disaster, and it was not until May 14 that General Secretary Mikhail Gorbachev addressed Soviet citizens on the matter.

The calculation of radiation dose estimates resulting from Chernobyl has sparked considerable controversy, but it is certain that most of the population of the Northern Hemisphere was exposed to some degree. By far the worst affected were the approximately 400 people on site at the time of the accident, including plant workers, firefighters, and medical crews. Of these, 31 died as a result of acute radiation syndrome. The 135,000 evacuees from the thirty-kilometer exclusion zone received significant doses, as did many of the 800,000 people involved in clean-up operations. About 270,000 people still live in contaminated areas, where radiocesium deposition is in excess of 555 kilobecquerels per square meter, the highest level considered safe. Populations outside the former Soviet Union received doses too low to be considered harmful.

The health implications of dose exposure from the Chernobyl accident vary. Those living in areas of contamination, especially children, have experienced increased incidence of carcinoma of the thyroid, which is expected to lead to many thousands of cancer deaths. The same areas have recorded no increases in leukemia, congenital abnormalities, adverse pregnancy outcomes, or any other radiation-induced disease. Over many years, however, public health officials expect increased incidence of genetic diseases, though these may not be statistically measurable or traceable to Chernobyl. The most serious long-term health impact continues to be psychological stress syndrome. Public fears about radiation, a mistrust toward public authorities, and the disruption of social networks and traditional ways of life has exacted a high psychological toll on populations in contaminated areas.

More serious than the direct health impact on humans is the long-term damage to food production and the environment. Large areas of agricultural land within the former Soviet Union must be excluded from productive use for many generations. Restrictions on animal slaughter and food distribution remain in place in some affected areas. Forest environments that lay in the path of fallout will constitute a radiological problem for many years. To date, contamination of ground water has been limited to the thirty-kilometer exclusion zone.

The residual risks posed by the Chernobyl accident are considerable. Seven months after the event, Soviet authorities completed the construction of the "sarcophagus," a massive concrete structure that encases the destroyed reactor. In recent years numerous cracks in the roof have allowed the penetration of rainwater, which is now radioactive. There is some concern that contamination of the water table in the thirty-kilometer zone could threaten the Dnieper River. An independent Ukraine awaits international assistance to repair the sarcophagus and eventually undertake the safe elimination of both the reactor and the large quantity of radioactive waste produced during postaccident countermeasures.

The destruction of the Chernobyl reactor, the worst industrial accident in European history, was and contin-ues to be an event of far-reaching significance. Aside from health consequences and environmental, industrial, and economic damage, Chernobyl has had a profound impact worldwide on public perceptions of nuclear power. After the accident the transboundary implications of nuclear disaster were better understood, and a global campaign in favor of international nuclear regulation and cooperation was launched. The Chernobyl disaster was also a harbinger of the coming demise of the Soviet Union. At Chernobyl, as with the collapse and dissolution of the Soviet empire, a poorly conceived experiment on a faulty system led to the destruction of the entire machine.

BIBLIOGRAPHY

Marples, David. *The Social Impact of the Chernobyl Disaster.* New York: St. Martin's Press, 1988.

Medvedev, Grigori. *The Truth about Chernobyl.* Tr. by Evelyn Rossiter. New York: Basic Books, 1991.

Medvedev, Zhores. *The Legacy of Chernobyl.* New York: Norton, 1990.

Mould, Richard. *Chernobyl: The Real Story.* New York: Pergamon, 1988.

Yaroshinskaya, Alla. *Chernobyl: The Forbidden Truth.* Tr. by Michèle Kahn and Julia Sallabank. Lincoln: University of Nebraska Press, 1995.

Daniel Kowalsky

Chernomyrdin, Viktor Stepanovich (1938–)

Russian prime minister. Viktor Chernomyrdin was born in the village of Cherny Ostrog in the Orenburg region, in 1938. He graduated from Kuybyshev Polytechnic Institute and received a Ph.D. in engineering from the School of Economics of the All-Union Correspondence Polytechnic Institute. He worked at an oil refinery before becoming a member of the staff of the City Committee of the Communist Party in Orsk. He subsequently served as the deputy of the engineer general at Orenburg gas refinery, and eventually became its manager.

From 1978 to 1982 Chernomyrdin served on the staff of the Central Committee of the Communist Party. In 1982 he was appointed a deputy minister of the gas industry and placed in charge of the All-Union Association on Natural Gas Production in the Tyumen region. From 1985 to 1989 Chernomyrdin was in charge of the Ministry of Oil and Gas. In 1989 he became manager of Gazprom, the state petroleum monopoly. He was appointed prime minister of the Russian Federation by President Boris Yeltsin in 1992.

Chernomyrdin advocated firing the minister of defense, Pavel Grachev; the minister of security, Sergey Stepashin; and the minister of interior, Viktor Yerin, after they had, with undue optimism, pushed for the crushing of the rebellion in Chechnya in December 1994. Though Stepashin and Yerin were fired, Yeltsin retained Grachev. In June 1995 Chernomyrdin successfully negotiated an end to a standoff with the leader of one hundred Chechen rebels who had stormed Budennovsk and seized a hospital there along with one thousand hostages.

In May 1995 Chernomyrdin founded the centrist political party, Our Home Is Russia. In the December 1995 Duma election winning 10.13 percent of the party list vote and 12.22 percent of the Duma seats, it became the second-largest faction in the Russian parliament. Despite Yeltsin's health problems, Chernomyrdin decided not to run for president against his boss in 1996, and both Chernomyrdin and Our Home Is Russia campaigned energetically for Yeltsin. After Yeltsin's victory, Chernomyrdin continued in the post of prime minister until Yeltsin's surprise shake-up of the entire government on March 23, 1998, which replaced the veteran Chernomyrdin with a young bureaucrat, Sergey Kiriyenko.

Chernomyrdin and Deputy Prime Minister Anatoly Chubais, the author of Russia's privatization program, had been at increasing loggerheads over economic policy. Chernomyrdin was closely tied to financier and media magnate Boris Berezovsky, who had heavily financed Yeltsin's 1996 presidential campaign but subsequently fell out with the president. Chernomyrdin supported Berezovsky in his opposition to aspects of Chubais's economic policy. Chernomyrdin also increasingly usurped prerogatives of the president during Yeltsin's recurrent illness.

Some analysts asserted that Chernomyrdin was complicit with Yeltsin in a decision that enabled the former to position himself better for the presidential election of 2000. Others saw the move as Yeltsin's revenge against Chernomyrdin's efforts to supplant him; they regarded Yeltsin's assignment to Chernomyrdin of preparation for the presidential campaign as Chernomyrdin's political and economic death warrant.

On August 23, 1998, a week after Kiriyenko's government devalued the ruble to avert financial collapse, Yeltsin dismissed him and announced that he was reappointing Chernomyrdin as prime minister. However, the Duma rejected Yeltsin's attempt. Rather than push the nomination for the third vote, which if rejected again would have plunged the country into a political campaign in the midst of an economic and social crisis and might have led to civil conflict, Yeltsin retreated. On September 10, following negotiations with the Communist-Party leadership, Yeltsin withdrew Chernomyrdin's nomination and nominated Yevgeny Primakov, the foreign minister, who was acceptable to both the Communists and Yeltsin.

Bernard Cook

SEE ALSO Gaidar, Yegor; Kirienko, Sergey; Primakov, Yevgeny; Yeltsin, Boris

Chervenkov, Vŭlko (1900–1980)

Bulgarian Communist leader. Vŭlko Chervenkov was born in Zlatitsa in 1900. He joined the Bulgarian Communist Party (BCP) following World War I. After participating in an attempted Communist coup, the September Uprising of 1923, he was sentenced to death but subsequently was allowed to emigrate to the Soviet Union. In Moscow he attended party schools and worked in the Comintern. Chervenkov was appointed to the Bureau of the Central Committee of the BCP in exile. In 1941 he was placed in charge of the Moscow radio station Christo Botev, which called on Bulgarian Communists and sympathizers to support the Soviet Union's war against Nazi Germany.

Chervenkov, who was the brother-in-law of BCP leader Georgy Dimitrov, was sent back to Bulgaria in October 1944 and, until 1962, was a member of the Politburo. He was a dedicated and convinced Communist who remorselessly pursued the political opponents of the BCP. He was also a dedicated Stalinist and opponent of the home Communists (those who had not spent World War II in the USSR), led by Traicho Kostov. Chervenkov is regarded as the architect of the purge that eliminated these "internal" Communists, who were charged with "national deviation."

After the death of Vassil Kolarov in 1950, Chervenkov became premier but, more important, was elected general secretary of the BCP. He presided over the forced collectivization of Bulgarian agriculture. The death of Stalin in 1953 undermined Chervenkov's position. Todor Zhivkov, with the support of Soviet General Secretary Nikita Khrushchev, progressively displaced Chervenkov from all his posts. Zhivkov, who had risen as a protégé of Chervenkov, replaced his mentor as first secretary of the BCP in 1954. In 1956 following Khrushchev's denunciation of Stalin at the Twentieth Party Congress in Moscow, Chervenkov, accused of promoting his own cult of personality, was replaced as chairman of the Council of Ministers by Anton Tahev Yugov. For a while Chervenkov was deputy chairman of the Council of Ministers, and he remained a member of the Politburo until 1962. Zhivkov not only removed him from the Politburo, but expelled him from the BCP in 1962. Chervenkov died in 1980.

BIBLIOGRAPHY

Lalkov, Milcho. *Rulers of Bulgaria.* Sofia, Bulgaria: Kibea Publishing Company, 1997.

Bernard Cook

SEE ALSO Dimitrov, Georgi; Zhivkov, Todor

Chichester-Clark, James Dawson (Lord Moyola) (1923–)

Ulster Unionist politician and prime minister of Northern Ireland, 1969–71. James Chichester-Clark was born in Castledawson in 1923. He was commissioned into the Irish Guards and served in the Army Staff College. After retiring from the army in 1960 he was elected to the seat in South Derry. He became assistant whip of the Ulster Unionist Party in 1963, chief whip from 1963 to 1969, leader of the house in 1966–67, and minister for agriculture from 1967 to 1969. The attempted reforms of his cousin, Captain Terence O'Neill, provoked Chichester-Clark's resignation from the government and helped to bring about O'Neill's own resignation on April 28, 1969. Chichester-Clark then became leader of the Ulster Unionist Party and also the new prime minister. When sectarian violence erupted in Belfast in August 1969, he requested British troops to help restore order. On August 29 Home Secretary James Callaghan promised reforms in response to demands by the Northern Ireland Civil Rights Association. Chichester-Clark proved unable to contain the increasing violence in 1970 between the Irish Republican Army and Protestant paramilitaries. He was severely criticized by the Rev. Ian Paisley, the militant Unionist leader, who demanded stronger action against the IRA. As the situation continued to deteriorate, Chichester-Clark requested more troops and when this was denied, he resigned on March 20, 1970. He was succeeded by Brian Faulkner.

Ricki Schoen

SEE ALSO Faulkner, Arthur Brian; O'Neill, Terence

Childers, Erskine Hamilton (1905–75)

President of Ireland from 1973 to 1975. Erskine Hamilton Childers was the son of Robert Erskine Childers, who was executed during the Irish Civil War of 1922–23. Childers was educated at Trinity College, Cambridge, then worked as the advertising manager of the pro–Fianna Fail *Irish Press* from 1931 to 1936. He then served as secretary of the Federation of Irish Manufacturers to 1944. He entered politics and was parliamentary secretary for the minister for local government from 1944 to 1948; minister for posts and telegraphs from 1951 to 1954; minister for lands, forestry, and fisheries from 1957 to 1959; minister for transport and power from 1959 to 1966; minister for transport and power, and posts and telegraphs from 1966 to 1969; and *tanaiste,* or vice-premier, and minister for health from 1969 to 1973. He succeeded Eamon de Valera as president of Ireland in 1973. Childers was the second Protestant to serve as president. Douglas Hyde, who was president from 1938 to 1945, was the first. Childers is noted for his condemnation of violence in Northern Ireland and his support for Ireland's membership in the European Community. He died in office and was replaced by Cearbhall O'Dalaigh.

Michael J. Kennedy

Chirac, Jacques (1932–)

French politician, prime minister 1974–76 and 1986–88, and president, 1995–. Born November 29, 1932, in Paris, Jacques Chirac attended the prestigious Lycée Louis-le-Grand. He went on to the Institut d'Études Politiques and the École Nationale d'Administration (ENA), which he left when drafted into the army. Chirac attended officer candidate school then served as an officer in Algeria. He returned to the ENA and graduated in 1959, briefly serving as a civil servant in Algeria. In April 1962, he joined the government secretariat and in November, Prime Minister Georges Pompidou's cabinet.

Chirac became a close associate of Pompidou but, to launch his own political career, in 1964 he went into rural administration in the Department of Corrèze, where he eventually served in a series of elective posts. These were the basis for a series of national ministerial positions that led to his being named premier in May 1974 by President Valéry Giscard d'Estaing, a post he held until his resignation in August 1976.

Chirac shared Charles de Gaulle's nationalist view of France's role in Europe and the world, and this led him in 1976 to found the Rally for the Republic, a political party to perpetuate the general's legacy. Although Chirac's Gaullists were part of Giscard's right-wing coalition in the National Assembly, in reality the two were rivals. In 1977 Chirac humiliated Giscard by easily defeating the president's hand-picked candidate for mayor of Paris.

In 1981 Mayor Chirac ran for the presidency against the incumbent Giscard, whom he attacked as being soft on the Soviet Union; he also condemned Giscard for his handling of the economy. Chirac proposed smaller government, fewer regulations for business, and paring the government bureaucracy. In the April balloting he came in third with 18 percent, behind President Giscard with 19 percent and Socialist challenger François Mitterrand with 26 percent. In the May runoff Mitterrand went on to beat Giscard.

After a March 1986 rightist victory in the National Assembly elections, Socialist President Mitterrand asked Chirac to form a government. He served as premier between March 1986 and May 1988 in an uneasy arrangement between Left and Right known as cohabitation.

In 1988 Chirac again ran for the presidency. Mitterrand let his three rightist opponents—Chirac, Raymond Barre, and ultrarightist Jean-Marie Le Pen—slug it out in preelection maneuvering so that he could appear as the nation's unifier. Chirac joined Mitterrand in the runoff but lost to him by 46 to 54 percent.

In 1993 Chirac could have claimed the premiership after the conservatives scored a smashing triumph in the March National Assembly elections, but he believed the post of mayor of Paris was a better platform for a presidential run. Édouard Balladur, also of the Rally for the Republic, became premier. Chirac expected Balladur to assist his campaign for the presidency, but Balladur decided he wanted the office as well, and both men ended up running in the presidential election of 1995 to replace the retiring President Mitterrand. In the process they split the rightist vote.

In the campaign Chirac presented himself as the agent of change and criticized Balladur, hurt by charges of corruption and wiretapping, as the candidate of "immobilism." Chirac also attacked Balladur for making control over French budget deficits and inflation a priority over solving unemployment.

Balladur led the early polling but Chirac overtook him. In the April elections Socialist Lionel Jospin came in first with 23 percent of the vote; Chirac was second with 21 percent, and Balladur was third with 19 percent. But Balladur urged his supporters to vote for Chirac, who easily won the May 7 runoff against Jospin to become the first Gaullist president of France since 1974.

President Chirac soon found himself in difficulty. He had come to power on a platform of reducing growing budget deficits. The economy was top-heavy, with government employees reaping such generous benefits that it was difficult for the private sector to create new jobs. Unemployment remained stubbornly high at 13 percent, and the annual budget deficit approached 6 percent of gross domestic product (GDP), twice the level allowed under the Maastricht Treaty, which had stipulated the economic prerequisites for participating in the common European currency.

Gripped by a sense of urgency, Chirac and Premier Alain Juppé attempted in the fall of 1995 to push through a series of reforms that would over a two-year period raise taxes and slash government spending by more than $55 billion. By far the most onerous task was to overhaul the French health-care system. Cuts were also scheduled in transportation, where there were thousands of miles of idle rural track and a large deficit. The government also announced a plan to increase the retirement age to sixty-five from sixty and increase to forty from thirty-seven the number of years a worker had to contribute to the system to receive its highest benefit. Juppé also promised to privatize France Telecom, the nation's telephone system, and Air France, the national airline. Social security taxes, the value-added tax, and corporate taxes were all to be increased.

The result was an explosion of labor unrest across France, with hundreds of thousands demonstrating their opposition. Mass transport workers went on strike and Paris became one vast parking lot. Many government workers and teachers also struck, and students demonstrated in Paris for increased spending on universities. Demonstrations and shutdowns were not confined to Paris, however, as tens of thousands of people followed suit in other cities. Although Juppé and Chirac initially announced they would hold firm, the intensity and longevity of the protests forced Juppé to announce in early December that he was willing to negotiate over the reforms, with the result that the demonstrations and strikes soon ended. Still, it was hard to see how the reforms could be enacted without considerable economic pain to French taxpayers.

Chirac did bring credit to himself for finally accepting France's responsibility for the Vichy government's World War II roundup and deportation of French Jews to German death camps. In foreign affairs Chirac supported Western intervention in Bosnia, where France had the largest number of peacekeepers on the ground, but he differed with the U.S. approach to bring the warring parties to the negotiating table through the use of air power. Chirac also restored France to NATO's military command (terminated by de Gaulle) and took steps toward integrating France's nuclear forces with those of its European and Atlantic allies.

Not all of Chirac's initiatives in foreign affairs went well. He ordered a series of nuclear tests in the South Pacific, ending a three-year moratorium proclaimed by Mitterrand. This resumption undermined efforts to restrain China from nuclear testing. The six nuclear explosions France set off over a five-month period provoked anger toward France in Europe, but particularly among Pacific Rim nations, and led Chirac to halt the program in December, two tests and four months earlier than planned.

In February 1996, Chirac, who professed deep affection for the United States, traveled to Washington in the first state visit by a French president there in twelve years. In a speech to a joint meeting of Congress, Chirac stressed the close relations between the two countries.

BIBLIOGRAPHY
Agulhon, Maurice. *The French Republic, 1879–1992.* Tr. by Antonia Nevill. Oxford: Blackwell, 1993.

Spencer C. Tucker

SEE ALSO Balladur, Édouard; Barre, Raymond; De Gaulle, Charles; Giscard d'Estaing, Valéry; Jospin, Lionel; Juppé, Alain; Le Pen, Jean-Marie; Mitterrand, François

Chornovil, Viacheslav Maksymovych (1938–99)

Ukrainian journalist, dissident, politician, and leading opposition figure. Viacheslav Maksymovych Chornovil was born on January 1, 1938, in Soviet, Ukraine. He received a degree in journalism from Taras Shevchenko Kiev State University in 1960. He worked in Lvov (Ukrainian, L'viv) as a journalist and editor of youth radio and television programming from 1960 to 1963. From 1963 to 1965 he was leader of the Komsomol (Communist Youth Organization) in Kiev. During that time he was section editor for the newspaper *Moloda Hvardia* and a literary critic while pursuing graduate studies at the Kiev Pedagogical Institute. He learned about the dissident movement during the course of his work by covering trials of dissidents. In 1965 Chornovil was fired from his job for his own involvement in the dissident movement. In 1967 he became a member of an environmental group in Lvov, and began the underground publishing of the *Ukrainian Herald*. He prepared a collection of materials about twenty Ukrainian dissidents who were imprisoned for protesting against the repression of the Ukrainian nationality by the Soviet Union, national oppression, which was entitled *Lykho z rozumu* and was subsequently published in Paris in 1978, then translated into English as *The Chornovil Papers*. He was arrested and imprisoned from 1967 to 1969, 1972 to 1979, and 1980 to 1983. Chornovil was a member of the Ukrainian Helsinki Group from 1979, and its co-leader from 1987. During this time he revived publication of the *Ukrainian Herald.* He was a leading figure in RUKH, the Ukrainian pro-democracy and pro-independence movement during the glasnost era in the Soviet Union Chornovil attended the founding congress of RUKH in 1989 and was elected to the leadership of the Lvov (L'viv in Ubrainian) parliament in the March 1990 elections. He became head of the democratic political movement in western Ukraine. An executive member of the Memorial Society from 1990, Chornovil came in second in the presidential race of December 1991. He was elected co-leader of RUKH 1992, after which he resigned his seat in Lvov and moved to Kiev. He was deputy head of the Parliamentary Openness and Information Committee from 1992 and editor in chief of RUKH's newspaper, *Chas.* Chornovil was reelected to parliament in the 1994 and 1998 elections, and after 1998 was head of the Parliamentary Committee on Historical and Cultural Heritage. He was replaced as the RUKH parliamentary faction leader in February 1999 and his position as RUKH leader was being challenged at the time of his death in an automobile accident on March 25, 1999. Chornovil's publications include *la nichoho u vas ne proshu* (I *Ask Nothing of You,* 1968) and *Budni mordovs'kykh taboriv* (*Daily Life in the Mordovian Prison Camps,* 1976).

Marta Dyczok

SEE ALSO Kravchuk, Leonid

Chubais, Anatoly (1955–)

Russian champion of privatization who served as first deputy prime minister from November 1994 to January 1996 and again in 1997. Anatoly Borisovich Chubais was born in 1955. He graduated from the Leningrad Institute of Technology and Engineering. From 1977 to 1982 he was assistant chairperson of the Institute of Economics and Engineering in Leningrad. In 1982 he became a member of the Municipal Council of Leningrad. In 1991 he became the first deputy chair of the Russian legislature. He left the Communist Party after the abortive coup of August 1991 against President Mikhail Gorbachev. That same year he was appointed minister of state property and as such was placed in charge of launching the program of privatization. In 1994 he became minister of economics and, after the resignation of reformer Aleksandr Shokhin, was appointed first deputy prime minister in November. Chubais, like his predecessor and mentor Yegor Gaidar, faced almost intractable problems of systemic corruption and tax evasion. The conservatives whom President Boris Yeltsin brought into the government in 1995 favored protectionist measures and continued subsidies to inefficient state industries. Economic problems, including inflation, were compounded by the futile and costly Chechen war. In January 1996 Yeltsin replaced Chubais with conservative Vladimir Kadannikov.

Chubais's star rose again as a result of his service to Yeltsin's presidential campaign in 1996, though serious questions were raised about his direction of the campaign. Yeltsin's campaign reputedly spent around $100 million when the campaign law allowed only $2.9 million. Chubais was accused of lying when two aides were caught carrying a box containing $538,000 out of the Kremlin. However, Yeltsin sided with Chubais and fired his security chief, Aleksandr Korzhakov, who had ordered the arrest of Chubais's associates. In July after Yeltsin's victory he was appointed Yeltsin's chief of staff and again made first deputy prime minister. In November 1997 he was taken to task by Yeltsin, reputedly for accepting an advance on a book concerning privatization, and fired from his post as finance minister. On March 22, 1998, he was ousted from the cabinet. However, in April he was appointed head of the state energy monopoly, Energy Systems. In summer 1998 he reentered the government as Russia's chief negotiator with the IMF. Yet he was ousted from that position in August. The IMF package, which he negotiated, was blamed by Russians for undermining the ruble, which had to be devalued. Chubais became one of the victims of the ensuing political crisis, which the conservatives blamed partially on him and he blamed on the policies and failures of his predecessors.

BIBLIOGRAPHY

Quinn-Judge, Paul, "Wolves on the Prowl: Men of Power are feasting on the Spoils of Russia," *Time* (Canadian Ed), July 7, 1999.
Reddaway, Peter. "Beware the Russian Reformer." *Washington Post*, August 24, 1997.
"Russia's Reforms in Trouble: the Humbling of Chubais," *Economist*, July 7, 1999.

Bernard Cook

SEE ALSO Gaidar, Yegor; Korzhakov, Aleksandr

Churchill, Winston (1874–1965)

Conservative prime minister of the United Kingdom, 1940–45 and 1951–55. Winston Leonard Spencer Churchill came to prominence as a soldier and author before the turn of the century, entering Parliament in 1900 and rising to home secretary in 1910. From 1911 to 1915 he was first lord of the Admiralty, and from 1924 to 1929 chancellor of the exchequer. Widely distrusted in the

1930s as a hot head, he warned against appeasing the fascist powers and returned to lead Britain through World War II. After his defeat in the 1945 election he warned of the dangers of Soviet expansion, though when reelected in 1951, he sought to end the Cold War. Churchill believed profoundly in the British Empire, the greatness of Britain, and the necessity of Anglo-American friendship. He built and sustained this alliance with his wartime speeches and diplomacy, and personified the determination and victory of the Allies.

Churchill was born November 30, 1874. Son of an American heiress, Jeanette ("Jennie") Jerome, and Lord Randolph Churchill, a Conservative politician, Churchill followed a career shaped by his parents. His father ignored him, and Churchill's relentless ambition and bouts with depression are thought to have owed much to his need to vindicate himself. He attended Harrow from 1888 to 1892, where he excelled in subjects that interested him but did poorly in those that did not, and the Royal Military College at Sandhurst from 1893 to 1895, which he found more congenial. He joined the Fourth Hussars, a cavalry regiment, and from 1896 to 1898 was posted to India, where he saw action on the North-West Frontier, an experience that provided the material for his first book, *The Story of the Malakand Field Force* (1898). Throughout his life, Churchill needed the income that his unceasing writing provided.

In 1898 Churchill's mother arranged his transfer to General Horatio Herbert Kitchner's army in the Sudan, which he joined in time to participate in the famous cavalry charge at the battle of Omdurman. In the fall of 1899 he went as a newspaper correspondent to South Africa, where the Boer War had just broken out. While accompanying an armored train into enemy territory, he was captured by the Boers. He soon escaped and made his way back to British territory, and hence to Britain, where he received a hero's welcome. He stood at Oldham as a Conservative in October 1900 and was elected.

Churchill had joined the Conservatives in deference to the memory of his father, but in his support for social reform and a vigorous foreign policy he was closer to the Liberal imperialists. When Joseph Chamberlain's crusade for industrial tariffs split the Conservatives, Churchill, a devout believer in free trade, joined the Liberals in May 1904. When that party came to power in December he received the post of undersecretary of state at the Colonial Office, where he worked to grant responsible government to his former captors in the Transvaal.

In 1908 Churchill married Clementine Hozier and, in the same year, joined the cabinet by accepting the office of president of the Board of Trade. In February 1910, after the Liberals gained a narrow election victory, he was promoted to home secretary, where he was a humanitarian reformer, though he was criticized by Labour for sending troops to a riot at Tonypandy in November 1910. During the Moroccan Crisis in the summer of 1911, triggered by the dispatch of a gun boat to the port of Agadir, he became worried by Germany's belligerence and the British navy's deficiencies. In October 1911 he moved to the Admiralty, where he worked to modernize and enlarge the navy.

When war broke out in August, 1914, the navy was ready. Churchill's attempt to hold Antwerp, Belgium, was ridiculed, but the navy transported the British Expeditionary Force to France without loss of life. This success could not counterbalance the failure of the attack on the Dardanelles in 1915. When this campaign led Admiral of the Fleet Lord Fisher to resign in May 1915, the ensuing political crisis resulted in the formation of a coalition government and Churchill's fall from power. For five months in 1916 he served in the trenches on the western front. He returned to office as minister for munitions in 1917–18 and held further posts through 1922, but his advocacy of intervention against the Bolsheviks in 1919 seemed to confirm the impression of many that his judgment was unsound.

From 1922 to 1924 Churchill lost three elections. The Liberal Party was disintegrating and Churchill rejoined the Conservatives in 1925, shortly after being elected for Epping in late 1924. When he returned to Parliament he was brought into the government as chancellor of the exchequer, a post he filled until 1929. Churchill was an indifferent chancellor; his most famous decision was to return Britain to the gold standard in 1925, which further strained the nation's already laboring economy.

When Labour won the 1929 election Churchill was consigned to the back benches, where he remained until 1939. From 1929 through 1935 he campaigned against the proposal, backed by both Labour and the Conservatives, to grant India central self-government. His description of Gandhi as a "seditious Middle Temple lawyer" alienated Labour; his attacks on Conservative leader Stanley Baldwin lost him the respect of his former colleagues. Churchill believed that "giving up" India would diminish the grandeur of Britain, and he felt an India divided by its religions was unfit for self-government.

His intemperate attacks slowed but could not stop the India Bill of 1935. They did, however, deprive him of his remaining credibility. Thus his warnings, which began in 1932, that Germany was rearming and would seek revenge for its loss in 1918 went largely unheard. Churchill was not opposed to revising the Versailles Treaty, which ended World War I, but wanted to do so from a position of strength and Allied unity. From 1932 onward he attacked the Baldwin and Chamberlain governments for their policy of appeasement, but his strictures were not always justified. Given the disparity between Britain's commitments and resources, a measure of appeasement was inglorious but necessary. Yet the essential fact remains that, far earlier than most, Churchill perceived the true nature of the Nazi regime.

After Churchill's prophetic speech against the Munich Pact on October 5, 1938, he began to win converts. When war broke out in Europe on September 1, 1939, after Germany's attack on Poland, Chamberlain reluctantly brought Churchill into the government and returned him to the Admiralty. Churchill urged that the war be prosecuted more vigorously, but the April 1940 campaign in Norway, which he backed, was a costly failure. It rebounded on Chamberlain, whose support in Commons was fading. Labour refused to serve in a coalition with him, and as German troops poured into France on May 10, 1940, Churchill became prime minister.

The first year of the war was Churchill's finest hour. He was a harsh taskmaster and prone to flights of strategy, but he kicked the government into high gear and inspired the nation with his call on May 13 for "blood, toil, tears and sweat." During the Battle of Britain—Germany's air assault on the British Isles—which raged over the summer, he spoke repeatedly to the Commons and the world, projecting indomitable purpose and unshakable confidence. This was more than rhetoric. It helped U.S. President Franklin Roosevelt win passage of the Lend-Lease Bill in March 1941. After the Soviet Union in June 1941 and the United States the following December entered the war, Churchill was sure that the defeat of the Axis powers was inevitable.

Churchill was right, but 1942 brought more defeats. Already expelled from Europe, Britain was threatened by German U-boat attacks on the convoys from America and pushed out of its empire east of India by the Japanese, a calamity that Churchill found particularly mortifying. Slowly, though, the resources of the Allies turned the tide. Churchill was always conscious of the need to maintain the alliance, but this meant that, as Britain's contribution to the war was surpassed by those of the emerging superpowers of the United States and the USSR, he was increasingly overshadowed. Yet in spite of serious disagreements over strategy and the future of the postwar world, the Allies stuck to the task at hand and Churchill, though exhausted and ill, remained the symbol of their determination.

When Germany surrendered unconditionally in May 1945, the coalition government broke up and, to the world's surprise, Churchill lost the ensuing election. The voters wanted Labour to direct the social reforms promised for the postwar years. From 1945 to 1951 Churchill worked on his war memoirs and allowed the younger figures in the party to refurbish its image. For his part, Churchill urged the creation of a "United States of Europe," including Germany, to resist the Soviet Union. He thus won a reputation as a founder of the European Union, even though he did not believe Britain was a European nation and did not suggest it should join this new "United States." Churchill's greatest cause was Anglo-American unity in the nascent rivalry with the USSR; in a speech at Fulton, Missouri, on March 5, 1946, he warned of the "iron curtain" that had descended across Eastern Europe. Protests were raised around the world against Churchill's supposed warmongering, but he proved as prescient as he had been in the 1930s.

In the election of October 1951 the Conservatives defeated Labour. In many respects it was unfortunate, both for Britain and for Churchill's reputation, that he served again as prime minister. Old and tired, he suffered from a stroke in 1953 that was concealed from the public. Without the war to provide direction, he allowed the government and nation to drift. At home and in the empire, his aim was essentially to keep things quiet; his return did nothing to puncture the illusions about Britain's place in the world that victory in the war had fostered. Churchill was created a Knight of the Garter in 1953 and in the same year won the Nobel Prize in literature.

Churchill thought little of the award; he wanted to win the Peace Prize. To the growing exasperation of his colleagues, he remained in office until April 1955, in the hopes of bringing about a four-power meeting with the Soviets and so ending the Cold War, a noble but unrealistic aim. Britain no longer had the necessary power to serve as the world's arbiter. After Churchill resigned he spent his last years writing his *A History of the English-Speaking Peoples* and receiving tokens of public recognition. On January 10, 1965, he suffered another stroke. He died two weeks later and was buried at the parish church at Bladon. His postwar successor, Clement Attlee, described him as "the greatest Englishman of our time."

By the time of his death many of Churchill's causes had failed or faded. The empire was gone and Britain had lost its greatness. These causes were of the Victorian Age into which Churchill was born; he could not save them. His hopes were anachronisms, but it was the very fact that he belonged to and sympathized with a bygone age that enabled him to rally Britain in the most critical year of 1940. In the course of his long political life he inevitably sustained more defeats and supported more lost causes than he won victories, but his victories helped save the Western democracies and shape the modern world.

BIBLIOGRAPHY

Addison, Paul. *Churchill on the Home Front, 1900–1955.* London: Jonathan Cape, 1992.

Blake, Robert, and William Roger Louis, eds. *Churchill.* New York: Norton, 1993.

Charmley, John. *Churchill, The End of Glory: A Political Biography.* London: Hodder & Stoughton, 1993.

Churchill, Randolph S., and Martin Gilbert. *Winston S. Churchill.* 8 Vols., 15 companion vols. London: William Heinemann, 1966–.

Churchill, Winston. *My Early Life, 1874–1904.* New York: Simon & Schuster (1930), 1996.

———. *The Second World War.* 6 Vols. Boston: Houghton Mifflin, 1948–1953.

Colville, John. *The Fringes of Power: Downing Street Diaries, 1939–1955.* London: Hodder & Stoughton, 1985.

James, Robert Rhodes. *Churchill: A Study in Failure, 1900–1939.* London: Weidenfeld & Nicolson, 1970.

Rose, Norman. *Churchill: An Unruly Life.* London: Simon & Schuster, 1994.

Young, John W. *Winston Churchill's Last Campaign: Britain and the Cold War, 1951–55.* Oxford: Clarendon Press, 1996.

Public and Personal Papers, 1874–1965, Churchill Archives Centre, Churchill College, Cambridge.

Ted R. Bromund

SEE ALSO Attlee, Clement

Chygir, Mikhail N. (1948–)

Prime minister of Belarus. Mikhail Chygir was born on May 24, 1948. He attended the Minsk State Institute of National Economy and the Financial Institute in Moscow. He worked in the banking system in Belarus between 1970 and 1986. In 1986 and 1987 he was the director of the Minsk branch of the USSR State Bank. From 1988 to 1991 he was first deputy chairman of the board of Agroprombank, and in 1991 he became chairman of the board of the commercial bank Belgagroprombank.

He served as prime minister of Belarus from July 1994 to 1996 when he was succeeded by Syarhei Linh.

Bernard Cook

Cimoszewicz, Włodzimierz (1951–)

On February 1, 1996, he became post-Communist Poland's seventh prime minister. Włodzimierz Cimoszewicz, an expert in international law and a farmer, was nominated on January 31, 1996, by the governing coalition of the Democratic Left Alliance and the Polish Peasants Party to replace Józef Oleksy, who was forced to resign after being accused of spying for the Soviet Union. Cimoszewicz at the time of his nomination was deputy speaker of parliament and a leader of the strong ex-Communist caucus, but he did not belong to a political party. He was considered to be independent of President Aleksander Kwasniewski's Social Democrats who dominated the Democratic Left Alliance. Following the victory of the right in the 1997 parliamentary election, Cimoszewicz was succeeded by Jerzy Buzek of Solidarity Electoral Action.

Bernard Cook

Claes, Willy (1938–)

Belgian politician and secretary-general of NATO. Willy Claes was born in Hasselt, Belgium, on November 24, 1938. An accomplished musician and conductor, Claes chose a career in politics. In 1964 he was elected to the city council of Hasselt and in 1968 entered the Belgian parliament as a Socialist deputy. In 1972 he was appointed minister of education in the government of Gaston Eyskens. He served a number of times as minister of economic affairs: during the 1973 Leburton-De Clercq-Tindemans coalition; in 1977 in the second Tindemans cabinet; from 1978 to 1982 in four governments headed by Wilfred Martens; and in the cabinet of Mark Eyskens, where he also held the position of deputy prime minister.

Claes was appointed minister of state by King Baudouin in December 1983. From 1988 to 1992, he served as deputy prime minister and minister of economic affairs in the government of Martens. In March 1992 Claes was appointed deputy prime minister and minister of foreign affairs in the government of Jean-Luc Dehaene.

In September 1994, following the death of Manfred Wörner, Claes was nominated by the NATO foreign ministers to become the new secretary-general of the organization. He assumed that position on October 17, 1994. Claes laid the groundwork for the expansion of NATO into Eastern Europe and for the replacement of U.N. forces in Bosnia with a fifty-thousand–person NATO peacekeeping force. Following accusations of involvement in a defense contract bribery scandal when he was a Belgian minister, the Belgian parliament removed Claes's parliamentary immunity. One day later, on October 20, 1995, he resigned as secretary-general of NATO. He was succeeded by Javier Solana. In December 1998 Claes was found guilty of authorizing the acceptance of a $1.37 bribe from an Italian manufacturer of helicopters. He was sentenced to a three year suspended prison sentence and forbidden to hold public office for five years.

BIBLIOGRAPHY

Claes, Willy. *Tussen droom en werkelijkheid: bouwstenen voor een ander Europa.* Antwerp: Standaard Wetenschappelijke Uitgeverij, 1979.

———. *Crisisbestrijding: een socialistische benadering.* Brussels: Studie-en Documentatiecentrum, Emile Vandervelde Instituut, 1975.

Whitney, Craig R., "Belgium Convicts 12 for Corruption on Military Contracts," *New York Times,* December 24, 1998.

Bernard Cook

SEE ALSO Cools, André; North Atlantic Treaty Organization; Solana, Javier; Wörner, Manfred

Claus, Hugo (1929–)

Belgian writer. Hugo Claus is generally considered the most important Flemish author since 1945. He has written poetry, novels, short stories, and plays. In addition he is a painter and has directed movies. Claus made his debut as a poet in 1948 and soon became the most important renewer of postwar Flemish poetry. His vital and spontaneous poetry was closely related to the work of his Dutch "experimental" contemporaries and friends, such as Lucebert and Gerrit Kouwenaar, and to the art of the Cobra movement, especially that of Karel Appel and Met Corneille. His poetic development after 1960 shows a great variety of styles and genres. Confessional lyricism, satire, and adaptations of older poetry alternate with intricate linguistic constructions.

In every literary genre Claus is a master in absorbing and adapting materials from high and low culture, from history and myth. He uses them to express his central theme, the oedipal relations between man and woman and child and father, and the human being confronting the power of law, fate, and God. In his most important novels, *De verwondering* (*The Astonishment,* 1962) and *Het verdriet van Belgie* (*The Sorrow of Belgium,* 1983, tr. 1990), he links this family theme with the social and political history of Flanders. His plays, which form the bulk of his work, show the same diversity of genres, from naturalist tragedy to burlesque satire, with an overall tragicomic tone. Here, too, many international influences can be traced, among them Antonin Artaud, Samuel Beckett, and Tennessee Williams. These are, of course, most evident in his many adaptations of the plays of others, including Euripides, Sophocles, Seneca, and Shakespeare. He has been awarded almost every literary prize in Holland and Flanders. The most important was the Prigs der Nederlandse Letteren in 1986.

BIBLIOGRAPHY
Claus, Hugo. *The Sorrow of Belgium.* Tr. by Arnold Pomerans. New York: Penguin, 1991.

Hugo Brems

Clay, Lucius D. (1897–1978)

Deputy military governor of the American zone of occupation in Germany (1945–47) and commander of U.S. forces in Europe and military governor of the U.S. zone of occupation (1947–49). General Lucius D. Clay played a pivotal role in the physical and political recovery of West Germany. After the Soviet Union severed land routes to West Berlin in June 1948, Clay organized and supervised the Berlin Airlift. He is credited with saving Berliners from starvation and saving the city for the West. Clay's participation in the 1948–49 airlift has overshadowed his accomplishments during the occupation of Germany.

Clay, the youngest child of Senator Alexander Stephens Clay of Georgia, was born on April 23, 1898. After graduating from West Point in 1918, Clay entered the Army Corps of Engineers. He developed his political skills in Washington, D.C., during the New Deal era while serving as the corps spokesperson on Capitol Hill and as assistant to Harry Hopkins at the Works Progress Administration.

In March 1942 General George C. Marshall selected Clay to direct the vast wartime military procurement program. This post secured his promotion to brigadier general, and at forty-three he was the youngest general in the U.S. Army. In November General Dwight D. Eisenhower called Clay to Europe to untangle supply. He then became deputy director of the Office of War Mobilization and Reconversion in December 1944.

In April 1945 General Marshall chose Clay to serve under General Eisenhower as deputy military governor of the American occupation zone in Germany; and in March 1947 Clay became commander of U.S. forces and military governor. In these posts he constantly fought to ensure humane treatment for the defeated German people. To better coordinate services, Clay secured the transfer of the military government from Army control to the War Department. Clay sought to establish a foundation for an enduring democratic society by overcoming massive food shortages and encouraging an early return to local German self-government. He believed that the German economy needed to be revived, the country unified, and the occupation terminated.

Clay initially held that cooperation with the Soviet Union in Germany was essential, but as Soviet intransigence toward Western economic proposals increased, he favored a "get tough" policy with the Soviets. Pressure mounted in early 1948, and on June 28, 1948, the Soviets closed the last rail link to Berlin, a move designed to leave the Allies no choice but to give up either Berlin or the plan to unify West Germany. Clay recommended a strong stance and initiated the airlift to Berlin on his own authority. Endorsed by President Truman, the airlift demonstrated Western resolve. During the airlift Clay pushed German politicians and Allied officials to compromise on the new constitution, known as the Basic Law. Clay returned to the United States and retired from active service in 1949.

Clay then pursued a successful corporate career. He also served a senior government adviser on German matters and acted as President Kennedy's personal representative to Berlin from September 1961 to May 1962. He died on April 16, 1978.

BIBLIOGRAPHY
Clay, Lucius D. *Decision in Germany.* Garden City, N.Y.: Doubleday, 1950.
———. *Germany and the Fight for Freedom.* Cambridge, Mass.: Harvard University Press, 1950.
Smith, Jean Edward, ed. *The Papers of General Lucius Clay, Germany 1945–1949.* 2 Vols. Bloomington: Indiana University Press, 1974.
———. *Lucius D. Clay: An American Life.* New York: Holt, 1990.

Mark Beasley

SEE ALSO Berlin Blockade; Germany, Federal Republic of

Clementis, Vladimír (1902–52)

Czechoslovak Communist and foreign minister from 1948 to 1950. Vladimír Clementis was born in Tisovec (Slovakia), Austria-Hungary on September 20, 1902. An early adherent of the Czechoslovak Communist Party, Clementis was a political journalist and served as editor of *Dav,* a journal that published the work of leftist writers and had broad influence, particularly among Slovaks. In 1935 Clementis was elected to the Czechoslovak parliament as a Communist delegate. When the Germans occupied what was left of Czechoslovakia in March 1939, Clementis crossed into Poland. When he arrived in Britain he was for a time interned in Scotland. In 1942 Clementis was appointed by Edvard Beneš to the Czechoslovak National Council operating in exile in London. After the liberation of Czechoslovakia Clementis became the Czech vice minister of foreign affairs. He played a leading role in the Czech Communist coup in 1948 and became foreign minister following the death of Ján Masaryk.

Clementis was a victim of the Stalinist purges. He was forced to resign as foreign minister in 1950. Together with Rudolf Slánský, secretary-general of the Czechoslovak Communist Party, and nine others, Clementis was convicted of "Titoism" and "national deviation," and hung on December 3, 1952. In 1963 he was posthumously rehabilitated by the Czechoslovakia Communist Party.

BIBLIOGRAPHY

Dubcek, Alexander. *Hope Dies Last.* Ed. and Tr. by Jiri Hochman. New York: Kondansha International, 1993.

Pelikan, Jiri, ed. *The Czechoslovak Political Trials, 1950–1954: The Suppressed Report of the Dubcek Government's Commission of Inquiry, 1968.* Stanford: Stanford University Press, 1971.

Bernard Cook

SEE ALSO Czechoslovakia

Clerides, Glafcos (1919–)

President of the Republic of Cyprus. Glafcos Clerides was born in Nicosia on April 24, 1919. His father, Yiannis Clerides, was a prominent lawyer. In 1939 Clerides volunteered for service in the British Royal Air Force. He was shot down over Germany in 1942 and spent the rest of the war in a German prisoner-of-war camp. After the war he studied law at King's College of the University of London. He practiced law in Cyprus from 1951 to 1960. He also served in the Greek Cypriot nationalist movement EOKA from 1955 to 1959 and defended captured EOKA members in court. He prepared an account of British human rights violations that was submitted by the Greek government to the Council of Europe's Human Rights Commission.

Clerides participated in the 1959 London Conference dealing with the issue of Cyprus and served as minister of justice in the transitional regime. After independence

he was elected to the Cypriot House of Representatives and was subsequently elected president of that body.

He again represented the Greek Cypriots at the 1964 London Conference on Cyprus. In 1974, when President Makarios was forced to flee in the face of an attempted coup, Clerides, in accord with the constitution, temporarily assumed presidential functions. He did this from July 23 until Makarios's return on December 7.

In February 1969 Clerides had founded the Unified Party, but in May 1976, with members of the Unified Party, the Progressive Front, and the Democratic National Party, he formed the Democratic Rally Party. He headed the parliamentary caucus of the Democratic Rally until his election as president on February 14, 1993.

BIBLIOGRAPHY

"Glafcos Clerides." ⟨http://www.cyprus-online.com/clerides/⟩

Bernard Cook

Cod Wars

Series of fishing disputes between Iceland and its neighbors, especially Britain. The first conflict over the Icelandic fishing grounds in the post–World War II years began in 1950–52, when the Icelandic government extended the Icelandic fishing limits from three to four nautical miles, in addition to closing off all bays and fjords around the country to foreign fishermen. Although a number of states that had traditionally fished around Iceland protested this action, only the British government acted directly against the extension, embargoing fish from Iceland. This seriously affected the Icelandic economy and the fisheries in particular, because Britain had been the most important export market for Icelandic fish products for most of the twentieth century. The long-term effect, however, was to divert Icelandic exports to the United States, which replaced Britain as Iceland's most important trading partner in the 1950s.

The next phase in this struggle for control over the Icelandic fishing grounds began in 1958, when the Icelandic government moved the fishing limits out to twelve nautical miles. The same year, the U.N. effort to revise the law of the sea broke down, and therefore the legal basis for the extension was doubtful at best. This time Britain used the Royal Navy to protect its fishermen inside the new Icelandic fishing limits, but fishing under the protection of warships proved to be impractical. The conflict came to an end in 1961 when Britain signed a treaty with Iceland, recognizing the Icelandic fishing limits in return for a temporary permission to fish inside the Icelandic limits.

Since the passing of the so-called Scientific Conservation of the Fisheries of the Continental Shelf Act in 1948, the official policy of the Icelandic government had been to expel all foreign fishing vessels from the fishing grounds around Iceland. This goal was fully realized in the 1970s, when the fishing limits were extended from twelve to two hundred nautical miles in two steps, first from twelve to fifty miles in 1972 and then to two hundred miles in 1975. Both these extensions were strongly opposed by the nations most seriously affected, in particular Britain and West Germany. The European Economic Community (EEC) responded to the first extension by embargoing imports of Icelandic fish in European harbors in 1972, and by suspending negotiated reductions in tariffs on Icelandic fish products imported to EEC countries. Moreover, in 1972 the British government dispatched a navy squadron to the Icelandic fishing grounds to protect British trawlers from harassment by the Icelandic Coast Guard. After threatening to cut diplomatic ties with Britain, Iceland negotiated a solution to the conflict in the fall of 1973. This respite lasted only two years. With the extension of the Icelandic fishing limits to two hundred miles in the fall of 1975, the British navy returned to Icelandic waters. As before, the objective was to prevent the Icelandic Coast Guard from disrupting British trawlers, but in spite of causing considerable damage to the small Icelandic gunboats, the British navy vessels were only partially successful. In February 1976 the Icelandic government suspended diplomatic relations with Britain, but the two nations ended hostilities with a negotiated settlement in spring of the same year.

The cod wars around Iceland were, in essence, a conflict over the use of limited natural resources in a territory that was not covered by international laws on property rights. This became crucial in the years following World War II, as increased catches threatened the rich Icelandic fishing grounds with depletion. Because Iceland's economy is totally dependent on the fish industry, the Icelandic government sought to gain exclusive control over Icelandic waters, both to enforce a scientific preservation policy and to provide the Icelandic fishing industry with monopoly over fishing around the country. This policy seems to have been successful, as the Icelandic share in the fishing catches around the country has risen from around 50 percent in the 1950s to over 90 percent in the 1980s, and as the catches of cod are finally increasing again after a prolonged period of stringent quota reductions in the Icelandic fisheries.

BIBLIOGRAPHY

Arnason, Ragnar. *The Icelandic Fisheries: Evolution and Management of a Fishing Industry.* Oxford: Fishing News, 1995.

Gudmundur Hálfdánarson

SEE ALSO Iceland

Cohn-Bendit, Marc Daniel (1945–)

German student revolutionary, politician, and writer. Daniel (Dany-le-rouge, "Danny the Red") Cohn-Bendit was born in Montauban, France, on April 4, 1945. His father was a Jewish lawyer who had emigrated from Germany in 1933. Cohn-Bendit moved to Germany in 1958 and holds German citizenship. In 1965 he completed his *Abitur.* He then returned to France to study sociology at the newly founded branch of the University of Paris at Nanterre. There he became one of the leaders of the student movement of the late 1960s. He initiated unrest at Nanterre by his protest against the strict separation of dormitories for male and female students. Then, the "Maoists," "Trotskyists," and "Dutschkists" (named after German student leader Rudi Dutschke) elected him as their spokesperson, and he quickly gained a reputation as a witty, powerful speaker and also an unconventional thinker.

On January 8, 1968, the French minister for youth and sports visited Nanterre to see the progress made in building the campus's swimming pool. On this occasion Cohn-Bendit gained notoriety by criticizing the minister's *White Book on Youth.* In mid-February Cohn-Bendit attended a huge international convention in Berlin, organized by German socialist students, and met Dutschke. On March 20 Communist students staged a protest in Paris against the Vietnam War. Several students were arrested for burning the American flag and throwing Molotov cocktails. Two days later several hundred students occupied the administrative building of Nanterre University. They demanded the release of arrested students and discussed their future actions. Cohn-Bendit's "Movement of the 22 March" was born. This event and the subsequent disciplinary actions against the students marked the beginning of the May riots of 1968, when students and workers combined in nationwide protests for societal change and clashed with the police forces sent by the de Gaulle government. The arrest of Cohn-Bendit on April 27 lasted only twenty hours but attracted the attention of the media. He was then expelled from France on May 21, and forbidden to return until 1978. But in September 1968, he was awarded his diploma in sociology without having had to pass any examinations.

In Germany Cohn-Bendit was active in the alternative circles of Frankfurt, published an alternative magazine, *Pflasterstrand* (literally, cobblestone beach, after the slogan of French students "Sous les pavés, la plage"). He made a living out of his rebel image, even though in 1978 he had publicly expressed his support for parliamentary democracy.

In 1984, Cohn-Bendit joined the Greens, and in 1986 he became their candidate for mayor of Frankfurt. In March 1989, he was named honorary head of the city's new Department for Multicultural Affairs. Since then he has advocated a policy to facilitate immigration to Germany using a quota system similar to that of the United States. After local elections in March 1993, Cohn-Bendit was confirmed in his honorary office. In June 1994 he was elected a member of the European Parliament for the Green Party.

BIBLIOGRAPHY

Cohn-Bendit, Daniel. *Heimat Babylon: das Wagnis der multikulturellen Demokratie*. Hamburg: Hoffmann und Campe, 1992.

———. *Nous l'avons tant aimée, la révolution*. Paris: Barrault 1986.

Cohn-Bendit, Daniel, et al. *Obsolete Communism: The Left-wing Alternative*. New York: McGraw-Hill, 1968.

Salvatore, Gaston. *Der Bildstörer: Gaston Salvatore im Gespräch mit Daniel Cohn-Bendit*. Berlin: Edition q, 1994.

Anjana Buckow

SEE ALSO Dutschke, Rudi

Cold War

Term that refers to the hostility between the United States and the Soviet Union from 1945 to 1991, a contest that pitted the capitalist West against the Communist East following the defeat of Nazi Germany in World War II. Though the tensions between the two dissipated during the era of *glasnost* (openness) ushered in after Mikhail Gorbachev became the general secretary of the Communist Party of the USSR in 1985, the formal end of the Cold War coincided with the demise of the Soviet Union in December 1991. The defeat of Nazi Germany, the common enemy of the United States and the USSR, led to the rapid emergence of fundamental differences concerning the administration of occupied Germany and the future of central, eastern and southeastern Europe, regions that had been occupied by the Soviet Army as it

drove out the Germans. The United States and the USSR avoided direct military action against each other during the Cold War, but there were three major conflicts between the main protagonists and surrogate forces: the Korean War (1950–53), in which the United States and United Nations forces supported South Korea against an invasion by Communist North Korea (later supported by Communist China); the Vietnam War (1955–74), in which the United States stepped in after France gave up its effort to restore French control over Vietnam in 1955 and provided support to South Vietnam in its struggle against the Communist Viet Cong in the south and, eventually, against the forces of Communist North Vietnam; and the Afghanistan War (1979–89), in which the Soviet Union attempted to preserve the Communist regime in Afghanistan against an anti-Communist guerrilla movement. In addition to these three conflicts, in which one or the other of the superpowers was directly involved, the United States and the USSR supported surrogates in a number of less intense conflicts around the world. Perhaps the most dangerous confrontation of the Cold War was the Cuban Missile Crisis of 1962, when the United States reacted to the placement by the Soviet Union of medium-range nuclear missiles in Cuba by imposing a naval quarantine around the island. Had Nikita Khrushchev of the USSR not agreed to withdraw the missiles, nuclear war might well have occurred between the United States and the USSR. Khrushchev's successor as general secretary, Leonid Brezhnev, determined that the USSR would not back down again, began a program to establish military parity with the United States. He simultaneously pursued a policy of détente, through which the USSR and the United States would respect each other's essential interests.

Some historians date the beginning of the Cold War from the dispute between the United States and the USSR over the composition of the Polish government following the Yalta Conference of February 1945. Winston Churchill, the former British prime minister, used the term "Iron Curtain" to signal the divide between the West and the Soviet-dominated East in a speech at Westminster College in Fulton, Missouri in March 1946. Bernard Baruch, the U.S. presidential advisor, used the term "Cold War," which had been suggested to him by the journalist Herbert Bayard Swope, in a speech in April, 1946, and the journalist Walter Lippmann published a book entitled *The Cold War* in 1947. The Cold War was definitely operative in 1947 as the Soviet Union pressed for a monopoly of Communist power in Poland, Romania, and Bulgaria, and the United States replaced Great Britain as the supporter of the conservative government in Greece against Communist guerrillas. U.S. President Harry Truman's called for military assistance and aid to Greece and Turkey in 1947 (the so-called Truman Doctrine) in an effort to contain the expansion of the Soviet Union. Following the enunciation of the Truman Doctrine, the Communists in Hungary moved against their coalition government partners and established a monolithic Communist government. With the threat of an extension of U.S. influence through Marshall Plan aid (1948), the Communists in Czechoslovakia consolidated their power and formed a clearly Communist dominated government (1948).

Historians have debated the cause of the Cold War. One group, often labeled "orthodox," place the blame on Stalin and Soviet aggression. They believe that he had a predetermined plan to impose monolithic Communist regimes on the states occupied by the Soviet Army, and that this led inevitably to a conflict with the West led by the United States "Revisionist" historians believe that the Cold War stemmed from mutual suspicions and mistakes made by both sides. "Radical revisionists" have argued that the actions of the United States, specifically the Truman Doctrine and the Marshall Plan, which were regarded by the Soviets as a challenge to the sphere of influence they had gained in Eastern and Central Europe, were the primary causes of the Cold War.

BIBLIOGRAPHY

Carlton, David, and Herbert M. Levine, eds. *The Cold War Debated.* New York: McGraw-Hill, 1988.

Dunbabin, J. P. D. *International Relations since 1945: A History in Two Volumes.* New York: Longman, 1994.

Judge, Edward H., and John W. Langdon, eds. *The Cold War: A History Through Documents.* Upper Saddle River, N.J.: Prentice Hall, 1999.

LaFeber, Walter. *America, Russia and the Cold War, 1945–1990,* 6th edition. New York: McGraw-Hill, Inc., 1991.

Lippmann, Walter. *The Cold War, A Study in U.S. Foreign Policy.* New York: Harper, 1947.

Maier, Charles S., ed. *The Cold War in Europe: Era of a Divided Continent.* Princeton, N.J.: M. Wiener, 1996.

May, Ernest R., ed. *American Cold War Strategy: Interpreting NSC 68.* Boston: Bedford Books of St. Martin's Press, 1993.

Bernard Cook

SEE ALSO Berlin; Cuban Missile Crisis; Détente; Kennan, George; Korean War and Europe; Marshall Plan; Peaceful Coexistence; Truman Doctrine

Colley, George (1925–83)

Irish politician. George Colley, a solicitor, was elected in 1961 to the Dail, the lower house of the Irish parliament, from the moderate party Fianna Fail. He was one of the new energetic figures brought into Irish politics in the 1960s by Sean Lemass. Colley was minister for education in 1965 and minister for industry and commerce from 1966 to 1970. On the retirement of Sean Lemass, the Fianna Fail prime minister, in 1966, Colley was the chief rival and opponent of Fianna Fail's controversial figure Charles Haughey. In 1966 Colley lost to Jack Lynch in an unsuccessful bid for party leadership. Following Haughey's dismissal as minister for finance after allegations that he had been involved in the illegal importation of arms, Colley took that post and held it until 1973. Colley stood fully behind Lynch in his campaign against extremist republicans. He served as *tanaiste* (or vice premier) from 1977 to 1981 and, again, as minister for finance from 1977 to 1979. After Lynch's resignation Colley lost the Fianna Fail leadership election by a narrow margin to Haughey. When Colley supported an attempt to unseat Haughey from the leadership following the 1981 election, Haughey responded by removing Colley from the post of tanaiste. Colley, who would not serve in a lower cabinet rank, left the government. The two men had never seen eye to eye since Haughey became leader in 1979. Until his death in 1983 Colley remained an important focus within Fianna Fail of discontent over Haughey's leadership.

Michael J. Kennedy

SEE ALSO Haughey, Charles; Lynch, John

Cominform

The Communist Information Bureau or Information Bureau of the Communist and Workers Parties (Cominform) was established by representatives of the Communist parties of Bulgaria, Czechoslovakia, France, Hungary, Italy, Poland, Romania, the Soviet Union, and Yugoslavia at their meeting at Wilizia Gora, Poland, between September 22 and 23, 1947. The official goal of the organization was to ensure the exchange of information and the possible coordination of the activities of the Communist parties involved. Andrey Zhdanov, the chief Soviet Communist Party ideologist, in a speech delivered at the inaugural meeting, developed the "two-camp" theory publicly for the first time, i.e., that the world was divided into a capitalist camp and a socialist camp. The Comintern also issued a declaration on October 5, 1947, in which the United States and the

United Kingdom were accused of supporting imperialism, opposing democracy, and preparing for another war. The declaration called on Communist parties worldwide to lead the opposition to U.S. policies, and it denounced left-wing parties other than the Communists as tools of the capitalists as well.

In reality the Cominform was intended to strengthen Soviet control over the Communist parties (CPs) in Eastern and central Europe. When the Yugoslav Communist Party under the leadership of Josef Broz (Tito) started to show signs of independence from Moscow, the Yugoslav CP was expelled from the organization on June 27, 1948, and its headquarters was moved from Belgrade to Bucharest. After Stalin's death in 1953, the role of the Cominform as a tool for controlling the satellite nations declined and the organization was finally dissolved on April 18, 1956, as a gesture toward the Yugoslavs in order to facilitate the reconciliation between the Soviet and Yugoslav CPs.

BIBLIOGRAPHY

The Cominform: Minutes of the Three Conferences, 1947/ 1948/1949. Milan: Fondazione Giangiacomo Feltrinelli, 1994.

Tamàs Magyarics

SEE ALSO Zhdanov, Andrei

Committee of Inquiry into the Growth of Racism and Fascism in Europe (European Parliament)

Committee set up after the June 1984 European elections on the initiative of the Socialist Group in the European Parliament. The trigger for the establishment of the committee was the meteoric rise of Jean-Marie Le Pen's Front National in France. Six months after the Front National performed unexpectedly well in a December 1983 by-election in Dreux, it achieved 10 percent of the French national vote. Consequently, on the initiative of the British Labour delegation, an obscure rule of the parliament, used only once before, was used to establish a Committee of Inquiry into the Growth of Racism and Fascism in Europe. This committee conducted its work between September 1984 and January 1986, despite a threat from Le Pen that he would use "all means possible" to stop the committee's work. Specifically, he filed a lawsuit in the European Court of Justice claiming that the parliament in setting up the committee had discriminated against the Front National. The initial committee report was presented to the public

in 1986. It was comprehensive, with a multitude of recommendations. However, apart from the signature in June 1986 of a solemn Declaration Against Racism and Xenophobia by the council, commission, parliament, and member states, nothing much came of the report outside of the parliament. Shortly after the report was published the European Court rejected Le Pen's case against the parliament.

The election to the European Parliament (June 1989) saw further advances by the far right in European elections, with the German Republikaner and Belgian Vlaams Blok gaining representation. Therefore, the Socialist Group demanded the establishment of a new committee of inquiry. The second report, published in 1990, contained seventy-seven recommendations based on the recognition that there were four million black Europeans and twelve to fourteen million third-country nationals living legally in the European Union (EU) and that all residents should have the same rights and same duties. The main recommendations included the following: (1) Establishment of a permanent committee dealing with racism in the EU; this was accomplished in January 1992 as the Civil Liberties and Internal Affairs Committee. (2) Declaration of a European Year Against Racism; 1997 was designated the European Year Against Racism with a budget at community level of five million ECU. (3) Establishment of a European Monitoring Center on Racism, Xenophobia, and Anti-Semitism. It was agreed at Amsterdam to establish the center in Vienna early in 1998, with an annual budget of five million ECU and a staff of twenty-five to thirty. (4) Amending the treaty to give the commission the unambiguous competence to tackle racism directly. That was done in Amsterdam and the Amsterdam Treaty took effect on May 1, 1999. (5) Introduction of a Race Relations Directive, which is still to be effected.

Andreas Sobisch

Commonwealth of Independent States (CIS)

A voluntary association of twelve (originally eleven) former union republics of the USSR, established at the time of the collapse of the USSR in December 1991. The attempted hard-line coup against Mikhail Gorbachev in the summer of 1991, which was launched to save the Communist Party and to preserve the Soviet Union, in its failure precipitated the very two things which its leaders had feared. Gorbachev was shoved to the sidelines by the Russian president Boris Yeltsin, who with Leonid Kravchuk, the political leader of Ukraine, and Stanislav

Schushkevich of Belorussia (Belarus) officially pronounced the death of the USSR on December 8, 1991, in Beloveshskaya Puscha, Belarus. At the same time through the Minsk Agreement they set up of a new interstate institutional body, the Commonwealth of Independent States (CIS), open to all other former union republics of the USSR. The framework of the CIS was vague since there were no formal and legal decisions concerning sharing of power and functions between the CIS and the independent member republics.

More detailed the goals and principles for the CIS were worked out and formulated in Alma-Ala Declaration of December 21, 1999. There eleven out of the fifteen former soviet republics of the USSR joined the CIS. Under this agreement, signed in the capital of Kazakhstan, the highest institutional body of the CIS, the Council of the Heads of the States, was set up.

On December 30, 1991, all the institutional structures of the former Soviet Union were abolished. At the same time a working group of the CIS was founded, and Minsk, the capital of Belarus, was declared as a headquarters of the CIS.

The Treaty on Collective Safety (Security) was signed by seven members of the CIS—Russia, Kazakhstan, Kyrgyzia, Turkmenistan, Tajikistan, Uzbekistan, and Armenia—in Tashkent, the capital of Uzbekistan, in May, 1992. An interparliamentary assembly of the CIS, including representative delegations of Russia, Belarus, Kazakhstan, Kyrgyzia, Tajikistan, and Armenia with competence in economic cooperation and the human rights started functioning in September, 1992. Finally, in January 1993, the charter of the CIS was promulgated with Armenia, Azerbaijan, Belarus, Georgia, Kazakhstan, Kyrgyzia, Moldova, Russia, Tajikistan, Turkmenistan, Ukraine, and Uzbekistan as members. The former Soviet Union republics that became independent states of Latvia, Estonia, and Lithuania did not enter the CIS.

Since that time up to no more than fifty interstate and intergovernmental institutional structures of the CIS were set, forty-one of which were founded according to the decisions of the heads of the states and heads of the governments of the CIS.

The most important CIS bodies deal with economic cooperation, monetary coordination, and collective security. The CIS has proven to be a feeble replacement for the USSR. It has produced an Agreement on Strategic Forces and an Agreement on Armed Forces and Border Troops, and it has served as the umbrella organization for member states to cooperate in attempting to seal the border of Tajikistan with Afghanistan in an effort to quell the civil war there.

BIBLIOGRAPHY

Suny, Ronald Grigor. *The Soviet Experiment: Russia, the USSR, and the Successor States.* New York: Oxford University Press, 1998.

Yelena V. Stetsko

Communist Fronts

In their war against capitalism the Soviets perfected the art of forming temporary alliances, or fronts, with fellow travelers, friends, and even opponents, uniting them in a common allegiance to Moscow, a common terminology, methods of organization, and strategy. These alliances had the advantage of gaining broad working-class support for the goals of Communists; the efforts of these groups were coordinated, worldwide, through the Communist International (Comintern, 1919), an association of national Communist parties to promote world revolution. In 1943, the Comintern was formally dissolved as a gesture of goodwill toward Soviet leader Stalin's Western allies, but Moscow continued to coordinate the pro-Soviet parties through a variety of devices, including the Communist Information Bureau (Cominform), formed in 1947.

The names of the fronts would fill a small encyclopedia; they included a plethora of bodies inspired by the genius of Willie Münzenberg, a veteran German Comintern agent during the 1930s. Among the most active were the League Against Imperialism (1927), World Federation of Trade Unions (WFTU, Paris, 1945), and World Council of Peace (Wrooław, Poland, 1948).

Some of the constituents of this network, which expanded during and after World War II, were not necessarily of Communist origin but were taken over later. The World Federation of Trade Unions, for example, began with a worldwide conference called by the British Trade Union Congress (TUC) in London in 1945. Sir Walter Citrine, the British TUC secretary, was elected president, but the post of secretary-general went to Louis Saillant, a French Communist, and the direction of the WFTU's press and information service went to a Soviet nominee. In 1947 differences between Communist members and their opponents became acute; two years later both the TUC and the American Congress of Industrial Organizations (CIO) withdrew from the WFTU and set up their own organization, the International Confederation of Free Trade Unions (ICFTU), leaving the WFTU as a Communist front. The Cold War thereafter spread to trade unionism. The WFTU, like all Communist fronts, pursued a line uniformly in accord with the Soviet Union's on every major question of foreign policy.

Some fronts were designed to appeal to particular occupational groups (International Organization of Journalists, set up in Copenhagen in 1946; World Federation of Scientific Workers, 1946; and International Association of Democratic Lawyers, 1946); others were designed to appeal to particular age groups (International Union of Students and World Federation of Democratic Youth, established in London in 1945 as a nonpolitical organization, but later taken over by Communists), or to people whose political experience might turn them into Communist allies (e.g., International Federation of Resistance Fighters, founded in Vienna, 1951), or to women (Women's International Democratic Federation, founded in Paris in 1945 through French Communist initiative). These bodies acted as the international equivalent of "transmission belts" within national parties and liberal–left-wing groups and so-called progressive causes, thereby attracting fellow travelers and assorted leftists. They were linked to a complex network of international commissions, conferences, congresses, friendship societies, and so on supported by radio broadcasts, a flood of printed propaganda, and overt and covert subsidies from the Soviet Union and its allies.

At the same time, the Soviets extended their espionage in the West. Soviet agents drew on the aid of some sympathizers and a few "moles" in Western academic, administrative, and scientific bodies. The careers of these infiltrators often outdid spy thrillers in melodrama; so did the stories of Soviet defectors, such as Igor Gouzenko or Viktor Kravchenko, whose accounts seemed so outlandish that many Western readers simply shook their heads in disbelief. These intelligence networks provided Moscow with information that supplemented knowledge gained through legitimate trade and investment. Espionage, disinformation campaigns, and Communist tactics of concealment, moreover, helped to create a new climate of controversy and distrust that both helped and hindered the Kremlin's cause.

The Cold War thus continued on many different fronts. Within the United States, the Communist Party of the USA, though loyal to Moscow, remained numerically small, electorally insignificant, and beset by a striking decline in membership and growing public distrust. The Communists responded to this challenge by perfecting their camouflage and also by their universal willingness to carry out those humdrum organizational tasks that their allies commonly shunned. One of the Communists' main targets was Henry Wallace's Progressive Party.

In addition to fronts, the Soviets also made use of many other left-wing bodies around the world. These Soviet friendship societies owed little to Soviet financial or organizational help but espoused left-wing, anticapitalist causes. Mention should be made of at least one such group—the National Council of Arts, Sciences and Professions (NCASP)—in the United States. Its members were distinguished, their purpose sincere if wrongheaded. Its masthead read like an excerpt from a Who's Who. Some were Communists, some fellow travelers, but all were sympathetic to communism.

Communist strategists paid particular attention to the intellectual community, to men and women regarded as opinion leaders, to writers, actors, and artists. And for a time the Communists seemed to be winning the ideological war. The World Peace Conference in Paris and the Waldorf Peace Conference held in New York City in 1949 turned out to be successes for the Communist cause and the United Front tactics inherited from the Spanish Civil War (1936–39). Luminaries such as Aaron Copland, Pablo Picasso, and Paul Robeson lent their prestige to the cause of peace, as interpreted by the far left, while the Soviets ravaged Eastern Europe. But it was the United States, not the Soviet Union, that stood in the dock, supposedly guilty of warmongering and capitalist exploitation. The Soviet Union, by contrast, was a peace-loving, socialist land, and Stalin a benevolent statesman. The Cold War echoed through Western lecture halls and the media, pitting not only right against left but also the democratic left against the pro-Communist left. Even Soviet Premier Khrushchev's 1956 revelation of Stalin's blood-stained rule failed to significantly shake the belief in communism of fronts, fellow travelers, and the pro-Communist left. Not until the 1968 revolt of the French left did Soviet communism suffer a major ideological defeat, but the international Communist movement had broken down earlier, after 1956, because of the Sino-Soviet split that year. Communist fronts lost influence and stature as they were recognized as "fronts" for the Soviet Union.

BIBLIOGRAPHY

Hollander, Paul. *Political Pilgrims: Travels of Western Intellectuals to the Soviet Union, China and Cuba, 1928–78*. Oxford: Oxford University Press, 1981.

Sworakowski, Witold, ed. *World Communism: A Handbook, 1918–1965*. Stanford, Calif.: Hoover Institution Press, 1973.

Peter Duignan

Communist Political System

The political system of communism consisted of both official and hidden elements. The former was the external part of the ruling Communist party: usually about 10 percent of the adult population, who paid dues, belonged to a party cell, possessed party cards, and attended meetings. This party was always victorious in very high-turnout elections (up to 99.9 percent of the electorate was usually recorded as voting in Albania), held a majority in parliament, formed the government, and controlled the administration. In Bulgaria, Czechoslovakia, East Germany, and Poland, satellite parties, together with the Communist party, formally created a multiparty system. Everywhere there were monolithic labor unions to which all employees belonged, one youth organization (except for Poland after 1956), one women's organization, one scientific society, and so on. All those organizations belonged to the structure commonly called the national front.

Voting, demonstrations, and celebrations commemorating May Day or the Russian Revolution were usually carefully staged, and even texts of official speeches had to be approved ahead of time; citizens were encouraged or forced to participate. This constant mobilization was a form of legitimizing the system. New patterns of speech, uniforms, systems of gestures, and alcoholism created the specific political culture of party officials, usually of peasant origin.

The hidden part was more complicated. There was a ban on founding any organizations, organizing meetings, publishing journals, or speaking in public without the consent of party authorities. All public speeches were controlled, censored, and self-censored by the speakers themselves, who were afraid of repression. Common fear and fear of revealing one's own feelings and deficiencies in the area of political thought were greater where the secret police functioned effectively. The police used the system of secret informants and the assumption that anyone who knew something about a political crime was a criminal himself unless he reported it to the secret police. Such a system, when fully effective, made independent individual or group activity impossible.

Communist party cells were present in all official structures. The only exception was satellite parties, founded and led by cryptocommunists. Candidates to parliament and local authorities were selected by the central and local leadership of the Communist party. All management positions in enterprises, public administration, and welfare organizations were filled through the recommendation of the Communist party.

The Communist party was constructed and functioned similarly to military structures, and making conspiratorial decisions demanded absolute loyalty from its members. As a result, under the illusory formal unanimity there was a fight for power, access to material goods, and the forbidden products of the cultural life of the West. Party officials who made decisions about filling various posts (secretaries, Politburo members) belonged to the inner party. According to a concept of group interest, the essence of the inner party was the existence of secret lobbies with mafialike and countermafia structures. They fought for maximization of resources and means of control, minimization of responsibility, and greater autonomy. As a consequence, a system of patron-client developed. Loyalty toward the patron, fulfilling all his or her instructions, created a path to advancement and access to goods. Decisions made on the central level depended on the results of a complicated fight between the highest patrons and the coteries surrounding them. A cult of personality was developed surrounding the party leader, and he could function successfully as long as he kept subordinates dependent on him and all coteries in a state of atomization and relative balance.

It is appropriate to speak of a new class division because a large part of society (including entire families of party members) belonged to the ruling class, separated from the rest of the society and possessing different and selfish interests. Milovan Djilas formulated the concept of a "new class" of exploiters and Leszek Nowak, a Polish philosopher of the Poznan school, developed the theory of the class of triple masters. Members of this class, according to Nowak, played the role of owners, rulers, and priests.

In the first phase of acquiring power, all efforts were directed toward destroying civil society. This period was characterized by the speedy creation of new institutions, a drive to centralization (except for Yugoslavia), and the adulation of charismatic leadership. The death of the leader prompted a period of struggle for power. In the second phase collective leadership developed, with professionalization of the party apparatus and short-lived attempts to decentralize. The third phase, that of decay, varied. It has been manifested as an attempt to keep authoritarian power with the introduction of a free-market economy (China) or a spontaneous attempt of transformation without free market (Belorus). There could also be a metamorphosis of the system through a "velvet revolution" (Poland, Czech Republic, Hungary). The decay of the system has also been associated with a decay of forced political ties and national wars (Yugoslavia and the Caucasus).

BIBLIOGRAPHY

Besanon, Alain. *The Rise of the Gulag: Intellectual Origins of Leninism.* New York: Continuum, 1981.

Ferdinand, Peter. *Communist Regimes in Comparative Perspective: The Evolution of the Soviet, Chinese, and Yugoslav Systems.* Hamel Hampstead U.K.: Harvester Whitsheaf, 1991.

Hazan, Baruch A. *The East European Political System: Instruments of Power.* Boulder, Colo.: Westwiev Press, 1985.

Holmes, Leslie. *Politics in the Communist World.* Oxford: Clarendon Press, 1986.

Nowak, Leszek. *Property and Power: Towards a Non-Marxian Historical Materialism.* Dotrecht, Netherlands: Reidel, 1983.

Roman Bäcker

Comprehensive Test Ban Treaty (CTBT)

Proposed nuclear testing agreement that would impose a comprehensive test ban (CTB) on all nuclear explosions. Negotiations among the United States, the USSR, and the United Kingdom have been sporadically carried out regarding this accord since the mid-1950s.

CTB discussions were initially implemented by U.S. President Dwight Eisenhower and continued over a forty-year period. Talks have been intermittent as the priorities of both the United States and the Soviet administrations shifted and tensions flared and eased. On the way to a comprehensive test ban, incremental bans have been reached, culminating in the Partial Test Ban, Threshold Test Ban, and Peaceful Nuclear Explosions treaties.

Two recent events have significantly influenced CTB negotiations. First, because of the tedious progress made toward a CTB over the years, many nonnuclear nations in 1988 pressured for an amendment to the Partial Test Ban Treaty that would transform it into a CTB. Such a proposed amendment, which was backed by the USSR and a number of Western states, was blocked by the threatened vetoes of the United States and the United Kingdom in 1991.

Second, during the last years of the Soviet Union, nuclear testing became limited, and in October 1991 a one-year test ban moratorium was implemented. This resulted in a U.S. policy enacted in August 1992 that established a nine-month moratorium and then severely limited both the number of nuclear tests and their yields over a multiyear period. Negotiations with the Russian Federation concerning a CTB continue, and the moratorium continued during the Clinton administration despite repeated Chinese testing of nuclear devices.

Criticisms of a CTB focus on the inability of the United States to maintain the reliability of its nuclear weaponry and to develop new generations of such. Concerns over verification of Russian compliance also exist.

On October 13, 1999, the U.S. Senate voted predominantly along party lines, with the Republicans being in the opposition, and failed to ratify the treaty by a vote of 48 to 51. Ratification would have required a two-thirds majority, or 67 votes. The opposition claimed that the treaty did not provide adequate verification and would harm the security interests of the United States. Some critics claimed that the vote was a reflection of Republican resentment over a series of victories by President Bill Clinton. Other critics claimed that Clinton and his administration had mishandled the issue and should have withdrawn the treaty in the face of what appeared to be certain defeat. International reaction was negative. British prime minister Tony Blair and German chancellor Gerhard Schröder had specifically appealed for the U.S. Senate to ratify the treaty. After the Senate rejection of the treaty there were warnings from Russia of the possibility of a new arms race.

BIBLIOGRAPHY
Fetter, Steve. *Toward a Comprehensive Test Ban.* Cambridge: Ballinger, 1988.

Lall, Betty G., and Paul D. Brandes. *Banning Nuclear Tests.* New York: Council on Economic Priorities, 1987.

Loeb, Benjamin S. "Test Ban Proposals and Agreements: The 1950s to the Present," in Richard Dean Burns, ed., *Encyclopedia of Arms Control and Disarmament.* Vol. 2. New York: Scribner, 1993.

Robert J. Bunker

SEE ALSO Arms Control Treaties and Agreements; Partial Test Ban Treaty

Conference on Security and Cooperation in Europe (CSCE)/Organization on Security and Cooperation in Europe (OSCE)

Agreement and then organization dedicated to cooperation and security. The idea of holding a European conference on peace and cooperation was originally a Soviet move in the early years of the Cold War. In the 1960s détente provided a basis for the European conference, which was arranged by Finnish initiative in 1975. The Helsinki Accords produced by the conference ironically did not prevent a peaceful change of the postwar status quo but, on the contrary, justified and made possible a fundamental political change in Eastern Europe by supporting human rights movements.

In 1954 the USSR, in all probability to cause disputes between Western European states and the United States, made a proposal that a European security conference be convened. The proposal was repeated periodically without any serious response. However, after the Cuban Missile Crisis of 1962, a new arms control process emerged, producing crisis management mechanisms between the United States and the USSR. The improved superpower relations, or détente, made a European conference feasible. In the mid-1960s the Warsaw Pact explored the willingness of the Western powers to have a European security conference to formalize the postwar territorial and political status quo. NATO members did not reject the initiative but tied it to the establishment of a conventional military balance between the alliances, to be negotiated at the same conference.

The Soviet-led Warsaw Pact invasion of Czechoslovakia in 1968 slowed the process for a while, but the idea survived. The USSR renewed its old proposal in April 1969. It is clear that the Soviets hoped that Finland and especially its president, Urho Kekkonen, would support their initiative. While the idea of the conference was welcome to Finland in its attempts to stabilize the security environment, Finland decided to make an independent initiatve.

When the Nordic foreign ministers supported the idea in April 1969, Finland in May published a memorandum, volunteering to host a preparatory meeting and the conference. Unlike the Soviet proposals, the initiative was sent, in addition to the European countries, to the United States and Canada, owing to their role in Europe; furthermore, Finland did not make the recognition of the German Democratic Republic (East Germany) a precondition. As a minor deviation from the NATO moves, Finland suggested that arms control measures not be included on the agenda.

Finland's special ambassador, Jaakko Iloniemi, collected the slow but favorable response to the initiative between 1970 and 1972. The final decision was made by American and Soviet leaders during President Nixon's May 1972 visit to Moscow; the Finnish initiative became part and parcel of the developing superpower détente. In September 1972 NATO decided to approve the planned conference.

Preparatory ambassadorial consultations in November 1972, and a foreign ministers' meeting in August 1973, were held in Helsinki. The foreign ministers of thirty-five countries, with Albania the only European country refusing to participate, agreed on areas the conference would address. Furthermore, a principle of consensus was adopted for decision making and the approval of documents.

After two years of preparatory discussions in Geneva the leaders of the participating countries met in Helsinki in July and August 1975 to sign the Final Act. It affirmed the inviolability against unilateral moves of European national borders as agreed on at Yalta at the end of World War II. The Helsinki Accords covered three "baskets" of security, economic issues, and human rights. Furthermore, it was agreed to have regular follow-up conferences in various European capitals. Finally, the accords encouraged a separate conference on confidence- and security-building measures in Stockholm.

After the Helsinki conference, détente became less popular in the United States; instead, a resumption of Cold War tensions followed at the end of the 1970s. The Western European states were more able to see some value in the Helsinki Accords. In any case, the fact remains that the accords became an important element in the Eastern European political change. Because of American insistence on including human rights in the third basket, without which no document could have been accepted, the Helsinki Accords gave a decisive impetus to and justification for human rights movements in Eastern Europe. This made the growth of a civil society possible, finally contributing to the collapse of the Communist system in and after 1989.

The Conference on Security and Cooperation in Europe (CSCE; later Organization on Security and Cooperation in Europe, OSCE) achieved considerable success in the follow-up conferences, four of which were held by 1992. However, the OSCE failed to find a peaceful solution to the Bosnian crisis. Many doubted that the OSCE would have any further role in the European security architecture. Nevertheless, it still exists as a single Pan-European forum including the old and new states in Europe, and it played a positive role in the Nagorno-Karabakh and Chechnya conflicts.

BIBLIOGRAPHY

Kavass, Igor I., Jacqueline Paquin Granier, and Mary Frances Dominick, eds. *Human Rights, European Politics, and the Helsinki Accords: The Documentary Evolution of the Conference on Security and Co-operation in Europe, 1973–1975.* 6 Vols. Buffalo, N.Y.: William S. Hein, 1981.

Maresca, John J. *To Helsinki: The Conference on Security and Cooperation in Europe, 1973–1975.* Durham, N.C.: Duke University Press, 1985.

Mastny, Vojtech. *Helsinki, Human Rights and European Security: Analysis and Documentation.* Durham, N.C.: Duke University Press, 1986.

Vihlo Harle

SEE ALSO Kekkonen, Urho

Congo Intervention

On June 30, 1960, Belgium granted independence to its African colony, the Congo, which was first renamed Zaire, and in 1997 the Democratic Republic of the Congo. Independence came after just five months' notice in what had been one of the most rapid decolonizations in Africa. This in turn set off a chain of events that led to the introduction of a U.N. peacekeeping force into the country. The Congo, however, was only the second large-scale U.N. peacekeeping operation. The proper role of peacekeeping, its limitations, and particularly the necessary conditions for its success were not fully understood. The U.N. Congo Operation (known by its French initials, ONUC) lasted from 1960 to 1964. In the process, U.N. troops faced with carrying out the mission were placed in impossible situations, and the United Nations itself was almost destroyed by internal political discord.

The speed of the Congo's decolonization process was caused partially by Belgium's desire to avoid a replay of the French experience in Algeria, and partially the result of a belief that the Congo was so dependent on the former colonial power that there would be no real change. The basis for future relations was formalized in a treaty of friendship, signed on June 29.

Among the various treaty provisions Belgium was allowed to maintain 10,000 regular troops and two military bases in the Congo. Belgium also provided 1,100 officers for the Congo's new 25,000-man army, the Armée Nationale Congolaise (ANC). On July 5 a small group of ANC soldiers mutinied in the capital city of Léopoldville (Kinshasa). Belgium proposed restoring order with its regular forces but could not obtain the approval of the Congolese government. Three days later the government summarily dismissed the ANC's entire Belgian officer corps and replaced them with soldiers from the ranks. Sergeant Major Joseph Mobutu was promoted to colonel and placed in command. As the situation deteriorated, Belgium on July 10 unilaterally deployed its regular troops to protect European lives and property. Seeing that as an act of aggression, the Congolese government began firing off simultaneous requests for military assistance to the United States, the United Nations, the USSR, and

Ghana. The United States immediately referred the Congolese to the United Nations.

Meanwhile, a power struggle broke out within the Congolese government between factions headed by President Joseph Kasavubu and Prime Minister Patrice Lumumba. On July 11 the situation became further muddied when the leader of Katanga (now Shaba) province, Moïse Tshombe, declared independence from the Congo. Located in the southwest of the country, Katanga is rich in minerals and natural resources. Tshombe was supported and encouraged by the powerful European mining interests operating there.

Lumumba reacted to the secession by increasing the requests for military aid to both the United Nations and the USSR. Tshombe, in turn, requested military support from Belgium, which already was providing over 200 seconded officers for the 10,000-man Katanga Gendarmerie. Tshombe also started importing his own mostly European mercenaries with the financial backing of the mining interests.

Against this backdrop of total chaos, the U.N. Security Council voted on July 14 to authorize Secretary-General Dag Hammarskjöld to provide the government of the Congo "with such military assistance as may be necessary." But even as the first contingent of U.N. troops (from Tunisia) reached Léopoldville on July 15, the USSR was already threatening unilateral intervention in support of Lumumba.

Further chaos reigned for almost a year. Lumumba and Kasavubu each sent rival delegations to be seated at the United Nations. Lumumba later was arrested, then transferred to U.N. protective custody, then "escaped" under still unexplained circumstances, and finally was murdered. ANC commander Mobutu seized control of the government. Belgium withdrew its regular troops and the ANC officers, but the cadre in Katanga remained. Tshombe mobilized to block the entrance of ONUC into Katanga.

Finally, in August 1961, a seemingly stable government emerged and the U.N. General Assembly quickly recognized it. Now that someone seemed to be "in charge," frustrated U.N. officials pushed for action. On August 28, 1961, the 16,000-strong ONUC force launched Operation RUMPUNCH, directed at ejecting all foreign mercenaries from Katanga. The operation stopped after twelve hours when the Belgian consul agreed to withdraw the gendarmerie's Belgian cadre. That turned out to be a bad move, because the professional Belgian officers had been a moderating influence. Now the European mercenaries were in control. RUMPUNCH was a failure.

On September 13 ONUC launched a second operation, MORTHOR. At the last minute, however, the

United Nation's chief representative in Katanga, Connor Cruise O'Brien, ordered the ONUC force commanders to execute arrest warrants for Tshombe and his key ministers as part of the operation. ONUC thus became a party to the Congo's internal struggle and lost the mantle of neutrality so essential to successful peacekeeping. Operation MORTHOR was a bloody failure. To make matters worse, Dag Hammarskjöld perished in a plane crash in Rhodesia while on his way to the Congo to personally attempt to negotiate a cease-fire.

On November 24 the Security Council issued a resolution that for the first time authorized a U.N. peacekeeping mission to initiate the use of force. The operation, ROUND TWO, started on December 5 and included the use of U.N. fighter aircraft. By December 18 the fighting was over. Most of the mercenaries escaped over the border to Angola, and Tshombe agreed to reunite Katanga with the Congo. But the Katangan Gendarmerie had not been disarmed completely. Tshombe started stonewalling almost immediately, and a long stalemate set in, dragging on for almost a year.

While Tshombe's troops slowly rearmed, many of the mercenaries infiltrated back. Then India announced it would have to withdraw its troops from ONUC in early 1963 because of China's attack on India's northern border. ONUC planners quickly drew up plans for Operation GRANDSLAM, which was launched on Christmas eve 1962. That operation ended on January 15, 1963, with complete defeat of the Katangan forces. Tshombe went into exile and the mercenaries left the country again. During the various operations in Katanga, ONUC suffered forty-two killed and about three hundred wounded. The Katangan Gendarmerie lost about three hundred killed.

The last U.N. soldier left the Congo on June 30, 1964. By that time the United Nations was in the middle of the worst financial crisis in its history, largely because of the political fallout from ONUC. Nine days after the U.N. pullout, Tshombe was back, this time as prime minister of the entire country. Despite his efforts to impose stability, the Congo suffered three armed insurrections in the last half of 1964 alone. The situation became so bad in November that the United States and Belgium mounted a joint military rescue mission of Europeans still in the Congo. That action brought cries of outrage and denunciation from both the Third World and the Communist bloc.

Tshombe was ousted for the final time in October 1965. Internal stability started slowly to return to the Congo only in the late 1960s and well into the 1970s. That the internal situation was just as bad after the se-

cession ended shows clearly that Katanga was not the main problem. The Congo's own army had been the main cause of the upheavals that brought in the United Nations, and it continued to be the major source of trouble after the United Nations left. ONUC had failed utterly in its mission to transform the ANC into a reliable instrument of government. Although retraining the ANC had been a key part of ONUC's original mandate, the Katanga problem quickly overshadowed that mission.

The Congo crisis can be understood only in the context of the Cold War and the broader superpower struggle. When the Security Council first took up the Congo situation on July 13, 1960, the Soviet Union and the rest of the East bloc considered the problem to be one of Belgian aggression. The United States and the majority of the Security Council's members, however, saw the problem as the Congo's chaotic internal conditions, which had prompted Belgian intervention. By the fall of 1960 the Soviets realized that rather than being directed against Belgium, ONUC was actually thwarting the Soviets' own ambitions in the region. At that point the USSR launched a bitter political assault against ONUC, the office of secretary-general, and Hammarskjöld personally.

The muddled mandate of ONUC was a direct product of this equally muddled political framework. Between July 14, 1960, and November 24, 1961, the mandate emerged from six separate U.N. resolutions that were vague and conflicting; were issued by more than one U.N. organ (Security Council and General Assembly); and were addressed at different times to the secretary-general, to various U.N. member states, and even to nonstate entities.

At the start of the operation ONUC had four main missions, as derived by Hammarskjöld from the first resolution: (1) Replace the Belgian forces that were maintaining what little order remained in the Congo; (2) bring the mutinous ANC under control, thereby eliminating the major source of the disorder; (3) help transform the ANC into a reliable, disciplined security force; and (4) establish and maintain ONUC's freedom of movement throughout the country.

As the internal situation continued to shift, the subsequent resolutions shifted emphasis accordingly, and so did ONUC's mission. Belgium cooperated in removing its troops, but the evolving Katanga crisis first shifted the emphasis to ejecting Tshombe's mercenaries, and then finally to "preventing civil war." In the end, ONUC prevented civil war and ended the secession under the guise of forcing its right of freedom of movement in Katanga. The mission of retraining the ANC fell by the wayside.

The Congo operation started as a peacekeeping mission but ended up as a peace-enforcement operation. In the early 1960s the entire concept of peace operations was in its infancy, and the distinction between peacekeeping and peace enforcement had not yet been articulated fully. This was one of the lasting lessons of ONUC. Perhaps the most important lesson to come out of ONUC is that a peacekeeping operation can work only if the force remains completely neutral, and if all parties to a dispute want the peacekeeping force there and want it to succeed. The absence of these conditions has been a major contributor to the failure of subsequent peacekeeping operations in Lebanon, Somalia, and, perhaps, Bosnia.

BIBLIOGRAPHY

Durch, William J., ed. *The Evolution of UN Peacekeeping: Case Studies and Comparative Analysis.* New York: St. Martin's Press, 1993.

James, Alan. *Britain and the Congo Crisis, 1960–63.* New York: St. Martin's Press, 1996.

Lefever, Ernest W. *Crisis in the Congo.* Washington, D.C.: Brookings Institution, 1964.

———. *Uncertain Mandate: Politics of the U.N. Congo Operation.* Baltimore: Johns Hopkins University Press, 1967.

David T. Zabecki

SEE ALSO Hammarskjöld, Dag

Congress for Cultural Freedom

The Congress for Cultural Freedom was an anti-Communist organization, headquartered in Paris, with many eminent writers, journalists, and public figures among its international membership. A creation of the American CIA, it sprang to life in 1949–50 at an intense stage of the Cold War, largely in response to the Cominterm's highly successful "peace" offensive of the late forties. The primary concern was to mobilize susceptible elements of what was loosely known as the "non-Communist left" to combat "neutralism" and anti-Americanism at first in Europe, then in Asia and other parts of the developing world.

In its heyday, from 1953 to 1962, the congress, through its numerous branch offices, magazines, conferences, and protest activities, was remarkably effective at winning friends for America and marginalizing its Cold War critics. Still, it stumbled badly at first, especially at its first large public gathering, which took place in beleaguered Berlin in June 1950. Organizing the affair was Melvin Lasky, a thirty-year old New Yorker and former

U.S. army captain, who in the midst of the Berlin Airlift had launched an intellectual monthly, *Der Monat,* with the backing of General Lucius Clay and the American military government. Delegates had been invited as "representatives of the intelligentsia of the free world," Lasky's prospectus said; Berlin would be a first attempt to formulate "an independent program for the defense of their democratic ideals." But at an opening session, it was bluntly made clear that the time for discussion had passed. Not debate but *action* was the order of the day: "You don't argue in the front line."

According to Arthur Koestler, James Burnham, Sidney Hook, and other ex-Communist firebrands in attendance, "action" required liberating the captive peoples of Eastern Europe. It required rescinding the rights of Western Communists. It especially required overcoming liberal inhibitions over the atomic bomb. So completely did these apocalyptic scenarios dominate the proceedings that a bitter floor fight ensued that, after a threatened walkout by British and Scandinavian delegates, eventuated in a toning down of the manifesto to be issued at the conclusion of the conference. But these last-minute efforts at unanimity did little to clear the air. The meeting broke up on a note of rancor that was echoed in negative reports in the French, Italian, and British press.

Clearly a frontal assault on the Western European drift toward "coexistence" had proved unavailing. How then was such "neutralism" to be combated? By the same token, how was America's "free world" leadership to be promoted? At Berlin, artists, musicians, and poets had been conspicuous by their absence. The decision to set up in Paris was to change all that, especially after composer Nicholas Nabokov's surprise appointment as secretary-general of the congress in 1951. With Koestler and Burnham in effect squeezed out and Hook marginalized in New York, there was consternation among anti-Communist hard-liners. Still, Nabokov's wide acquaintanceship in the worlds of music and ballet made him ideal for the new "nonconfrontational" congress that was taking shape. Besides, the CIA had apparently decided that one of its own, a nonintellectual, Michael Josselson, was needed at the center of the operation.

Born in Estonia in 1908, Josselson had worked in Paris as a buyer for U.S. department stores before emigrating to the United States in 1936 and being drawn into the Office of Strategic Services (OSS) during the war. After the war he supervised the American-licensed press in Germany. He also joined the CIA. Josselson had hovered in the background during the Berlin proceedings, letting Koestler, Burnham, Lasky, and a few others do the planning and take the bows. Now, with the great matadors of anticommunism sidelined and with Nabokov as a capable front, the anonymous Josselson could run things pretty much as he and the CIA wished.

That he surrounded himself with independent-minded advisers and collaborators is worth noting: Lasky, who adjusted to the new order, in Berlin; Raymond Aron in Paris; Ignazio Silone in Rome; Malcolm Muggeridge and Michael Polanyi in London; Edward Shills, Irving Kristol, and Daniel Bell in America. The first project of the new regime, a hugely expensive, monthlong festival of the arts that opened in Paris in April 1952, left hard-liners in shock. There were new and specially commissioned operas and ballets, works by sixty-five modern composers, and a vast exhibition of modern painting. Extended appearances of the Boston Symphony and the New York City Ballet were likewise featured. Publicly, the festival was trumpeted as an answer to Communist claims about the cultural bankruptcy of capitalist countries. The point, however, as a congress insider suggested, was not so much to put Western culture on display. It was to show off the best of U.S. artists and performers "in the teeth of European contempt for us as uncultivated."

Or as an ex-CIA division chief boasted years later: "the Boston Symphony won more acclaim for the U.S. in Paris than John Foster Dulles could have bought with a hundred speeches." With the overweening Dulles and Senator Joseph McCarthy both creating diplomatic havoc with America's allies, one can appreciate why an arts-oriented Congress flourished after 1952, especially as the principal battlegrounds of the Cold War began to shift elsewhere. It was in India and Japan that the first non-Western offices and subsidized publications were established. Later, Australia, Africa, and the Middle East all became sites of congress intervention.

In 1953 the London-based review *Encounter* was launched; part of its mandate was to focus on the Indian subcontinent, as well as to introduce India's leading writers to Western audiences. At Milan, in 1955, a substantial contingent of Asians and Africans was invited to meet with Americans and Europeans to explore economic developments in both old and new states. This emphasis on the "underdeveloped world" was repeated in a 1958 conference on the prospects for democracy in the new states. Milan also spawned an impressive series of smaller meetings, or "seminars," where leading experts, Western and non-Western alike, deliberated over policy issues in a similar, nonideological spirit.

By the 1960s the congress numbered almost three hundred employees. Its Paris Secretariat was dispensing over $2 million annually, with the greater share going to its offices and programs in the developing areas. That

Americans were felt to be at a disadvantage in winning Third World friends and imparting "Western values" helps account for this extensive program. In Europe, by contrast, with the fellow-traveling mentality largely vanquished, extending moral and material aid to intellectuals behind the Iron Curtain was now the first priority.

East-West exchange activity had proceeded fitfully, beginning with the thaw following Stalin's death in 1953. Then, after the brutal Soviet suppression in Hungary in 1956, the congress's Eastern contacts multiplied rapidly. There were meetings of Soviet-bloc editors and writers with their Western counterparts. Dissident writers were published in special editions of *Encounter* and other congress magazines. In Poland and Hungary, the most fertile sites of congress interventions, stipends were covertly extended to writers and scholars, and ways and means were found to facilitate their travel abroad.

By such artful clandestinity the congress won the gratitude of hundreds, if not thousands, of beleaguered intellectuals. With the Vietnam polarization in the mid-1960s, however, the possibility of exposure threatened. Josselson even started limiting his organization's involvement in anti-Soviet protests lest they be tarnished by association with the CIA. For years there had been rumors that some agency of the U.S. government had been behind the congress; but in the absence of hard evidence, these suspicions had seldom deterred anyone from writing for congress publications or attending one of its lavishly financed conferences. In 1966 proof finally materialized in the form of a series of *New York Times* articles on the CIA's vast communications empire; they were followed within a year by more sensational revelations.

In the aftermath, there was an attempt on the part of the Ford Foundation to continue some of the Congress's more estimable undertakings. This petered out after a few years. Josselson, in resigning, claimed that he alone was responsible for accepting CIA funds, and that the money had been offered with no strings attached. Few believed him. But despite recriminatory charges about an "underground gravy train," and about editors, writers, and conference participants chosen for their correct Cold War positions, few of the insiders' reputations suffered.

During the dark days of Stalinism there had been no other source for anticommunist liberals to turn to—so it was said in the organization's defense. Besides, the congress was simply helping its collaborators to do and say more effectively what they would have been inclined to do and say in any event. This made sense insofar as it cast attention on activities in Europe, especially the congress's outreach to East-bloc intellectuals. It left in the shadows America's more dubious Cold War initiatives outside of

Europe, which, in so many artful ways, had also been defended in congress forums.

In time, as the luster of Communist regimes the world over diminished, the congress's achievements came to be regarded in a more accepting spirit. That it initiated much that was culturally and politically valuable few would dispute. But by adopting, and sometimes improving on, the Leninist habits of organization long used by the enemy, there were costs associated with those achievements, costs that, owing to CIA secrecy, may never be judiciously reckoned.

BIBLIOGRAPHY

Coleman, Peter. *The Liberal Conspiracy: The Congress for Cultural Freedom and the Struggle for the Mind of Postwar Europe.* New York: Free Press, 1989.

Grémion, Pierre. *Le Congrès pour la liberté de la culture en Europe (1950–1967).* Paris: Centre National de la recherche scientifique, 1988.

Longstaff, S. A. "The New York Intellectuals and the Cultural Cold War, 1945–50." *New Politics* (new series) 2, no. 2 (Winter 1989): 156–70.

S. A. Longstaff

SEE ALSO Lasky, Melvin

Constantine II (1940–)

King of Greece from 1964 to 1974. Constantine II was born June 2, 1940, at Psychiko, near Athens, the only son of Paul I and Frederica of Brunswick-Hanover. After the 1941 German invasion, Constantine went into exile with his parents until September 1946. He attended the University of Athens and won an Olympic gold medal in 1960 as a yachtsman.

Constantine succeeded his father on March 6, 1964. He was soon faced with a crisis that pitted the government of Prime Minister George Papandreou against the army. It was disclosed that the Greek army had unconstitutionally intervened in the 1961 elections to thwart Papandreou and his Center Union Party, the expected winner, and to keep Prime Minister Konstantinos Karamanlis and his National Radical Union Party in power. Papandreou and his party had been victorious in the 1963 elections and won a smashing electoral victory in February 1964. The king quarreled with Papandreou over royal prerogatives, especially the king's leadership of the armed forces, and on July 15, 1965, Constantine deposed the government of Papandreou. Constantine claimed that he had moved to forestall a conspiracy in the armed forces that involved a number of younger officers under the political

leadership of the Greek Central Intelligence Service (KYP). The alleged objective of the Aspida (the Shield) conspiracy of leftist officers was the overthrow of the government, the banishment of the king, and the establishment of a dictatorship along neutralist and socialist lines. In fact Constantine had moved against Papandreou as a result of the prime minister's decision to take over the Ministry of National Defense. Papandreou's Center Union was replaced with two puppet governments before Stephanos Stephanopoulos and his government took power with a bare parliamentary majority in September. The king's actions, considered arbitrary and unconstitutional, caused mass demonstrations, rallies, and riots through the summer of 1965.

In the fall of 1966 it became clear that Papandreou's party would be restored to power. Constantine proposed a caretaker government to last until elections in May 1967. Both political parties would support the government in parliament and the Center Union would not attack the king or "excite the people." After the rejection of this proposal, Constantine and his circle determined to head a military coup that would forestall a victory by the popular Papandreou and his party in the May elections. An organization called IDEA, a generals' junta under the influence of Queen Mother Frederika, planned the coup for May 13, but the colonels' junta, EENA, under the leadership of Colonel Georgios Papadoupoulos, struck on April 21. The colonels' junta, with CIA backing, applied Plan Prometheus, a NATO plan for a military takeover designed to neutralize a Communist uprising in the event that Greece was attacked by a Soviet-bloc country. The coup established an authoritarian government in Greece. On December 13, 1967, Constantine tried to overthrow the colonels and reestablish his own power by rallying loyalist support in the north, but the army remained loyal to the dictatorship. The king gave up and within twenty four hours fled with his family to Rome.

At first the colonels claimed that Constantine II "voluntarily abstained" from his duties and was welcome to return to Greece, but the king refused to subordinate himself to the colonels. In June 1973 Papadoupoulos declared the monarchy abolished.

In 1974 the military regime fell apart during the Turkish invasion of Cyprus, and former prime minister Karamanlis formed a government. While the antimonarchical Karamanlis promised his support to the "legal head of state," he made no move to restore the monarch. On December 8, 1974, the government conducted a referendum in which 69 percent of those voting rejected the king's restoration and expressed their support for the establishment of a republic.

In August 1993, the former king and his family flew back to Greece for a vacation but were asked to leave the country. Upon their departure, Karamanlis, now Greek president, decided that "a definitive end must be put to this issue" with no recurrences that make "a mockery of this country." In April 1994 the Greek government denied Constantine his nationality, his passport, and his properties.

Constantine married Anne Marie of Denmark, daughter of Frederick IX, on September 18, 1964, in Athens. Their son, Crown Prince Pavlos (Paul), is the heir to the vacant Greek throne and is considered the probable replacement instead of his father if the Greek monarchy were to be restored.

BIBLIOGRAPHY

Kiste, John Van der. *Kings of the Hellenes.* Dover, N.H.: Alan Sutton, 1994.

Prince Michael of Greece. *The Royal House of Greece.* London: Weidenfeld and Nicolson, 1990.

Martin J. Manning

SEE ALSO Greece; Karamanlis, Konstantinos; Papadoupoulos, Georgios; Papandreou, Georgios

Constantinescu, Emil (1939–)

Professor of geology and geography and rector of the University of Bucharest, elected Romania's president in October 1996. Emil Constantinescu was born November 19, 1939, at Tighina in the former Romanian province of Bessarabia, where his parents were temporarily residing. He studied at the University of Bucharest, receiving a law degree in 1960, a degree in geology in 1966, and a doctorate in geology and geography in 1979. After practicing law in Pitesti briefly during 1961 and 1962, Constantinescu turned to geology because he felt that he would have to make too many compromises as a jurist. Nevertheless, he joined the Romanian Communist Party (RCP) in 1965, hoping, as did many intellectuals, to change things from the inside. In 1966 he was appointed to the University of Bucharest's Department of Geology and Geography and eventually became the department's RCP cell leader for organization and propaganda. He taught geology until 1990, when he became the university's prorector (vice president). From 1992 until his election as president of Romania in 1996, he was the rector or president of the University of Bucharest.

Like many intellectuals who had lost faith in communism, he welcomed the National Salvation Front when it replaced Nicolae Ceaușescu in December 1989, but

Emil Constantinescu, president of Romania. *Illustration courtesy of the Romanian Embassy, Washington, D.C.*

soon became disenchanted over its unwillingness to break decisively with Romania's past. His active involvement in the front's opposition began in the spring of 1990, when he granted opponents of President Ion Iliescu's regime permission to use the university's faculty balcony as a speaking platform during the April-to-June marathon demonstration that protesters held at the center of Bucharest in University Square. The Iliescu-approved violent suppression of the demonstration by Jiu valley miners between June 14 and 16 made Constantinescu an active opponent of Iliescu's regime. He became the president of University Solidarity, an organization dedicated to rallying academics and students to help secure the release of those arrested in June 1990. Constantinescu also helped found two political parties that opposed the front: the Movement of Civic Alliance in November 1990 and the National Convention of Romania in November 1991.

The National Convention coalesced the parties opposed to Iliescu's government, but personality conflicts within it made nominating a candidate for president difficult. The issue of the restoration of Michael as king also deeply divided the Convention's members during the spring of 1992. Given these problems, the Convention belatedly nominated the relatively unknown Constantinescu on June 27 as its compromise candidate for president. On the sensitive issue of Michael's restoration, he advocated a referendum but only because he felt that Romanians had not understood that they were voting for a republican constitution in December 1991. He also stated that if Michael visited Romania, he would welcome him "as kings must be received." Such positions on former King Michael, while necessary for nomination, left Constantinescu open to the charge that he was really a monarchist, not a republican, as he later claimed and a deliberately weak candidate who, when elected, would resign in favor of a restored monarchy.

The Convention's infighting had left Constantinescu too little time until the first round of the general election on September 27 to overcome his obscurity. While his campaign was convincing, it suffered from the Convention's political inexperience. At political rallies Constantinescu often lost the attention of audiences by delaying his speech for well over an hour until after a representative from every member of the Convention had spoken. He also campaigned on the ideological issues of his anti-communism versus Iliescu's "neo-communism" and the need to punish the Communists for their crimes while in power. These issues appealed to Romania's urban middle class, especially the professionals and intellectuals whom former dictator Nicolas Ceauşescu had despised, but the majority of Romanians—workers and peasants—were far more interested in economic than ideological issues. Despite these campaign weaknesses Constantinescu received 31.24 percent of the vote among the six candidates for president, second only to Iliescu's 47.34 percent in the September 27, 1992, election. Since no candidate received a majority of the votes cast, a runoff between the first two finishers took place on October 11, and Iliescu defeated him 61.43 percent to 38.57.

Between October 1992 and October 1996 Constantinescu remained the Convention's president. Now, as a nationally known political figure, he prepared to challenge Iliescu for the presidency a second time. During these four years he shed his monarchist label and worked to reduce the divisions within the Convention by replacing some of the coalition's members with new ones so that by 1996 the re-created Convention was capable of doing more than just opposing Iliescu.

In contrast to 1992, Constantinescu ran a positive campaign in 1996. Instead of demanding vengeance against former Communists, he promised to combat the widespread corruption that had embarrassed Iliescu dur-ing 1996, to pursue the truth about Romania's past, and to reform Romania's economy rapidly. Iliescu, rather than run on his record, pursued the scare tactics that had worked for him in past presidential elections. He charged that Constantinescu planned to restore the monarchy, return property the Communists had confiscated to its previous owners, stop paying pensions, and federalize Romania by catering to its Hungarian minority. The voters were not intimidated and expressed their confidence in Constantinescu by voting in November for the changes he offered. On the first ballot, held on November 3, sixteen candidates ran for president and Iliescu finished first with 32.25 percent, while Constantinescu finished second with 28.21 percent. Constantinescu won the November 17 runoff election with 54.41 percent of the vote. One week later he became Romania's new president, marking the first time since 1937 that an election had changed a Romanian government.

With the support of a Convention majority in the Romanian parliament, he immediately launched his reform program. To begin reducing Romania's decades-old ethnic strife, he granted a ministry and several state secretary positions to members of the Hungarian Democratic Federation of Romania, which overwhelmingly supported him during the election. While not seeking revenge against former Communists, he still removed many from office, such as the heads of Romania's state television and the national archives. Numerous members of cultural and educational institutions also lost their jobs, as did several county officials in Transylvania who were replaced by Hungarians. As a part of his war on corruption, Constantinescu ordered the police to investigate Miron Cozma, leader of the Jeu valley miners, for mob violence and involvement in organized crime. His economic reforms included privatizing numerous state enterprises, closing those that were unprofitable, and liberalizing energy and food prices partly owing to pressure from the International Monetary Fund. Unfortunately for Romanians these economic changes increased unemployment and inflation rather than their standard of living, which continued to decline.

BIBLIOGRAPHY

Banac, Ivo, ed. *Eastern Europe in Revolution*. Ithaca, N.Y.: Cornell University Press, 1992.

Robert Forrest

SEE ALSO Iliescu, Ion; Romania

Cook, Robert (1946–)

British foreign minister, 1997–. Robert "Robin" Finlay-son Cook was born in February 1946, and was educated at the University of Edinburgh. Cook was chair of the Scottish Association of Labour Student Associations in 1966–67 and was a tutor-organizer with the Workers' Education Association from 1970 to 1974. He entered politics as a city councilor for Edinburgh. Cook, who had served as the Labour MP for Edinburg Central from 1974 to 1983 and for Livingston since 1983, was named secretary of state for foreign and commonwealth affairs on May 2, 1997. Before Labour's 1997 electoral victory, Cook served in a number of shadow positions while Labour was in opposition, for social services from 1987 to 1992, for trade and industry from 1992 to 1994, and for foreign affairs from 1994 to 1997.

Cook is a member of Labour's National Executive Committee and its National Policy Forum. He was elected chair of the Labour Party in October 1996.

BIBLIOGRAPHY

"Cook, Robert (Robin) Finlayson." *International Who's Who 1997,* London, U.K.: Europa Publications, 1998, p. 318.

Bernard Cook

Cools, André (1927–91)

Belgian socialist politician. André Cools was born at Flimalle in the region of Liège on August 1, 1927. Cools's father, a steelworker and trade union militant, was deported and beheaded by the Nazis during the Second World War. At the end of the war Cools entered politics. He became secretary of the National Assistance Board in Flimalle and climbed the rungs of the Belgian Socialist Party (PSB). At the age of thirty-one he was elected to parliament, and he held his seat until his death on July 18, 1991. Cools actively participated in the general strike during the winter of 1960–61 and joined the Popular Walloon Movement (MPW). Because of this he was called to task by the leadership of the Belgian Socialist Party. In reaction, Cools shifted for a short time to the left wing of the party. His political career, nevertheless, continued successfully. In 1965 he became mayor of Flimalle and in 1968 received his first ministerial portfolio. He was appointed minister of the budget in a Socialist–Social Christian government, becoming one of the dominant figures in the Socialist Party. In 1969 he rose to the rank of vice prime minister and minister of economic affairs. When the president of the Socialist Party, Edmond Leburton, became prime minister, Cools became co-president of a Socialist Party troubled by Belgian national divisions. In 1978 the party split in two: the Walloon Parti Socialist (PS) and the Flemish Socialistische Partij (SP).

Cools became the first president of the PS. Criticized by the left wing of the Socialist Party and by segments of the Socialist trade union FGTB for his turn to the right, he abandoned the presidency of the strife-torn party. The heir whom he designated, Guy Spitaels, won the presidency.

Cools became president of the Walloon Regional Council (1981–85), an institution created by the agreement of August 8, 1980, and he was appointed secretary of state in 1983. Following the return of the Socialists to the government in 1988, Cools served as minister of local power, works and water. He resigned that post in 1990 to become president of the board of directors of the important Popular Mutual Insurance Company (SMAP). He was murdered in a parking lot in Liège on August 18, 1991.

On September 8, 1996, Alain Van der Biest, former pensions minister and leader of the Socialist faction in the Belgian parliament, and until 1992 interior minister in the government of Wallonia, was arrested in connection with the murder. An aid of Van der Biest, Richard Taxquet, who along with three others had been charged with involvement in the murder, informed the police that Van der Biest had ordered the murder. Cools was reputedly killed after threatening to reveal bribes paid by the Italian firm Augusta for a contract to provide helicopters to the Belgian military. On January 7, 1997, Van der Biest was released after his lawyer argued that there was insufficient evidence to justify his incarceration, but the charges remained intact. The disclosure of the bribery scandal after Cools's murder decimated the Socialist Party and led to the resignation of Willy Claes as secretary-general of NATO.

Pascal Delwit

SEE ALSO Claes, Willy

Coposu, Corneliu (1917–95)

Leading figure in opposition Romanian politics after 1989 and the only politically influential survivor of the pre-Communist interwar period. Born in 1917, Corneliu Coposu acquired early prominence in the National Peasant Party (PNT) and spent seventeen years in prison following the Communist seizure of power in 1947. A quarter of a century of police surveillance followed until 1989, when Coposu relaunched the PNT, adding the name "Christian Democrat" (CD) to the title. The PNTCD, however, lacked the milieu of private agriculture, urban commerce, and independent religious faith that had sustained it before 1945, and it did poorly in the 1990 elections. Nevertheless, Coposu became a symbol of moral integrity who encouraged reconciliation between Romanians and ethnic minorities, such as the Hungarians, and began the painful process of reconstructing the PNTCD. Under his leadership the party avoided the splits that blighted other opposition forces. Coposu was instrumental in forming an opposition alliance, known as the Democratic Convention, which did well in further elections held in 1992. It was unable, however, to supplant the ruling ex-Communists, and the reformist opposition's challenge to the government subsequently faded. In October 1995, Coposu was awarded the Legion of Honor by the French government in recognition of his defense of democracy. He died on November 11, 1995.

Tom Gallagher

Corfu Channel Incident

The Corfu Channel, the stretch of water that divides the Greek island of Corfu from the southern coastline of Albania, is between one and six miles wide. These waters were extensively mined by the Axis powers in World War II. Mine clearance operations initiated by the British Royal Navy in late 1944 continued throughout the following year. In November 1945 mine-sweeping operations throughout the world were regularized with the establishment of the International Central Mine Clearance Board in London. Albania, however, was not represented on the board.

On May 15, 1946, the Royal Navy ships *Orion* and *Superb,* the first warships to pass through the swept Corfu Channel following reopening of the straits, were fired on by an Albanian coastal battery. Neither British ship was hit, nor were there any casualties. This, the first of three incidents involving Royal Navy vessels in these waters during 1946, elicited a British demand "for an immediate and public apology from the Albanian Government for the outrageous action of the Albanian shore batteries concerned, and an assurance that the persons responsible have been severely punished." The Albanian government claimed the British vessels had intruded into Albanian territorial waters without its permission, and never submitted to the British demand.

The second and by far the most serious incident occurred on the afternoon of October 22, 1946, when a flotilla of four Royal Navy warships was steaming north through the Corfu Channel en route from the port of Corfu to Argostoli on the Greek island of Cephalonia, another of the Ionian islands, south of Corfu. Just before 3:00 P.M. the destroyer *Saumarez* struck a mine. The destroyer *Volage* was instructed to take the *Saumarez* in tow

and head back south through the channel to Corfu harbor. At 4:16 P.M. the *Volage* too hit a submerged mine. In the incident forty-four officers and men were killed or missing, and forty-two injured. The *Saumarez* was beyond repair while the HMS *Volage* could be put back in service.

The third incident occurred on November 12 and 13 of the same year, when the British navy carried out a further mine sweeping operation in the Corfu Channel. This resulted in telegrams of complaint being sent by Albanian Premier Enver Hoxha to the United Nations claiming unilateral intrusion into Albanian territorial waters. The British accused the Albanians of laying this new minefield. To compensate for the loss of men and matériel in the October incident the U.K. government demanded reparations. It placed the affair before the U.N. Security Council and, on May 13, 1947, filed an application with the International Court of Justice at the Hague, requesting that the court adjudicate on its claim against Albania. It was not until December 1949 that the court made its award in favor of Britain: Albania was instructed to pay £843,947 ($2,009,437) in damages. The Albanian government declined to accept the court's findings, and in retaliation, Britain held on to 7,100 kilos of Albanian gold looted by the Axis powers during the war and recovered by the Allies following the cessation of hostilities. The gold was allotted to Albania by the U.S.-U.K.-France Tripartite Commission in 1948 but retained in the vaults of the Bank of England. Only in 1996, following lengthy negotiations, was the Corfu Channel incident finally resolved with the return to Albania of the bulk of the looted gold. Controversy still surrounds the identity of those responsible for laying the mines that wrought death and destruction on that October afternoon in 1946 and that resulted in a five-decade-long diplomatic rupture between Britain and Albania.

Philip E. Wynn

SEE ALSO Albania

Corrigan, Mairead (1944–)

Cofounder of the Peace People in Northern Ireland in 1976 and recipient of the Nobel Peace Prize in 1976. Mairead Corrigan was born in 1944. She was the aunt of three children killed by a car driven by a paramilitary gunman that went out of control. She was one of three people who founded the group Peace People, partially in response to the deaths of the three children. Together with Betty Williams, another cofounder of the Peace People, Corrigan went on to win the Nobel Peace Prize in 1976.

She has continued to promote the goals of the Peace People in the 1990s and has been a welcome speaker at events that promote peace, not just in Northern Ireland but in general.

Ricki Schoen

SEE ALSO Northern Ireland; Williams, Betty

Corsican Nationalism

The island of Corsica, in the western Mediterranean north of Sardinia, is politically viewed as an integral part of France and yet is geographically closer to Italy. This ambivalence about the relationship of the island to either country and about its essential identity has shaped its history and politics. Corsica was a part of the Genoese empire throughout the medieval period, being incorporated into France only in 1769. The culture of the island prior to this date was essentially that of a somewhat remote Genoese province ruled by powerful families and clans. Much of Corsican language and culture date from this period. While incorporation into France had far-reaching political implications, the actual process initially involved little change at the village or town level, and the island remained both remote and little developed economically or politically. A pattern of rural depopulation, agricultural decline, lack of industries, and consequent emigration, with nearly half of native-born Corsicans now living outside the island, emerged as the dominant feature of Corsican society. Poor transportation, both within the island and between Corsica and France, worsened the situation, as did the endemic banditry that plagued the island for years. The occupation of Corsica by Italy in 1942 was reversed, largely as a result of popular efforts, in 1943 with Corsica being the first European département of France to be liberated from the Axis. Corsica was also the first European area of France to acclaim the overthrow of the Fourth Republic and the return of General Charles de Gaulle in May 1958.

Beneath this erstwhile integration into France, reaction toward the decline of the island's economy and its political domination by mainland France continued. The Parti Corse Autonomiste, founded in 1927, began the modern agitation for recognition, largely in cultural terms. The mass immigration of *pieds noirs* (French settlers from Algeria) after 1958, the deepening economic malaise of the island, and the various scandals associated with "development" efforts by the French government aggravated the situation and led to the foundation of the Action Régionaliste Corse in 1967. Continuing political agitation and dissatisfaction turned to violence in 1975, focusing on a wine adulteration scandal involving *pieds noirs*. This violent aspect of Corsican ethnonationalism has continued to the present with bomb attacks, individual assaults, trials of activists, and the banning of ethnonationalist movements. Despite this violence, which has recently degenerated into faction fights between rival groups supported by different Corsican clans, extended families, and various criminal elements, significant progress has been made toward fulfilling the cultural and political aims of the ethnonationalists.

Corsica was granted a "special statute" status in 1982 by the French government with a range of autonomous powers. Corsican language and culture have achieved a degree of recognition in communication and education, and the status of Corsican claims has gained a Europewide dimension since 1979, thanks to the efforts of the Union du Peuple Corse. While the demise of the Socialist government of François Mitterand and the ongoing violence associated with the Front de Libération Nationale de la Corse and various factions cloud the picture, the prospects for ethnonationalism in Corsica and for Corsican culture, especially in the context of the European Union, are better now than they have ever been.

Míchál Thompson

Čosič, Dobrica (1921–)

Serbian writer and novelist. Most of his works deal with the Second World War. Dobrica Čosič joined the Yugoslav Communist Party in 1941 and was a member until 1968, when he was expelled for "Serbian nationalism." During the 1970s and 1980s he was a nationalist opponent of the Tito regime. His support for self-government developed into greater Serbian chauvinism.

A member of the Serbian Academy of Arts and Sciences, he is a defender of the Serb cause. He was one of the authors of the "Memorandum," that played a significant role in inspiring the nationalist politics of Slobodan Milośevič. Čosič was president of the new Yugoslavia from June 15, 1992, to June 1, 1993, when he was removed by the parliament.

Catherine Lutard
(Tr. by B. Cook)

Cossacks

People who reside in parts of Russia and Ukraine. The Cossacks, Russian in speech and Orthodox in religion, settled along the rivers of the steppes, the Don and the Volga, as well as the Dnieper. Cossacks, who elected their leaders and distributed the land among themselves, played an important role in the development of Ukrainian identity and mythology.

A conglomeration of escaped serfs, soldiers, and Tartars, the Cossacks prided themselves on their independence and historical opposition to subjugation by landlords. Although Cossacks played a prominent role in seventeenth- and eighteenth-century rebellions, their elite military units served the Romanovs with distinction. When Ukrainian nationalists attempted to establish an independent state in 1918, Cossacks played an important military role in the struggle against the Bolsheviks.

During the 1930s Moscow tried to stamp out both Ukrainian and Cossack nationalism. The Soviet government ordered the destruction of important Cossack buildings, churches, and records, and, until recently, there were few accurate histories of either the Cossacks or Ukraine. Indeed, until the mid-1950s fiction and legends were the richest sources on the Cossacks.

Following the Second World War, Soviet Premier Joseph Stalin placed heavy restrictions on Ukraine and the Cossacks. Citing the cooperation of a number of Cossacks with the Germans, Moscow again tried to stamp out Cossack political organizations. A number of Cossacks were also sentenced to internal exile. This included much of their military leadership, involving thirty-five generals and some two thousand officers, some of whom managed to escape to other countries. Despite this, a Cossack Association survived to draw support from the estimated 120,000 Cossacks for the creation of a new "Cossackia."

By the 1950s and 1960s, as Ukrainian Communists permitted a limited program to restore Ukrainian culture and placed the Cossack at the center of that identity, there was renewed interest in the history of the Cossacks and Ukraine. In the 1980s and 1990s Cossack political groups pushed for autonomous status. Perhaps prompted by tensions with Ukraine, Russian leaders have made overtures toward the Confederation of Peoples of the Caucasus and the Union of Cossacks of Southern Russia. In 1992 Russian President Boris Yeltsin issued a decree rehabilitating the Cossacks and appointed a commission to consider their status in the new Russia.

BIBLIOGRAPHY

Longworth, Philip. *The Cossacks.* London: Sphere, 1969.

Quinne-Judge, Sophie. "The Cossacks are Coming: Revival of Cossacks in post-USSR Russia." *Far Eastern Economic Review* (August 27, 1992): 155.

Seaton, Albert. *The Cossacks.* Berkshire U.K.: Osprey, 1972.

Sysyn, Frank. "The Re-emergence of the Ukrainian Nation and Cossack Mythology." *Social Research* (Winter 1991): 58.

Jackie Stroud

Cossiga, Francesco (1928–)

President of the Italian Republic from 1985 to 1992. Born in Sassari, Sardinia, on July 26, 1928, Francesco Cossiga studied law at the University of Sassari. A scholar and authority in constitutional law, he taught at the University of Sassari. An active member in the Catholic Action movement and a national executive of the Italian Catholic University Association (FUCI), he joined the Christian Democratic Party (DC) in 1945. Between 1956 and 1958 he was provincial secretary of the Sassari branch of the DC. He was elected to parliament in May 1958, and was also group leader of the DC on the local council in Sassari until 1966.

Cossiga was appointed deputy minister of defense in the third Moro government in February 1966, an appointment that he held in the successive Leone and Rumor governments until 1969. He was minister for public administration in the fifth and sixth Moro governments from 1974 to 1976, and was appointed secretary for the interdepartmental committee for the coordination of public order. He was minister of the interior in the successive Moro government in February 1976, a post that he held in the two national unity governments headed by Andreotti. During this period he reformed the police and created the antiterrorism squads. It was in these years that Aldo Moro was kidnapped and murdered by the Red Brigades, and Cossiga presented his resignation following the murder.

After the elections of June 1979 he was charged by President Pertini with the formation of a new government. It was a center-left coalition characterized by the fight against terrorism through strict legislation and reduced sentences for informers. On February 19, 1980, Cossiga resigned because of parliamentary opposition, but on April 5 of the same year he began his second government. In May, however, he was involved in the scandal that followed the escape of terrorist Marco Donat Cattin. Cossiga was accused of having warned the father of his son's imminent arrest. The father, Carlo Donat Cattin, was DC vice secretary and a personal friend of Cossiga. Although the opposition continued with their accusations, a parliament inquiry committee exonerated Cossiga.

Cossiga's government fell on September 27, 1980, following a vote in the Chamber of Deputies against his economic policy. Elected senator in 1983, he became president of the Senate in July 1984. On June 24, 1985, he was elected president of the republic with 752 votes out of 977, obtaining even the support of the Communists.

Discretion was the fundamental characteristic of the first part of his tenure. In spring 1990, however, a new phase of his presidency began, characterized by Cossiga's outspoken positions. On March 21 he took issue with the Supreme Council of Magistrates and asserted the right of judges to belong to Freemasonry. In May he strongly criticized the behavior of Leoluca Orlando, ex-mayor of Palermo, who had denounced political intrigues for interfering with inquires into killings by the Sicilian Mafia. On June 13 Cossiga initiated a grave institutional crisis when he sent a letter to the Council of Magistrates expressing his doubts about the legitimacy of the judges' process of self-regulation.

In 1991 the climate became even more heated. Numerous disputes arose between President Cossiga and leading politicians, magistrates, and journalists exasperated with his continued "outbursts." Many of Cossiga's outbursts were motivated by his defense of the paramilitary organization Gladio. The legality of this organization was strongly contested by many, and there were grave suspicions that it had carried out numerous acts of terrorism. In May the Party of Democratic Socialism (PDS), the former Communist Party, demanded a parliamentary inquiry on Gladio, P2, and criminal activity. In answer Cossiga not only attacked the PDS but the whole Italian party system. He apparently hoped for an institutional reform that would lead to a second republic, founded on a presidential basis.

On December 4, some PDS deputies asked for the impeachment of the president. This time he was openly supported only by the extreme right and the carabinieri, the national police. On February 2, 1992, Cossiga dissolved parliament and announced his intention of leaving the DC. Then, on April 25, he announced on television his resignation as president of the republic.

By law, however, he remained a senator for life. His name was touted for a while as a possible government leader for a wide coalition to initiate a process of constitutional transformation.

He eventually formed a small center-right Christian Democratic party, the Democratic Union for the Republic. Following the collapse of Romano Prodi's government in October 1998, Cossiga led his party into a coalition with the Democrats of the Left, which ironically enabled Massimo D'Alema to form the first Italian government headed by a former-communist.

BIBLIOGRAPHY

Cossiga, Francesco. *Il torto e il diritto: quasi un'autobiografia personale.* Ed. by P. Chessa. Milan: Mondadori, 1993.

Galli, Giorgio. *Psicanalisi e politica: Francesco Cossiga dalle esternazioni all'esito del voto.* Milan: LeG, 1992.

Gambino, Michele. *Carriera di un presidente: biografia non autorizzata di Francesco Cossiga.* Rome: Edizioni associate, 1991.

Guzzanti, Paolo. *Cossiga uomo solo.* Milan: Mondadori, 1992.

Padellaro, Antonio. *Chi minaccia il presidente.* Milan: Sperling & Kupfer, 1991.

Dario Caroniti

SEE ALSO Gladio; Italy

Costello, John A. (1891–1976)

Irish prime minister, 1948–51 and 1954–57. John Costello was born in Dublin and was educated at University College, Dublin, and King's Inns. He served as attorney general from 1926 to 1932. From 1933 to 1938 he was member of parliament for Dublin. He became *taoiseach* (prime minister) of the interparty government in 1948 as a compromise choice. Costello will be remembered for declaring his government's intention to repeal the External Relations (Executive Authority) Act in 1948. This led to the 1949 Republic of Ireland Act, which declared Ireland to be a republic.

As *taoiseach* Costello was innovative but, partially owing to his lack of presence and partially because he had never held ministerial office before, was unsuited to managerial aspects of the office. Though there was a reduction in the *taoiseach*'s powers during this period because of the politics of his interparty government, Costello showed ability as a chairman of a powerful group of figures. He was more firmly in control during his 1954–57 term as *taoiseach*.

Costello was quite conservative and a staunch Catholic, as shown by his pro-Hierarchy stance over the 1951 Mother and Child Scheme welfare program, which brought down his government. In 1954 his disagreement with the economic policies of his minister for finance, Gerald Sweetman, led to the fall of his second government. He unsuccessfully opposed James Dillon for the leadership of the Christian Democratically oriented party Fine Gael and returned to the back benches in 1963, where he supported Fine Gael's radical Just Society program, which led to a conservative/progressive split in the party.

BIBLIOGRAPHY

Farrell, Brian. *Chairman or Chief?* Dublin: Gill and Macmillan, 1971.

Michael J. Kennedy

Coty, René (1882–1962)

French politician and president of the Fourth French Republic, 1953–58. Born on March 20, 1882, in Le Havre, René Coty graduated from the University of Caen and then practiced law. He was a soldier in World War I and afterward entered local politics. In 1923 he won election to the National Assembly from Le Havre, a post he held until 1935, when he became a senator. After World War II Coty was elected to both Constituent Assemblies and to the National Assembly in 1945. He was minister for reconstruction and town planning from November 1947 to September 1948, when he was again elected to the Council of the Republic, as the Senate was renamed. A member of the right-wing Independent Republicans, Coty was, however, known as a moderate and a conciliator.

In December 1953 Coty was completely unknown to the French public at large when he was elected president by the National Assembly and Council of the Republic meeting together. The proceedings were hopelessly deadlocked, and he was not even a candidate until the twelfth ballot. After an unprecedented thirteen ballots over six days, Coty won election and succeeded Vincent Auriol.

Described as courteous and charming, Coty made an admirable first citizen of France. The duties of president under the Fourth Republic were largely ceremonial, but he did have the important power of naming the premier, who then had to win confirmation in the National Assembly. Thus Coty played a key role in negotiating with Charles de Gaulle, beginning on May 5, 1958, over the terms of the latter's return to power. After the November 1958 approval by referendum of the new constitution of the Fifth Republic, Coty, who still had two years left in his term, informed de Gaulle that he was resigning. He then retired to Le Havre, where he died on November 22, 1962.

BIBLIOGRAPHY

Agulhon, Maurice. *The French Republic, 1879–1992.* Tr. by Antonia Nevill. Oxford: Blackwell, 1993.

Bell, David S., Douglas Johnson, and Peter Morris, eds. *Biographical Dictionary of French Political Leaders since 1870.* New York: Simon and Schuster, 1990.

Northcutt, Wayne, ed. *Historical Dictionary of the French Fourth and Fifth Republics, 1946–1959.* New York: Greenwood Press, 1992.

Spencer C. Tucker

SEE ALSO Auriol, Vincent; De Gaulle, Charles.

Council of Europe

Organization of European states to promote European unity, human rights, and social and economic progress. The council was initiated on May 5, 1949. Its founding members were Belgium, Denmark, France, Ireland, Italy, Luxembourg, the Netherlands, Norway, Sweden, and the United Kingdom. Austria, Cyprus, Finland, the Federal Republic of Germany, Greece, Iceland, Liechtenstein, Malta, Portugal, San Marino, Spain, Switzerland, and Turkey subsequently joined. After 1989 Bulgaria, the Czech Republic, Estonia, Hungary, Lithuania, Poland, Romania, Slovakia, and Slovenia were admitted. The Council of Europe has its headquarters at Strasbourg, France. Among its committees are the European Committee on Crime Problems, European Commission of Human Rights, European Court of Human Rights, Cultural Heritage Committee, Council of Europe Social Development Fund, European Committee on Legal Cooperation, and the Steering Committee on Local and Regional Authorities.

The council developed from the dual impulse of a desire for European unity following the calamity of World War II and the developing Cold War. The International Committee of the Movements for European Unity organized "The Congress of Europe" at the Hague on May 7, 1948, to promote the economic and political union of Europe. Though there were serious differences between the supporters of European federation and the proponents of intergovernmental cooperation, Georges Bidault, French foreign minister, called on the United Kingdom and the Benelux countries, which had joined France in the 1948 Brussels Treaty creating the European Union (later the Western European Union), to give substance to the Europeanist impulse of the Hague congress. His successor, Robert Schuman reiterated the call. Joined by Paul Henri Spaak, the prime minister of Belgium, Schuman called for the establishment of a European Assembly to be composed of members drawn from the respective national parliaments, to operate on a majority basis, and to have considerable power. The United Kingdom, however, wanted nothing more than a consultative forum. On January 27 and 28, 1949, the five foreign ministers of the Brussels Treaty countries agreed to establish the Council of Europe as a committee of foreign ministers with decision-making power and a purely consultative assembly. At first, on the insistence of the United Kingdom, the members of the assembly were to be appointed by the respective governments, but in 1951 it was decided that the respective parliaments would designate their representatives, and each representative was to be free to vote as he or she saw fit. The assembly consists of 286 members and an equal number of alternates, who are to proportionately represent the party division of their respective national assemblies. The council's secretary-general is elected for a five-year term by the assembly. He has a permanent staff. The Council of Ministers meets twice a year, while their deputies meet monthly. The assembly meets four times a year. There are also permanent staffs both for the Council of Ministers and for the assembly. By the end of the century the permanent Council bureaucracy numbered 1,500.

Another constituent body, the Congress of Local and Regional Authorities of Europe, was established to provide a voice and encouragement for local democracy and regionalism. This congress, like the Parliamentary Assembly, has 286 representatives and 286 alternates. It has two chambers, one to represent local authorities and the other to represent regions.

The treaty constituting the Council of Europe was signed in London on May 5, 1949, by the signatories of the Brussels Treaty joined by Denmark, Ireland, Italy, Norway, and Sweden. The structure and functions of the council were gradually elaborated. The first Parliamentary Assembly of the Council of Europe meeting at Strasbourg formulated the European Convention on Human Rights. This convention was signed in Rome on November 4, 1950, and entered into force on September 3, 1953. After the Federal Republic of Germany was admitted to the council, Schuman proposed that the council take a step toward economic integration by setting up the European Coal and Steel Community. The six countries where federalist sentiments were the strongest—France, Italy, Benelux, and West Germany—signed the agreement on May 9, 1951.

The structure and mechanisms of the council have been elaborated with the passing of time. In 1960 the European Court of Human Rights began operations. The Council of Europe has a unique judicial procedure that permits individuals to bring actions against governments if they believe they have been victims of a violation of the European Convention on Human Rights. On October 18, 1961, the European Social Charter was signed in Rome, and on February 25, 1965, it went into effect. It enumerated twenty-one fundamental rights covering such areas as the family, young workers, trade unions, and social insurance. It has produced reforms in individual countries, but it lacked an effective enforcement mechanism. The Convention for the Prevention of Torture, on the other hand, possesses an independent committee empowered to make unannounced inspections of places of detention in any member state. In 1961 a Council for Cultural Co-operation was set up and noncouncil members were allowed to participate. A Social Development Fund has been established to provide loans to members states for low-rent housing and infrastructure projects.

Following the Greek coup and the establishment of the colonels' regime in 1967, the council, after some hesitation, decided to exclude Greece. The Greek junta preempted the council, however, by repudiating the European Convention on Human Rights and quitting the council. Greece returned only after the reestablishment of democracy in 1974. The efforts of the council to find a solution to the Cyprus crisis, precipitated first by the proponents of union with Greece and then by a Turkish invasion, met with failure. In 1981 the assembly refused to allow Turkish delegates to sit following a coup in that country. They were denied their seats until free elections were held in Turkey in 1984. The Carnation Revolution of 1974 in Portugal led to that country's entry on September 22, 1976, and the restoration of democracy in Spain, following the death of Francisco Franco in 1975, led to Spain's entry on November 24, 1977. The same year the assembly moved into its new Palais de l'Europe in Strasbourg. The European Parliament of the EC/EU, a separate body with a separate agenda, shared those facilities until 1998.

In January 1985 on the initiative of Hans-Dietrich Genscher, foreign minister of the Federal Republic of Germany, then serving as the council's chairman of the Committee of Ministers, an extraordinary session was held on East-West relations. The council stressed a common European tradition and identity that transcended the old Cold War line of demarcation. It attempted to support democratization and human rights and to serve as a gatekeeper certifying the progress of the Eastern European states in these areas.

On July 6, 1989, Soviet leader Mikhail Gorbachev addressing the European Assembly proposed a unilateral reduction of Soviet short-range nuclear missiles, advanced his concept of a Common European Home in which he repudiated the Brezhnev Doctrine, and discussed human rights. The assembly then established the status of special guest for countries whose national assemblies adhered to the final act of the Helsinki CSCE Conference and the U.N. Covenant on Human Rights. The status was granted to Hungary, Poland, the USSR, and Yugoslavia. Following the collapse of the Berlin Wall on November 9, the secretary-general of the Council of Europe enunciated the new political role of the organization, stating that, once the countries of the East had begun democratic transformation, the council was the only organization capable of uniting all of the countries of Europe. When Hungary joined the council on November 6, 1990, its foreign minister echoed that sentiment, stating that the event marked the beginning of the restoration of European unity.

The council launched a series of programs, Demosthenes, Themis and Lode, to assist the former East-bloc nations in the transition to democracy. Consultation was provided on constitutional construction, legal underpinnings for human rights, bureaucratic reconstruction, and formation of an independent judiciary and an independent media. The Council of Europe has produced over 160 European conventions, the equivalent of 10,000 bilateral treaties, to serve as the foundation for legal harmonization on issues as diverse as the protection of computerized data, spectator violence at sporting events, conservation, prevention of torture, and minority rights.

On May 4, 1992, French President François Mitterrand proposed that the heads of state and government of Council of Europe countries meet every two years alternating with meetings of the CSCE, which in addition to council members includes the United States, Canada, and the Central Asian successor states to the USSR, and has as its main concern security and preventive diplomacy. At the 1993 Vienna summit the security implications of human rights were clearly recognized and enunciated. It was agreed to make the council's human rights mechanism more effective and to develop protections for minority rights and combating intolerance. To further this objective a single, permanent court was initiated on November 1, 1998.

The adhesion of Russia in February 1996 made the organization formally pan-European. The Council of Europe, expanded at the end of the century to forty member states, has become the principal political focus for cooperation between the states of Western Europe and the developing democracies of central and Eastern Europe.

BIBLIOGRAPHY

Council of Europe web site. ⟨http://www.coe.fr/index.asp⟩

Council of Europe. *The Council of Europe: A guide.* Strasbourg, France: Directorate of Press and Information of the Council of Europe, 1986.

Council of Europe, Directorate of Human Rights. *The Family: Organisation and Protection within the European Social Charter.* Strasbourg, France: Council of Europe Press/Croton-on-Hudson, N.Y.: Manhattan Publisher, 1995.

Harris, David John. *The European Social Charter.* Charlottesville: University Press of Virginia, 1984.

Hughes, John. *The Social Charter and the Single European Market: Towards a Socially Responsible Community.* Nottingham, U.K.: Spokesman for European Labour Forum, 1991.

Western European Union web site. ⟨http://www.weu.int/eng/info/info-0400.htm⟩

Bernard Cook

SEE ALSO European Union; Organization for Security and Cooperation in Europe; Schuman, Robert; Western European Union

Couve de Murville, Jacques Maurice (1907–)

French civil servant, foreign minister, and premier, 1968–69. Born in Rheims on January 24, 1907, Maurice Couve de Murville was raised in a Protestant family. After studying literature and law in Paris, as well as earning a diploma from the École Libre des Sciences Politiques, he joined the civil service in 1932. He attained a senior post in the Treasury in 1937 and emerged as an important figure in the wartime Vichy administration in 1940.

Couve de Murville continued with Vichy until 1942, when he transferred his allegiance to the National Liberation Committee in Algiers. Shortly after his arrival there, General Charles de Gaulle appointed him financial commissioner of the committee. After the war Couve de Murville worked in the French Foreign Ministry, rising to general secretary for political affairs. He was then in succession ambassador to Egypt, a French delegate to NATO, ambassador to the United States, and ambassador to the Federal Republic of Germany.

In 1958, when de Gaulle returned to power, Couve de Murville became minister of foreign affairs, and in this post he played an important role in implementing de Gaulle's controversial foreign policy, which included ending the Algerian War and granting independence to French Africa south of the Sahara. The good relationship he established with Chancellor Konrad Adenauer was vital in cementing the special relationship between France and the Federal Republic of Germany, which culminated in the 1963 Franco-German treaty of cooperation.

Couve de Murville opposed British entry to the European Economic Community (EEC), advocated diplomatic recognition of the People's Republic of China, and supported the French withdrawal from NATO's military command. He was instrumental in securing the 1966 Luxembourg compromise, which gave member states primacy over the commission in determining EEC affairs.

By 1967 it was evident that de Gaulle was grooming Couve de Murville to replace Georges Pompidou as premier. In the general election that year, however, Couve de Murville showed his political limitations. His awkward style led to ridicule and his defeat by Michel Rocard in a bid to represent Paris in the National Assembly.

After the May 1968 government crisis, Couve de Murville became de Gaulle's economics and finance minister. In June he was elected to the National Assembly in the Gaullist landslide, and in July de Gaulle appointed him premier. He was fiercely criticized by an embittered Pompidou, whom he replaced. After de Gaulle's April 1969 resignation, Couve de Murville served as premier under the interim presidency of Alain Poher. Couve de Murville left office with Pompidou's election as president that same year. He was elected to the National Assembly in 1973 and served there until 1986, when he was elected to the Senate.

BIBLIOGRAPHY

Agulhon, Maurice. *The French Republic, 1879–1992.* Tr. by Antonia Nevill. Oxford: Blackwell, 1993.

Northcutt, Wayne, ed. *Historical Dictionary of the French Fourth and Fifth Republics, 1946–1991.* New York: Greenwood Press, 1992.

Michael R. Nichols

SEE ALSO De Gaulle, Charles; Pompidou, Georges

Craig, William (1924–)

Ulster Unionist MP for East Belfast, 1974–79. William Craig was born in 1924. He became Ulster Unionist MP for Larne (1960–73) and was Unionist chief whip in 1962–63. As minister for home affairs from 1966 to 1968, Craig opposed concessions to the Northern Ireland Civil Rights Association (NICRA). During the NICRA demonstration in Derry on October 5, 1968, he ordered the presence of the Royal Ulster Constabulary, and a severe riot ensued in the city. He was dismissed by Captain Terence O'Neill shortly afterward and became a close associate of the Reverend Ian Paisley, the outspoken ultra-Unionist. In February 1972 he founded the Ulster Vanguard and a year later the Vanguard Unionist Progressive Party, which he led in the assembly and convention. He lost control of the party in 1975 when he appeared to suggest that power sharing with the Catholic minority might be acceptable in certain circumstances.

Ricki Schoen

SEE ALSO O'Neill, Terence; Paisley, Ian

Craxi, Benedetto (Bettino) (1934–)

Italian prime minister. Bettino Craxi was born in Milan. As a journalist he wrote numerous essays on the history, ideology, and politics of the socialist movement. After having participated in the socialist youth organizations, he was elected in 1957 to the Central Committee of the Italian Socialist Party (PSI). He served as a city councillor in Milan then was appointed in 1965 to the party directorate. In May 1968 he was elected to parliament from the electoral district of Milan-Pavia with over twenty-three thousand votes.

In 1976 Craxi, who had been formed politically under the influence of Pietro Nenni, became leader of the Italian Socialist Party, replacing Francesco De Martino. On his arrival Craxi found a party rent by internal conflicts and politically overwhelmed by the developing alliance of the Christian Democratic (DC) and Communist Parties (PCI). In a few years Craxi radically renewed the party leadership and set up a reform strategy based on the gradual abandonment of Marxism in favor of the European social democratic tradition. The new socialist course gained wide support not only from the party itself but also from center-left moderates who had never agreed with the political convergence of the two main Italian popular parties.

By the end of the 1970s Craxi had become one of the most dominant figures of the Italian political scene. During Aldo Moro's kidnapping the Socialist leader became deeply committed to Moro's release and opposed the firm line taken by the government. In the summer of 1978 he successfully led the fight to elect Sandro Pertini president. On July 9, 1979, Craxi was charged by the president with forming a new government, but two weeks later he was forced to give up because he could not reach an agreement with the DC. However, with the failure of the "historic compromise," the proposal to create a DC-PCI coalition government, the Socialist Party became the left-wing coalition partner of the Christian Democratic Party, which in the first part of the 1980s was still the largest party in parliament. From 1980 to 1983, under Craxi's leadership, the Italian Socialists took part in five of the six governing coalitions.

Reconfirmed as party leader during a succession of conferences, Craxi must be given credit for foreseeing the failure of "real socialism" and in particular the impossibility of applying the principles of the Russian Revolution to Italian politics. The liberal swing given to the party and, principally, the definitive distance taken from the Communists won the PSI a prominent position in the Italian political scene.

In 1983 Craxi was charged again by the president with forming a government, and he became the first Socialist premier of the Italian Republic. He led a center-left coalition including DC, Social Democrats, Liberals, and Republicans. During his three-year government, the inflation rate was kept under control and the country's economy grew because of favorable international conditions as well as a series of financial and fiscal reforms. During his tenure Craxi successfully supervised the revision of the agreement with the Holy See governing the relations between the Vatican and the Italian Republic. In the area of foreign relations he became one of the most reliable partners of the United States. Together with Alcide De Gasperi, a founder of the Italian republican system, Craxi was certainly the Italian politician held in the highest esteem abroad. In 1989 he was named personal representative of the U.N. Secretary General for matters concerning peace and development and as such undertook a number of international missions. He represented the Italian Socialists in the Union of European Socialists and held the office of vice president of the Socialist International from 1978 to 1993.

In 1992 the Clean Hands (*Mani pulite*) scandal put the most important politicians of the First Republic, including Craxi, before the bar. A many-decade system of corruption involving almost all Italian political parties and the principal entrepreneurial elements of the country was disclosed. The scandal prevented Craxi from again assuming leadership of an Italian government. In over eighteen judicial inquiries, the ex-Socialist premier was accused of being the main protector of the system of corruption. Craxi, who retired from political life and took refuge in Tunisia in 1994, declared himself a victim of a political conspiracy and firmly denied any involvement in illegal fund-raising for his party. Nevertheless, in November 1996, in the first judgment handed down in the corruption trials, Craxi was sentenced in absentia to five and a half years in prison for his role in accepting bribes for the PSI and the DC from an insurance company seeking to insure workers of the state oil concern, ENI. In January 1999 he was again found guilty of corruption in a case dealing with the state electric company and sentenced in absentia to another five and a half years.

BIBLIOGRAPHY

Bellu, Giovanni M., and Sandra Bonsanti. *Il crollo: Andreotti, Craxi e il loro regime.* Rome: Laterza, 1993.

La Navicella: I Deputati e i Senatori dell'11° Parlamento Republicano. Città di Castello: INI, 1992.

Mammarella, G., and Z. Ciuffoletti. *Il Declino: Le origini storiche della crisi italiana.* Milan: Mondadori, 1996.

Montanelli, Indro. *L'Italia degli anni di fango: 1978–1993.* Milan: Rizzoli, 1993.

Padellaro, Antonio, and Giuseppe Marsilia. *Processo a Craxi: Ascesa e declino di un leader.* Milan: Sperling & Kupfer, 1993.

Veltri, Elio. *Da Craxi a Craxi.* Rome: Laterza, 1993.

Fabio Marino

Cresson, Édith Campion (1934–)

First woman premier in French history. Born on January 27, 1934, in the Paris suburb of Boulogne-Billancourt, daughter of a civil servant, Édith Cresson worked closely with Socialist leader François Mitterrand for twenty-six years and was widely respected in the business world. She graduated from the Hautes Études Commerciales in Paris and subsequently wrote her dissertation for a doctorate in demographics on the life of women in a rural French canton. In 1979 she was elected to the European Parliament; two years later she won election to the French National Assembly from Vienne on the Socialist ticket.

Cresson had been minister for agriculture, industry, foreign trade, and European affairs, and was best known for her aggressive response to German and Japanese economic challenges and her desire to improve the competitiveness of French products. In late 1990 she resigned as minister for European affairs and criticized what she regarded as Premier Michel Rocard's weak industrial policy.

On May 15, 1991, President Mitterrand appointed Cresson premier to replace the low-keyed Rocard, who resigned in part to distance himself from the government in order to run for the presidency in 1995. Cresson was to the left of Rocard politically and was known for her direct, even combative manner. The French press called her "Mitterrand's Iron Lady."

On becoming premier, Cresson named five women to her cabinet. Her first action was to merge the ministries of economics and industry into a super ministry with the task of strengthening France's industrial power. Rather than solving France's pressing economic problems, the Socialist Party fell into disarray and infighting. Partly as a result, Cresson's approval ratings plummeted to the lowest of any French premier, but Mitterrand stuck by her until the Socialist Party suffered a stinging defeat in the March

1992 regional elections, which were widely regarded as a plebiscite on the Socialists' eleven years in power. The party won only 19 percent of the vote. Cresson resigned on April 2, 1992, and Pierre Bérégovoy replaced her as premier.

Cresson was appointed to the European Commission. As head of the Department of Research and Education she was accused of favoritism in the awarding of grants and triggered a scandal.

BIBLIOGRAPHY

Agulhon, Maurice. *The French Republic, 1879–1992.* Tr. by Antonia Nevill. Oxford: Blackwell, 1993.

Bell, David S., Douglas Johnson, and Peter Morris, eds. *Biographical Dictionary of French Political Leaders since 1870.* New York: Simon and Schuster, 1990.

Spencer C. Tucker

SEE ALSO European Commission; Mitterrand, François; Rocard, Michel

Crimea

Autonomous republic in southern Ukraine. Crimea consists of 10,400 square miles (27,000 sq km) and in 1991 had an estimated population of 2,549,800. Its capital is Simferopol. Soviet Premier Nikita Khrushchev, in honor of the three hundredth anniversary of the union of Russia and Ukraine, transferred Crimea to the Ukraine in 1954. After a January 1991 referendum in Crimea, the Ukrainian Supreme Soviet granted Crimea the status of an autonomous republic.

A movement toward autonomy and independence was opposed by the Tartars. The Crimean Tartars had been expelled by Stalin from the peninsula in 1944 for reputedly having collaborated with the invading Germans during World War II. With the onset of Mikhail Gorbachev's policy of glasnost, the Crimean Tartars began agitating to return to their home territory. They objected to the 1991 referendum since the 1991 population was approximately 70 percent Russian. In the opinion of the Tartars, the moves toward autonomy and, later, independence were the effort of Russians to prevent the "Ukrainization" of the Crimea and the return of the Tartars.

After the Russian Federation decided in January 1992 to reexamine the status of Crimea, the Crimean Supreme Soviet in February 1992 voted to transform the area into the Republic of Crimea. Ukraine offered extensive autonomy to the region, but in May 1992 the Crimean legislature declared the area independent and promulgated a constitution. Under threats from the Ukrainian govern-

ment of economic blockade and the imposition of direct rule, the Crimean parliament withdrew the declaration of independence. The autonomous status was confirmed by Ukraine in June 1992.

After the election as president of an ethnic Russian, Yuri Meshkov, head of the Republican Party of Crimea, in January 1994, the Ukrainian legislature passed a constitutional amendment empowering the president of Ukraine to nullify any Crimean laws that he regarded as contrary to Ukrainian law. Nevertheless, in March 70 percent of Crimean voters approved a referendum calling for greater autonomy. In May the Crimean parliament voted to restore the suspended constitution of 1992. This was tantamount to reassertion of independence. The Ukrainian government demanded that the action be rescinded within ten days. Early in June a compromise was reached when at a meeting between representatives of the Ukrainian and Crimean parliaments it was agreed that Crimea would continue to submit to Ukrainian law.

In September Ukraine asserted the right of its Supreme Council to nullify laws passed by the Crimean parliament in opposition to the Ukrainian constitution. In March 1995 the Ukrainian parliament decided to abolish both the Crimean presidency and the constitution of 1992. In April President Leonid Kuchma replaced Crimean autonomy with direct rule by Kiev, and the Ukrainian parliament debated the abolition of the Crimean parliament.

Local elections in the Crimea in the early summer of 1995 registered a decline in support for the pro-Russian parties. In July Yevhen Suprunyuk was elected chairman of the Crimean parliament, and he was more conciliatory toward Ukraine. A new constitution was approved in October by the Crimean legislature. However, it was attacked by Tartars, who complained that it ignored their cultural rights, and by the Ukrainian government for its separatist implications. It was approved by the Ukrainian Supreme Council in April 1996 only after revision. By the time a final version was promulgated, it had been further amended to recognize Ukrainian as the state language of the autonomous republic, even if Russian was the official language.

Discontent continued in Crimea, however, and the legislature served as the sounding board. Owing to lack of confidence among parliamentarians, Suprunyuk resigned in October 1996, and his successor, Vasyl Kiselev, faired little better. In February 1997 the parliament attempted to usurp from the Ukrainian president the role of appointing the Crimean prime minister. It ousted Kiselev from the presidency and prevailed over Kuchma to gain the prime ministership for its candidate, Anatoliy Franchuk.

BIBLIOGRAPHY

Developments in Crimea: Challenges for Ukraine and Implications for Regional Security. Washington, D.C.: American Association for the Advancement of Science, 1995.

Suny, Ronald Grigor. *The Soviet Experiment: Russia, the USSR, and the Successor States.* New York, N.Y.: Oxford University Press, 1998.

The Crimea: Chronicle of Separatism, 1992–1995. Kyiu, Ukraine: Ukrainian Center for Independent Political Research, 1996.

"Ukraine," *Europa World Year Book, 1997.* London: Europa Publications, 1997.

Bernard Cook

Croatia

Croatia was formerly the Socialist Republic of Croatia of the Socialist Federal Republic of Yugoslavia. It declared its independence on June 25, 1991, and, after fighting a war with Serbia, gained international recognition in January 1992. Croatia, located along the Adriatic Sea, is bordered by Slovenia, Hungary, Serbia, Bosnia-Hercegovina, and Montenegro. In April 1990 the population of Croatia was 4,760,344, of which Serbs constituted 12.2 percent. Some 153,000 Serbs resided in counties where they constituted a majority of the population. Croatia experienced a period of independence from the tenth to the eleventh centuries, but for much of its history it was tied to the

Croatia. *Illustration courtesy of Bernard Cook.*

Habsburgs. It fell under Turkish control for a time but was regained by the Habsburgs. Thus it escaped the long Turkish occupation that colored Serbian national consciousness. In contrast to the Serbs, Croatians received their Christianity from the West and utilized the Roman (Latin) alphabet when their common Serbo-Croatian language was written.

On December 4, 1918, Croatia became part of the Kingdom of Serbs, Croats, and Slovenes. But Croats objected to the predominance of the Serbs in the new state, which was organized along centralized lines. Croatian hostility to the kingdom intensified after the assassination of Stepan Radič the Croatian Peasant Party leader, during a meeting of the parliament in Belgrade. King Alexander, to forestall separatism, changed the name of the country to the Kingdom of Yugoslavia, substituted new administrative districts for the old traditional units, and established monarchical dictatorship. Yet as a Croatian nationalist movement, the Ustaša, led by Ante Pavelić, grew in strength, the king was assassinated in Marseilles in 1934. Efforts by the regent, Prince Paul, to placate the Croatians with regional autonomy failed. He offered too little, too late. After the Germans overran Yugoslavia in April 1941, they recognized a fascist Croatian state under the leadership of Pavelić. The Ustaša state included a large part of Bosnia-Hercegovina and carried out a policy of genocide directed at its Serbian inhabitants. Approximately 250,000 Serbs, Jews, and Rom were exterminated at the Jasenovac death camp before the regime collapsed with the retreat of its German patrons. Croatia was occupied by the victorious Partisans led by Tito and became part of his Socialist Federal Republic of Yugoslavia.

Expressions of Croatian nationalism were equated by the regime in Belgrade with fascism. When a nationalist movement developed in the 1960s with the support Croatian Communists, Tito responded with a purge of the League of Communists of Croatia (the Communist Party of Croatia). In 1972, 427 people, including leading Croatian Communists among whom was later President Franjo Tudjman, were convicted of political crimes. A new constitution was introduced in 1974 to emphasize the federalist principle for the state. Nevertheless, many Croatians continued to resent the predominance of Serbs in Yugoslavia. Croatia, after Slovenia, was the most prosperous and industrialized area of Yugoslavia. Its per capita output was approximately one-third above the Yugoslav average. Croatians resented that relatively prosperous Croatia was forced to contribute heavily to funds designed to assist the development of the poorer regions of the country but that were suspected of being wasted on display or on projects to benefit Serbia.

As communism began to crumble and as Slobodan Milošević played the nationalist card in Serbia, Tudjman formed the Croatian Democratic Union (CDU, HDZ in Croatian) in 1990, championing Croatian nationalism. In multiparty elections for the Croatian legislature on April 7 and May 6–7, 1990, the CDU emerged as the largest party, with 42 percent of the vote. It won 205 of the 356 seats in the Sabor (assembly). The Communist Party (League of Communists of Croatia–Party of Democratic Reform) received the second-largest number of votes. Tudjman was elected president. Although he appointed a Serb vice president, the Serbs of independent Croatia, especially those of the Krajina, the old military borderland to which the Austrians had invited Serbian warriors in the seventeenth century, feared Ustaša-like ethnic intolerance. Tudjman had spoken of a Croatia for the Croatians, and the new flag of Croatia bore the checkerboard *sahovnika* emblem utilized by the Ustaša.

In July 1990 a Serb National Council was formed at Knin in the Krajina. Despite the best efforts of the Croatian government, it conducted an overwhelmingly successful referendum in August and September on autonomy for the Serbs of Croatia. By October 1991, with the encouragement of the Serbian government, three autonomous Serbian regions had been proclaimed in the Krajina, Eastern Slavonia, and Western Slavonia. In December the Republic of Serbian Krajina was proclaimed.

Despite the resistance of Serbs, Croatian nationalists went forward. In August 1990 the Socialist Republic of Croatia was renamed the Republic of Croatia. The Sabor also recalled Croatia's Serb representative to the federal presidency, Stipe Suvar, and replaced him with Stipe Mesić, the Croatian premier. In December the Sabor declared Croatia's sovereignty, its right to control its own military (a Croatian National Guard was organized in April 1991), and its right to secede from the Yugoslav federation. In March it asserted that republican legislation took precedence over federal laws. On May 19, 94 percent of the 86 percent of Croatia's potential voters who voted (Serbs, especially outside the cities, boycotted the vote) expressed their support for a sovereign Croatia. Though willing to accept sovereignty within a loose confederation, 92 percent expressed their desire to end Croatia's participation in the existing Yugoslav federation.

On June 25 Slovenia and Croatia declared their independence. Serbia was unwilling to allow Croatia, or at least an intact Croatia, to secede without a fight. Despite an agreement by Croatia and Slovenia on July 7 to suspend secession for three months, full-scale war erupted in Croatia that very day. Croatian Serbs attacked Croatian defense forces at Tenja. Milošević encouraged the Serbs

of Croatia to resist and the Yugoslav People's Army (YPA), dominated by Serbs, went into action, ostensibly to prevent Croatian secession but arguably to facilitate the annexation of the rebellious Serb regions of Croatia into a greater Serbia. By November the YPA and Croatian Serb insurgents controlled approximately a third of Croatia. Although the YPA attacked the port of Zadar and besieged and bombarded Dubrovnik, the heaviest fighting was in Eastern Slavonia at Osijek, Vinkovci, and Vukovar. When the Serbs finally overran Vukovar, their victory was accompanied by atrocities.

Although the Sabor offered to guarantee minority rights to the Serbs of Croatia, the outbreak of hostilities and atrocities committed by both sides and the encouragement of Serbian separatism by Milošević made reconciliation improbable. Tudjman and the CDU came under intense pressure from the extreme nationalist right not to make concessions. In November the Supreme Council, chaired by Tudjman, ordered all Croatians to resign from any posts they held in the federal government or administration. On December 5 Stipe Mesić resigned from the Yugoslav presidency, and on December 19 Ante Marković stepped down as Yugoslav prime minister. Under German pressure, the European Community (EC) formally recognized the independence of Croatia on January 15, 1992.

On January 2, 1992, a U.N.-brokered cease-fire went into effect, and in February a 14,000-person United Nations Protection Force (UNPROFOR) was deployed to supervise the withdrawal of the YPA and to separate Croat forces from Serb irregulars in the U.N.-protected areas.

The first elections under the new constitution were held on August 2, 1992. Croatians living in Bosnia-Hercegovina were allowed to vote, as were persons with a Croatian parent. Tudjman, who was opposed by seven other candidates, received 56 percent of the vote, more than twice as many votes as his closest competitor, Drazen Budiša, the candidate of the Croatian Social-Liberal Party (CSLP). The CDU won 85 of the 138 seats in the Chamber of Representatives, and Hrvoje Sarinić was appointed prime minister. The government continued the harassment of opponents, using tactics that had already been employed by Tudjman. When elections were held for the second chamber, the Chamber of Municipalities, on February 7, 1993, the CDU won thirty-seven of the sixty-three seats. The CSLP and its allies won only 16 seats, and the Croatian Party of the Right (CPR) boycotted the election. In March 1993, owing to serious economic problems and financial scandals, Sarinić's cabinet resigned. He was replaced by Nikiča Valentić, who had previously headed Industrija Nafte, the Croatian petroleum industry.

In October 1992 David Owen, cochair of the European Union sponsored peace talks, threatened Croatia with sanctions if it did not withdraw its forces from Bosnia-Hercegovina, where they had recognized a Croat breakaway entity, the Croatian Union of Herzeg-Bosna. Supported by the Croatian National Guard, an independent Croatian state had been proclaimed in Hercegovina with Mostar as its capital on October 24, 1992. Owen accused the Croatians of practicing ethnic cleansing in the area of Bosnia under their control. Nevertheless, the Croatians decided, in light of the Owen-Vance plan's acceptance of ethnically based provinces, to stake out their claim to as much territory for Croatia as possible. A year-long conflict between Croats and Bosnian Muslims ensued. In 1993 fighting also occurred in Croatia proper. An offensive by the Croats succeeded in regaining the Maslenica bridge connecting Zagreb with the Dalmatian coast. In addition to securing a link to Zadar, the Croatian government moved against Dalmatian Action, which was seeking autonomy for Dalmatia. The Croatian government also opposed the autonomist Istrian Democratic Assembly, which won 72 percent of the votes cast in Istria in local elections in February 1993. In December a cease-fire was negotiated between the Croatian government and the Serbs of Krajina. Also, under pressure from the United States, Tudjman agreed to the establishment of a Bosnian-Croat federation in Bosnia-Hercegovina. There was also growing dissatisfaction with the performance of UNPROFOR. The Chamber of Representatives demanded that UNPROFOR disarm the Serb forces of Krajina, facilitate the return of Croat refugees to the area, and enforce the official frontiers of Croatia. In October the prime minister of the Serb Republic of Krajina, Borislav Mikelić, rejected the reintegration of Krajina into Croatia, and Tudjman under growing nationalist pressure threatened to let the UNPROFOR mandate lapse when it expired in March 1995. Under U.S. pressure he relented, but UNPROFOR was replaced by the U.N. Confidence Restoration Operation (UNCRO), which was stationed along the borders between Croatia and Bosnia and Serbia, largely cutting off the Serbs of Krajina from supplies.

In March 1995 a formal military alliance was concluded between Croatia and Bosnia. By April Tudjman announced Croatia's intention to liberate rebellious Serb enclaves within Croatia's frontiers. Bosnian and Croatian Serbs played into his hands. In April Bosnian Serbs shelled Dubrovnik and in protest against the cutting off of their supplies, Croatian Serbs blocked the principal road between Zagreb and Belgrade. On May 1 and 2

Croatians launched the first of their successful offensives against the Serb enclaves. They easily overran Western Slavonia, through which the Zagreb-Belgrade road ran. The Serbs of Krajina responded by shelling Zagreb and other cities and voting for a union of Serb territories in Croatia and Bosnia. In late July a preparatory campaign by Croat and Bosnian Croat troops seized the strategic Bosnian Serb town of Bosansko Grahovo, blocking the last supply line into Krajina. On August 4 the second offensive was launched and it quickly overran Krajina. The successful Croatian offensive precipitated the flight of 150,000 Croatian Serbs to Bosnia and Serbia. The victorious Croats continued into Bosnia and essentially altered the balance in the Bosnian war.

Fighting continued in Eastern Slavonia after the cease-fire was negotiated in Bosnia. On October 3 an agreement was signed by Croatia and Serb leaders from Eastern Slavonia. The agreement, mediated by U.S. Ambassador Peter Galbraith and U.N. negotiator Thorvald Stoltenberg, set up a transitional period under U.N. administration with a joint Serb-Croat police force. In November a further agreement was signed providing for the reintegration of Eastern Slavonia into Croatia. This agreement was a necessary pre-condition for peace negotiations among Croatia, Serbia, and Bosnia, and the formal signing of this agreement negotiated in Erdut, Croatia, occurred after the signing of the Dayton Peace Accord on December 14, 1995. On January 15, 1996, the U.N. Security Council set up the U.N. Transitional Administration for Eastern Slavonia, Baranja, and Western Sirmium (UNTAES), which took over from UNCRO. Jacques Paul Klein of the United States became the administrator of the region during the transition. In May demilitarization of the region commenced and was completed within a month.

In the elections of October 29, 1995, the CDU, buoyed by Croatia's military success, won approximately 45 percent of the vote. Despite severe limitations placed on opposition access to television, the CDU failed to win the two-thirds of the Sabor necessary to amend the constitution. Zlatko Matesa, minister of education, became the new prime minister. Harassment of the opposition continued. In January 1996 Tudjman, after a long dispute with the opposition, which had a majority in the Zagreb City Assembly, dissolved the assembly. The same month an independent newspaper that had criticized Tudjman was shut down. Subsequently the foreign ministers of the member states of the Council of Europe refused to admit Croatia because it did not meet EU democratic standards. Following the acquittal of an editor and journalist of charges of libel against Tudjman and Croatia's agreement to ratify the European Convention on Human Rights within a year, the Council of Europe agreed to accept Croatia as a member in October 1996.

Croatia in addition to the substantial problem of privatization suffered the destruction of a significant part of its infrastructure during its war with Serbia and the internal Serbian forces. Nearly 30 percent of its factories and 30 percent of its electricity-producing facilities were ruined during the fighting. Croatia was not only cut off from a third of its territory but had to devote considerable resources to the creation of an effective military force. It was forced to deal with and support a large nonproductive refugee population consisting not only of displaced Croats but refugees from the war in Bosnia. Industrial production, which contributed approximately 23.4 percent of GDP and employed 40.1 percent of the working population in 1995, had declined by 11.3 percent in 1990, 28.5 percent in 1991, 14.6 percent in 1992, 5.9 percent in 1993, and 2.5 percent in 1994. In 1995 the decline was reversed and production increased by 0.3 percent. The annual rate of inflation that had soared to 1,486.3 percent in 1993 declined to 107.2 percent in 1994 with the introduction of a new national currency, the kuna, in May 1994. In 1993 Croatia was allowed to join the IMF. It received loans conditioned on the progress of privatization, which had been slowed because of political considerations. The European Bank for Reconstruction and Development and private groups also provided development funds. Infrastructure repair enabled the government to reduce the unemployment rate, which had officially run at 15 percent in 1997.

BIBLIOGRAPHY

"Croatia." *The Europa World Yearbook 1997.* London: Europa Publications, 1998. I:1007–13.

Glenny, Misha. *The Fall of Yugoslavia: The Third Balkan War,* 3rd ed. New York: Penguin, 1996.

Tanner, Marcus. *Croatia: A Nation Forged in War.* New Haven, Conn.: Yale University Press, 1999.

Bernard Cook

Independence and War

Croatia until 1991 was one of the six republics of Yugoslavia. The rise of nationalism in Yugoslavia, combined with the collapse of communism, weakened the multinational state in the late 1980s and early 1990s. This led to the secession of Slovenia and Croatia in June 1991. A bloody war of rebel Serbs, supported by the Yugoslav army, ensued. Between 1991 and 1995 over a quarter of Croatia remained under control of Serb nationalists. While all of Croatia's national territories were regained

only in 1998, Croatia participated in the conquest of parts of Bosnia during the war of 1992–95.

After the breakup of the Yugoslav League of Communists in 1990 following controversies over the country's future and pressure from Slobodan Milošević, free elections were scheduled in all republics, but not on the federal level. In Croatia tensions rose sharply after the electoral victory in 1990 of the Croatian Democratic Community (HDZ) of Franjo Tudjman. Tudjman had been a Partisan during World War II and rose to the rank of general in the Yugoslav People's Army. He was sacked in 1967 for espousing Croatian nationalism and spent several years in the 1970s and 1980s in prison. As a historian he attempted to revise the number of Serb and Jewish victims of Ustaša rule in Croatia. Despite his status as dissident, he was allowed to travel abroad, where he fostered ties with nationalist Croatian émigré communities who helped fund the election of his nationalist party. The financial weight of the party combined with the policies of Milošević drove many Croatians to vote for the HDZ and Tudjman. Although it paid lip service to Yugoslavia, it intended to lead Croatia into independence. The party, once in power, began dismissing large numbers of Serbs from the civil service, introduced symbols from the past that provoked Serbian minorities, and revoked their status as a constituent nation. The resulting opposition of many of the 580,000 Serbs living in Croatia to the new regime was further fueled by the propaganda machinery of Serbia. Serbia and the Yugoslav army furthermore supplied many rural Serbs with weapons. The main Serbian party, the Serbian Democratic Party (SDS) under the leadership of Jovan Rasković, received substantial support from Belgrade and called increasingly for autonomy of the Krajina along the Bosnian border and Eastern Slavonia, along the frontier with Serbia. The party did not represent half the Serbian population, which lived in the larger cities and, despite discrimination, remained mostly loyal to the Croatian government. Areas held by the SDS withdrew increasingly from the control of the Croatian government, leading to skirmishes between rebel Serbs and Croatian police and the emerging Croatian army.

Proposals by Bosnian President Alija Izetbegović and his Macedonian counterpart, Kiro Gligorov, to transform Yugoslavia into an asymmetrical confederation failed to win the support of Serbia and its allied republics and provinces and Croatia. Instead, Croatia followed Slovenia's preparation for independence. A referendum on May 19, 1991, gave an overwhelming vote for independence, but the result was flawed as most Serbs boycotted the polls. A month later, on June 25, Croatia and Slovenia declared their independence. While a brief war ensued in

Slovenia that led to humiliating defeat and withdrawal of the Yugoslav army, a tense calm continued in Croatia until the intervention of the Yugoslav army. By July 7, 1991, the army, pretending to stop the fighting between Serbs and Croats, in reality took the Serbian side and waged war against Croatia.

For a long time few countries were ready to recognize the independence of Croatia. Both the EU and the United States attempted to preserve the unity of Yugoslavia. This consensus evaporated after the attack of the Yugoslav army on the civilian populations of Vukovar and Dubrovnik. While the EU insisted on better legal protection of Serbs preceding the recognition of Croatia, Germany announced in December 1991 that it would unconditionally recognize the independence of Croatia and Slovenia on January 15, 1992. This forced other EC members to follow suit to preserve unity.

The fighting ended in January 1992 after more than ten thousand Croats and Serbs had died, with a cease-fire brokered by the United Nations. It left one-third of Croatia in the hands of rebel Serbs, while U.N. soldiers stood between both sides. This Serb-dominated area became the "Serb Republic of Krajina," but its population comprised less than half of the prewar Serb population of Croatia.

Discrimination against Serbs continued and increased during the war in Croatia, while the Krajina was systematically "cleansed" of all non-Serbs (Hungarians and Rom as well as Croats). Already in 1993 Croatia had managed to conquer small but strategic parts of the Krajina, leading up to the capture of Western Slavonia in May 1995 and the Krajina in August 1995. The swift military offensive of August 1995 led to a mass exodus of the Serb population, with as many as 170,000 escaping to Bosnia and Yugoslavia. Although denying that it was engaged in ethnic cleansing, the Croatian army did nothing to stop the exodus and frequently encouraged it. The last Serb-held territory, Eastern Slavonia, along the Serbian border, was placed under U.N. administration in 1996 and was finally reintegrated into Croatia in January 1998.

As a consequence of the Dayton peace accords for Bosnia in November 1995, Croatia and Yugoslavia normalized their relations and mutually recognized each other. The large number of Serb and Croat refugees prevented complete normalization, and ethnic hostilities continued in mixed areas.

The Croatian quest for independence stood in a direct relationship to the stalemate in federal institutions in Yugoslavia caused by Serbian President Milošević, who sought to recentralize the country under Serbian predominance. Unlike Slovenia, Croatia declared independence unprepared, militarily as well as legally. By alienating the Serbian minority in Croatia it offered Serbia a pretext to conquer large parts of the country. While it took Croatia five years to reestablish control over all its territory, Croatia has only a few remaining Serbs. The leadership of the HDZ and Tudjman has been authoritarian, allowing little opposition in politics and media and engaging in military support for nationalist Croats in Bosnia. Although the independence of Croatia is no longer questioned, its small size as well as its awkward geographical location necessities cooperation with neighboring countries, including other former Yugoslav republics.

BIBLIOGRAPHY

Cohen, Lenard J. *Broken Bonds: The Disintegration of Yugoslavia.* Boulder, Colo.: Westview Press, 1993.

Glenny, Misha. *The Fall of Yugoslavia.* London: Penguin, 1993.

Magas, Branka. *The Destruction of Yugoslavia: Tracking the Break-Up 1980–1992.* London: Verso, 1993.

Markovich, Stan. "Ethnic Serbs in Tudjman's Croatia." *RFE/RL Research Report 2* (September 1993): 28–33.

Plestina, Dijana. "Democracy and Nationalism in Croatia," in *Beyond Yugoslavia: Politics, Economics, and Culture in a Shattered Community.* Ed. by Sabrina Petra Ramet and L. S. Adamovich. Boulder, Colo.: Westview Press, 1995, 122–54.

Silver, Laura, and Allan Little. *The Death of Yugoslavia.* London: Penguin & BBC, 1995.

Stikovac, Ejup. "Croatia: The First War," in *Burn This House: The Making and Unmaking of Yugoslavia.* Ed. by Jasminka Udovicki and James Ridgeway. Durham, N.C.: Duke University Press, 1997, 153–73.

Woodward, Susan L. *Balkan Tragedy: Chaos and Dissolution after the Cold War.* Washington, D.C.: Brookings Institution, 1995.

Florian Bieber

Republic of Serbian Krajina

Before the collapse of the Yugoslav state in 1991, Serbs constituted 12 percent of the population of Croatia. Their ancestors had settled in the Military Frontier (Vojna Krajina) of the Habsburg Empire in the seventeenth century, having been invited by Habsburg emperors to serve as border guards against the Turks and to provide the Austrians with a jumping-off point for attacks on the Ottoman Empire. These Serb frontier militiamen and their families were granted religious freedom and a degree of autonomy. The military tradition of the region combined with a tradition of banditry. To establish order in the area, Empress Maria Theresa removed much of the autonomy.

Though Banija was assigned to a Croatian *ban* (administrator) and Vojvodina to a *vojvode* (duke), the Vojna Krajna, to the dismay of the Croatian and Hungarian nobility, was ruled directly from Vienna. There was tension between Serbs and Croats during the era of the Kingdom of Serbs, Croats, and Slovenes (1918–29) and the Kingdom of Yugoslavia (1929–41), as well as genocidal persecution of the Croatian Serbs during the Ustaša regime of Ante Pavelić (1941–45).

Memories of the Ustaša and the ferocity of Croatian nationalists and politicians fueled Serb unease as Croatia moved toward independence. When the process of Yugoslav disintegration became evident in 1989, the leaders of the Serbs of Krajina demanded cultural autonomy from Croatia as the price for recognizing its sovereignty. Their leader at the time, Jovan Raskoviv, merely sought autonomy within the Croatian state, such as Serb control over the school system in the majority Serb areas. When the Serbian demands were rejected, the Serbs of Krajina demanded political autonomy. When that demand was ignored, under their new leader, Milan Babić, they repudiated the authority of the Croatian government. After the declaration of Croatian independence on June 25, 1991, and the eruption of the Croatian war in July, the Croatian Serbs, who had overwhelmingly voted in a plebiscite to remain part of Yugoslavia, set up the Republic of Serbian Krajina with its capital at Knin. It included the Croatian regions of Lika, Kordun, Banja, and East and West Slavonia.

Following the January 2, 1992, truce between Croatia and the Serb-dominated remnant of Yugoslavia, fourteen thousand troops of the United Nations Protection Force (UNPROFOR) were deployed in the areas of Croatia controlled by Croatian Serbs. Nevertheless, clashes continued. After serious fighting in January 1993 the Croatians secured the Maslenica bridge and the Peruca dam, which controlled access between Split on the coast and Zagreb. On March 30, 1994, Croatia and the Croatian Serbs signed an agreement to separate their forces and establish a two-kilometer buffer zone along the one-thousand–kilometer frontier between Croatia and the Serbian-controlled districts.

Between 1992 and 1995 Croatia, despite the U.N. embargo against the sale of arms to the countries of the former Yugoslavia, with at least the connivance of the United States, which wished to use Croatia as a counterpoint to Serbia, built up a credible military force. Croatia spent $5.5 billion on the purchase of arms and reorganized its military with the help of retired senior U.S. military officers. Unhappy with the continued Serbian separatist enclaves of Eastern and Western Slavonia and Krajina within

its pre-1991 frontiers, Croatia threatened to oust UNPROFOR after its mandate expired on March 31, 1995. On March 12 President Franjo Tudjman, meeting with U.S. Vice President Al Gore, agreed on a compromise that would drastically reduce the number of U.N. troops within Croatia. In April that number was cut in half, and the U.N. forces, now labeled U.N. Confidence Restoration Operation (UNCRO), were limited to the policing of Croatia's international frontiers. On May 2, 1995, with the U.N. buffer removed, Croatia attacked the Serb enclave of Western Slavonia and overran it in two days. In response President Slobodan Milošević of Serbia, who had been alienated by the independence of Milan Babić, sent General Mile Mrksić to reorganize the military forces of the Republic of Serbian Krajina. In effect he was sent to extract as much artillery as possible to save it from an impending Croatian attack.

On August 5, 1995, the Croatians launched a massive assault, Operation Storm, with 120,000 troops against Krajina. A month before the attack American Secretary of State Warren Christopher and U.S. Ambassador to Croatia Peter Galbraith reputedly gave the Croatians approval for the operation. The United States wanted to use Croatia to counter the Serbs in Bosnia and wished to reward the Croatians for ending their war with the Bosnian Muslims in 1994. On August 4, NATO aircraft had knocked out Serbian radar and antiaircraft defenses. U.S. electronic warfare aircraft then jammed Serbian military communications. After this preparation Croatian planes attacked Serbian military assets and towns. As Serbian Krajina defenses were overwhelmed and collapsed, a massive flood of refugees took to the road. By August 8 between 150,000 and 200,000 Serbs had fled to Bosnia and approximately 14,000 were killed in this single worst example of ethnic cleansing in the former Yugoslavia before the concerted Serbian action in Kosovo in 1999.

In the November 1995 Dayton peace accords ending of the Bosnian war, it was agreed that Eastern Slavonia would gradually be restored under international supervision to Croatian administration. On January 15, 1996, the U.N. Security Council approved the stationing of 5,000 U.N. peacekeepers in Eastern Slavonia for one year to supervise the transfer of the region to Croatia. By June 21 the United Nations had competed the demilitarization of the region. On August 23 Croatia and Serbia signed a treaty normalizing relations between each other and on September 9 established full diplomatic relations. On September 20 Croatia passed an amnesty law for all Croatian Serbs who participated in armed rebellion except for individuals accused of war crimes. On July 15, 1997, as the region was gradually integrated into Croatia, 2,000

U.N. troops were withdrawn. On October 20 another 1,700 were removed, leaving only 720 U.N. soldiers to guard U.N. facilities. On the recommendation of U.N. Secretary-General Kofi Annan the U.N. Security Council passed a resolution on December 19 to terminate the mandate of the U.N. Transitional Administration in Eastern Slavonia (UNTAES) on January 15, 1998.

BIBLIOGRAPHY

Bennet, Christopher. *Yugoslavia's Bloody Collapse: Causes, Course, and Consequences.* New York: New York University Press, 1996.

Elich, Gregory, "The Invasion of Serbian Krajina." ⟨http://www.iacenter.org/bosnia/elich.htm⟩

Glenny, Mischa. *The Fall of Yugoslavia: The Third Balkan War.* 3rd ed. New York: Penguin, 1996.

Bernard Cook

Crosland, Charles Anthony Raven (1918–1977)

Politician, cabinet minister, and intellectual spokesman for Britain's Labour Party. In 1950 Anthony Crosland gave up his academic career at Oxford to join Parliament on the Labour side. A classical scholar with interests in economics, he published *The Future of Socialism* in 1956. In this book Crosland accepted the theories of J. M. Keynes in favor of a government-managed economy dedicated to sponsoring economic growth. This policy, Crosland argued, would reduce class barriers and maintain programs promoting social welfare. It also provided an alternative to the nationalization of industries and the redistribution of wealth through taxation. The work influenced a generation of Labour leaders. It underlay Hugh Gaitskell's campaign to remove the Labour Party's commitment to nationalization from its constitution, and it set the agenda for the Labour governments of the 1960s and 1970s. Under the governments of Harold Wilson (1963–70, 1974–76), Crosland held junior-level ministerial posts, usually concerned with the economy and the environment. Although Wilson's successor, James Callaghan, made Crosland foreign secretary in 1976, he never fulfilled his aspiration to be chancellor of the exchequer.

Despite Crosland's effectiveness as a minister and cabinet member, his relations with Wilson were uneasy and his unwillingness in 1970 to support entry into the EEC cost him a chance at the party's leadership. These setbacks mirrored the larger difficulties that Crosland's *Future of Socialism* encountered. Economic recession, low productivity, and labor union militancy brought an end to Crosland's program and in 1979 ushered in Margaret Thatcher's Conservative government, dedicated to a free-market alternative to Crosland's ideas.

BIBLIOGRAPHY

Crosland, Susan. *Tony Crosland.* London: Coronet Books, 1983.

Jenkins, Peter. *Mrs. Thatcher's Revolution: The Ending of the Socialist Era.* New York: Random House, 1987.

Leonard, R. L., and David Lipsey, eds. *The Socialist Agenda: Crosland's Legacy.* London: Cape, 1981.

Robert D. McJimsey

SEE ALSO Callaghan, James; Gaitskell, Hugh; Wilson, Harold

Crvenkovski, Branko (1962–)

Prime minister of Macedonia. Born in Sarajevo, the son of an officer in the Yugoslav People's Army, Branko Crvenkovski heads the Social Democratic Union of Macedonia, the successor to the former League of Communists of Macedonia. Graduating as an engineer in 1986, he began a career in industry before being elected to the Macedonian legislative assembly. His rise to power has been meteoric. He became president of the Commission on Foreign Affairs and head of his party in 1991, and prime minister of Macedonia in 1992. Although his political success has been attributed to the patronage of President Kiro Gligorov, Crvenkovski demonstrated his undoubted political ability by successfully managing a coalition government that included the main Albanian party, the Party of Democratic Prosperity.

John B. Allcock

Csoori, Sándor (1930–)

Hungarian writer, poet, and president of the World Federation of Hungarians. Sándor Csoori became one of the leading dissident writers in the 1980s and was one of the founding members of the Hungarian Democratic Forum in 1987.

Csoori was silenced by the authorities after 1956 because of his participation in the revolution against Soviet domination. He was again allowed to publish his poems and prose works from the mid-1960s. Csoori emerged as one of the leading Hungarian dissident writers in the early 1980s. He played a central role in organizing the two most important meetings of the opposition to the Communist regime in the 1980s, at Monor in 1985 and at Lakitelek in 1987. He joined the right-of-center Hungarian Democratic Forum in 1987 and was a member of its presidium between 1988 and 1993. He was elected president of the World Federation of Hungarians in 1991.

Csoori has published some fifteen volumes of poetry, ten volumes of essays, and one novel, and has six film scripts. *Barbarian Prayer: Selected Poems of Sándor Csoori, Memory of Snow,* and *Selected Poems of Sándor Csoori* have appeared in English. Csoori received the most prestigious Hungarian prize for artistic achievements, the Kossuth Prize, in 1990.

Csoori is one of the foremost proponents of cooperation with and understanding of all Hungarians living within and without Hungary, and is a committed defender of the human and civil rights of Hungarian minorities living in such neighboring states as Romania and Slovokia.

BIBLIOGRAPHY

Csoori, Sandor. *Selected Poems of Sandor Csoori.* Port Townsend, Wash.: Copper Canyon Press, 1992.

Kiss, Ferenc. *Csoori Sandor.* Budapest: Magveto, 1990.

Tamás Magyarics

Cuban Missile Crisis

The October 1962 confrontation between the United States and the Soviet Union over the Soviet stationing of strategic nuclear missiles in Cuba, ninety miles from the Florida coast. Soviet military forces in Cuba were far more extensive than believed by U.S. policymakers at the time and were equipped with tactical nuclear missiles, which could be launched by local Soviet commanders in response to a U.S. invasion of the island. President John F. Kennedy immediately formed a group of experts known as the Executive Committee (ExComm) to advise him on U.S. responses to the presence of Soviet missiles in Cuba, demanded the withdrawal of the missiles, enforced a naval blockade of the island, and prepared for the Soviet response. Thus began the most perilous superpower confrontation of the nuclear age, the moment during the Cold War when these two powers came closest to crossing the threshold of nuclear war. While Soviet vessels did not effectively defy the blockade, it was only after a threat of U.S. invasion that the USSR consented to remove the missiles. The agreement was complemented by a pledge not to invade Cuba and Kennedy's covert guarantee to remove American Jupiter missiles from Turkey.

In the early morning hours of October 14, 1962, an American U-2 reconnaissance plane flew over Cuba, taking almost one thousand photos of the western region. During the next afternoon CIA photographic interpreters informed high-level CIA authorities that the sortie had

documented Soviet medium-range ballistic missile (MRBMs) bases under construction near San Cristóbol. The Deputy CIA Director provided the photographs to the White House. On the morning of October 16 National Security Adviser McGeorge Bundy warned the president that the United States faced a grave international crisis.

The recent intelligence furnished the first definitive evidence that Soviet missile sites were actually under construction in Cuba. During the summer of 1962 the president and his advisers observed with increasing alarm the rapid transport to the island of Soviet arms, including antiaircraft missiles, missile boats, advanced MiG fighters, and jet bombers. Yet the belief among most authorities in the administration was that the Soviets would not risk inciting Washington by deploying surface-to-surface missiles with nuclear capability. In conferences with Soviet authorities during September and early October, the United States solicited and secured pledges that "offensive" missiles were not being positioned on the island. The administration now learned that it had been deluded.

For most of the world this incendiary confrontation between the two major Cold War powers began on October 22, 1962. For President Kennedy, who that evening divulged the existence of Soviet missiles in Cuba, the crisis had thus begun nearly a week earlier. In his televised address he stated that the USSR had started to deploy medium- and intermediate-range nuclear missiles, maintaining that the objective of these bases was to supply a nuclear strike capacity against the United States. He asserted that by engaging in this activity, the Soviets confirmed that they had for many months distorted their strategy on the island. Kennedy demanded the immediate dismantling and withdrawal of the missiles under U.S. supervision and asserted that Washington was ready not only to blockade Cuba but also to do whatever would be required to remove the missiles. The president announced a naval quarantine on shipments of arms to Cuba. The United States would not unnecessarily risk a nuclear conflagration, he insisted, but neither would it back down from this danger whenever it must be confronted. He stated that a Soviet offensive on any target in the United States or Latin America would eventuate in "a full retaliatory response" against the USSR.

The Soviet determination to station missiles in Cuba made five months previously was forged both as a result of continual aggravation and a reckless wager. Kennedy also misunderstood Soviet Premier Nikita Khrushchev's intentions. Achieving a nuclear strike capability was not his sole purpose. Andrey Gromyko, Soviet foreign minister in 1962, maintained in 1989 that the purpose of the missile deployment was to intensify the defensive stability of Cuba and impede the threat against it. He insisted that this was the only intent. In reality, Khrushchev had convinced the Politburo that an American assault against Cuba was highly probable and could be thwarted by positioning medium-range R-12 ballistic missiles and intermediate-range R-14 ballistic missiles. These MRBMs and IRBMs stationed so near to North America would likewise be a factor in rectifying the nuclear balance by compensating for the underdeveloped nature of the Soviet arsenal of intercontinental ballistic missiles (ICBMs). The Soviet military quickly mobilized to carry out Khrushchev's plans for Cuba.

Khrushchev's convictions about American intentions toward Cuba were not without factual basis. Extensive covert action operations against Cuba included the notorious Operation Mongoose. These operations were connected with U.S. military contingency planning, which increased substantially starting in early 1962. This intensified planning followed not from Soviet conventional expansion on the island but from the covert program's inbred impetus and possibly from the enhanced aspirations of its directors that they might have a chance to facilitate an anti-Castro revolt.

On October 27 an American invasion fleet converged off the coast of Cuba. In Florida 850 combat aircraft awaited orders to assault Soviet missile sites and soldiers on the island. In the air more than 50 B-52 bombers transported 196 nuclear weapons bound for targets in the Soviet Union. The chairman of the Joint Chiefs of Staff in the White House communicated the Pentagon's recommendation to Kennedy: carry out the "big strike . . . no later than Monday morning the 29th." Fidel Castro's forces and 40,000 Soviet troops on the island prepared for what their leaders believed would be an impending attack. Units transported nuclear warheads out of their storage depots closer to missiles Washington ascertained as able to strike the U.S. mainland and to battlefield weapons U.S. intelligence had not yet observed.

Soviet ships moved toward a line of U.S. naval vessels designated to quarantine the island. Nearly at the last minute, on the morning of October 24, Soviet vessels headed for Cuba arrived at the blockade line and turned back. On October 27 the USSR and the United States a second time appeared on the verge of war as the Soviet missile sites came to completion, rockets shot down a U-2 spy plane over the island, killing its American pilot, and Kennedy mandated more than one hundred thousand combat-ready troops to southern Florida to prepare to invade Cuba. On the morning of October 28 Khrushchev announced in a broadcast over Radio Moscow that he

would accept the president's assurance not to invade the island in return for a Soviet promise to remove the missiles. This brought an end to the most mordant stage of the confrontation. President Kennedy consistently depended on negotiation before, during, and after the missile crisis. Kennedy and ExComm attempted to hide this diplomacy, subsequently affecting a facade of resoluteness. This posture involved leaking the allegation shortly after the crisis that U.N. Ambassador Adlai Stevenson, who supported negotiation, had "wanted a Munich," while in fact a number of officials, Kennedy among them, had endorsed this position.

The perception of the Cuban missile crisis has altered. Instead of a precipitous incident, the deadlock today appears as the climax of worsening relations between the USSR and the United States, and between the United States and Cuba. Likewise, it is no longer possible to view the conflict as limited to "thirteen days," starting on October 14 with the detection of Soviet missiles on the island and concluding with Khrushchev's decision to remove the missiles on October 28. Correspondence between Khrushchev and Kennedy, declassified and released to the National Security Archive in 1992, confirms that the conflict went on at least through late November 1962.

Both Kennedy and Khrushchev were moderates who were acutely alert to the perils of nuclear confrontation and ultimately tended to be accommodating. Yet both were also motivated by a necessity to mollify their own hard-liners, adept at swaggering, and barely mindful of each other's political environment and mores. What resulted from this was an escalation of misperception and distorted communication. The resolution of the crisis for Khrushchev resulted in his being subjected to ridicule from China and other Communist countries.

President Kennedy misunderstood Premier Khrushchev's January 1961 Wars of Liberation speech to be the introduction to an era of Soviet expansionism, not realizing that it was principally an attempt to fend off China's censure of his policies. Kennedy replied with an ominous State of the Union Address, which along with other of the administration's previous activities provided Soviet leaders with the perception that Washington's aims were belligerent. During the first months of the administration the disastrous Bay of Pigs invasion validated the Soviets' apprehension but induced them to believe that the president did not have the resoluteness and competence to complete the operation. In an attempt to capitalize on Kennedy's apparent lack of strength, Khrushchev forcefully challenged him over the question of Berlin at a June 1961 summit meeting in Vienna, galvanizing the president to promote America's superior strategic nuclear advantage. Khrushchev reacted by attempting to rectify the disparity, covertly stationing missiles in Cuba.

A subject of consequence is the relationship between Soviet operations in the Caribbean and its goals in Europe. The United States viewed the Berlin crisis and the Cuban crisis as comparable situations. It anticipated a forceful Soviet response in Berlin to any U.S. military engagement in Cuba. Yet Soviet authorities have asserted that they perceived Berlin and Cuba as two discrete situations with no immediate connection between them.

Divisions existed within the Kennedy administration over Cuba—between learning to live with Castro and avenging the Bay of Pigs defeat. These mixed signals confounded even the most astute observers in 1962. Both Havana and Moscow believed that a U.S. attack was being planned. The Pentagon command structure, for its part, had been demoralized by earlier conflicts with its civilian leaders and was eager to use overwhelming force against Cuba both to eliminate the external threat and to regain the president's confidence. For nearly thirty years after the Cuban Missile Crisis, the history of this perilous confrontation remained mostly secret. Because Soviet military doctrine held secrecy to be a vital element of national security, the diplomatic, political, and military archives of the USSR were concealed. U.S. sources were also fragmentary. The American public was thus compelled to see the crisis in terms of a drama pitting an adroit American president against an erratic Soviet leader. Yet because of archival material now available, a case may be made, for instance, for viewing ExComm not as the adept, judicious group of advisers ordinarily depicted in most of the literature on the missile crisis but the medium by which Kennedy established consensus for decisions at which he had previously arrived. Current documentary evidence also substantiates the importance of domestic politics in Kennedy's determination and his decision to establish the blockade.

The momentum that almost brought these two "ignorant armies" into conflict was potentially more destructive than political leaders understood at the time. Retired Soviet General Anatoly I. Gribkov, who was in charge of devising the USSR's covert nuclear deployment to Cuba, maintains that Soviet troops on the island during the crisis were armed not only with strategic nuclear missiles, which could strike Washington or New York, but also with shorter-range tactical nuclear weapons. Gribkov asserts that the USSR positioned Luna missiles in Cuba with nuclear warheads of fewer than one hundred kilotons, with a range of approximately twenty-five miles. There are Soviet claims that the commander in Cuba, General Issa Pliyev, had authorization from Khrushchev to launch

these missiles against a U.S. invasion without clearance from Moscow, even if contact with Moscow had been severed. While there still exists uncertainty about all the details of Pliyev's standing orders, even if it could be ascertained that Khrushchev strictly preserved nuclear release authority, no mechanism existed for guaranteeing control. These assertions, with their apparent insinuation that the crisis may have verged nearer to nuclear war than formerly believed, generated debate over the meaning and credibility of Gribkov's declaration. Based on newly declassified material from Soviet archives, Gribkov's account adds a new element of risk to the narrative of the Cuban Missile Crisis.

Is General Gribkov's assertion credible? The Russian Defense Ministry declassified documents from the "Andyr" file, the code name for the Cuban missile operation. Defense Minister Rodion Malinovsky's order imparted late September–early October 1962 to General Pliyev reads: "Only in the event of a landing of the opponent's forces on the island of Cuba and if there is a concentration of enemy ships with landing forces near the coast of Cuba, in its territorial waters . . . and there is no possibility to receive directives from the USSR Ministry of Defense, you are personally allowed as an exception to take the decision to apply the tactical nuclear Luna missiles as a means of local war for the destruction of the opponent on land and on the coast with the aim of a full crushing defeat of troops on the territory of Cuba and the defense of the Cuban Revolution."

There are correlative Russian assertions that Soviet military on the island possessed thirty-six nuclear warheads for the twenty-four intermediate-range missiles targeted on American cities. At the time, the CIA maintained that there were no nuclear warheads on the island. It has also been revealed that there were six dual-purpose tactical launchers bolstered by nine tactical missiles with nuclear warheads to be employed against a U.S. invasion combat force. If a U.S. assault had taken place, as many in the government were advocating, American landing forces would probably have been destroyed on the island with thousands of casualties. Though the U.S. military would not have transported tactical nuclear warheads, if nuclear warheads had been used against American forces, Washington would have used nuclear warheads in retaliation.

There has existed an inclination on the part of Western scholars to identify the Kennedy administration's conjectures and information with the complex reality of what the Soviets called the "Caribbean Crisis." This results in minimizing the degree to which decision making was marked by uncertainty. Archival materials today are severely damaging of overstated assumptions about "crisis management." One of the most important morals of the missile crisis is that governments need pay strict attention to how their adversaries might or do view their activities. The United States performed poorly on that score in advance of the actual crisis. Public pronouncements, military activities, covert operations—each gave the appearance of preparations for an incursion onto the island and the removal of Castro. High-level figures in the government, however, had no plans for such an incursion, though a number of civilian and military authorities hoped that this type of aggravation of Castro would force him to believe that his position was precarious. The intention was to compel him to concentrate his efforts on maintaining strength on the island rather than undermine governments in other Caribbean and Latin American countries.

It is impracticable to comprehend accurately how hazardous the Cuban Missile Crisis was, since it is not feasible to fix a probability to the prospect that the deadlock would have intensified to strategic nuclear war. Yet the crisis was absolutely the most ominous episode of the nuclear age. The deployment of Soviet tactical nuclear weapons on the island only intensified the hazard. An insouciant disposition toward nuclear risk, based in deficient awareness of military procedures, of command and control, and of civil-military alliances, is in itself extremely hazardous.

By the final forty-eight hours of the crucial stage of the crisis (from approximately October 26 to 28), the source of dread for the primary managers of the crisis had changed from nuclear attack to nuclear danger. This involved a certitude that while neither antagonist wanted to initiate nuclear war against the other, the exigency they were both part of might veer out of control into an unintentional war. Both Khrushchev and Kennedy repeatedly evinced the constraints on their influence of the organizations under their formal command. It is arguable that this dread of nuclear dereliction is what allowed the missile crisis to be resolved without war. Neither side had a real motive for taking on the other in a nuclear conflict. The crisis is saturated with episodes of misinformation, distortion, and miscalculation. It should be a lesson learned that when these types of misjudgments influence decisions relevant to nuclear forces, they can lead to the obliteration of nations.

For seven days the world lived with a foreboding that neither antagonist would compromise and that nuclear conflagration would result. The resolution of this monumental East-West confrontation was a defining moment in a fading epoch of the Cold War. It dramatized the closure of a period when an intense antagonism between two societies ended in a confrontation that might have resulted in nuclear war. The two world powers went to the threshold of nuclear war, peered over the crevasse, and determined to turn back. Both the USSR and the United States stumbled, frequently because of activities and responses initiated with minimal deliberation and circumspection, into conflict and near catastrophe.

BIBLIOGRAPHY

Allison, Graham. *Essence of Decision.* Boston: Little, Brown, 1971.

Allyn, Bruce, James Blight, and David Welch, eds. *Cuba on the Brink: Castro, the Missile Crisis and the Soviet Collapse.* New York: Pantheon, 1993.

Beschloss, Michael. *The Crisis Years: Kennedy and Khrushchev 1960–1963.* New York: HarperCollins, 1991.

Blight, James, and David Welch. *On the Brink: Americans and Soviets Reexamine the Cuban Missile Crisis.* New York: Hill and Wang, 1989.

Brugioni, Dino. *Eyeball to Eyeball.* New York: Random House, 1991.

Central Intelligence Agency. *The Secret Cuban Missile Crisis Documents.* Washington, D.C.: Brassey's (US), 1994.

Chang, Laurence, and Peter Kornbluh. *The Cuban Missile Crisis, 1962: A National Security Archive Documents Reader.* New York: New Press, 1992.

The Cuban Missile Crisis, 1962: The Making of U.S. Policy. Washington, D.C.: National Security Archive, 1992.

Gribkov, Anatoli I., and William Y. Smith. *Operation ANADYR: U.S. And Soviet Generals Recount the Cuban Missile Crisis.* Chicago: Edition Q, 1994.

Kennedy, Robert. *Thirteen Days: A Memoir of the Cuban Missile Crisis.* New York: Norton, 1969.

May, Ernest, and Philip Zelikow, eds. *The Kennedy Tapes: Inside the White House during the Cuban Missile Crisis.* Cambridge, Mass.: Harvard University Press, 1997.

Nathan, James A., ed. *The Cuban Missile Crisis Revisited.* New York: St. Martin's Press, 1992.

Thompson, Robert. *The Missiles of October: The Declassified Story of John F. Kennedy and the Cuban Missile Crisis.* New York: Simon and Schuster, 1992.

Kenneth Keulman

Cuccia, Enrico (1907–)

Italian banker. Enrico Cuccia was born in Rome to a Sicilian family on November 24, 1907. During the 1930s he worked at Banca d'Italia, Istituto per Riconstruzione Industriale (IRI), and COMIT (a commercial bank).

During World War II he was active in the antifascist and left-wing Partito d'Azione and in 1942 was sent to Lisbon on a mission. After the war in 1946 Cuccia was appointed general manager of Mediobanca. This commercial bank was founded by the three most important banks of the IRI (Banco di Roma, Credit, and Comit), and it has operated since then as a clearinghouse for deals between different Italian economic groups, the place where alliances, mergers, and acquisitions are engineered and where the most important financial operations are planned. Because of his position, Cuccia became the gray eminence of Italian finance. From Mediobanca the Sicilian banker governed the financial policies of the most important Italian economic groups. Mediobanca became, in fact, the most important Italian merchant bank and acquired interest in the major Italian business groups (Fiat, Generali, Montedison, and Pirelli). Cuccia maintained the bank's independence from political parties and led it to privatization in 1988.

Mediobanca became one of the most important centers of power in Italy, because it centralized de facto the control of a large part of the private economy. This position allowed Mediobanca to counterbalance the expansion of the public sphere and the influence of political parties over the private economy. Because of this, the bank suffered attacks from the political forces excluded from this play and from the economically ascendant forces who sought to enter the rigidly controlled market. Among the great enemies of Cuccia were Michele Sindona and Roberto Calvi, two important Italian bankers implicated with organized crime. One of the last decisive clashes was against Raul Gardini. Currently Cuccia is the honorary president of Mediobanca.

BIBLIOGRAPHY

De Cecco, Marcello, and Giovanni Ferri. *Le banche d'affari in Italia.* Bologna: Il Mulino, 1996.

Galli, Giancarlo. *Il padrone dei padroni.* Milan: Garzanti, 1995.

Tamburini, Fabio. *Un siciliano a Milano.* Milan: Longanesi, 1992.

Daniele Petrosino

SEE ALSO Gardini, Raul; Sindona, Michele

Cunhal, Alvaro (Barreirinhas) (1913–)

Militant of the Portuguese Communist Party (PCP) since the 1930s and secretary-general from 1961 to 1992. In the midst of Soviet leader Mikhail Gorbachev's reforms, Alvaro Cunhal refused to alter the PCP's orthodox commitment to the proletariat and Marxism-Leninism. After a long history of participation within the PCP, Cunhal continued to hold an influential position in the organization in 1998.

In 1931 he joined the PCP while a law student in Lisbon. He became secretary-general of the Portuguese Communist Youth (JC) in 1935, and this also gave him membership in the PCP's Central Committee. He advanced to the PCP's Secretariat in 1942 after playing a leading role in the reorganization of 1940–41, which gave the party its present orthodox character. Cunhal labeled himself "the adopted son of the proletariat" at the 1950 trial that sentenced him to eleven years in prison for Communist activity. Because his father was a lawyer-painter-writer and Cunhal received a master's degree in law, his origins were neither peasant nor worker but petit bourgeois. During his lifetime he spent thirteen years in prison, eight of them in solitary confinement. In 1960 he and nine other mostly Communist political prisoners made a spectacular escape from the Peniche prison and fled the country. Cunhal, the party's main theoretician, was elected secretary-general in 1961 and, along with other top leaders, directed the party from abroad while in exile.

In the aftermath of the 1974 Portuguese revolution, which terminated the Salazar/Caetano dictatorship and ushered in democracy, Cunhal ended his exile and returned home. He played important roles in post-1974 political events ranging from leader of the Communist offensive during the "hot summer" of 1975, positions of minister without portfolio in the first through fifth provisional governments, to his membership in parliament beginning in 1976.

At the PCP's Fourteenth Congress in 1992, Carlos Carvalhas was elected secretary-general, replacing Cunhal. Whatever official or unofficial position Cunhal held, however, automatically became a dominant position within the party. After stepping down as secretary-general he was elected to head the party's National Council, a post that, was eliminated in 1996.

Many political observers have argued that Cunhal purposefully picked a successor who could not outshine him. Carvalhas did not have Cunhal's humanistic savvy, lacked emotion, and was void of discourse. Cunhal continued to eclipse Carvalhas not only charismatically but also in his "jack-of-all-trades" accomplishments. Cunhal was known not only as a dynamic orator but also as an artist, novelist, and brilliant political tactician. He has admitted to writing under several pseudonyms, including Manuel Tiago, author of the well-known *Até Amanhã, Camaradas,* and the novel recently adapted for film *Cinco Dias, Cinco No-*

ites. And he recently published a book on art theory under his own name titled *A Arte, O Artista E A Sociedade.* He has also published several volumes of speeches and political treatises.

Although he was among the most orthodox leaders of the major Western European Communist parties, Cunhal was not a Soviet puppet as many claimed. His disdain for Gorbachev's policies of perestroika and glasnost clearly illustrated this. He was not only a major leader at home but also in the international Communist movement. His orthodoxy was especially useful to the Soviets in their struggle to maintain cohesion in a movement threatened by division from the Eurocommunists in the 1970s. To conclude that Cunhal was a Soviet puppet is to ignore his independent decisions during the Portuguese revolution (1974–75), when the Soviets reportedly tried to slow Cunhal's revolutionary strategy because it ran counter to détente and other Soviet strategies.

In many ways Cunhal's views are still locked in the past. His perception and analyses of modern Portuguese revolutionary conditions have not altered radically from his experiences and analyses of revolutionary conditions in the 1940s. To Cunhal, although some conditions have changed that require tactical shifts, the major conflict is the same one that led to the creation of the Communist Information Bureau (Cominform) in 1947. The world is still divided into two camps: American and Western imperialism on one side, and socialism, with its goal of achieving the fullest of democracies, on the other. Cunhal continues to believe that Marxism-Leninism and scientific socialism provide the solutions to resolving the problems of the world.

Despite the perceived changes at the 1992 congress, Cunhal has played a major, though not as public, a role in the political life of the PCP.

BIBLIOGRAPHY

Andringa, Diana. "Cunhal, Alvaro Barreirinhas," in Fernando Rosas and J. M. Brandão de Brito, eds., *Dicionário de História do Estado Novo.* Vol. 2. Venda Nova, Portugal: Bertrand Editora, 1996.

Cunha, Carlos A. *The Portuguese Communist Party's Strategy for Power, 1921–1986.* New York: Garland, 1992.

Ferreira, Francisco. *Alvaro Cunhal, Heroi Soviético.* Lisbon: Edição do Autor, 1976.

60 Anos de Luta. Lisbon: Ediçoes Avante, 1982.

Carlos A. Cunha

Curcio, Renato (1941–)

Founder of the Red Brigades with Margherita Cagol and Alberto Franceschini in 1970 in Milan. Curcio was the Red Brigades' principal theoretician and director. Though the authorities jailed him in 1976, Curcio continued to play a leading role in terrorist activities.

Renato Curcio was born in Monterotondo as the illegitimate child of Yolanda Curcio and Renato Zampa. A good student, Curcio had already received a degree in chemistry when he accepted a scholarship to study at the Institute of Sociology at the University of Trentino in 1964. There he met Margherita Cagol and began to study the writings of Marx, Lenin, and Mao. Trentino was a center for students of the radical left, and Curcio thrived in his new environment. He encouraged the students to begin a movement of the proletariat and rejected the revisionist politics of Italy's Communist Party. In 1969 Curcio and Cagol married and moved to Milan, where the political climate was especially tense. In the spirit of the worker and student movements, the young couple joined the Metropolitan Political Collective (MPC) to fight capitalism and bourgeois power. The MPC accepted violence as a legitimate tool in their struggle. By 1970 Curcio, Cagol, and Franceschini had formed their own revolutionary group, the Red Brigades. They claimed responsibility for their first action in September 1971, when they set fire to the automobile of a Sit-Siemens executive. A highly secretive and well-organized group, the Red Brigades under Curcio's leadership staged robberies, kidnappings, and maimings to attract attention to their cause. At first their targets included factory foremen and those with direct power over workers. They then went on to attack important public figures and journalists. Curcio was jailed as the result of an undercover operation in 1974, but Cagol rescued him in 1975. Shortly thereafter a police officer killed her during a raid on a Red Brigades hideout. Another investigation led police to Curcio in 1976. In 1994 Curcio was given permission to leave his jail cell during the day to work as a publisher in Rome. Many Italians have expressed outrage that a former terrorist has been allowed to pursue a career.

BIBLIOGRAPHY

Franceschini, Alberto, Pier Vittorio Buffa, and Franco Giustolisi. *Maria, Renato e io: storia dei fondatori delle BR.* Milan: Mondadori, 1988.

Meade, Robert C., Jr. *Red Brigades: The Story of Italian Terrorism.* New York: St. Martin's Press, 1990.

Moss, David. *The Politics of Left-Wing Violence in Italy, 1969–1985.* New York: St. Martin's Press, 1989.

Tessandori, Vincenzo. *Br. Imputazione: banda armata.* Milan: Garzanti, 1977.

Wendy A. Pojmann

Cyprus

Island (Greek, Kipros; Turkish, Kibris) located in the eastern Mediterranean Sea about 40 miles (60 km) south of Turkey and 250 miles (402 km) north of the Nile delta in Egypt. The island has an area of 3,572 square miles (9,251 sq km) and its population in 1993 was 764,000. The population is approximately 80 percent Greek and 20 percent Turkish. The Greeks are Eastern Orthodox Christians and the Turks are Sunni Muslims. Following the Turkish invasion of 1974 and the proclamation of the Turkish Republic of Northern Cyprus (TRNC), the island has been separated into two political units. The capital of the Republic of Cyprus (RC) is Nicosia. The capital of the TRNC is the Lefkosa section of Nicosia, on the Turkish side of the dividing line.

After Russia defeated the Ottoman Empire in the 1877–78 Russo-Turkish War, Cyprus was transferred to British administration at the Congress of Berlin in 1878. In 1914 Britain formally annexed the island, which became a crown colony in 1925. The British were initially welcomed by the Greeks of the island, who hoped that the British would turn the island over to Greece. Britain did offer Greece the island as a reward in 1915, if it would enter World War I on the Allies' side, but when Greece refused, the offer was dropped. An offer of greater self-government in 1947 was refused by the Greeks, who single-mindedly demanded unity with Greece (*enosis*). In 1955 Cypriot Greek nationalists led by Lieutenant Colonel Georgios Grivas, a Cypriot serving in the Greek army, launched a terrorist struggle against the British and Greek opponents of *enosis.* They called themselves the National Organization of Cypriot Struggle (Ethniki Organosis Kipriakou Agonos, EOKA). Archbishop Makarios III, head of the Orthodox Church on Cyprus, was the political leader of the movement for *enosis,* and in the minds of the British he was responsible for the terror. In March 1956 he and three other EOKA leaders were deported. Makarios was exiled to the Seychelles for a year. After he

was allowed to leave, he was forbidden to return to Cyprus. From Athens, however, he continued his political campaign. The Turkish Cypriot minority, led by Fazil Küçük, roused by the fear of a Greek-controlled Cyprus, began a campaign for the return of the island to Turkey or partition. Public opinion in Greece and Turkey became mobilized in support of their respective conationals. In the tense climate there were riots and expulsions of Greeks from Turkey.

In February 1959 the Greek and Turkish governments, attempting to defuse the increasingly tense situation, reached an agreement at Geneva that became the basis for a compromise agreed on in London by the British government, Makarios, and Küçük. Cyprus was to become independent, but Britain was to retain control of bases at Akrotiri and Dhekélia. Independent Cyprus would not be united politically or economically with any other state and would not be partitioned. Greece and Turkey both accepted the agreement.

In December 1959 Makarios was elected president and Küçük was elected vice president. Although decisions made by a Council of Ministers would be binding on the president and the vice president, either of them could veto decisions connected with security, defense, and foreign relations. The Turkish Cypriot community was guaranteed quotas in segments of the public arena that exceeded their percentage of the population, including. The Turks were guaranteed 33 percent of the seats in the House of Representatives, 30 percent of civil service posts, and 40 percent of the military, which was also to have a joint Greek and Turkish command.

The first parliamentary election took place on July 31, 1960. Supporters of Makarios won thirty of the thirty-five seats set aside for the Greeks. Five by prior agreement had been assigned to the Communist Progressive Workers Party (Anorthotiko Komma Ergazomenou Laou, AKEL). Supporters of Küçük won all fifteen seats set aside for the Turks. The London agreement was ratified by treaties signed in Nicosia, and Cyprus officially became independent on August 16, 1960. The United Kingdom agreed to provide £12 million in aid over a period of five years. Cyprus was admitted to the United Nations and became a member of the British Commonwealth.

There were difficulties in implementing the London agreement. In November 1963 Makarios proposed amendments to the constitution that were rejected by Küçük. The Turks withdrew from the government and in December fighting erupted between the two communities. In March 1964 the United Nations set up the U.N. Peace-Keeping Force in Cyprus (UNFICYP). The Turks, without any representation in the national government,

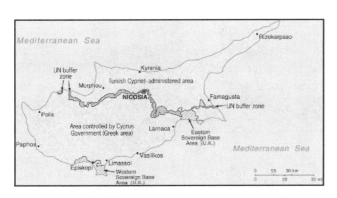

Cyprus. *Illustration courtesy of Bernard Cook.*

set up their own counteradministration in the Turkish-populated area. They sought a federational solution to the political impasse but the Greeks refused. Despite the presence of UNFICYP, fighting intensified and the Turkish air force became involved. Both Greece and Turkey surreptitiously sent troops to the island, and Grivas, who had been promoted to general in the Greek army, was sent to take command of the Greek-Cypriot National Guard. A 1967 incident provoked an ultimatum from Turkey, and the Greek junta responded by withdrawing the Greek military contingent and calling Grivas back to the mainland. Though a temporary peace followed, attempts to find a compromise solution to the interethnic conflict failed.

In 1968 Makarios was reelected president by a significant majority and had no opponent when he ran in 1973. He had been a leading proponent of *enosis,* but his opponents on Cyprus and in Greece believed that as president he had become comfortable with a separate Cypriot state. There were attempts to assassinate him in 1970 and 1973. The three other Cypriot bishops attempted to force him to renounce the presidency, but he appealed to a synod convened by the patriarch of Alexandria. With its support Makarios retained both his political and ecclesiastical offices.

In 1971 Grivas came back to the island, roused the EOKA militants, formed a more militant offshoot of EOKA called EOKA-B, and began a new terror campaign, now with the apparent support of the colonels' regime in Greece directed against Makarios's government. Grivas died in January 1974, but on July 15, 1974, a segment of the National Guard commanded by officers from Greece proper launched a coup. They wanted to assassinate Makarios and unite Cyprus with Greece. Makarios escaped but they named Nikos Sampson (1935–), an extreme Greek nationalist and former EOKA terrorist, president. Responding to an appeal from Rauf Denktas (1924–), leader of the Cypriot Turks, the Turkish government on July 20 landed troops at Kyrenia to overthrow Sampson and prevent the union of Cyprus with Greece. On July 23 Sampson resigned. Glavkos Klerides (1919–) became acting head of the RC, holding that post until Makarios's return in December. Following Sampson's resignation, the military regime in Greece, as a result of the failure of its machinations in Cyprus, fell. The Turkish force, despite discussions in Geneva among the United Kingdom, Greece, and Turkey, continued to advance. By August 15 they had seized 37 percent of the island and established a line running from Morphou to Famagusta. This "Attila" line ran through Nicosia and became the frontier between a new Turkish Cypriot para-state in the north and the rest of the island. In February 1975 the leaders of the Turkish Cypriots proclaimed the Turkish Federated State of Cyprus (TFSC) with Denktash as president. Denktash, however, stated that the goal of the Turks was still federation rather than independence. U.N.-sponsored talks in Vienna in 1975 and 1976 led to a 1977 agreement between Makarios and Denktash on conditions for a bizonal federation. Then Makarios died in August 1977.

Spyros Kyprianou (1932–), president of the House of Representatives since 1976, became acting president of the RC. He was elected to the presidency in January 1978. An electoral alliance between his Democratic Party (Dimokratiko Komma, DIKO) and AKEL secured his reelection in February 1983, but the Turks took part in neither election. A heated debate followed in 1985 on Kyprianou's leadership. He dissolved the House of Representatives and called for a general election. When that was held in December, Kyprianou's opponents, the Democratic Rally (Dimokratikos Synagermos, DISY) and AKEL won, respectively, nineteen and fifteen seats to the sixteen won by Kyprianou's DIKO. But they did not have the two-thirds necessary to amend the constitution to strip away some of the president's power. In 1988, however, Kyprianou lost the presidency to economist George Vassiliou (1931–), an independent unofficially supported by the Communist AKEL. Vassiliou had proposed reconvening Makarios's National Council composed of representatives of all Cypriot political parties to discuss a settlement of the ethnic standoff.

In May 1983 Denktash terminated the continuing talks with the Greek Cypriots and in November proclaimed the Turkish Republic of North Cyprus (TRNC). The U.N. Security Council condemned this initiative and demanded, as it had since 1974, that foreign troops be withdrawn from the territory of the RC. The Turkish Cypriots were unmoved and approved the constitution of their new republic in May 1985. The republic has been recognized only by Turkey but continues its de facto separate existence. Nejat Konuk (1928–), who served as prime minister of the TFSC from 1976 to 1978 and president of its legislative assembly from 1981 to 1983, headed an interim government. On June 9, 1985, 70 percent of the voters continued Denktash's tenure as president, and on June 23 the National Unity Party (Ulusal Birlik Partisi, UBP) won twenty-four of the fifty seats in the Legislative Assembly. Dervis Eroglu of the UBP became prime minister.

In July 1985 and April 1986 the U.N. secretary-general proposed a settlement based on a federal republic with specified ratios of participation in the federal government. The Turkish Cypriots rejected the first proposal, because they insisted that Turkey be a guarantor of the settlement and that Turkish troops remain on the island. The Greek Cypriots rejected the second because they insisted that in addition to the withdrawal of Turkish troops and the elimination of Turkey as a guarantor, Turkish settlers who had come from the mainland after 1975 be forced to leave the island. The Greek Cypriots wanted a meeting between Kyprianou and Denktash or an international conference. The Turkish Cypriots, however, refused to attend a conference that would treat the RC as the legitimate government and the Turks as only an aggrieved minority. They also refused to agree to demilitarization as a precondition to a settlement.

Despite face-to-face negotiations between Vassiliou and Denktash in 1988 and 1990, and a May 1989 "deconfrontation" agreement for the ethnic boundary, progress toward a settlement foundered on Denktash's demand that the right of the Turkish community to self-determination be recognized. The United Nations continued to support a nonpartitioned federal republic.

In April 1990 Denktash's retention of the presidency was supported by 67 percent of those voting. In May the UBP won thirty-four of the fifty seats in the TRNC's legislative assembly and Eroglu continued as prime minister.

In July 1990 the RC petitioned for EU membership. Denktash protested but the EU approved Cyprus's eligibility. The EU, however, demanded that membership be contingent on the success of U.N.-sponsored negotiations. Turkey responded by confirming its economic support of the TRNC. In 1994 the expenditures of the TRNC exceeded revenues by 25 percent, but Turkey subsidized approximately 38 percent of the deficit. Turkey also announced its intention to remove passport controls between the TRNC and Turkey, proposed a customs union for the two, and affirmed its continued guarantee of the TRNC's security. Efforts by the United States to encourage talks between the two Cypriot entities and Greece and Turkey failed when Greece and Turkey were unable to agree on preliminary conditions.

On May 19, 1991, elections to the House of Representative in the RC resulted in 35.8 percent and twenty seats for a coalition of DISY and the Liberal Party (Komma Phileleftheron), but AKEL won 30.5 percent and eighteen seats. On February 14, 1993, Glavkos Klerides of DISY defeated Vassiliou for president by less than 1 percent. In November Klerides and Greek Prime Minister Andreas Papandreou affirmed that Greece and the RC would make joint decisions on the issues involved in the Cyprus dispute. Greece also promised to provide the RC with land, sea, and air protection.

In February 1994 Denktash and Klerides had agreed to confidence-building measures proposed by the United Nations. But the talks broke down. Though some small positive steps were subsequently taken, there was no substantive agreement.

In July 1994 the EU refused to accept produce from the TRNC that had not been certified by the RC. This was a severe economic threat for the TRNC, where 23.4 percent of the workers were engaged in agriculture, predominantly growing citrus fruit. While manufacturing produced 14 percent of the gross domestic product in the RC, it accounted for only 8.5 percent in the TRNC. Tourism, the largest producer of income for the island, preponderantly benefits the RC, which had 2,069,000 tourists in 1994 compared with the 351,628, predominantly Turkish, tourists who visited the TRNC.

In July 1994 the United Nations also adopted a resolution for a Cyprus settlement on the basis of a single nationality and sovereignty, yet the legislative assembly of the TRNC rejected any peace based on even federation and called for closer integration with Turkey. The attempt of the EU to proceed with the consideration of membership for Cyprus also caused negative reactions in the TRNC.

BIBLIOGRAPHY

Borowiec, Andrew. *Cyprus: a Troubled Island.* Westport, Conn.: Praeger, 2000.

"Cyprus," *The Europa World Yearbook 1996.* London: Europa Publications Limited, 1996. I: 990–994.

Joseph, Joseph S. *Cyprus: Ethnic Conflict and International Politics: From Independence to the Threshold of the European Union.* New York: St. Martin's Press, 1997.

Spilling, Michael. *Cyprus.* New York: Marshall Cavendish, 2000.

Bernard Cook

SEE ALSO Ioannides, Demetrios; Makarios III

Cyrankiewicz, Józef (1911–89)

Polish politician and premier (1947–52, 1954–70). Under the leadership of Józef Cyrankiewicz, the Polish socialist movement was merged into the Communist-dominated Polish United Workers Party (PUWP) in 1948.

Cyrankiewicz, a lawyer, joined the Polish Socialist Party (PSP) in 1931. He was active in the Polish resistance and was interned in Auschwitz. His career took off after

World War II, when he shifted to a center-left position in the reemerging socialist movement. As general secretary of the Executive Committee of the PSP, Cyrankiewicz in 1948 gave in to pressure from Bolesław Bierut, the first secretary of the Polish Workers Party and head of the Polish state, and allowed for the absorption of the PSP into the structures of the Polish Workers Party. The PUWP resulted from this merger. Cyrankiewicz became a member of the Politburo of the new party (1948–71), and his skillful political maneuvering among the shifting political currents allowed him to remain premier for years though his function was mainly that of a figurehead. During the Stalinist period of postwar Polish history (1948–56), Cyrankiewicz held himself aloof from active involvement in party affairs. However, in June 1956, during disturbances in Poznan, he threatened to "cut off the hands" of those who opposed the "people's rule." He did not oppose pacification of the city by the police and the army. After 1956 he was totally loyal to Communist Party leader Władysław Gomułka. Cyrankiewicz served as chairman of the State Council from 1970 to 1972 and chairman of the Polish Peace Committee from 1973 to 1986. In 1986 he was elected honorary chairman of the World Peace Council, an organization founded in 1949 to oppose colonialism and support disarmament.

Energetic but compromising, Cyrankiewicz had an enormous intuition for political expediency. He avoided uncomfortable situations by avoiding responsibility for making sensitive decisions.

BIBLIOGRAPHY

De Weydenthal, Jan B. *The Communists of Poland.* Stanford Calif.: Hoover Institution Press, 1978.

Ryszard Sudziński

Czechoslovakia

Central European state that was divided into the Czech Republic and Slovakia on January 1, 1993. After the Second World War Czechoslovakia seemed the most likely of Eastern European states to follow a Western democratic political course. Between the wars Czechoslovakia had been one of the few success stories in Eastern Europe. It had the highest standard of living of the region and was the only democracy in the area. Czechoslovakia had also managed its minorities problems peacefully, but after the *Anschluss* between Austria and Nazi Germany in 1938, Hitler demanded the Sudetenland for Germany. In September 1938 at Munich, despite commitments to Czechoslovakia, Great Britain and France caved in to Hitler. In March 1939 Hitler broke his promise to respect

the remainder of the country. Germany made Bohemia and Moravia into German protectorates. Slovakia became nominally independent in a one-party fascist state headed by a Catholic priest, Monsignor Josef Tiso.

Postwar History: An Overview

When the Second World War began, ex-President Edvard Beneš's London-based Czech government-in-exile was recognized by the Allies as the legitimate government of the country. Beneš believed that after the defeat of Germany the dictates of reality would require a policy of friendship with the Soviet Union. He nevertheless hoped that his country could serve as a bridge between East and West. Internally, he hoped to combine Western-style democracy with socialism. In 1943 Beneš went to Moscow and signed a twenty-year alliance with the Soviet Union. The fate of the anti-Soviet Polish government in London provided Beneš ample warning of the need to cooperate with the Kremlin.

After the war Beneš authorized a popular front government made up of Social Democrats, Communists, his National Socialist Party (an anticlerical, bourgeois reform party that despite its name was not in any way related to the German Nazi Party), and others. In the May 1946 elections the Communists won 38 percent of the vote and became the largest single party in parliament. Communist strength was based on remaining resentment over Munich, gratitude for Soviet sacrifices in the war, Slavic solidarity, the perceived need for Soviet protection against a reemergent Germany, and the social measures sponsored by the Communists. The Communists, who had promoted a program of land redistribution, won the votes of many peasants. Workers, organized in Communist unions, also gave strong support to the party.

More than half a million Germans, predominantly from the Sudetenland, left immediately at the end of the war; two million others were expelled in the months that followed. The Communists, who held the Ministry of Agriculture, resettled Czechs on these lands and reallocated the acreage. Fear of possible future German retribution bound Czechoslovakia closer to the USSR. A half million Hungarians were also evicted from Slovakia. In June 1945, Moscow ordered the Prague government to hand over Ruthenia, the easternmost part of the country, to the Soviet republic of Ukraine.

As finally constituted Czechoslovakia's population was approximately two-thirds Czech. Another third was Slovak. There were also a half million Hungarians. Most Czechs lived in the western part of the country in Bohemia, where the capital, Prague, was located, and Moravia. Slovaks lived in the eastern province of Slovakia. The Hungarians lived in southern Slovakia.

The Czechs and Slovaks had a very different past. The Czechs had been dominated by Austria, whereas the Slovaks had been under Hungarian control. Czechs tended to be better educated and more liberal and secular in their outlook. Their part of the country was more industrialized. Slovaks tended to be conservative, rural, and Roman Catholic.

Although Beneš continued as president, after the 1946 elections Communist Party leader Klement Gottwald became premier at the head of a National Front coalition cabinet, which included Social Democrats and Democrats as well as Communists. Jan Masaryk, son of the founding president, was foreign minister.

For several years the Beneš experiment appeared to be working and proof that a Communist party could abide by parliamentary rules. This apparent lesson had its uses in other countries, most notably Italy and France.

As early as 1945 the Prague government nationalized about two-thirds of all industry. Economic recovery was not as difficult as in neighboring states because Czechoslovakia had suffered less war damage. The Czech-Slovak rivalry was eased by recognition of a separate Slovak nationality status; even the Communist Party had separate Czech and Slovak organizations.

Beneš's concept of Czechoslovakia as a bridge between East and West broke down as the Cold War developed. When Marshall Plan aid was announced in 1947, Prague expressed a desire to participate. But Gottwald and Masaryk were immediately called to Moscow and ordered to reverse their stance.

The Soviets were aware that the Communists would lose seats in elections scheduled for the spring of 1948. The loss of Czechoslovakia might endanger the new East European Communist regimes, and Moscow regarded Czechoslovak industrial production as essential. In addition, Czechoslovakia was strategically located, and its loss would create difficulties for the Soviet military and political position in the Soviet occupation zone of East Germany.

Czech Communist leaders worked to place their followers in key positions in the police, army, and information services. When Minister of the Interior Václav Nosek fired some police officials in Prague, on February 20, 1948, twelve Democratic cabinet ministers resigned in protest. Customary procedure called for the entire cabinet to resign, but Gottwald refused and demanded that President Beneš permit him to appoint new ministers. The Social Democrats decided to remain in the cabinet under Gottwald. During a four-day crisis the Commu-

nists sponsored demonstrations and the Communist-controlled confederation of labor threatened a general strike. The Communist-controlled media also provided a slanted view of events. Not by coincidence Soviet Deputy Foreign Minister Valerian Zorin was in Prague at the time on a trade mission. Under all these pressures President Beneš gave in.

On March 10, the body of Foreign Minister Jan Masaryk, who had remained in the Communist-dominated cabinet, was found beneath the windows of the foreign affairs building, the Cernin Palace. Although his death was ruled a suicide, many still believe that Masaryk was almost certainly killed.

A reign of terror followed in which Communists and their supporters ousted all opponents from positions of authority. Parliament agreed to approve a new constitution proposed by Gottwald's government. Beneš, ill and suffering from a stroke, resigned in June rather than sign it. The May 1948 elections, held on a single-ticket basis, gave the National Front nearly 90 percent of the vote. Gottwald now became president and Antonín Zápotocký, a trade union leader, premier. On June 8, 1948, Czechoslovakia was proclaimed a people's republic. Czechs were not enthusiastic about the changes. Factory absenteeism increased and production declined. Collectivization of land brought a food shortage. There were also purges and executions within the party.

In 1953 President Gottwald died while in Moscow attending Stalin's funeral. Zápotocký then became president and Antonín Novotný first secretary of the Communist Party. His decade in power was marked by Stalinist repression. When he died in 1957 he was succeeded by Novotný, who was also a Stalinist and retained his position as first secretary. Novotný faced growing difficulties stemming from deficiencies in the command economy and a growing desire for greater cultural freedom. By the 1960s Moscow was pressing for improved relations with the West. At the time Czechoslovakia was producing manufactured goods that met Western standards, but it needed new technology and equipment. West German Foreign Minister Willy Brandt's *Ostpolitk* was based on reducing tensions in Eastern Europe through increased financial ties, and Bonn planned to extend credits to Czechoslovakia, sell it machinery to produce goods, and then sell some of these finished products in the West.

In January 1968 Alexander Dubček replaced Antonin Novotný as first secretary of the Czechoslovak Communist Party. Dubček, an idealist, was pro-Soviet and believed in communism. He now ushered in what became known as the Prague Spring. In April 1968 he announced an "action program" that called for continued loyalty to the Soviet Union but also a "new economic model" providing for competition and decentralization of authority. Dubček promised a new era that he called "Socialism with a human face." This included easing travel restrictions. Czechs enthusiastically embraced the Dubček reforms.

Many Czech intellectuals were more idealistic than practical, pressing Dubček for complete freedom of expression and of political association, and he was swept along in the reformist tide. Dubček found himself trying to reassure the Kremlin that his free press would not write anything too objectionable and that his free elections would not topple the Communist regime. Moscow was unwilling to accept the possibility of these notions spreading to other satellites or to the USSR itself. What also made the situation impossible for the Kremlin was the growing contact between Czechoslovakia and the Federal Republic of Germany.

On August 3, 1968, at Bratislava in Slovakia, an all-day summit meeting took place between Soviet and Czechoslovak leaders, their second emergency meeting within a week: Soviet leader Leonid Brezhnev bear-hugged Dubček and referred to him as "Dear Comrade Sasha." The joint communiqué made no mention of a counterrevolutionary threat, and it pledged the signers to respect "equality, sovereignty, national independence, and territorial integrity." The Czech side was completely optimistic and paid little attention to a phrase in the communiqué about a "joint international duty" to protect socialist achievements.

Moscow had in fact been preparing for months to use force, if necessary, against the Prague reformers. As early as June careful plans had been drawn up by Soviet units that were in Czechoslovakia for Warsaw Pact "staff maneuvers" that had gone three weeks over schedule. On August 11, new Soviet "maneuvers" began on the border, but few Czechs worried. Two days earlier they had welcomed maverick Yugoslav President Tito on a euphoria-filled visit. But on August 17, civilian-clad Soviet military intelligence specialists arrived in Prague on a special Aeroflot airliner.

On August 20, shortly before 11:00 P.M., in the largest deployment of force in Europe since World War II, six hundred thousand men and two thousand tanks from five Warsaw Pact states—the Soviet Union, East Germany, Bulgaria, Poland, and Hungary—used some twenty crossing points to invade Czechoslovakia, and military aircraft landed at Prague's airport with light armor and elite airborne units.

When the invasion occurred, the Czech party leadership was meeting with Dubček in Communist Party headquarters. They immediately drew up a proclamation for radio broadcast that branded the invasion incompatible "with principles of international law." But they noted the "impossibility" of armed resistance.

Early on the morning of August 21, elite Soviet paratroops arrived at Czech party headquarters in armored vehicles. Bursting into Dubček's office, they held the party leadership at gunpoint for nearly five hours until plainclothes security agents took them away. Meanwhile, at the presidential palace Moscow emissaries tried in vain to talk President Ludvik Svoboda, seventy-three-year-old "Hero of the Soviet Union," into signing a prepared document recognizing a Kremlin-backed government. The Soviets claimed the invasion resulted from a request by Czechoslovak government leaders. In 1992, however, Russian President Boris Yeltsin released to the Czech government a letter dated August 3, 1968, and stamped "never to be opened." Signed by a minority, five members, of Czechoslovakia's ruling Politburo and given to Brezhnev during the Bratislava meeting, it asked him to use "all means available" to crush the anti-Communist "counterrevolution." On August 18, Brezhnev had shared this letter with other Communist leaders.

Warsaw Pact troops were unprepared for their reception in Czechoslovakia. Clandestine television and radio transmitters took the place of silenced stations. In Prague seas of humanity engulfed Soviet tanks, which youths painted with swastikas. The center of Czech resistance was Wenceslas Square, with its statue of the tenth-century national hero Bohemian king. Here Czech student Jan Palach burned himself to death in protest. But except for a few cases of soldiers losing control in the face of hostile crowds, there was no widespread violence. Police loudspeakers warned, "Don't provide the occupiers with pretexts." In all, the death toll was 186 people killed and 362 seriously wounded. Passive resistance made the country a labyrinth in which Soviet soldiers lost their way and could find neither food nor water. Hundreds of young men and women also practiced on the occupying soldiers the Marxist dialectic they had learned in school, and several demoralized military units had to be rotated out of the country.

President Svoboda, meanwhile, received Soviet agreement for a top-level Kremlin meeting. When Dubček and other party leaders joined him in Moscow, they were told that the alternative to "compromise" was a bloodbath. There were lengthy discussions, during which a furious Brezhnev thundered at Dubček: "Don't talk to me about 'socialism.' What we have we hold." The Soviets had no intention of giving up this portion of their security zone. Dubček and other Czech leaders, fearful of the threatened bloodbath and hopeful of salvaging something of the reform program, reluctantly signed a protocol consenting to "temporary" stationing of Soviet forces until the situation could be "normalized." Although Dubček was allowed for a time to continue as nominal party leader, it was the end of the Prague Spring.

The Communist camp did not greet the Soviet action with unanimous approval. Communist China denounced it. No Romanian forces participated, and President Nicolae Ceauşescu later condemned the invasion by calling it "a grave danger to peace in Europe and the fate of socialism in the world." A U.N. Security Council resolution brought by seven nations condemned the invasion and called for a troop withdrawal. The USSR vetoed the resolution.

Although not evident at the time, crushing the Prague Spring had an impact on the Soviet Union. It inspired a Red Square demonstration and sowed seeds of doubt among young Communists and intellectuals. These led to organized dissent and, much later, to change in the Kremlin itself. Mikhail Gorbachev told the Czech foreign minister in 1990: "We thought we were strangling the Prague Spring, but we were strangling ourselves."

In the spring of 1969 a Soviet ice hockey team was beaten by Czechoslovakia in a world title match in Stockholm. With KGB (Soviet secret police) connivance rioters stoned the Aeroflot office in Prague. This provided the pretext for Dubček's forced resignation in April 1969. He was replaced by fellow Slovak Gustáv Husák, who remained in power for the next twenty years. Unlike Hungary, which managed to knit itself back together after its much more violent 1956 revolution, Czechoslovakia seemed unable to heal its psychic wounds. It was as if eliminating the Prague Spring meant removing everything for which the nation stood.

Fearful of drawing down more Kremlin wrath on themselves, the new Czech leaders became more Soviet than the Soviets. Meanwhile, eighty thousand Soviet troops remained in occupation, although there was little for them to do. Followers of Dubček were condemned to a kind of bloodless punishment. Dubček himself was briefly given a diplomatic post in Turkey then demoted to a minor position in the Ministry of Forests in Bratislava. He seemed to display an almost superhuman self-abnegation, surfacing only after the advent of Gorbachev in the USSR. It was said in Moscow in the late 1980s that the difference between Alexander Dubček and Mikhail Gorbachev was twenty years.

Husák gutted the Communist Party; half a million members were drummed out and forced into jobs such as cleaning the streets or shoveling coal. Another 150,000 Czechoslovaks, mostly young and skilled, left the country.

Strong actions were taken against the Catholic Church. Some priests were arrested and dioceses were left without bishops.

Unlike János Kádár in Hungary, Husák made no gesture to the fallen reformers. Husák was, however, no Stalinist; indeed, he had spent ten years in Czechoslovak prisons during the 1950s, and many Czechoslovaks credit him with preventing mass arrests, and perhaps even executions, following the 1968 invasion. Meanwhile, the economy stagnated as Husák reinstalled the old centralized planning system. Husák's admirers claimed that he was about to embark on a program of cautious reform when in 1977 three hundred dissidents signed a petition known as Charter 77, which called on the government to respect human rights. This strengthened the hard-liners.

When Gorbachev came to power in the Soviet Union in 1985, he applied pressure on the Czechs for reforms. As elsewhere in the Soviet bloc, the leadership was split, but Husák announced publicly in 1987 that he welcomed limited reforms, including the secret ballot. In December 1986 Miloš Jakeš replaced Husák as first secretary of the Czechoslovak Communist Party, although Husák continued as president.

The Czech Communist leadership held out as best it could against the reforms sweeping Eastern Europe. Its leaders watched as reforms came to Poland, Hungary, and finally even to East Germany. Jakeš made concessions on travel, cultural matters, and religion, but not on major issues. The regime cracked down even harder on those who aired their dissatisfaction. This included playwright Václav Havel, one of the original signers of the Charter 77 manifesto. Havel had been arrested and imprisoned numerous times, but he continued to attack the regime by means of novels and poetry smuggled out of Czechoslovakia and published abroad. Havel was rearrested in January 1989 but was released in May after serving half his sentence. His trial made him a powerful symbol of opposition to the regime.

In November 1989 Gorbachev warned Jakeš not to delay further. Jakeš then announced modest economic reforms that would be followed later by minor political adjustments. This led to eight days of public demands for change. On November 17, some twenty-five thousand Czech students marched through Prague demanding democracy and free elections. Riot police brutally beat them. Instead of quelling unrest, this action inflamed it. Three days later more than two hundred thousand citizens swarmed into Wenceslas Square. After that came a rally of three hundred thousand and finally one of half a million people, nearly a third of the city's population and the biggest rally in the country's history. Jakeš faced the inevitable dilemma of declaring martial law and crushing the protest movement with force, possibly at great cost in lives, or giving in to popular will and resigning. At the end of November he and the entire Politburo stepped down. To succeed Jakeš as Communist Party secretary general the Central Committee quickly named Karel Urbanek, a little-known apparatchik.

In December Husák was forced to resign the presidency, and, under threat of a general strike, the Communists relinquished power to Havel and his Civic Forum organization. On December 9, one hundred thousand people in Wenceslas Square had shouted "We want Havel," and as the crisis widened, "Havel for President" buttons appeared all over Prague. The Communist Party now gave way, and on December 29 Havel became president. Czechs appreciated Havel's antipolitician stance. He never sought the presidency and seemed to be a reluctant politician. But he became president of a new, democratic Czechoslovakia, and the former dissident was now able to negotiate a Soviet military withdrawal from Czechoslovakia.

One of the interesting aspects of what became known as the Velvet Revolution was the rehabilitation of Alexander Dubček. He was jubilantly chosen chairman of the Federal Assembly, the country's third-highest office. In his last lost battle, Dubček fought against dismemberment of the federation, a divorce that became final shortly after he was fatally injured in an October 1992 automobile accident.

In June 1990 twenty-two political parties faced the voters. Civic Forum of the Czech Republic, headed by Havel, and its counterpart movement in Slovakia, Public Against Violence, gained the most support. But there were serious economic problems when the government moved rapidly to a free-enterprise system. With the removal of subsidies food prices soared.

The great tragedy was the breakup of the federation. Many Slovaks, who made up a third of the fifteen million people in the country, were unhappy. As a minority they resented being a junior partner. There were also economic reasons. Many lamented that the bulk of Western investment went to the Czech region of the country. Although the USSR had invested in new plants in Slovakia, these were inefficient by Western standards. As a result, Slovakia was harder hit than the Czech region in the transition to a free-market economy.

Havel did what he could to hold the country together, but Slovak Premier Vladimir Mečiar, a former Communist and leader of the Movement for Democratic Slovakia, was determined to play the nationalist card. A particularly disturbing sign was a growing cult movement in Slovakia embracing the memory of wartime leader Josef Tiso. In 1942 the Tiso government had deported fifty-one thousand Slovak Jews and an unknown number of Gypsies to German death camps, and Tiso himself had been executed after the war as a war criminal. Many Slovaks worried about Mečiar's commitment to human rights, and the half million Hungarians living in Slovakia were anxious about their future in the new nationalist state.

In June 1992 elections were held for the 300 deputies in the bicameral federal parliament. Czechs also elected 200 deputies to their regional parliament and Slovaks 150 to their regional parliament at Bratislava. During the campaign Havel repeatedly called for continuation of the federation and warned of people with "dictatorial tendencies." The elections saw right-wing reformers triumph in the Czech part of the federation and left-wing nationalists in Slovakia. In Slovakia Mečiar's Movement for a Democratic Slovakia was the big winner. Even though public opinion polls showed that a majority of Slovaks wanted to remain in the federation, Mečiar pressed for separation. Despite the questionable legality of this action, the Czechs accepted the inevitable. In the resulting "velvet separation," the two sides worked out a distribution of resources, and on January 1, 1993, the federation split into two completely independent states: the Czech Republic and Slovakia.

BIBLIOGRAPHY

Bradley, John F. N. *Politics: Czechoslovakia, 1945–1971.* Washington, D.C.: University Press of America, 1981.

Frantisek, August. *Red Star over Prague.* London: Sherwood Press, 1984.

Korbel, Josef. *The Communist Subversion of Czechoslovakia, 1938–1948.* Princeton, N.J.: Princeton University Press, 1959.

Krejci, Jaroslav, and Pavel Machonin. *Czechoslovakia 1918–92.* New York: St. Martin's Press, 1996.

Mlynar, Zdenek. *Nightfrost in Prague: The End of Humane Socialism.* New York: Karz Publishers, 1980.

Skilling, Harold G. *Czechoslovakia's Interrupted Revolution.* Princeton, N.J.: Princeton University Press, 1976.

Valenta, Jiri. *Soviet Intervention in Czechoslovakia, 1968: Anatomy of a Decision.* Baltimore: Johns Hopkins University Press, 1979.

Spencer C. Tucker

Kosice Program

Socialist program initiated by the Czechoslovak provisional government in 1945–46 that laid the foundation for the Communist success in the May 1946 election.

Zdeněk Fierlinger, ambassador to the USSR of the Czech government-in-exile, a left-wing Social Democrat favorably disposed to the USSR, helped to convince Eduărd Beneš, head of the Czech government-in-exile, that the Soviet Union would be dominant in eastern Europe and that, if Czechoslovakia had to choose between the West and the USSR, it had no choice but to go with the Soviets. Fierlinger returned to Czechoslovakia with Beneš in 1945 to head the provisional Czechoslovak government established at Kosice in Slovakia on April 3. The government contained six parties, but the Communists were given five of the fifteen ministries, including the key ministries of interior, information, agriculture, finance, and education. Klement Gottwald, secretary-general of the Communist Party of Czechoslovakia, was appointed deputy premier.

As a residual affect of the Munich Pact of 1938 and its aftermath, there was much popular support for the USSR in Czechoslovakia. During the Soviet liberation of Czechoslovakia from Nazi Germany, Communists, with the aid of the Red Army and the support of the Kosice government, were placed in key positions. Communists gained firm control over unions. Large industries, utilities, and financial institutions were nationalized and care was taken to win the support of the workers involved. Through the ministry of agriculture Sudeten German farms and large estates elsewhere were seized and redistributed to peasants. The Kosice Program banned "fascist" organizations and political parties that had "transgressed against the interests of the nation." The banned parties included the Czech organizations and political parties that had "transgressed against the interests of the nation." The banned parties included the Czech Agrarian Party because some of its members had collaborated with the Germans, and the Catholic Populists, previously the largest party in Slovakia, because its leaders had collaborated with the Germans.

When the USSR forced Czechoslovakia to cede to it Subcarpathian Ruthenia, Czechoslovakia was compensated with Teschen, (Cieszyn) which had been a bone of contention with Poland between the wars.

The measures taken by the Kosice government helped to lay the groundwork for the Communist success in the May 1946 election. The Communists, with 38 percent of the vote, won the largest number of seats in the Czechoslovak parliament, and Gottwald was appointed prime minister on July 3, 1946.

BIBLIOGRAPHY

Korbel, Josef. *The Communist Subversion of Czechoslovakia, 1938–1948: The Failure of Coexistence.* Princeton, N.J.: Princeton University Press, 1959.

———. *Twentieth-century Czechoslovakia: The Meanings of Its History.* New York: Columbia University Press, 1977.

Rothschild, Joseph, and Nancy M. Wingfield. *Return to Diversity: A Political History of East Central Europe Since World War II,* 3rd ed. New York: Oxford University Press, 2000.

Zinner, Paul E. *Communist Strategy and Tactics in Czechoslovakia, 1918–48.* Westport, Conn.: Greenwood Press, 1975.

Bernard Cook

SEE ALSO Gottwald, Klement

Communist Coup (February 1948)

The events that brought a Communist government under Klement Gottwald to power in Czechoslovakia. The coup of 1948 was an important milestone consolidating Communist dominance in Eastern Europe under Soviet leadership as well as the Cold War division of Europe. The new regime transformed Czechoslovakia into a one-party dictatorship.

On April 4, 1945, Czechoslovak political parties, led by president-in-exile Edvard Beneš, met in Kosice and formed a provisional government known as the National Front. The National Front included representatives from most of Czechoslovakia's prewar political parties. Two banned parties, the Slovak People's Party and the Agrarian Party, as well as ethnic German and Hungarian parties, had no representation. Though the prime minister was the Social Democrat Zdeněk Fierlinger, the Czech and Slovak Communist Parties were prominent in the National Front, reflecting genuine support for communism in Czechoslovakia, but also Beneš's decision to ally himself with the Soviet Union. After the Munich Pact of 1938, Benes felt that he could not trust France or England to protect Czechoslovakia's security. Beneš calculated that friendship with the Soviet Union was the best way to guarantee the future independence of Czechoslovakia.

After Germany's defeat, the National Front took several important decisions, notably the disenfranchisement and expulsion of most of Czechoslovakia's ethnic Germans, as well as some of its Hungarians. In elections held in May 1946, the Czech Communist Party did well, receiving 40 percent of the Czech vote and 31 percent of the total vote, the largest showing of any party. The National Socialist Party, which included many figures close to Beneš and had campaigned against the Communists, came in second, with 24 percent of the Czech vote. Of the other Czech parties, the Populists won 20 percent and the Social Democrats 16 percent. In Slovakia, the Democratic Socialist Party won an overwhelming 62 percent of the vote, 14 percent of the total vote. The Slovak Communist Party managed only 31 percent. The two Communist parties, together with their closest allies, the Social Democratic Party, had 153 parliamentary seats out of 300.

The National Front coalition continued after the election with Gottwald as prime minister. Beneš became president, and Jan Masaryk, the son of Czechoslovakia's first president and a powerful symbol of democratic Czechoslovakia, remained foreign minister. The Czech Communists kept the Ministry of the Interior, which gave them control of the police. The Slovak Communist Party received the Ministry of Agriculture and redistributed land seized from expelled Germans and Hungarians to ethnic Czechs and Slovaks.

Gottwald's government embarked on a "two-year plan" to increase Czechoslovakia's economic production. The results were poor: drought and a reviving German economy caused a severe economic downturn in 1947. Faced with a massive budget deficit, the Communist parties proposed a one-time "millionaire's tax," which all other parties in the National Front rejected. This was the first open conflict within the National Front, and it provoked a political crisis. The Communists mobilized street demonstrations for the tax, and eventually Fierlinger decided to support it. Because rank-and-file Social Democrats opposed this decision, the Social Democratic Party lost much of its credibility and internal cohesion. At the same time, the Communists began to manipulate the police for political ends. In Slovakia, leading Democratic Socialists were accused of "conspiracy" and arrested.

Throughout this period, the Soviet Union strongly influenced Czechoslovak affairs, though more through intimidation than direct intervention. In June 1945 Czechoslovakia ceded its eastern province of Sub-Carpathian Rus (Ruthenia) to the Soviet Union. It also placed the output of its uranium mine in Jachymov under Soviet control. These concessions brought results. The Red Army withdrew from Czechoslovakia in November 1945, at the same time as the U.S. army. Yet in 1947, when the United States offered financial assistance to Czechoslovakia through the Marshall Plan, Soviet disapproval convinced even non-Communist parties in the National Front to refuse American aid. After the meeting in Moscow in which Stalin made his displeasure known, Masaryk commented, "I went to Moscow a free minister and I'm coming back a servant of Stalin." Czechoslovak leaders felt too vulnerable to Soviet military power to stand up for Czechoslovakia's interests, and allowed themselves to be intimidated.

In February 1948 the National Front finally collapsed when twelve ministers, representing the National Socialist, Czech Populist, and Slovak Democratic Socialist Parties, resigned. They hoped the Social Democrats would resign as well, which would have meant new elections, and they assumed that Beneš would not accept their resignations if the Social Democrats remained. This was a major blunder. The Social Democratic ministers did not resign, which left Gottwald's government legally in power. Gottwald convinced Beneš to replace the departed ministers with Communists. Beneš withdrew from public life shortly afterward, and died in August 1948. Masaryk also died in suspicious circumstances that March. His fatal fall from a bathroom window was probably a murder, not a suicide as the Communists claimed. The Social Democratic Party dissolved itself and many of its members, including Fierlinger, joined the Communist Party. Without Beneš or Masaryk, opposition to communism had no rallying point. Leading National Socialist politicians fled the country, and Gottwald quickly assumed complete control.

The National Socialists missed many chances to unite in defense of democratic Czechoslovakia. Fear of Soviet intervention was a factor, as was the fear of violence from the Communist-controlled police or worker militias. Many also overestimated the strength of Czechoslovak democracy. The National Socialists assumed that all parties, including the Communists, would play by democratic constitutional rules, and were unsure how to react to Gottwald's extralegal political maneuvers.

The coup had a chilling effect on European and American governments. In 1949 fear that communism might spread to other European countries inspired the United States to abandon its traditional policy of neutrality and join the North Atlantic Treaty Organization (NATO), a military alliance that led to the permanent presence of American soldiers in Western Europe.

The seizure of power was mostly the achievement of Gottwald and the Czech Communists. The Soviet Union played no direct role in the Communists' seizure of power: Gottwald refused a Soviet offer to send troops on the grounds that none were needed. Nevertheless, the new government followed the Soviet line closely, and Czechoslovakia under Gottwald became a client state of the Soviet Union. Gottwald also copied the Stalinist system of semirandom arrests and executions to break any opposition to his rule, including the show trial and execution of Communist Party members.

The new regime also continued the dramatic social transformation of Czechoslovakia. It purged the government bureaucracy, with around half of state employees losing their jobs. They were replaced by individuals with working-class backgrounds, often lacking necessary skills or training. Nationalization continued, and by the early 1950s almost all small businesses were under state control, though only a third of farmers. These and other changes caused the Czechoslovak standard of living to decline, even as Western Europe experienced rapid economic growth. Finally, the government suppressed free and open public life in Czechoslovakia, not only politically but economically and culturally. Many years passed before civil society returned to Czechoslovakia.

BIBLIOGRAPHY

August, Frantisek. *Red Star Over Prague.* London: Sherwood Press, 1984.

Kaplan, Karel. *The Short March: The Communist Takeover in Czechoslovakia 1945–1948.* London: C. Hurst & Co, 1987.

Krejci, Jaroslav. *Czechoslovakia, 1918–92; A Laboratory for Social Change.* New York: St. Martin's Press, 1996.

Myant, M. R. *Socialism and Democracy in Czechoslovakia, 1945–1948.* Cambridge: Cambridge University Press, 1981.

Alexander Maxwell

SEE ALSO Beneš, Edvard; Fierlinger, Zdeněk; Gottwald, Klement; Masaryk, Jan

Slánsky Trial

The largest Stalinist purge trial of post-World War II Europe. In the trial held in Czechoslovakia in 1952, Rudolf Slánsky, general-secretary of the Czechoslovakian Communist Party, and thirteen other defendants were branded as bourgeois nationalists, Titoists, Zionists, or Western imperialist agents. Although there is little doubt that Slánsky was actually a loyal Stalinist, all were found guilty of treason and other high crimes against the state. Eleven, including Slánsky, were executed. The remaining three received sentences of life imprisonment.

From 1949 to 1954 Stalinist terror in the form of purge arrests and trials reached its height in Czechoslovakia. An estimated tens of thousands were arrested, and well over a hundred thousand lost jobs or governmental and party positions. Among the targeted "bourgeois nationalists" were Roman and Greek Catholic religious leaders, lawyers, doctors, small shopkeepers, merchants, and the leadership of the war-time Slovak Communist Party. Most accused "Titoists" were persons having extensive international contacts: Spanish Civil War veterans or foreign trade and foreign policy specialists assigned to the West during the 1930s and World War II. Jews who were seen as anti-state "Zionists" were then labeled, through Zionism, as agents of American foreign policy. Of the fourteen persons charged in the Slánsky trial, twelve were Jews. The state of Israel's alignment with the United States, along with Stalin's personal anti-Semitism, opened to suspicion all Czechoslovaks of Jewish ancestry.

Although purges often followed from power struggles within the East European Communist parties, the Slánsky trial, like the majority of the era's purges and show trials, resulted more broadly from Cold War pressures. Growing U.S. presence and power in Europe, seen in the Truman Doctrine, the Marshall Plan, and NATO, led Stalin to create Cominform, designed to unify the international communist movement and subordinate it to Moscow. Czechoslovakia's flirtation with the Marshall Plan, along with the failure evident in the late 1940s of its five-year plan and the Tito-led breakaway of Yugoslavia from Cominform, provoked in Stalin and the Moscow Politburo a fear of all national independence movements. Zhdanovism, the Soviet Union's version of McCarthyism, generated a need for internal enemies to pursue in order to bolster strict obedience within the bloc. The 1949 purge trial of László Rajk in Hungary had already set the tone for the Slánsky trial.

The fourteen Slánsky defendants were arrested in 1950 and 1951. From the time of their arrests until their trial in late 1952 they were physically, psychologically, and spiritually tortured. They were forced to confess and to memorize statements of guilt. The trial was conducted as a piece of theater, with scriptwriters, actors, and directors. Czechoslovak President Klement Gottwald was informed that the trial would begin at 9:00 A.M. on November 20, with sentencing to be handed down on the eighth day between 9:00 and 11:00 A.M. The State prosecutor charged Vladimir Clementis (1902–52), Otto Fischl (1902–52), Josef Frank (1909–52), Ludvík Frejka (1904–52), Bedrich Germinder (1901–52), Vavro Hajdu (1913–), Evzen Löbl (1907–), Artur London (1915–), Rudolf Margolius (1913–52), Bedrich Reicin (1911–52), André Simone (1895–1952), Rudolf Slánsky (1901–52), Otto Sling (1912–52), and Karel Sváb (1904–52) with sabotage, espionage, and high treason. Slánsky and ten others were hanged on December 30, 1952. Hajdu, Löbl, and London were given life sentences. All were legally exonerated in 1963. The Slánsky trial epitomized the brutality and inhumanity of Stalinism in Eastern Europe and sowed the seeds of rebellion against communism in the 1980s and 1990s.

BIBLIOGRAPHY

Kaplan, Karel. *Report on the Murder of the General Secretary.* Columbus: Ohio State University Press, 1990.

Loebl, Eugene. *Sentenced and Tried: The Stalinist Purges in Czechoslovakia.* London: Elek Books, 1969.

London, Artur. *On Trial.* New York: Morrow, 1970.

Zilliacus, Konni. *A New Birth of Freedom?: World Communism Since Stalin.* London: Secker & Warburg, 1957.

Ken Millen-Penn

SEE ALSO Clementis, Vladimír; Cominform; Rajk, László; Zilliacus, Konni

Prague Spring

A belated parallel to the Polish October of 1956, the Prague Spring was an attempt on the part of the Czechoslovak Communist Party (CzCp) and the Czechoslovak government to reform and liberalize socialism within the country. Between April and August 1968 sweeping changes in official policy and personnel combined with a genuinely democratic grassroots movement to create what became known as "socialism with a human face."

The initiative for reform came from within the party, where the lingering effects of de-Stalinization mingled with Slovak nationalism and a stagnant economy to spur a coalition opposed to the centralizing policies of President and First Secretary Antonín Novotný. Economic reform was on the table as early as 1963, when at the government's request Ota Šik, a Communist professor of economics, drew up a plan for decentralizing the economy to place more emphasis on consumer goods and markets. Officially endorsed by the CzCP in 1965, Šik's plan remained largely unrealized until 1968, when he became deputy prime minister of Czechoslovakia for the brief period of the Prague Spring.

At the Thirteenth Party Congress in 1967, the Slovak question and political liberalization were at the forefront. The reformers, headed by Zdeněk Mlynar, advocated a system of "one-Party pluralism" that they believed would be more just and humane than the Stalinist regime of Novotný. Slovak Communists seeking equal status and representation within the CzCP quickly threw their strength into the battle for internal reform, and Novotný was forced to resign as first secretary of the CzCP in January 1968. Alexander Dubček, a Slovak Communist with reforming tendencies, was elected to replace him.

Under Dubček's leadership, the "process of renewal," as it was officially known, moved rapidly forward. Expansion of the economic reforms begun in 1967 was approved by the party in February 1968, and in March Novotný resigned as president. His replacement, General Ludvik Svoboda, favored further reforms, and more personnel changes followed as Dubček's faction moved to consolidate its position. The minister of the interior, Josef Kudrna, and the prosecutor general were removed by vote of the newly vitalized National Assembly, and investigations were launched into the death of Jan Masaryk and the fate of many others killed or imprisoned during the Communist takeover in 1948. Censorship was lifted de facto, and the first grassroots political discussion groups emerged; K-231, founded by a group of former political prisoners, and KAN are only the most famous of many.

With a secure power base and public opinion squarely behind him, Dubček pressed further. On April 5 an "Action Program" outlining the aims and limits of the reforming movement was published by the government. The major objective was a revitalization of the party as the vanguard of a semiautonomous civil society. Workers' councils and state representatives would be given a voice in government, and the government in return would guarantee their rights and interests. While accepting the notions of a free press and nonpolitical spheres of action in society, however, the reformers never renounced the party's leading role in society or its monopoly of political power. The party would cease to exercise its nomenklatura rights unilaterally and consult with outside experts regarding political and economic policy, but would always retain ultimate control. This fact, as well as the socialist context of the reforms, was reaffirmed by a CzCP Plenum at the end of May 1968.

Nevertheless, the publication of the Action Program opened a period of liberalization in Czechoslovakia that stunned the world and sent tremors throughout the Soviet bloc, the true blossoming of the Prague Spring. Leaders of the Warsaw Treaty Organization (WTO, or Warsaw Pact) nations met in March 1968, probably at the instigation of East German leader Walter Ulbricht, to discuss developments in Czechoslovakia and send notice that reform anywhere in the socialist bloc was an international, as well as an internal, affair. Then, in mid-May, large-scale military maneuvers on the Czechoslovak border were planned to reinforce the message.

The Czechoslovaks plowed ahead, however, proclaiming loudly their loyalty to socialism and to the WTO. While their foreign policy explicitly called for closer relations with the West and with the breakaway Communist regimes in Yugoslavia and Albania, Czechoslovak leaders did not believe this was incompatible with their obligations to the Warsaw Pact or with their alliance with the Soviets, which, they insisted, remained as the cornerstone of Czechoslovak foreign policy. Never during the Prague Spring did either the Czechoslovak government or the leadership of the CzCP call for the withdrawal of the nation from either the Warsaw Pact or the socialist sphere.

Czechoslovak leaders decided at the end of May that an extraordinary party congress would be convened on September 9, 1968, to institutionalize the reform movement and consolidate changes in personnel. In June the National Assembly prepared laws that would make censorship illegal and called for the rehabilitation and compensation of political prisoners "wrongly convicted" between 1948 and 1965. In July the Central Committee of the Slovak Communist Party announced the decision to hold a separate Congress prior to the convening of the Fourteenth Extraordinary Congress of the CzCP in September to consult on the issues of cadre changes and federalization.

Threatened by these actions and concerned that Czechoslovak leaders were continuing their reforms without consulting Moscow, the Soviet government pressed the Czechoslovaks to discuss the situation. The publication of Ludvik Vaculik's "2,000 Words" manifesto in late June 1968 apparently convinced even those within the Soviet Politburo who sympathized with the Czechoslovak situation that things were getting out of control. When talks opened in the border town of Cierna nad Tisou on July 29 with nearly all the Soviet Politburo and Czechoslovak Presidium participating, the Soviets demanded that the Czechoslovaks reassert control over the mass media, including a ban on political discussion clubs such as KAN and K-231, and dismiss several key members of the reforming government. The Czechs held firm over several days, and no written agreement was produced.

Thereafter, the difference in views became more pronounced and threatening. On August 3, the leaders of the WTO met again and signed an agreement committing themselves to unified action regarding developments in Czechoslovakia. Seven days later the Czechoslovak leadership published the statutes for the extraordinary Fourteenth Party Congress; these allowed factions to form and to publicize their views, and provided for secret balloting within the party.

The response came in the early hours of August 20 as more than fifteen divisions of WTO troops crossed the borders into Czechoslovakia. Thirteen of the divisions were supplied by the Soviet Union, though all signatories of the Warsaw Pact save Romania contributed. The Czechoslovak army offered no resistance, and the general populace resisted only passively. By the morning of August 21, WTO forces had sealed the nation's western borders and achieved all military objectives.

Soviet-sponsored attempts to establish a hard-line government within Czechoslovakia failed, however, as the diverse Czechoslovak media continued to broadcast and publish news of the occupation. In the streets of Prague

and elsewhere citizens approached tanks not to fight but to argue with soldiers, waving copies of the "Action Program," "2,000 Words," and printed broadsheets, demanding to know why their socialist brothers were invading. The occupying troops were denied food and supplies whenever possible by the citizenry, and a one-hour general strike was held on August 22 in Prague and other cities across the nation to protest the invasion.

Meanwhile, the Czechoslovak leadership, with the exception of President Svoboda, had been arrested and flown to the Soviet Union in the early hours of August 21. Initially taken to KGB (secret police) camps, they were moved to Moscow when President Svoboda refused to legitimize the actions of the Warsaw Pact and public pressure against the occupation mounted. Communist parties throughout the world condemned the invasion, adding their voices to those of Western European and the U.S. governments. On August 24 Svoboda flew to Moscow to negotiate the release of the incarcerated Czechoslovak leaders. An agreement was reached on August 26.

In return for their release and restoration to their government posts, Dubček and the other Czechoslovak leaders promised to re-impose censorship and declare invalid the convening and statutes of the Extraordinary Fourteenth Party Congress. The Czechoslovaks were also forced to agree to the permanent, unlimited, and unconditional stationing of Soviet troops on their territory. Many among the Czechoslovak leadership were expelled from the party. Dubček remained as first secretary of the CzCP but was severely restricted in his scope of action. The Moscow agreement was approved by a revamped Czechoslovak National Assembly in October 1968, and the remaining political reforms were gradually repealed over the rest of the year as personnel changes continued throughout the government and the party apparatus. The debate on economic reform continued in muted fashion, and a last vestige of reform came at the end of October, when a bill federalizing the Czechoslovak Socialist Soviet Republic was signed in Bratislava.

Public protests against the invasion continued within Czechoslovakia through the early months of 1969. On January 16 a student named Jan Palach set himself afire in Prague's Wenceslas Square. Four more self-immolations followed that month. Demonstrations against the USSR after the Czechoslovak national hockey team defeated the Soviet team in the World Championships in March 1969 turned into riots, possibly the work of pro-Soviet provocateurs, and Warsaw Pact troops were moved in to quell the disturbances. Political and social controls were tightened further, though the Czechoslovak press still retained much of its relative freedom. In April

Dubček resigned as first secretary and was replaced by Gustav Husák, who proceeded to purge the Presidium of its remaining reforming members. The Prague Spring was at an end.

The legacy of the Prague Spring, however, extended far beyond 1969. The reform movement and its suppression established the boundaries of reform within the Soviet bloc for the next twenty years. Dissenting Communist parties were repelled, deepening the splits that had begun in 1949 within the movement. Albania broke away to follow the Chinese. Yugoslavia moved closer to the West. Western European Communists were left stranded, and socialism in general suffered a blow internationally with this demonstration of inflexibility and brutality. The belief that the Czechoslovak reformers had held and proclaimed—that socialism and humanity were not incompatible—had proven untenable. Their vision of a socialist society based on merit, civil freedoms, open relations with nonsocialist nations, and justice was crushed beneath the treads of Soviet tanks, not to resurface in Eastern Europe until Mikhail Gorbachev came to power in the USSR in 1985. For with the Velvet Revolution of 1989 came the reappearance of Alexander Dubček, the hero of the Prague Spring and the symbol of the "new course" and socialist opposition for two decades. He was elected as the first president of the newly democratic Czechoslovakia and proclaimed it a victory for the ideals of the Prague Spring.

BIBLIOGRAPHY

Dawisha, Karen. *The Kremlin and the Prague Spring.* Berkeley: University of California Press, 1984.

Kusin, Vladimir V. *The Intellectual Origins of the Prague Spring: The Development of Reformist Ideas in Czechoslovakia, 1956–1967.* Cambridge: Cambridge University Press, 1971.

Svitak, Ivan. *The Czechoslovak Experiment, 1968–1969.* New York: Columbia University Press, 1971.

Timothy Dowling

SEE ALSO Dubček, Alexander

Charter 77

Czechoslovak human rights group. Following the Soviet-led invasion suppressing the Prague Spring of 1968, Czech domestic politics entered a period of "normalization" in which public dissent was largely stifled. Charter 77 was formulated to publicize the failure of the Czech government to adhere to the human rights provisions of the Final Act of the Helsinki Accords signed in 1975. On January 6, 1977, the Charter 77 text became public. Bearing the names of 243 signatories from all walks of life, the document called for compliance with the Final Act and listed repeated violations of its provisions by Czech authorities.

Membership in the organization came from five segments of the population: intellectuals, artists, former Communist officials, the clergy, and young people. Thus playwright Václav Havel joined sociologist and former politician Rudolf Battek, dancer Jana Sternova, and sacked journalist Jiří Dienstbier in signing the charter and acting as a spokesperson for the group. Although Charter 77 could claim at least some support from all strata of Czech society, its main appeal was to urban intellectuals and students.

Charter 77 characterized itself as a humanitarian, rather than political, organization, carefully avoiding calls for reform or protest. Instead, the group published a limited number of declarations for distribution in the West as well as in Czechoslovakia each year, documenting human rights abuses that violated Czech law, which, after October 1976, included the human rights guarantees of the Helsinki Final Act. Charter 77 pronouncements recorded the systematic illegal harassment, detention, interrogation, and denial of employment for Czechs because of their beliefs or association with dissenters. As similar organizations arose in other Eastern European countries during the 1980s, Charter 77 established connections with them, as well as with Western antinuclear groups.

The Czech government first responded to Charter 77 with further repression as signatories were detained and questioned, falsely accused of "antistate activities," and even physically assaulted. Havel spent nearly four years (1977 and 1979–83) in prison before being released because of ill health. Chartist Zdena Tomovina, dismissed from her position at Charles University in 1978, faced continued harassment and intimidation by police; beaten by masked assailants in 1979, she emigrated to Great Britain in 1980.

Most Chartists, however, remained in Czechoslovakia and continued their activities. The government eased restrictions somewhat with a 1985 general amnesty for political prisoners. In 1989 the authors of a petition calling for release of all political prisoners received comparatively light sentences; nevertheless, that same year Havel was on trial once more, although not directly for Chartist activities.

In addition to drawing Western attention to human rights abuses, the members of Charter 77 provided a new generation of leadership for Czechoslovakia. In December 1989 after the Velvet Revolution, Havel became the first non-Communist president of Czechoslovakia since 1948.

BIBLIOGRAPHY

Bugajski, Janusz. *Czechoslovakia: Charter 77's Decade of Dissent.* New York: Praeger, 1987.

Bugergenthal, Thomas, ed. *Human Rights, International Law, and the Helsinki Accord.* Montclair, N.J.: Allanheld Osmun, 1977.

Havel, Václav. *Disturbing the Peace.* New York: Vintage, 1990.

Roger Tuller

Civic Forum (Občanké Fórum)

Political movement of anti-Communist human rights organizations in Czechoslovakia that became influential following the Prague street demonstrations of November 17, 1989, that ignited the Velvet Revolution. Civic Forum (OF) was forged as a broad opposition coalition, functioning as the coordinating body of pro-democracy organizations that overturned the Communist regime through weeks of massive popular protest. Its predominant standing in the 1990 Round Table conferences and the following elections allowed the creation of a mainly Civic Forum government, and the subsequent reelection of Václav Havel to the presidency. Maintaining unanimity on matters of civil liberties and democratic process, Civic Forum was incapable of reaching agreement on economic policy, the question that brought about the election of Václav Klaus as its chairman in October 1990, its eventual breach in March 1991, when OF split into the Civic Movement and the Civic Democratic Party. Civic Forum persisted as an umbrella for collaboration during the period before the mid-1992 elections and was the most significant political organization to issue from the Velvet Revolution.

Czechoslovakia from 1948 to 1989 exhibited circumscribed features of a multiparty arrangement through the National Front of the Czechoslovak Socialist Republic, regulated by the Communist Party, yet encompassing four lesser parties as well as farmer, trade union, and other organizations. The front became inactive late in 1989 with the exit of the Socialist and People's Parties. During the interim, grassroots support developed around the newly formed alliance of Civic Forum in the Czech regions and its Slovak equivalent, Public Against Violence (VPN).

Communism deteriorated rapidly in Czechoslovakia in late 1989, as was the case in other countries in Eastern Europe. Representatives of Charter 77, other autonomous groups, and a number of students and intellectuals in a gathering in a theater in Prague on November 19 spelled out mandates for comprehensive political reformation. The opposition of the autonomous organizations to Communist rule had previously been articulated in the context of regard for legal rights. Civic Forum was the coalition that its representatives constituted following the initial street demonstrations. On November 20, a day after the organization of Civic Forum headed by dissident playwright Václav Havel, 250,000 anti-Communist protesters marched in Prague and twenty-four hours later regime officials began talks with OF delegates. President Husák resigned on December 10 after swearing in the first non-Communist majority government in forty-one years, with Marián Calfa as premier. The assembly designated Havel head of state on December 29.

Civic Forum, which catalyzed the nation and abolished Communist rule, was radically distinct from the Communist Party. A far-reaching alliance, it avoided individual membership, corresponding more to a nondescript American-type party rather than to the structured European kind. In Czechoslovak elections held before the Second World War, it was not particular candidates but parties that were important. Civic Forum retreated from that custom with its tendency to advocate such well-known candidates as minister Václav Klaus. It was because of Civic Forum that the strife between the nation and its state was ultimately characterized as strife between citizens and the state.

June 1990 national elections encompassed twenty-three political parties and movements ranging from radical left to far-right. Civic Forum and Public Against Violence decisively won a majority of federal legislative seats, with Čalfa, who had resigned from the Communist Party on January 18, constituting a new administration on June 27. Havel was elected to a two-year term as president on July 5. For Civic Forum, whose public endorsement was thought to have been weakened, the success was a referendum on communism and a credit to OF, appropriately seen as the impetus for terminating the regime. The elections eventuated in a coalition government of Civic Forum and Christian Democrats that proceeded to follow a policy of privatization and transition to a market economy.

Havel considered Civic Forum as an impermanent alliance to facilitate the transition to a democratic regime. After coming to power subsequent to its success in the June 1990 general balloting, OF divided into two factions in March 1991: a right wing headed by Civic Forum Chairman Václav Klaus and a more amorphous wing affiliated with Foreign Minister Jiří Dienstbier, consisting mainly of veterans of the Prague Spring. Afterward, confronted with a legal impasse that allowed the forum's dissolution but not its actual reconstitution as a party, a majority of Civic Forum leadership voted to organize a new group, the Civic Democratic Party (ODS), which held its founding congress on April 20–21. The Dienstbier wing organized independently on April 20–21 as the Civic Movement (OH), adopting the name Free Democrats (SD [OH]).

In the first half of 1992 regional parties took on more importance than those striving to sustain federal constituencies. This paved the way for the dissolution of the federal system at the end of 1992. With the founding of the independent Czech Republic on January 1, 1993, the parties that had previously asserted a federal identity did so no longer.

BIBLIOGRAPHY

Ash, Timothy Garton. *The Magic Lantern: The Revolution of 89 Witnessed in Warsaw, Budapest, Berlin and Prague.* New York: Random House, 1990.

Glenny, Misha. *The Rebirth of History: Eastern Europe in the Age of Democracy.* London: Penguin Books, 1990.

Holy, Ladislav. *The Little Czech and the Great Czech Nation: National Identity and the Post-Communist Transformation of Society.* Cambridge: Cambridge University Press, 1996.

Leff, Carol Skalnik. *The Czech and Slovak Republics: Nation Versus State.* Boulder, Colo.: Westview Press, 1997.

Kenneth Keulman

SEE ALSO Havel, Václav; Klaus, Václav

Velvet Revolution

Political and social changes that were the harbinger of the downfall of the Czechoslovak Communist Party, one of the last Stalinist states to give way in Europe, and the advent of the pluralist, parliamentary democracy that displaced it. Politically active organizations made up of dissenters, intellectuals, and students prepared to work for the creation of new democratic political institutions won the backing of a large segment of the population. This nonviolent movement in Prague and other Czech cities overturned the Communist regime during ten days in November 1989. The elements of the revolution consisted of the police assault on Black Friday; the strike by university students and actors in Prague; the creation of Civic Forum; and the mobilization of resistance to the regime, which expanded into a mass movement with nationalist overtones.

The antecedents of the revolution developed during the Prague Spring of 1968. The Soviet invasion of Czechoslovakia in August of that year concluded the prime opportunity for basic reform of a socialist government and began the prolonged decline of communism

that was to climax in the Velvet Revolution two decades later. The suppression of the Prague Spring ended the expectations of a sizable segment of the country, whose participation in public life evidenced a reanimation of their commitment to both socialism and democracy. Another crucial event took place during 1977 with the signing of Charter 77, a document with over 250 signatories reproving the regime for not fulfilling human rights stipulations of documents it had agreed to, such as its constitution and the Helsinki Accords. The regime reacted by intimidating, oppressing, and imprisoning charter signatories and members of other dissident organizations. As political strains in Poland increased during the 1980s, the Czechoslovak Communist government, apprehensive of a ripple effect, became more overbearing.

Charter 77 and other new organizations denouncing the Communist Party initiated a number of nonviolent protests that brought out thousands in Prague during late 1988 and early 1989. The government used force to break up protests in January 1989 and imprisoned well-known human rights proponents, including playwright Václav Havel.

By summer 1989, the Soviet nomenklatura decided to disengage from Eastern Europe. This was signaled on June 12 by Mikhail Gorbachev's excursion to West Germany. His address to the Council of Europe in Strasbourg, France, on July 7 contained statements that repudiated the Brezhnev Doctrine, while also speaking favorably of structural changes in central Europe. Soviet leaders initially hoped that the burgeoning grassroots movement in Eastern Europe would eventually be satisfied with glasnost (openness) and perestroika (restructuring). But as the movement increased in intensity, the Soviet leadership's objective was no longer reform communism but a type of withdrawal that would avert disaster.

During summer and fall of 1989, the movement of dissent in Czechoslovakia grew in conviction because of the erosion of Communist authority in neighboring Poland and Hungary. Havel and other leaders signed a document challenging the regime to begin a process of democratization. Protests took place in Prague during August marking both the twenty-first anniversary of the invasion and the seventy-first anniversary of the establishment of the independent republic.

Gorbachev was discontented with party secretary-general Miloš Jakeš's performance as the leader who would initiate reform. Civil society began to resurface in Czechoslovakia in the atmosphere of Gorbachev's reform program and the growing challenges to the conservative leadership in the German Democratic Republic (GDR).

Further demonstrations began in Czechoslovakia on October 28. By November 1989 events in central and Eastern Europe were moving in a revolutionary direction, beginning with Poland and concluding with Romania. All these outbreaks not only influenced one another but also critically affected ensuing incidents in Czechoslovakia. Thus, while the Velvet Revolution was the accomplishment of dissidents and students, it was also the result of a transformed international environment.

On November 19 Havel established a new democratic party called Civic Forum, made up of a number of organizations of intellectuals, students, and liberal Christians. It advocated civil liberties and government reorganization. Civic Forum soon won the backing of a majority of the country, as did its Slovak counterpart, Public Against Violence.

By the time Czech security forces provoked popular resistance on November 17, 1989, by violently breaking up a large protest in Prague, the future of Czechoslovakia had by this time been settled by other circumstances. The initial event was the resignation in November of party leader Erich Honecker in the GDR, the strongest supporter of the Czech regime. The other was the denunciation by the Central Committee of the Soviet Communist Party of the 1968 invasion of Czechoslovakia by five Warsaw Pact countries as a serious political blunder. These two incidents obliterated any residual legitimacy that the Czech Communist Party leadership may have possessed. Communist officials in Prague seemed to be paralyzed by the Soviet disavowal of the old ideology and by events in East Germany. The ineffectual deployment of force against the protesters on November 17 further weakened the regime.

Alexander Dubček, who had been deposed as party leader in 1968, regained prominence on November 22 with a speech to a crowd in Bratislava. On November 24 Civic Forum organized a demonstration of three hundred thousand people in Prague, including industrial workers who made up 60 percent of the population. Following Havel's mandate to overturn the regime rather than reform it, the protesters demanded political democratization. On the same day, Communist officials ejected Jakeš and his Politburo associates in favor of Karel Urbánek, a moderate. But Urbanek and Prime Minister Ladislav Adamec were not adequately progressive for the dissenters and were quickly removed. President Husák on December 10 designated Marián Calfa, a Slovak reformer, as prime minister. Calfa immediately resigned from the CzPC and designated a cabinet consisting of opposition leaders. Grassroots demands for the termination of Communist rule persisted, resulting in Husák's resignation as state president. The Prague parliament on December 29 elected Václav Havel as president. Dubček became chairman of the federal asssembly.

The Central Committee of the Communist Party of Czechoslovakia (CzPC) was as startled as the populace when the revolution began. It had systematically discounted indications that society was ripe for disintegration, situating its confidence in security operations and sanctions. Aside from grave social and economic difficulties that regularly became more conspicuous and climaxed in public protests in 1988, the CzPC disregarded signs that important segments of party-backed organizations were opposing it and that widening fissures and sectional mobilizations were developing.

As evidenced by the initial public protests against the government in 1988 and 1989 and the destruction of the regime in 1989, resistance to communism was thus arguably Czechoslovakia's nationalist rebellion against foreign domination. The development of a nationalist disposition antedated the dissolution of the regime and originated from the recognition of socialism as a grotesque Soviet intrusion that had deformed the culture. In spite of an occasionally faltering resistance, the Czechs and Slovaks nonetheless succeeded in bringing about the most rapid reversal in Eastern Europe.

Early in 1990 the People's Militia, the armed section of the Communist Party, was abolished, and the operations of the CzPC in places of work, the police, and the army were prohibited. The majority of party assets were put to new utilization. The national political principle and the partition of the political situation along national lines continued post-1989, even though the political rhetoric underscored the significance of civil society. The constitutional law of 1991 specified once more that the Czech and Slovak Federal Republic was a willing alliance of two commensurate republics of the Czech and Slovak nations founded on the claim to self-determination. The state after the revolution preserved the prewar arrangement of distinct Czech and Slovak political aggregations.

A process of attrition and party political realignment within Civic Forum went on until autumn 1991 and was attended by other dilemmas. Aside from social pressures brought about by an unstable economic situation, the governing parties had to deal with issues connected with popular doubts about the electoral process, the political consequences from the proposed *lustrace,* law, or screening law that would exclude certain Power Communist officials from positions in public administration, and the issue of Slovak separatism.

BIBLIOGRAPHY

Ash, Timothy Garton. *The Uses of Adversity.* New York: Random House, 1989.

Banac, Ivo, ed. *Eastern Europe in Revolution*. Ithaca, N.Y.: Cornell University Press, 1992.

Bradley, John. *Czechoslovakia's Velvet Revolution*. Boulder, Colo.: East European Monographs, 1992.

Goldman, Minton. *Revolution and Change in Central and Eastern Europe*. New York: M.E. Sharpe, 1997.

Havel, Václav. *On Living in Truth*. Ed. by Jan Vladislav. Boston: Faber and Faber, 1986.

Historical Institute of the Czechoslovak Academy of Sciences. *Ten Days in Prague*. Prague: Academia, 1990.

Krejčí, Jaroslav, and Pavel Machonin. *Czechoslovakia, 1918–1991*. Boulder, Colo.: Westview Press, 1992.

Wheaton, Bernard, and Zdeněk Kavan. *The Velvet Revolution: Czechoslovakia, 1988–1991*. Boulder, Colo.: Westview Press, 1992.

Kenneth Keulman

SEE ALSO Havel, Václav; Husák, Gustav; Jakeš, Miloš

Economy

The relatively high level of industrial development and degree of prosperity present in Czechoslovakia in 1945 was not typical of the group of countries destined to become the socialist part of Europe. Though physical wartime damage had been less than in most other European countries, there were nevertheless serious reconstruction needs, and these would have to be tackled without Marshall Plan Aid.

The Kosice Program, initiated by the coalition government in April 1946, aimed to recover and surpass 1937 levels of industrial and agricultural output and address serious disparities between Slovakia and the significantly more developed Czech lands (Bohemia and Moravia). By the end of 1947 the economic prognosis was on balance favorable. Inflation had been brought under control, production was rising steadily, and Slovakia's disadvantages were being tackled.

Consolidation of Communist rule in February 1948 and the ensuing Sovietization of the country was a key turning point in every dimension of life in postwar Czechoslovakia, including the economy. Yet from the outset of the postwar period, there had been a general belief that a decisive break with the interwar period was necessary, both in terms of the economic structure at which reconstruction policies should aim and the economic system itself. Nationalization carried out immediately after the war was extensive. In 1946 about half of output already came from state-owned companies. It was accepted that the state should play a key role in steering economic development, though the assumption was that planning combined with economic levers rather than Soviet-type

directive planning would prevail. In addition, though the Kosice Program and the initial content of the First Five-Year Plan (1949–53) emphasized some reorientation of the economy toward heavy industry, this reflected the widespread view that overdependence on consumer and agricultural goods produced for Western European markets had proved a key weakness during the interwar period, rather than acceptance of socialist orthodoxy according to the Soviet script at this point.

The prevailing political situation prevented a specifically Czechoslovak pattern of socialist economic development from emerging. The Soviet-influenced first redraft of the initial Five-Year Plan in 1950 with emphasis on heavy industry entailed a considerable inversion of the country's economic configuration. A subsequent revision of targets ordered by Moscow in January 1951 required a further structural shift toward military industries. These were of a scale at which even the Gottwald team balked. The attempt to attain such unrealistic targets did fundamental damage to the Czechoslovak economy, not least because the government's fear of failure led it to hand over control to Soviet economic advisers, who proceeded to implement the Soviet planning and management model. Joining the Soviet system also meant becoming highly integrated into the "soft" markets of the socialist economic area dominated by the exchange of Soviet raw materials and energy in return for manufactures.

The outward successes of the Czechoslovak economy during the 1950s included impressive growth rates, with average annual national income increases of 8.2 percent for 1951–55 and 6.9 percent for 1956–60. There was also further progress toward eliminating regional inequalities. By 1958 Slovakia's contribution to national industrial output was 17.4 percent, double its prewar share, and there were positive developments in agricultural output as well as consumption, productivity, and the employment. Yet overall many adverse trends set in. Growth was not uniform across the economy, and even in sectors where output expanded rapidly, the typical quality-quantity trade-off emerged. The prewar level of agricultural production was not restored until 1965, while consumer industries lost their scale and stagnated technologically owing to low investment and isolation from the mainstream international economy. Living standards steadily slipped. Though monetary wages were high, the population experienced an estimated 4 percent fall in real consumption between 1952 and 1953 and were incensed by a currency reform of June 1953 that virtually wiped out household savings. The official intention to scale back priority to heavy industry in plans two and three failed as the imbalanced economic structure became embedded. By the end of the 1950s concerns about economic performance were already mounting.

The first set of reform initiatives, introduced in 1958, included amalgamating enterprises into large industrial associations, attempts to introduce financial criteria for planning, and very limited decentralization of decision making. These measures failed to stem the steady buildup of an economic crisis, and the imperative for fundamental reforms gained real momentum after the 3 percent fall in net material product recorded for 1963. Two other important developments around this time compounded the pressure on Czechoslovak policymakers. The first was the loss of Chinese markets. The second was the "scissors effect," which stemmed from Soviet demands for higher-quality industrial goods at a time when the capital-output ratio of the Czechoslovak economy was increasing and further undermining competitiveness in nonsocialist markets, which in turn reduced opportunities to acquire advanced technology. Under the intellectual leadership of Ota Šik, radical economists began to argue openly for an end to central planning. By 1966 a coherent reform concept had emerged and the party congress that took place in June of that year gave the go-ahead for the shift to a New Economic Model (NEM). The Czechoslovak NEM envisaged reintroduction of some capitalist principles. The main elements were devolution of key decisions to enterprise level, including the right to determine product mix and have some say in investment decisions; the requirement for enterprises to be profitable; progressive deregulation of a wide range of prices; more wage differentiation; and greater involvement with the world economy. While the time period was too short for NEM to become properly established, the economic agents responded to the new environment. Growth during 1966–70 averaged 6.9 percent, against 2.0 percent for the 1961–65 period. This reform experiment was officially terminated at the end of 1969, though it effectively ended in August 1968, a casualty of the Dubček government's aborted move toward wholesale abandonment of communism.

With a new leadership at the helm, centralized control of the economy was quickly restored. Soviet willingness to take poor-quality exports and supply energy at subsidized prices removed much of the immediate pressure from the Czechoslovak economy and shielded it from the oil shocks of the 1970s. This external support, together with a temporary reordering of priorities in favor of consumer goods, agriculture, housing and infrastructure, and some other favorable conjunctural factors, including repayment of earlier loans extended to developing states and some borrowing to finance imports from the West, under-

wrote relatively good economic performance in the first half of the 1970s. Thereafter gradual stagnation set in. Growth slumped from an average of 5.7 percent for 1971–75 to 1.8 percent for 1981–85, with absolute declines recorded for 1981 and 1982, and virtually halted by the end of the 1980s.

Further reform measures attempted in 1980 proved largely inconsequential. One conspicuous success appeared to be the harmonization of the economic levels of Slovakia and the Czech lands, yet even the progress of Slovakia was a mixed blessing. The region acquired what was by global standards a technologically retarded and backward-looking industrial base. Meanwhile, the emphasis on Slovakia in investment plans had left few funds to devote to the technological upgrading of those industries located in the Czech lands. Though the reform debate opened up again in Czechoslovakia during 1987, in the context of pressure to emulate the Soviet perestroika, or restructuring, being initiated by Soviet leader Mikhail Gorbachev, the traditional, unreformed Soviet-type economic system stayed intact until 1990.

The economic legacy of post-Communist Czechoslovakia was not totally negative. Serious foreign indebtedness was avoided, consumer goods markets were relatively balanced, and national income per capita, at $3,140 in 1990, was the highest in the socialist bloc. Moreover, though the industrial base had decayed, it nevertheless incorporated a diverse range of manufacturing possibilities, especially in the Czech part of the country. Intense debates over post-Communist reform strategy took place during the first half of 1990. Economic experts agreed on the priority of switching to a free market but generally divided over how rapidly to initiate internal and external liberalization of the economy. Some important transformation measures were possible at this stage. A two-tier banking system and unemployment compensation were introduced, and the Planning Commission, Prices Board, and state foreign trade monopoly were abolished. Legislation on formation and operation of new private business and joint stock companies, approximating Western practices, also appeared, and amendments to 1988 legislation greatly enhanced conditions for domestic investors.

In September 1990 the newly elected Czechoslovak government approved the "Scenario for Economic Reform." Essentially a blueprint for a fast-track road to a market economy, it represented a victory for the neoliberals led by Minister for Finance Václav Klaus. On January 1, 1991, 85 percent of retail and wholesale prices were decontrolled, and the koruna became convertible for current account purposes. The package also included a 20 percent import surcharge, tax-based measures to restrict wage growth, and reinforcement of the social safety net. A strict anti-inflationary stance, resting on restrictive fiscal and monetary policy, was confirmed as the principal macroeconomic goal. At the same time a fundamental reform of trade and payments arrangements among the former socialist countries came into effect, with trade-destroying consequences.

The usual set of negative economic results ensued. Inflation reached 58 percent in 1991, GDP plummeted by over 14 percent, industrial production by around 22 percent, and investment by 20 percent. The overall effects on the population were severe. Real earnings declined by 26 percent in 1991, personal consumption by 33 percent, and social consumption by 10 percent. Unemployment appeared, although at 4.1 percent it was comparatively mild in the Czech part of the country, compared with 11.8 percent for Slovakia. The recession continued into 1992, with GDP falling by a further 7 percent, though the rate of inflation slowed considerably. The main bright spot was foreign trade. The country achieved a rapid reorientation of its exports to the OECD area and by end of 1992 had managed to compensate completely for lost sales to markets of the former Council of Mutual Economic Assistance (CMEA), the organization formed in 1949 under the direction of the Soviet Union to foster the economic integration of eastern Europe. Export growth concentrated on the European Union (EU) and on Germany in particular, as Czechoslovak companies proved able to take advantage of improved market access included in the Agreement on Association concluded with the EU in December 1991.

The separation of Czechoslovakia as of January 1, 1993, prolonged the recession in both Slovakia and the Czech Republic. A substantial fall in what was now international trade was the main reason for the 0.3 percent decline in both Czech and Slovak GDP and for a subsequent rise in unemployment in both countries. The short-lived common currency lasted only until February 1993, at which time a customs union together with a clearing system to prevent hard currency shortages preventing further trade loss came into play. Both states are party to the Central European Free Trade Agreement (CEFTA), which began operating in April 1993. Mutual trade remains significant. Though small-scale privatization had been virtually completed, the split caused a delay in the process of large-scale "voucher" privatization. The latter is now virtually complete in the Czech Republic, but progress in Slovakia has been slower, reflecting a lack of political consensus over this dimension of reform.

Nowadays the Czech Republic is commonly regarded as having made the most effective transformation from socialism of all of the former "socialist" countries. In November 1995 it became the first post-Communist country to join the OECD. The Czech Republic had, at around 3 percent, the lowest rate of unemployment in Europe, had the best credit rating of the post-Communist world, and is at the front of the line for EU membership. By the mid-1990s the economic outlook for both the Czech Republic and Slovakia appeared promising. Both economies were growing healthily, at around 5–6 percent per annum in 1994 and 1995, inflation had fallen to manageable proportions, and real wages had recovered to 1989 levels. While Slovakia had been unable to emulate the Czech Republic's labor market miracle, the unemployment rate had been moving in the right direction since 1993.

Problem areas for both countries were growing trade deficits and worries that the absence of bankruptcies was indicative of a relatively slow pace of economic restructuring. The future economic prospects of both parts of the former Czechoslovakia may ultimately rest with their future economic orientations. It has always been clear that the Czech Republic's economic future is clearly tied to Western Europe. Slovakia's increasingly close economic relationship with Russia made an important contribution to the good growth performance of 1994 and 1995, given the contribution of favorable oil prices offered by the latter. However, the cancellation of this arrangement in 1996 raised questions about the sustainability of both Slovakia's economic recovery and its eastward agenda.

BIBLIOGRAPHY

Dangerfield, M. "The Czech Republic," in Bateman, M., ed., *Business Cultures in Central and Eastern Europe.* Oxford: Heinnemann Butterworth, 1996

European Bank for Reconstruction and Development. *Transition Report.* London: EBRD, 1995.

Paul, David W. *Czechoslovakia: Profile of a Socialist Republic at the Heart of Europe.* Boulder, Colo.: Westview Press, 1981.

Selucky, R. "From Capitalism to Socialism," in H. Gordon Skilling, ed., *Czechoslovakia 1918–88: Seventy Years from Independence.* London: MacMillan, 1991.

Martin V. Dangerfield

SEE ALSO Klaus, Václav; Sik, Ota

Catholic Church

The Roman Catholic Church came under intense pressure in Czechoslovakia after the Communist achieved a monopoly of power in February 1948. The Catholics of Czechoslovakia at the end of the Second World War numbered approximately ten million, or about 70 percent of the population. The Communists quickly moved to marginalize the church. Monasteries were suppressed, church land was nationalized, and religious instruction was banned. In 1949 church appointments were made dependent on state approval, sermons and pastoral letters were subjected to censorship, and many church organizations were outlawed. After 1948 public church ceremonies were forbidden, priests had to receive the approval of the regime to conduct their ministry, all but two seminaries were closed, priests could not be ordained without state authorization, many parishes were without priests, religious orders were forbidden to train novices, no new churches could be built, and bishops, priests, and nuns were subjected to arbitrary arrest and detention.

After the arrest of Archbishop Josef Beran of Prague, Pope Pius XII, without state approval, named two new bishops in Slovakia and in October 1949 appointed František Tomášek auxiliary bishop of Olomouc. The Communists responded in 1950 by arresting all the country's bishops and half its priests. Tomášek was released from a labor camp three years later but was refused permission to reassume his episcopal role. Instead he was sent to a rural parish in what amounted to internal exile. In 1979 there were thirteen dioceses in the country but only three resident bishops. Miloslav Vlk, who became archbishop of Prague in 1991, was stripped of his state approval to perform his priestly ministry in 1978. Until his license was restored in 1989, he was forced to earn a living as a window washer.

In 1968, during the Prague Spring restrictions that had hamstrung the church were removed. However, the Soviet-led Warsaw Pact invasion of that year and suppression of the Dubček regime brought about the reimposition of state controls. A state-sponsored organization of "Peace Priests" was organized, called Pacem in Terris after John XXIII's 1963 encyclical in an effort to give the movement the aura of the popular pope. The organization was intended, however, to co-opt and divide rather than evangelize. Tomášek, who had been appointed by Rome episcopal administrator of Prague in 1965, did not join but did not directly confront the organization. Some sincere priests apparently joined to gain state approval to conduct their ministries. The papacy even decided to appoint four Pacem in Terris members to vacant dioceses rather than leave them unserved.

Change began after Karol Wojtyla became pope in 1978 as John Paul II. Tomášek, apparently inspired by the new pope with whom he had become friends during the Second Vatican (1962–65) Council, abandoned his timidity and began to forthrightly denounce the repression of the regime. Tomášek condemned Pacem in Terris

in 1980. The group was formally condemned by the Vatican in 1982, and Tomášek announced that the organization's newspaper, *Catholic News,* the only "Catholic" newspaper allowed to be published in Czechoslovakia, did not represent the church.

In the 1980s Tomášek became an outspoken critic of the government. He supported lay opposition to the liberal 1986 abortion law and in 1988 gave his support to the massive petition launched by layman Augustin Navratil on behalf of religious freedom. By November 1989 Tomášek had clearly placed the church on the side of the developing Velvet Revolution.

BIBLIOGRAPHY
Corley, Felix. "Obituary: Cardinal Frantisek Tomasek." *The Independent* (London), August 5, 1992.
Dallas, Roland. *Reuters News Service,* April 29, 1979.

Bernard Cook

SEE ALSO Beran, Josef; Tomášek, František

Cinema

By far the most politically, economically, and culturally advanced country in Central-Eastern Europe during the interwar period (1918–39), Czechoslovakia established an independent and dynamic film industry in the early 1920s. Aided by the state, the country's first film production company and studio was founded in 1921. Inspired by a rich national literature and theater, the early Czech film industry produced thirty to thirty-five silent feature films per year during the 1920s. A key figure of this period was director Gustav Machaty, who made a trilogy of films based on Jaroslav Hašek's novel *The Good Soldier Schweik* in 1926–27. In 1929 Machaty produced a very successful and influential erotic film, *Erotika,* followed by a 1933 sequel, *Extase.* The first Czech sound film was released in 1930. Over the next decade, the Czechoslovak film industry expanded rapidly. Despite competition from imported Hollywood films and strong tendencies toward commercialism in domestic film output, filmmakers like Machaty created works of great originality at this time. In 1934 a group of Czech films, including *Extase,* won the Cup of the City of Venice. During the period 1935–38 the Czech film industry produced thirty-five to forty features per year for release in over two thousand, cinemas with an overall capacity of six hundred thousand seats. After Nazi Germany's annexation of Czechoslovakia in 1938–39, however, many prominent filmmakers went into exile, including to Hollywood. From 1939 to 1945 some local film production continued, mainly because most local studios survived the wartime period undamaged.

Although ruled by a Communist-dominated government after 1945, Czechoslovakia did not become a full "people's republic" until after the Communist coup of 1948. Only then was the Czech film industry nationalized and forced to make socialist realist films in support of Communist propaganda. Although not as free or as innovative as the Polish cinema of the mid-1950s, Czech filmmakers nevertheless made a number of interesting films at this time, notably Jiří Trnka's 1955 version of the *Good Soldier Schweik*. After de-Stalinization was launched in the Soviet Union in 1956, a new wave of younger and talented filmmakers came to the fore in Czechoslovakia and other countries in the region. In Czechoslovakia, these included Věra Chytilova, Miloš Forman, and Jiří Menzel, who later became the core group of a so-called Prague School of filmmaking during the 1960s. Influenced by developments in Polish cinema in particular and by the French New Wave in Western Europe, the Prague School filmmakers produced a remarkable body of innovative work at this time, including Forman's 1963 *Peter & Pavla*, *A Blade in Love* (1965), and *Fireman's Ball* (1967), Chytilova's *Daisies* (1966), and Menzel's *Closely Watched Trains* (1966). Based on sharp observation of the seemingly mundane and enlivened by a wry wit and subtle eroticism, films like Menzel's *Closely Watched Trains* were also sophisticated allegories that reflected on the recent past to illuminate a troubled present—an approach that could and was interpreted as being subversive by party censors.

With the flowering of the liberal Prague Spring of 1968, the Czech cinema briefly enjoyed an unprecedented freedom to reflect on, criticize, and ridicule "actually existing socialism." Cut short by the Soviet-led invasion of Czechoslovakia in August 1968, this remarkable period was quickly obliterated by hard-line censorship, the politics of the permanent purge, and the flight of many top filmmakers into exile. Of these new émigrés, Miloš Forman was to find fame as a top Hollywood director in the 1970s and 1980s. However, by the mid-1970s the post-1968 Czechoslovak cinema had begun to revive in the form of original films like *Seclusion in the Forest* (1980) and *Cutting It Short* (1980), both by Menzel, *Jara Cimrman, Lying Asleep* (1983) by Ladislav Smaljak, *Dimensions of Dialogue* (1983) *Down to the Cellar* (1983) by Jan Švankmajer, and *Pre-fab Story* (1979) and *Very Late Afternoon of a Fawn* (1983) by Věra Chytilova.

However, it was to be Slovak rather than Czech cinema that was to be at the forefront of local cinema during the 1970s and 1980s. Relatively insignificant during the mainly Czech "New Wave" of the 1960s, Slovak filmmakers were less vigorously censored than their Czech counterparts in Prague after the events of 1968. As a result newer filmmakers like Štefan Uher, Dušan Hanak, and Juraj Jakubisko were able to work relatively unimpeded during the 1970s and 1980s. One exception was the official banning of Hanak's 1969 film, *399*, which won an international award in West Germany in the same year but was not released locally until 1989. Of the many distinguished films produced in Slovakia at this time, probably the most significant was Jakubisko's *The Millennial Bee* (1983), an epic treatment of the fate of the Slovak people during this century. Outside of Czechoslovakia after 1968, émigré filmmaker Forman went on to Hollywood to make *The Last Picture Show* (1971), a masterly study of small-town American life and teenage rebellion in a dying Texas town, and *One Flew Over the Cuckoo's Nest* (1975), a big-budget Oscar-winning film with Jack Nicholson in the lead role. For *Amadeus* (1984), an international coproduction on the life of Mozart, Forman returned to his native Prague to film many of its visually stunning street and interior scenes.

With the end of communism and its system of subsidized film production and distribution at the end of the 1980s and early 1990s, Czechoslovak cinema experienced a sharp decline, with matters made worse by the dissolution of Czechoslovakia in 1993. Far more than was the case in nearby Poland, where some state-supported filmmaking continued in the 1990s, Czech and Slovak cinema was forced to rely on films made for TV and international coproductions in English for its economic survival at a time when local film going was dominated by films and TV programs from Hollywood. As things stand there are now serious doubts as to whether distinctive Czech and Slovak cinemas will survive in the future.

BIBLIOGRAPHY

Czechoslovak Cinema/Ceskoslovensky Film. Prague: Czechoslovak Film Institute, 1982.

Marko Milivojevic

Czech Republic

On January 1, 1993, Czechoslovakia split into the Czech Republic (Ceská Republika) and Slovakia. The Czech Republic, with its capital at Prague, had a population of 10.4 million people, twice that of Slovakia.

Economic trends in the Czech Republic were in marked contrast to those in Slovakia. Most noticeable were the differing approaches to privatization of state-owned enterprises. Unlike other governments in Eastern

Czech Republic. *Illustration courtesy of Bernard Cook.*

Europe, including that of Slovakia, the Czech government moved aggressively toward privatization. It offered its citizens books of vouchers for one thousand crowns (about $35, an average week's salary) that could be used to bid on shares. This program contrasted with the piecemeal approach in both Hungary and Poland, and particularly with that of Slovakia, where, a year after the breakup, only about 5 percent of state-owned enterprises had been privatized. By the end of 1993 more than six million Czechs had purchased shares in some of the hundreds of companies that were being privatized. By early 1994 fully 40 percent of state enterprises had been privatized (two thousand companies valued at $20.7 billion), and the expectation was that only about 10 to 15 percent of all Czech assets would be state-run by the end of 1994. In early 1994 fully 60 percent of the republic's production came from privatized companies. The distribution of additional voucher books in 1995 led to the privatization of approximately 80 percent of the economy. The republic was also very successful in attracting foreign investment. By the mid-1990 foreign investment in the Czech Republic totaled over $2 billion.

The Czech Republic also had much lower unemployment and inflation, and a higher rate of economic growth than Slovakia and other Eastern European states. In early 1994 unemployment was 3.5 percent in the Czech Republic versus 15.1 percent in Slovakia. Inflation was a problem, although at 18 percent it was less than the 22 percent in Slovakia and was the lowest in the region.

Also in contrast to Slovakia, the leaders of the Czech Republic were popular and the domestic political scene was stable. The Czech Republic possessed two key political leaders, both of whom were gifted communicators: the philosophical Václav Havel, the president, and Václav Klaus, a pragmatic conservative economist and member of the Civic Democratic Party, the prime minister.

Under the old Czechoslovak constitution the president held most of the executive power, but the 1993 constitution scaled back his powers somewhat and increased those of the prime minister. By early 1994 as Havel's prestige momentarily ebbed, that of Klaus rose. Klaus, the first post-Communist finance minister and prime minister from 1992 to 1997, was the only Eastern European leader to embrace market reforms and see his prestige rise, if only temporarily.

In 1996 the growth of the economy slowed and the new state experienced its first budgetary deficit. There were problems in the banking sector and by the middle of 1996 eleven banks had failed. In 1997 a number of bankers were charged with fraud and embezzlement. Because of the loss of public confidence in financial institutions and speculative attacks on the country's currency, the government was forced to take a more active role in managing the economy. The privatization of state-owned banks and energy companies was put on hold, public spending was cut, and measures were implemented to reduce imports and regulate the capital market. By the end of 1997 the trade deficit narrowed and industrial output was growing.

The Czech Republic has been very concerned to maintain close and friendly relations with Slovakia. After the split with Slovakia in January 1993, the Czech Republic, in an effort to foster broad cooperation in the areas of economics and defense, retained its status as a member of the Visegrad Group with Slovakia, Poland, and Hungary. Nevertheless, it has also sought to create close ties with Western Europe. It was one of the first Eastern European states to apply for membership in the North Atlantic Treaty Organization (NATO), and, as a temporary alternative, accepted the "Partnership for Peace" program with more grace than Poland. With the 1998 ratifications of a protocol signed with NATO in December 1997, the Czech Republic, along with Poland and Hungary, became the first of the old East Bloc countries to join the trans-Atlantic alliance. In March 1998 the Czech Republic was invited to begin negotiations concerning its possible entry into the European Union.

The Czech Republic has, in particular, fostered close ties with Germany, its principal trade partner and the principal foreign investor in its economy. On January 21,

1997, Havel and the German Chancellor Helmut Kohl signed a joint declaration condemning both the German occupation and partition of Czechoslovakia in 1939, and the Czechoslovak abuse of human rights during the expulsion of the Sudeten Germans in 1945–46. However, the Czechs, anxious to avoid claims for compensation by those expelled, refrained from admitting that the expulsion had been criminal. One problem, which temporarily exacerbated relations with a neighbor, was the Czech decision to complete with U.S. technical assistance, a Soviet-designed nuclear power plant at Tremelin, close to the Austrian border.

BIBLIOGRAPHY

Simon, Jeffrey. *Czechoslovaki's "Velvet Divorce," Visegrad Cohesion, and European Fault Lines.* Washington, D.C.: Institute for National Strategic Studies, National Defense University, 1993.

Symynkywicz, Jeffrey. *Vaclav Havel and the Velvet Revolution.* New York: Maxwell Macmillan International, 1995.

Spencer C. Tucker

SEE ALSO Czechoslovakia; Slovakia

Political Parties

The only genuine parliamentary democracy in East Central Europe during the interwar period, Czechoslovakia descended into dictatorship in 1939, first under Nazi German occupation then as a one-party Communist state allied to the Soviet Union after the coup carried out by the Communist Party of Czechoslovakia (CzCP) in 1948. In 1946, when the first free but not entirely fair postwar parliamentary elections took place, the CzCP gained 38 percent of the vote in the Czech lands but only 30 percent of the vote in Slovakia. Briefly ruled by a coalition government dominated by the CzCP from 1946 to 1948, Czechoslovakia thereafter became a one-party Communist dictatorship controlled by the Soviet Union for the next forty years. In 1968, however, a new reformist CzCP leader, Slovak Alexander Dubček, attempted to implement a reformist Prague Spring in Czechoslovakia. Brutally crushed by the Soviet-led Warsaw Pact invasion of the country in August 1968, this brief attempt to liberalize communism was followed by a so-called normalization of Czech and Slovak politics for the next twenty years. Involving mass purges of the CzCP and hard-line repression of all dissent, this policy turned Czechoslovakia into one of the most conservative, repressive members of the Warsaw Pact during the 1970s and 1980s. By the mid-1970s, however, a number of dissident groups had

emerged, foremost of which was Charter 77, a human rights initiative led by people who were to play a major role in Czech politics after 1989. Among others, these included a future Czech president, Václav Havel. After Mikhail Gorbachev came to power in the Soviet Union in 1985, the human and civic rights campaigners of yesteryear became the new rulers of Czechoslovakia after its Velvet Revolution of November 1989, when the power monopoly of the CzCP collapsed.

In the same month as the Velvet Revolution, a Civic Forum (Občanské Fórum) was founded in Prague to represent all democratic forces in the Czech Republic (a similar movement, Public Against Violence [PAV], then also emerged in the Slovak Republic). Closely bound together and popular throughout the federation, Civic Forum and PAV then pushed the discredited CzCP aside in December 1989, when they created a new "government of national understanding" that also included the Czechoslovak Socialist Party (CSP) and the Czechoslovak People's Party (CPP), two former splinter groups of the CzCP-dominated National Front after 1948. Also in December 1989, the venerated leader of the Prague Spring, Alexander Dubček, became chairman of the Federal Assembly, which then also elected the prominent Charter 77 leader, Haval, as the new president of Czechoslovakia. Following new federal and republican parliamentary elections in June 1990, Civic Forum and PAV became the largest parties in both the federal and republican assemblies. Under new electoral laws passed earlier in 1990, only eight of the twenty-two parties that contested these polls won parliamentary representation.

Other than Civic Forum, which events were to show was more a movement than a political party, the most significant parties in the Czech Republic at this time were former Communists or new parties of the social democratic left. In the case of the CzCP, which was later renamed the Communist Party of Bohemia and Moravia (CPBM) in 1992, it was only one of two parties to nominate candidates in both the Czech and Slovak Republics. Another significant party in the early 1990s was Coexistence (*Egütteles*), which aimed to attract support from all ethnic groups but proved to be mainly of interest to the large Rom and Hungarian minority communities. Of the center-left and anti-CzCP parties, the most significant later in the 1990s was the Czech Social Democratic Party (SDP), a major prewar party prohibited by the Communists in 1948 and one of the first to be reestablished in 1989. Led by Miloš Zeman, the SDP is now well on the way to becoming the party of government in the late 1990s. Of the prewar center-right parties, the Christian Democratic Movement (CDM) was similar to the SDP in that it did not have much of an electoral impact in 1990. More significantly, in 1990 at least, a number of regionally based parties then emerged. Of these, the Movement for Democracy–The Society for Moravia and Silesia (MAD–SMS) was a junior member of the first elected Civic Forum–led coalition government of June 1990, along with the CPP, which had earlier campaigned as part of the CDM.

More a broadly based national movement against the Communist past than a political party for future government, Civic Forum split apart in 1991. The split resulted in an expansion of new political parties in the Czech Republic. On the center-right, these included the Civic Democratic Party (CDP) led by Václav Klaus, a former Civic Forum chairman. Of the centrist parties that emerged out of Civic Forum, the most significant was Civic Movement, later known as Civic Democratic Alliance (CDA). In 1992 the CDM-CPP alliance that had contested the 1990 elections became a new party, the CDM-CPP. Following new parliamentary elections in the Czech Republic in June 1992, Klaus's CDP became the dominant Czech party, leading a new coalition government that also included the CDM-CPP and the CDA. As in 1990, the Communists remained the second-largest party in the Czech Republic, closely followed by the SDP. On the far, or fascist, right of Czech politics, a worrying development was the 6 percent of the vote gained by the Republican Party of Czechoslovakia (AFR) in 1992, or only three years after it was founded on a mainly anti-Rom and anti-German platform in 1989.

Following the formal dissolution of Czechoslovakia on January 1, 1993, when the Czech Republic became independent of the former Czechoslovak federation, Czech party politics became more unstable and controversial than hitherto. To begin with, Klaus's haste to reject Czechoslovakia caused problems with its president, Havel, who did not become president of the Czech Republic as automatically as he would have liked. Here the major problem was the often open hostility between Klaus and Havel for the next five years. In terms of generally effective government, however, Klaus's coalition proved to be cohesive, although it was to be undermined and then destroyed by the unfolding of a serious socioeconomic crisis

toward the end of its four-year term in 1996. This negative trend was also exacerbated by Klaus's abrasive political style and his overconfidence in free-market economics, the eventual failure of which was mainly to benefit the parties of the left led by the CPBM and then the SDP. The ODS remained the strongest party after the June 1996 general elections, but Klaus's coalition lost its majority in parliament and he was forced to form a minority government. Though his government survived votes of no confidence in June and November 1997, Klaus was undermined by economic difficulties and a ODS fund raising scandal. He resigned as prime minister at the end of November, and Havel appointed Josef Tosovsky, the head of the state bank, to lead a caretaker government. In an election in June 1998, the Social Democrats emerged victorious, with 74 seats in the 200 seat lower house of the Czech parliament. Klaus's CDP came in second with 63 seats. Zeman became prime minister but, in accord with an "opposition agreement" pact in which the CDP agreed not to initiate or support a vote of no confidence, Klaus was elected chairman of the lower house. The minor parties protested the agreement as an undemocratic move that would deny them a role in government.

However, the resurgence of the SDP in 1996 had as much to do with the decline of the traditional Czech left as with the failings of Klaus's CDP and the center-right more generally. Here the biggest loser was the CPBM. A move toward the center-left was then and remains part of a wider political trend in the region after the fall of communism. More than elsewhere in the region, the center-right became politically dominant in the early post-Communist period, but once the costs and problems of economic transition became too high, then the center-left reemerged to become the growing political force of the future. In sharp contrast to the situation in the nearby Slovak Republic during the 1990s, post-1989 party politics in the Czech Republic have generally been successful in establishing the roots of a durable and legitimate multiparty democratic system of governance.

Marko Milivojevik

SEE ALSO Havel, Václav; Klaus, Václav

Dagestan: Chechen Incursion

On August 7, 1999, approximately 1,200 Chechen fighters entered the Russian province of Dagestan and seized control of a number of villages in the mountainous Botlikh region.

Dagestan, located on the Caspian Sea bordering Chechnya, Georgia, and Azerbaijan, has a diverse population. Its two million inhabitants belong to thirty-three different ethnic groups, but an estimated 71 percent of them also speak fluent Russian. Despite the linguistic and cultural diversity, most of the groups are Islamic, and the Wahhabi fundamentalist sect has made significant inroads in the area. Islamic fundamentalism and opposition to Russian rule have been abetted by poverty and the inefficiency and corruption of the government. Dagestan possesses one of the highest provincial levels of unemployment in the Russian Federation. However, Mukhu Gumbatovich Aliyev, the chairman of the People's Assembly of Dagestan, has asserted that 90 percent of the Dagestanis desire to remain part of Russia. According to Aleksei Malashenko of the Carnegie Endowment for International Peace, "The Dagestanis don't want independence. They are a multiethnic, multinational society. For them, a struggle for independence means civil war."

Dagestan has great economic significance for Russia. Seventy percent of Russia's Caspian Sea shoreline is located in Dagestan. Russia's only all-weather Caspian port is the Dagestan capital city of Makhachkala, and the crucial pipelines that connect Russia to the oil fields of Azerbaijan run through Dagestan. For the Chechens, control of the Botlikh region would provide Chechnya with access to Islamic Azerbaijan and the outside world.

The rebel fighters were led by Shamil Basayev, the daring and tenacious Chechen commander, and Khattab, a Jordanian-born Chechen militant who fought against the Russians in Afghanistan and with Basayev against the Russians in Chechnya. Khattab, who is married to a Dagestani and is an adherent of Wahhabism, set up a guerrilla training camp in Chechnya to train Chechens and Dagestanis to fight for Islamic rule in the north Caucasus.

The incursion was preceded by growing tension both in Dagestan and Chechnya. In May 1998 the main governmental building in Makhachkala was briefly seized by gunmen, and in August of the same year the chief Muslim cleric in Dagestan was assassinated in a bomb attack. In September, Islamic oppositionists demanded that Chechen president Aslan Maskhadov resign. Maskhadov, who favors independence for Chechnya but resists the establishment of a conservative Islamic state, was, according to his opponents, too conciliatory to the Russians. In March 1999 there was an attempt on Maskhadov's life, and in the same month fifty people were killed by a bomb in the city of Vladikavkaz. On June 18, Russia shut down fifty of its sixty checkpoints on the Chechen frontier after overnight clashes left seven Russian policemen and interior ministry troops dead and fourteen wounded. The clashes occurred along the frontier between Chechnya and the Stavropol region in north and Dagestan in the east.

When the Russians responded to the incursion with artillery and air attacks in Dagestan and an air attack against reputed rebel camps in Chechnya, fear was expressed that Russia was resuming the same tactics that failed during the Chechen War. Critics said that Russia's reliance on air and artillery attacks on villages because of its inability to mount a organized ground effort could alienate Dagestanis and win the Chechen fighters wider support in Chechnya.

By August 24 the rebels withdrew back into Chechnya despite the assertion of the Russians that they would be crushed. Basayev said that they had not given up but were merely changing tactics. His prediction was fulfilled in

September. While the Russian military mounted an ill-conceived assault against several villages in central Dagestan that were controlled by the Wahhabis, the Chechen militants struck again. On September 4, a powerful car bomb demolished a military housing complex in Buinaksk, the second largest city in Dagestan. Over fifty officers and family members were killed. At the same time militants crossed into Dagestan, seized six villages, and engaged the Russians in heavy fighting.

In September, Russia was shaken by a bombing campaign that targeted apartment complexes and killed over three hundred Russian civilians. The Russian government responded by mounting air strikes on Chechnya. The raids in and around Grozny, the Chechen capital, drove tens of thousands of Chechen refugees into neighboring Ingushetia. The new Russian prime minister, Vladimir Putin, in a seeming repudiation of the August 1996 agreement between Russia and Chechnya, refused to negotiate with President Maskhadov, and announced that Chechnya was part of Russia. On October 1, Russian ground troops advanced from Dagestan into Chechen territory and the next day land links between Russia and Chechnya were cut. The original Russian support for action against Chechen rebels began to shatter as the prospect for a renewed war grew.

BIBLIOGRAPHY

Bohlen, Celestine, "Fighting in Dagestan Threatens to Spill over into Chechnya," *New York Times,* August 14, 1999.

———. "Russian Troops are in New Battle with Separatists in the Caucasus," *New York Times,* August 9, 1999.

———. "Russians Push Islamic Militants Out of Dagestan, but Threat Remains," *New York Times,* August 26, 1999.

"Chechen Says He Leads Revolt in Nearby Area," *Reuters,* August 12, 1999.

Gall, Carlotta, "Dagestan Skirmish is Big Russian Risk," *New York Times,* August 13, 1999.

Gordon, Michael R., "Widening Caucasus Conflict, Russia Bombs Chechnya Bases," *New York Times,* August 15, 1999.

"Russian Forces Pound Rebel Villages," *Associated Press,* August 16, 1999.

Bernard Cook

Dahrendorf, Ralf (1929–)

German sociologist, Bundestag deputy, and director of the London School of Economics, one of the great public intellectuals of the postwar era. Born in Hamburg, son of a Social Democratic Reichstag (parliament) deputy who was jailed in 1933 when the Nazis came to power, Ralf Dahrendorf himself was sent to a concentration camp in 1944 for anti-Nazi activities. After the war he studied philosophy and classical philology at the University of Hamburg, where he received a Ph.D. in 1952, and at the University of London, where he received a Ph.D. in sociology in 1956. He returned to West Germany as an instructor in sociology at the University of Saarbrücken (1954–57), then accepted various professorial appointments in Hamburg (1958–60), Tübingen (1960–65), and Constance (1965–69). He was elected to the Bundestag as a Free Democratic Party delegate and served a two-year term (1969–70), then became a member of the European Community Commission (1970–74). Dahrendorf subsequently served as director of the London School of Economics (1974–84) and in 1987 became Warden of St. Antony's College, Oxford. Dahrendorf has held numerous visiting appointments, headed many committees and professional societies, including the German Sociological Society, and has been awarded a remarkable array of honors, including the German Bundesverdienstkreuz in 1974 and a lifetime peerage from Elizabeth II in 1993.

His scholarly accomplishments extend to studies on Marxism, class conflict, education, economic crises, and the European Union (EU). Dahrendorf's most influential work remains *Gesellschaft und Democratie in Deutschland* (*Society and Democracy in Germany,* 1965), in which he examines the origins of postwar German democracy. He posed the thesis that the Nazis cleared the way by destroying the social bases of authoritarian government, particularly aristocratic hegemony, and analyzed Germany's "long road to modernity" with an equally masterful grasp of both history and sociological theory. His earlier goal "to stimulate, perhaps to provoke, critical thought about Germany's past, present, and future" has been extended beyond his place of birth in works such as his 1990 *Reflections on the Revolution in Europe.*

BIBLIOGRAPHY

Mastroeni, Giuseppe. *Analisi Critico-Storiografica del Homo Sociologicus di Ralph [sic] Dahrendorf.* Messina: Peloritana, 1977.

Jonathan Petropoulos

D'Alema, Massimo (1949–)

Italian premier, secretary of the Italian Democratic Party of the Left (PDS). Massimo D'Alema played an important role in the transformation of the Italian Communist

Party (PCI) into a democratic party of the left. He was born in Rome on April 20, 1949, and studied philosophy at the University of Pisa. He joined the Federation of Young Italian Communists (FYIC) in 1963 and the PCI in 1968. In 1975 he became the national secretary of the FYIC. At the Fifteenth Congress of PCI, D'Alema became a member of the Central Committee, and at the Seventeenth Congress in 1986 he also entered the Secretariat.

D'Alema wrote for *Rinascita, L'Unità,* and *Città Futura* before editing *L'Unità* from 1988 to 1990. He was one of the young leaders who assisted Achille Occhetto in 1989 as he transformed the PCI into the PDS. After the dissolution of PCI, D'Alema became a member of the directorate of PDS. He was elected to the Chamber of Deputies in June 1987, was reelected from the constituency of Lecce-Brindisi-Taranto in April 1992, and became president of the PDS parliamentary delegation. In July 1994 D'Alema was elected secretary of PDS, and he was again returned to the legislature from the twenty-first district of Puglia. On February 5, 1997, he was elected president of the parliamentary commission on constitutional reform.

He became premier of Italy following the collapse of Romano Prodi's center-left government on October 9, 1998, owing to the refusal of Communist Refounding to vote for his proposed budget. President Oscar Luigi Scalfaro asked Prodi to form a new government, but the Union of Democrats for the Republic (UDR), led by former Christian Democrat Francesco Cossiga, refused to support Prodi. Scalfaro then turned to D'Alema, leader of the largest party of Prodi's Olive Tree Coalition. D'Alema put together a coalition consisting of seven parties, including the UDR. The cabinet included a number of holdovers from Prodi's cabinet. Lamberto Dini was reappointed foreign minister; Carlo Azeglio Ciampi retained the Ministry of Treasury and Budget; and Vincenzo Visco continued at the Finance Ministry. Giuliano Amato, former socialist premier, was appointed minister of institutional reform.

BIBLIOGRAPHY

D'Alema, Massimo. *Il compagno Massimo: quando D'Alema era comunista: 1975–1990.* Milan: Kaos, 1998.

———. *Un paese normale: la sinistra e il futuro dell'Italia.* Milano: A. Mondadori, 1995.

———. *La sinistra nell'Italia che cambia.* Milan: Feltrinelli, 1997.

Fasanella, Giovanni. *D'Alema: la prima biografia del segretario del PDS.* Milan: Longanesi, 1995.

Rapisarda, Alberto. *Massimo D'Alema.* Rome: Viviani, 1996.

Spini, Valdo. *La rosa e l'ulivo: per il nuovo partito del socialismo europeo in Italia.* Milan: Baldini & Castoldi, 1998.

Bernard Cook

SEE ALSO Cossiga, Francesco; Italy

Dalla Chiesa, Carlo Alberto (1920–82)

Carabinieri (national police) officer and prefect of Sicily, assassinated by the Mafia in 1982. Carlo Alberto Dalla Chiesa was born in Saluzzo (Cuneo) on September 27, 1920. He obtained the rank of second lieutenant in the military branch of the Carabinieri in 1942. For his bravery during the war, including the partisan struggle, he was granted a permanent commission in the Carabinieri in 1945. During his long career he reached the highest possible rank for a general of Carabinieri when he was appointed the deputy chief commander of the institution (December 1981–May 1982).

Among his assignments, the most important were the command of the Legione of Palermo (1966–73) and the coordination of the Security Service for Jails, which also included the task of coordinating the police forces against terrorism (1978–79). In that post he reported directly to the minister of interior. He held that post when Prime Minister Aldo Moro was kidnapped and killed.

Dalla Chiesa, as a young captain, was sent to Corleone (Palermo) in 1949 to fight against bandits. Because of his deep knowledge of Sicily and of the extremely rewarding results he had obtained against terrorism, he was nominated prefect of Sicily, a difficult assignment, with the specific purpose of fighting the criminal organizations of the mafiosi. In Palermo Dall Chiesa, his young second wife (he was a widower), and his policeman driver were all killed by the Mafia in Palermo on September 3, 1982.

BIBLIOGRAPHY

Dalla Chiesa, Carlo Alberto. *In nome del popolo italiano.* Milan: Rizzoli, 1997.

Dalla Chiesa, Nando. *Delitto imperfetto: Il generale, la mafia, la societa italiana.* Milan: Mondadori, 1984.

Damato, Francesco. *L'ombra del generale: Diario di un servizio televisivo sulla mafia dopo Dalla Chiesa.* Milan: SugarCo, 1983.

Morte di un generale: L'assassinio di Carlo Alberto Dalla Chiesa, la mafia, la droga, il potere politico. Milan: Mondadori, 1982.

Maria Gabriella Pasqualini

SEE ALSO Mafia

Daly, Cahal Brendan (1917–)

Roman Catholic primate of Ireland. Cahal Brendan Daly was born in Loughgiel, near the Glens of Antrim, on October 1, 1917. He studied at St. Malachy's College and Queen's University in Belfast, at Maynooth in the Irish Republic, and at the Institut Catholique in Paris. He was ordained to the priesthood in 1941. He taught scholastic philosophy at Queen's University in Belfast from 1946 to 1967. He was consecrated bishop of Ardagh and Clonmacnois in 1967, and became the bishop of Down and Connor Belfast in 1982. He became the bishop of Armagh and primate of all Ireland in 1990, and was made a cardinal in 1991.

Daly, who wrote the appeal for peace delivered by Pope John Paul II when he visited Ireland in 1979, forcefully condemned the Irish Republican Army. However, the bishop also took the government in Northern Ireland to task for its failure to create the conditions for peace, stating that violence flourished in a political vacuum. He specifically called on the government to respect the rights of the Catholic minority. Daly's opposition to the IRA often led to verbal confrontations with members of his church in heavily IRA sections of Belfast. But when the IRA declared a cease-fire, Daly called for its inclusion in any dialogue.

The bishop opposed the revocation of the constitutional prohibition of divorce in the republic and opposed the legalization of contraceptives. Daly, following the 1994 jailing of the priest Brendan Smyth for sexual abuse, expressed his dismay over this betrayal of trust, issued a public apology on behalf of the church, and established a commission that apologized for covering up past incidents and promised to cooperate in the future with the police.

Daly retired on October 1, 1996, and was succeeded as archbishop of Armagh by Sean Brady.

BIBLIOGRAPHY

"Irish Cardinal Retires." *San Diego Daily Transcript*, October 1, 1996.

"Outspoken Critic of the I.R.A. Is Named Primate of Ireland." *New York Times*, November 7, 1990.

Pollak, Andy. "A dedicated, outspoken spiritual leader." *Irish Times*, October 2, 1996.

Bernard Cook

Damanaki, Maria (1952–)

Greek political figure. Maria Damanaki was born in Agios Nikolaos, Crete, in 1952. She attended primary school in Crete and moved to Athens after being accepted at the National Technical University of Athens in 1970 to study chemical engineering. There she joined the Communist Youth Movement of Greece (KNE) in 1972 and played an active role as a radio broadcaster for the besieged university students in the Athens Polytechnic in the turmoil that accompanied the collapse of the Greek military regime in 1974.

After the return of parliamentary democracy to Greece in August 1974, Damanaki continued her involvement in politics, serving as a member of the Secretariat of the Communist Youth Movement. In 1977 she was elected to parliament as a representative of the Athens area "B" for the Communist Party of Greece (KKE), a position that she held until 1990. During her tenure she served as fifth and then first vice president of parliament in 1981 and 1989. In 1990 Damanaki joined the Sinaspismos Party and became the first female party leader in Greek history. In 1993 she resigned as party head and dedicated her time to the newly formed social organization Citizens for Athens. In 1994 Damanaki became a candidate for mayor of Athens, securing 12 percent of the popular vote and a position on the city board.

In October 1996 Damanaki returned to the political arena as a parliamentary representative for the Sinaspismos Party. As a member of Sinaspismos she was responsible for the party's position and strategy on foreign policy and defense. She has written a widely read book, *Greek Women: The Female Aspect of Power*.

Stelios Zachariou

Danube Dam

Much-criticized Slovak dam at Gabcikovo on the Danube River, completed in November 1992, which came to symbolize Slovak nationalism. The Slovaks also announced their determination to preserve two large nuclear reactors that many Western experts thought were unsafe and should be dismantled. The dam project, which diverted the Danube River, produced acrimonious relations with Hungary.

The Slovaks were determined to produce as much electricity as possible, both for the country's own use and for sale to Western Europe. Slovakia was much poorer than the Czech Republic, with which it was linked as part of the former Czechoslovakia until 1993, and its leaders believed that the sale of electricity was critical for the country's economic survival. More than half the nation's electrical power had come from two nuclear reactors at Jaslovske Bohunice, which produced 440 megawatts each. The Gabcikovo dam generated 720 megawatts, almost as much as the two reactors together.

The Danube project was begun in 1977 as a cooperative venture between Czechoslovakia and Hungary. But in 1989, when the Communists were toppled in Hungary, the new government in Budapest announced its intention to end the project altogether, and its leaders bitterly criticized Slovak leaders for their decision to proceed. Budapest was soon joined by a chorus of environmental groups that charged the dam would destroy wildlife, flood valuable land, and damage one of Europe's largest underground water supplies. Nations downstream from the dam also worried about the effect of any reduction in the flow of the Danube on river transport.

The waters of the Danube were diverted in October 1992. In September 1997 the World Court ruled that both Slovakia and Hungary had violated international law and called on them to resume negotiations. Hungary still demands the diversion of 50 percent of Danube water through its Szigetkoez region.

BIBLIOGRAPHY

"Hungarian-Slovak Talks on Danube Damn Delayed," *BBC Worldwide Monitoring,* September 20, 1999.

Rothschild, Joseph, and Nancy M. Wingfield. *Return to Diversity: A Political History of East Central Europe since World War II.* 3rd ed. New York: Oxford University Press, 2000.

Spencer C. Tucker

Dassault, Marcel (1892–1986)

French industrialist. Marcel Dassault was born Marcel Bloch, son of a Jewish physician, in Paris on January 22, 1892. He studied electrical and aeronautical engineering at the École Nationale Supérieure de l'Aéronautique, and he designed propellers and airplanes for France in World War I. After marrying into a wealthy family in 1919 he built condominiums. In 1930, however, inspired by a call from the French minister of air for the construction of all-metal planes, he set up an aircraft company and had success in the production of both civilian and military aircraft. Despite the nationalization of the French aircraft industry by Premier Léon Blum's Popular Front government, Bloch was permitted to continue plane production at a small factory at Saint-Cloud. After the Germans overran France in 1940, they tried to force him to produce planes for Germany but he refused. He was sent to Buchenwald concentration camp in Germany, where his health was broken.

After the defeat of the Germans, he returned to France, converted to Catholicism, and changed his name to Dassault, which had been the Resistance nom de guerre of one of his brothers. When the war ended, the French aircraft industry was partially denationalized, and private companies were allowed to produce civilian planes. Dassault reestablished himself as an aircraft manufacturer and, with foreign contracts from the United States, moved again into production of military aircraft. His aircraft company, Générale Aéronautique Marcel Dassault, produced Europe's first supersonic aircraft, the Mystère. His delta-winged Mirages, produced from 1956, became the standard component of the air forces of many countries. In 1967 Générale Aéronautique merged with Breguet Aviation, a manufacturer of commercial aircraft.

A controversy arose over the sale of Mirages to Libya in 1970. The Mirage had been a standard element of Middle Eastern air forces before the 1967 war between Israel and Egypt, Syria and Jordan. The French government imposed an embargo on the sale of aircraft to 1967 belligerents, even though the Israeli government had paid for fifty Mirages that had not yet been delivered. France in 1970 decided to sell one hundred Mirages to Libya, which had not been a belligerent in 1967. Though Dessault was a supporter of Israel and had said that he would sell no planes to any Arab country until the boycott against sales to Israel was lifted, he declared the sale "the government's affair" and gave way.

Dessault, who also served as a deputy in the National Assembly, died in Paris on April 18, 1986.

BIBLIOGRAPHY

"Dassault, Marcel." *Current Biography Yearbook 1970.* 105–7. New York: H. W. Wilson, 1970.

Bernard Cook

De Beauvoir, Simone (1908–86)

French feminist and author, Europe's best-known postwar woman writer and activist. Her 1949 *The Second Sex* helped inspire the contemporary women's movement. Her public support of liberal causes and lifelong intellectual collaboration with philosopher Jean-Paul Sartre brought her international recognition.

Despite a conventional Catholic middle-class upbringing, recounted in her 1958 *Memoirs of a Dutiful Daughter,* Simone de Beauvoir abandoned religion in adolescence and pursued higher education. While achieving an outstanding record at the Institut Catholique, Sorbonne, and École Normale Supérieure, de Beauvoir established friendships with Maurice Merleau-Ponty, Claude Lévi-Strauss, and Jean-Paul Sartre, the last of whom became her lover and companion. Her score on the 1929 *agrégation* in philosophy was second behind Sartre's, but at twenty-one she was the youngest student ever to pass the examination.

By 1936 she and Sartre were both teaching in Paris lycées and active in cafe-based intellectual circles. Rejecting marriage or motherhood, de Beauvoir embraced Sartre's existentialism. Initially indifferent to the politics of the 1930s, she was politicized by the fall of France to the Germans in 1940 and the loss of her teaching post. After 1943 she devoted herself entirely to writing and by 1946 had published three novels and, with Sartre, founded and edited the influential monthly *Les Temps modernes.* As a public intellectual de Beauvoir opposed the Algerian War and the establishment of Charles de Gaulle's Fifth Republic. A prominent critic of the Vietnam War and the Soviet-led invasion of Czechoslovakia in 1968, she also supported French student demonstrators in that year. She collaborated politically with Sartre, but was much warier of French and Soviet communism than he.

The Second Sex brought de Beauvoir fame in her own right. Expanding on portrayals of female dependence and sexuality in her fiction and feminist elements of her hostility to capitalism and bourgeois culture, the long historical essay presented female subordination as a product of millennia of cultural and societal repression. Radical legal and educational changes would enable women to achieve the freedom and intellectual independence men enjoyed. The widely translated *The Second Sex* and her 1954 novel *The Mandarins,* which was awarded France's prestigious Goncourt prize, brought de Beauvoir financial security, international honors, and invitations to travel and lecture in the United States, China, Brazil, the USSR, and Africa. In the 1970s she joined the renascent French women's liberation movement that her writings had partly inspired, and signed the manifesto in which 343 prominent French women announced that they had undergone illegal abortions.

Five volumes of memoirs, a book on aging, and published reminiscences of Sartre preceded her death in 1986. Though criticized for emotional and intellectual dependence on Sartre, who seldom acknowledged her many contributions to his own work, and a feminism that urged women to embrace male models of accomplishment, de Beauvoir achieved a measure of independence and influence unequaled among women of her generation.

BIBLIOGRAPHY

Bair, Deidre. *Simone de Beauvoir.* New York: Simon & Schuster, 1990.

Evans, Mary. *Simone de Beauvoir: A Feminist Mandarin.* London: Tavistock, 1985.

Whitmarsh, Anne. *Simone de Beauvoir and the Limits of Commitment.* Cambridge: Cambridge University Press, 1981.

David Longfellow

SEE ALSO Sartre, Jean-Paul

Debray, Régis (1940–)

French intellectual and revolutionary theorist. Debray was a proselyte of Ernesto "Che" Guevara and popularized Guevara's legend and his type of guerrilla warfare. Régis Debray's imprisonment in Bolivia for alleged revolutionary activity became a cause célèbre among European intellectuals, many of whom protested his detention. After his release in 1970 he returned to France and established a career as a writer and political figure, serving as an adviser on Third World affairs to President François Mitterrand.

Debray studied at the École Normale Supérieure, where his professors included Marxist philosopher Louis Althusser. He made his reputation as a young French intellectual and influenced the political thought of Fidel Castro with the publication of *Revolution within the Revolution* (1967). The book, which gained Debray worldwide notoriety, was written after a sojourn in Havana, where he had lengthy conversations with leaders of revolutionary and Communist movements from Latin American countries. The same year that the book was published, he left Cuba for Bolivia to report as a journalist on the newly opened guerrilla fronts. In the course of his journalistic work there, he was arrested and charged with aiding the guerrillas. He served three years of a thirty-year sentence. After his release Debray traveled to Cuba and Chile, where he met with Socialist President Salvador Allende, then returned to France. For Debray, at that time, violence was a necessary component of revolution. In 1974, in *A Critique of Arms* and its successor volume, *The Revolution on Trial,* he articulated a "critique" of the use of violence. Debray eventually came to a more centrist political position.

Debray is also the author of a number of successful volumes of fiction, among them *The Undesirable Alien* (1975). His literary career has consisted of journalism, fiction, and nonfiction, often written in tandem with his service as a foreign affairs official in the Mitterrand government. Debray's writings reflect fashionable intellectual and political currents in contemporary French culture. These currents are mirrored in the titles of some of his books: *Critique of Political Reason* (1984); *Teachers, Writers, Celebrities: The Intellectuals of Modern France* (1985);

Le Puissance et les rêves (1985); *Les Empires contre l'Europe* (1986); *Vie et mort de l'image: Une histoire de regard en Occident* (1992).

BIBLIOGRAPHY

Huberman, Leo, and Paul M. Sweeney, eds. *Régis Debray and the Latin American Revolution.* New York: Monthly Review Press, 1968.

Ramon, Hartmuth. *The Marxism of Régis Debray: Between Lenin and Guevara.* Lawrence: Regents Press of Kansas, 1978.

Reader, Keith. *Régis Debray: A Critical Introduction.* London: Pluto Press, 1995.

Kenneth Keulman

Debré, Michel (1912–)

French Gaullist politician who served as the first prime minister of the Fifth Republic, 1959–62. In addition to being a competent leader, Michel Jean-Pierre Debré was respected for his intellect and knowledge of constitutional law. He was the chief architect of the constitution of 1958 and was author of more than a dozen books.

Debré was raised in a wealthy Parisian family and, after receiving a doctorate in law in 1934, obtained a position with the Council of State. Serving as lieutenant in the army, he was captured by the Germans during World War II but escaped to join the Resistance in Morocco and then to work with the underground in occupied France. In Charles de Gaulle's provisional government after the war, Debré was appointed to a commission to reform the civil service, and during 1947 he held an appointed office at the Foreign Ministry. An early member of de Gaulle's Rassemblement du Peuple Français (Rally of the French People), he was an elected senator from 1948 to 1958, acquiring a reputation as a Gaullist loyalist critical of the Fourth Republic's concentration of power in the Chamber of Deputies.

When de Gaulle became premier in May 1958, he appointed Debré minister of justice and head of the commission to draft a constitution for the Fifth Republic. The resulting document emphasized executive leadership and also incorporated Debré's preference for some separation of powers. When de Gaulle became president of the new republic in 1959, Debré served as prime minister for more than three years. Their collaboration established the model of a president firmly in control of policy, with the prime minister having a secondary role. Thus, while Debré personally opposed independence for Algeria, he loyally supported disengagement. Since Debré's earlier views on Algeria led to embarrassment for De Gaulle as he pre-

pared to recognize Algerian independence, the president unexpectedly requested his resignation in April 1962.

Debré was elected to the National Assembly in 1963 and remained a member until 1988. Under de Gaulle he held the positions of economics minister (1966–68) and foreign minister (1968–69), and under Georges Pompidou he was defense minister from 1969 to 1973. He was also elected mayor of Amboise in 1966 and to the European Parliament in 1979, but he failed in his bid for the presidency in the election of 1981. Debré retired from politics in 1992.

BIBLIOGRAPHY

Chariot, Jean. *The Gaullist Phenomenon.* New York: Praeger, 1971.

Debré, Michel. *Memoires.* Paris: Albin Michel, 1985.

Touchard, Jean. *Le Gaullisme, 1940–1969.* Paris: Le Seuil, 1978.

Williams, Philip, and Martin Harrison. *Politics and Society in de Gaulle's Republic.* London: Longman, 1971.

Thomas T. Lewis

Decolonization

Post–World War II process of colonial nationalists rejecting control by European imperialists. As Western European states recovered at home from the war, they lost their colonies abroad. In retrospect, decolonization takes on an air of inevitability, and of a single drama. Pressured alike by the Soviet Union and the United States and pushed by indigenous independence movements, the colonial powers of Western Europe came to realize that their colonial commitments had to end. Within three decades the flags of Great Britain, France, Belgium, Portugal, Spain, and the Netherlands were hauled down. The colonial powers failed to cooperate with one another in a common defense of empire, and the colonial cause no longer appealed to the mass of the people in the metropolitan countries. The ideological initiative during and after World War II passed to the critics of colonialism and Asian and African nationalists who were supported with different motives by both the United States and the Soviet Union. Colonial rulers encountered bitter, sustained criticism in the metropolitan parliaments, the media, the universities, the churches, and even within the ranks of their own colonial services. In consequence, the colonial warlords became increasingly apologetic. They compromised, and each reform and concession led to new demands. In Vietnam, Ho Chi Minh's Communist Party led the essentially nationalist struggle, whereas in Algeria the Front de Libération Nationale, attacking French governance, admitted Communists as individuals, not as Communist Party members. In parts of sub-Saharan Africa, the colonial powers were prepared to get out even before African nationalists asked them to leave; in other parts, such as settler Africa, whites fought to stay.

The imperial powers faced more practical considerations. Empire, it was realized, did not pay, either militarily or economically. But the European powers were not forced out of Africa by economic imperatives. On the contrary, decolonization came just at the time when African colonies were beginning to show a return for the metropolitan countries. But the cost of empire increased vastly—in both political and military terms. The British and French recognized this first, the Portuguese last. The French came to see that they were compounding their wartime losses by expensive colonial campaigns. The war in Indochina imposed great sacrifices on France. No sooner were the French rid of the Indochina commitment than they faced a serious struggle in Algeria that weakened France in Europe. The loss of Indochina in 1954, moreover, in no way injured the French economy. The French recovered from the disappearance of their East Asian empire as quickly as the Dutch got over the loss of their possessions and investments in Indonesia. With the exception of the Portuguese, who hung on in Africa until 1975; white Rhodesians, who gave up in 1980; and white South Africans, who continued to hang on until 1994, the rulers lost the will to rule.

President Roosevelt and advisers such as Harry Hopkins opposed Western colonialism. Roosevelt regarded the British system of imperial preferences as an obstacle to world prosperity and the British Empire as a potential threat to peace. The U.S. State Department looked to a policy of accelerated reform whereby the colonial regimes would become accountable to an international authority in which the United States would have a predominant voice. American pressure was far from negligible in its effects. The colonizers, especially the British, became more defensive; colonial reformers could point to this American anticolonialism to help improve conditions in the colonies. The colonial Development and Welfare Acts, passed by the British Parliament, were, in part, designed as a reply to American criticism of British colonial rule.

But Roosevelt's successor, Harry Truman, preoccupied with the Cold War, became much less interested in colonial issues. Black Americans, during the two decades following World War II, were, for the most part, too concerned with their own emancipation to take an active interest in countries such as the Gold Coast (Ghana) and Uganda, of which they knew little.

Decolonization in India and most of sub-Saharan Africa did not come from an armed struggle, nor was it carefully planned. The main cost of decolonization was not born by the great metropolitan companies that mostly managed to adjust to the new regimes. The principal costs fell on the colonizers' erstwhile local allies—white settlers, African chiefs, Indian princes, those many unhappy Muslim soldiers who had fought in the French army in Algeria, and their like. In most of "Black Africa," as opposed to Algeria and Rhodesia, the door to self-government was unlocked for African nationalists to push open. The British adopted this policy because they anticipated African nationalist pressure supported, by a bizarre combination of American anticolonialism, Indian nationalism, British economic need, and moral utopianism. The colonialists turned out to have been the unwitting state builders of a new Africa, its political map drawn by and legitimized through the European empires. Their demise aroused immense expectations that the successor states failed to meet. Africans of a subsequent generation had cause to remember the witticism current in France after the fall of Napoléon III: "how fair was the Republic under the Empire." With the burden of empire removed, all ex-colonialist nations prospered, to the shock of those Marxist theoreticians who held that only colonial superprofits kept capitalism from collapsing. The end of empire altered the global map but spelled neither the end of capitalism nor victory for the socialist cause.

BIBLIOGRAPHY

Duignan, Peter, and L. H. Gann. *The Rebirth of the West: The Americanization of the Democratic World, 1945–1958.* Oxford: Basil Blackwell, 1992, 436–52.

———. *The United States and Africa: A History.* Cambridge: Cambridge University Press, 1984, 284–93.

Robinson, Ronald. "Sir Andrew Cohen: Proconsul of African Nationalism," in L. H. Gann and Peter Duignan, eds., *African Proconsuls: European Governors in Africa.* New York: Free Press, 1978, 353–64.

Smith, Tony. "Decolonization," in Joel Krieger, ed., *The Oxford Companion to Politics of the World.* Oxford: Oxford University Press, 1993, 217–18.

Peter Duignan

SEE ALSO Algerian War; Congo Intervention

De Gasperi, Alcide (1881–1954)

One of the most important Italian political leaders and statesmen after World War II, Christian Democrat premier of Italy from 1945 to 1953. Alcide De Gasperi was born in 1881 in Pieve Tesino, in what was at that time the Austrian Tyrol. He completed his studies in philology at the University of Vienna in 1905. In the years before World War I he had been influenced by the uneasiness and expectations of the ethnic minorities of the Austro-Hungarian Empire. The year he graduated, De Gasperi founded the Popular Trentine Party (Partito Popolare Trentino, PPT) and became the chairman of *La voce cattolica* (*The Catholic Voice*), which later became *Il trentino* (*The Trentine*), and again changed its title to *Il nuovo trentino,* when Italy annexed the area following World War I. He held that position until 1925. After the war, with Trentino annexed to Italy, De Gasperi joined the Italian Popular Party (Partito Popolare Italiano, PPI), created by Luigi Sturzo. In 1921 De Gasperi was elected to the Italian Chamber of Deputies. When Sturzo resigned as leader of the PPI in May 1924, De Gasperi took charge.

The Exceptional Laws of 1926 initiated the transformation of the Fascist movement into a dictatorship. In the following year De Gasperi was arrested and accused of clandestine activities. After his release he worked in the Vatican Library, beginning a period of study and meditation. He pondered some of the fundamental questions of the time: the relationships between church and state, the significance of the corporate conception of social life, the autonomy of Catholics in political action, a plurality of unions within a context of solidarity. De Gasperi during this period came into contact with important people in the Curia and the international scene. He began to collaborate with *L'illustrazione vaticana,* writing editorials on the main political events between 1933 and 1938.

De Gasperi laid the intellectual groundwork for a postFascist lay Catholic political movement and the transformation of Italy in "Idee riconstruttive della democrazia cristiana" (Reconstructive Ideas of Christian Democracy). The text of this program was circulated on July 25, 1943, after the coup that ousted Mussolini. The Christian Democratic Party (Democrazia Cristiana, DC), therefore, did not begin in 1943, as has been asserted, as the "Church Party," and this new political organization also differentiated itself from the political ideas of the resistance. The new Catholic party offered its concept of democracy as an alternative to the social-communist conception of politics, with its Marxist ideology of class struggle and the necessity of revolution.

De Gasperi, rightly regarded as the principal representative of the Catholic party, had important positions in the first years after the war. He was prime minister in eight governments between 1945 and 1953. When the Italian monarchy fell in the referendum of June 1946, De Gasperi led the provisional republican government, in which were reflected the complexities and contradictions of the *Costituente*, the original convention for the elaboration of a constitution. The government was a heterogeneous temporary coalition, consisting of the DC, the Italian Communist Party (PCI), the Italian Socialist Party of Proletarian Unity (PSIUP), and the Italian Republican Party (PRI).

While De Gasperi was conducting negotiations to overcome the hostility of some of the Allies on matters concerning the peace treaty, he agreed with the Austrians to provisions concerning the Alto Adige–Süd Tirol areas on September 6, 1946. His earlier attitude toward national identities was evident in this agreement.

Before 1918 he had been concerned about protecting the Italian minority. Now consistent with his views, informed by Catholic solidarism, he favored measures protecting the German minority. He desired peaceful cohabitation and cooperation. His difficulties with the negotiations for the peace treaty in Paris were accentuated by the PCI's policy, which for ideological reasons favored territorial concessions to Yugoslavia. The contrast between the DC and the PCI, evident since November 1946, was a prelude to the rupture of the governing coalition. De Gasperi's trip to the United States in January 1947 was a turning point in Italian politics, both foreign (U.S. support for Italy in the peace treaty was relevant) and domestic. The visit had basically positive results for Italy, as the United States provided economic aid to the country and political support to the DC and De Gasperi.

The peace treaty was harsh for Italy, but De Gasperi had little room to maneuver, owing to the hostility of France and Britain and to Soviet aims supported by the PCI. On the other hand, U.S. aid was dependent on the expulsion of the left from the government. Thanks to his political skill De Gasperi succeeded in ousting the Communists from the government in May 1947.

The elections of April 18, 1948, which launched the first legislature of the republic, gave the DC an absolute majority, marking the definitive defeat of the Popular Front of the PCI and PSIUP. De Gasperi's government, which lasted from May 23, 1948, to January 27, 1950, was made up of a coalition of the DC, PRI, and Italian Social Democratic Party (PSDI). The same coalition formed De Gasperi's next government, from January 27, 1950, to July 26, 1951.

Italian foreign policy completely conformed to De Gasperi's views. Italy was the first country to accept the U.S. Marshall Plan in fall 1947. Italy also joined the Executive Committee of the Organization for European Economic Cooperation (OEEC) in April 1948. Italy signed on to the North Atlantic Treaty Organization

(NATO) on April, 4, 1949, and became a member of the Council of Europe, instituted in May 1949, as the first embodiment of a European parliamentary assembly, and the European Coal and Steel Community on April 8, 1950. International political considerations including the Korean War increased the difficulties of De Gasperi's third government, made up only of the DC and the PRI, which lasted from July 1951 to July 1953.

The election law for which De Gasperi struggled, against the opposition of the former leader of the IPP, Sturzo, was approved, yet the electoral results of June 1953 did not give the four center parties the absolute majority they needed to enable them to have 65 percent of the seats in parliament. The DC lost two million votes and dropped from 48.5 to 40 percent. Therefore, De Gasperi's fourth government, composed only of DC members, lasted just one month, from July 16 to August 7, 1953. After having led the government for seven and half years, De Gasperi had to resign. At the party congress held at Naples in June 1954, a new generation stepped forward lead by Amintore Fanfani and his group, Democratic Initiative. The new direction was confirmed at the DC National Council on July 16, 1954. Shortly thereafter, De Gasperi died on August 18, 1954, at his place of birth. His remains, by will of parliament, were returned to Rome and now lie at the foot of the porch of the Basilica of San Lorenzo Fuori le Mura.

BIBLIOGRAPHY

Andreotti, Giulio. *De Gasperi e il suo tempo.* Milan: Mondadori, 1964.

Baget-Bozzo, Gianni. *Il partito cristiano al potere: La DC di De Gasperi e di Dossetti, 1945–1954.* Florence: Vallecchi, 1974.

Catti De Gasperi, Maria Romana. *De Gasperi, uomo solo.* Milan: Mondadori, 1964.

———. *La nostra patria Europa.* Milan: Mondadori, 1969.

Fanello Marcucci, Gabriella. *Alle origin della Democrazia Cristiana (1929–1944). Dal carteqqio Spataro-De Gasperi.* Brescia: Marcelliana, 1982.

De Gasperi, Alcide. *De Gasperi scrive. Corrispondenza con capi di Stato, cardinali, uomini politici, giornalisti, diplomatici.* Ed. by M. R. Catti De Gasperi. Brescia: Morcelliana, 1974.

———. *Discorsi politici.* Ed. by T. Bozza. Romae: CinqueLune, 1976.

Gonella, Guido. *Con De Gasperi nella fondazione della DC (1930–1940).* Rome: Cinque Lune, 1978.

Scoppola, Pietro. *La proposta politica di De Gasperi.* Bologna: Il Mulino, 1978.

Paolo Pastori

SEE ALSO Italy; South Tyrol; Sturzo, Luigi

De Gaulle, Charles (1890–1970)

Professional French army officer, prominent theorist of armored warfare, head of the French government-in-exile during World War II, provisional president of the Fourth Republic, and president of the Fifth Republic from 1958 and 1969. Charles André Marie Joseph de Gaulle was arguably France's greatest twentieth-century statesman. From his youth he believed he was destined for greatness, and throughout his life he manifested a sense of drama, great personal intelligence, and a mystical faith in France, what one of his biographers called "his great agonizing devotion to France." Frugal in his habits, his one outside interest was reading.

Charles de Gaulle was born in Lille, France, on November 22, 1890. His family was staunchly Roman Catholic and conservative, and his father taught in a Parisian Catholic high school. In 1909 de Gaulle joined the Thirty-third infantry regiment and the next year entered the military academy Saint-Cyr. He graduated in 1912, thirteenth in a class of 211. He returned to his former regiment, now commanded by Colonel Henri Philippe Pétain, where he won both praise and promotion to full lieutenant.

In August 1914 de Gaulle received a severe leg wound during fighting in Belgium at the start of World War I. After seven months of recovery he rejoined his regiment as adjutant. Wounded again in March 1915, he spent five

President Charles DeGaulle of France greeting the citizens of Quebec City in Canada during a visit in July, 1967. *Illustration courtesy of UPI/Corbis-Bettmann.*

months recovering. Promoted to captain in September 1915, de Gaulle returned to the Thirty-third, which, in February 1916, was ordered to Verdun. In March near Fort Douaumont, de Gaulle was again wounded and this time captured. He later received the Legion of Honor for this action. While a prisoner in Germany de Gaulle made five attempts to escape. His 6′5″ height was one obstacle.

De Gaulle returned to France in November 1918 with a suitcase full of writings. Perhaps because he had spent so little time in actual combat, he retained a certain detachment and enthusiasm not shared by those who had gone through the entire ordeal of the war.

After the war de Gaulle published a short account of his experiences. He returned to Saint-Cyr as professor of history and, in 1920, went to Warsaw as part of the French military mission to Poland. He returned to France to study and later teach at the École de Guerre, then served for a time as aide-de-camp to French Army Commander in Chief Marshal Pétain. The two had a falling out because Pétain wanted de Gaulle to ghost his memoirs, which Pétain expected would secure him admission to the French Academy.

De Gaulle became an important theorist of the new armored warfare. He argued for six completely mechanized and motorized divisions that would have their own organic artillery and air support. These would be the blade to the French military spear, the shaft being the slower reserve divisions. With such a force, he argued, maneuver would come back into its own on the battlefield. In 1934 he published *Vers l'Armée de métier* (*The Army of the Future*); significantly, the book sold many more copies in Germany than in France. Another book, *Le Fil de l'épée* (*The Edge of the Sword*) revealed much about de Gaulle's concept of leadership and his belief that a true leader followed his conscience regardless of circumstances.

Far from learning from the Germans, de Gaulle was teaching them: the armored divisions of Hitler's Wehrmacht were almost carbon copies of those he proposed. Deputy Paul Reynaud sought without success to secure National Assembly approval for de Gaulle's proposals. The French army high command continued to think along World War I lines, emphasizing artillery and old-style infantry divisions. Tanks were regarded not as an independent maneuvering force but as a means to reduce obstacles impeding the passage of infantry. When World War II began the French actually outnumbered the Germans in tanks. The major problem with French armor was not the machines themselves but their tactical employment. The French army was slow to embrace the concept of tank divisions, and most French tanks were split up in small pockets along the frontier in static defense. Had de Gaulle's ideas been followed, the 1940 defeat of France might never have occurred.

De Gaulle was appalled by France's lack of offensive spirit in the Rhineland in September 1939, and after the defeat of Poland that month, he sought in vain to change his superiors' attitudes. His memorandum to the French inspector general of tanks on the lessons of the Polish campaign was rejected. When the battle for France opened, de Gaulle's knowledge of armor warfare secured him command of the Fourth Tank Division. Although in the process of formation when de Gaulle assumed command, the Fourth achieved one of the few successes scored by the French army. On June 1 he was promoted brigadier general and five days later Premier Paul Reynaud brought him into his cabinet as undersecretary of state for national defense.

As France collapsed, de Gaulle urged Reynaud to fight on, either from Brittany or North Africa. This advice was rejected, although in the process de Gaulle attracted the attention of British Prime Minister Winston Churchill. De Gaulle and the French diplomat Jean Monnet visited London and suggested to Churchill the plan for an indissoluble Anglo-French union that the French government rejected. When he returned to France, de Gaulle discovered that the government was prepared to surrender; on June 17, he determined to continue the fight, leaving Bordeaux on a British military aircraft for London. On June 18, 1940, this youngest general of the French army spoke to his countrymen over the BBC ("L'Appel du 18 Juin"), urging them to continue the fight. That de Gaulle became the most prominent leader of the French Resistance in World War II was because he was the only official of stature to escape abroad.

De Gaulle's wartime relations with the British and Americans were difficult. Though supported by the British financially, de Gaulle saw them as "malevolent and scheming." He constantly acted as if he were a head of state while the British and Americans persisted in treating him as an auxiliary. Particularly vexing was President Roosevelt's attitude, which was conditioned by French émigrés in the United State who suspected de Gaulle of being fascist and antidemocratic. The Free French seizure of the islands of St. Pierre and Miquelon fifteen miles of the coast of New Foundland, Canada, particularly angered Roosevelt, as did the botched September 1949 British–Free French assault on the Vichy-held port of Dakar, Senegal, which was falsely attributed to French security failures. De Gaulle for his part was embittered during the war by blatant British efforts to dislodge the French from their prewar positions of influence in Syria and Lebanon, by the failure of the Allies to inform him in advance of their landings in French North Africa, by their efforts to supplant him with General Henri Giraud, and by their failure to consult with him regarding the invasion of France. The United State was also slow to recognize de Gaulle's government as legitimate.

On August 25, 1944, de Gaulle returned to Paris in triumph even as the fighting was going on. For the next five months he ruled France as provisional president. No plebiscite was necessary to bolster his authority. But with the return of peace the old political parties of the Third Republic reasserted themselves and the general faced opposition where heretofore there had been only assent. When the parties rejected his plan for a strong presidency, de Gaulle abruptly resigned in January 1946.

He spent the next years in the political wilderness, writing what would be his much-heralded war memoirs. His brief fling with the new rightist opposition party, the Rally for the French People (RPF), went poorly. Meanwhile, the Fourth Republic, created after the war, was stumbling toward disaster.

In May 1958, having survived the long war in Indochina, the Fourth Republic finally collapsed under the weight of the Algerian imbroglio. Right-wingers, determined to retain Algeria as part of France, teamed up with the professional military to overthrow the Fourth Republic. De Gaulle, not their first choice, was the only logical figure and returned to power, technically as the past premier of the Fourth Republic but with virtual dictatorial powers to recast the constitution and save France.

De Gaulle's preservation of the democratic process was to be his greatest service to France. The most pressing problem remained that of Algeria, where a million European French who resided there insisted that it remain French. Although de Gaulle promised the French in Algeria and the military that he would not abandon them, he proceeded to do just that, working through a variety of options until finally giving Algeria its independence in 1962. De Gaulle claimed in his memoirs that he foresaw the necessity of this from the beginning, although this is highly questionable.

De Gaulle's Fifth Republic, what one historian called "the first serious attempt to institutionalize one man," brought France the strong presidential system that de Gaulle had long advocated. As a leader de Gaulle was difficult, often arrogant and vain. De Gaulle was at his best confronting danger; he stoically survived numerous assassination attempts, most of them the result of opposition to his Algerian policies. His successor, Georges Pompidou, who worked with him on the closest terms for a quarter century, once went out of his way to deny

a published report that de Gaulle had ever addressed him by his first name. Much like Konrad Adenauer of the Federal Republic of Germany, with whom he established a close working relationship, de Gaulle insisted on absolute support of his policies from within the government.

In foreign affairs de Gaulle was arguably less successful, largely because he sought to reassert a French greatness that was gone forever. He was determined to preserve his nation's independence of action and saw France taking the lead of a "third," European, force between the two superpowers. This produced the most contentious domestic issue of de Gaulle's years as president. After France tested an atomic bomb in the Sahara, de Gaulle pressed ahead with a nuclear strike force, the so-called *force de frappe*. This was partly because he distrusted the Anglo-U.S. alliance and resented its control over Western atomic warheads. He also believed the United State would not risk nuclear attack on its own soil to defend Europe. Opposition in France to the *force de frappe* stemmed not so much from philosophical disagreement as its extraordinarily high cost.

De Gaulle's entente with Adenauer's Germany was certainly a success, and he began the process of détente with the Soviet Union and Eastern Europe. More questionable was his withdrawal of France from NATO's military command (but not NATO itself), because he believed it to be dominated by the United State and Britain. Yet de Gaulle gave strong support when the West was pressured by the Soviets, as when he backed President Dwight Eisenhower during the May 1960 Paris summit. Perhaps in part bitter because of his treatment by the British and Americans during World War II and believing that London had not demonstrated commitment to the continent, he twice vetoed British entry into the Common Market. He also cut France's close ties to Israel after that country in 1967 rejected his advice and opted for preemptive war. He called on Quebec to seek separation from Canada, and he clashed with successive U.S. presidents. He warned President John F. Kennedy about involvement in Indochina. "You will find that intervention in this area will be an endless entanglement."

A student uprising in Paris in May 1968, followed by widespread general strikes, was the beginning of the end for the general. Rescued from the crisis by Premier Georges Pompidou, de Gaulle never forgave him this success and soon dismissed him from his post. On the defeat of a national referendum in 1969, which he had made a test of his leadership, de Gaulle again resigned, retiring to write his final set of memoirs. He had intended to write three volumes but completed only two and two chapters of the third before his death at Colombey-les-Deux Églises on November 9, 1970.

The man who had been denounced by many as a would-be Bonaparte was anything but; he restored domestic peace to a France on the brink of civil war and he gave his country a resilient political system that continues today. Even more than his leadership in the Resistance during World War II, this was de Gaulle's greatest legacy to France.

Today's French government follows the broad lines of de Gaulle's foreign policy, and his dream of a Europe "united from the Atlantic to the Urals" now at least seems possible. If the test of greatness in leaders is that they shape events rather than being shaped by them, de Gaulle was arguably great.

BIBLIOGRAPHY

Cook, Don. *Charles de Gaulle, a Biography.* New York: Putnam, 1983.

De Gaulle, Charles. *Memoirs of Hope: Renewal and Endeavor.* Tr. by Terence Kilmartin. New York: Simon and Schuster, 1972.

Lacouture, Jean. *De Gaulle: The Rebel, 1890–1944.* Tr. by Patrick O'Brian. New York: Norton, 1990.

———. *De Gaulle: The Ruler, 1945–1970.* Tr. by Alan Sheridan. New York: Norton, 1972.

Ledwidge, Bernard. *De Gaulle.* New York: St. Martin's Press, 1982.

Spencer C. Tucker

SEE ALSO Algerian War; France; Pompidou, Georges

Dehaene, Jean-Luc (1940–)

Prime minister of Belgium. Jean-Luc Dehaene was born in Montpellier, France, on August 7, 1940. After a classical education with the Jesuits in Aalst, he received licentiates in law and economics from the universities of Namur and Leuven. He was the leader of the Flemish League of Catholic Scouts from 1963 to 1967. He served as vice president of the youth organization of the Flemish Christian People's Party (CVP) from 1967 to 1971 and was appointed to the national bureau of the CVP in 1972. He was president of the CVP for the Brussels-Halle-Vilvoorde area from 1977 to 1981.

In 1972 Dehaene was appointed adviser to the cabinet of the minister of public works, J. De Saeger, and went with De Saeger to the Ministry of Public Health in 1973. From 1974 to 1977 he served first as adviser to and head of the cabinet of the minister for economic affairs. From 1977 to 1978 he was head of the cabinet to the minister of Flemish affairs. From 1979 to 1981 he was cabinet chief for Prime Minister Wilfried Martens. In 1981 he was successively appointed minister of institutional reforms and as such had to deal with the issues of national devolution in Belgium, and then minister of social affairs and institutional reforms. He held that post until 1988, when he became deputy prime minister and minister for communications and for institutional reforms.

Dehaene became prime minister on March 7, 1992. He succeeded his party colleague Martens, whose ministry had been weakened in the November 1991 election. Dehaene's appellations, the "Bulldozer" and the "Plumber," were put to the test as he kept together Martens's contentious center-left coalition, which consisted not only of socialists and Christian democrats but also of Walloon Socialists and Flemish Socialists and Walloon Christian Democrats and Flemish Christian Democrats. Dehaene's government established direct elections for regional and communal assemblies and worked to shift additional power to the regions. Following the election of 1995, he reorganized his cabinet and continued as prime minister.

BIBLIOGRAPHY

Platel, Marc. *Dehaene: van I tot II.* Leuven, Belgium: Davidsfonds, 1995.

Ridder, Hugo de. *Le cas Dehaene.* Brussels, Belgium: Racine, 1996.

Bernard Cook

SEE ALSO Martens, Wilfried

Dehler, Thomas (1897–1967)

German liberal politician. Thomas Dehler was a founding member of the Republican Reichsbanner organization during the Weimar Republic and a member of the left-liberal Democratic Party (Deutsche Demokratische [Staats-] Partei). After the Second World War Dehler became leader of the Free Democratic Party (FDP) in Bavaria from 1946 to 1956. Having served on the parliamentary council, or constituent assembly, Dehler was a member of the Bundestag (lower house of parliament) from 1949 until his death in 1967. He was justice minister of the Federal Republic of Germany (1949–53), chair of the FDP Bundestag Parliamentary Caucus (1953–57), and FDP party leader (1954–57).

Dehler espoused radical liberal ideas in home affairs. As justice minister he strongly opposed reintroduction of the death penalty. He was also keen to limit the role of churches in German society. Later, Dehler fought against the emergency laws (Notstandsgesetzgebung) that gave the government extensive police powers at a time of national crisis. However, Dehler is better known for his emotional patriotism, inspired by the German nation-liberal tradition, and for his increasingly fierce opposition during the 1950s to Chancellor Konrad Adenauer's political preference for Western integration over German unification. The conflict with Adenauer was one important reason why Dehler supported the FDP leadership in North Rhine-Westphalia in its decision to switch its allegiance from Adenauer's Christian Democrats (CDU) to the Social Democrats (SPD) in February 1956, resulting in the breakdown of the coalition with the Christian Democratic Union/Christian Social Union (the Bavarian counterpart of the CDU) at the national level and a split in the FDP party leadership and parliamentary caucus.

Although Dehler's moral integrity continued to be admired within the FDP, his German and European policy was widely regarded as outdated from the late 1960s onward. More recently, however, the revived national-liberal section of the FDP and some writers, like Rainer Zitelmann, have praised Dehler, alongside Karl Kaiser (CDU), Kurt Schumacher (SPD), and others for his opposition to Adenauer's German and European policy in the 1950s.

BIBLIOGRAPHY

Dehler's personal papers are located in the Archiv des Liberalismus (Archive of Liberalism) of the Friedrich-Naumann-Stiftung in Königswinter, Germany. Those papers related to his work as a lawyer and politician in Bamberg are located in the Stadtarchiv (city archive) in Bambert, Germany.

Dehler, Thomas. *Bundestagsreden.* Bonn: AS Studio Bonn, 1973.

Friedrich-Naumann-Stiftung. *Thomas Dehler: Reden und Aufsätze.* Cologne/Opladen: Westdeutscher Verlag, 1969.

Henning, Friedrich. *Theodor Heuss: Lieber Dehler! Briefwechsel mit Thomas Dehler.* Munich: Günter Olzog Verlag, 1983.

Rilling, Detlef. "Thomas Dehler—Eine politische Biographie: Ein Leben in Deutschland." Ph.D. diss., University of Augsburg, 1988.

Wolfram Kaiser

Deleuze, Gilles (1925–)

French philosopher and social critic. Gilles Deleuze is one of the most important contemporary French thinkers. A leader of the avant-garde, he has made notable contributions to social criticism, psychology, the history of philosophy (especially Nietzsche studies), and film criticism. With longtime collaborator Félix Guattari, Deleuze wrote his monumental *Capitalism and Schizophrenia,* which appeared in two volumes: *Anti-Oedipus* and *A Thousand Plateaus.* Although this work is extremely dense and at times opaque, it has attracted readers who find in it the development of a new understanding of psychological identity and sexual development, a criticism of psychoanalysis and Marxist theory, and a treatment of present-day society as a community of nomads. Deleuze's work constitutes some of the fundamental texts of postmodernism. Michel Foucault claimed that the current epoch in the future will be called the "Age of Deleuze."

BIBLIOGRAPHY

Boundas, Constantine, and Dorothea Olkowski, eds. *Deleuze and the Theatre of Philosophy.* New York: Routledge, 1994.

Hardt, Michael. *Gilles Deleuze.* Minneapolis: University of Minnesota Press, 1993.

Martin, Jean-Clet. *Variations: la philosophie de Gilles Deleuze.* Paris: Payot, 1993.

Nordquist, Joan. *Félix Guattari and Gilles Deleuze: A Bibliography.* Santa Cruz, Calif.: Reference and Research, 1992.

Daniel E. Shannon

SEE ALSO Guattari, Félix

Delle Chiaie, Stefano (1934–)

Italian neofascist leader and reputed international terrorist. Stefano Delle Chiaie was a key figure in both the Italian extraparliamentary right and the transnational neofascist paramilitary networks. He has been implicated in a host of terrorist crimes throughout southern Europe and Latin America but always managed to escape conviction and punishment.

Delle Chiaie was born near Rome in 1934 into a pro-Fascist family. After dropping out of school, he first became a rightist youth gang leader and then, in 1957, secretary of the local Movimento Sociale Italiano (Italian Social Movement, MSI) section in Appio. Within a year he grew so disillusioned with this "neofascist" party's moderate orientation that he and some of his loyal followers abandoned it to form the action-oriented Gruppi di Azione Rivoluzionaria (Revolutionary Action Groups, GAR). When this venture failed to attract wider support, Delle Chiaie temporarily joined Giuseppe ("Pino") Rauti's Ordine Nuovo (New Order, ON). This radical youth group, inspired by the ideas of conservative revolutionary philosopher Giulio Cesare ("Julius") Evola, also proved to be too tame for Delle Chiaie. In 1959 he broke with ON and formed Avanguardia Nazionale (National Vanguard, AN). AN immediately began forging links with international neofascist circles and soon gained notoriety for launching brutal "punitive expeditions" against Communist militants and left-wing students, sometimes with the tacit support of the antiriot police.

In response to the wave of student protests and workers' strikes in 1968 and 1969, Delle Chiaie and his group shifted tactics and began applying the more sophisticated infiltration and provocation techniques to which he had been introduced while attending a 1965 conference on French counterrevolutionary warfare doctrine in Rome. Both leftist and neofascist sources claim that Delle Chiaie began collaborating with the Interior Ministry's Ufficio Affari Riservati (Clandestine Operations Section, UAR) during this period, and one of his right-hand men, Mario Merlino, was directly involved in a complex "false flag" operation designed to implicate anarchist circles in the December 12, 1969, terrorist bombings in Rome and Milan. After an arrest warrant was issued for him in connection with the Piazza Fontana massacre, Delle Chiaie fled to Spain and took refuge with well-known Spanish ultras such as the duke of Valencia, former Francoist Labor Minister José Antonio Girón, Guerrilleros de Cristo Re (Guerrillas of Christ the King, GCR) leader Mariano Sanchez Covisa, Alberto Royuela, Luis Antonio Garcia Rodríguez, and Ernesto Milá. In 1970 he surreptitiously returned to Italy and played a crucial role in the abortive December coup organized by Prince Junio Valerio Borghese's Fronte Nazionale (National Front, FN), specifically by leading an AN commando group that took control of the Interior Ministry's armory with the help of UAR personnel.

Following the last-minute recall of this operation, Delle Chiaie returned to Spain. Along with other Italian neofascist fugitives, veterans from the French Organisation de l'Armée Secrète (Secret Army Organization, OAS), and members of the Alianza Anticomunista Argentina (Argentine Anti-Communist Alliance, AAA), he was recruited by several Spanish police and intelligence agencies to help organize "plausibly deniable" counterterrorist actions against Euskadi ta Askatasuna (Basque Country and Freedom, ETA) militants. These parallel commando groups operated under the cover of various rubrics and were direct forerunners of the now notorious Grupos Antiterroristas de Liberación (Anti-Terrorist Liberation Groups, GAL). In 1974 Delle Chiaie and Borghese met personally with General Augusto Pinochet in Chile to discuss collaborative ventures, and the following year Delle Chiaie (code name "Alfa") was recruited by Michael Townley, an American-born operative of the Chilean Dirección de Inteligencia Nacional (National Intelligence Directorate, DINA), to carry out the surveillance and assassination of prominent Chilean dissidents in Europe. On October 6 one of Delle Chiaie's chief lieutenants, Pierluigi Concutelli, shot and severely wounded Chilean Partido Demócrata Cristiano (Christian Democratic Party, PDC) leader Bernardo Leighton and his wife in front of their Rome apartment. In return Delle Chiaie was paid $100,000 by DINA.

In Spain he and several of his Italian and foreign comrades participated in the brutal May 1976 assault by rightwing Carlists on their reform-oriented colleagues at the Catholic movement's holy site on Montejurra. Perhaps against the wishes of Delle Chiaie, Concutelli returned to Italy in July and, using a machine pistol donated to the anti-ETA commandos by the Spanish police, assassinated Italian judge Vittorio Occorsio. The following year Delle Chiaie was linked to a brawl that left one Communist labor militant dead during a rally in Madrid. Soon after, he fled to Chile, where he set up the Agencia Internacional de la Prensa (International Press Agency, AIP), modeled on Yves Guérin-Sérac's Lisbon-based Aginter Press, under the aegis of DINA, for whom he carried out a number of covert missions in Argentina and Peru. Following Townley's 1978 arrest and extradition to the United States for his role in the 1976 assassination of Chilean dissident Orlando Letelier in Washington, D.C., Delle Chiaie moved on to Argentina. Making use of contacts he had previously made in Spain with members of exiled dictator Juan Perón's entourage, including AAA founder José López Rega, he was recruited as a contract agent by the Argentine Servicio de Información del Ejercito (Army Intelligence Service, SIDE). In that capacity he purportedly attended top-secret military intelligence meetings and visited other countries in Latin America to help coordinate continentwide collaboration in the struggle against leftist subversion.

In late 1979 SIDE sent him to Bolivia along with seventy Argentine intelligence officers, and together they worked to organize and carry out the July 1980 "cocaine coup," a putsch followed by a brutal wave of paramilitary repression. After actively participating in these *guerra sucia*–inspired parallel police activities, including "disappearances," he was sent to Europe to organize "friendship committees" in support of the new Bolivian military regime. Two years later, on the very day that this corrupt, drug-trafficking regime was compelled by international pressure to cede power, Delle Chiaie managed to avoid an Italian secret service effort to capture him in Bolivia and escaped across the Argentine border. For several years he laid low, presumably with the assistance of various comrades, but in 1987 he was finally captured in Venezuela and extradited to Italy, where he was placed on trial for his alleged involvement in the August 1980 Bologna train station bombing and other terrorist crimes. Eventually he was acquitted of all these charges, a further demonstration of his legendary "untouchability." While certain revolutionary neofascist circles see this as additional evidence that he had long been a tool of various "reactionary" forces, some younger ultras nowadays view him as a genuine hero who waged a long and noble struggle against both "bourgeois" democracy and Communist subversion.

BIBLIOGRAPHY

Bale, Jeffrey M. "The 'Black' Terrorist International: Neo-Fascist Paramilitary Networks and the 'Strategy of Tension' in Italy, 1968–1974." Ph.D. diss., University of California at Berkeley/Department of History, 1994.

Christie, Stuart. *Stefano Delle Chiaie: Portrait of a Black Terrorist.* London: Anarchy/Refract, 1984.

Ferraresi, Franco. *Minacce alla democrazia: La destra radicale a la strategia della tensione in Italia nel dopoguerra.* Milan: Feltrinelli, 1995.

Flamini, Gianni. *Il partito del golpe: Le strategie della tensione e del terrore dal primo centrosinistro organico al sequestro Moro, 1964–1978.* Ferrara: Bovolenta, 1981–85, 4 Vols. in 6 parts.

Laurent, Frédèric. *L'Orchestre noir.* Paris: Stock, 1978.

Linklater, Magnus, et al. *The Fourth Reich: Klaus Barbie and the Neo-Fascist Connection.* London: Coronet, 1985 (part 2).

Miralles, Melchor, and Ricardo Arques. *Amedo: El estado contra ETA.* Barcelona: Plaza & Janes/Cambio 16, 1989.

Sánchez Soler, Mariano. *Los hijos del 20-N: Historia violenta del fascismo español.* Madrid: Temas de Hoy, 1993.

Willan, Philip. *Puppetmasters: The Political Uses of Terrorism in Italy.* London: Constable, 1991.

Jeffrey M. Bale

SEE ALSO Borghese Coup; Rauti, Giuseppe: Terrorism, Right-wing

Del Noce, Augusto (1910–89)

Italian philosopher. Augusto Del Noce was born in Pistoia on August 11, 1910, into a family with both Piedmontese and Sicilian roots. He went to Turin in 1915 to attended the prestigious liceo (high school) D'Azeglio, where he returned as a teacher in 1948. He received a doctorate from the University of Turin with a thesis on Nicolas Malebranche.

In 1963, after teaching in the high schools of several cities, he was elected lecturer of moral philosophy at the University of Trieste. In 1970 he was appointed to the political science faculty of the University of Rome "la Sapienza," as professor of the history of political theory. In 1974 he was appointed professor of political philosophy, a post he held until the end of his teaching career in 1985. From 1984 until 1987 Del Noce, as an independent sponsored by the Christian Democratic Party, was a senator of the republic.

Del Noce's philosophical reflections centered on modernity. He approached it problematically as a process driven by rationalism and leading to the realization of a completely atheistic ambiance for humanity. In the history of modern philosophy he, in fact, traced the presence of two fundamental paths, modern rationalism and Christian realism. Starting from Cartesian thought, with Malebranche, Pascal, Vico, and, above all, Rosmini, he envisioned the growth and ripening of an ontological rethinking of Christian realism.

In the light of a rigorously philosophical interpretation, he understood contemporary history as having first moved in an atheistic direction, then through nihilism, and finally arriving at Marxism. His reflections were communicated through numerous essays and articles in newspapers and journals, which are still relevant today despite the collapse of communism, which Del Noce foresaw because of the structural and anthropological contradictions on which it was based.

In his speculation, rooted in a deep Christian faith, Del Noce analyzed the past to provide a continuous new perspective on the present. While engaging in a detailed examination of the human process through time, he recalled original sin and Providence as factors not to be ignored. Indeed, Del Noce, in his philosophical work, testified that to live as free individuals a real understanding of history was necessary. He died in Rome on December 30, 1989.

BIBLIOGRAPHY

Buttiglione, R. *Augusto Del Noce: Biografia di un pensiero.* Casale Monferrato: Piemme, 1991.

Del Noce, Augusto. *Il problema dell'ateismo: Il concetto di ateismo e la storia della filosofia come problema.* Bologna: Il Mulino, 1964.

———. *L'interpretazione transpolitica della storia contemporanea.* Naples: Guida, 1982.

———. *Riforma cattòlica e filosofia moderna.* Bologna: Società editrice Il Mulino, 1965.

Mauro Buscemi

Delors, Jacques (1925–)

Regarded by the world's presidents and prime ministers as an intimate and power broker when he served as president of the European Commission (1985–92), and engineered the European Economic and Monetary Union (EMU).

Born in 1925, Jacques Delors rose to the heights of national political ranks in 1981 as economics minister under France's first Socialist President, François Mitterrand. In 1983 Delors presided over the U-turn in French economic policy that departed from socialist economic orthodoxy to a more neoliberal view consisting of financial stringency. Eventually, Delors demonstrated at the European level that he was not afraid of bold policy initiatives. He was so successful in expanding the scope of the European Community (EC), now the European Union (EU), that his main opponent, Britain's Prime Minister Margaret Thatcher, sought political credit for opposing his creation of a "superstate." Previously, the EC had been criticized for its weaknesses.

At the commission, Delors transformed a little-noticed institution into a formidable policy initiator at regional and international levels. His successes consisted of strategically lining up EC member states in support of the single-market initiative, aimed at removing nontariff barriers and strengthening the EC as a competitor to the United States. Emboldened by this success, Delors made the case for replacing national currencies with a single European currency to reduce transaction costs in the regional market and enhance European influence in international monetary politics. The committee, chaired by Delors, presented the blueprint for EMU European leaders eventually accepted in the Maastricht Treaty on European Union in 1991. By 1998 a group of core countries had agreed to phase out national currencies and presided over the creation of a European central bank. Whereas Delors overcame British resistance to the EMU and even saw Thatcher's downfall related to her intransigence on this issue, his plans for balancing a neoliberal EU with socially active policies were watered down and partially defeated by the market emphasis Delors himself had embraced. Finally, Delors's ambitions for the EU to rival the United States in foreign policy influence and to develop security capacities also came to naught.

In the final analysis, Delors's dramatic policy successes earned him the name and legacy of "Mr. Europe." At root a technocrat, he fashioned a dramatic and effective leadership style. In this, he employed a mix of confrontational, special-interest, and French "haute" politics while showing the savvy of a U.S. politician in terms of manipulating media and public opinion. He paved the way for professional European politicians and gave definition to regional issues with the effect of mobilizing a transnational constituency. Consequently, one could speak of a "political" Europe after Delors.

BIBLIOGRAPHY

Delors, Jacques. *Our Europe: The Community and National Development.* Tr. by Brian Pearce. London: Verso, 1992.

Ross, George. *Jacques Delors and European Integration.* New York: Oxford University Press, 1995.

Mary Troy Johnston

De Maizière, Lothar (1940–)

Last prime minister of the German Democratic Republic (DDR) and a leader in the process of German reunification. Lothar de Maizière was born on March 2, 1940, at Nordhausen. He grew up with strong religious beliefs and joined the Christian Democratic Union of the DDR in 1956. De Maizière played the viola in the Berlin Radio Symphony Orchestra until an arm ailment forced him to stop performing in 1975. He studied law at Humboldt University and, as a lawyer, defended dissidents.

On October 11, 1989, Hans Modrow, the chairman of the Council of Ministers, appointed de Maizière minister of religious affairs in the new DDR government. However, under de Maizière's leadership the East German Christian Democrats asserted their independence from the Socialist Unity Party (SED). As a member of the old SED bloc, the Christian Democrats had been permitted to organize throughout the DDR and publish newspapers. With these advantages, the Christian Democrats, who supported unification and privatization, won 40.91 percent of the vote in the DDR's first free election on March 18, 1990. On April 12, 1990, de Maizière, who had formed a grand coalition with the Social Democrats and the Free Democratic Alliance, was elected prime minister of the DDR. His overwhelming desire was to bring about a rapid unification of East Germany with the Federal Republic of Germany.

De Maizière worked with Helmut Kohl to accomplish this. The Social Democrats, who objected to de Maizière's haste and to the terms of the July 1, 1990, monetary, economic, and social union with the Federal Republic, withdrew from the coalition. De Maizière, nevertheless, proceeded. On August 23, the DDR's Peoples Chamber voted to join the Federal Republic on October 3, and the Treaty of Unification was signed on August 31. In Moscow, on September 2, de Maizière signed the "2 plus 4" Agreement, which removed the last international impediments to unification. When Germany was reunited on October 3, 1990, de Maizière became a minister without portfolio in the government of the united Federal Republic.

On December 17, however, de Maizière resigned his position in Kohl's government and from the vice chairmanship of the Christian Democratic Union because of rumors that he had served as an informer for the Stasi, the East German Secret Police. De Maizière, who retained his seat in the Bundestag, denied the rumors and stated that he did not "want to burden the work of my party or the government with this unresolved situation."

With accusations still being circulated, de Maizière, claiming that his own party was attempting to discredit and humiliate him, resigned his Bundestag (parliamentary) seat in September 1991. An official investigation found no evidence that he had been a spy.

BIBLIOGRAPHY
Elitz, Ernst. *Sie waren dabei.* Stuttgart: Deutsche Verlags-Anstalt, "Last East German PM Quits," *Toronto Star,* September 7, 1991.

Bernard Cook

Demirkan, Renan (1955–)

German actress and writer. Renan Demirkan was born in Ankara on June 12, 1955. Her father, an engineer, was unable to support his family in Turkey, and the family left for Germany when Demirkan was seven. Reacting to her mother's strict observance of her Islamic religion, Demirkan grew up passionately desiring personal freedom. She belongs to the second generation of Turkish "guest workers" who had to cope both with the growing prejudices of their German environment and the demands of their family to stay loyal to their background. In her autobiographical *Black Tea with Three Pieces of Sugar,* Demirkan later described vividly her yearnings as a child to be like Germans, to celebrate Christmas, and to be allowed to socialize with her Christian school friends. She suffered from a dilemma still felt by many children of Turkish-German descent: the need to adapt to the German world around them and the sense of guilt toward their parents for having "betrayed" them. Demirkan finally decided against the traditional lifestyle prescribed for a Turkish girl and left home shortly before her *Abitur* examinations. For a while her family declared her an outcast, yet in the end even her marriage to a Christian was grudgingly accepted. Today she describes herself as "cosmopolitan."

After acting lessons at the Hochschule für Musik und Theater in Berlin, she started from the early 1980s onward to work as an actress at theaters in Nuremberg, Dortmund, and Cologne. Unlike some of her Turkish colleagues, she was not typecast for ethnic minority parts but played complex, ambitious young women, as in the award-winning *Reporters* in 1988 and in *Der große Bellheim* in 1993. After the birth of her first child she turned to writing. Her latest book, *A Woman with a Beard* (*Die Frau mit Bart,* 1994), portrays marriage difficulties. For her work as an actress she has been awarded several prizes, among them North Rhine Westphalia's theater prize for young actors, the Golden Camera, a prize sponsored by the most popular German television newspaper, and the prestigious Grimme Prize.

BIBLIOGRAPHY
Demirkan, Renan. *Die Frau mit Bart.* Cologne: Kiepenheuer & Witsch, 1994.
———. *Schwarzer Tee mit drei Stuck Zucker.* Cologne: Kiepenheuer & Witsch, 1991.

Karina Urbach

De Nicola, Enrico (1877–1959)

Italian politician, president of the republic from 1946 to 1948. Enrico De Nicola was born in Naples in 1877. He graduated with a degree in law when he was only eighteen. He was elected to parliament and entered the ministry of Giovanni Giolitti in 1913. In 1919 he was appointed minister of the treasury. He was elected president of the Chamber of Deputies from 1920 to 1924. During the Fascist period he was appointed senator, but he did not attended any sessions. After World War II De Nicola returned to politics, becoming temporary head of the Italian Republic after the fall of the monarchy. In 1956 he was elected president of the Constitutional Court but resigned because of his health after one year. In 1959 he died in Torre del Greco (Napoli).

BIBLIOGRAPHY
Delzell, Charles F. *Italy in the Twentieth Century.* Washington, D.C.: American Historical Association, 1980.

Dario Caroniti

Denktash, Rauf (1924–)

Leader of the Turkish Cypriots. Rauf Denktask was born on January 27, 1924, in Paphos, Cyprus. From 1944 to 1947 he studied law at Lincoln's Inn in London (one of four British Inns of Court responsible for educating barristers). Shortly after returning to Cyprus he entered the Consultative Assembly set up by the British colonial administration. He was solicitor general from 1956 to 1957.

Denktash was a founder of the Turkish Cypriot Youth (TMT), a paramilitary group, organized in opposition to the National Organization of Cypriot Struggle (Ethnikí Organosis Kipriakoú Agónos, or EOKA), the Greek Cypriot organization seeking union of the island with Greece. Turkish Cypriots countered the Greek demands for *enosis* (union) with Greece with the slogan *taksim,* or partition of the island into two geographically separate Greek and Turkish sections.

Denktash was elected chairman of the Federation of Turkish-Cypriot Associations in the late 1950s, and as such was second only to Turkish Cypriot leader Fadil Kuçuk.

In 1963 he affirmed his determination that "the Turkish Cypriot community will never become a minority, nor will the island become Greek." This affirmation guided his efforts in the years following the attempted coup by Greek nationalists in 1974. Denktash, as leader of the Turkish Cypriot community, asked the Turkish military to come to the aid of Turkish Cypriots. In February 1975 a Turkish Federated State of Cyprus was declared with Denktash as president, and he became president of the Turkish Republic of North Cyprus (TRNC) when it was established in 1983. He was formally elected president of the TRNC in 1985 and was reelected in 1990 and 1995.

Denktash in negotiations with Presidents Makarios and Glavkos Clerides of the Republic of Cyprus (RC) continued to support the establishment of a federated state, but he insisted on guarantees for the Turks in their zone to prevent the island's 160,000 Turks from being dominated by its 600,000 Greeks. No state besides Turkey recognizes the TRNC, and the Turks fear that EU talks with the RC might lead to the admission of the RC and the further marginalization of the TRNC.

BIBLIOGRAPHY

Denktash, Rauf. *The Cyprus Problem and Remedy.* Nicosia, Cyprus: Lefkoça, 1992.

———*The Cyprus Triangle.* 2nd ed. Nicosia, Cyprus: Lefkoça, 1989.

Dodd, C. H., ed. *The Political, Social and Economic Development of Northern Cyprus.* Huntingdon, England: Eothen Press, 1993.

Bernard Cook

SEE ALSO Cyprus

Denmark

Constitutional monarchy in northern Europe situated between the North and Baltic Seas with an area of 16,629 square miles (43,094 sq km) and a population of 5.2 million. The kingdom also includes the Faroe Islands, eighteen islands in the North Atlantic with a total of 540 square miles (1,399 sq km) and 43,382 inhabitants in 1996, and Greenland, the world's largest island, with a total area of 839,999 square miles (2,175,600 sq km) and a population of 55,863 in 1996. Denmark consists of the Jutland peninsula and 406 islands, of which 79 are inhabited. Of these, the largest is Zealand (Sjælland), on which the capital, Copenhagen, is situated. All the main islands are connected by bridges. Administratively Denmark is divided into 14 counties (*amter*) and 275 municipalities (*kommuner*).

Since the tenth century Denmark has been a united and independent country, making it one of the oldest states in Europe. The political system is a parliamentary democracy with a strong legislative body, the Folketing. Denmark is an active member of the European Union

Denmark. *Illustration courtesy of Bernard Cook.*

(EU), NATO, the Nordic Council, and the United Nations. It has a bridging function between continental Europe and the rest of Scandinavia.

Danish agriculture, which is highly developed, is the basis for the production of processed foods of which about 66 percent are exported. However, since the beginning of the 1960s industrial production has surpassed agriculture in its share of the Danish GNP as well as in the value of exports. Well-known Danish products are furniture, pharmaceuticals, beer, hearing aids, and windmills.

Only scarce deposits of minerals exist in Denmark. However, enough oil and natural gas have been found and exploited in the North Sea to cover most of the country's needs. Also, chalk is found and used in cement production. Agriculture and fisheries in the 1990s employed only 5 percent of the workforce. Industry and manufacturing employed 27 percent, and the service sector 68 percent. About 33 percent of the workforce is employed in the public sector in education, health, infrastructure, administration, and social services.

After the liberation from the Germans on May 5, 1945, Denmark was faced with three tasks: getting its political system to function, finding another security and defense policy to replace the neutrality of the prewar period, and getting the economy to work. The political system had been suspended after August 1943 when the government and the politicians stepped down and the German occupation authorities and the Danish bureaucracy took over. During and after the war there was serious tension between the so-called cooperative politicians, who, without sympathy for Nazism, cooperated with the Germans to make the best of a bad situation, and the members of the Freedom Council, the Danish underground movement. The first government after the liberation in 1945 was a compromise between the two groups and had ministers from both. This government consisted of all the Danish political parties including the Communists, but the government lasted only six months until a general election took place in November 1945. Following the election, Knud Kristensen, a farmer from the Liberal Party, formed a minority government. Gradually, the traditional politicians took over and pushed out the more radical elements of the wartime Freedom Council, the members of which desired to establish a new style of democracy after the war and felt betrayed by the old politicians. In 1947 the Social Democrats formed a government with Hans Hedtoft as prime minister.

The second task for postwar governments was to work out a new defense and security policy. The neutrality preferred by Denmark was not credible anymore. In 1945–46 the view in the government was that the United Nations, of which Denmark was one of the founding states in 1945, was the best organization to safeguard Danish security. The United Nations with its clauses on collective security and peaceful settlement of conflicts appealed to Danish politicians, who thought that the alliance between East and West would somehow continue after the war. But in 1946–47 it had become clear that the Cold War had started and stalemated the United Nations. The Danish government under Hedtoft preferred a Nordic option rather than siding with East or West. When the Swedish government in May 1948 invited Denmark and Norway to start negotiations for a Nordic defense alliance, Denmark happily agreed. Yet the plan failed, principally because Norway demanded that the proposed alliance be oriented toward the West and particularly the United States. Since neither a U.N. nor a Nordic defense arrangement worked out, the Folketing accepted an invitation to join the North Atlantic Alliance (NATO) in March 1949. The Social Democrats, Liberals, and Conservatives voted in favor, but the Social Liberals, a close partner of the Social Democrats and a coalition partner in most postwar coalition governments, voted against NATO together with the Communist Party. The Social Liberal Party (Radikale Venstre), founded in 1905 on strong antimilitaristic and pacifist ideas, continued to press for limiting the role of the military and participation in NATO. In 1953 Denmark decided not to allow foreign bases on Danish soil, and in 1957 it decided to exclude nuclear weapons as well, "under the prevailing circumstances."

Relations with West Germany improved considerably, and in 1955 a Copenhagen-Bonn declaration was issued specifying conditions for Danish and German minorities in the other country. Likewise, a Danish-German military command within NATO was established for NATO's northern area.

Although there was little physical destruction in Denmark, the third task after World War II was to rebuild and stimulate the economy. The big prewar level of agricultural export to the United Kingdom was gradually restored but at lower prices than Denmark had received during the war. Increasing wages in the agricultural sector prompted the mechanization of many farms. Production per person employed in agriculture increased 40 percent between 1945 and 1950. Industrial production also increased. After the war massive emigration took place from agriculture to industry in urbanized areas. Exports to a rebuilding Europe created intense demand in Denmark. Between 1945 and 1950 industrial production increased

50 percent, and 33 percent of Danish industrial production was exported.

The Marshall Plan helped to finance many projects through loans and grants, and helped primarily through the acquisition of foreign currency, which was used to modernize industry and agriculture. Also, membership in the Organization for European Economic Cooperation (OEEC), through which Marshall aid was channeled, pushed Denmark into the international economy through the dismantling of trade and currency restrictions. In trade relations Denmark retained close cooperation with the United Kingdom, which remained its largest trade partner in the 1950s. Denmark stayed out of initial negotiations in the late 1950s on formation of the European Economic Community (EEC). Instead, Denmark, Norway, Sweden, the United Kingdom, Portugal, Austria, and Switzerland established the European Free Trade Association (EFTA) in 1960. However, Denmark's exports were nearly equally divided between the EEC and EFTA. The Danish government, therefore, welcomed negotiations in 1961 for membership in the EEC together with the United Kingdom. This first attempt did not succeed. But ten years later, in 1972, negotiations were brought to a successful conclusion, and Denmark, the United Kingdom, and Ireland joined the EEC in 1973.

A pillar of Danish foreign policy has been cooperation with the other Nordic states—Finland, Iceland, Norway, and Sweden. In 1952 the Nordic Council was established with an assembly of eighty-seven Nordic representatives operating as a kind of miniparliament that passed recommendations for common legislation. The Nordic Ministerial Council was set up in 1971 as a governmental and administrative institution for Nordic coordination and cooperation. Two important results of this cooperation were an agreement to end passport controls for Nordic citizens and the establishment of a common Nordic labor market.

A major reform of the Danish constitution in 1953 included abolition of the upper house, the Landstinget, and the establishment of a one-chamber parliament with 179 seats; introduction of the post of ombudsman elected by parliament to oversee the executive branch; rules of succession making it possible for a woman to succeed to the Danish throne; and a rule to have a referendum if a third of MPs demanded it.

The period from 1958 to 1973 was characterized by strong economic growth. Productivity increased significantly in both industry and agriculture. The period also saw a strong reduction in the number of farms and agricultural workers, yet the surplus workforce was drawn into the expanding industry. Similarly, strong employment took place within the service sector, private and public. The demand for labor was translated into higher salaries and consequently a higher living standard. Single-family houses, private cars, and vacation travel became common features of Danish life.

But from around 1973, with the oil crisis, signs of economic instability appeared. Unemployment increased to the 10 to 12 percent range, and there were deficits in both trade and current accounts balances. These continued until the mid-1980s, when a brake was put on private and public consumption by the new center-right government led by Prime Minister Poul Schluter (1982–93). In the mid-1990s, an improvement took place in the economy resulting in an inflation rate of about 2 percent, a trade surplus, a surplus in current accounts balances, and a reduction of the unemployment rate to around 7.5 to 8 percent while maintaining moderate growth in GNP.

In the 1980s and especially in the 1990s, owing to Danish membership in the EU, Denmark's economy was strongly Europeanized. However, Danish attitudes toward various EU projects such as the single market, the Maastricht Treaty, and the Amsterdam Treaty have been deeply divided.

BIBLIOGRAPHY

"Denmark." Translation of the section of *Den Store Danske Encyklopfdi* (The Great Danish Encyclopedia). Copenhagen: Editors of the Danish National Encyclopedia, 1996.

Manniche, Peter. *Denmark, a Social Laboratory:* Oxford: Pergamon Press, 1969.

Miller, Kenneth E. *Denmark, a Troubled Welfare State.* Boulder, Colo.: Westview Press, 1991.

Jørn Boye Nielsen

SEE ALSO Faeroe Islands; Greenland

Denmark and the European Union

The Danish relationship to the European Common Market (EEC) and the European Union (EU) has been marked by controversy since 1993. It is the foreign policy issue that has most divided the Danes.

In the 1950s Britain and Denmark showed interest in the formation of the EEC but wanted to restrict it to a free-trade area without supranational institutions; Denmark traditionally followed Britain in trade orientation. This was unacceptable to the six core countries signing the EEC treaty in Rome in 1957: France, Germany, Italy, Netherlands, Belgium, and Luxembourg. As a reaction to the EEC, the European Free Trade Association (EFTA) was formed in 1960 by Britain, Denmark, Norway, Sweden, Switzerland, Austria, and Portugal. Later Iceland and Finland joined.

As early as 1961, however, Denmark, Britain, Ireland, and Norway started negotiations with the EEC on membership. But French President Charles de Gaulle vetoed Britain's membership in 1963, which stopped the whole process of unification of the two trading blocks for some years. In the late 1960s serious negotiations started again between the same four countries and the EEC. This time there was agreement on conditions for joining, but Denmark and Norway required a referendum. In Denmark the referendum was scheduled for October 2, 1972. After an emotional debate, 63.3 percent voted in favor of joining the EEC, and 36.7 percent voted against entering. In Norway, however, opponents of joining won, and since then no Norwegian government has succeeded in convincing a majority of the electorate of the benefits of membership. Greenland, which is owned by Denmark, followed the mother country into the EEC, even though a majority of voters there had voted against EEC membership. But when home rule was introduced in Greenland in 1979, the Greenland government decided to hold a new referendum on Greenland's connections to the EEC. Held in 1982, it resulted in a renewed majority against the EEC. The exit was effected in March 1985, but Greenland was recognized as an overseas territory associated with the EC; thus it retained free access to EC markets.

To revive the movement toward integration, the EEC agreed on the establishment of a single market in 1985. The Danish government called a new referendum in February 1986. The result was a narrow majority of 56.2 percent in favor, 43.8 percent against. In February 1992 a new transfer of sovereignty was on the agenda with the signing of the Maastricht Treaty, which changed the European Economic Community (EEC) to the European Union (EU), with the aim of a common currency; legal affairs, including immigration and police policy, decided by a majority; and military cooperation through the Western European Union. According to the Danish constitution, the Maastricht Treaty needed to be submitted to a referendum, which took place on June 2, 1992. Surveys showed many people felt that their politicians were selling out Danish institutions in favor of a federal Europe. The result shook the whole of Europe: 49.3 voted in favor, 50.7 against. The Maastricht Treaty was defeated, because all twelve EEC members had to agree for getting the treaty into force.

Yet the politicians decided soon after the referendum to propose to the EU that Denmark be exempted from four points in the Maastricht Treaty: 1. Denmark would not accept the concept of union citizenship; 2. Denmark would keep its kroner and not participate in the third phase of European Monetary Union; 3. Denmark would not participate as a member of the Western European Union; 4. Denmark would not be part of the legal cooperation envisioned by the Maastricht Treaty, for instance, a common European immigration and asylum policy. Those reservations were brought by Denmark to the EEC summit meeting in Edinburgh in December 1992, and they were accepted by the other eleven countries. There was a new Danish referendum on the Maastricht Treaty minus the four exemptions or reservations mentioned above. It was held on May 18, 1993, and resulted in 56.8 percent in favor and 43.2 percent opposed. The Maastricht Treaty as such was not changed, only the conditions of Danish adherence to it.

The recent official Danish position vis-à-vis the EU is to support fully the membership of eastern and central European countries; urge more emphasis on the environment and measures against unemployment in the EU; and support democratization of EU institutions.

Jørn Boye Nielsen

Political Parties

Between 1945 and the mid-1960s four parties dominated the political scene in Denmark: the Social Democrats, the Radical-Liberals, the Liberals, and the Conservatives. The political landscape was altered after 1960 by the appearance of a number of new parties.

The Social Democratic Party (S) has been the biggest political party in Denmark since 1913. It governed alone or in coalition with other parties for fifty years during the period 1924–96. It was formed in 1871 in a period with strong class barriers and social clashes, but gained representation in parliament in 1884 with two seats. It continued to grow in successive national and local elections. The original strategy of the party was not to take on government responsibility before it could bring together an absolute majority in parliament. However, it was decided at the time of World War I to give up this aim and cooperate with other parties for gradual reform of the existing social order.

In 1924 the Social Democrats formed their first government and started to work in cooperation with social-minded center parties gradually to build the welfare society, which guaranteed all members a high degree of social security in case of disease, old age, unemployment, and social problems. In the labor market the party worked with the trade unions and employers' organizations in a tripartite system to secure better conditions, including reduced working hours, sick pay schemes, and early retirement. Health care, education, and many cultural activities party of the large landowners and the conservatives, who favored keeping privileges, opposing liberal and democratic reforms, and thereby excluding the peasantry from the political arena. The Liberal Party was carried into parliament by peasants and farmers, who constituted the majority of the Danish population in the nineteenth century. It worked primarily for parliamentary democracy and universal suffrage irrespective of income, education, and gender. In 1901 parliamentary democracy was introduced in the constitution, and women were given the vote in 1915. The Liberal Party experienced many schisms between 1870 and 1905 as it struggled for democracy and popular reforms.

In this century the Liberal Party has more and more developed into a party for those favoring personal freedom, basic human rights, the right to own property, personal responsibility for one's own life, decentralization, and liberal democracy. After World War II the party has been Western oriented, strongly supporting NATO and the EU. The party has defined itself as the alternative to Social Democratic values and policies. Except for 1978–79 the party has always been in opposition to Social Democratic governments and presented itself as an alternative. It has been leader of or part of the government in 1901–09, 1910–13, 1920–24, 1926–29, 1950–53, 1968–71, 1973–75, 1978–79, and 1982–93. Uffe Ellemann-Jensen, who was minister for foreign affairs from 1982 to 1993, has been the leader of the Liberal Party since 1984.

The Conservative Party is the third-largest party in Denmark. It dates back to the *Højre* (Right), the party of big were made free. The Social Democratic reforms were, and still are, financed by a high income and value-added tax.

The Social Democratic Party did not nationalize industry or intervene to any major degree in the market mechanism. Its socialist strategy was not to change basically the capitalist way of working but, via high taxes, to redistribute resources to provide free services for all citizens in the fields of health, education, and culture. Since 1980 the party has given priority in its policies to fighting unemployment, protecting the environment, and building educational facilities adequate for the information age. But the Social Democrats have not had the same success in this endeavor as with their social project. Unemployment has been high since 1975.

The growing educated middle class has not identified with Social Democratic ideology and attitudes, which have emphasized social collectivity and solidarity. The industrial working class, which was the backbone of the

party, has diminished in size. However, a Social Democratic–led minority coalition government consisting of the Social Democrats, Social Liberals, and Center Democrats was formed in January 1993. Poul Nyrup Rasmussen, leader of the Social Democrats, headed this coalition.

The Liberal Party (Venstre, V) is the second-largest political party in Denmark. Its origin lies in the middle of the nineteenth century among Denmark's peasants and small farmers. Historically the party started as the United Left (Det Forenede Venstre) in 1870. The word *venstre* (left) was chosen to indicate its distance from *højre* (right), which was the name of the landowners and national liberals (higher middle class and civil servants) from the towns who tried to hinder the growing political influence of the farmers and the general democratization of society. They were confronted by the farmers party, Venstre (the left) in the so-called constitutional struggle from 1872 to 1901. *Højre* lost and a constitutional change introduced parliamentarism.

The Conservative People's Party (KF) was established in 1916 on the ruins of the old *Højre*. As a modern democratic party it is based on the middle class and the more wealthy sectors of society. It claims to be a party without ideology but with certain basic ideas: respect for differences and respect for individual and human rights. Freedom and responsibility are the watchwords of the party. It supports the welfare state as long as it is limited to assistance to the poor and weak, but it is opposed to the Social Democratic concept of welfare, which it considers too extensive and too costly. The party favors a balance between the individual and state, and, although it wants to strengthen the private sector, it is less hostile to state activities than the Liberal Party, with which it cooperates. In foreign policy it emphasizes Danish sovereignty but strongly supports membership in NATO and the EU. It participated in governments in 1940–43, 1945, 1950–53, and 1968–71, and its leader, Poul Schlüter, held the prime ministership between 1982 and 1993. In 1993 Hans Engell became party leader.

The Social Liberal Party (Radikale Venstre, RV) was founded in 1905 as the result of a splintering of the Liberal Party (Venstre). The Social Liberal Party was built on support from small farmers and socially oriented intellectuals in the towns. It defined itself as a social liberal party to the left of Venstre. The Social Liberal Party emphasized private enterprise and the market economy, on one side, and the responsibility of the state to intervene to help the weak and disadvantaged on the other. The party supported the Social Democratic Party in its endeavor to build up the welfare state since the

1930s and participated as a junior partner in several So-cial Democratic coalition governments. The RV has es-pecially emphasized disarmament and peace and has also given strong support to the United Nations and devel-opment assistance to the Third World. It has stressed the need for bridging the gap between the Social Democratic Party and the nonsocialist parties, but in practice the RV has often had to choose sides. From 1968 to 1971 and again from 1982 to 1993, it supported the liberal-conservative camp in the Folketing (parliament), mainly because of dissatisfaction over what it saw as Social Dem-ocratic economic irresponsibility. But in January 1993 it turned again to the Social Democrats and became part of the three-party coalition government. Its leader, Niels Helveg Petersen, held the Ministry for Foreign Affairs.

The first of the "new parties," the Socialist People's Party (SF) was founded in 1959 by Aksel Larsen, chair-man of the Danish Communist Party until 1958, from which he was expelled for being critical of Soviet domi-nation of national Communist parties. The new party won eleven seats and received 6.1 percent of the vote in its first national election in 1960. It has been represented continually in the Folketing, and since 1981 it has been the third- or fourth-largest of the eight or nine political parties in parliament.

The SF is to the left of the Social Democratic Party. Though it adheres to socialist ideals, it does so in a dem-ocratic fashion. Since the end of the 1970s it has in-creasingly seen itself as a "red-green" party with a strong environmental and ecological dimension. In the 1980s and 1990s it also became the party of grassroots move-ments, especially embracing the women's movement, green movement, and peace movement. It stressed the need for self-management and decentralization, thus dis-tancing itself from the Social Democratic orientation to-ward state solutions for many problems. It called for "more society, less state."

The SF kept a strong peace and disarmament profile, opposing NATO, the WEU, and all other military blocks but advocating a strengthening of the United Na-tion's capacity to intervene. As a consequence of its non-alignment policy, the SF opposed Denmark's entrance into the EEC and later the EU. However, in 1993 it softened its policy and accepted EU membership. At the second referendum on Maastricht in May 1993, the SF recommended a yes vote. Nevertheless, it opposes eco-nomic and monetary union, a common defense force, and the Maastricht clauses on European citizenship and legal cooperation. Holger K. Nielsen became leader of the SF in 1991.

The Progress Party was founded in 1971 by tax lawyer Mogens Glistrup with the primary aim of greatly reduc-ing the income tax. Glistrup himself demonstrated on a TV program in 1971 how he paid no taxes and how people could imitate him, if they knew the rules. His provoking appearances launched a big debate on the level and structure of the Danish tax system as well as the size of the state. In the 1973 national election Glistrup re-ceived 15.9 percent of the vote and the Progress Party became the second-largest party of the ten parties that presented candidates in that election.

Besides the tax issues, the party emphasized personal freedom and a market economy. It saw Denmark as a restrictive, bureaucratic system supported by both so-cialist and nonsocialist parties. The party has been char-acterized by many internal struggles, especially between "fundamentalists," who wanted no compromises, and a wing who wanted to cooperate with other nonsocialist parties. The latter was eventually victorious.

In the 1990s the party focused strongly on preventing the entry of refugees and asylum seekers into Denmark. The party rallied some support because of that policy but is seen by other parties as unacceptably hostile to immigrants. The party has also assumed a nationalist mantle in public debate. It was the only party in parlia-ment to recommend a no vote on the last Maastricht referendum in 1993. It wanted European cooperation to be only a cooperation of sovereign nation-states without a supranational elements for the EU.

The party split again at its general meeting in Sep-tember 1995, mainly over the question of leadership. Pia Kjaersgaard, party leader at the time, left the party and brought three other MPs with her. In October they founded a new party, the Danish People's Party. Its pro-gram closely resembled that of the Progress Party, ad-vocating strict laws on immigration and the expulsion of refugees, simplification and reduction of taxes, and lim-itation of the EU to cooperation on trade and the en-vironment.

The Unity List was founded in 1989 by three left-wing parties—the Communist Party (DKP), Left So-cialist Party (VS), and Socialist Worker's Party (SAP), a Trotskyite party. The idea was originally to unite for na-tional elections, because the election law require a group to receive 2 percent of all votes cast to be represented in parliament. In 1991 this cooperation was upgraded by the formation of a political organization with member-ship. The original parties have ceased to be active but exist formally. The new party, which has a collective lead-ership of twenty-one persons, calls itself the Unity List–The Red Greens. The party is situated to the left of the

Socialist People's Party. Like the SF, it distanced itself from Soviet Communist theory and practice, but it fundamentally criticizes the capitalist system for exploitation of people and nature and advocates a socialist democracy with a green dimension.

What probably brought the party into parliament for the first time in 1994 with six seats (out of 179) and 3.1 percent of the vote was its strong criticism and rejection of Danish membership in the EU. A year before, in 1993, the SF had for the first time recommended a yes vote in the second Maastricht referendum, despite the fact that its rank and file was still opposed to the EU.

The Center Democrats (CD) were founded in November 1973 by Erhard Jacobsen, who broke with the Social Democratic Party, for which he had held a seat in parliament from 1953 to 1973. He felt the Social Democrats had turned too much to the left. In the general election of December 1973 his party received 7.8 percent of the vote and fourteen seats. Though its support fluctuated between 2.2 and 8.8 percent, it has been continually represented in parliament. The party emphasized that it has no ideology but takes an ad hoc stand on issues. Nevertheless, it consistently opposed left-wing tendencies in schools and the media, especially TV and radio. It supported lower taxes for the owners of private houses and cars and strongly supported NATO and the EU. The CD depended heavily on Jacobsen's ability to use the media. After he resigned as party chairman in 1989, his daughter Mimi took over the leadership. A nonsocialist center party, DC participated in the liberal-conservative government of 1982–88, and in 1993 joined the Social Democratic–led government.

The Christian People's Party was founded in 1970 by Danish Christians who felt that an erosion of Christian values had taken place in the 1960s, as exemplified by the legislation of free abortion and the lifting of the ban on pornography in 1967. The party's program is based on Christian values and ethics. It emphasized strengthening the family and believes that infants should be cared for at home rather than in day-care institutions, which are widespread and heavily state-supported in Denmark. The party also advocated a green perspective on the environment.

The Christian People's Party was represented in parliament from 1973 until 1994, when it fell below the necessary 2 percent of the total vote. It participated in the Liberal-Conservative government of 1982–88, and later in the Social Democratic–led government of 1993–94.

BIBLIOGRAPHY

Miller, Kenneth E. *Friends and Rivals: Coalition Politics in Denmark, 1901–1995.* Lanham, Md.: University Press of America, 1996.

Jørn Boye Nielsen

SEE ALSO Jakobsen, Erhard; Larsen, Aksel; Nielsen, Holger K; Rasmussen, Poul Nyrup; Schlüter, Poul

Economy

Before World War II Denmark had a close commercial relationship with Great Britain based on the export of bacon, butter, and eggs. The 1945 trade agreement reopened the British market for these traditional Danish exports. However, the prices obtained were significantly lower than those paid by Germany during its wartime occupation of Denmark. Britain also promised iron, steel, and coal in exchange for Danish products but failed to deliver. As a result, Denmark accumulated a large surplus in sterling and had to import goods from outside the sterling area with scarce U.S. dollars.

By 1947 the Danish economy was in crisis, but the American European Recovery Program (Marshall Plan) proved to be particularly helpful in ameliorating it. Over the period 1948–53, Denmark received $236 million in Marshall Aid, used to purchase essential raw materials and industrial equipment, and to construct a modern electrical supply system. In 1947 the Bank of England demanded no further increase in Denmark's national debt after Denmark failed to make the kroner convertible to sterling. Hence Denmark introduced a policy of deflation that resulted in higher unemployment and lower growth. However, the establishment of the European Payments Union (EPU) in 1950 allowed the limited convertibility of Denmark's sterling surplus and permitted the Danes to set this surplus against its deficit with other EPU members.

Reconstruction saw the strong development of manufacturing industry, in particular sugar refining and brewing. Agriculture, on the other hand, took longer to recover from the effects of the war and did not begin to experience strong growth until 1948. One of the most serious problems in this period was a housing shortage, which remained unresolved throughout the 1950s.

After 1949 the Danish economy experienced three shocks. The first was the devaluation of the kroner in relation to the U.S. dollar, because Denmark imported more from dollar-area countries than it exported. The second was the liberalization of trade within the Organization for European Economic Cooperation (OEEC). Quantitative restrictions were removed but not customs duties. Denmark had relied more on quantitative restrictions than most other OEEC countries. The third shock was the outbreak of the Korean War, the main consequence of which was that raw material prices rose a great deal more swiftly than the prices of Danish foodstuffs and manufactured goods. The combined effect of these shocks was that the Danish terms of trade fell by one-third between 1949 and 1951 and remained at a unfavorable level until 1958.

During the period 1950–58, Denmark adopted a stop-go macroeconomic policy: the desire for expansion and higher employment had to be weighed against the concern for the balance of payments. As a result, in Western Europe only Britain had as low a growth rate as Denmark in this period. It became clear that agricultural exports were less and less profitable and needed to be supplemented by an export-oriented manufacturing industry. The most successful growth areas in manufacturing industry during the 1950s were engineering and electrical equipment and shipbuilding.

In 1960 Denmark found itself in a difficult situation when its two most important trading partners, Great Britain and West Germany, joined opposing trade blocs, the European Free Trade Association (EFTA) and the European Economic Community (EEC), respectively. Denmark decided to join EFTA, but in 1973 it was reunited with both its principal trading partners when both it and Great Britain joined the EEC.

Between 1959 and 1972 Denmark experienced rapid economic growth, low unemployment, and an unprecedented increase in real wages. In Western Europe only France and Italy experienced a higher rate of economic growth. The terms of trade were also highly favorable to Denmark. Agriculture continued its relative decline in this period and was replaced by manufacturing as Denmark's main source of export earnings. During this time Sweden became a major market for Danish manufactures. The housing crisis was also finally solved during the 1960s through the use of government subsidies. During this period Denmark also experienced a labor shortage directly linked to the growth of employment in the welfare state. The growth in welfare expenditures led to a significant increase in taxation.

The first oil shock in 1973 led to an instant 15 percent deterioration in Denmark's terms of trade. During the period 1973–80 Denmark experienced a low growth rate, insignificant investment, high unemployment, high inflation, and deficits in its balance of payments. In 1979 Denmark was affected by the second oil shock when it had still not fully adjusted to the consequences of the first one. The second oil shock caused a boom in private in-

vestment and consumption, but between 1979 and 1982, unemployment grew by almost 60 percent, to 9.8 percent of the labor force.

In 1982 a new coalition government tried to address Denmark's underlying economic problems by attempting "an economic reconstruction." Between 1982 and 1986 economic growth recovered and inflation fell. By 1986 the budget deficit, which had been 11 percent of gross domestic product (GDP) in 1982, had been eliminated but at the cost of large increases in taxation. In the mid-1980s most of Denmark's underlying economic problems remained unresolved. The trade deficit and unemployment remained high. The central government accounted for nearly 60 percent of Denmark's GDP. By 1986 the country had also had twenty-two consecutive years of current account deficits and a net foreign debt that was equivalent to 40 percent of its GDP.

After December 1985 Denmark adopted a deflationary domestic macroeconomic policy to slow the growth of incomes and consumer demand. In October 1986 the "potato diet" introduced further measures to control private consumption; seven years of near stagnation with low economic growth and high unemployment followed. On the other hand, both the large external deficits and budget deficits of the first half of the 1980s were brought under control, and exports grew by 5 to 6 percent a year until 1993. The *Frankfurter Allgemeine* described these latter achievements as a "quiet economic miracle."

During the first half of the 1990s Denmark had to make some difficult decisions with regard to its future in the European Union. In a referendum on June 2, 1992, the Danes rejected the Maastricht Treaty on the economic and monetary unification of the EU, partly because of fear of domination by their powerful southern neighbor, Germany, and partly because they were against a common EU currency. The Danish government subsequently negotiated various reservations and exemptions to those parts of the treaty to which the voters objected most strongly. In a second referendum on May 18, 1993, the Danes voted to ratify the treaty.

Denmark experienced a sharp downturn in its external trade in 1993 after the country was abruptly made uncompetitive through devaluations by some of its European trading partners. However, this setback proved to be temporary, even though the kroner came under attack from speculators in 1993 and was forced into a wider European Exchange Rate Mechanism band of 15 percent in August 1993. Unlike Great Britain and Sweden, Denmark prevented the depreciation of its currency. During the mid-1990s Denmark experienced a strong recovery in its rate of economic growth, but this was not accompanied by a fall in unemployment because there was a significant increase in productivity.

In 1993, with its per capita gross national product equivalent to $26,510, Denmark was the fourth-richest country in the world. Denmark retains a strong commitment to its welfare state, despite the fact that by 1994 government expenditure accounted for 64 percent of GDP, the highest level in Western Europe with the exception of Sweden.

In 1999 the Danish economy was experiencing its fifth year of expansion. However, growth slowed from 3 percent in 1998 to around 2 percent in 1999. The center-left coalition government concentrated on bringing down the unemployment rate, which was 6.5 percent in 1998; reducing the budget deficit; keeping inflation, which was 1.8 percent in 1998, low; and maintaining a current account surplus. The national budget produced a surplus in 1997, and the Danish debt-to-GDP ratio declined from approximately 80 percent in 1993 to less than 60 percent in 1998.

BIBLIOGRAPHY

Johansen, Hans Christian. *The Danish Economy in the Twentieth Century.* London: Croom Helm, 1987.
The OECD has published an annual survey of the Danish economy since 1960. ⟨http://www.oecd.org/eco/surv/esu-den.htm⟩

Richard A. Hawkins

Confederation of Danish Employers

The Confederation of Danish Employers (DA) was founded in 1896 as the main organization of employers within industry, trade, and commerce, and as a counterpart to the growing strength of the labor unions.

At the start of the Confederation there were only five member organizations and two individual companies represented. At the peak in 1965, there were 260 member organizations. Later many of the members merged. In 1996 DA had twenty-nine members, which represented twenty-eight thousand companies. After 1994 DA's aims were redefined. DA became the official representative and lobby organization for employers in public debate and in relations with the state. This left collective bargaining and sectoral agreements, which are negotiated normally every second year, to the twenty-nine member organizations. The most influential member organization is the Confederation of Danish Industries. Since 1994 the DA has placed more emphasis on EU relations and other types of international cooperation.

Jørn Boye Nielsen

Danish Confederation of Trade Unions

The Danish Confederation of Trade Unions (LO) was founded in 1898. It is the largest labor union in Denmark, organized as an umbrella organization with twenty-four (in 1996) affiliated trade unions with approximately 1.5 million members. The largest affiliated unions are the Union of Commercial and Clerical Workers in Denmark (HK), with 360,000 members; the General Workers' Union (SID), representing 310,000 mainly unskilled workers; the Danish Union of Public Employees, with 200,000 members; the Danish Metal Workers Union, with 140,000 members; and the Women Workers' Union, with 100,000 members.

The division into twenty-four unions is based on vocational criteria. To carry out more efficient and targeted labor union activities, the LO, together with its affiliated unions, has set up six confederations of labor unions, the so-called cartels, within important sectors to coordinate cooperation among various unions. The primary tasks of these cartels are to conduct collective bargaining, which takes place in six sectors: building and construction; trade, transport, and services; industry; the municipal sector; the state sector; and graphics and media.

The General Agreement between the LO and the Confederation of Danish Employers (DA), the so-called labor constitution, lays down the framework and regulations for collective bargaining and regulations regarding redundancy, dismissals, and the rights of shop stewards. The Cooperation Agreement between the LO and the DA establishes the parameters within which employers exercise their right to manage in cooperation with employees and their shop stewards. Individual management agreements are formulated by a joint consultation committee in each company of a certain size (in private-sector establishments with more than thirty-five employees) consisting of an equal number of representatives elected by management and employees. In the joint consultation committee, management is obliged to provide information on the company's financial situation and prospects, employment, major changes, and restructuring. The LO is also involved in supporting its representatives on company boards. In 1974 an act on representation on company boards gave the unions the right to elect two representatives to company boards. In a 1980 act further provisions allowed employees to elect a third of board members with a minimum of two representatives in all companies with thirty-five or more employees.

LO is represented in the International Confederation of Free Trade Unions (ICFTU), the European Trade Union Confederation (ETUC), and in the Nordic area in the Nordic Council of Trade Unions (NFS). There is close cooperation among the Social Democratic Party, the workers cooperatives (bakeries, canteens, housing societies, an insurance company, a bank, and a newspaper), and the LO. Each organization has representation in the others' bodies. Also, the LO is involved in various cultural organizations and labor colleges.

Unionization in the Danish labor market is very high compared with most other European countries. Approximately 85 percent of wage earners are affiliated with unions. The unemployment insurance system is administered by the labor unions in cooperation with the public employment services and heavily subsidized by the state.

Taxation

Characteristic of the Danish tax system are the many forms of taxes paid to different levels of the public system: income tax to the national level, county tax, municipal tax, church tax, and value-added tax (VAT). Income tax, paid to the state, is a progressive tax that increases with increasing income. Income tax in Denmark takes place at the source where it is earned. The employer deducts the tax from the salary of the employee and sends it to the tax administration. The highest incomes are taxed at 62 percent. This includes all taxes with the exception of the VAT and other indirect taxes.

Local taxes vary from county to county and from municipality to municipality. In 1996 the lowest percentage for municipal tax was 13.5 percent; the highest was 22.3 percent; the average was 19.8 percent. Combined local taxes, county plus municipal taxes, are on average around 30 percent. Local taxes finance approximately half of welfare expenses other than pensions and educational expenses. Local taxes are proportional, with the same percentage for all incomes.

Around 90 percent of Danes belong to the Lutheran Protestant Church, which is financed and administered by the state. The state collects a church tax of about 0.8 percent of taxable income.

The high tax percentages are modified by the deduction of certain types of expenditures from yearly income tax returns. From taxable income employees/wage earners can deduct a personal allowance, about one to two months' salary, expenses in connection with work, such as transportation, interest on nearly all kinds of loans, which especially benefits homeowners, and fees to professional associations and trade unions.

The tax reform of 1994 shifted the burden from income taxes, which are levied on work, to green taxes, which are laid on use of resources. Until 1998 the income tax decreased yearly by small percentages. Instead indirect taxes on gasoline, electricity, coal, water, plastic bags, and waste increased. The Danish government strongly has advocated harmonizing the tax systems in EU countries with these Danish initiatives. However, the private sector has complained that the heavy tax on resource use makes companies less competitive internationally. The green movements in Denmark welcomed the restructuring of the tax system.

In addition to the direct income and local taxes, there are indirect taxes such as a 25 percent VAT and special taxes on selected commodities like cars and luxury products. The indirect tax for a new car is 180 percent. However, there are no taxes for electric cars. The reason for the high tax on cars was not motivated originally by environmental concerns but the desire for higher state revenues.

Surveys show that a majority of Danes accept the high taxes and the welfare system, which they see as a necessity to finance a society with free health services; free educational opportunities at all levels, including scholarships for everyone older than nineteen, irrespective of parents' income; social services in case of sickness, unemployment, and old age; and leave systems for families with small children, for education, and for sabbaticals. Yet according to new surveys, the younger generation is critical of some aspects of the system. Many younger Danes object to its paternalism and high burdens on them, and seem to want a higher degree of individualism and economic freedom.

BIBLIOGRAPHY

The Danish Tax Reform: a Brief Description of the Most Important Acts Passed as Part of the Tax Reform. Copenhagen: Ministry of Taxes and Duties, 1986.

Olgaard, Anders. *The Danish Economy.* Brussels: Commission of the European Communities, 1979.

Jørn Boye Nielsen

SEE ALSO Glistrup, Mogens

Education

In Denmark from 1100 to 1700, education was seen as a task of the church. Around 1100 the first Catholic schools were set up. After the Reformation a new school law in 1536 still linked education to the church. New Latin schools were set up to prepare young males to become priests.

The first major educational law designed for the whole population was promulgated in 1814. This made education obligatory from ages seven to fourteen, the age of confirmation. The *folkeskole* (public school) was and still is paid for by local taxes. However, after 1856 the state also provided support. The *folkeskole* is an undifferentiated school with a one-year voluntary kindergarten class, a nine-year basic school, and a one-year voluntary tenth year for those who are not entering the gymnasium or leaving school. Children start kindergarten at six years of age and continue in the same class up to the ninth or tenth grade. The organization and curriculum is decided by the *folkeskole* law, and further regulations on the aims and contents of subjects taught are promulgated by the ministry of education. At the end of the ninth or tenth year, pupils can choose to sit for a leaving exam, which is voluntary but taken by nearly all pupils. Exams are not used in the *folkeskole* except for the leaving exam.

The municipal council has the overall control of the *folkeskole*. At each school there is a board a majority of whose members are parents. On many school boards there is also a representative for students. The board works out the guidelines for the educational activities and approves lesson plans and teaching methods.

About 12 percent of children between six and sixteen attend private schools, which receive state support covering about 75 percent of the costs of running the schools. Those schools follow special pedagogical (Steiner, Montessori, Little School), religious (Muslim, Catholic), or minority (German) traditions.

A student who completes the *folkeskole* or a private school has several options. The general gymnasium takes three years and prepares students for higher education. Within business and technical colleges there exists a similar gymnasium line taking three years, with emphasis on economic and technical subjects. There are about one hundred vocational programs in industry, commerce, transport, and agriculture. These are normally of three to four years' duration, with time divided between school attendance at technical schools and training/working in companies or institutions. All gymnasiums as well as vocational schools are, like the *folkeskole,* free.

An experimental approach to education in Denmark is the Free Youth Education, which started 1995. It is a two-year sequence consisting of at least three parts that students can put together with the help of an adviser. It might be a course in another country, training in an organization, or a folk high school. The main idea is that young people, who have not yet decided what to study, can put together short courses, visits, and training programs of their own choice and thus experience different environments to help them mature and motivate them for a final choice of education. The Free Youth Education is financed by the state, which pays course fees and finances scholarships.

Further and higher education takes place at different specialized schools such as teacher training colleges, the Danish School of Journalism, and colleges for librarians and other specialties. There are universities in Copenhagen, Aarhus, Aalborg, Odense, and Roskilde, and specialized institutions with university status such as the Technical University of Denmark (civil engineers), three business colleges, the Royal Veterinary and Agricultural University, the Royal Danish School of Pharmacy, the Royal Danish School of Educational Studies, two dental universities, and a school of architecture.

Unique educational and pedagogical institutions in adult education are the Folk High Schools, boarding schools for adults offering liberal and general education in a nonformal setting. The courses offered are from one week to about six months, but the normal course length for long courses is four months. The Folk High Schools originated in the nineteenth century. The idea was conceived by Danish theologian, historian, and writer Nicolai Frederik Severin Grundtvig in the 1830s. The first Folk High School was started 1844 in Rødding, in South Jutland. The schools are private but receive state support through the Folk High School law. At their start and up to the 1950s the schools were mainly frequented by young people and adults from the farming class, but in the last fifty years the schools have drawn students from all social groups in Denmark. In addition to the general "Grundtvigian" Folk High Schools, new issues-oriented Folk High Schools have developed within areas of sports, ecology, art, drama, health, and film. The Folk High Schools teach in Danish except for the International People's College in Helsingør (Elsinore), which accepts students from all over the world, has an international staff, and provides instruction in English.

BIBLIOGRAPHY

Denmark, Educating Youth. Paris: Organisation for Economic Cooperation and Development, 1995.

Jørn Boye Nielsen

Press

Denmark has fifty-five daily newspapers. Nearly a dozen are published in Copenhagen. Among the most respected of the large newspapers are *Politiken* and *Berlingske Tidende.*

Politiken, which has had considerable influence on political life, especially on social-liberal opinion, was founded in Copenhagen in 1884 by social liberals Viggo Hørup and Edvard Brandes as a sounding board against the Conservative government. Henrik Cavling, editor from 1905 to 1927, carried through a major program of modernization that had a big influence on the Danish press. *Politiken* became the model of a daily operating independently of party affiliation. However, it still espoused social-liberal viewpoints and was normally sympathetic to social democratic–social liberal coalition governments.

Berlingske Tidende, founded in 1749 by an immigrant German printer, Ernst Heinrich Berling, is the oldest existing daily in Denmark. From 1808 to 1831 it was the organ of the Conservative government but was subjected to censorship. In the beginning of the 1830s censorship was lifted. Freedom of the press was institutionalized with the Press Act of 1838. The free constitution of 1849, which transformed Denmark from an absolute to a constitutional monarchy, possessed a clause that still endures: "Everyone has the right to publish his ideas in print, but with responsibility before the law. Censorship and other preventive measures may never again be introduced."

In 1901 *Berlingske Tidende* broke all its government connections. By this time daily circulation was twenty-four thousand, and it had sufficient advertising to achieve full independent status. In the 1930s the newspaper stressed democratic conservatism and warned about Hitler's aims. After the war the newspaper devoted much coverage to foreign policy and business matters, as well as broad issues on family topics.

In 1977 *Berlingske Tidende* was hit by a 141-day strike by its technical staff, mainly printers, but survived. Until 1981 the newspaper was owned by the descendants of E. H. Berling, but in its latest reorganization the paper was changed to a corporation, the Berlingske Officin A/S. The new corporation also owns *BT,* a tabloid newspaper; *Weekendavisen,* a weekly newspaper; and several local or regional newspapers. The Berlingske Officin A/S is one of the three dominant newspaper groups in Denmark. The other two are the Politiken Group and Jyllands-Posten, which has the largest circulation.

Det Fri Aktuelt is a national newspaper published in Copenhagen by the Social Democrats in Denmark. It was founded in 1871 by Louis Pio, one of the pioneers of the Social Democratic Party in Denmark, and was published under different names as the main national organ of the Social Democratic movement. Since 1890 it has been one of the biggest dailies in Denmark. There were also about eighteen local and regional Social Democratic newspapers.

After 1911 the circulation of this Social Democratic organ stagnated at around fifty-five thousand copies. At the beginning of the 1950s circulation started to fall, and during the 1960s and 1970s most of the local and regional newspapers of the Social Democrats closed down. In 1959 the newspaper's name was changed from *Socialdemokraten* to the less political *Aktuelt* (what is of current interest). Since 1973 it has been published in tabloid format. In 1987 its name was again changed to *Det Fri Aktuelt,* adding the word *fri* (free), and it survives as the only Danish Social Democratic newspaper. It gets substantial financial support from the Danish Trade Union Congress. Its stated political aims are to change society in a democratic direction, be to the left of the center, and try to cover news and events with three questions in mind: What happened? Why did it happen? What does it mean?

Jyllands-Posten is an independent newspaper founded in 1871 in Aarhus, the second-biggest town in Denmark. It is still published in Aarhus but has editorial offices in Copenhagen. *Jyllands-Posten* is the only national newspaper published outside Copenhagen. In 1997 it had the widest circulation of all Danish newspapers. It provides broad coverage of events in western Denmark (Jutland), of business and economic issues, and the widest coverage of job advertisements. The newspaper is owned by an independent foundation. It is politically independent but conservative in orientation.

Social Services

The Danish welfare system provides a high degree of security for the aged, the sick, and the unemployed. It provides funding or support for social institutions for all, young and old, and free medical services through family doctors or hospitals, and home help. This system of income or service support is often referred to as the Scandinavian welfare system.

The public services are the same for all citizens regardless of occupational or family background. Recent welfare legislation rests on the Social Welfare Act of 1976, which was a product of the 1960s and early 1970s, a period of growth, optimism regarding the future, and dominance of the Social Democratic Party. The 1976 Social Welfare Act was based on the idea that each client should be treated individually by the local social office. It meant that support should be given on the basis of an evaluation of the client's needs and whole life situation—the individual judgment principle. All administration of social laws was centered in the municipal social administration.

With the 1976 law, nearly all insurance of one's person was rendered superfluous. The national, county, and municipal authorities became responsible for all kinds of social services. Citizens pay through taxes, relatively high compared with those of the rest of the world, then when they are in need they are provided for.

In 1987 the individual judgment principle was changed to a system of fixed rates—the legal principle. For each social event—unemployment, sickness, maternity—fixed rates were introduced. This was necessitated because of a rapid growth of social clients who made demands on the municipal social administrations. The growth stemmed from increased levels of unemployment, a growing number of pensioners, and many single parents, as divorce increased, who often needed support.

It is the state, through the Ministry of Social Affairs and the parliament, that established the framework for social services in the form of laws and regulations, but the actual administration of nearly all social welfare laws is carried out by the municipal councils and their social administration. Compared with other countries, Denmark has a very decentralized system. The financial resources come from state allocations and from municipal and county taxes. However, the health service, including hospitals and family doctors, is supported by the counties. Compared with the rest of Europe except for Scandinavia, in Denmark there are only small contributions from employers or insurance-based welfare schemes. The social system is based solely on state, county, and municipal taxes from citizens, and all citizens are eligible for income support or services independently of any connection to the labor market. In Denmark 87 percent of total social expenditures are financed by public direct or indirect taxes, mainly the value-added tax, compared with an average of 35 percent for other European countries.

Social expenses—social welfare, allowances, pensions, social institutions, health, and education—made up 64.2 percent of the total public budgets in 1997, including the state, counties, and municipalities. In the 1990s social expenses increased substantially, mainly because of the growth in expenditures for the unemployed; activation programs, such as job training courses, youth projects, support for people just beginning to live on their own; and different kinds of paid leaves, for families with small children, for education, or for sabbaticals. In 1995, 10.3 percent of the labor force was unemployed and receiving daily allowances or social assistance. In addition 9.9 percent of the labor force was involved in labor-training projects, on different paid leaves, or on early retirement pension for people between ages sixty and sixty-five.

In Scandinavia practically all women between eighteen and sixty-seven are in the labor market or studying, so the percentage of the total population connected to the labor market or in process of getting there is the highest in the world.

With regard to family support, there is paid maternity leave of two weeks before birth and twenty-four weeks afterward. The father has two weeks' paternity leave around the birth and can switch the last ten weeks of the leave with the mother and receive her payment. During maternity leave the daily allowance is paid by the municipality. However, in many collective agreements between employers and employed it is stipulated that the maternity leave payment consist of the worker's normal salary.

All families with children under eighteen years receive an allowance, "the children check," for each child every three months. There is strong public support for day-care institutions. There is also a general old age pension, "the folk pension" (folkepension). It is paid to all from age 67 onward, regardless of earlier labor market connection or income and is financed by taxes. But new forms of early retirement schemes have emerged. In 1979 the early retirement pension (efterløn) was introduced to let older people make way for the young unemployed. This early retirement pension pays the sixty-to-sixty-six group the rate of the unemployment daily allowance, which is relatively high compared with other European countries. This arrangement has been such a big success that about 70 percent of everyone between ages sixty and sixty-six have now gone on pension using one of the early retirement schemes.

The increase in social expenses due mainly to the unemployed, leave arrangements, and early retirement pensions has led to an intense debate in Denmark on the welfare system. There is a growing opinion that expenses have to be curtailed, otherwise a taxpayer revolt will arise. Basically, there is a consensus about the need to renew and restructure the welfare society. No political party would dissolve the welfare system. The conservative, nonsocialist parties—the Liberal Party and the Conservative Party—hold that certain allowance systems, such as paid leave arrangements and early retirement pensions, should be eliminated. They would also encourage more privatization, where possible, but would still keep the public health system. The Social Democratic Party, the Social Liberal Party, and the two Socialist parties to the left of the Social Democratic Party believe that the leave and early pension systems should be kept but that education and training should be emphasized much more to help qualify the unemployed so they can get work. The parties of the left would hope in that way to limit the amounts paid to the unemployed and to foster independence.

BIBLIOGRAPHY

Bjorkoe, Jens Aage. *Social Welfare in Denmark: The Danish Social Welfare System.* Copenhagen: J. A. Bjorkoe, 1986.

Marcussen, Ernst. *Social Welfare in Denmark.* 4th rev. ed. Tr. by Geoffrey French. Copenhagen: Danske Selskab, 1980.

Jørn Boye Nielsen

De Rossa, Prionsias (1940–)

Irish politician. Prionsias De Rossa was born in Dublin and graduated from the Technical College there. From 1980 to 1989 De Rossa was a member of the Workers Party (WP), formed as a result of a split in 1976 within Sinn Fein, the republican party that is the political arm of the Irish Rupublican Army. In 1988 he was elected president of the WP, the political arm of the "official" branch of the IRA in the republic. He was elected to the Dàil, the Irish parliament, as the WP representative of Dublin North West in 1982. From 1989 to 1992 De Rossa was a member of the European Parliament. In February 1992 he thwarted an effort by the WP's old guard to ram through antidemocratic amendments, a battle he described as one between democratic socialists and a group of Leninist advocates of so-called democratic centralism. He advocated a party conference to clearly define the organization as independent of the IRA, democratic rather than "revolutionary," and socialist rather than "Leninist." When he was unable to deter the old guard, De Rossa bolted in March 1992 and took about 80 percent of the WP's membership with him. Under his leadership they formed a new party, the Democratic Left. In 1994 he entered the Irish government of John Bruton as minister of social welfare. In that position De Rossa promoted increases in child benefits and community development projects.

In 1997 De Rossa successfully pursued a libel suit against journalist Eamon Dunphy for a December 13, 1992, article in the *Independent* that accused the Workers Party under the leadership of De Rossa of having engaged in criminal activity.

BIBLIOGRAPHY

Tynan, Maol Muire. "Eire: De Rossa Plans Purge of 'Old Guard' in Workers' Party." *Irish Times,* January 25, 1992.

Bernard Cook

Derrida, Jacques (1930–)

French philosopher. Born of Algerian Jewish parents near Algiers, Jacques Derrida traveled to Paris in 1948 to enroll in preparatory classes for admission to the École Normale Supérieure (ENS), to which he was admitted in 1952. An assistant to Gaston Bachelard, Georges Canguilhem, Paul Ricoeur, and Jean Wahl at the Sorbonne from 1960 to 1964, Derrida served as maître-assistant at the ENS from 1964 to 1984. In his defiance of academic professional norms, Derrida refused to complete a doctoral dissertation in philosophy until 1980, by which time he had already earned an international reputation. In 1974 Derrida founded the Research Group on the Teaching of Philosophy (G.R.E.P.H.) to resist a French government reform aimed at curtailing jobs in philosophy. Since 1984 he has been a director of studies at the École des Hautes Études en Sciences Sociales.

Like many in his intellectual generation, Derrida was greatly influenced by the later philosophical works of Martin Heidegger and the linguistic theory of Ferdinand de Saussure; yet unlike many of his colleagues, Derrida retained a deep interest in the phenomenology of Edmund Husserl. Though his first essays were published in philosophical journals and directed toward experts in phenomenology, Derrida gained greater recognition by shifting to journals in literary criticism during the 1960s. Linked to Georges Bataille's journal, *Critique,* and Philippe Sollers's *Tel Quel,* Derrida ascended to fame in the 1970s with his trenchant critiques of the structuralism of Claude Lévi-Strauss and Michel Foucault.

For Derrida the Western intellectual tradition is "phonocentric" insofar as it privileges the spoken over the written word: that is, the experience of hearing oneself speak seems to entail an immediate recuperation of meaning within its origin in human consciousness, whereas writing is typically viewed as a secondary and derivative phenomenon. Derrida radicalizes phenomenology by showing how, against Husserl, consciousness does not precede but is rather constituted by language. Thus, beginning with this speech/writing distinction, Derrida proceeds to "deconstruct" all the major binary opposites that characterize the Western philosophical tradition, including mind/body, interior/exterior, structure/event, culture/nature. By doing so he shows how the first term of each binarism requires the second for its very intelligibility. The second term is always a "supplement" that at once adds to and supplants the first term: the supplement stands for the missing parts within the whole. In Derrida's own words, the process of deconstruction involves "gaining access to the mode in which a system or structure, or ensemble, is constructed or constituted, historically speaking. Not to destroy it, or demolish it, nor to purify it, but in order to accede to its possibilities and its meaning; to its construction and its history."

BIBLIOGRAPHY

Bennington, Geoffrey, and Jacques Derrida. *Jacques Derrida.* Chicago: University of Chicago Press, 1993.

Culler, Jonathan. *On Deconstruction: Theory and Criticism After Structuralism.* Ithaca, N.Y.: Cornell University Press, 1982.

Derrida, Jacques. *Of Grammatology*. Baltimore: Johns Hopkins University Press, 1976.

———. *Writing and Difference*. Chicago: University of Chicago Press, 1978.

———. *Dissemination*. Chicago: University of Chicago Press, 1981.

———. *Glas*. Lincoln: University of Nebraska Press, 1986.

———. *The Post Card: From Socrates to Freud and Beyond*. Chicago: University of Chicago Press, 1987.

———. *Specters of Marx*. New York: Routledge, 1994.

Gasché, Rodolphe. *The Tain of the Mirror: Derrida and the Philosophy of Reflection*. Cambridge, Mass.: Harvard University Press, 1986.

Megill, Allan. *Prophets of Extremity: Nietzsche, Heidegger, Foucault, Derrida*. Berkeley: University of California Press, 1985.

Christopher E. Forth

Derycke, Erik (1949–)

Belgian minister of foreign affairs (1995–). Erik Derycke was born in Waregem on October 28, 1949. After receiving a law degree from the university of Ghent he became a lawyer in Kortrijk. He entered politics in 1975 as a provincial councilor in West Flanders. In 1984 he was elected to parliament. In 1988 he became a member of the municipal council in Waregem, where he led the Socialist Party. He became a member of the government in 1990 as secretary of state for science policy. In 1991 he was appointed minister for development aid and deputy minister for science policy. In 1992 he served as secretary of state for development aid assigned to the minister for foreign affairs. In 1995 Derycke assumed the leadership of the foreign ministry.

Bernard Cook

De Sica, Vittorio (1901–74)

Important post–World War II Italian film director. Vittorio De Sica was an acclaimed director of neorealism, a post–World War II movement in Italy that focused on the little people and real situations. A handsome, aristocratic demeanor characterized De Sica as a screen actor, and he starred in many films, Italian and foreign, that financed his filmmaking.

Shoeshine (1946), an important film of early neorealism, tells the story of two shoeshine boys during the Allied occupation of Italy and traces their downward spiral through black-market hustling to imprisonment and finally to murder of one by the other. Shot in the mean streets and jails of postwar Rome, it is a somber yet humane treatment of life's unpretty side. The film won a special award at the 1947 Academy Awards. The jury cited it as "proof to the world that the creative spirit can triumph over adversity."

The Bicycle Thief (*Ladri*, Thieves, in Italian, 1948), perhaps the most famous of all neorealist films, is the story of an unemployed man in postwar Rome who lands a job requiring a bicycle. He hocks family goods to purchase one only to have it promptly stolen. He and his son search for the bike, and in frustration the father steals a bike, gets caught, and is humiliated in front of his son. A sort of reconciliation between father and son concludes the film. Thinking about trying to pitch this story to a Hollywood producer gives an idea of the uniqueness of the neorealist movement.

Miracle in Milan (1951) has been described as a neorealist fable more whimsical than *The Bicycle Thief* but still focused on the human sprit. *Umberto D* (1952) is one of the masterpieces of the later neorealist films. It focuses on a pensioner and his dog who cannot survive on his inadequate monthly income. Umberto contemplates suicide but in the end opts for life. The film is a powerful story of one of the little people so beloved of the neorealists. In *Two Women* (1961) Sophia Loren won the Oscar for best actress for her spirited portrayal of a mother trying to shield her daughter from the cruelties of the departing German forces in war-torn Italy.

All the above films were products of an extraordinary collaboration between De Sica and the moving spirit and theorist of the neorealist movement, scriptwriter Cesare Zavattini.

Beyond neorealism, De Sica's *Garden of the Finzi-Continis* (1971), his first feature in color, tells the heartbreaking story of the intrusion of the Holocaust into the lives of a wealthy, patrician Jewish-Italian family during Mussolini's reign. The film's lyrical beauty is memorable, though some find it too pretty and perhaps discordant with De Sica's earlier neorealist style.

BIBLIOGRAPHY

Samuels, Charles Thomas. *Encountering Directors*. New York: Putnam, 1972.

William M. Hammel

Détente

Diplomatic term used for many years to denote relaxation of tension, détente was particularly applied to East-West relations from the late 1960s until the Soviet Union collapsed in 1991. Use of the term in this context may have been initiated by Josip Broz (Tito) of Yugoslavia in the late 1960s. Détente was a special hallmark of relations between the Nixon-Ford administrations and Leonid Brezhnev's USSR, and of the *Ostpolitik* of West German Chancellor Willy Brandt and his successor, Helmut Schmidt, of Germany directed toward the USSR. Détente as a process became closely identified with summitry, and there were numerous bilateral and some multilateral conferences involving the USSR and the Western powers.

The motives of the various states involved in détente differed, but the overall result was the achievement of a new, more favorable climate in East-West relations. The Soviet Union characterized its foreign policy toward the West under Premier Nikita Khrushchev as a policy of peaceful coexistence. It would be incorrect to say that détente supplanted peaceful coexistence, but it tended to refer to more positive manifestations of peaceful coexistence. The Soviet attitude toward and commitment to détente evolved over time but helped pave the way for Mikhail Gorbachev's "new thinking" in the 1980s.

Perhaps the high point of détente was the series of international meetings that culminated in the Helsinki Accords of 1975, which formally ended World War II. A series of discussions begun in 1972 were called the Conference on Security and Cooperation in Europe (CSCE). The Final Act signed in Helsinki in 1975 accepted existing boundaries as legal and provided for monitoring activities in Europe in the areas of security measures, economic cooperation, and greater freedom of information and movement of peoples. Western agreement to the Helsinki Final Act was a recognition of the status quo and of Soviet influence in Eastern Europe. At the same time the monitoring activities that emerged from the Helsinki Final Act committed the USSR to participating in a world that demanded greater commitment to human rights.

In the United States the policy of détente was developed during the Nixon administration while Henry Kissinger was national security adviser and secretary of state. It reflected not only an easing of Cold War tension but also various kinds of cooperation. The United States also developed the concept of linkage, in which positive Soviet behavior was rewarded with trade concessions. Détente between the United States and the USSR followed an uneven course. In the early 1970s there were several major developments, including the SALT I negotiations, the 1972 Brezhnev-Nixon Summit Conference, and negotiations for a comprehensive trade treaty. By the mid-1970s Congress was questioning whether détente had produced a real change in Soviet behavior. The U.S. Senate added two conditions to the trade treaty negotiated by the Nixon administration. One condition limited the amount

of credit to be extended to the USSR for purchases in the United States and the other tied trade to the emigration of Soviet Jews. The USSR refused the two conditions, and the treaty was never ratified by either side.

The downward slide away from détente in Soviet-American relations began about 1974 and continued throughout the 1970s. The American retreat was due to a number of factors including human rights' infractions in the USSR, the issue of Jewish emigration, Soviet intervention in Africa, and finally Soviet intervention in Afghanistan. The administration of Jimmy Carter was less committed to détente than were the Nixon-Ford administrations. Carter's emphasis on human rights caused the administration to look askance at Soviet behavior. Although negotiations for SALT II continued and a treaty was drafted, ratification never occurred. After the Soviet invasion of Afghanistan in 1979 relations further deteriorated, and the Carter administration boycotted the 1980 Olympics held in Moscow. In 1980 Ronald Reagan assumed the U.S. presidency with a distinctly anti-Soviet posture. He distanced himself from the Republican administrations of the 1970s, which had worked to improve Soviet-American relations.

Soviet-German cooperation proceeded gradually but steadily throughout the 1970s. Willy Brandt began the process but Helmut Schmidt continued it. In 1971 an agreement was reached among the four major allies of World War II to ensure better access to West Berlin from the Federal Republic of Germany (FRG). Although the status of Berlin was not finally resolved, and there were intermittent problems between East and West Germany, Soviet–West German cooperation improved significantly. When the American-Soviet trade treaty collapsed, West Germany stepped into the vacuum, and by the late 1970s West Germany became the largest Soviet trade partner outside the Soviet bloc. West Germany extended long-term credit to the USSR to buy technology and equipment in the FRG. Despite pressure from the United States to restrict cooperation with the USSR after the Afghan invasion, Germany refused to change its economic course. In the early 1980s the USSR tried to prevent West Germany from deploying American missiles but was rebuffed. Germany was pursuing its own course of détente, which sought to maintain its alliance with the United States and its economic relationships with the USSR. Détente between the FRG and the USSR was strained by Soviet attempts to influence the outcome of the 1983 FRG elections in which the Social Democrats, who had pursued *Ostpolitik,* were unseated by the more conservative Christian Democrats led by Helmut Kohl.

Détente between the USSR and the United States almost disappeared during the last days of Brezhnev's rule and the first Reagan administration. Except for the initiation of the Strategic Arms Reduction Talks (START) talks, which supplanted the early SALT process, there were no summit conferences and little progress in most forms of cooperation. Détente between West Germany and the USSR was interrupted during the early years of the Kohl government.

Détente resumed and flourished only after Mikhail Gorbachev came to power in the Soviet Union in 1985. The beginning of Reagan's second administration was closely followed by Gorbachev's succession to the position of general secretary of the Communist Party. To distinguish itself from prior administrations, the Reagan administration preferred the term "engagement" to détente and spoke of engaging the cooperation of the USSR. The Geneva summit conference in 1985 between Reagan and Gorbachev launched a new stage of détente, or engagement, which continued throughout the Reagan and Bush administrations until the collapse of the USSR. Cooperation expanded in all areas from science to trade, and a new spirit of cordiality characterized U.S.-Soviet relations.

Relations with the West German government led by the Christian Democrats improved in 1986 after German Foreign Minister Hans Dietrich Genscher visited the USSR. In 1989 the Gorbachev administration apparently decided to withdraw its long-term support of East Germany and to allow the reunification of Germany. This brought détente between the USSR and West Germany to a new level of cooperation as both sides took steps to facilitate the transition.

The end of détente between East and West was a natural result of the end of the Cold War. In the absence of the Cold War, there was no need for détente as the post-Soviet states and especially Russia redefined their foreign policies and put behind them the old foreign policy stance of the USSR.

BIBLIOGRAPHY

Garthoff, Raymond. *Détente and Confrontation,* rev. ed. Washington, D.C.: Brookings Institution, 1994.

LaFeber, Walter. *America, Russia, and the Cold War, 1945–1996.* New York: McGraw Hill, 1996.

Oudenaren, John Van. *Détente and Europe: The Soviet Union and the West since 1953.* Durham, N.C.: Duke University Press, 1991.

Rubinstein, A. Z. *Soviet Foreign Policy since World War II,* 4th ed. New York: HarperCollins, 1992.

Shearman, Peter, ed. *Russian Foreign Policy since 1990.* Boulder, Colo.: Westview Press, 1995.

Zwick, Peter. *Soviet Foreign Relations: Process and Policy.* Englewood Cliffs, N.J.: Prentice Hall, 1990.

Norma Corigliano Noonan

SEE ALSO Arms Control Treaties and Agreements; Brandt, Willy; Conference on Security and Cooperation in Europe; Strategic Arms Limitation Talks; Strategic Arms Reduction Treaty

de Valera, Eamon (1882–1975)

Fianna Fail politician; *taoiseach* (prime minister) 1932–48, 1951–55, and 1957–59; and president of Ireland, 1959–73.

With his political pedigree as the last surviving commandant of the 1916 Rising and a founding member of Fianna Fail, the center-right party that opposed the 1922 treaty between Great Britain and the Irish Free State, Eamon de Valera remained unassailable in the post-1945 Irish political landscape. Yet his star was waning, and he could no longer live up to his former glory in practice. By remaining *taoiseach* until 1959 he held back the ascendancy of Sean Lemass.

After 1945 de Valera lacked the drive and purpose exhibited in his domestic policy during the early interwar years. In international affairs, though psychologically pro-Western, he carried the burden of his ambivalent although neutral policy during World War II. Many of his actions were carried out with constant reference to the past, and he showed an increasing inability to come to terms with the modernization of Ireland. His performance showed that he could not understand the creation of an Irish society other than that which he himself saw as proper. His speeches and policies during the election campaigns of the 1950s bore a marked similarity to those he made in the 1920s and 1930s. His eyesight had also deteriorated to complete blindness, a metaphor for his political lack of vision.

In June 1959, he was elected president after defeating Fine Gael, the Irish party comparable to the Christian Democrats of Continental Europe, candidate Sean MacEoin in the first count, receiving 54.92 percent of the vote against MacEoin's 42.62 percent. In June 1966, de Valera was reelected by the barest majority, 50.036 percent, against Fine Gael's T. F. O'Higgins. As president, de Valera was by the definition of that office essentially confined to a ceremonial, nonpolitical role. Some argued that he had written the post into his own constitution as a retirement position.

The postwar years were de Valera's long decline. He will be remembered for his performance as *taoiseach* between 1932 and 1939, when he reformed the constitutional nature of the Irish state, attempted to industrialize Ireland as a self-sufficient state, and kept the country neutral during World War II.

BIBLIOGRAPHY

Coogan, T. P. *Long Fellow, Long Shadow.* London: Hutchinson, 1993.

Longford, Earl of, and O'Neill, T. P. *Eamon de Valera.* London: Hutchinson, 1970.

Ryle Dwyer, T. *Eamon de Valera.* Dublin: Gill & Macmillan, 1980.

Michael J. Kennedy

SEE ALSO Lemass, Sean

Devlin, Bernadette (1947–)

Militant civil rights activist and member of the British Parliament (1969–74) at the outbreak of civil unrest in Northern Ireland. As a student at Queen's University, Belfast, Bernadette Josephine Devlin participated in marches protesting restrictions on voting rights, gerrymandering of electoral districts, and discrimination in hiring—all directed against the Roman Catholic population. She helped to found the student movement Peoples' Democracy and entered the British Parliament from the Independent Unity Party. Devlin participated in the barricading of Catholic areas of Belfast in 1969, lauded the Black Panthers in the United States, and physically attacked Home Secretary Reginald Maudling in 1972. This attack followed the deaths of thirteen Northern Irish protesters in a skirmish with the British army. Her participation in the barricading of Belfast earned her a jail sentence of six months. In 1975 Devlin was a founder of the Irish Republican Socialist Party. In 1981 she and her husband, though wounded, survived an assassination attempt by members of the Unionist Ulster Defense Association. The next year she ran unsuccessfully against Prime Minister Charles Haughey for a seat in the Irish parliament.

Devlin's themes were common to the antiestablishment positions of the early 1970s: social radicalism, popular government, civil rights, civil disobedience, and feminism. Her emphasis on social justice diverged from the established themes of Irish nationalism: unification of Ireland and independence from British rule. Her career demonstrated both the volatility and variety of the Northern Irish political situation and the limitations of her particular message.

BIBLIOGRAPHY

Devlin, Bernadette. *The Price of My Soul.* New York: Vintage, 1970.

Target, G. W. *Bernadette: The story of Bernadette Devlin.* London: Hodden and Stoughton, 1975.

Robert D. McJimsey

SEE ALSO Northern Ireland

Dewinter, Filip (1962–)

Leader of the extreme-right Vlaams Blok (VB) of Belgium, member of the Antwerp city council, and member of the Belgian parliament. Filip Dewinter was born in Brugge on September 11, 1962. His father, a railroad administrator, was a Flemish nationalist and his mother was a conservative. After getting into fights with left-wingers, Dewinter quit the university but received a degree in journalism from a trade school. From 1987 to 1990 he was leader of the VB Youth League.

Dewinter was part of the electoral success of the Vlaams Blok in Antwerp, where it won 28 percent of the vote to become the largest party in 1995. According to Dewinter, "Belgium is an artificial state, there is only one imaginable solution: Flemish independence." He also espouses an anti-immigrant line. Ten percent of Belgium's ten million inhabitants are immigrants, and a third of them come from Islamic countries. Demanding that the "Islamic invasion" be stopped, Dewinter would deny the vote to non-European immigrants, segregate their children in separate schools, and deport as many as possible even if they were Belgian-born and citizens. Dewinter and the VB had their greatest success in Antwerp in mixed neighborhoods, where, in Dewinter's words, working-class Belgians felt "Islamicized."

BIBLIOGRAPHY

Carlander, Ingrid. "Marée de scandales, monté de l'extrême droite: Anvers la cosmopolite, Anvers la brune." *Le Monde diplomatique,* May 1995, 8–9.

Crouch, Gregory. "Three to Watch: Populists of the Hard Right." *New York Times,* April 21, 1996.

Bernard Cook

Diana, Princess of Wales (1961–97)

The death of Diana, the princess of Wales, in a car crash in Paris in 1997, was met by perhaps the deepest mourning of this century. An unprecedented amount of press covered every aspect of the funeral procession and service, which was viewed on television by more than two and one-half billion people worldwide. Why so many who had never met the princess would lament her death is part of the phenomenon that had grown up around her person in the years after her marriage in 1981 to Charles, the prince of Wales and heir to British throne.

Lady Diana Spencer was born on July 1, 1961, the third daughter of Viscount Althorp (who became the eighth Earl Spencer after his father died in 1975) and Viscountess Althorp. Her family was one of England's oldest, and her ancestry included five lines of descent from Charles II (1660–85). She went to a finishing school in Switzerland, the Institute Alpin Videmanette, but was unhappy there and convinced her father to allow her to come home.

After returning home she worked as a waitress, a charlady, and a babysitter. Diana soon found a job at the Young England kindergarten where she taught children drawing, dancing, and painting. She continued to supplement her income by working as a cleaner at her sister Sarah's house.

Diana first met Prince Charles in November 1977 on the Althorp estate. At the time he was dating her sister Sarah. It was not until July 1980 that Diana would see Charles again. Their engagement was announced on February 24, 1981. The wedding took place on July 29, 1981. The couple and the wedding became a national obsession as people marketed and sold Charles and Di mugs, plates, bookmarks, and coins. The wedding was televised and there was a mood of universal celebration as the beautiful, shy bride married what seemed to be her "prince charming."

In the early 1990s, Diana revealed that she had begun to suffer from bulimia shortly before her marriage, an eating disorder that would haunt her for much of her life. She became depressed and believed Charles was still seeing Camilla Parker Bowles, his former mistress. Her life was plagued by depression and apparent suicide attempts, but the marriage produced two sons.

Diana gave birth to Prince William, on June 21, 1982. Another son, Prince Henry, followed in September 1984. As Charles and Diana made official tours around the world, her popularity grew. Eventually, Diana overcame her shyness and grew more comfortable with photographers. Diana's public persona emerged as a warm and caring person who loved her children deeply. She also transformed her style of clothing and became one of the most glamorous women in the world.

Diana's marriage, however, disintegrated. Both she and Charles reportedly had affairs during their marriage. In 1991, the publication of excerpts from the book by Andrew Morton, *Diana: Her True Story*, shocked and horrified the royal family. Although Diana denied contributing to the book, it was widely believed by Charles—and was later confirmed—that she had cooperated with the author. The book portrayed Charles as a cruel and neglectful husband who flaunted his mistress. It also depicted the royal family as cold and indifferent. On December 9, 1992, the government announced that the two would separate, but not divorce. Diana did not suffer the humiliations that Charles did over the separation. She was elevated to a kind of secular sainthood as she toured orphanages, homeless shelters, and hospices, hugged lepers in Nepal, and touched the untouchables in India. People continued to be mesmerized by her warmth and beauty. Her involvement with charitable organizations raised hundreds of million of pounds annually.

Relations between Charles and Diana did not get any better, and in August 1996 they divorced, reportedly at the insistence of the queen. After the divorce, Diana continued her charity work, developing a special interest in ridding the world of land mines.

Diana had taken her sons with her on holiday in July 1997 to the south of France, where they stayed as guests of Dodi al-Fayed, the son of a wealthy Egyptian businessman who resided in London. On August 31, 1997, shortly after leaving the Ritz Hotel in Paris, Diana and Dodi's car crashed into a concrete dividing pillar inside the Alma Tunnel. The driver and Dodi Fayed were killed instantly. A bodyguard was seriously injured and Diana lay near death. Despite efforts to save her, she died two hours later. Later, investigators determined that the driver's blood contained four times the legal amount of alcohol permitted.

As news of her death spread, London became engulfed in flowers. People left them along the gates of Buckingham Palace, lamp posts, park benches, and monuments. Almost every flag in the kingdom flew at half mast. Diana's funeral was held at Westminster Abbey. In order to accommodate the 1,500,000 who were expected to line the route of the funeral procession, Charles ordered that the procession be doubled to two miles. The cortege began at Diana's home, Kensington Palace. Behind Diana's coffin walked Prince Philip; Earl Spencer, Diana's brother; Charles; William; and Harry. Behind them walked five representatives from each of the one-hundred ten charities Diana had supported. Diana's body was laid to rest on an island inside the grounds of Althorp.

Since her death, Diana has become an icon. Some believe that because Diana revealed herself as a normal, flawed person that people felt close to her. In comparison to the rest of the royal family, Diana seemed genuine and warm. Her compassion toward the sick and her insistence that her sons be raised as normal boys brought her even closer to people's hearts.

BIBLIOGRAPHY

Anderson, Christopher. *The Day Diana Died.* New York: Morrow, 1998.

Dimbleby, Jonathan. *The Prince of Wales: A Biography.* New York: Morrow, 1994.

Kelley, Kitty. *The Royals.* New York: Warner Books, 1997.

Merck, Mandy, ed. *After Diana: Irreverent Elegies.* London: Verso, 1998.

Morton, Andrew. *Diana: Her True Story.* New York: Simon & Schuster, 1992.

Spoto, Donald. *Diana: The Last Year.* New York: Harmony Books, 1997.

Rebecca Hayes

SEE ALSO Charles, Prince of Wales

Dienstbier, Jiří (1937–)

Czechoslovak foreign minister. Jiří Dienstbier was born in Kladno, Bohemia, on April 20, 1937. He received an M.A. from Charles University in Prague in 1960. He began working as a foreign correspondent in Asia in 1958, and at the time of the Warsaw Pact invasion of Czechoslovakia in August 1968 Dienstbier was a foreign correspondent in Washington, D.C., for Radio Prague. He was recalled to Czechoslovakia and fired in 1969, along with two thousand other journalists and commentators who had worked for and supported Alexander Dubček's reform government and refused to support the invasion. He worked as an archivist at the Design Institute from 1970 to 1979, then was jailed from 1979 to 1982 for his activities in the Czech human rights organization Charter 77. His original sentence of three to ten years was reduced to the minimum because of protests from abroad, which came from, among others, U.S. President Jimmy Carter, British Prime Minister Margaret Thatcher, and Georges Marchais, leader of the French Communist Party. When Dienstbier was released from prison he was first a night watchman. From 1983 to 1989 he earned a living shoveling coal for the Czech-Soviet combine that was constructing the Prague subway. Dienstbier sarcastically commented, "Here, it's punishment to be sent among the workers."

In December 1989, following the Velvet Revolution, Dienstbier became the first foreign minister of democratic Czechoslovakia. His chief priority was to work out an agreement with Russia to remove all the seventy thousand to seventy-five thousand Soviet troops stationed there within a year. Though his original goal was not met, the last of the Soviet troops left in June 1991. Dienstbier also advocated a new Marshall Plan to assist in the democratic, free-market transformation of Eastern Europe and Russia, whose movement toward democracy he viewed as crucial. In January 1990 Dienstbier announced that Czechoslovakia, for moral reasons, would cease to export arms. Owing to the economic importance of military production, however, especially in the Slovak part of the country, his promise remained unfulfilled. Yet Czechoslovakia did cut its arms exports by 1993 to 25 percent of their 1989 level. In December 1991 Czechoslovakia along with Poland and Hungary became an associate member of the European Community (EC). Dienstbier's goal was for eventual full membership.

On February 11, 1991, Civic Forum (CV), which on June 8, 1990, won the first free parliamentary elections in Czechoslovakia since 1946, split into two factions. One group was headed by Minister of Finance Václav Klaus, a long-time anti-Communist who had nevertheless not joined the dissident movement before November 1989. Klaus defeated the handpicked candidate of President Václav Havel to become chairman of CV in October 1991. The other CV group, the Liberal Club, which had the support of Havel's associates from Charter 77, was headed by Dienstbier, who now in addition to being foreign minister was deputy premier. Klaus said that the Liberal Club represented "1968 Communists," social liberals who opposed his advocacy of rapid introduction of free-market economic liberalism.

In 1992 Dienstbier became chairman of the Civic Movement. After Klaus's Civic Democratic Party was victorious in the June 1992 election, Dienstbier was replaced as foreign minister by Josef Zieleniec.

BIBLIOGRAPHY

Kamm, Henry. "Civic Forum, Prague's Leading Party, Splits in Two." *New York Times,* February 12, 1991.

Lewis, Anthony. "Abroad at Home; Leveraged Investment." *New York Times,* May 22, 1990.

Whitney, Craig R. "Upheaval in the East: Czechoslovakia: Prague Arms Trade to End, Foreign Minister Says." *New York Times,* January 25, 1990.

Bernard Cook

SEE ALSO Klaus, Václav; Sedivy, Jaroslav

Dillon, James (1902–86)

Leader of Fine Gael, the Irish political party comparable to the Christian Democratic tradition of continental Europe, from 1959 to 1965. James Dillon was born in Dublin. He served in the Dáil (Irish parliament) for Donegal from 1932 to 1937 and for Monaghan from 1937 to 1968. In 1932 Dillon founded the National Centre Party, which merged into Fine Gael in 1933. He then became a vice president of Fine Gael. Dillon was a constant critic of Irish neutrality during World War II. Advocating that Ireland join the Allies, he resigned from Fine Gael over the neutrality issue in 1941. An independent member of the Dàil from 1942 to 1948, Dillon rejoined Fine Gael in 1951. He was minister for agriculture from 1948 to 1951 and from 1954 to 1957. In the first interparty ministry, he was responsible for instituting the land drainage scheme funded by Irish portions of the U.S. Marshall Aid program. Dillon was leader of Fine Gael from 1959 to 1965, when he retired in favor of Liam Cosgrave.

BIBLIOGRAPHY

Foster, R. F. *Modern Ireland 1600–1972.* New York: Penguin, 1989.

Michael J. Kennedy

Dimitrov, Filip (1955–)

Bulgarian prime minister of the first wholly non-Communist government, November 8, 1991, to October 28, 1992, since World War II, formed after the victory of the Union of Democratic Forces (UDF) in the October 1991 general elections. Filip Dimitrov, born on March 31, 1955, became the second leader of the UDF after its chairman, Zheliu Zhelev, was appointed president of Bulgaria on December 11, 1990, by the National Assembly. Dimitrov was also the first leader of a Green party in Europe to gain the position of prime minister.

Prior to his activities as a post-Communist opposition leader, Dimitrov worked as a lawyer. He graduated from the Faculty of Law of Sofia University. In spite of the deeply hostile political environment and the reluctance of labor unions to support transition to the rudiments of a market economy, Dimitrov's government resumed payments on the national debt after the moratorium imposed on them by Andrei Lukanov's post-Communist government. Dimitrov also gave high priority to attracting foreign investments. Sustaining a balanced foreign policy and responsible home policy, Dimitrov worked strenuously to stabilize Bulgaria's collapsing economy and create a new image of a country on the road to Western-style democracy.

Under Dimitrov's leadership Bulgaria became a member of the Council of Europe on May 5, 1990; signed a treaty of security, cooperation, and friendship with Turkey on December 20, 1991; and on January 16, 1992, was the first country to recognize the independence of Macedonia, thus revealing its determination to contribute to the peaceful development of post-Communist states in the Balkans. Under Dimitrov Bulgaria also started reforming its system of taxation.

Dimitrov resigned on October 28, 1992, as leader of the UDF government after losing a vote of confidence in the National Assembly.

BIBLIOGRAPHY

Crampton, R. J. *A Short History of Modern Bulgaria.* Cambridge: Cambridge University Press–Open Society Foundation, Bulgaria, 1994.

Lyudmila Iordanova Dicheva

SEE ALSO Zhelev, Zheliu

Dimitrov, Georgi Mikhailovich (1892–1949)

Bulgarian Communist leader. Georgi Dimitrov was born at Kovachevsti on June 18, 1892. His father was a poor peasant who had migrated from Macedonia to become a factory worker in Bulgaria. Dimitrov, unable to attend the university because of poverty, went to work for a printer when he was fourteen. Already active in revolutionary movements, Dimitrov organized a union at his firm and in 1900 became the secretary of the Bulgarian Printers Union. He was elected to the Sofia city council in 1903 and to the National Assembly in 1913. He was a founder of the Bulgarian Communist Party and in 1909 became a member of its Central Committee. He helped to organize the Bulgarian Trade Union Federation, led strikes, and was jailed for his antiwar activity.

In 1921 Dimitrov became a member of the executive committee of Comintern, the Communist or Third International, an association of Communist parties established in 1919 to ostensibly promote world revolution but in fact to secure Soviet control over communist parties throughout the world. He led an armed insurrection against the Bulgarian government in 1923 and was sentenced to death in absentia for his reputed involvement in the bombing of a state funeral in the Sofia cathedral in 1925. Dimitrov, who was in Berlin on Comintern business in 1933, was arrested and accused of involvement in the "Communist plot" to burn the Reichstag (German parliament) building. At the trial he attacked the Nazis and rightly accused them of having done the deed themselves. Before the complete consolidation of Nazi power, Dimitrov, who had won worldwide support and had been granted Soviet citizenship, was acquitted and released on February 28, 1934.

From 1935 to 1943 Dimitrov served as general secretary of the Comintern in Moscow. He was a spokesperson for the popular front line, which sought to encourage cooperation between progressive elements of the bourgeoisie in Western Europe and Communists. He quickly altered his tack to accommodate the Nazi-Soviet Non-Aggression Pact of 1939, and then again following the German attack on the Soviet Union in June 1941.

From Moscow Dimitrov directed Communist activities in Bulgaria. In July 1942 he engineered the establishment of the Fatherland Front of anti-Fascist elements from the military and anti-Fascist political parties. On September 9, 1944, the Fatherland Front, with Kimon Georgiev serving as prime minister, took control of the country and surrendered to the Allies. In April 1945 Dimitrov returned to Bulgaria to lead the Communist Party. The party under Dimitrov consolidated its position in the Fatherland Front and the country. It branded its enemies and competitors as fascists and collaborators and eliminated them through people's courts or vilified them in the Communist press. Anti-Communists resigned from the Fatherland Front government and advocated a boycott of the October 1945 election. Though the Social Democrats and the Peasant Party refused to participate, the election took place and the government received 86 percent of the ballots that were cast.

Following a September 1946 referendum, conducted and controlled by the communist dominated government, the monarchy was abolished, and in October the Fatherland Front claimed 78 percent of the vote. Dimitrov became premier and Georgiev foreign minister and vice premier. In 1947 Dimitrov's government introduced a new constitution patterned on the Soviet constitution of 1936, and Bulgaria became a "people's republic." Dimitrov, however, roused the suspicion of Stalin by discussing with Tito the possibility of a Balkan federation. Though he fell in line after Tito broke with Stalin in 1948, he was summoned to Moscow, where he died under questionable circumstances on July 2, 1949.

Dimitrov was succeeded by Vasil Kolarov instead of by the heir apparent, Traicho Kostov, vice president of the Council of Ministers, who was purged for "national deviationism" and executed. When Kolarov died in early 1950, he was succeeded by Dimitrov's brother-in-law, arch-Stalinist Vulko Chervenkov.

BIBLIOGRAPHY

Crampton, R. J. *A Short History of Modern Bulgaria.* Cambridge: Cambridge University Press—Open Society Foundation, Bulgaria, 1994.

Dimitrov, Georgi. *Current Biography 1949,* New York: H. W. Wilson, 1949, 152–54.

Bernard Cook

SEE ALSO Chervenkov, Vŭlko

Dini, Lamberto (1931–)

Italian prime minister. Lamberto Dini was born on March 1, 1931. A Florentine economist, he worked for the International Monetary Fund (IMF) and then for the Banca d'Italia, where he was director general until he became minister of the treasury under Silvio Berlusconi's center-right government in 1994. When Berlusconi's government collapsed at the end of 1995, Dini was named prime minister and formed a "technicians" government. Dini was considered a political newcomer and a moderate who could therefore be accepted by most parties. However, he eventually depended on the support of the center-left parties, which created a coalition called the Olive Tree (Ulivo). Dini succeeded where others had failed in negotiating with the unions to curtail some of the escalating expenditure on pensions and started to reduce the huge deficit in the national accounts. Though he also tried to introduce some measures to make elections fairer by correcting or counterbalancing the political bias of the television stations belonging to Fininvest, an Italian media group, this was strongly resisted by Berlusconi's supporters and in practice was ineffective. Dini's cabinet of "nonpolitical technicians" had been intended as temporary, until new elections could be held in a calmer atmosphere. Dini did offer to resign in December 1995, but four months passed while the search continued for a successor whom parliament would accept. On February 16, 1996, Dini was confirmed in office pro tempore and elections were called for April 21, 1996. The elections were won by the Ulivo center-left coalition led by Romano Prodi. Dini, who had meanwhile formed a party called the Rinnovamento Italiano (Italian Renewal, RI), campaigned within the Ulivo coalition. Ulivo's leader, Prodi, an economist and university professor, became prime minister, while Dini was named minister of foreign affairs.

BIBLIOGRAPHY

Kadri, Françoise, "New Italian premier a technocrat, conservative," Agence France Presse, January 13, 1995.

Federiga Bindi Calussi

SEE ALSO Berlusconi, Silvio; Italy; Prodi, Romano

Di Pietro, Antonio (1950–)

Antonio Di Pietro initiated the legal investigation that exposed the most extensive bribery scandal in postwar Italy. As a deputy district attorney Di Pietro revealed a vast network of illegal financing used by political parties. The case, nicknamed *Tangentopoli* (Bribesville), contributed to the demise of the major political parties in Italy in 1993 and 1994.

Di Pietro was born in a poor peasant village in the Molise, of eastern Italy, in 1950. After secondary school and work as an immigrant laborer in Germany, he completed university studies in law in the late 1970s. He studied to be an investigator at the National Police Academy, and then worked as a police commissioner in both Milan and Bergamo before transferring to the state prosecutor's office in Milan in 1984.

In February 1991, Di Pietro began an investigation of kickbacks among Milan's business and political leaders. He discovered corruption on a large scale, and working with a pool of magistrates in an operation code named *Mani Pulite* (Clean Hands), the investigation soon moved out of Milan and spread through the rest of Italy, eventually involving most of the leading politicians of the country.

Di Pietro headed the prosecution in the first major trial of the *Tangentopoli* scandal. Carried on television over a six-month period in 1993–94, the trial showed how common corruption had become in Italian government. This court case also made Di Pietro for many the most admired man in Italy.

From spring of 1994 Di Pietro faced strong political pressure when the investigation focused on Prime Minister Silvio Berlusconi. At the end of the year, because of a campaign of slander directed against him, Di Pietro resigned from the judiciary. A judge in February 1996 cleared Di Pietro of charges of extortion and abuse of office, but other charges, which Di Pietro said were the result of a conspiracy by his enemies, remained.

He served as minister of public works in the government of Romano Prodi from May to November 1996. He was elected to the Italian parliament in a November 1997 by-election.

BIBLIOGRAPHY

" 'Clean Hands' Leader cleared," *The Gazette (Montreal),* February 24, 1996.

"Popular Italian Investigator says Craxi led conspiracy," Deutsche Presse–Agentur, December 16, 1996.

David Travis

SEE ALSO Berlusconi, Silvio; Craxi, Benedetto; Italy

Displaced Persons

As a result of Nazi German racial, labor, and military policies, between 2.5 million and 3 million non-German refugees and 3.5 million Soviet prisoners of war (POWs) found themselves in Germany and Austria at the end of World War II. Millions more joined them over the next few months. The Allies designated these individuals displaced persons (DPs) and established refugee camps segregated by national origin. The United Nations Relief and Rehabilitation Administration (UNRRA), created in 1943, cared for and repatriated them according to their prewar citizenship.

While most DPs wished to return to their home states, two million refused, posing a serious problem for zonal administrators. Initially, all Soviet citizens were to be repatriated regardless of personal wish, excluding citizens of the former Baltic states. During this period five million Soviets returned home, but many others feared doing so because their government had made capture by the Germans during the war a criminal offense. By late 1945 the Western Allies had ceased forcible repatriation of Soviet citizens, reflecting a deterioration in American-Soviet relations. Eastern Europeans refusing repatriation underwent an intense screening procedure during which many lost their DP status and were hence at risk of repatriation. Many were compromised by their collaboration with the Nazis and feared returning home. With restrictive immigration quotas from the 1920s still in force in the United States, non-Jewish DPs often immigrated to labor-poor countries like Canada, Britain, and Belgium. Eventually U.S. President Harry Truman convinced Congress to make a special exception for DPs, allowing 400,000 to enter before the end of 1951. An additional 185,000 were allowed to immigrate in the mid-1950s.

The Jews posed special problems for the Allies. Most concentration camp survivors had no homes to which they could return. Soon the Jewish DPs agitated for their own DP camps, which the Americans established after a scathing investigative report on camp conditions by Earl G. Harrison, Truman's personal envoy. Most wished to go to Palestine, but the British, who still ruled the mandated territory, vigorously resisted attempts at immigration. As Jewish DPs poured into the American zone of occupied Germany, the Americans pressured the British to reverse their policy. Only Israel's independence in 1948 resolved the issue.

Most DPs lived in camps located in former army bases or concentration camp barracks. They often faced squalid living conditions, little better than those they had experienced as camp inmates. Camp inhabitants soon formed self-contained communities, complete with their own religious, cultural, and governmental institutions. The DPs competed with Germans for scarce consumer goods. With special access to American goods, especially cigarettes, DP camps became known for their thriving black markets beyond the reach of German law, further straining relations between Germans and DPs.

With the onset of the Cold War and increased German-American amity, the position of the camps changed. They were now seen as an anachronism. In July 1947 the International Refugee Organization replaced UNRRA, later becoming the Office of the High Commissioner for Refugees. The West German government took over administration of the camps in 1951 and closed the last one in 1957. Those DPs unable or unwilling to emigrate remained behind, forming the core of West Germany's new Jewish and Slavic communities. After five years these former DPs became full German citizens.

BIBLIOGRAPHY

Jacobmeyer, Wolfgang. *Vom Zwangsarbeiter zum Heimatlosen Ausländer: Die Displaced Persons in Westdeutschland, 1945–1951.* Göttingen: Vandenhoeck & Ruprecht, 1985.

Proudfoot, Malcolm J. *European Refugees, 1939–52: A Study in Forced Population Movement.* Evanston Ill.: Northwestern University Press, 1956.

Wyman, Mark. *DP: Europe's Displaced Persons, 1945–1951.* Philadelphia: Balch Institute Press, 1989.

Jay Howard Geller

SEE ALSO Expellees-Refugees; Pire, Dominique

Djilas, Milovan (1911–95)

Yugoslav dissident. Milovan Djilas was born in the Kolasin region of Montenegro on June 12, 1911. His father, who served as an officer in World War I, was a landowning peasant who could hire others to work with him on his land. Djilas studied philosophy and law at the University of Belgrade. He had already been drawn to communism before entering the university, and there he became a revolutionary student leader. He was imprisoned from 1933 to 1935 for his radical activity. He met Tito in 1937, became a member of the Central Committee of the Yugoslav Communist Party in 1937, and was appointed to the Politburo in 1940.

During the resistance to the Germans during World War II, Djilas was a member of the supreme staff of the Partisan army and a member of the Presidium of the Partisan Assembly. He held a number of cabinet posts in the postwar Communist government. Tito valued Djilas's ad-

vice and he played a central role in Tito's decision to break with the Soviet Union in 1948. In January 1953 he became, with Edvard Kardelj and Aleksandar Ranković, one of the four vice presidents of Yugoslavia. However, Djilas's calls for increased liberalization of the party resulted in his condemnation by the party's Central Committee in January 1954. Djilas, who was ousted from all his party posts, was forced to resign from the presidency of the legislature. In April he renounced his party membership. He was handed an eighteen-month suspended sentence but was kept under police observation and lived in poverty. He was imprisoned for three years, however, following the publication of an article in the United States in 1956 in which he praised the Hungarian Revolution of 1956 and called it the "beginning of the end of Communism." Before his imprisonment he wrote *The New Class,* in which he decried the Communist leadership as a new class of privileged and parasitic exploiters. When the manuscript was smuggled out of Yugoslavia and published in the West, Djilas was sentenced to another seven years in prison. He was released from prison in 1961 but was sent back to jail after the publication of his *Conversations with Stalin.* He was granted an amnesty in 1966 but continued his critical writing. He died in Belgrade on April 20, 1995.

BIBLIOGRAPHY

Djilas, Milovan. *Fall of the New Class: a History of Communism's Self-destruction.* New York: Knopf, 1998.

———. *Land without Justice.* New York: Harcourt, Brace, 1958.

———. *Memoir of a Revolutionary.* New York: Harcourt Brace Jovanovich, 1973.

———. *The New Class: An Analysis of the Communist System.* San Diego: Harcourt Brace Jovanovich, 1983.

———. "The Storm in Eastern Europe." *New Leader,* November 19, 1956.

———. *The Unperfect Society: Beyond the New Class.* New York: Harcourt, Brace & World, 1969.

"Djilas, Milovan." *Current Biography 1958.* New York: H. W. Wilson, 1958, 118–20.

"Djilas, Milovan," Obituary from *New York Times,* April 21, 1995 in *Current Biography Yearbook 1995,* 618–19.

Reinhartz, Dennis. *Milovan Djilas, a Revolutionary as a Writer.* Boulder, Colo.: East European Monographs/ Columbia University Press, 1981.

Bernard Cook

Dobruja

Region on the Balkan Peninsula between the lower Danube river and the Black Sea, lying within present-day Romania and Bulgaria. Dobruja (Romanian, Dobrogea; Bulgarian, Dobrudzha) is composed largely of steppe with a total surface area of around 9,000 square miles (23,310 sq km). The population is mainly Romanian in the north and Bulgarian in the south, with small communities of Turks and Tartars scattered throughout. Its largest city, Constantsa (population 356,000), is an important Romanian port on the Black Sea.

Dobruja has long been of strategic importance. Roman Emperor Trajan's Wall ran along the region's southern border from the Danube to Constantsa (ancient Tomis). Claimed by both Bulgarian and Romanian princess, Dobruja was incorporated into the Ottoman Empire in the early fifteenth century. The Treaty of Berlin in 1878 awarded northern Dobruja to the independent Kingdom of Romania and the southern portion to Bulgaria, then an autonomous principality within the Ottoman Empire. At the close of the Second Balkan War the Treaty of Bucharest in 1913 transferred the southern region, known as the Quadrilateral, from Bulgaria to Romania. Under pressure from Nazi Germany, Romania was forced to cede the Quadrilateral to Bulgaria in the September 1940 Treaty of Craiova. This division was finalized in the postwar peace treaty of February 1947.

BIBLIOGRAPHY
Crampton, Richard. *A Short History of Modern Bulgaria.* Cambridge: Cambridge University Press, 1987.
Hitchins, Keith. *Rumania, 1866–1947.* Oxford: Oxford University Press, 1994.

Charles King

Dobrynin, Anatoly Fyodorovich (1919–)

Soviet ambassador to the United States, 1962–86. Anatoly Dobrynin, son of a worker, was born on November 16, 1919, in Krasnaya Gorka. He graduated from a technical college and earned a master's degree in history. He was an engineer in an aircraft factory during the Second World War. In 1944 he joined the Soviet diplomatic service. From 1949 to 1952 he was an assistant to the deputy foreign minister. In 1952 he posted abroad for the first time as a counselor at the Soviet Embassy in the United States. In 1954–55 as minister-counselor he was the second-ranking person at the embassy. In 1955 he returned to the Soviet Union as an ambassador extraordinary and plenipotentiary in the Foreign Ministry. He served for a while as assistant to Foreign Minister Dmitri T. Shepilov. In July 1957 he joined the Secretariat of the United Nations. The highest-ranking Soviet official serving on that level, Dobrynin developed a close working

relationship with Secretary-General Dag Hammarskjöld. In 1960 he returned to Moscow to head the American department. In the summer, however, he returned to New York to assist Foreign Minister Andrey Gromyko as he lodged complaints about the U-2 flights of the United States. In 1962 Dobrynin replaced Mikhail A. Menshikov as Soviet ambassador to the United States. His fluent English served him well and he provided a degree of continuity in Soviet relations with the United States during his twenty-four-year tenure. Because of the close contact he established with Robert Kennedy, brother of the president and U.S. attorney general, Dobrynin was able to accurately assess the U.S. administration's attitude during the Cuban missile crisis of 1962. His role as a calm conduit proved helpful in resolving the crisis.

Dobrynin was recalled to Moscow by Mikhail Gorbachev in 1986 to head the international department of the Secretariat of the Communist Party. He retired in 1988.

BIBLIOGRAPHY
"Dobrynin, Anatoly," *Current Biography 1962.* New York: H. W. Wilson, 1962, 103–5.

Bernard Cook

Dohnanyi, Klaus von (1928–)

West German economics minister (1968–69), minister of education and science (1972–74), and foreign minister (1976–81). Klaus von Dohnanyi was born on June 23, 1928, in Hamburg, the son of Hans and Christine (née Bonhoeffer) von Dohnanyi. His father, a lawyer, participated in the anti-Hitler resistance, and was arrested in 1943 and executed in April 1945. Dietrich Bonhoeffer, the noted theologian and prominent resistance figure murdered by the Nazis, was his uncle. Von Dohnanyi studied law at Munich, Columbia, Stanford, and Yale Universities. He started work with the Max Planck Institute in 1953, then served with the Ford Motor Company in Detroit, and was director of the Planning Division at the Ford plant in Cologne, Germany, from 1956 to 1960. Von Dohnanyi entered politics during the grand coalition as secretary of state of the Federal Ministry of Economy from 1968 to 1969. His performance was a boon to his Social Democratic Party, which won enough votes to form a coalition with the Free Democrats in 1969. Von Dohnanyi, who served as a Social Democratic member of the Bundestag (lower house of parliament) from 1969 to 1981, held a succession of offices in the federal government: parliamentary secretary of state for the Ministry of Education and Science (1969–72), minister of education and science (1972–74), and minister of state and parliamentary secretary of state of the West German Foreign Office (1976–81). From 1981 to 1988 he served as first bürgermeister and president of the Senate of Hamburg, a post his father held in 1928. While serving as minister of education and science, he angered Chancellor Willy Brandt by suggesting that Brandt needed a cochancellor for internal affairs. As foreign minister von Dohnanyi worked to improve relations between the Eastern and Western blocs. As mayor of Hamburg he was involved with the environmental and political activities of the Green Party.

Since 1990 von Dohnanyi has been chairman of the board of TAKRAF A.G., a company that supplies machines and systems for mining, in Leipzig, and has worked with the Treuhand, the German privatization agency. In 1994 he was appointed to a position with the Center for the Study of European Community Law at Harvard Law School. His brother, Christoph, a musician, became conductor of the Cleveland Symphony Orchestra in 1984.

BIBLIOGRAPHY

von Dohnanyi, Klaus. *Das deutschen Wagnis: Über die wirtschaftlichen und socialen Folgen der Einheit.* Munich: Knaur, 1991.

———. *Education and Youth Employment in the Federal Republic of Germany.* Berkeley, Calif.: Carnegie Council on Policy Studies in Higher Education, 1978.

———. *Regionale und Sektorale Strukturpolitik für die 80er Jahre.* Bonn: Friedrich-Ebert-Stiftung, Forschungsinstitut, 1984.

Daniel K. Blewett

Dolci, Danilo (1924–97)

Educator and founder of successful educational experiments in Sicily, Danilo Dolci led several nonviolent protests for the social and cultural development of Sicilian villages from 1950 to 1980, giving to education a central role in the fulfillment of human potentialities of development. Dolci, whose father was Italian and mother Slovenian, was born in Sesana (Trieste). He was brought up in multicultural surroundings that contributed to the main features of his personality: respect for and utilization of diversity. He soon showed his disapproval of authoritarianism and violence, which caused his imprisonment by the Fascists in 1943.

In 1952 he moved to Trappeto, a poor Sicilian village lacking almost everything, where he started his first nonviolent campaigns, fasting and promoting the people's consciousness of their needs as well as necessary changes through initiatives of popular self-analysis. Within a few years Trappeto had some public infrastructure such as roads, drainage, a library, and the Popular University. In this period Dolci wrote continuously to give voice to those who never had one as well as to report and denounce the social realities he observed: *Fare presto e bene perché si muore* (Act Quickly and Well because they are dying) (1953), *Banditi a Partinico* (Bandits at Partinico) (1955), *Inchiesta a Palermo* (Report from Palermo) (1958), which was awarded the Viareggio Prize, and *Una politica per la piena occupazione* (A Political Program for Full Employment) (1958). In 1957 he won the Lenin Prize, which provided the funds to open the Centro Studi ed Iniziative (The Center for Study and Action) in Partinico.

In 1965 he was asked by the Anti-Mafia Committee to initiate, in collaboration with his associate Franco Alasia, a campaign against the Mafia. On September 22, 1965, during a conference in Rome he denounced publicly, for the first time in Italy, the connection between politics and the Mafia, openly accusing some politicians. Despite the evidence, Dolci and Alasia were tried for slander and condemned to prison; nevertheless, Bernardo Mattarella, the Italian minister of foreign trade, and Calogero Volpe were forced to resign from the government. Dolci still continued his fight, publishing *Chi gioca solo* (The Man Who Plays Alone) in 1967. In 1968 he was awarded an Honorary degree in pedagogy by the University of Bern. He then founded an organic educational center in Mirto, in collaboration with children, adults, and pedagogists. In 1974 he published two important works: *Esperienze e riflessioni* (Experience and Reflection) and *Non esiste il silenzio,* (Silence does not exist), in which he discussed his maieutic (Socratic) method and his pedagogic theories. In addition to his social and educational commitment, he wrote poetry. *Il limone lunare* (The Lemon Moon) (1970) was awarded the Prato Prize for poetry, and in 1979 his *Creatura di Creature* (Creative of Creatures) was published.

By the 1980s his methodology had been adopted in several Italian schools, and maieutic groups of research sprang up around the world. Dolci died on December 27, 1997.

BIBLIOGRAPHY

Dolci, Danilo. *Sicilian Lives.* New York: Pantheon Books, 1981.

Mangano, Antonino. *Danilo Dolci educatore: Un nuovo modo di pensare e di essere nell'era atomica.* San Domenico di Fiesole: Edizioni Cultura della Pace, 1992.

Mangione, Jerre Gerlando. *A Passion for Sicilians: the World around Danilo Dolci.* New Brunswick, N.J.: Transaction Books, 1985.

Renda, Francesco. *Storia della Sicilia dal 1860 al 1970: Dall'occupazione militare alleata al centrosinistra.* Vol. 3. Palermo: Sellerio Editore, 1987.

Fabio Marino

Dönhoff, Marion Gräfin von (1909–)

One of the most influential publicists and journalists in West Germany from the mid-1960s through the *Wende* (collapse of Communist East Germany and the turn toward reunification) and into the late-1990s. Marion Dönhoff joined the major liberal Hamburg weekly paper *Die Zeit,* one of a handful of highly influential journals in Germany, in 1946, became political editor in 1955, editor in chief in 1968, and has been publisher since 1972.

Marion Dönhoff's childhood and early years were spent on her family's East Prussian estate, which she helped manage from the mid-1930s through the end of World War II, and her family had close connections to antifascist resistance groups. Her political commentary in *Die Zeit* has been at the heart of political dialogue in West Germany for decades, and she helped align the paper firmly with the Social Democrats. Her many books have addressed two main themes: politics and her East Prussian homeland. Her political works include studies of Konrad Adenauer, Willy Brandt, foreign policy, U.S. and South African politics, and German-Polish relations. In autobiographical and historical studies she has written elegantly and humanely about her own lost homeland. Yet this work, too, is directly political in the German context, since her essays and books on Masuria, Poland, and East Prussia are thoughtful and charitable, whereas much other literature about "lost" former German territories comes from the reactionary, revanchist right. Dönhoff has received many honors and awards, including the Theodor Heuss Prize (1966), the Heinrich Heine Prize (1988), and numerous honorary doctorates in the United States. Her latest works have addressed the problems of postunification Germany, the history of the Cold War, and her autobiography.

BIBLIOGRAPHY

Dönhoff, Marion. *Bilder, die langsam verblassen: Ostpreussische Erinnerungen.* Berlin: Siedler, 1998.

———. *Die Bundesrepublik in der Ara Adenauers.* Reinbek bei Hamburg: Rowohlt, 1963.

———. *Deutsche Auzenpolitik von Adenauer bis Brandt.* Hamburg: Wegner, 1970.

———. *Im Wartesaal der Geschichte: Vom Kalten Krieg zur Wiedervereinigung. Beiträge und Kommentare aus fünf Jahrzehnten.* Stuttgart: DVA, 1993.

———. *Kindheit in Ostpreuzen.* Berlin: Siedler, 1989.

———. *Polen und Deutsche: Die schwierge Versöhnung. Betrachtungen aus drei Jahrzehnten.* Frankfurt am Main: Luchterhand Literaturverlag, 1991.

———. *Weit ist der Weg nach Osten.* Stuttgart: DVA, 1985.

———. *Zivilisiert den Kapitalismus: Grenzen der Freiheit.* Stuttgart: DVA, 1997.

Dönhoff, Marion, et al., eds. *Weil das Land sich Ändern muss: Ein Manifest.* Hamburg: Rowohlt, 1992.

Schwarzer, Alice. *Marion Dönhoff: Ein widerständiges Leben.* Cologne: Kiepenheuer & Witsch, 1996.

Scott Denham

Douglas-Home, Alec Alexander Frederick, Baron Home of Hirsel (1903–)

British politician and prime minister. Home was elected to the House of Commons in 1931. From 1935 to 1940, he served as parliamentary private secretary to Prime Minister Neville Chamberlain. In 1951, he inherited the title Earl of Home. Home served the Conservative governments of the 1950s in ministerial posts dealing with Scottish and Commonwealth affairs. As foreign secretary from 1960 to 1963, he continued the postwar policies of the Conservative Party: alliance with the United States, maintenance of Britain's nuclear arsenal, and antipathy to socialism. When Harold Macmillan resigned as prime minister in 1963, Home's reputation for careful attention to detail, loyalty to his party's leadership, and good relations with his ministerial colleagues stood him in good stead. From the informal "soundings" taken from his colleagues he emerged as a consensus candidate of good judgment and reliable opinions. In accord with convention, he resigned his peerage and won election to the House of Commons. Facing a general election in 1964, Home's government appeared to be an extension of Macmillan's. However, it lacked the political promise that Macmillan's unsuccessful effort to join the EC had hoped to secure. The fears of his Conservative critics, that Home lacked the vigor and assertiveness to offer the electorate an appealing political image, proved to be well founded. His style of campaigning suffered from a lack of rhetorical flare, and his campaign's emphasis on British influence abroad failed to match Labour's theme of reviving the domestic economy. The election lost, Home found that his congenial temperament could not sustain the aggressive leadership needed for the political opposition. In 1965, he resigned as leader of the Conservatives. His successor, Edward Heath, was chosen on a vote of the Parliamentary Party, a reform carried out on Home's initiative. In 1975, Home headed a committee whose recommendation established that the party's leader be chosen annually by the Parliamentary Party.

From 1970 to 1974, Home served as foreign secretary in Heath's government. In 1975, Queen Elizabeth bestowed on him the title Baron Home of Hirsel, and he returned to the House of Lords. The transition from Home to Heath moved the Conservative Party's leadership away from a focus on foreign affairs flavored with upper-class gentility toward emphasis on the domestic economy and the later "conviction politics" of Margaret Thatcher.

BIBLIOGRAPHY

Jenkins, Peter. *Mrs. Thatcher's Revolution: The Ending of the Socialist Era.* New York: Random House, 1987.

Home, Alec Douglas. *The Way the Wind Blows.* London: Fontana, 1978.

Young, Kenneth. *Sir Alec Douglas Home.* Teaneck, N.J.: Fairleigh Dickinson University Press, 1970.

Robert D. McJimsey

SEE ALSO Heath, Edward; Macmillan, Harold; Thatcher, Margaret

Doyle, Roddy (1958–)

Irish dramatist and novelist. Roddy Doyle, born in Dublin, taught secondary school from 1980 to 1994. His first play, *Brownbread* (1987, published 1992), was followed by *War* (1989). Both were highly successful in Dublin theaters. His first novel, *The Commitments* (1988), was filmed by Alan Parker to worldwide acclaim, and it was followed by *The Snapper* (1990), a black comedy about the effects of an unexpected pregnancy on a Dublin family. It too has been filmed. Doyle's Dublin novels, including *The Van* (1991), are set in the fictional Dublin suburb of Barrytown. The three Dublin novels were published together in *The Barrytown Trilogy* (1992). His novel *Paddy Clarke Ha Ha Ha* (1993) won the 1994 Booker Prize.

BIBLIOGRAPHY

Paschel, Ulrike. *No Mean City?: the Image of Dublin in the Novels of Dermot Bolger, Roddy Doyle, and Val Mulkerns.* New York: P. Lang, 1998.

Michael J. Kennedy

Drach, Ivan Fedorovych (1936–)

Ukrainian poet, political figure, and civic leader. Ivan Fedorovych Drach was born on October 17, 1936, in Telizhentsi, Ukraine. Drach was the first leader of the People's Movement for Restructuring in Ukraine (RUKH), the glasnost-era pro-independence movement formed in September 1989 in Kiev. After serving in the army from 1955 to 1958, he studied philology at the Taras Shevchenko Kiev State University from 1959 to 1963 and screenplay writing at the State Film Studio of the USSR in Moscow in 1964. Drach then worked on the editorial staff of *Literaturna Ukraina* and *Vitchyzna* (Forward), and in the script department of the Kiev Artistic Film Studio. He was a member of the Shestedesiatnyky (Writers of the Sixties) (artists who came of age during the Khrushchev thaw). His poetry was criticized in the Brezhnev era for departing from the canons of socialist realism, but by the late 1960s he accommodated to the dictates of the regime. Active in the Writers' Union of Soviet Ukraine, Drach was elected to leadership positions and eventually became first secretary of the Kiev branch. He was a founding member of RUKH in 1989, and was elected the first leader of the organization. The Kiev office of the Writers' Union became the unofficial headquarters of the opposition movement. He was reelected leader of RUKH in 1991, and in 1992 was elected co-leader. In the March 1990 Ukrainian parliamentary elections he won a seat in the first round, representing the Artem district of Lvov (Ukrainian, L'viv). While a member of parliament, Drach sat on the Parliamentary Foreign Affairs Committee. In 1991 he was elected head of Tovarystvo Ukraina (the Ukranian Society), and in 1992 was elected head of its International Council. In 1995 Drach was elected head of the Presidium of the Congress of Ukrainian Intelligentsia. From 1997 he was a member of the President's Council on Language Politics. Drach's publications include the collections of poetry—*Soniashnyk* (*The Sunflower,* 1962), *Protuberantsi sertsia* (*Perturbances of the Heart,* 1965), *Poezii* (*Poems,* 1967), and *Vohon' z popelu* (*Fire from the ashes,* 1995), and several scripts that have been used as screenplays, including *Kaminnyi Khrest* (*The Stone Cross*), based on a story by Vasil' Stefanyk.

BIBLIOGRAPHY

Drach, Ivan. *Orchard Lamps.* Toronto: Exile Editions, 1989.

Marta Dyczok

Draghici, Alexandru (1913–93)

Romanian minister of the interior between 1952 and 1965 and staunch Stalinist who controlled the Communist Party's repressive apparatus, including its secret police (Securitate). Alexandru Draghici was born in Moldavia, had little formal education, worked for the railroad, and joined the Romanian Communist Party in the early 1930s. He was imprisoned from 1936 until 1944 with future leader Gheorghe Gheorghiu-Dej, who admitted him to his inner circle. Starting as a leader in the Communist youth movement after the war, he was a deputy to the 1946 National Assembly and advanced to the party's Central Committee in 1948. Between 1948 or 1949 and 1951 he was the party's first secretary in Bucharest and associated with the Ministry of the Interior as a "party instructor," where he discovered "bourgeois elements" that let Gheorghiu-Dej replace a dangerous rival, Minister of the Interior Teohari Gheorgescu, with Draghici in 1952.

After Gheorghiu-Dej's death in 1964, the new party leaders carefully eliminated Stalinists and their rivals from positions of power. Consequently, Draghici lost control of the Ministry of the Interior in 1965 and had to give up his seat on the Presidium in April 1968, which ended the career of a principal architect of Romania's police state. Immediately after the execution of Nicolae Ceauşescu in 1989, Draghici and his Hungarian wife fled to their daughter in Budapest. Hungarian authorities refused Romanian requests for his extradition. His death in December 1993 ended Romanian efforts to convict him in absentia.

Robert F. Forrest

SEE ALSO Gheorghiu-Dej, Gheorghe

Drašković, Vuk (1946–)

Serb novelist, journalist, and nationalist, proponent of a Greater Serbia. Born in Media, in the Banat region of Vojvodina on November 29, 1946, Vuk Drašković studied at the University of Belgrade and was one of the leaders of the student demonstrations of 1968. He worked for the Yugoslav press agency, Tanjug, as an international radio journalist, but returned from Africa to chair the Council of Trade Unions from 1978 to 1980. He was editor of the newspaper *Rad* from 1980 to 1985.

In 1990 Drašković founded the Serbian Renewal Movement (SPO), which he chaired. Nationalist statements and abrupt and short-lived political shifts characterized his political style. During the elections of 1990 he declared that every bit of soil on which a Serb had died belonged to the Serbian people. A controversial and contradictory personality, Drašković generally gave his ap-

proval to the policies pursued by Slobodan Milošević, the president of Serbia.

Drašković campaigned against Milošević in the 1990 election and played a central role in the anti-Milošević demonstrations of March 1991. He was also one of the leaders of the protests following Milošević's annulling of the municipal elections of November 1996. Following the retreat of Milošević in 1997, Drašković and Zoran Djindjić, the new mayor of Belgrade, with whom he led the anti-Milošević coalition, Zajedno, immediately parted ways over which of them would run against Milošević for president of Yugoslavia.

Drašković's penchant for the bizarre was displayed again in his campaign to restore the monarchy and his proposal to name the street on which Milošević lived after Draža Mihajlović, royalist leader of the wartime Chetniks who was executed by Tito after World War II.

Drašković, who at the time supported Milošević's hard-line approach to the Albanians of Kosovo, was appointed deputy premier of Serbia on January 19, 1999. He brought three members of his Serbian Renewal Movement into the Serbian government. However, on April 28, Milošević fired him because he had publicly called for an end to the conflict in Kosovo with the stationing of armed United Nations peacekeepers in the province. In early October he was almost killed in an automobile accident, which supporters claimed had been deliberately staged in an attempt to assassinate him.

Catherine Lutard
(Tr. by Bernard Cook)

Drnovsek, Ivan (1950–)

Prime minister of Slovenia. Ivan Drnovsek was born in Celje, Slovenia, on May 17, 1950. He received a Ph.D. in economics from the University of Maribor in 1986 and also studied in Norway, the United States, and Spain. After working as the financial officer of a construction company and as chief executive officer of the Ljubljanska Banka in Trbovlje, he was economic attaché at the Yugoslav Embassy in Egypt. In 1986 he was elected to the Slovene parliament and was then appointed to the Chamber of the Republics and Provinces of the Yugoslav Assembly.

On April 2, 1989, Drnovsek was elected the Slovenian representative to the collective presidency of Yugoslavia, and from May 1989 to May 1990 he was president of the presidency of Yugoslavia. As president he asked the Yugoslav parliament to allow a multiparty system. He advocated the introduction of a Western-style market economy and called for the release of all political prisoners in Yugoslav jails.

Drnovsek played a central role in the developments following Slovenia's plebiscite in favor of independence in December 1990 and the actual declaration of independence on June 25, 1991. He negotiated with the Yugoslav People's Army (JNA) during its intervention in Slovenia and was a principal representative of Slovinia during the Brioni negotiations that ended the fighting in Slovenia.

In April 1992, after the government of Lojze Peterle lost a parliamentary vote of no confidence, Drnovsek, now the leader of the Liberal Democratic Party (LDP), became prime minister. Key concerns of his government were privatization and restructuring of the banking system. In the December 1992 election, although the LDP secured the largest number of seats in the National Assembly, it fell short of a majority. In January 1993 Drnovsek, nevertheless, formed a coalition with the Slovenian Christian Democrats (SCD) and temporarily with the United List of Social Democrats (ULSD), the Greens of Slovenia, and the Social Democratic Party of Slovenia (SDPS). Drnovsek's new government helped to stabilize the economy and control inflation. Slovenia reoriented its markets toward the West and was allowed to join a number of international organizations including the United Nations, the International Monetary Fund, the World Bank, the European Bank for Reconstruction and Development, the Council of Europe, GATT, and the World Trade Organization.

Bernard Cook

Dubček, Alexander (1921–92)

First secretary of the Czechoslovak Communist Party (1968–69). A career Communist, Alexander Dubček rose to lead the 1968 reform movement in Czechoslovakia known as the Prague Spring. Forced to resign in April 1969, Dubček endured a long period of internal exile to emerge, at the insistence of post-Communist Czechoslovak President Václav Havel, as chairman of the Federal Assembly of the newly democratic Czechoslovakia in 1989. Ironically, chairman Dubček hailed the accomplishments of the Velvet Revolution in creating a pluralistic, multiparty society as the realization of the Prague Spring, even though he had denied such aims in 1968.

The Dubček family had a history of socialist activity when Alexander was born. His father, a carpenter, had been a member of a socialist group in Chicago, and was a founding member of the Czechoslovak Communist Party. Alexander spent most of his childhood in the USSR, returning to Czechoslovakia in 1938. He and his

brother fought as Czech partisans during the Second World War, and Alexander continued to work as a grassroots Communist activist for several years afterward. He became a party official in 1949, serving as secretary for his home district of Trenčin.

Dubček's rise through the party was steady, if unspectacular. He joined the organizational department of the Central Committee of the Slovak Communist Party in 1951 and became a regional secretary in 1953. In 1955 he enrolled at the Higher Political School of the USSR, and on his return in 1958 was elected regional secretary for Bratislava, the Slovak capital. He transferred to Prague in 1960 as secretary for industry to the Czechoslovak Central Committee and became first secretary of Slovakia in 1963. Still, Dubček's election as first secretary of the Czechoslovak Communist Party in January 1968 was surprising; he was virtually unknown outside Slovakia.

His selection rested on a broad coalition of Slovak nationalists and economic reformers who were more against the Stalinist policies of President Antonín Novotný than they were in favor of Dubček. As a Slovak who favored reform yet had an unquestionable Communist pedigree, Dubček was the candidate most acceptable to all groups, and he quickly assumed leadership of the reform movement. As first secretary of Slovakia, Dubček had been noted for allowing a relatively free press, and this, along with the economic policies of Ota Sik, became the fulcrum of Dubček's "action plan" to reform Czechoslovak politics and society.

The action plan aimed at combining an orthodox Communist dictatorship with a genuine popular pressure system in an open civil society, and it advanced rapidly. Hard-line Communists in all branches of government and the party were replaced by reformers throughout the spring of 1968. Novotný was forced to resign as president in March, and political discussion groups like K-231 and KAN emerged with the de facto suspension of censorship.

Though Dubček and his allies always reserved the "leading role" for the Communist Party and did not advocate withdrawal from the Soviet alliance system, the pace and direction of reform triggered fears of a chain reaction within the Soviet bloc. After a series of diplomatic meetings and conferences failed to produce a satisfactory solution, troops of the Warsaw Pact invaded Czechoslovakia in August 1968. Dubček and his allies were arrested by Soviet forces and taken, eventually, to Moscow for "negotiations." Dubček continued to serve as first secretary until April 1969; then he was removed from the Presidium and the Federal Assembly in September 1969.

Appointed ambassador to Turkey, Dubček was too potent a symbol to be trusted abroad by the new, conservative government led by Gustav Musák. Recalled in 1970, he was stripped of his membership in the Communist Party and given a job as a mechanic in the Forest Administration, a post he retained until his retirement in 1981. Dubček remained isolated and out of the public eye until the Velvet Revolution of 1989 brought democracy to Czechoslovakia. He was the presidential candidate of Civic Forum in 1989 and served as chairman of the Federal Assembly from 1989 to 1992. He was elected to parliament in June 1992 but died in October as a result of injuries suffered in an earlier automobile accident. The recipient of the 1990 Sakharov Prize awarded by the European Parliament, Dubček was a symbol of hope and humanity within the socialist bloc.

BIBLIOGRAPHY

Hochman, Jiří, ed. *Hope Dies Last: the Autobiography of Alexander Dubcek.* New York: Kodansha International, 1993.

Shawcross, William. *Dubcek and Czechoslovakia, 1968–1990.* London: Hogarth Press, 1990.

Timothy C. Dowling

SEE ALSO Novotný, Antonín; Sik, Ota

Duclos, Jacques (1896–1975)

French Communist leader. A founder of the French Communist Party (Parti Communiste Français, PCF), Jacques Duclos was a member of successive French legislatures and a candidate for president of France in 1969.

Born in southern France and trained as a pastry chef, Duclos was wounded and captured in World War I. A Socialist after the war, he joined the breakaway PCF in 1920. After two years at the Moscow Party School (1924–25), he joined the PCF Central Committee and was elected to the French Chamber of Deputies. Simultaneously a member of the Comintern Executive Committee, he carried out various international missions for the Soviets. A thirty-year sentence for subversion in 1927, soon annulled by the legislature, marked the first of several brief periods of imprisonment. In 1936 Duclos served as vice president of the chamber while the PCF supported Léon Blum's popular front government.

The Hitler-Stalin pact of 1939 obliged the party to oppose the French declaration of war against Germany in September 1939 after the Germans, and later the Soviets, invaded and occupied Poland, and it was outlawed. Party activists and deputies went underground while its con-scripted leader, Maurice Thorez, deserted the French army and fled to Moscow, where he remained until 1944. Left in effective control, Duclos edited the party newspaper, L'Humanité, throughout the war and helped lead the struggle against the Germans after Hitler invaded the USSR in 1941. An anti-Vichy proclamation, "Appeal," which he signed in June 1940 was proclaimed by the PCF, with strategic postwar editing, to be the first authentic act of the French Resistance.

With the Liberation and Thorez's reappearance, Duclos returned to the Chamber of Deputies after the Liberation. He also served as PCF delegate to the Cominform in 1947–49. When a stroke sent Thorez to the USSR for treatment, and de facto detention for angering Stalin, from 1950 to 1953, Duclos again assumed party leadership, delivering the official party eulogy on Stalin's death in 1953. Thorez's return again saw Duclos demoted and forced to undergo self-criticism at the 1954 party congress. With a seat in the Senate after 1958, Duclos saw his influence in the party decline, and the more moderate Waldeck Rochet took over from Thorez in 1964. Always a vigorous campaigner, Duclos was nominated as the PCF candidate for president in 1969, but his impressive 21.5 percent third-place showing in the first round did not seriously impede the election of Georges Pompidou.

In the labyrinthine politics of the PCF, Duclos with his Soviet training and Comintern background was widely seen as Moscow's mouthpiece in the PCF, and a rival to Thorez. Thorez's leadership was Stalinist and included a considerable personal popularity cult, but he saw the party's future in France as part of a popular front–style government, a goal the USSR and Duclos intermittently opposed. In addition, Duclos's habitual sarcasm, southern French accent, and pastry lover's girth did not fit the robust proletarian image Thorez had cultivated for the party's leadership.

BIBLIOGRAPHY

Duclos, Jacques. *Mémoires.* Paris: Fayard, 1972.

Robrieux, Philippe. *Histoire intérieure du parti communiste.* 5 vols. Paris: Fayard, 1981–85.

Wall, Irwin. *French Communism in the Era of Stalin.* Westport, Conn.: Greenwood, 1983.

David Longfellow

SEE ALSO Eurocommunism; Marchais, Georges; Thorez, Maurice

Duda-Gracz, Jerzy (1941–)

Controversial Polish artist especially popular with youth. Jerzy Duda-Graz was born on Mach 20, 1941, in Częstochowa. He studied there at the Fine Arts College and at the graphics department of the Academy of Fine Arts in Kraków.

Duda-Gracz calls himself a "journalist." He pokes fun at typical Polish vices and weaknesses by transforming painted figures and placing them in surreal landscapes and interiors. His fascination with Bruegel is visible.

His favorite technique is oil paining; less known are his engravings and sketches. The most frequently repeating motifs of Duda-Gracz's works are those of religion, patriotism, and silhouettes of ugly women. His best-known series of paintings are "The Compatriots" dealing with Poles from Silesia who immigrated to Germany; "The Polish Motifs," depicting the reality of the 1970s; and "The Jura Landscapes," depicting the artist's home region, Jura Krakowsko-Częstochowska. His early series, "The Ghetto," was not preserved.

Duda-Gracz teaches at the Academy of Fine Arts in Katowice and since 1992 also at the European Fine Arts Academy in Warsaw, the first private fine arts school of higher education in Poland.

BIBLIOGRAPHY

Duda-Gracz, Jerzy. *Jerzy Duda-Gracz*. Warsaw: Arkady, 1985.

Tomasz Marciniak

Dudayev, Dzhokhar Musayevich (1944–96)

Leader of the movement for Chechen independence. Dzhokhar Dudayev was born on April 15, 1944, in Soviet Kazakhstan. As a result of Soviet dictator Stalin's forced relocation of the Chechen and Ingush peoples, Dudayev's family was deported to Kazakhstan from their village of Yalkhori in what had been the Chechen-Ingush Autonomous Republic. Dudayev and his family returned in 1957 to a reestablished Chechen-Ingush Autonomous Republic after Premier Nikita Khrushchev had denounced Stalin's policy and rehabilitated the Chechens.

Dudayev attended evening school and qualified as an electrician. He entered the Soviet Air Force and graduated from the Tambov Military Aviation School for Pilots in 1966. He was stationed in Siberia and Ukraine with a heavy bomber unit. After joining the Communist Party in 1968, he studied at the Gagarin Air Force Academy in Monino, east of Moscow, from 1971 to 1974. By 1987 he had risen to the rank of major general and was placed in command of the strategic air base at Tartu, Estonia.

In May 1990 he retired from the air force and returned to Chechnya to enter the political fray amid the increasing political uncertainty and confusion gripping the late Soviet Union. In November 1990 Dudayev was elected head of the Executive Committee of the opposition National Congress of the Chechen People. He took advantage of the failed coup against Soviet leader Mikhail Gorbachev to oust the Supreme Soviet of the autonomous republic, which had supported the August coup attempt. On October 27 Dudayev was elected president by 84 percent of the electorate. Though the Ingush refused to go along, Dudayev declared Chechnya sovereign on November 1. President Boris Yeltsin declared a state of emergency and sent troops to Grozny, the Chechen capital. As they would do so many times, the Russians completely underestimated their Chechen opponents, and their attempt at force was a miserable failure.

Dudayev, whom many Chechens opposed because of the state of the economy or rampant crime, dissolved the Chechen parliament on July 4, 1993, and assumed dictatorial power. President Yeltsin sought to bolster his own waning popularity by forcefully reasserting Russian authority in Chechnya. Despite Dudayev's willingness to accept a degree of autonomy short of independence, Yeltsin tried to overthrow him with Russian Interior Ministry troops and Chechen collaborators on November 26, 1994. This fifth Russian use of force failed, as had the other four and as would subsequent efforts. However, the discovery that Russian personnel were involved in the November 28 effort to topple Dudayev coupled with Yeltsin's subsequent ultimatum demanding submission were enough to rally the vast majority of Chechens behind Dudayev as their national leader against the Russians.

Persuaded by Defense Minister Pavel Grachev that Russia's honor and, perhaps more significantly, Yeltsin's own position were at stake. Russian forces launched a major invasion on December 11, 1994. As their plans and estimates went awry, Grachev on December 30 sent Russian troops and tanks into Grozny in an ill-conceived effort that turned to disaster. Dudayev directed resistance from his presidential palace in the heart of the city. The Russians were not able to take the city until the end of January after their artillery and aircraft had leveled much of it. Dudayev and the Chechen fighters withdrew to the countryside, where they continued the struggle.

On the night of April 21–22, 1996, as the war between Chechnya and Russia continued, Dudayev was killed near the village of Geki Chu. The Russians claimed that his death was the result of intra-Chechen rivalries. Most believe that the Russians were responsible, though versions of the story vary from a rocket attack, a bomb planted in his car, to even a smart bomb targeted on his cell phone. On April 23 Zelimkhan Yandarbiyev, Chechen vice president, assumed the presidency, and in August, after a successful Chechen attack on the Russians in Grozny, the Russians signed a treaty with the Chechens that ended the war and granted, though the Yeltsin government would strenuously deny this.

The invasion of Dagestan by Chechen militants in the summer of 1999 and terrorist attacks in Russia was followed by a Russian invasion of Chechnya in October 1999.

BIBLIOGRAPHY

Gall, Carlotta. *Chechnya: Calamity in the Caucasus.* New York: New York University Press, 1998.

Lieven, Anatol. *Chechnya: Tombstone of Russian Power.* New Haven: Yale University Press, 1998.

Bernard Cook

SEE ALSO Chechnya; Dagestan

Dukes, Alan (1945–)

Irish politician. Alan Dukes, in a contest against Peter Barry and John Bruton, replaced Garret FitzGerald as leader of the centrist Fine Gael party in 1987. Dukes served as an economist with the Irish Farmers Association in 1967 and 1968; he was its chief economist from 1969 to 1972, director of the Irish Farmers Association in Brussels from 1973 to 1976, and personal adviser to the cabinet of European Commissioner Richard Burke from 1977 to 1980. Dukes was elected as Fine Gael member of the Dàil (Irish parliament) for Kildare in 1981. On his first day in the Dàil he was appointed minister for agriculture. In 1982 he became minister for finance and held that post until 1986. Though his hands were tied by Fine Gael's Labour coalition partners, Dukes tried to control Ireland's ailing public finances. He also played a role in international economic policy as a governor of the European Investment Bank, the International Monetary Fund, and the International Bank for Reconstruction and Development. In 1986 and 1987 he served as minister for justice. As leader of Fine Gail after 1987, Dukes attempted to broaden the party's base of support against encroachments by the Progressive Democrats. However, his 1987–1990 "Tallaght Strategy" of general support for the center-right Fianna Fail party's economic policies lost him party support and cost him the leadership of Fine Gael in 1990. Dukes, a technocrat, lacked the tact and diplomacy of a proper politician. Politically and economically he has been characterized as a liberal, centrist, and social democrat.

Michael J. Kennedy

Durzinda, Mikulas (1955–)

Slovak prime minister. Mikulas Dzurinda was born on February 4, 1955, in Spisska Stvrtka. He graduated in economics from the Advanced School of Transportation and Communication in Zilina, then worked as a manager on the state railway, where he helped to introduce computerization and automated systems. After the Slovak Transport and Communications Ministry was set up in 1991, he became the economic assistant to the minister. Dzurinda held that position until June 1992, when he was elected to the Slovak parliament, where he became the spokesperson for the Christian Democratic Movement (KDH) on economic issues. In March 1994 he became the minister of transport, communications, and public works in the government of Jozef Moravcik.

On September 27, 1998, Slovak voters rejected the government of Vladimir Mečiar. Although Mečiar's Movement for a Democratic Slovakia emerged as the largest party, it won only 27 percent of the vote and 43 seats in a 150-seat parliament. The Slovak Democratic Coalition (SKD), headed by Durzinda and consisting of the Christian Democrats, Greens, Social Democrats, Democratic Union, and Democratic Party, won 26 percent of the vote and 42 seats, but the three other opposition parties, the most important of which was the Party of the Democratic Left, headed by Jozef Migas, received 32 percent of the vote and 51 seats. This made an anti-Mečiar government, headed by Durzinda, possible and also made it feasible to elect a new president. Slovakia had been without a president since March 1998, when the term of Michal Kovač expired. The three-fifths of parliament necessary to elect a president could not be achieved, and Mečiar had merely assumed most of the powers of his political enemy Kovač.

Bernard Cook

SEE ALSO Kovac, Michal; Mečiar, Vladimír

Dutschke, Rudi (1940–79)

The most popular leader of West German student radicals in the 1960s. Rudi Dutschke was born on March 7, 1940, in Schoenfeld, later part of East Germany. In 1960 he fled to West Berlin, where for the next six years he studied sociology at the Free University. He also helped found the Sozialistische Deutsche Studentenbund (German Socialist Student League, SDS), and assumed leadership of its Berlin branch.

Dutschke aroused more emotion than any other postwar German political figure. Nicknamed "Red Rudi," he borrowed elements from Marx, Trotsky, Mao, Che Guevara, Herbert Marcuse, and the Bible, rejecting Soviet-style communism as hopelessly tainted by Stalinism.

Like his American counterparts, Dutschke began as a critic of university "authoritarianism," but soon his protest expanded. Dutschke's position as a preeminent radical student leader began when he led a 1967 protest against the visit of the Shah of Iran to West Berlin. He attracted thousands to his radical views by eloquently denouncing the shooting death of a student by the police. Subsequently he deplored the Christian Democrat–Social Democrat coalition government (1966–69), which, he charged, eliminated all meaningful parliamentary opposition. The Vietnam War also became a focus of his protest.

In Dutschke's view, West Germany was a sham democracy, with the politicians and their accomplices, especially conservative press magnate Axel Springer, using their power to manipulate the masses. For the moment, only students could offer an effective opposition. Dutschke advocated a determined, though nonviolent, agitation that he hoped would ultimately lead to the emergence of participatory democracy. His dream was of a new world order of such states.

On April 11, 1968, a young neo-Nazi shot and critically wounded Dutschke in Berlin. The incident sparked days of student rioting across West Germany. After successful surgery, Dutschke sought further medical treatment in Britain; he also enrolled at Cambridge University. But in 1971 the Conservative government expelled him essentially on the basis of his reputation. He resettled in Denmark, where the University of Aarhus hired him to teach sociology.

Dutschke returned to West Germany periodically to dabble in radical politics and journalism. By the late 1970s he was moving toward support of the environmentalist Green Party. On December 24, 1979, Dutschke, one of the most visible symbols of the radicalism of the 1960s, drowned in his bathtub, the result of a fainting spell related to his old wounds.

BIBLIOGRAPHY
Chaussy, Ulrich. *Die drei Leben des Rudi Dutschke: Eine Biographie.* Darmstadt; Neuwied: Luchterhand, 1983.
Shabecoff, Philip. "The Followers of Red Rudi Shake Up Germany." *New York Times Magazine,* April 28, 1968, 26–27, 115–19.

Sheldon Spear

SEE ALSO Springer, Axel

Dzemyantsei, Mikalai (1931–)

High-ranking official of the Communist Party of Belarus (CPB) who chaired the Presidium of the Supreme Soviet of the Belarusan SSR in 1990–91.

Born on May 10, 1931, to Belarusan peasants in Khotlina, Mikalai Dzemyantsei graduated from the Belarusan Agricultural Academy in 1959. The agronomist rose steadily in the CPB, which he joined in 1957. He held low-ranking positions in regional party committees in Vitebsk from 1958 to 1966. He was first secretary of the Ushachy raion party committee and head of the agricultural section of the Vitebsk district party committee from 1966 to 1970. Dzemyantsei then became inspector of the Central Committee of the CPB (1970–74) and secretary of the Vitebsk district party committee (1974–77). From 1977 to 1979, Dzemyantsei headed the agricultural department of the Central Committee of the CPB. In 1979, he became a full member and secretary of the Central Committee, of which he had been a candidate member from 1971 to 1976.

Under Soviet leader Mikhail Gorbachev, Dzemyantsei was people's deputy of the USSR and deputy chairman of the Presidium of the Supreme Soviet of the USSR. From 1989 to 1991 he was also a member of the Commission on Nationalities Policy and Intra-Nationalities Relations of the USSR. In July 1989 he became chairman of the Presidium of the Supreme Soviet of the BSSR. His failure to oppose the 1991 coup against Gorbachev cost him his post and ended his career as a conservative Communist.

Karel C. Berkhoff

SEE ALSO Belarus; Shushkevich Stanislau

E

Eanes, António dos Santos Ramalho (1935–)

President of Portugal from 1976 to 1986. General António dos Santos Ramalho Eanes had a distinguished military career as an officer in Portuguese Asia and Africa. During his presidency he was instrumental in the consolidation of Portuguese democracy and in the depoliticization of the Portuguese military.

Eanes was born in Alcains in 1935 to a family of modest means. In 1953 he enrolled in the Military Academy. After graduating in 1956 he continued his studies by attending class at the Lisbon Faculty of Law and the Institute for Applied Psychology. From 1958 to 1974 Eanes had a distinguished military career, serving in the Portuguese colonies in Africa and Asia. He served tours of duty as a commissioned officer in Portuguese India from 1958 to 1960, in Macau in 1962, and in Mozambique from 1962 to 1966. He also served as operations officer in Mozambique from 1966 to 1968, and as information officer in Guinea-Bissau from 1969 to 1973, and in Angola in 1973–74, where he held the rank of major.

Disillusioned with the hopelessness of the colonial conflict and the government's unwillingness to seek nonmilitary solutions, he joined in the Armed Forces Movement Conspiracy, which overthrew the Caetano government on April 25, 1974, but did not participate in the actual revolution as he was still in Angola. Shortly after the revolution, interim president General António de Spinola summoned him to Lisbon and made him a member of the ad hoc committee on the mass media in June 1974. Shortly afterward Eanes was promoted to director of programming and in September became chairman of the board of Portuguese Television. During his tenure he gained a reputation for scrupulous objectivity and neutrality, which brought him into conflict with the powerful Portuguese Communist Party. He was forced to reign his post in March 1975 because of his decision to permit impartial coverage of the March 11, 1975, coup attempt by conservative supporters of former President Spinola. Once cleared of the accusation of complicity, he resumed his military duties in the General Staff and was promoted to lieutenant colonel. As the political chaos intensified during the "hot summer" of 1975, Eanes aligned himself with the moderate officers (Group of Nine) whose activities challenged the leftist control of the government and the armed forces. During the far-left coup attempt in late November 1975, interim President Francisco Costa Gomes entrusted Eanes with organizing the resistance. He succeeded in crushing the coup with minimum violence. In December Eanes was appointed army chief of staff and promoted to general. He immediately began the process of reforming the army. He also served as a member of the Council of the Revolution, which approved the new democratic constitution in December 1975.

In May 1975 Eanes announced his candidacy for the presidency on a firm anti-Communist platform, while supporting the constitutional mandate for democratic socialism, restoration of law and order, strengthening the economy, and consolidation of democracy. He received the support of the three non-Communist parties and was elected president with 61.54 percent of the vote on June 27. After taking office on July 14, he appointed Socialist Party leader Mario Soares as prime minister.

During his two terms in office from 1976 to 1980 and from 1980 to 1986, President Eanes was instrumental in providing stability and in consolidating democratic institutions. After the election of April 25, 1976, the Portuguese parliament was divided among four major parties, with the Socialist Party holding only 107 of the 260 seats. President Eanes and a series of prime ministers faced the political instability resulting from two years of revolutionary excesses, a stagnant economy, and high trade deficits.

The inability of Soares's minority government to deal with these problems led to its collapse in December 1977. Eanes encouraged Soares to form a coalition with the Center Democratic Party, but it, too, fell apart in July 1978. In view of the inability of any party to form a government, Eanes named a nonpartisan technocrat, Alfredo Jorge Nobre da Costa, as premier. When he failed to receive parliamentary approval, Eanes again took the initiative by naming Carlos Alberto da Mota Pinto as prime minister. The new government won approval of its program but as the political bickering worsened, it resigned in June 1979. Eanes next appointed Maria de Lurdes Pintasilgo as premier, dissolved parliament, and called for new elections. In the elections that followed, a conservative coalition (Aliança Democratica) won a bare majority, and Eanes appointed its leader, Francisco de Sá Carneiro, as premier. In December 1980 Sá Carneiro was killed in a plane crash and Eanes appointed the new head of the coalition, Francisco Pinto Balsemão, as premier. Also in December 1980, Eanes won election to a second presidential term as a nonparty candidate, although with the informal support of the Socialists and Communists, despite the bitter opposition of the Aliança Democratica.

During his second term as President, Eanes saw his powers curtailed by the Constitutional Revision of 1982, especially with reference to his ability to appoint prime ministers by presidential initiative. This revision concluded the transition to democratic institutions indicated by the revolution of April 1974, when it abolished the Council of the Revolution and substituted for it the Council of State, thus ending the role of the military in politics. This was made possible by Eanes's efforts in reforming and depoliticizing the military during the period 1976–79, in which Eanes was both president and chief of the General Staff. In the winter of 1983 the Balsemão coalition fell apart and Eanes was forced to call early elections. The Socialists received only a plurality of seats but remained in office until June 1985 through an informal coalition with the Social Democrats. When in 1985 it became clear that within the context of the existing assembly it was impossible to form a government, Eanes again called elections. Unlike previous elections, in addition to the four established political parties, a new party, the Democratic Renewal Party, created with the support of President Eanes, fielded candidates. Despite this, the Social Democrats won a plurality and formed a government. Having served the two terms permitted under the constitution, Eanes turned power over to a new president on March 9, 1986. In 1986–87 he served as leader of the Democratic Renewal Party. Afterward, except for retaining his seat on the Council of State, he left the political scene.

While president, Eanes insured the consolidation of democratic institutions by serving as the center of stability amid the confusion of constantly changing governments and by reforming and depoliticizing the military. As head of state he also fostered better relations with the former Portuguese colonies by exchanging state visits with their presidents.

BIBLIOGRAPHY

Popovic, Dragisa. *Eanes entre o ontem e o amanha.* Lisbon: Nova Nordica, 1986.
Silva, Rola da. *Eanes e os misterios de Macau,* 2nd ed. Lisbon: Vozes da Tribo, 1985.

Paul Brasil

SEE ALSO Pintasilgo, Maria de Lourdes; Portugal; Soares, Mario

Eco, Umberto (1932–)

Italian philosopher and novelist. Umberto Eco studied philosophy at the University of Turin. His dissertation was on the problem of the aesthetic in Aquinas. Eco has been a collaborator in the cultural department of Italian Television (RAI); professor for aesthetics at the University of Turin and Milan; visiting professor at the universities of São Paulo, New York, Buenos Aires, as well as Northwestern University; and professor for semiotics and director of the Institute for Communication Theory and Theater Arts at the University of Bologna. In 1988 he became president of the University of San Marino. He was also cofounder of the avant-gardist "gruppo 63."

Although the novels *The Name of the Rose* (1980) and *Foucault's Pendulum* (1988) secured Eco's fame, his significance was already established by the publication of his numerous works on semiotics. In 1967 he published *La struttura asserte* (*Introduction to Semiotics*), in 1976 *A Theory of Semiotics,* and in 1992 *Limits of Interpretation.* In addition, he has published writings on aesthetics and history; essays in cultural criticism; and numerous columns, literary miniatures, and parodies. The connecting piece of all these heterogeneous projects has been semiotics as a fundamental philosophy of the sign. It implies the foundation of a theory of culture insofar as signs exist only in the context of culture and, in turn, culture is expressed through the production of signs. Correspondingly, his aesthetic and cultural-historical writings can be considered contributions to a theory of symbolic production, whereas his cultural-critical essays have to be understood as applicatory models toward a semiotics of everyday life. The novels, on the other hand, are to be read in terms of a "narrative semiotics," that is, an exemplification of theory and meta-narrative speculation according to the maxim: "What cannot be said theoretically, that has to be narrated."

Thus, Eco's position in philosophy places itself within the cultural conditions of the late twentieth century. Against the one-sidedness of both modernity and postmodernity, Eco warns that neither reason nor the desiderata of the nondiscursive form a conclusive answer, since both lead into impossible alternatives: either into destruction or madness. Correspondingly, Eco's position lies "between" modernity and postmodernity, for one can criticize the fatality of an independent reason without falling prey to the cult of an irrationalist counter-Enlightenment; and one can criticize the excesses of irrationalism without subscribing to sterile rationalism. And the theoretical program of semiotics, through its patient labor on the concrete and the respective social reality and culture, attempts to work within this narrow gap between a critique of rationality and a critique of the critique of rationality by following a logic of discovery founded in prudence as the kind of rationality always already marked by the insight into its own regionality and limitation.

BIBLIOGRAPHY

Bondanella, Peter E. *Umberto Eco and the Open Text: Semiotics, Fiction, Popular Culture.* Cambridge: Cambridge University press, 1997.

Erik Vogt

Eden, Anthony (1897–1977)

Conservative prime minister of Great Britain from 1955 to 1957. Anthony Eden earned his reputation as a foreign affairs expert through his three terms of service as Britain's foreign secretary (1935–38, 1940–45, and 1951–55).

After serving in the British army during the First World War, Eden studied at Christ Church, Oxford, before launching his public career in 1923, when he was elected to the House of Commons. Eden quickly demonstrated his interest in foreign affairs, and in 1931 he was appointed undersecretary of state for foreign affairs. In December 1935 Prime Minister Stanley Baldwin appointed him foreign secretary. Eden continued to serve in that capacity under Prime Minister Neville Chamberlain until 1938. He openly broke with Chamberlain when he denounced the prime minister's appeasement of Hitler's expansionism on the continent. In 1939 Eden returned to Chamberlain's government as secretary of state for the

dominions. By late 1940 Eden was once again foreign secretary in the coalition government led by Prime Minister Winston Churchill. After the Conservative defeat in July 1945, Eden served as the shadow foreign secretary and in October 1951 began his third term as foreign secretary, in Churchill's second ministry. Eden was also recognized as deputy prime minister and the person in line to succeed Churchill. During this term as British foreign secretary Eden made substantive contributions to solidifying the Western alliance by negotiating settlements over Trieste and Iranian oil. However, Eden's health declined notably in this period.

In April 1955 Eden became prime minister upon Churchill's resignation. Eden's tenure as prime minister focused on foreign affairs at the expense of mounting domestic problems. In 1956, Egypt announced that it would seize the Suez Canal; in response Eden entered into a secret alliance with France and Israel. In November the coalition attacked Egypt but was forced to bow to American pressure to have U.N. forces replace their units in the field; Suez remained under Egyptian control. While Eden enjoyed a measure of support from the British public, his effectiveness as a Western leader was gone after Suez. In January 1957 he resigned and was replaced as prime minister by Harold Macmillan.

BIBLIOGRAPHY

Carlton, David. *Anthony Eden: A Biography.* London: Allen Lane, 1981.

Dutton, David. *Anthony Eden: A Life and Reputation.* London: Arnold, 1997.

Peter, A. R. *Anthony Eden at the Foreign Office, 1931–1938.* New York: St. Martin's Press, 1986.

Rhodes James, Robert. *Anthony Eden.* New York: McGraw-Hill, 1987.

Rothwell, Victor. *Anthony Eden: A Political Biography 1931–1957.* Manchester: Manchester University Press, 1992.

William T. Walker

SEE ALSO Churchill, Winston; Suez Crisis

Einaudi, Luigi (1874–1961)

Italian economist and politician, president of Italy from 1948 to 1955. Born in Carrù (Piedmont) in 1874, Luigi Einaudi graduated from the University of Turin, where he subsequently taught science of finance and political economics. In 1919 his political activity led him to be appointed a senator of the kingdom. After the accession of Mussolini he remained faithful to his own liberal ideas, and in 1926 gave up his post at the university. The articles he contributed to some Italian and foreign papers, such as the *Economist,* expressed his opposition to fascism.

In 1943 he fled to Switzerland, returning to Italy after World War II when he was nominated governor of the Bank of Italy. In 1946 he was elected to the Constituent Assembly. He fought in favor of the adoption of a majority electoral system with uninominal constituencies, on the model of the British and U.S. systems. He predicted that the proportional system would increase the power of parties to the detriment of the independence of single deputies.

In 1947 Einaudi entered the fourth ministry of Alcide De Gasperi, acting as vice president and minister of finance. During his tenure he was able to leave his mark on the Italian economic policy of the era. The "Einaudi deal" was founded on the restriction of bank credit to balance the state deficit, enabling the government to curb inflation and stabilize the purchasing power of the lira. Einaudi's prestige was due to the success of his economic policy and to the consistency of his work, and was at the same time anti-Fascist and anti-Communist. He was elected president of Italy in May 1948. When his term of office expired in 1955, he became a life member of the Senate. He died in Rome in 1961.

Einaudi is to be numbered with the founders of the European Economic Community (EEC), as he often supported the idea of a federation of European states through his work and his political activity. Einaudi's financial theories and history of economic doctrines continue to have remarkable importance and place him among the masters of Italian liberal doctrine.

BIBLIOGRAPHY

Cressati, Claudio. *L'Europa necessaria: Il federalismo liberale di Luigi Einaudi.* Torin: G. Giappichelli, 1992.
Delzell, Charles F. *Italy in the Twentieth Century.* Washington, D.C.: American Historical Association, 1980.

Dario Caronitti

Eldjarn, Kristjan (1916–82)

Third president of Iceland. After studying archaeology at the University of Copenhagen, Kristjan Eldjarn completed a master's degree in Icelandic studies at the University of Iceland in 1944, and in 1957 he defended his doctoral dissertation. In 1945 Eldjarn became an assistant at the Icelandic National Museum and was appointed director in 1947. In that capacity he served as the leading authority on all archaeological research in Iceland for over two decades. Eldjarn held this position until he entered the presidential race of 1968.

The elections of 1968 marked a watershed in Icelandic presidential politics. Eldjarn's victory with nearly two-thirds of the vote demonstrated a clear preference for the principle of a nonpartisan president among the voters. He ran unopposed in 1972 and 1976, but retired at the end of his third term.

After Eldjarn retired, the University of Iceland awarded him an honorary professorship, but his death in 1982 prevented him from pursuing a further academic career.

Gudmundur Halfdanarson

Elizabeth II (1926–)

Queen of Great Britain (1952–), elder daughter and successor to George VI. Born on April 21, 1926, to George, duke of York, and Elizabeth, duchess of York, Princess Elizabeth was third in the line of succession to the throne after her uncle, Edward, prince of Wales, and her father. The possibility of her eventually ruling England seemed remote; however, with the abdication of Edward VIII in 1936, her father became King George VI, and Elizabeth became heir to the throne.

Elizabeth married Lieutenant Philip Mountbatten (known as Prince Philip of Greece until he was naturalized as a British citizen) on November 20, 1947. After becoming queen, she gave him the title of duke of Edinburgh in 1957. They had four children. The first, Charles, was born in 1948. He was followed by Anne in 1951, Andrew in 1960, and Edward in 1964.

Elizabeth was crowned on June 2, 1953, in Westminster Abbey. The first diplomatic crisis of the new queen's reign began on July 26, 1956, when Egypt nationalized the Suez Canal. The failed invasion of Egypt by British and French troops on October 29, 1956, made manifest Britain's loss of world power and signaled the beginning of imperial disintegration, a theme that dominated the queen's reign as most of her former colonies became independent.

Many of Elizabeth's problems have resulted from money and requests to increase the civil list, which provides the monarch and her family with a set annual income. The queen's vast personal wealth and her tax-exempt status caused friction, as opposition to the royal immunity from taxation grew. This crisis was temporarily put on hold with the 1977 Silver Jubilee, which marked the twenty-fifth anniversary of the queen's accession. The anniversary resulted in much public interest in the monarchy that was overwhelmingly positive.

A new and not entirely respectful attitude toward the monarchy emerged in the 1980s. Attention was especially focused on the antics of the queen's children, especially Prince Charles and Prince Andrew. The marriage of Prince Charles and Lady Diana Spencer in 1981 spawned a media frenzy. The audacity of the tabloid reporters grew, and criticisms of the royal family, though not so much of the queen, became frequent. The queen remained largely exempt from criticism except on the tax issue. Overall, she aroused much less interest and received less coverage than the younger generation of the royal family.

In November 1992, a fire at Windsor Castle caused heavy damage, and since the structure was uninsured, the government paid the repair bill of £20 – £40 million. This announcement caused an uproar and may have influenced the announcement in late November that the queen and her husband would pay tax on their private income from 1993 and that civil list payments to five members of the royal family would cease. Most people assumed that she agreed to pay taxes because of a tabloid campaign, and as a result, this concession was offered too late. Others were annoyed that neither the amount of tax paid nor the size of the fortune were revealed.

But the greatest crisis faced by the monarchy during Elizabeth's reign stemmed largely from the negative publicity surrounding the marriages and romantic pursuits of the princes Charles and Andrew. Both of their marriages ended in highly public, embarrassing divorces that heaped ridicule on the royal family and, indirectly, on the institution of the monarchy. The queen received the most intense criticism following the death in 1997 in an automobile accident of Diana, Princess of Wales, the ex-wife of Prince Charles. Diana had remained extremely popular with the British public, and her death created an outpouring of national grief. When the public felt overwhelmingly that the royal family's response to Diana's death was cold and uncaring, the queen was forced to give a nationally televised talk assuring her subjects of her devotion to the memory of Diana.

But Elizabeth weathered that storm and continued to perform her royal duties. Despite the embarrassing publicity surrounding her children and the inevitable periodic calls for the end of monarchy as an institution, the queen continues to enjoy the abiding respect of the British people.

Though her reign has not coincided with a period of rising national power or wealth, it is difficult to find major mistakes on her part. As she entered her mid-70s, Elizabeth showed no sign of slowing down or abdicating for her son, and it was assumed that she will continue to reign until her death.

BIBLIOGRAPHY

Pimlott, Ben. *The Queen: A Biography of Elizabeth II.* New York: John Wiley & Sons, Inc., 1996.

Hamilton, Willie. *My Queen and I.* London: Quartet Books, 1975.

Rebecca Hayes
Richard Steins

SEE ALSO Charles, Prince of Wales; George VI; Suez Crisis

Ellemann-Jensen, Uffe (1941–)

Danish journalist and politician. Born in 1941, Uffe Ellemann-Jensen worked successively as a journalist at *Berlingske Aftensavis* from 1967 to 1970, economic reporter at Danish TV (Danmarks Radio) from 1970 to 1975, and editor in chief of *Børsen,* the main organ of Danish business from 1975 to 1976. He was elected to parliament for the Liberal Party (Venstre) in 1977 and became party spokesman in 1978, then party chairman in 1984. He served as minister for foreign affairs from 1982 to 1993 in the liberal-conservative government of the same period. Subsequently, with his experience and talent for debate, he became the de facto leader of the opposition.

In the first part of the 1980s as minister for foreign affairs, Ellemann-Jensen had implement a decision by parliament to postpone the NATO deployment of middle-range missiles in Europe. A strong supporter of NATO, he did not fully agree with this decision. He relegated the parliamentary position to footnotes appended to many NATO communiqués from Denmark. As a result he was often the object of heavy criticism from the opposition and the peace movement.

Ellemann-Jensen's strong support for the European Union (EU) often brought him into conflict with the strong anti-EU opinion in Denmark. When a majority of Danes said no in a referendum on the Maastricht Treaty in June 1992, Ellemann-Jensen viewed it as a severe setback for his aspirations. However, he was able together with Prime Minister Poul Schlüter to convince the other EU leaders to grant Denmark certain exceptions to the Maastricht Treaty.

After the resignation of Willy Claes as secretary-general of NATO in the fall of 1995, Ellemann-Jensen was a strong candidate. He was supported by the United States, but his candidacy was defeated by the French government, which reputedly wanted to punish Denmark for strong protests against French nuclear tests and also desired a French-speaking candidate.

BIBLIOGRAPHY

Ellemann-Jensen, Uffe. *Et lille land, og dog—: Dansk udenrigspolitik i det nye Europa.* Copenhagen: Forlaget liberal, 1991.

Haag, Karsten. *Uffe: Et portraet.* 3d ed. Hojbjerg: Hovedland, 1994.

Rudiger, Mogens. *Pa kant: Et portraet af politikeren Uffe Ellemann-Jensen.* Copenhagen: Gyldendal, 1992.

Jørn Boye Nielsen

Engholm, Björn (1939–)

Social Democratic minister president of the Land (state) of Schleswig-Holstein of the Federal Republic of Germany from 1988 to 1993 and chairman of the Social Democratic Party (SPD) from 1991 to 1993. Björn Engholm was a moderate-left–oriented reformer who had to withdraw from all public offices before his candidacy for chancellor in 1994. Engholm's biographers have described him as a "failed hope" and thus emphasized the great discrepancy between his high moral pretensions as a political figure and his rather pitiful resignation. The resignation came as a result of a scandal, the so-called Barschel affair, that shook the German political caste as no other scandal since the Spiegel affair of 1962. This affair had such a large wake that Engholm was drawn into it six years later, a victim of spying by his opponent, Christian Democratic (CDU) Minister-President Uwe Barschel.

Engolm was born in Lübeck in 1939 and was thus one of the first of the postwar generation of German political leaders. He entered the SPD in 1963 and steadily pursued a party career. In 1965 he became chairman of the Young Socialists in his hometown and in 1969 was elected the youngest member of the Bundestag (lower house of parliament). In 1977 he served as parliamentary state secretary in the Ministry of Education and in 1981 department chief. Since educational policy in Germany is predominantly the domain of individual states, Engholm was little more than moderator. However, with regard to the question of further reductions of income supplements for students through federal allowances, the so called BaföG (grant), he prevailed against Chancellor Helmut Schmidt. A bit later he was the first SPD minister openly to oppose the NATO decision to close the missile gap with the USSR.

After the collapse of the social-liberal coalition, he shifted to the state parliament (Landtag) of Schleswig-Holstein and remained there until 1993 as the leading Social Democratic prospect for chancellor. He quickly achieved popularity in that Land, and in the 1987 state election engineered a tie with the governing parties—the CDU and the Free Democratic Party.

In the 1988 by-election necessitated by the arrest of Barschel in a vote manipulation scandal known, by analogy to U.S. President Richard Nixon, as the "Waterkandgate," Engholm brought the SPD to a comfortable majority, which established it as the ruling party for the first time in Schleswig-Hosltein. Barschel, who had resigned over Waterkangate, was shortly afterward found dead fully clothed in the bathtub of a Geneva hotel from a combination of barbiturates and alcohol. His death was at first thought to be a suicide but murder proceedings were later opened. Allegations had surfaced, fueled by files from the former East Germany, that Barschel had had contacts with Israeli and Iranian arms dealers. Speculation linked his possible murder to that act with.

After the resignation of Hans-Jochen Vogel, Engholm became chairman of the SPD in 1991.

When early in 1993 the Barschel scandal revived because intimate associates from Engholm's party had given bribes to a Barschel confident, it appeared that Engholm would not survive the crisis. He resigned from all his offices in a mixture of wounded vanity and frustration at his inability to succeed with his own party colleagues. Yet the ultimate reason was his belated admission that he had knowingly lied under oath when he told a parliamentary commission of inquiry investigating Barschel's death about the date he had learned that Barschel's staff was spreading falsehoods about him during the 1987 campaign.

BIBLIOGRAPHY

Burchardt, Rainer, and Werner Knobbe. *Björn Engholm. Die Geschichte einer gescheiterten Hoffnung.* Stuttgart: Deutsche Verlags-Anstalt, 1993.

Engholm, Björn. *Ethik und Politik Heute: Verantwortliches Handeln in der technisch-industriellen Welt.* Opladen: Leske und Budrich 1990.

Gertler, Alfred. *Björn Engholm im Gespräch: Perspektiven sozial-demokratischer Politik.* Bonn: Bouvier 1991.

Whitney, Craig R. "Lie trips up German party chief," (New Orleans) *Times-Picayune.* May 4, 1993.

———. "German Politician's Death is Reinvestigated as Possible Murder," *New York Times,* January 1, 1995.

Georg Wagner
(Tr. by B. Cook)

Environmental Degradation in Eastern Europe

In many ways, the environmental catastrophe that has befallen the Aral Sea basin is emblematic of the state of the environment in Eastern European countries. This is a result of the fact that the governmental imperatives of economic growth and industrial and agricultural self-sufficiency, which saw the Soviet Union implement a land-use policy that destroyed the Aral Sea ecosystem, characterized Communist policy making and planning in the post-1945 period. As a brief survey of the present condition of the environment attests, Communist agricultural and industrial production has left a legacy of environmental degradation that will inhibit the future economic growth of Eastern European nations as they continue along their path of political, social, and economic reform.

Situated on the border of Kazakhstan and Uzbekistan in the former Soviet Union, the Aral Sea was once the world's fourth-largest inland lake, with a surface area twice the size of Belgium. It was fed by over 120 major rivers and tributaries, including the Syr Darya and Amu Darya, which also supplied water for the surrounding agricultural areas. The sea was bountiful and sustained a large fishing fleet that operated out of a number of inland port towns. These agricultural and fishing industries provided most of the wealth for the region—until the Soviet Union changed its agricultural policy for Soviet Central Asia and aggressively pursued self-sufficiency in cotton production. In order to achieve this transformation, gigantic canals were built in the 1960s to divert water from the Syr Darya and the Amu Darya and take it to the desertlike fields that would soon yield cotton. The result was catastrophic for the Aral Sea ecosystem. The water level of the sea dropped by 13.5 yards (15 meters) and by the 1990s it had shrunk to almost half its former size. As evaporation continued to take effect, the salinity of the water sharply increased, contributing to the extinction of twenty of the twenty-four species of fish that were formerly caught in the sea. The fishing industry collapsed, decimating the villages and towns that it had previously supported. Wind storms now rake the exposed former lake, annually lifting seventy-five tons of salt, sand, and accumulated agricultural chemicals into the air before depositing them in other regions. Combined with the pesticides, herbicides, and fertilizers from the cotton fields, which leach into the irrigation channels, these chemicals find their way into the food chain and contaminate the drinking water. As a result, new mothers in the Kara-kalpak region of Uzbekistan are advised not to nurse their children because they carry pesticides in their breast milk. Indeed, the population of the Aral Sea basin suffers extraordinarily high incidences of eye disease and cancer of the digestive system and throat, and, just before the breakup of the Soviet

Union, had a life expectancy that was twenty years below the national average.

Water and soil pollution are two of the most visible and pressing environmental problems in Eastern Europe. Agricultural lands and waterways have become contaminated because of the overuse of pesticides and fertilizers, which were required because the soil under cultivation was often unaccustomed or unsuited to nourishing the particular crop varieties that were planted. There was little incentive to moderate the use of the agrochemicals that were supplied below cost in large quantities by the state. Similarly, industrial waste such as petroleum products, heavy metals, and sewage, which flowed untreated into rivers with little penalty, polluted water sources and leached into the soil. As a result, the lead content of Polish apples and lettuces now exceeds the United Nations' health standards by a factor of ten. Similar examples can be found for other Eastern European countries.

As one moves away from agricultural areas toward cities of Eastern Europe, the air becomes noticeably noxious, polluted by the gaseous by-products of industrial processes. In 1989, 126 cities in the Soviet Union exceeded UN air-quality standards by a factor of ten; yet, in terms of its level of sulfur dioxide emissions, the USSR still ranked behind East Germany and Czechoslovakia which led the world. Unsurprisingly, 71 percent of forests in Czechoslovakia and 44 percent of forests in East Germany sustained significant damage from acid rain. In an effort to diminish the effects of this poor air quality on the health of the population, children from the polluted areas of Czechoslovakia were often sent to "green classes" in the mountains for several weeks each year during the school term and to less-polluted areas for vacation in the summer.

The extent of the environmental degradation in Eastern Europe was virtually unknown in the West until the relaxation of censorship laws at the end of the 1980s and the fall of the Communist regimes in 1989 and 1990. An exception to this rule was the explosion and subsequent meltdown of a nuclear reactor at Chernobyl, in the Ukraine, in April 1986, which became the major news story of that year in the Western world. The subsequent radioactive fallout contaminated eight million acres of agricultural land, affecting two thousand towns and villages. Over 130,000 people had to be resettled. The Soviet Premier, Mikhail Gorbachev, was forced to send in 35,000 emergency workers to clean up the debris and secure the site. Half of these workers are now invalids; all of them live with the knowledge that their children are nearly six times more likely to be born with birth defects than those who did not come in contact with radiation.

Despite the magnitude of this disaster, the level of radiation that people living in Chernobyl and its surrounding areas were exposed to pales in comparison with the contamination that occurred in the 1940s and 1950s as the Soviet Union developed its nuclear weapons capabilities. Radioactive waste from the top-secret Mayak nuclear weapons production complex in the Ural mountains city of Chelyabinsk-40, for example, was dumped into a local river and then into a local reservoir. Officials were even forced to erase a number of contaminated villages from the map after a waste storage tank exploded at Mayak in 1957, casting radioactive material across the countryside. The total accumulated radiation in the region has been recorded as one billion curies, twenty times the contamination produced by Chernobyl.

The causes of these environmental catastrophes were familiar to many Western nations in the second-half of the twentieth century: a reliance on nuclear power, coal, and oil rather than investment in safer and cleaner energy alternatives; persistence with extensive rather than intensive agricultural practices that required vast inputs of resources such as land and agrochemicals; and a reluctance to invest in technology associated with pollution abatement. Soviet industrial planners, like their Western counterparts, also sought to take advantage of the economy of scale provided by clustering their enterprises in single cities, thus creating ecological "blackspots" while other regions remained pristine. This situation is epitomized by the Russian city of Norilsk, whose copper-smelting complex produced 52 percent of the Soviet Union's total sulfuric acid while releasing more sulfur dioxide into the atmosphere than that produced by the nation of Italy.

Other causes of environmental degradation in Eastern Europe were unique to the Soviet system of agricultural and industrial production. As centrally planned economies, most of the Eastern European countries set their prices administratively, according to political prerogatives rather than market forces. The price of a commodity, therefore, was rarely related to its actual cost of production. Such a system meant that indicators of a project's viability, such as the costs of inputs and the efficiency of their use, were skewed. Thus natural resources such as land, forests, and minerals were allocated to enterprises at virtually no real cost to the user, eliminating any incentive to use them wisely. The Soviet Union, for example, sold oil to its industries for about nine rubles a barrel, less than the price of a liter of vodka. Water for irrigation was provided virtually free. The end result was an economy that tended to maximize the use of inputs at great cost to the environment. This situation was exacerbated by the fact

that it was not uncommon for production plans to call for the manufacture of farming or industrial equipment, but not the production of the necessary "spare-parts" required for their maintenance. Thus storage lagoons with leaky valves allowed toxic waste to escape; sewage systems broke down, casting raw waste into rivers and lakes; and industrial and farming equipment were simply replaced instead of being repaired, requiring further expenditure of raw materials and energy. Not surprisingly, by the 1990s, countries such as Poland, Russia, and Hungary ranked last in Europe in terms of energy efficiency and conservation.

These things occurred despite the fact that by the 1980s, most Eastern European countries had developed sound environmental standards and legislation. Unfortunately, such legislation proved insufficient because the enforcement agencies were far weaker politically and financially than the enterprise managers they were trying to control. Fines imposed on managers, for example, were either nominal or paid by the relevant ministry. In fact, annual subsidies given to agricultural and industrial enterprises often included funds earmarked to pay fines. When money was allocated to factories for pollution abatement equipment it often went unspent, and when the equipment was installed, managers often refused to operate it as directed because it was easier to continue paying fines for exceeding the emission standards than to interrupt or curtail production.

Despite the enforcement of rigid censorship laws and the restraint placed on political dissidence by the Communist regimes of Eastern Europe in the post-1945 period, an environmental movement responding to the ecological crisis had begun to emerge by the late 1970s. It began in the republic of Slovenia in Yugoslavia, but really found its voice in Poland during the period of relaxed censorship and increased political freedom occasioned by the gains made by the independent labor union Solidarity in 1980 and 1981. Environmentalism went underground in Poland with the imposition of martial law in 1981, however, and did not seriously surface again until 1988. By this time, the impact of Chernobyl, and its toxic cloud, which drifted across national borders, had awoken many Eastern Europeans to the ecological peril that they faced. Environmentalists frequently formed alliances with nationalists and ethnic separatists to protest against teetering Communist regimes, and their movements proved to be mutually enforcing. In the Baltic states of Lithuania, Estonia, and Latvia, for instance, environmentalism was often couched in a broader anti-Russian feeling leading an official in the USSR Council of Ministers to observe in

1989 that "the degradation of natural areas which people identify with their national dignity, aggravates relations between ethnic groups." In Latvia, Dainis Ivans wrote a series of articles that appeared in the local press during 1986 and 1987 that criticized Moscow's plans to build a hydroelectric dam on the Daugava River. He became leader of the Latvian Popular Front, the movement that led the republic's drive for independence, and was eventually elected deputy chairman of the Latvian parliament.

Despite the fall of the Communist regimes in Eastern Europe and the rhetoric of the new "reformist" governments, environmentalists have not seen the revision in thinking about the environment for which they were hoping. While farmers and factory owners have been forced to adopt new production methods that minimize the use of resources in order to remain viable, few could afford to invest in equipment and techniques that would have produced less pollution and toxic residues. Moreover, while "reformist" leaders of the 1960s and 1980s proved adept at rehabilitating political prisoners and dissidents who were condemned by previous regimes, the likelihood that a new wave of political leaders will begin the long process of rehabilitating the environment seems remote while their attentions are diverted by perpetual economic crisis and the social problems caused by the transition from planned to market economies.

BIBLIOGRAPHY

DeBardeleben, Joan. *To Breathe Free: Eastern Europe's Environmental Crisis.* Washington: Woodrow Wilson Center Press, 1991.

Feshbach, Murray. *Ecological Disaster: Cleaning Up the Hidden Legacy of the Soviet Union.* New York: Twentieth Century Fund Press, 1995.

Feshbach, Murray, and Alfred Friendly. *Ecocide in the USSR: Health and Nature Under Siege.* New York: Basic Books, 1992.

Jancar-Webster, Barbara, ed. *Environmental Action in Eastern Europe: Responses to Crisis.* Armonk: M.E. Sharpe, 1993.

Jancar-Webster, Barbara, "Eastern Europe and the Former Soviet Union" in Sheldon Kamieniecki, ed., *Environmental Politics in the International Area: Movements, Parties, Organisations, and Policy.* New York: State University of New York Press, 1993.

Petersen, D. J. *Troubled Lands: The Legacy of Soviet Environmental Destruction.* Boulder, Colo.: Westview Press, 1993.

Singleton, Fred, ed. *Environmental Problems in the Soviet Union and Eastern Europe.* Boulder, Colo.: Lynne Rienner, 1987.

Savchenko, V. K. *The Ecology of the Chernobyl Catastrophe.* Paris: UNESCO, 1995.

Paul Sendziuk

SEE ALSO Chernobyl; Environmental Degradation in Western Europe

Environmental Degradation in Western Europe

Among Europe's significant environmental problems are atmospheric pollution; water conservation, protection, and management; and waste management. The overall quality of the European environment is mediocre, and there is a need to employ more effective and clean technologies. This type of undertaking is daunting in view of the number, size, and productivity of Western European enterprises.

Europe initiated the international economy, and the industrial and agricultural revolutions of the eighteenth and nineteenth centuries continue to alter the contours of the planet. In Europe during this century industrialization and increased population have polluted the atmosphere, contaminated seas and rivers, and damaged the countryside. An understanding of the environmental challenges connected with European Union (EU) integration is correlative with the realization that member states contrast with each other not only in socioeconomic qualities, population, and culture, but also in natural resources, topography, climate, and hydrology.

Europe and the other OECD countries represent 82 percent of world commercial energy use. Forty percent of this was consumed in Europe though Europeans accounted for only about 13 percent of world population in 1990. Europe and the other OECD countries also produced more than 70 percent of world industrial waste. The principal effects of energy use are tropospheric ozone and climate change, acidification, and local air pollution. Energy use was responsible for approximately 95 percent of human-induced sulfur dioxide emissions and 97 percent of nitrogen oxides in twenty European countries in 1990.

Anxiety over the environment intensified among Europeans because of calamities such as radiation ensuing from the Chernobyl nuclear accident in the USSR in 1986; the toxic chemical discharge into the Rhine River at Basel, Switzerland, during the same year; the *Amoco Cadiz* oil spill in the Atlantic Ocean; air emissions of sulfur dioxide from coal-fired power stations; and the tainting of southern Scandinavian acid-sensitive soils and lakes by airborne sulfur and nitrogen oxide discharged mainly by industrial processes and power plants in the United Kingdom and Germany. All these produced extensive damage to the European environment.

The quality of urban air is an ongoing concern. There has been progress since the 1970s in reducing the level of lead, sulfur dioxide, and particulate matter in urban air. Emissions of nitrogen oxides, though, are not declining. Tropospheric ozone is an accelerating problem because of emissions of volatile organic chemicals and nitrogen oxides. Europe is responsible for approximately 25 percent of global emissions of dioxide and nitrogen oxides. Emissions of these gases from power plants add 30 to 55 percent to total acid deposition. Nitrogen oxides increase the acidification of the environment. The European release of chlorofluorocarbons (CFCs) and halons, which endanger stratospheric ozone, amounts to 35 to 40 percent of world totals. Europe is responsible for about 25 percent of carbon dioxide and 16 percent of methane emissions from human activities around the globe.

Water protection, conservation, and management are issues crucial in international waters like the Baltic and North Seas, and rivers such as the Danube and the Rhine. While the pollution of lakes and rivers has been more successfully controlled than any other environmental problem, the concentration of water resources produces scarcity dilemmas in a number of regions in southern Europe. Approximately 15 percent of the entire renewable resource is consumed annually. Industry extracts more water than agriculture and personal use and consumption combined. However, water utilization for agricultural and domestic uses is expanding, while industrial utilization is lessening or constant. Sixty-five percent of Europe's inhabitants are supplied from ground water, the quality of which is at risk in numerous areas. Over-exploitation of ground water is an issue in almost 60 percent of urban and industrial areas, endangering as well 25 percent of principal wetlands areas. Lake and river nutrient enrichment brought about by surplus phosphorus and nitrogen from agriculture and domestic and industrial effluents is a serious predicament throughout Europe.

European seas exhibit a broad spectrum of environmental situations. Coastal zone pollution and contested uses of the coastal zone are problems in all regions. All seas, apart from the northern ones, confront eutrophication dilemmas in various regions. Contamination by organic micropollutants affects fauna in nearly all European seas. Over-exploitation of fish and shellfish stocks is also a typical predicament.

Soil erosion is accelerating throughout the EU, encompassing approximately 115 million hectares, resulting in water contamination and damage to fertility. Over 90 percent of the eroded area is in the Mediterranean region. Critical values for acidification are exceeded in approximately 75 million hectares of European forest soils. Excessive use of nitrogen and phosphorous fertilizers brings about runoff and leaching, resulting in the enrichment of natural waters by nutrients and pollution of drinking water.

In the period between 1984 and 1986 alone, 14 percent of Europe's forests showed signs of damage. In the past, forests covered 80 to 90 percent of the European area and now make up only 33 percent of land cover. Natural river sites have been impacted by the decline in forested watershed and are at risk. The majority of river ecosystems are affected by pollution and destruction of riparian ecosystem capacities. Numerous animal and plant species groups are also dwindling and face extinction.

Waste management is another crucial issue for Western Europe: disposal of toxic and dangerous wastes, dumping of refuse and a mixture of raw material and industrial wastes in rivers and at sea, recycling, and storage of radioactive wastes. Of 2,000 million tons of waste generated by Western Europeans, 80 percent is recyclable as energy or raw material.

The EC's environmental policy was initiated at a meeting in 1972 of heads of government and state. Yet it was not until the Single European Act, that environmental policy was given its own position in the treaties. The act provides that "action shall be based on the principles that preventive action shall be taken, that environmental damage should as a priority be rectified at source, that the polluter should pay" and that "environmental protection requirements shall be a component of the Community's other policies."

Starting in 1972 the Community developed a sizable body of environmental law to guard against air and water pollution and the damaging consequences of noise, and to manage hazards related to nuclear power, biotechnology, and chemicals. The EU is installing more exacting environmental regulations focusing on the polluter, guaranteeing the explicit implementation of legislation, developing investment to improve the environment, and assisting in the dissemination of information on the environment. The principal institutions involved in proposing, implementing, and enforcing environmental legislation are the Council of Ministers, the European Parliament, the European Commission, and the European Court of Justice. Legislation is ordinarily accomplished through directives or regulations.

At Maastricht, in February 1992, the twelve European Community (EC) member states signed the Treaty on European Union (TEU), which amended the EEC Treaty (including provisions on environment) with the goal of instituting a European Monetary and Political Union. The TEU mandated environmental protection as one of the basic aims of the union. According to the TEU, the union must strive for "sustainable and noninflationary growth respecting the environment." The Treaty also provided that "[e]nvironmental protection requirements must be integrated into the Community's other policies," rather than just being a "component," as has been mandated by the Single European Act (SEA).

In the climate deliberations, the European Council determined that provision for sharing responsibility through national emission goals was not suitable for a community in process of consolidation, and member governments requested that the EC prepare an EC-wide plan for converting the predictions of 12 to 14 percent emissions increase into a collective stabilization. The commission developed a strategy for doing so. Yet attaining compliance with a directive after it becomes part of national law is more complicated than merely consolidating union directives into national legal codes.

Although there have been improvements in some areas, such as emission controls, these activities are frequently inadequate by themselves to bring about restoration and enhancement of natural resources and environmental quality. This is because of the degree of deterioration and the intricacy and frequently circumscribed carrying capacity of the environment. Analyses and projections of the problems of European environmental change demand a systems approach joining mathematical modeling and other methods that can come to terms with complexity, nonlinearity, and coupling of diverse processes.

Western Europe today includes countries that have domestic environmental policies in place, while others have little or no national environmental legislation. Since 1995 three of the foremost countries in environmental policy making—Finland, Sweden, and Austria—have joined the EU. Their membership strengthens the environmental policies that have been advocated in the EU by Germany, Denmark, and the Netherlands.

The EU is striving to improve the environment during the course of political and economic integration. Environmental affairs are to be merged into EU policy at incipient planning stages. The union acknowledges that overseeing environmental issues efficiently is crucial to realization of the common market enterprise. If Western Europe is able to improve its environment at the same time that it liberalizes trade, the EU may become an example for other areas of the world.

BIBLIOGRAPHY

Anderson, Mikael Skou, and Duncan Liefferink, eds. *European Environmental Policy: The Pioneers.* Manchester, U.K.: Manchester University Press, 1997.

Baker, Susan, Maria Kousis, Dick Richardson, and Stephen Young. *The Politics of Sustainable Development: Theory, Policy, and Practice within the European Union.* London: Routledge, 1997.

Commission of the European Communities. *Report of the Commission of the European Communities to the United Nations Conference on the Environment.* Brussels: SEC (91) 2448 final, 1992.

———. *Toward Sustainability: A European Community Programme of Policy and Action in Relation to the Environment and Sustainable Development.* Brussels: COM (91) 23 Final, 11, 1992.

Höll, Otmar. *Environmental Cooperation in Europe: The Political Dimension.* Boulder, Colo.: Westview Press, 1994.

O'Riordan, Timothy, and Jill Jäger. *The Politics of Sustainable Development.* London: Routledge, 1996.

Stanner, David, and Philippe Bourdeau, eds. *Europe's Environment: The Dobrís Assessment.* Copenhagen: European Environment Agency, 1995.

Vellinga, Pier, and Michael Grubb, eds. *Climate Change Policy in the European Community.* London: Royal Institute of International Affairs, 1993.

Kenneth Keulman

SEE ALSO Environmental Degradation in Eastern Europe

Erhard, Ludwig (1897–1977)

Christian Democratic chancellor of the Federal Republic of Germany from 1963 until 1966, economics minister from 1949 to 1963. Leading formulator of economic policy for the Christian Democratic Party (CDU) from 1947, who played a significant role as the co-initiator of the German "economic miracle" (*Wirtschaftswunder*), but as chancellor was less successful. Compared with his predecessor, Konrad Adenauer, the second chancellor of West Germany appears pallid. His chronic indecisiveness and immobility and the absence of initiatives in internal and external policy made his three-year chancellorship a transition period with an uncertain conclusion, based merely on the inability of his party to find a suitable successor for the founding father of the republic.

Ludwig Erhard, economics minister of West Germany from 1949 to 1963 and federal chancellor from 1963 to 1966. *Illustration courtesy of the German Information Center.*

Ludwig Erhard was born in Fürth, Bavaria, in 1897. After completing his *Abitur* in 1916 he served as a soldier in the First World War. In 1919 he began the study of economics and sociology at the University of Frankfurt and received a doctorate under the direction of Franz Oppenheimer in 1924. Subsequently he joined the Nuremberg Institute Economic Forecast and became, in 1942, leader of the Institute for Industrial Research in the same city.

His long research experience on economic issues and his clean (i.e., non-Nazi) political record predestined Erhard for high government service in postwar Germany. From October 1945 until December 1946 he was economics minister in Bavaria. In 1947 Erhard became chairperson of the Special Authority on Credit and Money (Sonderstelle Kredit und Geld) in Bad Homburg, one of the numerous intermediate authorities during the occupation period, and oversaw the preparations for a currency reform in the three Western occupation zones.

As director of the Administration for the Economy of the United Economic Area (Trizonia) in Frankfurt, he set the exact date for the money changeover and ordered a simultaneous series of relaxations in the control of the prices of consumer and industrial goods. Both long-awaited measures intermeshed with and stimulated the economic boom. His success secured for the rest of Erhard's life the popular label "father of the economic miracle." The CDU also profited from this reputation. Erhard put the CDU's ability to draw votes into motion and established a lasting symbiosis between the party and economic liberalism. Erhard patterned his neoliberal economic theory after the ideas of economists Wilhelm Röpke and Alfred Müller-Armack. The economic system should as much as possible be freed from state intervention and given over to the free play of forces. First there should be full freedom of seller and consumer to secure from the market optimal chances for development. But in addition, in the paradoxical neologism "social market-economy," of which Erhard would speak, a social obligation arose to establish a state welfare policy for the bulk of the population. However, it remained unclear how this was to be accomplished. The modern intervention state is to be found only at the margins of his model.

Erhard as a neoliberal was assigned to the right wing of the CDU. As economics minister he struggled against every expansion of the welfare state because he wanted to keep the expenses to the state as low as possible. He appealed to the unions to observe moderation. Thanks to his authority and a general desire to rebuild the country, the unions in the 1950s and 1960s restrained their wage demands and thus made possible the exceptional growth rates of the German economy. The means to bring about reinvestment in and extensive modernization of industrial plants were supplied to a considerable extent through the delay of consumption by worker and employee. On the other hand, Erhard engaged in cartel politics, establishing a cozy relationship with business. He offered the captains of German industry, who retained a corporate tradition, no measurable opposition to the progressive building of cartels.

In the golden years of German economic policy between 1961 and 1964, the four goals of the "magic square" of political economy were reached: growth, price stability, full employment, and a foreign-trade balance. But it became quickly apparent that these years were exceptional in a long-term period of continuous prosperity. The growth crisis of 1966–67 showed that the chancellor did not provide an instrument to control growing inflation and increasing unemployment (from 300,000 to 650,000). Erhard had the ground cut out from under him when his coalition partner, the Free Democratic Party, no longer supported his budgetary policy. His own weakness, aside from his inability to intervene in the economic structure because of his monetary policy, became apparent. In the ensuing grand coalition of the CDU/Christian Social Union and the Social Democratic Party, the new minister of economics, Social Democrat Charles Schiller, overcame the crisis within a short period by utilizing state expenditures as economic incentives on the pattern of John Maynard Keynes.

Erhard possessed only a mediocre political world view. His foreign policy perceptions were limited to playing the part of a junior partner of the United States, which in his eyes alone guaranteed the military security of Germany and Western integration. As his social-political leitmotif he advanced the "formed society," his ideal of a satiated community of economic individuals, the harmony of which was accomplished solely by the operation of the economy. With his pot belly and a cigar in his hand, he was a perfect symbol of the satisfied citizens of the Federal Republic of the *Wirtschaftswunder* years.

Ludwig Erhard was not the sort to deal with political conflicts, let alone take advantage of them. As the "monolith" of the Deutsche Mark he was something of a relic, unable to deal with power-hungry competitors and a general desire within the CDU for change.

BIBLIOGRAPHY

Erhard, Ludwig. *Germany's Comeback in the World Market.* Westport, Conn.: Greenwood Press, 1976.

———. *Prosperity through Competition.* Westport, Conn.: Greenwood Press, 1975.

Luitenberger, Volkhard. *Ludwig Erhard: der Nationalökonom als Politiker.* Göttingen: Muster-Schmidt, 1986.

Schroder, Gerhard, ed. *Ludwig Erhard: Beiträge zu seiner politischen Biographie. Festschrift zum 75. Geburtstag.* Frankfurt/Main: Propyläen, 1971.

Georg Wagner
(Tr. by B. Cook)

SEE ALSO Adenauer, Konrad

Eriksen, Erik (1902–72)

Danish prime minister from 1950 to 1953. Erik Eriksen served as a member of the Danish parliament from 1935 to 1968. A farmer, he was chosen to serve as minister for agriculture from 1945 to 1947. He was chairman of the Liberal Party (Venstre) from 1950 to 1965. From 1950 to 1953 he was prime minister for a liberal-conservative government.

Eriksen is remembered for having led the extensive commission work that gave Denmark a new constitution in 1953. It modernized the political system by reducing the parliament from a two-chamber (Landstinget and Folketinget) to a one-chamber system (Folketinget only). Furthermore, it allowed women to become heirs to the throne, thus paving the way for the accession of Queen Margrethe II in 1972.

In 1965 Eriksen proposed the fusion of the Liberal and Conservative Parties, but this was rejected by his own party. After that he withdrew as chairman of the Liberal Party and its parliamentary group. He was president of the Nordic Council in 1953–54, 1956–57, and 1961–62. He died in Copenhagen on October 7, 1972.

Jørn Boye Nielsen

Erlander, Tage (1901–85)

Swedish prime minister from 1946 to 1969, principal architect of the Swedish welfare state. Tage (Fritiof) Erlander was born in Ransäter on June 13, 1901. He received a doctorate from the University of Lund in 1928, and for the next ten years worked as an editor for the encyclopedia *Svensk Uppslabok.* He was elected to parliament in 1933. From 1938 he held ministerial posts in various Social Democratic governments. At the death of Par Albin Hansson in 1946, Erlander became chairman of the Social Democratic Workers Party and prime minister. Following a strong electoral victory in September 1968, Erlander, who had served longer than any other democratic prime minister in the twentieth century, decided to resign. In 1969 he handed the leadership of the party and the post of prime minister to his protégé Olof Palme. In 1970 Erlander was elected to the new single-chamber legislature, of which he had been a proponent.

During Erlander's long prime ministership he oversaw the expansion of the Swedish welfare system. Old-age benefits, child allowances, and rent subsidies were all increased. Education was expanded with the extension of compulsory schooling and greater opportunities for advanced learning.

Erlanger died at Huddinge near Stockholm on June 21, 1985.

BIBLIOGRAPHY

Mitchell, George J. *Making Peace.* New York: Knopf, 1999.

Ruin, Olof. *Tage Erlander: Serving the Welfare State, 1946–1969.* Pittsburgh: University of Pittsburgh Press, 1990.

Bernard Cook

Esterhazy, Piter (1950–)

Hungarian writer. Piter (Peter) Esterhazy earned a diploma in mathematics in 1974, but he became a freelance writer in 1978. He became more widely known with his *Termelesi Regeny* (*A Novel of Production*, 1979), the first important postmodern novel in Hungary. In this book, as well as in his subsequent works, he mixed several characteristics of postmodern fiction, including citations, footnotes, self-references, and metalinguistic terms. Esterhazy has published several novels, volumes of short stories, and essays. By the late 1980s he established himself as the most popular representative of the generation of writers and men of letter who started their career in the 1970s. He was awarded various literary prizes in the 1980s and 1990s. Besides being arguably the most significant postmodern writer in Hungary, Esterhazy also participated in the activities of the democratic opposition to the Communist regime in the 1980s.

Some of his major works have also been translated into English and German. They include: *Fuharosok* (1983) (*Fuhrleute: Ein Roman*, 1988); *Kis ma pornografia* (1984; *A Little Hungarian Pornography*, 1995); *A sziv segedigei* (1985; *Helping Verbs of the Heart*, 1991); *Hrabal konyve* (1990; *The Book Hrabal*, 1994); and *Hahn-Hahn grofnu pillantasa* (1991; *The Glance of Countess Hahn-Hahn: Down the Danube*, 1994).

BIBLIOGRAPHY

Bernath, Arpad. "Literatur der Postmoderne in Ungarn." *Neohelicon* 16 (1990): 151–70.
Kulcsar, Szabs Ernu. *Esterhazy Piter.* Pozsony: Kalligram, 1996.

Tamàs Magyarics

Estonia

Baltic state that regained its independence from the Soviet Union in August 1991. Estonia (Eesti), a country of 18,370 square miles (47,549 sq km) and with 1.6 million inhabitants, is bordered by Russia, Latvia, the Baltic Sea and the Gulf of Finland.

Dominated in turn since the thirteenth century by Danes, Germans, Poles, Swedes, and Russians, native Estonians began nation building in the middle of the nineteenth century. The formation of national identity that had occurred only in the cultural sphere for half a century culminated in the establishment of the modern nation-state on February 24, 1918. From the very beginning of their own state, Estonians had to fight for their independence against the imperialist ambitions of both Germany and Bolshevik Russia. The war of independence ended

Estonia. *Illustration courtesy of Bernard Cook.*

successfully with the signing of the Tartu Peace Treaty on February 2, 1920. During the subsequent twenty years of peace Estonians managed to construct an economically and culturally successful small state. Politically it was a developing democracy that saw sporadic instability and then a period of moderate authoritarianism following the suppressing of a pro-fascist coup in 1934, when Estonia was led by President Konstantin Paets (1933–39). According to the census of 1934 the population of the Estonian Republic consisted principally of ethnic Estonians (88.2 percent). The largest minorities were Russians (8.2 percent), Germans (1.5 percent), Jews (0.4 percent), and Estonian Swedes (0.7 percent).

Under the secret protocols of the 1939 Nazi-Soviet Pact, Estonia was invaded and occupied by the Soviet Union on June 17, 1940. The seizure of power by Estonian Communists and social democrats, led by Soviet dictator Stalin's emissary, Andrey Zhdanov, was staged according to Moscow's scenario. A puppet government, completely dependent on the alien regime, was established, with a left-wing writer, Johannes Vares Barbarus, as prime minister. While ignoring direct democratic elections, Moscow officials arranged an election in which only Communists were eligible to run. Those elected formed an entirely new "representative" body on July 14. This Soviet creation then appealed for the incorporation of Estonia into the Soviet Union. This was carried out on August 6, 1940. In the first months of the first Soviet year, the majority of Estonians could not fully understand what had happened. The terror that was soon launched and the massive deportation of June 14, 1941, (more than ten thousand people) opened people's eyes to the new regime's animosity toward the native population.

After Hitler's Germany attacked the Soviet Union on June 22, 1941, Estonia was occupied by German armed forces from August 1941 until September 1944, when the Soviets again took over. During the German occupation Estonia became part of Ostland province of the Reich and was led by Commissar General K. S. Litzmann. The economy was subjugated to the interests of the Reich and nationalized property was not returned. Between the two occupations, Estonians tried to reestablish their independent state, but those attempts failed. The clash of two enemies on Estonian territory forced a great number of Estonians to make a choice. In 1941 about 68,000 citizens were forcibly conscripted into the Red Army (later the Estonian Rifle Corp) or joined the retreating Soviet administration. Approximately 5,500 citizens were executed in concentration camps. When the Soviets returned, 70,000 Estonians fled and most immigrated to Sweden, Canada, Australia, and the United States.

Estonia lost about 15 percentage of its population because of the war, deportations, and extermination. Twenty thousand Baltic Germans moved to Germany during the Hitler's *Umsiedlung* (resettlement) campaign, and Estonian Swedes were shipped to Sweden. Jews and Gypsies were killed. As a result of heavy Soviet bombardment in the last several months of German occupation, Estonia suffered extensive destruction to its cities and industry. Ninety-seven percent of the buildings of bordertown Narva and nearly half of those in the capital, Tallinn, and university town Tartu were left in ruins. The wartime devastation resulted in an overall decline of 45 percent in industrial productive capacity as compared with 1941.

When the Soviet forces drove the Germans out, they reamalgamated Estonia into the Soviet Union. The vehemently anti-Communist Estonian refugee communities in the Western countries never reconciled themselves to the Soviet occupation of their homeland. About a thousand armed men in the homeland found shelter in the woods to fight against the Soviet power as guerrillas. The so-called forest brethren continued to fight against Communist security forces until the beginning of the 1950s, by which time the majority of them had been killed.

In the postwar years, Estonia became fully integrated into the Soviet Union's economic system. The fuel industry was developed in the newly built up north Estonian towns to supply the energy needs of the northwestern region of the USSR. Estonian industry underwent important changes; whereas the major emphasis had been on textiles and foodstuffs, by 1950 a significant shift had taken place toward heavy industry such as oil shale and oil shale gas, electric power generation, and the machine industry. The Moscow administration started to bring in Russian-speaking workers in great numbers to be employed in heavy industry. Officially this was justified as supplementing the workforce depleted by the war. Thus forced industrialization was closely connected with a specific policy aimed at restricting the role of native Estonians in society.

The campaign to reorganize Estonian agriculture based on private farms was launched in 1947 but was carried out two years later, when a massive deportation was utilized to intimidate the rural population. In March 1949, 20,700 people were deported to Siberia to force those who remained behind to submit to working on the collective farms. In 1939 Estonia had approximately 140,000 farms, but by the end of Stalin's era there were 934 agricultural collectives and 84 fishing collectives in Estonia. The Stalinist model of "liquidation of the kulaks as a class" was also implemented in Estonia, and at least 1,200 families were deported as kulaks (well-to-do farmers) in 1947–48.

The main tool of the Soviet ideology was the Estonian Communist Party (ECP), which had a membership of 2,400 after World War II. By the end of the Stalinist era it had multiplied ten times. In the beginning its members were generally Estonians (90 percent), but by 1952 the percentage of non-Estonians in the ECP was 58.5. The Sovietization of the ECP reflected both Moscow's distrust of ethnic Estonians as well as a reluctance by Estonians themselves to take part in the administrative institution occupying their homeland. A coup was launched against the leadership of the ECP in March 1950. A decree was adopted by the Eighth Plenary Session of the Estonian Supreme Soviet that pushed aside the head of the ECP, Nikolai Karotamm, who had been born in Estonia and defended Estonians, and other national Communists. Thus, the leadership of the ECP was taken over by Estonians born in the Soviet Union and by Russians. Another decree of the same plenary launched a persecution campaign labeled the "fight against bourgeoisie nationalism," during which about 3,000 people were either deported or fired from leading positions.

The de-Stalinization and liberalization of Soviet society following the Twentieth Congress of the Communist Party of the Soviet Union ended the so-called severe class struggle period in Estonia and created the environment for social stabilization. Thousands of deportees returned to their homeland, first contacts with exile Estonians were established, travel was allowed to a limited extent, and the creative freedom of the intelligentsia widened. The impact of a Moscow-centered mentality on Estonian cultural life was reduced, and the new generation of young educated people sought to restore connections with their prewar cultural heritage. The opportunity to communicate with people from the socialist countries of central Europe expanded. A creative intelligentsia realized that under the canons of socialist realism one could moderately cultivate both nation-centered and current Western-style art. In the 1960s Estonia began increasingly became a center of dissident ideas. Especially noteworthy in the endeavor were young prose writers, graphic artists, and musicians.

Thanks to Soviet Premier Nikita Khrushchev's campaign to increase the role of the agricultural economy and to decrease the difference between rural and urban regions, agriculture prospered in Estonia. From the late 1950s Estonia followed the overall Soviet trend toward an increasingly greater role for state farms, or sovkhozes, especially through taking over the lands of weak collective farms. But by the beginning of the 1960s collective farm workers received normal wages rather than shares based on production. Although the mechanization and reorganization of agriculture was an ongoing process, recovery to the 1939 level in agricultural output was reached only in the early 1960s. By that time Estonian farmers had become accustomed to collective land ownership, their living standard was stable, and income was gradually surpassing that of industrial workers.

By the 1960s an industrial complex developed in northern Estonia, led by the capital Tallinn and followed by Kohtla-Järve and Narva. As the development of industry was carried out largely at the expense of immigrant labor, these regions consequently experienced a high level of Russification. According to the Soviet work distribution scheme, Estonia was assigned the processing of electric energy on the basis of oil-shale mining, and two-thirds of its oil-shale production was exported to other sites in the USSR. Roughly half the oil shale burned to produce electricity remained on the ground as inorganic ash, and the process contributed to both air and water pollution in the northeastern part of the country. The Sillamäe uranium plant, where half the raw material necessary for the Soviet nuclear industry was processed, was situated in northern Estonia. This also adversely affected the environment. In Tallinn machine industry, docks, and military industry predominated. The local textile industry depended on cotton produced in the Central Asian regions of the Soviet Union. By the 1960s Estonia had become thoroughly integrated into the economic life of the Soviet Union, but at the same time it was becoming an area of

Soviet economic experimentation because of its high level of worker efficiency. As a result of liberalization the attitude of native Estonians toward the ECP gradually changed, and the illusion spread widely that the leadership of the ECP was being turned over to native Estonians. In 1966 the membership of ECP was fifty-nine thousand, of whom 52 percent were native Estonians. The majority of these were high-level agricultural and industrial administrators, but the intelligentsia, who up to that moment had rejected communism, also entered the party ranks. Since 1950 the leader of ECP had been Johannes Köbin (1905–), an Estonian educated in the Soviet Union who had become sympathetic toward Estonians and had become rather tolerant toward manifestations of nationalism. But the Prague Spring in Czechoslovakia in 1968 resulting in the Soviet-led Warsaw Pact invasion destroyed the liberal illusions of Estonians about the opportunities of Eurocommunism in their home country.

By 1978 the ECP was led by so-called Estonian-minded Communists who had managed to soften ideological pressure and the directives of the centrally directed economy. But in 1978 there was another "palace revolution" in the ECP and power was seized again by Estonians born in the USSR who were loyal to the Kremlin. The new general secretary of the ECP, Karl Vaino (1923–), became the ideological force behind neo-Sovietization.

In the 1980s, Moscow managed more than 90 percent of Estonian industry; possibilities for extensive development were exhausted, and Estonia had fallen further behind developed countries. The amalgamation of state farms in the 1970s resulted in the destruction of many historic settlements and cultural traditions in the countryside. The Soviets started to treat Estonia as a huge plant for breeding pigs based on imported fodder. A system of colossal farms that depleted the local labor force was developed, with the aim of providing Leningrad and Moscow with meat and dairy products. By the beginning of the 1980s the deficient economy experienced a crisis: the supplies of electricity and heat were insufficient, and there was a serious lack of essential commodities and food.

Massive immigration worsened relations between ethnic groups. Although the population had reached 1.5 million, the percentage of native Estonians continually declined and by the 1985 census it barely reached 61. Rapid urbanization (71.3 percent of Estonia's population was urban in 1984) occurred mainly because of the imported non-Estonian labor force, while the percentage of Estonians in rural areas remained stable. Estonians developed deep resentment toward the determined Russification of Tallinn (according to the 1934 census, the percentage of

Russians in Tallinn was 5.8, in 1985 the Russian-speaking population had reached nearly 53 percent).

In cultural life there was a growth in Russification and ideological control. Censorship increased, and creative freedom was restricted. At the end of the 1970s the ECP, intending to increase the importance of the Russian language, began to restrict the use of Estonian in education and administration. All academic dissertations, including those on Estonian language and literature, had to be translated into Russian.

The dissatisfaction of native Estonians increased and in the 1970s cultural resistance developed. It was mainly expressed by hidden statements in works of art and literature that mocked Sovietism, but also in the emergence of grassroots national voluntary cultural associations. A neodissident generation evolved who started to write letters to the United Nations and to the Western powers publicizing the critical situation in Estonia. In 1980 spontaneous demonstrations of schoolchildren occurred in Tallinn to condemn the Soviet regime. Inspired by this, intellectuals wrote the "Letter of 40," an open but never published letter to Soviet Communist Party newspaper *Pravda* in which they drew attention to the unresolved nationalities problem. Persecution of the authors of the letter by the party and the KGB (Soviet secret police) seriously increased dissident sentiments among Estonians, strengthening the aspirations to achieve freedom from Moscow's control.

In the mid-1980s the general economic and political stagnation in the USSR deepened. In an attempt to revivify the Soviet system the new party leader Mikhail Gorbachev introduced the doctrines of glasnost (openness) and perestroika (restructuring). Although during the first two years the leaders of the old guard of the ECP managed to hinder the development of perestroika in Estonia, nationalist forces took the initiative in 1987. They managed to inform the public of Moscow's plan to establish new phosphorus mines in northern Estonia, which would have resulted in an ecological catastrophe as well as another influx of migrants. The looming danger mobilized the people, and massive protests of youth led by Green movement intellectuals occurred in the spring. On August 23, on the anniversary of the Molotov-Ribbentrop Pact of 1939, which assigned Estonia to the USSR, the second galvanizing episode took place. Dissidents organized the first political demonstration in Tallinn. Pressure for independence from the Kremlin developed rapidly, and native Estonians organized. In December 1987 the rapidly politicized Estonian Heritage Society was founded with the goal of restoring the historical memory of the people and de-Sovietizing of society. It also resurrected the blue,

black, and white Estonian national flag. In November the intelligentsia, who up to now had protested mainly via works of art, became overtly political and founded the Cultural Council of the Creative Unions. It organized a joint plenary session of the creative unions on April 1–2, 1988, at Toompea at the center of administrative power. Writers, artists, and scholars met to discuss publicly for the first time the necessity of stopping the disastrous economic hegemony of Moscow and the flow of immigrants, the need to extend Estonia's economic and political rights and rehabilitate the victims of Stalinism, to stop Russification, and to guarantee Estonians their cultural independence. These critiques were broadcast to the Estonian public over Estonian Radio.

Estonians became again aware that they were an independent nation, and a peaceful, romantic struggle to restore the independence of the country began. On April 13, 1988, the Popular Front was founded to unite thousands of people. In June spontaneous nightly song festivals occurred on the Song Festival Grounds, sacred to Estonians, where thousands of young Tallinners sang patriotic songs, and the liberation movement acquired the label the "singing revolution." The unprecedented political activity during the summer of 1988 pushed the ECP administration from power. Vaino Valjas (1931–) was appointed to be the new leader of the Communist Party. He had been removed from power in 1978 by Karl Vaino and dispatched to work as the Soviet ambassador to Venezuela. The Estonian-minded Communists broke off from Moscow-oriented party members, which in turn led to a split within the ECP on national grounds. In contrast to the Popular Front, Russians residing in Estonia organized an empire-minded Interfront, which opposed the aspirations of native Estonians. At the mass gathering at the Song Festival Grounds organized by the Popular Front on September 11 (with three hundred thousand participants, or a third of the Estonian population), radicals demanded independence for Estonia. A day earlier at the plenary session of the ECP, Estonian-minded Communists had demanded a new union (USSR) contract that would secure the existence of Estonians on their home territory and declare Estonian to be the official language. As a result of public pressure, the Supreme Council of Soviet Estonia, on November 16, 1988, passed a sovereignty declaration that acknowledged the supremacy of Estonian laws. The disintegration of the USSR by parliamentary methods had thus begun, and the Estonian problem began to receive attention in the world arena.

In the years 1989 to 1991, civic society was restored in Estonia: a free press was established, political parties were formed, several formerly prohibited associations and organizations were restored, free elections took place, and society became more open. The ECP broke up and lost its hold on power. In November 1989 the Supreme Council declared null and void the decisions of July 23, 1940, which incorporated Estonia into the USSR. The idea that Estonia could not leave the USSR because Estonia never voluntarily joined it became widely spread. Historical truth was the basis for the Citizens Committees movement, established on February 24, 1989. It proposed the restoration of independence on the basis of international law and Estonian citizenship. On August 23, 1989, the Popular fronts from the Baltic states organized a six hundred kilometer long human chain from Vilnius (Lithuania) to Tallinn, demanding freedom for the Baltic states. On December 24, 1989, the USSR Supreme Soviet declared null and void the secret protocols to the Nazi-Soviet Pact. The Congress of Estonia, a new institution representing all registered citizens of the republic, convened on March 11, 1990. The Estonian Committee became its permanent working body. On March 30, 1990, the newly elected Supreme Council declared Soviet power to be illegal in Estonia and proclaimed a transition period for the restoration of the Republic of Estonia. On May 8, 1990, the symbols of the Estonian Soviet Socialist Republic were abolished, and the official name of the country became again Republic of Estonia.

Independence from Moscow increased step by step: an Estonian police and the foundation for a defense force were formed, payments into the USSR state budget were reduced, and an economic border was established. Cooperation among the Baltic states intensified and the Baltic Council, a consultative and coordinating body, was established. Transition to a market economy began, prices were liberalized, many small enterprises were privatized, and private farms were reestablished. Negotiations between Estonia and the USSR were unsuccessful. In January 1991, when Soviet forces intervened in Latvia and Lithuania, there was deep uneasiness in Estonia. However, the crisis passed and Estonia's government remained in place. In the referendum of March 3, 1991, 77.8 percent of the population (including a third of immigrants) supported restoring the independence of Estonia.

The internal crisis of the Soviet Union culminated in August 1991 in the attempted coup by reactionary forces. A state of emergency was declared over the whole of Soviet territory and power was seized by the National State of Emergency Committee (ESSC). The Estonian Supreme Soviet and the government declared the ESSC's orders to be illegal. Late on the night of August 20, with the support of a number of political groups, the Supreme Soviet passed a resolution on the National Independence of Es-

tonia that reestablished the independent state both de jure and de facto. On August 21 the attempted coup in Moscow failed and the tanks that had been brought in to lay siege to Tallinn retreated. Estonian independence was recognized on August 24 by the USSR, on August 27 by EC members, and on September 2 by the United States. On September 10 Estonia became a member of the Conference on Security and Cooperation in Europe (CSCE) and on September 17 of the United Nations.

After the restoration of independence, state power had to be reestablished. A constitutional assembly was formed to work out a new constitution. The assembly finished drafting the constitution by the end of 1991. This was followed by a national debate. On June 28, 1992, a national referendum approved the new constitution overwhelmingly and it came into force on July 3, 1992.

On the basis of the Election Act, passed in April 1992, preparations for national parliamentary and presidential elections were also carried out. At the same time political parties prepared for the elections on September 20, 1992. On October 5, 1992, the Riigikogu (parliament) elected Lennart Meri the first president of the newly independent Republic of Estonia.

Toward the end of 1992, the Riigikogu appointed Rait Maruste as chief justice of the Supreme Court and Eerik-Juhan Truuvali as legal chancellor at the beginning of the next year. On May 27, 1993, the Supreme Court held its first session in Tartu. Thus by spring 1993, the basic state administration structures had been put into place in the form of legislative power (Riigikogu), executive power (government) and judicial power (Supreme Court).

Independence created the necessary conditions for the transition to a market economy. The principal basis for economic reform was the monetary reform carried out in June 1992. The Estonian kroon was tied to the German mark at the rate of 1 mark to 8 kroon. With this monetary reform, Estonia cut itself off from the ruble zone and started developing an Estonia-centered economic policy. Within a few months, an economic balance was achieved and inflation abated. One of the most difficult years was 1992: significant economic indicators were at a low level. Over the next year the economy showed signs of improvement, and in 1994 the privatization of industry and ownership reform proceeded more quickly. Positive changes were accelerated by the increased inflow of foreign capital and the reinvestment of the profits of Estonian enterprises. Besides privatization and ownership reform, an important role in the transition process was played by the development of banks and the transformation of Soviet-style grand-scale agriculture into a system founded on individual ownership of farms. All these processes, especially the reorganization of agriculture, caused occasional diffi-culties (e.g., problems connected with small towns and villages that entirely depended on one large enterprise). The speed of privatization has been remarkable: whereas in 1994 the private sector's share of the GDP was 67.5 percent, by 1996 it had reached 86.2 percent. The per-centage of the private sector engaged in wholesale and retail business was 98.6. Privatization of land, however, did not go so smoothly; by autumn 1996, only 10 percent had been privatized.

The Estonian economy opened itself to the West, and economic integration with Europe has become an irre-versible process. On January 1, 1995, the free trade agree-ment between Estonia and the European Union (EU) came into force. Today more than 60 percent of Estonian foreign trade is with EU members. In addition, Estonia has signed free-trade agreements with several other coun-tries (Norway, Latvia, Lithuania, Czech Republic, etc.). Creating a legislative environment for entrepreneurship and keeping the state budget in balance have both helped considerably to regulate the economy. Between 1992 and 1995, approximately twelve thousand to fourteen thou-sand enterprises were set up each year. A characteristic tendency has been the growth of small enterprises, the private sector, and foreign investments.

BIBLIOGRAPHY

Lagerspetz, Mikko. *Constructing Post-Communism: A Study in the Estonian Social Problems Discourse.* Annales Universitatis Turkuensis. Turku, Finland: Turkun Yliopisto, 1996.

Lauristin, Marju, and Peeter Vihalemm with Karl Erik Rosengren and Lennart Weibull, eds. *Return to the Western World: Cultural and Political Perspectives on the Estonian Post-Communist Transition.* Tartu, Estonia: Tarty Universityiet Press, 1997.

Raun, Toivo U. *Estonia and Estonians,* 2d ed. Stanford, Calif.: Hoover Institution Press, 1991.

Aili Aarelaid-Tart

Political Parties

The Popular Front of Estonia, founded in 1988, aimed to unite all the forces seeking reform, from reform Com-munists to environmentalists, from moderate nationalists to economic reformers. Initially it aimed to support Soviet leader Mikhail Gorbachev's reform policy, but it was grad-ually pushed by events into endorsing independence in autumn 1989. Though heterogeneous in its composition, the front was united in organizing the mass movement that culminated in independence in 1991. Even before then, however, the front began to split into a number of different parties that currently dominate Estonian poli-tics. The exception to this assertion was the Estonian Na-tional Independence Party (ENIP), which, like the Pop-ular Front, was founded in 1988 but was more radical than its rival on the issues of independence and economic reform, and unwilling to run candidates for the Supreme Council (a Soviet body), concentrating instead on sup-porting the Estonian Congress as an alternative and, in its view, legitimate parliament.

The successor parties to the Popular Front included the Pro Patria (Fatherland) National Coalition Party, led by Mart Laar, and the Moderates, which, with the ENIP, formed the broadly right-wing government after the elec-tion of 1992. The Moderates were an alliance of the Social Democratic Party and the Estonian Rural Center Party, which allied with the Right on the issue of the restoration of the Estonian First Republic.

With the election of 1995 a new coalition took power. It was composed of the Estonian Coalition Party (made up of reform Communists and Popular Front moderates formerly in the Kindel Kodu, or Secure Home Party) led by Tiit Vahi, the Estonian Rural Union led by Arnold Rüutel, and the Center Party of Edgar Savisaar, formed from the rump of the Popular Front and with strength among blue-collar urban workers. When Savisaar was forced to resign following a scandal involving charges of illegal surveillance, the Center Party's position in the gov-ernment was taken by the Reform Party, headed by former Bank of Estonia governor Siim Kallas. In all, eleven par-ties, including Our Home Is Estonia, representing Esto-nian Russians, passed the 5 percent voting threshold re-quired to obtain seats in parliament in 1995. Nine did not, among them the Estonian Labor Party, successor to the hard-line Communists.

In March 1997, Mart Siimann of the Coalition Party replaced Vahi, whose policies he pledged to continue. Vahi had been accused of unethical real estate transac-tions. As a result of a defeat at the polls in March 1999, the Coalition Party lost control of the government to Mart Laar of the Fatherland Union, which was formed through the merger of the National Coalition Party and the Estonian National Independence Party.

BIBLIOGRAPHY

Hiden, John, and Patrick Salmon. *The Baltic Nations and Europe: Estonia, Latvia and Lithuania in the Twentieth Century.* Harlow, U.K.: Longman, 1991.

Lieven, Anatol. *The Baltic Revolution: Estonian, Latvia, Lithuania and the Path to Independence.* New Haven, Conn.: Yale University Press, 1983.

Norgaard, Ole, et al. *The Baltic States after Independence.* Cheltenham, U.K.: Edward Elgar, 1996.

Smith, Graham, ed. *The Baltic States: The National Self-Determination of Estonia, Latvia and Lithuania.* Basingstoke, U.K.: Macmillan, 1994.

Taagepera, Rein. *Estonia: Return to Independence.* Boulder, Colo.: Westview Press, 1993.

Thomas Lane

Ise-Majandav Eesti
(IME: Self-Managing Estonia)

When Mikhail Gorbachev became Soviet leader in 1985, he tried to tackle the problem of economic stagnation that had bedeviled the Soviet economy since at least the 1970s. The Baltic states' long industrial tradition, skilled labor forces, and higher labor productivity made them ideal laboratories in which to test his economic restructuring (perestroika) proposals.

The Balts were receptive to the ideas behind perestroika. In particular, they favored regional self-management and economic autonomy. In 1987 the so-called Four-Man Proposal was published in Estonia, named after four of the ten authors who were prepared to be identified—Edgar Savisaar, later prime minister; Siim Kallas, later president of the Estonian National Bank; Tiit Made, TV political commentator; and Mikk Titma, distinguished sociologist. They advocated *ise-majandav Eesti* (self-managing Estonia, IME), which involved making Estonia responsible for economic activities within its borders. To achieve this they proposed the transfer of enterprises from all-Union control to Estonian administration, an increase of Estonian budgetary autonomy, and the possibility of substantial institutional reforms. At this stage political independence was not envisaged. Indeed, the local economy would still be managed in close association with Moscow.

In April 1988 the Kremlin agreed to transfer control of seven leading economic sectors to Estonia, and in 1989 it produced a draft law remitting substantial economic powers to the republic but retaining significant control at the Union level. In the subsequent discussions on implementing the law, Soviet bureaucrats dragged their feet, interpreting the legislation in a restrictive way. The failure to gain agreement on meaningful economic autonomy from Moscow mobilized the Estonian Popular Front until it joined the radicals in demanding the restoration of political independence. The IME proposal was one of the catalysts for accelerated political change in Estonia and a major stimulus to the creation of the Estonian Popular Front.

Thomas Lane

Ethnic Cleansing in Croatia and Bosnia

The term *ethnic cleansing* denotes the forcible removal of a civil populace from a territory during which armed men kill men of military age, imprison or execute prominent members of the community, carry out wholesale rapes of women, and drive out the rest of the population.

Ethnic cleansing acquired near-universal currency as the term to describe rebel Serb attempts to achieve their war aims in Bosnia after April 1992. However, the preceding conflict in Croatia during 1991–92 in which Serb forces seized one-third of the newly independent state also involved indiscriminate attacks on civilians, although on a much smaller scale. The most notorious act of the Croatian war was the leveling of Vukovar, one of the most prosperous cities in Croatia where one-third of local families were ethnically mixed. The city fell to the Serbs on November 17, 1991, and human rights organizations claim that many civilians, including many of the patients of the city's hospital, were then indiscriminately killed by the occupying forces.

Lightly armed, or more often unarmed, Muslim civilians were the targets of rebel Serbs in Bosnia. The rebel Serbs under the overall command of General Ratko Mladić went on the offensive in April 1992. In 1993 the human rights organization Helsinki Watch published a massive volume on war crimes in Bosnia replete with accounts of invading Serb troops separating men from women and older men from "combat age" ones, then carrying out large-scale summary executions, beatings, torture, and detention of the males. An integral part of the ethnic cleansing process was the elimination of Muslim community leaders such as mayors, teachers, businessmen, and intellectuals; systematic attempts were made to remove any signs of the centuries-long Muslim presence in the area by blowing up mosques and other buildings of historic significance.

Rape was also used as a technique to demoralize the Muslim civilian population. The number of female rape victims is a matter of dispute, but estimates range as high as 20,000 (European Union figures) to 50,000 (the Sarajevo State Commission for the Investigation of War Crimes). An Amnesty International report published early in 1993 documented the existence of "rape camps"—detention centers organized mainly for the sexual abuse of women.

In August 1992 Western television journalists located Serb-run detention camps in which, according to Western human rights groups, up to 170,000 Muslim and Croat men had been held and up to 20,000 killed. The television footage of emaciated survivors created worldwide shock and led to claims that U.N. officials had been aware of these camps for several months but had kept silent about them.

Helsinki Watch in August 1992 named nine Serbs against whom it had evidence of involvement in war crimes or serious violations of the Geneva Convention. They included Slobodan Milošević, leader of Serbia; Radovan Karadžić, the Bosnian Serb leader; General Ratko Mladić, and Serb warlord "Arkan" (Zelko Raznjatović), who, in April 1992, permitted a photographer from *Time* magazine to film his soldiers carrying out wholesale execution of Muslim civilians.

In October 1992 the U.N. Security Council authorized the creation of what became a war crimes tribunal to examine evidence of atrocities in former Yugoslavia, and to prepare criminal charges against alleged perpetrators. Leading civilian and military officials from the self-styled Bosnian Serb republic were indicted, but President Milošević was not mentioned, even though military chiefs received their orders from him when they shelled the civil populace in the besieged Croatian cities of Vukovar and Dubrovnik in 1991.

Britain was condemned in December 1993 by MPs from all British parties for trying to obstruct the terms of the tribunal and for withholding evidence. In 1994 Louis Gentile, head of the U.N. Commission for Refugees in northern Bosnia, condemned the inaction of the big powers toward "persecution . . . of non-Serbs that was beyond evil."

The United Nations record of protecting civilians suffered further discredit with the resignation, on July 27, 1995, of Tadeusz Mazowiecki, Poland's first post-Communist head of government who had been the United Nation's special investigator in the former Yugoslavia since 1992. Mazowiecki declared, "I cannot continue to participate in the pretense of the protection of human rights." Already, by the end of 1992, the war in Bosnia had resulted in the largest forced migration of civilian populations in Europe since the 1940s. Ethnic cleansing was also carried out by Croatian and government forces in Bosnia, but Mazowiecki's investigations concluded that the overwhelming number of cases were carried out by Serb paramilitary or regular forces.

When fighting resumed in Croatia in the summer of 1995 with the Croatian reconquest of its Krajina region, there were widespread allegations of ethnic cleansing by reliable press and humanitarian sources. The vast majority of Krajina Serbs fled in advance of the Croatian offensive, perhaps 150,000 people in all, resulting in the end of a community that had existed there since the seventeenth century. The few who remained, mainly the elderly and infirm, were often terrorized by Croatian forces to induce their departure.

BIBLIOGRAPHY

Bell-Fialkoff, Andrew. *Ethnic Cleansing.* New York: St. Matrin's Press, 1996.

Cushman, Thomas, and Stjepan G. Mestrovic, ed. *This Time We Knew: Western Responses to Genocide in Bosnia.* New York: New York University Press, 1996.

Tom Gallagher

SEE ALSO Bosnia-Hercegovina: Bosnian War; Croatia; Kosovo

Eurocommunism

Political ideology and movement particularly in Mediterranean states in the 1960s and 1970s that offered an alternative to Soviet-style communism. Eurocommunism represented an adaptation of communism to the politics of these states and their historical development.

Eurocommunism has its earliest intellectual roots in the "evolutionary socialism" of Eduard Bernstein, the participatory democratic theory of Rosa Luxemburg, and the theory of council and party politics of Antonio Gramsci. Adapting themselves to parliamentary conditions in Italy, France, Spain, and Portugal, Eurocommunist parties departed from an antisystem ideology and rhetoric and participated more fully in the mainstream political life of these countries.

While there was no founding manifesto or document proposing their program, Eurocommunists considered two texts as important sources of their principles—the declaration signed in Madrid in March 1977 by the leaders of the Spanish, Italian, and French Communist parties (PCE, PCI, and PCF), and Santiago Carrillo's book *"Eurocommunism" and the State.* The most important Eurocommunist leaders were Enrico Berlinguer in Italy, Georges Marchais in France, and Carrillo in Spain. The most important period of Eurocommunism was clearly the 1970s, when many of its main tenets were developed, and the Communist parties of these countries enjoyed influence within the governments of these states, e.g., the "historic compromise" in Italy in the mid-1970s, and the legalization of the Spanish party after the death of Franco.

Eurocommunist theory broke from Soviet Communist theory to argue that Communist parties in modern, industrialized, Western states could lead coalitions of political classes, including the working class, professionals, and students. Eurocommunist parties did not organize themselves in strict accordance with the Leninist principle of democratic centralism. These parties represented an alliance of the working and middle classes within democratic systems, and sought to reform those systems, thus providing an alternative to total revolution as the primary method of political change. Eurocommunist parties often expressed a willingness to work with Socialist parties in these states, and also cultivated special relationships with both industrial and service labor unions.

In recent years Eurocommunist parties have lost influence as they have lost support at the polls. Reasons for their decline include the success of Socialist governments in maintaining power, especially in France and Spain, the collapse of the Soviet system of government and power in Eastern Europe, the rise of rival political movements and parties on the Left, such as the Green and feminist movements, and the collapse of traditional bases of support as economies shifted from industrial to service-sector work. Symptomatically, in 1990 the Italian Communist Party changed its name to the Democratic Party of the Left.

BIBLIOGRAPHY

Antonian, Armen. *Toward a Theory of Eurocommunism: The Relationship of Eurocommunism to Eurosocialism.* New York: Greenwood Press, 1987.

Carrillo, Santiago. *"Eurocommunism" and the State.* Tr. by N. Green and A. M. Elliott. London: Lawrence and Wishart, 1977.

Kriegel, Annie. *Eurocommunism: A New Kind of Communism?* Tr. by Peter S. Stern. Stanford, Calif.: Hoover Institution Press, 1978.

Lange, Peter, and Maurizio Vannicelli. *The Communist Parties of Italy, France, and Spain: Postwar Change and Continuity.* London: George Allen and Unwin, 1981.

Leonhard, Wolfgang. *Eurocommunism: Challenge for East and West.* Tr. by Mark Vecchio. New York: Holt, Rinehart and Winston, 1978.

Narkiewicz, Olga A. *The End of the Bolshevik Dream: Western European Communist Parties in the Late Twentieth Century.* London: Routledge, 1990.

————. *Eurocommunism: 1968–1986, a Select Bibliography.* London: Mansell, 1987.

Schwab, George. *Eurocommunism: The Ideological and Political-Theoretical Foundations.* Westport, Conn.: Greenwood Press, 1981.

Eric Gorham

SEE ALSO Berlinguer, Enrico; Carrillo, Santiago; Napolitano, Giorgio

European Bank for Reconstruction and Development

Intergovernmental organization, an agency of the World Bank with a political- and economic-oriented mandate. Initially proposed by French President François Mitterrand in 1989 and established in 1990, the European Bank for Reconstruction and Development (EBRD) initiated its activities in 1991 with a starting capital of 10 billion ecus. The treaty to constitute the EBRD was signed by forty nations, the European Community (EC), and the European Investment Bank (EIB). Jacques Attali, Mitterand's adviser who had first recommended the venture, was designated the bank's president, with a secretariat in London.

The mandate of the EBRD is to aid in the reconstruction of the economies of central and Eastern Europe and the former Soviet Union and facilitate their transition to a market economy, on condition that the countries implement the principles of multiparty democracy, pluralism, and a market economy. The bank renders assistance by offering market-rate loans and making equity investments. Precedence is given to programs that undertake structural and sectoral reforms, including the breakup of monopolies, decentralization, and privatization of state enterprises to facilitate integration into the international economy. It similarly supports projects to restructure industry, increase international investment, improve the environment, and promote trade. Though the United States and the United Kingdom initially wanted lending to be restricted to the private sector, a bargain was struck allowing up to 40 percent of the bank's assets to be employed for public-sector programs.

The founding treaty of the EBRD stipulated that 60 percent of its lending be designated for private enterprise. The bank thus encourages private and competitive enterprises, specifically small- and medium-sized businesses, and aggregates national and international capital. It offers an array of financial services, such as loans, equity and guarantees. A low rate of utilization, though, has been an obstacle for the Bank.

At the EBRD's annual meeting in 1993, the Board of Governors formed an audit committee to probe the bank's financial procedures. The report of the committee censured inept lending practices and excessive internal use of funds. Attali resigned from the presidency. A new president, Jacques de Larosière of France, who had been managing director of the International Monetary Fund (IMF) from 1978 to 1987, was appointed. He set out to implement organizational adjustments to make the bank more efficient. This included termination of the political department and eradication of the division between merchant banking and development banking, which had formerly been responsible for the private and public sectors, respectively, in support of a more regional orientation.

The EBRD has a unique function available to it in the integration of Europe, the integration of central Eastern Europe into the international financial system, and in the formation of the private sector in recipient countries. If the bank is to be effective in facilitating transitions to democracy and market economies, it must discover a satisfactory alliance of private-sector orientations to investment banking with conventional public-sector issues concerning infrastructure.

BIBLIOGRAPHY

The Economics of Transition. Oxford: Oxford University Press for the European Bank for Reconstruction and Development, Vol. 1, no. 1.

Menkveld, Paul. *Origin and Role of the European Bank for Reconstruction and Development.* London: Graham and Trotman, 1991.

Shihata, Ibrahim F. I. *The European Bank for Reconstruction and Development: A Comparative Analysis of the Constituent Agreement.* London: Graham and Trotman, 1990.

Transition Report: European Bank for Reconstruction and Development. London: The Bank for Reconstruction and Development, 1994.

Kenneth Keulman

European Commission

Executive body of the European Union (EU). The European Commission was established in 1958 to draft and implement laws for the European Economic Community (EEC). After the expansion of the EU to fifteen members in 1995, the European Commission was expanded to twenty members, who are appointed by their individual governments for a five year term. France, Germany, Italy, Spain, and the United Kingdom each has two representatives. The other EU member states have one representative on the commission. The commission has a broad assortment of executive powers and operates as the civil service of the EU. It also proposes acts to the European Parliament and the Council of Ministers and enforces legislation enacted by that parliament.

The entire commission resigned on March 16, 1999. Although the commission had guided the EU through the process that preceded the introduction of the single European currency in January 1999, an inquiry by the European Parliament disclosed its inability to deal with problems of corruption and nepotism. The rebellion of the European Parliament was fueled by the accusation of favoritism in the awarding of grants by Edith Cresson, the head of the department of research and education.

Romano Prodi, the president-designate of the commission, announced on July 9, 1999, a new nineteen-member executive, consisting of fourteen men and five women. Despite the deficiency in female members, Prodi appointed the Spanish minister of agriculture, Loyola de Palacio del Valle Lersundi, to a vice presidency of the commission and commissioner in charge of transportation, energy, and relations with the European Parliament. Hoping to restore public confidence in the executive, Prodi retained only four members of the outgoing commission: Neil Kinnock of Great Britain, who moved from transportation to the new office of commissioner for administrative reform; Franz Fischler of Austria, who added fishing to his previous responsibility for agriculture; Mario Monti of Italy, who moved from single market and taxation policy to antitrust to replace the effective Karel Van Miert of Belgium, who chose to accept an academic post in the Netherlands; and Erkki Liikanen of Finland, who moved from budget to industry. Among the new commissioners, Chris Patten, the former governor of Hong Kong, was given foreign affairs, including relations with China, and Pedro Solbes Mira, the former finance minister of Spain, was assigned economic and monetary affairs, including the common currency. In order to avoid the criticism of "unhealthy national allegiances" and cronyism, Prodi stated that he would require commissioners to include officials from at least three nationalities in their private offices and pick an executive director from a nationality different from their own.

BIBLIOGRAPHY

"All Commissioners of European Union Give Resignations: Waste and Fraud Cited: Inquiry Reports Graft in Aid and Other Programs was 'Unnoticed' by Officials," *New York Times,* March 16, 1999.

At the Heart of the Union: Studies of the European Commission. New York, N.Y.: St. Martin's Press, 1997.

"A Hybrid Entity, With Worldwide Muscle," *New York Times,* March 16, 1999.

James, Barry, "Ethical Laxity Undermined EU Executive Body, Panel Finds," *International Herald Tribune,* July 23, 1999.

———. " 'New Era of Change' Arrives in Brussels," *International Herald Tribune,* July 10–11, 1999.

Bernard Cook

European Defense Community

Proposed supranational European military. The Korean War (1950–53) heightened fears in the West that the Soviet Union might exploit the engagement of the United States in other areas by taking advantage of its conventional military superiority in Europe. West German Chancellor Konrad Adenauer suggested to the United States that Germany would be willing to take part in the common defense of the West. In the latter part of 1950 the United States suggested that West Germany be admitted to NATO. The French were reluctant to see an independent German armed force. In 1952 France advanced the Pleven Plan for a European military that, with the assistance of the United States, would provide for the defense of Europe. The national forces of all the signatories to the European Defense Community (EDC) would be incorporated into the European force and be subjected to supranational control. Robert Schuman, French foreign minister, introduced the idea at a meeting of the Council of Europe in 1951. Despite the opposition of the U.S. Department of Defense the proposal was accepted by the NATO Council in May 1952. The United Kingdom showed the same distance that it had demonstrated and would demonstrate toward projects for European integration. The treaty providing for the EDC was signed by the same six countries that had joined the European Coal and Steel Community (ECSC): France, Italy, the Benelux countries, and West Germany. In early 1953 the Consultative Assembly of the Council of Europe proposed a directly elected European parliament that would exercise control over the ECSC, the EDC, and the proposed European Economic Community.

The development of the integrated NATO command with an American commander-in-chief and undergirded by substantial U.S. subsidies undercut the potential for an independent EDC and made it superfluous from a military point of view. Though the treaty was ratified by the Benelux countries and West Germany, Italy waited for France. And in France, the originator of the idea, serious doubts undermined the project. Many in France were concerned about the absence of the United Kingdom; national pride had been wounded by the failures of the French military in Vietnam—this was not seen as an opportune moment to forswear France's national military; and trouble was brewing in North Africa. Finally Premier Pierre Mendès-France brought the treaty before the French National Assembly without a recommendation. The National Assembly rejected the EDC on August 30, 1954, by a vote of 319 to 264.

With the collapse of the EDU the issue of a German military was solved through its integration into NATO. This was effected by the Western European Union (WEU). The Brussels Treaty of 1948 had produced the European Union (EU), a fifty-year alliance among the

United Kingdom, France, and the Benelux countries to provide for Western European defense. Though the EU had been superseded by NATO, it still existed. Anthony Eden, the U.K. Secretary of State for Foreign Affairs, proposed that Italy and West Germany become members and its name be changed to Western European Union. The WEU was incorporated into NATO. Germany joined the WEU and agreed that the size and armaments of its military would be determined by the WEU. This and the U.K. commitment to keep its forces in Germany indefinitely sufficiently soothed French concerns and Germany joined NATO.

BIBLIOGRAPHY

Fursdon, Edward. *The European Defence Community: A History.* New York: St. Martin's Press, 1980.
McGeehan, Robert. *The German Rearmament Question: American Diplomacy and European Defense after World War II.* Urbana: University of Illinois Press, 1971.

Bernard Cook

SEE ALSO North Atlantic Treaty Organization; Pleven, René; Schuman Plan; Schuman, Robert; Western European Union

European Free Trade Association

The European Free Trade Association (EFTA) was founded by Britain, Sweden, Norway, Denmark, Switzerland, Austria, and Portugal in 1959–60. The EFTA treaty came into force on May 3, 1960. Finland became associated with EFTA in 1961 through the FIN-EFTA treaty. The EFTA treaty provided for strictly intergovernmental market integration in the form of an industrial free-trade area with weak institutions. The treaty included limited provisions for majority voting to enforce treaty provisions, a general consultation and complaints procedure, escape clauses intended mainly for balance-of-payments problems, and a set of rules of origin. The EFTA treaty defined industrial commodities in a set of process lists and lists of basic materials. Commodities could claim EFTA treatment when containing more than 50 percent value added in EFTA. In agriculture the EFTA treaty merely included a general commitment to the removal of agricultural export subsidies and to consultations about the expansion of agricultural trade among member states.

The creation of EFTA was in response to the failure of the OEEC negotiations during 1957–58 about the creation of a wider free-trade area in Western Europe, encompassing the six member states of the European Economic Community (EEC), founded in 1957–58, and the so-called OEEC peripherals. Such a free-trade area had been proposed by the British government in 1956. Negotiations in Paris had, however, revealed substantial technical problems, particularly concerning rules of origin. Moreover, Britain's OEEC partners saw the proposal as uneven, especially in its exclusion of agriculture, and many in the EEC feared that it would dilute the political content of the newly founded organization. When Charles de Gaulle became French president in 1958, he also feared a reduction of French influence over European integration. He finally vetoed the proposal in November 1958.

With the creation of EFTA the so-called Outer Seven European states proved that an industrial free-trade area was technically feasible and could operate with a loose institutional framework. Moreover, the gradual reduction and eventual abolition by January 1, 1967, of internal tariffs in EFTA did lead to increased trade. From 1959 to 1969 EFTA's trade with the EEC grew by 130 percent, while intra-EFTA trade grew by 186 percent. EFTA's greatest economic success was to foster economic ties among Sweden, Norway, and Denmark, as intra-Scandinavian trade rose by 284 percent during the same period. But none of the member states regarded EFTA as an aim in itself. Rather, they hoped it would be a bridge to the EEC to reopen negotiations with that organization about a wider free-trade area in Western Europe.

Compared with the EEC, EFTA suffered from four main weaknesses. The first was its low degree of economic cohesion as a result of its lack of geographical coherence, of the inclusion of two peripheral states with a very weak industrial base (Portugal and Finland), and of the lack of reciprocal export advantages in agriculture, especially for Denmark. The second weakness was the lack of agreement on an alternative policy, once a quick agreement with the EEC proved illusory, which became evident when Britain applied for EEC membership for the first time in August 1961. EFTA also lacked a committed economic and political leadership by its strongest member, Britain. Finally, its fourth weakness was U.S. hostility to it and to a wider settlement between the EEC and EFTA that intensified with persistent U.S. balance-of-payments problems during 1958–61.

The conflict between EFTA and the EEC was finally resolved in 1972–73 when Britain and Denmark as well as Ireland became members of the EEC in its first round of enlargement. Norway stayed outside the EEC after a referendum that showed a slight majority against joining. Norway and the other remaining EFTA states concluded bilateral free-trade treaties with the EEC that safeguarded their core trade interests. What EFTA and its members had established politically during the 1960s was, most of all, that the contradiction between widening and deepening the EEC asserted by the protagonists of a tightly knit core Europe was artificial. It became clear that to manage internal interest mediation and succeed in enhancing the cohesion of the inner core of European integration, the EEC also needed to address its responsibility for all Europe and to allow for the economic and political interests of other European states on the periphery.

EFTA continued to exist after 1972–73, but it increasingly developed into a waiting room for future full EC membership. (In 1967 the EEC was combined with the European Coal and Steel Community and the European Atomic Energy Community to form the European Communities. The plural form was changed to the European Community in the 1980s.) Portugal joined the EC in 1986 and Austria, Finland, and Sweden in 1995. Only Switzerland, Liechtenstein, Norway, and Iceland, which had joined EFTA in 1970, remained in EFTA, with only Liechtenstein and Norway linked to the European Union (EU) through the European Economic Area. The revamped EFTA began to see its diminished future role as that of a lobby group for further liberalization of international trade, but it no longer played any significant role in European politics.

BIBLIOGRAPHY

Kaiser, Wolfram. "Challenge to the Community: The Creation, Crisis and Consolidation of the European Free Trade Association, 1958–72." *Journal of European Integration History* 3, no. 1 (1997): 7–33.

———. "A better Europe? EFTA, the EFTA secretariat and the European identities of the 'outer Seven,' 1958–72," in Marie-Thérèse Bitsch ed. *European Institutions and European Identity* (in press).

Malmborg, Mikael, and Johnny Laursen, "The Creation of EFTA," in T. B. Olesen, ed. *Interdependence versus Integration: Denmark, Scandinavia and Western Europe, 1945–1960.* Odense, Denmark: 1995, 197–212.

The EFTA archives can be consulted on request at the EFTA headquarters in Geneva, Switzerland.

Wolfram Kaiser

European Monetary Institute

The European Monetary Institute (EMI), a precursor of the European Central Bank, was established as Stage Two in the transition to Economic and Monetary Union (EMU) defined by the 1991 Maastricht Treaty (formally, the Treaty on European Union). Established in 1994, the EMI developed a coherent plan for the implementation of a European monetary union on January 1, 1999, with the creation of the Euro as a single currency of the eleven participating EU members.

The treaty has three pillars: a common foreign and security policy, common action in domestic and justice affairs, and economic and monetary union (common currency). The purpose of Stage 2, which began on January 1, 1994, was to prepare for a single monetary policy while monetary policy responsibility remained with national authorities. Countries also began, as agreed, to make their central banks independent in the second stage. This was a transitional period to a third (final) stage during which the basic organs and structure of the European Central Bank will begin operation and exchange rates will be permanently fixed. In 1998 the EMI was scheduled to play a pivotal role in the politically sensitive decision to select the nations that will participate in the introduction of the European Monetary Union.

For Stages Two and Three to exist it was necessary to revise the Treaty of Rome, which established the European Economic Community, (EEC), to create the necessary institutional structure. To achieve this an Intergovernmental Conference on EMU was convened in 1991. The final negotiations resulted in the Maastricht Treaty, which amended parts of the Treaty of Rome and incorporated the Protocols on the Statute of the European System of Central Banks and of the European Central Bank and the Protocol on the Statute of the European Monetary Institute.

The EMI coordinated monetary policy of the central banks of the member states within the European System of Central Banks (ESCB) to prepare Stage 3. Its objectives, tasks, and functions included; central bank cooperation and coordination of policies; preparatory work for Stage Three of the EMU; and advisory functions. The EMI consists of the EMI Council, a president, and an internal organization. In accordance with the EMI Statute, the Institute has its own budget of approximately $615 million to cover the administrative expenditure. The institute is headquartered in Frankfurt am Main, Germany.

BIBLIOGRAPHY

Bayoumi, Tamin A., Barry Eichengreen, and Jurgen von Hagen. *European Monetary Unification: Implications of Research for Policy, Implications of Policy for Research.* Berkeley: Center for German and European Studies, University of California, 1996.

Bayoumi, Tamin A., and Barry Eichengreen. *Shocking Aspects of European Monetary Unification.* Cambridge, Mass.: National Bureau of Economic Research, 1992.

Eichengreen, Barry J. *European Monetary Unification: Theory, Practice and Analysis.* Cambridge, Mass. MIT Press, 1997.

Eichengreen, Barry J., and Fabio Ghironi. *European Monetary Unification: The Challenges Ahead.* London: Centre for Economic Policy Research, 1995.

Kenan, Peter B. *Sorting Out Some EMU Issues.* Princeton, N.J.: Princeton University, International Finance Section, 1996.

Scobie, H. M., ed. *European Monetary Union: The Way Forward.* New York: Routledge, 1998.

Welfens, Paul J. J., ed. *European Monetary Integration: EMS Developments and International Post-Maastricht Perspectives,* 3d rev. ed. New York: Springer-Verlag, 1996.

————. *European Monetary Union: Transition, International, and Policy Options.* New York: Springer-Verlag, 1997.

Martin J. Manning

European Parliament

April 1951: A common parliamentary assembly was established for the European Coal and Steel Community (ECSC) through the Treaty of Paris. It was empowered to question and censure the high authority of the ECSC. It could also discuss the ECSC's reports and exercise limited supervision over the ECSC.

March 1957: With the treaties of Rome the ECSC's common assembly was replaced by the Assembly of the European Community. Its 142 members were appointed by the respective national parliaments, and it exercised an advisory function.

January 1973: The European Parliament was expanded to 198 members when Denmark, Ireland, and Britain joined the European Economic Community (EC).

December 1974: It was agreed by member governments that the members of the European Parliament would be elected by direct universal suffrage every five years.

June 1979: The first direct elections to the 410-member European Parliament were held. Sixty-three percent of eligible voters participated in the nine member countries.

January 1981: With Greece's admission to the EC, the number of European Parliament deputies was expanded to 434.

June 1984: Sixty-one percent of eligible voters participated in the second direct elections for the European Parliament.

January 1986: With the admission of Spain and Portugal the parliament was expanded to 518 members.

February 1986: The foreign ministers of the EC states signed the Single European Act. The role of the European Parliament in the making of laws was expanded and it was given the power to ratify the adhesion of new full and associate members.

June 1989: Only 50.5 percent of eligible voters voted in the third direct elections to the parliament.

March 1991: Eighteen representatives from the six Länder (states) of the German Democratic Republic were admitted to the European Parliament as observers.

February 1992: The Maastricht Treaty, agreed to in December 1991, signed in February 1992, and ratified in May 1993, empowered the parliament to veto some European laws and gave it a greater voice in matters of education, culture, health, and consumer protection.

May 1994: The parliament overwhelmingly approved the extension of European Union membership to Austria, Finland, Norway, and Sweden.

June 9–12, 1994: European nationals living in a member state other than their own were allowed to vote in the fourth direct election to the parliament. The parliament was increased to 567 members to take into account German reunification.

Bernard Cook

European Union

Fifteen-member European governmental organization resulting from successive efforts to create a United States of Europe after World War II, which formulates comprehensive regional planning in the areas of trade; agriculture; transportation; industrial, monetary, social, environmental, technological, and foreign policy; and security issues. Based on their successful cooperation in the European Coal and Steel Community (ECSC), started in 1952, the original six member governments—France, Germany, Italy, Belgium, Netherlands, and Luxembourg—negotiated a plan for a European Defense Community, accepted by five countries until its final defeat in the French parliament. Not to be dissuaded, in 1958 the six launched the European Economic Community (EEC), also known as the Common Market, and the European Atomic Energy Community (Euratom). Eventually they merged along with the ECSC, in 1967, under a single institutional structure, the European Community (EC). From 1993 the Maastricht Treaty expanded the organization's economic and political roles to create the European Union (EU). Denmark, Ireland, and the United Kingdom acceded to the EC in 1973, Greece in 1981, Portugal and Spain in 1986. Austria, Finland, and Sweden joined in 1995.

The EU is the product of creative thinking responding to the glaring needs of a particular time and of the sheer force of the personalities of individuals involved in its construction. It is like the animal designed by a committee: incomprehensible except to those who know how the parts were appended. Its institutional and constitutional history must be grasped to understand the attitudes, expectations, and politics that surround it today.

The term *integration* describes the process of organizing Europe for common tasks, started by the ECSC. Frenchman Jean Monnet was the first in a long line of technocrats whose passions focused on building Europe. Monnet's technocratic impulses found expression in the novel institutional structure he devised for the ECSC. He supplied the plans for the first so-called supranational organization: one that stands, figuratively, above the member countries and, literally, makes decisions that are legally binding. The institution called the High Authority was the supranational essence for the institutional designers and the institution most objectionable to more sovereignty—individual countries. Britain, in particular, would not submit to the decision-making powers of the High Authority, but Monnet refused to dilute the powers of this institution. He passionately avowed that countries needed to give up some of their sovereignty if they were to get along. According to Monnet's view, the power politics of the past based on furthering national interests had only produced wars. Instead of an onslaught against sovereignty, Monnet opted for a "sectoral" approach. Countries would be asked to give up some of their sovereignty in a vital sector, and once having learned and reaped the benefits of that cooperation they would want to expand the process into new sectors. In pursuit of peace Monnet initially targeted coal and steel, the industry that supplied France's and Germany's war efforts and represented the source of recurrent territorial disputes between them. In this way, countries' making decisions in common on select issues represented a broader plan for bringing about stability in Europe. In a negative vein, suspicious politicians have since spoken of "integration through the back door."

In the aftermath of World War II Monnet's fears about politics based predominantly on claims about sovereignty had wide support from partisans who had fought in the anti-Nazi Resistance. Concerned that history not repeat itself and convinced they had sacrificed for their right to influence European relations after the war, resistance fighters gained inspiration from the idea of uniting Europe through federalism. Altiero Spinelli (1907–86), an Italian communist and a founder of the federalist movement in Europe, led their cause with writings on European unification during imprisonment for his role in the resistance. Even though Monnet's plan was based on lower expectations, it justified itself to federalists as a plan to accomplish their objectives incrementally.

From the outset technocratic and popular dynamics mixed in the creation of Europe. While Monnet provided the institutional and legal planning, European elites and the public attached themselves to the idea, captured in the rallying cry "the United States of Europe." Even when French President Charles de Gaulle opposed the federalist conception of Europe in the mid-1960s, he substituted for it another idea, that of "Europe des Patries" (Europe of Nations) built on strong nation-states using their solidarity to maintain Europe's influence in the world. However, de Gaulle believed countries had to protect their vital interests and cultural distinctions. Britain neither shared the Europeanist view of the Federalists nor that of the Gaullists. Britain's perspective was entirely opposite: fearful of the loss of sovereignty, dismissive, and mistrustful of non-British institutions, and doubtful that Europe would ever recover from the humiliation and devastation of World War II. The term "special relationship" suggested the extent to which Britain linked its future with the United States. As a result Britain refused to join the EEC as it had the ECSC, leaving the original six to go forward with their plans.

The extent to which the Franco-German relationship gave identity and form to Europe should not be underestimated. French Foreign Minster Robert Schuman had proposed the ECSC and enlisted the personal and political commitments of the first postwar West German Chancellor Konrad Adenauer. Eventually, the policy focus of the early EEC represented a Franco-German compromise, the first of many more. A reindustrializing Germany aimed to secure an adequate market for its goods. France was also interested in stimulating industry, but it had a larger agricultural sector than that of Germany and the will to see it survive after the extreme food shortages of World War II. The Treaty of Rome, the founding document of the EEC, accommodated both France and Germany with measures and timetables for creating a customs union among the members states (MS) and a policy to protect European agriculture, eventually known as the Common Agricultural Policy (CAP). To consolidate the customs union, a common external tariff was agreed to in relation to non-EEC countries. The much-quoted line

from the preamble of the Treaty of Rome, the promise of "an ever closer union," signified that the EEC was an initial step in European integration. Indeed, the view that constructing Europe remained unfinished business dominated the development of the EEC and led to a pattern of European elites' initiating new common policies and institutional innovations at important junctures to push the development of Europe.

In the heady years of launching European unification, the institutions and policies tended to run on their own steam. The successor to the High Authority, the European Commission, had the exclusive right of proposition as well as of administering the bureaucracy. The Commission made its proposals to a Council of Ministers with the power of decision. These were ministers from national governments whose portfolios matched the issues under consideration—agricultural ministers dealing with farm issues, foreign ministers tackling the thornier questions, and so forth. As the institutions developed their characters, the supranational Commission framed the issues and controlled the agenda while the national-minded councils had the last word. If governments did not keep their obligations or institutions erred, there was the European Court of Justice, which was actually accorded great respect by MS. Deadlines were met ahead of time and consensus decision making tended to be the rule.

The first serious dispute among the MS involved de Gaulle's claim that the Commission, the EEC executive, had overreached by linking completion of the CAP to securing France's agreement on a peripheral issue. France felt betrayed by the Commission strategy of applying pressure on such an extrasensitive issue and maintained the CAP was not up for renegotiation. The French followed the "empty chair" policy in which they made themselves absent from community institutions for a six-month period and insisted on a price for their return. France succeeded in having the other MS accept the Luxembourg Compromise. Henceforth, a country could not be overruled in the council if it claimed it had a "vital" interest at stake, and, thus, the Treaty of Rome's provisions for phasing in majority voting were suspended. In the future, where disagreements existed, de Gaulle (and other members with similar fears) had stunted the development of procedures committing the countries to resolution.

Unfortunately, the decade of the 1970s was a time when disagreements abounded and procedures and institutions became increasingly impoverished as a result of a lack of legitimacy. Unresolved issues mounted as well as a lack of consensus over how the community should develop. Integrationists pitted themselves against anti-integrationists. Meanwhile, economic issues were fought over a wide ideological gap between the European Left and Right. The 1970s was not without accomplishments. Informal procedures for European political cooperation began to take root in the beginning of the decade as foreign ministers consulted on foreign policy questions. At the end of the decade two achievements in particular stood out. The first direct election of the European Parliament in 1979 meant that this institution had a popular basis for claiming new powers, and it has consistently done so to overcome its initial weakness. In addition, two monetary arrangements were attempted during the decade, one of which survived into the 1990s and, ultimately, provided the basis for European and Economic Monetary Union (EMU). In 1979 French President Valéry Giscard d'Estaing and German Chancellor Helmut Schmidt proposed the European Monetary System (EMS), a loosely structured regime. The countries that joined the Exchange Rate Mechanism of the EMS committed to minimize the fluctuation of their currencies within so-called bands.

Despite these bright spots, the community entered the 1980s with a backlog of unsettled issues in the council and economies badly shaken by the oil crises of the previous decade to which the Europeans could not mount a unified response. Various diagnoses for the sources of the "*immobilisme*" that afflicted the EEC ranged from structural flaws to the lack of political will. Constitution builders, especially among the federalists in the European Parliament still answering to the call of Altiero Spinelli, wanted to strengthen the community's pro-European institutions (i.e., the Commission and the European Parliament) and reintroduce majority voting. Opponents maintained that without political will institutional tinkering was of no avail. The British disdained blueprints in favor of institutions evolving, much as they had done in Britain, with experience creating necessity. This meant, in political terms, that the British tended to oppose the institutional schemes of the federalists and supplied the "lowest common denominator" on issues of constitutional reform.

The 1980s was a time when Britain tried to dominate the community, and almost succeeded, with Prime Minister Margaret Thatcher determined to treat the EC with a dose of her own policy mixture. Formidable German and French leaders, respectively, Helmut Kohl and François Mitterrand, both of whom eventually outserved Thatcher, provided counterweights to her. However, community decision making still suffered. Thatcher's primary concerns were initially financial. In simple terms, her view was that Britain contributed disproportionately to the community budget, which, in turn, was excessively allocated to agricultural spending and not of great benefit to Britain. When she took aim at CAP overspending (which in fact was the main EC budget item), she ran squarely up against the French and, often, their German allies. The so-called British budget dispute stymied action on other issues and eventually isolated Britain in the community. A compromise was reached in 1984 after four years of wrangling, and the community seemed ready for a fresh start.

The one issue Britain's leaders could wholeheartedly embrace was improving the market potential of the community. Impediments to trade in the form of nontariff barriers had mounted at the same time the community's institutions failed in the area of decision making. Many of the proposals blocked in the council were linked to creating a more efficient market. British Commissioner Lord Cockfield (1984–88) grasped both the strategy and the content of what was required to revitalize the community. He identified the great challenge of the community to be that of constructing a market rivaling that of the United States and scrupulously detailed the numerous concrete measures needed to accomplish his goal.

The political climate supported free-market initiatives. Thatcherism and Reaganism had gathered steam, ultimately to propel neoliberalism to ascendancy in the policies of international lending institutions and the economic approaches of the majority of the world's countries in the next decade. Furthermore, by the mid-1980s the "global economy" had made its presence felt with competition from Asia's "tigers"—countries in which aggressive export strategies had produced high rates of growth. Socialist economies had shown they could not compete. Even though France was under the Socialist leadership of President Mitterrand throughout the 1980s, and for that matter the community, with French Socialist Jacques Delors at the head of the Commission, both leaders personally committed themselves to market-based economics. They could not turn back the tide begun by Reaganomics in the United States and Thatcherism in Britain. Fortuitously, "creating the single market" unified the community's political heads at a time when all but Italy of the community's most influential members had politically secure and powerful leaders. Among the "*cinq grands*" Spain was anxious to prove its European credentials; Britain wanted to show a constructive approach after the "British budget dispute"; Italy kept its tradition of being pro-European; while France and Germany shared Italy's devotion to Europe and, as usual, worked in tandem. Elite support and serious stocktaking of Europe's global position produced an agreement that relaunched the community. Timely, topical, and fresh, the single-market initiative also appeared to provide direct solutions to identifiable problems, cutting through the contemporary tendency of obscurity in politics. Indeed, the idea proved to be a public relations dream and led to a massive advertising campaign built around the central topic of achieving the single market by "1992," the target year becoming a code word for the enormous project. Therefore, "1992" succeeded in mobilizing public opinion. As it turned out, the Single European Act (SEA), ratified in 1986, incorporated the single market, along with a variety of other commitments, into a constitutional document amending the Treaty of Rome.

The SEA succeeded in so far as it gave the community competency in new policy areas (i.e., the environment and research and development of new technologies) and, among institutional reforms, instituted majority voting in the council on matters related to completing the single market. More generally, it provided the decision makers with a wide area of consensus on which to build and connect to a vast area of linked issues. It cemented political goodwill and offered a model for future constitutional reforms. However, the process failed completely to incorporate public support and participation in an enterprise citizens increasingly came to see as excessively elite-governed, technocratic and far-removed from common concerns to the point that it was unaccountable in regular democratic terms. People began to regret the loss of influence through parliamentarians whose names they at least knew on issues they at least identified with. Eurocrats working hard to expand the scope of the community did not seem to inspire confidence; more integration through the "back door" eventually produced a backlash.

Looking forward to the 1990s, community decision makers emboldened by their successes with the SEA and other 1980s initiatives began to prepare for the next comprehensive negotiation. The prevailing logic suggested that a single market required a common currency. Experience had shown the extent to which currency instability produced distortions in the common market. Transacting in multiple currencies created inefficiencies and higher costs. Furthermore, European governments discovered early in the decade how extremely vulnerable their separate currencies were to traders after speculation had forced several currencies out of the Exchange Rate Mechanism of the EMS. Finally, in political terms, a common currency seemed to be a way around dependency on the U.S. dollar, a bone of contention for the French and a position unequal to the status of a unified Germany, but something Thatcher claimed she did not object to in the least. As earlier initiatives concerned themselves with currency stability, the bureaucratic dynamic assured the issue was not dead. Major political figures gave their support to the

single currency, notably Kohl and Mitterrand, while Thatcher's party removed her from office partly as a result of her playing the role of "spoiler" in European affairs. The 1989 Delors Report provided the blueprint for the EMU, which ultimately became the cornerstone of the Treaty on European Union (TEU), signed by the heads of government in Maastricht, the Netherlands, in December 1991 and popularly known as simply "Maastricht." This was also the point, apparently, at which Commission President Jacques Delors had overreached.

As a comprehensive agreement Maastricht was, by then, the tried-and-true formula for more federalism mixing institutional reforms and expanded competencies. In scope, however, Maastricht represented a huge leap, as it included three significant pillars. The first pillar expanded the content, especially with regard to the EMU, and reformed decision-making procedures of the European Community. The second pillar intensified and created new procedures for developing a common foreign and security policy (CFSP), most notable for strengthening the regional security apparatus in the context of developing a European pillar in NATO. The third pillar provided for a new area of cooperation on the European level on home and justice affairs among interior ministries. However, as a result of the political complications Maastricht faced, European leaders reached a compromise whereby they removed the "Social Chapter" from the first pillar and relegated it to the end of the text, where it became a semiofficial fourth pillar.

Boldly, governments committed to a plan in the first pillar for the EMU with specific deadlines for each objective resulting in phasing out of separate national currencies and their replacement with a single currency governed by a European central bank. Ideally, Maastricht would have marked the arrival of "federalism." It indeed did so according to the interpretation of the German Constitutional Court and as parlance adjusted to the new name of the community, that of the "European Union." But a rebellion against European federalism ensued in the ratification campaigns in various MS. Ratification succeeded by a narrow margin in France despite the broad support of French politicians. Ratification succeeded in Denmark and Britain only as those countries negotiated so-called opt-outs of the commitments to which their citizens objected. Denmark would be party neither to the monetary union nor to the political union that Maastricht entailed. British objections focused on monetary union, unless the British Parliament eventually consented (amounting to a reassertion of "parliamentary sovereignty" in Britain) and to the "Social Chapter," an obvious target of the Conservative government. Even though recently elected New Labour brought Britain into the "Social Chapter" in 1997, there was no illusion about, or even political support for, a progressive social policy.

In addition, the political aims of the union bitterly disappointed advocates of the integration process. Unfortunately, Maastricht looked forward to negotiating a common foreign policy simultaneously with the breakup of Yugoslavia. Divisions in the union over how to respond to the crisis and disagreements about Europe's role relative to that of the United States frustrated efforts. Even though the union engaged in humanitarian relief, cooperated through the United Nations to field peacekeepers (in the absence of U.S. participation, initially), and conducted intensive diplomacy, the military actions of the United States overshadowed Europe's extreme caution and failure to act decisively. Furthermore, US-led air strikes in Bosnia, though bringing the combatants to the negotiating table, could not turn back the clock on the massive killings and rapes in Croatia and Bosnia. During the atrocities the union rested on a technicality, that the organization did not have legal competency to intervene in the crisis. The new procedures of Maastricht, which did, indeed, provide a means for transferring foreign policy issues to the union, were of no use absent political will and precedents.

Up to now the essence of the union has been institutionalizing a particular kind of diplomatic relations among MS. Their technical, legal, and bureaucratic relations accord equal respect to individual MS and constitute the only form of cooperation they know. They focus a vast diplomatic network on problem solving, and their foreign ministry officials are trained to internalize the union's rules, procedures, and decision-making culture. Obviously, the EU is not an organization with the capacity to move decisively, or even to move in one direction, on issues for which there is no consensus and the union lacks legal and institutional capacities.

The union finds itself not only struggling for these capacities but operating with historical biases and modes that may not be helpful in responding to the new and pressing issues of the 1990s. In relation to the problem of Iraq in the 1990s, the U.S. preference for military intervention collided with the diplomatic reflex of the "EU collectivity" and the organization's incapacity in security matters outside of diplomacy. By 1998 the EU found itself sidelined as Britain militarily backed and supported U.S. policy in the U.N. Security Council, in contrast to France's cooperation with Russia to find a diplomatic solution to Iraq's latest transgression. In addition to being asked to come to terms with "the use of force" as an instrument of foreign policy, the EU has had to revise its

understanding of and responses to security threats. Increases in organized crime, arms trafficking, and drug smuggling accompanied the transitions to democracy in Eastern and central Europe and overflowed into Western Europe. Meanwhile instability in the former Yugoslavia, the Middle East, and North Africa threatened a situation in which persecuted and otherwise desperate peoples might overrun countries in Western Europe. France and Germany had special cause for concern as their citizens had already reacted strongly against foreign workers in the midst of those countries' unemployment woes. Maastricht made weak provisions for dealing with what are likely to be some of the most pressing issues. The treaty requires consensus decision making on issues interior ministers address as well as on issues under the CFSP that foreign ministers negotiate.

A further complication concerns the next enlargement process the EU has to face with the end of divisions between Eastern and Western Europe. Impending enlargement promises to add new strains to EU decision making, coinciding in timing with the sensitive politics of the EMU, and bringing up contentious issues, especially in terms of allocating EU resources already imperiled after almost a decade of economic hard times. For the most part, the EU prefers to take its time. There is opposition to bringing in less developed economies at a time the EU needs to underpin the common currency with strong economic performance. The United States, however, is preoccupied with enlarging NATO and afraid of embracing countries unable to pay their own way. From the U.S. perspective countries admitted to NATO should also receive the financial support of the EU, a position the United States may well stress with Europeans.

The EU seems most poised to compete in the global economy with the establishment of the EMU. The eleven participating states—Austria, Belgium, Finland, France, Germany, Ireland, Italy, Luxembourg, the Netherlands, Portugal, and Spain—met the criteria in 1998, and the single currency, the Euro, was launched on January 1, 1999. At that point the exchange rates of all participating currencies were irrevocably fixed and businesses could handle their accounts in Euro calculations. In January 2002, Euro coins and bank notes will be introduced and on July 1, 2002, national currency will be completely replaced by the Euro in the participating states. To qualify for the core group, countries had to meet stringent criteria to prove their economies are in balance. National governments carried out painful economic reforms but not without criticisms from their citizens, manifested in strikes and demonstrations and the repudiation of governments. EU issues have not fit into the traditional political categories of Left and Right in European politics. Therefore, it was difficult to frame opposition to, or for that matter support for, the EU in familiar political terms. This situation seems to be changing as the EU comes under challenge from Europe's political Left for placing economic over social priorities. It seems the public is prepared to vie for influence with organized lobbies in EU affairs.

In the final analysis, the animal constructed by a committee, and still under construction, has been able to adapt to the needs of the time and the specific requirements of its makers. However, recent reactions show that the public has begun to see the EU as disconnected, and even alien. Citizens suspect political executives and Eurocrats of imposing their hidden agendas to the neglect of national concerns. The politicization of the EU means more public scrutiny and, significantly, provides the EU with the possibility of mobilizing public support. Politicians and Eurocrats need to domesticate the EU animal if they are to reach for more powers.

BIBLIOGRAPHY

Archer, Clive, and Fiona Butler. *The European Union: Structure & Process,* 2d ed. New York: St. Martin's Press, 1996.

Delors, Jacques. *Our Europe: The Community and National Development.* Tr. by Brian Pearce. New York: Verso, 1992.

Dinan, Desmond. *Ever Closer Union? An Introduction to the European Community.* Boulder, Colo.: Lynne Rienner, 1994.

Johnston, Mary Troy. *The European Council: Gatekeeper of the European Community.* Boulder, Colo.: Westview Press, 1994.

Molle, Willem. *The Economics of European Integration: Theory, Practice, Policy,* 2d ed. Brookfield, England: Dartmouth, 1994.

Nugent, Neill. *The Government and Politics of the European Community,* 3d ed. Durham, N.C.: Duke University Press, 1994.

Piening, Christopher. *Global Europe: The European Union in World Affairs.* Boulder, Colo.: Lynne Rienner, 1997.

Sbragia, Alberta M., ed. *Euro-Politics: Institutions and Policymaking in the "New" European Community.* Washington, D.C.: Brookings Institution, 1992.

Treverton, Gregory F., ed. *The Shape of the New Europe.* New York: Council on Foreign Relations, 1992.

Urwin, Derek W. *The Community of Europe: A History of European Integration Since 1945.* New York: Longman, 1991.

Mary Troy Johnston

SEE ALSO European Commission; European Monetary Institute; Monnet, Jean; Schuman Plan; Schuman, Robert

Eurotunnel

The idea of a tunnel under the English Channel to connect France and Great Britain had been considered by Napoléon. The English South Eastern Railway had funded a tunnel project from 1874 to 1883, and there were abortive joint proposals in 1907–13 and in 1957. The vast increase of cross-channel trade following the entry of the United Kingdom into the European Economic Community prompted the consideration of improved connections between England and the Continent. While slow seaborne traffic across the English Channel could be expanded somewhat, the faster air routes were close to the saturation point. A land route, therefore, made economic sense. A bridge across the Dover Straits would be very expensive; operations could be hampered by the notorious weather in the channel; and there was the danger of ships hitting the bridge towers. These considerations made a tunnel (or "Chunnel") more desirable. An Anglo-French plan was formulated in 1973 but was cancelled in 1975 because of the projected costs. The four main options were to build (1) a tunnel for rail traffic only, (2) a tunnel to carry both trains and drive-through vehicular traffic, (3) a combination of vehicular bridge and tunnel, plus a separate rail tunnel, and (4) a drive-through tube bridge with a separate rail tunnel. Oppositon to the project, mainly from the British, centered on the cost, security concerns, and fears that disease-carrying rodents would invade Britain. On January 20, 1986, the British and French governments finally chose the first tunnel option. Construction of the 150-kilometer- (93-mile-) long tunnel was started the next year. The British terminus is at Cheriton near Folkestone, south of Dover, while the French station is at Frethun, south of Calais. It is formally known as the Eurotunnel, after its operating company, but is popularly known as the Chunnel. British Rail and the French state railway, Société Nationale des Chemins de Fer Français, are the primary railroad operators. However, a ten-nation consortium, TranMancheLink (TML), built the tunnel.

Modern engineering technology made this project much more feasible than in the past; monster boring machines dug through the stable, chalky soil from both sides of the channel. To avoid the trouble and expense of removing these machines, they dug their own graves under the channel, where they rest today. Ten thousand people were employed during the construction phase, and some eight thousand are employed for its operation. The Eurotunnel has two tunnels for trains going in opposite directions, plus a service tunnel between the other two. First projected at $3.8 billion (£2.5 billion), the final cost of this, Europe's largest construction project of the twentieth century, was closer to $15 billion (£9.8 billion). Government investment was very limited. The bulk of the capital was raised by an international consortium.

The Eurotunnel was officially opened by French President François Mitterrand and England's Queen Elizabeth on May 6, 1994, but continued problems forced further delays. The primary reason was poor British tracks that could not carry the high-speed French Train à Grande Vitesse (TGV). Freight rail service, composed primarily of trucks on flatcars, began in the summer of 1994, and passenger trains (Eurostar service) began in 1995. It is planned eventually to run passenger trains every fifteen minutes, with freight trains running every twenty minutes.

Although the French seemed to be generally in favor of the project, there was considerable anti-Chunnel sentiment among the British, some of whom have apparently enjoyed their isolation from the European mainland and wished to maintain their cultural and economic separateness. There was also fear that the Eurotunnel would take business away from the existing airlines and channel ferry services.

BIBLIOGRAPHY

Anderson, Graham, and Ben Roskrow. *Channel Tunnel Story*. London: E & F Spon, 1994.

The Channel Tunnel: A 21st Century Transport System. Kent, U.K.: Channel Tunnel Group Ltd., 1990.

Haining, Peter. *Eurotunnel: An Illustrated History of the Chunnel Tunnel Scheme*. London: New English Library, 1973.

Daniel K. Blewett

Expellees and Refugees

With Germany's defeat in 1945, millions of central and Eastern Europeans, mostly ethnic Germans, fled or were forced from lands that then came under the control of the Soviet Union and its satellites. Fearful of life under communism or of being victims of deliberate "ethnic cleansing," most of these refugees eventually settled in the western sectors of Germany. The social and political life of the Federal Republic of Germany was profoundly influenced by their presence.

As Germany lost a quarter of its prewar territory to the Soviet Union and Poland, a flood of uprooted humanity swept into the heartland of the country. Others were summarily expelled from Czechoslovakia, Hungary, and the Balkan states. The exodus began with the Soviet advance in 1944, reached its height between 1945 and 1950, but still totaled more than two hundred thousand per year until the construction of the Berlin Wall in 1961. In the 1990s the movement of ethnic Germans to Germany was given new impetus with the collapse of the Soviet system. While exact figures remain elusive, informed estimates place the total number of refugees and expellees between twelve and fourteen million, not counting hundreds of thousands of displaced Eastern Europeans who had been deported to Germany under Hitler and now refused to return to their native countries. Most of the refugees, often after personal ordeals, ended up in West Germany, where Schleswig-Holstein, Lower Saxony, and Bavaria absorbed proportionally the most. Four million individuals alone left the new Polish territories beyond the Oder-Neisse line, while refugees from Soviet-dominated territories, including the future German Democratic Republic, numbered even more. A significant number were young, relatively skilled, and more easily absorbed into West German society than older individuals whose recollection of a better life in earlier times remained paramount.

The integration of refugees and expellees produced enormous stress on the resources of the Federal Republic. Housing, education, and social services remained strained for many years even as the reconstruction of Germany's economy and infrastructure progressed rapidly. During the 1950s and 1960s a small but influential political party, the League of Those Expelled from their Homelands and Those Deprived of their Rights (Bund der Heimatvertriebenen und Entrechteten, BHE), catered to the refugees' special concerns, especially their desire to regain the lost territories or at least prevent any de jure recognition of their loss by the West. The refugee vote tended to support the conservative governments of Konrad Adenauer and Ludwig Erhard, whose antisocialist platforms, strong commitment to German reunification, and special Ministry for Refugees exerted a greater appeal than the ideology of the Social Democrats. Successful long-term assimilation of the refugees into West German society, a decline in numbers over time, and political realism eventually combined to pave the way for Chancellor Willy Brandt's *Ostpolitik* in the 1970s. Unification of all remaining German territories in 1990 softened or eliminated resentments of the aging refugee population while offering ethnic Germans still residing in the East the opportunity to relocate peacefully in the West.

BIBLIOGRAPHY
De Zayas, Alfred M. *Nemesis at Potsdam: The Expulsion of the Germans from the East,* 3d rev. ed. Lincoln: University of Nebraska Press, 1989.
Lattimore, Bertram G. *The Assimilation of German Expellees in the West German Polity and Society since 1945.* The Hague: Nijhoff, 1974.
Schoenberg, Hans W. *Germans from the East: A study of Their Migration, Resettlement, and Subsequent Group History since 1945.* The Hague: Nijhoff, 1970.

Eric C. Rust

Eyskens, Gaston (1905–88)

Belgian prime minister, 1949–50, 1958–61, and 1968–72. Gaston Eyskens was born in Lier on April 1, 1905. He received doctorates in economics and political science from the University of Louvain and an M.A. from Columbia University in New York City. Eyskens taught economics at the University of Louvain. He was elected to parliament in 1939 as a representative of the Catholic Party. During the Second World War Eyskens worked in the Ministry of Economic Affairs of the Belgian government-in-exile in Great Britain. From 1945 to 1949 he was minister of finance and in 1949 became premier of the coalition government formed by his Christian Social Party (successor to the Catholic Party) and the Liberals. He resigned in 1950 when the Liberals withdrew from the cabinet over the proposed return of Leopold III.

During his prime ministership from 1958 to 1961, Eyskens's government solved a bitter controversy over education by granting equal support to state and church schools. In 1960 Eyskens presided over the granting of independence to the Belgian Congo. The March 1961 election, however, brought down his government. The electorate was soured by the chaos following Belgium's exit from the Congo and by economic difficulties at home.

Eyskens, who spoke Flemish and French, headed the government in 1970 when a revision of the constitution granted a degree of autonomy to Flanders and Wallonia. His government fell in 1972 when the Flemish wing of his Christian Social Party bolted over what it believed to be an inadequate application of Flemish language and cultural prerogatives to a Flemish enclave in Wallonia. Eyskens withdrew from politics and became chairman of the board of Credietbank.

Eyskens's son, Mark Eyskens, was finance minister in the government of Wilfried Martens, 1979–81, and following that, briefly, prime minister in 1981. Eyskens died on January 3, 1988, in Louvain (now called Leuven).

BIBLIOGRAPHY
"Gaston Eyskens Dies at Age 82; Led Six Governments in Belgium." *New York Times,* January 5, 1988.

Bernard Cook

SEE ALSO Belgium; Congo Intervention; Leopold III

Fabius, Laurent (1946–)

French prime minister, 1984–86. After his appointment as junior budget minister in 1981, Laurent Fabius became identified with the moderate wing of the Socialist Party (PS). As a dynamic young prime minister he emphasized modernization of industry and generally pursued liberal, free-market policies.

Following graduation from the École Nationale d'Administration in 1973, Fabius worked as an auditor in the Council of State. In 1978 he was elected a Socialist deputy of the National Assembly, where he vigorously supported the left-wing economic policies then espoused by the PS leader François Mitterrand and criticized the social democratic views of Michel Rocard. Following the Socialist victory of 1981, Fabius first supported the policies of ideological socialism, but when the economy worsened he advocated austerity and compromise. Appointed minister of industry and research in March 1983, he cooperated with business leaders and endorsed less government control over nationalized industries.

In July 1984 Fabius succeeded Pierre Mauroy as prime minister. The appointment symbolized President Miterrand's decision to abandon ideological socialism in favor of restructuring rundown industry and combating inflation, even if this meant an increase in unemployment. The left wing of the PS, led by Lionel Jospin, opposed the change in direction, but the party congress of 1985 endorsed the government's policies. Two incidents of 1985 harmed Fabius's popularity: his poor performance in a televised debate with Jacques Chirac and his unclear involvement in the Greenpeace affair. In the parliamentary election of March 1986 the conservatives won a narrow majority, and Fabius immediately resigned. In 1988 he failed in his bid for first secretary of the PS, but that same year he became president of the National Assembly. Although Fabius continued to be a significant figure within the social democratic wing of the party, many members remained critical of his rapid departure from a leftist vision of socialism.

BIBLIOGRAPHY

Fabius, Laurent. *C'est en allant vers la mer.* Paris: Seuil, 1990.

Gino, Raymond, ed. *France During the Socialist Years.* Dartmouth, N.H.: Aldershot, 1994.

Morray, Joseph. *Grand Disillusion: François Mitterrand and the French Left.* Westport, Conn.: Praeger, 1997.

Thomas T. Lewis

SEE ALSO Jospin, Lionel; Mauroy, Pierre; Rocard, Michel

Faeroe Islands

Self-governing group of eighteen islands between Scotland and Iceland associated with the Kingdom of Denmark. Although seventeen of the islands are populated, one third of the islands' 47,310 inhabitants live on the principal island, Streymoy. The capital, Tórshavn, located on Streymoy, has a population of 16,223. Schooling is conducted in Faeroese, which is akin to Icelandic and western Norwegian, but Danish is a compulsory subject.

The Faeroe Islands (Danish, Føroyar), under Danish administration since 1380, were occupied by the United Kingdom after Denmark was overrun by Germany in 1940. Control was restored to Denmark at the end of World War II, but in 1948 a Home Rule Act gave the islanders control over their internal affairs. There is a local parliament, the Løgting, and the Faeroese send two representatives to the Danish parliament. The Løgting, consisting of at least twenty-seven members, is elected by all the Faeroese over age eighteen on the basis of proportional

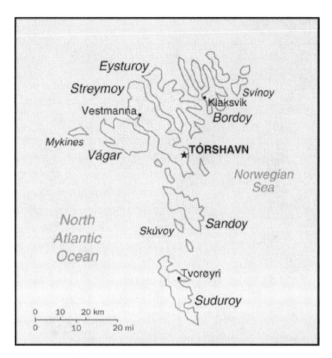

The Faeroe Islands. *Illustration courtesy of Bernard Cook.*

representation. Denmark is responsible for foreign policy, defense, and the courts. The Faeroes issue their own stamps and paper money (krona), tied to the value of the Danish krone, but use the coins of Denmark. Denmark, besides setting the value of the islands' currency, provides approximately one-third of public expenditures.

Politics on the Faeroes has spawned a surprising number of political parties for an entity with fewer than fifty-thousand inhabitants. The principal parties have been the Social Democratic Party, the Union Party, and the conservative People's Party. Jógvan Sundstein, chairman of the People's Party, was prime minister of a coalition government from January 1989 to January 1991. The Social Democrats then provided the prime minister, first Atli Dam, then two years later Marita Petersen. In September 1994 Edmund Joensen of the Union Party replaced Petersen. In addition to the three main parties, there are a number of smaller ones: Republican Party, Home Rule Party, Christian People's Party, Progressive and Fishing Industry Party, and Labor Front. Since all Faeroe governments since 1975 have been coalition governments, these smaller parties have often played a crucial role in the formation of governing majorities.

Agriculture, principally sheep, potatoes, and vegetables, has been surpassed by fishing as the dominant economic activity. In 1987 fishing accounted for 23 percent of GDP, 26 percent of employment, and 80 percent of exports. The Faeroese's concern over their fisheries and potentially rich sea bottoms led them to reject EEC mem-

bership when Denmark joined in 1973. The islands control fishing within their territorial waters. In 1977 a 370-kilometer exclusive zone was established around the islands, and in September 1992 Denmark acceded to Faeroe demands that the islands control access to their sea bottoms. A dispute continues with the United Kingdom, however, concerning the demarcation between the Shetland Islands and the Faeroes.

Free trade exists between the Faeroes and the Nordic countries, and the islands enjoy favorable trading terms with the European Union (EU). It is a member of the Nordic Council, and Denmark represents it in the United Nations and in NATO, but in 1983 the Løgting unanimously declared the islands a nuclear-free zone and in 1987 requested that U.S. naval vessels cease visiting there. The Faeroes, like Greenland, are represented in international fisheries organizations. In July 1992 the Faeroes challenged the International Whaling Commission's (IWC) criticism of its whaling practices. In 1986 whale meat constituted half of the islands' meat production and a third of meat consumption. In September 1992, because of their disagreements with the IWC, the Faeroes, Greenland, Iceland, and Norway established the North Atlantic Marine Mammal Commission.

To reduce vulnerability to fluctuations in the supply of fish, the Faeroe government has encouraged fish farming and economic diversification. Although only 25 percent of the islands' power is provided through a hydroelectric facility, the Faeroese, fearing threats to their culture and way of life, have been reluctant to permit development of their petroleum potential. Yet in 1994 the Løgting, in hopes of offsetting depletion of its fisheries, a decrease in fish prices, and austerity measures imposed by Denmark, authorized seismic studies for offshore oil.

BIBLIOGRAPHY

"The Faroe Islands." *The Europa World Year Book 1997.* London: Europa Publications, 1997, 1098–99.

Jackson, Anthony. *The Faroes: The Faraway Islands.* London: Robert Hale, 1991.

Sanderson, Kate. *Whales and Whaling in the Faroe Islands.* Tórshavn, Faroe Islands: Dept. of Fisheries, 1990.

Thompson, Wayne C. *Western Europe 1996.* Harpers Ferry, W.Va.: Stryker-Post, 1996.

West, John Frederick. *Faroe: The Emergence of a Nation.* London: C. Hurst; New York: P. S. Eriksson, 1972.

Wylie, Jonathan. *The Faroe Islands: Interpretations of History.* Lexington: University of Kentucky Press, 1987.

Bernard Cook

Falange

Spanish Fascist political organization. José Antonio Primo de Rivera, son of former Spanish dictator Miguel Primo de Rivera, founded the Falange in 1933 to encourage national unity and pride and to combat the Left and liberal Republicans. Although personally opposed to violence, he collected arms for his organization and permitted terrorist activities. The Falange advocated abolition of all political parties and establishment of a nationalist dictatorship. Despite these objectives it lacked a specific plan of action. In February 1934 the Falange merged with another Fascist group, the Junta de Ofensiva National Socialista (JONS) with Primo de Rivera as leader.

The Falange attracted only a small following initially and it was driven underground after the February 1936 election by the left-wing Republican government that it opposed. However, the Falange gained greater importance during the Spanish Civil War (1936–39). When the Spanish army organized its revolt against the government, the Falange, which did not have the strength to lead its own revolt, joined the army's rebellion. Membership in the Falange swelled from five thousand in February 1936 to two million during the war.

Francisco Franco's military dictatorship needed a right-wing political theory on which to base its criticism of the Left. The anticlerical Falange proved to be only one of the viable choices. On April 19, 1937, Franco merged the Falange and the ultraclerical Carlist traditionalists to create the Falange Española Tradicionalista y de las Juntas de Ofensiva Nacional Sindicalista. He fused the ardent Catholicism and Spanish pride of the Carlists with the Falange's social ideals of interclass cooperation and egalitarianism. The result was an organization suited to his own needs. Franco declared that the head of state would become the leader of the Falange, as well as commander of the military forces. Weakened by internal differences, the Falange was easily dominated.

This new Falange became the only political party permitted in Spain, but it did not represent a united front. A minority of members wanted a syndicalist revolution in which labor cooperatives would gain authority equal to that of management. Others advocated reactionary terrorist measures, such as assassinating liberals. Catholic university students and former anarchists and Communists completed the mix. These divergent groups could only agree that the war should bring radical change to Spain.

After the Civil War Falange members held positions in Franco's government and Falangism continued to furnish the regime with a political theory. Party members obtained bureaucratic positions. Despite these jobs Franco insured that the Falange would not become too radical by keeping conservatives and army officers on the Falange National Council. Members were now more apt to be opportunists rather than revolutionaries.

The party's influence declined after 1943 as fascism waned in Europe. To diminish the party's Fascist ideology, Franco's regime stressed the Catholic aspects of Falangism and admitted that liberal regimes had achieved some success. The antiroyalist Falange was further weakened in 1947 when Franco appointed a member of the Spanish Bourbon family to succeed him upon his retirement or death.

The Falange, however, remained part of Franco's regime. Franco used it to prevent monarchist influence from becoming too strong. In 1951, in an attempt to quiet dissatisfied workers and university students, he appointed a new cabinet that reflected the social interests of the Falange and displaced the conservative monarchists.

The Falange was further eclipsed after 1955 when official statements began referring to the organization as the Movimiento. Because Spaniards had used this term to refer to the entire Nationalist cause, the new name essentially stripped the Falange of its identity as a political party. In 1956 and 1957 an official commission defined Falangism and none of its original precepts remained. The new definition instead stressed Catholicism and a willingness to support a moderate form of capitalism. In 1967 Falangists gained a victory when the Organic Law promoted the National Council of the Movimiento to the status of an upper house in parliament with the power to rule on the constitutionality of laws. But the Falange never regained its influence from Civil War days.

BIBLIOGRAPHY

Crow, John A. *Spain: The Root and the Flower, an Interpretation of Spain and the Spanish People.* Berkeley: University of California Press, 1985.

Herr, Richard. *An Historical Essay on Modern Spain.* Berkeley: University of California Press, 1971.

Jackson, Gabriel. *The Spanish Republic and the Civil War, 1931–1939.* Princeton, N.J.: Princeton University Press, 1972.

Payne, Stanley G. *Falange: A History of Spanish Fascism.* Stanford, Calif.: Stanford University Press, 1961.

Shannon L. Baker

Falcone, Giovanni (1939–92)

Italian magistrate assassinated for his anti-Mafia campaign. Giovanni Falcone was born on May 15, 1939, in Palermo, Sicily. Falcone entered the magistracy in 1964 and after a short period in Lentini he was posted to Trapani, where he stayed for twelve years as a substitute district attorney. His main interest was criminal law. In 1979 he was transferred to Palermo after Judge Cesare Terranova was killed by the Mafia. There he launched his investigation of the Mafia under Rocco Chinnici, chief of the Strategic Investigation Bureau of the Tribunal of Palermo.

One of Falcone's first investigations dealt with boss Rosario Spatola. This case involved American criminality and pointed toward Falcone's later activity. During this investigation Falcone realized for the first time that to curb the Mafia criminal organization, it was necessary to draw an accurate map of the connections, both domestic and international, related to drugs and weapons. This required a thorough investigation of the financial and personal connections of all suspected Mafia members. After Chinnici was assassinated in 1983, a team of experts was set up, including Falcone, Paolo Borsellino, and other colleagues known in Italy and abroad as the Antimafia Pool. It earned an international reputation for its work.

In July 1984, when Falcone started questioning the Mafia leader Tommaso Buscetta, this was the marking point in gaining knowledge of the inner structure of Cosa Nostra. (Our Thing, the Sicilian Mafia). When later, in the summer of 1985, after two of Buscetta's collaborators were killed and the threat to his life was evident, he was transferred to the island of Asinara, off the northern coast of Sardenia, to a highly secure jail compound. Nonetheless, the pool went on investigating and in November 1985 indicted 475. Two years later, on December 16, 1987, the Court of Assizes of Palermo presided over by Alfonso Giordano, the so-called *Maxi Processo* (twenty-two months of hearings and thirty-six days of Council Chamber) acquitted 114 but condemned 19 of the accused to life imprisonment and sentenced the others to a total of 2,500 years of imprisonment. The trial involved the most important men of Cosa Nostra, an all-encompassing criminal organization, with results achieved after many years of thorough and painstaking investigation. It was an important victory for anti-Mafia magistrates, among whom Falcone had been one of the most determined.

Falcone had brought Buscetta back to Italy and knew how to talk to him and understand and interpret his revelations. Buscetta opened the way for the confessions of other important Mafia bosses and Falcone had succeeded in obtaining all this.

The pool had achieved an invaluable success in the *Maxi Processo,* but simultaneously a negative public relations campaign was launched against Falcone. Antonio Caponnetto, a respected anti-Mafia judge, because of his age, stepped down from the post in Palermo, but the Superior Council for the Magistracy denied Falcone that important post. The magistrator Antonio Meli was preferred to the younger Falcone, although Meli and the pool heatedly differed over their assessments of the character of the Mafia. When in 1988 in the Court of Cassation the magistrates decided that the Mafia could not be considered a unitary body but a series of different groups, all enjoying an autonomous power of decision, the Antimafia Pool was dissolved.

Nevertheless Falcone continued with his approach, becoming a member of a successful Italo-American investigating team and obtaining brilliant results in collaboration with the U.S. Federal Prosecutor Rudolph Giuliani in the Iron Tower operation, against the Gambino and Inzerillo crime families. In the meantime his case had not been going well at the Palermo Tribunal. As a result, in March 1991 Falcone accepted an offer to become director general of the Penal Department at the Justice Ministry in Rome. When under his pressure the anti-Mafia Investigative Force Direzione Investigativa Antimafia was set up in November 1991, he was supposed to head it, but the Superior Council had not yet decided on his name when he was assassinated at Capaci outside Palermo on May 23, 1992, with his wife, Francesca, and three policemen assigned for his personal security. Salvatore Riina, then the boss of bosses of the Sicilian Mafia, has been accused of ordering the murder.

BIBLIOGRAPHY

Galluzzo, L., F. Nicastro, and V. Vasile. *Obiettivo Falcone.* Naples: T. Pironti, 1992.

La Licata, F. *Storia di Giovanni Falcone.* Milan: Rizzoli, 1992.

Lodato, S. *Diciotto anni di mafia.* Milan: Rizzoli, 1996.

———. *Dieci anni di mafia: La guerra che lo stato non ha saputo vincere.* Milan: Rizzoli, 1992.

Maria Gabriella Pasqualini

SEE ALSO Borsellino, Paolo; Bucsetta, Tommaso; Mafia

Falklands War

War between Britain and Argentina over the Falkland (Malvinas) Islands, April to June 1982.

The Falkland Islands are located east of the southern tip of South America, 272 miles (438 km) off the coast of Argentina. They could be an important springboard for any country seeking to expand its influence in the Antarctic. Britain's first crisis over the Falklands occurred

The Falkland Islands. *Illustration courtesy of Bernard Cook.*

in 1769 during an ownership dispute with Spain. At that time Samuel Johnson, writing to support London's efforts to avoid war, described the Falklands as "thrown aside from human use, stormy in winter, barren in summer, an island which not even the southern savages have dignified with habitation." Two hundred years later the islands were still of little value to Britain in either strategic or economic terms. The problem was that in the interim they had acquired an English-speaking population of some 1,800 people, and the islanders did not wish to be taken over by Argentina.

The Argentine military junta forced the war. Already guilty of massive civil rights abuses and detested by most Argentineans, the unpopular government sought to stay in power by playing the "nationalist card." The issue of the Malvinas presumably would appeal to all Argentineans, especially as the British government had been delaying negotiations regarding the future of the islands. But rousing nationalist emotions also meant that the junta would have a hard time reversing itself when prudence demanded it.

Hardly anyone in Buenos Aires or London actually believed there would be a war over the Falklands. President Leopoldo Galtieri and other members of the Argentine junta were confident that the British would not regard occupation of the islands as a casus belli and would merely give way. British intelligence was woefully inadequate; London had no idea of the reality of the Argentine

threat until too late. British intelligence dismissed the junta's statements as mere posturing and a device to shore up its sagging popularity. As a result Margaret Thatcher's government failed to dissuade the junta by making it clear that it would fight to resist an Argentinean takeover of the islands.

The Argentine military operation was actually launched prematurely when a trivial incident on South Georgia, a dependency of the Falklands 800 miles (1290 kilometers) to the east, caused it to be speeded up. Had the invasion occurred later, as had been planned, some of the British warships involved in the fighting would have been transferred to other nations and, therefore, would have been unavailable for battle.

On April 2, 1982, Argentina landed troops on the Falklands. The British cabinet responded by ordering a task force to the South Atlantic to retake them. Also on April 2, in what came as a considerable surprise to the junta, the U.N. Security Council passed Resolution 502 demanding Argentine withdrawal. Three days later a British carrier task force sailed from Portsmouth.

The war was short. When it was over Britain had salvaged its honor, the junta was discredited, and much of the world was left wondering what the war was about and why it had been fought. One of the unique aspects of the war was extensive coverage by the Cable News Network (CNN). The war was also somewhat unusual in that it was fought with remarkable decency on both sides.

Winter weather conditions in the South Atlantic were extremely difficult and a major hurdle for the British. The distance of the war from Britain—eight thousand miles—was another problem. In a deliberate campaign of misinformation London bluffed Buenos Aires into believing that the Royal Navy already had a nuclear-powered submarine in place off Argentina when the war began. After the British submarine *Conqueror* sank the old heavy cruiser *General Belgrano* on May 2 with a loss of 368 lives, the Argentine navy stayed in port. In 1984 there was something of a political scandal in Britain, when it was revealed in Parliament that the *General Belgrano* was actually outside the two-hundred-mile exclusion zone proclaimed by the British around the Falklands and was moving away from the islands when it was torpedoed.

In a remarkably short time, the British converted four merchant ships to aircraft ferries with operational flight decks and maintenance facilities. This achievement was especially notable because before the outbreak of war there had been no plans for this conversion. The war also saw the first use of a vertical short-takeoff-and-landing fighter (VSTOL), the Harrier, to engage high-performance aircraft.

The Argentinean air force was superb; its pilots flew their French-built Super Entendards almost at wave top and switched on their radars at the last possible moment to attack Royal Navy ships in Stanley (also called Port Stanley) harbor. Had more French manufactured Exocet missiles been available or the Argentinean bombs been properly fused, the war might have ended differently. Even so, the British lost two destroyers (*Coventry* and *Sheffield*), two frigates (*Ardent* and *Antelope*), a requisitioned merchant ship acting as a carrier (*Atlantic Conveyor*), and a landing vessel (*Sir Galahad*). Ten other vessels were damaged. The British also lost fourteen aircraft to combat and ten in accidents. The British claimed Argentine losses amounted to more than a hundred aircraft.

Once the Royal Navy had cut off the Falklands from resupply, British infantry, paratroops, and commandos went ashore to deal with the occupying land forces. The difference was superior British training, leadership, and initiative, even among conscripted troops, rather than superior technology. The Argentine army had not fought an international war in more than a hundred years; morale was low, the men were poorly trained and woefully supplied, and their officers tended to run away under fire. The result was a foregone conclusion. The last of Argentine forces surrendered on June 13.

Most of world opinion sided with Britain in the war. U.S. support was extremely important. The war was a great fillip to the British, although the public response was more subdued than that of British leaders. The big winner was Margaret Thatcher. Lost in the euphoria of victory was her failure to avoid the war. What the British public chose to remember was her Churchillian stance when the conflict began: "Defeat—I do not know the meaning of the word!" In June 1983 the British electorate went to the polls and returned the Conservatives to power by an overwhelming margin in the House of Commons. This was attributable in part, however, to the British election system: more Britons, 58 percent, voted against Thatcher than for her, 42 percent. The war also led London to shelve plans, for the time being, to reduce further the size of the Royal Navy. The government ordered four new frigates and announced plans to keep the Royal Navy at fifty-five frigates and destroyers. The aircraft carrier that was to have been sold was also retained.

The war was in fact both absurd and expensive. It cost Britain 255 dead and 777 wounded. Argentina's exact losses are unknown but Buenos Aires announced a provisional total of 652 men dead and missing in the war. The war cost British taxpayers $1.1 billion. Another $1.5 billion would have to be spent by 1985 to replace the lost Royal Navy ships and aircraft. That was only the beginning. In order to hold the Falklands the British government had to lengthen Port Stanley runway and station a squadron of twelve F-4 Phantoms for air defense. In the long run defense of the Falklands would require a new runway at a cost of several hundred million dollars, one thousand infantry troops, six destroyers, and a submarine. Maintaining the garrison would cost $650 million a year. All this meant that the British "defense of sovereign rights" cost at least $1.5 million per Falklander.

BIBLIOGRAPHY

Brown, David. *The Royal Navy and the Falklands War.* Annapolis: Naval Institute Press, 1987.

Dillon, George M. *The Falklands, Politics and War.* New York: St. Martin's Press, 1989.

Hastings, Max, and Simon Jenkins. *The Battle for the Falklands.* New York: Norton, 1983.

Middlebrook, Martin. *The Fight for the "Malvinas": The Argentine Forces in the Falklands War.* London: Viking, 1989.

Moro, Rubén O. *The History of the South Atlantic Conflict: The War for the Malvinas.* New York: Praeger, 1989.

Villar, Roger. *Merchant Ships at War: The Falklands Experience.* Annapolis: Naval Institute Press, 1984.

Spencer C. Tucker

SEE ALSO Thatcher, Margaret

Fälldin, Thorbjörn (1926–)

Swedish prime minister from 1976 to 1978 and from 1979 to 1982. Nils Olof Thorbjörn Fälldin was born at Högsjö on April 24, 1926. He was self-educated and passed his secondary education exam in 1945. He became active in the Agrarian (Center) Party as a teenager and became its leader in 1971. He was elected to the parliament (Riksdag) in 1958. He lost his seat in 1964 but was reelected in 1967. He made environmentalism and an adamant antinuclear stance central concerns of the Center Party.

In the wake of the oil crisis of 1973, the Social Democratic Workers Party (SAP) had planned to build twenty-four nuclear power plants. This became a key issue, strenuously opposed by the Center Party, and cost the SAP votes. Other voters were disenchanted by the high level of taxation necessary to fund the elaborate Swedish welfare state. The nuclear issue, which had provided the opposition with its victory, proved to be its downfall.

As leader of the Center Party, Fälldin formed a center-right coalition in October 1976, Sweden's first non-

Socialist government since 1936. As prime minister he refused to approve the fueling and start-up of the country's seventh and eighth nuclear power plants. This led to serious differences with the Center's coalition partners, the Liberals, or People's Party (Folkspartiet, FP) and the Moderate Unity Party (Moderata Samlingspartiet, MS). The FP and the MS endorsed a recommendation by an independent commission to continue to use nuclear power and rejected Fälldin's proposal to submit the issue to a referendum. Fälldin's government resigned in October 1978 and Ola Ullsten, leader of the FP, formed a minority government. After the September 1979 election Fälldin returned as head of a government consisting of the Center, the MS, and the FP. Their majority, however, consisted of one seat. A referendum on nuclear power was held in March 1980. Fifty-eight percent of the voters approved the completion of twelve reactors at four plants, but all reactors would be shut down at least by 2010. In 1995 a parliamentary commission recommended that the 2010 deadline be dropped, owing to the cost of alternative energy, but it also recommended that one reactor be decommissioned before 1998.

Unemployment, intensified by the economic slump of 1980–83, was a central issue in the 1982 election, and this favored the SAP. The SAP won 45.6 percent of the vote and 166 of the Riksdag's 349 seats, a three-seat majority over the three non-Socialist parties. Fälldin was forced to resign and Olof Palme of the SAP formed a new minority government. Fälldin also resigned as leader of the Center Party in 1982. Since the mid-1980s he has served on the boards of cultural and commercial institutions.

BIBLIOGRAPHY

Elmbrant, Bjorn. *Fälldin*. Stockholm: Fischer, 1991.

Fälldin, Thorbjörn. *Battre samhalle, tryggare manniskor.* Solna: Seelig, 1976.

Hammerich, Kai Ewerlof. *Kompromissernas koalition: person-och maktspelet kring regeringen Fälldin.* Stockholm: Raben & Sjogren, 1977.

Strand, Dieter. *Palme mot Fälldin: rapporter fran vagen till nederlaget.* Stockholm: Raben & Sjogren, 1977.

Vedung, Evert. *Karnkraften och regeringen Fälldins fall.* Stockholm: Raben & Sjogren, 1979.

Bernard Cook

SEE ALSO Palme, Olof

Fanfani, Amintore (1908–)

Christian Democratic politician who served as premier of Italy five times. Amintore Fanfani was born at Pieve Santo Stefano near Arezzo on February 6, 1908. An economic historian, Fanfani taught first at the Catholic University of Milan and then at the University of Rome, authoring a number of economic studies. He was active in the Italian Catholic University Federation during the Fascist regime of Benito Mussolini and became one of the youngest leaders of the Christian Democratic Movement in 1946. He was elected to the Constituent Assembly in 1946 and served as minister of labor and social security in the governments of Alcide de Gasperi from 1947 to 1950. In 1951 he served as the minister of agriculture and forestry in the eighth De Gasperi government. He subsequently served as minister of the interior, 1953 and 1987–88; minister of foreign affairs, 1965 and 1966–68; minister of the budget, 1988–89; and prime minister, January 1954, 1958–59, 1960–63, 1982–83, and April–July 1987. As minister of labor and social security he produced a plan for urban and rural reconstruction. He promoted a plan for housing for workers and the formation of non-Communist labor unions. Fanfani was president of the Senate in 1968–73, 1976–82, and 1985. He was appointed one of five senators for life in 1972 and from 1992 to 1994 was president of the Senate's standing committee on foreign affairs. He also served as president of the U.N. General Assembly in 1965–66.

Fanfani became secretary-general of the Christian Democratic Party (DC) in 1954 and held that post until ousted by opponents of his policy of "opening to the left" in 1959. In February 1962 Fanfani formed the first center-left government. Although the Socialists (PSI) did not participate in the Council of Ministers, they voted their approval of the government and its policies, which included nationalization of electric energy, regional decentralization, and economic planning. Fanfani was ousted by conservative Christian Democrats in May 1963, but under his successor as secretary-general of the DC, Aldo Moro, the PSI was brought into the government in December 1963. He had hoped to become president in 1971. Although that bid did not succeed, Fanfani served as caretaker president in 1978 after the resignation of Giovanni Leone.

BIBLIOGRAPHY

"Fanfani, Amintore." *Dictionary of Modern Italian History,* Ed. by Frank J. Coppa. Westport, Conn.: Greenwood, 1985.

Ottone, Piero. *Fanfani*. Milan: Longanesi, 1966.

Bernard Cook

SEE ALSO Italy; Moro, Aldo

Fassbinder, Rainer Werner (1946–82)

Immensely prolific West German film and theater director who, along with Werner Herzog, Alexander Kluge, Volker Schlöndorff, Margarethe Von Trotta, and Wim Wenders, was one of the key figures of the New German Cinema that emerged in the late 1960s and 1970s. In a film career that began in 1969 with his first feature, *Love Is Colder Than Death,* and ended with his untimely death in 1982, Fassbinder completed roughly forty feature-length films and multi-episode series for theatrical release and television broadcast.

Although the figure of the auteur was central to the success of the New German Cinema, with Fassbinder the notion of the director as artist and celebrity was taken to extremes. Of all the New German Cinema directors, Fassbinder's body of work received the greatest amount of acclaim and attention during the director's lifetime, both for its artistry and vision, as well as for its frequently outrageous, confrontational, and controversial nature. Fassbinder's personal life was also riddled with controversy. His bisexuality, drug use, and leftist/terrorist associations made him not only the "bad boy" of the New German Cinema, but also one of the most notorious public figures in Germany at the time and a fixture of the West German tabloids.

Early experimentation with genres such as the gangster film, *Love is Colder than Death* and *The American Soldier* (1970), led to an embrace of Hollywood melodrama of the 1940s and 1950s that would become a defining characteristic of his oeuvre. Using the conventions of this genre, Fassbinder created a distinctive film style that could be approachable and appealing, yet also subversive, much in the same way as the work of Douglas Sirk and other Hollywood masters of the melodrama. Fassbinder's interest in the Hollywood melodrama not only informed his storylines and thematics but also his formal concerns, and much of his work displays a mastery of color, lighting, and mise-en-scène akin to that of the Hollywood directors he so admired.

Fassbinder's homages to the Hollywood melodrama include *The Bitter Tears of Petra Von Kant* (1972), *Ali/Fear Eats the Soul* (1973), a loose version of Sirk's *All That Heaven Allows* (1955), *The Marriage of Maria Braun* (1978), and *Veronika Voss* (1981).

Fassbinder also gained notoriety for producing a number of unconventional adaptations of literary classics for West German television. These adaptations include an unsettling version of Theodor Fontane's *Effi Briest* (1974), and his monumental, and disturbing fourteen-part serialization of Alfred Döblin's *Berlin Alexanderplatz* (1980), which many consider to be the director's masterpiece.

Fassbinder died in 1982 of an apparent drug overdose.

BIBLIOGRAPHY

Elsaesser, Thomas. *Fassbinder's Germany: History, Identity, Subject.* Amsterdam: Amsterdam University Press, 1996.

Fassbinder, Rainer Werner. *The Anarchy of the Imagination: Interviews, Essays, Notes.* Ed. by Michael Töteberg and Leo A. Lansing. Trans. by Krishna Winston. Baltimore: Johns Hopkins University Press, 1992.

Shattuc, Jane. *Television, Tabloids and Tears: Fassbinder and Popular Culture.* Minneapolis: University of Minnesota Press. 1995.

Anthony Kinik

SEE ALSO Herzog, Werner; Schlöndorff, Volker; Wenders, Wim

Faul, Denis (1932–)

Priest and teacher at St. Patrick's Academy, Dungannon, Northern Ireland. Denis Faul was born in County Louth in 1932. In 1969 he claimed that most Roman Catholics felt that the judicial system in Northern Ireland was prejudiced against them. This was the first time his statements attracted attention. He has been critical of the Royal Ulster Constabulary Special Branch and also of the British army. However, he also extended this criticism to the actions of Republican paramilitaries. Father Faul also spent much time trying to improve the treatment of persons interrogated by security forces.

Ricki Schoen

Faulkner, Arthur Brian Deane (1921–77)

Ulster Unionist politician and Prime Minister of Northern Ireland (1971–72). Brian Faulkner (Lord Faulkner of Downpatrick) was born in County Down in 1921. Upon his election to the Northern Ireland parliament or Stormont as MP for East Down in 1949, he became the youngest member of the Northern Ireland parliament. He was chief whip in 1956 and became minister for home affairs in 1959 at the height of the Irish Republican Army (IRA) campaign that he suppressed with internment under the Special Powers Act. As minister for commerce in 1963 he inaugurated a new era for the Northern economy, persuading companies such as ICI, Ford, Michelin, Goodyear, and Du Pont to set up plants there. He opposed concessions to the Northern Ireland Civil Rights Association. On January 23, 1969, he resigned in protest at the attempts by Captain Terence O'Neill to introduce reforms at the request of the British government and at the appointment of the Cameron Commission, which was set up to investigate the sources of Unionist violence. When James Chichester-Clark became prime minister of Northern Ireland in May 1969, Faulkner returned to serve as minister for development, declaring that he now favored a policy of reform. Chichester-Clark proved unable to handle the deteriorating situation as more clashes occurred between the IRA and Protestant paramilitaries, and Faulkner succeeded him as prime minister on March 23, 1971. He also held the post of minister of home affairs. His commitment to reform incurred Protestant-Unionist suspicions and his past association with internment, the Orange Order, and previous opposition to reforms made him unattractive to Catholics. His announcement on May 25 that any soldier could shoot to kill on suspicion provoked a strong attack from the Social Democratic and Labour Party. He later sought their support when he announced the establishment of three committees for social, environmental, and industrial affairs, two to be chaired by Opposition MPs. On August 9 he introduced internment, which, in the beginning, was directed at the Catholic population and led to increased support for the Provisional IRA. During the following month he engaged in unproductive tripartite talks with Edward Heath and Jack Lynch. In October the British government published a green paper, *The Future of Northern Ireland: A Paper for Discussion,* which implied the abolition of the Stormont system, through which the Protestant Loyalist community controlled the government of Northern Ireland and dominated the Catholic, largely Republican minority. While Faulkner resisted this, he did not reject the measure out of hand but his position was badly impaired by the events of Bloody Sunday (January 30, 1972), in which fourteen Catholic demonstrators were killed by British troops in Londonderry. In March 1973 the right wing of his party founded the Vanguard Unionist Progressive Party, of which William Craig became leader. On March 22 Faulkner met with Heath again in London, where he refused to agree to a transfer of security to Whitehall and also rejected Heath's suggestion of power sharing. Two days later Heath announced the abolition of Stormont and the introduction of direct rule by the British government. During the next year Faulkner supported the Ulster Defence Association, a Unionist paramilitary organization. In December 1973, having by now lost hard-line Unionist support, Faulkner was a party to the Sunningdale Conference, joining representatives of the British and Irish governments and the incoming executives of Northern Ireland in an effort to promote harmony. He became chief executive of the As-

sembly of Northern Ireland and following the collapse of the executive he formed his own party, the Unionist Party of Northern Ireland, which held five seats in the fruitless 1975 Northern Ireland Constitutional Convention. Toward the end of 1975 he announced his retirement from politics and was raised to the peerage in January 1977. On February 28, 1977, two days after he was received into the House of Lords, he was killed in a hunting accident.

Ricki Schoen

SEE ALSO Chichester-Clark, James; Craig, William; Faulkner, Brian; Ireland, Northern

Faure, Edgar-Jean (1908–88)

French premier, 1952 and 1955–56, and holder of eleven cabinet posts. Edgar Faure played a prominent role in both the Fourth and Fifth French Republics. President François Mitterrand said of Faure, "he was one of the most lucid in seeing the necessity of decolonization, encouraging disarmament and with instilling better East-West relations."

Edgar Faure was born in Béziers on March 30, 1908. Faure studied Russian at the Paris School of Eastern Languages and earned a law degree from the University of Paris. Before the Second World War he practiced law in Paris and was active in the Radical Party. After the German occupation of France in 1940, Faure participated in the Resistance until 1943, when he joined General Charles de Gaulle's Committee of National Liberation in Algiers as director of legislative services.

After the war Faure served as an assistant to Champtier de Ribes, the French jurist who represented France on the International Military Tribunal at Nuremberg. Faure was elected to the assembly of the Fourth French Republic in 1946. In 1947 he was placed in charge of a legislative committee investigating responsibility of French citizens for war crimes and collaboration, but though masses of testimony and files were accumulated, there were few results. Critics claimed that the responsibility of various individuals was purposely submerged in the mass of information.

Faure assumed his first cabinet post as budget minister in 1950. In January 1952 he became premier for the first time. Faure's cabinet, which succeeded the second cabinet of René Pleven, has been derided as "the government of 40." It had 40 ministers; it lasted 40 days; and it reputedly cost France 40 billion francs. He formed a second ministry, the twenty-first of the Fourth Republic, after the collapse of the government of his friend Pierre Mendès-

France in February 1955. Faure's government lasted until 1956. It successfully supported measures that gave French support to the arming of West Germany and provided for the return of the Saar to Germany in 1957. Faure lost his parliamentary seat in November 1958.

Beginning in 1962 Faure was sent to China by de Gaulle on a special mission that reestablished diplomatic relations with the Chinese. He was appointed minister of agriculture in 1966, and minister of education following the events of May 1968. In the year after the student upheavals, Faure introduced important reforms of the university system. Overcrowding was eased by an increase in the number of universities, from twenty-two to sixty-five. Students received a vote through representatives in the management of universities. Finally universities were freed to a certain extent from the rigidly centralized administration of the Ministry of Education. Following the resignation of de Gaulle in 1969, however, Faure was dismissed from the Education Ministry. Georges Pompidou and the Gaullists objected to what they perceived to be the rewarding of student disrupters. From 1973 until 1978 Faure was president of the National Assembly. He refused to accept a cabinet post in François Mitterrand's government because of the participation of the Communist Party, but he did agree to serve as the organizer of the bicentennial celebration of the French Revolution.

Faure, whose writings include history, legal and political studies, and detective stories published under the pen name Edgar Sanday, was elected to the French Academy in June 1978. He died on March 30, 1988.

BIBLIOGRAPHY

"Edgar Faure, 79, Dies in France; Twice a Postwar Prime Minister." *New York Times,* March 31, 1988.

Bernard Cook

Fellini, Federico (1920–93)

Italy's most famous filmmaker. Federico Fellini has had an enormous impact on motion pictures; he has influenced other filmmakers, and he has revised the way we see movies. "Felliniesque" has come to mean a certain Italian sophistication yet earthiness, a fascination with the bizarre yet a love of simplicity all wrapped in a flamboyant Mediterranean approach to life and art. The words *ciao* and *paparazzi* have entered everyday English through Fellini movies.

Fellini began his film career near the end of the neorealism period, that legendary post–World War II Italian film movement that stressed real people in real places doing real things, as opposed, for example, to the escapism

of the typical Hollywood fare of the day. Three films especially stand out in this vein. *I Vitelloni* (*The Spivs* 1953) is the semiautobiographical story of provincial loafers. *La strada* (*The Road,* 1954), one of the classics of world cinema, traces the adventures of Zampano (Anthony Quinn), a petty circus strongman, and the unforgettable Gelsomina (played by Gulietta Masina, Fellini's wife), his human but dim assistant. *Le notti di Calabria* (1956, *Nights of Calabria*) (1956) is the story of a simple Roman prostitute (Masina) who keeps getting up after life slaps her down. These films also contain magic moments that transcended realism, and they introduced the world to a certain flamboyant lyricism we now label Felliniesque.

La dolce vita (*The Sweet Life,* 1960) was a *cause de scandale.* Condemned by the Vatican as immoral, it remains one of the century's most impressive morality plays. In seven segments we follow Fellini's alter ego, Marcello (Mastroianni), a Roman gossip reporter, as he wanders the glitzy haunts of Rome's rich and famous. *8 1/2* (*Otto e mezzo,* 1963), considered by many Fellini's finest film, again stars Marcello and is a portrait of the artist as a disintegrating middle-aged man. Fellini's structure here is his boldest, weaving elements of reality, the past, and fantasy.

Juliet of the Spirits (*Giulietta degli spiriti,* 1965) can be read as *8 1/2* told from the long-suffering wife's standpoint. Fellini's first color feature is a baroque feast for the eyes with its outrageous costumes and suggestive use of color. *Fellini Satyricon* (1969), as its title suggests, is as much Fellini as it is Petronius, and its over-the-top visuals and treatment of Roman decadence were controversial indeed. *Amarcord* (1974) was in a gentler mode: a nostalgic look at the town of Fellini's birth.

If later Fellini films did not elicit the reverence and awe of the work of his earlier days, few filmmakers in the history of the art have produced a body of work as individual, visually memorable, and ultimately humane.

BIBLIOGRAPHY

Alpert, Hollis. *Fellini: A Life.* New York: Marlowe, 1988.
Baxter, John. *Fellini.* New York: St. Martin's Press, 1994.
Bondanella, Peter. *The Cinema of Federico Fellini.* Princeton, N.J.: Princeton University Press, 1992.
Burke, Frank. *Fellini.* Old Tappan, N.J.: Twayne, 1966.
Murray, Edward. *Fellini, the Artist.* New York: F. Ungar, 1976.

William M. Hammel

Fenech-Adami, Edward (1934–)

Prime minister of Malta, 1987–96, and 1998–. Edward Fenech-Adami, son of a customs officer who for a time had emigrated to the United States, was born in 1934 in Malta. Fenech-Adami received a law degree from the University of Malta and entered parliament in the early 1960s as a representative of the Christian Democratic Nationalist Party (PN). He was elected to succeed dr. George Borg Olivier as party leader in 1977. In the first general election after assuming the party leadership, Fenech-Adami led the PN to a popular vote victory over the Labor Party (MLP) with 50.9 percent of the vote. But Labor retained the government with a three-seat majority in parliament.

In the May 1987 elections the PN won 50.9 percent of the vote to the MLP's 48.9 percent. A constitutional amendment adopted in January provided that any party winning over 50 percent of the vote should have a majority in the House of Representatives. Therefore the PN was awarded four additional seats. With a majority of one seat the PN ended the MLP's sixteen-year hold on power. Fenech-Adami became prime minister and led his party to another electoral victory in 1992 with 52 percent of the vote, and a similar one in 1998 after two years in opposition.

Fenech-Adami had announced in 1992 that his government, though it would continue its nonaligned status and maintain diplomatic relations with Libya, would strengthen its ties to the United States and other Western nations and would seek full membership in the European Community (EC). The EC responded favorably and negotiations on Malta's membership began. In April 1995 Malta entered NATO's Partnership for Peace.

These steps toward integration with Europe, however, were dealt a blow by the September 1996 election. Called in advance by Fenech-Adami to broaden his mandate, the election was won by the MLP with 50.7 percent of the vote. The MLP's victory was due to its promise to abolish the value-added tax introduced by the Fenech-Adami government as a prerequisite to EU membership. The MLP, led by Alfred Sant, formed a new government. In fewer than two years, however, Fenech-Adami's pro-EU party was back in office with a comfortable majority, thus rendering Sant's MLP the first Maltese political party to have lost an absolute majority of the popular vote in so short a time.

Bernard Cook
Henry Frendo

SEE ALSO Borg Olivier, Giorgio; Malta

Fidelbo, Anna Finocchiaro (1955–)

Italian politician. Anna Finocchiaro Fidelbo was born in Modica, Sicily, on March 31, 1955. A lawyer, Fidelbo

served as a magistrate and secretary of the Democratic Magistrature in eastern Sicily, and achieved distinction for her efforts against the Mafia. She was elected to parliament for the first time in 1987 on the Communist (PCI) list. She became a member of the Justice Commission and of the leadership committee of the PCI's parliamentary caucus. She was reelected to parliament in 1992 on the list of the Democratic Party of the Left (PDS), and became vice president of its parliamentary caucus. She was a member of the Justice Commission and the special commission empowered to study a reform of the law on parliamentary immunity.

On April 21, 1996, she was reelected to the Chamber of Deputies as a proportional representative of the PDS for the second district in Sicily. She became a member of the cabinet of Romano Prodi in May with responsibility for the ministry of equal opportunity. Fidelbo was replaced as head of the ministry of equal opportunity by Laura Balbo with the formation of Massimo D'Alema's government on October 21, 1998.

Bernard Cook

Fierlinger, Zdeněk (1891–1976)

Czechoslovak politician who facilitated the Communist seizure of power in 1948. Zdeněk Fierlinger was born in 1891. His family was Sudeten German but Slavophile in sentiment. His father was a professor at the University of Olmütz (Olomouc). Fierlinger graduated from the School of Economics and was a colonel in the Czechoslovak army during World War I, fighting first in Russia then in France against the Central Powers. With the formation of the Czechoslovak state, he served as a Czech diplomat.

Fierlinger was posted in Moscow at the time of the German occupation of the remainder of the Czech state in March 1939. He remained there and served as the ambassador of the Czech government-in-exile from 1942 to 1945. Fierlinger, a left-wing Social Democrat favorably disposed to the USSR, helped to convince Edvard Beneš, head of the Czech government-in-exile, that the Soviet Union would be dominant in Eastern Europe and that, if Czechoslovakia had to choose between the West and the USSR, it had no choice but to go with the Soviets. Fierlinger returned to Czechoslovakia with Beneš in 1945 to head the provisional Czechoslovak government established at Kosice in Slovakia on April 3. The government contained six parties, but the Communists were given seven ministries, including the key ministries of interior, information, agriculture, finance, and education.

When the Communists won the largest number of seats in the Czechoslovak parliament in May 1946, Beneš appointed Czech Communist leader Klement Gottwald prime minister. The Communists, however, did not control a firm majority in the Council of Ministers despite the consistent support of Fierlinger and his left Social Democrat allies. In late 1947 the Social Democrats ousted Fierlinger as their chairman and announced that they would no longer participate in the National Front coalition with the Communists after the May 1948 election. In February 1948 the Communists, realizing that their control of the government was slipping, introduced a number of measures in the Council of Ministers that they knew would be unacceptable to their opponents. Twelve ministers tried to topple Gottwald's government by resigning. The Communists organized demonstrations by their union supporters, and Gottwald demanded that Beneš appoint him leader of a new, more loyal government. Gottwald was supported by Fierlinger, who entered the new clearly Communist government with some of his left Social Democratic allies. The Social Democrats bowed to Communist and union pressure and reinstated Fierlinger as chairman of the party.

Fierlinger continued to serve as a minister until September 1953, when he became president of the National Assembly, a post he held until his retirement on June 14, 1964. Fierlinger died in Prague on May 2, 1976.

BIBLIOGRAPHY

Rothschild, Joseph, and Nancy Merriwether Wingfield. *Return to Diversity: A Political History of East Central Europe Since World War II*. 3rd ed. New York: Oxford University Press, 1999.

Bernard Cook

SEE ALSO Beneš, Edvard; Gottwald, Klement

Figl, Leopold (1902–)

Austrian chancellor, 1945–51, and foreign minister, 1953–59. Leopold Figl was born into a rural, Catholic-conservative environment in 1902. During his studies at the Hochschule für Bodenkultur (a graduate school for soil sciences) he became a member of Norica, a Catholic student fraternity. In 1927 he was assigned to the post of secretary of the Lower Austrian Association of Farmers. In 1931 he advanced to the position of deputy director and in 1933 to that of director. In 1936 as an agricultural engineer, he helped organize a conference on agriculture for Richard N. Coudenhove-Kalergi's Paneuropäische Wirtschaftszentrale (Central Office of the Pan-European Economy). In 1937 he was appointed director of the Association of Farmers (Reichsbauernbunddirektor) in the

Austrian corporate state, the conservative regime established by Engelbert Dollfus and continued under Kurt von Schuschnigg. As the farmers' representative Figl was part of the Austrian Federal Economic Council (Bundeswirtschaftsrat) between 1934 and 1938.

On March 12, 1938, following the Anschluss (or forced union of Austria with Germany) Figl was arrested by the Nazis for being an exponent of the corporate state system, a socio-economic regime based on the anti–laissez-faire but also anticommunist system advocated by Pope Pius XI in his encyclical *Quadragesimo Anno*. On April 1 he was transported to Dachau concentration camp. On May 8, 1943, Hilde Figl succeeded in her efforts to procure her husband's release. His friend and later Austrian Chancellor Julius Raab provided him with a position in a construction firm.

On May 4, 1944, Figl cofounded the Association of Farmers. In October 1944 Figl was again detained. One month later he was taken to Mauthausen concentration camp for interrogations. Only the rapid advancement of the Red Army prevented him from perishing in the notorious camp.

No politician of the Second Austrian Republic founded in 1945, held as many top positions simultaneously as Figl did in 1945. The Soviet occupation authorities, who controlled the eastern third of Austria, entrusted him with the governorship of Lower Austria, and he later served as permanent undersecretary without portfolio in the provisional Karl Renner government established with permission of the Soviet authorities in April 1945. He was also a representative of the Austrian People's Party (ÖVP) and became chancellor because of the ÖVP's success in the November 25 National Council elections.

Figl's political activities were characterized by sophisticated negotiations above all as far as the Soviet occupying power was concerned. He furthermore excelled at improvisation. Figl's policy between 1945 and 1947 often resembled fortunate improvisation rather than planned action.

Despite the polemics of the Soviets and the Austrian Communist Party, the Figl government opted for participation in the U.S.-sponsored Marshall Plan and became a founding member of the Organization for European Economic Cooperation (OEEC). The Figl government was the only government of a country partly occupied by Soviet forces to take that step.

The Figl era ended in 1951 when Raab was appointed acting federal representative of the ÖVP, a position that became definitive in 1952. In March 1953 Raab replaced Figl as chancellor. In November 1953 Figl was made foreign minister. Although he spoke no foreign languages, he understood the Soviet mentality. On May 14, 1955, one day before the signing of the State Treaty, which ended the low-power occupation of Austria by establishing the country as a sovereign but neutral nation, Figl had a passage deleted that pointed toward a "certain Austrian responsibility" for World War II in the preamble of the document. In 1956 Figl as well as Raab publicly approved of Austria's membership in the European Coal and Steel Community, but in the wake of the repression of the Hungarian Revolution of that year, and fearful of a possible Soviet reaction to this tie with Western Europe, they reconsidered. In 1958 Figl persuaded the Soviets to agree to a decrease in the oil transfers to the USSR, which had been agreed on as part of the State Treaty settlement, by 3.5 million tons.

As a reaction to the founding of the European Economic Community, Figl advocated the creation of a large free-trade zone within the framework of the OEEC. The latter would have secured Austria's export interests and allowed the policy of "permanent neutrality." Yet France's resistance caused the failure of the Wide Free Trade Area project in autumn 1958. In 1959 Figl became first National Council president. Figl's departure from the Foreign Ministry signaled the end of the Raab era. In 1962 Figl became provincial governor of Lower Austria. He was regarded as an advocate of the grand coalition, combining closeness to the people, geniality, and determination.

BIBLIOGRAPHY

Kraus, Therese. "Leopold Figl," in Friedrich Weissensteiner and Erika Weinzierl, eds., *Die österreichischen Bundeskanzler: Leben und Werk.* Vienna: Österreichischer Bundesverlag, 1983.

Kriechbaumer, Robert. "Leopold Figl," in Herbert Dachs, Peter Gerlich, and Wolfgang C. Müller, eds., *Die Politiker: Karrieren und Wirken bedeutender Repräsentanten der Zweiten Republik.* Vienna: Manzsche Verlags- und Universitätsbuchhandlung, 1995.

Mantl, Wolfgang. "Leopold Figl," in *Staatslexikon der Görres-Gesellschaft,* 7th ed., Vol. 2. Freiburg: Herder, 1986.

Seltenreich, Susanne. *Leopold Figl—Ein Österreicher.* Vienna: Metten, 1962.

———. *Leopold Figl: Dokumentation einer Erinnerung.* Vienna: Lischkar [Rust], n.d.

Trost, Ernst. *Figl von Österreich.* Vienna: Molden, 1980.

Michael Gehler

SEE ALSO Raab, Julius; Renner, Karl

Filbinger, Hans (1913–)

West German politician. Hans Filbinger, son of a bank employee, was born in Mannheim on September 15, 1913. He studied law as well as political economy in Freiburg, Munich, and Paris. In 1937 he was awarded a doctorate in law from the University of Freiburg. His dissertation dealt with the legal constitution of joint-stock companies and could be interpreted as an attack on the then "machinations" of Jewish shareholders allegedly detrimental to the German economy. After he passed his second public examination he became an assistant of the faculty of law and lecturer for law of civil procedure at the University of Freiburg.

Drafted for military service in the Second World War in 1940, he initially served as a naval officer on small vessels in the North Atlantic and in the Arctic Ocean. From March 1943 Filbinger was a naval judge, an office he continued to hold as POW in camps in Norway after the German capitulation in 1945.

Released from captivity in 1946, he settled down as solicitor in Freiburg. In 1947 he was appointed a member in the Commission on Decartelization. He was active in pan-European societies, among them the German-French Association in Freiburg and the Association for Supranational Cooperation. Filbinger joined the Christian Democratic Union (CDU) in 1951 and was elected city councilor in Freiburg two years later. In 1958 he was appointed privy councilor to the government of Baden-Württemberg, which was led by the CDU. In 1960 Filbinger was elected a member of the State Assembly of Baden-Württemberg and was appointed secretary of the interior in the cabinet of the Land's (State's) Prime Minister Kurt Georg Kiesinger. Among his personal secretaries in those years was Manfred Rommel, who later became mayor of Stuttgart. When Kiesinger became federal chancellor in December 1966, Filbinger succeeded him as prime minister of Baden-Württemberg. Similar to Kiesinger in the federal government, Filbinger formed a grand coalition with the Social Democratic Party (SPD) for the state's government. Successful in the Baden-Württemberg elections in 1968, 1972, and 1976, Filbinger continued to hold office as the state's prime minister; after 1972, when his party won an absolute majority for the first time, he formed a government relying on the CDU alone.

Filbinger also held various posts within his party on the regional and national levels. Moreover from 1971 until 1974 he acted as plenipotentiary of the Federal Republic of Germany for cultural affairs within the treaty of German-French cooperation. From November 1, 1973, until October 31, 1974, he also officiated as chairman of the German Federal Council (Bundesrat), the upper house of parliament. Until 1976 Filbinger was held in high esteem because of a thoroughgoing reform of Baden-Württemberg's administrative subdivisions.

Filbinger, a rather dogmatic conservative close to Franz Josef Strauß, the right-winghead of the Barvarian Christian Social Union, enjoyed a reputation in the 1970s as an advocate of a strictly confrontational opposition by the CDU against the federal government of the Social Democrats and the Free Democrats. He was well known as one of the most strident critics of the government's *Ostpolitik*, a new approach toward Eastern Europe. Filbinger's renown deteriorated quickly when his role as a naval judge in the Second World War became public in the summer of 1978. Rolf Hochhuth, a playwright (*Der Stellvertreter, The Deputy, 1963*) who was already noted for his charges against the collaboration of the Roman Catholic Church with the Nazis, initiated the whole affair. It soon came out that Filbinger had imposed and enforced capital sentences in the National Socialist era; as late as in April 1945, he participated in a case ending with the death sentence against a sailor accused in absentia. Filbinger only reluctantly admitted the facts about his involvement in several cases that had ended with a death sentence. He emphasized the legality of the procedures under laws valid at that time and he claimed a loss of memory. In August 1978 he was forced by his own party to resign from as prime minister of Baden-Württemberg, and he was deprived of all his offices within the CDU the following year.

Subsequently he confined his political activity to the Studienzentrum Weikersheim. This institution, founded in 1979, aims at ethical renovation on a Christian basis through meetings and publications and is generally regarded as a highly conservative think tank. In 1997 Filbinger lived in seclusion in Günterstal near Freiburg.

BIBLIOGRAPHY

Bossle, Lothar, ed. *Deutschland als Kulturstaat: Festschrift für Hans Filbinger zum 80. Geburtstag.* Paderborn: Bonifatius, 1993.

———, ed. *Hans Filbinger, ein Mann in unserer Zeit: Festschrift zum 70. Geburtstag.* Munich: Universitas, 1983.

Filbinger, Hans. *Bildungspolitik mit Ziel und Mass: Wilhelm Hanh zu seinem zehnjahrigen Wirken gewidmet.* Stuttgart: Klett, 1974.

———. *Die geschmahte Generation.* Munich: Universitas, 1987.

———. *Freiheit:Strukturen und Werte.* Stuttgart: Seewald, 1976.

———, ed. *Identität und Zukunft der Deutschen: Klaus Hornung zum 65. Geburtstag.* Frankfurt am Main/New York: P. Lang, 1992.

Hurten, Heinz. *Hans Filbinger, der "Fall" und die Fakten: eine historische und politologische Analyse.* Mainz: von Hase und Koehler, 1980.

von dem Knesebeck, Rosemarie, ed. *In Sachen Filbinger gegen Hochhuth: Die Geschichte einer Vergangenheitsbewaltigung/Originalausgabe.* Reinbek bei Hamburg: Rowohlt, 1980.

Neubauer, Franz. *Das öffentliche Fehlurteil: der Fall Filbinger als ein Fall der Meinungsmacher.* Regensburg: Roderer, 1990.

Bernd Leupold

Fini, Gianfranco (1952–)

Italian right-wing politician. Gianfranco Fini was born in Bologna on January 3, 1952. His father was a civil servant and his mother a teacher. Though his paternal grandfather had been a Communist, Fini's father was for a time an ardent, though soon to be disillusioned, Fascist, and his maternal grandfather had participated in the Fascist March on Rome in 1922.

When he was sixteen Fini joined the Youth Front of the Italian Social Movement (MSI), the neofascist party founded in 1946, after left-wing demonstrators had prevented him from entering a cinema where the American film *The Green Berets* was showing. After his family moved to Rome, where his father opened a service station, Fini attended the University of Rome and received a degree in psychology. In 1977 he became secretary of the Youth Front. In 1983, after working as a journalist, he entered parliament as a member of the MSI. In 1987 Fini became party secretary and in 1991 party leader. Though as late as 1994 he called Mussolini "the greatest statesman of the twentieth century," Fini quickly began to distance the party from the legacy of fascism and in 1995 renamed it the National Alliance. In the European Parliament to which he was elected in 1989, he withdrew the MSI from the right-wing caucus led by French right-winger Jean-Marie Le Pen after a dispute with the Republican Party of Germany over the predominately German-speaking areas of northeastern Italy. Fini identified his post-fascist party as "a reformist right, based on the necessity of modernizing the Italian state . . . a political right comparable to Chirac in France." The party, he says, supports "traditional values" such as opposition to abortion and state-sanctioned homosexual unions. Unlike the right in the United States, Fini is positive about the "social market economy" concept of the Bavarian Christian Social Union. While the National Alliance calls for a reduction in size of the Italian government and bureaucracy, it pragmatically supports subsidies and job creation in the poorer south, where it has strong support.

With the support of Silvio Berlusconi, the Italian businessman turned politician, in 1993, Fini came in a close second in the mayor' race in Rome, and in March 1994 the party won the vote of one out of every seven Italian voter, emerging as the third-largest party and a member of the victorious coalition Freedom Alliance, assembled by Berlusconi. The National Alliance with 13.5 percent of the vote won 105 of the right's 366 seats. Its allies Berlusconi's Forza Italia won 155 and the Northern League 106. As part of the Freedom Alliance, Fini and four other members of the National Alliance entered Berlusconi's government.

Following the rapid collapse of the Berlusconi government in December 1994 and the victory of the Olive Tree coalition of the center-left in 1996, Fini, whose party received a respectable six million votes in 1996, concentrated on the continuing rehabilitation of his party and the demonstration that he and the party deserve to be regarded as mainstream. The effort has met with success. According to post-Communist leader Massimo D'Alema of the Democratic Party of the Left, Fini, the post-Fascist, is his counterpart on the democratic right.

BIBLIOGRAPHY

Caprettini, Alessandro. *La nuova destra: e quindi uscimmo a riveder le stelle.* Palermo: Edizioni Arbor, 1995.

Crouch, Gregory. "Three to Watch: Populists of the Hard Right." *New York Times,* April 21, 1996.

"Fini's nice new suit." *Economist,* February 21, 1998.

Lewis, Anthony. "At Home Abroad; 'A Reformist Right'." *New York Times,* June 30, 1995.

Locatelli, Goffredo. *Duce addio: la biografia di Gianfranco Fini.* Milan: Longanesi, 1994.

Ravaglioli, Fabrizio. *Italia, mia: un saggio sulla destra: con un intervista a Fini.* Rome: SEAM, 1995.

Bernard Cook

SEE ALSO Berlusconi, Silvio

Finland

Finland (Suomi), a Nordic country of five million inhabitants, covers 130,119 square miles (338,145 sq km). Western and southern Finland came under Swedish dominion around 1200. In 1808–9 Sweden lost the area to Russia. Finland became an autonomous grand duchy, and the Russian tsar, as the grand duke of Finland,

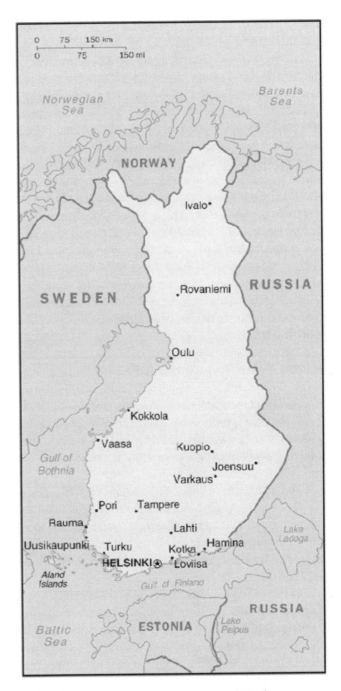

Finland. *Illustration courtesy of Bernard Cook.*

promised to uphold the constitutional laws and rights of Finland. Finland declared itself an independent republic on July 20, 1917, after the Russian Revolution of 1917.

After the 1918 civil war with Finnish Communists supported by their Soviet counterparts, Finland was declared a constitutional monarchy by the Eduskunta (parliament). On October 8, 1918, a German prince, Karl Friedrich, was elected the first king, but he never received the crown because of Germany's defeat in World War I. In

1919, Finland became a republic with political power vested in the people, represented by the Eduskunta.

The president's status descends directly from that of the Swedish kings of the eighteenth century. The highest executive power is vested in the president, assisted by the Council of State (the government). The president presents laws and other proposals to the Eduskunta, ratifies laws, issues statues, appoints top civil servants and judges, leads foreign policy, and is commander in chief of the armed forces. The president is elected for a six-year term, and since 1988 one successive term is allowed. The president was formerly elected by an electoral college formed by 300 electors (301 after 1981). In 1987 a mixed system was applied; the people voted for both presidential candidates and electors. In 1991 direct election of the president was established. If no candidate receives more than 50 percent of the votes in the first round of an election, voters choose between the two candidates receiving the most votes.

Legislative power is vested in the Eduskunta, consisting of 200 members. It enacts laws and supervises the actions of the government body, which must enjoy its confidence. There are 199 members elected for four years (until 1954, three years) by proportional from the Åland Islands by majority vote. Earlier the president had the right to dissolve the Eduskunta, but since 1991 the prime minister must ask the president to do so.

For regional administration, the country is divided into twelve lääni (provinces), led by a governor appointed by the president. The kunta (municipality) represents local self-government separate from the state administration. Judicial institutions at all levels are independent of political ones.

Finland is linguistically, religiously, and ethnically an exceptionally homogeneous country. There are two official languages. Finnish (a Finno-Ugric language) is spoken by 95 percent and Swedish (a Germanic language) by 5 percent of the population. About 99 percent of the population expressing religious conviction belong to the Lutheran Church; the Greek Orthodox Church (1 percent). The Orthodox Church together with the Lutheran Church constitute the state religions. Lapps, Gypsies, Russians, and some recent, mainly European immigrants represent around 1 percent of the total population.

Although the Bolshevik regime in Russia recognized the independence of Finland on January 2, 1918, Finland had to fight a war with the Soviet government from June 1919 to October 1920 in order to retain the Finnish-inhabited area of Karelia. Following the Nazi-Soviet pact of August 23, 1939, the Soviet Union extended its control over eastern Poland and the Baltic states. It demanded that Finland cede it the Viipuri (Viborg) isthmus near Leningrad. When the Finns refused, the USSR attacked on November 30, 1939. Though the Finns were victorious in the first part of this war, called the Winter War, they were eventually overwhelmed by Soviet numbers and had to agree to the Soviet terms on March 12, 1940. The war cost Finland the Viborg isthmus, the southeastern part of Karelia, and Pechenga (Petsamo), Finland's access to the Barents Sea in the north. Though Finland never signed a formal agreement with Germany, following the German conquest of Norway (April-June 1940) the Finns allowed German troops to cross and be stationed on their territory. When the German invasion of the USSR began on June 22, 1941, Finland joined the war, which it called the War of Continuation, in order to regain its lost territory.

Finnish postwar history can be divided into two main periods: the years 1944–61, a time of political crises, and the period 1962–94, a time of consensus. Politics formed the essence of the first period and the economy that of the second; indeed, the development of a political consensus has been made possible by economic growth.

The first period started with the years of danger (1944–48), when Finland narrowly escaped the fate of Eastern Europe—absorption into the Soviet sphere. In the first parliamentary elections after the war in 1945, the Finnish People's Democratic Union (SKDL), an alliance of the Communist Party and left-socialists, became one of the three big parties and obtained a strong position in a coalition government. Communists attempted extra-parliamentary measures to change the political system. In 1948 they planned to carry out a coup d'état, but President J. K. Paasikivi placed the Finnish police and army in the Helsinki area on alert, preventing the attempt. Furthermore, Paasikivi restricted Soviet influence by convincing the Soviet Union to accept Finland's neutrality in the preamble of the Treaty of Friendship, Cooperation and Mutual Assistance between the two countries in 1948. Finally, Finns strongly reacted to the extraparliamentary measures and the open Soviet support of the Finnish Communists. As a result the SKDL lost eleven seats in the 1948 parliamentary elections and was left out of the new government.

Economic and social recovery were also of central concern between 1949 and 1955. The recovery started immediately after the war and was carried out in a surprisingly short period. Finland's imports and exports reached prewar levels by 1950. Finland joined the International Monetary Fund in 1948 and the General Agreement on Tariffs and Trade in 1950. Finally, the return by the USSR of the Porkkala naval base in 1955 formally ended the war for Finland, making it fully sovereign. Finland became a member of the United Nations and the Nordic Council in 1955.

The final period of political crises culminated in the period 1956–61. There was no danger to democracy, but a drama evolved around exceptionally heated political fights over hegemony, not only within and between the political parties but also among the president, the government, and the Eduskunta. In addition, there were two major crises in Finnish-Soviet relations: the "night frosts" in 1958 and the "note crisis" in 1961.

The second major period, the years of consensus (1962–94), started with a transitional period (1962–66) when relations between the Social Democratic Party (SDP) and President Urho Kekkonen were improved and political breaches within the social democratic movement healed. In the 1966 parliamentary election, the SDP and the Communists won a majority, forming a new government together with the Center Party (KESK). The government launched a consensus-building project, first reflected in 1968 in comprehensive collective bargaining agreements between the unions and representatives of business. Finland began its transformation into a welfare state, mainly through social security pension and health insurance, as well as comprehensive school reforms. Finland became an affluent service economy; foreign trade expanded, and trade agreements were concluded with the European Free Trade Association (EFTA) in 1961 and the European Community (EC) in 1973.

The years from 1974 to 1990 can be called the time of mature consensus. Rapid economic growth and low unemployment made it possible to complete the welfare-state project by 1980. As a great historical achievement by President Kekkonen, the Conference on European Security and Cooperation convened in Helsinki in 1975. In 1981, Kekkonen resigned because of illness, and in the 1982 presidential elections Mauno Koivisto was elected the first Socialist president in Finland's history. The disintegration of the Communist movement became so advanced that Communists had to leave the government in 1983. Consequently, a growing tension between the Center and the SDP anticipated the end of their coexistence. A new alternative emerged: the conservatives had been gaining additional support, especially because they were excluded from governments because of the informal veto exercised by the USSR. In 1987 the Conservative Party (KOK) became the second-largest party and formed a government with the Social Democrats without the Center. The new coalition lost the 1991 parliamentary elec-

tions, however, when the Center became the biggest party.

If the time of consensus started with a transitional period (1962–66), it is ending in another (1991–). A deep economic recession took Finns by surprise in 1991. Not understanding the severity of the situation, the new government went from one political failure to another, becoming even less popular than its predecessor. Consequently, a grass roots movement supported Martti Ahtisaari as the SDP's presidential candidate and elected him Finland's new president in 1994.

Finnish-Soviet relations occupied a central position in Finnish foreign policy until the 1980s. As a consequence of international détente in the 1970s and the collapse of the Soviet Union in the 1990s, Finland has become less interested in neutrality and more active in relations with Europe since the end of the 1980s. First Finland became a partner in the European Economic Area (the agreement between the EFTA and the EC, in force since the beginning of 1994), then applied for membership in the European Union (EU) in 1992. The negotiations were concluded in March 1994, and the agreement between Finland and the EU was signed on June 24, 1994. The agreement was ratified by the Eduskunta after a consultative referendum on October 16, 1994, and was approved by 57 percent of voters.

Finland at the end of the Second World War had had difficulty maintaining its independence and multiparty democracy against attacks by the Soviet Union and the Finnish Communists. Domestic fights over political hegemony did not make things easier. However, Finland was ultimately successful both in the political and economic spheres. By 1980, Finland become a Nordic welfare state. On the other hand, the future of the welfare state is uncertain, owing to economic difficulties. If the general hope for its survival is not realized, the economic basis of consensus is likely to disappear.

BIBLIOGRAPHY

Constitution Act and Parliament Act of Finland. Helsinki: Ministry for Foreign Affairs, 1967.

Häikiö, Martti. *A Brief History of Modern Finland.* Helsinki: University of Helsinki, Lahti Research and Training Center, 1992. Häikiö's work includes an extensive bibliography of English-language books on Finland.

Jutikkala, Eino, and Kauko Pirinen. *A History of Finland.* London: Heinemann, 1979.

Kanninen, Ermei, et al., eds. "Aspects of Security. The Case of Independent Finland." *Revue internationale d'historie militaire,* no. 62 (1985).

Nousiainen, Jaakko. *The Finnish Political System.* Cambridge, Mass.: Harvard University Press, 1971.

Vilho Harle

Finland and the Soviet Union

After Finland's declaration of independence on December 6, 1917, Finnish-Soviet relations were hostile. The War of Independence broke out when Finnish soldiers tried to disarm Russian troops in Finland. Afterward Finnish volunteers occasionally penetrated into Soviet Karelia. A peace treaty was concluded in Tartu in 1920, but Finns remained suspicious toward the Soviets. In 1933 Finland signed a nonaggression pact with the USSR, but this reflected only a minor improvement in Finnish-Soviet relations.

The Molotov-Ribbentrop Pact of August 23, 1939, left Finland in the Soviet sphere of interest. However, the Soviet Union failed to occupy Finland, which it attacked in the Winter War 1939–40. When Germany attacked the Soviet Union in 1941, Finland joined the Germans in what the Finns call the Continuation War (1941–44). Finland soon occupied all the areas it had lost in the Winter War, and also Soviet Karelia. A massive Soviet attack in June 1944 caused the Finnish army to withdraw in panic. With material aid from Germany, however, Finland stopped Soviet troops from occupying Finland in July 1944. An interim peace agreement with the USSR was signed in September 1944 and was confirmed by the final peace treaty in Paris in 1947. Finland lost 12 percent of its area to the Soviets and had to fulfill many other obligations: expel German forces from Finland, rent the naval base at Porkkala to the USSR, pay huge war reparations, and bring to trial wartime political leaders considered responsible for Finland's involvement in the Continuation War. An Allied Control Commission (ACC) consisting of British and Soviet representatives, but actually led by the Soviets, was stationed in Helsinki.

Finland's position was precarious. The USSR controlled Finnish politics through the ACC. In 1948 Finland had to refuse U.S.-sponsored Marshall-Plan-aid and sign a ten-year Treaty of Friendship, Cooperation and Mutual Assistance (FCMA) with the USSR. While Finland was obligated only to defend Finnish territory should Germany or any power allied with it attempt to invade the Soviet Union through Finland, a real danger was included in the obligation to consult with the USSR about military cooperation if such an invasion was anticipated. On the positive side, the preamble to the treaty stated that Finland had the right to remain outside of big-power conflicts; moreover, it was understood in Finland that the improvement of Finnish military capabilities would be important in preserving Finnish independence.

Attempts in 1948 involving pressure by the USSR and Finnish Communists and demonstrations by Finnish Communists failed to make Finland a Communist country. This led to a period of adaptation, when relations between the two different systems had to be rebuilt. A Social Democratic (SPD) minority government, formed by K. A. Fagerholm (1948–50), became a test case. Fagerholm's government was heavily criticized by the USSR, which applied economic sanctions to force Fagerholm to resign. However, President Paasikivi gave his full support to the government and the USSR changed its line in December 1948, accepting a trade deal favorable to Finland. Yet as a consequence of the crisis, the USSR perceived the SDP as hostile to Finnish-Soviet friendship; in domestic politics the Communists (SKDL) and the Agrarian Union (ML) became closer to each other.

After the first crisis, relations improved and trade increased: the FCMA Treaty was extended by twenty years and Porkkala was returned to Finland in 1955. The USSR and Finnish Communists were satisfied when Kekkonen defeated Fagerholm in the 1956 presidential elections. But, for the USSR President Kekkonen alone was not sufficient to guarantee the continuation of Finnish-Soviet friendship. On the contrary, domestic power struggles directly and indirectly challenging Kekkonen made the USSR suspicious. This caused two major crises in Finnish-Soviet relations.

In 1957 the SDP elected Väinö Tanner, a convicted war criminal, its chairman. Against warnings from Kekkonen's son and friends in the Agrarian Union (ML), the ML decided to form a government with the SDP. Kekkonen appointed Fagerholm prime minister. Furthermore, the Communists (SKDL) were excluded from the new government. The result was the "Night Frost" crisis of 1958, in which the USSR openly expressed its disapproval of the Fagerholm majority government and applied economic sanctions against Finland, cutting off imports from Finland completely. Consequently, Foreign Minister Johannes Virolainen (ML) resigned, and the other Agrarian Union ministers soon followed him. A minority government formed by the Agrarian Union was appointed, and relations between the two countries immediately improved.

Domestic tensions did not disappear, however, but grew stronger as a consequence of the Night Frost crisis. In 1961 cooperation among the SDP, the Conservatives (KOK), and the centrist People's parties (KP and SFP) against Kekkonen developed into a formal coalition, which hoped to prevent his reelection by supporting the candidacy of Olavi Honka, former chancellor of justice but a largely unknown figure. The USSR did not remain passive, concerned as it was about the possibility of such a right-wing coalition during the whole postwar period.

On October 30, 1961, the Soviet Union sent a diplomatic note to the Finnish government, which launched the "note crisis." Referring to the rearmament of Germany and its increased naval presence in the Baltic Sea, the note proposed consultations for a common defense effort against this alleged military threat. President Kekkonen, who was in the United States at the time, tried to postpone negotiations as long as possible. But Finland had to give the Soviets guarantees that its foreign policy would continue unchanged. Taking this as his justification, Kekkonen dissolved the Eduskunta on November 14. Then, he went to Novosibirsk to meet Soviet Premier Nikita Khrushchev on November 22. They agreed that the consultations were to be postponed until the indefinite future and that future consultative initiatives would have to come from both countries. During the visit, Honka withdrew from the presidential elections, and the coalition collapsed.

Several factors were likely behind the note, but the Soviets believed it would help Kekkonen in the fight against the Honka coalition. The management of the conflict went smoothly, proving that Kekkonen alone could shepherd Finnish-Soviet relations. The question of whether Kekkonen requested the note or had some role in planning it still remains a bone of contention, but he at least knew a note was coming. On the other hand, even without the justification provided by the note, Kekkonen was determined to dissolve the Eduskunta to weaken the Honka Coalition. It is also true that a number of politicians from various parties, as well as eminent nonpartisan figures, were accepted on the ML lists as candidate electors for Kekkonen's in the spring and the summer, well before the note.

After the note crisis, the anti-Kekkonen and anti-Soviet movements died. The SDP improved its relations with Kekkonen and the Finnish and the Soviet Communist parties. Above all, Kekkonen became an unchallenged figure as the leader of Finnish foreign policy. He made all his initiatives fully acceptable to the USSR: proposals for a Nordic nuclear-free zone in 1963, a Finnish-Norwegian border peace agreement in 1964, and strong criticism in 1964 against a planned multinational NATO fleet armed with nuclear weapons. Finnish defense capabilities were increased by purchasing antiaircraft missiles and MiG fighters in 1961.

Minor episodes were caused by Soviet ambassadors in 1969 and 1979 when they played an active role in power struggles within the Finnish Communist Party. Both, however, were quickly recalled from Finland. In 1972 the USSR warned Finland that an agreement with the EEC could destroy valuable political ties and economic achievements and make Finland lose a share of its trade with the USSR. Kekkonen gave his personal guarantee of the continuation of Finnish-Soviet friendship and trade, and the Soviet criticism was withdrawn. A final minor episode occurred in late 1978 when Soviet Defense Minister Dimitri Ustinov proposed joint military exercises during peacetime to improve readiness for military cooperation in case of needs anticipated by the FCMA Treaty. Kekkonen rejected the proposal immediately.

Meanwhile, a real struggle was going on regarding the question of Finnish neutrality. While the policy had been formally approved by the Western powers in 1961–62, the USSR emphasized a policy of peace and friendship instead. This became conspicuous after the occupation of Czechoslovakia in 1968, when official Finnish-Soviet statements, published mainly during state visits, became the decisive battleground over whether the Finnish preference for "neutrality" or the Soviet preference for "friendship" would prevail. The struggle over the selection and definition of words was carried out with careful moves from both sides, with the Soviets suggesting "peace and friendship" but the Finns "neutrality." Kekkonen's "peace-loving policy of neutrality" was acceptable to the USSR for some time. Finnish foreign policy was defined as the "Paasikivi-Kekkonen Line," which rested on the 1948 mutual assistance pact and on Finland's desire to pursue a "peace-loving policy of neutrality."

In the post-Kekkonen 1980s, Finland returned to a "policy of neutrality" and avoided the complex Soviet formulations in official Finnish documents. Because of the changes in the USSR that followed Soviet leader Mikhail Gorbachev's ascendancy in 1985, this remained a minor domestic debate without much further reaction from the USSR. In 1989 Gorbachev was finally willing to call Finland "a neutral Nordic country."

The USSR did interfere in Finland's domestic politics, but it is difficult to distinguish the role of the USSR from Kekkonen's use of power. Finnish politics and society became distorted or even corrupted. Because conservatives were left out of the government for foreign policy reasons, political opposition in Finland was shut out of power, and Kekkonen and his allies enjoyed a privileged and secure hold on government. Voters reacted by increasingly supporting to the conservatives, and a growing desire developed to separate domestic affairs from foreign policy. The USSR recognized this trend and did not criticize or support any candidate in the 1982 presidential elections. To prove that there were no problems in Finnish-Soviet relations, the FCMA treaty was extended by the traditional twenty years in 1983.

The importance of Finnish-Soviet relations from both countries' point of view decreased conspicuously toward the end of the 1970s. The Finnish-Soviet FCMA treaty went out of existence at the end of 1991; a new treaty, without any military obligations, was signed between Finland and Russia in 1992 but was soon forgotten. In the wake of the collapse of the Communist system, Finland carefully followed a wait-and-see policy. Finland was among the latecomers in recognizing the independence of the Baltic states, but it openly supported democratic development in Russia after 1992.

Finnish-Soviet relations reflected Soviet strategic interests and Finland's wish for security. Trade was also an important factor, the economic value of their trade being considerable for both partners. Finnish businesses involved in exports to the USSR employed around 300,000 persons annually, and until the 1970s Finland was the largest non-Communist trading partner of the USSR. Therefore, Finland had to balance moves toward European integration with concessions to the Soviets. When the USSR found other trading partners in the West in the 1970s, Finland's exports to the Soviet Union decreased from 28 percent of total exports in the 1970s to 5 percent in 1989, and remained close to zero in 1990–91. However, the continuing importation of energy from Russia had to be paid for in hard currency. From 1992 to 1993 Finnish exports to Russia increased, reaching 7 percent of Finnish exports in 1994.

BIBLIOGRAPHY

Allison, Roy. *Finland's Relations with the Soviet Union, 1944–1984.* Oxford: Macmillan, 1985.

Jakobson, Max. *Finnish Neutrality.* New York: Praeger, 1969.

Kekkonen, Urho K. *Neutrality, the Finnish Position.* London: Heinemann, 1973.

Maude, G. *The Finnish Dilemma.* London: Oxford University Press, 1976.

Möttölä, Kari, et al., eds. *Finnish-Soviet Economic Relations.* London: Macmillan, 1983.

Väyrynen, Raimo. *Conflicts in Finnish and Soviet Relations.* Tampere: University of Tampere Press, 1972.

Vloyantes, John P. *Silk Glove Hegemony.* Kent, Ohio: Kent State University Press, 1975.

Vilho Harle

SEE ALSO Kekkonen, Urho; Koivivsto, Mauno; Porkkala

Political Parties

Under Swedish rule (1200–1809), Finns were represented among the four Swedish Estates. As a grand duchy, Finland was granted an autonomous legislature, Säätyvaltiopäivät (the Estates). In 1907 the Estates was abolished and replaced with a democratic, unicameral parliament (Eduskunta), elected by universal suffrage. Finnish women were the first in Europe to be enfranchised. Several parties won seats in the Eduskunta.

The Finnish Workers Party, later called the Finnish Social Democratic Party (SDP), was founded in 1899. It became the largest political party in the first elections. Because of the civil war of 1918, the Communists were ousted from the SPD and communism was outlawed. The Social Democrats (SDP) remained in the Eduskunta and won eighty-five seats in 1939. In 1945, owing to the resurgence of the Communists, the SDP was reduced to fifty seats. After a party crisis in 1957–59 a minority left the party and established the Workers and Small Farmers Social Democratic Union (TPSL). Consequently, in the 1962 elections the SDP won just thirty-eight seats. In 1973 the TPSL was abolished when the majority rejoined the SDP and the minority (called the Socialist Workers Party) did not survive. Between 1966 and 1991 the SDP was the largest party, and it regained that position in the 1995 elections. Two Social Democrats, Mauno Koivisto and Martti Ahtisaari, have been elected president of Finland. SDP voters are found among blue-collar workers but also among civil servants in the public sector. The party believes in the welfare state and strongly supports Finland's integration into the EU.

The Finnish Communist Party (SKP) was established in Moscow in 1918. The Interim Peace Treaty of 1944 legalized the party, but in elections it operated through the Finnish People's Democratic Union (SKDL), an alliance between the Communists and leftist Socialists. The SKDL won forty-nine seats in 1945; in 1958 it was the biggest party with fifty seats. In the 1960s support started to decrease because of the rise of the SDP and splits within the Communist movement. While the SKDL still had forty MPs in 1975, the number fell to nineteen by 1991. The Stalinist minority founded the Democratic Alternative (DEVA) in 1986. In 1990 the Left Alliance (VAS) was established, including all the Communist MPs in the Eduskunta. The SKP literally went bankrupt on November 15, 1992, leaving the VAS the single Communist force in Finland, with the support of around 10 percent of the electorate. The communists have obtained support from two different groups: blue-collar workers in cities and agricultural workers or small farmers in eastern and northern Finland. The communists supported close friendship between Finland and the USSR and still oppose EU membership and the new Western orientation in Finnish foreign policy.

The political center is occupied by several parties. The largest is the Finnish Center (KESK), established as the Agrarian Union (ML) in 1908 but renamed the Center Party in 1965 and the Finnish Center in 1988. Since 1945 the party has been one of the three largest, and between 1991 and 1995 the biggest with fifty-five seats. Farmers still have a leading role in its policy making, but 70 percent of its electoral support comes from new voters, mainly from the middle class. In the big southern cities, however, the party wins less than 4 percent of the vote. The KESK leadership supports EU membership, but 70 percent of its voters opposed it in the referendum.

In 1958 the Agrarian Union ousted Veikko Vennamo, who had joined anti-Kekkonen forces after 1956. He established the Finnish Small Peasants Party in 1959, called since 1966 the Finnish Rural Party (SMP). A majority of its parliamentary representatives established a short-lived Finnish People's Union Party (SKYP) in 1972. The SMP was a protest party, but in 1987 it participated in government in place of the KESK. In the 1991 elections the SMP collected seven seats, but four of its elected representatives left the party.

The Swedish People's Party (SFP), a nonideological party of Swedish speakers, has remained an important small party (fifteen seats in 1945, and twelve in 1991). Liberalism has had various successive representatives. The Finnish People's Party (KP) was founded in 1951 through a fusion of the Progressive Party and the Independent Middle Class; in 1964 it formed the Liberal People's Party (LKP) with the Free-Thinkers League. The Finnish Christian Union (SKL) was established as a political party in 1970. The SFP and the LKP support EU membership, but the SKL and the SMP strongly oppose it.

Among the conservative parties, the Finnish Party was founded as early as the 1860s. In the first parliamentary elections in 1907 it was divided into two formal parties, the Old Finns and the Young Finns. In 1918 the Old Finns became the National Coalition Party (KOK), while the Young Finns formed the National Progressive Party (EP). From 1945 to 1975 the KOK had twenty-four to thirty-seven MPs, but in 1979 it became the second-largest party, defeating the Center Party. In 1987 the KOK formed the government with the SDP. While losing in 1991, it remained in the government, now with the Center. The KOK evolved from a strictly conservative party to a more moderate one after the beginning of the 1970s. A conservative member of parliament, reacting to this change, resigned and formed the Constitutional Peo-

ple's Party (PKP), which did not long survive. The KOK has received its support from white-collar workers and the upper middle class. The party was critical of Finnish-Soviet friendship and President Kekkonen, and fully supports EU membership.

Certain Finnish parties have always been difficult to locate along the conventional ideological continuum (e.g., the SMP and the SKL). They have often but not always remained short-lived and small. Among such groups, the so-called Koijärvi Movement, together with other environmental groups, elected two representatives in 1983. Finally, these groups established the Green Union (VIH) in 1987. In 1991–95 the VIH had ten representatives, but in 1994 its support declined.

The postwar years witnessed a power struggle between two informal constellations of parties that never became formal alliances. The first consisted of the Agrarian Union/the Center (ML/KESK) and the Communist Party (SKP/SKDL), which agreed on Finnish-Soviet friendship. The second was formed by the SDP and the Conservatives (KOK). The KESK/SKDL constellation won the 1956 presidential elections and remained in power for twenty-five years. Between 1966 and 1983 the KESK and the SKDL, even when they lost their combined parliamentary majority around 1970, were able to restrict the SDP's power in coalition governments.

The rival constellation, consisting of the SDP and the KOK, was clearly anti-Kekkonen and anti-Soviet until the Note Crisis of 1961, when Kekkonen smoothly managed a crisis resulting from a Soviet note to the Finnish government that was perceived as a military threat. Since 1962 the SDP changed its policy toward Kekkonen and the Soviet Union. It entered the government in 1966 together with the ML and the SKDL. While this left the KOK in opposition for two decades, conservative voters preferred Mauno Koivisto (SDP) to any non-Socialist candidate in the 1982 and 1988 presidential elections. This was even more conspicuous in 1994, when Martti Ahtisaari (SDP) was elected, although an acceptable non-Socialist alternative existed. In 1979 the SDP and the KOK together gained 99 MPs, for the first time enabling them to join together to form a governing coalition. However, such a coalition was unacceptable to Kekkonen. In 1983 they won 101 seats, but at the very beginning of Koivisto's first term such a coalition was again deemed inopportune. When the parties won 109 seats in 1987, President Koivisto finally gave his support, and the SDP/KOK government was formed. The coalition lost the 1991 elections. In the March 1995 elections the SDP again became the largest party, and on April 13 Paavo

Lipponen became premier after reconstructing the coalition among his SDP, the KOK, and three smaller parties.

Another major trend is the emergence of small, mainly centrist or nonideological parties that may have a considerable role in shifting basic constellations. This trend has acquired new power from antipolitical feelings since the end of the 1970s. Furthermore, EU membership has caused serious cleavages within all the parties, especially the KESK. All in all, the heyday of the old parties is coming to an end. Differences within the parties have grown bigger than those between them. This makes future developments hard to predict. Shifting antipolitical protest voters may channel their support to the old parties in opposition (e.g., the KESK 1987–91 and the SDP in 1991–95), to new parties (e.g., the VIH) but most likely to nonpartisan and independent candidates on all the party lists.

BIBLIOGRAPHY

Hodgson, John H. *Communism in Finland*. Princeton, N.J.: Princeton University Press, 1967.
Mylly, Juhani, and Michael Berry. *Political Parties in Finland*. Turku: University of Turku Press, 1987.

Vilho Harle

SEE ALSO Ahtisaari, Martti; Kekkonen, Uhro; Koivisto, Manuo; Lipponen, Paavo

Economy

Postwar reconstruction, resettlement of refugees from the areas annexed by the USSR and of war veterans, and war reparations projects required a huge effort by the Finns. Foreign assistance was needed to satisfy basic needs; Sweden's assistance in 1944–45 and loans from the United States were invaluable. However, the Finnish economy recovered and was modernized surprisingly soon after the war. The resettlement of Karelians was carried out from 1944 to 1948 through redistribution of arable lands and forests, and war reparations were paid to the USSR by the deadline of 1952. In war reparations the Finns lost, in per capita figures, as much as Western Europeans received in U.S. Marshall Plan aid.

Until 1948 the annual rate of growth remained below the prewar level of 3 percent but rose above it between 1949 and 1957 to 4 percent. Growth remained high until the end of the 1980s. However, the growth rate in Finland remained lower than in Western Europe for a quarter of a century after the war. After the 1973 oil crisis, triggered by the embargo on the sale of oil to Western Europe by Arab states during the Yom Kippur War between Israel and Egypt, and continued through limits placed on pro-

duction agreed to by Oil Producing and Exporting Countries (OPEC), which drove up the price of oil, the Finnish economy grew slightly faster than that of Europe as a whole. Consequently, at the end of the 1980s Finland reached the level of per capita gross national product (GNP) of the leading twelve Organization of Economic Cooperation and Development (OECD) countries. In general, Finland has developed a wealthy economy, with a per capita income of some $18,000 in 1990. A deep economic depression in the early 1990s did not alter this general picture.

Finland became an industrial and service economy in a surprisingly short period of time after 1944. Agriculture and forestry employed 43 percent of the total workforce in 1948, industry 31 percent, and service 26 percent, but as early as 1958 the three sectors were equal. In 1992 agriculture and forestry employed 8 percent, industry 30 percent, and services 59 percent. In recent years, the service sector has grown, while agriculture has continued to decline, joined in the 1980s by industry.

The development from an agricultural to an industrial and then service economy implies fundamental social and structural changes. The percentage of the population living in urban areas grew from 32 percent in 1950 to 80 percent in 1992. An exceptionally rapid and dramatic change took place between 1960 and 1975; during that time a million Finns moved from northern and central Finland to the southern part of the country. Furthermore, since the World War II, but principally from 1960 to 1975, about 450,000 Finns moved to Sweden. Some provinces, as a result, lost around one-third of their populations.

Exports have been a decisive factor in Finnish economic development. War reparations had an unexpected side effect. The Soviet Union demanded payment in modern industrial products, which forced Finland to launch an advanced metal industry, especially shipbuilding. This was possible through conversion of military industry to civilian production, giving the state a major role in industrial development. Furthermore, exports provided a basis for the development of the Finnish paper industry, which enjoyed the benefits of the so-called Korean expansion, a high increase in Finnish exports during the Korean War from 1950 to 1953.

Finland's imports and exports reached prewar levels, respectively, in 1948 and 1950. Wood and paper products have occupied a central position in Finland's foreign trade. They accounted for 80 percent of Finland's total exports in the 1950s but decreased toward the end of the 1960s to 40 percent. Between 1960 and 1975 the share of metal industry exports increased from 15 to 33 percent of total exports, but this trend did not continue.

Until the 1970s Sweden and the Soviet Union, together accounting for 25 to 30 percent of Finnish foreign trade, were Finland's most important trading partners. Since 1989, trade with both, but especially with the Soviet Union, has declined. Whereas the Soviet share of Finnish exports was still around 20 percent in the mid-1980s, in 1989–90 it collapsed to almost zero, and Germany became Finland's most important trade partner. Germany accounted for 16 percent of Finnish exports in 1992, Sweden 13 percent, the United Kingdom 11 percent, France 7 percent, and the United States 6 percent. Russia held tenth place, with less than a 3 percent share. Even Norway was higher at 3.5 percent, and Spain was almost equal at 2.6 percent. Germany's share of Finland's imports was 17 percent; Sweden was second with 12 percent, and the United Kingdom third with 9 percent, followed by Russia with 7 percent, the United States with 6 percent, and Japan with 5 percent. Finland trades mainly with OECD countries, with OECD trade accounting for 79 percent of imports and 82 percent of exports in 1992. Trade with the European Community (EC/EU), accounting for 47 percent of imports and 53 percent of exports, was more important than trade with the European Free Trade Association (EFTA), which accounted for 19 percent of both Finnish imports and exports.

Because of the importance of foreign trade to the Finnish economy, and especially the role of Western Europe, Finland's interest in European economic integration is not difficult to understand. Owing to Soviet sensitivity, Finnish integration policy was based on small steps balanced by political guarantees to the Soviet Union. Finland negotiated associate membership in EFTA in 1961 and became a member of the OECD in 1969. Finland negotiated a free-trade agreement with the EC in 1972, ratified in January 1974.

In 1989, Finland joined the negotiations to establish a European Economic Area (EEA) of the EFTA and EC member countries. The agreement came into effect on January 1, 1994. Meanwhile, Austria and Sweden applied for direct membership in the EC in 1991, and Finland followed suit in March 1992. A membership agreement was reached in March 1994; it was accepted by the European Union (EU) in April 1994 and signed by the participants in June 1994. In Finland the agreement was submitted to a consultative national referendum on October 16, 1994. It was approved by a vote of 57 to 43 percent.

From the point of view of the average Finn, the most important feature of the postwar societal change has been a sustained rise in the standard of living. The real purchasing power of wage earners increased fourfold by 1989. The postwar inflation, which ran 30 to 60 percent annually from 1945 to 1948, was brought under control in 1949 at 2 percent. While inflation generally remained low until 1973, it occasionally rose to vary between 12 and 16 percent. From 1973 to 1982, that high level prevailed. Since 1983 inflation has remained below 6.5 percent and in 1992–94 even below 2 percent.

Devaluations have been common in Finland, owing to its dependence on a single export, wood and paper. In 1957 the Finnish mark was devaluated by 39 percent, and in 1967 by 31 percent; there was also a minor devaluation in 1976. In the 1980s the avoidance of devaluations became a governmental goal. Since the economic downturn in 1990, devaluation has been viewed by many as a way to give a new impetus to exports. However, the inexperienced Aho government gave in to the will of the Bank of Finland, the policy of which was strongly supported by President Koivisto. It was decided to tie the mark to the European Currency Unit in June 1991 to prevent further devaluation. Nevertheless, a 14 percent devaluation was carried out in November 1991. As this was not enough, in September 1992 the mark was allowed to float, and a 24 to 27 percent devaluation took place.

Unemployment was usually about 3 percent until 1973, when it grew temporarily to 7 percent during the oil crisis. It subsequently returned to some 3 percent, where it remained until the onset of depression in 1990. In 1992 unemployment was 13 percent and increased to about 21 percent during the winter of 1993–94, when there were about 520,000 unemployed. At the end of 1994 unemployment was a little bit lower at 17 percent, or 460,000. By October 1997 it had declined to 13.1 percent.

The depression reduced tax revenues and was a final blow to the public savings, which had been spent generously for years to avoid tax increases. Simultaneously, the costs caused by the public sector and social security payments soared. Therefore, to cover budget deficits (some 60 billion marks in 1994), the state debt, especially foreign indebtedness, had to be increased rapidly. Until 1990 the state debt had remained at 50 billion marks but climbed to 260 billion at the beginning of 1993, and is projected to grow to 400 billion in 1995. The share of the debt amounted to 10 percent of GNP up to 1990, but rose to 78 percent by 1994, causing a huge increase in interest payments. These payments amounted to 8 billion marks in 1992, and 20 billion, or 10 percent of the state budget, in 1994. Over all budget deficits declined in the late 1990s and the state debt had ceased its dramatic expansion. In September 1997 it stood at 426 billion marks.

In short, the GNP still had a growth rate of 2 percent in 1990, but it decreased to −7 percent in 1991. In 1992 the figure was −4 percent and in 1993 −3 percent. In 1994 the economic situation improved and the GNP rate reflected a strong growth of over 4 percent. It grew by 4.2 percent in 1995 and 3.7 percent in 1996. Export earnings have increased, mainly because of the devaluations, and foreign trade has produced a considerable and increasing surplus since 1992, amounting to 15 billion marks in the first half of 1994. On the other hand, as export companies have been paying their foreign debts, the expected positive effects on the economy have remained small.

The deep depression was caused by many factors. External ones include the collapse of Finnish-Soviet trade; economic recession in the OECD countries; and a severe global overcapacity in wood and paper production. But the domestic side was even more decisive. A free flow of loans from banks to entrepreneurs and individuals since 1987 led to unproductive and ill-considered investments and overconsumption. Unpaid loans and the devaluations made it impossible for the banks to pay back their foreign debts; to prevent the collapse of the banking system, the state had to subsidize them with sums amounting to over 10 percent of the annual budget between 1991 and 1993. Furthermore, the rate of exchange of the Finnish currency had been kept artificially high for years by the Bank of Finland, thus increasing imports but reducing exports. Finally, public spending exploded because of unemployment compensation, which increased tenfold between 1989 and 1993, and other social security benefits. In addition, the amount of personnel in the municipal sector increased from 314,000 in 1960 to 683,000 in 1988, this during a period when the state sector had grown from 177,000 to just 215,000. Thus, despite recent improvements, the economy of Finland in the mid-1990s faced a number of serious problems requiring attention.

BIBLIOGRAPHY

Häikiö, Martti. *A Brief History of Modern Finland.* Helsinki: University of Helsinki, Lahti Research and Training Centre, 1992.

Koivisto, Mauno, and Pertti Paasio. *Finland in a Changing Europe: Major Speeches.* Helsinki: Ministry of Foreign Affairs, 1990.

Solem, Erik. *The Nordic Council and Scandinavian Integration.* New York: Praeger, 1977.

Vilho Harle

Taxation

In Finland public expenditures as a percentage of gross national product increased from 26 percent in 1950 to 63 percent in 1993. Therefore, increases in taxation rates have been inevitable. All income, including pensions and unemployment benefits and some bank savings, have been subject to taxation. However, taxes on profits are relatively low, at 25 percent, while the tax rate for wages and salaries in 1995 was about 49 percent. In the 1990s taxes were increased by eliminating inflation corrections in progression tables and especially by transferring an increasing amount of unemployment and pension costs to the employed.

The state collects direct and indirect taxes. State income tax is progressive. Municipalities collect a nonprogressive tax on earned income, varying between 15 and 23 percent. Similarly, the Lutheran and Orthodox Churches collect a nonprogressive income tax of 1.5 percent from their members. Indirect taxes are collected by the state on goods and services. As of 1961 they were paid on business turnover, but in 1994 a new value-added tax was applied to all products and services. In general this value-added tax is 22 percent, but in some special cases it is lower.

While high taxes have been criticized, in a welfare state like that of Finland they are legitimized as a public insurance system and a source of benefits in the areas of education, unemployment, health, and old age. The gross tax percentage, including income taxes, sales taxes, and social security and pension payments by the employed, has increased from 29 percent in 1950 to 34 percent in 1980, and further to 49 percent in 1993. But the net tax percentage (taking into account transfers from the public sector to individuals) has been decreasing, especially during the 1990s. Furthermore, Finland's gross level of taxation has remained lower than that of the other Nordic countries.

Yet the welfare system has become the central and increasing factor for increasing taxes and is burdensome for those who pay income taxes and social security insurance but do not collect social security benefits. In 1993 two million working people supported three million nonworkers. The present level of taxation is not likely to survive the desire of voters to have more to say about government spending, especially when they fear that there will be too few persons to pay for their own old-age pensions.

To avoid public criticism caused by increasing taxes, the state and municipalities have spent public savings. Public savings decreased between 1960 and 1980 from 40 to 10 percent, and have been exhausted in the 1990s.

Furthermore, a steadily increasing sum has been borrowed from foreign countries. This has merely postponed the decision either to increase taxes or to reduce public spending dramatically.

BIBLIOGRAPHY
Häikiö, Martti. *A Brief History of Modern Finland.* Helsinki: University of Helsinki, Lahti Research and Training Centre, 1992.

Vilho Harle

Education

Finns were made literate by the Lutheran Church, which required a modest reading ability as a precondition for marriage. Grammar school became compulsory at the end of the nineteenth century. In the postwar period the entire Finnish educational system experienced fundamental reforms.

In 1950 there were 640,000 students in all levels of Finnish education. By 1992 the number exceeded a million. The percentage of the population with more than a comprehensive school education increased from 12 percent in 1950 to 51 percent in 1991. About 10 percent of the population has received a university-level education. The number of university students in Finland increased from 15,000 in 1950, to 25,000 in 1960, to 58,000 in 1970, and up to 113,000 in 1993.

In the period from 1944 to 1972, compulsory primary education consisted of eight years, normally begun at the age of seven. There were two alternatives for the compulsory years: either primary school for the whole period or four years in primary school and five in junior high school.

In 1968 a reform of Finnish education was enacted to be implemented gradually between 1972 and 1977. A nine-year comprehensive school, consisting of six years of primary school and three years of intermediary, became compulsory for all children; it was financed by the municipalities. A three-year high school was available for those aiming at a matriculation examination, a precondition for university studies. Vocational schools were an alternative to high school and university training.

At the end of the 1970s, to reduce unnecessary high school studies, entrance to universities was opened to applicants with vocational training but without high school diplomas. In practice, however, high school education and the matriculation examination still offer the most typical route to university studies.

The first university was founded in 1640 in Turku, but when Turku was destroyed by fire in 1812, Helsinki was made the new capital and the university was moved there.

New universities were later established in Turku for Finnish- and Swedish-speaking students. In addition, Jyväskylä had a teacher's college. As a systematic part of a new regional policy the University of Oulu was established at the end of the 1950s, and in the 1960s universities in several other cities, especially in the eastern part of the country, were founded. The newest university, that of Lapland (Rovaniemi), was started in 1979. Currently there are twenty universities, including those for arts and music. The University of Helsinki with 28,500 students has the biggest enrollment, while the universities in Turku and Tampere each have a student population of 11,000, and the smallest ones in Vaasa and Rovaniemi each have some 2,000 students.

Earlier there were private universities in Tampere and Turku. However, they were financially supported by the state and formally became state universities, as the others already were, in the 1970s. Semester fees were abolished by the end of the 1960s; proposals to return to this system in universities failed in 1994.

Finnish universities were earlier administered exclusively by professors, all of whom participated with full rights in faculty meetings. Reforms in university administration begun in 1969 attempted to reduce the administrative responsibilities and power of professors and the faculties. But the original proposal raised a heated debate by suggesting that members of three new councils (university, faculty, department) were to be elected by a one-person, one-vote principle, in which everybody studying or working at a university was allowed to vote for any candidate. Consequently, a modified version of the proposal was adopted, giving a third of the seats to each of three groups: professors, other teachers and staff, and students. Rules were also added to exclude unqualified persons from making decisions on academic competence.

The universities formerly gave four degrees: candidate, master, licentiate, and doctorate. During the 1970s the candidate degree was abolished, but it was restored in 1994 to make international comparisons easier. The new candidate degree corresponds to the B.A. It is likely that the licentiate degree will gradually disappear and that the doctoral degree will become less demanding than it has been traditionally. Earlier licentiate and doctorate were earned by submitting an acceptable thesis to a faculty. Since the end of the 1980s licentiate and doctoral students have had to complete a certain number of credits planned for postgraduate education. In 1994 the first attempts to create graduate schools in the universities that required seminars and classes rather than research projects alone, were launched. The Academy of Finland has had a considerable role in financing postgraduate research training.

Vilho Harle

Press

The first newspapers in Finland were published at the end of the eighteenth century. In the 1830s the press began to play an important role in forming the national identity. The press maintained its central political role until the end of the 1960s, when television usurped its leading position.

A total of 227 newspapers and about one thousand weekly and monthly publications of one sort or another were published in Finland in 1993. Fifty-six newspapers were published at least four times a week, and twenty-six of them appeared every weekday. The latter numbered 1.7 million copies, one for every third citizen. In per capita figures, Finland holds third place after Norway and Japan for the total circulation of newspapers.

Newspapers are privately owned, but ownership has been strongly concentrated in a decreasing number of national and local publishers. The state subsidizes postal costs of the newspapers to guarantee that copies can be delivered to subscribers early in the morning. Evening tabloids are sold mainly by the copy at newsstands.

For commercial reasons the number of newspapers affiliated with various political parties has declined. In 1946 there were thirty nonaffiliated newspapers, accounting for 35 percent of total newspaper circulation. The remaining circulation was divided between various political groups. The nineteen conservative newspapers accounted for 24 percent of newspaper circulation, the sixteen Agrarian 15 percent, the fourteen Social Democratic eight percent, the eleven Communist seven percent, the three Liberal six percent, and the ten Swedish five percent. By 1985 there were sixty independent newspapers, accounting for 65 percent of total newspaper circulation. Only the Center Party, formerly the Agrarians, despite losing one paper, still kept its 15 percent share. In the 1990s, however, even the Center lost a number of its newspapers.

Of the ten major newspapers in 1993, the largest was *Helsingin Sanomat,* with a circulation of 476,163. It used to be the organ of the Progressive Party but became independent in 1932. The second-largest newspaper, *Ilta-Sanomat,* circulation 212,854, was published as an evening tabloid by the Helsingin Sanomat publishing house, which has a considerable role in influencing public opinion.

The third-largest newspaper, *Aamulehti,* circulation 135,194, published in Tampere, was earlier affiliated with the Conservative Party. The fourth was the independent *Turun Sanomat,* circulation 119,004, published in Turku. The fifth, *Maaseudun Tulevaisuus,* circulation 110,951, was published by the Central Organization of Agricultural Producers in Helsinki. The sixth was *Iltalehti,* circulation 105,059, an independent evening tabloid published in Helsinki. The seventh was the nonaffiliated *Kaleva,* circulation 95,118, published in Oulu. The eighth, *Keskisuomalainen,* circulation 80,600, published in Jyväskylä, was earlier affiliated with the Center Party. The ninth was *Kauppalehti,* circulation 78,705, a business paper owned by the publishers of *Aamulehti* and published in Helsinki. The tenth was *Savon Sanomat,* circulation 70,028, affiliated with the Center and published in Kuopio.

A special feature of the Finnish press is that some regional newspapers account for at least 80 percent of the newspaper subscriptions in the region in which they are published. Consequently, as many as five of them—*Aamulehti, Turun Sanomat, Keskisuomalainen, Kaleva* and *Savon Sanomat*—are among the ten biggest newspapers in Finland.

The state-owned Finnish Broadcasting Corporation (YLE) had a monopoly over the electronic mass media until the 1980s but because of the intrusion of TV satellites lost that position. In the 1980s the establishment of competing commercial radio and television stations was permitted.

BIBLIOGRAPHY

Häikiö, Martti. *A Brief History of Modern Finland.* Helsinki: University of Helsinki, Lahti Research and Training Centre, 1992.

Vihlo Harle

Social Services

In Finland the first state measures in social policy were carried out by redistributing plots of land to workers in the countryside after the civil war of 1918. Modern social policy was started before the Winter War with the USSR (1939–40). Finland, however, was transformed into a welfare state between 1962 and 1980. The achievements of social policy have been considerable. Wage differentials became smaller until the beginning of the 1990s and poverty declined. But the future of the welfare system looks dreary.

The national pension law, enacted in 1937 and revised in 1957, extended basic old-age pensions to the entire population. During the first half of the 1960s, employment pensions and health insurance were created, and at the end of the same decade a Family Pensions Act was passed. In the early 1970s, the employment pension system was expanded to cover entrepreneurs and farmers.

Social insurance includes statutory pension insurance, health insurance, accident insurance, and unemployment insurance. The purpose of Finland's compulsory social insurance is to insure all persons for old age, disability, sickness, unemployment, and financial losses resulting from the death of a family provider. Voluntary additional policies supplement the public social security.

Social insurance guarantees a minimum income to all. The work pension is paid only to those who have earned a wage or salary, and depends on the number of work years and the amount earned. It represents approximately 60 to 66 percent of the individual's average wage during the four years preceding retirement.

In addition, the social security system has guaranteed accident and health insurance benefits to everybody since 1964 through a comprehensive health insurance law. In 1972 Finland began to establish a system of national health centers whose services were generally free of charge. In the 1990s minor fees for the service could be charged, but some municipalities do not collect them.

Everyone, excluding entrepreneurs and farmers, is guaranteed basic unemployment compensation. If the worker has been a member of an unemployment fund, usually maintained by labor unions, the benefits are tied to wages or salary earned during the six months preceding unemployment.

The so-called child allowance system, giving actual financial support to parents with children under seventeen years of age, was created to encourage the birth rate, especially after the Continuation War (1941–44). Furthermore, expectant mothers and newborn babies must regularly visit doctors and nurses for consultation. Compulsory education and a daily meal on school days are provided free of charge.

The government has encouraged housing construction through different kinds of tax deductions, which have gradually become more and more restricted. The Arava system, created in 1949, extended low-rate and long-term state credits to subsidize the construction of private homes and apartments. The municipalities subsidize rent and other housing costs if a person's income does not exceed a certain limit.

The social security system has been financed by compulsory social security and pension payments and by tax revenues. Payments are collected partly from employees through taxes and personal social insurance payments, and partly from employers, who must pay, in addition to wages and salaries to their employees, an amount equal to approximately 35 percent of the wage to the state in social security and pension payments.

The social security system has required increasing infrastructure and welfare investments. The percentage of the gross national product (GNP) in the public sector doubled between 1950 and 1980, from 7 to 15 percent. The share of GNP consumption in the public sector increased from 12 to 18 percent, and public-sector consumption as a percentage of total consumption went from 15 to 25 percent. The percentage share of welfare (health and social security, education, science, and culture) in the state budget increased from 29 to 38 percent, and income transfers from the public sector to individuals as a percentage of GNP increased from 8 percent in 1950 to 30 percent in 1993.

Welfare and social security responsibilities, including Finnish aid to developing countries, presuppose an affluent society. The economic depression since 1990 has challenged this assumption, and the system ran into serious difficulties. Social security and unemployment costs soared while tax revenues declined. About 36 percent of GNP in 1994 went for social security services and a further 26 percent for education. Some cosmetic attempts have been carried out to save the system. Furthermore, the growth of the public sector has been dramatically reduced, especially at the local level. But, it is likely that further savings will be required to stop a soaring increase in the foreign debt. Simultaneously, growing international competition will demand sharp reductions in labor costs.

BIBLIOGRAPHY

Kiviniemi, Markku. *Perspectives on Structure, Culture and Action: Studies in the Public Administration of the Welfare State.* Helsinki: Painatuskeskus, 1994.

Social Insurance in Finland. Helsinki: Ministry of Social Affairs and Health, Government Printing Centre, 1992.

Vilho Harle

Finnbogadóttir, Vigdis (1930–)

Fourth president of the Republic of Iceland. After studying French literature, drama, and English at the universities of Grenoble, the Sorbonne, Copenhagen, and Iceland, Vigdis Finnbogadóttir served as a secondary-school teacher in Reykjavík from 1962 to 1972. In 1972 she was appointed director of the Reykjavík Theater Company, one of the two professional theaters in Reykjavík at the time. Eight years later, Finnbogadóttir ran for president and was elected in June 1980 in a close four-way race. In her sixteen years in office, she faced an opposition candidate only once and received over 90 percent of the votes cast in 1988. Finnbogadóttir retired in 1996, at the close of her fourth term.

The election of Finnbogadóttir to the country's highest office was a significant victory for advocates of gender equality in Iceland because, as the first woman to be elected to this post, she demonstrated that women can reach the highest levels of Icelandic social and political life. Moreover, she was exceptionally popular as president among Icelanders, and highly respected abroad. During her tenure as president, the office became more visible than before in Icelandic social and cultural life, and she traveled extensively to promote the interests of the Icelandic nation. Finnbogadóttir followed the policy formulated by her predecessors however, of limited involvement in the government.

Gudmundur Halfdanarson

Fischer, Joschka (1948–)

Pragmatic leader of Germany's Green Party (Die Grünen) in the state of Hesse who broke with party idealists (Fundis, or fundamentalists) at the national level in 1985 by entering a coalition government with Hesse's Social Democratic Party. As Hesse's minister of the environment, Joschka (Joseph Martin) Fischer became the first Green to hold a ministerial post in any state government. After Fundis leaders were ousted in 1988, Green Party politics fell into the hands of the political realists (Realos), led by Otto Schily and Fischer. Under Fischer's influence the Greens were integrated into mainstream politics and accepted as a integral component of German political life.

Fischer was born on April 12, 1948, in Gerabronn, Baden-Württemberg. His politics evolved through his involvement with student demonstrations in the 1960s and perception of a residual authoritarianism in contemporary German life. Fischer's own activism escalated in 1967 following the fatal shooting by German police of student leader Benno Ohnesorg in West Berlin.

In 1983 Fischer entered the Bundestag (lower house of parliament) as the Green Party won 5.6 percent of the vote. Taking a softer line than party Fundis on Germany's use of nuclear energy, labor policy, the military, and its participation in NATO, Fischer lost political clout with the 1986 Chernobyl nuclear disaster in the USSR and the 1987 breakup of the coalition government in Hesse. As the Green Party matured, its rank and file accepted Fischer's piecemeal pursuit of Green objectives through political compromises. In the 1990s Fischer moved further to the political center by advocating a German role in the United Nation's peacekeeping mission in Bosnia. Fischer became foreign minister in the Social Democratic-

Green coalition government formed by Gohard Schröder in October 1998.

BIBLIOGRAPHY
Fischer, Joschka. *Risiko Deutschland: Krise und Zukunft der deutschen Politik.* Cologne: Kiepenheuer & Witsch, 1994.
———. *Die Linke nach dem Sozialismus.* Hamburg: Hoffman und Camps, 1992.
———. *Der Umbau der Industriegesellschaft.* Frankfurt am Main: Eichborn, 1989.
———. *Regieren geht über Studieren: Ein politisches Tagebuch.* Frankfurt am Main: Eichborn, 1987.
Markovits, Andrei S., and Philip S. Gorski. *The German Left.* New York: Oxford University Press, 1993.

David A. Meier

FitzGerald, Garret (1926–)

Leader of the moderate Fine Gael party (1977–87) and Irish prime minister (1981–82, 1982–87). Garret FitzGerald was born in Dublin and educated at University College, Dublin. He joined the national airline, Aer Lingus, from 1950 to 1958 as research and schedules manager. He was a lecturer in economics at the UCD Economics Department from 1959 to 1973, as well as freelance economist and journalist. FitzGerald joined Fine Gael in 1964 and was involved with Declan Costello's "Just Society Programme" that sought to redefine the party in the social democratic mold. In 1969 he was elected to the constituency of Dublin South East after which he was involved in an unsuccessful attempt to topple Liam Cosgrave as party leader. FitzGerald then became minister of foreign affairs in the 1973–77 coalition government. In this post he built up his reputation as an international statesman, holding Ireland's first presidency of the European Economic Community (EC) and having a major involvement in the Lomé Convention to provide aid for developing countries.

FitzGerald was central to the redefining and restructuring of Fine Gael following his election as party leader in 1977. As prime minister he saw economic affairs as the major issue facing the country. His handling of the situation was later highly questioned, specifically by himself. He had devoted much attention to the development of Fine Gael as a party but little to its policies. As such the party's handling of the depression of the early 1980s seemed to lack focus. His domestic policies did little to improve the drastic economic situation facing Ireland. Foreign affairs, especially the Anglo-Irish Agreement of 1985, consumed him to the detriment of domestic policies. As party leader, however, he made a huge impact on the electoral success of Fine Gael, which greatly increased its number of seats in parliament. The subsequent slump in the party's support may be an indication that this was just a blip. Socially FitzGerald tried to institute what he called a "constitutional crusade," but its social democratic values were not in tune with the majority of the people; FitzGerald was seen as a hectoring intellectual by some and as a bumbling academic by others. He had a large degree of personal support but less for the austerity policies his governments implemented. His duels with Charles Haughey, the leader of the traditionalist Fianna Fáil party, on the national media will link both men as the key Irish politicians of the early to mid-1980's. On his resignation in 1987 he was replaced by the technocratic Alan Dukes.

BIBLIOGRAPHY

FitzGerald, Garret. *All in a Life*. Dublin: Gill and Macmillan, 1991.

O'Byrnes, Stephen. *Hiding behind a Face: Fine Gael under FitzGerald*. Dublin: Gill and Macmillan, 1987.

Michael J. Kennedy

SEE ALSO Dukes, Alan; Haughey, Charles

Five, Kaci Kullmann (1951–)

Conservative Norwegian politician. Kaci Five was born in Oslo on April 13, 1951. He entered politics as a member of the municipal council of Baerum, a post he held from 1975 to 1981. In 1980–81 he was the executive officer of the Norwegian Employers Federation. He was a deputy member of parliament from 1977 to 1981, and has been a member of parliament since 1981, serving as minister of trade and shipping in 1989–90. He rose through the ranks of the leadership of the Conservative Party, becoming deputy chair of the party from 1982 to 1988, vice chair of the party's parliamentary group from 1985 to 1989, and party leader from 1991 to 1994. In 1994 he became the party's spokesperson for foreign affairs and the European Union.

BIBLIOGRAPHY

Hvem er Hvem? 14th ed. Oslo: Kunnskapsforlaget, 1994.

International Who's Who 1996–1997. London: Europa Publications, 1998.

Bruce Olav Solheim
Bernard Cook

Fock, Jenő (1916–)

Prime minister of Hungary from 1967 to 1975. Jenő Fock was one of the major supporters of economic reforms implemented in Hungary in and after 1968.

Fock joined the social democratic movement in the 1930s, then in the mid-1940s became a member of the Hungarian Communist Party. He served in various positions, especially in the industrial leadership in the 1950s, and was promoted to deputy prime minister in 1961. He was prime minister from 1967 to 1975. Fock was a member of the Central Committee of the Hungarian Socialist Workers Party (the official name of the Hungarian Communist Party) between 1956 and 1989 and was a member of the party's top decision-making body, the Political Committee, from 1957 to 1980.

Fock was one of Hungary's Communist leaders in the 1960s who helped end the Soviet-type command economy and introduced elements of a market economy in the form of production incentives and toleration of private enterprise on a small scale in retailing and agriculture. The orthodox wing of the Communist Party managed to abort these experiments with a mixed economy in the mid-1970s and forced Fock out of power as well.

BIBLIOGRAPHY

Fock, Jenő. *A szocializmus epitesenek gazdasagpolitikaja: beszedek es cikkek, 1963–1972*. Budapest: Kossuth Konyvkiado, 1972.

———. *Riforma economica e sviluppo della democrazia socialista: [rapporto del presidente del Consiglio sull'attivita del governo]; Internazionalismo e lotta per la coesistenza pacifica: [intervento del ministro degli esteri alla sessione d'autunno dell'Assemblea nazionale: Budapest, 16–18 ottobre 1968]*. Rome: Ufficio stampa della Ambasciata della Republica popolare ungherese, 1968.

Tamás Magyarics

SEE ALSO Hungary; Kádár, János

Foot, Michael (1913–)

Journalist, socialist, and leader of the British Labour Party from 1980 to 1983. Michael Foot was active in left-wing politics and journalism from an early age. He entered Parliament in 1945, and apart from the period 1955–60, remained a Labour MP until he retired in 1992. He became leader of the Labour Party in 1980 and was unfortunate enough to preside over the party's disastrous defeat in the 1983 general election.

Educated at Wadham College, Oxford, Foot was president of the Oxford Union and contested Monmouth for the Labour Party at the age of twenty-two. He embarked on a career in left-wing journalism and first came to general notice with his coauthorship of *The Guilty Men* (1940), an indictment of British "appeasers" of Hitler. Later, he was an active backbencher and a strong advocate of nuclear disarmament. He held office in the 1974 Labour government as secretary of state for employment, following which he became deputy leader of the party under James Callaghan. The defeat of Labour at the 1979 general election led to a period of infighting in the party, and Foot became leader in 1980. A principled parliamentary socialist, Foot was widely attacked by the conservative press, and his personal leadership style and commitment to the antinuclear cause were seen to be partly responsible for the election defeat of Labour in 1983. Following that defeat, Foot was replaced as leader by Neil Kinnock, and the process of party "modernization" began.

BIBLIOGRAPHY

Foot, Michael. *Aneurin Bevan, A Biography.* 2 Vols. London: Davis-Poynter, 1973.
Jones, Mervyn. *Michael Foot.* London: Gollancz, 1994.
Wainwright, Hillary. *Labour: A Tale of Two Parties.* London: Hogarth Press, 1987.

Stephen M. Cullen

SEE ALSO Kinnock, Neil

Forlani, Arnaldo (1925–)

Prime minister of Italy from September 1980 to July 1981. Arnaldo Forlani was born in Pesaro on December 8, 1925. He rose quickly through the ranks of the Christian Democratic Party (DC), serving ultimately as party secretary and president. He was known for his patience and his ability to build parliamentary alliances, which were so useful to his party, especially during the Andreotti period (1976–79). A chief achievement in this regard was Forlani's participation in the formation of the *pentapartito* (five-party) parliamentary alliance, consisting of the DC and the Italian Socialist Party (PSI), Italian Liberal Party (PLI), Italian Social Democratic Party (PSDI), and Italian Republican Party (PRI). Forlani's ability to form an alliance with the so-called *polo laico,* or "lay" group, of center parties (PSI, PRI, PSDI, PLI), as well as his skill in navigating through the issues of party factionalism and through the informal power structure of Italian government and politics, made him the choice as a stopgap prime minister during a crucial period of Italian history. Yet within just nine months, suffering under the enormity of the P2 Masonic lodge scandal (in which P2's leaders

had attempted to use the secret society to gain a controlling influence over the Italian government and economy) that shocked the nation, his government collapsed.

BIBLIOGRAPHY

Ginsborg, Paul. *A History of Contemporary Italy: Society and Politics, 1943–1988.* New York: Penguin, 1990.
Hine, David, *Governing Italy.* Oxford: Clarendon Press, 1993.

William Roberts

SEE ALSO Andreotti, Giulio

Foucault, Michel (1926–84)

French philosopher and social critic, professor of the history of systems of thought at the Collège de France, and genealogist of language/knowledge/power. Michel Foucault emerged as a major voice in French postmodern philosophy with *Madness and Civilization: A History of Insanity in the Age of Reason* (1961). In this book, the outlines of themes that run consistently through his thinking are evident: knowledge in any historical epoch is constituted through discursive formations; "man" as a rational and moral subject is a construct of modern discourse; language, knowledge, and power are closely linked in producing the order of things and in silencing difference and otherness. One of the late-twentieth-century heirs of Friedrich Nietzsche, Foucault pursued his project of critical analysis, what he referred to as "effective history," with the desire to uncover the groundlessness of discourse, problematize accepted "truth" as socially constructed, and show the grand liberation narratives of the Enlightenment tradition to be stories of human subjugation.

The son of a medical doctor in Poitiers, Foucault was educated at public and Catholic schools there, and at the Lycée Henri IV in Paris, where he studied philosophy with Jean Hyppolite. He gained entrance to the École Normale Supérieure in 1946, studied with Louis Althusser, and received degrees in both philosophy and psychology. He continued to study psychoanalysis at the Hospital Sainte Anne in Paris while he held an assistantship in the philosophy faculty of the University of Lille. He then accepted a position to teach French at the University of Uppsala, Sweden, where he began research for *Madness and Civilization,* submitted in 1960 as his doctoral thesis under the direction of Georges Canguilhem. From Uppsala he moved to direct the French Institutes in Warsaw (1958) and Hamburg (1959), and then returned to France, to the University of Clermont-Ferrand, to teach psychology and philosophy.

As something of a companion volume to *Madness*, which examines the rise of the asylum for treatment of the insane, Foucault wrote *The Birth of the Clinic* (1963), a study of the emergence of the modern medical discourse. Perhaps his most difficult work, *The Order of Things* (1966), his history of the human sciences, became enormously popular and established him as a major intellectual figure rivaling Sartre. Teaching in Tunisia after 1966, he missed the May-June days of Paris 1968, but returned following the events to head the philosophy department at the experimental university at Vincennes. A theoretical essay, "The Archaeology of Knowledge," appeared in 1969, and in 1970 Foucault accepted a chair at the Collège of France.

He continued to decipher discursive formations, institutions of subjugation, and knowledge/power relations in *Discipline and Punish: The Birth of the Prison* (1975), and *The History of Sexuality: An Introduction* (1976), the first of a proposed multivolume project. At the same time he became instrumental in the "Groupe d'information sur les prisons," an organization established to promote reform of the French prison system. Two collections of essays and interviews appeared: *Language, Counter-Memory, Practice* (1977), containing the influential essay "What Is an Author?", and *Power/Knowledge* (1980). And two more volumes of *The History of Sexuality* were published before his death: *The Use of Pleasure* (1984) and *The Care of the Self* (1984).

Foucault's studies center on language, which, he argued, is not a transparent medium for communication about the world and does not grasp things in themselves; rather, it creates and invents. Knowledge, reality, truth, even human subjectivity are all configurations of historically specific language practices and discursive structures. Initially he called his methodology "archaeology": the laying bare of the modes of representation (or "epistemes") that regulate the thinkable and sayable in an historical period (his works primarily examined the Renaissance, the Enlightenment, and the nineteenth century). History is not continuous but a series of discrete epistemes. Later he emphasized "genealogy" as the method by which to examine how discourse arises and functions in a period, and to reveal discourse as contingent, groundless interpretation.

Archaeology and genealogy discern in the creation of knowledge and truth the "biopolitics" and microtechnologies of the cultural practices of power. Foucault discarded the notion that power is best understood in terms of centralized state authority. Further, power/knowledge is at once productive and repressive; it constitutes the normative human subject by encoding the body, limiting and disciplining it and marginalizing alternative articulations. Modern "man" he argued, has represented itself as rational, sane, healthy, and normal and at the same time has constituted and sought to eradicate madness, illness, criminality, deviance, and perversion.

Foucault offered his "histories of the present" as fictions that reveal all discourse as fictional. And he called for resistance, offering his "specific intellectual" whose task is not to universalize but to challenge, question, and seek to alter the practices and production of "truth" in a given, local domain and to promote new forms of subjectivity. Foucault refused to prescribe or construct a new liberation narrative, for any new discourse, like all discursive structures, is at once creative and disciplining. In this, Foucault's thought and critical position are deeply ironic. Still, his dramatic announcement of the "death of Man" is a call to rethink human subjectivity, and in his last two volumes the human subject, earlier dispersed in language, is granted agency. Examining the ethical self-constitution of the self in the societies of ancient Greece and Rome, he announced an "aesthetics of existence," the endeavor to free oneself from oneself, to become (following Nietzsche) what one is, and to create one's life as a work of art. Often described as a troubling and elusive writer, for he defies easy categorization and his prose is sometimes difficult, Foucault, nevertheless, moves his reader to think differently about the self, subjectivity, and the world and to see the familiar in new ways.

BIBLIOGRAPHY

Dreyfus, Hubert, and Paul Rabinow. *Michel Foucault: Beyond Structuralism and Hermeneutics.* Chicago: University of Chicago Press, 1983.

Eribon, Didier. *Michel Foucault.* Tr. by Betsy Wing. Cambridge, Mass.: Harvard University Press, 1991.

Gutting, Gary, ed. *The Cambridge Companion to Foucault.* Cambridge: Cambridge University Press, 1994.

Macey, David. *The Lives of Michel Foucault: A Biography.* New York: Pantheon Books, 1993.

William E. Duvall

Fraga Iribarne, Manuel (1922–)

Spanish conservative politician. Manuel Fraga Iribarne is one of the most successful and influential conservative politicians in modern Spain. He played an important role in the successful transition to democracy following the death of Francisco Franco. Fraga helped draft the 1978 constitution and his support insured its acceptance by all but the most hard-line conservatives.

A lawyer, Fraga taught law at the University of Valencia from 1945 to 1948. Later, he abandoned teaching in favor of a political career. His first important position was as minister of information and tourism (1962–69). From 1973 to 1975 he was Spanish ambassador to the United Kingdom. Fraga was part of a new generation of Francoist politicians unaffiliated with the traditional sources of political power in the Franco dictatorship: the army, the Fascist party, the Falange, and the religious organization Opus Dei. While in office he was considered one of the most progressive ministers. His Law of the Press (1966) eased censorship regulations. However, Fraga's attempts at liberalization were viewed by Franco as going too far, and Franco eventually dismissed him. He was named vice president in the first government after Franco's death in 1975, although his term in that position lasted less than a year because the government was asked to resign.

In 1976 Fraga formed a political party called Popular Alliance. Originally founded as a hard-line rightist party, the group's poor showing in the 1977 elections forced it toward the political center. Fraga was named part of the subcommittee charged with drafting the 1978 constitution. His participation virtually guaranteed that the document would have widespread conservative support. By 1982 Fraga was leader of the opposition and his Popular Alliance Party was the second-largest in Spain.

Owing in part to his connections with the Franco regime, Fraga was never able to successfully challenge the Spanish Socialist Workers Party for control of the government. In 1987 he resigned as president of the Popular Alliance in favor of José María Aznar and the party officially changed names, becoming the Popular Party. In 1990 Fraga became head of the local government in the northwestern province of Galicia.

Fraga, a career politician although not necessarily in favor of a democratic regime, recognized it as inevitable. His conservative party played a key role in the passage of the 1978 constitution and helped establish a system of parliamentary opposition. After leaving national office he continued to wield significant power and influence among conservatives in Spain.

BIBLIOGRAPHY

Coverdale, J. F. *The Political Transformation of Spain after Franco.* New York: Praeger, 1979.

Fraga Iribarne, Manuel. *Memoria breve de una vida política.* Barcelona: Planeta, 1980.

Payne, Stanley G. *The Franco Regime, 1936–1975.* Madison: University of Wisconsin Press, 1987.

Preston, Paul. *The Triumph of Democracy in Spain.* New York: Methuen, 1986.

Brian D. Bunk

SEE ALSO Franco, Francisco

France

France, République Française, historically one of the most important European countries, is located on the western coast of Europe. It is bordered by Belgium, Luxembourg, Germany, Switzerland, Italy, Monaco, the Mediterranean Sea, Spain, Andorra, the Atlantic Ocean, and the English Channel (known to the French as La Manche). The Alps in the east and the Pyrenees in the southwest form natural frontiers. The island of Corsica in the Mediterranean is an integral part of France. France, including Corsica, has an area of 210,026 square miles (543,965 sq km), and in 1999 had nearly 59 million inhabitants. Its capital, Paris, had approximately 2.5 million inhabitants, but nearly ten million people live in the greater metropolitan area.

Remnants of France's former colonial empire, which crumbled in the 1950s and 1960s, have been organized into four overseas departments: Guadeloupe and Martinique in the West Indies, French Guiana on the northern coast of South America, and Réunion in the Indian Ocean. These departments have the same status as the European departments of France. Their inhabitants are

France. *Illustration courtesy of Bernard Cook.*

citizens and elect representatives to the French parliament. St. Pierre and Miquelon, a 93-square-mile (242-sq km) group of islands 15 miles (25 km) south of Newfoundland, Canada, became an overseas territory in 1946 and an overseas department in 1976, but it was transformed into an overseas collectivity (*collectivité*) in 1986. The inhabitants of the islands are French citizens and vote in French elections, but have their own assembly. Mayotte (Mahoré) in the Indian Ocean has the same status. The only remaining overseas territories are French Polynesia, which includes Tahiti; New Caledonia, which has a strong independence movement; the Wallis and Futuna islands in the Pacific Ocean; and Adélie Land in Antarctica.

France, one of the victorious powers in World War I (1914–18), suffered so many casualties that its postwar population was smaller than it had been in 1914. The heavy toll of the war placed a tremendous psychological burden on the country. Its birth rate remained flat from the end of World War I until World War II (1939–45). In addition to this psychological malaise, France was afflicted by economic difficulties and deep political divisions. It sought security from another German attack by building a network of defensive positions, the Maginot Line, but was unwilling to take preventive action when, in the late 1930s, the German dictator Adolf Hitler blatantly violated the provisions of the Versailles Treaty (1919) that had ended World War I.

When Germany attacked France in 1940, the Maginot Line was outflanked and France was overwhelmed in six weeks. A collaborationist regime, headed by Marshal Philippe Pétain, was established in the town of Vichy. On June 18, 1940, as Pétain prepared to sign an armistice with the Germans, General Charles de Gaulle issued a call from Great Britain for the French to continue to resist. De Gaulle formed the Free French Movement, but since Pétain had the support of a majority of the French, its initial impact was minimal. Eventually, the failure of Germany to subdue Britain and Hitler's ill fated decision to invade the Soviet Union (1941), coupled with the murderous behavior of the German occupiers, inspired the emergence of a Resistance movement. Nevertheless, the liberation of France came from abroad. It commenced with the Allied landing at Normandy on June 6, 1944. Though the invasion began the liberation of France, it intensified the feeling of de Gaulle that he was being ignored and shoved to the sidelines by the British and Americans. However, de Gaulle was able to assert himself and the Free French by directing the commander of the Free French Forces, once they had been transported to France, to advance on Paris and liberate the capital from the Germans.

On the night of August 24, 1944, General Jacques Philippe LeClerc's Second Armored Division tanks rumbled into Paris. The next day, amid the shots of German snipers, the leader of the Free French, General Charles de Gaulle, marched down the Avenue des Champs Élysée. De Gaulle needed no plebiscite to legitimize his authority; all factions accepted him as interim president.

The French Fourth Republic lasted for twelve years, from 1946 to 1958. Although it ended in the threat of civil war, much was accomplished during its existence. France carried out one of the first experiments in national economic planning through the democratic process, the economy registered solid gains, the birthrate rose, social reforms were implemented, and a possible Communist attempt to seize power was thwarted. The republic, however, also suffered a host of serious setbacks in foreign policy.

From August 1944 to October 1945, de Gaulle was dictator by consent. But the euphoric idealism and fraternity of the liberation did not last long. Political parties revived even before the end of the war, although there was no political Right because it had been discredited during the Vichy regime under the German occupation.

The Communists held the far Left. Although they had entered the struggle against the Germans only after the 1941 invasion of the Soviet Union, they claimed more dead in the Resistance than any others. The Communist Party also benefited from the new prestige of the Soviet Union, and in December 1944 de Gaulle signed a twenty-year treaty of alliance with the USSR. He also named two Communists to his provisional government and allowed party leader Maurice Thorez to return to France from Moscow. In the immediate postwar period the Communist strategy was to stress patriotism and to work within the democratic system.

The Socialist Party was the other leading party on the Left. It was led by Léon Blum, longtime party leader who spent much of the war in a German concentration camp. To the right of the Socialists was the Popular Republican Movement (MRP), the most important new political party, led by Resistance leader Georges Bidault. It championed social reform and a directed economy. If they had merged, the Socialists and MRP might have governed France and brought political stability, but the heritage of distrust between Catholics in the MRP and anticlerical Socialists ran too deep. This and de Gaulle's reluctance to form a party meant a fragmented center.

After its return to Paris the provisional government concentrated on liberating the rest of the country, and on the invasion of Germany. There was no protest of de Gaulle's decision to postpone elections until prisoners of war and forced workers could return home. Restoring the economy was a major problem. Food production was 40 percent of prewar levels and the transportation system was in a shambles. The minister for national economy, Pierre Mendès-France, tried to convince de Gaulle to issue new bank notes and freeze accounts. He claimed that these measures would halt inflation, end the black market, and provide data on profits from collaboration with the Germans. Accompanying this would be an austerity program. Finance Minister René Pleven and other advisers opposed the plan. When de Gaulle rejected it, Mendès-France resigned.

In October 1945, elections were held for a constituent assembly. Although the Communists were the largest party with nearly 27 percent, the Socialists and the MRP followed closely. Together the three parties gained three-quarters of the total vote. There was strong desire for a different constitutional system but no agreement on the type. Some wanted a British- or American-style political system with a strong executive. Others sought an all-powerful unicameral legislature. The problem was that de Gaulle sought the former and the Communists the latter. In January 1946, de Gaulle abruptly resigned. If he thought this unexpected action would force the parties to abdicate to him, this did not occur. Some of his followers called on him to lead a new political party, but de Gaulle refused and retired to write his war memoirs.

In May 1946, the new constitution was presented to the voters. With concerns about a lack of effective checks and balances, the constitution was rejected. In June 1946, elections were held for a second constitutional assembly. Its draft was only a slight modification of the first. De Gaulle denounced it as having too weak an executive, but in October it was approved by the barest of margins. Only about a third of eligible voters voted for it. Almost as many opposed it and another third stayed away.

The Fourth Republic turned out to be almost an exact copy of the Third. There was a two-house legislature, consisting of a National Assembly and a Council of the Republic. The lower house, the National Assembly, the members of which were elected to five-year terms, held most power. The president was chosen by the two houses together and the premier came from the assembly. Unfortunately, the Fourth Republic continued the instability that marked its predecessor. From September 26, 1944, to June 1, 1958, there were twenty-six premiers. Another characteristic of the Fourth Republic was a steady movement from the political Left to the Right. From the beginning the Left was badly splintered, especially between

Communists, who regularly got a quarter of the vote, and non-Communists.

Early in 1947 the Communists were expelled from the cabinet and a new "third force" coalition was formed. It included the Socialists, MRP, and Radicals. In 1951 the Socialists left the cabinet, and France was ruled by a coalition of MRP, Radicals, and the Independent-Peasant bloc. The Socialists returned to the coalition in 1956 but the balance of political power continued to be right of center until the end of the Fourth Republic.

In 1947 and again in 1948 the Communists threatened the government. Minister of the Interior Jules Moch stood firm and used the threat of armed force to keep order during Communist-sponsored general strikes, perhaps intended as the prelude to a coup d'état. Despite the political turmoil France began a significant economic recovery. This recovery owed much to state planning directed by Jean Monnet and $2.3 billion in U.S.-sponsored Marshall Plan aid.

In 1947 the Right began to reemerge politically. That spring de Gaulle, disgusted by the weakness of the republic, lent his name to a new political movement known as the Rally of the French People (RPF). In the 1951 elections the RPF barely edged the Communists to become the largest party in the National Assembly, but splits developed and de Gaulle withdrew his support. A small number of Gaullists continued in parliament but the party itself lost national significance after 1953. The threat from the Right did force the other parties to come together in coalition, but they were so badly divided as to be unable to bring about meaningful change. Its critics charged the government with *immobilisme,* or stagnation.

In June 1954, Radical Party leader Pierre Mendès-France became premier. He had been playing a Cassandra-like role in the assembly, warning his countrymen that pressing social, economic, and colonial problems had to be addressed. His immediate task was to end the war in Indochina. Mendès-France promised to end the war in sixty days or resign; he was successful on the last day of the deadline. This achieved, he took steps toward granting independence to Morocco and Tunisia, which would be accomplished in 1956. Mendès-France then turned to domestic problems. His plan for the economy was economic liberalism, but he immediately ran into entrenched special interests and was forced to resign in February 1955.

Another interesting episode of the mid-1950s was the Poujade movement. Pierre Poujade was a small shopkeeper who opposed the laissez-faire economic modernizing advocated by Mendès-France. Poujade's Association for the Defense of Shopkeepers and Artisans enjoyed rapid growth, especially in rural areas and among small shopkeepers. In the 1956 elections it won three million votes and fifty seats in the assembly. Poujade, however, proved an inept politician; although it did reveal the depth of sentiment against modernization, his organization soon fell apart.

Following the 1956 election the Socialists returned to the governing coalition and their leader Guy Mollet became premier. His tenure from February 1956 to May 1957 was the longest in the Fourth Republic. By this time, however, the assembly was so badly fractured that no cabinet could govern without a coalition of four parties. This meant even more *immobilisme.* When Mollet finally attempted meaningful reform, his cabinet was overthrown.

Government along these lines might have continued indefinitely in normal times, but the Fourth Republic faced serious problems overseas. From 1946 to 1954 France fought an increasingly costly war in Indochina. By the early 1950s this was consuming 40 percent of the defense budget and about 10 percent of the national budget. The war was also intensely unpopular at home and no government dared send out conscripts. For all intents and purposes it was fought by professional officers and noncoms. Finally the 1954 French military defeat at Dien Bien Phu allowed the politicians to shift the blame to the army and end the war.

Almost immediately after the French withdrew from Indochina, fighting broke out in Algeria in November 1954. French forces were transferred there to deal with the growing Muslim nationalist rebellion. Led by Muslim nationalists known as the National Liberation Front (FLN), the fighting ultimately destroyed the Fourth Republic.

There seemed good reason for France to hold onto Algeria. While there had been only forty thousand Europeans in Indochina, a million lived in Algeria. This also precluded a solution à la Morocco or Tunisia. Algeria, a part of France since 1830, was divided into three departments and considered an integral part of France. Many in France came to believe that the nation's future rested on its development. Socialist Guy Mollet spoke of Algeria as France's "California."

The European population that dominated Algeria's economic and political life would neither allow meaningful reform, which would have granted equal rights to Algeria's Muslim inhabitants, nor independence. Ultimately one million French troops served there in what became an imbroglio defying solution. The failure to adopt meaningful reform meant that the vast majority of the Muslims, once politicized, sided with the rebels.

In February 1956, Mollet, who had talked of compromise, visited Algiers and received a rude reception. He hastily backtracked and soon sent the bulk of the army, including conscripts, to Algeria. When the rebels resorted to terrorism, the French army responded with its own atrocities and torture. Revelations of this further divided Europeans in Algeria from metropolitan France. By 1958, two hundred to five hundred French soldiers were dying each month in a war that seemed without end.

The army's role in bringing down the Fourth Republic marked the first time it had intervened in politics since the era of Napoléon III. Since 1940 the French army had experienced only defeat. Its professionals were determined that they would not again be "betrayed" as they believed had happened in Indochina. Fervent anti-Communists, they also believed that they were fighting to save France from itself.

A host of plots was developed to overthrow the government. These were put into motion when MRP deputy Pierre Pflimlin became premier on May 13, 1958. Rumors reached Algiers that Pflimlin intended to appoint a foreign minister known to favor negotiations to end the war. Extremists in Algiers called for a massive demonstration. This event on May 13 turned into a riot, which the plotters used as a pretext to set up a Committee of Public Safety. For the next two weeks there were frantic negotiations between Paris and senior officers in Algiers. The plotters had the advantage that the bulk of the army was in Algeria and they had support from the political Right in France.

The flow of support away from Pflimlin became a flood when de Gaulle announced he would be willing to take power under certain conditions. While many Europeans in Algeria thought him too moderate, he soon emerged as the only possible choice. Aided by key generals in Algiers, de Gaulle's negotiators finally secured a peaceful transfer of authority, but civil war was only narrowly averted. Plans were already underway for Operation Resurrection, a paratroop operation against Paris.

President René Coty arranged a formula for the transfer of power. The National Assembly was induced on June 1, 1958, to name de Gaulle the last premier of the Fourth Republic. He was invested with dictatorial powers for six months, during which time he was to draw up a new constitution for the Fifth Republic. Many saw a parallel to Marshal Philippe Pétain in 1940 and feared a return of fascism. It was to de Gaulle's credit that he did not resort to authoritarianism. In fact he saved parliamentary democracy in France.

In contrast to 1945 de Gaulle showed some flexibility in his leadership. Long-standing Gaullist and constitutional lawyer Michel Debré was the key figure in drafting the new constitution. The ease with which cabinets could be overthrown was curtailed by requiring an absolute majority for votes of no confidence, and the trend toward legislative irresponsibility was reduced by giving the president the power to dissolve the National Assembly. The upper house, or Senate, was given increased powers. The most pronounced change, however, was the increase in presidential powers. The president, elected indirectly, served a seven-year term. He selected the premier and presided over the cabinet, and he possessed extraordinary emergency powers under controversial Article 16. In October 1958, almost 80 percent of those voting approved the constitution of the Fifth Republic. In the November legislative elections the Right triumphed. De Gaulle's party, the Union for the New Republic (UNR), was the largest in the assembly. In December de Gaulle was elected president.

The new constitution created a new arrangement between France and its former colonies. The French Community replaced the old French Union. If a colony voted against the constitution, it would immediately be independent, a course chosen only by French Guinea. De Gaulle soon announced a new program of economic development for Algeria. Unfortunately, the Constantine Plan came four years too late. In September 1959, de Gaulle, promising free elections after four years, called on the Algerian rebels to lay down their arms. In January 1960, resentment by Europeans in Algeria to de Gaulle's "compromises" led to new barricades in Algiers. Although army sentiment clearly favored the rebels, de Gaulle refused to budge and the rebellion collapsed. With this affair, however, the close relationship between de Gaulle and the Right ended. Subsequent negotiations with the FLN failed and the fighting continued.

In 1962 de Gaulle brought the Algerian War to an end by granting that country independence. Options had gradually been ruled out and in April 1961 de Gaulle crushed another attempted putsch led by disgruntled army officers in Algiers. The diehards formed the Secret Army Organization (OAS) and resorted to a campaign of terror and assassination, including attempts on the life of de Gaulle himself. These drove a further wedge between them and moderate elements in France.

The attempts on his life convinced de Gaulle and his advisers of a need to regularize the succession. In October 1962 French voters narrowly approved a constitutional referendum providing for direct election of the president, and in November de Gaulle's party, the UNR, won a smashing victory and an absolute majority in National Assembly.

In France the old political parties seemed paralyzed as de Gaulle governed as a benevolent despot. He insisted on unity. Where possible he remained above the fray, stepping in only when intervention was necessary. While de Gaulle pushed economic modernization, he also looked back to an age when France was a great power. Resenting what he regarded as the domination of the Atlantic alliance by the Anglo-Saxon powers, de Gaulle developed a close relationship with Chancellor Konrad Adenauer of the Federal Republic of Germany. To further emphasize its independence, France, in 1960, exploded an atomic bomb in the Algerian desert.

The most fractious issue of the de Gaulle presidency was the *force de frappe*, or nuclear strike force. Most of the opposition to it was not on philosophical grounds but rather due to its high cost, which bled money from domestic programs. In part the *force de frappe* was based on de Gaulle's concept of France as leader of a "second" Western force cooperating with but not subservient to the Anglo-Americans. He also did not believe the United States would risk nuclear war on its own soil to defend Europe.

De Gaulle reached out to Eastern Europe and the Soviet Union. He lectured Washington on its Vietnam policy, extended full diplomatic recognition to Communist China, and sought to expand ties with Latin America and French-speaking Canada. Twice, in 1963 and 1967, he vetoed British entry in the Common Market. In 1967 de Gaulle ended the long-standing close French relationship with Israel after that country rejected his advice.

By the mid 1960s de Gaulle's power had begun to erode. In 1965 he ran for a second presidential term but was opposed by a number of candidates, especially Socialist Party leader François Mitterrand. In a field of six candidates, Mitterrand won 32 percent of the vote against 42 percent for de Gaulle. De Gaulle won the runoff, but only by 9 percent.

De Gaulle was further shaken by the so-called Events of May in 1968. These began with student agitation at Nanterre, a suburban branch of the University of Paris, and the protest soon spread to the Sorbonne. Students fought battles with the police in downtown Paris and were joined by workers. On May 14, de Gaulle left for Romania on a prearranged visit but was forced to cut short his trip. By the end of May it appeared that the opposition might soon come to power.

On the advice of Premier Georges Pompidou and after having assured himself of army support, de Gaulle dissolved the assembly and called for new elections. The voters, alarmed by the continuing violence, gave de Gaulle his greatest assembly majority ever. However, de Gaulle soon made a major miscalculation. He announced that a hotly contested April 1969 referendum over regional autonomy would be a test of his leadership as well. If it were rejected, he would resign. The opposition coalesced. When the referendum was defeated, de Gaulle kept his word.

The proof of de Gaulle's work was that the Fifth Republic survived him. In June 1969 Georges Pompidou, whom de Gaulle had rewarded for handling the May 1968 crisis by dismissing him as premier, was elected president. He served as president from 1969 to 1974 and proved Gaullism could survive without de Gaulle.

Pompidou concentrated more on domestic matters such as economic advances and social and educational reform. He was also less dogmatic and more flexible than de Gaulle. He let Great Britain into the Common Market and improved French relations with the United States. In April 1974 Pompidou died in office, of cancer.

Pompidou was followed by his minister of finance, Valéry Giscard d'Estaing, leader of the Independent Republicans. Although Mitterrand led all candidates on the first presidential ballot with 43 percent of the vote, Giscard beat him in the runoff, 51 percent to 49.

Rightist moderates won a majority in the assembly and D'Estaing and Mitterrand worked closely together. Both men were staunch Europeanists and their policies seemed close. Mitterrand, although attempting to maintain an electoral alliance with the Communist Party, favored the *force de frappe* and the Atlantic Alliance, and Giscard announced his support for social reform.

In 1981 Giscard fell prey to a scandal relating to gifts to the president from Jean-Bídel Bokassa, the dictator and self-proclaimed emperor of the Central African Republic. Mitterrand at last secured the presidency, defeating Giscard by a scant 3.5 percent. Mitterrand marginalized the Communist Party within his cabinet and proved a reliable and consistent friend of the United States and NATO. He supported the entry of Portugal and Spain into the EC. The 1986 assembly elections, in which the Socialists took a beating because of the poor performance of the economy, placed Mitterrand in a situation never previously encountered in the Fifth Republic: a president faced an assembly controlled by his opponents. This "cohabitation" saw Mitterrand appoint a conservative, Jacques Chirac, as premier.

In early May 1988, however, Mitterrand, taking advantage of a divided Right, easily defeating Chirac and won a second term as president. This encouraged Mitterrand to seek early parliamentary elections in the hope that momentum from the presidential victory would enable him to break the power-sharing arrangement with the Right in place since 1986. It was not to be. The Socialists were the largest party but nonetheless fell 13 seats shy of the 289 required for a majority in the National Assembly. While Mitterrand could dissolve the assembly and call new elections, the constitution specifies that at least one year must elapse after the last elections.

There were a number of signs of political malaise, the foremost of which was the right-wing racism of former paratrooper Jean-Marie Le Pen. With the cost of social services high, Le Pen's National Front Party tapped a well of support in opposition to the liberal French immigration policies. French farmers also protested EC agreements with the United States that cut agricultural subsidies. The September 1992 referendum on the Maastricht treaty became a focal point for discontent and was approved by only 51.05 percent.

The tottering economy and government scandals had their effect in the March 1993 elections when a strong conservative vote returned the Right to power. The Union for France coalition and other conservatives won more than 84 percent of the vote, while the Socialists fell to less than 12 percent. Gaullist Édouard Balladur became premier and seemed the likely candidate to succeed Mitterrand in the 1995 presidential elections. But with the economy stagnant and inflation rising, there was a general feeling of discontent and politicians in power suffered from this. When the election finally came, the Socialists' leading prospect, Jacques Delors, declined to run. Balladur and Chirac to the delight of the Socialist candidate, Lionel Jospin, divided the conservative vote after an acrimonious campaign. Ultra-rightist Le Pen captured 15 percent, but Chirac won second place with 20.8 percent. In the runoff, however, Chirac easily emerged victorious over Jospin.

BIBLIOGRAPHY

Ardagh, John. *France Today.* New York: Viking Penguin, 1987.

De Gaulle, Charles. *Memoirs of Hope: Renewal and Endeavor.* Tr. by Terence Kilmartin. New York: Simon and Schuster, 1991.

Ehrmann, Henry, and Martin A. Schain. *Politics in France,* 5th ed. New York: HarperCollins, 1992.

Larkin, Maurice. *France since the Popular Front: Government and People, 1936–1986.* Oxford: Oxford University Press, 1988.

Werth, Alexander. *France, 1940–1955.* New York: Holt, 1956.

Spencer C. Tucker

France and Indochina

The first phase of a twenty-nine-year struggle for Vietnamese independence and unity. While there were other explosions of nationalist sentiment in the French Empire after World War II, most notably in Algeria in 1945 and Madagascar in 1947, the most damaging by far to France was in Indochina, where France fought from 1946 to 1954.

World War II signaled the end of European colonialism. French leaders chose not to see the inevitable, however, and failed to seek accommodation with nationalist leaders. In Indochina the result was missed opportunity for orderly transition to self-rule and a close relationship with France. World War II itself was a principal reason why Paris refused to compromise. It is hard for the weak to be generous, and only with its empire intact did France believe it would continue as a great power.

From 1862 to 1887 France established control over Indochina: first Cochin China, then Cambodia, Annam, and Tonkin. In 1887 Paris formed them into French Indochina. Laos was added in 1893. Only Cochin China was an outright colony; technically the others were protectorates. The reality was that all were ruled by a French governor-general responsible to the minister of colonies in Paris.

French administration in Indochina was haphazard. Ministers of colonies and governors-general changed frequently. Also, Indochina did not attract the best administrators, and many of those sent there never bothered to learn the local language. Administrative salaries ate up what little money was available in the colonial budget and life in the countryside changed but little. The small French community of forty thousand to fifty thousand dominated the economy of what was France's richest colony.

Following World War I moderate nationalists who took their cue from China's Kuomintang, the nationalist political movement founded by Sun Yat-Sen and headed after 1925 by Chiang K'ai-shek, had sought reform in association with France. Paris rejected this and in 1930–31 there were uprisings in northern Vietnam that the French easily crushed. In the process, however, France opened the way for the more radical Communists, and by World War II they were the dominant nationalist force in Indochina.

World War II brought the Japanese in 1940. France, having been crushed militarily by Germany, was in no position to resist Tokyo's demands for bases. The Japanese left the Vichy French colonial government in place. As the war neared its end the French were determined to liberate themselves, but the Japanese struck first, and, on March 9, 1945, arrested virtually all French administrators and military personnel. At the end of the war Japan created a further problem for France by declaring the region independent.

Vietnamese nationalist and Communist leader Ho Chi Minh moved into this vacuum. On August 16, 1945, in Hanoi, Ho declared himself president of a "free Vietnam," and on September 2, he proclaimed the independence of the Democratic Republic of Vietnam (DRV). Even before the end of the war the French government had planned to make concessions and grant more freedom to Indochina, but only if Paris retained ultimate authority.

In January 1946, Ho carried out elections in north Vietnam. Although they were neither free nor democratic, there was no doubt that Ho had won. There remained the problem of dealing with France, and in March 1946, Ho worked out an agreement with French diplomat Jean Sainteny. According to its terms Paris recognized the DRV as a free and independent state within the French Union. France would be allowed to send a limited number of troops to the north to protect its interests there, although all were to be withdrawn over a five-year period. Paris also accepted the principle of a united Vietnam by agreeing to a plebiscite in the south on the question of joining the north.

Meanwhile, following the release of French troops from Japanese camps and the arrival of reinforcements from France, French control was reasserted in the south of Vietnam, Cambodia, and Laos. French High Commissioner for Indo-China Thierry d'Argenlieu, with his position strengthened, refused to allow the promised southern plebiscite. In a direct appeal to Paris Ho led a delegation to France. By the time it arrived the French government had fallen and it was weeks before a new one was formed. Unfortunately, the Socialists lost seats in the June 1946 elections and the Communists, who were in the government, were trying to demonstrate their patriotism. As a result, at the Fontainebleau Conference the French made no concessions to the Vietnamese nationalists. D'Argenlieu had on his own initiative, meanwhile, proclaimed the independence of the south as the "Republic of Cochin China."

D'Argenlieu's action clearly violated the Ho-Sainteny agreement and left Vietnamese leaders feeling betrayed. Although there is still disagreement on this point, Ho Chi Minh, who led the nationalist Vietminh coalition, was probably more nationalist than Communist, and, given Vietnam's long antagonistic relationship with China, he might have become an Asian Tito. In September Ho left Paris and forecast the outbreak of fighting. He also correctly predicted how the war would be fought and how it would end.

The war began following the November 23, 1946, shelling, ordered by d'Argenlieu, of the port of Haiphong by the French cruiser *Suffren*. The fighting lasted for eight years. The Vietminh rebels were quickly forced out of the cities and into the countryside. There was some talk in Paris of ending the war through peace talks, but the steady drift of the coalition French government to the right and increasing bloodshed prevented this.

The Vietminh, led by General Vo Nguyen Giap, steadily grew in strength and controlled more and more territory. In March 1949, Paris concluded the Élysée Agreements with former Emperor Bao Dai. Paris conceded that Vietnam was one country, and the agreement recognized the state of Vietnam. The new political entity allowed the French government to portray the war as a conflict between a free Vietnam and the Communists. Washington, which needed French military support in Europe, claimed to be convinced.

The Indochina War changed dramatically in the fall of 1949 when the Communists came to power in China. The United States, which had backed the losing side there, now reaped the whirlwind. The Chinese Communists sent military supplies to the Vietminh by land across their common border. The Korean War, which began in June 1950, also affected the U.S. attitude toward the war in Indochina. Korea and Vietnam were seen as mutually dependent theaters in a common struggle against communism. The United States recognized Vietnam and increased its military aid to the French forces in Indochina.

The Vietminh secured the backing of virtually all Vietnamese nationalists. As Paris refused to concede real authority to the state of Vietnam, they had no other recourse. The war itself seemed an endless quagmire. By 1950 it was costing France between 40 and 45 percent of its entire military budget, which accounted for more than 10 percent of the national budget.

In 1950 Giap won control of Colonial Highway 4, the rue sans joie, in the far north. Since the Vietminh thus secured access to China, the French perhaps lost the war at that point. However, in 1951 Giap went over to conventional warfare and Vietminh units were stopped cold by French forces led by General Jean de Lattre de Tassigny, probably the most capable of French commanders in the war.

The culminating act of the Indochina War was the Battle of Dien Bien Phu. The new French commander, General Henri Navarre, set up a blocking position in a valley astride the principal Vietminh route into Laos. He also hoped to draw enemy forces into a set-piece conventional battle where Navarre believed they could be destroyed by French artillery and air power. The siege of Dien Bien Phu lasted from March to May 1954 and was decided by the Vietminh's ability to transport artillery to the heights by hand, and by the inadequacy of French air support. On May 7, the French garrison surrendered, allowing Paris to shift the blame to the generals and bring the war to an end. Some 1,500 French troops were killed in the battle, and of the 10,000 captured, half were wounded. Vietminh losses were 8,000 killed and 15,000 wounded.

Attention now turned to a conference previously scheduled in Geneva to deal with a variety of Asian problems. The new French premier, Pierre Mendès-France, imposed a sixty-day timetable for an agreement, threatening to resign if one was not reached; the Geneva Accords were signed on the last day of the deadline. The Vietnamese were in fact pressured by their supporters, China and the Soviet Union, into an agreement that gave them less than they had won on the battlefield. Cambodia and Laos were declared independent, but the key provision was recognition of the unity of Vietnam. Pending unification there was to be an armistice and a temporary dividing line at the seventeenth parallel. The agreements also provided for the compulsory regroupment of troops and the free movement of civilians. Free nationwide elections were to be held in two years, but ultimately a new government in South Vietnam headed by Ngo Dinh Diem refused to permit the elections and the United States supported Diem in his stand. Ultimately this led in the late 1950s to a renewal of the war in an American phase.

This "First Indochina War" probably claimed half a million Vietminh casualties and 172,000 French Union casualties. The French forces suffered 92,000 dead, 20,000 of whom, almost all of them officers and noncommissioned officers, were from metropolitan France. Perhaps 250,000 civilians lost their lives. For France the struggle had been a distant one. Paris had not dared send draftees to Indochina, and the conflict had been fought largely by the professionals. Paris almost immediately transferred these men to Algeria, where another insurrection had broken out. Many of these professional soldiers felt they and their Vietnamese allies had been betrayed and were determined that the politicians would not repeat this in Algeria.

BIBLIOGRAPHY

Duiker, William J. *The Communist Road to Power in Vietnam.* Boulder, Colo.: Westview Press, 1981.

————. *The Rise of Nationalism in Vietnam, 1900–1941.* Ithaca, N.Y.: Cornell University Press, 1976.

Dunn, Peter M. *The First Vietnam War.* New York: St. Martin's Press, 1985.

Fall, Bernard B. *Hell in a Very Small Place: The Siege of Dienbienphu.* Philadelphia: J.B. Lippincott, 1966.

————. *The Two Vietnams.* New York: Praeger, 1964.

Hammer, Ellen J. *The Struggle for Indochina.* Stanford, Calif.: Stanford University Press, 1954.

Kelly, George A. *Lost Soldiers: The French Army and Empire in Crisis, 1947–1962.* Cambridge, Mass.: M.I.T. Press, 1965.

Lacouture, Jean. *Ho Chi Minh: A Political Biography.* New York: Random House, 1968.

Sainteny, Jean. *Ho Chi Minh and His Vietnam: A Personal Memoir.* Chicago: Cowles, 1972.

Spencer C. Tucker

Pieds Noirs

European settlers in French Algeria, one-tenth of its total population. The *pied noir* minority controlled the colonial economy, society, and local government. When a war for independence broke out in 1954, the *pieds noirs* overwhelmingly supported military efforts to help repress it. When these failed, most *pieds noirs* emigrated to France in 1962.

French settlers in Algeria usually came as refugees, political prisoners in 1848, Alsatians after 1871, and wine growers ruined by phylloxera in the 1880s. Large numbers of Spaniards, Italians, and Maltese, mostly poor, joined them, and by 1917 only 20 percent of the European population was of French origin. By 1945 it numbered nearly one million, compared with nine million Muslims. The name "*pied noir*" was derived from the black shoes of French soldiers or, perhaps, the settlers' skin, tanned "black" by the African sun.

The French government granted settlers former Turkish state properties or Arab farms expropriated for noncultivation or rebellion. Settlers also took advantage of the Arabs' unfamiliarity with French law to acquire additional arable land cheaply. Occasional legislative efforts to protect native landholders were easily circumvented, and most Arabs eventually became rural wage laborers for Europeans. The best land and major businesses—wine, shipping, banking, and publishing—were controlled by a handful of wealthy families, and many *pieds noirs* were working class but most lived far more comfortably than their Muslim neighbors. The best-known *pied noir* author, Albert Camus, chronicled their leisurely Mediterranean lifestyle in his novels, stories in which the Arab majority is usually conspicuous by its absence.

By 1950 the European minority controlled 90 percent of the colony's wealth. *Pieds noirs* clustered in the coastal plain and port cities of Algiers, Oran, and Constantine, whose European neighborhoods resembled French metropolitan ones. Eighty percent of the Muslim population lived in the desolate interior districts, but rapid population growth and rural poverty drove many Arabs to the coast in search of work, and the major cities had crowded Muslim quarters and shantytowns. All *pied noir* children attended primary schools, and one-third completed secondary education, but only 15 percent of Muslims were educated. Muslim doctors, lawyers, pharmacists, teachers, and engineers were rare, while 95 percent of manual laborers were Arabs.

Though no legal system of segregation kept Arabs and Europeans apart, there was little assimilation, with fewer than one hundred mixed marriages recorded a year. Race, religion, and language combined to divide the two peoples that lived in close proximity. *Pieds noirs* practiced a casual racism, addressing Muslims familiarly or with epithets, while insisting on deference in return. Rapid Arab population growth and unemployment, while *pied noir* numbers remained stable, contributed to a stereotype of Arabs as lazy and idle but sexually active and threatening.

Administratively Algeria was run by an appointed governor-general and three departmental prefects, but Algerians could choose political representatives for the National and Algerian assemblies in two separate electoral colleges, one European and one Muslim. Since the two colleges chose equal numbers of delegates, Europeans were overrepresented, and they, in addition, were usually able to control the outcome of Muslim voting. Given French multiparty politics, the Algerian legislative bloc in the National Assembly, sixteen senators and thirty deputies, was usually able to obstruct any legislation that threatened *pied noir* dominance.

The outbreak of the Algerian War for independence in 1954 united virtually all *pieds noirs* behind French military efforts to defeat it. *Pied noir* propaganda and agitation often shaped government policy. In February 1956 Socialist Prime Minister Guy Mollet, suspected of favoring a negotiated peace, was mobbed in Algiers and thereafter adopted a more hard-line policy. Similar suspicions fueled the *pied noir* general strike and military uprising that initiated Charles de Gaulle's return to power in May 1958. When he in turn appeared ready to abandon French Algeria, the "Day of the Barricades" in January 1960 and *pied noir* support for the "generals' putsch" in April 1961 underlined their opposition to any negotiated settlement.

De Gaulle adopted a policy of self-determination for Algeria in 1961, a position most mainland French also supported. After the Evian agreements were signed with the National Liberation Front, the revolutionary organization that had led the struggle for Algerian independence against France, in February/March 1962, *pied noir* extremists joined the terrorist campaign of the Secret Army Organization (OAS), but most prepared to emigrate. In the course of the summer nearly one million *pieds noirs* hastily abandoned North Africa for France. Many lost everything, and subsequent government assistance was meager, but most were gradually absorbed into the expanding French economy of the 1960s.

BIBLIOGRAPHY

Horne, Alistair. *A Savage War of Peace: Algeria 1954– 1962.* New York: Viking, 1977.
Nora, Pierre. *Les Français d'Algérie.* Paris: Julliard, 1961.
Tillion, Germaine. *Les Ennemis complémentaires.* Paris: Éditions de Minuit, 1960.

David Longfellow

SEE ALSO Algerian War; De Gaulle, Charles

Secret Army Organization (OAS)

Underground terrorist organization opposed to Algerian independence from France. In 1961–62 the Secret Army Organization (Organisation de l'Armée Secrète, OAS), composed of disaffected army officers and Algerian *pieds noirs* (European settlers), determined to prevent the government of Charles de Gaulle from negotiating an end to the Algerian War with the National Liberation Front (Front de Libération Nationale FLN). It conducted a terrorist campaign in Algeria and metropolitan France but collapsed when an independent Algeria was established in the summer of 1962.

The OAS was organized in February 1961 in Madrid. Some military officers, convinced that the Fifth Republic intended to "betray" the army by granting Algerian independence, allied themselves with existing *pied noir* terrorist organizations that had been active in the struggle against the FLN. Its titular head was General Raoul Salan, a former commander of the French forces in Algeria. General Edmond Jouhaud; Colonels Antoine Argoud, Jean Gardes, and Yves Godard; and *pied noir* activists Pierre Lagaillarde, Jean-Claude Perez, and Jean-Jacques Susini were among the organization's most influential leaders and tacticians. The OAS had its base of support in the European Community in the cities of Algiers, Oran, and Constantine, but it also raised funds from bank robberies and recruits from veterans' groups, French right-wing parties, and Catholic organizations.

Modeling itself on the nationalist guerrillas the French army had fought in Indochina and Algeria, the OAS created specialized units for propaganda, intelligence, fundraising, bombings, and assassination. Its leaders hoped that a campaign of terror against Arab civilians and French and Muslim moderates who favored negotiations would provoke FLN reprisals. In response, the French army would force a French government already weakened by selective OAS assassinations to maintain French control of Algeria. As de Gaulle moved toward a diplomatic settlement of the war, the terrorism campaign became increasingly indiscriminate. OAS "commandos" and bombs killed bureaucrats, journalists, police and security officers, doctors, lawyers, members of leftist political parties, and several thousand Arab civilians. Repeated efforts to assassinate de Gaulle and his ministers failed, some narrowly.

The government responded with repressive measures, many of dubious legality. Informants led to the arrest of Generals Salan and Jouhaud in the spring of 1962. As its officers and enlisted men became OAS targets, the army largely turned against the terrorists. Massive *pied noir* emigration from Algeria after pro-independence referenda there and in France deprived the organization of its base of popular support in the summer of 1962, and its last act was a scorched earth campaign of arson and bombing before the new Algerian government took power. Though several low-ranking members of the OAS were tried and executed for treason, most of those apprehended, including the generals, were imprisoned. All those still in jail or exile were granted amnesty by de Gaulle during the disturbances of May 1968 to assure the president the support of the army for armed action if necessary.

BIBLIOGRAPHY

Henissart, Paul. *Wolves in the City: The Death of French Algeria.* New York: Simon and Schuster, 1970.
Horne, Alistair. *A Savage War of Peace: Algeria 1954– 1962.* New York: Viking, 1977.
Kelly, George. *Lost Soldiers: The French Army and Empire in Crisis, 1947–1962.* Cambridge, Mass.: M.I.T. Press, 1965.

David Longfellow

SEE ALSO Algerian War; De Gaulle, Charles; Salan, Raoul

Force de Frappe

French term for France's independent nuclear strike force. On February 13, 1960, France joined the atomic club when it exploded its first atomic bomb in the Sahara desert. This successful test paved the way for the development of delivery systems.

President Charles de Gaulle justified the *force de frappe* because the United States and Great Britain had a nuclear monopoly within the Western alliance and refused to share atomic secrets with France. In the early 1990s, however, it was revealed that the U.S. government did indirectly provide hints to French scientists that enabled them to realize substantial savings in money and time in the development of nuclear weapons. De Gaulle rejected U.S. President Dwight D. Eisenhower's appeal for an integrated NATO military command and Secretary of State John Foster Dulles's efforts to persuade France to forgo the development of nuclear weapons. The United States, on the other hand, rebuffed de Gaulle's calls for a NATO tridirectorate to oversee defense policies. De Gaulle believed that such an arrangement was impossible without France's having nuclear weapons.

Owing to mistrust extending back to World War II, de Gaulle believed that France could not count on the two Anglo-Saxon powers. He and many other French citizens saw Britain as unreliable and not committed to Europe. The French also believed the United States would not risk Soviet nuclear attack on its own soil to employ nuclear weapons in the defense of Western Europe. De Gaulle's resolve on this point was strengthened during the Cuban Missile Crisis, when the two superpowers went to the brink of war and the United States imposed a naval blockade without consulting France. De Gaulle's guiding axiom was "The defense of France must be French."

In addition de Gaulle was moved by French nationalism. As he put it in an April 1962 news conference: "It is the duty and the right of . . . European powers to have their own nuclear defense. It is intolerable to a great nation that its destiny be left to the decisions . . . of another nation, however friendly." De Gaulle's vision, however, ran beyond narrow nationalism. He saw French possession of nuclear weapons not merely as a defensive measure but as a positive contribution to the establishment of a new balance of forces in the world. France would be the leader of a "second" Western force. Working in partnership with Konrad Adenauer's Federal Republic of Germany, de Gaulle sought a new Europe that would embrace Eastern Europe and be a third force between the two superpowers—a Europe in partnership with, but not a pawn of, the United States. A French nuclear weapons capability would enhance the power of his proposed second force.

In his *Memoirs of Hope: Renewal and Endeavor,* written after his final retirement, de Gaulle listed the development of a nuclear deterrent as one of his principal policy goals when he returned to power in May 1958. On November 3, 1959, in a speech at the École Militaire in Paris, he publicly announced that France would have its own nuclear strike force, the *force de frappe.*

On July 25, 1960, after two successful French atomic bomb tests, Premier Michel Debré presented to the National Assembly a four-year $2.3 billion plan for an independent atomic and hydrogen bomb strike force. Debré said the choice for France was between becoming a nuclear power or a "satellite." On November 22, after a censure motion failed, a bill providing $1.2 billion through 1964 for development of the nuclear strike force passed the National Assembly on its second reading. The bill, rejected by the Senate on November 10 in a 188-to-83 vote, was returned there on November 22. The Senate could not block a measure after its third passage in the assembly. On November 30 the Senate rejected the measure for a second time. When it came before the National Assembly on a third reading and a censure motion opposing it failed with only 215 of 277 required votes, the bill became law on December 6.

The *force de frappe* was one of the most fractious issues in French domestic politics during the de Gaulle presidency. This was not so much the result of differences in philosophy. Public opinion polls showed that a majority of the French supported an independent nuclear strike force; even the French Communist Party announced that it favored an independent nuclear deterrent. The issue was rather the high cost to be borne by taxpayers. Military expenses were approximately a quarter of the total French budget and nuclear armaments claimed a quarter of that. De Gaulle's opponents also used the issue as a rallying point to attack him personally.

Beginning in 1962 French armed forces were radically reshaped into three types of units. The first, an interior defense force, was intended solely for the defense of France; the second was an intervention force for emergency deployment beyond French borders; the third was the *force nucléaire stratégique,* a strategic nuclear force of fifty Mirage IV bombers. The first French nuclear bomber units became operational in 1964, and delivery systems came to embrace a triad of submarine-launched and ground-to-ground ballistic missiles in underground silos. On March 7, 1966, de Gaulle informed President Lyndon Johnson that he was withdrawing French forces from NATO's integrated Command Structure. The development of the *force de frappe* was speeded up, and in August 1968 France achieved its first thermonuclear explosions in a series of South Pacific tests.

The *force de frappe* survived de Gaulle's presidency and is now supported by virtually the entire French political spectrum.

BIBLIOGRAPHY

De Gaulle, Charles. "Tenth Press Conference." New York: French Press and Information Service, July 23, 1964.

Diamond, Robert A. *France under de Gaulle.* New York: Facts on File, 1970.

Hoffmann, Stanley. *Decline or Renewal? France Since the 1930s.* New York: Viking, 1974.

Kulski, W. W. *De Gaulle and the World: The Foreign Policy of the Fifth French Republic.* Syracuse, N.Y.: Syracuse University Press, 1966.

Spencer C. Tucker

SEE ALSO Debré, Michel; De Gaulle, Charles; Mitterrand, François

May 1968

Massive student protests followed by huge workers' strikes that nearly brought down President Charles de Gaulle's government. When authorities at the Sorbonne called on the police to end a militant demonstration, the situation quickly escalated into violent confrontations between students and the police. Labor unions supported the students, and eventually nine million workers went on strike. By early June, however, public condemnation of the disorder was clear, and the unions' acceptance of wage agreements marked the end of the crisis.

The May rebellion began as part of an international youth movement. Students in France had long tended to sympathize with leftist politics, and American policies in Vietnam promoted a sense of righteous indignation. The large baby-boom generation, having experienced a revolution of rising expectations, was frustrated by overcrowded universities and decreasing prospects for future employment. Leaders of the New Left movement were generally distrustful of orthodox Marxist-Leninist ideology, and they articulated a variety of socialist, anarchist, and Third World perspectives. Despite their differences, militants such as Daniel Cohn-Bendit agreed that students should exercise more direct control over the universities.

Early in 1968 a number of incidents occurred at the suburban Nanterre campus of the University of Paris. On March 21 a group of Nanterre students were arrested for smashing the windows of an American Express building to protest the Vietnam War. The next day Cohn-Bendit mobilized about two hundred students to occupy the administration building. With the motto "provocation, re-

pression, solidarity," leftists called on students to boycott their final exams. Serious disturbances really began on May 2, when student protesters occupied a lecture hall. In response, Nanterre administrators suspended classes and initiated disciplinary actions against Cohn-Bendit and other leaders. On May 3 several hundred students assembled at the university's Sorbonne campus to contest the disciplinary proceedings. When police tried to remove the demonstrators, more than 1,000 students were soon engaged in street fights. After 573 students were arrested, university officials closed the Sorbonne in an effort to prevent further violence. The National Union of French Students, backed by the National Union of University Teachers, called for a general strike of all students and university teachers throughout France. During the "night of the barricades" on May 6, an estimated 10,000 students repelled police charges reinforced with armored trucks and water cannons. By midnight more than 700 students were injured and 437 were arrested.

On May 10 some 30,000 students demanded that the police withdraw from the Sorbonne, and confrontations of that night resulted in 367 injuries and 468 arrests. The police were forced to withdraw, and militant students occupied most of the Latin Quarter. The students then used the lecture halls to debate educational reform, and they decorated the buildings with red flags and left-wing graffiti. Throughout France sympathetic students in provincial universities showed their solidarity by staging sit-ins and holding demonstrations.

On May 13 several unions, including the Federation of National Education, supported the students with a twenty-four-hour general strike. Concurrently, labor unions in Paris staged a four-hour march with a crowd of about 400,000 workers. The next day sit-in strikes began in an aircraft factory in Nantes, and within a week an estimated nine million workers, one-third of the labor force, were occupying factories and other places of work. Most trains stopped operations, and there were few mail deliveries. On May 20 the Communist Party called for a new popular front government, and two days later the Gaullist government of Premier Georges Pompidou narrowly survived a parliamentary vote of censure. Pompidou promised both educational reforms and wage concessions for workers. The worst rioting erupted in Paris on May 24–25, when more than 1,000 were injured and one man, Philippe Matherion, was stabbed to death. On May 28 leftist leader François Mitterrand proposed the formation of a transitional government.

With these anarchical conditions, informed observers expected that de Gaulle's regime could not survive. On May 29 de Gaulle disappeared, secretly going to West

Germany to ascertain the loyalty of army units stationed there. On May 30 de Gaulle gave an emotional radio speech in which he announced that parliamentary elections would be held in June. Many workers were already returning to their jobs, and the great differences between the workers and New Left students were becoming increasingly apparent, especially the incompatibility between the wage demands of workers and the students' attacks on modern civilization. By June 6 train and mail services were resumed, and most of the labor unions had agreed to settlements based on large wage increases. Although the street battles of June 10–11 resulted in the drowning of one student in the Seine, the police finally regained control of the Sorbonne on June 16.

The immediate impact of the May-June incidents was to fortify the status quo. In the election held on June 23, de Gaulle and his Gaullist party benefited from the backlash of a frightened and angry public. For the first time in French history a single party received an absolute majority of seats in the National Assembly. The crisis, nevertheless, damaged de Gaulle's image, contributing to the rejection of his constitutional proposal the following year. Likewise, Mitterrand's behavior during the crisis temporarily ended his chances for the presidency. In contrast, Pompidou emerged as a strong and respected leader. The student revolts did promote decentralization and other reforms of the university system, as recommended by Edgar Faure's report. At the same time, the crisis highlighted the limited appeal of the quasi-anarchist ideas of the New Left, and it demonstrated that French workers were primarily interested in better salaries and working conditions.

BIBLIOGRAPHY

Aron, Raymond. *The Elusive Revolution: Anatomy of a Student Revolt.* Tr. by Gordon Clough. New York: Praeger, 1969.

Cohn-Bendit, Daniel, and Gabriel Cohn-Bendit. *Obsolete Communism: The Left-Wing Alternative.* Tr. by Arnold Pomerans. New York: McGraw-Hill, 1968.

Johnson, Richard. *The French Communist Party Versus the Students: Revolutionary Politics in May–June 1968.* New Haven, Conn.: Yale University Press, 1972.

Reader, Keith, and Khursheed Wadia. *The May 1968 Events in France.* New York: St. Martin's Press, 1993.

Rohan, Marc. *Paris 68: Graffiti, Posters, Newspapers and Poems of the Events of May 1968.* London: Impact, 1968.

Touraine, Alain. *The May Movement.* Tr. by Leonard Mahlew. New York: Random House, 1971.

Wylie, Laurence, et al. *France: The Events of May–June 1968; A Critical Bibliography.* Pittsburgh: Council for European Studies, 1973.

Thomas T. Lewis

SEE ALSO Cohn-Bendit, Marc Daniel; De Gaulle, Charles

Election of 1997

Decisive victory of the French Left in legislative elections of May 25 and June 1, 1997. An alliance of leftist parties—Socialists, Communists, and Greens—gained a solid majority in the National Assembly, overturning the massive majority that the center-right had held since 1993. The outcome meant that conservative President Jacques Chirac was forced to accept several years of "cohabitation" with a leftist assembly.

With the center-right's legislative victory of 1993, combined with the election of Chirac in 1995, it appeared that the French Left had been almost totally repudiated. On April 21, 1997, Chirac announced early elections to the National Assembly, about a year ahead of schedule. He wanted to avoid an election in 1998, the target date for the European Union's (EU) decision about which countries might participate in the single currency. His goal was to secure a mandate for the government to impose the unpopular spending cuts required for participation. The ruling coalition, consisting of the Gaullist Rally for the Republic and the right-of-center Union for French Democracy, controlled 465 seats of the 577-member assembly, but its popularity had declined because of serious economic problems exacerbated by the pain from reductions in social programs. The unemployment rate was nearly 13 percent, producing massive protests and work stoppages. Polls indicated that the ruling coalition would probably lose about 125 seats but maintain its majority.

Lionel Jospin, leader of the Socialist Party, vowed to create seven hundred thousand new jobs, half in the public sector, and to cut the work week to thirty-five hours without reducing wages. Jospin skillfully forged an electoral coalition with the Communist Party and the Green Party. The right-wing National Front Party, led by Jean-Marie Le Pen, tended to blame high unemployment on an influx of African and Asian immigrants.

In the first round of elections on May 25, the leftist alliance unexpectedly out-polled the conservative coalition, about 41.5 percent to 36.4 percent. The National Front took 15 percent of the vote. Prime Minister Alain Juppé, in an effort to increase the coalition's chances in the runoff election, announced that he would resign even if the coalition maintained control of parliament. Although Juppé had received much of the blame for France's economic problems, opposition leaders claimed that his announcement was an admission that conservative policies had failed.

In the runoff elections of June 1 the leftist parties won a decisive victory. Although the Socialist Party, with 274 seats, was about 30 short of a majority, the Communists won 38 seats, and the Green Party obtained seven seats. The National Front won just one seat, but clearly it had taken many votes from the center-right coalition. The main message of the election appeared to be that the French public was not ready to sacrifice jobs and social programs for a common currency. Jospin, in his victory statement, declared that France needed a more "humane" approach to economic policy, and he pledged to give priority to employment, which would require new negotiations about the conditions of European unity. On June 2, President Chirac named Jospin the new prime minister.

BIBLIOGRAPHY

Hoffman, Stanley. "Look Back in Anger." *New York Review of Books* 44 (July 17, 1997): 45–50.

Javetski, B., and G. Edmondson. "Long Live the Welfare State! Will the French Revolt Cripple Reform Throughout France?" *Business Week,* June 16, 1997, 48–50.

Schain, Martin, and John Keeler. *Chirac's Challenge: Liberalization, Europeanization, and Malaise in France.* New York: St. Martin's Press, 1996.

Thomas T. Lewis

SEE ALSO Chirac, Jacques; Jospin, Lionel; Juppé, Alain

Decentralization

Under the Fourth French Republic (1944–58) the balance between national integration and local autonomy shifted toward a greater level of national direction over local affairs; and during the Fifth Republic (1958–) the pendulum began swinging the other way as both local governments and regions gained control over taxation and spending.

At the end of World War II powerful new bureaucracies were created to manage the economy and to provide for a greater measure of social welfare, social security, and national health care. These institutional changes reduced the power of elected representatives to the national legislature to secure special benefits and privileges for their constituents. In the private sector a comparable wave of industrial and commercial consolidation created large, nationwide enterprises that wiped out small businesses such as neighborhood groceries. One reflection of the social

discomfort produced by this wave of consolidation was the right-wing protest movement, Poujade's rebellion of 1956, in defense of the petite bourgeoisie. Both Gaullists and Socialists welcomed the greater centralization after the Second World War. Socialists saw the welfare state and economic planning as a step toward socialism; Gaullists saw the same institutions as a well-oiled machine by which to modernize French capitalism and to compete effectively with the United States in the domestic marketplace.

By the 1960s, however, critics of centralization abounded. From the New Left centralized socialism was subjected to withering criticism. Among the Gaullists and among businessmen the inefficiencies of overregulation were beginning to cast doubt on the whole logic of Keynesian-style economic management.

The first wave of decentralization was initiated by General de Gaulle in 1969 with his referendum to create corporate assemblies at the regional level and to devolve some centralized bureaucratic tasks to these bodies. Voters resoundingly rejected the plan, many fearing that corrupt provincial elites would be worse than Parisian cadres. De Gaulle resigned as president in disgust.

The next major attempt at decentralization came in the middle 1980s when Socialist President François Mitterrand successfully created regional assemblies with limited powers to tax and spend revenues on projects of regional interest such as road improvements.

BIBLIOGRAPHY

Belorgey, Gerard. *La France decentralisée.* Paris: Berger-Levrault, 1984.

Peggy Anne Phillips

Political Parties

Few events in a nation's history have as much political impact as a revolution. Revolutions are upheavals that by definition mark major historical discontinuities. So overwhelming in the minds of the French was their Revolution of 1789 that to this day its impact is manifested in the French political system, and recognizable in that arena where political parties compete for governmental power.

In the first instance, the Revolution swept away the absolutist, divine right monarchical system developed by Louis XIV and his Bourbon successors. The Revolution also reoriented relations with the Roman Catholic Church. The privileged, intimate relationship of the church to the rulers was destroyed as its lands and wealth were confiscated and, symbolically, street names in Paris with saints' names were renamed to reflect the secularized mood of the new citizen-rulers. Finally, the Revolution marked a turning point in the French view of the political economy. The rampant middle class valued work and a no-frills approach to life. Their fierce sense of individualism was not evident in the motto of the Revolution, Liberté, Égalité, Fraternité, but in their reaction to the overbearing state created by the Bourbons at Versailles. Distrust in what was centralized and big carried over into the next century's growth of industrialism, which spawned urbanization and labor unions, among other things. Profound mutual distrust became evident among capital, labor, and the rurally oriented and small-town bourgeoisie. These social, political, and economic cleavages were to form the major benchmarks in the creation of the French political party system.

National consensus on a legitimate form of government has been difficult to achieve in France. Currently in its fifth republic, including the one established after the Revolution and another lasting only three years, France has had two empires, a monarchical restoration, and one "regime" at Vichy during the German occupation of World War II. As France enters the twenty-first century there seems to be little question about the populace's commitment to participatory politics. Questions still arise in election campaigns, however, as to who are legitimate participants and what their relative influence is and what it should be. In many ways France is one of the most socioeconomic, class-oriented political systems in Europe, trapped by its history.

The role of the Roman Catholic Church remains ambiguous. Legally, today France has a secular political system. But as in most of Europe, the legacy of the religious question lingers as subtext in National Assembly debates over aid to church-related schools and to some extent, immigration policy. In the 1995 presidential election Jean-Marie Le Pen, leader of the National Front, indicated that if North African immigration were not halted and indeed reversed, France would soon become an Islamic republic rather than a Catholic nation. His comment was designed to play to the overwhelmingly Catholic population whom he may have believed to be clerically oriented. In fact most French are at least nominally Catholic, but of this group many are also anticlerical, reflecting the historically negative attitudes toward the church as a political rather than a religious force in France. So profound is this distrust of the political role of organized religion that France is one of the only nations on the European continent that does not have a political party with some variant of "Christian Democrat" in its name.

Direct political action in defense of social and especially economic terrain is part of the French political landscape. Actions by French governments, regardless of ideological stripe, can provoke strikes or similar work disruptions where unions are not evident. The art of the political demonstration by disaffected groups, however, seems to have been perfected by French labor unions through the general strike that virtually shuts down the whole nation. Other groups such as farmers close down rural roads and interurban highways when they feel their interests threatened. In 1968 students, who began an antigovernment demonstration in suburban Paris, in the ensuing days found the event joined by various groups nationwide. A few days later a counterdemonstration took place of nearly similar magnitude. These events almost brought down the Fifth Republic. Lack of trust in the political brokerage process, usually fostered by political parties, and a foreboding sense of exploitation by other socioeconomic groups drives the disaffected into the streets. This, in turn, has led to capital flight to more stable political environments. Politics in France can be very class-oriented as is manifested in the political process by class-oriented parties.

The historical period that best illustrates the development of political parties' orientation is that of the Third Republic, from the end of the Franco-Prussian War until World War II. After Louis Napoléon's defeat by Prussia in 1870 France was in turmoil. Various groups blamed one another and each seemed to have a solution to fix the system. The Third Republic was proclaimed by the barest of majorities, with those opposed waiting for the first opportunity to push their solution at the expense of others' interpretation of what was best for France at the end of the nineteenth century. Instead of a bona fide constitution, the elected assembly produced three "organic laws" that became the basis of one of the longest-lived and arguably, one of the least effective French governmental systems. It lasted sixty-five years, enduring World War I and the Great Depression, and was an incubator for current French political parties whose antecedents, however, went back to the Revolution. During the Third Republic a number of economic and social groups colonized the National Assembly to enhance their specific interests, or, at a minimum, prevent their interests from being damaged. The interplay among interest groups and assembly members strained the development of all but the most ideological political parties and led to marked instability in governments' tenure. The average was more than one per year.

By the end of World War I a left to right political configuration was evident. On the left were the Communist (PCF) and Socialists (SFIO), both Marxist and anticlerical but differing on the means to achieve a classless state. Becoming a virtual appendage of the Bolsheviks in Russia, the PCF supported world revolution as a means to world communism. The bourgeois Third Republic was an impediment to achieving this goal and was, consequently, expendable. These sentiments carried forward until the mid-thirties, when Moscow signaled a change through the latest version of the Communist International, the Cominform, for Communist parties to form "popular front" governments to thwart the newly created Rome-Tokyo-Berlin anti-Communist Axis. This position, with the exception of the nonaggression pact interlude, held until the founding of the Fourth Republic after World War II, and the beginnings of the Cold War. By then the PCF was the largest party in France with over a million members and able to garner a quarter of the popular vote. Ironically, the PCF would have formed a "negative coalition" with the conservative party founded by supporters of Charles de Gaulle, leader of the wartime Free French in London, had not the center parties changed the electoral system to favor themselves in the 1952 election. The only thing these diametrically opposed parties had in common was their distaste for the Fourth Republic and a wish to see it replaced.

The Socialists, who originally considered themselves to be the French Section of the International Workers Movement (SFIO), competed for the same voters as the PCF. Their electoral campaigns during the Third, Fourth, and much of the Fifth Republics were laden with images of class struggle and state ownership of the means of production, i.e., nationalization. Although they were able consistently to draw a sizable minority of voters of almost 25 percent and participate in governments, the PS, as they later became known, did not have the discipline, support from Moscow, or influence in the General Workers Union (CGT) that enabled the PCF to dominate the left. PS voters tended to be left-wing intellectuals and a variety of white-collar workers, such as teachers, who could not deal with the PCF's dogmatism. At times the PCF and PS cooperated, as they did in the common fronts of the thirties and during the 1973 election, when both supported what was called the Common Program. The latter was an attempt to bring together the Left to confront a coalition of rightist forces revolving around the resuscitated Gaullist party. Led by François Mitterrand in the early 1970s with fewer than eighty thousand members, the PS pulled back from the abyss of obscurity to become a force once again in French politics. By 1978 they received more than a third of the vote and by 1981 captured the presidency for Mitterrand. Socialist successes included reestablishing their legitimacy among manual workers at the expense of the apparently outdated PCF and deepening their appeal throughout the country, not just in the industrial areas. With the death of Mitterrand during his last presidential term, one of the PS unifying forces died. With no provisions for the succession of a vice president, new presidential elections were held and a Gaullist, Jacques Chirac, took the helm in 1995. The new leader of the PS, Lionel Jospin, came in second with 47.7 percent of the runoff vote. Down but not out, in early elections called in 1997 by Chirac to bolster the Gaullist position in the assembly, the PS roared back with enough votes to capture the premiership for Jospin, creating a strangely French phenomenon, *cohabitation,* in which the president of the republic is of one party and the government leader is of another.

As their name makes clear, Gaullists follow what they perceive to be thoughts on governing developed by the founder of the Fifth Republic, Charles de Gaulle. In 1958, the year the Fourth Republic disintegrated, Michel Debré tailored the constitution of the Fifth Republic to de Gaulle's specifications. Leader of the Free French in London and a former general of the army, de Gaulle had little positive to say about political parties, which he blamed for the chaotic politics of the Third Republic; this in his mind led to German occupation and national humiliation. Ironically, many of the most heroic Resistance fighters on the continent were members of the PCF and PS. The uniting agenda item, however, was to liberate France from German domination. Below that priority, the agendas of each differed markedly and became evident after the war. An interim government was established with de Gaulle as president and premier, while a constitutional convention concocted the fundamental laws of the Fourth Republic. After initial rejection by French voters, a revision was adopted by a plurality of voters. With an assembly-dominated government driven by political parties, de Gaulle saw a replay of the Third Republic, only now much more dangerous with the onset of the Cold War and France with a well-organized Communist party. He denounced the Fourth Republic and encouraged his followers who formed the first Gaullist party, the Rally of the French People (RPF), to work to revise this seemingly unworkable system. De Gaulle, abhorring political parties as divisive and destructive to the nation, never formally joined this or any other political party. After 1952 de Gaulle retreated from the political arena to await what he was sure would come, namely, a call to straighten out France after the factions could no longer deal with circumstances. This call came in 1958. De Gaulle took command of France as president and premier, ruling with emergency powers until "his constitution" had been fashioned. De Gaulle's supporters created another party from which he could draw members to run "his governments."

Since de Gaulle was again not a member, leaders could vary party structure and indeed some policies to suit their own political ambitions as long as they adhered to a theme of strong leadership representing France. The name of Gaullist supporters has changed three times so far during the Fifth Republic. Originally they were the Union pour la Nouvelle République (UNR). By 1968 they had become the Union des Démocrates pour la République (UDR), and in 1976, under the ambitious and energetic direction of Jacque Chirac, took their current name, the Rassemblement pour la Républic (RPR).

Even though they have acted very much like other political parties, in their own minds Gaullists claim to be a popular movement rather than an ordinary party. In spite of a desultory end to his reign, de Gaulle's death in 1970 removed a living symbol of what his followers saw as a united, powerful, and therefore respected France. Few postwar politicians could evoke national pride and the glory of France in the way de Gaulle could. Self-appointed, Jacques Chirac took on the task. After much maneuvering and infighting, he was elected to the long-vacant position of mayor of Paris. As a consummate member of the "political class" and Gaullist insider, he had the means to rally former Gaullist supporters at a symbol-laden gathering at Versailles to launch the RPR. Original Gaullist political thinking was nationalist and catered to a broad center-right spectrum. Although conservative in nature, as president, de Gaulle was not captured by ideology of the Right and certainly not of the Left. De Gaulle's variety of supporters found something in what he called "national societal goals" to which they could be loyal. Chirac's RPR has had a more determined and narrow appeal to the wealthier elements in France without the broadly appealing grandeur that previous Gaullist leaders displayed in spite of their conservatism. Under the last RPR government privatization and market efficiency were stressed along with reform of the expensive social welfare programs of France as it prepared to enter the European currency union. French voters were not impressed by the potential increase in unemployment and cuts in state benefits, and, in 1997, voted to replace the RPR government with that of Lionel Jospin, a Socialist and political heir of Mitterrand who now cohabits politically with President Jacques Chirac.

Other French political parties are strewn about the political spectrum and add needed votes to coalitions of the dominant parties. Some are historical artifacts, others are very new. In some cases they can exert influence well beyond their assembly numbers, determining how governments will be constructed and what policies they will pursue. One in particular, the Radicals (Parti Radical Socialiste, PRS), was a linchpin party during the Third and Fourth Republics. Put together after the Franco-Prussian War, the Radicals represented avant-garde thinking in the late nineteenth century that included anticlericalism and universal suffrage. As part of the untenable middle during the twentieth century, they moved to the right and occasionally to the left to maintain governing positions. By the end of World War I they could lay little claim to being radical or socialist. During the twelve years of the Fourth Republic they contributed premiers to seventeen governments. This number demonstrates the instability of that republic as well as the political opportunism of the Radicals.

Another component of the political center revolved around what many called political "notables." A classic example in the Fifth Republic is the Republican Independents (PR). Their leader, Valéry Giscard d'Estaing, an assembly member in the Fourth Republic and a finance minister in various Fifth Republic Gaullist governments, negotiated enough political concessions to be elected president in 1974. Accelerated by the eclipse of Giscard, the PR formed "federations" to deal with the complex French voting system to gain assembly representation. In the 1997 assembly elections they were part of one such grouping called the Union pour la Démocratie Française (UDF), which managed to garner 14.2 percent of the popular vote and 108 seats, third behind the PS and RPR. Within the UDF were components from a Christian Democratic reform movement, economic conservatives with liberal social views, and supporters of the European Union. Positions in this part of the French political spectrum reflect the images held by the notables and vary within a narrow framework of centrist, pragmatic politics with little or no cosmological guidance.

On the far left and right are parties with very specific points of view. Some have gained representation in the assembly, while most, such as the Maoists, have not. Twenty-one seats are distributed among radical left groups. The Greens (Verts) in combination with Génération Écologie (GE) currently hold seven seats. Monarchists and other right-wing groups held fourteen seats as a result of the 1997 assembly elections.

Most prominent of the smaller right-wing parties is the National Front (FN). Led by Jean-Marie Le Pen, it gained 14.9 percent of the popular vote in 1997, coming in third. It holds only one assembly seat because of other parties' unwillingness to join in electoral coalitions with it. Its message is clearly anti-immigrant, specifically anti–North African Muslim. Le Pen sees many of France's economic woes such as unemployment as a result of immigrants, and he offers to repatriate them. His narrow world view imagines French Christian culture under siege by Islam and North African culture. FN voters come from the petite bourgeoisie and from those who are unhappy with their current circumstances, whatever they happen to be. In the 1998 regional elections Le Pen offered to make electoral alliances with RPR candidates. Anxious as Chirac was to recoup political status from the previous year's assembly election losses, he warned his partisan compatriots against any such temptations. FN's appeal resonates in other European nations as well, where a persistent, and occasionally well-organized, ultranationalist minority party taps into the sentiment of the disaffected, causing more notice than they are probably worth.

Conrad Raabe

Poujadists

French populist movement of the 1950s. Led by thirty-three-year-old Pierre Poujade, the Poujadists appeared on the French political scene in 1953. Espousing a right-wing, populist cause, the Poujadists mixed rowdy street politics with surprising success in the 1956 general election. However, the inexperience and poor quality of their deputies brought parliamentary failure, and the Poujadists faded with the passing of the Fourth Republic in 1958.

Poujade was a small shopkeeper in St. Céré in the south of France. Although he fought with the Royal Air Force in World War II, he had a history of involvement with fascist and right-wing parties. In 1952 he was elected to the municipal council as a Gaullist, but he soon turned his attention to a wider political stage. Incensed by the deteriorating economic position of small shopkeepers and artisans, Poujade in 1953 formed the Union for the Defense of Merchants and Artisans (Union de Défense des Commerçants et des Artisans, UDCA). The new pressure group attacked the rich, technocrats and officials, while attempting to defend the interests of "the small men." As a result, the UDCA was, at first, seen as a left-wing movement, and was supported by the French Communist Party (PCF).

But at the UDCA's first conference, held in Algiers in November 1954, the movement moved right. Continuing his populist, antitax, antigovernment campaign, Poujade added support for French Algeria, xenophobia, and anti-Semitism to his litany. This led to his condemnation by the PCF and to the nickname "Poujadolf." But his movement continued to grow. Poujade held a monster rally in Paris in January 1955, attended by one hundred thousand, most of whom had come from the provinces. In mid-1955 Poujade decided to contest the next election and began to campaign against Pierre Mendès-France's government, which he characterized as being one of

"muddle and treason." The Poujadists ran a violent and empty campaign, under the slogan "throw the rascals out" (*sortez les sortants*). The result surprised everyone. The Poujadists, reorganized as French Union and Brotherhood (Union et fraternité française, UFF), won 2,476,038 votes, nearly 12 percent, and captured fifty-one seats in the National Assembly.

The Poujadists had support in the poorer regions of France south of the Saint-Malo–Geneva line. They had also benefited from the electoral collapse of the Gaullists, some defections from the PCF, and nationalists worried about French Algeria. The Poujadists' vote was, in addition, a protest against politicians, modernization, foreign competition, and "the system" in general.

The Poujadists, however, were unable to convert electoral success into parliamentary success. They could not prevent their opponents from unseating eleven of their deputies in a procedural move, and the remaining forty UFF members proved to be a vocal but ineffective and isolated group. Poujade himself had not stood for parliament, and failed to win a subsequent by-election. Outside the National Assembly, the Poujadists continued their violent protests. They were heavily involved in the February 6, 1957, riots in Algeria against Premier Guy Mollet. But Poujade found that he was unable to control the parliamentary UFF, and there was major disagreement when Poujade attempted to force his deputies to vote against the Anglo-French-Israeli Suez operation of 1956. This parliamentary confusion was mirrored by the movement's decline in the country. The final act came when, against their leader's wishes, Poujadist deputies voted for Charles de Gaulle and his new constitution. Thus, the end of the Fourth Republic also marked the end of the Poujadists.

BIBLIOGRAPHY

Etwell, Roger. "Poujadism and neo-Poujadism: From Revolt to Reconciliation," in Paul Cerny, ed., *Social Movements and Protest in France*. London: Frances Pinter, 1982.

Giles, Frank. *The Locust Years: The Story of the Fourth French Republic, 1946–1958*. London: Secker & Warburg, 1991.

Hoffmann, Stanley. *Le Mouvement Poujade*. Paris: Colin, 1956.

Rioux, Jean-Pierre. *La France dela Quatrième République*, Vol. 2, *L'Expansion et l'impuissance, 1952–1958*. Paris: Éditions du Seuil, 1983.

Williams, Philip. *Crisis and Compromise: Politics in the Fourth Republic*. London: Longmans, Green, 1964.

Stephen M. Cullen

Economy

The French economy enjoyed rapid growth and considerable modernization during the decades immediately after World War II. This era of prosperity contrasted sharply with the prewar depression, when many of the pivotal French ideological notions about economic life and policy were forged. Fitful and clearly slower growth in the 1980s and 1990s eroded some of the earlier gains, and economic policy faced unprecedented challenges by the end of the twentieth century.

The interval of rapid real growth and development after World War II was the result in part of broad trends in the industrialized world without respect to political and economic systems. Expansion was most widespread in the Western countries such as the United States and France and far less complete in the Soviet Union and its East bloc. In France sophisticated long- and short-range economic planning played an important role in controlling the features of this general wave of prosperity within the domestic marketplace. During the 1950s and 1960s economic planning and high levels of regulation enjoyed widespread support among French political leaders. While differences of opinion separated the Right with its loyalty to private ownership and the Left, which generally favored state ownership of key industries, both ends of the spectrum shared the common assumption that the state could increase the level of general prosperity through policy.

After World War II France completed the transition from a developing economy based heavily on the agricultural and industrial sectors to a fully developed system with industry and services as the dominant sectors. Less than 8 percent of the labor force made its living directly from farming in the postwar period. In the immediate aftermath of the liberation of France from the Germans, widespread nationalization brought under direct state control a vast array of industries from electricity to rails and airlines to automobile manufacture. Many of these state-owned enterprises played a crucial role in modernizing the structure of the French economy. France also became urban, with more than half the population living in towns after World War II. The shift between sectors, a baby boom, and the growth of urban centers produced a strong demand for new housing in the 1950s and 1960s. National five-year plans for economic growth and comprehensive urban planning became hallmarks of the French system, which was widely recognized as a hybrid of regulated capitalism and socialist-style nationalized industry: a mixed economy.

French growth in the 1950s and early 1960s attracted workers from Italy, Portugal, and North Africa as well as other parts of the world. The influx of tens of thousands of guest workers each year allowed French industries to maintain a large pool of low-paid workers and encouraged labor-intensive strategies of industrial organization. In the long run France's failure to invest in new technologies during the 1960s made its products less competitive in the world market.

The postwar boom ran out of steam during the Fifth National Plan in the mid-1960s. Birthrates began declining as general growth slowed in the late 1960s. The famous Thirty Glorious Years were in fact an interlude of about two and a half decades. In 1973 a powerful external shock, the OPEC oil crisis, sent energy prices to unprecedented levels, sapping the strength of the entire economy. The huge increase in energy costs came at the expense of general consumption. France fell into a interlude reminiscent of the fin de siècle when demand for goods plummeted, production fell, unemployment rose, and prices skyrocketed. By 1976 unemployment and inflation climbed to three times their levels during the era of prosperity.

Probably the most important consequence of the era of rapid inflation and high unemployment during the late 1970s was the damage it did to the foundations of economic theory and policy that might be loosely described as Keynesianism. France, like most of the Western capitalist-style systems after World War II, shared the expectation that states could reduce the level of unemployment by inducing job creation at the cost of stimulating a rise in general price levels. During the presidency of Valéry Giscard d'Estaing, a conservative, in the late 1970s unemployment levels did not respond to the government's stimulation policy, while inflation jumped into the double-digit range, thus cutting consumers' ability to purchase major durables like automobiles and to secure home mortgages.

In 1981 Socialist François Mitterrand defeated Giscard in his bid for reelection as president, and a Socialist-led coalition swept into control of parliament. Mitterrand's initial recovery program of nationalization in the financial industries and direct job creation in the public sector drove inflation rates even higher as capital fled abroad but failed to stem rising unemployment rates. By 1983 he was forced to abandon old Socialist doctrines and cast his policies along more market-responsive lines similar to policies being pursued by conservative governments in Britain and the United States. Planning and regulation were reduced. Public expenditures declined and government borrowing fell. Eventually interest rates and inflation fell as the state placed less demand on domestic capital markets. These changes positioned France to take advantage of the recovery in the United States, which in turn fueled job creation in France and other parts of the developed world.

The decade between 1976 and 1986 dealt a mortal blow to many long-held assumptions about socialism and Keynesian capitalism by the ineffectiveness of both approaches to policy. By 1985 and 1986 French inflation had been broken, falling to the 3 to 5 percent range, though unemployment remained high. For lack of a more convincing explanation, greater reliance on marketplace norms became the central force shaping French economic policy by the 1990s. Policymakers were quick to discern the large impact that external factors played on French marketplace equilibrium.

In 1989 the fall of the Berlin Wall and the burden of German reunification reduced the ability of France to sell goods to this key trading partner. As Germany suffered, so did all of Europe and especially France. The crumbling of Eastern European regimes in the early 1990s gave impetus to the trade negotiations among the modernized states, the G7, who ultimately ratified in 1993 and 1994 a series of pacts to regulate many aspects of international trade and minimize fluctuations: the General Agreement on Tariffs and Trade (GATT) accord. The European Community (EC) working independently attempted to forge a common monetary system for Europe in hopes of stabilizing its financial markets. France played a key role in both international movements.

By the end of the twentieth century the French economy had become a fully modernized industrial and service market-driven system with a labor force including nearly half the women in their active labor force years, with moderate levels of inflation, stable unemployment rates concentrated heavily among young and unskilled workers, and a sophisticated plan to advance the country's interests within the world marketplace.

BIBLIOGRAPHY

Carré, J. J., P. Dubois, and E. Malinvaud. Abrégé de *La Croissance français: un essai d'analyse économique causale de l'après-guerre*. Paris: Le Sevil, 1972.

OECD. *France*. Country Survey series, published every three years.

Tuppen, John N. *France under Recession, 1981–1986*. Albany: SUNY Press, 1988.

Peggy Anne Phillips

Labor Unions

The French labor movement is divided into three principal labor federations: the Communist General Confederation of Labor (Confédération Générale du Travail, CGT), the Socialist General Confederation of Labor-Workers' Force (Confédération Générale du Travail-Force Ouvrière, CGT-FO), and the moderate French Democratic Federation of Labor (Confédération Française Démocratique du Travail, CFDT). Some teachers belong to an independent union, the National Education Federation (FEN), and some two hundred thousand white-collar workers belong to the Confederation of Supervisory Grades (Confédération Générale des Cadres, CGC).

Despite radical rhetoric and ideological militancy, labor relations in France have traditionally been characterized by fewer strikes than in the United States or Great Britain. In Western Europe only Austria, Switzerland, the Netherlands, and West Germany, all of which were without a tradition of strikes, lost fewer workdays to strikes. Between 1977 and 1988 the number of workdays lost to strike per one thousand workers in France averaged fewer than one hundred. France's social welfare system has helped to placate workers. In 1980 only 18 percent of French wage earners belonged to unions. By 1990 the percentage had fallen to 10. Unions, however, continue to maintain their support among French white-collar workers. In 1985 the CGT had approximately two million members, and the CFDT, which had surpassed the CGT-FO in size, nearly a million. In the 1990s threats of privatization, downsizing, and reduced benefits led to a costly strike at Air France in 1993 and a transportation workers strike that largely crippled Paris in late 1996.

Workers in particular branches of the public or private economy can choose to be represented by competing unions. Interunion competition, ideological differences, and personal rivalries are reflected in competing lists advanced by the different unions in the work-site elections for factory councils and social security committees. This interunion rivalry has also impeded efforts at union organization and has prevented mergers that might have strengthened the position of workers.

The strength of unions and workers in France has been impacted by the establishment of a single market in the European Union (EU). Workers who are too militant or demanding risk seeing their jobs exported to lower-wage areas of the EU.

BIBLIOGRAPHY

Safran, William. *The French Polity*, 2d ed. London: Longman, 1985.

Wegs, J. Robert, and Robert Ladrech. *Europe since 1945: A Concise History*, 4th ed. New York: St. Martin's Press, 1996.

Bernard Cook

French Democratic Confederation of Labor. One of the three major French labor federations. The French

Democratic Confederation of Labor (Confédération Française Démocratique du Travail, CFDT) was originally called the French Confederation of Christian Workers (Confédération Française des Travailleurs Chrétiens, CFTC). It was organized by social Catholics in 1919 to provide workers with an alternative to the Socialist orientation of the General Confederation of Labor (Confédération Générale du Travail, CGT). It was reorganized after World War II but was far overshadowed by the CGT. In 1964 the CFTC, which had been associated with the Christian Democratic Popular Republican Movement (MRP), dropped its "Christian" appellation in favor of "Democratic" to broaden its appeal. In 1968 it assumed a more radical stance than the Communist-led CGT. While a conservative rump of one hundred thousand to two hundred thousand members continued to retain the label CFTC and to support moderate politicians, the CFDT's advocacy of the socialization of the means of production, democratic planning, and worker self-management (*autogestion*) aligned it ideologically with the reorganized French Socialist Party of the 1970s. By the mid-1980s the CFDT had surpassed the moderate General Confederation of Labor-Workers' Force (Confédération Générale du Travail-Force Ouvrière, CGT-FO) to become France's second-largest labor union federation with nearly a million members.

Bernard Cook

General Confederation of Labor.

Largest labor federation in France. The General Confederation of Labor (Confédération Générale du Travail, CGT) was established in 1895 and joined with the Federation of Labor Exchanges in 1902. It sought immediate goals through collective bargaining and the general strike, but its ultimate goal was a revolutionary transformation of society to be achieved through class struggle. In 1919 Catholic workers bolted and formed the French Confederation of Christian Workers. In 1921 the CGT expelled the unions dominated by Communists and anarchists. The Communists then founded the Unitary Confederation of Labor, which rejoined the CGT in 1936 during the era of the Popular Front. After its reconstitution following World War II, the CGT was dominated by Communists. The general secretary, Léon Jouhaux, and four other members of the CGT executive board left the CGT in 1947 and founded the General Confederation of Labor-Workers' Force in 1948.

The CGT is the largest of the three major French labor federations. It has approximately two million members with particular strength among factory workers and blue-collar government workers. However, it has experienced a loss of members to the French Democratic Confederation of Labor and the Confederation of Labor-Workers' Force.

Bernard Cook

General Confederation of Labor—Workers' Force.

One of the three major French labor union federations. The General Confederation of Labor-Workers' Force (Confédération Générale du Travail-Force Ouvrière, CGT-FO) was founded in 1948 when Léon Jouhaux, general secretary of the General Confederation of Labor (Confédération Générale du Travail, CGT), and four other members of the executive board of the CGT resigned and organized a new federation. They were opposed to Communist domination of the CGT and to the use by the Communists of the CGT to advance the interests of the French Communist Party. Jouhaux and the others believed that the general strike of 1947 was being waged for Communist political interests rather than to advance the job-site interests of workers. In response to an appeal from the veteran French Socialist and statesman, Léon Blum for support for an anti-Communist labor union movement, financial assistance came from the United States. The support at first came from, or was at least channeled through, American unions, but eventually it was provided directly by the CIA.

Initially the CGT-FO was socialist in its outlook, but it joined the Western-oriented International Confederation of Free Trade Unions. Though the CGT-FO eschewed direct involvement in politics, during the late 1940s and 1950s many CGT-FO leaders and members were linked, at least ideologically, to the Socialist Party (SFIO). The CGT-FO supported the Fourth Republic and sought to advance the interests of its members through collective bargaining and lobbying for legislative reform.

The moderation of the CGT-FO resulted in its eventual replacement by the French Democratic Confederation of Labor (Confédération Française Démocratique du Travail, CFDT) as the democratic socialist alternative to the CGT. By the early 1980s the CFDT had surpassed the CGT-FO as the second-largest labor federation in France.

Bernard Cook

Mitterrand's Economic Policy

President François Mitterrand's initial commitment to socialist change was abandoned in favor of "economic realism." With the victory of the Left in 1981, Mitterrand enacted an ambitious program to nationalize private businesses, expand the welfare state, and redistribute the nation's wealth. Within a year, however, economic difficulties forced him to move in a more centrist direction. This shift intensified after the defeat of the Left in the legislative elections of 1986.

Mitterrand was largely responsible for the formation of the new Socialist Party (PS) in 1971, and as first secretary he skillfully mediated differences between the party's left wing and its moderate reformist factions. His support for a Union of the Left with the French Communist Party (PCF) culminated in an alliance, the Common Program of 1972, that envisioned nationalizations, redistributive taxation, additional benefits for labor, and an increase in social services. But Mitterrand refused to run on this left-leaning program during his unsuccessful attempt at the presidency in 1974, and the PS-PCF alliance came to an end three years later.

In his campaign for the presidency in 1981, however, Mitterrand incorporated many elements of the Common Program into his platform, the 110 Propositions. Following an unprecedented triumph by the Left, Mitterrand spoke of a "break with capitalism," and his first prime minister, Pierre Mauroy, put together a cabinet that contained Communist ministers. During their "state of grace" (May 1981–June 1982), Mitterrand and Mauroy successfully implemented a four–pronged economic program. The centerpiece of the program was the Nationalization Act of 1982, bringing about the public ownership of thirty-six large banks, twelve industrial firms, and two financial corporations. As a result the state controlled virtually all the country's credit, and the public sector increased from about 10 percent to about a quarter of France's industrial capacity. This extension of nationalization was accompanied by egalitarian reforms, including an increase in benefits for the elderly and the handicapped, a tax on wealth, and labor reforms that reduced the work week to thirty-nine hours, extended vacations to five weeks, lowered the retirement age to sixty, and increased the minimum wage. Simultaneously, the Mitterrand-Mauroy government tried to reduce the unemployment rate (then at 8 percent) by a Keynesian-style increase in government spending, including the addition of one hundred thousand jobs in the public sector.

After the euphoria of Mitterrand's first year in office, it became evident that his economic program was greatly enlarging the budget and trade deficits, leading to serious inflation. Finance Minister Jacques Delors and other moderates insisted on a "pause" in socialist reforms, and Mitterrand reluctantly agreed to an austerity program that was implemented in two stages. In June 1982 the government instituted a temporary freeze on wages and prices, while also devaluing the franc for the second

time. In March 1983 Mitterrand made the crucial decision to remain within the European Monetary System (EMS), which required a deflationary plan of new taxes, reduced spending, and a third devaluation of the franc.

In 1984 Mitterrand moved even further to the center, with the theme of modernization replacing discourse about the injustices of capitalism. In February the Council of Ministers announced an "industrial restructuring" plan that meant huge job losses in several of the nationalized industries. After the elections to the European Parliament in June, Mitterrand selected a new prime minister, Laurent Fabius, a technocrat not committed to the classic model of socialism. At the congress of Toulouse in 1985, the PS proclaimed that it was in the social democratic tradition, but this moderation did not prevent the right-wing parties from winning control of the parliament in the elections of 1986. During the cohabitation of the next two years, conservative Prime Minister Jacques Chirac inaugurated massive privatization of state-owned businesses, cut corporate taxes, reduced the budget deficit, and pursued financial deregulation. Mitterrand could only voice his disapproval.

In the presidential election of 1988, Mitterrand's "Letter to the French People" accepted the status quo and called for modernization, national unity based on compromise, and continued development of the European Community (EC). After Mitterrand's second victory, voters elected the PS the largest party in the National Assembly, but without a majority. Mitterrand's choice for a new prime minister, Michel Rocard, was the incarnation of the social democratic wing of the PS. The Rocard government cautiously reformed tax policy to make it more progressive, but Rocard continued Chirac's anti-inflationary fiscal and monetary policies. The next two prime ministers, Édith Cresson and Pierre Bérégovoy, also followed the path of austerity, and Mitterrand championed the cause of the Maastricht treaty, despite its anti-socialist implications.

The legislative elections of 1993 were a disaster for the Left; during the resulting two-year cohabitation with Édouard Balladur as premier, Mitterrand exercised little influence over economic policy. The victory of Jacques Chirac in the presidential election of 1995 was interpreted as a repudiation of both Mitterrand and the socialist message.

By 1995, most of the radical reforms of 1981–82 had been reversed, and it appeared doubtful that there would be a repeat of such experiments in the foreseeable future. By objective measurements Mitterrand's economic policies were not very successful. Unemployment grew from 7 percent in 1981 to 12 percent during the last years of his second term. Inflation and budget deficits, however, had compared favorably with other EC countries, and under Mitterrand the Socialists had demonstrated that they could responsibly manage a capitalistic economy. Probably Mitterrand's most important legacy was the purging of Marxist, revolutionary ideology from the PS, so that the party might conform to the model of socialist and social democratic parties elsewhere in Europe.

BIBLIOGRAPHY

Cole, Alistair. *François Mitterrand: A Study in Political Leadership.* London: Routledge, 1994.

Friend, Julius. *Seven Years in France: François Mitterrand and the Unintended Revolution.* Boulder, Colo.: Westview Press, 1989.

Raymond, Gino, ed. *France During the Socialist Years.* Dartmouth, N.H.: Aldershot, 1994.

Ross, George, Stanley Hoffman, and Stanley Malzacher, eds. *The Mitterrand Experiment.* Oxford: Polity Press, 1987.

Singer, David. *Is Socialism Doomed?: The Meaning of Mitterrand.* New York: Oxford University Press, 1988.

Truppen, John. *Chirac's France, 1986–1988.* New York: St. Martin's Press, 1991.

Thomas T. Lewis

SEE ALSO Chirac, Jacques; Delors, Jacques; Fabius, Laurent; Mauroy, Pierre; Rocard, Michel

Taxation

The French have always resisted taxation. In the eighteenth century the venal capitation sometimes led to the decapitation of tax collectors. In modern times taxpayers routinely flaunted the income taxes of the Fourth and Fifth Republics. As a consequence French taxation schemes have always relied on a mix of individual taxes like the income tax and more easily collected indirect taxes on goods and property.

Income taxes have been used in the post–World War II era as policy instruments in addition to being revenue devices. For instance, the 1948 tax surcharge on incomes attempted to dampen income by shifting it from consumption to savings. In the 1950s special tax exemptions were created to encourage large families with three or more children, and a decade or so later welfare benefits came to be pegged to "large" families with three or more children. Late in the Fourth Republic many taxes on industrial production and wealth were replaced with a simpler broad-based value-added tax (sales tax). In 1966 the value-added tax was extended to services.

Inflation troubles in the 1970s and 1980s brought a return to the use of income taxes as a vehicle to control all economic performance with far less success than was the case during the Fourth Republic. Income tax rates were adjusted and taxes on business increased, yet government revenues lagged far behind expenditures. This problem was especially pronounced with a shrinking base of taxpayers supporting an increasing group of old age pensions. Between 1979 and 1982 the percentage of the gross domestic product (GDP) devoted to all forms of taxation including social security rose from 39.5 to 43.9 percent.

By the end of the twentieth century income taxes yielded about 20 percent of total tax revenues, while the value-added tax yielded over 40 percent. In addition, the French pay a variety of fees and other direct taxes. These include taxes on gasoline that serve primarily as a policy instrument to encourage conservation by raising prices. Nearly 10 percent of all revenues come from such indirect taxes and fees. French tax and social spending policies taken together place a large amount of economic power in the hands of the state.

BIBLIOGRAPHY

Deloitte, Haskins & Sells. *Taxation in France.* New York: Deloitte, Haskins & Sells, 1982.

Peggy Anne Phillips

Education

Contemporary French education reflects postwar society and politics. Increased equality of opportunity, decentralization of the state and democratization of institutions have modified the rigid, uniform system of education inherited from Napoléon. However, French education continues to be highly organized and essentially controlled by the Ministry of Education in Paris. Administrators, faculty, and staff, appointed by the ministry, are *fonctionnaires* of the state. The same programs, textbooks, and, as much as possible, teaching methods are used in all French schools. France spends approximately 20 percent of the national budget on education. In contrast, only a very small portion of the federal budget in the United States is spent on education, but total governmental expenditures on education in the United States in 1992, as a percentage of the GDP (4.9 percent), exceeded those of France (4.8 percent). However a much larger percentage was spent in France on pre-primary education, 0.6 percent versus 0.2 percent.

Compulsory schooling is from ages six to sixteen, although most children attend state-supported nursery schools, which begin receiving children at age two. These *écoles maternelles* are among the best preschool systems in Europe. The remaining phases of education are primary (*écoles primaires*), lower secondary (*collèges*), higher secondary (*lycées*), and higher education (universités, institutes, and *grandes écoles*). The primary and secondary phases have reverse numbering of grades: six-year-olds begin at the twelfth level, and those who continue through the *lycée* end thirteen years of schooling with the *seconde, première,* and *terminale.* One of the 1975 Haby Reforms was the creation of the *collège* (CES), which begins theoretically at age eleven. The *collège* consists of four years of common core subjects organized into three "tracks": Modern I, Modern II, and Transitional III. In higher secondary education, from age fifteen to eighteen-nineteen, there are basically three options: the classical *lycée d'enseignement général,* leading to the competitive national examination (*baccalauréat*) required for entrance to the university, the vocational *lycée technique* leading to the *baccalauréat professionnel* and the higher-education option, and the *lycée d'enseignement professionnel* terminating in a *brevet de technicien.*

Most primary and secondary schools are secular institutions administered by the state. Approximately 17 percent of children attend private schools, which are predominately Catholic. In recent years the debate over public versus private education has been intense. One of the goals of Mitterrand's Socialist government was the "unification of education." However, as a result of the massive June 1984 demonstration in Paris, by supporters of religious schools, the government withdrew its proposal for secularization of all education. The "contracts of association" between private education and the state, resulting from the 1959 Debré law, provide financial support for teachers' salaries and administrative costs in exchange for state control of study programs.

Since the 1960s increasing numbers of individuals, including those of lower-middle- and working-class families, have gained access to higher education. There are basically four options: some students continue in a higher *lycée* to prepare a *brevet de technicien supérieur* (BTS) or to prepare qualifying examinations for the *grandes écoles,* the two-year *instituts universitaires de technologie* (created in 1965 to train students for technical jobs in business and industry), the université, and the *grandes écoles.*

The largest system in higher education is the université. The student revolt of May 1968, resulting later in the primary and secondary Haby reforms, produced even more significant changes in the université. Edgar Faure's Law of Orientation created new regional universitiés and reorganized the traditional *facultés* into multidisciplinary *unités d'enseignement et de Recherche* (UER). These have more flexible curricula and are governed more autonomously, with participation of staff and students. Small individualized groups (*travaux dirigés*) and continuous assessment of students' progress have been integrated with the traditional lectures and anonymously graded terminal examinations. There is more human contact between students and teachers, especially in the *travaux.* Presently there are more than eighty state universities, of which thirteen are in Paris and its environs. There are also five important Catholic institutions of higher education.

The universities are organized into three cycles. Created in 1973, the *diplôme d'études universitaires générales* (DEUG) is awarded following two years of broad interdisciplinary studies. The second cycle requires an additional one to two years, completion of which is recognized by the *licence* and *maîtrise* diplomas. The third cycle consists of specialization and research leading to the *doctorat.* The third-cycle studies were changed by Alain Savary's 1984 Law. The previous dual system, consisting of the two-year *doctorat de troisième cycle* and the more prestigious *doctorat d'état,* which took many years to complete, has been replaced by a single two-level doctorate. Lasting three to five years, the French *doctorat* now corresponds more to the English and American Ph.D. To teach at the university level, candidates must pass a demanding state qualifying examination, the *agrégation.*

The *grandes écoles* are specialized institutions that offer demanding courses of study leading to particular professions, notably in the armed forces, the higher ranks of public administration, post-*baccalauréat* teaching and research, and high-level industry and commerce. Access to them is limited by competitive examinations (*concours*) that students prepare one to three years after the *baccalauréat.* Among the best known and most prestigious are the École Polytechnique, École Nationale d'Administration, École Normale Supérieure, and the École des Hautes Études Commerciales. As with other educational institutions in France, most are state-operated; however, some, primarily schools of engineering and institutes of formation of managerial professionals (*cadres*), are private. Having educated many important political leaders and elite professionals, the *grandes écoles* maintain their high status as the "pinnacle of the French education system."

In the 1990s French education continued to be scrutinized. Far too many students repeated grades, sometimes the same grade two or three times. The dropout rate was extremely high; those who left the system before completing a qualifying program faced the prospect of unemployment. In addition, there was much dissatisfaction among teachers, who felt their salaries and prestige were lower than in comparable professions. In 1995 Minister of Education François Bayrou proposed a *"contrat"* to modify primary and secondary programs. Despite the existing problems, France's system of education is a model for its organization, classical rigor, and, over the last thirty years, its striving, with significant reforms, to meet the changes and challenges of an emerging European Community.

BIBLIOGRAPHY

Ardagh, John. *France Today.* London: Penguin Books, 1990.

Edmiston, William, and Annie Duménil. *La France contemporaine.* New York: Holt, Rinehart and Winston, 1997.

Halls, W. D. *Education, Culture and Politics in Modern France.* Oxford: Pergamon Press, 1976.

Hollifield, James F. *Searching for the New France.* New York: Routledge, 1991.

Lewis, Howard Davies. *The French Education System.* New York: St. Martin's Press, 1985.

Reviews of National Policies for Education: France. Paris: Organisation for Economic Co-operation and Development (OECD), 1971.

Cassandra P. Mabe

Press

With the liberation of France in 1944 from German occupation, a new French press emerged with, principally, new newspapers and new rules. After a few years news dailies settled into patterns that would last until the spread of television in the 1960s. Readership declined from 1969, and a new generation of more business-oriented leadership guided the industry through mergers and partial integration with the new media.

When France was liberated in 1944, Resistance figures and papers immediately dominated the new French press. Many were initiated as clandestine papers during the Resistance: *Combat* (Albert Camus), *Défense de la France* (later *France-Soir*, Pierre Lazareff), *Franc-tireur, France libre, Front national* (with ties to Communists and the Right), and *Libération* (Communist ties, Emmanuel d'Astier de la Vigerie). New national newspapers included *Le Monde* (news in general, Hubert Beuve-Méry, center-left) and *Les Échos* (economy, Émile and Robert Servan-Schreiber). Only a handful of interwar papers reemerged in, or survived into, the postwar period: *L'Humanité* (Communist Party), *Ce Soir* (Communist ties), *Le Populaire* (Socialist Party), *L'Aurore* (Socialist ties), *L'Aube* (Christian Democrat), *Le Figaro* (independent but upper middle class), and *La Croix* (Catholic). *Le Canard enchaîné*, founded during World War I, resumed its uniquely satirically critical role.

Indeed, of 206 interwar dailies, only 28 published in liberated France, and these under new legislation governing their functioning. Many of the rest were banned owing to Vichy ties and/or corruption under the Third Republic. One perceived malignancy of the interwar press had been pervasive yet hidden ownership by financiers and their manipulations of the press. New legislation in 1944 overturned many liberal aspects of the 1881 press law and mandated transparency in a newspaper's ownership, finances, and direction. The legislation furthermore created a national press agency (Agence France de la Presse, later Agence France-Presse) and state subsidies, direct and indirect.

The French press grew tremendously from 1944 to 1946 despite economies that restricted paper consumption and transportation. French readers, starved for uncensored news, devoured the new, inexpensive papers; total daily circulation rose from 12.1 million in 1945 to a historic peak of 15.1 million in 1946. Papers were limited first to two and then four pages, and newspapers persistently pressed for more. *Le Monde* was permitted extra pages to print official documents, a fact that enhanced its prestige. The general ration increased gradually to six pages between 1948 and 1951, and then jumped to eight pages in 1956.

Despite the initial politicization of several national dailies, the collective postwar press was less politicized than it had previously been. One reason for this was its decentralization; with transportation limited at the end of the war and afterward, national newspapers had difficulty extending themselves beyond Paris, the invariable base. Regional and local newspapers filled the void. From interwar parity between Parisian and provincial newspapers, the latter attained 61 percent of the market share by 1946, and 72 percent by 1990. In 1976 the regional *Ouest-France* became the highest-circulating French daily, which it remains. Several regional papers have two dozen or more local editions, varying in local news sections.

A monthlong newspaper strike in early 1947 ruined several of the new newspapers, and a spate of mergers and closings ensued. By the late 1940s the basic patterns for the next fifteen years had emerged. After the 1946 peak of newspaper reading at 370 dailies in circulation for every 1,000 people, the highest such ratio in Western Europe, French news reading declined steadily. One cause for this was the increase in real newsstand prices.

While dailies consolidated, news weeklies continued to evolve. Many followed Anglo-American models, and their success stemmed in part from the lack of substantial Sunday newspapers. The most prominent weeklies included *Paris Match* (circulation of 1.8 million in 1957), *L'Express* (Jean-Jacques Servan-Schreiber), and *France Observateur* (later *Nouvel Observateur*).

These last two focused especially on criticism of the decolonization wars in Indochina and Algeria, which regularly landed them in trouble, as the state (Fourth and Fifth Republics) exercised various forms of censorship. The most striking such episode occurred on October 17, 1961, when Parisian police banned journalists before massacring two hundred, or perhaps many more, Algerians peacefully demonstrating against a discriminatory curfew—an event then underplayed in the French press and population.

The 1962 conclusion of the Algerian War, and the spread of television during the same decade, yielded a brief third stage in the postwar French press. Several national papers became more descriptive than prescriptive, and newspapers briefly coexisted with television without suffering circulation losses. While the percentage of households with television sets increased from 27 percent in 1963 to 62 percent in 1968, national daily circulation rose steadily to a second peak in 1968 of thirteen million, after having hovered around ten to eleven million in the 1950s.

The situation changed dramatically after 1974, when television was allowed more advertising. Much advertising revenue flowed away from the press, which in France depends on advertising for more than half its revenues, unlike the press in Great Britain or Germany, which depends more on sales. At the same time, Western European economic growth decelerated dramatically. Daily circulation dropped to below 10 million dailies in the late 1980s, by which time French per capita newspaper consumption had fallen below northwestern European averages, while it remained higher than other Mediterranean ones. The only new national daily since the 1940s to reach a wide audience, *Libération,* was founded in 1973, just before this downturn. (It was unrelated to the previous paper of the same name, which closed in 1964.) The sale of traditional weeklies, however, remained steady, and new television guides, similar to the American *TV Guide,* became some of the most popular publications.

During the same period some newspapers became part of growing multimedia conglomerations. Next to the older Hachette group, Robert Hersant acquired several titles in the later 1970s, including *Le Figaro* and *France-Soir.* In 1984 the new Socialist government aimed legislation against the Hersant group to limit press ownership to 10 percent of all French dailies, which would have forced Hersant, a former Gaullist deputy, to discard many

of his holdings; but the Constitutional Council then restricted application to new acquisitions. The new center-right government of 1986 passed legislation limiting ownership to 30 percent, or approximately the amount owned by Hersant. (Also in the 1980s, *Le Monde* and *L'Express* moved to the center-right and right, respectively.)

After revenue gains, without circulation growth, in the later 1980s, newspapers again suffered when income from classified advertisements dropped in the 1990s with rising unemployment. French newspapers continue to receive state subsidies and to struggle financially.

BIBLIOGRAPHY

Albert, Pierre. *La Presse française.* Paris: La Documentation Française, 1990.

Bellanger, Claude, et al. *Histoire générale de la presse française,* Vols. 4–5. Paris: Presses Universitaires de France, 1975–76.

Cazenave, Elisabeth, et al. *Presse, radio et télévision en France de 1631 à nos jours.* Paris: Hachette, 1994.

Eveno, Patrick. *Le Monde, 1944–1995.* Paris: Le Monde-Éditions, 1996.

Kuhn, Raymond. *The Media in France.* London: Routledge, 1995.

Jeffrey William Vanke

Resistance Charter

Program of action adopted by the organized resistance movement of France and espoused by all the major parties of the country prior to the general elections of October 1945. It called for a genuinely democratic political system as well as sweeping social and economic reforms. Accordingly, in addition to guaranteeing all basic human rights for every citizen, the charter called for a more just social order.

In its economic provisions the charter postulated a three-tiered system. Heavy industry and credit were to be largely nationalized. The subordination of private interests to the common good was to be assured through state direction of the national economy. Within this framework, the free-enterprise system would then be operative.

In its social reforms the charter basically provided for a modern welfare state. The rights of individual workers to job security, collective bargaining, and guaranteed wages were to be complemented by the participation of labor unions in the formulation of national economic and social policy. Social security, old age pensions, and accident compensation were to be mandated. Agricultural labor was to be justly compensated, and a system of reforms to benefit farmers as well as to promote rural life was to be undertaken.

The main goals of the Resistance Charter were subsequently implemented by the Provisional Government and the Fourth Republic.

BIBLIOGRAPHY

Aron, Robert. *De Gaulle Before Paris.* London: Putnam & Co., 1962.

Shennan, Andrew. *Rethinking France: Plans for Renewal 1940–1946.* New York: Oxford, University Press, 1989.

Thomson, David. *Democracy in France since 1870.* New York: Oxford University Press, 1969.

Francis J. Murphy

SEE ALSO Bidault, Georges; De Gaulle, Charles

Social Welfare Policy

France has one of the most comprehensive and expensive social welfare systems in Europe. The system is the legacy of decades of social reform beginning in earnest under the early Third Republic (1820–1940) and accelerating under the tripartite governments that laid the foundations of the postwar reconstruction in the late 1940s. By the time of the Fourth Republic (1946–1958) a broad political base had been established for the notion that the state should play a large, direct role in ameliorating the economic conditions of the poor, the disabled, and the elderly. Both social democrats and conservative Gaullists supported the creation of the modern, elaborate system of old age pensions, family allowance, unemployment compensation, and health care.

Leftist-dominated governments created the first modern social security programs in 1945 and 1946. The programs were intended to be comprehensive, extending benefits to all citizens without regard to income. The initial plan quickly became embedded in a more elaborate system, however, which assigned pension benefits on the basis of the political clout of different constituencies in the labor force and the electorate. By the end of the Fourth Republic the old age pension system included special agencies for miners, railroad workers, craftsmen, government workers, farmers, and so forth. The state set the terms for the collection and disbursement of old age funds. At the same time a variety of private and semipublic entities, employers, mutual aid societies (insurance companies), and labor unions handled the administration of the funds.

Family allowances and general welfare were added to the social security system in the 1950s. Basic welfare assistance came under the administrative umbrella of state agencies and private family associations. Family policies contained mixed messages throughout the Fourth and Fifth Republics. Haunted by the meager birth rates of the previous century and by three wars with fecund Germany, the makers of French family policy encouraged mothers to have as many children as possible. Families with three or more children were guaranteed special allotments for baby needs. This and widespread state-subsidized day care was intended to stimulate the birthrate. At the same time, one of the criteria for awarding welfare benefits was unusually large numbers of children. By the 1990s being a member of a large family was considered a risk factor for learning disabilities in the French public schools. Welfare and social policy goals appeared at odds with social norms during the Fourth and Fifth Republics.

Health care is state-subsidized in France. Patients choose their own doctors and receive a partial reimbursement for their expenses from the national health insurance fund. A copayment by patients is required and intended as a check on uncontrolled costs. Medicines are also covered in the same shared-cost way. On the whole the health-care system has brought medical care to most segments of society, though it is difficult to persuade doctors to practice in rural areas. Public clinics and state programs to subsidize doctors' incomes in less favored areas meet some of the need for health care in these areas.

Social security and health care have created enormous deficits in the current budgets during the Fifth Republic. Cost sharing in health care has not appreciably reduced the growth in medical expenditures. Special interest groups within the pension system have proven tenacious in fighting to hold on to their privileges. During his first presidential term Jacques Chirac launched a campaign to prune social benefits in hopes of bringing the French budget in line with the goals of the European Community for a unified currency at the end of the twentieth century. Howls of protest and massive strikes forced Chirac to abandon his efforts.

By the next century France will have only one and a half active workers for each retired worker receiving pension benefits. The welfare state in France was created in the late 1940s when life expectancy was below the retirement age in the pension system, and when effectively seven or eight active workers contributed to the benefits of the tiny number who drew them. The key question facing France in the next century is what level of social benefits can be maintained under the altered demographic patterns of the labor force.

BIBLIOGRAPHY

Rodgers, Barbara N., Abraham Doron, and Michael Jones. *The Study of Social Policy: A Comparative Approach.* Boston: Allen & Unwin, 1979.

Peggy Anne Phillips

Franco, Francisco (1892–1975)

Nationalist generalissimo in the Spanish Civil War (1936–39) and head of state in Spain, 1939–75. After leading Nationalist forces to victory over the second Spanish republic, Francisco Franco established an authoritarian regime in Spain that persisted until his death in 1975. Despite his ideological sympathies, Franco avoided full alliance with Hitler and Mussolini in the Second World War, and during the 1950s established himself as an anti-Communist ally of the West. The final decades of Franco's rule brought rapid economic growth to Spain but no parallel increase in political participation, and the regime maintained its repressive character until the end.

Spanish dictator Francisco Franco in the 1960s.
Illustration courtesy of Popperfoto/Archive Photos.

Franco was born on December 4, 1892, in El Ferrol, the second son of a family with a tradition of naval service. The boy was intended for a naval career but could not secure a place in the cadet program; instead he entered the Infantry Academy in 1907. He graduated in the bottom third of his class in 1910 and was posted to Morocco in 1912. Franco saw action against Riff rebels and was seriously wounded in 1916. He won battlefield promotions for bravery, rising quickly to major. Franco returned to Spain in 1917 to serve in the Oviedo garrison. There he participated in quelling a miners' strike and met his future wife, María del Carmen Polo y Martínez Valdés, the daughter of a wealthy local family. (They would marry in 1923.) In 1920 Franco returned to Morocco as a battalion commander in the newly formed Tercio de Extranjeros (Spanish Legion), organized by Lieutenant Colonel José Millán Astray on the model of the French Foreign Legion. Millán Astray was a bizarre figure, obsessed with notions of redemption through violence, but also an inspirational leader who shaped the Tercio into a crack unit of shock troops who regarded themselves as "the bridegrooms of death." In Morocco the legionaries fought well and spread terror by mutilating captives and slaughtering villagers, behavior condoned by their officers. Franco was Millán Astray's closest collaborator and won respect as a cold-blooded commander and harsh disciplinarian.

Millán Astray left the Tercio in 1922, and when his successor died the next year Franco rose to command. In September 1923 General Manuel Primo de Rivera seized power in Spain with the collusion of Alfonso XIII. Franco opposed the dictator's proposed disengagement from the Moroccan war but served loyally nonetheless and was promoted to colonel early in 1925. In September 1925 Franco's legionaries triumphed in a perilous amphibious operation at the bay of Alhucemas. This success palliated Spanish humiliation over previous colonial debacles and earned Franco a promotion to brigadier general in 1926; just thirty-three, he became the youngest general in any European army.

Franco returned to Spain to command a brigade in Madrid. There he made contacts in the highest military and governmental circles. By 1926 support for Primo de Rivera's regime was dwindling. On the right, the dictator had been discredited by his moderation; meanwhile republican sentiment was on the rise among liberals and leftists. Franco steered clear of military plotting against the dictator though, and in 1928 his loyalty earned him command of the new Academia General Militar (General Military Academy, AGM) in Zaragoza. The AGM drew on a French model—in fact, in the planning stages Franco traveled to Saint-Cyr to consult its commandant, Marshal

Philippe Pétain—and was meant to enhance esprit de corps by providing a common two-year curriculum for all army cadets before they began specialized training. Under Franco, the AGM earned an excellent reputation. Cadets were drilled in stern military values, while the commandant developed ties to the men who would be his line officers in the civil war.

During Franco's years in Zaragoza the Primo de Rivera regime collapsed, and the dictator fell in January 1930. The weak successor administrations could not stem discontent with the monarchy, and a groundswell of republican sentiment culminated in a strong electoral showing in the local elections of April 1931. Franco had played a role in suppressing the rising of republican officers at Jaca in December 1930; his actions demonstrated continued loyalty to the crown despite his younger brother Ramón's highly visible involvement in republican plotting. When Alfonso XIII abdicated in April 1931, giving way to a provisional republic, Franco was careful to keep his distance from the new regime while signaling his willingness to serve it. As a conservative soldier, Franco was distressed by the republic's anticlericalism and its sympathy for Catalan and Basque regionalism. He was personally affronted by the army reforms initiated by Manuel Azaña as minister of war in 1931; as a consequence of Azaña's policies, Franco's seniority as a brigadier was revised downward, and the Academia General Militar was closed. The disgruntled Franco was transferred to provincial La Coruña.

He regained some credit with the regime by refusing to join the abortive coup led by General José Sanjurjo in August 1932. His loyalty stemmed from self-interest rather than attachment to the republic—he is said to have remarked, "when I rise, it will be to win"—but nonetheless it earned him a better posting, to the Balearic Islands, in early 1933. Franco's star rose further after the resurgence of the Right in the elections of November 1933. He won promotion to major general, became a close adviser to Minister of War Diego Hidalgo Durán, and was the latter's choice to direct the military suppression of the October 1934 revolutionary rising in Asturias. Franco, his passion for order compounded by a growing hatred for the radical Left, directed a ruthless campaign, employing the Tercio and even Moroccan auxiliaries to crush Asturian resistance. Military operations, including reprisals and torture of prisoners, left about four thousand dead and another twenty thousand to thirty thousand rebels and sympathizers imprisoned. Franco's role earned him hatred on the Left but the gratitude of conservatives, manifested in his appointment to command the Army of Africa and then, in May 1935, as chief of the General Staff under the new minister of war, rightist *supremo* José María Gil Robles.

Franco worked with Gil Robles to improve the equipment and professional development of the army, and to undo Azaña's reforms by restoring anti-Republican officers to key posts. For example, General Emilio Mola, later to mastermind the military rising of 1936, was reinstated in the army, assigned important commands in Morocco, and even called to Madrid to help with plans for the deployment of African troops in the peninsula should the revolutionary violence of 1934 recur. Franco's collaboration with Gil Robles ended late in 1935, when the president of the republic, Niceto Alcalá-Zamora, reshaped the cabinet preparatory to general elections. Although he was by now the military darling of the Right, Franco refused to participate in the anti-Republican plotting that proliferated in the weeks before the election of February 16, 1936. He did, however, undertake cautious soundings for a coup attempt on the morrow of the popular front's victory, but found support too tepid to move ahead.

The new government tried to cripple military plotting by dispersing unreliable commanders to peripheral posts; Franco was sent to the distant Canary Islands. This had little effect, though, and within a few weeks a conspiracy was underway, coordinated by Mola. The plotters regarded Franco's participation as crucial, but he continued to waver, maintaining close contact with the conspirators while balking at an irrevocable commitment to rebellion. Franco's partisans regard this hesitation as proof of his respect for legality, while his detractors ascribe it to caution and careerism. Exasperation with his coyness earned Franco the mocking title of "Miss Canary Islands 1936" among Mola's correspondents. Meanwhile, conditions in the country strengthened the plotters' conviction that the republic could neither maintain order nor resist the revolutionary demands of the far Left. Mounting political violence culminated in July with the police assassination of hard-line monarchist José Calvo Sotelo. This event triggered the implementation of Mola's conspiracy and convinced Franco to join the rising, now scheduled to begin on July 18, 1936.

Flawed coordination was evident in the unfolding of the *pronunciamiento;* for example, the Moroccan garrisons rebelled too soon, on July 17, while Franco did not arrive from the Canaries to direct the African rising until July 19. Despite these problems, the plot succeeded in Morocco, but on the peninsula the rebels failed in most major cities and might have been crushed had the government reacted vigorously. Instead, a stalemate ensued, with control of the national territory rather evenly split between the republic and its military enemies. Franco's Moroccan forces might tilt the balance if they could cross the straits to Andalusia, a passage hindered by Republican control of most naval and air assets. Franco approached the Italian and German governments for aerial support to gain control of the straits and assist in ferrying his troops. Before the end of July both Hitler and Mussolini agreed to help. Their aid facilitated the passage of about eight thousand soldiers by early August. Franco's ability to procure foreign aid propelled him to the forefront of the rebellion.

Only civil war could now resolve the situation. The insurgents, calling themselves "Nationalists," planned an advance on Madrid. Mola's forces, reinforced by Carlist militiamen, would strike from the north, while Franco's army of Morocco moved toward the capital from the southwest under the battlefield command of Colonel Juan Yagüe. Yagüe's columns met little effective resistance as they advanced through Extremadura, instituting a fierce repression in each fallen town—in Badajoz alone, perhaps four thousand "Reds" were massacred in the assault or executed afterward in the bullring. By early September the advance had reached Talavera in the Tagus valley, and by July 21 the road north to Madrid seemed open. Franco decided to divert his forces to Toledo, however, to relieve its Nationalist garrison. This expedition delayed the advance long enough for the Republicans to bolster Madrid's defenses. Consequently the capital was able to hold out in heavy fighting against the Nationalist onslaught in October and November. The costly decision to relieve Toledo was in part a product of Franco's military experience in the Moroccan counterinsurgency. Tactics there had dictated that the army secure its rear and flanks before moving forward, and all Franco's campaigns in the Spanish Civil War respected this cautious doctrine. In September 1936, however, political considerations also weighed heavily in Franco's decision making. Since late August the insurgents and their Italian and German allies had wanted to establish a single command in the Nationalist zone. On the same day that Franco ordered his columns to Toledo, the chief rebel generals met in Salamanca and voted to name Franco head of all their forces. Because some opposition remained, this decision was tabled until a second meeting on September 28. As it happened, the Toledo garrison was delivered that same day; Franco, acclaimed the savior of heroic defenders, won confirmation from his peers not just as generalissimo but also "Head of the Government of the Spanish State." There can be no doubt that Franco aspired to such control, and the relief of Toledo both enhanced his stature in the Nationalist camp and assured that Madrid would not fall nor the war end before he could gain supremacy among the insurgents.

Franco's elevation and his subsequent ability to maintain unity in the insurgent zone contributed significantly to the eventual Nationalist victory over the internally divided Republicans. The scales were further tipped by the fact that Axis aid to the Nationalists outweighed Soviet assistance to the Republic, which was abandoned by the Western democracies in the name of "nonintervention."

The military rebellion of 1936 arose from the traditional notion among Spanish officers that the army was the ultimate guarantor of civil order and the unitary state, but the aspirations of the political Right—Bourbon monarchists, Carlists, traditional Catholics, and fascist fringe groups like the Falange—were also pinned to the success of the July 18 rising. As a soldier to the core and supreme commander within the insurgency, Franco had no intention of yielding the prospective spoils of victory to a restored monarch or civilian politicians. Nor could he tolerate internal bickering and disunity. In April 1937 he engineered a shrewd solution to the political divisions within the Nationalist camp, decreeing the fusion of the Falange and the Carlists into a single party with the unwieldy name of FET y de las JONS (Falange Española Tradicionalista y de las Juntas de Ofensiva Nacional Sindicalista). Franco himself would be the party chief, and all other rightist political formations would meld into the new single party. Obviously the party could have no coherent ideology, since it comprised the forced amalgamation of two incompatible extremist groups—Carlists and Spanish fascists—who dominated the FET y de las JONS at the expense of the more mainstream right of Bourbon monarchists. Just as clearly, this arrangement suited Franco's interests perfectly since his control of the army made him the only feasible leader for the hybrid party, whose members in turn would never countenance a Bourbon restoration despite strong support for that solution among Franco's officer colleagues.

In the sphere of Nationalist internal politics, then, Franco paved the way toward a postwar single-party state under his personal control. Meanwhile, in his conduct of the war, Franco proceeded to victory through grinding campaigns of attrition. In northern Spain in 1937, and in the subsequent fighting around Madrid and in the east, Franco steadfastly rejected all proposals for a mediated peace and, to the chagrin of his officers and Axis allies, repeatedly failed to seize opportunities for rapid conquest. Paul Preston argues persuasively that this slow road to victory was not merely the result of Franco's shortcomings as a strategist, but that he in fact intended "the total annihilation of the Republic and its supporters." More than a quick decision, the generalissimo wanted to destroy the Republican army in detail and to conduct thorough purges of leftists in conquered regions so that Nationalist triumph would mean the definitive end of "Red" Spain. When the war finally ended in the spring of 1939, by conservative estimate it had cost the lives of 268,500 Spaniards (other respectable computations reach half a million deaths), but resistance had effectively been crushed and Franco emerged as undisputed leader of a shattered nation.

Two complementary but distinct propaganda images of Franco were forged in the course of the war. One is encapsulated in the title caudillo, a Spanish version of the Italian duce or German führer, with similar connotations of the fascist leadership principle. The second envisioned the generalissimo as the leader of a crusade, a reincarnated warrior of the Reconquest, defender of the Catholic faith and Christian Spanish identity against godless leftism—most notably Bolshevism—and secular liberal democracy, the latter hopelessly infected, in Franco's world view, with the contagion of Freemasonry. These images provide a way to understand the perpetuation of Franco's regime for three-and-one-half decades after the Nationalist victory in the Spanish Civil War. Internally, the twin images of the head of state were kept alive throughout Franco's life; as the caudillo and chief of the Movement—as the FET y de las JONS came to be known—Franco could maintain the support of Falangists and party operatives, while the crusader appealed to the more traditional Spanish Right—Catholic conservatives and monarchists of various stripes. Simultaneously, the prestige of the military victor placed Franco largely above partisan sniping from the Right, while his unhesitating recourse to repression quelled any serious opposition threat. As one would expect, the regime's repressive efforts were most vigorous in the immediate postwar era and declined substantially thereafter. Large numbers of executions for political "crimes" continued through 1944, and totaled at least 28,000 (with the regime's enemies providing estimates of up to 200,000). Meanwhile, the prison population, nearly 271,000 in 1939, dropped to about 125,000 by 1942 and to fewer than 30,000 by 1950, according to official statistics. But while the mass punishments of the immediate postwar era dwindled over time, Franco's regime never lost its hard edge. In the dictator's last year, 1975, for example, efforts to repress violent Basque opposition led to 4,625 arrests, and the mortally ill Franco ordered the execution of five convicted revolutionaries on September 27, 1975.

The caudillo image defined Spain's face to the world in the early years of the regime. Placing heavy reliance on his brother-in-law Ramón Serrano Suñer, a Falangist and Axis sympathizer, and aspiring to an honored role in a fascist world order, Franco stayed close to his civil war allies Hitler and Mussolini as the Second World War unfolded. Despite his tilt to the Axis, though, Franco kept Spain officially neutral and restricted his military contribution to the dispatch of the Blue Division of "volunteers" to the Soviet Front. While detractors see dumb luck in Franco's failure to strike an open deal with Hitler, there is much to commend the view that the caudillo was wary, as before 1936, of committing himself too soon to a cause that might fail. In any case as the Allies turned the tide, he retreated into a truer if grudging neutrality. If the war's victors were not entirely convinced by Franco's graceless pirouette—after 1945, Spain was a pariah nation, excluded from the United Nations—they had no appetite for military intervention to overthrow him.

Responding to Allied victory, Franco deemphasized the caudillo to become more fully the crusader. The Falange lost prominence in his postwar cabinets, and, portraying himself as Spain's defender against foreign meddling, Franco turned international denunciations to his internal advantage. Over the next years he worked to curry favor with the Vatican and the United States. In Spain, reanimated Catholic support could make up for the disgruntlement of fascist militants. Franco also had his eye on conservative Catholic opinion in the United States as a potential ally in his campaign to convince Washington that the crusader—a prescient anti-Communist—could be a useful Cold Warrior. His plans were crowned with success in 1953 with the signing of a Concordat Holy See (Vatican) that recognized the regime and conveyed episcopal patronage rights to it in return for reconfessionalization of the state. Weeks later, Franco concluded the Pacts of Madrid with the United States, granting the Americans air and naval bases in Spain in return for aid and, most important, legitimation as a friend of the West. From this bilateral agreement it was a short step to Spanish admission to the United Nations in 1955.

The Pacts of Madrid marked an economic as well as a diplomatic watershed for Franquist Spain. Direct American military and construction expenditure was a boon to a nation grimly impoverished by a destructive conflict, international sanctions, and the regime's disastrous policies of autarky. Washington's imprimatur also attracted foreign investment to Spain, where the stabilized dictatorship could offer cheap labor, protection from strikes, and security for foreign assets. Franco seems to have been an economic dullard, but from the late 1950s at least he turned the management of internal development over to ministerial technocrats, many of them tied to the Catholic lay fraternity Opus Dei, and these men guided the so-called Spanish economic miracle of the 1960s. Impressive rates of industrial growth and a sizable improvement in personal income were accompanied by an ill-managed migration to the cities. Rapidly sprouting slums overstressed urban infrastructure, while much of the Mediterranean coast was disfigured by resorts hastily developed to serve the tourist boom of the regime's final decade.

Rising prosperity moderated popular discontent with the sclerotic regime of Franco's final years but could not squelch a dissatisfaction manifested in mounting labor turmoil, eruption of Basque separatist violence, clandestine growth of leftist political opposition, and, widely discernible in the popular culture, a sardonic disdain for Franquism's myths, values, and protagonists. Outside the so-called bunker of the regime's diehards, there seems to have been little expectation that Franquism could outlive Franco. Having avoided a commitment about the succession for over thirty years, the dictator in 1969 chose the option of a belated Bourbon restoration by recognizing Prince Juan Carlos as his eventual successor. Franco entrusted considerable power to Admiral Luis Carrero Blanco, perhaps envisioning him as the Franquist backbone of the successor monarchy, but the admiral's 1973 assassination by Basque terrorists ended the last realistic chance for a continuation of dictatorship. On November 20, 1975, thousands of Spaniards toasted Franco's death (after a prolonged agony) with champagne carefully hoarded for the occasion; within fourteen months, a negotiated opening to democracy paved the way to free elections and the total dismantling of the Franquist apparatus.

Evaluating Franco's place in history is difficult because of the partisanship that pervades the study of his life and times. His enemies (whose loathing for the dictator is understandable and perhaps commendable) have not been satisfied to disapprove of his actions but often insist that his undeniable accomplishments—leading the Nationalist victory and ruling Spain without serious opposition for nearly forty years—were owed entirely to blind luck and not at all to skill or shrewdness. His sympathizers, their numbers by no means confined to the geriatric veterans of the "bunker," are not content merely to praise the caudillo-crusader for his military and political prowess and the "values" of his regime, but insist that he deserves credit for the astounding rebirth of Spain as a vibrant and prosperous democracy since 1977. Egoist that he was, it seems unlikely that the generalissimo would care to take responsibility for developments that amount to an utter repudiation of his life's work.

It is perhaps more just to see Franco for what he incontrovertibly was, a skilled and cruel soldier and a master of authoritarian politics, and to recognize that as time passes his era will likely be perceived as an historical parenthesis, bracketed not by achievements but by failures. In the Spanish Civil War, Franco engineered the destruction of a failing experiment in democracy, but despite all his recourse to violence and propaganda, despite a succession of powerful friends in Rome, Berlin, and Washington, and despite his remarkable personal persistence, the dictator could not breathe lasting life into the hierarchical and obscurantist "eternal" Spain that was the desideratum of the Right.

BIBLIOGRAPHY

Bennassar, Bartolomé. *Franco.* Paris: Perrin, 1995.

Boor, Jakin (pseudonym of Francisco Franco). *Masonería.* Madrid: privately printed, 1952.

Carr, Raymond, and Juan Pablo Fusi Aizpurúa. *Spain: Dictatorship to Democracy.* London: Allen and Unwin, 1981.

Ellwood, Sheelagh. *Franco.* London: Longman, 1994.

Franco Salgado-Araujo, Francisco. *Mis conversaciones privadas con Franco.* Barcelona: Planeta, 1976.

Fusi Aizpurúa, Juan Pablo. *Franco.* Madrid: El País, 1985.

Payne, Stanley. *The Franco Regime, 1936–1975.* Madison: University of Wisconsin Press, 1987.

Preston, Paul. *Franco: A Biography.* London: HarperCollins, 1993.

Suárez Fernández, Luis. *Francisco Franco y su tiempo.* 8 Vols. Madrid: Ed. Fundación Nacional Francisco Franco, 1984.

James M. Boyden

Franco-German Brigade/Corps

Franco-German military cooperation started in the mid-1950s with agreements for joint licensed production of aircraft. On January 22, 1963, West German Chancellor Konrad Adenauer and French President Charles de Gaulle signed a friendship treaty that contained provisions for cooperation in security matters. From these beginnings the French and the Germans sought to overcome their long history of animosity by inching closer together on security issues. Although the French withdrew from the NATO unified command in 1966, they signed an agreement with the Germans on December 21, 1966, for the continued stationing of French forces on German soil.

In the summer of 1987 both governments agreed to establish a joint brigade numbering some 4,200 German and French troops. Officially activated on December 12 of that year, the Franco-German Brigade held a special status in both armies, belonging neither to the West German Field Forces nor to the French First Army. The German units in the brigade were not withdrawn from the

NATO force structure but rather came from the German Territorial Command. Initially, the German units came from Fifty-Fifth Home Defense Brigade, which was disbanded as a headquarters, and the Franco-German Brigade assumed the territorial defense mission of the Fifty-Fifth Brigade.

The headquarters of the Franco-German Brigade was first established in Boblingen, south of Stuttgart. Its first commander was French Brigadier General Jean-Pierre Sengeisen. A few years later the headquarters relocated to Müllheim, between Freiburg and the Swiss border. Command of the brigade rotates every two years between a German and a French general.

The brigade's French units consisted of a reconnaissance company, the 110th Infantry Regiment, and the Third Hussar Regiment, armed with AMX-10RC light, wheeled tanks. The German units were the 552nd Light Infantry Battalion, the 555th Field Artillery Battalion, the 553rd Heavy Anti-tank Company, and an engineer company. The brigade's headquarters company and support battalion are mixed organizations. All the brigade's units are stationed within the German state of Baden-Württemberg.

The brigade became fully operational just as the Cold War was ending. This immediately threw its territorial defense mission into question. Initially there was some discussion of giving the unit a rapid-response-force role for out-of-area missions. There was some logic to this because the brigade was equipped predominantly with lighter armored vehicles. The brigade did not, however, have the necessary organic mobility necessary for such a mission. Another problem was the German constitutional restriction against the use of its forces outside NATO territory.

Originally touted as a test for binational integration, the individual units of the Franco-German Brigade remained wedded to the equipment, tactics, organization, and administrative procedure of their parent armies. True integration occurred only at the level of the headquarters, and many observers felt that a brigade was too low an organizational level for such integration to be effective.

In October 1991, Paris and Bonn went a step further by announcing the formation of a Franco-German Corps, which, like the Franco-German Brigade, would be outside the NATO force structure. Although the new corps would ultimately absorb the Franco-German Brigade, there would be no additional attempts to create integrated units at such a low level. Essentially, the 35,000–40,000-person corps consisted of one French division, the First Armored, and one German division, the Tenth Panzergrenadier. Both divisions were stationed in Germany, but the corps

headquarters was located in the French city of Strasbourg. With the establishment of an integrated corps headquarters, German soldiers were stationed on French soil for the first time since World War II.

The creation of the Franco-German Corps caused no little consternation within NATO. The Americans and British saw it as a French ploy to establish a European security structure that excluded the United States. The Germans, on the other hand, insisted that the German units earmarked for the new corps would remain "dual-hatted" under NATO, and, moreover, the corps itself would be available for NATO contingencies. Thus, the Germans saw the Franco-German Corps and the Franco-German Brigade as a means to bring the French army back into the NATO unified command through the back door. The French, for their part, started referring to the organization as the Eurocorps, and invited other nations to participate.

BIBLIOGRAPHY

Feld, Werner J. "International Implications of the Joint Franco-German Brigade." *Military Review* (February 1990): 2–11.

Foster, Edward. "The Franco-German Corps: A Theological Debate?" *RUSI Journal* (August 1992): 63–67.

Johnsen, William T, and Thomas-Durell Young. "Franco-German Security Accommodation: Agreeing to Disagree." *Strategic Review* (Winter 1993): 7–17.

Laird, Robbin, ed. *Strangers and Friends: The Franco-German Security Relationship.* New York: St. Martin's Press, 1989.

von Wolff Metternich, Dominik. "The Franco-German Brigade: A German Perspective." *RUSI Journal* (Autumn 1991): 44–48.

David T. Zabecki

SEE ALSO North Atlantic Treaty Organization

Frankfurt School

Influential school of critical social theory led by the German philosophers Max Horkheimer (1895–1973) and Theodor W. Adorno (1903–69). The independently endowed Institute for Social Research was founded in Frankfurt in 1924 to reexamine Marxist theory in the wake of the division of the socialist movement after World War I and the Russian Revolution. Exiled during the Nazi period, the institute was reestablished as a part of the University of Frankfurt in 1951. The critical theory of the Frankfurt School exercised significant influence on the

New Left that emerged in Germany and other European countries in the 1950s and 1960s.

From its beginnings, the Frankfurt School rejected orthodox Marxism and other closed or deterministic philosophical systems in favor of radical, open-ended, unfinished philosophical critiques of various forms of cultural, political, and ideological domination in twentieth-century societies. Besides Horkheimer and Adorno, leading figures of the Frankfurt School before the war included Friedrich Pollock, Herbert Marcuse, Walter Benjamin, Leo Lowenthal, Erich Fromm, Otto Kirchheimer, and Franz Neumann. Although differing widely in their specific interests, methods, sources, and publications, the intellectuals of the Frankfurt School were committed to the development of a "critical theory" of society that examined its own assumptions and biases in an ongoing process of self-reflection and did not claim a neutrality independent of its social origins and purposes. Its practitioners contrasted critical theory with both metaphysics, which assumes an eternal order of reality, and positivism, which conceals its bias in favor of the given behind a supposedly value-neutral commitment to scientific method and empirical fact. Guided by practical interest in change toward a society that meets all human needs, critical theorists recognized the socially conditioned character of human thought and therefore its lack of finality without thereby abandoning the traditional distinction between truth and error. Though never affiliated with any specific party, the Frankfurt School sought to reinvigorate the critical perspectives of the nondogmatic political Left. Their work, drawing on Kant, Hegel, Freud, and Weber as well as Marx, provided wide-ranging and incisive critiques of fascism, state capitalism, and state socialism as well as of the totalitarian potential in liberal society.

After relocating the institute to New York City in the mid-1930s, Horkheimer and Adorno became increasingly pessimistic about the chances of effecting meaningful emancipatory change in the contemporary age of epidemic conformism and "total administration." Their classical text, *Dialectic of Enlightenment,* written during World War II, expressed their despair at the pervasive effects of reason and rationality instrumentalized in the service of technocratic and bureaucratic control. The modern search for knowledge promised enlightenment and freedom but has produced domination and barbarism as well. The domination of nature and society through science and technology has given rise to a new form of domination of human beings. The impersonal force of technological rationalization now shaped society and held sway over individuals' beliefs and impulses. Culture, they

maintained, has become an "industry" that was managed and controlled to produce the "social cement" for the existing order, encouraging an unreflected affirmation of society and conveying the message always to adapt, submit, and conform.

Returning to Germany at the height of the Cold War in 1950, Adorno and Horkheimer rebuilt the institute and devoted themselves to educating a new generation of German students. Their commitment to Marxism, a function of their belief in the 1920s and 1930s that only revolutionary change could prevent the triumph of fascism, weakened under the changed conditions of the postwar era. Their work, increasingly preoccupied with the protection and extension of individual freedom, reflected their growing skepticism about any positive alternative to the inexorable trend toward scientific-technological rationalization in advanced industrial societies and the consequent loss of personal autonomy. Adorno developed a theory of "negative dialectics"—the title of a book he published in 1966—in which the critical and subversive potential of avant-garde works of art assumed a central importance. Only Marcuse, no longer formally affiliated with the Frankfurt School, retained a vestigial faith in the possibility of revolutionary opposition to the domination of scientific-technological rationality in the "totally administered societies" of East and West. His exhortation to "grand refusal" became a major inspiration for the anti-authoritarian student movement of the 1960s, from which Horkheimer and Adorno quickly disassociated themselves. In the minds particularly of those who opposed the protest movements of the 1960s, however, the generational revolt against "the establishment" and "the system" was strongly linked to the teachings of the Frankfurt School.

With the deaths of Adorno in 1969 and Horkheimer in 1973, a major phase of the Frankfurt School came to a close. But the philosophical tradition of critical theory was carried on by a second generation of thinkers, the most important of whom is Jürgen Habermas. More optimistically than his predecessors, Habermas continued to pursue the philosophical underpinnings of critical theory and explore emancipatory alternatives to the extension of instrumental reason (reason concerned solely with the adequacy of means for the attainment of predetermined ends) and the manipulation of the culture industry. His overriding concern has been to examine and develop the norms of critical and rational discourse and consensus formation in the public sphere under the conditions and procedures of democratic pluralism.

Habermas, who succeeded to Horkheimer's chair in philosophy and sociology at the University of Frankfurt in 1964 and served as director of research at the Max Planck Institute in Starnberg from 1972 to 1981, developed a theory of communicative action that seeks a rational grounding of freedom in argumentative discourse in an ideal speech situation free from domination. While continuing the Frankfurt School's critique of positivist social science, Habermas has defended the Enlightenment tradition against radical "postmodernist" critiques of Western "logocentrism," particularly those of the French "poststructuralists." His work has also focused on broad crisis tendencies intrinsic to the structure of advanced capitalism. As one of Germany's leading public intellectuals, Habermas has been embroiled in a number of political controversies, including the *Historikerstreit* of the 1980s, which pitted German historians and other intellectuals against one another with regard to their interpretations of the Nazi phenomenon.

BIBLIOGRAPHY

Alway, Joan. *Critical Theory and Political Possibilities: Conceptions of Emancipatory Politics in the Works of Horkheimer, Adorno, Marcuse, and Habermas.* Westport, Conn.: Greenwood Press, 1995.

Bottomore, Tom. *The Frankfurt School.* Chichester, U.K.: Ellis Horwood, 1984.

Held, David. *Introduction to Critical Theory: Horkheimer to Habermas.* Berkeley: University of California Press, 1980.

Hoy, David Couzens, and Thomas McCarthy. *Critical Theory.* Cambridge, Mass.: Blackwell, 1994.

Jay, Martin. *Adorno.* Cambridge, Mass.: Harvard University Press, 1984.

———. *The Dialectical Imagination: A History of the Frankfurt School and the Institute of Social Research, 1923–1950.* Berkeley: University of California Press, 1996 (1973).

Wiggershaus, Rolf. *The Frankfurt School: Its History, Theories, and Political Significance.* Cambridge, Mass.: MIT Press, 1994.

Rod Stackelberg

SEE ALSO Adorno, Theodor; Habermas, Jürgen; Germany; Horkheimer, Max; Philosophy; Pollock, Friedrich

Friuli-Venezia Giulia

The Italian region of Friuli-Venezia Giulia borders Slovenia and the Austrian province of Kärnten (Carinthia). The indigenous population of the region is heterogeneous. It includes people speaking not only standard Italian (and Venetian) but also Friulan (a linguistic relative of the Rhaeto-Romansch of Switzerland), Slovene, and isolated dialects of German. The physical borders of the region have been long disputed. Friuli became part of the new united Italy in 1866; the city of Trieste was added after World War I; and the frontiers with Austria and Yugoslavia were resolved only after World War II. There was extensive Slovene partisan activity in the area during World War II, and following the war international arbitration over the frontier lasted until 1954. The "special statute" region of Friuli-Venezia Giulia was finally established only in 1963. Territorial disputes, especially over the city of Trieste and its hinterland, have meant that the region has attracted public controversy and that this international dimension has impacted, frequently negatively, the claims of indigenous peoples to full cultural and social rights. The efforts of both Italy and Yugoslavia to validate their attempts to "Italianize" or "Slavicize" the population, along with the added complexity of Yugoslavia's being a postwar Communist state, channeled and diverted ethnonationalism in the region and especially complicated the struggle for recognition of a separate Friulan cultural and ethnic identity. Electorally, this meant that ethnonationalist parties had to struggle not only to clarify their distinctiveness from Italian "national" parties, which often possessed a strong local base, but also to assert their legitimacy, that they were not proxies for any "disloyalty" or weakness. The Slovenes of the region have been divided between parties of the Left, which won the vast majority of their votes, and the Slovenska Skupnost (Slovene Union), which has more localized goals. The Movimento Friuli and the Lista per Trieste, representing Friulans and inhabitants of Trieste, respectively, have likewise had to struggle hard to establish themselves as both viable and "loyal." The recent rise of the Lega Nord (the Northern League) in this region, as throughout northern Italy, has simplified issues for the last two parties though not as yet for the Slovenes. The collaboration of Friulans and Slovenes with European Union (EU) organizations for "lesser used languages" has, along with the increasing recognition accorded both communities in Italy and with the demise of Yugoslavia, helped to validate their claims. The "deinternationalization" of the border and the political crisis that engulfed Italy after 1992 with the demise of the former dominant parties and the formation of new political alliances offers the best chance in many decades that the various minorities of the region will be allowed to work out their future amicably and with mutual respect.

BIBLIOGRAPHY

Greco, Massimo, and Alberto Bollis. *Carroccio a nord-est.* Trieste: MGS Press, 1994.

Stranj, Pavel. *La communità sommersa.* Trieste: Editoriale Stampa Triestina, 1992.

Mícheál Thompson

Fulbright Scholarships

U.S.-sponsored program for international study and research. U.S. government involvement in international cultural and exchange programs began in 1938 when the State Department established a Division of Cultural Cooperation and an Interdepartmental Committee on Scientific Cooperation. On September 27, 1945, a young Arkansas congressman, James W. Fulbright, introduced a bill "authorizing the use of credits established through the sale of surplus properties abroad for the promotion of international good will through the exchange of students in the fields of education, culture, and science." Against opposition, especially by older congressmen who thought such a program would make its participants forget America and acquire radical ideas, he introduced a second bill in November, similar to the first one, an amendment to the Surplus Property Act that would turn "swords into plowshares" and use a percentage of the surplus property revenue to establish an educational exchange program. The bill was signed by President Truman on August 1, 1946. In 1948 the Fulbright program got underway when thirty-five students and one professor came to the United States and sixty-five Americans ventured overseas.

In 1948 Congress also approved the United States Information and Educational Exchange Act, which authorized the State Department to seek appropriations to pay some dollar expenses of foreign grantees, as well as to carry out academic exchanges in countries with minimal surplus property sales. This responsibility was transferred to the United States Information Agency (USIA) in 1953. Also in 1953 and in 1954 the House and the Senate gave permission to use other foreign currencies owed the United States, most notably from surplus agricultural commodity sales abroad, to finance educational exchange. This was an important step because in some countries surplus property proceeds were already exhausted. In the mid-1950s Congress also authorized the extension of exchanges to additional countries. Finally, in September 1961, the Mutual Educational and Cultural Exchange Act (Fulbright Hays Act) brought together the various pieces of legislation affecting educational exchanges.

At the end of the year the Bureau of Educational and Cultural Affairs was established in the State Department to administer the educational exchange programs. It did so until April 1978, when the bureau was abolished and its programs were transferred to the USIA as part of President Carter's new U.S. International Communication Agency, which reverted to USIA in 1982.

By 1993 there were 130 Fulbright commissions around the world; of these, more than half shared in the costs of the program. The USIA coordinates the Fulbright program with foreign governments and private agencies, either cooperatively with binational commissions in forty-five countries or directly in the eighty-five "noncommission" countries. Binational commissions design and operate Fulbright programs that address the educational needs and resources of both the host country and the United States. Commissions comprise equal numbers of Americans and citizens of the host country, representing both public and private sectors. Under cooperative agreements with the USIA, private organizations such as the Council for International Exchange of Scholars, Institute of International Education, America-Mideast Educational and Training Services, and Latin-American Scholarship Program of American Universities recruit and screen American senior scholars and American students, and monitor Fulbrighters in the United States. In addition, the U.S. Department of Education funds and administers a portion of the Fulbright program that aims to support research and training efforts abroad, focusing on non-Western foreign languages and world area studies. Awards are available to American doctoral candidates and university faculty to conduct research abroad. Short-term grants are available for participation in overseas seminars and workshops. The department also, under separate legislation, supports foreign area studies centers at U.S. universities.

There are approximately 5,000 grants awarded each year for Americans to study, teach, lecture, or conduct research abroad, and for foreign scholars to engage in similar activities in the United States. The presidentially appointed J. William Fulbright Foreign Scholarship Board (formerly Board of Foreign Scholarships) sets policies and has final responsibility for awarding grants. The USIA executes the program through its overseas posts and forty-six bilateral Fulbright commissions established by government agreements. With nearly 200,000 alumni, over 90,000 from the United States and 120,000 from abroad, and hundreds of thousands more who have participated in related programs, the Fulbright program has built goodwill among scholars around the world and has served the national interest. The term "Fulbright Program" encompasses a variety of exchange programs, including several types of individual and institutional grants: U.S. Scholar Program, which sends scholars and professionals to lecture and/or conduct research; Fulbright Student Program for U.S. and foreign graduate students to study and to do research abroad; Visiting Scholar Program and the Scholar in Residence Program; Fulbright Teacher Exchange Program; Hubert H. Humphrey Fellowship Program for midcareer professionals; and the College and University Affiliations Program.

BIBLIOGRAPHY

Arndt, Richard T., and David L. Rubin, eds. *The Fulbright Difference, 1948–1992.* New Brunswick, N.J.: Transaction, 1993.

Gayner, Jeffrey. *The Fulbright Program After 50 Years: From Mutual Understanding to Mutual Support.* Washington, D.C.: Capital Research Center, 1995.

Martin J. Manning

Fyodorov, Boris (1958?–)

Russian investment banker and free-market finance minister, 1993–94. Boris Fyodorov was born in Moscow and received a doctorate in economics from the Moscow Institute of Finance. He worked under Viktor V. Gerashchenko at the Soviet Central Bank from 1980 to 1987. He then joined the influential Soviet Institute for World Economics and International Relations (Imemo). In 1990 he helped to author the radical "500-day Program" for economic reform, which Soviet leader Mikhail S. Gorbachev refused to implement. Following the collapse of the USSR, he worked for a time at the European Bank for Reconstruction and Development and at the World Bank. His wages were not taxed and he bought up high-interest-bearing Russian treasury bills and in the process became wealthy. He and Charles Ryan then founded the investment bank United Financial Group. In December 1992, after Boris Yeltsin was forced to oust Yegor T. Gaidar, the architect of radical free-market reform, he appointed Fyodorov deputy prime minister. On March 27, 1993, Fyodorov became minister of finance and in that post battled with Gerashchenko, head of the central bank and a proponent of increasing the money supply. After resigning on January 27, 1994, Fyodorov attacked Prime Minister Viktor Chernomyrdin as a do-nothing and labeled Gerashchenko as the world's worst banker. Fyodorov complained of "the domination in the Cabinet of the lifeless and illiterate ideology of . . . Red economic managers, which, in a market economy, inevitably dooms the country to collapse and the people to a fall in living standards. 'Ukrainization' has crossed the border of Russia."

On June 18, 1996, there was an attempt on Fyodorov's life. The attack came after he was dismissed as head of the Sports Fund in May and replaced by an associate of Aleksandr Korzhakov the chief of presidential security for Yeltsin from 1991 to July 1996. While Fyodorov was recovering from a shot to his abdomen (the assailant's gun jammed after the first shot) and nine knife wounds, journalist Alexander Minkin attempted to lay the blame for the assault at the feet of a number of President Boris Yeltsin's friends and associates, who according to Minkin were deeply involved in corruption.

Fyodorov in May 1998, after sending Yeltsin a letter in which he criticized the lack of a coherent financial policy, was appointed deputy prime minister in the government of Sergey Kiriyenko and placed in charge of Russia's tax service with the task of directing an aggressive drive to collect taxes. He personally joined the police in raiding tax evaders and launched an effort to collect back taxes from Gazprom, the state natural gas monopoly with close ties to the government and its cronies. Access to export pipelines was denied to four delinquent oil companies, and he threatened to seize the assets of the tax-delinquent United Energy Systems headed by Anatoly B. Chubais.

Fyodorov continued to hold those posts when Yeltsin sacked Kiriyenko in August, and he drew up a program for dealing with Russia's economic crisis. However, when the president was unable to persuade the Duma to accept his reappointment of Chernomyrdin as prime minister, he nominated Yevgeny Primakov as prime minister and dismissed Fyodorov on September 28 from his posts. In response Fyodorov, an ardent advocate of the free market, appealed to the International Monetary Fund not to lend additional funds to Russia unless Primakov's government took decisive steps to develop a market economy in Russia. Fyodorov had wanted to peg the ruble to the dollar, but Primakov made overtures to the Communists, who were at odds with the free-market proponent. Yury Maslyukov, a Communist, was appointed first deputy prime minister and placed in charge of economic issues, and Gerashchenko, responsible for devaluing the ruble in 1994, was returned to the central bank.

BIBLIOGRAPHY

Bohlen, Celestine. "Key Economic Reformer Said to Quit Primakov Government." *New York Times,* September 16, 1998.

Erlanger, Steven. "Russian Reformer Picked as the Finance Minister." *New York Times,* March 27, 1993.

Gordon, Michael R. "Brash Russian Tax Chief Takes on Land of Evasion." *New York Times,* July 4, 1998.

———. "I.M.F. Urged by Russian Not to Give More Aid." *New York Times,* October 1, 1998.

———. "Kremlin Ousts Its Most Outspoken Reformer." *New York Times,* September 29, 1998.

Hockstader, Lee. "Scandal Shrouds Kremlin Figures; Tape Is Said to Reveal Corruption Among Close Yeltsin Associates." *Washington Post,* August 5, 1996.

"Russian Reformer's Words: 'Economic Coup.'" *New York Times,* January 27, 1994.

"Yeltsin Names New Aide." *The Herald* (Glasgow), January 27, 1994.

Bernard Cook

Gadamer, Hans-Georg (1900–)

German philosopher. Hans-Georg Gadamer was born in Marburg in 1900. He studied philosophy and classical philology in Marburg under such renowned professors as Paul Natorp, Nicolai Hartmann, Martin Heidegger, and Paul Friedländer. He completed his doctorate with a dissertation on Plato in 1922, and held university posts in Marburg (1929–37), Leipzig (1938–47), Frankfurt (1947–49), and Heidelberg (1949–68). He retired in 1968. His numerous essays on Greek philosophy, philosophical hermeneutics, language, art, and poetry are gathered in Gadamer's collected works in German, which are projected to fill ten volumes.

Gadamer, along with Paul Ricoeur, the other champion in philosophical hermeneutics, demonstrates that "understanding," the key concept of hermeneutics, is always mediated linguistically and historically. By mobilizing certain arguments in Heidegger's *Being and Time* concerning the "pre"-structure of all understanding, Gadamer rehabilitates the notion of prejudice against its discrimination since the Enlightenment. According to Gadamer it is pre-understanding that makes our encounter with history possible. This indicates the importance of tradition that, together with the different interpretations to which it has been subjected, form a historical continuum. Thus, Gadamer emphasizes the importance of what he called "effective history" that underlies any potential "fusion of horizons" that could be brought about. "Effective history" is Gadamer's response to historical objectivism; it designated the fact that understanding is rooted in its own history, but that we are nevertheless able to understand. "Effective history" is, in fact, the very condition of the possibility of understanding.

This fusion of horizons, however, is not to be understood in terms of the romantic (psychologistic) approach of nineteenth-century hermeneutics, such as that of Friedrich Schleiermacher. In other words, the fusion of horizons is not to be conceived of as a collapse of historical distance by promoting "empathy" with the mental dispositions and worlds of the authors of the traditional texts being interpreted.

In his 1960 opus magnum, *Truth and Method,* Gadamer's elaboration of a philosophical hermeneutics with claims to universality avoids the Scylla of Enlightenment and the Charybdis of romanticism. However, he also criticized Wilhelm Dilthey's application of a methodology somehow derived from the natural sciences to the historical or human sciences (*Geisteswissenschaften*). For Gadamer, there is a gap (already expressed in the title of his book) between the transmission of culture and the understanding of ourselves as human beings, a gap that he saw all too often falsely closed by positivistic methodologies.

Finally, it is in Gadamer's version of philosophical hermeneutics that language acquires a prominent and central place. Informed by reflections on language by the later Heidegger, Gadamer stressed the role and function of linguisticality (*Sprachlichkeit*) in our encounters with tradition and with each other. More and more, the notion of "dialogue" comes to the fore, a notion that Gadamer tested not only with regard to poetry but also in the context of encounters and conversation with other philosophical theories.

BIBLIOGRAPHY

Bullock, Jeffrey Francis. *Preaching with a Cupped Ear: Hans-Georg Gadamer's Philosophical Hermeneutics as Postmodern Wor(l)d.* New York: P. Lang, 1999.

Gadamer, Hans Georg. *Hans-Georg Gadamer on Education, Poetry, and History: Applied Hermeneutics.* Albany: State University of New York Press, 1992.

How, Alan. *The Habermas-Gadamer Debate and the Nature of the Social: Back to Bedrock.* Brookfield, Vt.: Avebury, 1995.

Kogler, Hans-Herbert. *The Power of Dialogue: Critical Hermeneutics after Gadamer and Foucault.* Cambridge, Mass.: MIT Press, 1996.

Wachterhauser, Brice R. *Beyond Being: Gadamer's Postplatonic Hermeneutical Ontology.* Evanston, Ill.: Northwestern University Press, 1999.

Erik Vogt

Gagauz

Turkic ethnic group living mainly in Moldova and southwestern Ukraine, in the historic region of Bessarabia. The 1989 Soviet census reported 197,768 Gagauzi in the Soviet Union, of whom 153,458 (78 percent) lived in Moldova. Smaller communities are scattered throughout Romania, Bulgaria, Turkey, and Greece. The Gagauz (Romanian, Gagauzi, Turkish, Gagauzlar) are traditionally Orthodox Christians whose ancestral language is part of the southwest division of Turkic languages; in its spoken form the language is very similar to Anatolian Turkish but with many Slavic, especially Bulgarian and Russian, influences. Although their precise ethnic origin is the subject of considerable debate, most scholars agree that the Gagauzi migrated to Bessarabia from Bulgaria in the late-eighteenth and early-nineteenth centuries. In the late 1980s the Gagauzi in Moldova began to demand greater control over local resources as well as increased attention to education, culture, and infrastructure in the poor and arid Gagauz regions in the south of the republic. Local Gagauz elites declared a separate Gagauz Autonomous Soviet Socialist Republic on August 19, 1990, and the relationship between the Moldovan authorities and the Gagauzi was extremely tense over the next several years, with the Gagauzi often cooperating with separatists in Transnistria in eastern Moldova. In 1995, however, the Gagauzi were given their own autonomous territorial unit within Moldova, Gagauz Yeri (literally, Gagauz land) with a locally elected executive and legislature and local control over education, trade, and other spheres.

BIBLIOGRAPHY

Gradeshliev, Ivan. *Gagauzite.* Dobrich, Moldava: Izdatelska kushta Liudmil Beshkov, 1994.

Güngör, Harun, and Mustafa Argunsah. *Gagauz Tükleri: tarih, dil, folklor ve halk edebiyati.* Ankara: Kültür Bakanligi, 1991.

King, Charles. "Minorities Policy in the Post-Soviet Republics: The Case of the Gagauzi." *Ethnic and Racial Studies* 20, no. 4 (1997): 738–56.

Kuroglo, S. S., and M. V. Marunevich. *Sotsialisticheskie preobrazovaniia v byte i kul'ture gagauzskogo naseleniia MSSR.* Chisinau, Moldova: Stiinta, 1983.

Charles King

SEE ALSO Moldava, Republic of

Gaidar, Yegor (1956–)

Russian politician and proponent of free-market economic reform. Yegor Timurovich Gaidar was born in Moscow in 1956, the grandson of Russian revolutionary Arkady Petrovich Gaidar. He worked as a journalist at the Soviet Communist Party newspaper *Pravda* and the magazine *Komunist* before joining the Institute of Economic Policy of the Soviet Academy of Economic Sciences, of which he became the director in 1990. In 1991 he was appointed vice premier of the Russian Republic, and in early 1992 he was promoted to first vice premier and finance minister. He was the architect of a radical free-market program of economic transformation. When he lifted most price controls, a serious wave of inflation was unleashed. He nevertheless remained committed to the "shock therapy." In June 1992 he was appointed acting premier, becoming the first prime minister of the Russian Republic under President Boris Yeltsin, but in December he was forced from office when the Communist-dominated Congress of People's Deputies refused to ratify his nomination. Yeltsin appointed Soviet-era manager Viktor Chernomyrdin to replace him.

In September 1993 Gaidar was again appointed minister of economics but resigned in January 1994, owing to his frustration with the opposition of Prime Minister Chernomyrdin to his free-market reform policy.

Bernard Cook

Gaitskell, Hugh Todd Naylor (1906–63)

Politician and leader of the British Labour Party, 1955–63. A university lecturer in political economy at Oxford, Hugh Gaitskell entered politics in 1935. During World War II he held a number of administrative posts and under the postwar Labour government rose to become chancellor of the exchequer in 1950. Committed to social reform through nationalization of key industries, he nonetheless embraced the tactics of piecemeal improvement and gradual change. His budget of 1950 also demonstrated his acceptance of political necessities; it placed charges on certain prescriptions to fund a rearmament program supporting British participation in the Korean War. Upon assuming the Labour Party's leadership in 1955, Gaitskell embraced the revisionist proposals of such future party leaders as Anthony Crosland, Denis Healey, and Roy Jenkins. They argued that a combination of government and private enterprise had not only replaced the socialist goal of public ownership but also provided the key to the future elimination of poverty and the attainment of social equality. Following Labour's defeat in the general election of 1959, Gaitskell argued that the party's viability depended on the modification of its traditional commitments to the nationalization of the means of production, distribution, and exchange, embodied in Clause IV of the party's constitution. The ultimate rejection of his proposal underlined the Labour Party's ideological divisions and revealed the limitations of Gaitskell's leadership. Although he possessed a gregarious manner, Gaitskell's precise and rational approach to problems often aggravated disagreements. His ultimately successful opposition to left-wing efforts to commit the party to unilateral nuclear disarmament in 1960–61 further illustrated the split between the traditional socialists and the pragmatic leadership of the next generation. His opposition to British entry into the European Community (EC) in 1961–62 helped him make peace with the traditional left wing but also showed his leadership to be transitional, fluctuating between the state-ownership socialism of the traditionalists and the mixed-economy pragmatism that was to dominate the party throughout the 1960s and 1970s.

BIBLIOGRAPHY

McDermott, Geoffrey. *Leader Lost: A Biography of Hugh Gaitskell.* London: Frewin, 1972.

Rodgers, W. T., ed. *Hugh Gaitskell, 1906–1963.* London: Thames and Hudson, 1964.

Williams, Philip. *Hugh Gaitskell.* Oxford: Oxford University Press, 1982.

Robert D. McJimsey

SEE ALSO Crosland, Anthony; Jenkins, Roy

Galicia

Region of Spain consisting of the provinces of Lugo, La Coruña, Pontevedra, and Orense. With an area of 11,154 square miles (29.575 sq km), its population was estimated to be 2,812,962 in 1997. Situated in the northwestern-most corner of Spain, Galicia is bordered by Portugal to the south, the Atlantic Ocean to the west, the Bay of Biscay to the north, and the region of Asturias to the east. Historically, fishing and agriculture have dominated the Galician economy; however, as of 1997 the Galician provincial government described its workforce as 45 percent service-oriented, 19 percent industrial, 18.5 percent agricultural, and 14 percent construction and fishing.

Galicia has been defined for much of its history by its Celtic identity and its pilgrimage center, Santiago de Compostela. In the post–World War II era, Galician identity politics and land reform have shaped the region. Though Francisco Franco was a native of Galicia, he was equally punitive in his treatment of both leftists and regionalists there. Perhaps as a result, regional identity became associated with leftist parties in what was a traditionally conservative region. Franco's agricultural reforms failed to ease the economic woes of Galicia, and thus the region has suffered a steady exodus of its rural population to Western Europe, Latin America, or Spanish cities, especially Madrid.

Galician regionalism was resurgent in the 1960s and 1970s and autonomy was granted to the region, along with Spain's other regions, by the constitution of 1978. But in the post-Franco era, Galician nationalism has continued to suffer from its association with the Left. Finally, in the elections of 1993, the Galician nationalist bloc moved toward the center and won nearly 20 percent of the regional vote, a significant accomplishment in a conservative region.

BIBLIOGRAPHY

Beramendi, Justo G. *O nacionalismo galego.* 2nd ed. Vigo, Spain: Ediciones a Nosa Terra, 1996.

Garcia Perez, Basilio. *O nacionalismo galego e o futuro do nacionalismo.* Pontevedra, Spain Ediciones "O Gato da Moureira". 1996.

Maiz Suarez, Ramon. *A idea de nacion.* Vigo, Spain: Ediciones Xerais de Galicia, 1997.

Stephen P. James

SEE ALSO Spain

Gamsakhurdia, Zviad (1936–93)

First president of the Republic of Georgia. Zviad Gamsakhurdia, a Mingrelian, was the son of Georgia's most imminent novelist, Konstantin Gamsakhurdia. Gamsakhurdia was himself an author, professor, and translator of Shakespeare and T.S. Eliot. A romantic nationalist dissident, he was first arrested when he was seventeen. With Merab Kostava, Gamsakhurdia founded the Georgian branch of Helsinki Watch in 1975. They were arrested in

1977. While Kostava served a twelve-year sentence, Gamsakhurdia, after incarceration in a psychiatric ward, was released following a humiliating recantation on All-Union television. Kostava after his release, to the dismay of many dissidents, again began working with Gamsakhurdia. They decided to pursue a radical nationalist course that led to war and disaster. There were ethnic clashes in the Azerbaijani districts of Marneuli and Dmanisi to the south of Tbilisi (Russian, Tiflis) in July 1989. Subsequent clashes later that month in Abkhazia caused fourteen deaths and served as the opening act of a scenario that would lead to full-scale warfare. However, it would be Gamsakhurdia rather than Kostava who would attempt to lead the "cleansing" campaign. Kostava was killed in a mysterious automobile wreck in October 1989, but Gamsakhurdia led the Round Table-Free Georgia, a coalition of the major political parties, to victory in the October 1990 elections.

In the May 26, 1991, presidential election Gamsakhurdia won 86.5 percent of the vote. In second place was Valerian Advadze, who asserted that Gamsakhurdia was intent on establishing a personal dictatorship. Though by December many would agree with Advadze, in May Gamsakhurdia received only 7.6 percent of the vote. Because of his authoritarian proclivities, however, Gamsakhurdia alienated many earlier supporters. This apparently benevolent attitude toward the August coup against Mikhail Gorbachev in the Soviet Union led to a break with Prime Minister Tengiz Sigura and Foreign Minister Gyorghi Khoshtaria. Gamsakhurdia in the aftermath of the coup dismissed both. When demonstrators massed in Tbilisi to oppose their ouster, Gamsakhurdia ordered the National Guard to fire. When he directed Tengiz Kitovani, commander of the guard, to repress further demonstrations with fire, Kitovani refused. Gamsakhurdia ordered his dismissal but Kitovani refused to accept the order. Meanwhile fighting had erupted in South Ossetia after Gamsakhurdia revoked its autonomous status. As more and more members of the government coalition defected, Gamsakhurdia jailed Georgi Chanturia, head of the National Democratic Party, and warlord Dzhaba Ioseliani, accusing both of consorting with Eduard Shevardnadze, the former foreign minister of the USSR who would eventually replace Gamsakhurdia. Mass demonstrations were organized to force Gamsakhurdia to resign, but he retreated to the parliament building as Tbilisi was gripped by turmoil for three months. Full-scale fighting broke out in December, and Gamsakhurdia had to flee on January 6, 1992. His escape took him to Armenia, but he eventually sought refuge in the Chechen capital of Grozny.

After the victory of the Abkhazians Gamsakhurdia returned to Mingrelia and his forces seemed ready to march on Tiblisi and restore him to power. But Shevardnadze, who had fled Sukhumi during the conflict in Abkhazia, submitted to Russian protection. The Russians with Georgia in their pocket routed the Zviadists in Mingrelia, in northwest Georgia next to Abkhazia. Gamsakhurdia at this point died. He reputedly committed suicide in Grozny, after having been surrounded by Georgian forces. But his wife asserted that Shevardnadze had infiltrated agents into his bodyguard who killed him in Mingrelia.

BIBLIOGRAPHY

Montefiore, Simon Sebag. "Zivad." *New Republic* vol. 210 (February 21, 1994) 8:9.

Shoemaker, M. Wesley. *Russia, Eurasian States, and Eastern Europe 1994.* Harpers Ferry, W.V.: Stryker-Post, 1994.

Bernard Cook

SEE ALSO Abkhazia; Georgia; Shevardnadze, Eduard

Gardini, Raul (1933–93)

Leader of the Ferruzzi family's vast industrial empire, he came to represent the "New Italy" of the 1980s.

Raul Gardini grew up in Ravenna in Italy's Romagna region. Though known as Il Contadino (the Peasant), Gardini came from a landowning family. He married grain mogul Serafino Ferruzzi's daughter Idina after having worked for Ferruzzi's company for several years. Following Ferruzzi's death in 1979 Gardini inherited his company and fortune. Under Gardini's leadership during the 1980s, the Ferruzzi company grew to become Italy's second-largest company after FIAT. Gardini took control of the chemical and pharmaceutical company Montedison in 1987. He then forged an alliance with ENI, Italy's main oil company, to create Enimont. Gardini forged these ventures largely outside the realm of the Salotto Buono, a group of Italy's long-standing industrial leaders, but the Enimont deal was problematic for Gardini. There were rumors that officials had been paid off to secure the initial venture. When ENI bought Gardini's stake in the company in 1990 at seemingly inflated prices, an investigation led to the discovery of a vast payoff network. Among other violations, Gardini is alleged to have paid $140 million to party officials to have the government buy out his Enimont shares. Five Ferruzzi executives were indicated on corruption charges. Yet it was not until Gardini's successor at Montedison, Giuseppe Garofano, revealed the details of Gardini's involvement in the bribery scheme that a warrant was issued for his arrest. Rather than face the embarrassment of a trial and imprisonment, Gardini shot himself in his Milan palazzo on July 23, 1993.

BIBLIOGRAPHY

Kramer, Jane. "Dirty Hands." *The New Yorker* 70 (1994):70–76.

Moody, John. "Death Before Disgrace." *Time* 142 (1993):39.

Turani, Giuseppe, and Delfina Rattazzi. *Raul Gardini.* Milan: Rizzoli, 1991.

Wendy A. Pojmann

SEE ALSO Italy

GATT

See General Agreement on Tariffs and Trade

Gelli, Licio (1919–)

Licio Gelli, leader, or as he was called, "venerable master," of the secret Masonic lodge Propaganda 2 (P2), was born in Pistoia on April 21, 1919. A Fascist sympathizer and active member of the party during Mussolini's regime, Gelli collaborated with the occupying Germans and served as an SS Oberleutnant (lieutenant) in the H. Göring Panzer Division during the Second World War. As the war drew to a close, he changed sides and collaborated with partisan groups from Pistoia and in particular with members of the Communist Party, thereby saving himself from prosecution and extemporaneous vendetta during the tormented years immediately after the war. In 1963 he joined the main branch of the Italian Freemasons, the Grande Oriente d'Italia di Palazzo Giustiniani.

In 1971, Gelli became the organizational secretary of Propaganda 2, an ancient and prestigious lodge whose members remained secret even to other Masons. Gelli accentuated the secretive character of the lodge and set up a personal administration that was often contrary to Masonic rules. Until 1981, he worked fervently to convince as many politicians, generals, bankers, and editors as possible to join the P2 lodge. In addition to high-ranking politicians and important financiers, he recruited prominent members of the secret services and media. In this way Gelli created a highly efficient system capable of affecting both Italian politics and the Italian economy.

In 1981, during the course of the trial of banker Michele Sindona, the Italian magistracy discovered numerous documents among which were the secret lists of members of Propaganda 2 lodge. The order went out immediately for Gelli's arrest, but he had already fled to Switzerland. When he was eventually arrested in Geneva, he managed shortly afterward to escape to South America.

In 1982, the Italian parliament set up a commission to look into the P2 lodge, and two years later the commission revealed its findings regarding the subversive aims and illegal methods of the lodge and its head.

Gelli turned himself in to Swiss authorities in September 1987. In December 1987 he was convicted by an Italian court of financing right-wing terrorists, and was also under indictment for helping to plot the bombing of the Bologna train station in 1982 that killed 85 people. However, the extradition agreement with Switzerland that brought him back to Italy in February 1988 stipulated that he would not be tried or jailed for political but only crimes. He was tried in 1995, convicted as an accessory to fraudulent bankruptcy, and sentenced to twelve years in prison. When the sentence was confirmed in 1998, Gelli again fled to avoid incarceration, but he was apprehended after four months and jailed. On May 3, 1999, he was released from jail because of poor health.

BIBLIOGRAPHY

Piazzesi, Gianfranco. *Gelli.* Milan: Garzanti, 1983.

Yallop, David. *In God's Name.* London: Cape, 1984.

Aldo Nicosia

SEE ALSO Gladio; Sindona, Michele

General Agreement on Tariffs and Trade (GATT)

Document signed in 1947 by twenty-three nations that agreed to reduce tariffs through multilateral negotiations. Originally GATT was to be a step toward creating a new regulatory body, the International Trade Organization (ITO). However, the 1948 Havana charter, which formally established the ITO, was not ratified by the United States. Thus the GATT document itself became the basis for eight distinct "rounds" of multilateral trade negotiations: Geneva, 1947; Annecy, France, 1949; Torquay, England, 1951; Geneva, 1956; Dillon round, 1960–62; Kennedy round, 1964–67; Tokyo, 1973–79; and Uruguay, 1986–94.

GATT's origins can be traced to the close diplomatic cooperation between the United States and Great Britain during World War II. At the Bretton Woods conference in 1944, American and British officials established a framework for a new international financial system. These officials also hoped to reduce, if not eliminate, tariffs through a process of multilateral negotiations after the war. At the time it was widely believed that the Great Depression and the rise of fascism in the 1930s had been caused at least partly by the high tariffs many countries had adopted to alleviate unemployment. Moreover, at the start of the Cold War, American officials hoped that free trade among the Western nations would help block the spread of Soviet communism.

GATT is often referred to as an international organization, but the document itself provides only a general secretary with sharply limited responsibilities. Nor does GATT provide for effective enforcement. Rather, it simply calls for "joint action" based on a set of common principles that are outlined in GATT and are its only source of diplomatic authority. First, GATT establishes the nondiscrimination, or most favored nation (MFN), principle, which states that any bilateral agreements to reduce tariffs must also apply to all other members of GATT. A second principle is "reciprocity," which means that tariff agreements must be designed to benefit all sides equally. This principle has led to disagreements between the Western powers and developing nations whose economies are at a competitive disadvantage in exports. Third, GATT calls for nontariff barriers, such as import quotas, to be abolished all at once, instead of being reduced gradually through ongoing negotiations. Some countries have circumvented the ban on quotas by agreeing to a voluntary export restraint (VER). Fourth, GATT allows so-called safeguards that enable countries to restrict imports in periods of economic distress or to protect infant industries. Finally, GATT affirms the idea that "commercial considerations," i.e., free-market forces, should take precedence over other national interests. In general, GATT principles are a historic affirmation of free trade as a means to further economic development and world peace.

GATT has been highly successful in reducing world tariffs. The Kennedy and Tokyo rounds each reduced world tariffs by about one-third. By the early 1980s world tariffs were about one-quarter as large as when the GATT was signed in the late 1940s.

In fact, the early rounds were almost exclusively concerned with tariffs. The Kennedy and Tokyo rounds did witness an increasing concern with nontariff issues like export dumping, but it was not until the Uruguay round that nontariff issues assumed a make-or-break importance in the GATT system. The Uruguay round broke new ground in GATT by including talks on emerging markets for services, including financial transactions, intellectual property, and technology transfers.

Even so, nontariff issues have proven much harder to resolve under the GATT framework than tariffs. The

Uruguay round nearly collapsed over the issue of agriculture subsidies, which had been a prime source of tension between the United States and Europe since the 1960s. The round was supposed to have been completed in late 1990, but the meeting at which the final agreement was to have been reached broke up over disagreements on agricultural issues.

The Uruguay negotiations were also complicated because 117 nations were involved, and the developing countries were able to demand a more active role than in the past. The Tokyo round had involved 99 countries, but in the final agreement the United States and the European Community (EC) vetoed requests by a number of developing countries for safeguards for emerging industries. By the 1980s, however, the emergence of rapidly developing nations, particularly in Asia, threatened to undermine the GATT system unless these countries were fully represented in the final agreement, and so the Uruguay round was more genuinely multilateral than the previous rounds.

In this context the Uruguay round led to what is perhaps the most significant event in the history of GATT—an agreement to form a new international body, the World Trade Organization (WTO). This came into existence in 1995, with 117 members. The new organization promised to further broaden the GATT agenda on nontariff issues. Even more important, the WTO has genuine enforcement powers; member countries are legally bound by the decisions of arbitration panels that are to be chosen by the WTO itself and not by member countries. But this new system will not eliminate bilateral trade negotiations, since the penalty for violating WTO decisions will be retaliatory trade sanctions imposed by member countries, with WTO blessing, on the offending country.

BIBLIOGRAPHY

Baldwin, Robert. *Trade Policy in a Changing World Economy.* Chicago: University of Chicago Press, 1988.

Low, Patrick. *Trading Free: The GATT and U.S. Trade Policy.* New York: Twentieth Century Fund Press, 1993.

Preeg, Ernest. *Traders in a Brave New World: The Uruguay Round and the Future of the International Trading System.* Chicago: University of Chicago Press, 1995.

Shonfield, Andrew, ed. *International Economic Relations of the Western World, 1959–1971.* Oxford: Oxford University Press, 1976.

Winham, Gilbert. *The Evolution of International Trade Agreements.* Toronto: University of Toronto Press, 1992.

Peter Botticelli

Genscher, Hans-Dietrich (1927–)

German politician and leader of the Free Democratic Party (FDP) from 1974 to 1985. Hans-Dietrich Genscher was born on March 21, 1927, in Reideburg, near Halle. He studied law at the universities of Halle and Leipzig and received a degree from Hamburg University in 1954. In 1946, while still living in the Soviet occupation zone, Genscher entered the Liberal Democratic Party. In 1952 he fled to the Federal Republic of Germany and became a member of the FDP. Genscher started his professional career as an attorney and his political career in Bremen, but as early as 1956 he was engaged by Thomas Dehler, leader of the FDP in Bonn, to work for the FDP parliamentary group in the Bundestag (lower house of parliament). From 1962 to 1964 he was party secretary, and in 1965 he was elected to the Bundestag. During the grand coalition from 1966 to 1969 the FDP was the only opposition party, and Genscher became one

Hans-Dietrich Genscher, leader of the Free Democratic Party (FDP) and foreign minister of West Germany under Chancellor Helmut Schmidt. *Illustration courtesy of the German Information Center.*

of its main spokespersons. In 1968 he was elected one of three deputy party chairmen. In October 1974 he succeeded Walter Scheel as party chairman. Genscher continued in that post until 1985, and was mainly responsible for his party's course. His role in 1982, when the Social Democrat–FDP coalition broke down and a conservative-liberal coalition was formed (the *Wende*), is still in dispute.

From December 1969 until May 1974 in the first and second social liberal ministries under Willy Brandt, Genscher was minister of the interior. After Brandt's resignation, the new chancellor, Helmut Schmidt, assigned Genscher the post of foreign minister and named him vice chancellor. Genscher kept these offices until his voluntary retirement on May 17, 1992.

During his long term in office, Genscher endeavored to ease East-West tensions. Although he advocated a hard line toward Moscow after the Soviet invasion of Afghanistan in 1979, he worked for continuance of the East-West dialogue. It was Genscher who first demanded that the West trust Soviet leader Mikhail Gorbachev. After the fall of East German Communist Party General Secretary Erich Honecker and the opening of the Berlin Wall, Genscher worked for German reunification. He was convinced that this could be achieved only with the consent of the four wartime Allies and of Germany's neighbors and within the context of European integration. Helmut Kohl eventually received most of the credit for German reunification, but Genscher contributed significantly to the process. Mainly because of Genscher's popularity, the FDP was highly successful in the December 1990 parliamentary elections. His hometown, Halle, is in Saxony-Anhalt, and in this federal state the FDP received an exceptional 19.7 percent of the vote.

Genscher has been criticized for his wavering. His reluctance to be tied down led Richard Burt, the U.S. ambassador to Germany from 1985 to 1989, to call him "this slippery man." He was also criticized because of his free-spending policy and his precipitate recognition of Croatia and Slovenia in 1992, after those former Yugoslav republics broke away from the mother country. He has been hailed, however, for his tactical skills, best seen in his handling of the reunification process while making sure that European integration was not halted. Whereas in earlier years Western leaders sometimes viewed his policy of détente toward the East with suspicion, his presence was later seen as the guarantee of stability and continuity in German foreign policy.

BIBLIOGRAPHY

Filmer, Werner, et al. *Hans-Dietrich Genscher.* Rastatt: Moewig bei Ullstein, 1993.

Genscher, Hans-Dietrich. *Unterwegs zur Einheit: Reden und Dokumente aus bewegter Zeit.* Berlin: Siedler, 1991.

Schulze, Helmut R., et al. *Hans-Dietrich Genscher: ein deutscher Außenminister.* Munich: Bertelsmann, 1990.

Anjana Buckow

George II (1890–1947)

King of Greece (1922–24, and 1935–47) whose turbulent reign reflected the struggle between republicans and monarchists in his country.

The eldest son of Constantine I and Sophie of Prussia, George was born at Tatoi, near Athens, on July 19, 1890. When his father was forced out by the Allies in 1917, because of his suspected sympathy for the Central Powers, the well-trained and highly capable George was excluded from the throne because of alleged pro-German sympathies, and his younger brother, Alexander, became king. After Alexander's death in 1920, Constantine was returned to the throne. Two months before the death of Alexander, the victorious Allies had imposed the Treaty of Sevres on Turkey. Greece was awarded the city of Smyrna and the territory around it. The Turks, however, led by Mustapha Keimal, repudiated the treaty and launched a military offensive against the Greeks. A few days after the fall of Smyrna to the Turks in September 1922, the Greek army revolted and Constantine as the scapegoat was forced to abdicate. George II replaced him. Chaos reigned, and after a failed monarchist coup, George left the country in January 1924. Three months later the Greek National Assembly voted to end the monarchy and proclaimed the country a republic. The failure of the republic to achieve stability and support from Britain led to George's return. In October 1935 the conservative Populist Party, supported by the army, restored the monarchy, an act confirmed the following month by a rigged plebiscite. In April 1936 George appointed General Ioannis Metaxas premier. Metaxas soon banned political parties, dissolved parliament, suspended constitutional rights, and strengthened censorship while the king remained a shadowy background figure.

After the German invasion of April 1941, George and his government narrowly escaped and established themselves in Egypt. For the next five years the king lived in exile, moving among Egypt, South Africa, and London, while his government enjoyed recognition without power. To some George II was a symbol of Greek resistance during the German occupation. But Communists and republicans challenged the status of the exiled monarch. After the war republican feelings again threatened his throne, but George was restored in September 1946 by a plebiscite supervised by the Allies. The king returned to Greece to confront a rapidly deteriorating situation. Fighting had broken out in the north the previous May and in the Peloponnisos in November; reconstruction of wartime damage and economic recovery stopped but inflation continued, and the black market flourished. When Britain proved unable to continue to provide support to the conservative cause in Greece, the United States stepped in. In January 1947 an American economic mission arrived to assess Greece's needs; two months later, the Truman Doctrine, which provided military and economic aid to Greece, was announced. Shortly afterward on April 1, 1947, George suddenly died of a heart attack and was succeeded by his brother, Paul.

BIBLIOGRAPHY

Kiste, John Van der. *Kings of the Hellenes.* Dover, N.H.: Alan Sutton, 1994.

Michael of Greece. *The Royal House of Greece.* London: Weidenfeld and Nicolson, 1990.

Martin J. Manning

SEE ALSO Constantine II; Greece: Civil War; Truman Doctrine

George VI (1895–1952)

King of the United Kingdom (1936–1952), successor of Edward VIII, his older brother. King George VI, christened Albert Frederick Arthur George, but known in the family as Bertie, lived in the shadow of his dashing elder brother Edward until he was thrust into the spotlight after the abdication crisis in 1936. Born at Sandringham on December 14, 1895, he grew up under the stern and temperamental eye of his father, George V. His shy and reserved mother, Queen Mary, kept her distance from the children. Bertie's childhood was marked by stammering, gastric disorders, and problems with his knees, all of which followed him into adult life. His education was sporadic at best until he enrolled at the Royal Naval College in 1908, where he finished near the bottom of his class. However, he served in the Royal Navy from 1913 until 1916 and saw action in the battle of Jutland. He was the only British monarch in recent times to have been on active service. The future king rose to the rank of lieutenant, but because of chronic seasickness he was transferred to the nascent Royal Air Force at the close of the war. He received his wings as a certified pilot but as a result of his health problems, he was unable to fly solo. Upon leaving the service he spent a year at Trinity College, Cambridge with his younger brother Henry, where he took varied courses including history, economics, and civics.

After becoming Duke of York in 1920, he became keenly involved in industrial relations and trade unions. He served as president of the Industrial Welfare Society and toured industrial centers, factories, and mines. While serving in this capacity the press nicknamed him the "Industrial Prince" and he was affectionately called "the Foreman" by his brothers. It was also during this time that he fell deeply in love with Lady Elizabeth Bowes-Lyon. They were married on April 26, 1923. They had two daughters: Elizabeth and Margaret. One of the duke's major undertakings during the 1920s was establishing the Duke of York's Camp in New Romney, Kent. The prince made sure that there was an even social mix among the campers between public schools and industrial firms.

The duke of York had greatness thrust upon him after the abdication crisis, when his brother Edward gave up the throne in order to marry the American divorcee Wallis Simpson. He himself was appalled at the idea of succeeding to the throne and also faced public doubts about his ability to be king. He survived the ordeal of his coronation on May 12, 1937, and one of his first acts as king was naming Edward the Duke of Windsor. In 1939 the king and his wife visited Canada and the United States, the first time a reigning British monarch had visited either country. George VI heartily supported Prime Minister Neville Chamberlain and his policy of appeasement because he did not want to see a repeat of the carnage of World War I. However, when war did come in 1939, the royal family stayed in London and symbolized the national spirit by remaining throughout the German bombardment of the capital. Buckingham Palace was hit by several bombs but the royal family was unhurt. At Windsor Castle the gardens turned into crop fields and the king took his turn at the plow.

George VI had a close and cordial wartime relationship with Prime Minister Winston Churchill, and he was disappointed when Labour won the 1945 election.

In November 1947, the king gave his eldest daughter Elizabeth away at her wedding to Prince Phillip Mountbatten of Greece. However, George VI was already experiencing diminished health. In September 1951 he had his left lung removed as a result of cancer. His condition did not improve, and he died in his sleep on February 6, 1952 at the age of 56. He was succeeded by his elder daughter, who assumed the throne as Elizabeth II.

BIBLIOGRAPHY

Bradford, Sarah. *The Reluctant King: The Life & Reign of George VI, 1895–1952*. New York: St. Martin's Press, 1989.

Judd, Denis. *King George VI, 1895–1952*. New York: Franklin Watts, 1983.

Warwick, Christopher. *King George VI & Queen Elizabeth: A Portrait*. New York: Beaufort Books, 1985.

Ziegler, Philip. *Crown and People*. London: Collins, 1978.

David Lilly

SEE ALSO Elizabeth II

Georgia

Independent successor state to the Georgian Soviet Socialist Republic of the former USSR. The Republic of Georgia (Sakartvelos Respublika) consists of 26,831 square miles (69,492 sq km) of Transcaucasian territory. It is surrounded by Russia, Azerbaijan, Armenia, Turkey, and the Black Sea. It is located between the Caucasian Mountains on the north and the Lesser Caucasus on the south; the Surami mountain range runs through the country from the northeast to the southwest. The western part of Georgia is humid and subtropically warm. Tobacco, tea, and citrus fruit are intensively cultivated in this region, and Georgia is noted for its wines and cognacs. The eastern part of the country, on the other hand, is dry and continental in character. It is utilized for grazing and the growing of grain, vegetables, and fruit. In 1995, agriculture accounted for 45.2 percent of Georgia's gross domestic product (GDP) and employed 31.9 percent of its work force. Industry made up 20.7 percent of Georgia's GDP and employed 22.8 percent of its workers. The agro-processing industry is its most important industrial sector. Georgia possesses reserves of manganese as well as petroleum, low-grade coal, barite, copper, and silver. The Black Sea port of Batumi is a center for petroleum refining. Georgia, nevertheless, depends on imports of electricity and petroleum from its neighbors for most of its energy needs. Rustavi in the east is an important metallurgical center.

Georgia. *Illustration courtesy of Bernard Cook.*

The population of Georgia in 1996 was approximately 5,361,000. It is currently faced with the de facto independence or autonomy of three of its regions: Abkhazia, Ajaria, and South Ossetia. The Georgians, who speak a non–Indo-European language written in their own script, are mostly Christians. They call themselves Kartveli. The English usage "Georgians" comes from the Turkish *Gurcu* or Russian *Gruziny*. A Georgian state was established in the fourth century B.C. Georgia was conquered by the Mongols in 1236 and later divided into principalities under Turkish and Persian suzerainty. The Persian-controlled principalities were incorporated into the Russian empire in 1801. In 1878, Russia annexed the rest of Georgia from Turkey. An independent Georgian state was established on May 26, 1918, and the Menshevik government of Georgia was recognized by the Russian Bolshevik government in May 1920.

Georgia was invaded by Bolshevik troops in early 1921, and on February 25, 1921, the Georgian Soviet Socialist Republic was proclaimed. Georgia was absorbed into the Transcaucasian Soviet Federative Socialist Republic in December 1922, and on December 22, 1922, the Transcaucasian Republic became a founding member of the USSR. Resistance to the Soviets continued until 1924, when the last uprising was brutally repressed, leading to the execution of 4,000 rebels and the imprisonment of many more. The Georgian SSR became a full Union Republic in 1936, when the Transcaucasian SFSR was disbanded.

The role that Georgians played in the development of the Soviet Union far exceeded the fact that they constituted only 1.4 percent of the Soviet population. The most prominent Soviet Georgians were undoubtedly Joseph Stalin, the Soviet dictator, Lavrenti Beria, the head of the Soviet secret police, and Eduard Shevardnadze, Soviet foreign minister under the last Soviet leader Mikhail Gorbachev. In addition, 3.2 percent of the members of Gorbachev's Congress of Peoples' Deputies and 5.7 percent of the members of the last Supreme Soviet were Georgians.

During the Soviet period the Georgians retained a strong national identity. Their language and script were never suppressed. Georgian, rather than Russian, was the language of instruction through the university system in Soviet Georgia. The Georgians lived physically and spiritually far removed from the center and chose to survive and prosper not by following the rules, but by relying on family and friends and taking advantage of the system. Their attitude toward the Russians was both condescending and contemptuous.

Georgian nationalism and opposition to the perceived threat of Russification was manifested in anti-Russian riots in 1956 and 1978. The 1956 demonstrations, which led to the deaths of several protesters, were prompted by the de-Stalinization campaign begun by Nikita Khrushchev, which was regarded as an affront to Georgia and its native son. The mass demonstrations in 1978 were staged in protest against a perceived weakening of the status of the Georgian language. With Gorbachev's glasnost, the increased freedom of expression led to the formation of groups that focused on linguistic and environmental issues. In November 1988 these groups organized demonstrations against Russification in Georgia. In February 1989, Abkhazians renewed their campaign for secession from Georgia. Demonstrations were organized in Tbilisi to demand the preservation of Georgia's territorial integrity and the restoration of Georgian independence. On the night of April 8–9, 1989, Soviet security forces attacked demonstrators in Tbilisi with spades, clubs, and toxic gas. Twenty people were killed and many more injured. The incident fired anti-Soviet sentiment and exacerbated interethnic conflict.

In November 1989, the Georgian Supreme Soviet (GSS) declared the primacy of Georgian laws over those of the USSR. In February 1990, the GSS asserted that Georgia was "an annexed and occupied country." Since Georgia refused to allow parties limited to one area of the country to participate, many non-ethnic Georgians boycotted the 1990 elections to the GSS. In November 1990, Zviad Gamsakhurdia, whose father, a writer, had romanticized and propagandized Georgian nationality, was elected chairman of the GSS. Georgia was re-named the Republic of Georgia without any reference to Socialist or Soviet, and the 1918 white, black, and carnelian colored flag was proclaimed the official flag. The GSS outlawed the conscription of Georgians into the Soviet armed forces and on January 30, 1991, established a Georgian National Guard.

In March 1991, Georgia refused to participate in the all-Union referendum on the future of the USSR. Against the instructions of the Georgian government polling stations were opened in South Ossetia and Abkhazia. In South Ossetia, 43,950 people voted and only nine opposed the preservation of the USSR. In Abkhazia practically all non-Georgians voted to preserve the USSR. The Georgian government would not take part in negotiations for a new union treaty. On March 31, 1991, a referendum on independence was supported by 93 percent of the 95 percent of the electorate who voted. And on April 9, 1991, the GSS formally restored Georgia's independence.

Gamsakhurdia, a champion of "Georgia for the Georgians," was elected president in direct elections held on May 26, 1991. He received 86.9 percent of the vote, but voting was not held in South Ossetia or Abkhazia. Despite Gamsakhurdia's overwhelming victory, he was ousted by political opponents in January 1992 for his authoritarianism and his reputed sympathy for the attempted Soviet coup in August. Gamsakhurdia had at the time of the coup dismissed Tengiz Kitovani, the head of the Georgian National Guard. Kitovani, as a result, joined the opposition led by Tengiz Sigua, who had resigned as chairman of the Council of Ministers. Opponents of Gamsakhurdia staged demonstrations in September, during which forces loyal to Gamsakhurdia clashed with those loyal to Kitovani. Gamsakhurdia ordered his supporters among the National Guard to fire on demonstrators, and this alienated many who had not yet joined the opposition. However, Gamsakhurdia, supported by the workers and rural people, imposed a state of emergency. Through arrests of opponents and control of the media, Gamsakhurdia appeared to consolidate his position, but his behavior created greater disaffection among the Georgian public and alienated some of his own supporters. The opposition mounted an armed effort in December. Kitovani's men were joined by the paramilitary Mkhedrioni (knights) of the warlord Dzhaba (Jaba) Ioseliani. More than one hundred were killed in the fighting in Tbilisi before Gamsakhurdia fled on January 6, 1992. A Military Council, headed by Kitovania and Ioseliani, which had declared Gamsakhurdia deposed, named Tengiz Sigua (1934–) to temporarily lead the Council of Ministers. This Council sought to gain legitimization and international acceptance of its unconstitutional act by calling upon Eduard Shevardnadze, who had been previously regarded by Georgians as a mere apparatchik but was highly regarded in the West. In March 1992, Shevardnadze, who had served as first secretary of the Georgian Communist Party from 1972 to 1985, returned to Georgia from Russia. He organized the Mshvidoba bloc consisting of former Communist officials, members of the intelligentsia, and those who advanced a center-left politics out of conviction or opportunism. A State Council replaced the Military Council. It had both legislative and executive competence and was composed of fifty representatives of various political groups, including Sigua, Kitovani, and Ioseliani. Shevardnadze was appointed head of the State Council, but was immediately thrown into a struggle with Gamsakhurdia and his supporters in the Mengrelian region of Western Georgia.

Gamsakhurdia's supporters in Abkhazia, the Zviadists, exacerbated the situation by committing acts of violence against their opponents. Shevardnadze attempted to reach an accommodation with the Abkhazians. His Defense Minister, Kitovani, however, using the kidnapping of Georgian officials by Zviadists as an excuse, sent three thousand of his men to Abkhazia. There were clashes with the Abkhaz militia, and Kitovani's National Guardsmen, now joined by paramilitary gangs, committed atrocities. Georgian successes and excesses in Abkhazia turned into an utter rout when Russians provided military support to the Abkhazians.

As the conflict in Abkhazia unfolded there were elections to the Supreme Council (the former Supreme Soviet) on October 11, 1992. The largest bloc in the 235-member legislature was the 29-seat Mshvidoba contingent. Many who voted for former Communists hoped that the Communists might ease the economic hardship that was afflicting most Georgians. In addition, 95 percent of the 75 percent of the electorate who voted, voted at the same time for Shevardnadze as chairman of the legislature. In November the Supreme Council made him chairman of the Council or head of state. Sigua was again chosen chairman of the Council of Ministers. One of Shevardnadze's objectives was to create a new Georgian military that would be controlled by the government. In May 1993, when it was rumored that Kitovani was plotting a coup, Shevardnadze dismissed him as minister of defense and suspended the Council of National Defense and Security. After the legislature rejected a budget proposed by the Council of Ministers, the ministers resigned and Shevardnadze appointed Otar Patsatsia (1929–), a former communist, to head a new cabinet. In mid September, after criticism that he was acting in a dictatorial fashion, Shevardnadze submitted his resignation as head of state. Crowds, however, surrounded the parliament and forced the Supreme Council to refuse his resignation.

At the end of September the Abkhaz routed the Georgians, and in October the Zviadists captured the port city of P'ot'i and the strategic center Samtredia, near K'ut'aisi. With the rail line to Tblisi blocked and the Zviadists advancing, Shevardnadze convinced the Supreme Council to join the Commonwealth of Independent States, the association of independent states of the former Soviet Union organized in 1991 to promote common economic and security interests, in order to gain Russian support. The day after Georgia's submission Russian troops were dispatched. In early November the Zviadists were crushed. On December 31, 1993, Gamsakhurdia reputedly committed suicide after having been surrounded by Georgian forces.

Despite the victory over Gamsakhurdia and the formation by Shevardnadze of a party, the Citizens' Union of Georgia, 1994 was a year of political turmoil, economic hardship, political violence, and escalating lawlessness. Georgia's economy was damaged by the demise of the USSR and by internal conflict. Imports of energy and basic commodities were impeded. The gross domestic product declined by 40 percent in 1993 and an additional 35 percent in 1994. Consumer prices rose by 913.1 percent in 1993 and an additional 7,380 percent in 1994. Much of the population was dependent on humanitarian aid. At the end of 1993, 93 percent of the population was living below the official Georgian poverty level. The number of unemployed and "hidden unemployed" in September 1994 totaled 780,000. Factional rivalries pitted the Ministry of Defense and the Ministry of State Security against each other. Sigua and Kitovani organized a National Liberation Front (NFL) to restore the territorial integrity of the country. In 1994, the United Communist Party was formed. In December of that year, Giorgi Chanturia, leader of the National Democratic Party of Georgia (NDGP), was assassinated. In January 1995, following a private effort by Kitovani and his followers to invade Abkhazia, Kitovani was arrested and the NLF outlawed.

Shevardnadze intensified his efforts to restore civil order. Ioseliani's "Rescue Corps," as the Mkhedrioni had been re-christened, was ordered to turn in its arms. On August 29 there was an attempt to assassinate Shevardnadze as he departed the parliament for the signing ceremony for Georgia's new constitution. He survived the attack and the constitution, which provided for a strong president, was signed on October 17. The office of prime minister was abolished and the cabinet, coordinated by a minister of state, became an advisory body to the president. The country, the name of which was changed from the Republic of Georgia to simply Georgia, was declared to be a unitary state, but the status of Abkhazia and South Ossetia was not defined. Pending the settlement of those issues the parliament was to be unicameral, but after the hoped for settlements with those regions there would be a Council of the Republic and a Senate, representing the constituent elements.

Following the attempted assassination, Igor Giogadze, the minister of state security, was dismissed. He was subsequently named as the chief conspirator but apparently fled to Russia with Temur Khachisvili, his deputy, and Gia Gelashvili, a leader of the Rescue Corps.

The parliamentary and presidential elections of November 1995 reinforced the position of Shevardnadze. He won 75 percent of the vote of the 64 percent of Georgians who voted. His closest competitor was Jumber Patiashvili, former first secretary of the Georgian Communist Party,

but Patiashvili received only 19 percent of the vote. In the concurrent parliamentary election only three parties gained the requisite five percent required for the 150 seats that were to be assigned proportionately. Of the three, Shevardnadze's CUG won 90, the NDPG 31, and the Ajarian leader Aslan Abasidze's All Georgian Union for Revival 25. Zurab Zhvania, the general secretary of the CUG, was elected chairman of the parliament, and Shevardnadze appointed Nikoloz Lekishvili minister of state. The subsequent arrest of Ioseliani and members of his paramilitary criminal force provided the opportunity for the development of political and economic stability. Assassinations ceased and crime abated. In October 1996, Kitovani was sentenced to eight years imprisonment for his attempt in January 1995 to invade Abkhazia. In November Loti Kobalia, the commander of the military units that had supported Gamsakhurdia after his ouster, was sentenced to death and three of his subordinated were sent to prison for fifteen years.

In 1996 the economic improvement that had begun in 1995 continued. In 1995 hyperinflation had ended and structural reforms had been introduced. Although energy shortages persisted and still stifled 45 percent of industrial operations, growth occurred for the first time since 1988. Production grew at a rate of between eight and ten percent, inflation fell to 30 percent per annum, and the lari, the Georgian unit of currency, held its value in relation to the dollar.

However, the Abkhazian issue still remained a sore point. Georgia felt that Russia had not lived up to its agreement to assist Georgia in reasserting its control over Abkhazia and South Ossetia in exchange for establishing four military bases on Georgian soil.

BIBLIOGRAPHY

Batalden, Stephen K., and Sandra L. Batalden. *The Newly Independent States of Eurasia: Handbook of Former Soviet Republics.* Phoenix, AZ: Oryx, 1993.

"Georgia." *The Europa World Year Book.* 1996 London: Europa Publications, 1996. I:1328–1333.

Goldenberg, Suzanne. *Pride of Small Nations: The Caucasus and Post-Soviet Disorder.* London and New Jersey: Zed Books, 1994.

Bernard Cook

SEE ALSO Abkhazia; Ajaria; Chanturia, Georgi (Gia); Gamsakhurdia, Zviad; Ingoroqva, Pavle; Kostava, Merab; Shevardnadze, Eduard; South Ossetia

Mkherioni (Horsemen) Militia

Georgian paramilitary force that played a controversial and violent role in the wars and political instability that very nearly destroyed the Republic of Georgia between 1989 and 1994. Created and thereafter commanded by an extreme anti-Communist and anti-Russian nationalist, Iaba Ioseliani, the Mkherioni (Horsemen) militia was ostensibly set up to help safeguard the territorial integrity of Georgia in the face of separatist armed revolts covertly supported by Russia in the Georgian regions of South Ossetia and Abkhazia. Other than a weak Georgian National Guard (GNG), Georgia had no official armed forces to defend the independence it had formally declared from the Soviet Union in 1991. Even more so than the GNG commanded by Tengiz Kitovani, however, the Mkherioni was never more than a semicriminal gang of a few thousand men intent in the main on profiting from the endemic chaos that had enveloped Georgia by 1991. At that time, Ioseliani, Kitovania, and the then Georgian Premier Tengiz I. Sigua used the unruly paramilitary forces under their nominal control to oust independent Georgia's first elected president, Zviad Gamsakhurdia, in January 1992, when this triumvarate seized power and established a Military Council dominated by the GNG and the Mkherioni. To give their unconstitutional regime some political credibility, its leaders installed former Georgian Communist Party leader and Soviet Foreign Minister Eduard Shevardnadze as the new Georgian president. When, in 1993, Shevardnadze attempted to curb the criminal and other questionable activities of the GNG and the Mkherioni in particular, their leaders turned against him when Sigua quit the ruling State Council.

Acting under a so-called National Liberation Front (NLF), Georgia's warlords then mounted a disastrous attack against the rebel province of Abkhazia in late 1993. Covertly well supplied by Russia, the Abkhaz rebels then drove every ethnic Georgian out of the strategic Black Sea province, which then became de facto independent of government-controlled Georgia. After this fiasco and subsequent warlord intrigues against Shevardnadze, the GNG was brought under official government control, whereas the Mkherioni was banned altogether in February 1994. However, many of its members entered a so-called Rescue Corps, of which Ioseliani remained head. In 1995, when Shevardnadze was attempting to negotiate a way out of the Abkhaz crisis, the Rescue Corps mounted another disastrous raid into Abkhazia. Accused of wrecking these peace talks and later attempting to assassinate Shevardnadze, the Rescue Corps was banned and disarmed by the GNG in late 1995. At the same time, Ioseliani was arrested, thereby dealing a serious blow to former Mkherioni elements. Although no longer the force they once were, these disgruntled elements were later suspected of being behind a number of plots to kill Shevardnadze, es-

pecially after he effected a rapprochement with Russia in 1994–95.

Marko Milivojevic

SEE ALSO Abkhazia; Sigua, Tengiz

Georgiev, Kimon (1882–1969)

Bulgarian politician and statesman. A graduate of the Military School in Sofia, Kimon Georgiev took part in the Balkan Wars (1912, 1913) and World War I, rising to the rank of colonel in the Bulgarian army. An MP in the National Assembly from 1923 to 1931, he became minister of railway transport, post office, and telegraph services in the cabinet of Andrei Lyaptchev (1926–28). Following the foundation of the Zveno Military League, Georgiev became one of its most active members and prominent leaders. After the split in Zveno in January 1934, Georgiev headed its most radical wing and took an active part in the preparation of the coup d'état of May 19, 1934. As prime minister during the authoritarian government established as a result of the coup, he called for the abolition of all political parties and for a renewal of Bulgaria. His unclear vision of the future political and economic development of the country, coupled with his incompatibility with the monarch and the military regime forced on Bulgaria after January 1935, led him into the camp of the democratic forces, represented by the Pladne Group of the Bulgarian Agrarian Union and the Workers Party.

During the years preceding and following World War II he ardently supported the idea of Bulgaria joining the world antifascist bloc. In 1942 he responded enthusiastically to the call of the Bulgarian Workers Party to establish the Fatherland Front, the Bulgarian version of the popular front. Participating actively in the preparation and successful engineering of a new coup d'état on September 9, 1944, Gorgiev headed the first and the second Fatherland Front governments and laid the groundwork for the establishment of the totalitarian state that was to be in existence until 1989. He held posts as chairman of the Committee for Construction and Architecture, deputy prime minister, vice chairman of the National Council of the Fatherland Front, and was also a member of the Presidium of the Bulgarian National Assembly. Winner of the People's Republic of Bulgaria Award (1947), he was consecutively decorated (1952, 1957, 1959, 1962, 1967) with the Georgi Dimitrov Medal for his dedicated and faithful service to the Communist regime.

BIBLIOGRAPHY

Staar, Richard F. *Communist Regimes in Eastern Europe.* Stanford, Calif.: Hoover Institution Press, 1988.

Swain, Geoffry, and Nigel Swain. *Eastern Europe Since 1945.* New York: Macmillan, 1993.

Lydmila Iordanova Dicheva

Georgievski, Ljupco (1966–)

President of the Internal Macedonian Revolutionary Organization–Democratic Party for Macedonian National Unity (IMRO–DPMNU). Ljupco Georgievski's career as a poet was interrupted by his diversion into politics only when a plurality of parties became possible in 1990, with the developing collapse of Yugoslavia. His brand of strident nationalism would have been totally unacceptable during the Communist period, and his descriptions of the Tito era in terms of oppressive dictatorship would certainly have earned him a prison sentence. Nevertheless, his authoritarian methods within his own party are reminiscent of the League of Communists (Yugoslav Communist Party). Georgievski represents in his opposition to the mainstream of Macedonian nationalism one of its major contradictions in that he is highly critical of the tradition of Macedonian autonomism established after 1945 and looks back to the late nineteenth century, when the original IMRO was often openly pro-Bulgarian.

John B. Allcock

Geremek, Bronislaw (1932–)

Polish medievalist and politician. Bronislaw Geremek was born in Warsaw in 1932. After studying at Warsaw University and the École Pratique des Haute Études in Paris, he worked at the Institute of History of the Polish Academy of Sciences. From 1962 to 1965 he was director of the Polish Culture Center in Paris and lectured at the Sorbonne on the history of Poland. Dismissed from the Polish Academy of Sciences in 1985 for political reasons, Geremek regained his post in 1989. He has authored many historical works, including *People of the Margin in Medieval Paris, Mercy and Gallows,* and *The Culture of Medieval Poland.*

Geremek was a member of the Polish United Workers (Communist) Party between 1950 and 1968. He left the party after the Soviet-led Warsaw Pact armies invaded Czechoslovakia in 1968. In 1980 he became a political adviser to the National Committee of Solidarity, the independent trade union that challenged the power of the Communist Party in Poland. At the first national congress of the trade union in Gdansk-Oliwa, he presided over the program group that promoted the idea of "an Autonomous Republic," a democratic state based on independent institutions in all spheres of social life. Interned between December 1981 and December 23, 1982, when General Wojciech Jaruzelski, under Soviet pressure, imposed martial law and outlawed Solidarity, Geremek became an adviser to the Provisional Coordination Committee of Solidarity and then to Lech Wałęsa himself. Arrested again in May 1982, Geremek was amnestied in July. He was a supporter of the so-called Anti-Crisis Pact, a national agreement of all social forces that sought economic reforms and democratization of public life. In 1989, when Jaruzelski agreed to talks with Solidarity as a prelude to its re-legalization, Geremek was chosen copresident of the Round Table talks that led to the elections that ultimately ended the domination of the country by the Communists. An MP since 1989, he led the Parliamentary Constitutional Committee and headed the Foreign Affairs Committee. From 1989 to 1990 Geremek was chairman of the Civic Parliamentary Club, later the Parliamentary Club of the Democratic Union and then the Parliamentary Club of the Union of Freedom. In 1991 he was a candidate for the post of prime minister. His political attitudes can be defined as a mixture of moderate social democracy and liberalism. Following the victory of Solidarity in the fall 1997 elections, Geremek was appointed foreign minister in the center-right government.

BIBLIOGRAPHY

Ascherson, Neal. *The Struggles for Poland.* New York: Random House, 1988.

Perlez, Jane. "Trying to Make the Twain of East and West Meet." *New York Times,* April 17, 1998.

Jaroslaw Tomaszewski

SEE ALSO Jaruzelski, Wojciech

Gerhardsen, Einar (1897–1987)

Social Democratic prime minister of Norway, 1945–51 and 1955–65. After Prime Minister Gro Harlem Brundtland, Einar Gerhardsen has been the most significant Norwegian political leader of the twentieth century. No one has served longer as prime minister in Norway.

Of working-class origin, Gerhardsen became active in the Labor Party early in life, holding key positions in the party in the 1920s and 1930s; he was mayor of Oslo in 1940 and again in 1945. During World War II he was active in the resistance movement. After he was captured by the Germans, he spent much of the war in a concentration camp.

In June 1945 Gerhardsen headed the first postwar Norwegian government. The Labor Party won a majority in the first postwar elections in October 1945, and Gerhardsen formed a new Labor government. This marked a new phase in Norwegian political history, as Gerhardsen was only forty-eight and the average age of his cabinet ministers was less than forty-five, making this the youngest government in Norwegian history.

Gerhardsen was one of the architects of the Norwegian "bridge-building" policy from 1945 to 1949. The idea was to avoid confrontation with either superpower through dampening the strategic rhetoric in the high north. The U.S. State Department described Norwegian bridge building in this way: "Norway has adopted a foreign policy which may be described as being pro-USA and UK to the greatest extent it dares, pro-Soviet to the extent it must, and pro-UN to the greatest extent it can."

Gerhardsen reluctantly led Norwegians into NATO in 1949 in the aftermath of the Soviet-backed coups in Eastern Europe. He resigned for personal reasons in November 1951, understanding that Norway's policies of neutrality and noninvolvement in European affairs needed to be changed. He returned to the prime ministership in 1955 and served until 1965, with a brief time out of office in 1963 when his government was defeated in a no-confidence vote.

Gerhardsen continued to be a moderating influence within the Labor Party, especially during the 1972 debates over Norway's membership in the European Community (EC). While he dominated Norwegian politics, Gerhardsen defined Norway's special NATO membership and opposition to nuclear weapons and foreign basing, which became the cornerstones of postwar Norwegian foreign policy. He guided Norwegian society through the effects of war and into a strong system of social welfare.

BIBLIOGRAPHY

Cole, Wayne S. *Norway and the United States 1905–1955: Two Democracies in Peace and War.* Ames: Iowa State University Press, 1989.

Derry, T. K. *A History of Modern Norway, 1814–1972.* London: Oxford University Press, 1973.

Lundestad, Geir. *America, Scandinavia, and the Cold War, 1945–1949.* New York: Columbia University Press, 1980.

Nyhamar, Jostein. *Einar Gerhardsen 1897–1945.* Oslo: Tiden Norsk Forlag, 1982.

Udgaard, Nils Morten. *Great Power Politics and Norwegian Foreign Policy: A Study of Norway's Foreign Relations, November 1940–February 1948.* Oslo: Universitetsforlaget, 1973.

Bruce Olav Solheim

SEE ALSO Borten, Per; Norway

German Democratic Republic

Regime established in 1949 in the Soviet zone of occupation in Germany. It ceased to exist in October 1990 when the East German states entered the Federal Republic of Germany.

Early in 1946 the Soviets forced the Social Democratic Party (SPD) in their zone of occupied Germany to merge with the Communist Party (KPD) to form the Socialist Unity Party (SED). This plan to take advantage of SPD strength in East Germany was not successful. In the October 1946 elections the new SED won fewer than half the votes in the Soviet zone and far fewer than that in Berlin.

The Soviet occupation authorities then suspended free elections and resorted to "people's congresses." By designating, but not electing, representatives, these provided the illusion of mass support. The SED, other parties, and organizations were joined into the Anti-Fascist Democratic Bloc, which was used as the basis for People's Congresses. The first of these met at the end of 1947. In 1948 a second congress chose a People's Council of four hundred delegates, which appointed a committee to draw up a constitution. In May 1949 a third People's Congress ratified the constitution and elected a new People's Council, or parliament. The constitution, allegedly for all Germany, was held in abeyance pending events in West Germany. After the establishment of the Federal Republic of Germany (BRD), on May 23, 1949, and its official recognition by the Western occupying powers on September 21, 1949, the People's Council on October 7, 1949, declared the constitution in effect. Western powers and the Bonn government refused to extend de jure recognition to the German Democratic Republic (DDR), although the two rival German governments did deal with each other on a de facto basis. The Soviets in recognizing the DDR did not impose any occupational limitations. Moscow assumed that Communist control of the SED and a large Soviet troop presence would be sufficient.

Although the constitution appeared liberal and democratic, it did not provide for separation of powers or judicial review. Also, despite a facade of federalism, the DDR was a unitary state. The lower house, Volkskammer (People's Chamber), dominated the Länderkammer, the upper house, and the states. But it was really the party elite who controlled the government. Contrary to the Four Power agreement on the occupation of Berlin, East Berlin was incorporated into the new state, the capital of which was Pankow, a Berlin suburb.

The hallmark of the regime was centralization. Pankow exerted complete control over the economy, education, even cultural activities. Other parties were permitted, but they were tolerated to broaden support rather than to provide an opposition. All East Germans could vote but no one could vote no, so the only recourse was to cast invalid ballots. As most voting was compulsory and public, the result was a series of near unanimously affirmative votes.

Otto Grotewohl was the first premier of the DDR. As in all Communist states, real authority lay in the party politbureau and its secretary-general, Walter Ulbricht. A dependable Moscow-trained Communist, Ulbricht in 1960 assumed new powers when the presidency was abolished after the death of Wilhelm Pieck. Because of Ulbricht's opposition to the regularization of relations with the BRD, he was replaced by Erich Honecker in 1971.

The DDR's foreign policy mirrored that of the USSR. Moscow forced Pankow to settle the border dispute with Poland. In June 1950 Poland and the DDR recognized the Oder-Neisse line as their permanent boundary. The BRD, the United Kingdom, and the United States all protested this action as contrary to wartime agreements.

The most pressing problem for the new government was rebuilding the economy. This imitated Soviet practice through a series of plans, each of which covered every aspect of the economy. The government instituted a system of productive associations and semiprivate cooperatives in both agriculture and industry, and by 1953 some 85 percent of the economy had been removed from private ownership.

During a July 1952 SED conference party leaders called for speeding up communization. This decision produced widespread public opposition. The death of Soviet leader Stalin in 1953 forced Ulbricht to adopt a "new course." It eased demands of the new plan, shelved the elimination of private enterprise, and lowered quotas. Ulbricht's retreat did not forestall the June 1953 uprising, however, the most spectacular unrest in the history of the DDR.

After the restoration of order, economic recovery in the DDR remained slow. A chief reason was the flight of 3.2 to 3.7 million East Germans to West Germany, where they were immediately eligible for government financial benefits. The only real escape route was from East Berlin to West Berlin. During the 1961 Berlin crisis, increasing numbers of East Germans fled. The DDR responded on August 13 by closing the border and erecting the Berlin Wall. To the leaders of the DDR the Wall was absolutely essential to halt the exodus that had bled off some 20 percent of the population, and they justified their actions as "protective measures" to "end subversive activities," including espionage and a "regular slave traffic."

The Wall in fact stabilized the DDR, reducing the flow of refugees to a trickle. Through 1986 only 4,902 Easterners made it over, under, or through the wall, and only 64 of these escaped in 1986. Data after reunification showed that 588 people died trying to flee East Germany's borders, 172 of these in Berlin. This included 25 border guards. After reunification Honecker was charged with having issued shoot-to-kill orders, but he escaped conviction because of poor health and was granted asylum in Chile, where he died in 1994.

The Wall forced East Germans to live with the regime. Within ten years the DDR had become the Communist bloc's second-, Europe's sixth-, and the world's eighth-largest industrial power. This economic miracle was, in many ways, more impressive than that achieved by the Federal Republic, for at the same time that the United States was pouring in $3 billion in aid to West Germany, the USSR was taking out of the DDR an estimated $20 billion in reparations, including 40 percent of its prewar industrial capacity, and this in a country that was largely agrarian.

The DDR became the world's largest producer of soft coal and lignite and one of the world's largest producers of potassium fertilizer. It was also a major producer of plastics and artificial rubber, as well as cameras and optical goods. It also excelled in shipbuilding and possessed a large state-owned merchant fleet. Few in the West were at the time aware of the high cost of this growth, particularly in pollution.

East Germany's living standard was the highest in the Soviet bloc. Luxuries were available, and by 1970 10 percent of East Germans owned automobiles, versus only 7 percent in the USSR. Many East Germans were reconciled to the regime and proud of what they themselves had accomplished, and they were comfortable with the trade-off of freedom for economic security. There was also a sense of glorification of the German past with its military virtues of discipline, obedience, and courage. Most visitors to the DDR came away convinced that the majority of citizens were loyal to their country and would not leave it permanently, even if this were permitted.

Credit for much of this achievement went to the new attitude of making do that gripped East Germany after the Wall. But it was also the result of the economic decentralization introduced by Ulbricht at the 1963 SED

Party Congress. This "market socialism" included incentives, production of consumer goods, and regulation through supply and demand.

In the early 1980s the DDR had an industrial growth rate averaging 4.5 percent and was the Soviet Union's biggest trading partner. The USSR usually traded goods for goods, and imports of Soviet oil helped ease reliance on lignite and led to the establishment of a petrochemical industry. But the economy was heavily dependent on exports and it lagged in technological developments. By the late 1980s it was apparent that East German goods could not compete with those of the West. Ironically the DDR's second-largest trading partner was West Germany. The BRD allowed tariff-free trade and purchased 10 percent of the DDR's exports. However, by 1989 the DDR had a trade deficit and its economic growth had slowed to 3.4 percent. Gross national product was $155 billion, compared with $870 billion for the BRD.

Most observers did not expect to see the reunification of Germany in their lifetimes, a view undoubtedly shared by East and West German politicians despite all the lip service they paid to it. Soviet leader Mikhail Gorbachev determined its timing. In 1988, Gorbachev renounced the Brezhnev Doctrine, which had asserted the right of the USSR to intervene in "Socialist" states if they were threatened by internal subversion or external aggression, and declared that the Soviet Union would not use force to intervene in the internal affairs of its former satellites. In 1988 Gorbachev renounced the Brezhnev Doctrine and declared that the Soviet Union would not use force to intervene in the internal affairs of its former satellites. This was a death sentence to the Communist regimes of Eastern Europe.

Tensions had been building in the DDR. The regime was clearly uncomfortable with Gorbachev's reform policies of glasnost (openness) and perestroika (restructuring), and sought to reduce their impact as much as possible. In the summer of 1989 the DDR and the other Soviet-bloc countries embarked on increasingly divergent paths. Freedom of expression became the watchword in the USSR, a non-Communist government took power in Poland, and Hungary permitted non-Communist parties to organize. In the DDR there were no official moves toward greater freedom and pluralism. On the contrary, in June the DDR went out of its way to praise the brutal suppression of the Chinese student reform movement and the massacre in Tiananmen Square.

To persist in a course of action opposed to developments among its neighboring states and unpopular with its own people, the DDR needed strong leadership. But in the spring of 1989 Honecker fell ill. He was not seen in public for weeks, and this led to rumors of serious health problems. The decision-making apparatus was paralyzed as Honecker's associates were unwilling to act in his absence. The combination of paralysis at the top and dissatisfaction at the bottom generated a process of dramatic change in East Germany.

In July and August, taking advantage of Hungary's decision to open its border with Austria, thousands of East Germans vacationing in Hungary decided to flee to Austria and from there to West Germany. After travel to Hungary was banned, many sought to leave through Czechoslovakia. By the end of 1989 some four-hundred thousand East Germans, mostly young families and skilled workers, had fled their homeland.

While the flight of refugees was an embarrassment to the East German regime, massive antigovernment demonstrations beginning in October endangered its very existence. In Leipzig more than one-hundred thousand people took to the streets in what became weekly "Monday night" demonstrations. The situation was reminiscent of June 1953, but with a fundamental difference. When Gorbachev was in East Germany for the DDR's fortieth anniversary celebrations on October 7, 1989, he stressed the need for change and made it clear to leaders of the DDR that Soviet troops would not intervene in any conflict between the regime and its people.

Honecker, who had returned to work, was undaunted. Taking Tianamen Square as his model, he ordered the army to be ready to break up the next anticipated Monday night demonstration in Leipzig on October 9, with live ammunition if necessary. Egon Krenz, the Politburo member in charge of its implementation, countermanded this order. Long regarded as Honecker's protégé, Krenz is generally credited with averting a bloodbath. Confronted with ever-larger demonstrations, increasing criticism from leaders of the usually subservient non-Communist parties, and fast-growing new political groups such as New Forum and the Social Democratic Party, the regime now jettisoned its leaders and their policies. In mid-October 1989 the Politburo forced Honecker and other top leaders to resign. Krenz succeeded Honecker as party chief and head of state.

Other changes followed. In early November 1989 the entire Politburo and all members of the East German cabinet resigned. The new prime minister was Hans Modrow, SED chief in Dresden and a longtime advocate of economic and political reforms. On November 9 the new DDR government announced freedom of travel for citizens of the DDR. This meant the end of the Berlin Wall. On the following weekend some two million East Berliners and East Germans visited West Berlin and West Germany for the first time in twenty-eight years.

Any hope that these changes would be sufficient to appease the East Germans were soon shattered. Revelations by the now-free press of widespread corruption and a lavish lifestyle among higher party officials soon led to further personnel and policy changes. Krenz was swept from political power after only forty-eight days in office. His long association with Honecker had made him a political liability.

At a hastily called mid-December special party congress, delegates voted to rename the SED the Party of Democratic Socialism (PDS). A democratically elected executive committee replaced the dictatorial Central Committee and Politburo. On March 18, 1990, East Germany held its first genuinely free elections. The campaign was dominated by parties that were all sister organizations of major West German parties. The Alliance for Germany was the amalgam of three groups closely associated with the West German Christian Democrats. The Social Democratic Party was linked to the West German Social Democrats, and the Union of Free Democrats had the support of the Free Democratic Party. Prominent West German politicians also campaigned throughout the DDR.

Political observers had expected the Social Democrats to lead in the balloting, but the Alliance for Germany was the runaway victor, vigorously supported by West German Chancellor Helmut Kohl. He and the Alliance campaigned on a platform of rapid unification with West Germany. Kohl repeatedly stated that the process would be easy and painless. The Social Democrats favored a go-slow approach to reunification and were hurt by the PDS's siphoning off of left-wing votes. The Alliance gained 48 percent of the popular vote, the Social Democrats 22 percent, and the former SED, now the PDS, came in a poor third, with only 16 percent. Modrow's days as prime minister were clearly numbered. His successor, with a mandate to bring about union with the Federal Republic, was Lothar de Mazière, head of the East German Christian Democrats.

On July 1, 1990, the DDR, by then in dire economic straits, officially agreed to surrender its economic and monetary sovereignty to the BRD. Gorbachev sought to prevent the DDR from joining NATO but gave way to the inevitable and the promise of financial assistance, ostensibly for the relocation of Soviet troops back to the USSR. On October 3, the two Germanies were officially reunited in one state of seventy-eight million people.

BIBLIOGRAPHY
Ardagh, John. *Germany and the Germans: An Anatomy of Society Today.* New York: Harper and Row, 1987.

Childs, David. *The GDR: Moscow's German Ally,* 2d ed. Boston: Unwin Hyman, 1988.

Craig, Gordon. *The Germans.* New York: Putnam, 1982.

Dennis, Mike. *Social and Economic Modernization in Eastern Germany from Honecker to Kohl.* New York: St. Martin's Press, 1993.

Dornberg, John. *The Other Germany.* New York: Doubleday, 1968.

Lippmann, Heinz. *Honecker and the New Politics of Europe.* Tr. by Helen Sebba. New York: Macmillan, 1972.

McAdams, A. James. *Germany Divided: From the Wall to Reunification.* Princeton, N.J.: Princeton University Press, 1993.

Turner, Henry Ashby. *Germany from Partition to Reunification.* New Haven, Conn.: Yale University Press, 1992.

Spencer C. Tucker

SEE ALSO De Maizière, Lothar; Honecker, Erich; Krenz, Egon; Stoph, Willi; Ulbricht, Walter; Wolf, Markus

Human Rights Groups

The most significant form of critical dissent in the Honecker era in the late 1970s materialized within the "alternative political culture," that is, the articulation outside official channels of a series of peace, ecological, human rights, women's, and gay issues. These issues were propagated by individuals and small groups who, owing to the restrictions imposed by the Socialist Unity Party (SED) on autonomous activities in the public domain, were largely confined to the protective space afforded by the Protestant Church. The autonomous groups tended to have a cultural rather than a political-power orientation and favored grassroots democracy. Their activities, together with popular discontent over restrictions on travel, were all aspects of a common theme: denial of human rights. This issue received a powerful boost from Mikhail Gorbachev's accession to power in the USSR and from the attempts to establish a civil society in Poland and Hungary.

A key role in human rights issues was played by the tiny Initiative for Peace and Human Rights (IFM), founded in 1986, which cultivated contacts with dissidents elsewhere in Eastern Europe and deliberately pursued activities outside the restricting confines of the church. Despite the higher profile of the autonomous groups in the later 1980s, they were still located on the periphery of society and had the direct support of only between ten thousand and fifteen thousand activists. Their limited appeal can be attributed to their relatively underdeveloped institutional and communications networks; coercion by the state, including forcible deportation of dissidents to the West; comprehensive surveillance and infiltration by Stasi informers; and the reluctance of ordinary East Germans to run the risk of involvement in politically sensitive issues.

During the fall of 1989, a crucial form of opposition to the SED regime emerged from the chrysalis of the alternative political culture in the shape of small citizens' movements and protopolitical parties such as Democratic Awakening, Democracy Now, New Forum, and the Social Democratic Party. New Forum was the most significant of these groups and its "September Manifesto" attracted two-hundred thousand signatures. Despite some important differences between them, the new opposition groups advocated a democratic, sovereign German Democratic Republic (GDR) based on positive socialist principles.

While the citizens' movements were crucial to the dismantling of SED rule, their idealistic notions of grassroots democracy and many aspects of their economic and ecological policies lacked the powerful appeal of the West German system. Although most of the citizens' movements soon abandoned their goal of an independent GDR, one of them, Democratic Awakening, joined Chancellor Kohl's Alliance for Germany, in the March 1990 Volkskammer (parliamentary) election in the GDR, which proved to be a great disappointment. Alliance 90, comprising New Forum, Democracy Now, and the IFM, scored a mere 2.91 percent of the vote and the electoral pact of the Greens and the Independent Women's Association only 1.97 percent. Other elections in 1990, at local, regional, and national level, brought no significant improvement in the fortunes of these groups.

BIBLIOGRAPHY

Jarausch, Konrad H. *The Rush to German Unity.* New York: Oxford University Press, 1994.

Joppke, Christian. *East German Dissidents and the Revolution of 1989: Social Movements in a Leninist Regime.* London: Macmillan, 1995.

Mike Dennis

SEE ALSO Honecker, Erich

Stasi

Negative term used in the German Democratic Republic (GDR), referring to the Ministry of State Security (Ministerium für Staatssicherheit der DDR), or MfS in official jargon. Officially, the MfS served to protect the GDR against spies and provided an internal control function against sabotage and counterrevolutionary activities. The MfS modeled itself after the Soviet KGB and other Soviet security organs.

Internally the MfS became the most feared instrument of control employed by the leadership in the GDR. Its extensive network of agents worked in all aspects of public and private life. Its arsenal included incarceration in psychiatric clinics, influence over the judicial system, expulsion of political dissidents, and manipulation of promotions and transfers in the workplace. The MfS's unsettling effect on citizens largely sustained the existing political system.

Internationally the MfS served a variety of purposes. It assisted Soviet agencies in developing security instruments in Third World nations. Within West Germany, Stasi agents were involved in the 1950s in hundreds of kidnappings. Stasi agents were also detected among Chancellor Willy Brandt's advisers, within the Department of Defense and later within the West German counterintelligence office in Pullach. In addition, the MfS supported the activities of various individuals and terrorist groups, including the Red Army Faction, Libyan terrorists, the Palestine Liberation Organization (Abu Nidal in particular), and the international terrorist "Carlos." Descriptions of these and other activities were revealed after the collapse of the Communist Regime in East Germany in the MfS's own 112 miles (180 kilometers) of files, one million photographs, and 200,000 tapes of recorded conversations.

The MfS's origins can be traced back to the early postwar years. First, the Soviet Military Administration in Germany organized an independent agency, Dezernat 5, within the East German criminal police devoted to political crimes. On October 7, 1949, the East German Ministry of the Interior was established, and it inherited Dezernat 5, which was now headed by Wilhelm Zaisser. Erich Mielke's Committee for the Protection of Public Property within the German Economic Commission added the second element with the creation of the Ministry of State Security on February 8, 1950. During 1952–53, Zaisser attempted to steer his own course within the GDR. However, when Zaisser attempted to use the 1953 uprising against Walter Ulbricht, Ulbricht countered, calling the MfS to task for failing to root out counterrevolutionary activity that had supposedly been eliminated. Ulbricht worked quickly to end the threat to the party's dominant position. Zaisser's supporters were arrested while Zaisser himself was replaced by Ernst Wollweber, and expelled from the Socialist Unity (Communist) Party. Ulbricht brought the Stasi under closer supervision by raising Wollweber to the level of state secretary within the Ministry of the Interior. In 1955 Ulbricht upgraded the security organ to the ministerial level. During these years the MfS swelled from 8,800 employees to roughly 19,000 by 1961. In light of the uprising in Hungary in 1956, Ulbricht used the MfS to guard the GDR's borders against the spread of so-called counter-revolutionary activities from Hungary.

Army General Mielke succeeded Wollweber in 1957 and directed the MfS until 1989. Under Erich Honecker, the size and scope of the MfS grew. By 1975 it had 75,000 employees. By 1989 its informers constituted an average of one out of every 120 citizens of the GDR, roughly 142,000 individuals adding to the long arm of the Stasi in an unofficial capacity by writing reports about their friends, neighbors, and co-workers. At its peak the Stasi employed 105,000 individuals, including the 11,000 soldiers of the Watch Regiment Felix E. Dzerzhinski. With the opening of the Berlin Wall and the decline of the Socialist Unity Party (SED) in November 1989, the MfS became the Office for National Security (AfNS). Only a month later, the Volkskammer (People's Chamber) ordered the AfNS dissolved.

BIBLIOGRAPHY

Fricke, Karl Wilhelm. *Die DDR-Staatssicherheit.* Cologne: Verlag Wissenschaft und Politik, 1984.

Friedrich, Ebert Stiftung. *Wie wird die DDR-Bürger überwacht?* Bonn: Verlag Neue Gesellschaft, 1984.

Gill, David, and Ulrich Schröter. *Das Ministerium für Staatssicherheit.* Reinbek bei Hamburg: Rowohlt, 1991.

Mitter, Armin, and Stefan Wolle. *Ich liebe euch doch alle!* Berlin: Basis Druck, 1990.

Pechmann, Roland, and Jürgen Vogel. *Abgesang der Stasi.* Braunschweig: Steinwag, 1991.

Schell, Manfred, and Werner Kalinka. *Stasi und sein Ende: Die Personen und Fakten.* Frankfurt am Main: Ullstein, 1991.

David A. Meier

Uprising of 1953

Popular revolt against the Communist regime of the German Democratic Republic (GDR) on June 17, 1953. The uprising had its genesis in the exceptionally harsh Soviet reparations and removal policy following World War II. These required the imposition of ever-increasing production norms on workers by the East German puppet regime headed by Walter Ulbricht and Otto Grotewohl. Until the death of Soviet leader Joseph Stalin in spring of 1953, workers had grimly acquiesced in the mercilessly increasing burdens placed on them. However, a new edict

imposed by the government on May 28, 1953, required a 10 percent increase in production. This portended a significant deterioration in the standard of living and evoked an immediate and profoundly negative reaction among East German workers.

In response to this unprecedented manifestation of opposition, the Council of Ministers of the GDR and the Central Committee of the Socialist Unity Party (SED) admitted on June 11, 1953, that some mistakes had been committed by the government in the past and that some of the criticism being voiced was valid. An attempt was made to defuse the growing wave of open resentment by promising greater availability of small loans to businesses, relaxation of exit visa restrictions for travel to West Germany, and easing of restrictions on religious organizations. But the government grimly insisted on maintaining the 10 percent increase in production, calling it an indispensable weapon in the struggle against Western Cold War ambitions.

In this atmosphere of rapidly growing tension, the spark that touched off the uprising was a deeply sarcastic article appearing on June 16 in the newspaper of the official union. It argued that the workers should stop whining and that more hard work would make them more perfect human beings. The effect was immediate and spontaneous. More than ten thousand demonstrators in East Berlin took to the streets, demanding an immediate apology from Ulbricht and Grotewohl. There was no response from either of them and the growing crowd now demanded the resignation of the government and new elections. A general strike was threatened if these demands were not met. Late that afternoon the government urgently broadcast the revocation of the new production requirements. By then, however, the surging crowds would no longer be placated; government buildings were surrounded, confidential files were thrown from windows, and newsstands selling the hated party paper, *Neues Deutschland,* were set on fire. Sporadic attacks against government offices continued throughout the night.

At dawn on June 17, East Berlin was paralyzed by a general strike. Huge columns of demonstrators moved toward the center of the city, and protest marches spread to all other major cities of the GDR. In response the Soviet garrison in Berlin with its six hundred tanks and fourteen thousand soldiers was placed on high alert. By 1:30 P.M. the Soviet military commander of Berlin realizing that the government of the GDR had slipped into a state of horrified paralysis, declared a state of siege, ordered a stop to all public gatherings, and threatened violators with summary justice according to Soviet military law. Tank columns moving into Berlin and later into other large cities were attacked by demonstrators with their bare hands, cobblestones, and wooden clubs. A number of civilians were machine-gunned or crushed under tank treads. These confrontations were nearly exclusively between Germans and the Soviet occupiers. The East German People's Police had shown themselves reluctant to attack the demonstrators and were ordered back to their barracks. The government of the GDR remained in hiding throughout this day and the following, when nearly all East Germany was involved in riots and attacks on government installations. It took regular Soviet army troops until June 19 to completely suppress the demonstrations by the use of force and massive arrests. According to secret files of the former GDR, first located in March 1994, 125 civilians lost their lives in the uprising, and of that number 41 were killed on June 17 and 18 by summary executions.

To justify their actions, the Soviets and their client government in East Berlin declared that Western reactionary elements led by a West Berliner, Willy Gottling, had exploited the difficult economic situation in the GDR and incited workers to riot against the authorities. Gottling was among those executed in a summary proceeding by the Soviets on June 17, 1953. As the first significant revolt against Communist oppression since the end of World War II, the common people of East Germany forced the regime to drop its mask.

BIBLIOGRAPHY

Baring, Arnulf. *Uprising in East Germany.* Ithaca, N.Y.: Cornell University Press, 1972.

Burant, Stephen. *East Germany: A Country Study,* 3d ed. Washington, D.C.: Government Printing Office, 1988.

Gottlieb, Manuel. *The German Peace Settlement and the Berlin Crisis.* New Brunswick, N.J.: Transaction Publishers, 1960.

McCauley, Martin. *The German Democratic Republic Since 1945.* New York: St. Martin's Press, 1986.

Turner, Henry A. Jr., *The Two Germanies Since 1945: East and West.* New Haven, Conn.: Yale University Press, 1987.

————. *Germany from Partition to Reunification.* New Haven, Conn.: Yale University Press, 1992.

Werner G. C. Voigt

SEE ALSO Ulbricht, Walter

The Collapse

The Berlin Wall came down in the midst of cheerful crowds in November of 1989. In the late 1980s reforms were enacted in Poland, Hungary, and the USSR, with fresh leaders bringing new hope. The East German leaders however, resisted all attempts to relax the hold of the communist state. If the GDR were to lose the ideological foundations, it would lose its legitimacy to exist. Growing reform movements existed in the GDR itself, organized by ordinary citizens and opponents under the protective wings of the church. These movements became more visible after Mikhail Gorbachev began his program of reform in the USSR, despite the efforts of the Stasi (security forces of the GDR) and the police to suppress them.

Gorbachev's new policies led to a general improvement of the relations between the East and West and between the GDR and FRG (Federal Republic of Germany). The general climate of détente led to increasing demands for freedom and reform in the GDR. But Erich Honecker, the leader of the GDR, and his government resisted and called instead for a stronger Warsaw Pact and the retention of the Berlin Wall. The Tiananmen Square massacre in China was used by GDR leaders as a warning to any East German who thought of voicing criticism.

The Evangelical church in East Germany enjoyed a degree of independence, and open discussion could be sustained within the church. Over the years the dialogue between the church and government leaders also grew. The church supported Gorbachev's reform measures in the 1980s and served as a shelter to government opposition. But the church was not able to absorb the growing frustrations of young people in East Germany. Church leaders appealed to the government to let people leave. In the first six months of 1989 more than 125,400 people had formally applied to leave the GDR.

On May 2, 1989, the Hungarian and Austrian governments agreed to open their borders. A growing number of East Germans left via this opening in the summer of 1989 by traveling first to Hungary (which was legal), then crossing into Austria. Hundreds of others jumped the fences of the West German embassies in Eastern Europe and refused to return. On September 11, Hungary suspended its 1956 agreement with the GDR to return East Germans caught escaping.

Attempts to persuade people to stay no longer worked. East German leaders seemed puzzled by the events but were paralyzed. On September 10, 1989, the reform movement Neue Forum (New Forum) was organized to unite all the reform efforts in the GDR. Local chapters met in churches for open discussion of political events. Thus, more demonstrations were encouraged, and in October, massive street protests erupted.

On October 7, 1989, the GDR celebrated its fortieth anniversary. Gorbachev, visiting Berlin, announced in a speech that those who resist change will be left behind.

The masses perceived that as a go-ahead from Moscow to press for reform. Attempting to halt the mass movements, Honecker ordered the use of force to stop a demonstration in Leipzig on October 9. Rumors that the government was planning a violent crackdown were confirmed by the reported movement of tanks and army troops. Nevertheless, 70,000 people took to the streets of Leipzig that evening, and violence was prevented by local party officials. The next Monday, 150,000 people were on the streets, then 200,000, and by November 6, there were more than 500,000.

By then the GDR government was undergoing great changes. Erich Honecker was forced to resign in an attempt to save the GDR. He was replaced by Egon Krenz, who had been groomed for this position. Krenz paid a visit to Moscow on October 31 to meet with Gorbachev, where he declared that the GDR was open to reform as long as the German reunification was not on the agenda.

On November 5, Czechoslovakia opened its border to West Germany. Immediately, thousands of East Germans went to wait in line at the West German embassy in Prague to reach to the West. Many young people in the GDR had lost any hope of reform. A mistaken announcement by the East German Communist Party secretary Günter Schabowski about the easing of travel restrictions was meant to control travel to West Germany and to save the legitimacy of the GDR. Instead, masses of East Germans crossed over to the other side on the night of November 9, 1989. The authorities and the police could only watch, since they had not received orders to stop anyone. The Berlin Wall was breached.

At the time the Wall came down, it became apparent that the government had lost control. Some East Germans then realized that the chances of a real reform of the GDR were slim. Calls for reform were over run by calls for reunification. West German chancellor Helmut Kohl hurried to Berlin to speak to the masses and to thank Gorbachev and Germany's Western allies for their support.

In East Germany, increasing pressure led to the resignation of the entire Politburo and the council of ministers on December 3, and of Egon Krenz on December 6. A new government under Hans Modrow was installed, which lifted all travel restrictions to and from West Germany.

On March 18, 1990, free elections were held in East Germany, and the new government moved quickly with Kohl to effect German unification on October 3.

BIBLIOGRAPHY

Gedmin, Jeffrey. *The Hidden Hand*. Washington, D.C.: The AEI Press, 1992.

Keithly, David M. *The Collapse of East German Communism*. Westport and London: Praeger Publishers, 1992.

McCauley, Martin. "Gorbachev, the GDR and Germany," in *The German Revolution of 1989*. Eds. Gert-Joachim Glaessner and Ian Wallace. Oxford, U.K.: Berg Publishers Limited, 1992.

Naimark, Norman M. "Ich will hier raus: Emigration and the Collapse of the German Democratic Republic," in *Eastern Europe in Revolution*. Ed. by Ivo Banac. Ithaca: Cornell University Press, 1992.

Sybille Reinke de Buitrago

Germany, Federal Republic of

Postwar West German state (Bundesrepublik Deutschland) established in 1949 and expanded to include the states of the former German Democratic Republic (GDR) in 1990. The most populous nation in Europe except Russia, the Federal Republic of Germany (FRG) owes much of its influence in the world to the strength of its economy and the stability of its currency. Its history falls into several stages: The period of military government and the founding of the FRG, 1945–49; the Adenauer era of conservative restoration and reintegration, 1949–63; the ascendancy of the Left, 1963–69; the era of the social-liberal coalition, 1969–82; the neoconservative revival, 1982–89; and reunification in the 1990s.

Germany after unification in 1990. *Illustration courtesy of Bernard Cook.*

The founding of the Federal Republic resulted from the inability of the victorious powers to agree on the form and structure of the German government and economy after World War II. Although wartime plans for the dismemberment of Germany had been rejected by the Big Three (United States, USSR, and United Kingdom), both at the Yalta Conference in February 1945 and at the Potsdam Conference in July–August 1945, no central government was established in Germany after the war. Supreme authority rested with the military commanders of the four occupation zones (American, British, French, Soviet) and the four sectors of Berlin. Their policies and decisions were to be coordinated through an Allied Control Council, formed by the military governors, each of whom possessed a veto. But the divergent social systems of the Western Allies and the Soviet Union made agreement on central governing and administrative institutions for Germany impossible. As the Cold War intensified, the Western Allies quickly moved from a punitive policy toward Germany to a policy of reconstruction. On January 1, 1947, the United States and the United Kingdom joined their occupation zones to form Bizonia, with France merging its zone into what then became Trizonia in early 1948. The Soviet commander walked out of the Allied Control Council in March 1948 to protest the six-power talks among the United States, United Kingdom, France, and the Benelux countries in London on the structure of a future West German state. The introduction of a new currency, the deutsche mark, in the Western zones and Western sectors of Berlin led the Soviets to block Allied road and rail access to Berlin in June 1948 in an effort to prevent the formation of a West German state or, failing that, to force the Western powers out of Berlin. However, the Berlin Blockade only accelerated the formation of a separate West German state. A Parliamentary Council of sixty-five delegates from the individual West German states (Länder) meeting in Bonn, the future capital of the Federal Republic, drew up a provisional constitution known as the Basic Law (*Grundgesetz*) in May 1949. That same month the USSR called off the counterproductive Berlin Blockade, and, after acceptance of the Basic Law by the occupying powers and its ratification by the individual West German Länder (Bavaria, Baden-Württemberg, Rhineland-Palatinate, North Rhine-Westphalia, Lower Saxony, Hesse, Schleswig-Holstein, Hamburg, and Bremen), the Federal Republic of Germany came into being on May 23, 1949.

The adoption of the Basic Law was intended to leave the door open for German reunification under an all-German constitution at some later date. The Basic Law sought to avoid the weaknesses of the Weimar constitution on which it was patterned. To avoid the proliferation of parties in an electoral system in which half the parliamentary deputies are elected by proportional representation, a party that does not win in any constituency has to receive at least 5 percent of the nationwide vote (before 1953 statewide) or receive a direct mandate from at least three electoral districts to enter the Bundestag (lower house of parliament). The Bundesrat (upper chamber composed of delegates of the Länder governments), must approve all legislation affecting the rights of the Länder. To avoid the instability that characterized politics in the Weimar period, Article 67 provides for a "constructive vote of no confidence." The head of government, the chancellor, can be dismissed in midterm only if a majority of Bundestag deputies vote a successor into office. The president serves as head of state but enjoys no special executive powers and is elected indirectly by a special Federal Assembly made up of Bundestag members and Länder delegates. The Parliamentary Council adopted the black-red-gold colors of the 1848 revolutionary movement and the Weimar Republic to symbolize the commitment of the new state to liberal democracy. The founding of the Federal Republic ended military government in West Germany, but the occupying powers retained important rights over foreign affairs and the economy through the Statute of Occupation, which remained in force, with important modifications in 1952, until 1955. Until 1952 German laws could come into effect only if no objections were raised by the Allied High Commission within twenty-one days.

The FRG claimed to represent all Germany (*Alleinvertretung*), including the Soviet zone, where the German Democratic Republic (GDR) was established in October 1949. The first Bundestag elections, of August 1949, resulted in a narrow victory for the moderately conservative interdenominational Christian Democratic Union (CDU) and its Bavarian Catholic-based counterpart, the Christian Social Union (CSU). The CDU/CSU received 31 percent of the vote to 29.2 percent for the nominally Marxist (until 1959) but in practice reformist Social Democratic Party (SPD). These two parties along with the economically conservative but socially liberal Free Democratic Party (FDP), which received 11.9 percent of the vote, would become the dominant parties in the Federal Republic. Although the FDP never received more than 12.8 percent of the vote, its best result in 1961 in a Bundestag election, it played a key role in determining which of the two major parties would govern the Federal Republic. From 1949 to 1957, 1961 to 1966, and again from 1982 on, the FDP participated in coalition governments with the CDU/CSU. From 1969 to 1982 the FDP joined in coalition governments with the SPD. The Bundestag met for the first time in September 1949 and chose as chancellor Konrad Adenauer, head of the CDU and a leading member of the Catholic Center Party before 1933. The leader of the FDP, Theodor Heuss, was elected the first president of the FRG.

Adenauer, who was reelected by sizable margins in the Bundestag elections of 1953, 1957, and 1961, governed Germany until 1963. Critics of his authoritarian executive style referred to the Federal Republic under Adenauer as a "chancellor democracy." The intensifying Cold War furthered Adenauer's aim of gaining full rehabilitation for the FRG through economic and political integration into Western Europe and strong anti-Communist policies. The FRG sought to isolate the GDR through the Hallstein Doctrine, which provided for the severance of diplomatic relations with any state, except the USSR, that recognized the legitimacy of the GDR. After the outbreak of the Korean War Adenauer supported American demands for West German rearmament. The plan for a European Defense Community (EDC) that would have integrated West German units into a Western European army had to be abandoned in 1954 when France refused to ratify it. The Soviets had tried to block the EDC and the rearming of the FRG by proposing a plan to reunify and neutralize Germany in 1952, which Adenauer and the Western powers rejected out of hand. In May 1955 the FRG joined the North Atlantic Treaty Organization (NATO) and gained full internal sovereignty, although the Allies reserved the right to resume their occupation authority if an emergency should arise. The FRG also accepted restrictions on its new military force, the Bundeswehr, by renouncing the production and use of atomic, biological, and chemical (ABC) weapons.

Economic integration was achieved through membership in a number of organizations to promote economic reconstruction and growth in Western Europe. The FRG joined the Organization for European Economic Cooperation (OEEC), formed in April 1948 for the administration of U.S.-sponsored Marshall Plan aid and replaced in 1961 by the Organization for Economic Cooperation and Development (OECD), which would become the leading economic forum of the advanced industrial nations. The European Coal and Steel Community (ECSC), established in 1951, created a semi-independent High Authority to administer the coal and steel industries of the FRG, France, Italy, and the Benelux countries. The institutional framework of the ECSC provided the model for the European Economic Community (EEC), founded in 1957 to create a common market and coordinate economic policies among the six participating countries. The

FRG subsequently played a leading role in the expansion and transformation of the EEC into the European Community (EC) in 1967 and the European Union (EU) in 1993.

Unabashed embrace of Western materialist culture constituted an important aspect of postwar West German identity. Under the leadership of Ludwig Erhard, economics minister from 1949 to 1963, the FRG adopted a highly successful "social market economy"—a form of welfare capitalism combining free-market principles with limited state intervention to insure stability and extensive social benefits. The FRG also adopted innovative labor policies, including "codetermination" (*Mitbestimmung*) in 1951, which gave labor unions representation on the supervisory boards of industrial companies. The FRG enjoyed unparalleled economic growth throughout the 1950s. Between 1952 and 1958 West German GNP rose by an average of 8.2 percent per year. Besides the German traditions of technological innovation, skilled craftsmanship, and a disciplined work ethos, a number of other factors contributed to this "economic miracle" (*Wirtschaftswunder*): the currency reform of 1948; Marshall Plan aid, most of which was invested in industrial productivity; huge pent-up demand for goods as a result of wartime destruction and deprivation; a favorable exchange rate, as a result of the undervalued deutsche mark, helping to make German goods competitive in the world market; increased demand for German exports during the Korean War; and a large labor pool resulting from the influx of close to ten million expellees and refugees from Eastern Europe between 1945 and 1950. The German economy received an additional boost by the return of the Saar on January 1, 1957, after a popular referendum rejecting economic integration with France. By the early 1960s the booming West German economy produced a labor shortage, leading to the recruitment of guest workers (*Gastarbeiter*) from predominantly southern European countries, including Italy, Spain, Greece, and Yugoslavia. The largest contingent of foreign workers came from Turkey. By 1973 the share of foreign workers in the labor force reached an all-time high of 11.9 percent. Between 1950 and 1975 the average real income of West German citizens more than tripled. Despite brief economic downturns in the mid-1960s and again following the rise in world oil prices as a result of the 1973 Arab-Israeli war, the GNP of the Federal Republic quadrupled in thirty-five years. West German economic growth was largely export-driven. More than 80 percent of German exports consisted of manufactured products such as machinery, motor vehicles, electrotechnical goods, precision instruments, metal goods, and chemical goods. In the mid-

1980s the FRG became for a time the leading exporting nation in the world, with balance-of-trade surpluses averaging more than deutsche marks (DM) 110 billion a year from 1986 to 1989. Although GNP growth rates dropped after 1975 to an annual average of 2.5 percent in the 1980s, the economy grew steadily from the founding of the FRG in 1949 until the postunification recession of 1993–94.

The decision in 1952 to make restitution payments (*Wiedergutmachung*) to the state of Israel and to Jewish victims of Nazi persecution contributed to the international rehabilitation of the FRG. In 1955 Adenauer visited the Soviet Union to negotiate the opening of diplomatic relations and the release of the last German POWs in Soviet captivity. Economic prosperity, the securing of virtually complete sovereignty in 1955, and the popularity of his firm anti-Communist stance led to Adenauer's greatest electoral triumph in 1957. With 50.5 percent of the vote the CDU/CSU won an absolute majority, the highest total of any party in any Bundestag election in the history of the FRG. The gap between the major parties narrowed again in 1961 as the CDU/CSU lost close to 5 percent of its 1957 vote while the SPD, which had adopted a liberal, non-Marxist program at its party convention at Bad Godesberg in 1959, gained more than 4 percent. Adenauer had lost some popularity by withdrawing his candidacy for the presidency after the completion of Theodor Heuss's second five-year term in 1959 to block the succession of Ludwig Erhard to the chancellorship. An obscure member of Adenauer's cabinet, Heinrich Lübke, was then elected to the presidency for two terms. Adenauer was also criticized for his detached response to the Berlin Wall, erected by the East German regime on August 13, 1961, to stem the tide of refugees to the west. The Wall brought to an unhappy end both the steady flow of East German refugees—more than three million between 1945 and 1961—and the standoff precipitated by Soviet Premier Nikita Krushchev's demand, first proclaimed in November 1958, that West Berlin be put under U.N. control. The end of the Adenauer era was hastened by the role of government officials, particularly the controversial head of the CSU, Defense Minister Franz Josef Strauss, in the arbitrary arrest of journalists and subsequent cover-up attempt in the Spiegel affair in 1962, which cast doubt on the Adenauer government's commitment to civil liberties and democratic process. Adenauer's last main achievement was the Franco-German Friendship treaty of January 1963, which called for regular consultations and close cooperation between the two governments. The inauguration of a special Franco-German relationship came at a time when some West German leaders, particularly Strauss, who was forced to resign as a result of the Spiegel affair, expressed concern that U.S. President John Kennedy's policy of "flexible response" and moves toward détente, temporarily interrupted by the Cuban Missile Crisis in October 1962, might leave Germany without sufficient protection. However, the FRG did not follow French President Charles de Gaulle's lead in opposing British membership in the EEC or in reducing participation in or commitment to NATO. After Adenauer's departure the primacy of the West German–American partnership was again reaffirmed.

Adenauer resigned on October 15, 1963, and was replaced by Ludwig Erhard. The CDU/CSU again emerged victorious in the 1965 elections with 47.6 percent of the vote, but the increase of the SPD vote to 39.3 percent signaled a shift of the political climate to the left as economic growth rates declined. Disagreement on how to overcome the budget deficit led to the breakup of the CDU/CSU coalition with the FDP and the formation of a great coalition with the SPD under CDU chancellor Kurt-Georg Kiesinger in 1966, with former West Berlin mayor Willy Brandt, the SPD's candidate for chancellor since 1961, as foreign minister. The stabilization law (*Stabilitätsgesetz*) of 1967 gave the government broad powers to counter cyclical fluctuations in the economy. But the marginalization of parliamentary opposition under the great coalition contributed to the growth of the extraparliamentary Left in the late 1960s. This was primarily a generational, student-based protest movement against the Vietnam War and in support of democratizing reforms in higher education and government. Student militancy reached its height when one of the leaders of the movement, Rudi Dutschke, was partially paralyzed in an assassination attempt in Berlin in April 1968. The student movement also challenged the repression of the Nazi past by members of the parental generation who had lived through the Third Reich. In March 1965 the Bundestag abolished the twenty-year statute of limitations on Nazi crimes. The question of overcoming the Nazi past (*Vergangenheitsbewältigung*) remained an important issue in the Federal Republic from that time on and led to a furious dispute among West German historians (*Historikerstreit*) in 1986–87. The extraparliamentary opposition's challenge to conservative values contributed to a pronounced shift of the political mainstream to the left in the late 1960s and early 1970s. One segment of the student movement was eventually integrated into Willy Brandt's rejuvenated SPD, while another strand culminated in the founding of the environmental Green Party in 1979. The most radical elements of the generational revolt turned to terrorism in the 1970s with the formation of the Red Army Faction (RAF) led by Andreas Baader (1943–77) and Ulrike Meinhof (1934–76), both of whom died in prison. The government sought to cut off the terrorists' base of support with a controversial decree on extremists (*Radikalenerlass*) in 1972, barring radicals from civil service employment. The government's anti-terrorist campaign reached a climax in the so-called German autumn (*deutscher Herbst*) of 1977, when German commandos freed a hijacked Lufthansa airliner in the Somali capital of Mogadishu, and three RAF leaders, including Baader, committed suicide in the high-security Stammheim prison.

The leftward trend of the 1960s contributed to the formation of the first SPD-led government in the FRG in October 1969 with Willy Brandt as chancellor and Walter Scheel of the FDP as foreign minister. The two parties had already voted together in March 1969 to elect Gustav Heinemann to the presidency, the only SPD nominee to serve in that office in the history of the FRG. The "social-liberal" coalition carried out a major reorientation of West German foreign policy toward the East bloc based on the new realities created by the stabilization of the GDR after the Berlin Wall and the interests of the superpowers in global détente. Brandt's new Eastern policy (*Ostpolitik*) accepted the political reality of German division and marked the official end of the Hallstein Doctrine. Its goals were to induce liberalizing change in the GDR through closer contacts and to improve relations with East bloc countries through acknowledgment of the postwar status quo. Germany's adherence to the Nuclear Non-Proliferation Treaty in November 1969 set the stage for better relations with the East.

In treaties with the Soviet Union and Poland in 1970 the FRG in effect recognized the Oder-Neisse line by renouncing the use of force to change the post-1945 borders. In return the Soviet Union recognized Western rights in West Berlin in the Four-Power Agreement of September 1971, thus finally removing Berlin as a major site of Cold War confrontation. After hard-liner Walter Ulbricht was replaced by the more flexible Erich Honecker as East German leader in 1971, the FRG and the GDR signed a Basic Treaty formally acknowledging the existence of two separate states within a single German nation. The two states exchanged "permanent representations" rather than embassies, and the FRG continued to grant automatic citizenship to all Germans. A treaty between the FRG and Czechoslovakia in December 1973 renounced the German claim to the Sudetenland in the 1938 Munich Pact. Both the FRG and the GDR joined the United Nations in 1973.

The German public endorsed *Ostpolitik* as the SPD achieved its best postwar results in the 1972 election, for the first and only time outpolling the CDU/CSU, 45.8 to 44.9 percent. Brandt, who won the Nobel Peace Prize in 1971, was forced to resign in May 1974 when one of his aides turned out to be an East German agent. In the same year his coalition partner, FDP leader Walter Scheel, was elected to the presidency. Brandt was succeeded by his more pragmatic finance minister, Helmut Schmidt, while Hans-Dietrich Genscher of the FDP succeeded Scheel as foreign minister. The coalition's majority was narrowed to only ten seats in the 1976 elections just as the FRG was emerging from a recession induced by the 1973 OPEC oil embargo. In 1979 Schmidt strongly advocated NATO's "dual-track" decision to deploy Pershing and Cruise missiles in Germany by 1983 while simultaneously pursuing negotiations to dismantle Soviet intermediate-range SS-20 missiles targeted on Western Europe. Despite protest demonstrations against Schmidt's nuclear energy policy and the stationing of nuclear weapons in the FRG, the government's margin of victory rose again in the 1980 elections, partly as a result of voter skepticism about the confrontational personality of Franz Josef Strauss, the chancellor candidate of the CDU/CSU. However, FDP conservatives led by Economics Minister Count Otto Lambsdorff, a strong supporter of free-market principles, were now increasingly at odds with the Keynesian policies of the SPD as the government resorted to increased borrowing in the late 1970s. The government was also weakened by a widening internal rift within the SPD on defense, welfare, and antiterrorist policies.

Opposition to government spending on social services led the FDP to terminate its coalition with the SPD and once again form a governing alliance with the CDU/CSU in October 1982. Helmut Kohl, head of the CDU, was elected chancellor by the Bundestag. Elections in 1983 confirmed the general realignment to the right as the CDU/CSU outpolled the SPD by 48.8 to 38.2 percent, while the FDP received 6.9 percent. The Green Party gained votes from the disaffected left wing of the SPD and became the first new party to enter the Bundestag since 1949, with 5.6 percent of the vote. In 1984 the CDU's candidate, Richard von Weizsäcker, was elected president. He served two terms and was succeeded by the CDU's Roman Herzog, president of the Constitutional Court, in 1994.

Kohl was to become the longest-serving chancellor in the history of the FRG, breaking Adenauer's fourteen-year record in 1997. In the mid-1980s he presided over a moderate rightward turn as his government cut back on welfare spending and revived Cold War rhetoric while continuing to extend generous economic credits to an increasingly stagnant GDR. His decision to commemorate the fortieth anniversary of the end of World War II in a ceremony with U.S. President Ronald Reagan at the Bitburg military and SS cemetery in April 1985 was widely criticized for abetting neoconservative efforts to "normalize" Germany's Nazi past. Kohl nonetheless emerged victorious from the polarized 1987 elections in which the CDU/CSU enjoyed a comfortable 44.3 to 37 percent lead over the SPD, while the FDP and the Green Party improved their totals to 9.1 and 8.3 percent, respectively.

Having revived the issue of German unification in domestic politics, Kohl was poised to take the initiative after Honecker's fall in the GDR on October 18, 1989, and the unexpected opening of the Berlin Wall on November 9. On November 28 Kohl issued a Ten-Point Declaration that envisioned a confederation of the two German states and eventual unification. The decisive victory of the East German CDU and parties allied with it in the parliamentary (Volkskammer) elections of March 18, 1990, induced Kohl to force the pace of the unification process. The "two-plus-four" negotiations involving the two German states and the four victorious Allies of World War II, who still enjoyed sovereign powers in Berlin, began in Bonn on May 5, 1990. On May 18 a treaty between the two German states established a monetary, economic, and social union to come into effect on July 1. On that date the deutsche mark was introduced as the official currency of the now virtually defunct GDR. On August 23 the Volkskammer approved the accession of the five resurrected East German Länder—Mecklenburg, Brandenburg, Saxony, Saxony-Anhalt, and Thuringia—to the Federal Republic in accordance with Article 23 of the Basic Law. The Unification Treaty between the two states was signed on August 31. Kohl's pledge of massive economic aid to the Soviet Union overcame Soviet President Gorbachev's objections to a united Germany's continued membership in NATO, a condition of Western support for unification. The final "two-plus-four" treaty, signed in Moscow on September 12, rescinded the wartime four-power rights in Berlin and provided for the withdrawal of all Allied troops by 1994. Berlin once again became the German capital and the sixteenth Land of the FRG. The two German states were officially reunified on October 3, 1990. A treaty with Poland in January 1991 gave final recognition to the Order-Neisse boundary.

The Kohl government won public endorsement in the first all-German elections in December 1990 as the CDU/CSU defeated the SPD, which had advocated a more cautious approach to unification, by more than 10 percentage points, while the other governing party, the FDP, recorded their third-best showing in history with 11 percent of the vote. The integration of the former GDR into the FRG proved more difficult and expensive than anticipated, however. While pent-up demand for Western goods brought about a short-lived economic boom in western Germany, the collapse of the markets for eastern German products in Eastern Europe and the inability of eastern German industry to compete in Western markets caused massive unemployment and disaffection in the east and forced the government to provide large transfer payments for social services and economic reconstruction. Unsettled property claims in the east inhibited private investments. The German economy went into recession as the all-German GDP fell by 1.1 percent in 1993 and unemployment rose to well over 15 percent in the former GDR. The German central bank's (Bundesbank) high interest rate policy to control inflation was blamed for slowing recovery in neighboring countries. Economic tensions contributed to the growth of extreme right-wing organizations and widespread hostility and acts of aggression against foreigners, including a five-day riot in the eastern German city of Rostock in August 1992. The problem was exacerbated by the steady increase of immigrants from Africa, Asia, and Eastern and southern Europe seeking political asylum under the FRG's liberal constitutional guarantee. The number of asylum seekers rose from 129,318 in 1989 to 438,191 in 1992. A new law adopted in 1993 and upheld by the Federal Constitutional Court in 1996 no longer granted asylum to emigrants coming from or arriving from countries with good human rights records.

Partial economic recovery enabled the government parties to retain a narrow majority in the 1994 elections despite a 6.5 percent decline in their combined vote. The former ruling party in the GDR, now renamed Party of Democratic Socialism (PDS), emerged as a formidable voice of regional protest, with thirty parliamentary seats. The PDS capitalized on resentment generated by the virtually total dismantling of the institutional structures of the former GDR under western auspices. Despite the transfer of DM 525 billion to the new Länder between 1990 and 1995, bridging the differences between the two parts of Germany continues to pose a major challenge to the new Federal Republic. Because of the lag in productivity in the east, the target date of 1996 for the equalization of wages with the west had to be postponed for at least a decade. Despite the return of modest economic growth in 1995–96, unemployment continued to be significantly higher in the east than in the west.

Reunified Germany was prepared to play a greater international role in the 1990s. Germany became the first major nation to recognize the independence of Slovenia and Croatia from the former Yugoslavia in 1991. In 1994 the Federal Constitutional Court ruled that German participation in international military operations outside the territory of NATO did not violate the constitution. In 1996 German personnel in the NATO-led IFOR peacekeeping mission in Bosnia became the first German combat-ready forces to serve outside the country's borders since World War II. German economic preponderance makes it inevitable that the FRG will continue to play a leading role in the European Union. Despite considerable internal opposition, the government firmly supported a single European currency as agreed on in the Maastricht treaty in 1991. The FRG also became the leading advocate of the eastward expansion of the EU in the post-Communist era. Commitment to European unification is perhaps the best indicator of the FRG's decisive break with Germany's pre-1945 legacy of nationalism and ethnocentrism.

BIBLIOGRAPHY

Bark, Dennis L., and Gress, David R. *A History of West Germany.* Vol. 1, *From Shadow to Substance, 1945–1963;* Vol. 2, *Democracy and Its Discontents, 1963–1991,* 2d ed. Oxford: Oxford University Press, 1993.

Benz, Wolfgang, ed. *Die Geschichte der Bundesrepublik,* Vol. 1, *Politik;* Vol. 2, *Wirtschaft;* Vol. 3, *Gesellschaft;* Vol. 4, *Kultur.* Frankfurt am Main: S. Fischer Verlag, 1989.

Bögeholz, Hartwig. *Die Deutschen nach dem Krieg: Eine Chronik.* Reinbek bei Hamburg: Rowohlt, 1995.

Glees, Anthony. *Reinventing Germany: German Political Development Since 1945.* Oxford: Berg, 1996.

Hanrieder, Wolfram F. *Germany, America, Europe: Forty Years of German Foreign Policy.* New Haven, Conn.: Yale University Press, 1989.

Kettenacker, Lothar. *Germany Since 1945.* Oxford: Oxford University Press, 1997.

Larres, Klaus, and Panikos Panayi, eds. *The Federal Republic of Germany Since 1949: Politics, Society and Economy before and after Unification.* New York: Addison Wesley Longman, 1996.

Nicholls, A. J. *The Bonn Republic: West German Democracy, 1945–1990.* New York: Addison Wesley Longman, 1997.

Pulzer, Peter. *German Politics, 1945–1995.* Oxford: Oxford University Press, 1995.

Steininger, Rolf. *Deutsche Geschichte seit 1945: Darstellung und Dokumente in vier Bänden.* Vol. 1, *1945–1947;* Vol. 2, *1948–1955* (4 Vols. projected). Frankfurt am Main: Fischer Taschenbuch Verlag, 1996.

Turner, Henry Ashby, Jr. *Germany from Partition to Reunification,* rev. ed. New Haven, Conn.: Yale University Press, 1992.

Rod Stackelberg

Allied Control Council

First meeting provisionally in Berlin on June 5, 1945, and officially installed on August 30, the four-power Allied Control Council assumed supreme administrative control over defeated Germany. It consisted of the military commanders of the occupying powers, each of whom enjoyed veto power. The United States was represented first by Dwight D. Eisenhower and later by Lucius D. Clay; Great Britain, first by Bernard L. Montgomery, later by Brian Robertson; France, first by Jean de Lattre de Tassigny, later by Pierre Koenig; and the Soviet Union, first by Georgy Zhukov, later by Mikhail Dratvin and Vassily Sokolovsky. While the council's overall jurisdiction remained poorly defined throughout its existence, day-to-day governing responsibility rested with a Coordinating Committee composed of the deputy military commanders of the four occupation zones and sectors into which Germany and Berlin had been divided. In addition, the Control Council delegated specialized responsibilities to 12 directorates and some 170 lower administrative units that operated with little common coordination or clear central guidelines.

There were several reasons for Stalin's support for the creation of the Allied Control Council. A quadripartite system would facilitate the extraction of German reparations, including 25 percent of the industrial equipment of the rich Ruhr district in the west that was to be shipped to the Soviet Union under the Potsdam agreement. A joint governmental structure promised relatively unimpeded Communist political activity and agitation, not just in Soviet-occupied territory but in all Germany. A centralized government would also make denazification easier and more effective, especially since Stalin had portrayed himself in part as an antifascist crusader.

The Allied Control Council turned out to be an ineffective instrument of government for postwar Germany. While relations were closest between the United States and Great Britain and led to the establishment of the American-British Bizone in January 1947, the French, belatedly elevated to equal status with the other occupying powers on May 2, 1945, and not a party to many other Allied agreements, including Potsdam, refused to sanction a strong centralized administration for Germany, especially with regard to infrastructure and the economy. This policy, which also envisioned the detachment of the Saarland and the Ruhr from the rest of Germany, their ruthless economic exploitation by France, and the creation of a buffer zone along the Rhine, echoed French concerns expressed a quarter century before. The zonal divisions, moreover, tended to preclude the free movement of officials and hindered enforcement of a common policy.

As ideological and territorial conflicts, for instance, over Poland's sovereignty and western border, or over Berlin's peculiar status, increasingly alienated Stalin from the Western leaders and their objectives, the Soviets, too, became disenchanted with the arrangements they had helped create. The Soviets also reneged on promises to ship agricultural goods from their zone to the West. In practice the Allies exercised little power except in their own occupation zones as political and economic reconstruction gained momentum and millions of refugees, expellees, and displaced persons from Germany's eastern territories and various Eastern European countries had to be accommodated. Among the few concerns for which the council found common ground were denazification, the International Military Tribunal in Nuremberg, disarmament, limitation of German steel production to approximately one-third of prewar levels, a step reflecting the widespread desire to weaken and pastoralize Germany's economy, and official dismantling of the former German state of Prussia in February 1947.

After years of paralysis, impasse and confrontation, the currency reform in the western zones, the imminent establishment of a West German state, the Berlin Blockade by the Soviets, and the West's resolve not to succumb to Stalin's pressure occasioned the Soviet Union's permanent withdrawal from the council on March 20, 1949. On that day the Soviet military commander, Marshal Vassily Sokolovsky, walked out of what would be the last regular meeting of the council, as American General Lucius D. Clay along with his French and British counterparts stuck unwaveringly to their positions. Within months the founding of the Federal Republic in the West and the creation of the German Democratic Republic under Soviet auspices rendered obsolete any joint Allied arrangements for postwar Germany.

BIBLIOGRAPHY

Botting, Douglas. *From the Ruins of the Reich: Germany 1945–1949.* New York: Dutton, 1986.

Gimbel, John. *The American Occupation of Germany 1945–49.* Palo Alto, Calif.: Stanford University Press, 1968.

Morgan, Roger. *The United States and West Germany 1945–1973.* Oxford: Oxford University Press, 1975.

Roy, Willis F. *The French in Germany, 1945–1949.* Palo Alto, Calif.: Stanford University Press, 1962.

Turner, Henry A., Jr. *Germany from Partition to Reunification,* rev. ed. New Haven, Conn.: Yale University Press, 1992.

Eric C. Rust

Basic Law

Constitution of the Federal Republic of Germany ratified in 1949 and in 1990 extended to the states (Länder) formed from the territory of the former German Democratic Republic. The constitution, besides a specification of basic rights, contained rules governing the relationship between the state structure and the constitutional institutions. Although indebted to German constitutional history, it also drew on elements of the French and American constitutions, especially in the expansion of basic rights. The preparation of the constitution in 1948–49 took place under the direct influence of Germany's defeat in World War II and the loss of state sovereignty by Germany. To accentuate its preliminary character until the achievement of the political reunification of Germany, the parliamentary council, which met under the leadership of later federal chancellor Konrad Adenauer in the Bonn König museum, called the new German constitution the Basic Law (Grundgesetz).

The Basic Law of the Federal Republic of Germany was in accord in many aspects with Western European constitutional constructs as well as with the North American constitution. Nevertheless, this relationship does not obscure that it is a German constitution, which can be looked on as a further development of the Weimar Constitution of 1919, which in its turn was based on the imperial constitution of 1871 and the Frankfurt (Paulskirche) constitution of 1849. In 1948–49 the parliamentarians had the task of removing the fateful provisions that in the Weimar constitution allowed the president and the chancellor to weaken or even abolish other constitutional institutions. Therefore the constitution contains an irrevocable core that defines the federal republic as a democratic and social constitutional state with a division of powers. However, this unusual a priori provision in no way prevents amendments to the constitution. Between 1949 and 1989 details of the constitution have been altered altogether thirty-five times, in each case with a two-thirds majority of the Bundestag (lower house of parliament). The constitution of 1949 contains a catalogue of basic rights. They define the main constitutive principles of the state and determine the spirit in which its basic functions are performed.

Article 1, paragraph 1, states: "The dignity of the person is sacrosanct." If the sixty two framers of the constitution established the dignity of the person as the leading cornerstone of a new state, they did this in the certainty that an ethical decision in favor of the citizen was fundamental to defining his or her new relationship to the state. The state does not exist as an end in itself in the polity, for it is only the formal expression of a reasoned act of state organization. Rather, the person is the center of the polity. The protection of the dignity of the person is the most important task of political organization, which as a result serves as a means to an end rather than as an end in itself.

Rooted in Article 1, the freedom and equality of the citizens is postulated and more precisely defined in Articles 2 and 3. Thus in Article 3, paragraph 2, is the equality of man and woman expressly fixed. This paragraph was much debated in the deliberations of the parliamentary council. It is due to the persistent insistence of Social Democratic (SPD) politician Elisabeth Selbert that the legal equality of the sexes was embodied in the constitution. She set herself against opposition within her own party but especially from the Christian Democratic Union/Christian Social Union (CDU/CSU), which favored a solemn reiteration of the traditional role of women.

How far the reality of the constitution can differ from its text is demonstrated by the history of the legislative debates in subsequent decades. The constitution had conferred on the legislators a binding charge by 1953 to change definitively all regulations offensive to the principle of equality. It took until 1957 before the Bundestag enacted a so-called equal rights law, but even this law contradicted in essential points the spirit of the constitution, so firmly imprinted was the type of the married housewife according to which she alone supervised the household and the education of the couple's children, while the husband pursued his occupation and thus secured the economic support of the family. The retrograde determination, that the father alone has legal competency in questions concerning children, and that he alone possesses the power of decision in family issues, was annulled by the Federal Constitutional Court. Nevertheless, a conservative view of marriage and the family militated against the legal rights of women and was overcome only with the marriage rights reform of 1976. The unsuccessful fight over wage-parity for women and men is also a mirror of the contradictions of this reactionary outlook.

Further basic rights in accord with a general elaboration of human rights and rights of the private and public sectors follow: freedom of religious practice; freedom of opinion and assembly; the right to found organizations and to advance one's interests through the organization of associations and parties (Article 9). The special character of the basic rights included in Articles 1 to 19 of the Basic Law is that they were given the claim of absolute validity and exercised an a priori influence on legislation. Also, though no justification was given for the existence of the rights, they were nevertheless clearly delineated. This approach was new to German constitutional understanding. The German constitutions of the nineteenth century were different from the American constitution of 1787 and the French constitution of 1791. Human rights were not perceived as predating the establishment of the state but subordinated to its jurisdiction. As a consequence of a constitutional construction rooted in reform rather than revolution during the state formation of Germany, basic rights were bestowed by the state and could, as a consequence, also be withdrawn by it.

This constitutional construction had fatal consequences for the first German republic, even though numerous basic rights were included in the Weimar constitution, more in fact than in the Basic Law. Alongside individual human rights the constitution of 1919 contained a whole catalogue of basic social rights and elaborations of political intent and elevated for the first time in German constitutional history the principle of the social state to the level of a constitutional declaration. However these basic rights were not absolutely binding. The claim to a basic right in the constitution of 1919 was not buttressed by the ability to seek a supporting court decision, so that lawmakers could ignore it with impunity. This grave flaw acquired immediate political significance as Adolf Hitler transformed the German republic into a dictatorship. After 1933 he restricted through a series of laws the rights of individuals and the constitutional institutions to a lamentable extent, without formally abandoning the framework of the constitution.

After the basic rights, specifics concerning federalism and the functions of legislative, executive, and juridical jurisdiction are enumerated in the constitutional text. As the constitutive principles of the German state, Article 20 specifies its republican and democratic, social, and federal character. Therefore the Federal Republic of Germany is a more democratic and social federal state. While the elaboration of the social-state component was relegated to the legislature—among the milestones on the path to the social state in the 1950s were legislation on social housing construction, retirement insurance, and the equalization of burdens with regard to expellees—the organization of the state was clearly delineated.

There is a double division of power: power is divided horizontally into legislative (Bundestag), executive (federal government and administration), and judicial (Federal Constitutional Court and independent jurisdictions) branches and vertically between the federation (Bund) and the states (Länder), so that the Bundesrat as the representative of the governments of the states (Länder) has the power to veto almost all Bundestag bills dealing with internal affairs (in fact, every bill that deals with the authority of Land administration). Notable is the strength of the government (*Bundesregierung*) in relation to the parliament and the strength of the chancellor in relation to the cabinet. The chancellor can in important questions exercise the right of personal decision (*Richtlinienkompetenz*) and thereby forgo collegial cabinet decision making, but will take this path only in such unique cases in which the coalition of ruling parties is not endangered.

Unlike the French and the U.S. presidency, the federal president has been transformed into a purely representative function. He corresponds rather to the powerless British monarch as a republican constitutional institution in the field of the balance of power. This power displacement in favor of the prime minister is also a consequence of the lopsided balance of political powers in the Weimar Republic. The complete lack of political power of the federal president is critical insofar as there is really no legal justification why this office ought to exist at all. His complete powerlessness is emphasized by the fact that he is not directly elected by the people but by the Bundestag and the Bundesrat, together by a vote based on party proportionality. This signifies a lack of trust in the constitution rather than an emphasis on the representative principle. Completely in contrast to that is the fact that with the Federal Constitutional Court powerful control authority has been set up that examines each law and if need be can declare it unconstitutional. If this is done, as a result, there must be without exception a new legislative deliberation. In the constitutional framework opposition is relegated to two places. In the Bundestag parties that are not part of the governing coalition are ranged against the government and the parliamentary majority (but never a situation of the whole parliament against the governing administration, as in the United States), and in the Bundesrat the governments of the Länder can organize a coalition different from that of the Bundestag. If a majority of votes in the Bundesrat can be found in opposition to the Länder that support the government—the predominant case in the 1970s, 1980s, and 1990s—the Bundesrat assumes a uniquely stronger position in legislative battles with the government than the actual opposition in the Bundestag. This arrangement is rooted in the special German tradition of federalism. The Bismacrkian Reich was more strongly stamped with a federative component than the unitary Weimar Republic, which had strong individual states but a weak Federal Council. From 1871 to 1918 the German states maintained numerous competencies: the postal sovereignty of Bavaria, control over education and police, their own sovereigns (kings in Württemberg, Saxony, and Bavaria), and armed forces. The Bundesrat (Federal Council) of that time consisted of the representatives of the particular sovereigns led by Prussia and formed a second ruling council personally headed by the chancellor. This field of forces was again launched in 1949 with quite different conditions of birth.

The Basic Law included in the concluding sentence of its preamble the summons to "the entire German people . . . in free self-determination to bring about the unity and freedom of Germany." After the nonviolent revolution of 1989 in the former German Democratic Republic, this was accomplished within a single year. There were two ways to accomplish this, both of them indicated by the constitution: Article 23 provided for the accession of German states to the territory of the Federal Republic, and Article 146 provided the possibility of an all-German constitutional convention in a German national constituent assembly. The first way implied the acceptance of the existing state system of the Federal Republic of Germany by the acceding areas, while the second implied the crafting of a new constitution with a new state order for both sections of Germany. Owing to the pressure for unification in the German Democratic Republic and foreign policy considerations, the quicker path of Article 23 was chosen.

BIBLIOGRAPHY

Hesse, Joachim, and Thomas Ellweini. *Das Regierungssystem der Bundesrepublik Deutschland.* Vol. 1. Op-Waden: Westdeutscher Verlag, 1992.

Karpen, Ulrich, ed. *The Constitution of the Federal Republic of Germany: Essays on the Basic Rights and Principles of the Basic Law with a Transition of the Basic Law.* Baden-Baden: Nomos, 1988.

Schroder, Gerhard, and Hans Peter Schneider. *Soziale Demokratie—Das Grundgesetz nach 40 Jahren.* Heidelberg: Müller, 1991.

Starck, Christian, ed. *Main Principles of the German Basic Law.* Baden-Baden: Nomos, 1983.

Stern, Klaus. *Der Staat des Grundgesetzes: Ausgewählte Schriften und Vorträge.* Ed. by Helmut Siekmann. Cologne: Carl Heymanns Verlag, 1992.

Georg Wagner
(Tr. by B. Cook)

Trials Against War Criminals

In view of the number and nature of the crimes committed in Germany and elsewhere in Europe by the Nazi regime and its accomplices before and during World War II, the question arose among Germany's opponents as to how to treat the offenders after Germany's military defeat. During the war the Allies agreed to take responsibility for the elimination of National Socialism and the punishment of its leaders. According to the Moscow Declaration, published by the United States, the United Kingdom, and the USSR on November 1, 1943, persons who participated in war crimes were to be punished by courts of the nations in which they committed their crimes. The main war criminals, whose crimes could not be limited to a special geographic area, were specifically excepted from that decision. They were to be punished according to the London Agreement of August 8, 1945. A statute added to this agreement called for an international law court established by the United States, the United Kingdom, the USSR, and France to judge the accused criminals. Twenty-four officials were accused at the Nuremberg International Military Law Court of preparing war of aggression, crimes against peace, war crimes, and/or crimes against humanity, which were defined in the statute. After more than ten months of trial, twenty-two of the accused were sentenced to death or prison. Additionally, the Allies charged war criminals in the areas occupied by them.

In contrast, the German juridical system collapsed after the Allied victory and Germany's occupation by Allied troops. The Allied Military Government banned party and special courts and closed ordinary German courts until the reopening of individual courts through the military government's special permission in the late summer or autumn of 1945.

Another law assigned the German courts only a small sphere of responsibility. Criminal proceedings committed against citizens of Allied nations or their properties were excepted from the courts' responsibilities. In addition, German courts were allowed to judge only crimes committed by Germans against Germans or, only by special permission, crimes committed against stateless persons. Besides the imposed restrictions, other circumstances caused by the specific German situation stood in the way of a fast and effective prosecution of war crimes. There was a massive shortage of police, judges, and district attorneys with clean records. Many files had been lost or destroyed during the war. And there was decreasing interest among Germans in pursuing war criminals. The prime concerns of the population were food and housing. They tried to forget and to displace the war and its con-

sequences. Moreover, denazification turned out as a farce in public opinion and the trials were seen as political.

Despite that, the majority of German trials against war criminals (5,228) were concluded by 1950, although only about 100 cases dealt with capital crimes. In the first years after the founding of the Federal Republic of Germany (FRG) in 1949, the Western Allies loosened the restrictions on the German courts, and remaining restrictions were removed by the so-called Treaty of Transferal (Überleitungsvertrag) between Germany and the United States, the United Kingdom, and France on May 5, 1955. The FRG's juridical system, however, had to face a constitutional problem. Conflicts emerged between the state's desire to sentence offenders and the constitutional principle of *nulla poena sine lege* (no punishment without a law). Therefore only a few offenses that were punishable under pre-1945 laws were prosecuted. In effect, the number of preliminary proceedings declined. The number of indictments decreased as minor offenses came under the statute of limitations, district attorneys were overburden with everyday criminality, and many prosecutors lacked historical knowledge. In addition, the end of denazification, amnesties by the Western Allies, and the FRG's integration into the West and its efforts for rearmament left the impression that the past had been mastered.

The situation changed when Chancellor Konrad Adenauer returned from his Moscow visit in September 1955 and brought about fifteen thousand German prisoners of war back to Germany. The behavior of these returnees had not been reviewed earlier and a criminal accusation that came to light accidentally in Ulm in 1958 indicated that many crimes, especially those committed in Eastern Europe, had not been prosecuted. As a result the attorneys general of the federal states assumed responsibility for prosecuting Nazi crimes. In contrast to the district attorneys' examinations, their investigations were broader and initiated when information about a possible war crime was received. They then examined the case to find possible offenders and sent the files to the district attorneys. To push their work forward they organized an integrated system for records, and their offices pursued research in archives abroad, especially in Eastern Europe.

As a consequence, the number of preliminary proceedings increased again, but with the passing of time more and more crimes came under the statute of limitations. To prevent this the statute of limitations for manslaughter was extended until December 31, 1969, and the statute of limitations for murder was abolished in 1979. However, other problems existed. Victims, witnesses, or offenders were older now or deceased. Evidence was hard to obtain, and the public interest in prosecuting war crimes was not that high, because many people were of the opinion that this chapter of German history was far behind them. Public interest in prosecuting war crimes increased only occasionally, when outstanding charges were brought before the courts. For example, the German Auschwitz trial of the chief SS officers who had worked at the death camp, was held in Frankfurt from 1963 to 1965, and the largest German trial, the Majdanek trial, took place between 1975 and 1981.

BIBLIOGRAPHY

Ruckerl, Adalbert. *NS-Verbrechen vor Gericht: Versuch einer Vergangenheitsbewältingung.* Heidelberg: C.F. Muller, 1982.

Christoph Priller

SEE ALSO Nuremberg Trials

Reparations after World War II

Policy adopted by the Allies of World War II to punish Germany for having caused untold human and material losses in the war. The program began in 1945 and ended in 1954. According to the most conservative estimates, approximately $26 billion was exacted from all four allied zones of occupation in Germany. The underlying philosophy of the reparations program essentially derived from the experience of the post–World War I era, when, according to the Treaty of Versailles, Germany was obligated to pay huge sums in currency and goods each year to the victors, principally France and Great Britain. Disappointingly, the hoped-for restitution was never achieved then. Therefore, following the end of World War II, the Allies adopted a new restitution policy. It centered around dismantling the existing industrial and communications infrastructure and physically transporting much of it to the territories, principally the USSR, France, and Great Britain, as well as many smaller nations that had suffered in the war from German aggression. In addition, large amounts of goods were to be taken out of current German production and, in the case of the USSR, German forced labor was used. This policy was made possible and could be effected rapidly because after 1945, in contrast to the situation after World War I, the four Allied powers physically occupied the whole of German territory and could implement the agreed upon measures without having to struggle against German obstructionism.

The first comprehensively detailed plan for post–World War II reparations was prepared by U.S. Secretary of the Treasury Henry Morgenthau in 1944. He proposed the total "deindustrialization" of Germany, making it in effect an agrarian nation functioning at a bare subsistence level in perpetuity. The Morgenthau Plan's philosophy, however, was perceived as being so retributive that Presidents Roosevelt and Truman refused to consider it as a basis for official U.S. policy.

The reparations issue was first seriously discussed at the insistence of the USSR by the Allied leaders at the Yalta Conference in February 1945. Joseph Stalin asserted that his country had sustained $128 billion in losses during the war and therefore demanded that reparations be included in any postwar settlement. Roosevelt and British Prime Minister Winston Churchill, taken aback by this enormous claim, tried to bring Stalin to reason. In the ensuing discussions Roosevelt casually, and to the extreme consternation of Churchill, proposed a figure of $20 billion, of which the USSR would receive 50 percent because it had clearly suffered the far greatest losses of all combatants. At Churchill's insistence, however, negotiations with respect to amounts were to be left to a future conference. In the final protocol of the Yalta Conference on February 11, 1945, the Allies agreed to make Germany pay in kind in three different ways for the losses it caused the Allies. First, within two years following the end of the war and at the election of the Allies, the transfer of any manufacturing equipment, machine tools, railroad cars and locomotives, and ships, as well as all German investments abroad would be handed over. On September 20, 1945, a codicil was added that required the surrender of all gold and silver in coin or bullion form and all platinum held by any person or authority in Germany. Further, all foreign currency as well as all patents and research data relating to militarily useful products or processes would be ceded to the Allies. Second, annual deliveries of goods from current production would be requisitioned. Third, at their election, the Allies would have the use of German forced labor.

These matters were discussed at much greater length and in much more detail at the Potsdam Conference in July 1945. At Potsdam the USSR immediately insisted that Roosevelt at Yalta had promised the Soviets $10 billion in reparations, and Stalin tenaciously insisted on this despite the arguments of President Truman. The conference ended on August 1, 1945, with the understanding that the USSR to satisfy its reparations claims would be permitted to remove property from both East and West Germany and to seize German assets abroad. The entire oceangoing merchant fleet and all remaining naval vessels would be divided equally among the USSR, Britain, and the United States. The remaining elements of the Yalta protocol were incorporated with the exception of the use of German forced labor, which was dropped from the agreement. To supervise the removals and make an orderly accounting, an Allied control council was to be created. This council would see that all nations in the war against Germany that made reparations claims would receive an agreed-upon percentage of the removals.

By January 14, 1946, the Inter-Allied Reparations Agency had established, exclusive of reparations claimed by the USSR, the following percentage allotments: Albania, 0.05 percent; Australia, 0.70; Belgium, 2.70; Canada, 3.50; Czechoslovakia, 3.00; Denmark, 0.25; Egypt, 0.05; France, 16.00; Greece, 2.70; India, 2.00; Luxembourg, 0.15; Norway, 1.30; New Zealand, 0.40; Netherlands, 3.90; South Africa, 0.70; Great Britain, 28.00; United States, 28.00; and Yugoslavia, 6.60. The entire arrangement, however, was already thrown into disarray before an orderly administration could be put into place. The United States between May and August 1945, without oversight, dismantled large numbers of industrial plants to aid in its final war effort against Japan. At the same time, France began to transfer the entire coal production of the Saar region to its industries. The USSR, for its part, refused to give any accounting of its campaign of removals, dismantling, and, in violation of the Potsdam agreement, its large-scale use of German forced labor. It is estimated that in the first two years of the program more than 2,500 industrial plants were stripped of production equipment under the supervision of the Inter-Allied Reparations Agency, but no reliable value has ever been placed on the hundreds of tons of patent documents the Allies removed from the German Patent Office and made freely available to their business sectors. In addition, armed forces personnel freely and without much fear of punishment "liberated" huge amounts of private property, art treasures, and other valuables for their personal use and profit. On the other hand, there is a substantial corpus of anecdotal evidence attesting to substantial sabotaging of equipment slated for removal by German workers, which would have drastically lowered the actual value of such equipment.

By 1946, against this backdrop of growing chaos, first indications were detected that the harsh terms of the Yalta and Potsdam agreements would be unsustainable if a repeat of the German socioeconomic collapse of the 1920s and 1930s was to be avoided. U.S. Secretary of State James Byrnes, at the second meeting of the Council of Foreign Ministers in Paris on May 20, 1946, called for substantial reductions in the amount of reparations, but the USSR categorically refused to entertain such ideas and proceeded to take ever-increasing amounts of goods out of current East German production while absorbing a large part of the industries under its control into Soviet state-owned concerns. At the same time the Inter-Allied Reparations Agency compounded the problem by ordering most industrial production in Germany not to exceed 50 percent of prewar levels, with the intention of assuring that the German standard of living would remain at a level of relative impoverishment into the foreseeable future.

As a result of these policies Germany was very nearly deindustrialized by the end of 1946. Large-scale starvation set in, and to avoid a humanitarian catastrophe of unimaginable proportions, the United States and Great Britain sent in food shipments on a large scale but paid for these by taking more German assets. This, coupled with the cost of Allied occupation fully charged to Germany, amounted to $1.5 billion annually.

With the beginning of the Cold War in 1947 it became increasingly obvious to the Western Allies that a prostrate, starving West Germany would be of no use whatever in meeting the threat of Soviet expansionism, and West Germany was made the primary beneficiary of aid under the Marshall Plan. Paradoxically, in spite of this changed attitude, especially Britain and to a lesser degree France continued to make large reparations demands with respect to ongoing production of consumer goods until widespread popular demonstrations in West Germany in 1949 caused the Western Allies to announce on November 22, 1949, the termination of further dismantling of industries.

During 1949–51 most other reparations were gradually phased out in the American, British, and French zones of occupation. In the Soviet zone removals continued unabated until January 1, 1954. This resulted in serious economic weakness in the German Democratic Republic and necessitated repeated demands for production increases. This led directly to the bloody uprising of 1953 throughout East Germany. According to records declassified in the Russian Federation in 1994 and confirmed by files from the former German Democratic Republic, the approximate total of reparations exacted by the USSR in East Germany was most likely $16 billion. The full value of what the USSR received from the western zones of Germany during 1945–46 is not known. It is estimated that reparations obtained by the Western Allies from their zones of occupation in West Germany amounted to slightly less than $10 billion.

BIBLIOGRAPHY

Bark, Denis L. *A History of West Germany.* London: Blackwell, 1992.

Diefendorf, Jeffry M., ed. *American Policy and the Reconstruction of West Germany, 1945–1955.* New York: Cambridge University Press, 1.

Fulbrook, Mary. *The Two Germanies, 1945–1990.* New York: Humanities Press, 1992.

Malzahn, Manfred. *Germany 1945–1949: A Sourcebook.* New York: Routledge, 1991.

Sharp, Tony. *The Wartime Alliance and the Zonal Division of Germany.* New York: Oxford University Press, 1975.

Werner G. C. Voigt

SEE ALSO Wartime Conferences

Foreign Policy

Germany did not initially have a foreign policy after 1945. When the Federal Republic of Germany was created in 1949, the first Adenauer government had no foreign ministry, and matters of European and foreign policy were largely dealt with by the chancellor himself. The Western Allies granted sovereignty to the Federal Republic in the German Treaty (*Deutschlandvertrag*) of 1952, which, however, was linked to the project for a European Defense Community (EDC). After the EDC failed in 1954, the Federal Republic finally became sovereign in May 1955, when it also joined NATO. The Allies retained residual rights over "Germany as a whole" and Berlin that were finally abolished only in the context of German reunification in 1990. In contrast, the German Democratic Republic (GDR) had a foreign ministry from its creation in 1949, but its freedom to maneuver in foreign policy was extremely limited inside the Soviet bloc. Historical studies published since the opening of various Eastern European archives have shown, however, that the GDR leadership did play an important role in bringing about Soviet Premier Nikita Khrushchev's decision in 1961 to build the Berlin wall to stop the exodus from the GDR and stabilize its satellite state. The GDR leadership under Erich Honecker also refused to adopt Soviet leader Mikhail Gorbachev's policy of perestroika (restructuring) after 1985, out of fear that it would undermine the Socialist Unity (Communist) Party's control over the GDR.

The dominant foreign policy controversy in the Federal Republic after 1949 was over Western integration versus German reunification. Chancellor Konrad Adenauer followed a policy of clear preference for full integration into European and transatlantic organizations, from the 1950 Schuman Plan, which led to the creation of the European Coal and Steel Community (ECSC) in 1951–52, to the EDC and West German membership in NATO and the Western European Union (WEU) in 1955, to the creation of the European Economic Community (EC) and Euratom in 1957–1958. He was severely criticized, especially over the Stalin notes of March 1952 (in which Joseph Stalin seemed to offer the possibility of German

reunification as a neutral state), for not trying hard enough to come to an understanding with the Soviet Union over reunification. Among the critics were Jacob Kaiser (1888–1961), the minister for all German issues (Bundesminister für Gesamtdeutsche Frage), whose principal political goal was reunification, and others in his own Christian Democratic Union; sections of the Liberal coalition partner; and opposition Social Democrats, whose first postwar leader, Kurt Schumacher, at one point denounced Adenauer as "Chancellor of the Allies." However, Western integration soon became a crucial part of the Federal Republic's postwar consensus when the Social Democrats revised their European and foreign policy after 1955.

Within the Western world, the Federal Republic's most important bilateral relationships have been those with the United States and France. During the Cold War the Federal Republic depended on the United States for its external security. Moreover, most West Germans were grateful to the United States for having played a crucial role in the establishment of what was becoming an increasingly stable parliamentary democracy and for having facilitated, through the Marshall Plan, the economic reconstruction of West Germany. The bilateral relationship with the United States remained of crucial importance throughout the postwar period, despite policy conflicts, such as over German payments toward the stationing costs of American troops in the Federal Republic during the 1960s, over international monetary policy during the 1970s, and over the possible stationing of short-range nuclear missiles in the Federal Republic in the late 1980s.

The bilateral relationship with France was crucial not only for historical reasons and in the context of some more immediate postwar problems, such as the Saar question, solved only in 1955–56. It was seen, especially by Adenauer, as essential for the integration of the Federal Republic into the Western democratic world as an equal partner and as the precondition for and the driving force behind the process of European integration. The ever closer cooperation and consultation mechanisms were formalized in the Élysée treaty of 1963, which provided, for example, for two annual summits between the German chancellor and the French president and prime minister. From French President Charles de Gaulle's attempt in the early 1960s to create a European foreign policy under his direction and largely independent of the United States to the 1998 conflict over the first president of the European Central Bank, the Franco-German partnership was never without frictions. However, often facilitated by close personal relationships between German and French leaders, such as Adenauer and Schuman, Helmut Schmidt and

Giscard d'Estaing, and Helmut Kohl and François Mitterand, it always proved crucial for bringing about progress in European integration and for the internal politics of the European Union (EU).

In the 1960s de Gaulle's foreign policy created frictions in German politics between the Atlanticists, who wanted to rely more closely on U.S. leadership, and the Gaullists, who were prepared to risk greater Western European independence in foreign and defense policy. But the basic consensus remained intact—that both relationships were crucial and had to be harmonized. Moreover, the issue was soon superseded by the new conflict over West Germany's *Ostpolitik*. The Federal Republic had not only not recognized the GDR; in accordance with the Hallstein Doctrine, with the exception of the Soviet Union it had no formal diplomatic relations with third countries recognizing the GDR. West German policy became less rigid under the grand coalition of 1966–69. After 1969 the Social-Liberal government led by Chancellor Willy Brandt then pursued a new policy of détente that led to the conclusion of the Moscow and Warsaw treaties with the Soviet Union and Poland, respectively, in 1970 and the German-German Grundlagen treaty in 1972. These treaties involved the de facto recognition by the Federal Republic of Germany's post-1945 eastern borders and of the GDR as well as the simultaneous U.N. membership of both German states in 1973. Like Western integration, *Ostpolitik* soon became part of the foreign policy consensus, and its basic direction remained unchanged when the Kohl government took office in 1982.

The breakdown of the Soviet bloc and German reunification necessitated the adaptation of German foreign policy. Most important, the Kohl government realized, especially over the Gulf War, that a reunited Germany would have to accept greater international responsibilities, including the out-of-area use of German troops, such as in Somalia and Bosnia. In return, the German Foreign Office has worked diplomatically for a restructuring of the United Nations to include a German seat on the Security Council. Germany also advocated enlargement of NATO eastward and expansion of the EU. However, key elements of the postwar foreign policy consensus have remained in place. They include, most of all, the continued importance of the transatlantic relationship and NATO; the Franco-German partnership; and, despite the global role of the mark/Euro and the international orientation of the German economy, the primarily European focus of German foreign policy.

BIBLIOGRAPHY

The papers of the (West) German Foreign Ministry are accessible in the Political Archive of the Foreign Ministry (Politisches Archiv des Auswärtigen Amts), Bonn, and the papers of the GDR Foreign Ministry in the Federal Archive (Bundesarchiv), Berlin.

Ash, Timothy Garton. *In Europe's Name: Germany and the Divided Continent.* London: Jonathan Cape, 1993.

Hanrieder, Wolfgang. *Deutschland, Europa, Amerika: Die Auẞenpolitik der Bundesrepublik Deutschland 1949–1994.* Paderborn: Schöningh, 1995.

———. *Germany, America, Europe: Forty Years of German Foreign Policy.* New Haven, Conn.: Yale University Press, 1989.

Schöllgen, Gregor. *Geschichte der Weltpolitik von Hitler bis Gorbatschow 1941–1991.* Munich: Beck, 1996.

Wolfram Kaiser

SEE ALSO Adenauer, Konrad; Brandt, Willy

Hallstein Doctrine Guiding principle of the Federal Republic of Germany's foreign Policy from 1955 until 1969. From the foundation of the Federal Republic in 1949, its government asserted the sole right of representation (*Alleinvertretungsanspruch*); that is, it claimed to be the only democratic, legitimated representation of the German people. It refused to recognize the authorities of the German Democratic Republic and even refused to recognize the very existence of East Germany as a political entity.

After the Federal Republic had been granted autonomy in foreign affairs by the three Western Allied powers of World War II (Britain, France, United States) and joined NATO through the Treaty of Paris in May 1955, a German delegation led by Chancellor Konrad Adenauer paid its first state visit to the Soviet Union in mid-September 1955. In return for the release of the last German prisoners of war still held in the USSR, the establishment of diplomatic relations between these two countries was agreed upon. The Soviet Union had since 1954 pursued a policy in favor of diplomatic recognition of the two German states and had already recognized the German Democratic Republic as a sovereign state in March 1954. Thus the Soviets established diplomatic relations with two German states, a condition in clear contradiction to the Federal Republic of Germany's commitment to German unity and the claim to have the sole right of representation. The West German government conceded that this had to be tolerated with regard to the leading power of the socialist countries, the Soviet Union, but this erosion of the sole right of representation should not be conceded elsewhere. In view of this, West German foreign office adviser Wilhelm Grewe elaborated the Hallstein Doctrine, which was named after then State Secretary of Foreign Affairs Walter Hallstein.

Proclaimed in an official declaration of the Federal Republic on September 22, 1955, the Hallstein Doctrine stated that the diplomatic recognition of the East German regime by a third country would be regarded as an unfriendly act against the Federal Republic of Germany and that the Federal Republic would consider appropriate countermeasures. The originally flexible proclamation soon developed into a rigid dictum, that the Federal Republic would not establish or maintain diplomatic relations with any country, apart from the USSR, that maintained or established diplomatic relations with East Germany. Relying on its economic potential, the country's economic aid to developing countries, and the diplomatic support of its Western partners, the Federal Republic succeeded for about a decade in internationally isolating the East German regime. The Hallstein Doctrine was applied to Yugoslavia in October 1957 and to Cuba in January 1963 after each country diplomatically recognized the German Democratic Republic and the Federal Republic broke off diplomatic relations with each of them. Until then the diplomatic relations of East Germany had remained confined to thirteen mainly socialist countries.

A visit of the East German leader of the ruling socialist party and head of state Walter Ulbricht to Egypt coupled with the establishment of diplomatic relations between the Federal Republic of Germany and Israel led to the rupture of diplomatic relations between the Federal Republic and most Arab countries in May 1965. The erosion of the *Alleinvertretungsanspruch* and its main instrument, the Hallstein Doctrine, continued when, after the end of the Adenauer era, the new vice chancellor and secretary of state for foreign affairs, Willy Brandt, agreed to establish diplomatic relations with Romania in January 1967. This in fact ended the Hallstein Doctrine, even though West Germany declared that it had intended to exempt only those countries from the doctrine that had established diplomatic relations with the East German regime as early as 1949. With regard to these cases, it asserted, there existed a conceptual mistake when the Hallstein Doctrine was created. The governments of the East bloc countries had no choice and could not abstain from recognizing East Germany diplomatically when they themselves were established by order of the USSR or at least under strong Soviet influence. The Federal Republic resumed diplomatic relations with Yugoslavia in January 1968, and with the *Ostpolitik* of the social-liberal coalition, which came to power in West Germany in 1969, the Hallstein doctrine was completely abandoned.

BIBLIOGRAPHY

Booz, Rüdiger Marco. *"Hallsteinzeit" Deutsche Auβenpolitik 1955–1972*. Bonn: Bouvier, 1995.

Loth, Wilfried, William Wallace, and Wolfgang Wenzel, eds. *Walter Hallstein: The Forgotten European?* New York: St. Martin's Press, 1998.

Bernd Leupold

SEE ALSO Brandt, Willy

The United States and West Germany (1945–55)

The initial postwar relationship between the United States and Germany was that between victor and vanquished. After the unconditional surrender of Nazi Germany in May 1945, no German government existed and the United States, together with its allies France, Great Britain, and the Soviet Union, exercised supreme authority over the defeated enemy. Much of Germany, divided into four military occupation zones, was a scene of utter destruction in the midst of a devastated Europe.

One of the most striking features of the first decade of postwar U.S.-German relations was the change from occupation to alliance within a relatively short time. Explanations for this rapid transformation of the German position in the postwar international system are to be found particularly in the context of German-American relations. The speed with which the transformation was achieved in less than a decade was largely due to the increasing polarization of the international system, the efforts of a number of key players on the American and German sides, and the conceptual link between America's global strategy of containment and the German question.

During the first four years up to 1949, Germany was occupied and stripped of national sovereignty. America's official Germany policy in the immediate aftermath of the war was defined by demilitarization, denazification, decartelization, and democratization with the goal of preventing Germany from ever becoming a threat to world peace again. The punitive aspects of the occupation were soon replaced by a cooperative and conciliatory policy.

The Office of Military Government for Germany, United States (OMGUS) under the leadership of General Lucius D. Clay was faced with the daunting tasks of providing considerable amounts of foodstuffs to avert famine, deal with large numbers of refugees and displaced persons, ensure denazification, punish war criminals, and organize and support the revival of political, economic, and cultural life through a program of democratization.

America's approach to reeducation, the size of its programs, and the missionary zeal with which they were carried out made Washington's contribution to the postwar development of German democracy the most unique, comprehensive, and lasting among the German policies of the three Western allies. The U.S. program encompassed virtually every facet of German life and concentrated not only on institutional reforms (i.e., reforms of the education system and the civil service) but also on teaching democratic procedures and thus the establishment of behavioral patterns aiming at the creation of a stable, democratic political culture.

The democratization program was accompanied by substantial efforts to improve the material situation of the population. In 1947 the United States launched the Marshall Plan to revitalize the devastated Western European economies. Washington's policies raised the level of industrial production and merged the British and American zone of occupation. In 1948 the German currency reform took place and in May of 1949, amid severe disagreement between the Western powers and the USSR, two German states were founded, the Federal Republic of Germany (West Germany) and the German Democratic Republic (East Germany), thus finalizing the postwar division of Germany for the next four decades.

West Germany was brought into existence as a subordinate partner of the Western powers and of the United States in particular. But the central theme of the U.S.-West German relationship between 1949 and 1955 was the way in which the worsening of the Cold War made America increasingly build up the status of its West German partner, whose first chancellor, Konrad Adenauer, was in turn able to count on American support to improve the position of his country.

The return of Germany to the international community of nations through membership in the Council of Europe, the World Bank, the European Economic Organization (OEEC), and finally NATO was made possible from the German side through close association with the United States. On the U.S. side, the transformation of the German-American relationship from occupation to alliance was made possible by the conceptual links between the German question and America's global strategy of containment of communism and the work of a number of key players on both sides of the Atlantic. Conceptually the readmittance of Germany into the community of sovereign nations was the consequence of America's strategy to contain the USSR through the integration of the non-Communist world into an alliance system under U.S. leadership. Western Europe was the geostrategic core of this approach. In Western Europe, Washington faced the dual challenge of preventing the Soviet Union from expanding its sphere of influence and

at the same time keeping Germany from ever endangering world peace again.

Washington's conceptual answer to this challenge focused on Western European integration. With the economic and military strengthening, political integration, and psychological uplift of the devastated continent, America aimed at the stabilization of Europe and with it at an adequate answer to the dual challenge.

The key to both concepts was the German question. America's Germany policy was thus characterized by what we call today the strategy of dual containment. The Federal Republic was strengthened for the containment of the Soviet Union in central Europe and at the same time tightly integrated into the collective political, economic, and military structures of an emerging North Atlantic community under the leadership of the United States. Wolfram Hanrieder has described this policy as "the containment of the Soviet Union at arm's length, and of West Germany with an embrace."

During the six years of German semisovereignty (1949–55), West Germany was allowed to reestablish itself in Europe. This phase culminated on May 5, 1955, with the resumption of sovereignty and NATO membership, almost exactly ten years after the unconditional surrender of Nazi Germany in May 1945.

The polarization of the international system, the conceptual link between the German question and America's strategy of containment, and the work of advocates for a strong American-German alliance (Konrad Adenauer, John J. McCloy, from 1949–52 the high commissioner representing the Western occupying powers in West Germany, John Foster Dulles, U.S. secretary of state from 1953–59) on both sides of the Atlantic fostered and enabled change from occupation to alliance and laid the foundations for more than five decades of transatlantic cooperation.

BIBLIOGRAPHY

Diefendorf, Jeffrey M. et al., eds. *American Policy and the Reconstruction of West Germany, 1945–1955.* New York: Cambridge University Press, 1993.

Ermarth, Michael, ed. *America and the Shaping of German Society, 1945–1955.* Providence, R.I., 1993.

Hanrieder, Wolfram F. *Germany, America, Europe: Forty Years of German Foreign Policy.* New Haven, Conn.: Yale University Press, 1989.

Morgan, Roger. *The United States and West Germany, 1945–1973.* New York: Oxford University Press 1974.

Schwartz, Thomas. *America's Germany: John J. McCloy and the Federal Republic of Germany.* Cambridge, Mass.: Harvard University Press, 1991.

Frank Schumacher

Rearmament and NATO

The most fractious domestic issue during the chancellorship of Konrad Adenauer in the Federal Republic of Germany. Adenauer's decision for German rearmament, which necessitated a constitutional amendment, sharply divided the country, and the Social Democrats (SPD) fought it until the end.

Adenauer believed emphatically in inextricable ties with the West. As early as December 1949 he stated his concerns over the security of the Federal Republic and his desire to see it make a contribution to the defense of Western Europe. Adenauer knew full well that Western interest in rearming Germany was related to the Cold War. Yet at the end of World War II it was a capital offense for Germans to possess firearms, and they were being taught by the occupying powers that militarism was evil.

Western interest in German rearmament was sparked by a North Atlantic Treaty Organization manpower shortage and events in Asia. France was fighting a protracted war in Indochina, but Korea was the catalyst. Divided Korea offered parallels with Germany, and when North Korea invaded South Korea in June 1950, it raised anxieties in the Federal Republic. This led Adenauer to make a renewed effort for German rearmament in the expectation that this would bring concessions from the Western powers.

In August 1950, without consulting with his cabinet, Adenauer proposed to the Allied High Commission the creation of a federal police force and a possible German contribution to the defense of Western Europe in return for revision of the Occupation Statute. This led to a storm of protest within the government and the resignation of Minister of the Interior Gustav Heinemann, who later joined the SPD. Opposition was not simply because Adenauer had acted on his own; the SPD worried especially that Federal Republic rearmament would render German reunification impossible.

The resulting parliamentary and electoral battles on this issue were the most bitterly contested in the history of the Federal Republic. If there had been federal elections in 1950, the government probably would have fallen. The opposition helped Adenauer in one respect; it made it easier for him to secure concessions from the Western Allies.

Having been invaded by the Germans three times in the past eighty years, the French feared German rearmament. To counter this they came up with a plan for a European army. Proposed by the French Premier René Pleven, the plan envisioned a force in which there would be no national military unit larger than a battalion or brigade. Such an arrangement would allow German rearmament without a general staff or armaments industry. In May 1952 a draft treaty for the European Defense Community (EDC) was signed, providing for no national unit larger than a division. Adenauer much preferred the EDC arrangement for German rearmament, but ultimately the EDC failed. Ironically the French killed it. The armistice in Korea (July 27, 1953), the death of Stalin (March 5 1953), and the end of their involvement in Indochina (1954) all led the French Chamber of Deputies in August 1964 to reject the treaty.

Opinion in the Federal Republic gradually shifted to Adenauer's side. A strong argument was the formation in East Germany of a quasi-military force known as the "people's police." Following the collapse of the EDC, a compromise was worked out to allow the West Germans to rearm within NATO to a maximum strength of twelve divisions. In return, the three Western Allies ended the Occupation Statute and the Federal Republic of Germany received full sovereignty. The Bonn Convention, signed in May 1952, went into effect on May 5, 1955. The United States, Britain, and France all signed status-of-forces agreements with the Federal Republic. These allowed the three countries to keep control over their own armies in the Federal Republic and retain their rights in Berlin. They also retained the right to invoke emergency powers in the event of a collapse of German democracy.

Rearmament of the Federal Republic proceeded rapidly. Within a decade the Bundeswehr, or Federal armed forces, constituted the largest single European contribution to NATO and was Europe's second-largest military establishment after that of the Soviet Union. It grew to a strength of half a million men and included twelve army divisions, sixteen air squadrons, and some two hundred warships.

A unique feature of German rearmament was that the Federal Republic was the only member of NATO to place all its combat-ready elements under direct NATO command and not retain any independent military establishment of its own. The amendment to the Basic Law of March 1956 ensured civilian control. It gave command of the Bundeswehr to the minister of defense in times of peace; in war command was assigned to the chancellor.

The Federal Republic renounced the use of force to achieve reunification or to modify its existing boundaries. It also renounced the production and possession of atomic, biological, or chemical weapons. Although the Bundeswehr had nuclear weapons delivery systems, the weapons themselves remained under exclusive American control in accordance with NATO agreements. Finally, the Basic Law unequivocally limited the task of the Bundeswehr to defense. This constitutional provision has come under question in recent years, largely because of the Gulf War (1990) and fighting in the former Yugoslavia in the late 1990s.

BIBLIOGRAPHY

Adenauer, Konrad. *Memoirs.* Tr. by Beate Ruhn von Oppen. Chicago: Henry Regnery, 1966.

Bark, Dennis, L., and David R. Gress. *A History of West Germany,* Vol. 1, *From Shadow to Substance, 1945–1963.* Oxford: Basil Blackwell, 1989.

Hiscocks, Richard. *The Adenauer Era.* Philadelphia: Lippencott, 1966.

Kelleher, Catherine McArdle. "Germany and the Alliance," in Viola Herms Drath, ed. *Germany in World Politics.* New York: Cyrco Press, 1979.

Prittie, Terence. *Adenauer: A Study in Fortitude.* Chicago: Henry Regnery, 1972.

Riste, Olav, ed. *Western Security: The Formative Years.* Oslo: Norwegian University Press, 1985.

Spencer C. Tucker

Grenzschutzgruppe 9

West German counterterrorism group. Grenzschutzgruppe 9 (GSG-9) was formed in reaction to the killing of eleven Israeli athletes by Black September terrorists during the 1972 Munich Olympics. The German handling of the situation drove home the point that the Federal Republic needed an organization specifically trained for counterterrorism and hostage rescue. One of the reasons the German government decided to make such an organization a police rather than a military unit was to avoid potential charges of creating a new version of the dreaded SS of the Third Reich.

Hans-Dietrich Genscher, the then minister of the interior, was given permission to form the new unit as the ninth group of the paramilitary Bundesgrenzschutz (BGS), the Federal Border Police. GSG-9's first commander was Police Colonel Ulrich Wegener, who immediately formed close ties with the leading counterterrorist organizations of major Western Nations, including the British Special Air Service (SAS) and the U.S. Army's Delta Force. Wegener, in fact, reportedly accompanied Israeli commandos on their rescue mission at Entebbe, Uganda, in 1976 to rescue hostages who had been hijacked by Arab terrorists.

GSG-9 came to the attention of the world on October 17, 1977, when a twenty-nine man team successfully stormed a hijacked Lufthansa airliner at Mogadishu, Somalia. During the rescue three of the ninety hostages were wounded, but none seriously; three of the four terrorists were killed, and the fourth seriously wounded. GSG-9

has carried out other missions since, most of which have been so successful that the general public never learned about them.

With an authorized strength of 188, GSG-9 originally was organized into three strike units, supported by a communications and intelligence unit, an engineer unit, a weapons unit, a research and equipment unit, a maintenance and supply unit, and a training unit. In 1983 a fourth strike unit was added. Each strike unit consists of 30 to 42 commandos, further organized into 5-man teams. GSG-9's intelligence support is provided by a sophisticated antiterrorist computer system located in Wiesbaden. In 1979 GSG-9's strength was increased to 219. In 1981 Wegener was promoted to the rank of police brigadier general and assumed command of BGS West.

Recruiting for GSG-9 is highly selective, and the training program is demanding. Candidates must have several years of experience in the BGS with a good record. The initial screening process, which includes intelligence and psychological evaluations, eliminates approximately two-thirds of applicants. Another 10 percent fail to make it through the five-month basic training phase, which heavily stresses individual skills such as marksmanship and the martial arts. The three-month secondary training phase focuses on teamwork and assault tactics.

In July 1993, GSG-9 came under severe criticism and scrutiny for mishandling the arrest of two Red Army Faction terrorists at a train station in eastern Germany. During the ensuing shoot-out, one GSG-9 officer died. Wolfgang Grams, one of the suspected terrorists, also died from a gunshot wound to the head at point-blank range. Much of the evidence at the time seemed to suggest that Grams was summarily executed after being subdued by GSG-9 officers. Grams's death was later ruled a suicide and the officers involved were never charged. The incident, however, cast a long shadow over GSG-9.

In August 1993, GSG-9 successfully ended the hijacking of a Dutch KLM airliner that had been diverted to Düsseldorf. Normally this type of operation would have been handled in a low-key manner. Its wide play in the press may have been part of a campaign to restore GSG-9's image in the wake of the Grams incident.

BIBLIOGRAPHY

Smith, G. Davidson. *Combating Terrorism.* New York: Routledge, 1990.

Thompson, Leroy. *The Rescuers: The World's Top Anti-Terrorist Units.* Boulder, Colo.: Paladin, 986.

David T. Zabecki

SEE ALSO Germany: Red Army Faction

Red Army Faction

West German terrorist organization, also known as the Baader-Meinhof gang, which attempted to incite revolution in the German Federal Republic during the 1970s and 1980s by engaging in a series of spectacularly violent acts. The Red Army Faction (Rote Armee Fraktion, RAF) was one of many splinter groups that emerged from the radical student movement of 1968. Organized and directed by Andreas Baader (1943–77), the RAF dedicated itself to oppose "reactionary oppression," Germany's postwar materialism, and "American Imperialism." The RAF's political ideology embraced some elements of Marxism and anarchism but never became a clearly defined platform. The RAF was certainly not a strictly Marxist-Leninist organization as its name implied; the designation "Red Army" served to indicate connections with similar groups abroad (Italy, the Middle East, and Japan).

Despite its sometimes populist rhetoric, the RAF itself acknowledged that the German Federal Republic's social and political basis was not conducive to revolutionary activities. The RAF borrowed the concept and tactics of "urban guerrillas" from radical Latin American groups and engaged in wave of sensational and brutal actions, including kidnappings, bank robberies, bombings, and a half dozen murders between 1968 and 1972, hoping to incite widespread revolutionary sentiment. These activities helped make Europe the world's leading region of terrorist activities at that time. The RAF sought to provoke West German authorities into resorting to police-state tactics to counter the revolutionary threat, a move calculated to "expose" the government as fascist and reactionary. The RAF's escapades received much media attention, and for a brief time elements of the German Left supported the terrorists. Baader was arrested in 1968 but managed to escape underground shortly before entering prison to serve his sentence. Captured again in April 1970, he was freed the following month by Ulrike Meinhof (1934–76), a renowned left-wing journalist, in a dramatic operation. Henceforth Meinhof worked closely with Baader. In 1972 both fugitives were apprehended by West German authorities. Meinhof, sentenced in 1974 to eight years' imprisonment, was found dead in her jail cell in 1976. The official verdict was suicide but many RAF followers and fellow travelers contended that in fact she had been murdered by the police. In the spring of 1977 Baader himself was sentenced to life imprisonment; he too died while in Stammheim prison in Stuttgart, committing suicide following an unsuccessful attempt by the RAF to force his release by holding a Lufthansa airliner hostage at Mogadishu, Somalia.

While in prison Baader continued to direct RAF activities through a network of sympathetic lawyers and above-ground contacts. Following his death it became apparent that the RAF was broken but not eradicated. An estimated core of fifteen to twenty RAF members remained underground, organized in hard-to-detect clandestine cells that continued to engage in violent actions. The remaining RAF personnel increased collaborative efforts with foreign terrorist groups (the Italian Red Brigades and the French Action Directe, among others), which raised the specter of "Euroterrorism," but their joint efforts failed to precipitate any significant changes in the political and social structures of Western Europe.

Following a lull in the mid-1980s, the RAF reemerged, claiming credit for the November 1989 assassination of Alfred Herrhausen, a prominent German banker. Charges that the German Democratic Republic (DDR) was involved in harboring and outfitting the RAF were confirmed after the collapse of the DDR in 1990. Although most of the RAF leadership had already died in prison by suicide or through hunger strikes, several fugitives were apprehended following the collapse of the DDR. The RAF continued a shadowy existence into the 1990s, but its activities have been by and large obscured in the public eye by the emergence of neo-Nazism and right-radical terrorist groups. The RAF has so far failed to inspire Germans to support revolutionary change; indeed, their brutal tactics have been counterproductive, in that any residual support from the early 1970s had disappeared by the late 1980s.

BIBLIOGRAPHY

Laqueur, Walter. *The Age of Terrorism*. Boston: Little, Brown, 1987.

Laqueur, Walter, and Yonah Alexander, eds. *The Terrorism Reader: A Historical Anthology*. New York: Meridian, 1987.

Mark P. Gingerich

Historikerstreit (Historians' Controversy)

Conflict among West German historians about the "historicization" and "normalization" of National Socialism and the Holocaust. Provoked by conservative efforts to revise the Nazi past to make it seem more a part of the "normal" history of the twentieth century, the *Historikerstreit* (Historians' Controversy) eventually involved virtually every major historian of modern German history in the Federal Republic of Germany as well as a number of prominent journalists. Originally focused on the issue of whether the Holocaust was uniquely evil, the controversy evolved into a fierce polemical debate about the appropriate interpretation of the Nazi past and its meaning for contemporary Germans. The *Historikerstreit* received wide publicity in the months leading up to the Bundestag elections of January 25, 1987, and for some time thereafter. The controversy occurred in a political climate that had taken a rightward turn after the transition from Social Democratic to Christian Democratic rule in the Federal Republic in 1982. The government of Helmut Kohl had already been accused of attempting to rehabilitate the Nazi past and relativize Nazi crimes in the Bitburg controversy of 1985, when Kohl and U.S. President Ronald Reagan visited a cemetery in which some of the interned had been SS members. Conservatives would charge that the *Historikerstreit* was started by left-wing intellectuals to counteract the loss of their dominance since the 1960s. The dispute began with an article by social philosopher Jürgen Habermas in the liberal weekly *Die Zeit* on July 11, 1986, attacking apologetic tendencies in recent conservative historiography. The main target of his criticisms was historian Ernst Nolte, whose article "The Past That Will Not Go Away" in the June 6, 1986, issue of the conservative *Frankfurter Allgemeine Zeitung* (*FAZ*) asserted that Nazi atrocities were no worse than the earlier Bolshevik and Stalinist crimes on which they were allegedly modeled and that the Holocaust represented an understandable preemptive response by the Nazis to the perceived Communist threat. Habermas also criticized historian Andreas Hillgruber for the unabashedly nationalist perspective of his book *Two Kinds of Downfall: The Destruction of the German Empire and the End of European Jewry* (1986). Habermas accused Nolte, Hillgruber, and historian Michael Stürmer, an adviser to the Kohl government, of rewriting history to build a national consensus in support of neoconservative policies. Stürmer had contended that the left-wing fixation on Germany's historical guilt threatened to weaken the NATO alliance and strengthen the "antifascist" ideology of the German Democratic Republic. The ensuing controversy divided the West German historical profession along political lines. Besides Nolte, Hillgruber, and Stürmer, the most prominent defenders of conservative positions included Klaus Hildebrand, Hagen Schulze, and Joachim Fest, a historian who was also editor in chief of the *FAZ*. Their critics included historians Hans Mommsen, Wolfgang Mommsen, Eberhard Jackel, Jürgen Kocka, Heinrich August Winkler, and Hans-Ulrich Wehler, doyen of the influential Bielefeld school of social historians. Some historians, such as Imanuel Geiss, defended Hillgruber and Stürmer but joined in criticizing Nolte's more extreme formulations. While some of the political issues lost their relevance with the collapse of communism and the re-

unification of Germany, the historiographical debate continued as part of the cultural wars of the 1990s. Although rejected by the mainstream of the German historical profession, Nolte's revisionist paradigm, according to which National Socialism must be understood as an at least partially justified reaction to the supposedly greater evil of Soviet communism, attracted some followers among a younger generation of "new right" historians and publicists. On the whole, however, the *Historikerstreit* reinforced public awareness both in Germany and abroad that the Nazi era cannot be viewed as part of "normal" history. The major documents of the *Historikerstreit* have been published in a single volume under the title *Historikerstreit*. The English translation is flawed, however, and should be used with caution.

BIBLIOGRAPHY

Augstein, Rudolf, et al. *"Historikerstreit": Die Dokumentation der Kontroverse um die Einzigartigkeit der nationalsozialistischen Judenvernichtung.* Munich: Piper Verlag, 1987. (English translation by James Knowlton and Truett Cates. *Forever in the Shadow of Hitler? Original Documents of the Historikerstreit, the Controversy Concerning the Singularity of the Holocaust.* Atlantic Highlands, N.J.: Humanities Press, 1993.)

Baldwin, Peter, ed. *Reworking the Past: Hitler, the Holocaust, and the Historians' Debate.* Boston: Beacon Press, 1990.

Evans, Richard J. *In Hitler's Shadow: West German Historians and the Attempt to Escape from the Nazi Past.* New York: Pantheon, 1989.

Habermas, Jürgen. *The New Conservatism: Cultural Criticism and the Historians' Debate.* Cambridge, Mass.: MIT Press, 1991.

Hillgruber, Andreas. *Zweierlei Untergang: Die Zerschlagung des Deutschen Reiches und das Ende des europäischen Judentums.* Berlin: Siedler, 1986.

Low, Alfred D. *The Third Reich and the Holocaust in German Historiography: Toward the Historikerstreit of the Mid-1980s.* New York: Columbia University Press, 1994.

Maier, Charles S. *The Unmasterable Past: History, Holocaust, and German National Identity.* Cambridge, Mass.: Harvard University Press, 1988.

Moeller, Robert G. "War Stories: The Search for a Usable Past in the Federal Republic of Germany." *American Historical Review* 101 (October 1996): 1008–48.

Nolte, Ernst. *Der europäische Bürgerkrieg 1917–1945: Nationalsozialismus und Bolschewismus.* Frankfurt: Ullstein, 1987.

———. *Das Vergehen der Vergangenheit: Antwort an meine Kritiker im sogenannten Historikerstreit*. Berlin: Ullstein, 1987.

Wehler, Hans-Ulrich. *Entsorgung der deutschen Vergangenheit? Ein polemischer Essay zum "Historikerstreit"*. Munich: Verlag C.H. Beck, 1988.

Rod Stackelberg

Social Integration of the Two Germanies

East Germany's passage to capitalism, unlike that of other Eastern European countries, has been determined by reunification with a major Western power. Much effort was devoted to the development of infrastructures designed to achieve long-term conditions for equality in the six new Länder, but meanwhile old identities have hardened as the new states remained the home of Germany's second-class citizens. By 1998 the Helmut Kohl government had not created the "blooming landscape" the chancellor had promised that reunification would bring to East Germany within just a few short years. Furthermore, some aspects of social unification, which in any case would not have been resolved quickly through the Christian Democrats' (CDU) predominantly economic policies for domestic reunification, would persist for more than one generation.

The Germans, who had been together through the unification of 1871, as well as the Great Depression and two world wars of the twentieth century, could not unify quickly following four decades on opposite sides of the Iron Curtain. During the two generations since 1949 during which citizens of the Federal Republic of Germany (FRG) had been learning the challenges of the capitalist *risiko Gesellschaft* (competitive society), East Germans had been chided into assuming that the state would take care of them and assure everyone a job. Torn suddenly from their familiar environment with the collapse of communism, East Germans were expected to slough off familiar truths in exchange for fully foreign structures of capitalism. Not surprisingly, the widespread perception of former East Germans in western Germany was of a people unable to take the risks capitalism demanded, and prone to blame others for their discontents, instead of assuming personal responsibility.

Problems of reunification were aggravated by early government promises of a relatively easy process. Early official optimism about unification created images of the long-established sense of East German inferiority vanishing almost as quickly as the Communist government itself. At the time of reunification in 1990, most East Germans, expecting to become assimilated as "West Germans" themselves, did not resent that reunification was defined totally by the FRG. West Germans, or Wessis, however,

considered their superior way of life to be the fruit of hard labors and (especially the younger West German generation, which had no personal experience with or expectation of a reunified Germany) resented the unification-triggered increase in taxes. To western Germans the mass of East Germans, who had little preparation for the ways of Western capitalist democracy, were laborious and at best dutiful, hardly their equals in the marketplace. East Germans in turn came to perceive their new fellow citizens as arrogant *Besserwissers* (know-it-alls) who unrealistically expected them to change into West Germans overnight.

As East Germans discovered how different they were from West Germans, the birthrate dropped precipitously, and many indulged in *Nostalgie,* the tendency to remember only the good things about life in former East Germany. By the mid-1990s as many Ossis realized that official promises of economic (and implied social) equality would remain out of reach for some time, the Ossi-Wessi syndrome of inferiority-superiority complexes hardened into unfriendly fronts, with one identity continuing to reinforce the other. Surveys revealed that former East Germans seldom visited the former West Germany or even talked to West Germans, and vice versa. By 1998 there was evidence that even those who were in elementary school at the time of reunification had taken on an identity as "former East Germans," where, in their recollections, as provided by their parents, everyone had a job, people had more time, and they helped each other more willingly.

Paradigms of Western superiority and Eastern inferiority will continue as long as individual Germans continue to derive separate identities from their conceptions of the two former Germanies, upheld especially by diverging opportunities for employment. Despite Kohl's promises to cut unemployment in half by the year 2000, the number of unemployed virtually doubled since 1991 to nearly five million by early 1998, with no immediate changes in this trend expected. Angst over unemployment weighed much heavier over the former East Germany, where the unemployment rate was double that of former West Germany (21 percent and 10.4 percent, respectively, in February 1998), and where a civil service job paid just 85 percent of what the same position pays in the territories of the former FRG. In addition to more jobs and superior pay, a third factor in the workplace maintained western German superiority: superior positions. In 1994 just 134,000 eastern Germans were civil service managers as compared with 3,775,000 from the former FRG. In the private sector, the Treuhandanstalt (the organization established to preside over privatization) sold nearly 90 percent of GDR businesses to West German companies, which often preferred to increase productivity in the west, where productivity per hour of labor was considerably higher, than to maintain old plants or build new ones in eastern Germany. The FRG privatized German Democratic Republic (GDR) businesses in a manner that former Chancellor Helmut Schmidt described as "nearing psychological colonization."

In the context of so much change so rapidly, there were bound to be many injustices and dissatisfaction with government. Confidence in democracy as a form of government declined after reunification, especially in the territories of former communism but also in the old FRG states. An initial spate of extreme-right violence following unification culminated in 1992, but 1997 registered a troubling renewed increase in extreme-right violence, 45 percent of which was in the new German states, which made up just 20 percent of the German population. In addition, by 1998 cases of Treuhandanstalt corruption had surfaced. Court trials revealed that the Treuhandanstalt in Halle, one of its fifteen regional offices, had destroyed thousands of eastern jobs and caused damages of some $700 million through betrayal, false representations, and bribes. Certain social groups in the new German states were hit especially hard by reunification. Unemployment was especially high among women, who were used to full employment, and intellectuals, especially academics in social sciences and humanities tainted by the Communist party line. Women who in the GDR always had access to child care now often found it harder simultaneously to work and take care of family, and access to abortion became more restricted.

The question persists as to whether eastern Germany will remain the poor cousin of the western FRG, less developed and industrialized in the character of southern to northern Italy. In election year 1998, with the cost of social welfare now taking up over 42 percent of gross state expenditures, leading German politicians, including Social Democrats, wondered whether the cost of unemployment payments must be reduced, and the large, wealthy states of Bavaria and Baden-Württemburg opposed renewing the existing mandate for a "sharing of wealth" among states, measures that would entrench the differences between Germany's east and west. With continuing massive government injections of an average of $70 billion per year since 1991, the former GRD had been registering steady economic growth year by year. In 1997, however, government transfers were cut back, and for the first time the yearly level of economic growth in the new states of the FRG was lower than that in western Germany. In the longer run, economic growth could succeed in bringing about social unification, but this would require continuing massive government subsidies to the east.

BIBLIOGRAPHY

Fuchs, Peter. *Westöstliche Divan.* Frankfurt: Suhrkamp, 1995.

Hancock, M. Donald, and Helga A. Welsh, eds. *German Unification: Process and Outcomes.* Boulder, Colo.: Westview Press, 1994.

Maier, Charles S. *Dissolution.* Princeton, N.J.: Princeton University Press, 1997.

Rueschemeyer, Marilyn, ed. *Women in the Politics of Postcommunist Eastern Europe.* Armonk N.Y.: M. E. Sharpe, 1994.

Schmitz, Michael. *Wendestreß: Die psychosozialen Kosten der deutschen Einheit.* Berlin: Rowohlt, 1995.

Nathan Stoltzfus

Two-plus-Four Treaty (1990)

International agreement between the two German states and the four Allied powers prior to German reunification. The treaty was signed September 12, 1990, in Moscow by the foreign ministers of the United States, the Soviet Union, the United Kingdom, France, the Federal Republic of Germany, and the German Democratic Republic. It was subsequently endorsed by the Conference on Security and Cooperation in Europe at its Washington meeting on October 1. This Treaty on the Final Settlement with Respect to Germany granted reunification and full sovereignty to Germany while attaching the reunited nation closely to already existing Western political, economic, and military organizations. It represented a legally and diplomatically indispensable precondition to actual German reunification and came after intense international negotiations, including a series of summit meetings in the summer of 1990.

The treaty reflected both the desire of the major powers to end forty-five years of confrontational Cold War arrangements in the heart of Europe and the skill of German Chancellor Helmut Kohl in translating a unique political opportunity into reality. It also strengthened détente as Germany's neighbors, especially Poland, and its allies and associates could anticipate new levels of cooperation in an increasingly integrated Europe.

BIBLIOGRAPHY

Jarausch, Konrad H. *The Rush to German Unity.* Oxford: Oxford University Press, 1994.

Maier, Charles. *Across the Wall: Revolution and Reunification of Germany.* Princeton, N.J.: Princeton University Press, 1994.

Neckermann, Peter. *The Unification of Germany: Anatomy of a Peaceful Revolution.* Boulder, Colo.: Colorado University Press, 1992.

Eric C. Rust

Denazification

Process carried out by the four occupying powers to remold Germany after twelve years of Hitler's dictatorship. The goal of denazification was to eliminate remnants of the Nazi ideology that had permeated German society. Carried out during the years 1945–49, this process incorporated reeducation, purges of Germany's major institutions, and trials of war criminals. At the Potsdam Conference from July 17 to August 2, 1945, Soviet leader Joseph Stalin suggested simply shooting fifty thousand of Nazi Germany's leaders. American president Harry Truman and British Prime Minister Clement Attlee refused to go along with this suggestion, and each occupying power developed its own style of denazification.

The Americans were the most determined denazifiers. Hoping to end their occupation of Germany within two years, they zealously set about reforming and democratizing German society. Directive 1067 of the Joint Chiefs of Staff in April 1945 called for a purge from public life of all Germans who had joined the Nazi Party before 1937. The Americans assumed that anyone who joined after that date probably did so to keep a job and was not a convinced Nazi.

All Germans over the age of eighteen in the American zone had to fill out a questionnaire (*Fragebogen*) consisting of 131 questions dealing not only with issues of party affiliation but also with income, education, and employment status during the Third Reich. The Americans assumed that anyone who ran a large business, owned a great deal of land, or had been an officer in the military had been a Nazi sympathizer. Altogether over thirteen million Germans living in the American zone filled out the form. Each respondent was placed in one of five categories: major offender, offender, lesser offender, follower, or exonerated. Making use of these questionnaires, American occupation authorities tried over 169,000 Germans, and a further 761,000 were administered lesser sentences that did not require a trial. By the end of 1945, for example, 141,000 had lost their jobs as a result of their wartime activities.

In June 1946, the Law for the Liberation from National Socialism and Militarism ordered Germans in the American zone to create a Special Ministry of Political Education, which would establish German denazification courts. The Germans established 545 denazification tribunals, which charged three million Germans, of whom only 930 were tried, convicted, and sentenced. The Germans were not as determined in their denazification efforts as the Americans had been.

Another component of the American denazification scheme was a purge of the German school system. Over 80 percent of Germany's teachers lost their jobs, as did most administrators. Textbooks adopted during the Third Reich were replaced and a curriculum developed designed to indoctrinate German students about the advantages of freedom and democracy.

In March 1945, Great Britain's Adjutant General's Office established a special office to deal with denazification and war crimes. From the beginning of their efforts, however, the British faced several obstacles, not the least of which was a shortage of resources assigned to the denazification campaign. Also, unlike the Americans, the British were convinced that National Socialism had been a natural product of German history and that denazification would involve a long-term commitment on their part. Finally, the British military was unwilling to make denazification a top priority of its occupation efforts. During the first year of British occupation, for example, only 91 Germans in the British zone were tried for war crimes.

The French, unlike the Americans and British, were unwilling to distinguish between the Nazi leadership and the German people. This affected their attitude toward denazification, and many considered the process a waste of time. The French, therefore, put the least effort of any of the occupiers into remolding German society. While the French maintained the categories established by the Fragebogen, they were less strict in their interpretation than the Americans. The French occupiers were more willing to judge each case individually, which slowed down the process. Altogether the French tried only 17,353 Germans for crimes committed during the Third Reich. Like the Americans, the French handed over the denazification process to the Germans in 1946 but did not provide the extensive oversight of the process that the Americans did.

The Soviets also developed their own style of denazification that they put into practice in their zone. In the Soviet zone, denazification was much more violent, and it was not uncommon for former SS members to be executed without a trial and dumped into the street as a warning to their fellow Germans. At the same time, the Soviets were much more tolerant of even high-ranking Nazis who were willing to assist in Soviet occupation efforts, especially if they were willing to join the communist Socialist Unity Party. For example, Heinrich Müller, former chief of the much-feared Gestapo, escaped denazification in the Soviet zone because of his willingness to cooperate with the Soviets. In spite of this tendency, the Soviets did try about 18,000 Germans, of whom around 10,000 were convicted and received sentences. It remains unknown how many former Nazis the Soviets executed without the benefit of a trial.

By 1949 the denazification process had ended. Denazification was, at best, a partial success. All four of the occupying powers soon discovered that they could not completely do without the expertise of the millions of former Nazis in Germany. These people had been the elite of the Third Reich, and it was simply impossible to carry out the occupation effectively without their help. Finally, denazification became a secondary concern as the former Allies began to turn on each other in the emerging Cold War.

BIBLIOGRAPHY

Gimbel, John. *The American Occupation of Germany: Politics and the Military, 1945–1949.* Stanford, Calif.: Stanford University Press, 1968.

Nettle, J. P. *The Eastern Zone and Soviet Policy in Germany, 1945–1950.* New York: Octagon Books, 1977.

Oppen, Beate Ruhm von, ed. *Documents on Germany Under Occupation, 1945–1954.* London: Oxford University Press, 1955.

Tent, James F. *Mission on the Rhine: Reeducation and Denazification in American-Occupied Germany.* Chicago: University of Chicago Press, 1982.

United States Department of State. *Documents on Germany, 1944–1985.* Washington, D.C.: Department of State, n.d.

Willis, F. Roy. *The French in Germany, 1945–1949.* Stanford, Calif.: Stanford University Press, 1962.

Wolfe, Robert, ed. *Americans as Proconsuls: United States Military Government in Germany and Japan, 1944–1952.* Carbondale: Southern Illinois University Press, 1984.

Russel William Lemmons

SEE ALSO Nuremberg Trials; Wartime Conferences

Berufsverbote (Vocational Ban)

German administrative practice of excluding from the civil service those applicants deemed politically unreliable, i.e., lacking in loyalty to Germany's constitution, the Basic Law. Until 1972, Article 52(2) of the Federal Civil Service Law, which requires that candidates for appoint-

ment to the civil service "be able to guarantee" that they "will at any time defend the free democratic basic order in the spirit of the Basic Law," was hardly noticed. But in that year the federal government, in conjunction with the Land (state) minister presidents, circulated a memorandum (often mistakenly termed the "Radicals' Decree" as it was not a decree) reminding public authorities of their responsibility to enforce the Civil Service Law. It was at that time that many left-wing activists were first entering civil service professions.

While the total number of persons excluded from the civil service on the basis of Article 52(2) is relatively small (about one thousand), many more, perhaps as many as a million, were investigated by the Verfassungsschutz (Office for the Protection of the Constitution). Moreover, the practice almost certainly had a "chilling," and thus illiberal, effect on many actual or potential civil servants, who may have refrained from any political activity so as not to attract the attention of the authorities. From the beginning the "vocational ban" was highly controversial, and not just among leftists, its primary victims. It also attracted considerable international attention, and critics were often quick to accuse Germany of reviving its undemocratic past. What added to the problem was that in Germany public servants make up a very large proportion of the workforce (19 percent), with half of them having the coveted "civil servant" status. Even mail carriers and train engineers could be, and actually were, removed from their chosen occupations because of the ban.

Because of a combination of factors, the practice of "routine inquiries" (*Routineanfragen*) in an applicant's background was largely discontinued after 1985. Yet the law remains in effect and continues to be applied in a small number of cases, especially in Bavaria, where the removal of several members of the Church of Scientology has recently caused considerable controversy. Moreover, in extreme cases, especially those involving hard-core neo-Nazis, the authorities have additional constitutional means at their disposal, such as Article 18 of the Basic Law, which allows for a person to be stripped of his or her civil liberties. In 1995, the European Court of Human Rights ruled that the "vocational ban" violated its Fundamental Charter on Human Rights as well as the principle of proportionality.

While it is almost certainly true that German officials were overzealous in enforcing the Radicals Decree (the large number of investigations testifies to that), it is important that it be seen in the proper historical and political context. The Weimar Republic (1919–33), Germany's first attempt at democracy, failed, many historians and constitutional scholars believe, because the state lacked the constitutional means to defend itself against extremist forces. In particular, the Weimar civil service, largely a holdover from the illiberal *Kaiserreich* (Empire), was widely regarded as having been deficient in its loyalty to the democratic state. It is precisely because of these experiences that the Federal Republic was designed by its founders to be a "militant democracy" (*Wehrhafte Demokratie*). This constitutional theory obliges state authorities to play an active role in protecting democracy against its enemies, i.e., political extremists intent on undermining, overtly or covertly, the "democratic-constitutional state" (*demokratischer Verfassungsstaat*). The Federal Constitutional Court, in a landmark ruling upholding the vocational ban, held that "the Constitution is not morally neutral but grounds itself on certain central values, takes them into its protection and gives the state the task of protecting and guaranteeing them. It establishes a militant democracy."

Andreas Sobisch

Office for the Protection of the Constitution

Agency charged with helping to protect the German constitution (Basic Law) against internal extremists and external agents. The Federal Office for the Protection of the Constitution (Bundesamt für Verfassungsschutz, BfV) is accountable to the minister of the interior. In 1996 it had a staff of 2,215 and an annual budget of about DM 225 million ($150 million). Its responsibility consists exclusively of collecting information on radical and subversive parties, groups, and organizations; it has no police powers. To open an investigation on an organization suspected of having extremist goals, German law requires that there exist "factual evidence of concrete, purposeful activities" aimed at "destroying the free democratic basic order" or "endangering the existence or security" of the country or any of its constituent states. The BfV publishes an annual report (*Verfassungsschutzbericht*) that is made available to the public (www.government.de/inland/index_d4.html) and that documents all its major findings. The BfV cooperates with similar agencies at the Land (state) level, and the data gathered are used not only by executive authorities in carrying out their constitutional duty of "safeguarding the Free Democratic Basic Order", but also by the courts in deciding relevant cases brought before them, as well as by academic researchers.

The BfV has often been criticized by civil libertarians for being overzealous in carrying out its responsibilities and by leftists for "selective persecution" of them while, at the same time, allegedly turning a blind eye to the threat from the extreme right. Although some of these charges probably held merit during the 1970s and early 1980s, in recent years the laws governing the BfV's activities have been clarified and privacy protections have been strengthened. Moreover, there can be little doubt that during the early 1990s the agency has played an important role in the government's efforts to curb the violence perpetrated by right-wing extremist activists against foreigners and other minorities.

The BfV should be understood in the context of Germany's "militant democracy" (*Wehrhafte Demokratie*), a constitutional theory that obliges state authorities to play an active role in protecting democracy against its enemies, that is, political extremists of various colors who are intent on undermining, overtly or covertly, the "democratic-constitutional state" (*demokratischer Verfassungstaat*). The Federal Constitutional Court in a landmark 1976 ruling held that "the Constitution is not morally neutral but grounds itself on certain central values, takes them into its protection and gives the state the task of protecting and guaranteeing them. It establishes a militant democracy." The concept of militant democracy was developed during the early years of the Federal Republic in an explicit effort to learn from the mistakes of the past, specifically the Weimar Republic (1919–33). That first attempt at democracy in Germany was doomed, many historians and constitutional scholars believed, because the state lacked the ability to use constitutional means to snuff out extremist forces in the early stages of their development.

Andreas Sobisch

Political Parties

Hitler's National Socialists ended the Weimar Republic's pluralist democracy in 1933 and forced all forms of political competition underground. Twelve years later Hitler's Third Reich lay in ruins and support for National Socialism had all but evaporated. Defeated and occupied, the Germans and their occupiers sought to create a new political system. West German political parties after 1945 provided a degree of political stability in a democratic state unmatched in most other European democracies. The East German political system, on the other hand, remained dominated by the Marxist-Leninist Socialist Unity Party until 1990.

Under Allied supervision Germany's postwar political recovery began. By 1945 it became clear that each of the occupying powers had its own unique vision of German political life. Soviet authorities sanctioned the de facto creation of political parties within their occupation zone in June 1945. Shortly thereafter, Western Allied authorities, fearing a loss of credibility among the German populace, accepted during the Potsdam Conference of July-

August, the re-creation of German political parties. Thus, just as four-power cooperation in the Allied Control Council in Berlin declined and ended with the Berlin Blockade, distinct socioeconomic and political systems developed within East and West Germany.

Political parties in the Federal Republic of Germany (FRG) differed substantially from their Wilhelmine and Weimar counterparts. The Basic Law (Grundgesetz), the FRG's constitution, bound political parties to the constitution by obligating them to support the democratic order or risk dissolution by the Federal Constitutional Court. This power was used by the court against the Socialist Reich Party, a neo-Nazi group, in 1952 and against the German Communist Party in 1956. According to Article 21, political parties advocating the overthrow of the democratic order are in violation of the Basic Law. The Weimar constitution, in comparison, made no provision for handling political institutions advocating the dissolution of the democratic order.

Major political parties in the FRG represented a broad spectrum of public interests rather than those of a single religious confession or social class. On the other hand, the political landscape is dotted with smaller parties not represented in parliament. Formally integrated into the political process through the Basic Law, the concept of the party-state (*Parteienstaat*) acknowledged the close relationship between political parties and the state. The two dominant political parties—the Christian Democratic Union (Christliche Demokratische Union, CDU, and its Bavarian affiliate, the Christian Social Union, Christliche Sozial Union, CSU, thus CDU/CSU) and, since its 1959 transformation at the Bad Godesberg Party Conference, the Social Democratic Party (Sozialdemokratische Partei Deutschlands, SPD)—also represent substantial departures from their Weimar counterparts. While linked with the Weimar's Catholic Center Party, Christian Democratic and Christian Socialist groups created the CDU in 1946, though it did not have its first FRG-wide convention until 1950. Chancellor Konrad Adenauer pulled together the multitude of conservative parties by focusing on Ludwig Erhard's concept of a social market economy. Adenauer's economic planning was guided by a belief in free enterprise supported by the state. Adenauer coupled his economic policy with a vision of a state motivated by a belief in basic Christian principles and morality. Such a state, Adenauer held, would also assume greater responsibility for the welfare of its inhabitants. Adenauer's competition on the political left, the SPD, pursued a platform espousing a Marxist orientation, the concept of class struggle, rejection of capitalism, and support for land reform and extensive economic planning. Although Social

Democrats held to a Marxist-oriented vision of politics and political objectives, in 1959 the SPD moved into the ranks of the catchall parties when it altered its party platform, dropped its Marxist rhetoric, accepted the basic principles of the social market economy, and coupled its historical links with the working class to those of the middle class. The political center fell to Theodor Heuss's Free Democratic Party (Freiheitliche Demokratische Partei, FDP, or Liberals). These Liberals advocated unfettered free enterprise. Emerging from its ecological-left origins of the early 1980s, the Greens (Die Grünen or, since 1992, Alliance 90/The Greens, Bündnis 90/Die Grünen) under Joschke Fischer in the 1990s tempered their stand on nonviolence, the military, and ecology, and moved into the political middle. These parties are best described as *Volksparteien,* or broad-spectrum popular parties.

Since reunification these political parties have been joined by the Party of Democratic Socialism (Partei Demokratischer Sozialismus, PDS), the successor party to the East German Socialist Unity Party (SED). First led by Gregor Gysi, the PDS was represented in parliament in 1990 and won a place there again in 1994. It has also played an important roll in state politics in eastern Germany. In addition, a number of splinter parties have dotted the political landscape. On the radical right, the National Democratic Party (Nationaldemokratische Partei Deutschlands, NPD) in the 1960s and the Republicans (Republikaner, REP) in the 1980s and 1990s took extremely nationalistic and xenophobic stands. Parties on the radical left, including the Marxist-Leninist Party (Marxistisch-Leninistische Partei Deutschlands, MLDP) and the PDS, have identified with rigidly Marxist world views.

Obtaining a seat in the lower house of parliament (Bundestag) is regulated by Articles 38 and 41 of the Basic Law and the first Election Law (Bundeswahlgesetz). According to the Election Law in June 1949, a party needed 5 percent in a Land (state) or direct mandates from one or more election districts to be represented in the Bundestag. The law changed in 1953 to demand 5 percent of the overall vote or one direct mandate. In 1956 the conditions for entry into the Bundestag were raised to 5 percent in the overall vote or three direct mandates.

The FRG's political system moved through six distinct phases since 1945. During the occupation (1945–49) political parties were established under the watchful eyes of the occupying powers. Directed by Chancellor Konrad Adenauer then Ludwig Erhard, the Christian Democrats dominated political life through 1966. Following the three-year era of the CDU-SPD grand coalition (1966–69), two Social Democratic chancellors, Willy Brandt and

Helmut Schmidt, and their coalition partner, the FDP, took the FRG into the era of social democracy lasting until 1982. When the FDP abandoned the coalition in 1982, Christian Democrats, under Helmut Kohl, established a new governing coalition with the FDP. Public sentiment moved against Kohl in the mid-1980s; however, the demise of the GDR and subsequent German reunification in 1990 reinforced popular support for Kohl and the CDU. After 1990 voter support for Kohl's Christian Democrats again waned. But federal elections in 1994 returned a governing majority for the Christian Democratic–Liberal coalition.

Political parties in the German Democratic Republic (GDR) evolved in a more one-sided manner. Two weeks after the formation of Konrad Adenauer's governing coalition in the FRG, East German politicians announced the promulgation of the constitution of the GDR on October 7, 1949. The creation of the GDR represented the end of a process whose origins were to be found in the breakup of the wartime coalition and consequent polarization of central Europe. Paralleling and furthering Germany's polarization were the distinctive economic and political occupation policies implemented by the Soviet Military Administration (SMAD) located in Karlshorst. SMAD directed the methodical transformation of the economy into the mold of the planned economy practiced in the Soviet Union. Under SMAD's supervision four political parties came into existence: the Communist Party (Kommunistische Partei Deutschlands, KPD), the Social Democratic Party (Sozialdemokratische Partei Deutschlands, SPD), the Christian Democratic Union (Christliche Demokratische Union, CDU), and the Liberal Democratic Party (Liberaldemokratische Partei Deutschlands, LDPD). After the forced fusion of the Socialist and Communist Parties in 1946 in the Socialist Unity Party (Sozialistische Einheits Partei Deutschlands, SED), all other political parties and mass organizations, namely, the Free German Unions (Freier Deutscher Gewerkschaftsbund, FDGB), Free German Youth (Freie Deutsche Jugend, FDJ), Cultural Union (Kulturbund der DDR, KB), Union of Democratic German Women (Demokratischen Frauenbund Deutschlands, DFD), Farmers' Mutual Aid Association (Vereinigung der Gegenseitigen Bauernhilfe, VdgB), and Union of Oppressed under National Socialism (Vereinigung der Verfolgten des Nazi-regimes, VVN), were forced to acknowledge the leading role of the SED. Until 1990, this political configuration remained unaltered.

The elections for positions in the People's Chamber (Volkskammer) closely followed the Block principle. The percentage of seats slotted for the various parties and mass organizations were set before the elections. Accordingly, the SED was guaranteed roughly 25 percent of the seats, the Christian Democrats, Liberal Democrats, National Democratic Party (Nationaldemokratische Partei Deutschlands, NPD), and the Democratic Peasants Party (Demokratische Bauernpartei Deutschlands, DBD) 10 percent each, and roughly 30 percent were allocated to the various mass organizations. As all mass organizations and the DBD were intimately linked with the SED, even the relative independence of the smaller parties diminished in significance.

The decline of communism in Eastern Europe spelled the end of the SED and, eventually, the GDR as well. Tearing down the Berlin Wall in November 1989 and the March 1990 elections set the stage for the currency union of July 1990 and German reunification in October. The question of German reunification dominated the March 1990 elections, the first and only free elections to take place in the GDR. Political parties linked with the former GDR lost to those directly linked or sympathetic with Kohl's CDU.

Despite a growing weariness of party politics that some analysts noticed, Germany's unified electorate in 1994 state and federal elections confirmed continued popular support for the CDU, SPD, and FDP. The system also demonstrated flexibility with continued representation for the PDS and renewed representation for the the Greens.

BIBLIOGRAPHY

Andersen, Uwe. *Handwörterbuch des politischen Systems der Bundesrepublik Deutschland.* Bonn: Bundeszentrale für Politische Bildung, 1995.

Hofmann, Robert. *Geschichte der deutschen Parteien.* Munich: Piper, 1993.

Mintzel, Alf, and Heinrich Oberreuter, eds. *Parteien in der Bundesrepublik Deutschland.* Bonn: Bundeszentrale für Politische Bildung, 1992.

Rogers, Daniel E. *Politics after Hitler: The Western Allies and the German Party System.* New York: New York University Press, 1995.

David A. Meier

SEE ALSO German Democratic Republic: Human Rights Groups

Bad Godesberg. Reforms that transformed the German Social Democratic Party (SPD). By the adoption of the 1959 Bad Godesberg Program, the SPD formally renounced its Marxist past and identified itself as a non-ideological, mass people's party. The new program enabled the SPD to broaden its electoral support and assume the leadership of a coalition government in 1969.

The adoption in 1959 of the Godesberg Program by the Social Democratic Party may be viewed as an acceptance of the changed historical and demographic realities of postwar Germany. It represented nothing less than a formal recognition of the SPD's transformation from a narrow, ideologically based working-class party to a popular mass people's party. The Godesberg socialism that followed from it meant that the SPD no longer attempted to unify the party faithful by emphasizing its historical heritage, as expressed in the Marxist-based Heidelberg Program of 1925. Instead, the SPD emphasized a hierarchy of shared values as the guide for the party's program and policies. No attempt was made to define the ultimate basis, secular or religious, of those values. Thus the way was cleared for the SPD to open the party to electoral support from Christians, especially Roman Catholics, and in so doing come to power in 1969.

In the initial postwar years the Social Democrats were confident of success in their own right. They turned a deaf ear toward talk among Christian labor leaders of founding a labor party that would embrace Protestants and Catholics and include the former Social Democrats. SPD leaders wanted to begin more or less where they left off in 1933. Thus the Heidelberg Program was carried over unaltered as the basic program of the postwar party. This left the party burdened with a program containing a traditional Marxist analysis of history, economics, and society, as well as such standard Marxist concepts as class struggle, international solidarity of the working class, and the inevitability of the classless society.

Orthodox Marxism, like the militant atheism of the interwar years, was no longer characteristic of a majority of the party's supporters. Still many retained a deep affection for Marxism and regarded it as a very important analytical tool. In short, although the party was no longer truly Marxist, it was unable officially and programmatically to renounce Marxist ideology. This meant that the SPD was an ideological foe of those who desired the reconstruction of postwar German society according to specifically Christian principles.

The breakthrough to a new non-Marxist party program in November 1959 was preceded by a decade of dialogue between pragmatic-minded politicians within the SPD and leading Catholic social reformers, left-wing Catholic publicists, and progressive Catholic lay leaders, who felt that the church-supported Christian Democrats (CDU/CSU) were more "liberal" than Christian. They believed that if the SPD would abandon its Marxist remnants and make concessions on such key issues as confes-

sional schools, then it could become an acceptable alternative for Catholic voters.

In the new Godesberg Program, Marxism was not even mentioned, and any claim to ultimate truth was specifically disavowed. Rather, the new Godesberg socialism was to be based on certain fundamental values, such as individual freedom growing out of a mutual respect for right and justice derived from a common heritage that included Christian ethics, humanism, and classical philosophy. The new attitude toward the churches and the refusal to ground itself in any specific ideology or historical theory were regarded by the party leadership as the two major changes in the new program.

The decade following adoption of the new program was devoted to "selling" the Godesberg socialism by both word and deed. The attempt to make the SPD an acceptable alternative to the CDU/CSU meant altering the party's position on two key issues, confessional schools and foreign policy. The latter was accomplished beginning with a surprise speech before the Bundestag on June 30, 1960, by Herbert Wehner, a former Communist who since the mid-1950s was the dominant force in the SPD. By identifying the new SPD with Konrad Adenauer's successful foreign policy, Wehner eliminated the foreign policy issue as a barrier to wider support.

Perhaps the most crucial issue of the post-Godesberg era was the question of confessional schools, schools operated by religious groups. The "Cultural and School Policy" section of the Heidelberg Program demanded the removal of all religious influence from the school system. The Godesberg Program simply ignored the issue, a move interpreted by defenders of confessional schools as an affirmation of the party's traditional opposition. Recognizing that the school issue stood in the way of the successful selling of Godesberg socialism to Catholic voters in particular, the party leadership resolved to act positively, although belatedly, to remove this final barrier to electoral success. This they did by adopting the "Guidelines to Educational Policy" at a special meeting of the party leadership in Berlin on July 2, 1964. A further step was taken in May 1965, when the SPD-led government of the predominantly Protestant state of Lower Saxony signed the Lower Saxon Concordat with the Vatican. The concordat recognized the continuing validity of both the Prussian Concordat of 1929 and the Reich Concordat of 1933. By so doing, the SPD accepted in principle the continued validity and existence of confessional schools.

The wisdom of the new Godesberg socialism was evident in the party's performance in subsequent federal elections. In September 1961 the SPD broke through the "one-third barrier" for the first time by capturing 36.2

percent of the vote. In 1969, it obtained 42.7 percent of the vote, and with it, the right to lead the governing coalition. Since then, the SPD has been accepted by German voters as an acceptable alternative to the Christian Democrats.

BIBLIOGRAPHY

Childs, David. *The SPD from Schumacher to Brandt: The Story of German Socialism, 1945–1965.* New York: Pergamon, 1966.

Graf, William D. *The German Left Since 1945.* New York: Oleander Press, 1976.

Parness, Diane L. *The SPD and the Challenge of Mass Politics: The Dilemma of the West German Volkspartei.* Boulder, Colo.: Westview, 1991.

Spotts, Frederic. *The Churches and Politics in Germany.* Middletown, Conn.: Wesleyan University Press, 1973.

Waibel, Paul R. *Politics of Accommodation: German Social Democracy and the Catholic Church, 1945–1959.* Frankfurt am Main: Verlag Peter Lang, 1983.

Paul R. Waibel

SEE ALSO Brandt, Willy; Schumacher, Kurt; Wehner, Herbert

German People's Union.   Extreme right-wing party. The German People's Union (Deutsche Volksunion, DVU) was founded by Gerhard Frey, a multimillionaire and well-known right-wing extremist, in 1971 as "a movement for all right-wing extremists in every party who are faithful to the Constitution of Germany." He established a publishing firm known as DSZ in the late 1950s, and through it by the late 1960s he had become the owner of the largest consortium of radical right-wing newspapers in the Federal Republic of Germany.

Frey had supported the National Democratic Party (NPD) in the 1960s but decided to form a party of his own, following the defeat of the NPD in the 1969 elections. He stated that a new party was necessary because of "the policy of total surrender to the East practiced by the red government and reflected in the treaties of Moscow and Warsaw in particular." The DVU's main organ throughout its existence has been the *Deutsche National Zeitung* (DNZ), owned by Frey himself, which had a circulation of approximately one hundred thousand in the 1980s. The paper trumpeted German nationalism, attacked Allied "war crimes," and decried the presence of foreign workers in Germany.

In spite of their similar political positions, the DVU and NPD did not actively cooperate until November 1986, when the DVU-Liste (German People's Union—

Democratic List) D was created. In addition to its hostility against immigrants, the DVU-Liste D demanded that "the constant accusations against the German people" stop. In 1987 the DVU and NPD together called for Germany to sever its ties with other Western countries and become neutral, refusing to participate in any political bloc.

The DVU's first electoral success was in local elections in Bremerhaven in 1987, where it gained 5.4 percent of the vote, followed by 6.2 percent in Tuttlingen in Baden-Württemberg. Frey invested a total of DM 18 million in the Euroelections of 1989. Liste D electoral material was sent to a large number of people, chiefly veterans of World War II and first-time voters. Despite its anti-immigrant rhetoric, the Liste D suffered a bitter defeat.

Owing to the poor outcome of the elections, Frey ended his electoral cooperation with the NPD in 1990. In 1991 the party exceeded the 5 percent threshold in local elections in Bremen, receiving 6.2 percent of the vote for its platform of "Houses instead of refugees." This was followed in 1992 by figures of 10.3 percent in Bremerhaven and 6.3 percent in Schleswig-Holstein. In addition to racist anti-immigrant attitudes, the DVU's ideology espouses anti-Semitism and anti-Americanism. During the Gulf War, Frey's papers sympathized with Iraqi dictator Saddam Hussein and made forceful attacks on the United States and Israel. The DVU claimed that American policy was controlled by the "Israeli lobby."

One of the key issues for the DVU since its foundation has been the notion of Greater Germany. Its demand for a change in the Oder-Neisse line and the return of former German areas now in Poland have become more vociferous following reunification. At the same time, the concept of Greater Germany is also taken to include Austria and the eastern Tyrol. Another central theme for the party in the 1990s was opposition to all multinational institutions, particularly the European Union (EU), which it perceived as "an attempt to subordinate Germany to a multicultural, multinational state governed by a bureaucracy in Brussels". The DVU claimed in particular that the existence of the EU led to an increase in the number of crimes committed by foreigners in Germany.

The DVU maintained extensive contacts with the radical right in Western Europe, the United States, and South Africa. Frey made a point of developing his contacts with Vladimir Zhirinovsky, the right wing Russian nationalist who visited the DVU in Germany in August 1992. Frey has also visited Zhirinovski in Russia. In August 1994 Frey and the Republicans' Franz Schönhuber agreed on cooperation to repel the "leftist people's front."

As a result Schönhuber was forced to step down as chairman of his own party.

The DVU can be regarded as Frey's personal project. Its focus on Nazi nostalgia and Frey's controversial personality prevent it from becoming a major power among right-wing radicals in Germany or achieving any permanent success in elections. The DVU gained 5.7 percent of the vote in the Bremerhaven local elections of September 1995 and fell just below the 5 percent threshold in Schleswig-Holstein provincial elections, where it won 4.3 percent. In 1997 the DVU had some twenty-two thousand members, and its main significance lay in its ability to recruit new members for extremist, right-wing organizations, especially neofascist ones.

BIBLIOGRAPHY

Childs, David. "The Far Right in Germany since 1945," in L. Cheles et al., eds. *Neo-Fascism in Europe.* London: Longman, 1991.

———. "The Far Right in Germany," in L. Cheles et al., eds. *The Far Right in Western and Eastern Europe,* 2d ed. London: Longman, 1995.

Linke, A. *Der Multimillionär Frey und die DVU.* Essen: Klartext, 1994.

Jouko Jokisalo

Green Movement. The Green movement (Die Grünen) in Germany emerged as a fundamental alternative to existing means of political expression and restructured the political Left in West Germany. Focusing on the individual and the individual's relationship to society, the Green movement pursued a diverse and idealistic agenda. It linked environmental protection with economic, ecological, and social issues, including support for human rights, women's issues, fighting hunger and poverty in the Third World, adhering to the principle of nonviolence, addressing the problem of growing unemployment, and rejecting all forms of military confrontation. The Green movement pulled ecological and grassroots democratic forces into an effective political opposition. It tapped a new means for participation in the political process, in which the interests of the citizenry were given first priority through citizens' initiatives groups. These groups represented a new form of political activism. The Green movement placed a premium on the principle of active dialogue as part of a nonviolent course of action. As for relations with East Germany, the Green movement sought a complete normalization of relations on the diplomatic level, and advocated elimination of the Ministry for German-German Relations. It proposed a nuclear- and chemical-free zone in the two German states and downplayed human rights violations by East German authorities.

The Greens' constituency consists of educated, post-materialistic, middle-class elements with a strong interest in ecological and political issues. Ideologically, this group stands slightly left of center, supports left-wing agendas, and is usually in agreement with the Social Democrats on social policy, the welfare state, and improved treatment of foreigners, political refugees, and other minorities. It supports Third World liberation movements. Supporters are primarily under thirty-five who are either employed in white-collar, service-industry jobs or are trained to perform them. Greens tend to live in university towns or urban areas where people are particularly affected by modern lifestyles and associated consequences, namely, pollution and crowded living conditions.

The Green movement's origins trace back to the early years of the Federal Republic. As the fervor of 1968 cooled, the demand for democratization continued to be expressed by a variety of alternative means. Beginning with the citizens' initiatives of the 1970s, the Greens pulled together ecological and alternative political groups. One of the key forces in the founding of the Green Party was the antinuclear movement and the movement for environmental protection in general. The government's decision in the wake of the OPEC oil shocks of 1973–74 to develop West Germany's nuclear energy production capacity prompted loud protests. People feared the wider implications of nuclear energy for the environment and reconsidered the benefits of West Germany's ongoing economic growth. The fact that all the established parties supported the move to nuclear energy, despite the hesitancy of the general electorate, made the issue perfect for the extraparliamentary arena throughout the 1970s. In the late 1970s and early 1980s the Greens brought the fragmented left together under one umbrella organization.

State-level organizations began with the founding in May 1977 of Lower Saxony's Environmental Protection Party (USP), the first statewide Green party. Green parties dotted the political landscape by 1978 throughout West Germany. The Green movement in Hamburg organized in early 1978 and drew 7.7 percent of the vote in the mayoral campaign in 1982. By the end of 1978 Green organizations were active in State-level elections throughout West Germany.

Momentum toward a national Green party began in 1979. Delegates from state and local Green parties, drawn primarily from the Hamburg and Berlin Alternative Lists, met at conferences in Offenbach in 1979 and in Karlsruhe in 1980 to discuss the formation of a new national party to be called Die Grünen (the Greens). Clashes over radical and conservatives' political approaches to ecological issues prompted conservatives to withdraw from the party soon after it was formally established. As the right wing dwindled, the left swelled with an influx of dogmatic leftists. Although the general party membership and corps of supportive voters was composed primarily of moderates, they tended not to be as motivated to take part in party functions. Thus the new infusion of radical leftists quickly gained a voice in the new party that was louder than their actual numbers would suggest.

The Greens became in 1983 the first new postwar German political party to break the 5 percent hurdle required for participation in the Bundestag. Reaching only 1.5 percent of the vote in 1981, in 1983 they took 5.6 percent of the national vote and held twenty-seven seats in the Bundestag. In 1987 electoral support rose to 8.3 percent and forty-two seats.

After a momentary success in linking Berlin's Social Democrats with the Alternative List (Greens) in 1989, Green political fortunes took a turn for the worse. Internal division and the addition of former East Germans to the list of eligible voters resulted in a proportional loss of overall support for the Greens in 1990. With only 4.8 percent, West German Greens were eliminated from the Bundestag. In April 1991 the Green's left wing Fundis were ousted and replaced by the less dogmatic Realos, who were determined to make the Greens into a respected component of the German political establishment.

In January 1993 the Greens merged with Alliance 90, the former East German political party with roots in the human rights movement. Officially listed as Alliance 90/Greens, it is informally referred to as the Greens. Initially opposed to dispatching German troops to foreign lands as well as the overturning of ecological policies and the cutting of social programs for the sake of former East Germany's economic recovery, the Alliance 90/Greens made particular headway in the West, and the Greens reentered parliament in 1994.

Under the leadership of Joschka Fischer the Greens recovered from their divisions and weakness. Fischer pushed for a German military contribution to a peacekeeping force in Bosnia and a revision in Green policy on nonviolence. The Greens moved from the left to center-left in the political spectrum, thus preparing themselves to be a potential junior partner for a future coalition with either of the two mainstream political parties.

In the September 27, 1998, Bundestag elections the Greens won 6.7 percent of the vote. They formed a coalition with the Social Democrats, led by Gerhard Schröder, who won 40.9 percent of the vote and thus entered into a federal German governing coalition for the first time. The Greens contributed three of the sixteen cabinet ministers. Joschka Fischer, leader of the Greens, became vice chancellor and foreign minister. Andrea Fischer became minister of health, and Jürgen Trittin was appointed minister of the environment, conservation, and reactor safety.

BIBLIOGRAPHY

Markovits, Andrei S., and Philip S. Gorski. *The German Left: Red Green and Beyond.* New York: Oxford University Press, 1993.

Mettke, Joerg R. *Die Grünen: Regierungspartner von morgen?* Reinbek bei Hamburg: Rowohlt, 1982.

Raschke, Joachim. *Die Grünen, wie sie wurden, was sie sind.* Cologne: Bund-Verlag, 1993.

David A. Meier

SEE ALSO Fischer, Joschka

National Democratic Party. Extreme right-wing German party. The National Democratic Party (Nationaldemokratische Partei Deutschlands, NPD) was founded in November 1964 to unite a number of small, extreme right-wing breakaway groups into a single group capable of raising the extreme Right from political obscurity to a position of influence. The aim of its leaders was to disengage the party from the legacy of Nazism and give it a "conservative image." Among the holders of the twenty leading positions in the party, twelve were former Nazi activists, and some 20 percent of party members in 1966 had formerly belonged to the Nazi Party.

The party received only 2 percent of the votes in the federal elections of 1965 but made its breakthrough in 1966 when it gained a total of sixty-one representatives in seven regional parliaments. Its support during the period 1966–69 was of the order of 5.6 to 9.8 percent. This expansion was attributable first to the shock caused by the first postwar economic crisis, which left seven hundred thousand unemployed and created a wave of bankruptcies among small businesses. The NPD exploited the uncertainty caused by the economic crisis to point to the 1.3 million migrant workers in the country as scapegoats for the high rate of unemployment. Second, the NPD cashed in on the dissatisfaction felt by many for the grand coalition government of the Social Democrats and Christian Democrats, and particularly with *Ostpolitik,* West Germany's opening to the East. Third, It called for "law and order" and suppression of the "anarchy and chaos" embodied in the student movement of 1968.

The members and supporters of the NPD were typically men forty-five to sixty years old who had formed their world view during Hitler's time. Middle-class professionals formed the backbone of its membership, and the proportion of professional soldiers was eleven times larger than that in society as a whole. The ideology of the NPD was based on a biological view of the world according to which a hierarchical, authoritarian society was the only "natural" one and any ideas of equality were simply unnatural. It demanded that the mass migration of foreigners be stopped and called for the establishment of a homogeneous national community (*Volksgemeinschaft*). It also played down the magnitude of Nazi war crimes, even to the extent of denying the existence of Auschwitz death camp.

A total of 1.5 million Germans voted for the NPD in the 1969 elections, representing some 4.3 percent of the votes cast, which fell short of the 5 percent threshold required to gain seats in parliament. This defeat can be traced to the economic recovery and the transfer of the Christian Democrats to the opposition, so that the NPD lost its role as the "nationalist" opposition. The NPD was unable to recover from its loss in the 1969 elections. Its support dropped to less than 1 percent of the electorate and its membership from almost 40,000 to 21,000 in 1970. Its electoral defeat and political decline led to major controversies within the party over policy, as a result of which Adolf von Thadden, who had been elected chairman in 1967, resigned in 1971.

The NPD attempted to raise its profile in the federal elections of 1980 with the anti-immigrant slogan "Germany for the Germans—foreigners out," but it captured only 0.2 percent of the vote, and 0.8 percent in the European parliamentary elections of 1984. The party concluded an electoral pact with the German People's Union (DVU) in 1987, benefiting in particular from the financial support provided by the latter. It also reformed its platform in 1987 to throw off its neofascist image. In the regional elections of 1988 the NPD received only 2.1 percent of the vote in Baden-Württemberg and 1.2 percent in Schleswig-Holstein. It did, however, make a temporary breakthrough in local elections in Frankfurt am Main in 1989, gaining 6.6 percent of the vote.

The NPD was unsuccessful in its attempts to expand into the five new Länder (States) following integration with East Germany, gaining only 0.3 percent of the total vote in the first elections to be held in reunited Germany at the end of 1990. This disappointment led to the abandonment of cooperation between the NPD and DVU. Aggressive nationalism and racist anti-immigrant attitudes gained ground in NPD policies in the early 1990s

as reflected in the choice of Günther Deckert as party chairman in the summer of 1991. A year later Deckert was sentenced to a year's probation and fined DM 10,000 for incitement to racial hate and defamation of Holocaust victims. The sentence was later increased to two years' imprisonment and Deckert eventually had to resign as chairman because of irregularities in the party finances. He was replaced in March 1996 by Bavarian Udo Voigt.

In spite of being again sentenced to seven months' imprisonment for incitement in that same year, Voigt continued as vice chairman of the NPD. The party strengthened its connections with militant neo-Nazis in the 1990s. NDP members have attended meetings of proscribed neofascist organizations and members of the latter have found a new home in the NPD. On the other hand, the NDP lost some members to the Republicans and the DVU during the same period, so that its members numbered only 2,800 in 1996. Likewise the readership of the party magazine, *Deutsche Stimme,* is evidently on the decline. In general, the NPD has become increasingly a political home for neofascist forces.

BIBLIOGRAPHY

Childs, D. "The Far Right in Germany," in L. Cheles et al., eds. *The Far Right in Western and Eastern Europe.* London: Longman, 1995.

Nagle, J. D. *The National Democratic Party: Right Radicalism in the Federal Republic of Germany.* Berkeley: University of California Press, 1970.

Jouko Jokisalo

Republican Party.   Extreme right-wing party in Germany. The Republican Party (Die Republikaner, Rep) was set up in 1983 by two former Christian Social Union (CSU) Bundestag deputies, Franz Handlos and Ekkehard Voigt, together with Franz Schönhuber, who had served in the Waffen SS in World War II and had worked as a journalist after the war. The formation of the party was a protest against the policies of the CSU leadership with regard to the German Democratic Republic (DDR), which were seen as too compliant. The original intention was not to create a movement that would gather together right-wing extremists, as was the case with the National Democratic Party (NDP) or the German People's Union (DVU), but rather to set up a new right-wing conservative party.

Internal disputes erupted soon after the foundation of the party because of disagreements between conservatives and right-wing extremists over the line to adopt. The position of the latter was strengthened by the selection of Harald Neubauer, an NPD activist and reporter on Gerhard Frey's newspaper, the *Deutsche National Zeitung* (the organ of the German People's Union), as secretary-general in 1985. Neubauer, who was also elected to the European Parliament in 1989, had connections with neofascist groups.

In 1986 Handlos and Voigt resigned when Schönhuber took over as chairman. With continuing strife over policy and personalities within the party, the Republicans fared badly in elections from 1986 to 1988. Racist, anti-immigrant policies and extreme nationalism gained a stronger foothold in the party at its 1987 annual conference. Migrant workers and asylum seekers were held up as scapegoats for practically all Germany's social and economic ills. The party wanted an amendment to Article 16 of the Basic Law, which embodied the right to political asylum. The demand for a strong national identity and "a healthy national pride" became a core theme in Republican policy. The party called for a revision of existing notions of history and an end to "reeducation." It was time for the German people to rise from "the shadow of Hitler." The Republicans believed that the history books should forsake "the war propaganda of the Allied forces" and that a campaign should be mounted against the "criminalization of the German culture, history and people." Other key Republican issues were opposition to the European Union (EU) and the call for disengagement from NATO, a theme that became party policy in 1988. The eventual aim was a neutral, nuclear-armed Greater Germany.

The Republicans also tried to present themselves as an environmental party. Their concept of environment was tinged with an element of nationalism and antipathy toward foreigners. Schönhuber stated in 1987, "We are national conservers of nature. If you love your fatherland, you will not let its environment deteriorate." The Republicans regarded national identity and love for one's home district as the only firm foundation for a love of nature and a desire to protect the environment, and they were of the opinion that these sentiments were inaccessible to outsiders with an alien culture and identity. They also maintained that the presence of foreigners in the country and the poor sense of national identity were the primary reasons for the ecological crisis. Neubauer asserted, "Parties that aim to enhance the national identity are natural conservers of nature."

The Republicans did not achieve their political breakthrough until the election for the West Berlin House of Deputies in 1989, when they received 7.5 percent of the vote. They were also successful in the European Parliament elections in the same year, gaining 7.1 percent of the vote and six representatives. Typical Republican voters in those elections were men, former supporters of the Christian Democratic Union/CSU, who lived in the southern part of the Federal Republic. They were also predominantly young, so that as many as 14.3 percent of people eighteen to twenty-three years old in West Berlin voted for them. Another distinctive feature was the relatively high number of members of the West Berlin police force drawn to the party.

By the end of 1990, however, the Republicans attracted as little as 1.5 percent of the vote in the first parliamentary elections to be held in reunited Germany, and this aggravated disagreements within the party. Neubauer resigned from the party and Rolf Schlierer was elected vice chairman at the annual conference of that year. The political decline was halted in 1992 by provincial elections in Baden-Württemberg, in which the party gained 10.9 percent, and local elections in Berlin, in which it won 8.3 percent.

In December 1992 the party was defined by the Federal Office for the Protection of the Constitution (BfV) as a "right-wing extremist" organization requiring continuous surveillance. According to Erich Uhrlau, head of the Hamburg branch of the BfV, the party did not differ in its policies from the NPD and the DVU to any appreciable extent, and its grassroots members were engaged in cooperation with neofascists.

The Republicans received only 3.9 percent of the vote in the European Parliament elections of 1994, and similarly failed to pass the 5 percent threshold in parliamentary elections that year. As a result Schönhuber attempted to initiate cooperation with the DVU. This led to accusations of fascism from within the party, and Schlierer became chairman in December 1994. Schönhuber left the party entirely in 1995. The Republicans consolidated their position somewhat in regional terms in 1996 when they took 9.1 percent of the vote in the Baden-Würtemburg provincial elections.

The party had a membership of some sixteen thousand in 1995, and its annual conference at Hanover in 1996 endorsed a policy of opposition to European integration and its replacement with a "Europe of the Fatherlands," German hegemony in central Europe, and a campaign for preservation of the German mark in the face of the movement toward a European currency (Euro). The party rejected the notion of a multicultural society and supported instead ethnic cleansing.

In 1997 the Republicans constituted the most notable right-wing extremist party in Germany. The main problems for its leaders were to fill the gap left by the charismatic Schönhuber, who had steered the party's course in an authoritarian manner up to 1995, and to consolidate the party's support. It enjoyed good relations with the right-wing extremist Austrian Freedom Party and its leader, Jörg Heider, and revived its connections with the French National Front of Jean-Marie Le Pen.

BIBLIOGRAPHY

Jaschke, H. G. *Die Republikaner: Profile einer Rechtsaussen-Partei.* Bonn: J.H.W. Dietz, 1993.

Saalfeld, T. "The Politics of National Populism: Ideology and Politics of the German Republikaner Party." *German Politics* 2 (1993).

Veen, H. J. *The Republikaner Party in Germany: Right-Wing Menace or Protest Catchall?* Westport, Conn.: Praeger, 1993.

Jouko Jokisalo

Neo-Nazism

The defeat of Nazism, the Allied occupation of Germany, and the formation of the Federal Republic of Germany marginalized neofascism in postwar German politics. In 1949 former Nazi activists established the Socialist Reich Party (Sozialistische Reichspartei, SRP), but it was proscribed in October 1952 as a neofascist organization. Neofascism was only a peripheral aggravation in the West Germany of the economic miracle, and it was chiefly the political demise of the National Democratic Party (NPD) in the 1960s that led to the organization of a neofascist movement.

The National Socialist German Workers Party/Abroad and Organizational Committee (Nationalsozialistische Deutsche Arbeiterpartei/Auslands—und Aufbauorganisation, NSDAP/AO) was founded in 1972 to create a network for neofascist cadres in West Germany. The organization was and still is led from Germany, but its publicity center is located in the U.S. state of Nebraska. Since 1973 the distribution of propaganda has been organized from there by Gary Rex Lauck (1953–). Lauck was arrested in Denmark in March 1995 at the request of the German authorities. In 1993 the organization's magazine, *NS-Kampfruf* (*National Socialist Battle Cry*) proscribed as a call to arms. In spite of its small membership of only about 150, the organization has played an important role in the neofascist movement. It distributes Nazi propaganda to some twenty thousand addresses in Germany and possesses its own illegal worldwide propaganda network.

Michael Kühnen (1955–91), an official of the NSDAP/AO and one of the key figures in postwar neofascism, founded another organization in 1977, the Action Front of National Socialists (Aktionsfront Nationaler Sozialisten, ANS), the key objectives of which were to educate a "fighting elite" and to legalize the NSDAP. Kühnen was sentenced to prison for four years in 1979 for distributing neofascist propaganda but resumed his party leadership position on his release. The organization changed its name to Action Front of National Socialists/National Activists (Aktionfront Nationaler Sozialisten/Nationale Aktivisten, ANS/NA) in 1983. Kühnen also set up an electoral campaign organization, Operation Repatriation—Popular Movement against Foreign Dominance and Destruction of the Environment (Aktion Auslanderrückführung—Volksbewegung gegen Überfremdung und Umweltzerstorung, AAR), the program of which was a combination of racist, antiforeigner attitudes and attention to ecological problems. Its "eco-racism" became a main theme of right-wing extremists and neofascists.

Both the ANS/NA and the AAR were proscribed in December 1983, and Kühnen escaped abroad. He was arrested in Paris in October 1984 and returned to Germany, where he was sentenced to more than three years' imprisonment for neofascist activities. The outlawed ANS/NA was replaced in 1984 by the Political Society of the New Front (Gesinnungsgemeinschaft der Neuen Front, GdNF), which developed into the most significant neofascist group following German reunification. Its organ, *Die Neue Front,* describes the GdNF as "the legal arm of the new generation national socialist movement and the seed of a new, future NSDAP." The GdNF became the center of the movement represented by Kühnen and the focus for the creation of a network of neofascist organizations, including the National Coalescence (Nationale Sammlung, founded July 15, 1988, proscribed February 9, 1989), the German Alternative (Deutsche Alternative, founded May 5, 1989, proscribed December 10, 1992), the Nationale Liste (founded March 13, 1989, proscribed February 24, 1995), and the Nationale Alternative (founded February 1, 1990).

The GdNF is a "cadre movement" organized on the leadership principle. The cadre was responsible for ensuring that the GdNF would be able to continue its work despite prohibitions imposed on it against establishing new organizations. The strategy of the GdNF was to give the impression of being a loosely formed group united only by a common ideology. This proved successful. The legal authorities have been unable to press charges against the actual cadre center but only against individual organizations.

Following the death of Kühnen, reportedly from an AIDS-related illness, in April 1991, Christian Worch (1956–), Austrian Gottfriend Küssel, and Arnulf Winfried Priem (1948–) became the de facto leaders of the organization. Its role has diminished drastically, however, as a number of its organizations have been closed down and its leading figures sentenced to long prison terms. Worch, one of the most experienced activists in the German neofascist movement, was sentenced to 2.5 years in November 1994, a sentence he managed to have postponed until February 1996, and Küssel was given ten years for "national socialist activities" in Vienna in 1994. Priem, who represented the militant wing of the neofascist movement in the 1970s, was sentenced to three years in prison in May 1995, and was suspected of having been involved in letter bomb assassination attempts in Austria.

Another organization that grew in importance until its proscription in February 1995 was the neofascist Free Workers Party (Freiheitliche Deutsche Arbeiterpartei, FAP). The party was established in 1979, though it did not achieve major importance until 1984, when Kühnen advised his supporters to join it following the abolition of the ANS/NF. It was plagued with internal disputes in the late 1980s. When Friedhelm Busse (1929–) was elected chairman in 1988, Kühnen's supporters left the party because of Kühnen's homosexual behavior. The FAP contributed actively to the organization of the "antiantifa (antifascist) campaign" in the early 1990s. Announcing its proscription, Interior Minister Manfred Kanther said that the FAP "had contempt for human rights, defamed democratic institutions and spread racist and anti-Semitic propaganda." The organization was, he said, "closely linked to the Nazi Party and practiced Nazi rituals." Following the proscription of the party, some of its members moved to the NPD, and the rest continued their activities under the auspices of apparently independent groups.

The acts of violence committed by neofascists in the 1970s were largely the work of the Defense and Sporting Group (Wehrsportgruppe Hoffmann) formed by Karl-Heinz Hoffman. A former member of the group, Gundolf Köhler, blew himself up while placing a bomb at the 1980 Munich Beer Festival, killing another 12 people and injuring 211.

The racist violence launched by the neofascists in 1991–93, following the reunification of Germany, reached a crescendo with incidents at Hoyeswerda in September 1991, Rostock in August 1992, Mölln in November 1992, and Solingen in May 1993. A total of some 2000 acts of violence against foreigners were recorded in Germany in 1992, resulting in 25 deaths.

GdNP leader Worch launched the antiantifa campaign in 1992 with the dual aims of maintaining connections within the neofascist movement following the abolition of its local organizations and terrorizing the antifascists.

This led to publication of *Der Einblick* (*The Glance*), which listed the names, addresses, and personal details of more than 280 antifascists. A response to the increasingly stringent measures adopted by the authorities has also been the attempt to establish an underground terrorist network, Werwolf, with the aim of creating a capability for armed action. This meant the construction of a tightly organized "dormant" network of cadres capable of armed intervention in the event of a social crisis. Part of this cadre system is made up of the 150 German and Austrian neofascists who served as mercenaries in the Croatian army in its war against Serbia after the break-up of Yugoslavia.

The neofascists have been quick to take advantage of the opportunities offered by advanced technology. Activists having connections with the NPD constructed the Thule network in March 1993, which enables neofascists in different parts of Germany to communicate with each other and aims at intellectualizing the whole neofascist movement. Strategic papers drawn up by members of the NPD student organization have acted as a theoretical basis for developing a concept of urban guerrilla activity adapted to conditions prevailing in Germany. The Thule network also provides opportunities for establishing and strengthening contacts between different groups and serves as a means for hampering the operations of the authorities. Its motto is "We are inside, the government is outside." The aim is to create "free zones" in which activists can operate. In addition, neofascists have made use of Internet connections to expand their international cooperation.

The German neo-Nazis have suffered serious setbacks in the 1990s, with the proscription of the main neofascist organizations and the imprisonment of the cadres. There are currently just over forty thousand militant neofascist activists and some seventy five neofascist publications, with a total circulation of perhaps as many as seven million. Neofascists make a point of exploiting social and economic crises through slogans such as "jobs and houses for the Germans," with the aim of introducing a racist, antiforeigner element into every aspect of the social struggle.

Although the neofascist groups were a politically marginal power in Germany of the late 1990s, they were a catalyst in the discussion of social affairs. Neo-Nazi Heinz Reiz, assessing the strategies and achievements of the right-wing extremist parties, stated that gaining power "would be [an] unrealistic [objective]. Our duty is rather to push the existing parties to the right. What we have accomplished is that the statements of the CDU [Christian Democratic Union], and particularly of the CSU

[Christian Social Union], are as far to the right today as the NPD was twenty years ago." As Hamburg Verfassungschutz (Protection of the Constitution) president, Ernst Uhrlau, stated, "the themes of the 1990s will be right-wing extremism, xenophobia, nationalism and self-absorption. . . . More than 20 percent of the younger generation sympathizes with the right-wing parties. Once they have established themselves they will change society, although with opposite goals, more significantly than the leftists of 1968 ever hoped." (*Der Spiegel,* September 14, 1992).

BIBLIOGRAPHY

Hasselbach, Ingo. *Führer-Ex: Memoirs of a Former Neo-Nazi.* New York: Random House, 1996.

Husbands, C. T. "Militant Neo-nazism in the Federal Republic of Germany in the 1990s," in L. Cheles et al., eds. *The Far Right in Western and Eastern Europe.* New York: Longman, 1995.

Schmidt, M. *The New Reich: Violent Extremism in Unified Germany and Beyond.* New York: Pantheon, 1993.

Jouko Jokisalo

SEE ALSO Terrorism, Right-Wing

Economy

Germany is, with a combination of a relatively large population and a high per capita income, the predominant economic power in Europe, and possesses one of the leading economies in the world. In 1996 Germany had a population of 82 million and a gross domestic product per capita of 42,800 deutsche marks, or $27,633 at the exchange rate of the time.

In the early postwar years the economic outlook was bleak. The Nazi regime and the war had left a legacy of death, destruction, and misery. When the two German states were founded in 1949, however, recovery was already underway. The Federal Republic was the larger and more dynamic part of Germany. From 1950 to 1989, its population increased from 51 million to 69 million, owing to a high birthrate in the 1950s and early 1960s, a large number of refugees from East Germany until 1961, and since the 1960s many immigrants from southern Europe. At the same time, from 1950 to 1989, the population of the German Democratic Republic declined slightly from 18 million to 17 million. In recent years the German population has stagnated, except for a small number of immigrants.

In the 1950s and 1960s, the industrial sector was the vanguard of economic development in both German states. In 1970 the primary sector of agriculture, forestry, and fishing employed 9 percent of the West German labor force, the secondary sector of industry and mining 49 percent, and the tertiary sector with services of any kind 43 percent. East Germany was more agricultural, and the service sector was less developed. Thus in 1970 the primary sector employed 13 percent of the East German labor force, the secondary sector 49 percent, and the service sector 38 percent. Since the 1970s West Germany has become a postindustrial society with the majority of the labor force employed in the service sector. The trend continued in the enlarged Federal Republic. In 1996 only 3 percent of the German labor force was in the primary sector, 35 percent in the secondary sector, and 62 percent in the service sector.

In both German states, economic recovery turned the early 1950s into a long period of economic growth. In West Germany net domestic product per capita by 1953 exceeded the prewar level of 1938. From 1950 to 1973 real gross domestic product per capita increased by an average yearly growth rate of 4.9 percent. Unemployment, still a problem in the early 1950s, was reduced by vigorous expansion of the economy. In the late 1950s the West German economy attained full employment and began to attract a great number of workers from southern Europe. The hunger and destitution of the war and the early postwar years were soon forgotten. Economic growth was the foundation of West Germany's high living standard; vast public investment in infrastructure, urbanization, and education; and an expanding welfare state.

In international comparison, the growth of the West German economy was not unique. In most of the advanced capitalist countries, the years from 1950 to 1973 were a "golden age"—a time when economic growth surpassed all historical records. The golden age was due to a constellation of favorable factors, rather than a single cause: population growth, social stability, economic policies that emphasized price stability, capital accumulation, and growth, an expanding world economy, and, both in Western Europe and in Japan, the transfer of technology from the United States.

East German figures are difficult to compare, as there was not only a different price system and a divergent method of national accounts but also a tendency to manipulate official statistics. According to recent estimates, the growth rate of real income per capita was from 1950 to 1973 in the range of 3.2 to 4.7 percent. Living standards in East Germany improved, too, but the population there was well aware of the considerable economic gap between the two German economies.

German economic growth slowed down after 1973. In West Germany the crisis of 1974–75 is regarded as a turning point, though the change was structural rather than cyclical. From 1973 to 1989 real gross domestic product per capita increased by an average of only 2.0 percent per year. As growth slackened, unemployment increased to 8 percent of all employees. In historical perspective, the transition from the golden age of the 1950s and 1960s to the slower growth rates of the 1970s, 1980s, and 1990s was an adaptation to the long-term growth path of capitalist economies. From the industrial revolution, when modern economic growth began, to 1950, the growth rate of real income per capita even in the most advanced countries rarely exceeded 1.5 percent.

The Communist economies were apparently not exempt from the trend of the capitalist world economy. In East Germany the growth rate of real national income per capita in 1973–89 was probably in the range from 1.3 to 2.3 percent. The economic gap between the two German states remained. At the time of reunification in 1990, the productivity of the East German economy was in the range of 40 to 60 percent of the West German level, depending on the estimates. Reunification created a short boom in the West Germany economy, which was offset, however, by the collapse of the East German economy. From 1992 the deceleration of economic growth continued in the enlarged Federal Republic of Germany. Real gross domestic product per capita increased by only 0.6 percent per year, and unemployment increased from 7 percent of all employees in 1991 to 12 percent in 1996. Slow growth and rising unemployment put pressure on consumer spending, on the budgets of federal, state, and local governments, and on the welfare state.

In their foreign economic relations the two German states were integrated into the rival spheres of capitalism and communism. West Germany's integration into the capitalist world economy began with the European Recovery Program of 1948–52, widely known as the Marshall Plan, and was subsequently fostered by the rapid economic growth of the 1950s and 1960s. The Federal Republic of Germany was one of the leading members of the Organization of European Economic Cooperation (OEEC) of 1948, precursor to the Organization for Economic Cooperation and Development (OECD), the European Coal and Steel Community (ECSC) of 1951, and the European Economic Community (EEC) of 1957, which became in 1993 the European Union (EU). West Germany was also an important partner in the General Agreement on Tariffs and Trade (GATT), the recently founded World Trade Organization (WTO), and the international monetary system. The West German currency, which was created in 1948, the deutsche mark, earned a reputation for its stability. East Germany was a prominent member of the now defunct Council on Mutual Economic Assistance (CMEA), sometimes known as Comecon. The contrast in their international orientation duplicated the domestic divergences in economic policy and performance between the two German states. The West German economy expanded in an environment that emphasized competition and comparative advantage, whereas East Germany was fettered to the cumbersome CMEA.

BIBLIOGRAPHY

Giersch, Herbert, Karl-Heinz Paqué, and Holger Schmieding. *The Fading Miracle: Four Decades of Market Economy in Germany.* Cambridge: Cambridge University Press, 1992.

Hoffmann, Walther G. *Das Wachstum der deutschen Wirtschaft seit der Mitte des 19. Jahrhunderts.* Berlin: Springer, 1965.

Maddison, Angus. *Phases of Capitalist Development.* Oxford: Oxford University Press, 1982.

Ritschl, Albrecht. "Aufstieg und Niedergang der Wirtschaft der DDR," in *Jahrbuch für Wirtschaftsgeschichte,* 1995/II.

Statistisches Jahrbuch für die Bundesrepublik Deutschland. Wiesbaden: Statistisches Bundesamt, 1997.

Gerd Hardach

Kreditanstalt für Wiederaufbau (Reconstruction Loan Corporation).   The Kreditanstalt für Wiederaufbau was founded in November 1948 as a state-owned bank to manage the "counterpart funds" of the European Recovery Program (ERP) in West Germany. The European Recovery Program was suggested by Secretary of State George C. Marshall in 1947 and was implemented from 1948 to 1952. The United States and sixteen European countries, including West Germany, participated in the Marshall Plan, as the program came to be known after its initiator. The Marshall Plan provided a framework for the liberalization of trade and payments in Western Europe, and the United States supplied $14 billion in foreign aid to finance the balance of payments deficits of their European partners. West Germany received $1.6 billion in ERP funds, 10 percent of the total. One-third of that amount was paid back in later years, two-thirds were given as grants.

The proceeds from the sale of ERP imports on the German market were accumulated in a special investment fund. With these "counterpart funds" the Kreditanstalt für Wiederaufbau financed credits at preferential interest rates for investment projects in industry and infrastructure. With continuous redemption and interest payments

Germany, Federal Republic of

the ERP investment fund increased in volume. In 1996
it had a volume of 26 billion deutsche marks. When recovery turned into economic growth in the early 1950s,
the activities of the Kreditanstalt became more varied. It
supported modern industries, commerce, and small business; began in the 1960s to finance development programs in the Third World; and recently turned to modernization projects in East Germany and Eastern Europe.

BIBLIOGRAPHY

Hardach, Gerd. *Der Marshall-Plan: Auslandshilfe und Wiedraufbau in Westdeutschland 1948–1952*. Munich: Deutscher Taschenbuch Verlag, 1994.

Kreditanstalt für Wiederaufbau. *Die KfW 1948 bis heute*. Frankfurt: Kreditanstalt für Wiederaufbau, 1997.

Pohl, Manfred. *Wiederaufbau. Kunst und Technik der Fin-
anzierung 1947–1953*. Frankfurt: Knapp, 1973.

Gerd Hardach

SEE ALSO Marshall Plan

Confederation of German Employers' Associations

The first employers' associations in Germany came into
being at the end of the nineteenth century in almost all
cases as a reaction to the organization of labor unions.
Their task was the defense of the employer's interests
against collective labor union action. The employers' organizations soon recognized, however, that they should
also participate in the debate of the social questions of
their time. In 1913 numerous professional and regional
organizations established the Association of German Employers' Organization, the precursor of the Confederation
of German Employers' Associations (Bundesvereinigung
der Deutschen Arbeitgeberverbünde, BDA). The advantage of this merger soon became evident in a more effective representation of employers in dealing with labor unions, the government, and the general public, as well as
uniting the various sociopolitical considerations of different employers to form a unified sociopolitical outlook.

Today the BDA represents the interprofessional and
interregional interests of German employers in the field
of social policy. The BDA's main tasks are to provide information, advice, and coordination to members and to
act as spokesman of employers in all social questions. The
BDA transcends the interests of a particular branch or
region vis-à-vis the government, the parliament, and the
public. The BDA also represents employers in the self-
administration bodies at the national level of the social
security system and sends honorary judges to the Federal
Labor Court and the Federal Social Security Board. The

confederation also acts as the representative of German
employers internationally within the field of its competence, especially with regard to international organizations
such as the International Labor Organization (ILO), the
Organization for Economic Cooperation and Development (OECD), and the European Union (EU).

The BDA is dedicated to a free-market economy based
on private ownership and competition among entrepreneurs as well as on the responsible cooperation among
free organizations of employers and labor unions. BDA
members represent practically all branches of the German
economy: industry, crafts, agriculture, wholesale and export trade, retail trade, banking, insurance companies,
transports, and other trades. It is a private organization
and membership is voluntary. Members are exclusively
employers' associations or federations, not individual
companies. In 1996 membership consisted of forty-seven
branch associations and fifteen interprofessional regional
or state associations. Through these direct-member associations an additional one thousand employers'
associations—either regional interprofessional or regional
branch associations—are indirectly members of the BDA.
Thus the Confederation of German Employers' Associations represents German employers who employ about 80
percent of German workers and employees employed by
private businesses.

There are four organs of the Confederation: the General Assembly, Executive Board, Presidential Board, and
Executive Office. The General Assembly consists of representatives of associations directly affiliated with the
BDA. It elects the president and vice presidents as well as
the members of the Executive Board. The General Assembly furthermore approves the budget, fixes membership
fees, and decides about changes of the statute. It normally
convenes once a year. The Executive Board of the BDA
is mainly composed of the presidents of member associations and additionally up to 18 other members. It is
responsible for the determination of the basic lines of policy of the confederation. The Presidential Board consists
of the president, up to eight vice presidents including the
treasurer, and 23 further members, of whom 16 are at the
same time members of the Executive Board. The Presidential Board guides the Executive Office according to
the policy fixed by the Executive Board. The Executive
Office is directed by one director general, three deputies,
and a number of directors. It attends to the BDA's current
business, assisted by a staff of about 150, 60 of them
having a university education. The policy decisions are
taken by the competent bodies of the confederation, i.e.,
the Executive Board and the General Assembly; the preparatory work is done by about 20 committees and several

working groups, which consist of business people, top executives, and experienced experts from the management of member associations.

The BDA maintains two foundations: the Walter Raymond Foundation is established to examine the factors governing social and economic life and to form a platform for free discussion between employers and other groups of society; the Hanns Martin Schleyer Foundation promotes science and academic research about fundamental principles of economic and social order.

The most important periodicals published by the BDA are *Kurznachrichtendienst der Bundesvereinigung,* published twice a week, and *Arbeitgeber,* published fortnightly.

BIBLIOGRAPHY

Simon, Walter. *Macht und Herrschaft der Unternehmerverbünde BDI, BDA und DIHT.* Cologne: Pahl-Rugenstein: 1976.

Bernd Leupold

Federation of German Industries

At the end of the nineteenth century, German industrial employers were organized in two highly competing associations: the Central Federation of German Industrialists (Centralverband Deutscher Industrieller), founded in 1876, and the Union of Industrialists (Bund der Industriellen), established in 1895. After World War I in 1919, both associations merged into the Reich Federation of Industry (Reichsverband der Industrie), which was renamed the Reich Industry Group (Reichsgruppe Industrie) in 1934. Thus the organization of German industry had a tradition, even though it was interrupted, comparable to the tradition of labor unions when it was reorganized in 1949 as the Federation of German Industries (Bundesverband der Deutschen Industrie, BDI), with its headquarters in Cologne.

In 1997 the Federation of German Industries was the umbrella organization for thirty-five industrial trade associations in Germany. Its members represent about eighty thousand private industrial enterprises employing over ten million people. Thus it includes about 90 percent of German private industry. The BDI is a voluntary association of associations, i.e., the enterprises themselves are not its actual members. Membership is confined to industrial trade associations and working groups acting as umbrella organizations representing German industrial groups. The BDI covers branches of German industry such as motor vehicles, chemicals, electrical and electronic engineering, machinery manufacture, building, mining, steel, textiles, printing, foodstuffs, precision mechanics, and optics.

The BDI represents the economic policy interests of German private industry in dealings with parliament, government and the parliamentary opposition, political parties, labor unions, other social groups, institutions of the European Union (EU), and other national and international bodies. With the exception of social policy, where it has assigned all competencies to the Confederation of German Employers' Associations (Bundesvereinigung der Deutschen Arbeitgeberverbände, BDA), the BDI acts as spokesman for its members and assists them by providing information on different issues in various fields such as foreign trade, taxation, monetary and environmental policy, infrastructure, energy, transport, research and development, as well as higher and vocational education.

There are three decisive organs of the federation: the Executive Board, Presidential Board, and Executive Office. The Executive Board consists of the president, six (as of 1997) vice presidents, the chairmen of the attached associations, and sixteen chairmen of regional state federations, each representing the industries of one of the sixteen states. The Executive Board annually appoints the fourteen members of the Presidential Board, which is entitled to enlarge itself by co-opting up to ten further members, primarily experts on special subjects. The Presidential Board formulates the principles of the federation and installs standing and special committees. It jointly with the Executive Board also directs the Executive Office, which totals about two hundred mainly university-educated staff who deal with current business. In 1997 the federation's decisions were prepared by eight independent working groups of the BDI and sixteen standing committees. Usually each member association delegates at least one representative to each committee. Besides other boards, for instance, the one responsible for the accountancy of the BDI, there are up to two dozen committees and working groups appointed by the BDI jointly with other organizations such as the BDA and the Association of German Chambers of Industry and Commerce (Deutscher Industrie- und Handelstag, DIHT). The most important of these committees and working groups deal with the promotion of German trade to particular geographical regions such as Eastern Europe, Latin America, or North Africa.

At the national level the BDI keeps in close touch with other umbrella organizations of trade and industry, above all with the BDA and the DIHT. Additionally, the BDI cooperates with the Institute of German Private Enterprises (Institut der Deutschen Wirtschaft), which is jointly sponsored by trade associations, employers' associations, and businesses. The BDI is also represented in numerous international organizations, and the Federation of German Industries maintains liaison offices in Brussels, Washington, D.C., and Tokyo.

Regarding party politics the BDI is officially not dedicated to a single party. Nevertheless the federation is regarded as a rather conservative association, an assumption also underlined by the fact that its first president, Fritz Berg, has been reelected for more than two decades. It is accused of principally representing the interests of big industry, which can be explained because only large companies are able to assign qualified managers and staff to the federation. The few branches of industry not attached to the BDI characteristically have a rather small turnover or number of employees. Moreover, influence within the BDI depends on the amount of the member's financial contribution. Big industry is thought to exert more influence in the federation than do other branches or enterprises, even though financial reports of the BDI are not published.

The BDI is very influential but not omnipotent or omnipresent. For instance, it proved unable to reach its aim in the early 1960s when trying to establish a privately financed national TV program that would be subject to the guidance of the federal government. It likewise failed in a campaign to prevent a devaluation of the mark early in the 1960s. On the other hand, the BDI succeeded in hindering principal changes in the vocational education system in the 1970s and limited the right of codetermination (Betriebliche Mitbestimmung) of workers and employees in the management of enterprises.

BIBLIOGRAPHY

Mann, Siegfried. *Macht und Ohnmacht der Verbände: Das Beispiel des Bundesverbandes der Deutschen Industrie e.V. (BDI) aus empirisch-analytischer Sicht.* Baden-Baden: Nomos, 1994.

Simon, Walter. *Macht und Herrschaft der Unternehmerverbände BDI, BDA und DIHT.* Cologne: Pahl-Rugenstein, 1976.

Bernd Leupold

Economic Miracle. The "economic miracle" (*Wirtschaftswunder*) is an image that contemporary observers, both in Germany and abroad, used between 1948 and 1965 to describe West Germany's surprising recovery and subsequent economic growth.

The discourse on the economic miracle began when the reform triad of 1948—with the U.S.-sponsored Marshall Plan, the currency reform, and the decision for a market economy—accelerated the reconstruction of the West German economy. In August 1948 Hermann Pünder, head of the German administration for the combined American and British occupation zones, described the rise in production that followed the currency reform and economic reform of June 1948 as a "miracle." The rapid recovery from World War II and its consequences, and the subsequent years of unprecedented economic growth, made the economic miracle a popular concept in Germany and abroad. Recovery turned into economic growth as West Germany's real per capita income grew by 1953 beyond the German prewar level of 1938. Real gross social product increased from 1950 to 1965 by an average rate of 7.4 percent per year, and in per capita terms by 5.8 percent. The deutsche mark became internationally renowned for its stability. Consumer prices rose from 1951, just after the boom from the Korean War, to 1960 by an average rate of 1.2 percent, from 1960 to 1965 somewhat faster by 2.8 percent, which would still pass as price stability by present standards. Unemployment, which was very high in the early 1950s, had vanished by the end of the decade. Depending heavily on American and British subsidies in 1948, the West German economy achieved since 1951 a persistent trade surplus that was interrupted only in 1965.

Notwithstanding its popular success, the concept of an economic miracle met with some criticism. Ludwig Erhard, minister of economics from 1949 to 1963 and chancellor of the Federal Republic from 1963 to 1966, who became the popular personification of the miracle, did not like the concept, insisting that sound economic policy and hard work were the real causes of economic progress. And Ludwig Rosenberg, at that time vice chairman of the German Federation of Labor (Deutscher Gewerkschaftsbund, DGB), declared in 1959 that the German miracle was not a miracle but the result of hard work by millions of industrious people.

In the early 1960s the economic miracle vanished from public discourse. A slight rise in the rate of inflation, increasing government deficits, and dwindling trade surpluses brought home the truth that there was nothing miraculous about the German economy. Thereafter, the term reappeared only as a nostalgic and often ironic reference to the blissful 1950s.

West Germany's economic miracle may have been particularly impressive, but it was not unique. In Japan contemporary observers would go back to the mythical origins of the country to find appropriate names for the "Jimmu" boom of 1956–57, the "Iwato" boom of 1959–61, and the "Izanami" boom of 1967–69. "Economic miracles" happened in many countries within the long phase of rapid economic growth and expanding international trade from 1950 to 1973, particularly in continental Europe and Japan, less pronounced in the United Kingdom and the United States. Explanations for this unusual expansion include—beyond a qualified labor force, high investment, and economic policy—an exceptional combination of structural factors such as the transfer of advanced technology from the United States, population growth, and successful integration into the world market. The theoretical interpretation may vary, but there is general agreement now that the period of high growth, in Germany as in other countries, was a historical exception from the moderate long-term rate of economic expansion of capitalist market economies.

BIBLIOGRAPHY

Abelshauser, Werner. *Die Langen Fünfziger Jahre: Wirtschaft und Gesellschaft der Bundesrepublik Deutschland 1949–1966.* Düsseldorf: Schwann, 1987.

Giersch, Herbert, Karl-Heinz Paqué, and Holger Schmieding. *The Fading Miracle: Four Decades of Market Economy in Germany.* Cambridge: Cambridge University Press, 1992.

Hardach, Gerd. *Der Marshall-Plan: Auslandshilfe und Wiederaufbau in Westdeutschland.* Munich: Deutscher Taschenbuch Verlag, 1994.

Maddison, Angus. *Economic Growth in the West: Comparative Experience in Europe and North America.* New York: Twentieth Century Fund, 1964.

Nakamura, Takafusa. *The Postwar Japanese Economy: Its Development and Structure.* Tokyo: Tokyo University Press, 1981.

Statistisches Bundesamt, ed. *Bevölkerung und Wirtschaft 1872–1972.* Stuttgart: Kohlhammer, 1972.

Wallich, Henry C. *Mainsprings of the German Revival.* New Haven, Conn.: Yale University Press, 1955.

Gerd Hardach

Fiscal and Monetary Policy. Fiscal and monetary policies in Germany are intrinsically connected with the different political and economic systems that the country has had since 1945. Under Allied occupation rule, Germany had a planned economy from 1945 to 1948. The major instruments of the planning system were control of prices, wages, and rents; central allocation of labor; rationing of raw materials, energy, investment, and consumer goods; and the direction of foreign trade. Fiscal and monetary policies complemented the planning system. Tax rates were high to extract sufficient revenue for the Allied military governments and the German administration. The Nazi methods of financing the war had left an excessive money supply and suppressed inflation,

which the Allies increased by printing fresh reichsmarks. Any serious monetary policy would have to start with currency reform—a problem the Allies eschewed for three years.

From 1948 the economic systems of West Germany and East Germany diverged. In West Germany planning was abandoned in favor of a capitalist market economy. In East Germany postwar planning was transformed into a rigid system of state socialism. The establishment of two German states in 1949 confirmed the economic partition for the next forty years, until the reunification in 1990 extended the social market economy eastward from the Elbe to the Oder.

In the Federal Republic of Germany functional specialization among federal, state, and local governments was, and still is, less specific than in the United States. The Federal Republic inherited this tradition from the imperial constitution of 1871 and the republican constitution of 1919. German federalism aimed to combine the political advantages of decentralization with a strong preference for the economic and social homogeneity of the national market. In a typical arrangement, the central government legislated a framework, while policies were implemented by state and local governments. The major source of revenue for the different tiers of government was their share in the major taxes that were jointly appropriated, such as the personal income tax, the corporate tax, and the turnover or, later, value-added tax. With shifting functions, the parameters of revenue sharing were changed. In addition, federal, state, and local governments levied some exclusive taxes, and local governments drew a substantial part of their income from fees for specific services. The federal, state, and local budgets included welfare programs, but Germany's comprehensive social security system with compulsory health, old age, unemployment, and work accident insurance programs was independent of the government and administered by separate organizations.

During the neoliberal period of the social market economy from 1948 to 1966, the official doctrine was that fiscal policy should play only an accommodating role in economic development. But the reality was more complex. Tax incentives were used to foster economic growth, while the progressive income tax and social expenditure created the foundations of the modern welfare state. During the Keynesian era of the social market economy, from 1966 to 1982, the government assumed a more active stance. In the economic stabilization law of 1967, the fiscal policies of federal, state, and local governments were defined as elements of a comprehensive macroeconomic policy that should be directed toward price stability, full employment, external balance, and steady growth. The assumption that careful macroeconomic management could keep the capitalist market economy on a steady growth path gave rise to a vast program of social reform.

Slow economic growth, rising unemployment, and increasing government deficits led to a new policy change in 1982, with less confidence in macroeconomic management and more emphasis on deregulation and competition. This was not, however, a return to the neoliberal regime of the 1950s and 1960s. Fiscal policy is, in theory and in practice, an essential element of the modern social market economy. Total expenditure by federal, state, and local governments amounted to 31 percent of Germany's gross domestic product in 1996. If the social security system is included, the government expenditure ratio rises to 50 percent.

West Germany's central bank, the Bank Deutscher Länder, was founded in 1948, before the establishment of the Federal Republic. The Allied reformers established a two-tiered system of central banking that was a compromise between the centralized tradition of the old German Reichsbank and the decentralized model of the U.S. Federal Reserve System. Thus the Bank Deutscher Länder rested on a regional structure of independent state central banks (Landeszentralbanken) that advised the central bank and implemented its policy in the different states. In 1957 the central bank was reorganized as the Deutsche Bundesbank, and the influence of the state central banks was reduced. A new currency, the deutsche mark, replaced the old reichsmark in 1948. The government debt was canceled, and monetary assets were sharply reduced, on average by 93.5 percent, to end the suppressed inflation. The currency reform was followed by a short inflationary boom during the second half of 1948, but during the 1950s and early 1960s prices remained relatively stable. Prices increased again in the 1970s, when an expansive fiscal and monetary policy was applied to fight unemployment.

In the German Democratic Republic, fiscal and monetary policies were instruments of economic planning. For three years East Germany had a federal structure, similar to that of West Germany. In 1952 the states were abolished, and the new districts were integrated together with the local governments into a rigidly centralized administrative system. The task of fiscal policy was much wider than in a market economy. Beyond the traditional functions of government, the state budget was an instrument for redistribution of resources among different segments of the economy. The main sources of government finance were contributions by state-owned corporations. The income tax and other personal taxes played only a minor role. The government used a large part of its income to subsidize the prices of food and other necessities and to finance new investment in the corporate sector. As the government determined not only its own revenues and expenditures but also prices, output, and incomes, the financial delineation among corporations, most of them state-owned, households, and the state was to some extent arbitrary. Social security was administered as a separate institution but was heavily subsidized from the general budget.

The Soviet zone carried out its own currency reform in 1948, following the currency reform of the Western occupation zones, with a similar depreciation of monetary assets. The East German mark was managed by the Deutsche Notenbank, which became in 1968 the Staatsbank der Deutschen Demokratischen Republik. Unlike the central bank in a capitalist economy, East Germany's central bank was not only a policy-making institution but also the top of the centrally controlled banking system. The planned economy was a money economy, and monetary policy faced some of the choices that are known from capitalist countries. Ideally the money supply would have been adjusted to the development of the real economy. Eager to accommodate to the liquidity needs of the economy, however, the East German banking system increased the money supply substantially beyond the growth of money incomes. Prices were held under control by the planning system, but there was some indication of a moderate suppressed inflation. In July 1990, three months before reunification, the deutsche mark was introduced in East Germany. A limited amount, roughly one-third, of East Germany's monetary assets was converted at an exchange rate of one mark east for one mark west, while two-thirds of the assets were depreciated by 50 percent to skim off the excess liquidity.

In Germany the European Economic Community (EC), which was founded in 1957 and became the European Union (EU) in 1992, has had an increasing influence on fiscal and monetary policy. The creation of the European Central Bank in 1998 and the introduction of the Euro in 1999 introduced a single monetary policy for Austria, Belgium, Finland, France, Germany, Ireland, Italy, Luxembourg, Netherlands, Portugal, and Spain. The monetary union has exerted strong pressure toward harmonization of the fiscal policies in participating nations.

BIBLIOGRAPHY

Berger, Helge. *Konjukturpolitik im Wirtschaftswunder.* Tübingen: Mohr, 1997.

Deutsche Bundesbank. *Fünfzig Jahre Deutsche Mark: Notenbank und Währung seit 1948.* Munich: Beck, 1998.

Giersch, Herbert, Karl-Heinz Paqué, and Holger Schmieding. *The Fading Miracle: Four Decades of Market Economy in Germany.* Cambridge: Cambridge University Press, 1992.

Gutman, Gernot, ed. *Basisbereiche der Wirtschaftspolitik in der DDR.* Stuttgart: Edition Meyn, 1983.

Statistisches Jahrbuch der Deutschen Demokratischen Republik, Berlin: Staatsverlag, 1990.

Statistisches Jahrbuch für die Bundesrepublik Deutschland, Wiesbaden: Statistisches Bundesant, 1997.

Gerd Hardach

Labor Movement

The principal German labor organization, the German Federation of Labor (Deutscher Gewerkschaftsbund, DGB), was established in 1949. The formation of a single labor federation not tied to any political party and dedicated to the improvement of wages and working conditions rather than revolutionary social transformation was encouraged by the Western occupying powers, especially the United States. This unitary, nonpolitical, and nonrevolutionary trade unionism was a departure from the type of unionism that had existed in the Weimar Republic (1919–33), when the union movement had been divided into competing Socialist, Communist, Catholic, and Liberal unions.

The DGB unites seventeen unions with a membership of approximately eight million. The metalworkers union, which represents workers in the automobile and steel industries, is the largest of the component unions.

The DGB's initial program called for nationalization of West Germany's principal industries and for economic planning, but in practice the unions concentrated on pragmatic labor union issues. In the DGB's 1963 program most of the earlier socialistic goals were abandoned. Though the DGB has utilized collective bargaining to improve workers' conditions and has been reluctant to resort to strikes, it has been a firm proponent of codetermination through which workers have been given a voice in the decision making of their firm.

Though the DGB is independent of political parties, the influence and sympathy of the unions has been with the Social Democrats (SPD) rather than the Christian Democrats. A significant number of SPD members of parliament have been union members, 35 to 40 percent in 1963. Unions also indirectly provide a large portion of the financial support for the SPD.

Union membership has declined in Germany but not as drastically as in the United Kingdom. In the early 1950s approximately 45 percent of the West German workforce was unionized. By 1961 the percentage had slipped to 36, remaining at that level until the late 1980s. In 1990 it was 34 percent of the labor force and in 1994 approximately 32 percent.

The German Basic Law prohibits the closed shop. Thus union membership is voluntary. Since the government provides unemployment, health, disability, accident, and pension programs independent of union membership, unions have sought to capture the interest of prospective members through union representation on company boards (codetermination) and through union enforcement and administration of labor and social welfare laws.

Relations between labor and management, which were very cordial in West Germany, have become more conflictual since the late 1970s. Globalization of competition and economic stagnation produced record unemployment. German unions have begun to campaign for a thirty-five-hour week as a means to increase jobs. This issue led to a 1984 strike of metalworkers. Owing to the legality of the "lockout," management has provoked laborers by shutting out whole sectors of workers from their jobs when faced with selective strikes by the unions. The union also displayed its organized hostility in the 1990s to proposed cutbacks in Germany's generous welfare system.

BIBLIOGRAPHY

Conradt, David P. *The German Polity,* 3d ed. New York: Longman, 1986.

Markovits, Andrei S. *The Politics of West German Trade Unions: Activist Challenges and Accommodationist Responses.* Cambridge: Cambridge University Press, 1985.

Markovits, Andrei S., and Christopher S. Allen. "Power and Dissent: The Trade Unions in the Federal Republic of Germany Re-Examined." *Western European Politics* 3 (1980):68–86.

Wegs, J. Robert, and Robert Ladrech. *Europe since 1945: A Concise History,* 4th ed. New York: St. Martin's Press, 1996.

Wiley, Richard J. "Trade Unions and Political Parties in the Federal Republic of Germany." *Industrial and Labor Relations Review* 28 (October 1974):38–59.

Bernard Cook

***Mitbestimmung* (Copartnership).** West German practice of giving workers organized representation in the administration of large corporations. Copartnership arose from the demand for democracy in economic and public affairs. At an earlier time the concept of a representative system (*Rätesystem*) was developed. The manner in which economic democracy can be affected has often been discussed. According to Walter Weddingen it can be viewed as "the participation of labor through their representatives, in teamwork with employers, in decision making of regulations and measures which mainly concern social or personnel policies or economic control."

The demand for copartnership by workers in companies was caused by the noticeable discrepancy between capital and labor and the conditions of laborers. The first efforts in this direction came from socially minded people, in most cases with a Christian background, and from the liberal bourgeoisie. Thus, Catholic social philosopher Franz von Baader in 1834 recommended workers' committees (*Arbeiterlandräte*) as corporate representative bodies for laborers. Similar ideas were shared by public law specialist and social scientist Robert von Mohl, who in 1835 suggested workers' committees to limit the power of company owners. In parliament, too, scholars made attempts at reforms: Franz Josef von Buz, a member of the Representative Assembly of Baden in Freiburg in 1837, and industrialists Carl Degenkolb, a member of the 1848 Frankfurt Assembly, were among the first to demand factory trade regulations (*Fabrik-Gewerbe-Ordnung*). It was not until the time of the German Empire (1871–1918), however, that copartnership of laborers was translated into action, encouraged principally by industrialists like Carl Zeiss, Robert Bosch, and Ernst Abbé. Nevertheless, the majority of industrialists still opposed such notions. A memorandum written by the Central Association of German Industrialists in 1887 asserted that "the worker is not the equal participant of the employer . . . , but instead his inferior, who must show him respect."

In 1891 the government passed a new law, the so-called *Gewerbeordnungsnovelle,* followed by the creation of workers' committees that were duly recognized by the German Empire. As the workforce was suspicious of these models of copartnership, the unions required from industrialists the recognition of unions with equal rights as the representatives of the interests of the working classes. During World War I, as the military situation of Germany deteriorated and dissatisfaction among the population increased, the government was forced to make domestic concessions. The Labor Service Law of December 15, 1916, stated that companies with more than fifty laborers could establish elected workers' and employees' committees, but their influence was weak. Of much more importance were the decisions taken by industry and government in 1918–19, influenced by the German revolution of November 1918. Committees of workers and soldiers demanded more socialization and the estab-

lishment of a democracy where government consisted of a series of representative committees (*Rätedemokratie*). There was an agreement between industrialists and unions on November 15, 1918, and a government declaration on March 5, 1919, accepted workers' committees (*Arbeiterräte*) as official representatives of the economy. These agreements served as a basis for the acceptance of unions as the corporate representatives of the workforce, the introduction of the eight-hour workday, and the establishment of codetermination on the basis of parity of representation. These regulations were also adopted into the constitution of the Weimar Republic and elaborated by the February 4, 1920, law of works councils (*Betriebsrätegesetz*), and a February 15, 1922, law on workers' representation. However, the National Socialists' coming to power in 1933 put an end to copartnership and democracy.

After World War II the development of copartnership started again. This time it was sponsored by the Allies, who opposed giving big companies too much economic power and did not desire a new, economically strong Germany. As a result of the political situation in Europe after 1945, the Federal Republic of Germany and the former German Democratic Republic went their separate ways. The first step in West Germany consisted of a law on April 10, 1946, that provided the legal basis of works committees. In 1947 codetermination on the basis of parity of representation in the coal and steel industries followed. The first models of copartnership founded on the principle of equality of capital and labor were supported by the British military government.

In the 1950s the fight for the retention and extension of copartnership continued, especially in the coal and steel industries, through the May 21, 1951, law of copartnership in the coal and steel industry and the November 14, 1952, law of company constitution. Since then the right of copartnership has undergone many elaborations. Workers and employees are organized into committees, and both have representatives on the board of trustees. The May 4, 1976, law of copartnership, however, did not establish copartnership of labor on the basis of parity of representation.

BIBLIOGRAPHY

Nagel, Bernhard. *Mitbestimmung in öffentlich-rechtlichen Unternehmen und Verfassungsrecht: Rechtsgutachten für die Hans-Bockler-Stiftung.* Baden-Baden: Nomos, 1990.

Niedenhoff, Horst. *Mitbestimmung und Betriebsverfassungsgesetz.* Cologne: Deutsche Industrieverlags, 1972.

Annette Biener

Social Market Economy.   The social market economy (*Soziale Marktwirtschaft*) is a political program, as well as an empirical concept used since 1949 to describe West Germany's economic system and subsequently a reunited Germany's economic system since 1990. There are different interpretations, and as an economic system the social market economy has gone through various stages. Essentially, the social market economy means a capitalist market economy where, in contrast to the liberal paradigm of the nineteenth century, imperfections of the market are compensated for by systematic economic and social policies.

The social market economy was established in 1948, even before the Federal Republic of Germany was founded the following year. In April 1948 the European Recovery Program, also known as the Marshall Plan, began to integrate the reconstruction of the West German economy into the overall economic recovery of Western Europe. Two months later, in June 1948, the military governments of the three Western occupation zones carried out a currency reform, designed by American experts. The reichsmark was replaced by a new currency unit, the deutsche mark. Monetary assets were drastically reduced to create a functioning currency. At the same time the American and British military governments allowed the German administration of their combined occupation zones to combine the monetary reform with a sweeping economic reform. The head of the economic reform of June 1948, which replaced the planned economy of the early postwar years with a market economy, was Ludwig Erhard, a liberal economist who had in March 1948 become director of the "Administration for the Economy of the United Economic Area" (Trizonia formed from the three Western occupation zones) in Frankfurt. The free-market doctrine was established as the new guideline for economic policy, and a number of price controls were immediately abolished. In the election campaign of 1949 for the first West German parliament, the conservative Christian Democratic Union (CDU) and Christian Social Union (CSU) Parties adopted Erhard's free-market doctrine as their economic program under the name of "social market economy" to emphasize that it was a socially responsible policy, not a new mis-en-scène of nineteenth-century Manchesterian classical capitalism. The concept was borrowed from a theory that German economist Alfred Müller-Armack had published in 1946 in his *Wirtschaftslenkung und Marktwirtschaft*.

When the conservatives won the elections of 1949 by a small margin to form the first West German cabinet in September 1949, the social market economy became the economic philosophy of the Federal Republic of Germany. The concept was vague enough to allow for different interpretations. Erhard, who shaped West Germany's economic policy as minister of economics from 1949 to 1963, and other liberals would argue that the market economy was inherently "social" as it optimized the allocation of resources. The prevailing opinion, however, shared by Konrad Adenauer, chancellor from 1949 to 1963, was that the social market economy was a new approach that combined a market economy with systematic social policy. The social market economy became the West German variety of the European welfare state, reconciling the dynamics of a market economy with a high level of social security.

When the Social Democrats came to power as junior partners in the great coalition government of 1966–69, and as senior partners in the social-liberal coalition government from 1969 to 1982, they propagated their own model of a social market economy. The market mechanism was accepted as the basic regulator of the economy, but it would have to be complemented by systematic fiscal and monetary policies to achieve economic stability. The stabilization law of 1967, designed by economics minister Karl Schiller (1911–96), defined price stability, full employment, economic growth, and balance-of-payments equilibrium as objectives of economic policy.

The conservative-liberal government that replaced the social-liberal coalition in 1982 promised yet another reform of the social market economy. In tune with developments in the United Kingdom and the United States, more emphasis was placed on private initiative, market forces, and deregulation. Reunification in 1990 confirmed the political attractiveness of the social market economy, but the economic performance was disappointing in following years. Rising unemployment, increasing government debt, and globalization of the economy have presented serious challenges to the social market economy of our time.

BIBLIOGRAPHY

Ambrosius, Gerold. *Die Durchsetzung der Sozialen Marktwirtschaft in Westdeutschland 1945–1949*. Stuttgart: Fischer, 1977.

Giersch, Herbert, Karl-Heinz Paqué, and Holger Schmieding. *The Fading Miracle: Four Decades of Market Economy in Germany*. Cambridge: Cambridge University Press, 1992.

Wallich, Henry C. *Mainsprings of German Revival*. New Haven, Conn.: Yale University Press, 1955.

Gerd Hardach

Economic Integration of East Germany.   The reunification of Germany in 1990 brought together two economies that had been separated by differences in economic institutions, size, and productivity yet linked by a strong feeling of national identity. Economic integration turned out to be more difficult than most people expected in 1989–90, but it was inevitable. An endogenous transformation of the German Democratic Republic toward a democratic state with its own market economy, which the Modrow government attempted hesitantly from November 1989 to March 1990, never had democratic legitimation. The Christian Democratic Union (CDU) won the election in March 1990 with a clear mandate for reunification, and the new government under prime minister Lothar de Maizière immediately opened negotiations to integrate East Germany into the Federal Republic of Germany.

The conditions for economic integration were negotiated between the two German governments in the Agreement on the Economic, Monetary, and Social Union of May 1990, which became effective in July 1990, and the Unification Treaty of August 1990, which became effective on October 3, 1990. It was a merger between two partners that were quite unequal in economic strength. West Germany had 62 million inhabitants, against East Germany's 17 million, or 27 percent of the west's population. The difference in the labor force was somewhat smaller, with 30 million people in West Germany and 9 million in East Germany, or 30 percent of the western level. The labor force participation ratio was higher in East Germany, 53 percent against 48 percent in the West. The main reason for the difference was that East German women usually sought gainful employment, while West German women would still frequently give up their job after marriage. The difference in the number of those actually employed was again somewhat smaller, with East German employment attaining 32 percent of the western level. The reason was that two million West Germans, or 7 percent of the total labor force, were registered as unemployed in 1989, while the East German economy traditionally guaranteed full employment. West German society put a smaller portion of its people to work, but those who did work were on average much more productive than their East German colleagues. West German per capita income was 36,300 deutsche marks in 1989, compared with 21,500 East German marks in the German Democratic Republic. If the purchasing power of the two different marks is assumed as equal, East Germans attained only 59 percent of the West German per capita income. This estimate implies that the East German economy, given the relatively larger labor input, attained 49 percent of the West German productivity level. The pro-

ductivity gap was, and still is, the major problem in the integration of the two economies.

West Germany's currency, the deutsche mark, was introduced in East Germany in July 1990, three months before political reunification. At the same time the monetary and fiscal policies were integrated, and the German Democratic Republic reorganized its social security system in the West German pattern. The exchange rate in current prices, wages, and rents was fixed at one East German mark for one deutsche mark. This was based on a reasonable comparison of the purchasing power. Food, housing, public utilities, as well as other necessities were cheaper in East German marks than in deutsche marks, but industrial consumer goods were much more expensive. The Deutsche Bundesbank, West Germany's central bank, warned that the application of the par exchange rate to monetary assets would create inflationary pressure as the money supply, including savings accounts, was much larger in East Germany in relation to gross domestic product than in West Germany. Therefore a dual exchange rate was applied. A basic amount of monetary assets was converted into deutsche marks at par to protect the average household savings. The amount that exceeded the limit was depreciated by 50 percent. As the favorable exchange rate applied to only one-third of the total volume of monetary assets, there was a considerable devaluation.

The transition from socialism to capitalism entailed a vast privatization program, as forty years of purposeful socialization of private property had to be unraveled. The expropriations that the East German government had effected since 1949 were to be repealed by restitution in kind, rather than monetary compensation. Restitution in kind was also applied to expropriations under the Nazi regime from 1933 to 1945. This historical redress was necessary as the German Democratic Republic had not repealed the theft of property, essentially from Jewish Germans, that public authorities or individuals had committed between 1933 and 1945. The expropriations by the Soviet Military Government from 1945 to 1949, however, were confirmed. This was not only a concession to the Soviet Union but also a political decision. The early expropriations in East Germany comprised essentially the large industrial corporations and the agrarian reform that had divided the large estates into small farm holdings. In both cases a restitution to the previous owners would have been highly unpopular in East Germany. Restitution in kind applied essentially to urban real estate or smaller businesses. The land and other assets of the agrarian cooperatives, which had replaced individual farming since the 1950s, were divided among their members.

East Germany's large industrial, commercial, and financial corporations, expropriated in 1945–49 or founded in later years, were inherited by the Federal Republic as successor to the German Democratic Republic. Most of this huge public domain was to be transferred to private owners. This part of the privatization program was implemented by the Treuhandanstalt (Trust Corporation) from 1990 to 1994. The Trust Corporation had been founded by the Modrow government in March 1990 in an attempt to replace the traditional command structure of the East German economy with a more flexible instrument of public control. The idea was to create a holding company, similar to state-owned companies in capitalist countries, which would manage East Germany's state-owned corporations. When the new government prepared East Germany for integration into the social market economy, the Trust Corporation was commissioned in June 1990 to transfer the state-owned corporations to private ownership, or in some cases to local governments. Companies that were not competitive in the market were to be liquidated, rather than stabilized with government subsidies. The privatization program was vigorously implemented. When the Trust Corporation was dissolved in 1994, most of the heritage of East Germany's state socialism had been either sold to private owners or liquidated. The result, however, was disappointing. In 1990 the property that the Trust Corporation managed was optimistically estimated at 600 billion deutsche marks. But the assets depreciated rapidly as East Germany's once prestigious large corporations were unable to compete in a capitalist market. In the end, the proceeds from the sale of the public domain were far outweighed by administrative costs, subsidies, and other expenditures. Contrary to the expected benefits, the Trust Corporation incurred severe losses that had to be covered from the federal budget. After 1994 the privatization program was to be completed by three successor organizations: the Bundesanstalt für Vereinigungsbedingte Sonderaufgaben to liquidate uncompetitive companies, the Treuhand-Liegenschaftsgesellschaft to administer the remaining real estate, and the Beteiligungs-Management-Gesellschaft to manage, and ultimately sell, the firms that might survive under private ownership.

After the reunification of October 1990, the German government promised that economic conditions in East Germany would be brought within five years to the West German standard. This was much too optimistic. The sudden integration into the capitalist world market threw the East German economy into a deep crisis from which it had not recovered by 1998. East Germany's industry had been competitive within the socialist Council on Mutual Economic Assistance (CMEA), and to some extent in the Third World, but it was unable to compete with the industries of West Germany and other advanced capitalist countries. From 1990 to 1992 there was a sharp decline in production and a steep rise in unemployment. Production recovered after 1993, but unemployment remained high. Fifteen percent of the East German labor force were unemployed in 1996, and when the hidden unemployed—those not registered at the Labor Offices—are added, the number might be as high as 26 percent. In West Germany, the respective figures were 9 percent for registered unemployment and 12 percent if estimated hidden unemployment is included. Starting from the low point in 1992, economic growth was somewhat faster in East Germany than in West, but there was still a considerable gap in productivity and incomes in the late 1990s. Considerable transfer payments from West Germany were made and will still be needed in the future to maintain a reasonable standard of public administration, social security, and welfare in East Germany. If economic integration implies that economic conditions in East Germany should be comparable to the West German level, the task is not yet completed.

BIBLIOGRAPHY

Bähr, Johannes, and Dietmar Petzina, eds. *Innovationsverhalten und Entscheidungsstrukturen: Vergleichende Studien zur wirtschaftlichen Entwicklung im geteilten Deutschland 1945–1990.* Berlin: Duncker & Humblot, 1996.

Fischer, Wolfram, Herbert Hax, and Hans Karl Schneider, eds. *Treuhandanstalt: Das unmögliche Wagen.* Berlin: Akademie Verlag, 1993.

Hickel, Rudolf, Ernst-Ulrich Huster, and Heribert Kohl, eds. *Umverteilen: Schritte zur sozialen und wirtschaftlichen Einheit Deutschlands.* Cologne: Bund, 1993.

Sachverständigenrat zur Begutachtung der gesamtwirtschaftlichen Entwicklung: *Reformen voranbringen. Jahresgutachten 1996/97.* Stuttgart: Metzler-Poeschel, 1996.

———. *Wachstum, Beschäftigung, Währungsunion—Orientierungen für die Zukunft. Jahresgutachten 1997/98.* Stuttgart: Metzler-Poeschel 1997.

Sinn, Gerlinde, and Hans-Werner Sinn. *Jumpstart: The Economic Unification of Germany.* Cambridge, Mass.: MIT Press, 1993.

Gerd Hardach

Trust Agency. The Trust Agency (Treuhandanstalt, THA), also called the Treuhand (Trust), was founded on March 1, 1990, by the German Democratic Republic

(GDR) with its head office in Berlin and fifteen branches to transform state-owned enterprises into competitive corporations (*Kapitalgesellschaften*) or into public ownership on the basis of a "free-market socialism." On June 16, 1990, the first democratically elected people's chamber of the GDR enacted the law on privatization and reorganization of social property, which came into force together with the economic and monetary union of July 1990. The legal framework of the trust was approved and modified by the Unification Treaty of August 31, 1990. The federal minister of finance became responsible for the technical and legal supervision of the Treuhand in conjunction with the minister of economic affairs. The trust law was amended on August 9, 1994, and renamed the Federal Office for Special Tasks Associated with Unification (Bundesanstalt für Vereinigungsbedingte Sonderaufgaben) on January 1, 1995.

The organizational management of the Trust Agency was in the hands of an executive committee headed by a president. The members of the executive committee were elected by an administrative council, which was also the supervisory and supporting authority, to which each of the five new federal states sent one representative.

The Treuhand immediately became the largest economic holding company in the world. There had never been a historical parallel to this accumulation of economic power in the hands of a few people. The trust agency became administrator of eighty thousand individuals' enterprises, 17.2 million square meters of agricultural area, 19.6 million square meters of forest area, 25 million square meters of real estate, 40,000 retail shops and restaurants, 14 department stores, and a great number of cinemas, bookshops, drugstores, and hotels. Nearly 3.6 million people worked in these enterprizes. As a consequence of the creation of competitive structures, many of these jobs were lost and the unemployment rate rose to 14.8 percent in 1992. Former East Germans had no experience with enterprises oriented toward a free-market economy, so most leading positions were given to West Germans. For example, Lothar Späth, a Christian Democratic politician and minister president of Baden-Württemberg from 1978 to 1991, became the consultant for the Carl Zeiss Jena Werke, the famous manufacturer of optical equipment and precision tools.

Difficulties in privatizing and reorganizing the people's enterprises (as the Communists called the state enterprises) arose especially in the area of retrocession. This concerned expropriations made between 1933 and 1945 (the Nazi era), as well as those made after 1949. Restitution took precedence over compensation; however, this was modified by a law of July 14, 1992. The restructuring

(*Sanierung*) of GDR enterprises was another point of contention. Uncompetitive enterprises were simply closed. From the beginning the calculation of the total value of the GDR public property was contested. At the time of the foundation of the trust agency the national property in the GDR was estimated to be 1.6 billion deutsche marks. In the course of time the number had to be recalculated. The overall balance of Treuhand property on October 15, 1992, was calculated to be 260 billion deutsche marks in fixed and circulating assets. On the other side, liabilities amounted to 520 billion deutsche marks.

The first president of the trust agency, Detlev Carsten Rohwedder, had already held key political and economic functions in the Federal Republic. He was murdered on April 1, 1991, by left-wing Red Army Faction (RAF) terrorists in front of his house in Düsseldorf. The former general secretary of the Christian Democratic Union (CDU), Heiner Geissler, had accused Rohwedder of "failure and incompetence" in autumn 1990. And in view of the severe criticism of the Trust Agency by right-wing as well as left-wing parties, the terrorists had thought they would be supported by the public. The murder was also intended to symbolize an attack on the capitalist system. Yet the idea of reform of the economy in the GDR through a trust had originated in a working group of eleven people during the Hans Modrow interim government. Birgit Breuel, who succeeded Rohwedder, was the daughter of Hamburg banker Alwin Münchmeyer, and a Christian Democratic economic expert with experience in state administration.

Despite accusations that the agency had been dominated by old power structures and was part of a rapacious conspiracy, it had been assigned a gigantic economic task and had been staffed by qualified personnel. When the trust was dissolved at the end of 1994, Breuel asserted, "Quick privatization was the only right way, and structural mistakes had not been made."

BIBLIOGRAPHY

Bichlmeier, Wilhelm, and Hermann Oberhofer. *Das Gesamtvollstreckungsverfahren in Ostdeutschland.* Cologne: Bund, 1994.

Breuel, Birgit, ed. *Treuhand intern: Tagebuch.* Frankfurt am Main: Ullstein, 1993.

Brezan, Jurij. *Die Leute von Salow: Roman.* Leipzig: G. Kiepenheuer, 1997.

Bundesministerium der Finanzen Treuhandanstalt. *Die Tätigkeit der Treuhand, Dokumentation 1990–1994.* 15 Vols. Berlin: Treuhandanstalt, 1994.

Christ, Peter, and Ralf Neubauer. *Kolonie im eigenen Land. Die Treuhand, Bonn und die Wirtschaftskatastrophe der fünf neuen Länder.* Berlin: Rowohlt, 1991.

Hommelhoff, P., ed. *Treuhandunternehmen im Umbruch.* Cologne: Verlag Kommunikationsforum Recht, Wirtschaft, Steuern, 1991.

Schulz, Werner, ed. *Entwickeln statt abwickeln, wirtschaftpolitische und ökologische Umbau-Konzepte für die fünf neuen Länder.* Berlin: Ch. Links, 1992.

Suhr, Heinz. *Der Treuhandskandal.* Frankfurt am Main: Eichborn, 1991.

Annette Biener

Media

Talking about Germany in the second half of the twentieth century means talking about two different political and ideological systems that have existed and developed in two separate states for over forty years. This section concentrates on the mass media: the press, radio, television, with a brief discussion of the computer and the Internet. The pluralistic character of the media in West Germany automatically leads to a focus on developments in the Federal Republic, though East Germany's media are considered too. Since German reunification in 1990, structures and approaches of the media in East and West Germany have largely realigned.

Roughly, the history of the mass media in West Germany, and to a certain degree in East Germany, can be divided into three phases: (1) the postwar years up to the late 1950s, which in the fields of the press, broadcasting, film, and television were also a period of construction and reconstruction; (2) the 1960s up to the mid-1970s, which saw an accelerated process of expansion and concentration of existing media; and (3) from the mid-1970s onward, a postindustrial phase characterized by the supremacy of information and the plurality of mass media.

For the media in Germany, having been firmly integrated into the National Socialist system of propaganda and indoctrination, the end of World War II marked a notable break. Even before the war was over, papers and radio stations began to resume their work freed from the restraints of Nazi dictatorship. The *Aachener Nachrichten,* reissued on January 24, 1945, was the first newspaper to appear in a German area already under Allied control. To the Allies, the Nazis owed much of their success to the regime's total control of the media. Consequently, a free press, radio and later television reporting was a central aim in the attempt to win the peace. In fact, the Allies exerted an immeasurable effect on the reconstruction of the media in their four zones of occupation. When the Federal Republic of Germany and the German Demo-

cratic Republic were created in May and October 1949 respectively, the bases on which people in the newly formed states could operate were laid.

Until 1949, newspapers, magazines, and broadcasting stations in the Western zones needed a license issued by the Allies before they could resume business. Allied media control made way for the restoration of a decentralized, federal system. Local and regional papers got a license first, and broadcasting stations were located in towns and cities where they had been during the Weimar years. At the same time broadcasting was put on a different footing, since it was recreated as an institution based on public law. To ensure a break with the past in media contents, the Allies attempted a change not only in structures but in personnel too, although they did not keep to their policy of exclusion of Nazis too consistently. In addition, news presentation itself was to follow Anglo-American principles more closely, for example, objective reporting and the separation of facts and comments. Parallel to these transformations in the Western part of the country, the Russians reorganized the media in their zone of occupation to become an organ of Communist Party and, later, state interests.

In West Germany press and broadcasting entered a new phase in 1949. In September of that year, the requirement that journals obtain an Allied license was repealed. This gave a new impetus to publishers to start or restart a host of additional papers and magazines. The Allies' influence on German broadcasting was considerably reduced and vanished altogether when the Federal Republic gained sovereignty in 1955. Article 5 of the country's constitution (Basic Law) saw to it that the legal basis of the media corresponded to the principles of a liberal democracy. Whereas the press came under the influence of a market economy, the broadcasting system was more subject to political influences. Thus, it was a political decision to split the regional broadcasting organization Nordwestdeutscher Rundfunk in two in 1956: NDR (Norddeutscher Rundfunk) and WDR (Westdeutscher Rundfunk). Until that time, there had been six organizations. They had constituted themselves as the Association of Public Law Broadcasting Organizations (Arbeitsgemeinschaft der Öffentlich-rechtlichen Rundfunkanstalten Deutschlands, ARD) in 1950, an organization that was to broadcast the first TV channel in West Germany from December 1952 onward. Four years later the age of television began in East Germany. Both the West German states (*länder*) and the federal government were involved in the elections of personnel to the committees that controlled the organizations for licensing new channels and broadcasting organizations. However, Public

Law Broadcasting was and is supposed to be politically autonomous. For many years, radio and television programs were mainly financed by fees paid by the audience. Commercials were first shown on West German television in November 1956.

For the press, the 1960s were a time of consolidation that lasted until the mid-1970s; number of daily and weekly papers, approaching a daily circulation of 20 million, was markedly reduced during these years. While circulation of specialist journals went down continuously until 1990, magazines catering for a mass readership, including the yellow press and new types of journals such as computer magazines, managed to occupy an ever larger segment of the market. Their circulation rose from 60 million copies in 1960 to more than 120 million in 1991.

Content changed as well. From the late 1950s on, more and more articles accentuated the emotional or speculative. Scandals have become increasingly important to the press. In a way, this change can be attributed to mounting competition not only between different segments of the press but between different kinds of media. The rise of television inevitably had its repercussions on the printed media, on their contents, structure, layout, topicality. The latter was boosted when new technologies such as offset printing and desktop publishing became available in the mid-1970s. At the end of the twentieth century, the contents of printed media had become even more heterogeneous, local or regional sections had acquired a greater relevance, and advice and services offered to readers had been extended. What is more, the press became a televised medium too after commercial channels were launched in 1984. Papers and journals are even less printed media in the traditional sense, since a great number of them are now simultaneously issued on paper and on the Internet.

In a similar way, expansion has been the most conspicuous characteristic of television broadcasting. At first, it was the number of viewers and hours of broadcasting per day that proliferated. The number of licensed viewers, those who purchased the TV tax certificate, rose from one million in October 1957 to more than two million in December 1958. For decades, transmission was limited to the early and late evening hours. Only in 1981 did the first and second channels begin to broadcast programs on weekdays before noon, the program then being interrupted from noon until early afternoon. Starting in 1989, this gap was filled by a variety of programs. Over the years, additional stations and channels went on the air. A second television channel, the Zweites Deutsches Fernsehen (ZDF), was created in 1961 and began to broadcast in April 1963. A third, regionally based channel went on air

in September 1964 in Bavaria and a year later in four other regions of the Federal Republic. Television soon overtook radio broadcasting and the cinema as the most popular mass media turned to by Germans in their leisure time, though since the 1980s the radio has regained some of the territory it had lost.

Nothing has transformed broadcasting in West Germany so dramatically as the initiation of commercial channels. From the first commercial experiments, the number of channels and, consequently, of programs has soared. The first private channel financed exclusively by commercials to start broadcasting was RTL plus in February 1984. More were to follow from 1986 onwards. The first pay-TV channel, Premiere, went on air the same year that the European joint venture, ARTE, began to broadcast its mainly culturally oriented programs in 1991. Since the inception of the dual public/private system, broadcasting has diversified and, simultaneously, has become less varied. Single channels now cater to specific interests or audience groups.

As with the printed media, broadcasting has gone on line. For instance, in 1997 the ZDF presented information of its news program "Heute" (Today) for the first time on the Internet as well. Technologically, television broadcasting has advanced from the first live programs via magnetic recording available in Germany since the end of the 1950s and live programs transmitted via satellite from other continents, in 1958 from the United States, and in 1969 from the moon, to color TV in the late 1960s and the beginnings of digital broadcasting today. In July 1996 the digital channel DF 1 started to operate.

In contrast to developments in West Germany, the media in the German Democratic Republic were firmly controlled by the party and state so that the changes they underwent were not the result of technology or economics but of ideology. Within the socialist system, the media were a pillar of party rule and functioned as a political guide and an instrument of the ideological education of the people. Whereas the media in West Germany had to fulfill a mixture of functions—economic, political, and educational as well as to entertain the audience—the socialist state first and foremost intended its media to concentrate on political aims, with entertainment and non-ideological education coming second or even third in order of rank. As a result, many programs were monotonous, such as the repeated reports of successes of the East Germany's dubious economy.

Despite the controlled media, East Germans were avid readers of papers and journals even before reunification. In 1984, circulation of daily papers, most of them party organs with a few church magazines specially licensed by the state, nearly touched the mark of 9 million, compared to 21 million in West Germany, with an additional circulation of 9 million for weeklies and magazines. The youth paper *Junge Welt* (Young World), issued by the youth organization Freie Deutsche Jugend (Free German Youth, FDJ) and the TV guide *FF-Dabei* were the most popular publications in the mid-1980s. As in West Germany, television in East Germany was very popular. In 1967, eleven years after the initiation of regular TV broadcasting, 60 percent of East German households had a TV set compared to 62 percent in the Federal Republic. By 1976 the number of East German households with TV sets had grown to 83 percent and by 1985, 93 percent. In the early 1980s, structures and program planning of the two TV channels were reorganized in order to raise viewer acceptance and to lure East Germans away from watching West German TV programs. The increase in entertainment programs and movies, though popular, failed to achieve this goal. In fact, West German broadcasts, reporting on the events before the collapse of the Berlin Wall in November 1989, led East Germans to increase the pressure they exerted on the Communist government, thus accelerating the process of tearing down the Iron Curtain between the two German states.

Reunification in 1990 produced a sort of alignment of the media in West and East Germany. The five new states that were created on the territory of the former GDR adopted the West German system of public law broadcasting supplemented by commercial organizations, who were soon to outrun the former in attendance figures. As in the period between 1945 and 1949 in West Germany, there has been no clean sweep with the past, since a considerable number of journalists formerly loyal to the Communist regime have remained within the field of journalism, a field more heterogeneous than ever in the new Federal Republic of Germany. Nevertheless, the country's transformation from the literate culture centered on printed media that it had been at the end of World War II, to a culture of rapidly expanding and diversifying multimedia is complete.

BIBLIOGRAPHY

Hickethier, Knut. *Geschichte des deutschen Fernsehens.* Stuttgart: Metzler, 1998
Klingler, Walter, Gunnar Roters, and Maria Gerhards, eds. *Medienrezeption seit 1945. Forschungsbilanz und Forschungsperspektiven.* Baden-Baden: Nomos Verlagsgesellschaft, 1998
Noelle-Neumann, Elisabeth, and Ruediger Schulz. "Federal Republic of Germany. Social Experimentation with Cable and Commercial Television" in Lee B.
Becker, and Klaus Schoenbach, eds. *Audience Responses to Media Diversification.* Hillsdale, NJ: Erlbaum, 1989.
Wilke, Juergen, ed. *Mediengeschichte der Bundesrepublik Deutschland.* Cologne: Boehlau, 1999.

Angela Schwarz

Education

The educational history of post–World War II Germany provides insight into the development and founding of two separate German states and their later reunification. The opening of German-German borders and reunification necessitated the unification of the school systems, which allowed for some innovation in former East German schools and universities.

The Occupation Powers (United States, Great Britain, Soviet Union, and later France) and Germans agreed that schools should be directly involved in the "reeducation" and "democratization" of Germans, beginning with the purging of Nazi influences from the educational system. This included developing new teaching materials and curricula, training new teachers, and making structural changes in the school system itself.

Article 7 of the Potsdam Treaty (August 1945) assigned a significant role to schools in the restructuring of German society. The Occupational Powers in both the Soviet Occupied Zone and the three Western zones, which became the German Democratic Republic (GDR) and the Federal Republic (FRG), respectively, in the fall of 1949, gave Germans broad latitude to develop and implement education reforms. The resulting two systems thus represented an interplay between German and Allied Command educational philosophies.

The Soviet Occupied Zone implemented an "antifascist democratic" educational program that drew on ideas from the progressive educational plans of 1848 and the Weimar era. As continued to be the case throughout the GDR, the system was centrally organized and directed from a single educational body in East Berlin. The resulting *Einheitsschule* (unified school) was a compulsory, comprehensive, nontracked, coeducational eight-year school, followed by either three years of vocational training or a four-year secondary school. The Law for the Socialist Development of the School System in the GDR (1959) called for the ten-year General Polytechnic Upper School (*Allgemeinbildende Polytechnische Oberschule,* POS), which combined theoretical instruction with practical training. The option of a two-year upper secondary school (*Erweiterte Oberschule,* EOS) followed the POS, whose school-leaving examination, the *Abitur,* provided the most common means of continuing to the university. This system remained largely in place until the end of the

GDR. Other educational institutions existed outside this official unified realm, such as the "special schools" that provided specialized training in subjects such as Russian language, sports, and mathematics. Educational opportunities remained consciously linked to socialist goals, including loyalty to the state and socialist community, indicated by such considerations as membership in the official youth groups, the Pioneers, until the seventh grade and the Free German Youth (Freie Deutsche Jugend) after the eighth grade. In spite of some persistent structural and ideological differentiations in the "unified concept" of GDR education, the tendency throughout the GDR generally continued to be a commitment to secular, common education for all students.

Like the elementary and secondary schools, universities were centrally administered. Postwar university programs aimed to facilitate entrance to university studies for the children of workers and farmers. The most significant institution for this purpose, named the Workers' and Farmers' Faculty (Arbeiter-und-Bauern-Fakultät) in 1949, offered special university preparatory courses beginning in 1946. The 1960s brought about a wave of reforms to meet the "scientific and technological revolution," including expanding the number of students in relevant departments and some attempts to bring students more actively into the learning process. This period also saw a stronger orientation toward Marxist-Leninist philosophy as the official ideological basis of university studies.

The federal Länder (states) in West Germany maintained control of their school systems, so that any discussion of education assumed regional variations. For all the Länder, though, one of the most debated questions in West German educational history remains whether postwar reforms were merely a restoration of the traditional system or a new construction that drew on the positive aspects of German educational concepts, the centerpiece of which was a Christian humanist approach. In opposition to the U.S. desire for a comprehensive, nontracked school, the West German Länder left the three-tiered tracked secondary system in place, which followed a four- or six-year elementary school and continued to provide confessional instruction as part of the standard curriculum. After the fifth or the seventh grade in elementary school, students attended either the academically oriented Gymnasium (through the thirteenth grade), which offered the Abitur, necessary for entrance to the university; the more modern and practically focused Realschule (through the tenth grade); or the general-education Hauptschule (through the ninth grade).

This three-tiered system has been criticized for institutionalizing socioeconomic inequalities as well as praised

for its contributions to the postwar West German "economic miracle" by creating qualified intellectuals and skilled workers. However, the system has not retained its postwar rigidity and stark, elitist character. The 1960s saw many societal changes that culminated in an expansion of the educational system, driven by two ideas: instrumentalization of educational resources for economic gains and promotion of education as a fundamental right of all citizens. The more lasting of these reforms included more flexibility to move between the three tiers of the secondary school and the creation of alternative means for obtaining an Abitur. One of the most notable results of this period, the Gesamtschule (comprehensive school), is an alternative secondary school whose goal is to provide increased educational equality by not tracking students. The organizational structure, which loosely resembles a U.S. high school, did not succeed in replacing the three-tiered system, although it has retained popularity in some Länder.

The university system drew largely on prewar organizational structures, making one significant change by guaranteeing autonomy in researching, teaching, and studying—a response to the policies of the Nazi era. A massive higher education expansion program began in the 1950s, motivated in part by the perceived link between institutions of higher learning and workforce needs. Whether or not the student protests of 1968 initiated entirely new reforms or merely encouraged tendencies already in place, it is clear that the late 1960s marked a new phase in the university system. More democratic organizational structures softened a rigid professional hierarchy, the various academic disciplines took on a more praxis-oriented character, and a larger critique of the university's complicity during the Nazi era began to take place.

The opening of German-German borders in November 1989 and the subsequent process of reunification in October 1990 put enormous pressure on the former GDR to align its institutions with those of West Germany as quickly as possible. The five Länder of the former GDR—the new Länder—have adopted the general outline of the elementary and secondary school structures of the old Länder but have made some adaptations to respond to demographic and sociocultural needs. One issue, the decision in some new Länder to continue the Gymnasium only through the twelfth grade, has resparked a debate throughout Germany about the advantages of shortening the time that students remain in school, as is the case in many other European countries. The more secular culture of the new Länder has also prevented full implementation of religious instruction in schools.

Universities in the new Länder have also been decentralized and harmonized to fit within the Western university structure. Here, too, some flexibility and innovation in universities in the new Länder have created the opportunity for experimentation with different degree options and programs. Creative solutions to current university problems, which include overcrowding, limited resources, and uncertain employment prospects for graduates, will become increasingly important as unified Germany addresses the challenges that it faces in the new Europe.

BIBLIOGRAPHY

Fishman, Sterling, and Lothar Martin. *Estranged Twins: Education and Society in the two Germanys.* New York: Praeger, 1987.

Führ, Christoph, and Carl-Ludwig Furck. *Handbuch der deutschen Bildungsgeschichte: 1945 bis zur Gegenwart,* Vol. 6 (1–2). Munich: C.H. Beck, 1998.

Hearndon, Arthur. *Education in the two Germanies.* New York: Oxford University Press, 1974.

Rodden, John. *Repainting the Little Red Schoolhouse.* New York: Oxford University Press, 1999.

Rust, Val D., and Diane Rust. *The Unification of German Education.* New York: Garland, 1995.

Tent, James F. *Mission on the Rhine: Reeducation and Denazification in American-Occupied Germany.* Chicago: University of Chicago Press, 1982.

Benita Blessing

Religion

German religious adhesion consists of the Roman Catholic Church and the union of Protestant provincial churches (*Landeskirchen*) through the Evangelical Church (Evangelische Kirche Deutschland), and smaller denominations including the Jehovah's Witnesses, Methodists, and in recent years, Mormons, Pentecostals, and above all, Muslims.

Both major churches exerted strong cultural and political influences after the war but declined thereafter. Membership dwindled, and the Protestant church in the German Democratic Republic was weakened by prolonged conflict with the state. In 1948 approximately 44 percent of the West German population was Catholic; the remainder was either Protestant or belonged to no church. In 1950, 80.5 percent of the population in the East was Protestant, 11 percent Catholic, and the remainder not affiliated with either denomination. By 1997 approximately 40 percent of the population officially remained Catholic, 40 percent Protestant, and the rest unaffiliated. The percentage of regular churchgoers was much lower.

In the wake of the collapse of National Socialist rule in May 1945, the American and British occupation ar-

mies looked to the churches to assist their efforts to demilitarize and democratize German society; the Catholic Church, in particular, had been an opponent of Nazi rule. Kurt Schumacher, leader of the Social Democratic Party, subsequently referred to the Catholic Church as a fifth occupation power. The Allies, however, encountered many difficulties in their partnership with the churches. Both churches strongly opposed policies of the Allied program of denazification and reeducation, and petitioned military officials to release German POWs from internment camps. The most prominent leaders of the church included, on the Catholic side, Cardinal Joseph Frings of the archdiocese of Cologne, Cardinal Michael Faulhaber of the archdiocese of Munich-Freysing, and, from the Protestant side, Theophil Wurm of Stuttgart and Reverend Martin Niemöller, who had spent years in Nazi concentration camps. These leaders denounced many Allied policies as examples of "victors' justice," and argued that God alone, not foreign authorities, had the right to pass judgments of guilt and innocence on their countrymen. These leaders saw themselves as spokesmen for the German national cause at a time of grim defeat.

The churches wielded strong influence in West German politics through the Christian Democratic Party (CDU) and its counterpart in southern Germany, the Christian Social Union (CSU). Unlike Catholic political parties prior to 1933, the CDU was interconfessional (not limited to a single church), even though most of its leaders were Catholics. Throughout the 1950s the Catholic Church supported social and cultural legislation that sought to promote family values in German society. Some laws were intended to protect youth from immoral and unseemly influences in society, while others provided stipends and subsidies to those with children. Yet the CDU was hardly a puppet of the church. The first chancellor of the Federal Republic, Konrad Adenauer, though a loyal Catholic from the Rhineland, frequently distanced himself from the church hierarchy, in part to avoid allegations of clericalism.

Rearmament divided the churches in the 1950s. Adenauer proposed building a new German military force that would be bound into larger European defense structures under NATO. Many Protestant church leaders bitterly opposed this policy, not just because it opened the specter of Germans in uniform but because it dashed their hopes for reunifying the country. The Catholic Church, in contrast, drummed up consistent, though by no means unanimous, support for the rearmament effort.

The Protestant churches in the East were often in conflict with the state. Although the church was less critical of the Communist regime than the Catholic Church in

Poland or Hungary, the state nonetheless sought to diminish its influence. Teenagers were encouraged to take part in a coming-of-age ceremony (*Jugendweihe*) that was a surrogate for the Protestant rite of confirmation. Under tremendous pressure, the church ultimately defined itself as a "church within socialism" and sought a rapprochement with an anticlerical East German state: its membership rapidly fell off during those years.

By the late 1960s and 1970s the fortunes of the Catholic Church in the West had likewise begun to ebb. The children of many once-loyal Catholics rebelled against the church, or by the 1980s and 1990s, treated the church as irrelevant to their daily lives. The church had hitherto relied on a strong network of ancillary entities—charity, youth, mothers', workers', and sports organizations—to rally members behind the cross. This network, the "Catholic milieu," sought not just to instill religious values but to protect young Catholics from potentially corrupting and subversive influences. By the late 1960s this foundation was in jeopardy, once the church in the wake of the Second Vatican Council opened its doors to mass culture, mass entertainment, and "modern society." Some of these organizations ceased to exist, while others were forced to redefine their purpose. The Protestant church in the twentieth century, on the other hand, had never displayed such strength, as many Protestants had left it at the turn of the century.

The 1980s saw two flurries of political activism in the churches. The Protestant church, as well as many lay Catholic organizations, took an active role in the German peace movement to protest the installation of new American nuclear missiles on German soil. Other church groups became active in the German environmental movement. In the East, the Protestant church became a venue for pleas for democracy and protests against the policies of the Communist state.

These movements did not reverse the membership loss of both churches, however, or put a stop to the larger processes of secularization. In the 1990s many German church members, burdened with a new tax to finance reunification, officially left the churches, since a percentage of members' paycheck was automatically deducted and distributed to the national churches. The Catholic Church also witnessed heated disagreements between a more conservative church hierarchy and a laity who disagreed with official policies on priestly celibacy, abortion, and other issues. Smaller denominations—Pentecostals and Mormons—have grown rapidly as a result, while the Muslim faith has reached out to large numbers of Turkish immigrants. In response, Christian leaders have engaged in much soul searching but to date have yet to record an upswing in their membership and fortunes.

BIBLIOGRAPHY

Damberg, Wilhelm. *Abschied vom Milieu? Katholizismus im Bistum Münster und in den Niederlanden, 1945–1980*. Paderborn: F. Schoningh, 1997.

Goeckel, Robert. *The Lutheran Church and the East German State: Political Conflict and Change under Ulbricht and Honecker*. Ithaca, N.Y.: Cornell University Press, 1990.

Ruff, Mark Edward. "Catholic Youth Work and Secularization in the Federal Republic of Germany, 1945 and 1962." Ph.D. diss., Brown University, 1998.

Spotts, Frederic. *The Churches and Politics in Germany*. Middletown, CT.: Wesleyan University Press, 1973.

Von Hehl, Ulrich. *Der Katholizismus in der Bundesrepublik Deutschland 1845–1985: eine Bibliographie*. Mainz: Matthias-Grunewald-Verlag, 1983.

Mark Edward Ruff

Gerö, Ernö (1898–1980)

Hungarian Communist politician. Ernö Gerö was a soldier during the short-lived Communist dictatorship in Hungary in March–August 1919. He had to flee abroad at the end of 1919, going first to Vienna, then to Bratislava and Bucharest. On returning to Hungary he joined the underground Communist movement, but he was arrested and sentenced to prison in 1922. He was extradited to the Soviet Union in 1924. He worked in various capacities and in various other countries in the international Communist movement, then he was sent by the Communist International (Comintern) to Spain as a political commissar in 1936. He became an adviser to the Communist International during the Second World War. In 1945, at the end of war, he returned to Hungary and worked in various governments in the late 1940s as a minister and a deputy prime minister. He became a member of the secret, top decision-making body in the company of Mátyás Rákosi and Mihaly Farkas. When Rákosi was deposed as secretary-general of the Hungarian Workers (Communist) Party (MDP) in the summer of 1956, Gerö succeeded him. After the outbreak of the Hungarian Revolution on October 23, 1956, Gerö made a futile attempt to calm the popular outburst of anger. He then fled to the Soviet Union on October 25. He was allowed to return to Hungary in 1960 but was expelled from the Communist Party. He retired and made a living as a translator.

Gerö was one of the most orthodox Stalinist politicians in Hungary in the postwar years, and his inflexible, dogmatic views and behavior contributed to a large extent to the outbreak of the Hungarian Revolution in 1956.

BIBLIOGRAPHY

Gerö, Ernö. *The Results of the First Year of the Five-Year Plan and Our Future Tasks in Building a Socialist Economy: Report to the Second Congress of the Hungarian Working People's Party, February 25, 1951.* London: Hungarian News and Information Service, 1951.

Kopacsi, Sandor. *In the Name of the Working Class: the Inside Story of the Hungarian Revolution.* New York: Grove Press, 1987.

Molnar, Miklos. *Budapest 1956: A History of the Hungarian Revolution.* London: George Allen and Unwin, 1971.

Tamàs Magyarics

SEE ALSO Hungary: Revolution; Nagy, Imre; Rákosi, Mátyás

Gheorghiu-Dej, Gheorghe (1901–65)

Head of the Romanian Communist Party from 1944 and ruler of Romania from 1952 until his death on March 19, 1965. Gheorghe Gheorghiu-Dej was born in Barlad. His early life is shrouded in myth, but it is certain that he came from a working-class family, attended school until the age of eleven, when he started working, and joined the Romanian Communist Party (RCP) in 1929. For his role in the violent February 1933 railroad workers' strike, he received a twelve-year prison sentence, which he served with other imprisoned Communists until the Soviets arranged for their release on August 9, 1944, but he and his associates had nothing to do with the August 23 coup against facist dictator Marshall Ion Antonescu, that resulted in King Michael's almost exclusively non-Communist coaltion government.

The Romanian Communists Gheorghiu-Dej led seemed far less trustworthy to Stalin than those who had lived in the USSR throughout the war and, led by Ana Pauker and Vasile Luca, were accompanying the Red Army into Romania as the Germans retreated. Nevertheless, Antonescu's fall made Gheorghiu-Dej's ethnic Romanian Stalinists useful to Stalin as a liaison with his new Romanian ally. Gheorghiu-Dej filled that role unquestioningly and in the process so impressed the Soviets with his leadership skills that Stalin tapped him as the RCP's general secretary in October 1945. Gheorghiu-Dej encouraged Stalin to avoid civil war in Romania by seizing power gradually through a coalition government in which Gheorghiu-Dej subsequently served as minister of communications (1944–46) and minister of industry and commerce (1946–49). In the latter post he introduced Stalinist heavy industrialization and collective agriculture into Romania, which included the destruction of the property-owning classes, three-hundred thousand peasants were tried as kulaks, and the Soviets initiated the Danube–Black Sea Canal in 1949 to make use of political prisoners. In June 1950 he began to undermine the Moscow Stalinists by charging that Pauker had allowed numerous anti-Communists to join the RCP who must be purged, and that she had mishandled collectivization. By mid-1951 Gheorghiu-Dej had manipulated party membership to the point that he controlled the party rank and file. By late summer 1951 Stalin, convinced of Gheorghiu-Dej's trustworthiness, ordered him to purge the Moscow Stalinists, which occurred on May 29, 1952. Then Gheorghiu-Dej, copying Stalin, added head of state to his control of the party by assuming the premiership on June 2, 1952, so that he could accelerate Romanian industrialization.

Stalin's death in March 1953 left Gheorghiu-Dej with two major problems. He feared that Romanians, unhappy over their low standard of living, might revolt and that the new Soviet leaders might try to depose him. To prevent the first eventuality, he perpetuated Stalinist political methods by strengthening Romania's security forces, who arrested thousands more victims, and by quickly adopting Moscow's new course, which lessened the pressure on rapid industrialization and offered Romanians more consumer goods. Political survival required him to imitate Moscow's collective leadership principle in April 1954 by transforming his office of general secretary into a four-member secretariat, while he remained the premier. The secretaries supported Gheorghiu-Dej, so although only head of state, he still strengthened his hold on the party by purging it and executing Lucretiu Patrascanu (a popular Communist and member of the politburo of the RCP, who had angered Stalin by placing the interests of Romania above those of the Soviet Union) in April 1954 before the party could rehabilitate this anti-Stalinist. By October 1955 the increasing prosperity and his hold on the party made him feel secure enough to reclaim control of the party as its first secretary. He appointed a crony, Chivu Stoica, as premier. Although Gheorghiu-Dej helped Soviet Premier Nikita Khrushchev quell the Hungarian Revolution in 1956, the latter still believed that Gheorghiu-Dej was an unrepentant Stalinist and encouraged Miron Constantinescu's bid to oust Gheorghiu-Dej, which failed in July 1957. Gheorghiu-Dej then purged the party of any possible remaining adversaries and governed unchallenged until his death in 1965.

In 1958, Khrushchev seemingly resigned himself to Gheorghiu-Dej and withdrew Soviet troops from Romania, but Khrushchev continued to press for Comecon (Council for Mutual Economic Assistance), which had been set up to coordinate the economic plans of the Soviet bloc countries, to avoid the development of redundant productive facilities in each member country. Khrushchev's plan, announced in 1956, called for Romania to reduce its industrialization and become a supplier of raw materials and food to the more industrialized Comecon members. Since Gheorghiu-Dej had sought in 1955 to use economic incentives to make the RCP popular with Romanians, he refused to allow Comecon to interfere in Romania's domestic affairs. Although he promised to accept Soviet leadership of the socialist camp in 1956, the controversy worsened until June 1962, when Gheorghiu-Dej proclaimed Romania's external autonomy. He took advantage of the situation and used "national deviation" to increase his popularity among intellectuals by ending Romania's isolation from the West and among Romanians in general by appealing to their strong nationalism. He succeeded so well that Khrushchev would have had to use force to bring him into line.

Once again, the Romanian leader displayed his skill at political maneuvering. With cunning and ruthlessness he had seized control of the RCP and the Romanian government. As Romania's first Communist dictator, he followed Stalin's policies to the letter. In the era of de-Stalinization he clung to a less intense version of Stalinist industrialization and sought autonomy from Moscow by placing Romanian national interests over those of the socialist camp without violating Communist principles or threatening Soviet security.

BIBLIOGRAPHY

Deletant, Dennis. *Communist Terror in Romania: Gheorghiu-Dej and the Police State, 1948–1965.* New York: St. Martin's Press, 1999.

Gheorghiu-Dej, Gheorghe. *Articles and Speeches, June 1960–December 1962.* Bucharest: Meridiane Publishing House, 1963.

Robert F. Forrest

SEE ALSO Ceauşescu, Nicolae; Patrascanu, Lucretiu; Pauker, Ana; Romania

Gibraltar

British colony at the entrance to the Mediterranean Sea. Gibraltar is virtually a city-state—a 2.5 square mile rock

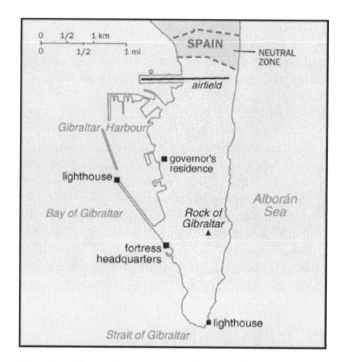

Gibraltar. *Illustration courtesy of Bernard Cook.*

strategically located at the entrance of the Mediterranean and attached by land to Spain. The rock has no agriculture and not even a natural supply of fresh water. Occupied by Britain in 1704 during the War of the Spanish Succession, Gibraltar passed to formal British control in the Treaty of Utrecht (1713). Over the next two and a half centuries it was an important base for the Royal Navy. During the Second World War the entire civilian population of the island, except for some three thousand adult males involved in essential work, was evacuated as a precaution against an attack by Spain or Germany. Those evacuated were finally returned in 1946–47.

The population of Gibraltar is a mélange of descendants of immigrants from all over the Mediterranean. Virtually all thirty thousand Gibraltarians are bilingual in English and Spanish. Two-thirds of the inhabitants are Catholics, and there are six hundred Jews.

The Spanish government very much wants to regain Gibraltar. Public opinion in Gibraltar has been almost unanimous in its opposition to this, and successive British governments have vowed not to hand it over. To pressure Great Britain to relinquish control, between 1969 and 1985 Spain closed its land border to the colony and began an economic siege, cutting off the supply of cheap Spanish labor. Rather than discourage Gibraltarians, the Spanish action gave fresh impetus to Gibraltarian nationalism.

After the 1985 reopening by Spain of the land border, it was British policy that alarmed Gibraltarians. This was reinforced in the late 1980s by London's refusal to grant

British citizenship to residents of Hong Kong and a sense that, as London reduced its armed forces and naval presence around the world, it no longer had a strategic interest in holding onto the colony. Actions such as Britain's decision to reduce military strength on Gibraltar by 1991 to little more than one thousand men prompted Gibraltarians to seek greater political and economic autonomy. Any movement toward independence was tempered, however, by the awareness that this would be rejected by Spain and would necessitate a British military presence that London would be unwilling to provide.

There is no longer any direct British economic aid to Gibraltar. Britain controls foreign affairs, but a local legislature makes tax policy. This legislature has also been allowed to write its own banking laws. When Britain joined the European Economic Community (EC) in 1973, Gibraltar was not required to make tax contributions to the community or even to follow its customs regulations. It is a recognized part of the European Union (EU), however, although not an individual member. This special status has allowed it to avoid the tariffs and sales taxes of other member nations.

Under Chief Minister Joseph Bossano, who was elected in March 1988, Gibraltar made an effort to stimulate tourism and promote itself as an offshore financial center. Bossano, a longtime labor union organizer who earned a degree from the London School of Economics while working nights in a bakery, founded the Gibraltar Socialist Labor Party in 1976. Despite his professed socialism, Bossano made his political platform one of very low taxes and free enterprise.

Each year some four million visitors come to Gibraltar, many of them to buy duty-free goods without value-added taxes. From 1989 to 1993 bank assets quadrupled and the value of the economy doubled to about $460 million. A banking secrecy law guaranteed confidentiality, although numbered accounts were not allowed.

Rapid economic growth enabled Gibraltar to provide first-class health care and education to residents. Any graduate of high school accepted at a British University was granted free tuition and travel expenses. Gibraltar also reorganized a money-losing shipyard inherited from Great Britain. To lure shipping business from nearby Spanish ports, there was no tax on fuel. Gibraltar was actually a net exporter of oil in monetary terms, given the price it paid for oil and the price at which it resold it.

By the 1990s the inhabitants of the Rock saw themselves first as Gibraltarians and only secondly as Britons. The principal political challenge was to keep Gibraltar free of Spanish control. Toward that end Chief Minister Bossano became a leading spokesman for the self-determinations of peoples.

BIBLIOGRAPHY

Denis, Philip. *Gibraltar and Its People.* Newton Abbot, England: David and Charles, 1990.

Jackson, W. G. F. *The Rock of the Gibraltarians: A History of Gibraltar,* 3d ed. Grendon, England: Gibraltar Books, 1990.

Morris, D. S., and R. H. Haigh. *Britain, Spain, and Gibraltar, 1945–1990: The Eternal Triangle.* New York: Routledge, 1992.

Shields, Graham J. *Gibraltar.* Santa Barbara, Calif.: Clio, 1987.

Spencer C. Tucker

Gide, André (1869–1951)

French winner of the Nobel Prize in literature in 1947 whose themes dealt with morality, man's place in the universe, and humanism. His most famous works are Les Nourritures terrestres (1897), Paludes (1895), Succès d'estime-El Hadj (1899), Le Prométhée mal enchaîné (1899), L'Immoraliste (1902), Oscar Wilde (1910), Les Caves du Vatican (1914), La Porte étroite (1909), Isabelle (1911), Numquid et tu? (1926), Les Faux Monnayeurs (1926), Voyage au Congo and Retour du Tchad (1927), and Saul (1928). He wrote his autobiography in 1926, Si le Grain ne meurt (If I Die: An Autobiography). André Gide's Huguenot father and his Norman heiress mother sent him to be educated at the École Alsacienne and the Lycée Henri IV in Paris. In 1895, oppressed by a feeling of guilt imparted by his strict Protestant upbringing, Gide, despite his homosexual inclinations, married his cousin Madeleine Rondeaux, whom he had loved since he was thirteen and in whose home he had spent many family vacations at Cuverville. The next year he was chosen mayor of La Roque. He was spiritually affected by the great loss of life during World War I and was concerned with promoting the cause of humanity and the commonalty of the human experience. He encouraged respect for other cultures, especially those in the French colonies, concern for the underprivileged, and humane treatment for criminals. Gide supported the ideals of socialism after the success of the 1917 Russian Revolution. He spent a great deal of time in North Africa, where he saw the failures of colonialism and the suffering and inhumanity that were its by-products. He was also greatly affected by World War II as he saw in its wake the destruction of tradition and the past. As both a novelist and a dramatist, the passion that permeated his writing was the betterment of all peoples.

BIBLIOGRAPHY

Cordle, Thomas. *André Gide.* New York: Twayne; Toronto: Maxwell Macmillan Canada, 1993.

DuBois, Charles. *Le Dialogue avec André Gide.* Paris: Correa, 1947.

Gide, André. *If I Die: An Autobiography.* Tr. by Dorothy Bussy. New York: Vintage Books, 1963.

————. *Journal 1889–1939.* Paris: Éditions de la Nouvelle Revue Française, 1940.

————. *The Secret Drama of My Life.* Tr. by Keene Wallis. Paris: Boar's Head Books, 1951.

Barbara Bennett Peterson

Gierek, Edward (1913–)

First secretary of the Central Committee of the Polish United Workers Party (PZPR, 1970–80), or Communist Party. While in power Edward Gierek was a cynical technocrat who, by enjoying relative popularity achieved by his populist policy, tried to use it to sustain the disintegrating Communist system in Poland.

Gierek's personality was shaped during the long periods when he worked in France (1923–34) and Belgium (1937–48); as a seventeen-year-old miner he joined the French Communist Party and, later, the Communist Party of Belgium. When, in 1948, French authorities expelled him, he returned to Poland. He was a member of the Polish Workers Party as of 1946, and in 1948 he joined its successor, the PZRP.

For helping to avert strikes in Silesia in 1951 he was promoted to the rank of organizational secretary and later economic secretary of the district committee of the PZRP. During the political struggle after the death of Bolesław Bierut in 1956, he remained neutral. As chairman of a special committee of the Politburo of the Central Committee of the PZRP established to investigate the June 1956 riots of workers in Poznan against shortages, low wages, and incompetent management, Gierek labeled them counterrevolutionary.

As first secretary of the district committee of the PZRP in Katowice (1957–70), the most industrialized region in Poland, he created there a powerful political and economic lobby, earning the reputation of being a good manager. He helped further the economic development of Upper Silesia by creating new factories, especially for women, as well as developing the social infrastructure. His popularity grew as that of First Secretary Władysław Gomułka diminished.

After the repression of student disturbances in March 1968, Gierek was promoted by the Kremlin as Gomułka's successor. Commenting on the March events, Gierek backed up the authoritarian regime, threatening to "break the bones" of its opponents. He did accept Gomułka's offer to become premier. Gomułka, in Gierek's opinion, wanted to pacify him and Moscow. In December 1970, as a result of the bloody suppression of workers' protests in Gdansk and the subsequent political crisis, Gierek became first secretary of the Central Committee of the PZRP, with Soviet leader Leonid Brezhnev's full support.

Owing to rapid economic growth in the West and cheap credits in the first half of the 1970s, Gierek could pursue a pro-consumer policy. He sought to increase living standards and freeze prices of basic goods. Poland's opening to the West and Gierek's attempts to promote economic growth won the goodwill of many Western leaders. On the other hand, Gierek belittled economists' warnings and, probably under Soviet pressure, made gigantic industrial investments that soon led to the collapse of the supply of consumer goods. Though conducting this shortsighted policy, he counted on sustaining his power through strengthening of the Party nomenklatura.

Pushing for constitutional changes despite public disapproval, party technocrats who enjoyed the backing of the USSR ensured themselves of the leading role in society. Price hikes in June 1976 led to public unrest in Ursus and Radom. Faced with workers' protests, the government recalled the price increases, but it did not cease its brutal repression of protesters. These factors were the direct impulse for the creation of the Worker's Defense Committee.

Irreversible economic crisis and the growth of democratic opposition forces discredited Gierek in party circles. As a result of the August 1980 victory of the striking workers of Solidarity, the independent trade union, Gierek, who agreed to their demands for pay raises, price rollbacks, the legalization of strikes, and the right to form independent trade unions, was removed from power. Later he was also removed from the party ranks and subjected to political exile.

BIBLIOGRAPHY

Rothschild, Joseph, and Nancy M. Wingfield. *Return to Diversity: A Political History of East Central Europe since World War II.* New York: Oxford University, 2000.

de Weydenthal, Jan B. *The Communists in Poland.* Stanford, Calif.: Hoover Institution Press, 1978.

Wozniuk, Vladimir. *From Crisis to Crisis: Soviet-Polish Relations in the 1970s.* Ames: Iowa State University Press, 1987.

Ryszard Sudzinski

SEE ALSO Gomułka, Władysław; Kania Stanisław

Gilson, Étienne (Henry) (1884–1978)

French philosopher. Étienne Gilson studied at the University of Paris, the Sorbonne, and later became professor at the Sorbonne (1921–32) and professor at the Collège de France (1932–51). A member of the Académie Française, Gilson was also founder of the Pontifical Institute of Medieval Studies (PIMS) at the University of Toronto in 1929.

Gilson's intellectual interests ranged from the relationship of painting and metaphysics to the intersection of politics and education. His dissertation argued against the standard historical account of Descartes as a sharp break with the preceding Jesuit neoscholasticism. Rather, according to Gilson, Descartes's method, language, and substantive philosophical positions reflect a deep, if not always acknowledged, indebtedness to his scholastic predecessors. Gilson also offered a number of attempts at synthesizing and explaining the development of Augustine of Hippo's thought, particularly the Augustinian epistemology of divine illumination. The fruitfulness of Augustine's thought led to the diversity of views characteristic of the thirteenth century, which was perhaps the period to which Gilson devoted his greatest attention. The prominent Franciscan doctors Bonaventure and Scotus prompted major books by Gilson, who sought to contextualize these thinkers within the spirit of the Franciscan order. Gilson's greatest efforts, however, were spent on the thought of Thomas Aquinas, to whom he devoted a number of books and ongoing attention. Gilson sought to distinguish Thomas from his neoscholastic successors and emphasize the Scriptural roots of Thomistic "philosophy."

Common to all these projects, as well as Gilson's many other contributions on lesser-known figures of the Middle Ages and philosophers from other epochs, was a concern for reading authors comprehensively and in historical context. Gilson uncovered the diversity and dynamic character of philosophical and theological thought of the medieval period. He sought to disengage his chosen texts from the prevalent Kantian, Hegelian, and neo-Thomist misreadings. It was his method of close textual reading within historical context that led to what is known as "medieval studies," a vision that was crystallized in Gilson's directorship of PIMS.

BIBLIOGRAPHY
Shook, Laurence K. *Étienne Gilson.* Toronto: Pontifical Institute of Medieval Studies, 1984.

Christopher Kaczor

Giscard d'Estaing, Valéry (1926–)

President of France, 1974–81, founder and leader of a major political party, Union pour la Démocratie Française et du Centre (UDF), and creator, with German Chancellor Helmut Schmidt, of the European Monetary System (EMS) in 1979.

Born in 1926, Valéry Giscard d'Estaing continued his family's political line. In 1959 he joined the Finance Ministry as a junior minister and rose to its top position in just three years. Eventually as president of the French Republic, Giscard and German Chancellor Schmidt had in common their backgrounds as former finance ministers, which also entailed dealings with the European Community (EC) prior to becoming heads of their respective countries. Franco-German cooperation supplied the basis for European cooperation, which Giscard and Schmidt modeled in their joint sponsorship of the EMS, their initiative to stabilize the national currencies of EC member countries. The EMS lasted well into the 1990s and became an important stage in the European journey to full Economic and Monetary Union (EMU). Giscard remained dedicated to European integration, serving as a member of the European Parliament (1989–93) and swinging critical support to the ratification of the Maastricht Treaty of European Union in France, which committed that country to the EMU in 1992.

As France's third president during the Fifth Republic, Giscard played an important part in defining that office. He emphasized his international role, having ample opportunities for visibility, owing partly to institutions he himself helped establish. Several times a year he attended European councils comprising EC leaders, after having personally launched this institution with a surprise announcement to the press in 1974. He actively involved himself in world politics ranging from issues related to France's former African colonies to the Group of Seven of the world's richest countries. In domestic politics he showed the same active interest, giving detailed direction to his premier, officially France's head of government, instead of delegating internal matters, as other French presidents had been prone to do. Though he was competent in policy making, the public image of Giscard as an elitist stood out and ultimately led to his defeat by Socialist François Mitterrand in 1981. Toward the end of his term scandal cast suspicion on him. Furthermore, catering to big business put him at odds with the party's small shop-keepers, the UDF he created to capture the political center. A catchall party meant to resemble U.S. political parties in terms of diverse membership and loose ideological affiliations, the UDF defined itself mostly in terms of supporting Giscard. In the final analysis, Giscard's brand of politics helped stabilize the Fifth Republic in the rejection of ideological politics and application of a technocratic approach to policy making.

BIBLIOGRAPHY

Frears, J. R. *France in the Giscard Presidency.* London: Allen & Unwin, 1981.

Giscard d'Estaing, Valéry. *Démocratie française.* Paris: Fayard, 1976.

Safran, William. *The French Polity,* 5th ed. New York: Longman, 1997.

Mary Troy Johnston

SEE ALSO Chirac, Jacques; Mitterrand, François

Gizikis, Phaidon (1917–99)

Ranking member of the military coup d'état of April 21, 1967, that overthrew the caretaker government of Panayiotis Kanelopoulos and held control of the government for the next seven years. Phaidon Gizikis studied at the Military Academy of Athens and continued his education at the National Defense Institute, where he gradually rose to the rank of lieutenant general. Following the second coup of General Demetrios Ioannides, on November 25, 1973, Gizikis, who at the time was in command of Army Group A, assumed the position of President of Greece. He retained that position even after Constantine Karamanlis was sworn in as premier of Greece on July 24, 1974. Gizikis stepped down in December 1974, retired from the armed forces, and was given the distinction of honorary commander of Army Group A. In 1976 a military court dropped charges against Gizikis and eighty-eight other officers who had been accused of treason for cooperating with the military junta. He died on July 26, 1999.

Stelios Zachariou

SEE ALSO Ioannides, Demetrios

Gladio

Code name for the Italian branch of a network of clandestine stay/behind organizations set up all over non-Communist Europe during the height of the Cold War.

These organizations were ostensibly designed to function as behind-the-lines resistance cells in the event of a Soviet military invasion, but certain "gladiators" were later implicated in a wide variety of anticonstitutional domestic activities.

These stay-behind groups were initially created during the late 1940s and early 1950s, typically under the aegis of elements of U.S. intelligence working in close cooperation with proven pro-Atlantic colleagues in the security services of various European nations. Most of their original members were recruited from preexisting anti-Communist paramilitary formations. They were provided with additional training by members of the Central Intelligence Agency's Office of Policy Coordination (OPC), the U.S. army's Special Forces (Green Berets), or the British Secret Intelligence Service (SIS, or M16), and provided with secret caches of arms, explosives, and communications equipment. By the middle of the 1950s such organizations, which in 1951 had officially come under the control of an Atlantic Alliance supervisory agency, the Clandestine Planning Committee (which itself operated after 1954 under the authority of the Allied Coordination Committee), existed in most NATO and neutral European countries, including Austria (Austrian Hiking, Sporting, and Social Club, Österreichische Wander-, Sport-, und Geselligkeitsverein; plus elements of the B-Gendarmerie); Belgium; Denmark; Finland; Great Britain; Greece; Italy (controlled by the autonomous Training Section, Sezione Addestramento, ISAD, administratively attached to the Armed Forces Intelligence Service Research Division, Servizio Informazioni Forze Armate Ufficio Ricerche); Netherlands (Operations and Intelligence Organization, Operaties en Inlichtingen); Norway (Section E-14 of the Defense Intelligence Staff, Forsvarets Etterretningsstab); Sweden; Switzerland (first the Intelligence and Defense Section, Üntergruppe Nachrichten und Abwehr; then Projekt 26, P26); Turkey; and West Germany. In France the first stay-behind network, successively called "Compass Rose" ("Rose des Vents"), "Mission 48," and "Rainbow" (Arc-en-Ciel), was set up in 1948. After being dismantled in 1958 by President Charles de Gaulle, who feared it might be used to undermine his own power, it was then reconstituted in 1970, rechristened "Sword" (Glaive), and integrated into the wider network by Premier Georges Pompidou and his pro-Atlantic secret service chief, Count Alexandre de Marenches. Similar organizations were also apparently set up by the dictatorial regimes in Spain and Portugal, as well as by anti-Soviet Yugoslav Premier Tito and Shah Muhammad Reza Pahlavi of Iran.

The existence of this clandestine Europe-wide paramilitary network was first officially acknowledged in 1990 by Italian Prime Minister Giulio Andreotti, who issued a public statement emphasizing Gladio's crucial national security functions and overall democratic legitimacy, if not its strict constitutional legality. But these reassuring claims, which were subsequently echoed by government spokesmen elsewhere, failed to forestall the development of major political scandals in several European countries. Nor did they assuage the suspicions of the political Left, whose concerns that these organizations were linked to anticonstitutional initiatives, including political terrorism and coup plots, were soon substantiated by the results of diverse judicial and parliamentary investigations.

Much information that has since become available about the national stay-behind organizations directly contradicts the overly benign picture provided by various government officials, and raises a number of serious and disquieting questions about their legitimacy, democratic reliability, and defensive orientation. For example, formerly classified documents reveal that, contrary to Andreotti's assertions, countering internal pro-Communist subversion had always been one of the Italian Gladio network's primary tasks, and members of other national stay-behind groups also regularly carried out internal security functions. One illustration of this pattern is that members of these groups in several European countries surveilled and collected extensive files on both real and imagined domestic enemies who were thence slated to be "neutralized" if necessary.

Much more serious are the revelations that elements of these organizations were linked to serious acts of anticonstitutional political violence. Perhaps best-documented examples of this relate to the participation of certain Italian "gladiators," including "Nazi-Maoist" Enzo Maria Dantini, neofascist activists Gianni Nardi and Manlio Portolan, and apparently both phony "anarchist" bomber Gianfranco Bertoli and army intelligence officer Amos Spiazzi in the systematic campaign of secret service–manipulated right-wing terrorism carried out between 1968 and 1975, the "strategy of tension." Others were apparently mobilized to participate in a number of "coup" plots, such as Carabinieri chief and ex-SIFAR head Giovanni De Lorenzo's 1964 anti-insurrection plan, the "Tora Tora" operation launched by Prince Junio Valerio Borghese's Fronte Nazionale and its allies in December 1970, and the Compass Rose (Rosa dei Venti) plot in 1974. Key stay-behind personnel were also directly or indirectly involved in campaigns of internal repression elsewhere. In Greece the stay-behind group, code named "Red Fleece," consisted largely of specially trained commandos from the elite Mountain Pursuit Companies (Lochoi Oreinon Katadromon, LOK), which participated in both the April 1967 military coup and in the brutal November 1973 crackdown on protesting students at the Polytechnic University in Athens. Even more notorious was the systematic involvement of members of the Turkish stay-behind group, the Counter-Guerrilla (Kontr-Gerilla, KG) organization attached to the Special Warfare Department (Özel Harp Dairesi, ÖHD) of the Armed Forces General Staff, in terrorist actions during the 1970s that helped to precipitate the 1980 military coup. More recently, evidence has appeared that links personnel affiliated with the Belgian stay-behind group, the Eighth Section of the Intelligence and Action Service (Service de Renseignements et d'Action, SDRA-8), a branch of the military's General Intelligence Service (Service General de Renseignements, SGR), to the August 1950 assassination of Communist Party of Belgium (Parti Communiste de Belgique, PCB) leader Julien Lahaut and, less reliably, to coup plots and terrorism in the 1970s and early 1980s.

Furthermore, in several cases it is now clear that unreconstructed fascists or their neofascist followers were among the "politically reliable" personnel recruited into these stay-behind networks. This has already been documented for West Germany, where the original stay-behind group—the Technical Service (Technische Dienst) section of the German Youth League (Bund Deutscher Jügend, BDJ) consisted almost entirely of ex-Nazis; for Turkey, where the bulk of the civilian recruits were drawn from the neofascist Nationalist Action Party (Milliyetcilik Hareket Partisi, MHP); and for Sweden, where members of the pro-Nazi and collaborationist wartime organization Sveaborg were recruited.

Despite this recent flood of revelations, the historical role and significance of these stay-behind networks remains difficult to assess. While it is certain that official efforts to cover up or minimize the documented crimes of various "gladiators" are indefensible, attempts to attribute the bulk of the major postwar acts of right-wing political violence and anticonstitutional subversion to stay-behind personnel are almost equally misplaced. Even apart from the likelihood that some of the actions carried out by these recruits were not officially sanctioned, a host of other official and quasi-official clandestine networks, some of which had little or no connection to Gladio, have likewise been implicated in such operations.

BIBLIOGRAPHY

Bettini, Emanuele. *Gladio: La repubblica parallela.* Rome: Ediesse, 1996.

Brozzu-Gentile, Jean-Francois. *L'Affaire Gladio: Les réseaux secrets américains au coer du terrorisme en Europe.* Paris: Alhin Michel, 1994.

Bye, Ronald, and Finn Sjue. *Norges hemmelige haer: Historien om Stay Behind.* Oslo: Tiden Norsk, 1995.

Deger, Emin. *CIA. Kontr-Gerilla ve Turkiye.* Ankara: Caglar, 1977.

Dudek, Peter, and Hans-Gerd Jaschke. *Entstehung und Entwicklung des Rechtsextremismus in der Bundesrepublik: Zur Tradition einer besonderen politischen Kultur.* Opladen: Westdeutscher, 1984.

Ferraresi, Franco. "A Secret Structure codenamed 'Gladio.'" *Italian Politics* 7 (1992): 29–49.

Flamini, Gianni. *Il partito del golpe: Le strategic della tensione e del terrore dal primo centrosinistro organico al sequestro Moro.* Ferrara: Bovolenta, 1981–85.

Gijsels, Hugo. *Netwerk Gladio.* Louvain, Belgium: Kritak, 1991.

Graft, Bob de, and Cees Wiebes. *Gladio, der vrije jongens: Een particuliere geheime dienst in Koude Oorlogstijd.* The Hague: Koninginnegracht, 1992.

Inzerilli, Paolo. *Gladio: La verità negate.* Bologna: Analisi, 1995.

Müller, Leo A. *Gladio—das Erbe des Kalten Krieges: Der NATO-Geheimbund und sein deutscher Verlaufer.* Reinbeck: Rowohlt, 1991.

Serravalle, Gerardo. *Gladio.* Rome: Associate, 1991.

Ussel, Michel van. *Georges 923: Un agent du Gladio beige parle.* Paris: Longue Vue, 1991.

Willems, Jan, ed. *Gladio.* Brussels: EPO/Retlex, 1991.

See also the parliamentary reports published in Belgium, Italy, Switzerland, and Turkey (on the Susurluk Affair).

Jeffrey M. Bale

SEE ALSO Borghese Coup; Terrorism, Right-Wing

Glemp, Józef (1929–)

Catholic primate of Poland (1981–). Józef Glemp, who was made a cardinal in 1983, received a doctorate in law and canon law at the Lateran University in Rome. He was a member of Stefan Cardinal Wyszyński's secretarial staff from 1967 to 1978. In 1979 he became bishop of Warmia and in 1981 metropolitan archbishop of Gniezno and Warsaw and the president of the Main Board and Conference of the Episcopate of Poland. He contributed to the work of a legislative group founded by the Common Committee of the Government and Episcopate. He also played a leading role from 1981 to 1991 in the Congregation of Churches of the East concerning the Orthodox and Armenian churches in Poland.

In an effort to prevent bloodshed during the imposition of martial law in Poland in December 1991 by Wojciech Jaruzelski, head of the Communist Party and Polish state, who was attempting to crush the Solidarity independent trade union and political movement, Glemp called for understanding and social stability through cooperation with the authorities. Many Polish Catholics criticized him for this initially muted response to the attack of the state. His sympathies, however, were with Solidarity, which had a dedicated Catholic contingent among its leadership. Solidarity, which continued to operate underground from 1981 to 1989, could rely on Glemp and the church for moral support. Thanks to its primate and status as the only social institution with unquestioned authority, the church took part in the Solidarity-government negotiations dubbed the "round table" talks.

The status of the church and its theological functions are the main focus Glemp's priestly work. Far from outright involvement in political activity, he has a clearly defined concept of the church's place in the public life of the country. According to him the new constitution of Poland should include recognition of the superiority of Christian values and totally ban abortion. State and church should be independent and autonomous bodies, the coexistence of which should be regulated through a concordat, assuming a democratic system with respect.

BIBLIOGRAPHY

Micewski, Andrzej. *Katolicy w potrzasku: Wspomnienia z peryferii polityki.* Warsaw: BGW, 1990.

———. *Między dwiema orientacjami.* Warsaw: Verum Press, 1990.

Michal Maliszewski

Gligorov, Kiro (1917–)

First popularly elected president of the independent Macedonia. Born in the eastern Macedonian town of Stip, Kiro (Kiril) Gligorov completed his secondary education in Skopje and graduated in law from the University of Belgrade in 1938. While attending the university, he became involved in the Communist movement. He worked as a lawyer until 1941, when he became a member of the Anti-fascist Assembly of the National Liberation Movement of Macedonia (ASNOM) and the Anti-fascist Council of the National Liberation of Yugoslavia (AVNOJ). From 1945 he held several posts in the Yugoslav government dealing with finance and the economy, becoming known as a leading advocate of a market economy during the 1960s. In 1974 he became a member of the federal presidency and speaker of the federal parliament. In 1978 he retired to engage in more theoretical writing but returned to active politics in 1989 to take a position in the reform government of Ante Marković. A proponent of the idea of multiparty elections in Macedonia, he successfully stood for election as president of the republic in January 1991. Gligorov played an energetic role in the final attempts to negotiate a new constitutional settlement for the Yugoslav federation and presided over the peaceful transition of Macedonia to independence in November 1992. The victim of an assassination attempt by unknown assailants on October 3, 1995, he partially recovered his health and resumed his duties as president at the end of November 1995.

BIBLIOGRAPHY

Ackermann, Alice. *Making Peace Prevail: Preventing Violent Conflict in Macedonia.* Syracuse, N.Y.: Syracuse University Press, 1999.

Lazarov, Risto. *This Is the Republic of Macedonia.* Skopje: Ministry of Information of the Republic of Macedonia, 1993.

John B. Allcock

SEE ALSO Macedonia

Glistrup, Mogens (1926–)

Danish lawyer and politician. A lecturer in tax law at Copenhagen University from 1956 to 1963, Mogens Glistrup advised clients on how to reduce their taxable income and thus reduce their taxes. In 1971 he participated in a TV program in which he declared that those who evade paying taxes could be compared to the freedom fighters during the Second World War. He also pointed out that it was possible to avoid paying taxes if one knew the tax laws.

His skill and populist aura led him to form the Progress Party (Fremskridtspartiet) in 1972. The core of its program was abolition of the income tax and of most state institutions. In 1973 in its first election it became Denmark's second-biggest party. It represented a protest against the relatively high income taxes in Denmark, and by its election victory gave a strong warning to the established parties of Denmark's welfare society not to raise taxes further.

Glistrup's personal efforts to avoid paying taxes, however, landed him in court in 1972. In 1974 he was partly acquitted but had to pay a fine. In 1981 he was taken to court, again accused of tax evasion. In a 1983 supreme court judgment he was given three years in prison, fined one million kroner, and deprived of the right to practice

law until further notice. He had to leave his seat in parliament and go to prison. He was returned to parliament again in 1987 but was soon involved in a power struggle in his party between a hard-line group unwilling to compromise, to which group he himself belonged, and a more flexible and traditional right-wing group that wanted to cooperate with other conservative and nonsocialist parties. The latter faction won, and Glistrup left the party he had founded. In 1990 he founded a new party, the Prosperity Party (Trivselspartiet), but it did not receive enough votes to enter parliament, and Glistrup withdrew from politics.

BIBLIOGRAPHY

Glistrup, Mogens. *Glistrup om Glistrupsagen.* Copenhagen: Stig Vendelkaer, 1983.

Robdrup, Jens. *Omkring Glistrup.* Copenhagen: Stig Vendelkaer, 1977.

Jørn Boye Nielson

Globke, Hans (1898–1973)

German politician. Hans Globke was born into a Catholic family in Düsseldorf on September 10, 1898, and grew up in Aachen. After completing secondary school during World War I, he joined an artillery unit in 1916. After the war he studied at Bonn and earned a law degree in 1921. One year later Globke joined the Catholic Center Party. He was employed at the court of justice in Cologne and at the police department of Aachen.

In 1929 Globke began working at the Prussian Ministry of the Interior in Berlin. From 1934 he was a councilor of the government at the Ministry of Interior. There he was engaged in constitutional problems, the Saar question, and issues before the Department for Legal Status.

After the National Socialists' decree of the Nuremberg racial laws in 1935, Globke, in cooperation with State Secretary Wilhelm Stuckart (1902–53), wrote an official commentary elaborating on its prohibitions.

Globke's request for admission to the National Socialist Party was refused because of his contacts with Catholic circles. Later he also kept contact with resistance groups involved in the July 20, 1944, plot against Hitler. In 1945 Globke was interned by the U.S. because of his position with a Reich ministry and became a witness at the Nuremberg trials.

In 1946 he was employed again in administration in the British zone of occupied Germany. He joined the Christian Democratic Party and became acquainted with future Chancellor Konrad Adenauer. After the foundation of the Federal Republic of Germany in 1949, Globke became state secretary and Adenauer's most important adviser. He influenced Adenauer's European policy and the foundation of a new German intelligence service. Globke was attacked especially by the Left and the German Democratic Republic because of his political activities during the Third Reich. But only when Adenauer resigned in 1963 did Globke retire. He moved to Switzerland and died on February 13, 1973.

BIBLIOGRAPHY

Ausschuss fur Deutsche Einheit. *Globke, Adenauer's State Secretary and the Extermination of the Jews: On the Criminal Past of Dr. Hans Globke, State Secretary in the Office of Federal Chancellor Adenauer.* Berlin: Committee for German Unity, 1960.

Der Prozess gegen Dr. Hans Globke. Dresden: Verlag Zeit im Bild, 1963.

Gotto, Klaus, ed. *Der Staatssekretär Adenauers: Persönlichkeit und politisches Wirken Hans Globkes.* Stuttgart: Klett-Cotta, 1980.

Jacobs, Norbert. *Der Streit um Dr. Hans Globke in der öffentlichen Meinung der Bundesrepublik Deutschland 1949–1973: Ein Beitrag zur politischen Kultur in Deutschland,* 2 Vols. Bonn, 1992.

Jürgen Streller

Godard, Jean-Luc (1930–)

Controversial French film director. Jean-Luc Godard was the most political (i.e., Marxist) director of the French New Wave (*Nouvelle Vague*) of the late 1950s and early 1960s, a prominent movement that sought to break the established rules of filmmaking. Godard began as a critic for the influential journal *Cahiers du Cinéma* and has continued his critical writing throughout his career.

His first feature, *Breathless* (À Bout de souffle, 1959) was an instant classic that overturned traditional notions of what film is and does. Equal parts film noir and gangster film, *Breathless* traces the adventures of a two-bit hoodlum (Jean-Paul Belmondo) and an American girl in Paris (Jean Seberg). The film's irreverence toward social conventions was a decade ahead of its time.

The 1960s was a prolific decade for Godard with such films as *My Life to Live* (*Vivre sa vie,* 1962), *A Married Woman* (*Une Femme mariée,* 1964), and *Alphaville* (1965). In 1966 he released three films: *Masculine-Feminine, Made in the USA,* and *Two or Three Things I Know About Her* (*Deux ou trois Choses que je sais d'elle*). In these films about "the children of Marx and Coca Cola," as Godard put it, prostitution becomes a prominent metaphor for the compromises of modern life.

Contempt (*Le Mépris,* 1964) is Godard's biggest film and features an international cast: Brigitte Bardot as the wife of a film writer who comes to have contempt for her husband's passivity toward moves by a crass American producer (Jack Palance). Fritz Lang, the famous German-American director, plays himself.

Pierrot le fou (1965) many consider Godard's finest film. Ferdinand (Belmondo again, the perfect Godard hero) leaves his wife at a boring party, where most of the people talk in sound bites of consumerist society, and escapes with a young woman he once knew. Disaster follows.

Weekend (1967), one of Godard's most widely seen films, was a savagely funny attack on capitalism and consumerism that ranges from the longest traffic jam on film to carnage and ultimately cannibalism.

After *Weekend,* Godard downscaled to make small films and TV programs that would extend the effects of the 1968 student riots in Paris. He saw these films as the blackboard of the coming revolution he desired. But they found little circulation in America other than on university campuses.

With *Tout va bien* (1972) Godard returned to the mainstream—in his fashion. Starring Jane Fonda and Yves Montand as a journalist and film director caught up in a strike, the film was typical political Godard. *Hail Mary* (1985) saw Godard back in the news with a modern retelling of the Mary and Joseph story. The film was picketed in the few U.S. cities where it appeared.

Godard filled his films with literary and philosophical quotations and his own aphorisms, and this became as much a Godard signature as his leftist politics, outsider/rebel protagonists, and radical New Wave style.

BIBLIOGRAPHY

Bellour, Raymond. *Jean-Luc Godard: Sound-Image, 1974–1992.* New York: Abrams, 1992.

Dixon, Wheeler Winston. *The Films of Jean-Luc Godard.* Albany: SUNY Press, 1997.

Loshitzky, Yosefa. *The Radical Faces of Godard and Bertolucci.* Detroit: Wayne State University Press, 1955.

Narboni, Jean, and Tom Milne, eds. *Godard on Godard.* New York: Da Capo Press, 1988.

Stam, Robert. *Reflexivity in Film and Literature: From Don Quixote to Jean-Luc Godard.* New York: Columbia University Press, 1992.

William M. Hammel

Godmanis, Ivars (1951–)

Popular Front prime minister of Latvia, 1990–93. Ivars Godmanis maintained his position by moving to the right and sacrificing most of his original former-Communist ministers. The economic policies associated with the transition to independence from the former Soviet Union produced a significant decline in living standards and an alienation of the population from his government. His conciliatory policies on citizenship for Russians who had been living in Latvia lost him support among ethnic Latvians. He remained in office until the election of 1993.

Godmanis was a research physicist at the University of Latvia. In the late 1980s he helped to found the Popular Front, an organization formed within the Communist Party of Latvia to promote Latvian sovereignty within the USSR, and he became a lecturer for its Political Committee, promoting the front's political program. In 1989 he was elected deputy chair of the front and successfully coordinated its campaigns in the local elections of 1989 and the general election of 1990, when he was elected an MP. He became chair of the front's pro-independence group in the Supreme Council, the former Supreme Soviet, and was elected prime minister on May 4, 1990.

Godmanis had never been a member of the Latvian Communist Party and had no previous government experience. He was criticized for making snap decisions and for using authoritarian methods. Most members of his first cabinet were reform Communists; the gap between them and the Popular Front representatives in the Supreme Council and supporters in the country grew increasingly wide. To maintain his position Godmanis gradually sacrificed these ministers and moved to the right.

However, his popularity continued to decline. He had sought an alliance of the different national groups in Latvia, adopting a conciliatory approach to the question of citizenship for Russians and supporting a policy of equal rights. Unfortunately for him the Popular Front abandoned this approach after the achievement of independence in 1991 in favor of an increasingly nationalist position. Godmanis was forced to move in the same direction in the following year and became close to the new political faction, Latvia's Way.

Godmanis's position was also weakened by the increasing economic hardship for the mass of the population resulting from rising inflation, shortages, and unemployment. After a period of drift in economic policy, by the end of 1992 his government adopted a coherent economic strategy underwritten by the International Monetary Fund (IMF), involving, as a central element, the creation of a stable Latvian currency. This was one of the fundamental achievements of his administration.

Godmanis attempted to remain loyal to the early equal rights ideals of the Popular Front, but the rapid movement to a policy of ethnic Latvian nationalism after in-dependence left him increasingly isolated. He lost power after the elections of 1993 and has played no major role in Latvian politics since then.

BIBLIOGRAPHY

Dreifelds, Juris. *Latvia in Transition.* Cambridge: Cambridge University Press, 1996.

Lieven, Anatol. *The Baltic Revolution: Estonia, Latvia, Lithuania and the Path to Independence.* New Haven, Conn.: Yale University Press, 1993.

Misiunas, Romnald, and Rein Taagepera. *The Baltic States: Years of Dependence 1940–1990.* London: Hurst, 1993.

Norgaard, Ole, et al. *The Baltic States after Independence.* Cheltenham, England: Edward Elgar, 1996.

Smith, Graham, ed. *The Baltic States: The National Self-Determination of Estonia, Latvia, and Lithuania.* Basingstoke, England: Macmillan, 1994.

Thomas Lane

Golding, William (1911–)

British novelist, poet, and playwright, winner of the 1983 Nobel Prize in literature. William Golding's first novel, *Lord of the Flies* (1954), gradually established itself as one of the few genuinely enduring works of fiction to be produced by a member of the generation of English writers who came to creative maturity in the 1950s. Its use of realistic techniques to produce a decidedly modern allegory on the subject of the chaos that resides beneath the veneer of technological civilization won an international audience, influenced many younger writers, and came to define the moral vision at the heart of all Golding's subsequent work.

Golding was born on September 19, 1911, in Cornwall to Alec and Mildred Golding, conventional Victorian parents steeped in the scientific rationalism of their time. His father, a schoolmaster, was the greatest influence on his life and convinced him to pursue the study of science, which he did for a time after entering Brasenose College, Oxford, in 1930. But Golding's interest in literature and music caused him to switch to the study of English literature after two years of academic work in the sciences. While at Oxford, he produced a small volume of poems (*Poems,* 1934) that was published by Macmillan. After graduation in 1934, Golding worked as a social worker and an actor and producer of plays at a small London theater until 1939, when, realizing that he would never become a professional actor, he married Ann Brookfield and began a teaching career at a school in Salisbury, where he stayed, with time off for wartime service, until 1961.

But it was his service in the Royal Navy from 1940 to 1945 that was the defining event in his life.

His wartime experience, Golding has often said, stripped him of his naive, idealistic vision of human nature and replaced it with the certainty that civilization is merely a veneer of order cast precariously over a deep and abiding cosmic chaos. This is the basic theme of all his fiction, although "softened" a bit in his later work, and it finds its most influential formulation in *Lord of the Flies*, written in a few months when Golding was forty-three years old. Although couched in terms of an almost Calvinistic idea of "original sin" that seemed old-fashioned to many readers even at the time, Golding's allegory of lost innocence and the grief that attends the knowledge of that loss found a huge audience and, in one way or another, informs all his best work since then, including *The Inheritors* (1955), *Pincher Martin* (1957), *The Spire* (1964), *Darkness Visible* (1979), and the later works, such as *The Paper Men* (1984) and *Fire Down Below* (1989), which show a fine but aging creative talent at the end of its career.

While many critics complain about Golding's "old-fashioned," "moralistic," "Christian" vision, his novels have found a worldwide audience. And his thesis—that modern humanity's simplistic faith in technocratic rationalism is unfounded and fated to fail in its effort to understand the cosmic condition in terms of simple, mechanical patterns of explanation—continues to exert its spell even over unsympathetic critics. The success of Golding's fiction is probably best understood by way of an appeal to modern history, which, at least at present, seems to confirm his dark view. Perhaps it is best, finally, to take Golding at his word when he says that his novels have always been intended to create a sense of "the numinous," the mysterious and unpredictable, as a corrective to our modern faith in the "demystifying" power of reason as well as to our naive faith in the technological civilization it has created and that, his novels argue, continues to produce its share of irrationality.

BIBLIOGRAPHY

Baker, James R., ed. *Critical Essays on William Golding.* Boston: G.K. Hall, 1988.

Biles, Jack. *Talk: Conversations with William Golding.* New York: Harcourt Brace Jovanovich, 1970.

Dickson, L. L. *The Modern Allegories of William Golding.* Tampa: University of South Florida Press, 1990.

Friedman, Lawrence S. *William Golding.* New York: Continuum, 1993.

Gindin, James. *William Golding.* New York: St. Martin's Press, 1988.

Twentieth Century Literature 28 (Summer 1982): Special Golding issue.

R. E. Foust

Gombrowicz, Witold (1904–69)

Polish novelist and playwright. Witold Gombrowicz was born on August 4, 1904, in Maloszyce near Opatow in Russian Poland, the son of a landowner and industrialist. In 1927 Gombrowicz graduated in law from the University of Warsaw and then studied at the Institut des Hautes Études Internationales in Paris. After returning to Poland he devoted himself to literary work and published his first collection of stories, *Pamietnik z okresu dojrzewania* (*Memoirs of Adolescence*) in 1933. It was reedited as *Bakakaj* in 1957. His first successful novel was *Ferdydurke* (1937). It was followed by a play, *Iwuna, Kcieznicrka Burgunda* (*Ivona, Princess of Burgundia*), published in the magazine *Skamander* in 1938. The following year Gombrowicz left for Buenos Aires, where he stayed after World War II broke out but was very much an outsider.

When his *Trans-Atlantic* was published in 1953, Gombrowicz became the leader of a group of younger writers associated with the journal *Kultura* published by the Polish émigre Instytut Literacki (Literary Institute) in Paris. Gombrowicz's *Dziennik* (*Diary*) was originally published by *Kultura,* and it subsequently published all his books. He gained international fame in the early 1960s when much of his fiction was translated and numerous plays were performed. Gombrowicz lived briefly in West Berlin but spent the last five years of his life in Venice, where he died on July 24, 1969.

The only values that mattered in Gombrowicz's world were those born in human interaction. Chief among these seemed to be youthful nudity, a symbol of existence not adulterated by social and moral patterns, and rebellion against the ideological follies of history. His 1965 novel *Kosmos* is a study of the individual who rejects clichés about reality and shows how human consciousness and sexual desire create something unique in the universe.

Gombrowicz's books, hardly known to average readers in the Polish People's Republic, were a great source of inspiration for several generations of writers and lovers of his fiction. They were a glorification of human freedom and dignity threatened by Communist collectivism.

BIBLIOGRAPHY

Georgin, Rosine. *Gombrowicz.* Lausanne: L'Âge d'homme, 1977.

Jelenski, Constantin, and Dominique de Roux, eds. *Gombrowicz.* Paris: Éditions de l'Herne, 1971.

Kurczaba, Alex. *Gombrowicz and Frisch: Aspects of the Literary Diary.* Bonn: Bouvier Verlag Herbert Grundmann, 1980.

Jerzy Speina

SEE ALSO Institute Literacki

Gomes, Francisco da Costa (1914–)

Interim president of Portugal from 1974 to 1976. General Francisco da Costa Gomes had a distinguished military career. He also served as undersecretary of state for the army from 1958 to 1961, commander for Mozambique from 1967 to 1969, commander for Angola from 1969 to 1972, and chief of the General Staff from 1972 to 1974. During his presidency, he was instrumental in preventing violence during the "Hot Summer" of 1975. He was promoted to army marshall in 1982.

Born in Tras-os-Montes, Costa Gomes pursued a military career and became one of the first Portuguese officers to receive NATO training in the early 1950s. In the aftermath of the heated presidential elections of 1958, he was nominated undersecretary of state for the army. He held that post until 1961, when he was fired for his involvement with the ministers of defense and the army in the April Conspiracy (*Abrilhada*) to depose dictator António Salazar.

Despite his critical attitudes toward the regime and his sympathies toward a negotiated settlement of Portugal's colonial wars, he was named by Salazar as military commander for Mozambique in 1965 and as military commander for Angola in 1969, where he was instrumental in destroying the chemical weapons the regime had prepared for possible use. Under his command the Popular Movement for the Liberation of Angola (MPLA) guerrilla activity in Angola was significantly reduced. He was named chief of the General Staff in 1972 and was instrumental in publishing General Antonio de Spinola's book *Portugal and the Future,* which undermined the regime. In March 1974 he was fired for his lukewarm support of Prime Minister Marcelo Caetano in the aftermath of the failed March attempt at a military coup.

With the collapse of the Caetano regime in the successful April 25, 1974, coup, Costa Gomes again became chief of the General Staff. A major supporter of the junior offices who led the coup of April 1974, Costa Gomes replaced Spinola as interim president on September 30, 1974. During the turbulent year of 1975, despite a reputation for hesitancy, he was instrumental in preventing civil war in the aftermath of the counter-coup attempt led by Spinola. In November 25, 1975, he declared martial law in the Lisbon area and supported Colonel Remalho Eanes's coup that ended the influence of the radical elements of the Armed Forces Movement (MFA) and began the stabilization of Portuguese democracy. During his final six months in office, the new democratic constitution was approved and the first completely democratic elections were held for parliament and the presidency.

He left the presidency in July 1976 and retired from the military and from politics. He briefly returned to public attention in 1997 when he revealed that the Salazar/Caetano regime had chemical weapons ready for use in Angola. Despite his association with that regime, Costa Gomes was a key promoter of its demise with his support of Spinola's book and the MFA, and he was instrumental in ensuring the triumph of Portuguese democracy by his careful maneuvering during 1975.

BIBLIOGRAPHY

Gomes, Francisco da Costa. *Sobre Portugal: dialogos com Alexandre Manuel.* Lisbon: A Regra do Jogo, 1979.

Machado, A. J. de Mello. *Aviltados e traidos (resposta a Costa Gomes).* Queluz, Portugal: Literal, 1978.

Murias, Manuel Maria. *De Salazar a Costa Gomes.* Lisbon: Nova Arrancada, 1998.

Paul Brasil

SEE ALSO Caetano, Marcelo; Eanes, António; Salazar, António

Gomułka, Władysław (1905–82)

Leader of the Polish Workers Party (1943–48) and first secretary of the Polish United Workers Party (PZPR, 1956–1970). After World War II Władysław (pseud. Wiesław) Gomułka became a proponent of an evolutionary transition to communism, thus opposing the speedy implementation of Stalinism in Poland. In 1956 he saved the country from a very likely Soviet intervention. Yet he never consented to deeper changes in Communist model of the state. Signing the treaty of normalization of relations between Poland and the German Federal Republic was his greatest diplomatic success.

As a twenty-year-old locksmith, Gomułka was introduced to the ideology of which he quickly became a convinced disciple. While a member of the Polish Communist Party (1926–38), he initially worked in the labor movement, organized strikes, and conducted agitation. Arrested in 1936 and sentenced to seven years' imprisonment in Poland, Gomułka avoided Stalin's bloody purge (1935–38), through which the Soviet leader sought to ensure his absolute dominance within both the Communist Party of the USSR and the worldwide communist movement. In 1938, Stalin ordered the Polish Communist Movement, which he regarded as too independent, dissolved. Most of its leaders who were in the USSR were executed. Following the invasion of Poland by Nazi Germany and the USSR in September 1939, he was briefly in the area occupied by the Soviets (Białstok and Lvov). He was not, however, sent to the political training organized for Communist activists. He returned to Poland and helped organize the Polish Workers Party (PWP). In 1943 as a result of internal conflicts within the party and the elimination of its two leading figures (Marceli Nowotko and Bolesław Molojec), Gomułka as an experienced Communist, even though unknown apart from the region of Upper Silesia and the labor movement, quickly progressed to the top of the party leadership. In November 1943, without Stalin's knowledge, Gomułka became the party's secretary (1943–45). He became general secretary in 1945. Gomułka revised the party's program in 1943, attempting to hide its real character, especially its close ties to Moscow and the Comintern (the Communist International), the body through which the Communist Party of the USSR exercised control over other communist parties. He also questioned the legality of the Polish émigré government exiled in London and the underground authorities, rejecting their right to represent the Polish nation. Without consulting Stalin he formed the National Home Council, an authority opposed to the London government-in-exile and its local structures. His advance was aided in November 1943 by the Nazi Gestapo's arrest of leading Communists in Poland, among them Pavet Finder and Matgorzata Fornalska. Gomułka, pressing his own point of view, clashed with the party's elite, Bolesław Bierut and his followers, who considered Moscow the ultimate authority. After some hesitation Stalin agreed to Gomułka's leadership of the party, even though he treated him with suspicion and reserve, and Bierut became Stalin's representative among Poland's ruling Communist elite.

With the creation of the Provisional Government of National Unity in June 1945, Gomułka took over the post of deputy premier. In November 1945 he also became minister of recovered territories. In that position he played an important role in the forced displacement of Germans and settlement of Poles in the new western and northern territories acquired from Germany after the war.

As a dogmatic supporter of Communist doctrine Gomułka was constantly faced with discrepancies between ideology and everyday life. He dreamed of a Polish road to socialism. According to Communist propaganda of the time, he associated this process with the establishment of a so-called people's democracy. In relations with Stalin, on the one hand, he fought the deporting of Poles to the Soviet Union; on the other hand, he fully accepted the loss of territory in the east to the USSR. He declared that transferring Soviet models to Poland and efforts to establish the dictatorship of one party ("dictatorship of the proletariat") were harmful; but in practice, by eliminating legal opposition he did everything to prevent the creation of a stable democratic system. For instance, the opposition centered around Stanisław Mikołajczyk, the Peasant Party leader and prime minister of the Polish government in exile in London from 1943 to 1944, was considered by Gomułka to be "reactionary and fascist"; he had a similar attitude toward the pre–World War II Polish government. In June 1945 he declared, "Communists will never give up power." He criticized activities of the security apparatus and was against revolutionary methods of widening Communist authority, but he could not accept parliamentary democracy and pledged "without any scruples" to destroy political opponents. Gomułka shares the responsibility (along with the Soviet Secret Police and other members of the Communist ruling elite) for abuse of authority and crimes against Polish democracy and its freedom fighters in the first years of "People's Poland." He opposed Stalinism because of tactical rather than theoretical reasons.

Stalinism was forced on Poland and other countries with the help of the COMINFORM, created by Stalin in September 1947. In the summer of 1948 Stalin removed Gomułka as general secretary of the PWP. Bierut became the new general secretary and accused Gomułka of "rightist and national deviation." Gomułka, by not agreeing to Stalin's request to stay in the party central leadership, condemned himself to banishment. Charged without foundation in November 1949 of being a spy within the party ranks, especially during the war (and as a consequence responsible for the killing of Nowotko, and the arrests of Finder and Fornalska), Gomułka was stripped from all posts and arrested in 1951 and removed from the party. He was the only prominent Communist Party official in the countries of the so-called people's democracies who was not sentenced to death and executed. Gomułka was saved by the death of Stalin in March 1953 and rehabilitated as a result of the Soviet leader Nikita Khrushchev's campaign of de-Stalinization. Released from prison in December 1954, he was banned from political life until spring 1956. In mid-1956 Gomułka regained his party membership and was rehabilitated.

In the wake of riots by workers in Poznań in June 1956, prompted by shortages, low wages, and disgust with the shipment of food to the USSR, Gomułka, with his reputation as a "national communist," appeared to be a person who might be able to mollify the Polish workers. Gomułka resumed power as first secretary of the Central Committee of the PZPR in October 1956. He asserted Poland's right to direct its own path to socialism but managed to appease Khrushchev, and, at the last moment, to avert Soviet military intervention. During the eighth plenum of the party's Central Committee in October 1956, Gomułka criticized the Stalinist system but failed to describe a new model of the party and the state. The rejection of Stalinism and an attempt to create equal relations with the Soviet Union (e.g., loosening economic ties, new methods of calculating coal exports, agreements on stationing Soviet army forces in Poland, and repatriation of Poles from the Soviet Union) created enthusiasm and hope throughout Polish society. The nation came to associate Gomułka with hope for a better future, especially for the return of democracy and independence to Poland. These hopes as well as more radical demands were a threat for Gomułka, an orthodox Communist who from the beginning treated all attempts at change with suspicion. He was also blackmailed by the Kremlin. By agreeing to some concessions demanded by the Polish people, he pacified the public and slowly returned to the authoritarian style of rule. He regarded independent thought as a "slandering of socialism"; likewise he eliminated all free criticism and discussion, identifying them with "revisionism." Instead he stressed development of heavy industry and limiting consumption.

With time Gomułka intensified his criticism of various social groups, thus alienating them. He had conflicts with the Catholic Church, with the intelligentsia, who were antagonized by limiting freedom of speech and tightening of censorship, with students, who were provoked to demonstrate in March 1968, and finally with workers, whom his forces fired on in December 1970. Until the end he remained a Communist doctrinaire, and despite his critical approach to the Soviet model of socialism, he never permitted the introduction of democracy in Poland. He left in dramatic circumstances in December 1970, alienated from the party and society, without the Kremlin's support.

Gomułka was moderately successful in international policy, but even there he was directed by Communist doctrinal considerations. For instance, he regarded the Prague Spring of 1968 as a "peaceful counterrevolution using revisionist slogans" and agreed to send Polish troops to participate in the Soviet-led Warsaw Pact invasion of Czechoslovakia. He signed limited partnership agreements with the Soviet Union but came close to asking the Soviet army to suppress workers' unrest in December

1970. His biggest diplomatic success was signing in December 1970, after long negotiations, the treaty normalizing relations between Poland and West Germany in which Germany recognized Poland's border on the Oder and Neisse Rivers (Oder-Neissa line).

BIBLIOGRAPHY

Bethel, Nicholas. *Gomulka*. London: Penguin, 1972.

de Weydenthal, Jan B. *The Communists of Poland.* Stanford, Calif.: Hoover Institution Press, 1978.

Hissocks, Richard. *Poland's Bridge for the Abyss? An Interpretation of Developments in Post-war Poland.* London: Oxford University Press, 1963.

Ryszard Sudzinski

SEE ALSO Bierut, Bolesław

Gonçalves, Vasco (1921–)

Most senior member of the Armed Forces Movement and prime minister of the second, third, fourth, and fifth provisional governments in Portugal following the April 25, 1974, coup. He studied engineering at the University of Lisbon and also attended the Portuguese Military Academy in Lisbon. He taught at the Military Academy and served in the Portuguese colonial wars in Mozambique and Angola.

An admirer of the Communist Party and of the Soviet Union, Gonçalves sought to implement leftist solutions to Portugal's political and economic problems. Following the failed March 11, 1975, right-wing coup organized by General Antonio de Spinola against the MFA, the Armed Forces Movement and the Gonçalves government jailed many conservatives and nationalized many businesses. Many property-owners fled the country at that time, and he faced opposition from many groups who feared the influence of the Communist Party in his administration. Notably, Socialist leader Mario Soares criticized Gonçalves, warning of the dangers of communism throughout the so-called Hot Summer of 1975. Eventually, Soares's moderate allies in the MFA successfully removed Gonçalves from power in September 1975.

Gonçalves represented the danger of Soviet-style communism gaining a beachhead in Portugal, and many were relieved after he was dismissed. He retired from political and military life shortly after, and has since resided in Lisbon.

BIBLIOGRAPHY

Brito, Rui de. *Anatomia das palavras: Vasco Goncalves.* Lisbon: Liber, 1976.

Gonçalves, Vasco. *Citacoes de Vasco Gonçalves.* Amadora, Portugal: Fronteira, 1975.

Paul Christopher Manuel

SEE ALSO Gomes, Francisco da Costa; Spínola, António de

Göncz, Árpád (1922–)

President of Hungary (1990–). Árpád Göncz studied law and agricultural engineering. He joined the Independent Smallholders Party in 1945. He was employed as a manual worker from 1948 to 1951, and worked in various jobs while studying at the Agricultural University in Gödöllö in the early 1950s. He was active in the anti-Communist Peasants Alliance during the Hungarian Revolution in 1956. In 1958 he was sentenced to life in prison for his activities during the revolution, but he was amnestied in 1963. Afterward he was a freelance writer and translator until 1990. He joined the Network of Free Initiatives, an underground opposition movement, in 1981, then became one of the founding members of the Alliance of Free Democrats, the democratic opposition during the reign of the Communist leader János Kádás. After 1989 it was organized as a party in the social democratic tradition, and its call for rapid privatization of the economy gave it a rightist appearance. Göncz was elected president of Hungary in 1990 and was reelected in 1995.

Göncz is an intellectual-political figure characteristic of central Europe, comparable to Václav Havel in the Czech Republic. Göncz published novels, plays, and short stories; translated a number of books from English into Hungarian; and received several awards for his literary output both in Hungary and abroad. Some of his plays have been staged in various countries including the United States.

BIBLIOGRAPHY

Goncz, Arpad. *Plays and Other Writings.* New York: Garland, 1990.
———. *Voices of Dissent: Two Plays.* Lewisburg, Pa.: Bucknell University Press, 1989.

Tamàs Magyarics

SEE ALSO Antall, József; Boross, Péter; Horn, Gyula; Németh, Miklós

Árpád Göncz, president of Hungary. *Illustration courtesy of the Embassy of Hungary, Washington, D.C.*

González Marquez, Felipe (1942–)

Spanish premier from 1982 to 1996. Felipe González, son of a livestock handler, was born in Seville on March 5, 1942, and raised in Andalusia. The only one of five siblings to attend college, he studied engineering and then law at the University of Seville and later at the University of Leuven in Belgium. As a student he became involved in anti-Francoist politics. Later, he taught labor law as an adjunct at Seville, founded a legal practice that specialized in labor cases, and was active in the socialist Unión General de Trabajadores. In 1966 he joined the outlawed Spanish Socialist Workers Party (Partido Socialista Obrero Español, PSOE), leading a movement of young Socialists attempting to relocate control of the PSOE to Spain from its long exile in France. He was instrumental, along with Alfonso Guerra, in building the Socialist presence locally in Seville and was active in European-wide Socialist politics, becoming a protégé of German Socialist leader Willy Brandt.

González was elected executive secretary of the Seville provincial branch of the PSOE in 1970 and served in that capacity until 1974. During that time the Spain-based PSOE gained control of the party and eventually severed ties with the party's leadership-in-exile controlled by Rodolfo Llopis in Toulouse. González became a member of the party's Executive Commission and in 1974 was elected first secretary of the redesigned PSOE at a congress in Paris.

With the aid of his telegenic good looks, an adaptable political philosophy, and the able assistance of Guerra, he gradually consolidated his control of the party and expanded its popularity and significance. He moved the PSOE's ideology gradually toward the center and focused its attention on democracy and politics more than on economic or social goals. When the PSOE was legalized after the death of Francisco Franco in 1975, it rapidly grew into a national political force. After Spain's first free, post-Franco elections were held in 1977, the PSOE became the second-largest party in the reconstituted Cortes. González, as the de facto leader of the opposition, used his platform to criticize the remnants of Francoism that he observed in the policies of premier Adolfo Suárez. When Spain's economy slumped and regionalist violence escalated in the early 1980s, Suárez resigned. Seizing on the uncertainty, a rightist conspiracy attempted to take power in an ill-devised coup. The coup failed when the king, Juan Carlos I, clearly signaled his refusal to support it. The failed coup and the king's strong affirmation of the young constitution paved the way for González's electoral success the following year.

In the elections of October 1982, the PSOE won a large plurality, 47 percent, and was the only party in a position to form a government. González was appointed premier by Juan Carlos. The peaceful transition of power to a Socialist government under the auspices of the constitutional monarchy in 1982 was an important step in the stabilization of Spanish democracy. Juan Carlos is often and rightfully credited for his unwavering commitment to democratic reform, but González helped facilitate his own smooth accession through strategic adjustments such as easing the PSOE's longtime antimonarchist stance and dropping the adjective "Marxist" from the official description of his party.

As premier, González moved Spain toward membership in the European Economic Community (EC). Spain's formal membership came in 1986 and, in the short term, eased the economic woes of the early 1980s. Spain experienced a miniboom and González and the PSOE were reelected to power in 1986, 1989, and 1993, though the last government was based on a much smaller plurality and a much more tenuous coalition than the earlier ones. Indeed, the later years of González's premiership were increasingly plagued by crisis, scandal, and division. In December 1988 he faced the first major labor walkout of his regime. In 1990 the EC-fueled boom began to wear off, and in the early 1990s Spain's unemployment swelled to over 20 percent. His support of liberal economic policies caused rifts within his party, which endured several major scandals in 1991 and 1992. Regionalist violence continued to plague democratic Spain. On the right, the Popular Party (Partido Popular, PP), a conservative heir to the Popular Alliance (Alianza Popular, AP), grew steadily in electoral popularity.

The fragile coalition of 1993 would be González's last. In 1994 the worst scandal of his long reign dealt a severe blow to his government. González and the PSOE were linked in press and judicial reports to the Anti-terrorist Liberation Group (GAL). GAL allegedly carried out at least twenty-seven extrajudicial executions of suspected Basque terrorists, mostly in France, between 1983 and 1987. According to some judges and reporters, González may have been involved in this "dirty war." This matter remained unresolved even after González left political life. To make matters worse for him, in 1995 the Cortes rejected the budget submitted by his government. This marked the first time the Cortes had rejected a budget in the post-Franco era. His coalition was shattered. González pledged to hold elections early the following year, and in May 1996 the PP under the leadership of José María Aznar Lopez won an electoral victory that ended the long reign of González and the PSOE. After thirteen years as premier and twenty-four as leader of his party, González resigned as secretary-general of the PSOE in 1997, closing the most important chapter of a long, successful career.

The scandals and struggles of the 1990s may have irrevocably damaged González's reputation in Spain, but he continues to be respected in international political circles. Perhaps above all, he should be associated with Spain's successful transition to democracy. Although his governments began seven years after Franco's death, González's careful, pragmatic focus on democratic goals helped ensure the survival of democratic Spain.

BIBLIOGRAPHY

Cierva, Ricardo de la. *El PSOE de Felipe Gonzalez: adios al marxismo.* Madrid: ARC Editores, 1997.

Gillespie, Richard. *The Spanish Socialist Party. A History of Factionalism.* Oxford: Oxford University, 1989.

Gonzalez, Felipe. *Socialismo es libertad.* Barcelona: Galba Edicions, 1978.

Navarro, Julia. *Entre Felipe y Aznar, 1982–1996.* Madrid: Ediciones Temas de Hoy, 1996.

Stephen P. James

SEE ALSO Aznar Lopez, José María

Gorbachev, Mikhail Sergeyevich (1931–)

General secretary of the Communist Party of the USSR (1985–91) and president of the USSR (1988–1991),

Gorbachev led the reform of the USSR from 1985 until its collapse in 1991.

Mikhail Gorbachev will be remembered as an important Soviet leader who tried but did not succeed in transforming the USSR. His efforts to change the USSR may have accelerated the demise of the Soviet system, but his program of glasnost (openness) and perestroika (restructuring) was a monumental effort to reform the Soviet system, while preserving its best features.

Gorbachev was born into a peasant family in the village of Privolnoe in the Stavropol region in 1931, a difficult time in Soviet history as the countryside was in the throes of forced collectivization. Peasants who resisted were arrested and deported to Siberian labor camps. Among those arrested was Andrey Gorbachev, Mikhail's grandfather, a fact that Gorbachev apparently never forgot. The talents of the young Mikhail were recognized at an early age, and he pursued a secondary education even while working in the fields. Politically active in the Komsomol, the Communist youth organization, at an early age and a star student at his secondary school, Gorbachev was accepted at prestigious Moscow University to study in the Law Faculty, a rare honor for a rural youth. Perhaps as important as his academic achievements was that he had received the Order of the Red Banner of Labor (1949) for his outstanding contribution to the harvest.

Gorbachev's Moscow years were an important formative period. He studied in Moscow from 1950 to 1955, the end of the Stalin era and the beginning of the Khrushchev era, when many changes were beginning in Soviet society. In Moscow he met people of varying backgrounds, and his education progressed, both inside and outside the classroom. His tastes in literature and the arts were cultivated during this period. An active member of the Komsomol, Gorbachev joined the Communist Party in 1952 at the age of twenty-one. While at the university, he met Raisa Maksimovna Titarenko, who was also a student there. They fell in love and were married in 1953.

After graduation, the couple went to Stavropol, where he worked for the Komsomol. His political career progressed from the Komsomol to the Communist Party organization. The Gorbachevs had one daughter, Irina, born in 1957. The family enjoyed a happy life in Stavropol, where they lived in relative comfort and had time to pursue their intellectual interests.

As the years passed, Gorbachev gradually rose to the position of first secretary of the Communist Party of the Stavropol region. Several developments distinguished his career from that of other regional party secretaries. During his years in Stavropol he acquired a degree in agriculture, cognizant that knowledge of agriculture was essential in that region. His wife, meanwhile, pursued an advanced degree in sociology and taught at a local institute. As part of her research for the candidate's degree, she surveyed farm families. The results of her research were significant in informing Gorbachev about peasant opinion and assisted him in conducting agricultural reforms in the region. The success of his agricultural policy gained the attention of Moscow and was a factor in the Kremlin's decision in 1978 to invite him to the capital. Perhaps even more significant was his growing acquaintance with high-level officials. The Stavropol region has a number of health spas frequented by the government's elite, and among visiting officials whom the Gorbachev's came to know well was Yuri Andropov, head of the KGB and a member of the ruling Politburo. In the last years of the Brezhnev era, later known as the period of *zastoi* (stagnation), the Kremlin was governed by an aging leadership more interested in the status quo than progress. Andropov, scouting for talented younger men to be of assistance in his own plans to succeed Brezhnev, is credited with bringing Gorbachev to Moscow.

The Gorbachevs moved to Moscow in 1978, when Gorbachev was appointed party secretary for agriculture; he was promoted to candidate status on the Politburo in 1979 and full membership in 1980. The transition to life at the center of Soviet politics was an important one for Gorbachev's career but not a happy one for the family. The elitist Kremlin circle regarded the Gorbachevs as provincials, and it took some time for the new arrivals to adjust to their new life.

To be the member of the Secretariat of the CPSU entrusted with the oversight of agriculture was always a precarious position, since agriculture had long been the Achilles' heel of the Soviet economy. Gorbachev appeared able to handle the challenge, and by the early 1980s was recognized as one of the few bright spots in an otherwise aging and dull Soviet leadership.

After Brezhnev's death in November 1982, Andropov became general secretary of the CPSU. Andropov was already in poor health, which deteriorated sharply during his short tenure. Gorbachev's role in the Secretariat was expanded as he unofficially assumed the role of second secretary of the party. When Andropov died in February 1984, Gorbachev nominated the ailing Konstantin Chernenko as general secretary. Chernenko, who owed his career to the patronage of Brezhnev, had few new ideas to offer the USSR, and Gorbachev used this period to consolidate his own position within the party.

Gorbachev's rising prominence did not go unnoticed in the outside world. In December 1984 the Gorbachevs made an official visit to the United Kingdom, where they met with Prime Minister Margaret Thatcher. Thatcher recognized that Gorbachev represented a new breed of Soviet leader and uttered the prophetic words: "This is a man that we can do business with."

A few months later, Chernenko died. Gorbachev was selected by the Politburo as general secretary in March 1985 and began consolidating his position within the Soviet hierarchy. He began systematically to retire aging officials in the ministries and party, many of whom had been appointed in the late Khrushchev or early Brezhnev era.

In the early stage of reform, Gorbachev introduced the policy of glasnost (openness), selectively revealing past Soviet misdeeds. Glasnost may be seen as the harbinger of political and economic reform, since it was necessary to reveal past wrongs before launching a program of change. Glasnost also ushered in an era of greater openness in literature and the arts. During this early period Gorbachev also launched a campaign against the excessive drinking that debilitated Soviet society. The goals of Gorbachev's antialcohol campaign were several: improve labor productivity, reduce problems in the family, and diminish the massive health problems caused by alcohol dependency among so many Soviet men. The number of places where alcohol could be sold was restricted and the hours when alcohol could be sold were sharply curtailed. Initially, the crackdown on drinking appeared to work, but soon people found ways around it. Long lines formed during the hours alcohol was for sale as workers left their jobs early to be certain to buy a supply of alcohol. Soon vodka became more valuable than currency as a means of exchange. A bootlegging industry developed in the countryside, contributed to a shortage of sugar, and increased deaths from wood alcohol, but there was no real decrease in alcohol consumption.

In 1986 Gorbachev discussed economic changes at the twenty-seventh Party Congress, but in 1987 he introduced the overall program of change that he now called perestroika. Launched in optimism, his program featured gradual evolution of the economy, limited free enterprise, and self-management in state enterprises. As of 1988 enterprises were to operate on a sound financial basis without government subsidies. They were free to set their own policies and hire their own employees so long as they met the state's general targets. Such policies were easier to enunciate than to practice.

Other reforms were proposed, including leasing land to collective farm peasants. With each new idea Gorbachev met resistance within the party leadership. Reform proved harder to promulgate than he had thought, and the party emerged as the source of change and of resis-

tance to reform. Even within the Politburo, these two tendencies were apparent. Yegor Ligachev, who headed the Communist Party's department of ideology and personnel, was inclined to proceed more slowly, objecting strongly to breaking up the collective farms and leasing land to peasants. On the other side, Boris Yeltsin, one of the regional officials wanted by Gorbachev to come to Moscow to help him reform the USSR, argued that reform was progressing too slowly. A showdown between Gorbachev and Yeltsin in 1987 resulted in the latter's removal from the Politburo. Despite occasional moments of cooperation, a permanent enmity developed between Yeltsin and Gorbachev, which time has not erased.

In 1988 Gorbachev expanded perestroika into political reform with a reorganization of the Supreme Soviet. A new, expanded body was introduced—the Congress of People's Deputies, a three-chamber parliament, two chambers of which were to be elected in competitive elections. The party nominated candidates for most of the places and was stunned when in selected cases some of its best-known candidates were defeated. From the large Congress of People's Deputies a smaller Supreme Soviet was selected as a standing parliamentary body. Although Gorbachev tried to influence the selection process, a number of opposition leaders won election to the Supreme Soviet, including the leading dissident Andrey Sakharov, Boris Yeltsin, and younger reformers. The new Supreme Soviet was a lively chamber whose proceedings were televised. For the first time the Soviet people witnessed democratic debate and discussion, and attention was riveted on the proceedings of the Supreme Soviet. The new Supreme Soviet elected Gorbachev chairman of its Presidium (president of the USSR), and the new position was entrusted with more power than the earlier, more ceremonial presidency.

Gorbachev increasingly functioned as president of the country and less as general secretary of the party. Although it would be impossible to separate the two in the Soviet system, it became clear that Gorbachev was gradually distancing himself from the party as he sought to transform the Soviet political system. He was resistant, however, to permitting political parties other than the Communist Party. Within the Supreme Soviet Sakharov led the struggle to legalize other political parties, and the stress may have contributed to his heart attack and death in late 1989. In 1990 the constitution was finally changed to permit the existence of other political parties. Gorbachev was caught between those who sought ever more rapid change and those who wanted to slow down its pace. While he managed to emerge victorious at the special Nineteenth Party Conference in 1988, he faced greater setbacks at the Twenty-eighth Party Congress in 1990. Gorbachev made his peace with party conservatives and co-opted several of them into his administration in key positions within the party and the government.

Ironically, Gorbachev grew increasingly unpopular at home while his international popularity crescendoed. His successes abroad were due both to his political style and to his foreign policy program. Together with his foreign minister, Eduard Shevardnadze, Gorbachev was the global ambassador of a new Soviet Union prepared to be a partner in world politics rather than a rival in the Cold War. Gorbachev talked of global interdependence rather than competition. In the West in particular, he was especially acclaimed, his popularity growing after the fall of the Berlin Wall in 1989. The Soviet Union under Gorbachev encouraged reform in Eastern Europe, and one by one the states of that region asserted their independence from Soviet domination and undertook their own reforms.

The paradox of Gorbachev's international acclaim and his domestic unpopularity was hard to reconcile. He used his international reputation to bolster his faltering domestic image, but the strategy had limited success. By 1991 his popularity at home had fallen.

In the winter and spring of 1990–91 Gorbachev vacillated between liberal and conservative policies. In the spring of 1991 a group of conservatives began to plot Gorbachev's overthrow to recapture the old Soviet Union. The plot was put into effect on August 19, 1991, while Gorbachev was on vacation with his family in the Corinea. He was placed under house arrest, and the seven leaders of the coup in Moscow including Vice President Valentine Pavlov announced that Gorbachev was stepping down because of ill health.

In St. Petersburg nearly 200,000 people took to the street in opposition to the coup. In Moscow resistance mounted to the coup, led by Boris Yeltsin, president of the Russian Republic. The forces of resistance obtained the release of Gorbachev and the coup leaders were arrested. In the aftermath of the coup, many changes occurred. Yeltsin forbade the Communist Party, which he blamed for the coup, to operate on the territory of the Russian Republic. Since Moscow was the capital of both the USSR and the Russian Republic, for all practical purposes Yeltsin was outlawing the national operations of the Soviet Communist Party. Gorbachev was pressured to resign as general secretary, and since certain leaders of the Supreme Soviet were implicated in the coup, Gorbachev called upon the Central Committee to dissolve itself and he issued a decree suspending all functions of the party.

For Gorbachev, the dissolution of the Supreme Soviet and the prohibition of the CPSU on Russian soil were the beginning of the end. He was a president elected by a Supreme Soviet that no longer existed, and a former general secretary of a now defunct CPSU. As the fall of 1991 progressed, the Soviet republics increasingly functioned independently of the central government. In December 1991 Russia, Ukraine, and Belarus formed the Commonwealth of Independent States, which a majority of the republics later joined. Gorbachev's authority evaporated, and on December 25, 1991, he formally announced his resignation as president of the USSR. On January 1, 1992, the USSR ceased to exist.

After his retirement from politics, Gorbachev extensively lectured abroad, headed a research foundation, and made an unsuccessful bid to become president of the Russian Federation in 1996. History will probably record a mixed evaluation of this innovative leader who initiated reform from above, only to find the system disintegrate beneath him.

BIBLIOGRAPHY

Desai, Padma. *Perestroika in Perspective: The Design and Dilemmas of Soviet Reform.* Princeton, N.J.: Princeton University Press, 1989.

Doder, Dusko, and Louise Branson. *Gorbachev: Heretic in the Kremlin.* New York: Penguin, 1991.

Goldman, Marshall. *What Went Wrong with Perestroika.* New York: Norton, 1991.

Gorbachev, Mikhail. *Perestroika: New Thinking for Our Country and the World.* New York: Harper and Row, 1987.

Gorbacheva, Raisa. *I Hope.* New York: HarperCollins, 1991.

Juviler, Peter, and Hiroshi Kimura. *Gorbachev's Reforms: U.S. and Japanese Assessments.* New York: Aldine de Gruyter, 1988.

Wieczynski, Joseph L., ed. *The Gorbachev Encyclopedia.* Salt Lake City: Charles Schlacks, 1993.

Norma C. Noonan

SEE ALSO Andropov, Yuri; Yeltsin, Boris

Gorbunovs, Anatolij (1942–)

Chair of the Supreme Council of Latvia and head of state, 1988–93. Anatolijs Gorbunovs fulfilled an important role during Latvia's transition to independence from the former USSR; personally popular and appearing to stand above politics, he acted as a conciliator among various political groupings—Soviet loyalists, local Russians, and ethnic Latvians—and retained his leading political position after the elections of 1990. Replaced as chair of the

Supreme Council in 1993, he continued to occupy a prominent position in politics.

Born in the Latgale region of Latvia into a farming family, Gorbunovs had an early career in civil engineering. From 1974 he held various posts in the Latvian Communist Party, becoming its secretary in the central district of Riga between 1980 and 1985, and then the secretary on ideology. In these posts he came into contact with and was influenced by moderate nationalists and reformers such as Janis Peters, poet and secretary of the Writers Union.

Gorbunovs first came into public prominence in 1988, when he openly supported the Popular Front of Latvia, a protest movement that first advocated sovereignty within the USSR and then independence, and took part in several demonstrations. In this he was anticipating the recommendations of Mikhail Gorbachev's emissary to Latvia, Boris Yakovlev, that local Communist parties should become more involved in the reform movement. Gorbunovs fit the bill of a loyalist Communist identified with reform and personally popular among both ethnic Latvians, who represented only some 52 percent of the total population, and local Russians. Although Janis Vagris became the new party general secretary, Gorbunovs was chosen chair of the Supreme Council (Soviet) in 1988, becoming, in effect, head of state.

In the period of intensified reform and heightened nationalist feelings between 1988 and 1990, Gorbunovs attempted to act as mediator among reformers in the Popular Front, the Communist Party, and the large Russian minority, as well as to keep on good terms with the Kremlin. In the pursuit of ethnic harmony he supported a generous citizenship policy for Russian immigrants. His own personality, particularly his so-called anodyne style, fitted him well for the role of conciliator. Like Arnold Rüütel in Estonia, the chairman of the Presidium of the Supreme Soviet of the Estonian Soviet Socialist Republic (1983–90) and Chairman of the Supreme Council (March 29–May 8, 1990), Gorbunovs finally severed his links with the party.

In the elections of 1990 the Popular Front gained two-thirds of the seats in the Latvian Supreme Council, which shortly afterward declared the renewal of Latvian independence. Although a new government was elected, Gorbunovs, now a reform Communist, was retained as chair of the council in an attempt to reassure the local Russian population and the radical Latvians. In the tense, confrontational months leading to independence in August 1991, Gorbunovs tried to maintain his role as mediator, sometimes by absenting himself from critical votes in the council.

After independence Gorbunovs moved in a nationalist direction, taking a more exclusionist position on citizenship and joining Latvia's Way, a party composed mainly of members of the Popular Front and reform Communists. In the parliamentary elections of 1993 under the new constitution, Gorbunovs was elected an MP and subsequently speaker of parliament. He was succeeded as president by Guntis Ulmanis. He later became a minister in the government led by Andris Skele. As minister of transport in the government of Vilis Kristopans (1998–99) he unsuccessfully ran for president in 1999, but the Latvia's Way vote was split between Gorbunovs and Kristopans, and Gorbunov's Communist past was held against him by some.

BIBLIOGRAPHY

Dreifelds, Juris. *Latvia in Transition.* Cambridge: Cambridge University Press, 1996.

Lieven, Anatol. *The Baltic Revolution: Estonia, Latvia, Lithuania and the Path to Independence.* New Haven, Conn.: Yale University Press, 1993.

Misiunas, Romuald, and Rein Taagepera. *The Baltic States: Years of Dependence 1940–1990.* London: Hurst, 1993.

Norgaard, Ole, et al. *The Baltic States after Independence.* Cheltenham, England: Edward Elgar, 1996.

Smith, Graham, ed. *The Baltic States: The National Self-Determination of Estonia, Latvia and Lithuania.* Basingstoke, England: Macmillan, 1994.

Thomas Lane

Goria, Giovanni Giuseppe (1943–94)

Italian Christian Democratic politician and premier. Giovanni Giuseppe Goria was born on July 30, 1943, in Asti. He became a member of the Christian Democrat Party in 1960. Goria was elected to the Chamber of Deputies from the electoral ward of Cuneo, Alessandria, and Asti in 1976 and was reconfirmed through the elections of 1979 and 1983.

As a deputy he was a member of the Committee of Finance and Treasury. In the period 1978–79, during Giulio Andreotti's governments, Goria was financial counselor to the premier. He was undersecretary of budget and financial planning during the first government of Giovanni Spadolini in 1981, but one year later he left office to take charge of the Financial Department of the Christian Democratic Party. In December 1982, during Amintore Fanfani's government, he was minister of the treasury, an office he retained during the Bettino Craxi and Fanfani governments.

Goria was elected deputy for the fourth time in June 1987. On July 19, 1987, he formed a new government and became premier and minister of extraordinary interventions in southern Italy. In 1989 he was elected to the European Parliament and in 1991 became agriculture minister in the Italian government. One year later he again became finance minister but resigned from the cabinet in 1993 after being caught up in the investigations of government corruption. Brought to trial in February 1994, Goria always denied any guilt. He died of lung cancer on May 21, 1994, at his home Asti while the trial was still in progress.

BIBLIOGRAPHY

La navicella: I deputati e i senatori del 10° parlamento repubblicàno. Città di Castello: INI, 1988.

Santarelli, Enzo. *Storia critica della Repubblica: 1946–1996.* Milan: Feltrinelli, 1996.

Fabio Marino

SEE ALSO Andreotti, Giulio

Gottwald, Klement (1896–1953)

Czechoslovak premier, 1946–48, and president, 1948–53. Klement Gottwald presided over the Communist seizure of power in Czechoslovakia. The illegitimate son of a peasant, he was born in Dedice, Moravia, on November 23, 1896. When he was twelve he was apprenticed to a carpenter and cabinetmaker in Vienna. He became a socialist at sixteen. Gottwald was in the Austro-Hungarian army in the First World War but he deserted to the Russians. After the war he was active in the left wing of the Czechoslovak Social Democratic Party, and participated in the transformation in 1921 of that faction into the Communist Party of Czechoslovakia. He edited the party newspaper *Hlas Ludu* (Voice of the People) in Bratislava and then *Pravda* (Truth). He was elected to the Central Committee of the party in 1925, and was elected secretary-general in 1929. He was elected to the Czechoslovak parliament in 1929.

Following the Munich Pact of 1938, he emigrated to Moscow, returning to Czechoslovakia with Czechoslovak President Edvard Beneš in 1945 and serving as deputy premier in the provisional government headed by left Social Democrat Zdeněk Fierlinger to head the provisional Czechoslovak government. Communists were given only a few ministries, but Fierlinger assigned them the key ministry of information. Gottwald, who became chairman of the Communist Party of Czechoslovakia in March 1946, worked to solidify support of Communists among Czechoslovakia workers.

When the Communists won the largest number of seats in the Czechoslovak parliament in May 1946, Beneš appointed Gottwald prime minister on July 3. The Communists did not control a firm majority in the Council of Ministers, however, despite the consistent support of Fierlinger and his left Social Democrat allies. In late 1947 the Social Democrats ousted Fierlinger as their chairman and announced that they would no longer participate in the National Front coalition with the Communists after the May 1948 election. In February the Communists, realizing that their control of the government was slipping, introduced a number of measures in the Council of Ministers that they knew would be unacceptable to their opponents. Twelve ministers tried to topple Gottwald's government by resigning. The Communists organized demonstrations by their union supporters, and Gottwald demanded that Beneš appoint him leader of a new, more loyal government. Gottwald was supported by Fierlinger, who entered the now clearly Communist government with some of his left Social Democratic allies. After Beneš resigned the presidency on June 14, Gottwald assumed the presidency. Antonín Zápotocký became premier.

Gottwald presided over the Stalinization of Czechoslovakia. Purges launched by him led to the execution of approximately 180 party leaders, among them Vladimír Clementis, the foreign minister, and Rudolf Slánský, the first secretary of the party and a Gottwald rival.

Gottwald died of pneumonia in Moscow on March 9, 1953, five days after Stalin's funeral, and was succeeded by Zápotocký.

BIBLIOGRAPHY

Korbel, Josef. *The Communist Subversion of Czechoslovakia, 1938–1948: The Failure of Coexistence.* Princeton, N.J.: Princeton University Press, 1959.

Zinner, Paul E. *Communist Strategy and Tactics in Czechoslovakia, 1918–48.* Westport, Conn.: Greenwood Press, 1975, c1963.

Bernard Cook

SEE ALSO Fierlinger, Zdeněk; Slánský, Rudolf

Gouin, Félix (1884–1977)

French premier, January 1946–January 1947. Félix Gouin was born into a middle-class family at Peypin on October 4, 1884. Both his parents were teachers. Gouin joined the Socialist Party in 1904 while he was still a student. He studied law at Aix-en-Provence. In 1911 he was elected councilor general of the department of Bouches-du-Rhône. After serving in World War I he entered parliament in 1924 and became vice president of the Socialist parliamentary group. During World War II he was one of eighty members of parliament who opposed the Vichy regime. He defended Léon Blum, the former Socialist premier who was accused of treason by the Vichy government, then joined the Free French under the Charles de Gaulle in London in 1942 as the representative of the Socialist Party. Gouin headed the French Parliament Group in London in 1943–44. He was elected president of the Consultative Assembly in Algiers in 1944 and was elected to the same post when a new assembly was set up in Paris on November 8, 1944.

De Gaulle retired from public life for the first time on January 20, 1946. He objected to the constitution being prepared by the left-dominated Constituent Assembly and its opposition to an increased military budget. The Communist Party, the largest party in the assembly, proposed a Communist-Socialist coalition headed by Communist leader Maurice Thorez. The Socialists, unwilling to give such power to the Communists, refused to participate in a government without the Christian democratic Popular Republican Movement (Mouvement Républicain Populaire, MRP). The MRP was unwilling to join any coalition headed by a Communist. As a compromise Gouin, a Socialist and president of the Constituent Assembly, was chosen to head the cabinet as president of the Council of Ministers.

Gouin was an ineffectual leader, described as a person of goodwill rather than of will. He succeeded, however, in forcing the acceptance of a deflationary budgetary program similar to one the parties had previously rejected. But the assembly's first constitution, which, in accord with the preferences of the Communists and the Socialists, provided for a strong, unicameral parliament, was defeated in a May referendum. Gouin stepped down and Georges Bidault of the MRP established a new tripartite government in which Gouin served as vice premier. The second draft of the constitution, which incorporated the MRP desire for a stronger executive and a second legislative house, passed in a November referendum, but a third of the electorate did not vote.

Though the Communists regained the plurality they had lost in the June election, their desire for Thorez to become premier was again thwarted. For one month Blum headed a caretaker government composed solely of Socialists. In January 1947 Socialist Vincent Auriol was chosen president; he appointed Socialist Paul Ramadier to head a new tripartite government in which Gouin served as minister of the four-year plan for economic recovery.

BIBLIOGRAPHY
Wegs, J. Robert, and Robert Ladrech. *Europe since 1945: A Concise History,* 4th ed. New York: St. Martin's Press, 1996.

Bernard Cook

SEE ALSO Blum, Léon

Grachev, Pavel (1948–)

Russian minister of defense and army commander from 1992 to July 1996. Pavel Grachev was born in the Tula region on January 1, 1948. He attended paratrooper school, joined the Communist Party, and became a battalion commander in Soviet Lithuania. He commanded a parachutist regiment in Afghanistan from 1981 to 1983, was made chief of staff of the Seventh Army in Lithuania from 1983 to 1985, and commanded a division in Afghanistan from 1985 to 1988. Grachev was the first deputy commander of Soviet parachute forces in 1990–91. He became first deputy minister of defense in 1991 and minister of defense in May 1992.

During the attempted coup against Soviet President Mikhail Gorbachev in August 1991, Grachev refused to fire on Boris Yeltsin and the supporters he had rallied at the Russian parliament (White House) to resist the coup. Yeltsin out of gratitude appointed him minister of defense. Nevertheless, when a clash between Yeltsin and his political opponents in the Russian parliament reached an absolute impasse in 1993 and they seemed ready to seize power, Grachev initially hesitated to order a military assault against the parliament. He was apparently persuaded to do so by General Aleksandr Korzhakov, Yeltsin's bodyguard and confidant.

Grachev was frustrated by the failure of several efforts to topple the separatist regime in Chechnya. Grachev pushed for a full-scale invasion of Chechnya and grossly underestimated the difficulty of the task. He continually downplayed Russian casualties in that war and was taken to task for his toleration of corruption in the military and for its disastrous performance in Chechnya.

In the June 1996 Russian presidential elections, the political independent and popular military officer Aleksander Lebed finished in third place in the first round, receiving 14.5 percent of the vote. To secure Lebed's support in the second round, Yeltsin appointed Lebed chairman of the Russian Security Council and agreed to dismiss Grachev, Lebed's main rival within the government.

Bernard Cook

SEE ALSO Chechnya: Russo-Chechen War

Grass, Günter (1927–)

Noted German novelist, winner of the Nobel Prize for Literature in 1999. Günter Grass was born and raised in a suburb of Danzig (now Gdansk, Poland), a city that played a prominent role in his writings, particularly the "Danzig trilogy" of books that made him famous: *Die Blechtrommel* (*The Tin Drum*), *Katz und Maus* (*Cat and Mouse*), and *Hundejahre* (*Dog Years*). Grass's father was a German Protestant grocer, and his mother was a Roman Catholic of Kashubian descent. As a matter of course Grass became a member of the Hitler Youth when he was fourteen, and in 1944 he began serving as a tank gunner on the eastern front. In 1945 he was wounded and eventually captured by the Americans. Grass's confrontation with his Nazi past began at a prisoner-of-war camp in Bavaria.

After the war he trained as a stone mason and sculptor, and he has maintained an interest in plastic and graphic arts throughout his life. Grass began his literary career as a lyric poet and dramatist in the mid-1950s, first gaining stature by participating in the famous group of postwar German writers known as Gruppe 47. The turning point in his career was clearly the success of *The Tin Drum*, which he completed in the spring of 1959. Told from the perspective of Oskar Matzerath, who as a three-year-old child in Danzig refuses to grow any more and communicates by banging on a toy drum, the picaresque novel recounts the National Socialist era by concentrating on the details of ordinary petit bourgeois life. As was to become a pattern with Grass's books, it was hailed by many as a monumental work of world literature, while others were outraged by its themes and shockingly grotesque passages. By all accounts, though, Oskar has established himself as an unforgettable character, made even more famous by Volker Schlöndorffs' Oscar-winning film adaptation (1979). *Cat and Mouse* (1961) and *Dog Years* (1963) were similarly both praised and vilified, but were ultimately clear successes.

During the early 1960s Grass began his political association with the Social Democratic Party (SPD) and with future Chancellor Willy Brandt. By the end of the decade Grass's literary work was turning to current political issues as well. The 1969 novel *Örtlich betäubt* (*Local Anesthetic*), for example, deals with the student protest movements of that era. *Aus dem Tagebuch einer Schnecke* (*From the Diary of a Snail*, 1972) describes the snail-like progress experienced in Brandt's campaign for chancellor in 1969. In 1986–87 Grass addressed another concern shared with Willy Brandt, the postcolonial Third World, by spending several months in the suburbs of Calcutta, India, and reporting on the experience in *Zunge zeigen* (*Show Your Tongue*).

Grass's later novels have remained politically topical but have returned to a somewhat broader scope. *Der Butt* (*The Flounder*, 1977) treats issues associated with feminism. *Die Rättin* (*The Rat*, 1986), which like *The Flounder* has strong fairy-tale elements and contains poems scattered throughout, presents an apocalyptic vision of nuclear or environmental disaster. *Unkenrufe* (*The Call of the Toad*, 1992) treats German-Polish relations. Grass's most recent novel, *Ein weites Feld* (*A Broad Field*, 1995), deals with German reunification. Both the novel and Grass's public comments on that topic have been typically controversial. Citing the memory of Auschwitz death camp, he called for a federation of the two states rather than a single enlarged republic.

BIBLIOGRAPHY

Hayman, Ronald. *Gunter Grass*. London: Methuen, 1985.

Hollington, Michael. *Gunter Grass: The Writer in a Pluralist Society*. London: Marion Boyars, 1980.

Keele, Alan Frank. *Understanding Gunter Grass*. Columbia: University of South Carolina Press, 1988.

Lawson, Richard H. *Günter Grass*. New York: Ungar, 1985.

O'Neill, Patrick, ed. *Critical Essays on Gunter Grass*. Boston: G.K. Hall, 1987.

———. *Gunter Grass Revisited*. New York: Twayne, 1999.

Thomas, Noel. *The Narrative Works of Gunter Grass: A Critical Interpretation*. Amsterdam: John Benjamins, 1983.

Robert Dewell

Greece

Country in southeastern Europe, officially known as the Hellenic Republic (*Elliniki Dimokratía*), occupying the southernmost part of the Balkan Peninsula. The Aegean, Mediterranean, and Ionian seas form the country's eastern, southern, and western borders. Greece has historically been poor and has endured periods of political instability throughout the twentieth century, but in the period after World War it has undergone rapid economic and social change.

Greece. *Illustration courtesy of Bernard Cook.*

Overview of Postwar History

The threat of civil war between nationalist and Communist undergrounds, a possibility in a number of countries during World War II, became reality in Greece.

When Italy invaded Greece from neighboring Albania in 1940, Great Britain came to Greece's assistance and sent troops there. Adolf Hitler, who had already decided to invade the USSR, believed that he needed to drive the British from Greece before advancing to the east. The Germans attacked Greece on April 6, 1941. Greek resistance collapsed on April 23, and the Greek king George II and his ministers fled into exile in Egypt along with the retreating British forces. The German occupation of Greece lasted three years. The Germans requisitioned resources and supplies with no concern for the fate of the Greek people, who, even in the best of times, were obliged to import most of their food. As a result, famine and disease decimated the country. The underground fought the Germans with sabotage and ambush and tied down perhaps 120,000 Axis troops. In reprisal the Germans and their Italian allies burned whole villages and executed as many as fifty Greek hostages for every one of their own killed. The largest Greek resistance movement was the National Liberation Front (EAM), with the National Popular Liberation Army (ELAS) as its military wing. As in Yugoslavia, the Communist-dominated EAM seemed to enjoy wider support than the nationalist underground and eventually held most of the country.

In October 1944, British Prime Minister Winston Churchill went to Moscow to confer with Soviet leader Josef Stalin. In his proposed Balkan settlement, accepted by the Soviet dictator, Britain was to have 90 percent predominance in Greece after the war. The Greek Communists understandably were unwilling to accept this arrangement.

When the Germans withdrew in October 1944, a new government of national unity was set up in Greece headed by George Papandreou, a left-of-center statesman. Fearing the Communist-dominated underground, however, he requested British troops, who began arriving in October 1944. When the British called on the guerrilla forces to disarm and disband, EAM deputies quit the cabinet, called a general strike, and held demonstrations. In this serious situation Churchill and Foreign Minister Anthony Eden visited Athens on Christmas Day 1944. Though the government and EAM reached accord early in 1945, it quickly broke down. EAM members took to the hills with their weapons.

In 1946 in Greece's first postwar elections the Royalist Peoples Party was victorious and consequently a royalist ministry was installed. A September 1946 plebiscite saw a majority vote for the king's return. George II, who was not popular in Greece, died the following April and was succeeded by his son Paul.

By the end of 1946 Communist rebels were ready for a comeback. Neighboring Communist Yugoslavia, Albania, and Bulgaria provided arms and sanctuaries. Some thirteen thousand Greek rebels were ably led by General Markos Vaphiades, who in late 1947 proclaimed the establishment of the First Provisional Democratic Government of Free Greece. Stalin, in fact, ordered Tito to halt aid to Markos, and Tito's failure to do so was one of the factors behind the 1948 Yugoslav break with the USSR. Despite Stalin's opposition (a result of his fear that a Communist victory might strengthen Tito in Yugoslavia), the Communists came close to winning in Greece.

That Greece, unlike its northern neighbors, did not become Communist was because of British and U.S. aid. London was determined that Greece, with its strategic control of the eastern Mediterranean, would not become Communist. But in February 1947, having spent $250 million to shore up the Greek loyalists and now deep in its own economic problems, Britain informed its American ally that it could no longer bear the burden. President Truman agreed to take over the responsibility, and Congress supported the March 1947 Truman Doctrine, appropriating $400 million for both Greece and Turkey. Ultimately the United States spent about $750 million in Greece on the final three years of the war. Over time,

Greek army commander General Alexander Papagos turned the military tide. Another important factor was Tito's defection from the Soviet bloc. He was forced to concentrate on resisting Soviet pressures, which cut off much of the Yugoslav supplies for the rebel cause. By the end of 1949 Communist rebels had been driven back into Albania and Bulgaria.

The cost of the civil war to Greece was as heavy as the years of World War II and Axis occupation. Thousands of hostages had been taken and disappeared, and a million Greeks had been uprooted and displaced by the fighting. Actual casualties may have been as high as half a million. After the war purges and bloodletting continued for some time.

In the March 1946 elections the center and conservative groups had won a two-thirds majority in parliament, but the Communists boycotted the proceedings. In the next years government leaders were drawn from the old order, and their overriding objective was to prevent any revival of Communist power. Basic reforms were sorely needed; had they been carried out, they might have weakened the Communist appeal, but little was done.

Thanks to the abolition of proportional representation, General Papagos's Greek Rally Party won an overwhelming victory in the 1952 national elections, gaining 239 seats to 61 for the opposition. During the three years of his strongman rule and the following eight years of his successor, Constantine Karamanlis, the government moved to deal with basic national problems, including the resistant vested interests, entangling red tape of an entrenched bureaucracy, and chronic corruption in high places.

Karamanlis, premier from 1955 to 1963, was a competent economist, and the United States provided some $3 billion in aid by 1962. Few countries are as deficient in natural resources as Greece. The majority of the population was rural, and agricultural products made up the bulk of exports, yet only 27 percent of the land was cultivable. American technical assistance and a five-year plan increased production and made food imports unnecessary. Although Greece lacks most minerals, plans targeted new industries: sugar refineries; food and fruit processing; shipyards; and bauxite, steel, and aluminum plants. The return of tourism was an economic boost and new roads were built to carry the tourist trade. Another boon came in 1966 with associate membership in the European Common Market (EC).

In 1963 Karamanlis suddenly resigned in a dispute with King Paul over the crown's powers. The preceding elections had been fought between the National Radical Union (NRU), the former Greek Rally headed by Kara-manlis, and, to its left, the Progressive Center Union (EPEK) of the now aging George Papandreou. The EPEK tended toward neutralism. Although the Communist Party had been outlawed since 1947, it supported a third grouping, the Union of the Democratic Left. In the 1963 elections the government coalition lost by a narrow margin.

Papandreou now became premier and abruptly called for new elections. Held in 1964, these gave him a majority of 175 seats to 105 for the NRU and 22 for the Democratic Left. Karamanlis promptly went into self-imposed exile. In 1965 an apparently solid majority crumbled when Papandreou tried to dismiss some right-wing army officers, only to meet the opposition of twenty-year-old Constantine II, who had succeeded his father, Paul I, in March 1964. Soon thereafter Papandreou collided directly with the king over the Aspida (Shield), a secret society of leftist officers stationed in Cyprus and allegedly led by Andreas Papandreou, son of the premier. When Constantine insisted on a full-scale investigation, Papandreou resigned. A government crisis of several months ensued in which Papandreou and his followers took to the streets. Demonstrations and rallies failed to budge Constantine, but his intervention in politics had raised the question of the role of the monarchy.

Finally some members of the Papandreou coalition broke off. Supported by the right, they formed a ministry led by Stephanos Stephanopoulis. However, Papandreou's EPEK was expected to win the May 1967 parliamentary elections. All through the 1960s Greek liberal and radical forces had been growing increasingly restive. George Papandreou had hoped to climax his stormy political career by extensive reform. His planned shake-up of senior ranks in the army while he had been premier was designed to make this possible. With a EPEK victory iminent, the generals struck first. To some observers it was a classic case of reckless leftists led by Papandreou provoking equally reckless rightist army leaders. But many liberals saw it as a classic case of the military using a Red scare to prevent necessary economic and social reforms in a developing country.

Ironically, the brilliantly executed coup (later well documented in the film *Z*) used a plan, Prometheus, that had been held in secret reserve by NATO to thwart a possible Communist takeover. The so-called Spring Cleaning that followed the coup was thorough. Hundreds of liberal and radical leaders were rounded up and jailed. George Papandreou was arrested and Andreas, who was then in the United States, was condemned in absentia. The military junta sharply curtailed both freedom of press and assembly, and it abolished parliament until "stability had been restored."

The new regime was sharply puritanical. There was stern censorship of exhibitions, plays, and music. Melina Mercouri, the popular actress who was also in the United States at the time of the coup, denounced the dictatorship and was stripped of her citizenship. The junta banned the music of Mikis Theodorakis, who had composed the scores for *Zorba the Greek* and *Z,* and prohibited miniskirts and frowned on long hair. When George Papandreou died, forty demonstrators at his funeral were arrested and given long prison terms. In fact the ESA, the military police, arrested thousands of political opponents and shipped them to various Greek islands.

King Constantine had opposed Papandreou's projected reforms because he thought they went too far, but he was equally opposed to the junta and the way it had seized power. In December 1967 he too tried a coup, but his efforts to win over part of the army leaked out or were betrayed to the junta, and his radio broadcast to the Greek people was jammed. To escape capture, he and his family flew to Rome.

Premier George Papadopoulos, the junta's strongman, sponsored a new constitution. Promulgated in 1968, it reduced the power of the crown (a regent had been named for Constantine) and strengthened the executive at the expense of parliament. It was approved in a managed election by a 92 percent vote.

The European democracies sharply criticized the junta, and the Council of Europe undertook an investigation of torture by the Athens government. The junta responded in 1969 by withdrawing from that body. More harmful was the expulsion of Greece from associate membership in the Common Market, which cost the country some $300 million in agricultural benefits.

The junta leadership took all this in stride, reasoning that as soon as there was another threat to NATO, the Americans would beg Greece to accept aid. Indeed, when the USSR built up its strength in the eastern Mediterranean, President Richard Nixon authorized the shipment to Greece of small arms and trucks, although jets and tanks remained embargoed. When there was an outcry in the United States over this support of the Greek dictatorship, the junta in 1971 authorized the return to Cyprus of Cypriot firebrand General Georgios Grivas, who had fought against the Germans, been invaluable in the struggle against the Communists during the civil war, and waged bloody guerrilla warfare against the British on Cyprus. The implication was that without U.S. financial assistance there would be no peace on Cyprus. Greece was a dictatorship but it was extraordinarily important to

NATO and the security of the eastern Mediterranean, and Washington tried to play for time.

Mounting opposition and economic problems forced Papadopoulos to relax slightly the repressive nature of the regime, and in 1973 he hinted at the possibility of elections the next year. Perhaps this slight shift was responsible for student riots in November 1973. Workers joined in and thousands of Greeks were arrested. These first extensive riots since the junta came to power led to a government reshuffle. General Phaidon Gizikis replaced Papadopoulos as president and General Demetrios Ioannides became the key figure in the regime. The junta seemed more firmly entrenched than ever, that is, until unexpected developments from Cyprus.

Cyprus, only forty miles south of Anatolia, is much closer to Turkey than to Greece. Acquired by Britain from Turkey in 1878, it was formally annexed by the United Kingdom in 1914, and until 1959 was part of the British Commonwealth of Nations. Its half million inhabitants were about 80 percent Greek and 20 percent Turkish, and the history of the island was one long record of friction. Its villages were so intermingled that partition did not appear to be a practical solution. For Greek Cypriots the objective was *enosis,* (union) with Greece. The Turkish Cypriots, who had suffered greatly as a minority, vowed to resist to the end any such union, and Turkey sided with them.

In 1963 violence on Cyprus almost led to war, and Turkish aircraft actually strafed Greek Cypriot positions. Despite U.N. efforts at mediation, resentment boiled over again in 1967 when the Greek Orthodox primate and the island's president, Archbishop Makarios, tried to eliminate the Turkish veto. Full-scale war threatened and there were violent outbreaks and deaths. Turkey then mobilized. U.S. President Lyndon Johnson, trying to avoid a disastrous conflict between two NATO allies, sent U.S. Deputy Secretary of Defense Cyrus Vance to the area. As a result, Athens pledged that there would be an end even to indirect activity to achieve *enosis.* Makarios was probably relieved by this outcome because it was apparent he was becoming reconciled to a separate republic. By 1972 he had become militantly Cypriot and resented the slightest Greek intrusion.

This was the situation when in July 1974 there was an uprising on the island. Greek Cypriots, with the encouragement and aid of the Athens Junta, attempted to seize control and oust Makarios. In August a substantial Turkish force landed and easily defeated the Greek Cypriot national guard. They took some 30 percent of the land in the north and expelled the Greeks from it. In 1999 the Cyprus situation remained frozen, with the island divided along a line that ran through the center of Nicosia. Turkey ultimately stationed some twenty-five thousand troops on the island and proclaimed a Turkish Cypriot state, which the United Nation refused to recognize. Athens said it would never agree to partition. The two sides are separated and kept apart by some two thousand U.N. peacekeeping troops.

The Turkish success led to the collapse of the junta in Athens. The junta expected a groundswell of support for an even more militantly hard-line government, which is why it had fished in troubled waters. To the surprise of the generals, however, there was little enthusiasm in Greece for war with Turkey, and discontent over the years of military rule now surfaced. Shaken by this, the junta then withdrew its support from the Greeks on Cyprus. This further discredited the generals, and in August 1975 the junta collapsed.

Konstantinos Karamanlis, the one Greek leader capable of stabilizing the situation, now returned from exile in Paris. When he had been premier, Greece had made significant gains. Cyprus gained its independence from Great Britain and there was rapid economic development in Greece. Karamanlis was a left-of-center moderate reformer; as he put it, his policy was "to pursue a left-wing policy with a right-wing government." In October 1974 Karamanlis lifted a twenty-seven-year ban on Communist Party activity and announced his intention to punish the junta "traitors." A December election saw him emerge with a clear mandate. A referendum on the monarchy, however, dealt a setback to King Constantine; by a two-to-one majority Greeks rejected his bid to return to the throne.

Difficult problems lay ahead for Karamanlis, however. In 1974 inflation was running at 32 percent and Greece had a $1.2 billion deficit in its balance of payments. Relations with the United States were also at a new low. Many Greeks blamed Washington for having known about the 1967 coup in advance and not having done anything about it, and they were angry over U.S. support for the junta. There was also Cyprus. Choosing not to remember their own role in triggering the Turkish invasion, Greeks blamed the United States for failing to restrain Turkey and not forcing the Turks to remove their troops. Greek resentment toward the United States took the form of pressure on the four U.S. military bases in Greece. In 1974 Greece also withdrew its force of 120,000 men and 160 jet fighters from the NATO military command, although it did not withdraw from NATO itself. In October 1980, after a six-year absence, Greece returned to the NATO military command structure, and the United States has sought to adhere to a ten-seven ratio in Greek-Turkish military assistance.

Karamanlis also faced problems with the military. In February 1975 the government announced the arrest of thirty top officers on charges of plotting a coup. Despite these economic and political problems, Karamanlis established Greek democracy on a firm footing. There was a smooth transition when in the October 1981 national elections, Andreas Papandreou's Panhellenic Socialist Movement (PASOK) won a decisive victory, and Papandreou became the first Socialist premier in Greek history. He had attacked his predecessor as too servile to the United States and for failing to resolve the impasse over Cyprus. Papandreou, a Harvard-educated economist and one-time U.S. citizen, came to power on promises of "socialization"; pressure on the West to resolve the Cyprus impasse; loosening Greek ties with NATO and the EC, which Greece had joined under Karamanlis in 1981; and closing U.S. military bases. But much of his support had come from those who desired change rather than from those attached to any particular program. With 172 of the 300 seats in parliament, PASOK had the necessary majority to carry out its program. However, the sheer scale of Greece's economic problems forced Papandreou to go slowly with socialism. Wage and welfare increases added to the high rate of inflation, and Papandreou then shifted to a pragmatic economic program that emphasized recovery rather than social welfare.

Papandreou's threats to withdraw Greece from NATO were not carried out because the United States would then have had to strengthen Turkey, and this would put additional pressure on Greeks in Cyprus. Still, relations with the United States were severely strained. Although Papandreou signed a new base lease arrangement with Washington in 1983, in August 1984 Greece abruptly canceled joint military maneuvers and announced that no American troops would be allowed to take part in future military maneuvers on Greek soil.

After two election victories and eight years in power, Papandreou came under attack for corruption involving high government officials. He had undergone open-heart surgery in 1988 and there were attacks on his judgment, the result of an affair between the sixty-eight-year-old premier and a thirty-three-year-old flight attendant. In addition, Papandreou had estranged Greece from its European partners by flirting with Cuba and Libya. In the June 1989 election Papandreou's PASOK retained only 125 of 300 seats, while his main opponent, the center-right New Democratic Party, led by Konstantinos Mitsotakis, took 145.

Mitsotakis had fought the Germans in World War II and was elected to parliament in 1946. Critical of George Papandreou's policies, he had withdrawn from the government in 1965. Leftists charged that this had started a period of instability that led to the 1967 military coup. Mitsotakis had been detained briefly after the coup and then went abroad. He returned as a cabinet minister in the Karamanlis government, and in 1984 became leader of New Democracy.

Following the 1989 election, the Communist-dominated Coalition of the Left and Progress with 29 seats was in a position to broker power. Mitsotakis formed a coalition government with the Communists but this soon fell apart. New elections in November were inconclusive. With 148 seats, New Democracy fell 3 seats short of a working majority. The Socialists (PASOK) had 128 and the remaining 22 went to the Communist coalition and independents. Mitsotakis then formed a coalition of all parties, but it too did not last. In April 1990 new national elections were held, the third in ten months. This time Mitsotakis's New Democracy won 150 seats and PASOK 123. With the support of one independent, Mitsotakis had his majority to govern. He set as his principal task improving Greece's international image. But in September 1993 Mitsotakis was forced to call early elections when his protégé, Foreign Minister Antonis Samarus, led a parliamentary revolt.

In the ensuing October 1993 elections Papandreou's PASOK scored a stunning upset, capturing 170 seats in the 300-member parliament. Now married to his former mistress, Papandreou changed course, adopting Mitsotakis's rigorous program of fiscal austerity and pursuing a more conciliatory approach in foreign policy. His health took a serious turn for the worse, however, and in November 1995 he was confined to a hospital for lung and kidney ailments. In January 1996 Papandreou finally resigned as premier. The PASOK chose one of his chief critics, Costas Simitis, as his successor. Greek politics now seemed ready to move into a new era of less contentious relations with Western Europe.

But relations with Turkey remained seriously strained. The two countries nearly went to war in 1987 over Aegean seabed mineral rights, and in January 1996 they again threatened war over the tiny uninhabited island of Imia (known as Karnak to Turks) in the eastern Aegean Sea four miles off the Turkish coast. This rising tension at a time of political uncertainty in both countries raised fears of miscalculation that could have led to war. However, U.S. pressure helped to defuse the crisis. In August 1996 Greek relations with Turkey again deteriorated after two Greek demonstrators trying to cross the dividing line

between the Republic of Cyprus and the Turkish Republic of North Cyprus were killed. Simitis went to Cyprus and, pledging continued Greek military support, joined the Cypriot President Glafcos Clerides in a declaration that any further Turkish encroachment on the island would mean war. In 1997 tensions over the island increased. When Turkey issued threats against a proposed purchase of ground to air missiles by Cyprus from Russia, Greece said that any preemptive strike by Turkey would lead to a Greek declaration of war. Tensions were later somewhat eased when Simitis engaged in talks with President Suleyman Demirel of Turkey during a NATO summit in July, but the problem of Cyprus remained an impediment to better Greek-Turkish relations at the end of the century.

BIBLIOGRAPHY
Clogg, Richard. *A Short History of Modern Greece,* 2d ed. New York: Cambridge University Press, 1986.
Dobratz, Betty A. *A Profile of Modern Greece: In Search of Identity.* New York: Oxford University Press, 1988.
Legg, Keith R. *Modern Greece.* Boulder, Colo.: Westview Press, 1995.

Spencer Tucker

Aspida Affair

Scandal linked to the discovery of a secret association within the Greek army officer corps. This association was portrayed by right-wing military and political circles as a subversive organization whose goals were to weaken the armed forces, overthrow the existing government, and install a "socialist-neutralist" dictatorship. The ASPIDA affair was the direct outgrowth of a largely subterranean struggle over political control of the armed forces, and was initiated and sustained to discredit the main center-left political party.

In early 1965 General Georgios Grivas, former leader of the paramilitary right-wing Organization X and the Cypriot guerrilla group National Organization of Cypriot Fighters (Ethnike Organosis Kyprion Agoniston, EOKA), who was subsequently appointed as military commander of the Greek forces on Cyprus, wrote letters to King Constantine and Defense Minister Petros Garouphalias to warn them about the potential threat posed by a secret "leftist" society that had been established within the officer corps in the fall of 1964. This organization, whose acronym was the Greek word for "shield," was officially known as "Officers, Save Fatherland, Ideals, Democracy, and Meritocracy" (Axiomatikoi Sosate Patrida Idanika Demokratia Axiokratia). In his letters Grivas identified the leader of Aspida on Cyprus as Captain Aristodemos

Bouloukos, a former member of X. Grivas then quoted directly from the secret oath taken by Aspida members, which required them to promote a Greater Greece, protect the nation from external enemies and internal Communist subversion, defend Greek democracy, do whatever was necessary to promote meritocratic procedures, and offer "blind and unlimited obedience" to Aspida, the "only carrier of legal authority" in the event that it became necessary to act. Although Grivas did not recommend that any action be taken against ASPIDA members, he strongly implied that Andreas Papandreou, son of Prime Minister George Papandreou, leader of the center-left Center Union (Enosis Kentron, EK) Party, was one of the secret leaders of the organization. In May Colonel Giorgios Papadopoulos, a key figure the Central Intelligence Service (Kentrike Yperesia Plerophorion, KYP), falsely claimed to have uncovered a Communist conspiracy to sabotage the Twelfth Infantry Division's military vehicles in Evros, a sensational charge linked by the rightist press to the earlier revelations about Aspida.

Political pressures thence constrained George Papandreou to authorize an investigation of ASPIDA, which he assigned to a royalist opponent of EK, Lieutenant General Ioannis Simas. Simas concluded that Grivas's charges had been exaggerated, since Aspida was an association consisting of only two dozen officers out of an officer corps totaling ten thousand, and there was no evidence indicating that any political figures were behind it. He therefore advocated only light disciplinary penalties for six of its members, but King Constantine at once demanded that the matter be investigated officially by a military court of inquiry. The fallout from this affair, which brought about a political confrontation between the prime minister and the king after the former attempted to replace Garouphalias and further investigate the illegal rightist "Perikles Plan" to influence the 1961 elections, ultimately led to George Papandreou's resignation in July.

In October 1966 the preliminary investigative report on Aspida was released. It had been prepared by Colonel Laganis, a member of the Sacred Bond of Greek Officers (Ieros Desmos Ellenon Axiomatikon, IDEA), a right-wing secret society within the officer corps with which Papadopoulos had long been associated. The report named Bouloukos and twenty-five other junior officers as members of the organization and identified one of the three senior ringleaders as KYP Deputy Director Colonel Alexandros Papaterpos. Papaterpos, on whose personal staff Bouloukos had previously served, was an opponent of IDEA and a George Papandreou appointee who had headed the commission investigating the Perikles Plan. These men were then arrested, charged with forming a subversive association and treasonably conspiring against the government, and remanded for court-martial. The most sensational and unsubstantiated of Laganis's claims were that Andreas Papandreou and other leading members of the EK secretly directed the organization, and that George Papandreou had sought to cover up his son's role in it. Although the evidence cited to buttress these accusations was based almost entirely on hearsay testimony obtained fraudulently from untrustworthy witnesses, the king pressured the new conservative government to bring the case to trial on November 14. Although the trial proceedings increasingly exposed the flimsiness of the prosecution's case, in February 1967 chief prosecutor Konstantinos Kollias sought to have Andreas Papandreou's parliamentary immunity lifted so that he too could be formally brought to trial, a request rejected by a parliamentary legal commission on March 15. The very next day the court sentenced fifteen members of Aspida, including Papaterpos, to jail terms ranging from two to eighteen years, but they were all granted amnesty and released in the wake of the military takeover on April 21, 1967. The Colonels' uncharacteristic leniency in this matter may have been due to their pressing need to heal rifts within the armed forces, but it also raises the suspicion that at least some members of Aspida may have secretly worked for rightist circles linked to Papadopoulos all along.

Although Aspida certainly had unconstitutional features, in retrospect it seems clear that the group's primary goals were to promote meritocratic advancement within the officer corps and serve as an organizational counterweight to the far more powerful rightist secret associations that operated within the armed forces, in particular IDEA and the Greek Union of Young Officers (Ellenike Enosis Neon Axiomatikon, EENA), which Papadopoulos himself had founded in 1956. This second objective coincided perfectly with the designs of the Papandreous, who sought whenever possible to replace rightist officers in key positions with their own supporters. Nevertheless, Aspida's political significance was due not so much to its own actions as to its secretive existence, which was exploited by the right to undermine parliamentary democracy, thereby laying the groundwork for the EENA-sponsored military coup of April 1967. Not coincidentally, several of the individuals involved in fanning hysteria about the subversive threat allegedly posed by Aspida were among the chief beneficiaries of that putsch.

BIBLIOGRAPHY

Bouloukos, Aris G. *Hypotheses ASPIDA: He aletheia pou kaiei.* Athens: A.E. Typos, 1989.

Chrondokoukes, Demestres. *Hoi anentimoi kai ho "ASPIDA."* Athens: Kedros, 1976.

Karagiorgas, Giorgios. *Apo ton IDEA ste chounta.* Athens: Papazeses, 1975.

Katris, John A. *Eyewitness in Greece: The Colonels Come to Power.* St. Louis: New Critics, 1971.

Papandreou, Andreas. *Democracy at Gunpoint: The Greek Front.* Garden City, N.Y.: Doubleday, 1970.

Papandreou, Margarita. *Nightmare in Athens.* Englewood Cliffs, N.J.: Prentice-Hall, 1970.

Paralikas, Demetrios K. *To alethino prosopo tou I.D.E.A. kai tou A.S.P.I.D.A., 1944–1974.* Athens: Gramme, 1978.

Stavrou, Nikolaos A. *Allied Politics and Military Intervention: The Political Role of the Greek Military.* Athens: Papazeses, 1977.

Jeffrey M. Bale

SEE ALSO Papandreou, Andreas; Papandreou, Georgios

Cinema

Greek cinema barely existed before World War II and then got off to a late start in the 1950s because of the Greek civil war that ended in 1949–50 but whose effects lasted much longer. The late 1950s, however, saw the birth of a vibrant "studio" film industry as newly formed studios such as Finos Films discovered that there was a great demand for Greek-language light romantic comedies and village melodramas throughout the country, especially in small towns and on isolated islands. Thus from around 1959 to 1969 a country of fewer than nine million people was producing roughly 150 feature films a year, which was not far beyond Hollywood's production for the same period. During the 1960s Greece was one of the most movie-attending nations anywhere, for Athens alone had over six hundred cinemas at its peak, and it was not unusual for many Athenians to attend four or five films a week. Much admired and loved stars emerged in these films, coming for the most part from the Greek stage and the Greek version of vaudeville called the *epitheorisis*. Ali Vouyouklaki managed to be both a Greek Brigitte Bardot and Jane Fonda rolled into one, and a whole series of Greek male comedians such as Dinos Eliopolis but especially Thanasis Vengos drew enthusiastic crowds for freewheeling satirical comedies that film historians will surely find have echoes of Aristophanes and ancient satirical farce.

Cinema as a serious art form was slow to develop in Greece, in part because of the heavy dominance of the literary tradition from Homer on down to Nikos Kazantzakis. But Cypriot-born theater and film director Michael Cacoyannis changed all that, managing to combine his love of ancient tragedy, particularly Euripides, with clear-sighted realism influenced by Italian neorealist films of the late 1940s and early 1950s. Cacoyannis was blessed with powerful actresses whose cinematic careers he launched including the late Melina Mercouri (*Stella,* 1955), Elli Lambeti (*A Girl in Black,* 1956), and Irene Pappas, who became internationally known in Cacoyannis's excellent screen adaptations of Euripides' tragedies: *Electra* (1962), *The Trojan Women* (1975), and *Iphigenia* (1976). But it was Cacoyannis's adaptation of Nikos Kazantzakis's feisty novel, *Zorba the Greek* (1962), with Antony Quinn in the lead role, made with American studio money, that won him a major world audience.

Ironically a "New Wave" of younger directors brought up on the French New Wave, Hollywood, and world cinema including Russian and East European models came into its own during the junta dictatorship of 1967–75. Some were graduates of the Greek film school—the Stavrakos Film School—but others studied abroad and returned home, including the best known of the group, Theo Angelopoulos, who finished his studies in France.

Angelopoulos focused on presenting what he calls "the other Greece," that part of Greek history, including the Greek civil war of 1945–49, and culture, especially the areas of northern Greece that border other Balkan countries, that has not been "told." His third feature, *The Traveling Players* (1975), focused on Greek history from 1937 to 1952, blending ancient myth and tragedy to become a film at the time seen by more Greeks than any other Greek film and to win countless film festival awards, including a British Academy Film Award as "The Most Important Film in the World for the 1970's." With Angelopoulos, Cacoyannis, and a handful of other directors including Tania Marketaki, Pandelis Voulgaris, and Nikos Kounderos, Greek cinema came of age and began to be taken seriously at festivals and by audiences around the world.

Yet the Greek film industry virtually dried up as television took over during the 1970s. Cinemas have closed, video shops opened, and television channels multiplied, leaving film production to basically a few art films supported, in part or wholly, by the Greek Film Centre, a state-funded agency. Attention continues to be called to Greek films through two important festivals, the Thessaloniki film Festival in October for feature films and the International Festival of Short Film in Drama, a northern Greek city, in September.

BIBLIOGRAPHY

Georgakas, Dan. "Greek Cinema," in William Luhr, ed., *World Cinema Since 1945.* New York: Fredrick Ungar, 1987.

Horton, Andrew. "Theodor Angelopulos and the New Greek Cinema." *Film Criticism* 6 (Fall 1981).

Slide, Anthony, ed. *The International Film Industry: A Historical Dictionary.* New York: Greenwood Press, 1989.

Andrew Horton

Civil War, 1944–49

Greece was the only country in Europe where communism tried to assume the reigns of power through armed struggle after the end of World War II. While Western Europe was making strides toward economic and social recuperation, Greece was embroiled in a bloody civil war that would scar Greek society and stifle economic progress for years to come.

There were three successive attempts by the Greek Communist Party (KKE) to overthrow republican Greek governments. The first occurred during the occupation of the Axis forces in 1943–44, in anticipation of an early end to the war. The second attempt erupted in Athens in December 1944, and the final, and longest, effort, which would also end Communist aspirations to power, lasted from 1946 to 1949.

The KKE was formed in November 1918 and was at first known as the Socialist Labor Party of Greece. In 1924 it adopted the name Kommounistiko Komma Ellados (KKE). In 1920 the KKE became a member of the Comintern, the Soviet Communist International, and followed the official policy as dictated by Moscow. The leader of the KKE, Nicholas Zakhariades, was nominated secretary by the Comintern in 1921.

At first the members of this small organization were intellectuals and students inspired by the success of the Russian Revolution. Following the Marxist-Leninist line, the party looked for support from workers rather than farmers and peasants.

In the Balkans, particularly in Greece and Yugoslavia, the task of creating proper political conditions for the eventual showdown with Britain was entrusted by the Soviet leadership to the underground movements of national resistance. The British, who had sent support to Greece when it was invaded by Germany in 1941 and maintained contacts with the anti-German resistance in Yugoslavia, were particularly interested in Greece because of its strategic position across from the Suez Canal, Britain's lifeline to India. The German conquest had destroyed the prewar political framework and opened the way to the formation of new political forces. Communist parties were able to achieve political predominance by leading the virtually headless nations in their struggle against the conqueror and, thus, emerging in the postwar period as the most powerful political and military organizations. In turn, they hoped to impose their political system and help advance the Soviet ideological and political principles to the Aegean shores. Should this fail, the Soviet Union would use the Communist position to manipulate other Allied powers to make concessions in other contested areas.

The surrender of the Italian occupation army in Greece on September 8, 1943, deeply affected the balance of forces in the country. The army of the Communist guerrilla movement (ELAS) had detachments in most parts of the country and obtained most of the Italian military equipment. This made up for the suspension of supplies by the Allied Military Mission, which realized the potential of a hostile conflict between ELAS and the anti-Communist Greek National Republican League (EDES). Early in October 1943 the reinforced ELAS army openly attacked EDES forces in Epirus in a last attempt to eliminate the only significant armed opposition to their objective. Their attempt was unsuccessful, initiating the race for supremacy between the two opposing political and military factions. In February 1944 an uneasy truce was signed by ELAS and EDES at Placa, by giving ELAS control of the entire countryside while EDES maintained control of a small area in Epirus.

In May of the same year, a conference of the representatives of all Greek political parties, including the Greek Liberation Front (EAM)–ELAS, convened in Lebanon. The conferees decided on the formation of a Government of National Unity, reorganization of the Greek armed forces in the Middle East, unification of the resistance organizations under the command of the Government of National Unity, and official condemnation of all terrorist activities of underground organizations in Greece. Shortly after the agreement EAM made new demands following accusations by British Prime Minister Winston Churchill that EAM bore the responsibility for the failure to bring about unity in Greek politics.

In September, in a final effort to forestall the gradual occupation of the country by EAM-ELAS, Premier George Papandreou summoned General Napoleon Zervas, chief of EDES, and General Stefanos Sarafis, military head of ELAS, to find a solution to the dangerous divide. The agreement was not a comforting one for EAM-ELAS. It placed the guerrilla forces under the command of the Greek government, which in turn delegated authority to British General Ronald Scobie. By December 1944 the political situation in Greece was explosive, as EAM reacted strongly to government efforts to contain the influence of EAM-ELAS and restrict their wartime gains. A revolt broke out on December 3, 1944, when ELAS guerrillas attempted to seize Athens. This effort failed because of the staunch resistance of the British and Greek troops. Following the failed armed revolt, EAM-ELAS agreed to a truce on January 15, 1945, by signing the Varkiza agreement. The armistice placed stringent stipulations on EAM-ELAS, guaranteeing its failure.

In June 1945 Zakhariades returned to Greece from the German concentration camps where he had been held prisoner and resumed his former position as secretary-general of the KKE. His return sparked anew the effort by the Communists to seize a political role. The preparations of the "third round," as the Communists called their third attempt, started in the spring of 1945. By December riots under Zakhariades's direction were instigated in Salonika, Volos, Kavalla, Kalamata, and other Greek cities. The third round was based mainly on the reorganization of an insurgent army that was to fight the Greek government. Yugoslavia promised massive material aid, and it was hoped that the Soviet Union would help materially too. At first this force was known as the Republican Army, and it was not until a year later that the title Democratic Army was adopted. Markos Vaphiadis was to take control of the Democratic Army and organize it properly. He arrived at Bulkes, Yugoslavia, and assumed command.

The actual material aid given to the Democratic Army in the first place was small and restricted mainly to food, but its unlimited freedom to move unhampered across the Albanian border into Greece and back again to security whenever harried by the Greek National Guard was of inestimable value. Bulgaria also gave the Democratic Army a little material aid. Like Tito, Georgi Dimitrov was a nationalist as well as a Communist, and he did not exclude the possibility that Thrace, which was taken from the Bulgarians at the end of World War I, might one day merge with Bulgaria. Both Yugoslavia and Bulgaria would have liked an outlet to the Aegean Sea. By the end of 1946 Albania, Yugoslavia, and Bulgaria were all Communist in principle and practice. They signed bilateral agreements of friendship, and economic and mutual aid, and thus were an ominous, unfriendly block to the north of Greece. Foreign help for the KKE came mainly from Yugoslavia but was provided only at a cost. Markos had agreed, despite staunch opposition from the political branch of the KKE, to turn over territory to the three northern supporting neighbors if the Communists succeeded in assuming power in Greece.

The Greek political scene was not any better than the military situation. In December 1946, George Papandreou, Sophoklis Venizelos, and Panayiotis Kanellopoulos agreed to enter a coalition on the condition that Britain would provide more arms. The political imbroglio, combined with the low moral and disorganization in the armed forces, created a state of despair in the country. Accentuating the situation was the death of George II in April 1947.

The dramatic situation was quickly alleviated when President Truman pledged to assist Greece in maintaining its democratic institutions and assist the Greek government in the war against the Communist guerrillas. The Truman Doctrine and American involvement in the Greek civil war brought new hope to a struggling government and demoralized army. In the meantime KKE leaders were now ready to proclaim a Communist government. Markos was appointed prime minister and minister of defense, while an additional eight members completed his cabinet. Zakhariades, secretary-general of the KKE and the top man in the Greek Communist hierarchy, was not included in the new "government," preferring to remain in the background.

During 1947 Democratic Army units dominated large areas of Greece but had failed to seize major towns. The Greek National Army (GNA) went on the offensive in 1948 determined to stifle Communist resistance enclaves. With the military supplies provided by the American aid mission to Greece and the counseling and training by American military specialists, the GNA was able to claim victory in the fall of 1949. The success of the army can be attributed to the GNA's strategy during its campaign, systematically clearing areas of the Communist threat first by relocating part of the population so that the communist army was deprived of information and supplies from sympathizers. This together with the defection of Yugoslavia from Moscow's orbit and the gradual closing of its frontiers to the guerrillas led to the Communist defeat.

The closing of the Greek-Yugoslav border was the outcome of the decision made by Greek Communist leaders to support Moscow in the Tito-Stalin split. General Markos favored Tito's nationalist line, while Zakhariades was known to be a supporter of the USSR. As a result, Tito began slowly but progressively to reduce his assistance to the Democratic Army. In the Markos/Zakhariades dispute, General Markos was dismissed from his position and Zakhariades himself took command of the Democratic Army. He then switched from guerrilla to conventional warfare, exposing the few available forces to the GNA and the air force. The final closing of the Yugoslav border on July 10 was the final blow to the Communists, who three months later decided on a cease-fire.

The civil war had been successfully won by General Papagos and the Greek National Army at a dear cost in human lives and material resources. Moreover, Greece did not make the significant progress that other European nations had achieved through the U.S.-provided Marshall Plan aid. The civil war left a deep scar on Greek society, dividing families and communities, and accentuating the poverty and devastation that World War II had inflicted.

BIBLIOGRAPHY

Close, David. *The Origins of the Greek Civil War*. New York: Longman, 1995.

O'Ballance, Edgar. *The Greek Civil War, 1944–1949*. New York: Praeger, 1966.

Vlavianos, Haris. *Greece, 1941–49: From Resistance to Civil War: the Strategy of the Greek Communist Party.* New York: St. Martin's Press, 1992.

Stelios Zachariou

SEE ALSO Truman Doctrine

Economy

Greece was predominantly a poor agricultural economy with high levels of emigration for most of the period after it gained independence from the Ottoman Empire in 1830. It did not experience meaningful economic development until after World War II and the related Greek civil war of 1946–49. Externally financed by U.S. Marshall Plan and other economic aid during the 1950s and 1960s, the Greek economy then underwent high economic growth, based on the modernization of its agricultural sector, rapid urbanization, and limited industrialization, and an exponential expansion of service sectors led by shipping and mass tourism. Although aborted by the colonels military junta of 1967–74, full membership in the European Economic Community (EC/EU) was agreed to in principle as early as 1961, though it did not come about for political reasons until 1981. As one of the poorest of the EC countries, Greece has greatly benefited from large financial transfers from Brussels over the last fifteen years. On a more negative note, the survival of statist and isolationist economic policies under successive Greek governments of both the Left and the Right meant that the country's economic performance was less than optimal during the 1980s and 1990s. Only by the mid-1990s did meaningful economic reform begin in Greece, mainly under pressure from its richer partners and creditors in the EU. Assuming that these ongoing reforms are successful, then Greece could enter full European Monetary Union (EMU) by around 2002.

At $85.5 billion in 1997, nominal Greek GDP then produced a GDP per capita of $8,500. Greek GDP per capita is still well below the all-Union average and toward the bottom of the income scale in the EU. Very low or even negative at times during most of the 1980s and 1990s, real GDP growth began to take off only in 1995, reaching 2.6 percent in 1996 and a record 3.1 percent in 1997. Negative until as recently as 1994, gross fixed investment reached a record annual growth rate of 11.7 percent in 1997.

On a more negative note, new investment remained relatively low at only 21 percent of GDP in 1997. In recent years savings ratios have been low in Greece, where private consumption accounted for a very high 74 percent of GDP in 1997. Because of ongoing rigidities in the Greek labor market and a still economically significant state sector, new job creation remains low or highly seasonal, as in the tourism services sector. At 10.2 percent of the working population in 1997, unemployment was relatively high and likely to increase still further in line with the privatization and restructuring of the over-manned state sector. In contrast to richer EU countries, welfare provision in Greece is basic and often highly inadequate.

Although still relatively significant at 11 percent of GDP in 1997, agricultural output was declining, mainly because many of its key products were produced to excess in the EU. Accounting for a relatively low 14.5 percent of GDP, or about half the EU average, industrial output increased by only 0.8 percent in 1997. Only partially industrialized in the pastwar period, Greece's limited industrial sector sharply declined during the 1980s and 1990s, mainly owing to low investment, poor profitability arising from price controls, and increased import penetration and competition after entry into the EU in 1981. Direct foreign investment (DFI) has also been low in Greece in recent years. Economically central at over 50 percent of GDP in 1997, services of all types are now the real motor of the Greek economy. Accounting for 15 percent of GDP in 1997, tourism then earned $7.5 billion, based on eleven million visitor arrivals from the rest of the EU. In 1997 the second-largest service sector, shipping, earned Greece around $2.5 billion. At around $1.5 billion in 1997, émigré hard currency remittances remain significant for Greece, which has a larger émigré diaspora than its current population of 10.2 million. In 1997 the fastest-growing domestic service sector was construction, based on ambitious infrastructure development financed principally by the EU.

As recently as 1992, the state sector generated as much as 60 percent of GDP. With a national debt in excess of 100 percent of GDP in 1997, when the budget deficit equaled a negative 5 percent of GDP, Greek inflation then remained relatively high at 5.7 percent. Although well down from the 15.8 percent inflation rate in 1992, this must be reduced to an annual rate of no more than 2.6 percent if Greece is to qualify for full membership in the EMU by 2002. Here the main problem is excessive public spending in a country where tax revenues are low and tax evasion is rife. Greece's poor public finances and inflationary tendencies have traditionally resulted in a weak currency. In recent years the drachma has sharply depreciated against stronger EU currencies led by Germany's Deutsche mark. In April 1998 the drachma was devalued by 15 percent when it entered the EU's Exchange Rate Mechanism (ERM), the essential precondition for eventual membership of post-2000 EMU. Although still relatively undeveloped by wider EU standards, the Greek financial system has been much improved in recent years. With EMU fast approaching, however, a major shakeout among Greek commercial banks is now underway. Most remain uncompetitive internationally, with matters made worse by the continuation of high real interest rates in Greece as part of a policy to support the weak drachma from foreign speculators.

Although pre-EMU macroeconomic stabilization has begun successfully in Greece, a wider structural reform of its economy is still producing very slowly for essentially social and political reasons. Here the main problem is a bloated and largely economically unviable state sector. So far, the government has only partially privatized a number of key public corporations, led by OTE, the telecommunications monopoly. Paradoxically, Greece's need to reduce public spending and its national debt to qualify for EMU is now at odds with the generosity of EU Community Support Framework (CSF) outlays. Under the current CSF II funding period for 1994–99, these outlays have been around $5 billion per annum. The 1997–98 government budget allocations for capital spending thus remain very high, mainly because Greece wishes to secure all the CSF II funding it can. EU capital inflows therefore reduce the incentive to cut capital spending, given that such funds are provided on a matching-funding basis. For 1998 the government aims to increase substantially privatization revenues, mainly through further sales of equity in OTE and the proposed sale of 20 percent of the equity in the uniquely profitable Public Petroleum Corporation. For 1998–99, up to $10 billion could be raised from such sales, most of which will be used to reduce the size of Greece's large national debt.

Externally, Greece's foreign trade and payments remain in serious imbalance, with imports now exceeding exports by a factor of nearly two in 1997. At $11.7 billion in 1997 exports were then equal to only 40 percent of the country's imports. At $27.5 billion in 1997, these imports were at record levels. With over 50 percent of its foreign trade with the rest of the EU, Greece recorded a record foreign trade deficit of $15.8 billion in 1997. On the current account, Greece's deficit reached another record of $4.7 billion in 1997. On the services balance, where Greece has a large surplus, tourism, shipping, and émigré hard currency remittances together earned $11.5 billion in 1997. In the same year outward service payments in the form of foreign investors' profit dividends and foreign debt interest payments were $6 billion and rising. On the capital account, CSF II inflows of $5 billion in 1997 were exceeded by new foreign borrowings from foreign commercial banks worth around $6 billion in that year. At nearly $90 billion the Greek national debt is excessive in relation to both GDP and local hard currency reserves, which were around $18 billion at the end of 1997. At below $500 million in 1997, the new DFI (Direct Foreign Investment) is low, although it may increase substantially through greater foreign investor participation in local privatization. If it were outside the EU, therefore, Greece would almost certainly be internationally insolvent and incapable of financing its present national debt and balance of payments. In practice if not in name, therefore, Greece remains a developing rather than a developed European economy, with everything now dependent on ever closer relations with the EU for its future economic prosperity.

BIBLIOGRAPHY

Pirounakis, Nicholas G. *The Greek Economy: Past, Present and Future.* New York: St. Martin's Press, 1997.
Tsaliki, Persefoni V. *The Greek Economy: Sources of Growth in the Postwar Era.* New York: Praeger, 1991.

Marko Milivojevic

The 1996 Election

Andreas Papandreou, who served as prime minister from 1981 to 1989 and from October 13, 1993, to January 15, 1996, died on June 23, 1996. He founded PASOK in 1974, which gained 48 percent of the vote on 1981 and formed the first non-ND government since the restoration of democracy in 1974. Its message was a mixture of populism and nationalism. It lost control of the government from 1989 to 1993 because of the drop in Papandreou's popularity in reaction to his affair with Dimitra Liana young divorcee and a financial corruption scandal associated with banker George Koskotas. Following the June 1989 election, a coalition of conservatives and Communists came to power to prosecute political figures accused of corruption. When a subsequent election in November again failed to give any party enough seats to govern, an all-party coalition was formed under the former head of the Bank of Greece, Xenophon Zolotas.

In the 1990 election ND received 46.9 percent of the vote and 150 seats. It was given a bare majority in the 300-seat parliament when it was joined by a right-wing independent member of parliament and a ND government was formed under Konstantinos Mitsotakis. His effort to address Greece's economic problems through a program of economic austerity disenchanted many voters and brought enough support to PASOK to return it to power in 1993.

In the September 22, 1996, parliamentary election, the Panhellenic Socialist Movement (PASOK) won 41.49 percent of the vote and 162 seats in parliament. New Democracy (ND), the conservative party led by Miltiades Evert, won 38.12 percent and 108 seats; the Communist Party of Greece (KKE), led by Aleca Papariga, won 5.61 percent and 11 seats; the leftist Progressive Left Coalition, led by Nicos Constanopoulos, won 5.12 percent and 10 seats; the socialist Democratic Movement of Social Equality, led by Dimitris Tsovolas, won 4.43 percent and 9 seats. Kostas (Constantinos) Simitis of PASOK, who became prime minister when the leader of PASOK, Andreas Papandreou, resigned as prime minister on January 18, 1996, formed a new PASOK government on September 25.

Bernard Cook

Greenland

World's largest island, with an area of 839,999 square miles (2,175,600 sq km). Greenland (Kalaallit Nunaat), located in the North Atlantic, is separated from Canada at one spot by only 14.5 miles. The island is a self-governing part of Denmark. Denmark, which remains responsible for defense, foreign affairs, and justice, is represented by a high commissioner (*rigsombudsmand*), who resides in the capital, Nuuk (Godthåb/Godtheb). Greenland elects two members to the Danish parliament but internal affairs are conducted by the Home Rule Government. There is a thirty-one-member legislature, the Landsting, elected every four years by proportional representation. The executive is selected by the legislature.

Greenland, which was settled by the Norwegian Eric the Red in 985, came under Danish control in 1380. The original Norse settlements, which had declined as a result of climatic changes, disappeared in the fifteenth century. In 1721 a Danish trading company set up a post and mission near present-day Nuuk. Between 1776 and 1950, Denmark forbade foreign access to Greenland. An attempt by Norway in 1931 to claim sections of the eastern

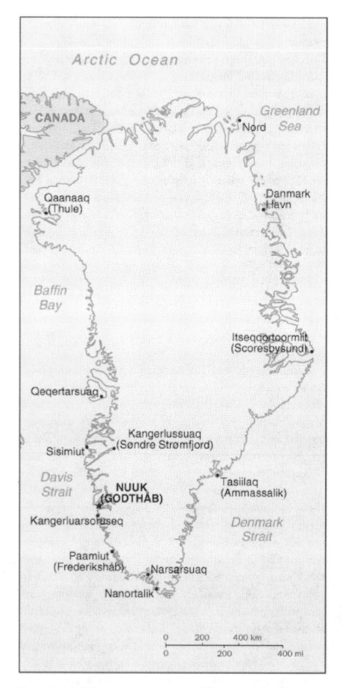

Greenland. *Illustration courtesy of Bernard Cook.*

and southern coast of the island, where Norwegian fishermen had established posts, was decided in Denmark's favor by the Court of International Justice in 1933. After the occupation of Denmark in 1940, the Germans established weather stations on Greenland. These were later ousted by American and Danish forces. NATO, in 1951, assumed responsibility for the defense of Greenland.

In 1953 the island became an integral part of the Kingdom of Denmark with the status of a county and began electing representatives to the Danish parliament. The

Greenland Provincial Council in 1967 began selecting one of its members as council chairman to perform the functions previously exercised by the Danish governor. In October 1972 Greenlanders opposed Denmark's entry into the European Community (EC/EU) by a vote of 9,658 to 3,990. Denmark's subsequent entry fueled resentment against Danish domination. The center-left nationalist party, Siumut, was formed in 1977. In November 1978 a home rule law was adopted by the Danish parliament. In January 1979, 73.1 percent of those voting in a referendum approved home rule, and Greenland received its own legislature, the Landsting, and its own administration, the Landsstyre. In April, Siumut, led by Jonathan Motzfeldt, won thirteen seats in the Landsting, which originally consisted of twenty-one seats but in 1987 expanded to twenty-seven, and in 1995 to thirty-one. In May 1979, Motzfeldt became Greenland's first prime minister, and held that post until 1991.

In a February 1982 referendum 53 percent of voters approved Greenland's withdrawal from the EC. The exit was effected in March 1985, but Greenland was recognized as an overseas territory associated with the EC, thus retaining free access to EC markets. Although Greenland lost development aid, this loss was offset by annual payments from the EC countries for fishing rights in Greenland waters, which were extended in June 1980 to 370 kilometers. Denmark also provides ample financial support, which in 1990 constituted 43.5 percent of the revenues of Greenland's government.

In 1987 Siumut received fewer votes than the leftist Inuit Ataqatigiit, which opposed modernization of the U.S. radar base at Thule (Qaanaaq). In May 1988 Siumut regained its preponderance. In 1991 Siumut retained its plurality but its share of the vote dropped to 37.3 percent. Motzfeldt, who had retained the post of Qaanaaq prime minister through various coalitions, was replaced by Lars Emil Johansen, the new chairman of Siumut, who formed a coalition with Inuit Ataqatigiit. In March 1991 the United States agreed to hand over one of its bases, Kangerlussuaq (Danish, Søndre Strømfjord) to Greenland but retained the right to reactivate it in the future.

In the March 1995 legislature election Siumut gained 38.4 percent of the vote and increased its representation to twelve in the Landsting. Atassut, the Liberal Party, with 30.1 percent, had ten seats, and Inuit Ataqatigiit, with 20.3 percent, received six. A coalition was formed between Siumut and Atassut. Johansen continued to serve as prime minister, and Daniel Skifte of Atassut became minister of finance and housing. Johansen resigned on September 19, 1997, to become vice director of Royal Greenland, one of the large publicly owned companies in

Greenland. He was succeeded by Motzfeldt as prime minister.

The 341,700 miles (549,914 km.) of coastal territory that are habitable were home to 55,385 people in 1991, of whom 12,233 resided in Nuuk. More than 80 percent had been born in Greenland. Most of the others were from Denmark. Native Greenlanders are principally Inuit, but the long contact with Danes has produced a pronounced mixing of peoples. Fishing is the principal economic activity, producing 83.5 percent of Greenland's export revenue in 1990. There are also sheep farms and herds of domesticated reindeer. Mining accounted for 13 percent of Greenland's export income in 1990, but a Swedish firm, which mined lead, zinc, and silver at Marmorilik, in the northwest, ceased its Greenland operation that year. Johansen, nevertheless, expressed the hope that Greenland could gain complete independence and economic self-sufficiency through exploitation of its petroleum, natural gas, and mineral resources. State companies dominate Greenland trade through the Greenland Company for external trade and Kalaallit Niuerfiat for internal trade.

Danish, which has been declared an official language, is widely used, but, despite the shortage of Inuit-speaking teachers, Greenlandic, an Inuit language, is the official medium of instruction. There is universal free health care. In 1989 education accounted for 17 percent of the expenditures of the Greenland government and social programs accounted for 23.2 percent.

BIBLIOGRAPHY

Anderson, Madelyn Klein. *Greenland, Island at the Top of the World.* New York: Dodd, Mead, 1983.

Faegteborg, Mads. *Grønland i dag: en introduktion, 1993.* Copenhagen: Artic Information, 1993.

Kalaallit Oqaluttuarisaanerat 1925-p tungaanut. *Grønlaendernes historie for 1925.* Nuuk: Namminersornerullutik Oqartussat: Atuakkiorfik, 1991.

Lidegaard, Mads. *Grønlands historie.* Copenhagen: A. Busck, 1991.

Thompson, Wayne C. *Western Europe, 1995.* Harpers Ferry, W.V.: Stryker-Post, 1995.

Bernard Cook
Jørn Boye Nielsen

Grimsson, Olafur Ragnar (1943–)

Fifth president of the Republic of Iceland and former politician and professor of political science at the University of Iceland. Grimsson sat on the steering committee of the Progressive Party (center party) from 1971 to 1973, but joined the Union of Liberals and Leftists in 1974. He served as chairman of its steering committee in 1974–75 before he changed parties again, now for the People's Alliance (socialist party), serving as its chairman from 1987 to 1995. Grimsson sat in parliament for the People's Alliance from 1978 to 1983, and from 1991 to 1996, serving as minister of finance from 1988 to 1991. Although he was not a member of parliament at the time, Grimsson was elected chairman of Parliamentarians for Global Action, an international organization of parliamentary representatives in 1984. In 1996 Grimsson ran for the presidency, winning the election with a comfortable margin.

Olafur Ragnar Grimsson's election to the presidency was a reversal of the established trend in Icelandic presidential politics, because the preceding two presidents were cultural figures but not politicians. Grimsson's education and political experience, especially in the field of foreign affairs, served him well in the campaign, however, and therefore his support extended far beyond the party he represented in parliament.

Gudmundur Halfdanarson

SEE ALSO Finnbogadóttir, Vigdis

Grivas, Georgios (1898–1974)

Greek Cypriot nationalist. He helped to win independence for Cyprus in 1960 but failed to accomplish his goal of Cypriot union (*enosis*) with Greece. Georgios Theodoros Grivas, son of a prosperous grain merchant and grocer who was a leader in the Greek Orthodox Church and an adviser to the British colonial administration, was born in Trikomo in the Famagusta district of east Cyprus. Grivas attended the Orthodox Pancyprian Gymnasium, a hotbed of Greek nationalism, in Nicosia. In 1916 he entered the Royal Hellenic Military Academy in Athens. He assumed Greek citizenship and as a lieutenant fought in the 1922–23 campaign against the Turks in Asia Minor. He became a staff officer in the Greek army and graduated from the École Supérieure de la Guerre in Paris. Toward the end of 1939 he became the operational officer of the Greek army's general staff. As chief of staff of the Second Army, he fought in Albania during World War II and was promoted to lieutenant colonel. During the resistance he led the underground organization X. After the withdrawal of the Germans, X under Grivas fought the Communists.

In 1952 he laid the groundwork in Cyprus for a struggle to drive the British out. He returned in October 1954 and founded the National Organization for Cypriot Struggle (Ethniki Organosis Kipriakou Agonos). EOKA, commanded by Grivas, who adopted the nom de guerre

of Greek hero Dighenis Akritas, launched its first attack on the British on April 1, 1955. Four years of terror and guerrilla warfare prompted the British to agree on February 19, 1959, to independence for Cyprus. Grivas, under the terms, was forced to leave Cyprus, but he was received as a hero in Athens on March 17, 1959, and promoted to lieutenant general. Although his subsequent effort to gain political power in Greece failed, he returned to Cyprus in December 1963 to work for *enosis*. He became the commander of the Greek-Cypriot National Guard in August 1964 and worked against his former ally, Cypriot President Archbishop Makarios III. Despite Grivas's death on January 27, 1974, his supporters continued his effort and staged a coup against Makarios in 1974 that resulted not in union with Greece but a Turkish invasion and partition of the island.

BIBLIOGRAPHY

Anagnostopoulou, Lilian. *Hoi dyo Digenedes tes E.O.K.A.* Athens: Ekdoseis S. Vasilopoulos, 1984.

Dodd, Clement Henry. *The Cyprus Imbroglio.* Huntingdon, Cambridgeshire, England: Eothen Press, 1998.

Grivas, Georgios. *Apomnemoneumata agonos E.O.K.A., 1955–1959.* Athens: [s.n.], 1984.

Heinze, Christian. *Cyprus Conflict, 1964–1985.* London: K. Rustem, 1986.

Leonidou, Leonidas Philippou. *Georgios Grivas Digenes: viographia.* Leukosia, Cyprus: Philokypros, 1997.

Bernard Cook

Gromyko, Andrey (1909–89)

One of the best-known Soviet diplomats and political figures of the post–World War II era. Andrey Andreyevich Gromyko served for many years as Soviet foreign minister (1957–85) before assuming the primarily symbolic Soviet presidency in 1985. Until he was retired from the presidency by Mikhail Gorbachev in 1988, Gromyko had been continuously involved in international politics since World War II. Gromyko revealed little about himself during the decades of his career. Only his memoirs, written shortly before his death, reveal a little more about him. Gromyko always portrayed himself as a cog in the Soviet system.

Gromyko was well educated, completing his candidate's degree, roughly equivalent to an American bachelor's degree, in 1936. Initially he worked at the Institute of Economics of the USSR Academy of Sciences. In 1939 he was invited to enter the diplomatic service and began working for the People's Commissariat for Foreign Affairs (later Ministry of Foreign Affairs). Shortly thereafter he was assigned to the Soviet Embassy in Washington as second in command. In 1943, at the age of thirty-four, Gromyko was appointed ambassador to the United States. From 1943 onward he was involved in the key diplomatic conferences of the war and in planning for the postwar United Nations. Despite the turmoil in Soviet politics from 1945 to 1957, when many political careers ended abruptly, Gromyko progressed in the Soviet system. After World War II he was the Soviet representative to the United Nations (1946–48) and deputy minister of foreign affairs. From 1949 to 1952 he was first deputy minister of foreign affairs under Andrei Vyshinsky, the Soviet minister of foreign affairs, 1949–53. He served briefly as ambassador to Great Britain (1951–53) and in 1953 was appointed first deputy foreign minister.

A member of the Communist Party (CPSU) since 1930, Gromyko progressed through the party ranks as his career developed. In 1952 he was elected a candidate member of the Central Committee of the CPSU and in 1956 a full member. In 1973 he was appointed to the Politburo, the ruling body of the CPSU, where he remained until 1988.

In 1957 Gromyko was appointed Soviet foreign minister, a position he held through the Khrushchev and Brezhnev eras, until Michail Gorbachev came to power in 1985. There were some consistencies in Soviet foreign policy, but also changes during that long period. Relations with the West ebbed and flowed. Relations with the Third World generally improved, with occasional setbacks. The maintenance of the Soviet spheres of influence in Eastern Europe and Asia were a high priority, although the intensity of the commitment to specific countries varied. Gromyko was foreign minister during the period of détente with the West, the Sino-Soviet split, the Warsaw fact invasion of Czechoslovakia, the war in Afghanistan, the revived Cold War of the early 1980s, and the beginning of the thaw in U.S.-Soviet relations in the mid-1980s.

One can argue that during his years as minister of foreign affairs Gromyko was only a spokesman for Soviet foreign policy, reading a script prepared in the Politburo. Such a conclusion would be a superficial assessment of his contribution. However loyally he served the foreign policy of the Politburo, he was an important instrument of Soviet foreign policy. His dour execution of Soviet policy during the Cold War, stoic acceptance of his assignments, and ability to survive through several different administrations attest to his skills and ability to adapt to the current line of the Soviet leadership.

His years in the Politburo (1973–88) were perhaps the most important of his career. As a member of the top decision-making organ of the Soviet political system, he

could hardly be regarded as a cog. In the 1980s, after President Leonid Brezhnev's death and before Gorbachev's accession, Gromyko was perceived as a key figure in the Soviet decision-making hierarchy. In 1984, during Konstantine Chernenko's administration, he participated in a rare instance of foreign policy initiative when as foreign minister and member of the Politburo, he visited President Ronald Reagan in the White House in what may have been a turning point away from the Cold War to a revival of détente, or engagement. During his career Gromyko rarely expressed his personal views on foreign policy, although an occasional statement indicates that he sought an improvement in East-West relations and thought of himself as an optimist who desired world peace.

When Gorbachev came to power, he wanted to break with the past in Soviet domestic and foreign policy. Gromyko was removed as foreign minister but was made chairman of the Presidium of the Supreme Soviet (titular presidency of the USSR). Although a largely symbolic position, it reflected respect for his judgment, experience, and power. Gorbachev was intent on promoting a new image for Soviet foreign policy, which he called "new thinking," and a leader identified with the old Soviet foreign policy could prove an embarrassment in a central role. Gorbachev and his foreign minister, Edvard Shevardnadze, brought an urbane and genial style to Soviet foreign policy, which was a distinct departure from Gromyko.

Gromyko's tenure as president and as a member of the Politburo ended in 1988 when Gorbachev assumed the presidency. Subsequently, the Soviet presidency was redefined as the chief executive of the government, rather than titular chief of state. In 1989, Gromyko, along with other elder statesmen, was retired from the Central Committee. Shortly afterward he died at the age of eighty.

Gromyko was married to the former Lydia D. Grinevich and they had two children. His wife frequently accompanied him on trips abroad, unlike the wives of many other Soviet officials.

Gromyko was one of the most durable of Soviet politicians because of his ability, unswerving loyalty to the Soviet leadership, good health, and political resilience. He served the Soviet system well and was rewarded with honors and career longevity. He was always a strong advocate of the Soviet position in world affairs, arguing that what was best for the USSR was the only logic in international relations. Although a Politburo member, he never sought the very top positions. Gromyko may be aptly described as the head bureaucrat of Soviet foreign policy for almost three decades rather than as one of the top decision makers; however, during his Politburo years, he unquestionably contributed to the decision-making process in Soviet foreign policy.

BIBLIOGRAPHY

Goldgeier, James M. *Leadership Style and Soviet Foreign Policy: Stalin, Khrushchev, Brezhnev, Gorbachev.* Baltimore: Johns Hopkins University Press, 1994.

Gromyko, A. A. *Only for Peace.* Oxford: Pergamon Press, 1979.

———. *Pamyatnoe (Memoirs),* 2 Vols. Moscow: Politizdat, 1988.

Powaski, Ronald E. *The Cold War: The United States and the Soviet Union, 1917–1991.* New York: Oxford University Press, 1998.

Rubinstein, A. Z. *Soviet Foreign Policy,* 4th ed. Boston: Little, Brown, 1992.

Ulam, Adam B. *The Rivals: America and Russia since World War II.* New York: Viking, 1971.

Norma C. Noonan

Gronchi, Giovanni (1887–1978)

President of the Italian Republic from 1955 to 1962. Giovanni Gronchi's presidential office coincided with the critical stage of transformation from centrism to the birth of the center-left policy.

Involved in Catholic associations since his youth, Gronchi joined the initial Christian Democratic Movement and was one of the leaders of Catholic unionism. Member of parliament for the Italian Popular Party as of 1919, Gronchi took part in Mussolini's first ministry but resigned a few months later, sharing Luigi Stuzo's (the founder and leader of the Catholic Popular Party) decision to withdraw support from the government.

After the fascist years he returned to active political commitment. He was a member of the national Liberation Central Committee and, with other former members of the Popular Party, contributed to the growth of the Christian Democratic Party. From 1944 to 1946 Gronchi was minister of industry. He was actively involved in the Constituent Assembly. He worked for a party of reform and progress, free from the influence of the church hierarchy and able to establish contacts with the left-wing parties.

BIBLIOGRAPHY

Gronchi, Giovanni. *Discorsi parlamentari.* Rome: Tipografia del Senato, 1986.

Malgeri, Francesco. *Storia della Democrazia Cristiana,* 5 Vols. Rome: Cinque Lune, 1987–89.

Merli, Gianfranco. *Giovanni Gronchi: Contributo per una biografia politica.* Pisa: Giardini, 1986.

Merli, Gianfranco, and Emo Sparisci. *Giovanni Gronchi: "Una democrazia più vera."* Rome: Studium, 1994.

Merli, Gianfranco, and Nicola Antonetti. "Gronchi, Giovanni," in *Dizionario storico del movimento cattolico in italia (1860–1980).* Francesco Traniello and Giorgio Campanini, eds. Vol. 3, no. 1 Casale Monferrato: Marietti, 1984–, 268–74

Spadoni, Ugo. *Giovanni Gronchi nell'Azione Cattolica, nel Partito Popolare, nella Confederazione Italiana dei Lavoratori,* 2 Vols. Florence: Libreria Editrice The Courier, 1992–1998.

Walter E. Crivellin

SEE ALSO Tambroni, Fernando

Grossu, Semion Kuzmich (1934–)

First secretary of the Communist Party of Moldova (CPM) from 1980 to 1989, the last republic-level first secretary to be replaced by Soviet Communist Party General Secretary Mikhail Gorbachev.

Semion Grossu was born in 1934 to a peasant family in the Moldovan Soviet Socialist Republic (MSSR). He joined the Communist Party in 1961. From 1959 to 1967 he worked at a variety of posts in the Moldovan agricultural sector, and from 1967 to 1970 held the post of first secretary of the Criuleni district party committee of the CPM. After working his way up through the local party hierarchy, he was appointed to the first secretary post in December 1980 and was, at the time, the youngest republican first secretary in the Soviet Union.

Under his aegis Moldova drifted further into economic stagnation and corruption, and despite repeated calls for reform from party officials in Moscow, Grossu was criticized for inaction. As the 1980s progressed his refusal to implement Gorbachev's policies of glasnost (openness) and perestroika (restructuring) caused increased discontent in both Kishinev (Romanian, Chisinau) and Moscow. Under a cloud of scandal, he was replaced by Petru Lucinschi in November 1989. After leaving the Moldovan party post, Grossu joined the Soviet diplomatic corps, holding the position of agricultural attaché at the Soviet Embassy in Mexico City. He settled in Russia after the collapse of the Soviet Union.

Charles King

SEE ALSO Moldavian Soviet Socialist Republic

Grosz, Károly (1930–96)

Hungarian politician. Károly Grosz succeeded János Kádár as secretary-general of the Hungarian Socialist Workers (Communist) Party in 1988; previously, he was the prime minister of Hungary from 1987 to 1988.

Grosz first worked as a printer, then became a soldier. From 1954 he worked in regional organizations of the Communist Party in the field of propaganda until the early 1960s. He was secretary of the Communist Party committee at the Hungarian State Radio and Television service from 1962 to 1968. After 1968 he was deputy head of the party's Department of Public Information, then first secretary in Fejor and Borsod counties. He was promoted to head the Budapest organization of the party in 1984 and was nominated prime minister in 1987. After Kádár was removed from his post as secretary-general of the Communist Party and given the honorific title of party president, Grosz was elected secretary-general in 1988. He was unable to arrest the party's decline and was to preside over its dissolution in the fall of 1989. After its collapse he retired from political life and died of cancer at age sixty-six in January 1996.

Grosz was a classic example of a manual worker's career in Communist Hungary. The undereducated, orthodox Communist Grosz was not able to respond to the challenges posed by reform Communists within the party such as Imre Pozsgay and those of the emerging opposition in the late 1980s. However, he acted with good judgment when, after his initial harsh rhetoric that threatened the opposition with armed suppression, he handed over power peacefully and stepped down from the political stage.

BIBLIOGRAPHY

Grosz, Karoly. *Nemzeti osszefogassal a reformok sikereert.* Budapest: Kossuth, 1989.

———. *Szocializmus es korszeruseg: nemzeti es tortenelmi felelosseg.* Budapest: Kossuth, 1987.

Tamàs Magyarics

SEE ALSO Kádár, János; Pozsgay, Imre

Grotewohl, Otto (1894–1964)

Minister president of the German Democratic Republic (GDR) from 1949 to 1964. The son of a Brunswick worker, Otto Grotewohl joined the Social Democratic Party of Germany (SPD) in 1912, served in the army during World War I, and became chairman of a Workers and Soldiers Council in 1918. During the Weimar Republic (1919–33) he held several ministerial posts in Brunswick and was a Reichstag (parliament) deputy between 1925 and 1933. After Hitler came to power, Grotewohl joined an illegal SPD resistance group. Imprisoned during 1938 and 1939, he subsequently spent most of the war as the manager of a small business in Berlin.

After the collapse of the Third Reich in 1945, Grotewohl became co-chairman of the SPD's Berlin Central Committee. Initially an advocate of a united working-class party in postwar Germany, he soon became disillusioned with the Soviet military authorities' palpable discrimination in favor of the Communist Party (KPD). He protested vigorously against the fierce pressure exerted against the SPD once the Soviet Union had decided on a merger between it and the KPD. He failed, however, to adhere to the position that he had reached by fall of 1945, that is, of an autonomous SPD in the Soviet zone, and he became one of the two cochairmen of the newly founded Socialist Unity Party (SED). Between 1949 and 1964, he held the post of minister president of the German Democratic Republic and was an influential member of the SED Central Committee and Politburo. The main power, however, rested in the hands of Walter Ulbricht, who until 1950 officially held only the post of deputy premier.

Grotewohl's motives for cooperating with the Soviet authorities and the German Communists are still a subject of considerable controversy, but he seems to have been influenced by a desire to retain some influence for his SPD constituency within the increasingly unfavorable political climate in the Soviet zone, as well as by his desire to advance his own career. As he became ever more enmeshed in the SED system, the latter motive seems to have become more significant. Grotewohl did not offer strong resistance to the much stronger-willed Walter Ulbricht and to the decline in the influence of former SPD members, especially after the SED's reconfiguration as a Marxist-Leninist party after 1948.

BIBLIOGRAPHY

Vozke, Heinz. *Otto Grotewohl: Biographischer Abriz.* Berlin: Dietz, 1979.

Mike Dennis

SEE ALSO Ulbricht, Walter

Grotowski, Jerzy Maria (1933–)

Polish actor and stage manager. Jerzy Maria Grotowski was born on August 11, 1933, in Rzeszow. He developed the conception of the "poor theater," utilizing entirely new techniques in his work with actors centering around theater-ritual bonds. His book *Ku teatrowi ubogiemu* (*Toward the Poor Theater*) has been translated into many languages.

He made his debut as a stage director in 1957 at Opole. His first period is characterized as "theater of spectacles." It was succeeded in 1969 by "theater of participation or para-theater," in 1976 by his "theater of sources" and "objective drama," and in 1985 by "theater as vehicle."

Grotowski started with the concept of the "poor theater" in which he rejected theatrical staging and the Wagnerian idea of drama as "universal art," a looking glass in which the social structure of the world is reflected. For him theater was no longer divided into stage and audience; it was a place where, having a spectator as a witness, an actor makes a spontaneous but well-ordered public confession. This confession is to voice spiritual truth of both the actor and the audience. The performance itself becomes a ritual, e.g., *Książę Niezłomny* (*The Unbroken Prince*) by Julius Slowacki, based on Calderón's work *Apocalypsis cum Figuris.*

Grotowski sought to make an actor integrate his physical and spiritual potentialities. He declared that an actor-creator consciously shapes his own internal mental and physical processes and penetrates his own life experiences in search of lively organic reactions, so-called body impulses. These impulses build up the "structure" or score of signs in a performance that is coherent with the individual truth of the actor, a truth convergent with the collective feeling. Through primeval, ritual unity the performance achieves a dimension of a human "myth newly incarnated."

In the second period traditional spectacles were replaced by "meetings," "workshops," "festivals," or "special projects." Grotowaski's team created nonfictional symbolic "meetings" both inside and in the open air at different times of day. This para-theater was to stimulate the collective processes of individualization, as C. G. Jung described them, in its participants and to create "utopias in practice" to preserve and defend human interior life threatened by "inhuman" modern civilization.

In the third period, although Grotowski returned to the theater, it was the theater of inter- or overcultural dramatic structures. His work took an intercultural form. Haiti, Bangladesh, Nigeria, and Mexico became the sites where he searched for archetypal theatrical techniques going back to the past when "ritual and artistic creation were inseparable." He aimed to "reestablish these archaic values of the theater" through such culturally universal elements as movement, voice, rhythm, sound, and "use" of space.

In the latest period of his theatrical work Grotowski adopted Brook's concept of "theater as a vehicle" and concentrated on archaic ritual plays as a source of his scripts of action. Theater reduced to elements of action and community has become "only" an instrument to experience ritual. The philosophical legitimation of his explorations was presented in a 1987 essay, "Performer."

Throughout these four phases of his work, Grotowski has tried to use theater as a tool to transform man.

Janusz Skuczński

Groza, Petru (1884–1958)

Prime minister of Romania, 1945–52, and president of the Presidium of the Grand National Assembly, 1952–58. Petru Groza was an ambitious, wealthy lawyer and landowner from Deva who sought fame through politics. Romania needed agrarian reform in the interwar years, and Groza sought to base his political career on a platform of moderate reform that would not threaten order. He joined the conservative People's Party, headed by war hero General Alexandru Averescu, to accomplish his goals and held a minor post in that party's 1926–27 government, but the poorly organized People's Party faded into obscurity after 1927.

The Great Depression caused severe problems for Romanian agriculture, which presented Groza with another chance for achieving political prominence. He concluded that Romania's rural crisis required a more radical solution than he had advocated in the 1920s. Since Romania's major political parties ignored the problem, he founded the Ploughman's Front at Hunedoara in 1933 to solve it by distributing land equally, promoting cooperation among peasants regardless of nationality, reducing peasant debt, raising taxes on the wealthy, and granting the poorest peasants free medical care plus an exemption from paying taxes. The party failed to attract even one percent of the vote despite allying itself in 1935 with a group representing Hungarians living in Romania and a small segment of the Romanian Socialist Party. Carol II abolished the Ploughman's Front along with all other political parties in 1938, but Groza's political career had not ended.

During World War II he opposed fascism and the Vienna Award, which gave part of Transylvania to Hungary. Groza revived the Ploughman's Front in 1944 and attracted enough dissatisfied peasants that Moscow ordered the Romanian Communists to include it in their National Democratic Front formed in October 1944. Furthermore, Groza's credentials as an antifascist, non-Communist leftist and agrarian reformer made him attractive to the Communists. Moscow wanted Groza appointed premier of Romania's coalition government in November 1944, but he had to settle for vice premier. In February 1945 Moscow insisted, and he became premier on March 6, 1945.

The Communists knew that Groza would help them establish their dictatorship. He realized that he had to become a puppet for the Communists to hold high political office, but his collaboration amounted to more than base opportunism. Since the 1930s he had believed that only a radical approach to rural Romania's problems had any chance of success. Collective farms fulfilled his criteria, even if most Romanian peasants disliked them. Gheorghe Gheorghiu-Dej, general secretary of the Romanian Communist Party, welcomed Groza's cooperation, which helped the Communists seize control of Romania. When Gheorghiu-Dej became Romania's ruler in 1952, he did not discard Groza, who worked very well with him, but rewarded Groza's service and loyalty with the ceremonial post of president of the Presidium of the Grand Nation Assembly.

BIBLIOGRAPHY

Focseneanu, Eleodor. *Doua saptamani dramatice din istoria Romaniei: 17–30 Decembrie 1947.* Bucurest: All Educational, 1997.

Groza, Petru. *Groza Peter Emlekere.* Budapest: Kossuth, 1984.

Puscas, Vasile. *Dr. Petru Groza, Pentru o "Lume Noua."* Cluj-Napoca, Romania: Editura Dacia, 1985.

Rothschild, Joseph, and Nancy M. Wingfield. *Return to Diversity: A Political History of East Central Europe since World War II.* 3rd ed. New York: Oxford University, 2000.

Wolf, Robert Lee. *The Balkans in Our Time.* New York: Norton, 1978.

Robert F. Forrest

SEE ALSO Gheorghiu-Dej, Gheorghe

Gruber, Karl (1909–)

Austrian foreign minister, 1945–53. Born in Innsbruck on May 3, 1909, Karl Gruber earned a degree in electrical engineering in 1927 then studied law and political science at Innsbruck University. In 1934, Gruber moved to Vienna and left the Social Democrats for the Fatherland Front (Vaterländische Front). In Vienna he entered the Viennese Catholic fraternity "Austria." Political conviction had prompted his transfer from the social democratic camp to the Christian-social one.

In 1936 he received a doctorate in law. As a member of the Christian trade unions he worked for the mail and telegraph service as well as serving as a scientific assistant at Vienna University. In 1938 he moved to Berlin, where he was first employed with Allgemeine Elektrizitätsgesellschaft and then with Telefunken. He managed to be classified as an "indispensable" worker because he was employed by companies important to the German war economy. Ultimately he found employment as a high-frequency engineer engaged in the development of radar.

Apart from being in touch with Austrian resistance groups in Vienna, from the autumn of 1944 onward he established contacts with the U.S. Office of Strategic Services (OSS) in Bern via a Liechtenstein confidant. During the dispersal of weapons factories by the Nazis to avoid Allied bombers, Gruber moved to the Tyrol and contacted the Tyrolian resistance. From April to the middle of May 1945 he assumed control of the Executive Committee of the Tyrolian Resistance Movement. At the beginning of the postwar occupation the French and Americans recognized him as provincial governor.

In May Gruber participated in the formation of the Austrian Democratic State Party (Demokratische Österreichische Staatspartei) in Innsbruck. He then advocated merging it with the Tyrolian People's Party to avoid a split within the bourgeois faction. At the two preparatory conferences of the Austrian People's Party (Österreichische Volkspartei) held in Salzburg in July and August 1945, he played a leading role. Thus, Gruber contributed to the establishment and consolidation of the People's Party in the western states of Austria and distinguished himself as "speaker of the West."

Gruber became the deputy foreign undersecretary in the government organized by Karl Renner. After the November 25, 1945, National Council elections, he was appointed foreign minister. At the same time, as an ÖVP politician, he represented the Tyrolian Association of Farmers on the National Council.

The September 5, 1946, Gruber–De Gasperi agreement on the Tyrol was defined as a "European solution" that addressed the concerns of both the Italians and the German speaking Tyrolese by leaving South Tyrol in Italy but guaranteeing the cultural rights of its German-speaking inhabitants and promising eventual autonomy. However, considerable obstacles hampered the agreement's implementation of the agreement. While autonomy for the province of Bolzano could be realized only later, the return of the relocated South Tyrolians from Germany and Austria to the Italian Tyrol occurred during the 1950s.

Gruber pressed for a quick signing of the Austrian State Treaty, which restored Austrian sovereignty, but, he did not want a treaty "at all costs." Between the Communists' coming to power in Czechoslovakia and the Berlin Blockade (1948–49), Gruber did not view the completion of the State Treaty as the most urgent objective. He saw new opportunities with the ending of the Berlin Blockade. In the summer of 1949 Gruber came close to concluding the treaty yet growing obstruction by the superpowers delayed the conclusion of the treaty to May 15, 1955.

During the Korean War (1950–53) and with the worsening of the East-West conflict, maintenance of the integrity of the Austrian state remained central to Gruber's policy. The "abbreviated treaty" presented to the Soviets on March 13, 1952, was rejected because it denied them a buy-out for the German industrial assets that would be returned to the Austrian government. Gruber followed the Austrian policy favored by the United States, which was to reject reparation payments to the USSR as the price for the withdrawal of the Soviet army. With Brazil's assistance he brought the Austrian question before the United Nations in December 1952.

From 1953 onward, under Julius Raab, the Austrian chancellor, there was a new orientation in foreign policy. Contacts with the Soviets were intensified. This new course generated exploratory talks concerning a "nonalignment" policy. At the meeting with Indian leader Jawaharlal Nehru at Bürgenstock in 19XX, this policy took shape. The purpose of the meeting was for India to sound out the Soviets on the nonalignment question. Austria, however, wished to be linked to the West and preserve the integrity of the state. Thus, Gruber's policy was a constant act of balance.

In 1948 under Gruber's leadership Austria became a founding member of the Organization for European Economic Cooperation (OEEC) and participated in trade liberalization within Europe. For the time being, Austria was only an associate member. Between 1949 and 1954 Gruber advanced to the position of OEEC vice president. As of 1950 the country benefited from the multilateral clearing of the European Payments' Union. As far as European integration was concerned, however, Gruber objected to a further commitment of Austria to European unification projects as long as Soviet troops still occupied part of Austria.

Gruber pushed for Austrian admission to the United Nations, the International Monetary Fund (IMF), and the General Agreement on Tariffs and Trade (GATT). Austria was accepted by the IMF in 1948 and GATT in 1951. In 1953 diplomatic relations with West Germany were established. Gruber also played an important part in collaborating with the Western powers in the formation of the B-Gendarmerie, precursor of the Austrian federal army, and the rearmament of the Western zones.

After Gruber resigned as foreign minister because of the failure of his state treaty policy and because of a controversy stirred by the publication of his book on recent Austrian politics, he was appointed ambassador to the United States. This enabled him to create an environment of confidence and to render Vienna's neutrality acceptable to the United States.

After serving as ambassador to the United States (1954–57), Gruber was special adviser to the International Atomic Energy Agency in Vienna (1958–61); between 1961 and 1966 ambassador to Spain; and in 1966, ambassador to West Germany. Between 1966 and 1969, he was the undersecretary responsible for administrative reform in Chancellor Josef Klaus's cabinet. From 1969 to 1972 he was again ambassador to the United States, and between 1972 and 1974 ambassador to Switzerland. As chairman of the state electric power corporation Association of Energy from 1978, Gruber supported the opening of the controversial nuclear power station Zwentendorf near Vienna, but voters rejected commissioning the completed facility in a referendum.

Sociopolitical balance and consensus sustained Gruber's political program. As a consequence he advocated the grand coalition. In foreign policy Gruber was accused of lacking negotiating skills and making decisions too swiftly.

During the Waldheim controversy in 1987, when Austrian President Kurt Waldheim's activity in World War II as a lieutenant in the German army was called into question, Gruber assumed the role of special ambassador to the United States. Because of his harsh criticism of the findings of the commission of historians, which asserted that Waldheim knew of German atrocities in the Balkans and facilitated the execution of these activities even if it could not be established that he was personally involved in war crimes, Gruber again found himself in the limelight. Until the end, Gruber in vain advocated a second Waldheim candidacy for president.

BIBLIOGRAPHY

Bischof, Günter. "The Making of a Cold Warrior: Austrian Foreign Policy à la Gruber, 1945–1953." *Austrian History Yearbook,* Vol. 26. Minneapolis: Center for Austrian Studies, 1995, 99–127.

Bischof, Günter, and Josef Leidenfrost, eds. *Die bevormundete Nation: Österreich und die Alliierten 1945–1949.* Innsbruck: Haymon-Verlag, 1988.

Gehler, Michael. "Karl Gruber," in Herbert Dachs, Peter Gerlich, and Wolfgang C. Müller, eds. *Die Politiker: Karrieren und Wirken bedeutender Repräsentanten der Zweiten Republik.* Vienna: Manzsche Verlags- und Universitätsbuchhandlung, 1995, 192–99.

———. *Karl Gruber: Reden und Dokumente 1945–1953. Eine Auswahl.* Vienna: Böhlau-Verlag, 1994.

———. " 'Die Besatzungsmächte sollen schnellstmöglich nach Hause gehen.' Zur österreichischen Interessenpolitik des Auzenministers Karl Gruber 1945–1953 und zu weiterführenden Fragen eines kontroversen Forschungsprojekts." *Christliche Demokratie.* 12 (1994): 27–78.

Steininger, Rolf. *Los von Rom? Die Südtirolfrage 1945/46 und das Gruber–De Gasperi-Abkommen.* Innsbruck: Haymon-Verlag, 1987.

Stourzh, Gerald. *Geschichte des Staatsvertrages 1945–1955: Österreichs Weg zur Neutralität,* 3d ed. Graz: Styria-Verlag, 1985.

Michael Gehler

SEE ALSO South Tyrol; Waldheim Affair

Grusa, Jiří (1938–)

Czech poet, translator, and political figure. Jiří Grusa was born on November 10, 1938. He began writing as a secondary school student, but his work was quickly condemned for "slandering the achievements of socialism." During the relatively more relaxed 1960s he attended Charles University, in Prague, and published some of his work. He was an editor at the literary magazines *Tvar (Face), Sesity (Notebooks), Nove knihy (New Books),* and *Zitrek (Tomorrow).* During this period he became acquainted with Václav Havel and other dissidents. After the suppression of the Prague Spring in 1968 by invading Warsaw Pact forces, he held a number of jobs. In 1970 after the publication of a novel, he was prosecuted for publishing "pornography." The novel *Dotaznik (Questionnaire),* published eight years later, brought Grusa prizes abroad but two months of jail in Czechoslovakia.

Grusa was an original signer of Charter 77, a document protesting the failure of the Czechoslovakian government to adhere to the human rights provisions of the 1975 Helsinki Accord. When he went to the United States in 1980 to study, he was stripped of his Czechoslovak citizenship. He then emigrated to West Germany and resided there until the collapse of communism in Czechoslovakia in 1989. He had been given German citizenship but relinquished it during the Velvet Revolution (1989) and his Czechoslovak citizenship was restored. Grusa was appointed Czechoslovak ambassador to Germany in 1991. He was subsequently accused by Zdeněk Mlynár, honorary chairman of the Left Bloc (LB), of having dual citizenship, and his role in negotiating German-Czechoslovakian relations was questioned. Grusa, nevertheless, continued as ambassador and played a key role in the negotiation of the Czech-German declaration that the two countries ratified in January and February 1997.

In October 1996 the Central Election Commission (UVK) rejected the registration of Grusa as a senatorial candidate because of his failure to submit documentation of his Czech citizenship. Although the Supreme Court upheld the UVK ruling, the Constitutional Court ultimately gave him approval to run. His electoral slogan, "Do not fear Germans, they are easy to speak with, one must only be frank," was perhaps more suited to ambassador than candidate, and he lost.

When Grusa was proposed as minister of education by the Civic Democratic Party in 1997, he stepped down as ambassador and was replaced by František Cerny. Grusa replaced Education Minister Ivan Pilip, who became minister of finance. Pilip had roused the anger of the teachers' union by increasing the hours of instruction without any pay increase. Grusa, who announced his desire to strip ideological cant from Czech textbooks, held the post from June 1997 until the fall of Václav Klaus's government on November 30 of that year. The new premier, Josef Tosovsky, replaced Grusa despite the minister's success with the teachers' union and the universities. Grusa was replaced because of his close connection with Klaus. Grusa's replacement as education minister was Jan Sokol, a lecturer at Charles University and also an original signer of Charter 77.

BIBLIOGRAPHY

Grusa, Jiri. *Franz Kafka of Prague.* New York: Schocken Books, 1983.

———. *The Questionnaire, or, Prayer for a Town & a Friend: A Novel.* Normal, Il.: Dalkey Archive Press, 2000.

Skilling, H. Gordon. *Charter 77 and Human Rights in Czechoslovakia.* Boston: Allen & Unwin, 1981.

Bernard Cook

Guattari, Félix (1930–92)

French clinical psychologist and social critic. With his longtime collaborator Gilles Deleuze, Félix Guattari has written a series of works that present postmodern criticism of Marx, Freud, modern social norms, and philosophy. Guttari was one of the leaders of the avant-garde in France. His chief works include *Capitalism and Schizophrenia: Anti-Oedipus* (1972) and, the second part of this work, *Thousand Plateaus* (1980). His last work with Deleuze was *What Is Philosophy?* (1991). These works are extremely dense, at times even impenetrable, but their influence has been significant in areas of literary criticism, social science, and continental philosophy. In their work on psychoanalysis Guattari and Deleuze criticized Freud's method and focus, contending that Freud mistakenly took the neurotic individual as the model of repression. To them, the schizophrenic, or bipolar individual, represented a more interesting and provocative case, because the schizophrenic shows how the individual is capable of adapting and altering his or her individuality. Repression, they argued, should be replaced with the idea of social oppression. They believed that Freud also used an overly simplified system for interpretation. Every neurosis could be traced to the "Mommy-Daddy-Me" structure. Guattari, in particular, believed that one had to look for the source of dysfunction in socialization, which he understood as being formed through capitalism and its consumer desires. In *Thousand Plateaus* Guattari attempted to show how individuals continuously change their character. He used an analogy of a rhizome (a tuber) to demonstrate that individual character is not static but a layered, growing organism.

BIBLIOGRAPHY

Bogue, Ronald. *Deleuze and Guattari.* London: Routledge, 1989.

Massumi, Brian. *A User's Guide to Capitalism and Schizophrehenia.* Cambridge, Mass.: MIT Press, 1992.

Nordquist, Joan. *Felix Guattari and Gilles Deleuze: a Bibliography.* Santa Cruz, Calif.: Reference and Resource Services, 1992.

Daniel E. Shannon

SEE ALSO Deleuze, Gilles

Gulag

The Soviet system of forced labor camps established in 1919 under the Cheka. The use of the term "Gulag," taken from the Russian acronym for Chief Administration for Correction Labor Camps, was popularized by Alekandr Solzhenitsyn's *The Gulag Archipelago* in the mid-1970s. The Gulag contained common criminals as well as political dissenters, but also many people who were simply caught up in the system. Located in Siberia and the far east of Russia, the Gulag contributed to the Soviet economy. Forced laborers of the Gulag constructed the White Sea-Baltic Canal, the Moscow-Volga Canal, the Baikal-Amur railway, as well as roads and industrial enterprises. Additionally, much Gulag labor was devoted to the timber and mining sectors.

It was Solzhenitsyn's work that brought the harsh working conditions in the camps to light. Prisoners received inadequate food and clothing, and overwork, exposure, and abuse took a terrible toll. The Gulag system was altered after Stalin's death in 1953. The prisoner population declined markedly and conditions in the camps became less harsh. Nikita Khrushchev, the first secretary who consolidated his power in 1955, equated the Gulag system with Stalinism and released prisoners to gain popular support in the power struggle with Stalinist hardliners in the Presidium. However, dissidents were again sent to camps during the era of Leonid Brezhnev (1964–82). The Gulag system continued to exist into the period of Mikhail Gorbachev, but under Gorbachev dissenters were no longer sent to camps.

BIBLIOGRAPHY

Jakobson, Michael. *Origins of the GULAG: The Soviet Prison Camp System, 1917–1934.* Lexington: University of Kentucky Press, 1993.

Solzhenitsyn, Alexander. *The GULAG Archipelago, 1918–1956.* New York: Harper & Row, 1974–1978.

Todd Alan Good

SEE ALSO Solzhenitsyn, Aleksandr

Gurvitch, George (1894–1965)

Philosopher and sociologist. George Gurvitch was born in Novorossiysk, Russia. His acute intellect and bad temper led to his exclusion from the Tout Paris Philosophical circle, while his severe strictures of his colleagues' works and his high expectations for his students caused his work to sink into oblivion after his death. Yet his spirited insights have endured the test of time and offer fresh foundations for an epistemology of the social sciences.

A student in Russia and Germany during the brilliant period of philosophical scholarship that preceded World War I, Gurvitch discovered Hegel, Marx, Stirner, Husserl, the post-Kantians, Bergson, and Fichte. His dissertation on political philosophy (*The Political Doctrine of Prokopovitch,* 1917) attracted public notice. Gurvitch was one of the few sociologists to witness and participate in the Russian Revolution and to incorporate his observations of that event in his sociological theory. He met such Soviet leaders as Stalin and Trotsky, participated in the movement with a group of students who split from the Bolsheviks (the Mensheviks and the anarchists), and observed with dismay the growth of centralism. Considered a left-wing oppositionist, he left his homeland in 1920.

He taught at the University of Prague, Czechoslovakia, from 1921 to 1924, then settled in France. After teaching courses at the Sorbonne in Paris, he obtained the chair of sociology at the University of Strasbourg. During World War II he joined the École Libre des Hautes Études in New York City, and afterward returned to Strasbourg. His promotion to a professorship at the Sorbonne in 1949 offered him an opportunity to visit and teach in Europe, Asia, and the Americas. He also founded the Centre d'Études Sociologiques and the journal *Cahiers internationaux de sociologie*. In spite of his poor health, he devoted his energy to renewing the French school of sociology that in his opinion, was the only one capable of a theoretical understanding of the modern world.

For Gurvitch, the grasp of "reality" is neither purely immediate nor totally constructed but, rather, a synthesis of both. There can therefore be no univocal theory of experience, because there always remains the multifarious, the unpredictable, and the unexpected. The appropriate approach consists of a "hyperempirical dialectic," which continually overturns its paradigms. Empiricism cannot be understood as a philosophical attitude, destined to justify some prior hypothesis. It is a work of removal of all obstacles between human relations and the multiple dimensions of reality.

According to Gurvitch, the social structure is in perpetual process of structuration and destructuration with a multiplicity of social times, a mobile hierarchization of its multiple levels, the ecological and morphological bases, signs, patterns, symbols, organizations, forms of knowledge, affects, mental states, works of civilization, and so on. Society must therefore be apprehended through a variety of perspectives.

Gurvitch also suggested new approaches to microsociology. He contributed to the sociology of law, seeing it as the creation of various social groups, and introduced an original analysis of Proudhon.

BIBLIOGRAPHY

Bosserman, Phillip. *Dialectical Sociology: An Analysis of the Sociology of Georges Gurvitch*. Boston: P. Sargent, 1968.
Gurvitch, Georges. *The Bill of Social Rights*. New York, International Universities Press, 1946.
———. *Sociology of Law*. New York: Philosophical Library and Alliance Book Corporation, 1942.
———. *The Spectrum of Social Time*. Tr. and ed. by Myrtle Korenbaum, assisted by Phillip Bosserman. Dordrecht, Netherlands: D. Reidel, 1964.
Gurvitch, Georges, and Wilbert E. Moore, eds. *Twentieth Century Sociology*. New York: Philosophical Library, 1945.
Swedberg, Richard. *Sociology as Disenchantment: The Evolution of the Work of Georges Gurvitch*. Atlantic Highlands, N.J.: Humanities Press, 1982.

Ronald Ceagh

Gysi, Gregor (1948–)

Leader of the German Party of Democratic Socialism. Gregor Gysi was born on January 16, 1948, in Berlin. He received a law degree from Humboldt University and worked as a defense lawyer in the German Democratic Republic (GDR). Gysi took the helm of the East German Communist Party as the German Democratic Republic and the party were in the process of self-destructing. From December 9, 1989, to January 1990 he was the chairman of the Socialist Unity Party/Party of Democratic Socialism. From February 1990 to January 1993 he was chairman of the Party of Democratic Socialism (PDS). Since January 1993 he has been a permanent member of the party's executive committee. He was elected to the Volkskammer (parliament) of the German Democratic Republic on March 18, 1990, and since October 3, 1990, has been a member of the Bundestag (federal parliament) and chairman of the PDS faction. Under Gysi's leadership the PDS retained or gained the support of nearly a fifth of the voters in the area that had been the GDR.

In the September 27, 1998, Bundestag election the PDS won 5.1 percent of the national vote, thus winning the right to representation in the Bundestag by the normal 5 percent rule. In the Land (state) of Mecklenburg-Vorpommern, where it won 24.4 percent of the vote, 1.7 percent more than it won in 1994, it entered into a coalition government with the SPD, which won 34.3 percent. The previous Land government has been a grand coalition between the SPD and the Christian Democrats. The Christian Democrats in 1998 saw their percentage of the vote drop from 37.7 to 30.2 percent. The PDS, which held many local offices in the East, demanded that limits on state borrowing be eased so that additional assistance could be provided to local governments.

BIBLIOGRAPHY

Gysi, Gregor. *Gregor Gysi: Freche Spruche.* Berlin: Schwarzkopf & Schwarzkopf, 1995.

Hoff, Peter. *Der rote "Verfuhrer": Gregor Gysis Wahltour '94: Beobachtungen und Bemerkungen.* Frankfurt au der Oder: Frankfurter Oder Editionen, 1994.

Sabath, Wolfgang. *Gregor Gysi.* Berlin: Elefanten Press, 1993.

Bernard Cook

SEE ALSO Honecker, Erich; Krenz, Egon

Haavelmo, Trygve M. (1911–)

Norwegian economist, assistant secretary in the Ministry of Commerce (1947–48), professor in economics and statistics at the University of Oslo (1948–79), and winner of the Nobel Prize in economics (1989).

Trygve Haavelmo started his academic career as an assistant to economist Ragnar Frisch, who received the first Nobel Prize in economics in 1969. In the 1930s Frisch initiated a change in economic science, from a commonsense-based science to a science with a clearer basis in theory and methodology. Haavelmo built on the work of Frisch and linked economic theory and economic data by means of mathematical statistics. He worked in the United States from 1939 to 1946 and came to be recognized as one of the leading econometrists of the world.

As a professor at the University of Oslo, Haavelmo had considerable influence on the education of other economists. In 1989 he won the Nobel prize in economics "for his clarification of the probability theory foundation of econometrics and his analysis of simultaneous economic structures."

In his most recent articles Haavelmo has concentrated on global poverty and the environment. He argues that natural capital (environment and resources) and man-made capital are incommensurable. Limited natural capital also limits certain economic activities, but the traditional ways of measuring growth are incapable of calculating negative effects on natural capital such as pollution or over-use of water.

BIBLIOGRAPHY

Haavelmo, Trygve. *On the Dynamics of Global Economic Inequality.* Oslo: Memorandum from Institute of Economics, University of Oslo, 1980.

Gisle Aschim

Habermas, Jürgen (1929–)

German philosopher. Jürgen Habermas was born in 1929 in Düsseldorf. From 1949 to 1954 he studied philosophy, history, psychology, German literature, and economics at Göttingen, Zürich, and Bonn. His most important teachers were Erich Rothacker and Oskar Becker. In 1954 Habermas received a doctorate after writing a dissertation on Schelling. From 1956 until 1962 Habermas was an assistant at the Institut für Sozialforschung in Frankfurt. He received his *Habilitation,* which qualifies a person to teach in a university, with his work *Structural Transformation of the Public Sphere.* In this text Habermas attempted to elucidate the conditions of the Federal Republic (West Germany) through a social-philosophical focus on the decline of the public sphere.

From 1962 to 1964 Habermas was a professor of philosophy at the University of Heidelberg. He published his first theoretical study of the relation between theory and practice (*Theory and Practice,* 1963), in which he developed a critique of positivism and the status of the empirical-analytic sciences. He introduced a distinction that would remain fundamental to his thought: that between labor (understood as purposive, rational behavior) and communicative action.

From 1964 to 1971 Habermas was a professor of philosophy and sociology at the University of Frankfurt. At the end of the 1960s and the beginning of the 1970s, Habermas focused on the currently dominant sociological theories to clarify his own methodological approach. He criticized both the empirical-analytic and the historico-hermeneutical sciences and their respective claims to universality. He tied hermeneutic interpretation to a critique of ideology. From this position he criticized Niklas Luhmann's system theory and began to integrate into his own theory elements of Anglo-American theories of language and developmental psychology. Important works by Habermas during this period were his *Knowledge and Human Interests* (1968), *Legitimation Crisis* (1970), and *On the Logic of the Social Sciences* (1982).

From 1971 to 1981 he was codirector with Carl Friedrich Weizäcker of the Max Plank Institute in Starnberg. With his major work, *Theory of Communicative Action* (1981) and his *Moral Consciousness and Communicative Action* (1983), he confronted the issue of the normative foundation of social critical theory and attempted to show that the concepts of truth, freedom, and justice are involved in the structures of linguistic communication as quasi-transcendent norms closely tied to one another, and how they must be integrated in the still unfinished project of modernity.

Since 1982 Habermas has again held a professorship at the University of Frankfurt. His major enterprises in the 1980s and 1990s have been brusque critiques of postmodern thought through his *Philosophical Discourses on Modernity* and his numerous political interventions in the so-called historians' debate (*Historikerstreit*). In *The New Conservatism: Cultural Criticism and the Historian's Debate* (1989) and his Post-Metaphysical Thinking (1988), he castigated revisionist theories of National Socialism and their attempts to create a new positive identity for Germans of the Federal Republic, which would have relegated National Socialism to the past.

BIBLIOGRAPHY

Habermas, Jürgen. *Jürgen Habermas on Society and Politics: A Reader.* Ed. by Steven Seidman. Boston: Beacon Press, 1989.

———. *The New Conservatism: Cultural Criticism and the Historians' Debate.* Ed. and tr. by Shierry Weber Nicholsen; Intro. by Richard Wolin. Cambridge, Mass.: MIT Press, 1989.

Teigas, Demetrius. *Knowledge and Hermeneutic Understanding: A Study of the Habermas-Gadamer Debate.* Lewisburg, Pa.: Bucknell University Press, 1995.

Thompson, John B. *Critical Hermeneutics: A Study in the Thought of Paul Ricoeur and Jürgen Habermas.* Cambridge: Cambridge University Press, 1981.

Erik Vogt

Hagen, Carl I. (1944–)

Norwegian politician, economist, member of parliament (1974–77, 1981–), and chairman of the Progress Party (1978–). Carl Hagen is the personification of the right-wing populist Progress Party. Founded in 1973 as "Anders Lange's Party for Promoting a Strong Reduction in Taxation, Duties and Official Intervention," the party was based on individual responsibility and freedom from excessive taxation and government regulation.

Hagen argued that the Scandinavian welfare state model was far too expensive and did not produce the security it promised. According to Hagen the welfare state destroyed a sense of personal responsibility. Besides reducing taxes, the main focus of the party has been on stopping immigration and maintaining law and order.

After more than ten years as "untouchables," the Progress Party entered the center of political life in 1985. Neither of the two major political blocks, the socialist or the center-to-right coalition, had a majority in parliament without support from Hagen and his one fellow member of parliament from the Progress Party. After one year with the non-socialists, Hagen joined the socialists in a vote of no confidence, clearing the way for a social democratic government, led by Gro Harlem Brundtland.

Hagen is a charismatic leader with a well-developed sense of public relations. He is often accused of stimulating racist undercurrents. The Progress Party experienced considerable growth in local elections in 1987 and in general elections in 1989, becoming the third-largest party, with approximately 13 percent of the vote. In 1993 the party received only 6.3 percent of the vote. Its support is usually attributed to xenophobia and contempt for established political leaders.

BIBLIOGRAPHY

Hagen, Carl I. *Frlighet varer lengst: Politiske erindringer.* Oslo: Aventura, 1984.

Teigene, Ingolf Hekon. *Carl I. Hagen og Fremskrittspartiet.* Oslo: Cappelen, 1988.

Gisle Aschim

Haider, Jörg (1950–)

Austrian politician, chairman of the Freedom Party (Freiheitliche Partei, FPÖ). Born in 1950 in Upper Austria, Jörg Haider became active in the youth organization of the FPÖ in the 1970s. After graduating in law from the University of Vienna in 1973 and a short period as an assistant at the university, he became secretary of the FPÖ's provincial branch in Carinthia in 1976 and member of the Austrian National Council (upper chamber of parliament) in 1979. In 1983 he was elected chairman of the Carinthian FPÖ and joined the Carinthian government as minister (Landesrat). In 1986 he was elected federal chairman of the FPÖ.

Haider represented the right wing of the party. He emphasized pan-German issues, like the "German" character of bilingual Carinthia, and defended the "war generation," a position traditionally seen as favoring the Wehrmacht and even the National Socialist tradition. When he became federal chairman of the party, he implemented a populist strategy using any possible topic to criticize the government. The FPÖ had joined with the Social Democrats (SPÖ) in 1983, but because of Haider's rightist image, his party was forced to leave the coalition cabinet.

Haider's populistic politics, which included an appeal to xenophobic resentments, led to electoral success: The FPÖ quadrupled its share in national elections and challenged the conservative People's Party (ÖVP) for the number-two position behind the SPÖ. But the FPÖ had to pay for this strategy; the party became increasingly isolated. Haider, state governor (Landeshauptmann) of Carinthia between 1989 and 1991 owing to a coalition with the ÖVP, lost this position after he made a statement in the Carinthian diet regarding the "proper employment" policy of the Nazi regime. The statement was widely seen as pro-Nazi and provoked the ÖVP to join the SPÖ in a vote of no confidence. The FPÖ had to leave the Liberal International, the bloc of liberal parties in the European Parliament. After Austria joined the European Union (EU) in 1995, a step much opposed by Haider, the FPÖ's member of the European Parliament was not invited to join any European party group.

Haider's career is seen as an example for "postfascist" politics. He is usually compared with Gianfranco Fini of Italy and Jean-Marie Le Pen of France. In his political statements he has used a combination of traditional fascist elements such as xenophobic and exclusivist attitudes, specific reminders of the Nazi past such as the "honor" of the Waffen SS, and antielitist approaches expressed as "we" against "them." He turned his party's pro-European outlook into anti-European resentment, appealing to the anxieties of those who fear modernization. His career depends very much on the probability of adding to his electoral successes the ability to convince public opinion and other political parties that he can be a reliable coalition partner.

In the Austrian parliamentary election of October 3, 1999, Haider's FPÖ came in second with 26.9 percent of the vote, 415 votes ahead of the ÖVP. Before the election Wolfgang Schüssel, the leader of the ÖVP, had said that if his party received fewer votes than the FPÖ, he would withdraw from the grand coalition with the SPÖ. Austrian Chancellor Viktor Klima of the SPÖ, which received 33.2 percent of the vote, said that he would "Never, never" form a coalition with Haider.

But Haider's party was ultimately asked to join the government when Schüssel formed a government with the FPÖ. The uproar in Europe and the United States led to Austria's diplomatic isolation. The president of Austria, in an attempt to quell the disturbance required Haider to sign a public pledge endorsing democracy and renouncing intolerance.

BIBLIOGRAPHY

Bailer-Galanda, Brigitte. *Haider wörtlich: Führer in die Dritte Republik.* Vienna: Löcker, 1995.

Bailer-Galanda, Brigitte, and Wolfgang Neugebauer. *Haider und die "Freiheitlichen" in Österreich.* Berlin: Elefanten Press, 1997.

Scharsach, Hans-Hennig. *Haiders Kampf.* Vienna: Orac, 1992.

Anton Pelika

SEE ALSO Austria; Fini, Gianfranco; Le Pen, Jean-Marie

Hallgrimsson, Geir (1925–90).

Mayor of Reykjavík, prime minister, and director of the Central Bank of Iceland. After studying law at the University of Iceland and at Harvard Law School, Geir Hallgrimsson practiced law in Reykjavík. He served as mayor of Reykjavík from 1959 to 1972, but was elected to the Icelandic parliament for the Independence Party (a center-conservative party) in 1970. After becoming chairman of the party in 1973, Hallgrimsson served as prime minister of Iceland from 1974 to 1978 and as minister of foreign affairs from 1983 to 1986. He completed his public career as director of the Central Bank of Iceland from 1986 to 1990.

Hallgrimsson, a cautious politician, was highly respected as mayor of Reykjavík. He lacked the necessary charisma, however, to direct the largest party of Iceland, and failed to be reelected to parliament in 1983. Under his tenure as prime minister Iceland extended its fishing limits to two hundred nautical miles, and his government completed successfully the so-called Cod Wars with Britain in 1976.

BIBLIOGRAPHY

Hallgrimsson, Geir. *Peirra eigin or?; kynni? ykkur kommúnisma, og dagar hans eru taldir.* Reykjavík: Heimdallur, 1953.

Gudmundur Halfdanarson

SEE ALSO Cod Wars

Hallstein, Walter (1901–82)

West German Christian Democratic politician, jurist, and promoter of European integration, president of the EC Commission from 1959 to 1967. Walter Hallstein was born in Mainz on November 17, 1901. He studied law in Bonn, Munich, and Berlin, where he obtained a doctoral degree in international civil law in 1925. Four years later he acquired the *Habilitation,* or right to lecture in a university, and he was given a chair at the University of Rostock in 1930. In 1941 he became a professor at the University of Frankfurt. While serving in the German army in World War II, he was captured in 1944 and sent to a U.S. prisoner of war camp, where he set up a "camp university" to teach the inmates about the U.S. political system. When he returned to Germany in 1946, he worked successfully to speed up the reopening of Frankfurt University, and he resumed his professorship. He also lectured at Georgetown University in Washington, D.C., and was involved in the negotiations for Germany's entrance to UNESCO.

In 1950 Hallstein headed the German delegation to the Paris Conference on the Schuman plan that led to the establishment of the European Coal and Steel Community; he became state secretary of the chancellor's office; and he, together with Herbert Blankenhorn, represented West Germany at the meeting of the Council of Europe's Committee of Ministers in Rome in November. When the German Foreign Office was reestablished in March 1951, he became deputy foreign minister under Chancellor Konrad Adenauer, and he kept this position when Heinrich von Brentano took over the Foreign Office in 1955. In those years the Hallstein Doctrine was developed. Although it bears Hallstein's name, it was formulated by Wilhelm Grewe. It stated that the Federal Republic was the only legitimate representative of the German people, including those Germans who lived in the Soviet-controlled German Democratic Republic (GDR) and the formerly German territories in Eastern Europe now belonging to Poland and the Soviet Union. It also stated that diplomatic relations would not be established or upheld with any country that recognized the GDR except for the USSR. The doctrine was first applied to Yugoslavia in 1957. Although the doctrine was sharply criticized from its inception, it was one of the guiding principles of German foreign policy until it was abandoned by Chancellor Willy Brandt's *Ostpolitik* in the mid-1960s.

Hallstein's endeavor was the building of a united democratic Europe. To achieve this aim he vigorously worked for the implementation of the 1957 Treaty of Rome, which established the European Common Market, and the advancement of European collaboration from the economic to the political sphere. His vision of a united Europe extended far beyond the original members of the Common Market.

From 1969 to 1972 Hallstein was a member of the Bundestag (lower house of parliament) a position he used as a forum to press for further European integration. He continued to promote the idea of a united Europe. He died on March 29, 1982.

BIBLIOGRAPHY

Hallstein, Walter. *Die Europäische Gemeinschaft.* Düsseldorf: Econ, 1979.

———. *Europäische Reden.* Stuttgart: Deutsche Verlags-Anstalt, 1979.

———. *Europe in the Making.* London: Allen and Unwin, 1972.

Loch, Theo M. *Walter Hallstein: Ein Porträt.* Freudenstadt: Eurobuch-Verlag Lutzeyer, 1969.

Anjana Buckow

SEE ALSO Adenauer, Konrad; Brandt, Willy; Germany: Foreign Policy

Hammarskjöld, Dag (1905–61)

Swedish political economist, statesman, and secretary-general of the United Nations. Dag (Hjalmar Agne Carl) Hammarskjöld effectively led the U.N. General Assembly through the early 1950s with Cold War crises such as Suez and the Congo, which ultimately claimed his life.

Hammarskjöld was born in Jönköping, Sweden, son of Hjalmar Hammarskjöld (1862–53), who served Sweden as prime minister during the First World War. Hammarskjöld studied law, as had his father, but was attracted to economics while studying at Uppsala and Stockholm Universities. The latter university invited him in 1933 to stay on as professor of political economy. Three years later he entered government service as undersecretary of the Ministry of Finance. After serving as chairman of the board of the Bank of Sweden, Hammarskjöld made politics and government his career.

In 1947 he joined the Ministry of Foreign Affairs. Here he was lauded for his work in international finance at a time when the United States was rebuilding Western Europe through the Marshall Plan. In 1951 Hammarskjöld became deputy foreign minister and in 1952 leader of the Swedish delegation to the United Nations. His interest in world diplomacy paralleled that of his father, who had been the Swedish delegate to The Hague and served after 1904 on its international board of arbitration.

In 1953 Hammarskjöld was elected for five years as secretary-general of the United Nations. His election occurred during the Korean War, and he wished to foster peace and harmony between East and West. This was perhaps why Hammarskjöld from neutral Sweden was selected to lead the United Nation during this time of turmoil. He was instrumental in balancing the interests of the United States and the USSR within the international organization during the 1950s.

Hammarskjöld mediated the Suez crisis in 1956–57. His skill and dexterity in diplomacy led eventually to an end to the dispute and his reelection as secretary-general. Shortly before Soviet Premier Nikita Khrushchev's visit to the United States in the fall of 1959, Hammarskjöld visited him at Sochi in the USSR. There he strove to reinforce the ideas of peaceful coexistence and the spirit of Geneva, which had developed between Khrushchev and U.S. President Dwight Eisenhower.

Had Hammarskjöld lived beyond his mid-fifties, perhaps he, like his father, might have become Sweden's prime minister. He was killed, however, while on a U.N. peacekeeping mission to the Congo in 1961. The Congo crisis led to bitter dissension within the United Nation because, while the United States had supported General Joseph Mobutu, the Soviets had supported Patrice Lumumba. Khrushchev construed the U.N. actions in the Congo as pro-Western and demanded a change in U.N. leadership. He demanded that Hammarskjöld resign so a tripartite leadership could be established with a delegate from the West, the East bloc, and a neutral country. Before this challenge to his power could result in any change, Hammarskjöld perished in a plane crash in Northern Rhodesia (Lambia) near Ndola.

BIBLIOGRAPHY

Dayal, Rajeshwar. *Mission for Hammarskjöld: The Congo Crisis.* Princeton, N.J.: Princeton University Press, 1976.

Hammarskjöld, Dag. *Markings.* New York: Knopf, 1966.

Henderson, James Lewis. *Hammarskjöld: Servant of a World Unborn.* London: Methuen Educational, 1969.

Lash, Joseph P. *Dag Hammarskjöld: Custodian of the Brushfire Peace.* Westport, Conn.: Greenwood Press, 1974.

Urquhart, Brian. *Hammarskjöld,* 2d ed. New York: Harper & Row, 1984.

Zacher, Mark W. *Dag Hammarskjöld's United Nations.* New York: Columbia University Press, 1970.

Barbara Bennett Peterson

SEE ALSO Congo Intervention

Hansen, H. C. (1906–60)

Danish Social Democratic politician, prime minister from 1955 to 1960. Hans Christian Hansen, a printer, served as chairman of the Social Democratic Youth from 1933 to 1937. He was a member of the Folketing (parliament) from 1936 to 1960. He served as minister for finance from May to November 1945, and again from 1947 to 1950. He was minister for foreign affairs from 1953 to 1958. In 1955 he became prime minister and chairman of the Social Democratic Party. He held both these posts until his death in 1960.

Hansen, known for his tactical capacities and realistic approach to politics, was the main architect in the 1950s of the shift to the right in the Social Democratic Party, especially with regard to Denmark's security policy. He led Denmark to a pro-NATO and pro-Western orientation in the early Cold War period of the 1950s.

BIBLIOGRAPHY

Fitzmaurice, John. *Politics in Denmark.* New York: St. Martin's Press, 1981.

Jørn Boye Nielsen

SEE ALSO Hedtoft, Hans

Hansson, Per Albin (1885–1946)

Swedish Social Democratic prime minister. Per Albin Hansson was born near Malmö on October 28, 1885. He had little schooling, but after joining the Social Democratic Youth Association in 1903 he became editor of the association's weekly, *Fram (Forward).* He became a writer for the party weekly, *Social-Demokraten,* and became its editor in 1917. He entered parliament in 1918, serving as minister of defense in the governments of Karl Hjalmar Branting and Rickard Sandler. When Branting died in 1925, Hansson was chosen to lead the Social Democratic Party. In 1932 he became prime minister and, with the support of the Agrarian Party, enacted a vigorous program to combat the economic depression and laid the basis for Sweden's welfare state. At the time of the Soviet-Finnish Winter War of 1939, Hansson formed a coalition government that lasted for the duration of World War II. It pursued a policy of neutrality. Following the war Hansson formed a purely Social Democratic government. He died in office on October 5, 1946.

BIBLIOGRAPHY

Andersson, Sven. *Pa Per Albins tid.* Stockholm: Tiden, 1980.

Johansson, Alf W. *Per Albin och kriget: samlingsregeringen och utrikespolitiken under andra varldskriget.* Stockholm: Tiden, 1984.

Hadenius, Stig. *Swedish Politics during the 20th Century.* 3d rev. ed. Stockholm: Swedish Institute, 1990.

Hansson, Per Albin. *Fran Fram till folkhemmet: Per Albin Hansson som tidningsman och talare.* Solna, Sweden: Metodica Press, 1982.

Isaksson, Anders. *Per Albin.* Stockholm: Wahlstrom & Widstrand, 1996.

Klockare, Sigurd. *Den unge Per Albin, marxisten.* Stockholm: Tiden, 1974.

Bernard Cook

SEE ALSO Erlander, Tage

Harmel Report

By accepting the "Report on Future Tasks of the Alliance," or Harmel Report, at its December 14, 1967, meeting, NATO's North Atlantic Council recognized, "Military security and a policy of détente are not contradictory but complementary." From this point on, détente, or the search for peaceful ways to manage East-West tensions, would be the second task for the alliance, next to deterrence of Soviet aggression.

When in December 1966 Belgian Foreign Minister Pierre Harmel proposed to undertake a broad-ranging examination of NATO's future tasks, the alliance was going through a difficult time. Six months earlier, French President Charles de Gaulle had withdrawn his country from NATO's military structures; disagreement existed over the new strategy of "flexible response," especially between the United States and West Germany; and a political stabilization in East-West relations in Europe since 1961, as well as increased Soviet nuclear capabilities, had led to calls for alternative approaches to dealing with Moscow. In the West, deterrence alone appealed to a dwindling number of people.

The Harmel Report alone did not revitalize NATO. Many organizational improvements in NATO in 1966 and 1967 were actually facilitated by the departure of the French. However, the Harmel study found a formula that accommodated the often diverging ideas of members such as the United States, France, and West Germany on the need for détente. The new resolve, clear enough to signal a change of course while also conveniently vague, would be the leading principle for NATO until the end of the Cold War.

BIBLIOGRAPHY

Haftendorn, Helga. "Entstehung und Bedeutung des Harmel-Berichtes der NATO von 1967." *Vierteljahrshefte für Zeitgeschichte* 40, no. 2 (1992):169–221.

Kaplan, Lawrence S. *NATO and the United States: The Enduring Alliance.* Boston: Twayne, 1988.

Text of Final Communiqués 1949–1970. Brussels: Ministerial Sessions of the North Atlantic Council, the Defence Planning Committee, and the Nuclear Planning Group, 1970. (The text of the Harmel Report can also be found in *Department of State Bulletin,* January 8, 1968).

Ruud van Dijk

SEE ALSO North Atlantic Treaty Organization

Harney, Mary (1953–)

First woman to lead an Irish political party. Mary Harney was born in Ballinasloe in March 1953. She attended convent schools in Dublin and graduated from Trinity College. She became the first female auditor of the College Historical Society in Trinity. She was nominated to the Senate by the prime minister, Jack Lynch, in 1977. In 1979 Harney became a member of the Dublin County Council, where she served until 1991. She was elected to the Irish parliament in 1981. She broke with her party, Fianna Fáil, and voted for the Anglo-Irish accord in October 1985 that gave the Republic of Ireland some voice in the affairs of Northern Ireland for the first time. In 1985 she and Desmond O'Malley cofounded the Progressive Democrats (PD) for members of Fianna Fáil opposed to the party's anti-British Northern Ireland policy. PD for a time displaced Labour as the third-largest Irish party. In 1989 Harney was appointed minister for environmental protection. In October 1993 she replaced O'Malley as the party leader, and in 1997 she became the first woman to lead a party into a coalition government. She became minister of trade employment in the Fianna Fáil–led government of Bertie Ahern.

BIBLIOGRAPHY

Collins, Neil. *Irish Politics Today.* 3d. ed. New York: St. Martin's Press, 1997.

Hadden, Tom. *The Anglo-Irish Agreement: Commentary, Text, and Official Review.* Dublin: E. Higel, 1989.

Owen, Arwel Ellis. *The Anglo-Irish Agreement: The First Three Years.* Cardiff, U.K.: University of Wales Press, 1994.

Bernard Cook

SEE ALSO Ahern, Bertie; Ireland, Northern; Lynch, Jack

Haughey, Charles (1925–)

Irish prime minister, 1979–81, 1982, and 1987–92. Charles Haughey was a controversial, wily politician who, despite being publicly disgraced during the 1970 Arms Crisis, rehabilitated his image in the 1970s to become leader of Fianna Fáil image in 1979. He held this position through the 1980s with ultimate control, despite many challenges to his leadership and rumors about financial scandals. He resigned after severe pressure on his leadership in 1992 and left parliamentary politics after that year's general election. Haughey was perhaps the most controversial figure in Irish politics since Eamon de Valera.

Haughey was born in Castlebar and was educated at University College, Dublin. He became an accountant and married the daughter of Sean Lemass. He was first elected to parliament in 1957 and rose swiftly in the 1960s. He was minister for justice from 1961 to 1964 and introduced a radical law reform program. His Succession Bill contributed to women's rights, and the appointment of Brian Walshe to the Supreme Court was at Haughey's instigation. Walshe was a liberalizing force in Irish society of the 1960s and gave substance to the articles on individual rights in the constitution. Haughey also was instrumental in ending the 1956–61 Irish Republican Army (IRA) campaign by introducing the Special Criminal Court.

Haughey was minister for agriculture from 1964 to 1966 during a period of militant protests by farmers. Following the 1965 general election, a party leadership contest began. Jack Lynch won, and became prime minister, but Haughey was supported by younger, brasher elements of the party. He was minister for finance from 1966 to 1970. Lynch did not manage his cabinet well during these years and Haughey dominated it. At Finance his giveaway budgets during a prosperous period earned him a reputation for decisiveness, acumen, and inspired judgment. His ascendancy was stopped in its tracks over allegations that he used government funds to buy arms then smuggle them to the IRA in Northern Ireland. Haughey had complete control over Northern policy, and Lynch was not involved. Haughey was dismissed from his post along with two other cabinet ministers in May 1970. He was later arrested under this charge, but the charges were dismissed in October 1970.

After spending the early 1970s building up local support, Haughey became minister for social welfare in the 1977–79 government. He defeated George Colley for party leadership, and there was much expectation about his potential performance as prime minister. Through the 1980s, despite his projection of power, Haughey never fulfilled that potential. He never led Fianna Fáil to the overall majority he promised in election campaigns. The many attempts to dislodge him as leader diverted attention to power politics rather than the solution of the republic's spiraling economic problems. The 1980s saw numerous short-term plans by Fianna Fáil that seemed to be based more on the politico-economic cycle than on an effective strategy for long-term economic growth and financial retrenchment. In Anglo-Irish relations his traditionalist stance and bad relationship with British Prime Minister Margaret Thatcher did little to solve the Northern problem after the 1985 Anglo-Irish agreement that gave the Republic of Ireland a voice in the affairs of Northern Ireland for the first time. In 1991 and 1992 growing rumors and evidence of financial and business scandals in which Haughey was implicated by association or default brought increasing calls for his removal as prime minister and party leader. His position as head of a coalition government with his old rival Desmond O'Malley of the Progressive Democrats weakened him further. After intense media speculation and debate, he resigned to be replaced by Albert Reynolds both as prime minister and party leader.

BIBLIOGRAPHY

Joyce, Joe. *The Boss.* Dublin: Poolbeg, 1983.
Mansergh, Martin, ed. *The Spirit of the Nation: The Speeches of Charles J. Haughey.* Cork: Mercier, 1986.

Michael J. Kennedy

SEE ALSO Lynch, John; Reynolds, Albert

Havel, Václav (1936–)

Playwright and politician, president of Czechoslovakia, 1989–92, and president of the Czech Republic, 1993–. Václav Havel, whose father was a commercial real estate developer, was born in Prague on October 5, 1936. He was introduced to books from childhood and said that he began writing almost as soon as he learned the alphabet. Because of his class background, after the Communist coup in 1948, he was denied access to ordinary secondary school. After he completed his secondary education at night school while working as a laboratory technician, Havel was denied entry to the university to study history, philosophy, or cinema. He had to settle for economics at the Czech University of Technology. Poet Jan Zabrana gave him entrée into the literary underground. Havel and his literary friends became regulars at Jiří Kolár's table in Prague's Café Slavia.

Czech president Václav Havel joins hands with other on a platform after a rally marking the forty-sixth anniversary of the Slovak uprising during World War II. Prague, 1990. *Illustration courtesy Reuters/David Brauchi/Arhive Photos.*

He left the Technical University for two years of military service in 1957. While in the army he cofounded a regimental theater. After the completion of his service he applied for admission to the drama school of the Academy of Music and the Arts in Prague but was rejected. As he gained fame as a playwright, the institution granted a contemptuous Havel an "external" degree in 1966. In 1959 he became a stagehand at Prague's ABC Theatre. In 1960 he joined the Theatre on the Balustrade, where he received a firm grounding in all aspects of theater.

Havel's first independent full-length play, *The Garden Party* (1963), denounced the absurdity of mindless bureaucracy. *The Memorandum,* produced in 1965, is a Kafkaesque study of the distortion of language by a regime bent on depersonalization of its subjects. During the Prague Spring of 1968, Havel's passport was restored and he traveled to the United States, where he was deeply impressed by the counterculture. Following the Warsaw Pact invasion of his country in August 1968, Havel's works were banned. Because of his open resistance to the conservative regime, Havel was arrested a number of times during the 1970s and jailed twice. Out of jail, he was forced to earn his living stacking barrels in a brewery. As one of the principal spokespersons for Charter 77, which took the government of Czechoslovakia to task for not living up to the Helsinki Declaration on Civil and Political Rights, Havel was arrested in January 1977 and jailed for four months. The authorities twisted a letter from Havel to the public prosecutor to make it seem that he had repudiated the Charter 77 movement. His de-

spondency at this misrepresentation can be seen in his letter to his wife, Olga (*Letters to Olga: June 1979– September 1982*). In October 1977 Havel was sentenced to four months' suspended sentence for "subversion" because he had sent writings abroad for publication. In 1978 he and other Charter 77 members founded the Committee for the Defense of the Unjustly Persecuted. As a consequence in October 1979 he was sentenced to four and a half years of hard labor. Owing to serious health problems and international protests, his sentence was suspended in February 1983.

After his release Havel responded to Samuel Beckett's *Catastrophe,* based on Havel's imprisonment, with his *Mistake* (1983), which echoed Paolo Fiere's pedagogy of oppression and took Western liberals to task for their obsession with trivial rights while remaining rather oblivious to violations of basic human rights. Havel bared his own ambivalence and crises of conscience in his 1986 *Largo Desolato.*

In January 1989 Havel was sentenced to jail for the final time for provoking antigovernment demonstrations. In November 1989 he joined in the founding of Civic Forum, which together with the Slovak Public Against Violence brought down President Gustav Husák and forced the Communists to agree on December 10 to a coalition cabinet, which scheduled free multiparty elections. The interim government unanimously elected Havel president on December 29, 1989. He gained an agreement from Soviet President Mikhail Gorbachev for a rapid withdrawal of the Soviet forces that had been stationed in Czechoslovakia since 1968. Following the expiration of his first presidential term on June 5, 1990, the newly elected parliament by a vote of 234 to 50 reelected Havel president on July 5, 1990.

In June 1992 Vladimír Mečiar's nationalist Movement for a Democratic Slovakia fell just short of winning a majority in the Slovak parliament and gained the second-largest bloc in the Czechoslovak parliament. Slovak nationalists blocked the reelection of Havel and prepared for the "Velvet Divorce" of Slovakia from its Czech counterpart in the Czechoslovak state. The largest group in the federal parliament consisted of the right-wing Civic Democratic Party of Václav Klaus. The Right objected to Havel's preference for an "industrial policy," or state economic planning, and to his opposition to the "lustration" law, which indiscriminately revoked the civil rights of all former Communist officeholders. Faced with this situation, a depressed Havel resigned from the presidency on July 20, three months before the official end of his term.

Following the splintering of Czechoslovakia on January 1, 1993, Havel was asked to accept the presidency of the Czech Republic. Though he failed to gain the approval of parliament for an increase in presidential powers, including a veto and the power to dissolve parliament, he agreed and was elected to a five-year term by the Czech parliament on January 26, 1993.

Havel's first wife, Olga, died of cancer in January 1996. Havel's own health—he also suffered from cancer—has been problematic. In December 1996 half of his right lung and a malignant tumor were removed. Despite health problems he was regarded as indispensable by many Czechs as the surest advocate for Czech entry into the European Union (EU). In addition, he was seen as an assurance of stability in the midst of political uncertainties that developed in the country during fall of 1997.

The government of Václav Klaus, which had been in power since 1990, collapsed in November as a result of financial scandals. Rising trade deficits and economic stagnation had undermined the popularity of Klaus's government, but the fatal blows were the revelations that former tennis star Milan Srejber had funneled $200,000 to the Civic Democratic Party before the 1996 election, a month after he had been awarded a privatization agreement for a steel mill, and that corporate donors had created a party slush fund of millions of dollars squirreled away in a Swiss bank. Klaus resigned on November 30 and on December 17 Havel appointed Josef Tosovsky, former governor of the Czech National Bank, the country's central bank, as caretaker prime minister until the June elections. Owing to the opposition of Klaus's party, Havel only narrowly won reelection on January 20, 1998. After Klaus resigned Havel bitterly criticized the former prime minister, with whom he had serious differences. He described the Klaus government as being "in the hands of untrustworthy figures whose primary concern is their personal advancement instead of the interests of the people." On the first ballot Havel needed an absolute majority in each house to gain reelection. But he received only 91 of the 200 deputies' votes and 39 of the 81 senatorial votes. Stanislav Fischer, backed by the Communist Party, won 31 votes and Miroslav Sladek, the Republican leader, won 23 votes, while approximately 100 deputies and senators abstained. On the second ballot only an absolute majority of those parliamentarians present was needed. Havel received 47 senatorial votes and 99 votes from the deputies, the absolute minimum number needed. In April while on vacation in Austria, Havel had an emergency operation on a perforated intestine. Despite these problems, he continued to serve as a symbol of moral authority in the Czech Republic. On July 23, 1998, Havel appointed a left-center cabinet headed by Miloš Zeman,

whose Social Democratic Party won 74 of the 200 lower house seats in the June parliamentary election.

BIBLIOGRAPHY
Havel, Václav. *The Art of the Impossible: Politics as Morality in Practice, Speeches and Writings, 1990–1996.* New York: Fromm International, 1998.
———. *Disturbing the Peace: a Conversation with Karel Hvizdala.* New York: Vintage Books, 1991.
———. *Letters to Olga: June 1979–September 1982.* New York: Henry Holt, 1989.
———. *Open Letters: Selected Writings, 1965–1990.* New York: Vintage Books, 1992.
———. *Politics and Conscience.* Stockholm: Charta 77 Foundation, 1986.
———. *Selected Plays, 1984–87.* London: Faber and Faber, 1994.
Kriseova, Eda. *Václav Havel: The Authorized Biography.* New York: St. Martin's Press, 1993.
Simmons, Michael. *The Reluctant President: A Political Life of Václav Havel.* London: Methuen, 1991.
Bernard Cook

Heath, Edward (1916–)

Conservative prime minister of Great Britain (1970–74). Edward Heath was committed to establishing British links with Europe and led Britain into the European Economic Community (EEC/EC) in 1973. Confronted by economic problems and his government's inability to stifle mounting violence in Northern Ireland, Heath's government was defeated in the elections of 1974. In 1975 he was replaced by Margaret Thatcher as leader of the Conservative Party.

Educated at Balliol College, Oxford, Heath served in the army during the Second World War. For five years after the war Heath worked briefly in civil aviation and as an editor of *Church Times,* but he spent most of his time in banking and working for the Conservative Party. He was elected to the House of Commons in 1950 and moved quickly into the inner circle of Conservative power. From 1955 to 1959 Heath served as the Conservative chief whip during the governments of Anthony Eden and Harold Macmillan, and from 1959 to 1960 Heath was minister of labor. During the brief ministry of Sir Alec Douglas-Home (1963–64), Heath held cabinet rank as minister for trade and industry. After the Conservative defeat in the elections of 1964 and Douglas-Home's withdrawal from politics, Heath moved to seize the leadership of the party. In 1965 a turbulent contest for the Conservative leadership developed among Enoch

Powell, Reginald Maudling, and Heath; Heath prevailed and led his party's opposition to the government of Prime Minister Harold Wilson until the elections of 1970. While continuing to recognize the "special relationship" with the United States, Heath during the late 1960s began to move the Conservative Party closer toward membership in the EEC; earlier efforts to gain British entrance to the EEC were blocked by British nationalists and by French President Charles de Gaulle.

With the Conservative electoral victory in June 1970, Heath became prime minister and launched a range of policies he intended to result in economic and social progress for Britain and a new, more progressive identity for the Conservative Party. Yet with the exception of Britain's entry into the EEC in 1973, Heath's policies led to economic confusion and distress. His 1971 Industrial Relations Act resulted in further straining the relationship between the government and labor unions. A major coal strike resulted in blackouts, and inflation was met with government attempts to limit wages. The economic crisis of 1973–74 reached its nadir when in January 1974 Heath placed the nation on a three-day workweek because of the lack of energy supplies. Besides these economic problems, Heath's government failed to suppress violence in Northern Ireland. In February 1974 the British elected a Labour majority. The following year Heath's leadership of the Conservative Party was challenged and overturned by Margaret Thatcher. Heath continued to hold a seat in the House of Commons and criticized the policies of Prime Ministers Margaret Thatcher and her successor, John Major. His reputation has been based on his loyalty to the Conservative Party, not his effectiveness as prime minister.

BIBLIOGRAPHY

Ball, Stuart, and Anthony Seldon, eds. *The Heath Government, 1970–1974: A Reappraisal.* London: Longmans, 1996.

Campbell, John. *Edward Heath, A Biography.* London: Jonathan Cape, 1993.

Hurd, Douglas. *An End to Promises: Sketch of a Government 1970–74.* London: Collins, 1979.

Hutchinson, George. *Edward Heath, A Personal and Political Biography.* Harlow, U.K.: Longmans, 1970.

Roth, Andrew. *Heath and the Heathmen.* London: Routledge and Kegan Paul, 1972.

William T. Walker

SEE ALSO Thatcher, Margaret

Hebrides

More than 40 islands and over 450 islets stretching in a 150-mile arc off the west coast of Scotland. The total land mass of the Hebrides is 2,596 square miles (6,724 sq km). The Hebrides are divided into the Outer Hebrides and the Inner Hebrides, which are separated by the North Minch and Little Minch channels. The most important islands of the Outer Hebrides are Lewis and Harris, North and South Uist, Benbecula, Barra, Saint Kilda, and the Flannan Islands. The most important islands of the Inner Hebrides are Skye, Mull, Islay, and Jura. The Outer Hebrides, consisting of 1,119 square miles (2,298 sq. km.) were organized in 1975 as the Western Isles, with an area council with more authority than that of comparable bodies on the mainland. The area council is located at Stornoway on the island of Lewis and Harris, the largest, most populous (23,390 inhabitants), and most northerly of the Outer Hebrides group. The council administers the area and region. Stornoway, the largest town in the Outer Hebrides, with over 13,000 inhabitants, is a port and the center for the manufacturing of Harris tweed. The Inner Hebrides are divided into three administrative districts, which are tied to the mainland regions of Highland and Strathclyde.

There has been a progressive depopulation of the Hebrides over the past 150 years, as well as a movement of people from the small islands to the larger ones. The total population of 29,350 on the Outer Hebrides is only about 20 percent of what it was a century and a half earlier. Tenant farming (crofting), limited to sheep and cattle raising and the growing of fodder, potatoes, and some vegetables, along with fishing and weaving, provides the economic base of the outer islands. Distilling, cheese making, and tourism are also significant. Gaelic is widely spoken.

BIBLIOGRAPHY

Ennew, Judith. *The Western Isles Today.* Cambridge: Cambridge University Press, 1980.

Parman, Susan. *Scottish Crofters: A Historical Ethnography of a Celtic Village.* Fort Worth, Tex.: Holt, Rinehart, and Winston, 1990.

Rosemary Cook

SEE ALSO Orkney Islands; Shetland Islands

Hedtoft, Hans (1903–55)

Danish prime minister. Hans Hedtoft, a litographer, worked his way up through the Social Democratic Youth, which he joined as a full-time party member in 1922. He served as chairman for the youth organization from 1927 to 1929, and was elected to parliament in 1935. Hedtoft became chairman of the Social Democratic Party (SP) in 1939, but was forced to resign in 1942 after pressure from the German occupation authority during World War II. In the last years of the occupation he was in contact with the Danish resistance movement and undertook a secret mission to neutral Sweden, where he obtained weapons for the Danish resistance.

After the liberation in 1945 he became the national president of the SP and prime minister in a SP minority government from 1947 to 1950. He wanted Denmark to follow a nonaligned course in the late 1940s, and pushed for a Nordic Security Pact among Denmark, Sweden, and Norway. He did not succeed, and Denmark joined NATO in 1949. In his last years he worked hard for Nordic cooperation through the Nordic Council, which was established in 1952.

BIBLIOGRAPHY

Fitzmaurice, John. *Politics in Denmark.* New York: St. Martin's Press, 1981.

Kjersgaard, Erik. *A History of Denmark.* Copenhagen: Royal Danish Ministry of Foreign Affairs, 1974.

Jørn Boye Nielsen

Hegedüs, András (1922–)

Prime minister of Hungary (1955–56). András Hegedüs was chosen by the leadership of the Hungarian Workers (Communist) Party (MDP) because, as a young Communist, he had not been compromised by the Stalinist policies of the late 1940s and early 1950s.

Hegedus studied engineering and became the general secretary of the Communist youth organization (MADISZ). He filled various positions within the party until 1956. He was a member of the Central Committee from 1950 to 1956 and a year later also joined the party's Political Committee. At the same time, he served in the government in various positions. He became prime minister in 1955 and was one of the politicians who officially "requested" Soviet military assistance for putting down the "counterrevolution" in October 1956. After the suppression of the revolution he was stripped of his government and party positions. Hegedüs spent two years at the Institute of Philosophy of the Soviet Academy of Sciences in Moscow 1957–58 and, on returning home, started working at the Hungarian Academy of Sciences. He was employed at various research institutions afterward, until he was dismissed from his job in 1973 because of voicing dissident political views. He became a freelance

intellectual and also worked at different research institutions. His autobiographical volumes, *A Life in the Shadow of an Idea* (1985) and *Under the Spell of History and Power* (1988), were important contributions to contemporary samizdat literature and helped undermine the ideological monopoly of the Communist Party. Hegedüs also published a number of studies and essays on questions concerning the structure of socialist societies and technological development under socialism.

Hegedüs's career was typical of a relatively large number of central European intellectuals who became committed to Communist ideas early in their life but who, after bitter experiences, such as the ruthless suppression of the Hungarian Revolution of 1956 by the Soviets, became disillusioned first with the practices and later the ideology of communism and ended their career opposing the system.

BIBLIOGRAPHY

Hegedüs, András. *A tortenelem es a hatalom igezeteben: eletrajzi elemzesek.* Budapest: Kossuth, 1988.

———. *Socialism and Bureaucracy.* New York: St. Martin's Press, 1976.

———. *The Structure of Socialist Society.* London: Constable, 1977.

———. *Rendhagyo eletek: szubjektiv reflexiok.* Budapest: BFI-Budapest, 1994.

Tamás Magyarics

SEE ALSO Gerö, Ernö; Kádár, János; Nagy, Imre

Heidegger, Martin (1889–1976)

German philosopher. Born in 1889 into a Roman Catholic family in Baden, Martin Heidegger received a doctorate in philosophy from the University of Freiburg in 1913. After briefly serving in World War I, Heidegger returned to Freiburg in 1920 as assistant to philosopher Edmund Husserl. A full professor at the University of Marburg by 1923, Heidegger published his masterwork, *Being and Time,* in 1927. After this Heidegger became increasingly concerned with political issues, going so far as to join the Nazi Party and to extol publicly its virtues as rector of the University of Freiburg in 1933–34. Compelled to resign the rectorship in 1934 because of political differences with the party, Heidegger withdrew from political matters generally. After the war Heidegger was reinstated as a professor at Freiburg with the help of his friend philosopher Karl Jaspers. While a lingering criticism of Heidegger has been his unwillingness to address his Nazi involvement, his complex philosophy resists being reduced to his shifting political allegiances.

In *Being and Time* Heidegger declared that while the Western philosophical tradition has concerned itself with beings, it has never adequately inquired into the problem of Being itself; that is, it has never asked the question posed by Friedrich Wilhelm Schelling: "Why is there anything rather than nothing?" Human reality is for Heidegger no disembodied Cartesian *cogito* but the simple fact of "being there" (*Dasein*) in the world. Inexplicably "thrown" into the world, *Dasein* is the only being to concern itself with the problem of its own existence, and thus must continually act to find answers to the recurrent question: "What am I?" Many factors in the world compromise *Dasein*'s quest for "authenticity," especially being reduced to a social category (*das Man*) by the anonymous collective "They." *Dasein* can recover from its "Fallenness" into unthinking "average everydayness" only by taking hold of itself and facing the reality of its own eventual nonbeing through concrete choices concerning self-identity.

BIBLIOGRAPHY

Heidegger, Martin. *Being and Time.* New York: Harper and Row, 1962.

Megill, Allan. *Prophets of Extremity: Nietzsche, Heidegger, Foucault, Derrida.* Berkeley: University of California Press, 1985.

Ott, Hugo. *Martin Heidegger: An Intellectual and Political Portrait.* New York: Basic Books, 1993.

Christopher E. Forth

Heinemann, Gustav (1899–1976)

Interior minister of the Federal Republic of Germany from 1949 to 1950, justice minister from 1966 to 1969, and president from 1969 to 1974. A lawyer and prominent representative of Germany's Confessing Church during the Hitler years, Heinemann became a founding member of the Christian Democratic Party (CDU) and interior minister in Chancellor Konrad Adenauer's first cabinet. In September 1950 he resigned over the question of West German rearmament, founded and led the ill-starred neutralist All-German People's Party, and in 1957 found his permanent political home in the Social Democratic Party (SPD). After winning election to the Bundestag (lower house of parliament), Heinemann served as justice minister in Kurt Kiesinger's grand coalition, in which capacity he pushed through a general liberalization of the penal code. Because of his political experience, independence of mind, and unblemished personal integrity,

Heinemann emerged by 1969 as the leading SPD candidate to replace Heinrich Lübke as president. His election, symbolically held in Berlin and won with a majority of only six votes over his CDU rival, Gerhard Schröder, anticipated the chancellorship of Willy Brandt, whose *Ostpolitik* Heinemann as president generally supported. Heinemann was succeeded in 1974 by the Free Democratic Party's Walter Scheel, who had helped him gain the presidency five years before.

BIBLIOGRAPHY

Braun, Joachim. *Gustav Heinemann: The Committed President.* London: Wolf, 1972.

Lindemann, Helmut. *Gustav Heinemann: Ein Leben für die Demokratie.* Munich: Kosel, 1978.

Lotz, Martin, ed. *Gustav W. Heinemann: Bibliographie.* Bonn: Archiv der Sozialen Demokratie, 1976.

Eric C. Rust

Heitmann, Steffen (1944–)

German politician and minister of justice in the Land (state) of Saxony. Steffen Heitmann was born on September 8, 1944, in Dresden. After completing the *Abitur* in 1963, he started working in the administration of the Protestant church. From 1964 to 1969 he studied theology and classical languages at the University of Leipzig. He then served as a priest, educator, and administrator of the Lutheran Church of Saxony. After training as a jurist at a church institute, he became an adviser to East Germans applying for exit permits or who had come into conflict with the regime. Through this work he became actively involved in the opposition movement and its mobilization of resistance in Dresden. He gave legal advice, assisted in the dissolution of the local State Security Service, and became a member of the Dresden city council. In 1990 he played a leading role in the constitutional reform of Saxony. On November 8, 1990, the new Christian Democratic minister president of Saxony, Kurt Biedenkopf, appointed Heitmann minister of justice. In December 1991 Heitmann joined the Christian Democratic Union (CDU).

In 1993 Heitmann gained notoriety when Chancellor Helmut Kohl proposed him as candidate for president, principally because he was from East Germany. Measured against then president Richard von Weizsäcker, who had been highly praised for his eloquence and noble stature, Heitmann was judged gray, awkward, and narrow-minded. Even inside the CDU, both in the East and the West, Kohl's choice was severely criticized. During interviews Heitmann made some unfortunate and controversial statements about the German nation and its history, and the role of women, which showed him as, at best, rather conservative. These were used by the media and competing political camps to demolish his presidential candidacy, which he withdrew on November 25. Still, the ill-fated candidacy did not harm his reputation as a tough but able minister of justice in Saxony. When Heinz Eggert had to resign as minister of the interior of Saxony and as deputy party chairman of the federal CDU in July 1994, Heitmann was appointed to both offices.

In March 1995, Heitmann was awarded the Freedom Prize by the conservative Stiftung Demokratie und Marktwirtschaft (Foundation for Democracy and Market Economy) for his "straightforwardness" and "civic courage."

BIBLIOGRAPHY

Heitmann, Steffen. *Die Revolution in der Spur des Rechts: Verdienst und Schwache des Umbruchs in der früheren DDR.* Dresden: Reuter and Klockner, 1996.

Anjana Buckow

SEE ALSO German Democratic Republic

Herbert, Zbigniew (1924–1998)

Polish poet, playwright, and essayist. Zbigniew Herbert was born in Lwow. He made his debut in 1956 with his first collection of poems, *Struna Shwiatka* (String of Light). His work raises important existential, aesthetic, and ethical questions. His thoughtful, weak, noble auto-ironical poetic "self" faces a multiform evil of the world. To defend the values of truth and courage he refers to the tradition of European culture, as in his most famous poetical series, *Pan Cogito.*

Greco-Latin tradition, in particular, is a source of Herbert's stoicism and inspiration for his poetic images, which often take the form of parables. No less important seem the questions the poet asks about central issues of art, its cognitive limits and moral functions, as well as the violations and distortions that literature suffered under totalitarianism. The language of his poetry combines both modern and traditional elements, accurate in their brevity, reserved and ironical. Herbert published eight volumes of poems, two volumes of essays, including *Barbarzyńca w orrodzie* (A Barbarian in the Garden), and a collection of dramas, including *Jaskinia filozofów* (The Cave of Philosophers), and *Lalek* (The Dolls).

BIBLIOGRAPHY

Herbert, Zbigniew. *Selected Poems.* Tr. by C. Milosz and P. D. Scott. New York: Oxford University Press, 1977.

Levine, Madeline G. "Zbigniew Herbert: In Defense of Civilization," in Madeline Levine, *Contemporary Polish Poetry 1925–1975.* New York: Twayne, 1971.

Krystyna Jakowska

Herling-Grudziński, Gustaw (1919–)

Polish writer, literary critic, and publicist. After World War II Gustaw Herling-Grudziński was an émigré and his work was censored in Poland. He was a shrewd analyst of the situation in Poland, of communism, and of the transformation of 1989 to a market economy. In his literary works he searched for a sense of history and for values that made sense of human existence.

Born in Kielce on May 20, 1919, Herling-Grudziński studied Polish literature at Warsaw University and made his debut as literary critic in 1935. During World War II he was arrested by the Soviets and sent to a labor camp at Jertsevo, in the Archangel district. He was eventually allowed to join a Polish army sponsored by the Soviets and fought against the Germans in Italy. After the war, Herling-Grudziński collaborated with émigré cultural institutions such as the Paris Kultura and Radio Free Europe. In 1955 he moved to Naples, where he edited a Polish language weekly.

His experiences in the Soviet labor camp were described in *Inny Swiat* (A World Apart, English edition, 1951; Polish edition, 1953), the most discerning book about the Soviet penal camp system before Aleksandr Solzhenitsyn's *Gulag Archipelago.* In his short stories, *Skrzydla oltarza* (1960) and *Opowiadania zebrane* (1990), he portrays exile and separation. *Książę niezłomny* (1963) is a discussion on the meaning of emigration, for Herling-Grudziński a painfully personal issue. His reflections on political and cultural problems of Europe were described in *Dziennik pisany noca* (The Journal Written at Night, 1980–93). Herling-Grudziński's works were published principally by Instytut Literacki in Paris; in Poland they circulated in the underground. *Wieza i inne opowiadania* (1988) was his first book published officially in Poland.

BIBLIOGRAPHY

Bolecki, Włodzimierz. *Ciemy staw: trzy szkice do portretu Gustawa Herlinga-Grudzinskiego.* Warsaw: Plejada, 1991.

Kudelski, Zdzisław. *Pielgrzym Swietokrzyski.* Lublin: Wyd. FIS, 1991.

Przybylski, Ryszard K. *Byc i pisac: o prozie Gustawa Herlinga-Grudzinskiego.* Poznan: Wyd. 5a, 1991.

Wyslouch, Seweryna, and Ryszard K. Przybylski, eds. *Etos i artyzm: rzecz o Gustawie Herlingu-Grudzinskim.* Poznan: Wyd. 5a, 1991.

Andrzej Stoff

Hermannsson, Steingrimur (1928–)

The most influential Icelandic politician of the 1980s. Son of a former prime minister of Iceland, Steingrimur Hermannsson was elected to parliament for the first time in 1971. That same year he became secretary of the Progressive Party (center party) and in 1979 its chairman. He served various ministerial posts in coalition governments from the late 1970s to the early 1990s. Thus, he was minister of justice, ecclesiastical affairs, and agriculture from 1978 to 1979, minister of fisheries and communications from 1980 to 1983, and minister of foreign affairs from 1987 to 1988. Moreover, he served as prime minister from 1983 to 1987 and again from 1988 to 1991. When appointed director of the Central Bank of Iceland in 1994, Hermannsson retired from politics.

The 1980s are often called the decade of the Progressive Party in Icelandic politics, and the party's influence can, to a great extent, be attributed to Hermannsson's popularity and political skills. As the party of the center, it has frequently led coalition governments, sometimes with the parties on the left and sometimes with the Independence Party, on the right. Through his ability to negotiate among those holding diverse political opinions, Hermannsson utilized this strategic position to give his party a leading position in Icelandic political life.

BIBLIOGRAPHY
Hjalmarsson, Jon R. *History of Iceland: From the Settlement to the Present Day.* Reykjavik: Iceland Review, 1993.

Gudmundur Halfdanarson

SEE ALSO Palsson, Thorsteinn; Thoroddsen, Gunnar

Hermlin, Stephan (1915–97)

East German writer whose central theme was resistance to fascism. Stephan Hermlin was born Rudolf Leder on April 13, 1915, in Chemnitz. His father, a Romanian Jew interned in Germany during World War I, became a successful businessman, but contrary to the myth advanced by Hermlin, was not killed in a Nazi concentration camp. After spending six weeks in Sachsenhausen in 1937, he emigrated to Great Britain. Hermlin's mother, contrary to his assertion, was a Galician Jew rather than English. Hermlin joined the Communist Party of Germany (KPD) when he was sixteen. Having to leave secondary school to become an apprentice printer in 1933, Hermlin said that he had fought in an underground struggle against the Nazis from 1933 to 1936. He then emigrated to Palestine. Though he claimed to have fought in the Spanish Civil War, upon arriving in France in 1937 he was interned. In 1943, before being deported, he escaped to Switzerland. At the end of the war he went back to Germany and worked at Radio Frankfurt.

In 1947 he went to the east and joined the Socialist Unity Party (SED). He was lauded by Stalin for his stories and poems dealing with the antifascist effort. Though he was a member of the Central Committee of the SED and vice president of the East German Writers Union, he developed and expressed a critical perspective. In 1957 he published *Kommandeuse,* a laudatory account of the 1953 uprising of East Germans against the Soviets. Though penalized for this, he followed up with *Der Leutenant York von Wartenburg,* in which he portrayed the 1944 plot against Hitler without a Communist slant. In 1976 Hermlin together with Stefan Heym persuaded other intellectuals to protest the revocation of the East German Song writer and dissident Wolf Biermann's citizenship. His pseudoautobiographical 1979 *Abendlicht* (*Evening Light*) was denounced in the West as a fabrication.

Hermlin was loyal to the German Democratic Republic as long as it lasted and praised its accomplishments after its demise. He became a member of the successor party to the SED, the Party of Democratic Socialism, and the Committee for Justice, which protested legal action against former functionaries of the DDR. He died on April 6, 1997.

BIBLIOGRAPHY
Ertl, Wolfgang. *Stephan Hermlin und die Tradition.* Bern: P. Lang, 1977.
Hermlin, Stephan. *Die Zeit der Gemeinsamkeit: Erzahlungen.* Munich: Deutscher Taschenbuch Verlag, 1991.
———. *Evening Light.* San Francisco: Fjord Press, 1983.
———. *In den Kampfen dieser Zeit.* Berlin: Wagenbach, 1995.
———. *Nachdichtungen.* Berlin: Aufbau-Verlag, 1987.
Schlenstedt, Silvia. *Stephan Hermlin: Leben und Werk.* Berlin: Verlag das Europäische Buch, 1985.

Bernard Cook

SEE ALSO Biermann, Wolf

Herzog, Roman (1934–)

Elected president of the Federal Republic of Germany on May 23, 1994, he assumed office on July 1. Roman Herzog was born on April 5, 1934, in Landshut. He studied and subsequently taught law at the University of Munich. From 1965 to 1969 he was professor of constitutional law and politics at the Free University of Berlin. He then served as rector of the College of Administrative Science in Speyer. He joined the Christian Democratic Union in 1972 and was elected to the Bundestag (lower house of parliament), where he served from 1972 to 1978. In 1978 he was appointed minister of culture and sport in the Land (state) government of Baden-Württemberg, and in 1980 he became minister of the interior. In that post he gained a reputation as a hard-liner by requiring participants in unauthorized demonstrations to pay for police costs and approving the use of rubber bullets to quell disturbances.

In 1983 he was appointed to the Federal Constitutional Court in Karlsruhe and in 1986 became its president. There he surprised some by his declaration that the freedom of assembly guaranteed by the Basic Law, the constitution of the Federal Republic of Germany was more important than the concern of the state for maintaining order. Yet he demonstrated what might be called strict constructionism by decrying the tendency of many to seek from the courts decisions that were more appropriately the domain of the Bundestag.

After the withdrawal of Steffen Heitmann, Chancellor Helmut Kohl's first choice to succeed President Richard von Weizächer, Herzog became the Christian Democratic candidate and defeated his Social Democratic rival, Johannes Rau, by 696 votes to 605. During the campaign Herzog called for the repeal of Germany's restrictive citizenship law and stated that the Germans of the east were "not a burden to us but a windfall." He added that they had brought with them " experiences that we in the west did not have, in a world where many things were more humane than they were with us."

BIBLIOGRAPHY

Beitlich, Klemens. *Roman Herzog: Ansichten eines Prasidenten.* Munich: C. Bertelsmann, 1998.

Reker, Stefan. *Roman Herzog.* Berlin: Edition Q, 1995.

Wiedemeyer, Wolfgang. *Roman Herzog: der Erste Gesamtdeutsche Präsident.* Munich: Bonn Aktuell, 1994.

Bernard Cook

SEE ALSO Weizsäcker, Richard von

Herzog, Werner (1942–)

German filmmaker. This idiosyncratic artist's preoccupation with lives beyond the fringes of normality has established him as one of the most well-known directors of postwar German cinema. Similar to other directors of the New German Cinema, such as Rainer Werner Fassbinder, Alexander Kluge, and Volker Schlöndorff, Werner Herzog produced many films that address his generation's unwanted Nazi legacy.

After studying in Munich and Pittsburgh, Herzog began making documentaries. He has said that his poetically visual films must be understood through his earlier documentaries. Herzog's films are marked thematically and formally by a relentless quest for "authenticity." His latest work, *My Best Fiend* (1999), a candid documentary about his ongoing, tumultuous collaboration with the actor Klaus Kinski, marks a return to these origins.

In his early films, Herzog addresses the level of fantasy and primordial drives to build allegories of barbarism. His films feature epics in which individuals approach mythic dimensions as they struggle against the bounds of humanity and nature. All of his films end in the apocalyptic defeat and usually the death of the main characters. His first film, *Signs of Life* (1968), won the Silver Bear at the Berlin Film festival. Shot on location on a Greek island, the film depicts one German soldier's rebellion against the army in World War II.

His second film, *Even Dwarfs Started Small* (1971) shocked viewers with its loosely connected scenes of chaos and destruction. Shot in the Canary Islands with an entire cast of little people, the film depicts the takeover of a correctional institution by its inmates. Dwarves destroy symbols of both civilization (equipment, typewriters, cars, dinnerware) and nature (trees, flowers, and animals) to increasingly greater mayhem and no specified resolution. An unconventional plot line sustains the allegory of imprisonment and rebellion. There are unnerving acts of barbarism, such as a crucifixion of a monkey, repeated scenes of cannibalistic and carnivorous chickens, and a five-minute sequence of a dwarf's cackling at a lamed camel.

Aguirre, The Wrath of God (1972), Herzog's first international success, transcends a one-dimensional critique of civilization. Shot in the Peruvian jungle, *Aguirre* allegorizes imperialism and is based on a historical event. A mad, disfigured conquistador leads a faction of rebels on a suicidal quest through the Amazon for the fabled El Dorado. Other films featuring the flawed nature of humanity, uncontrollable drives, and obsessional urges were *Fata Morgana* (1971), *Heart of Glass* (1976), and *Fitzcarraldo* (1982). *Fitzcarraldo* depicts the clash of east and west, of high and low culture in its epic depiction of a man obsessed with bringing opera (high European culture) to the Iquitos, an indigenous Latin American people living in an inaccessible region of the Amazon rainforest. The film's riveting portrait of a man on a dangerous, unrealizable colonialist mission, particularly his determination to haul a ship over a mountain through hostile Indian territory, won Herzog a best director award at the Cannes Film Festival. Herzog's insistence on enacting the central metaphor of the film, that is, actually moving a ship over a South American mountain, delayed the film's completion by four years. Like *Fitzcarraldo* and *Aguirre, Enigma of Kaspar Hauser* (1974) tells of a man more comfortable outside of the confines of humanity. A dungeon prisoner for the first eighteen years of his life, Kaspar Hauser appears in a nineteenth-century town without knowing how to talk or interact with others. He is educated according to Enlightenment ideals of rationality only to fall into despair and ultimately be murdered by the man who was his mentor.

Herzog's has also made films that follow the tradition of Weimar expressionism. *Nosferatu the Vampyre* (1979), for example, is a beautiful and melancholy homage to F. W. Murnau's 1920 masterpiece. Unpredictable camera angles, vivid lighting, luminescent make-up, and unusual framing devices illustrate the perceptual distortion of the characters. Long-time collaborator, Klaus Kinski, brilliantly plays the hideous vampire cursed with immortality and plagued with unquenchable loneliness.

Stroszek (1977) features a quiet unassuming alcoholic who has spent most of his life in prisons. Together with a prostitute (played by Eva Mattes) and an old eccentric, Stroszek journeys to the U.S. Midwest. Simultaneously bleak and amusing, this film portrays three misfit pilgrims from Berlin trying to reconcile their fantasy of the American way of life with the forsaken reality that meets them. Herzog's themes often involve the failures of the human psyche rather than the problems with social institutions. The emotional and physical extremes his characters face match inhospitable and marginalized geographic settings. His protagonists revolt against the conventions of civil society, seek a life of extreme challenge, and ultimately fail to transcend this challenge. The thematic consistency of Herzog's thirty-year long career in filmmaking can best be summarized by a fascination with the consequences and challenges faced by the marginalized, dispossessed, and deviant.

BIBLIOGRAPHY

Cook, David A. *A Short History of Narrative Film.* New York: W. W. Norton, 1981.

Corrigan, Timothy, ed. *Herzog: Between Mirage and History.* New York: Methuen, 1986.

———. *New German Cinema: The Displaced Image.* Revised Edition. Bloomington: Indiana University Press, 1994.

Jill Gillespie

SEE ALSO Fassbinder, Rainer Werner; Schlöndorff, Volker

Heseltine, Michael (1933–)

Conservative member of the British Parliament since 1966. Michael Heseltine held various offices of state including secretary of state for the environment (1979–83, 1990–92), for defense (1983–86), for industry and president of the board of trade (1992–95); and deputy prime minister and first secretary of state (1995–97).

Following a successful career in property development and publishing, Heseltine entered parliament in 1966 as member for Tavistock. In 1974 he became the member for Henley. In Edward Heath's Conservative government he served in several minor ministerial positions, and during the years in opposition was his party's spokesman on industry (1974–76) and the environment (1976–79). When Margaret Thatcher assumed the prime ministership in 1979, Heseltine was appointed secretary for the environment. He took a keen interest in the plight of Britain's inner cities, notably Liverpool, following rioting there in 1981. Friction with Thatcher over domestic policy led to his "reassignment" to Defense. There he tackled the implementation of the NATO decision to improve battlefield nuclear weapons in Europe (1979) and ensuing conflicts with Britain's antinuclear arms movement. He resigned from this post following the Westland Affair in 1986, in which he strongly favored the sale of the British firm Westland Helicopters to a European consortium rather than an American company, a view not shared by Thatcher. The resignation of Geoffrey Howe, the deputy prime minister, in November 1990 and divisions within the Conservative Party over European monetary union triggered Heseltine's long-expected challenge for the party leadership. John Major won the contest for the leadership and appointed Heseltine as environment secretary in his new cabinet, with the task of reforming the highly unpopular poll tax. Within months Heseltine announced that it was replaced by a new council tax based on property values. He left government when the Conservatives were defeated by Labour in the general election of 1997.

BIBLIOGRAPHY

Critchley, Julian. *Heseltine.* London: Andre Deutsch, 1987.

Heseltine, Michael. *Where There's a Will.* London: Hutchinson, 1987.

———. *The Challenge of Europe.* London: Weidenfeld and Nicholson, 1989.

Eileen Groth Lyon

Heuss, Theodor (1884–1963)

President of the Federal Republic of Germany (1949–59). Theodor Heuss was born in Brackenheim, Württemberg, on January 31, 1884. He studied at the Universities of Munich and Berlin and received a Ph.D. in 1905. He was an editor of the journal *Hilfe* of his mentor, Friedrich Naumann. In 1912 he became editor in chief of the *Neckarzeitung.* From 1918 to 1922 he was involved in the labor movement. He became a professor at the Deutsche Hochschule für Politik in 1920. Heuss was elected to the parliament of the Weimar Republic in 1924 and was leader of the Democratic Party until it was suppressed by Hitler in 1933, even though Heuss and other Democratic delegates voted for the March 23, 1933, Enabling Act, which gave Hitler dictatorial power. Heuss's book, *Hitlers Weg* (*Hitler's Way*), was condemned and publicly burned by the Nazis. He continued to write articles under the pseudonym Thomas Brackenheim for the *Frankfurter Zeitung* until that paper was suppressed. Because of his public objection to the Nazis' anti-Semitic policy, he was forced into retirement in 1936. He could not work for the remainder of the Nazi period, and his wife supported the family.

Under the American occupation Heuss was minister of public worship and education for Württemberg-Baden from September 1945 to December 1946. He was approved as editor of the Heidelberg *Rhein-Neckar Zeitung* in 1945. In 1946 both Heuss and his wife, Elly Knapp Heuss, were elected to the Württemberg legislature. In 1948 Heuss became professor of constitutional law at the Stuttgart Polytechnic Institute.

As head of the Free Democratic Party (FDP), the successor to the pre-Nazi Democratic Party, he played a key role in the constituent assembly. Heuss's contribution to the Basis Law (the constitution) of the Federal Republic gained him the title "father of the Bonn constitution." His retort was that rather than father, he had been the "obstetrician."

Heuss was elected the first president of the Federal Republic on September 12, 1949. His candidacy was opposed at first by conservative Catholics because he was a Protestant and by the Communists, who voted for Social Democrat Kurt Schumacher because Heuss had voted for the 1933 Enabling Act. Heuss, who had been supported by Konrad Adenauer, the leader of the Christian Democrats, for the presidency, then nominated Adenauer to become the first chancellor of the Federal Republic. This was confirmed by the Bundestag on September 17 with the indispensable support of the FDP. Heuss contributed to the positive image of the Federal Republic. His Protestantism offset the perceived Catholic influence of the Christian Democrats and his literary and academic reputation merited respect. He was reelected to the presidency in 1954 and retired from politics at the end of his second term. Heuss died on December 12, 1963.

BIBLIOGRAPHY

Fussmann, Klaus. *Theodor Heuss: ein Leitbild des Liberalismus.* Sankt Augustin, Germany: COMDOK, 1989.

Hamm-Brucher, Hildegard. *Gerechtigkeit erhoht ein Volk: Theodor Heuss und die deutsche Demokratie.* Munich: Piper, 1984.

Heuss, Theodor. *Theodor-Heuss-Lesebuch.* Tübingen: R. Wunderlich and H. Leins, 1975.

Moller, Horst. *Theodor Heuss: Staatsmann und Schriftsteller.* Bonn: Bouvier, 1990.

Nicholls, A. J. *The Bonn Republic: West German Democracy 1945–1990.* London: Longman, 1997.

Pikart, Eberhard. *Theodor Heuss und Konrad Adenauer: die Rolle des Bundespräsidenten in der Kanzlerdemokratie.* Stuttgart: Belser, 1976.

Sieckmeyer, Doris. *Theodor Heuss, der Zeichner.* Sankt Augustin, Germany: COMDOK, 1993.

Winter, Ingelore M. *Theodor Heuss: ein Portrait.* Tubingen: R. Wunderlich, 1983.

Wurtzbacher-Rundholz, Ingrid. *Verfassungsgeschichte und Kulturpolitik bei Dr. Theodor Heuss: bis zur Grundung der Bundesrepublik Deutschland durch den Parlamentärischen Rat 1948–49.* Frankfurt am Main: Lang, 1981.

Bernard Cook

SEE ALSO Adenauer, Konrad

Hillery, Patrick J. (1923–)

President of Ireland from 1976 to 1990. Patrick Hillery was born in County Clare in 1923 and was educated at University College Dublin. In 1951 he was elected as a member of Fianna Fáil to parliament for Clare. He held this seat until he represented Ireland on the European Economic Community (EEC) Commission in 1973.

From 1973 to 1976 he served as a vice president of the commission with responsibility for social affairs. Hillery held many government posts: minister for education (1959–65), minister of industry and commerce (1965–66), minister for labor (1966–69), and minister for foreign affairs (1969–72). He was on the negotiating team for Ireland's entry into the European Community (EC).

Hillery replaced Cearbhall O'Dalaigh as president in November 1976, following the latter's resignation. He was a low-key president who represented the state in line with his formal constitutional position. During the 1990 presidential election there were accusations that Fianna Fáil politicians had improperly pressured him not to dissolve the 1982 Fianna Fáil minority government. Hillery remained unscathed, however, and handed over the office to Mary Robinson following that election.

BIBLIOGRAPHY

Collins, Neil. *Irish Politics Today.* 3rd ed. New York: St. Martin's Press, 1997.

Hillery, Patrick. *Community Social Policy: Progress and Prospects.* Geneva: International Institute for Labour Studies, 1975.

Michael J. Kennedy

SEE ALSO Childers, Erskine; Robinson, Mary

Hochhuth and *The Deputy*

The dramatist Rolf Hochhuth's *Der Stellvertreter,* which premiered at the Freie Volksbühne (Free People's Theater) in West Berlin on February 20, 1963, precipitated a widespread and heated public debate concerning the conduct of Pope Pius XII during the Holocaust. The title of the play, translated into English first as *The Representative* and then as *The Deputy,* carries a double meaning, referring first to the pope as the vicar, or representative, of Christ on earth and secondly to the drama's fictional protagonist, the young Jesuit Riccardo Fontana. Having failed in Rome to effect a public protest on behalf of Hitler's victims at the height of the Nazi Holocaust, Riccardo, wearing the yellow star of David, accompanies a group of deported Italian Jews to the gas chambers at Auschwitz, thereby filling as a deputy the representative office refused by the pope. Although Pius XII appears personally in only one scene of Hochhuth's play, the fact of his silence provides the background for the action and dialogue of the other characters and emerges as the work's dominant theme. It was above all this allegation of culpable silence on the part of the Vatican during the Holocaust that gen-

erated the controversy following the publication and performance of *The Deputy* in Europe and the United States.

The Deputy, which has remained Rolf Hochhuth's most successful play, was also his first, bringing to world attention a German author almost entirely unknown prior to its publication. Born in 1931 in Eschwege just to the west of what later became the inner-German border, Hochhuth grew to adulthood under the Third Reich and the American military occupation. Leaving high school early at seventeen, he worked for several years as a bookseller's apprentice in Eschwege, Marburg, Heidelberg, and Munich before becoming a reader for the publishing house Bertelsmann in 1955. Although Hochhuth's experiments with writing during this period remained for the moment unpublished, the years were formative in his development not only as a writer but also as a student of contemporary history and politics. His deep interest in the unresolved issues of his country's recent past and particularly his fascination with the enigmatic Kurt Gerstein, a Protestant dissident who joined the elite Nazi corps, the SS, in order to combat Hitler's regime from within, would ultimately lead him to the sources from which he constructed *The Deputy.*

Having abandoned earlier plans for a short story centering on Gerstein, Hochhuth began daily work on his play in 1959. Although Gerstein, who had approached both Protestant and Catholic leaders in Germany during World War II with details of the Nazi death camps in the East, remained a major character in *The Deputy,* the playwright chose as his central figures the young Jesuit Riccardo and Pope Pius XII, whose moral authority made him the ideal antagonist of the drama. Drawing on published sources and interviews conducted in Rome, Hochhuth researched the role of the Roman Catholic Church during the Holocaust and constructed *The Deputy* as both a work of fiction and documentation of fact. In addition to the meticulous detail incorporated into his stage directions, Hochhuth compiled his research in a lengthy commentary entitled "Historical Sidelights" and appended to the text of the play.

Hochhuth completed *The Deputy* in 1961 and received a Gerhart Hauptmann Prize for his work the following year, but the controversial nature of the play initially prevented its publication. His first publisher, an affiliate of Bertelsmann, had already begun preparations for printing the work when a higher office in the company intervened. One of the proofs, however, found its way to the Heinrich Maria Ledig-Rowohlt of the Rowohlt publishing house, who not only agreed to publish *The Deputy* but also contacted Erwin Piscator about the possibility of staging it. Piscator, an established director best known for his communist-oriented "political theater" in Berlin during the 1920s, became an enthusiastic champion of Hochhuth's work, which he promoted as both a new departure in theater and a vital breakthrough in confronting repressed problems of Europe's recent history. A significant obstacle to production, however, remained the daunting length of the play, which would extend to about seven or eight hours if performed in its entirety. Committed in principle to the full text but recognizing the difficulties of presenting it, Piscator staged a significantly abridged play while arranging for its premiere to coincide with Rowohlt's publication of the complete work.

Notwithstanding the remarkable diversity of the play's productions, *The Deputy*'s climactic fourth act, and thus its central theme, remained essentially consistent. Although the portrayal of Pius XII naturally varied with the visions of actors and directors, Hochhuth's script is unambiguously indicting, and his personal views, as related in the appendix to the play, are even less sympathetic. The pope's concern for the Catholic Church's finances and his protests against the Allied bombing of Rome are set in sharp contrast to his equivocal posture toward Hitler, whom he regards as an awkward but vital instrument against the advance of Soviet armies across Europe. Hochhuth's Pius rejects Riccardo's pleas not as a moral coward but as a cautious and experienced diplomat. Pressed to respond to the deportation of Jews from Rome, he dictates a vague statement, based on an actual text from the Vatican's *L'Osservatore Romano,* which expresses his solidarity with the suffering but avoids mention of the Jews by name. The heated exchange between the pope and Riccardo culminates in mutual outrage, as Riccardo pins the yellow star on his cassock and the pope, repelled by this gesture, stains his hand with ink in signing the ambiguous proclamation. Following the intervening fifth act, the play closes with a text from Ernst von Weizsäcker's 1943 memo to Berlin, in which the German ambassador reports the Vatican's self-restraint during the deportations, cites the text from the Vatican newspaper, and notes with approval the lack of any direct reference to the Jews. Before the final curtain, the voice of an announcer explains that the mass murder of Jews thus continued, reaching its height the following summer, until the last prisoners of Auschwitz were freed by Soviet troops.

For over a year following its Berlin premiere, *The Deputy* enjoyed popularity and notoriety unmatched by any other postwar German drama. Beginning even before the first production, the public controversy surrounding the play took on international dimensions as producers in major European cities as well as New York followed Piscator in rushing the work to the stage. Expressions of outrage and opposition came primarily from Catholic critics, but opinion was divided here as elsewhere. Most remarkable among reported reactions to *The Deputy* was a rumor in Rome, published by Hannah Arendt, according to which the dying Pope John XXIII, Pius XII's successor, was said to have found the play compelling. The official reaction of the Vatican, however, was less in doubt. In a letter to an English Catholic periodical just before election as Pope Paul VI in 1963, Cardinal Giovanni Battista Montini described Hochhuth's work as inept and suggested a possible lack of "ordinary human integrity" on the part of the author. Having worked closely with Pius XII during the period in question, Montini praised both the courage of the pontiff and the wisdom of his decisions. Open protest, he argued, would merely have resulted in further suffering. Hochhuth, replying that Montini had accepted and represented this same view at the time of the deportations, claimed that it was precisely this posture which had played into the hands of Hitler. Maintaining that even the rumor of possible protest had caused German officials to hesitate, he also rejected the suggestion that the suffering of the Jews could have been substantially worsened.

The debate between the champions and detractors of *The Deputy* played itself out for the most part on the pages of journals and newspapers but also took on more dramatic forms. The largest demonstration against the play occurred in Basel, Switzerland, where some two hundred police officers were required to restrain approximately six thousand Catholic and right-wing demonstrators. Hochhuth subsequently moved to Switzerland, inspired by the determination of the Swiss to allow the performance of his work under these conditions. In West Germany, where the papal nuncio weighed the possibility of legal action on charges of sacrilege or defamation of character, Hochhuth also faced the possibility of prosecution. Although this course was abandoned, it was in part the work of Vatican diplomacy that brought about a kind of censure against Hochhuth by the government of the Federal Republic of Germany. Responding to a question formally moved in the West German parliament, the government, while not mentioning Hochhuth or *The Deputy* by name, expressed its regret for recent aspersions against Pius XII.

In the end, Hochhuth undoubtedly benefited not only from the favor of celebrated intellectuals but also from the reaction of his more prominent critics. The controversy over The Deputy, to the extent that it pitted the author against religious or state authority, evoked one of the play's major themes, and several of Hochhuth's subsequent works have continued very much in this vein. Although some of these have provoked notable controversies of their own, none has achieved the extraordinary success of *The Deputy*. This, of course, is primarily because of the play's subject and the timing of its allegations. Recognized in the early postwar period for his leadership of the Catholic Church through war and persecution under totalitarian regimes, Pius XII has received public attention since Hochhuth's drama primarily in connection with the Holocaust. Saul Friedländer's *Pius XII and the Third Reich* in 1964 and the Pope Paul VI's decision the same year to begin publishing Vatican records from World War II marked the beginning of a debate among historians that has continued to the present. Although this scholarship has yielded important new insights, the controversy, which has reemerged recently with efforts toward Pius XII's beatification and canonization, is only in part a dispute of fact. Pius XII's opposition to National Socialism and the rescue efforts of Catholic institutions under his leadership are well-established, as are the Vatican's awareness of the Nazi genocide and its decision not to denounce Hitler's government openly. At issue, rather, remain the more elusive questions, rendered dramatically by Hochhuth in *The Deputy*, of the Pope's motives, his capacity for action, and the effect to which he might have spoken out against the Holocaust.

BIBLIOGRAPHY

Bentley, Eric, ed. *The Storm over The Deputy*. New York: Grove, 1964.

Blet, Pierre. *Pius XII and the Second World War: According to the Archives of the Vatican*. Tr. by Lawrence J. Johnson. New York: Paulist Press, 1997.

Cornwell, John. *Hitler's Pope: The Secret History of Pius XII*. New York: Viking, 1999.

Friedländer, Saul. *Pius XII and the Third Reich: A Documentation*. Tr. by Charles Fullman. New York: Knopf, 1966.

Hinck, Walter, ed. *Rolf Hochhuth—Eingriff in die Zeitgeschichte: Essays zum Werk*. Reinbek bei Hamburg: Rowohlt, 1981.

Hochhuth, Rolf. *The Representative: A Christian Tragedy*. Tr. and with a preface by Robert David MacDonald. London: Oberon, 1998.

Joel Dark

SEE ALSO Paul VI; Pius XII

Hoffmann, Karel (1924–)

Czechoslovak Communist functionary. After secondary school, Karel Hoffmann worked as a helper at the Skoda Works in Pilsen from 1942 to 1945. He joined the Communist Party in 1945, and from 1945 to 1949 studied at the Advanced School for Politics and Social Sciences. An opponent of the 1968 Prague Spring, or loosening of control by the Communist Party under Alexander Dubček, Hoffmann lost his position as minister of culture and information in April 1968. He supported the Warsaw Pact invasion of Czechoslovakia in August and the ensuing Soviet suppression of what he regarded as a counterrevolution. He was rewarded for his stance. Early in 1969 he was appointed minister of post and telegraph, and in January 1971 he was elected a candidate member of the Communist Party's Politburo.

On August 10, 1995, Hoffmann was arrested and accused of treason for collaborating with a foreign power at the time of the Soviet-led Warsaw Pact invasion. The charges were subsequently dismissed, however, as politically motivated rather than criminal.

BIBLIOGRAPHY

Hoffmann, Karel. *Zkouska zralosti revolucniho odboroveho hnuti: vybrane projevy a stati 1971–1983*. Prague: Prace, 1984.

Bernard Cook

Hoist, Johan Jorgen (1937–94)

Foreign minister of Norway (1993–94). Johan Jorgen Hoist facilitated top-secret talks in Norway between Israel and the Palestine Liberation Organization (PLO) that led to the September 1993 peace agreement on limited Palestinian self-rule in the Gaza Strip and the West Bank.

Hoist was born in Oslo on November 29, 1937. He studied at the University of Oslo and Columbia University in New York City. Considered the preeminent Scandinavian scholar on strategic considerations in the region, he was a key academic and political figure in Scandinavia and wrote many articles and books. Hoist served in the Defense Ministry and the Foreign Ministry before becoming defense minister in 1986, a position he held until 1993.

Already well known in northern Europe, he played his greatest role as peace negotiator in the Israeli-PLO agreement that served as his crowning achievement. He used unorthodox strategies to facilitate that historic settlement. For example, he hosted meetings in his own home, where Israeli and Palestinian officials divided their time between intense negotiating and playing on the floor with his young son.

Ironically, Hoist, like so many other Norwegians, preferred to stay in the background and not take credit for this historic accomplishment. In fact, the grueling schedule of his shuttle diplomacy may have caused the stroke that ended his life.

BIBLIOGRAPHY

Holst, Johan J. "Norway's Search for a Nordpolitik." *Foreign Affairs* 60 (Fall 1981): 63–86.

———. "The Pattern of Nordic Security." *Daedalus* 113 (1984): 195–226.

———, ed. *Five Roads to Northern Security.* Oslo: Universitetsforlaget, 1973.

———, ed. *Norwegian Foreign Policy in the 1980s.* Norwegian Foreign Policy Studies No. 51. Oslo: Universitetsforlaget, 1985.

Bruce Olav Solheim

Honecker, Erich (1912–94)

Head of state of the German Democratic Republic (GDR), 1971–89. Erich Honecker, general secretary of the Central Committee and chair of the State Council, was the son of a miner born in Wiebelskirchen (Saarland) on August 25, 1912. At the age of ten Honecker joined the Young Spartacus Union. While working as a farm laborer from 1926 to 1928, he joined the Communist Youth League (KJVD) and the General German Trade Union. Beginning in 1928, Honecker trained as a roofer. As a member of the Communist Party (KPD) in 1929, Honecker focused on the KJVD in the Saar, where he held the position of political director. After receiving additional political training at Moscow's International Lenin School (1933–35), Honecker returned to Germany to

East Germany's leader Erich Honecker (right) shaking hands with former West German chancellor Willy Brandt in East Berlin, September 19, 1985. *Illustration courtesy Reuters/Bettmann Newsphotos.*

lead various Communist youth activities in the Rhineland, Hesse, Baden-Württemberg, the Pfalz, and Berlin. In 1935 he was arrested and held in Moabit prison Berlin's. In 1937 he was sentenced to ten years in prison in Brandenburg-Görden.

Released after the Second World War, Honecker quickly blended into the emerging East German Communist nomenklatura. In May 1945 he held the position of secretary of youth of the Central Committee of the Communist Party while chairing the Central Anti-Fascist Youth Committee. In 1946 he cofounded the Free German Youth (FDJ) and served as its chair until May 1955. From 1946 a member of the party's Executive Committee (later called the Central Committee of the Socialist Unity Party after the Social Democratic Party in the Soviet zone of occupation (East Germany) was forcibly merged with the Communist Party to form the Socialist Unity Party (SED) in April 1946), Honecker secured a place on the Presidium of the German People's Council, the consultative assembly of the Soviet Zone, from 1948 to 1949 and became a member of the Provisional People's Chamber (Volkskammer) of the German Democratic Republic in 1949.

A candidate member in 1950, Honecker became a full member of the party's Politburo in 1958. Standing by the East German leader Walter Ulbricht during the 1953 uprising against the Soviets, Honecker also supported Ulbricht's plan to build the Berlin Wall in August 1961. Beginning in 1965 Honecker pushed a policy of re-Stalinization through "socialist realism." When Christa Wolf publicly criticized Honecker's attempt to purge the intellectual community of critics, she lost her seat on the Central Committee.

In May 1971 Honecker replaced Ulbricht as head of the SED. Unlike Ulbricht, Honecker accepted without question the leading role of the Soviet Union in the Eastern Bloc (Warsaw Pact). Furthermore, Honecker accepted the leading role of the Communist Party of the Soviet Union (CPSU) in both foreign and domestic policy. To that end, Honecker engineered the Politburo's acceptance by East Germany of the CPSU party program. Overall, the Ulbricht-Honecker transition underscored the junior partner position of East Germany to the Soviet Union. Thereafter, Honecker continued to concentrate power in his hands. Beginning in 1971 he chaired the Council for Defense, after October 1976 the State Council, and, finally, the post of general secretary of the SED in May 1976. Centralization of authority under Honecker reduced the Central Committee, other political parties, and mass organizations to the role of applauding the Politburo's decisions.

Honecker's foreign policy focused on improving the GDR's legitimacy and expanding diplomatic contacts throughout the world. The Basic Treaty of 1972, a result of West German Chancellor Willy Brandt's *Ostpolitik,* or "Eastern Policy," based on the premise that a better future for all Germans depended on improved relations with the USSR and the Eastern bloc, served just that purpose. At Helsinki in 1975, Honecker accepted for East Germany the Helsinki Accords alongside West German Chancellor Helmut Schmidt. Honecker's straightforward reasoning considered the Helsinki documents as international acceptance of the GDR and its territorial integrity. On the other hand, Helsinki also called on the GDR to respect basic human rights. Expectations and hopes aroused among the populace were not realized. The Helsinki package encouraged artists, intellectuals, and youth to push for greater freedom of expression. East German stability, on the other hand, depended on Soviet support for the SED. East Germans appeared increasingly skeptical, however. Honecker allowed a period of flexibility in East German cultural policies until the arrival of Eurocommunism in 1976. Thereafter, he repressed all calls for reform, imprisoned political dissidents, or exiled them to the West. Honecker outlawed the distribution of any materials critical of the GDR or the Soviet Union. During the tenth SED Party Convention of April 1981, Honecker evaluated the balance of events concerning the SED since 1976 as positive, announcing that the GDR would witness the realization of "developed socialism" in the 1980s and prepare for the transition to communism. However, he feared the spread of the Polish democratic movement Solidarity to East Germany in 1980 and secretly advocated the invasion of Poland by Warsaw Pact forces.

As the Soviet Union under General Secretary Mikhail Gorbachev contemplated extensive political reforms during the 1980s, Honecker and other East German leaders distanced themselves from the USSR. Concurrently, Honecker attempted to build warmer relations with West Germany. The two Germanies concluded a number of agreements in the 1980s that enhanced contacts between them and addressed mutual ecological concerns. In the wake of improved relations, Honecker visited Bonn and his former home in the Saarland in September 1987.

Inspired by poor economic growth, a discredited ideology, and open displays of corruption by party leaders, opposition to Honecker's rule grew dramatically from 1987 to 1989. Honecker planned to incarcerate the political opposition, diplomats, journalists, and all foreigners in emergency internment camps. But public demonstrations, proved to be beyond the control of the state. Having lost the support of his own SED and the Soviet Union, Honecker resigned in 1989 from all offices and fled to Moscow in March 1991. Pressured by the Russians and the Chilean government, in whose embassy he had taken refuge, Honecker returned to Germany on July 29, 1992, where he was charged with misappropriation of funds and manslaughter for giving a standing shoot-to-kill order to guards along the border between the two German states. Because he was suffering from liver cancer, Honecker's lawyers convinced the German court in 1993 to drop all charges against him. Honecker then was allowed to emigrate to Chile, where members of his family lived. He died there on May 29, 1994.

BIBLIOGRAPHY

Honecker, Erich. *From My Life.* Oxford, England: Pergamon Press, 1981.

Lippmann, Heinz. *Honecker and the New Politics of Europe.* New York: Macmillan, 1972.

Weber, Hermann. *DDR: Grundriss der Geschichte 1945–1990.* Hannover, Germany: Fackeltraeger, 1991.

David A. Meier

SEE ALSO Bahro, Rudolf; Biermann, Wolf; Brandt, Willy; Ulbricht, Walter

Hong Kong

Former British crown colony returned in 1997 to Chinese rule after the expiration of a 150-year lease. An exceedingly profitable capitalist territory. Hong Kong is considered the economic gateway to Southeast Asia, a center of both industry and finance. Its return to the control of the People's Republic of China has been met with intense controversy.

The territory of Hong Kong consisted of three different political entities, acquired by Britain at different times. The actual island of Hong Kong was ceded to British colonial control in the Treaty of Nanking; it was the British prize for winning the first Opium War with China in 1842. It was a prime center for importing opium into the Chinese mainland and exporting Chinese tea. After the second Opium War Britain also acquired the Kowloon Peninsula on the mainland in 1860. With the growth of European imperial expansion in east Asia in the late nineteenth century, Britain leased the "New Territories," also on the mainland, for a 99-year period in 1898 to provide defense for Hong Kong and Kowloon. The expiration of this lease prompted the return of all three territories to Chinese rule on July 1, 1997.

Always a major port in southern China, the combined territories of Hong Kong proved remarkably prosperous following World War II. Numerous Chinese citizens flooded the colony in the late 1940s as the Chinese Communists took over mainland China in 1949. Soon after, Hong Kong closed its borders to further immigration and used its new supply of cheap labor to build a booming industrial trade in textiles, electronics, and shipping. Along with Tokyo, the colony also became one of the two major financial markets of the east Asian world, as well as a major banking center. Its prosperity and that of Taiwan was marked in contrast to that of either the Communist mainland or British industry and finance itself. By the 1990s Hong Kong had achieved a higher gross domestic product than its former colonial overlord.

In December 1984, in preparation for the eventual return of capitalist Hong Kong to Communist Chinese control, the Thatcher government negotiated an agreement with China in a Sino-British Declaration. It was agreed that all three territories constituting British Hong Kong would be turned over to Chinese rule at the end of the New Territories lease in July 1997, in return for certain concessions to Hong Kong's capitalist economic orientation. Under a policy of "one country, two systems," China agreed to treat Hong Kong as a "special administrative region" for fifty years after 1997, with a capitalist economy and a British legal system. This agreement was welcomed in Hong Kong and also prompted the growth of market reforms in China itself. Today, a full 60 percent of all new investment in China comes from Hong Kong.

However, since 1984, the turnover of Hong Kong to Chinese rule has been marred by controversy. In June 1989 the Thatcher government denied British residency to Hong Kong holders of British passports. Also, some developments before the turnover ceremony raised considerable question about China's ultimate commitment to the one country, two systems policy. In 1996 the Chinese government established a constitution, the Basic Law, for Hong Kong that subjects press and other criticism of Chinese policies to government scrutiny. Also, a postcolonial chief executive, businessman Tung Chee-hwa, was appointed to preside over an appointed 400-member legislative body to run Hong Kong's political affairs. There were no elections to these offices, and most of Hong Kong's liberal politicians were excluded from the government. Also, the prominence of relatives of important Chinese government figures in Hong Kong's business community led many to speculate that corruption will be rampant under Chinese rule.

Nevertheless, on July 1, 1997, Hong Kong reverted to Chinese control as the last British governor, Chris Patten, turned over control of the government. According to a timetable established by treaties, Britain's consultative role in Hong Kong's government will end in 2000, Hong Kong will be given over to the Basic Law in 2007, and in 2047, the policy of one country, two systems will officially end.

BIBLIOGRAPHY

Blyth, Sally, and Ian Wotherspoon. *Hong Kong Remembers.* New York: Oxford University Press, 1996.
Buckley, Roger. *Hong Kong: The Road to 1997.* Cambridge: Cambridge University Press, 1997.

David Simonelli

Horáková, Milada (1901–50)

Czech lawyer, politician, fighter for human rights, member of parliament for the Socialist Party, and head of the Office for Social Affairs in Prague. Milada Králová, born in Prague on December 25, 1901, studied law and became an expert in labor law, family law, and women's rights. She played a significant role in constitutional matters in Czechoslovakia.

Frantiska Plamínková, member of parliament from the Socialist Party, chairperson of the National Council of Women, and confidante of President Thomas Masaryk, recommended the young Králová, now Milada Horáková following her marriage to Bohuslav Horák, as her possible successor. Consequently, Horáková became one of the central figures of the feminist movement.

The German occupation interrupted Horáková's work in 1939. In 1940 she and her husband as well as Plamínková were imprisoned by the Germans. Plamínková was put to death in 1941. Horáková also received the death sentence, but it was commuted to imprisonment. She spent the war years in various Czech and German prisons, including Terezín (Theresienstadt), where she occupied the same cell in which Gavrilo Princip, assassin of Austrian Archduke Franz Ferdinand, spent his last years.

After the liberation of Czechoslovakia in 1945, Horáková helped organize the Association of Czechoslovak Resistance Fighters and Survivors of the Nazi Period. She was deputy chair of this organization until 1948. The Czechoslovak Republic awarded her one of the most distinguished decorations for her fight against the occupation. She was again a member of parliament, member of its foreign relations committee, and chairperson of the Council of Czechoslovak Women. In that capacity she had many international contacts.

Between 1945 and 1948 Czechoslovakia was a country with democratic structures. But Communist influence and pressure became increasingly stronger. In February 1948 the Communist Party succeeded with a putsch, and the opponents of this newly established dictatorship became victims of political repression. Horáková protested against the putsch and resigned from her parliamentary seat, declaring, "I am going the straight way." Immediately afterward she became more and more subject to official criticism. In 1949 twelve prominent opponents of the regime were imprisoned, among them Horáková. Her husband managed to escape, however. After a show trial she was found guilty and together with three others of the group of twelve—Závis Kalandra, Oldrich Pelcl, and Jan Buchal—sentenced to death. Despite a wave of international protest, including from Albert Einstein and Winston Churchill, the four were executed.

This show trial was typical of the Stalinist repression to which Eastern Europe was subjected in the postwar period. To underline the monstrosity of this execution, the following data are instructive. Between 1918 and 1938 five persons were sentenced to death in Czechoslovakia, all of them for first-degree murder. But between 1948 and 1952, 233 persons were sentenced to death by Czechoslovak courts and 10,790 persons were imprisoned. The death penalty was under the complete control of the Communist Party's leadership.

Most of Horáková's legal work was integrated by the Communists into their constitution, but they claimed it for themselves. In 1968, Horáková was rehabilitated, but the last letters that she wrote from prison (eleven letters of eighteen pages) were not given to her family until 1990.

BIBLIOGRAPHY

Horáková, Milada. *Dopisy Milady Horákove*. (*Correspondence, Selections*) Prague: Lidove noviny, 1990.

Ivanov, Miroslav. *Justicni vrazda, aneb, smrt Milady Horákove*. Prague: Betty, 1991.

Milada Horáková: k 10. vyroci jeji popravy. Washington, D.C.: Council of Free Czechoslovakia, 1960.

Proces s vedenim zaskodnickeho spiknuti proti republice. (*The Trial Against the Bandits Who Conspired Against the Republic*). Prague: Ministerstvo spravedinosti, 1950.

Marta Marková

SEE ALSO Slánský, Rudolf Salzmann

Horkheimer, Max (1895–1973)

German philosopher. Max Horkheimer, son of conservative Jews from the upper middle class, was born in Stuttgart-Zuffenhausen in 1895. In 1911 he became friends with the economist Friedrich Pollock, who later helped him establish the contacts to form the circle around the Institute für Sozialforschung (Institute for Social Research) in the 1920s. In 1913 Horkheimer began his reading of Schopenhauer, whose philosophy was to have a decisive impact on his later work. From 1916 to 1918 Horkheimer performed military service as a medic.

After obtaining his *Abitur* he studied psychology, philosophy, and political economy, first for one semester in Munich, then in Frankfurt. In 1921 he went to Freiburg to attend Edmunt Husserl's lectures. From 1920 on Horkheimer pursued his reading of Marx. Both his dissertation and his *Habilitation* deal with Emmanuel Kant's *Third Critique.*

In 1931 he became professor for social philosophy and director of the Institut für Sozialforschung in Frankfurt. In 1933, after Adolf Hitler came to power, he moved to Geneva, in 1934 to New York City, and in 1940 to southern California.

During the thirties he published many articles in the *Zeitschrift für Sozialforschung*, (Journal for Social Research), as well as thoughts, notes, and aphorisms collected under the title *Dämmerung*. He also published *Eclipse of Reason, Dialectic of Enlightenment*, written with Adorno, and *Critique of Instrumental Reason.* These texts formulate the task of philosophy as not only social diagnosis but also the further development of critical and dialectical thought. Both texts interweave a critique of instrumental (subjective) reason and the diagnosis of the decline of individuality caused by changes in socialization. Thus the replacement of the idea of objective reason by instrumental-subjective reason is closely linked to the transformation of individuals into social atoms. This critique of instrumental-manipulative reason is supplemented and motivated by reflections on "administered society" and "culture identity" characteristic of late capitalism, as well as on the precarious status of nature, that is, its omnipresent suppression in contemporary society. This is framed not as a total critique or farewell to the Enlightenment, however, but rather as enlightenment about the Enlightenment.

In 1949 Horkheimer finally returned to Germany and accepted the chair for sociology and philosophy at the University of Frankfurt. From 1951 to 1953 he was rector of the university; at the end of his term of office he received the Goethe badge, the highest award of the city of Frankfurt. In 1954 he was visiting professor at the University of Chicago.

His continuing ambivalence toward the Germany, whose antisemitism he had fled, was symbolized in the great significance of American citizenship for Horkheimer. In 1952 President Harry Truman signed a special law enabling Horkheimer to keep his U.S. citizenship despite his return to Germany.

In the 1950s and 1960s Horkheimer published a number of articles that, despite their interesting content, cannot be considered as important as his earlier works. In 1958 he moved to Switzerland, and in 1970 he received the Lessing prize of the city of Frankfurt. Horkheimer's late thought is commonly described as a turn toward conservatism and pessimism reminiscent of Arthur Schopenhauer. Horkheimer abandoned any expectation that a "just society" could be created. Revolution, rather than being a harbinger of liberty, became catastrophic. The late Horkheimer embraced the concept of solidarity with all creatures and a theological longing that this world not be the end—so that the innocent might ultimately triumph over their murderers. He died in 1973.

BIBLIOGRAPHY

Alway, Joan. *Critical Theory and Political Possibilities: Conceptions of Emancipatory Politics in the Works of Horkheimer, Adorno, Marcuse, and Habermas.* Westport, Conn.: Greenwood Press, 1995.

Grimminger, Michael. *Revolution und Resignation: Sozialphilosophie und die geschichtliche Krise im 20. Jahrhundert bei Max Horkheimer und Hans Freyer.* Berlin: Duncker & Humblot, 1997.

Held, David. *Introduction to Critical Theory: Horkheimer to Habermas.* London: Hutchinson, 1980.

Honneth, Axel. *The Critique of Power: Reflective Stages in a Critical Social Theory.* Cambridge, Mass.: MIT Press, 1991.

Stirk, Peter M. R. *Max Horkheimer: A New Interpretation.* Lanham, MD: Barnes & Noble, 1992.

Tar, Zoltan. *The Frankfurt School: The Critical Theories of Max Horkheimer and Theodor W. Adorno.* New York: Wiley, 1977.

Erik Vogt

SEE ALSO Frankfurt School

Horn, Gyula (1932–)

Prime minister of Hungary (1994–98). Gyula Horn was also foreign minister from 1989 to 1990. Horn studied at the Don-Rostov College of Economics and Finance in the Soviet Union from 1950 to 1954. On returning to Hungary he was employed at the Finance Ministry. In 1957 he joined the Communist paramilitary forces that were intended to protect the Kádár regime from domestic opposition forces in the wake of the Hun-

garian Revolution of 1956. He was transferred to the Foreign Ministry in 1959 and worked at the Hungarian Embassy at Sophia, Bulgaria (1961–63) and at Belgrade, Yugoslavia (1963–69). He was employed at the Foreign Policy Section of the Hungarian Socialist Workers (Communist) Party from 1969 to 1983. He was then promoted to be head of the same body. He was secretary of state for foreign affairs from 1985 to 1989, and then was appointed foreign minister. He became leader of the Socialist Party (SP) after the collapse of communism in Hungary in 1989. At the parliamentary elections in spring 1994, the SP received an absolute majority of the votes (54 percent), and Horn formed a coalition government with the Alliance of Free Democrats.

Horn belongs to the generation of Communist politicians who were not so strongly committed to Marxist-Leninist ideology as the members of the older generation. They were able to discard Communist ideology at the end of the 1980s and adopt a social democratic platform. Once in power, they pursued a liberal, free-market economic program, including strict monetary policies and privatization programs. Horn's personal reputation as a reform-Communist politician was founded in 1989 when the Hungarian government decided to open Hungary's border with Austria to let tens of thousands of East German tourists flee to Austria, thus undermining the East German regime under the leadership of Erich Honecker.

BIBLIOGRAPHY

Horn, Gyula. *Colopok.* Budapest: Mora Ferenc Ifjusagi Konyvkiado, 1991.

———. *Itt vagyunk, Europa: portre Horn Gyularol.* Budapest: Brainman, 1990.

Kis, Janos. *Politics in Hungary: For a Democratic Alternative.* Boulder, Colo.: Social Science Monographs, 1989.

Tamás Magyarics

SEE ALSO Boross, Péter; Göncz, Árpád

Howe, Geoffrey (1926–)

British barrister and Conservative politician. Geoffrey Howe was a Conservative member of parliament from 1964 to 1966 and from 1970 to 1992. He held a number of key cabinet appointments including chancellor of the exchequer and foreign secretary. He was a strong advocate of monetarism and European integration.

While active in Conservative politics since his university days, Howe did not enter parliament until 1964, when he was returned for Bebington (Cheshire). After he lost the seat in the general election two years later, Howe focused on legal work. His handling of a number of sensitive, high-profile cases greatly enhanced his reputation both in legal and Tory circles. He reentered parliament in 1970 as the member for Reigate (Surrey) and was appointed solicitor-general by the new prime minister, Edward Heath. In this capacity, he was responsible for handling the highly contentious Industrial Relations Bill and guiding the necessary legislation through the Commons for Britain's membership in the European Community (EC). Howe subsequently served as minister for trade and consumer affairs (1972–74), and opposition spokesman for social services (1974–75) and for treasury and economic affairs (1975–79). On the Conservatives' return to power, he served in Prime Minister Margaret Thatcher's government as chancellor of the exchequer (1979–83) and foreign secretary (1983–89). As chancellor, he implemented strict monetarist policies to curb inflation and the power of the trade unions. His achievements at the Foreign Office included the negotiations for the return of Hong Kong to China, facilitation of the arms reduction talks between the United States and the USSR, and Britain's enhanced standing in Europe. In 1989, following disagreements with Thatcher over European monetary union, Howe was demoted to the post of leader of the House of Commons and deputy prime minister. Continued dissent from the prime minister's views on Europe led to his resignation in a highly critical speech to the House of Commons in November 1990. This speech laid bare the deep divisions in the Conservative Party over Europe, an integration that contributed to Thatcher's decision to resign the prime ministership three weeks later. In 1991, Howe announced his intention to stand down as an MP after the next general election. He as made a life peer in 1992.

BIBLIOGRAPHY

Hillman, Judy, and Peter Clarke. *Geoffrey Howe: A Quiet Revolutionary.* London: Weidenfeld and Nicholson, 1988.

Howe, Geoffrey. *Europe Tomorrow: Five Speeches.* London: HMSO, 1985.

———. *Conflict of Loyalty.* New York: St. Martin's Press, 1994.

———. *Nationalism and the Nation-State.* Cambridge: Cambridge University Press, 1995.

Eileen Groth Lyon

Hoxha, Enver (1908–85)

Albanian Communist leader. Enver Hoxha brought his Communist Party to power in Albania with little external assistance. As leader of Albania he pursued a xenophobic policy of isolation. His legacy was four decades of Stalinist government and a poorly developed economy.

Hoxha came from a landowning family and was educated at the French lycée in Korçë. He won a scholarship to study law in Montpellier, France. As a student he became active in politics, writing articles against the Albanian monarch for the French Communist newspaper, *L'Humanité.* As a result, his scholarship was withdrawn, and he was forced to continue his legal studies in Paris and Brussels. Returning to Albania in 1936, he taught in Tirana, then in Korçë. However, following Italy's annexation of Albania in April 1939, Hoxha was dismissed from his post by the fascist authorities. He returned to Tirana and became an underground Communist leader.

Germany's invasion of the Soviet Union in June 1941 signaled the beginning of Communist attacks on Axis forces and their allies. At first the Albanian Communists under Hoxha were able to mount only small attacks against the Italians and their Albanian collaborators. By July 1943, however, Hoxha was head of a National Liberation Army (NLA) of 10,000 partisans. After the Italian armistice in September 1943, 1,500 Italians joined his army as the Antonio Gramsci Brigade and more Albanians allied themselves with the Communists. In the winter of 1943–44 the Germans forced Hoxha and 35,000 of his fighters into the mountains. But by the summer of 1944 the NLA was on the offensive again, with Hoxha able to field 70,000 partisans. They captured Tirana in November and pursued the retreating Germans into Yugoslavia.

Military victory enabled Hoxha to establish a Stalinist regime in the country. Hoxha's Democratic Front claimed 93 percent of the vote in the December 1945 election. Agriculture was collectivized and all major economic assets were nationalized. The Communist party was the only legal political group, with a membership of approximately 50,000 out of a population of 1,122,000. Rigorous internal security was in the hands of 15,000 special police under Koci Xoxe, the interior minister. Xoxe was later accused of treason and executed in 1949. He was one of four interior ministers to be so accused, an indication of the paranoia that afflicted Hoxha throughout his rule. Finally, Hoxha instituted a drive to wipe out all vestiges of religion, which enabled Albania to declare itself the world's first atheist country in 1967. At the same time an associated campaign was launched to bring women into the social and political life of the country.

Economic and social conditions were far from favorable for Hoxha. Albania was the poorest country in Europe and possessed no rail links with any of its neighbors.

The country had little industry, and over 90 percent of the population lived on the land. Much of the low-lying ground of Albania was marsh, and rich mineral and oil deposits remained untapped. In addition, the country's gold reserves, looted by the Germans and Italians in World War II, were in the hands of Britain, and Hoxha was never able to recover them. In the face of such difficulties, Hoxha quickly established a policy that was to remain unchanged throughout his long rule. Essentially he believed in a form of communism in one country that could be described as autarkic nationalism carried to its limits. In pursuit of this policy Hoxha adopted the tactic of developing close links with a single external power designed to extract the maximum economic benefit at the minimum cost in terms of interference in Albania's internal affairs.

From November 1944 until June 1948, Hoxha allied Albania with Tito's Yugoslavia. Even in the straitened economic circumstances following the end of the war, Hoxha managed to extract aid from the Yugoslav government. However, Tito's break with the Soviet Union in 1948 led Hoxha to focus even more intently on the USSR, which needed a base in the region following Tito's assertion of independence and the Communist defeat in Greece's civil war in 1949.

The de-Stalinization of the Khrushchev period in the Soviet Union precipitated Albania's next switch in international relations. Hoxha remained an avid Stalinist, denounced Soviet Premier Nikita Khrushchev, and established ties with China in 1960. Apart from ideological considerations, it may well have been Hoxha's dissatisfaction over the nature of Soviet assistance that led to the break. Hoxha was more successful with China, obtaining aid for several heavy industrial projects, thereby giving Albania new industrial capacity. By the mid-1970s Albania had also become self-sufficient in agriculture. But by the end of that decade Hoxha had, once again, split with his patron as China began to establish closer links with Yugoslavia. Thereafter Albania made limited and tentative approaches to Japan, Italy, and Canada.

Hoxha maintained himself and his party in power for forty years. But his regime did not long survive the passing of its architect in April 1985.

BIBLIOGRAPHY

Amery, Julian. *Sons of the Eagle: A Study in Guerrilla War.* London: Macmillan, 1948.

Hoxha, Enver. *The Artful Albanian: The Memoirs of Enver Hoxha.* Ed. by Jon Halliday. London: Chatto and Windus, 1986.

Pipa, Arshi. "The Political Culture of Hoxha's Albania," in Tariq Ali, ed., *The Stalinist Legacy: Its Impact on Twentieth Century World Politics.* Harmondsworth, England: Penguin, 1984.

Stephen M. Cullen

SEE ALSO Alia, Ramiz; Corfu Channel Incident; Hoxha, Nexhmije

Hoxha, Nexhmije (1921–)

Nexhmije Hoxha (née Xhulini) was born in Monastir (Macedonia) in 1921. In 1927 persecution by the Serbs forced her family to move to Tirana, where she eventually became an elementary school teacher. She joined the Albanian Communist Party at its foundation in 1941 and became a leading member of its youth organization. During World War II she fought against the Italian and German occupiers, first in Tirana, and from 1944, in the Vlorë and Gjirokastër districts. In February 1945 she married Enver Hoxha. From 1946 to 1955 she was president of the Union of Albanian Women. From 1948 she was a member of the Party's Central Committee and a deputy to the People's Assembly (parliament). In 1952 she became head of the Agit-Prop directorate and subsequently director of the Institute of Marxist-Leninist studies.

Following Hoxha's death in 1985, she succeeded him as president of the Democratic Front, a mass organization, and held the position until her enforced retirement in December 1990. Although never a member of the Politburo, as Hoxha's widow she wielded considerable power behind the scenes.

There were many rumors about her abuse of power. Though she was arrested by the new non-Communist government in December 1991, she was subsequently convicted in January 1993 only of misappropriating $3,000 in public funds. In May of the same year the Appeals Court reassessed the amount as $55,000 and increased her prison sentence from nine to eleven years.

BIBLIOGRAPHY

Hoxha, Nexhmije. *Some Fundamental Questions of the Revolutionary Policy of the Party of Labour of Albania about the Development of the Class Struggle.* Tirana: Nentori, 1977.

Skendi, Stavro, ed. *Albania.* New York: Praeger, 1957.

Kirk West

SEE ALSO Hoxha, Enver

Hrabal, Bohumil (1914–97)

Czech novelist. Bohumil Hrabal was born in Brno in southern Moravia on March 28, 1914. He grew up in Nymburk, a town near Prague, where his father managed a brewery. His university studies were interrupted by the German occupation. During World War II he worked as a clerk, an unskilled worker, and a railroad employee. He received a law degree from Charles University in Prague in 1946 but never practiced law. Hrabal held a variety of jobs, and after the Communists came to power in 1948, he worked at the Kladno steel mill and then at a warehouse. Before he became a full-time writer in 1962, he worked at the S.K. Neuman Theater in Prague as a stagehand and an extra. In 1963 he published his first work, the short story "Little Pearl on the Bottom." Hrabal's masterpiece, *Closely Watched Trains* (1965), with a heroic comic character at its center, Miloš Hrma, the assistant station master, has been compared to the work of the Czech writer Jaroslav Hašek. His writing was not primarily a protest against the totalitarianism of Soviet-style communism but a story of the lives of the common people, engaged in a common human struggle, with a subtext of traditional Czech protest against foreign domination. *Closely Watched Trains* was made into a film in 1966 by Jiří Menzel; Hrabal worked closely with Menzel on the screenplay. The film won an Oscar as best foreign film of 1967. A translation of the novel was published in English in 1968.

With the suppression of the Prague Spring in 1968, all of Hrabal's works were banned and two galley proofs of as yet unpublished novels were destroyed. Until 1975 only typewritten versions of his works were circulated. That year in an interview Hrabal made some positive statements about the regime of Gustav Husák. This led to a partial lifting of the ban against his work. He was criticized by some after the Velvet Revolution of 1989 for submitting to the regime, but his popularity as a writer remained undiminished. Unfazed by this change in fortune, he continued to frequent his favorite haunt, Prague's Golden Tiger pub, and listen to the stories of common people that had always provided him with insights and themes.

Hrabal, called by Milan Kundera "our greatest writer" and by Ivan Klima "the greatest Czech prose writer," died on February 3, 1997. He fell, in an apparent accident, from a fifth-floor window in Prague's Bulovka hospital.

BIBLIOGRAPHY
Gotz, Alexander. *Bilder aus der Tiefe der Zeit: Erinnerung und Selbststilisierung als ästhetische Funktionen im Werk Bohumil Hrabals.* New York: P. Lang, 1998.
Hrabal, Bohumil. *A batons rompus avec Bohumil Hrabal: entretiens.* Paris: Criterion, 1991.
———. *Closely Watched Trains.* Evanston, Ill.: Northwestern University Press, 1995.
———. *Dancing Lessons for the Advanced in Age.* New York: Harcourt Brace, 1995.
———. *The Little Town Where Time Stood Still and Cutting It Short.* New York: Pantheon Books, 1993.
Bernard Cook

Human Rights

Despite glowing contributions to the conceptualization and legalization of human rights, European states have participated in and witnessed some of the most criminal violations of human rights: imperialism, totalitarianism, violation of the rights of ethnic minorities, and genocide.

Western Europe has played a leading role in the development of human rights concepts dating from the French Declaration of the Rights of Man and Citizen in 1789. As Europeans tried to resurrect civil life and values after the inhumanities committed during the Second World War, the occupation zones in West Germany underwent denazification. The Nuremberg Tribunal forcefully demonstrated international law existed not only as an instrument of states but also to protect individuals. The justice meted out maintained that violations of human rights were indefensible even if national laws pretended otherwise; international law on human rights was supreme. The crimes against humanity carried out by the Nazi regime in Germany found an institutional response in the United Nations Universal Declaration of Human Rights, the fundamental and most comprehensive international legal text on human rights. A fragile Western Europe proceeded to put in place a human rights regime after the war. Only ten countries launched the Council of Europe in 1949. Subsequently, the organization concluded the European Convention on Human Rights with the goal of implementing select rights contained in the Universal Declaration. To interpret human rights law and apply it, the European Court of Human Rights in Strasbourg, France, convened for the first time for a public hearing in 1960. Progressively, it established itself and became fully operational. Following the precedent of Nuremberg, the creators of the court gave individuals access to that institution. Political intimidation and fear of retaliation did not stop states from taking each other to court. National systems attempted to bring their domestic laws into conformity with regional and international human rights commitments through legislation, administrative supervision, and court rulings. Furthermore, the

Council of Europe system had the support of the European Economic Community (now European Union, EU) in effecting a human rights regime. Whether at the level of the United Nations or the Organization of American States, in most places supranational human rights institutions met more resistance from sovereignty-conscious politicians and subordinated themselves to other geopolitical goals.

After the consolidation of Soviet control in Eastern and central Europe by the late 1940s, Communist leaders installed regimes based on the Soviet model of communism. Contemptuous of the political liberalism the West ascribed to, regimes under the sway of Stalinism represented themselves as proponents of a "socialist" view of human rights. In international discussions on human rights, these regimes claimed to promote so-called socioeconomic rights as opposed to the "civil-political rights" that Western countries advanced. The impasse lasted until the conclusion of the Helsinki Final Act of 1975, a seminal text in which the two parts of Europe, Canada, and the United States formally committed themselves to protecting the same human rights. Ironically, Communist governments increased their vulnerability by accepting international legal obligations in the human rights area under Helsinki. Indeed, Helsinki provided legitimacy for dissidents who claimed their governments violated international human rights laws and, at the same time, raised expectations in central and Eastern European.

Throughout the 1980s the theme of human rights was prominent in political discourse throughout Europe. The European Community attempted to emphasize human rights in regions where it pursued a common foreign policy. The community's European Parliament emerged as an outspoken advocate of human rights. National parliaments in Western Europe contributed their voices to the movement. In West Germany parliament went so far as to refuse to sell weapons to Turkey because of the latter's persecution of its Kurdish minority, even though both countries shared membership in NATO. When Eastern and central Europeans took to the streets and moved against their regimes to demand democracy, the human rights movement achieved an incredible victory.

Unfortunately, the collapse of Communist regimes in Eastern Europe did not usher in an era that secured the pursuit of human rights in foreign policies. Rather, a succession of situations in which foreign regimes abused human rights presented itself, begging a response from a European Union bent on positing itself as a foreign policy power. In 1989 Chinese Communist authorities assaulted prodemocracy demonstrators in Tiananmen Square. Toward the end of the 1990s the West pursued business as usual with China, partly as a result of the U.S. approach of "constructive engagement." Policymakers in the United States maintained that isolating China was detrimental, even to that country's human rights performance. Rather, if the West was to have any bases for influencing the Chinese leadership, the goal should be to develop a balanced relationship with China, consisting of commercial and diplomatic links. Commercially, Western countries competed with one another for market access and investment opportunities in China. Meanwhile the prospect of a common political approach evaporated. Significantly, no coalition supported even presenting a resolution against China's human rights violations in the U.N. Human Rights Commission in 1998. Extending this policy approach, the Europeans couched their human rights concerns in a more complex relationship with Iran against the U.S. preference for punitive measures against this "rogue" country. Europeans called the policy adopted in relation to Iran "critical dialogue." The two cases above show the extent to which European countries have reevaluated their foreign policy priorities, giving more important consideration to bilateral economic relations than multilateral measures in favor of human rights.

Occurring as it did in Europe's backyard, the horrific breakup of Yugoslavia starting in 1991 demoralized EU human rights aspirations and foreign policy. The decision makers who referred to the massive numbers of murders, torture, and rapes that various ethnic groups committed against each other as "genocide" spoke purposefully. They favored enforcing the Genocide Convention and applying international legal sanctions, even military intervention. However, the description of the situation that seemed to predominate in diplomatic counsels was "ethnic cleansing," a term that did not have the same ramifications in international law. From the outset, the EU and the United States were uncomfortable with the use of force to stop such crimes, however heinous. Even though the United States preferred for the EU to act alone, in reality, Europeans had no organized military capacity outside of NATO. Members of the EU were willing to become engaged in a "peacekeeping role" and to supply humanitarian assistance. However, with no peace to keep, the troops they sent under U.N. auspices were at the mercy of the combatants, and their presence lacked credibility as the United States refused to cooperate. Eventually, the policy shifted to that of "peacemaking," in which the United States took a leading role through NATO air strikes to punish the Serbs. As the Serbs experienced military setbacks, they were finally brought to the negotiating table. After years of European negotiating efforts, a U.S.-brokered settlement prevailed with the 1995 Dayton accords, which the parties warring over Bosnia signed. With the failure of the EU to coordinate an effective response to ethnic conflict in the former Yugoslavia, the so-called Contact Group,—United States, Britain, France, Germany, and Russia—informally assumed leadership in decision making and diplomacy on this issue.

Europeans are in the process of coming to terms with the security and foreign policy failures of the EU. But the precedent established in the Bosnian war of ultimately relying on U.S. direction and NATO capacity has complicated their efforts. The most important deficiency to remedy is the absence of an independent EU military capacity. Presently, the Western European Union (WEU), an exclusively European security organization, is striving to improve operational capacity. Already it is participating in small-scale actions, especially to provide humanitarian assistance. Ideally, it should develop as a military organization that can be utilized by the EU and the Organization for Security and Cooperation in Europe, a pan-European political organization in which Canada, the United States, and the Asian successor states to the USSR participate. Even though the logic of strengthening the WEU seems clear, the concern that it will undermine the authority of NATO and give the United States a reason to withdraw from Europe inhibits its development.

For the time being, an enlarging NATO, solidified by its decisive intervention in Bosnia, seems to hold sway in the politics of European security. NATO has demonstrated initiative through Partnership for Peace, a program to associate Eastern and central European countries with NATO and to involve them in responding to "new" security threats, including human rights violations and other kinds of emergencies. Furthermore, NATO enlargement has initiated human rights advances insofar as prospective members have had to guarantee the legal protection of their national minorities to be accepted by the alliance.

As European regional policy on foreign and security matters shows strains and bows to U.S. leadership, the process of the Dayton accords has been innovative for humanitarian policy. Dayton put in place in Bosnia a Commission on Human Rights, an ombudsman, and a Human Rights Chamber and enhanced the International Tribunal on War Crimes in the Former Yugoslavia located in the Hague. Despite the proliferation of such structures, the tragedy of Yugoslavia exposed the difficulties of implementing foreign policies based on human rights and dimmed optimism about humanitarian interventions.

During the 1990s the collapse of Communist regimes changed the foreign policy priorities of Western countries, especially the United States. Indeed, the Clinton admin-

istration's emphasis on trade tended to treat human rights as an evolutionary goal dependent on democratization and free-market economics. Moreover, the Clinton administration saw itself as adopting a European approach in giving so much importance to commercial policy. This perspective tended to work against activism on the part of Western governments in favor of human rights, while relying on the efforts of nongovernmental organizations and an unpredictable process of political development in countries uncommitted or opposed to Western-style human rights. Whereas European governments and the United States have been most influenced by the practical obstacles they encounter and economic considerations, other political institutions have unpredictably interjected human rights into foreign policy considerations. This has been true of parliaments and courts in Europe that have sometimes forced difficult human rights issues onto the political agenda that governments acting alone might have preferred to keep quiet or subordinate to "more important" relations with foreign countries. In this vein, a German court ruled in 1997 against the government of Iran for killing Iranians in Germany who opposed the Islamic fundamentalist regime, thus complicating EU relations with Iran. When governments do privilege human rights in foreign policies, they often have in mind accomplishing other goals with the same stroke. For instance, on the initiative of the European Parliament, the EU rejected Turkey's application to join it because of the latter's human rights record. In doing this, the EU also avoided putting Greece in a position of unilaterally blocking Turkey's application, thus avoiding an escalation in hostilities over Cyprus between the two countries. In conclusion, foreign policies will not be completely without human rights emphases. However, human rights are more likely to be considered when the use of force is not required to accomplish goals, when important diplomatic and commercial relationships are not at risk, and when human rights fit into an overall strategy of managing foreign relations with a particular country.

While much is lacking in international and regional efforts to influence regimes opposed to international human rights law, Europeans can celebrate the conversion of most Eastern and central European countries to the establishment of a continental human rights regime. Between 1989 and 1998, the membership of the Council of Europe swelled from twenty-three to forty members. In addition, the Council of Europe has expanded its conceptions of human rights in light of its new members. The Framework Convention for the protection of national minorities was drawn up as a result and opened for signature on February 1, 1995. Unfortunately for the new members, most of which are concerned about the economic uncertainties that free markets entail, the machinery for making progress in social and economic rights lags behind that for civil and political rights. Essentially, there is no institution equivalent to the European Court of Human Rights on the social side. Yet the Council of Europe's Social Charter, which began operation on February 26, 1965, boasts legal achievements in rights for workers, family policies, and other social protections. As with the EU, an organization that also strives to be active in the social field, national politicians tend to predominate in an area that involves "money" matters for which politicians stand to be rewarded or punished by their local electorates. Finally, the Council of Europe, in conjunction with the EU, provides economic aid in the difficult transitions of the new European democracies.

The institutional success of Europeans in the human rights field provides a model for institution building in other regions and on the international level. It contributes to socializing the general public, politicians, and officials about human rights, a less dramatic demonstration than military intervention in defense of human rights, but one not to be undervalued. After all, by the late 1980s the call to human rights succeeded in mobilizing people to denounce Communist regimes in the countries of Eastern and central Europe.

BIBLIOGRAPHY

Forsythe, David P., ed. *Human Rights in the New Europe: Problems and Progress.* Lincoln: University of Nebraska Press, 1994.

Fry, John. *The Helsinki Process: Negotiating Security and Cooperation in Europe.* Washington, D.C.: National Defense University Press, 1993.

Laqueur, Walter, and Barry Rubin, eds. *Human Rights Reader.* New York: New American Library, 1989.

Piening, Christopher. *Global Europe: The European Union in World Affairs.* Boulder, Colo.: Lynne Rienner, 1997.

Mary Troy Johnston

SEE ALSO Council of Europe; Nuremberg Trials; Western European Union

Human Rights: The European Convention on Human Rights and the European Social Charter

Until the end of World War II most nations considered the relationship between state and citizen as an internal matter not subject to international law. It required the policy of the Nazi state in Germany, which disdained human rights systematically, to initiate new reflections about the role of international law in the protection of human rights.

The Charter of the United Nations mentions the aim of supporting and consolidating respect for human rights and basic freedoms for all people regardless of race, sex, language, or religion. The U.N. Declaration on Human Rights of December 10, 1948, influenced the 1949 European Convention on Human Rights (ECHR).

There were efforts to formulate a European charter on human rights before the U.N. declaration. This was evident at a congress of the European Movement in May 1948. On May 5, 1949, ten nations met in London and established the European Summit. The summit sought to establish a closer connection among those nations to preserve and support the ideas and principles seen as their common inheritance and to promote both their economic and social progress. By May 1998 the European Summit consisted of forty members, including the former Communist Eastern European nations. The decisions of the European Summit concerning its members' affairs are advisory only. Summit decisions are formulated through summits of ministers, consisting of the members' secretaries of state (foreign ministers) or their deputies and through advising summits, whose members are sent by the nations' parliaments. The statute of the European Summit obligates every member nation to accept human rights and basic freedoms, so in effect a nation can become a member of the European Summit only if it signs the ECHR.

On September 9, 1949, a summit approved the ECHR draft formulated by French Attorney General Pierre-Henri Teitgen and it was signed in Rome on November 4, 1950, after the summit of ministers and a Conference of Senior Officials had made some modifications. It came into force when ten nations ratified it on September 3, 1953. On March, 18, 1992, Czechoslovakia became the first former Communist country to ratify the ECHR, and Russia was the last, signing it on May 5, 1998.

The ECHR obligates the contracting parties to assure all of their citizens the rights specified in the text and subsequent amendments without regard to sex, race, color, language, religion, political or other opinions, national or social origin, membership in a national minority, property, or birth. Included in the convention are the right to live complemented by the prohibition of the death penalty in times of peace, the ban of torture and inhuman or humiliating punishment or treatment, the ban of slavery, the right of freedom and security, the right of access to court, the right of fair trial, the principles of *nullem crimen sine lege* (no crime without a law), *nulla poena sine lege* (no punishment without a law) and *ne bis in idem* (no double jeopardy); furthermore, the rights of property, respect for private and family affairs, freedom of thought and conscience, religious freedom, freedom of speech, assembly and coalition, the right of effective legal protection in case of violation of one of these rights, the right of education, the right to vote and be counted, and equality between husband and wife.

Those rights in special circumstances, however, can be regulated or restricted. For example, political rights can be restricted by law in special cases and the ECHR, except for an inviolable core, can be suspended in times of war or states of public emergency. But restrictions are allowed only for special, foreseen purposes. Finally, no one can claim the ECHR's and the amendment's rights in order to abolish them.

The ECHR's system of legal protection is unique. The ECHR was the first international convention on human rights to give individuals the possibility to accuse their native country if they feel violated in their rights. For that purpose the ECHR installed a European Commission on Human Rights and a European Law Court on Human Rights. To attain legal protection, a party of contract, a citizen, or a group of citizens can appeal to the commission or they can bring a charge to the law court. Despite some weaknesses of the ECHR system, the commission and the law court did their share to extend and strengthen the protection of fundamental rights in Europe. In view of the attitude of Europeans toward the ECHR, the judgments of the highest national courts have lost their formerly undisputed character, and the ECHR's system of legal protection is evolving into the institution of a European constitutional court.

The ECHR must be separated from the system of human rights within the EC. Because the ECHR is an international legal agreement, which the EC did not sign, it does not formally bind it. The EC is not even allowed to join it, because according to the ECHR statutes only members of the European Summit are entitled to membership. Despite this the European Law Court has taken the ECHR into consideration in many of its decisions. The EC's agreements contain no written catalogue of human rights. The EC's basic rights were formulated by the judges of the European Law Court. The court considers the EC's sovereignty committed to basic rights, which have developed from the constitutional traditions of EC members. In this context the court also refers to the ECHR, but according to the European Law Court's point of view, the ECHR does not bind the EC. It is rather a source for the community's members when formulating human rights. In the meantime basic rights formulated by the European Law Court obligate the community's administration.

Another guarantee of human rights in Europe is the European Social Charter (ESC). It can be seen as the counterpart to the ECHR. The ESC's genesis dates from 1951, when the advising summit of the European Summit suggested the formulation of a statement about a common social policy among member nations. In 1953 the European Summit's general secretary presented a memorandum that suggested the formulation of European social policy in a European Social Charter. In the following years different bodies of experts devoted themselves to the project until it was finally formulated and signed on October 18, 1961, in Turin. The ESC came in force on February 26, 1965, when it was ratified by five European nations.

The ESC enunciated the following social rights: the right to work; fair, secure, and healthy working conditions; fair loans; the right of organization for employers and employees; the protection of children, young persons, women, and families; the right of social security; and the right to care and integration for handicapped persons. All these rights are formulated as a political program by the ESC, and every party to the contract is obligated to pursue them with all suitable methods. However, as with the ECHR, the ESC's rights can be restricted. The conditions for a restriction are comparable to those of the ECHR. The system of legal protection in its basics is comparable too, but in effect it is not as powerful.

A large number of private human rights initiatives were also established in Europe. Well known for their international activities are the League for Human Rights (Ligue pour la Défense des Droits de l'Homme et du Citoyen), which was founded in Paris in 1898 and in 1922 developed into an international federation, and Amnesty International, which was founded in London in 1961.

BIBLIOGRAPHY

Bleckmann, A. *Europarecht: das Recht der europäischen Gemeinschaft,* 6th ed. Cologne: C. Heymanns, 1997.

Frowein, Jochen, and W. Peukert. *Europäische Menschenrechtskonvention, EMRK-Kommentar,* 2d ed. Berlin: Springer, 1996.

Christoph Priller

Hume, John (1937–)

Northern Irish Social Democratic and Labour Party MP for Foyle (1983–); member of the European Parliament for Northern Ireland (1979–). John Hume was born in Derry City in 1937. Formerly a teacher and a businessman, he put his administrative abilities to use in founding a housing association and a credit union, which he pioneered among the Derry Catholic population. He was also president of the Credit Union League of Ireland (1964–68). Although a pacifist, he was a member of the Northern Ireland Civil Rights Association (NICRA) and was present at the riot that ensued when NICRA members were attacked by police in Derry on October 5, 1968. Four days later he cofounded and became vice chairman of the Derry Citizens' Action Committee. Hume, who won the Foyle seat to the Northern Ireland parliament from Eddie McAteer in 1969, played a leading role in the prevention of rioting in Derry on November 16, 1969. A founding member and deputy chairman of the SDLP, he was returned as MP for Londonderry to the Assembly of Northern Ireland (1973–74) and was minister for commerce in the power-sharing Executive (January–May 1974). He held his seat in the election to the convention to draft a constitution (1975–76). Following the failure of the convention, he took up a position in the Commission of the European Economic Community (EC). In June 1979 he was one of the members elected to represent Northern Ireland in the first directly elected European Parliament, and he has retained his seat ever since. He was elected leader of the SDLP to succeed Gerry Fitt, who resigned in November 1979. In 1983 he was elected as MP for Foyle in the general election, another seat he has retained ever since. Beginning in 1988 he has been in contact with Gerry Adams, paving the way toward the eventual signing of the Good Friday Agreement in 1998. The path was not always smooth and Hume suffered through much criticism, both from the unionist and also from the nationalist community. He remained steadfastly committed to persuading Sinn Fein to steer away from militant republicanism toward pursuing goals through exclusively peaceful means.

BIBLIOGRAPHY

Drower, George M. F. *John Hume, Peacemaker.* London: V. Gollancz, 1995.

Hume, John. *A New Ireland: Politics, Peace, and Reconciliation.* Boulder, Colo.: Roberts Rinehart, 1997.

———. *Personal Views: Politics, Peace, and Reconciliation in Ireland.* Dublin: Town House, 1996.

Murray, Gerard. *John Hume and the SDLP: Impact and Survival in Northern Ireland.* Dublin: Irish Academic Press, 1998.

Routledge, Paul. *John Hume: A Biography.* London: HarperCollins, 1998.

White, Barry. *John Hume, Statesman of the Troubles.* Belfast: Blackstaff Press, 1984.

Ricki Schoen

SEE ALSO Adams, Gerry

Hungary

Country in central Europe. Hungary lost 65 percent of its territory as a result of World War I (1914–18). Nazi Germany won the support of revisionist Hungary by allowing it to annex the mostly Magyar-populated territories of Ruthenia (from Czechoslovakia), Bácska (now Vojvodina, part of Serbia), and parts of Slovakia and Transylvania (from Romania). Hungary participated in the 1941 Axis attack on Yugoslavia. Regent Miklós Horthy went along reluctantly while Prime Minister Count Pál Teleki committed suicide rather than dishonor himself. Despite adverse public opinion, Hungary also participated in the German invasion of the Soviet Union in June 1941. By 1943, however, Budapest was trying to leave the war, and in March 1944 the German army occupied Hungary and forced Horthy to appoint a Nazi sympathizer as premier.

In October 1944 Horthy announced that Hungary would seek an armistice. In the occupied parts of the country, the Germans responded by replacing Horthy with Ferenc Szálasi, leader of the small Hungarian fascist organization, Arrow Cross. After Horthy was ousted, General Béla Miklós, commander of Hungarian forces on the eastern front, went over to the Soviets and set up a pro-Allied provisional government.

It took the Red Army forty-nine days to take the Buda heights overlooking the Danube River. German resistance ceased on February 13, 1945, and in April the Miklós government moved into Budapest. It remained in power until the November 1945 elections.

In Hungary, as in the rest of Eastern Europe, the immediate postwar government was a United Front coali-

Hungary. *Illustration courtesy of Bernard Cook.*

tion, the Hungarian Independence Front. It consisted of a number of parties. Communists held the ministries of interior and agriculture. People's courts, meanwhile, dispensed justice to "fascists" and war criminals and terrorized the opposition. The Communists also managed to infiltrate all major political parties save the Smallholders.

It appeared that the November 1945 elections would see a pro-Communist victory, but with word that the Smallholders were the only political party not controlled by the Soviets, Hungarians gave them 57 percent of the vote and a majority in the new one-house assembly. Also working against the Communists was the memory of the brief and violent Communist regime of Béla Kun in 1919.

A coalition government now ruled Hungary. Smallholders held the two leading posts, including the premiership under Ferenc Nagy. However, the new constitution, providing for a democratic republic, was doomed to a brief existence. Secretary of the Communist Party and Vice Premier Mátyás Rákosi controlled the police and the Soviet army occupied Hungary. Expropriation of German monetary assets in Hungary also provided the Soviets with a strong economic lever.

Minister of the Interior and Police Chief László Rajk directed a reign of terror, while Rákosi embarked on what he called "salami" tactics, slicing off one segment of the opposition after another. The Communists also moved against the Smallholders Party. Its leader, Béla Kovacs, was arrested and accused of plotting to restore the Habsburgs. In May, Nagy, on vacation in Switzerland, was forced to resign by threats from Moscow. The 1947 parliamentary election, tainted by Communist election fraud, reduced the strength of the Smallholders and in March 1948 the Social Democratic Party was forced to merge with the Communist Party to form the Hungarian Workers Party, renamed the Hungarian Socialist Workers' Party in 1956. In 1949 Hungary became a so-called people's republic.

The Roman Catholic primate of Hungary, József Cardinal Mindszenty, refused to recognize the government's confiscation of church lands and nationalization of its schools. Mindszenty also refused to hide his conservative social and political views. Accused of being a monarchist, he was arrested in December 1948, tried, and found guilty the following February and sentenced to life in prison.

Within a few months Rajk was himself on trial. A nationalist revolutionary rather than a Moscow-trained bureaucrat, he was found guilty and executed. Rákosi, a pure Stalinist subservient to Moscow, assumed formal control and was premier until 1953.

Hungary's economic restructuring progressed rapidly after the war. By 1948 most of the economy had been socialized, including banks and enterprises employing more than one hundred people. In 1950 the regime inaugurated a five-year economic plan. Economic, recovery was retarded, however, by the costs of maintaining the Soviet army of occupation, paying $200 million in reparations, and the unequal character of trade with the USSR.

In 1945 Minister of Agriculture Imre Nagy carried out land reform. Although about half of the land was owned by peasant proprietors, a few hundred wealthy noble families held nearly a third of the total acreage and some seven hundred thousand peasants had no land whatsoever. The Communists parceled out new farms with a maximum size of twenty-one acres, too small for viability. Probably the Communists thought this would force peasants to settle for collective farms. Meanwhile, the economy deteriorated as Rákosi sought to turn Hungary into a country of heavy industry despite the lack of natural resources to sustain such a plan.

By 1955 the intellectual elite of Hungary were demanding change. An emerging new leadership in the Kremlin prevented Rákosi from suppressing a rising chorus of protests during the spring and summer of 1956. The dissidents were not anti-Communists but merely demanded that the government align its policies and practices with stated Communist ideals.

In July 1956 Moscow forced Rákosi to resign as party secretary. His Stalinist replacement, Ernö Gerö, was no improvement. Hopes then centered on Imre Nagy. He had been premier from 1953 to 1955, at which time he attempted to reduce or abolish forced labor, achieve accommodation with religious authorities, curtail the secret police, amnesty political prisoners, slow collectivization of land, and reduce economic strains caused by overly rapid industrialization. In general, these were the demands of the 1956 reformers. Party Secretary Rákosi had prevented implementation of Nagy's reforms, however, and then convinced Moscow to oust him.

Revolution of 1956

By 1956 there was widespread dissatisfaction in Hungary. Under Rákosi the economy had deteriorated. Agriculture had stagnated as a result of collectivization and a lack of investment, and the government had endeavored to transform the economy into a heavy industrial, base, despite a lack of natural resources to sustain it. A poor harvest and fuel shortage in the fall of 1956 added to the already serious economic problems.

At the same time there was rising discontent among Hungary's intellectuals, who had come to enjoy some freedom in the "thaw" following the death in March 1953

Budapest, October 2, 1956. A large statue of the Soviet dictator Stalin is toppled and removed from Stalin Square in Budapest. Among the graffiti scrawled on the statue are the letters "W.C." (water closet, or toilet) and "Striki" (low gigolo). *Illustration courtesy UPI/Bettmann Newsphotos.*

of Soviet dictator of Joseph Stalin. In 1955 nearly sixty of them signed the so-called Workers' Memorandum, which demanded an end to rigid state regimentation of cultural life. Although most were later forced to retract this daring gesture, the de-Stalinization campaign in the USSR saved them from further punishment. Certainly the Kremlin's changing approach prevented Rákosi from suppressing what became a rising chorus of protests during the spring and summer of 1956.

The principal outlet for the intellectuals was a debating society known as the Petőfi Club, named for Sándor Petőfi, nationalist poet and hero of the Revolution of 1848. The dissidents were not anti-Communists; rather, they demanded that the government bring its policies and practices into line with true Communist ideals.

June unrest in Poland and Władysław Gomułka's return to power there encouraged the Hungarian reformers. The situation within Hungary, meanwhile, had deteriorated to the point that Soviet Premier Nikita Khrushchev ordered Rákosi to resign as party secretary on July 18, 1956. But Rákosi's Stalinist replacement, Ernö Gerö, was not acceptable to party "moderates," who favored greater liberalization.

For months the opposition had been demanding the return to power of Imre Nagy. Nagy had served as minister of agriculture on his return from Moscow in 1944. He then became minister of the interior before being replaced by László Rajk. In June 1953, following worker strikes in Budapest, the new Kremlin leadership demanded change in Hungary. Rákosi was allowed to remain as party general secretary but the Kremlin forced him to relinquish the premiership to Nagy. While in office

Nagy attempted to reduce or abolish forced labor, work out an accommodation with religion, curtail the power of the secret police, provide amnesty for political prisoners, slow down collectivization of land, and relax economic controls. These were the same demands of the rebels in 1956.

Hard-liners headed by Rákosi thwarted implementation of Nagy's reforms and, in April 1955, ousted him as premier. In November 1955 Rákosi, once more in full control, expelled Nagy from the party. Reformers within the party warned that if Nagy did not return and the government was not reorganized under his leadership, there would be an explosion. The party leadership, however, resisted these steps.

Stimulated by news of unrest from Poland, students in Budapest began openly to demand reforms. On the night of October 22, 1956, they held meetings and began formulating demands. In Budapest on the following afternoon a large crowd of students, soon joined by thousands of other people, defied a ban on meetings and demonstrations to gather at the statue of General Józef Bem, hero of the Polish revolution of 1830 and the 1848–49 Hungarian struggle for independence. Originally planned as an expression of sympathy for the Polish movement, the march reflected acute dissatisfaction with the Hungarian government.

At first members of the crowd were merely onlookers to the student demonstration, but as time went by their mood changed. After laying a wreath at the Bem statue, the crowd, instead of disbanding, moved across the Danube Chain Bridge to Kossuth Square in front of the parliament building. A series of events that evening transformed the reform movement into a rebellion.

Another crowd gathered in front of the radio station where Party Secretary Gerö was scheduled to address the nation at 8:00 P.M. He had recently returned from a meeting with Khrushchev in the Crimea and most in the crowd assumed he would announce concessions. They were disappointed. Gerö's remarks, recorded earlier and carried to the crowd over loudspeakers, were uncompromising. This stemmed either from his misunderstanding of the mood in Budapest or his desire to provoke a presumably easily suppressed revolt.

The students gathered at the radio station demanded that a resolution they had drafted be read over the air. A riot ensued, and the first shots of the revolution rang out as the state security police (the AVH) fired from the radio building on the unarmed crowd below. Despite this AVH attack the crowd did not disperse. Many soldiers and police sent by the government to put down the disturbance soon joined the demonstrators.

Its possession of arms gave the crowd a sense of power. The people were soon swept up in an effort to destroy the symbols of the hated regime. One crowd cut down a huge statue of Stalin and hauled it through the streets. Demonstrators wrecked the party headquarters and newspaper office. Crowds lit bonfires with Communist literature and tore down hated red star emblems. Above all, the people attacked AVH posts and the people manning them.

The revolution entered a new phase when Gerö proclaimed martial law and called in Soviet troops. Early in the morning of October 24 Soviet tanks and troops entered the city of Budapest and took up positions. Bringing in the Soviets was a mistake because the uprising now took on a frankly anti-Soviet, nationalist character. Bewildered Soviet soldiers, told they would be fighting fascists, were confronted by a solidly hostile populace. The most frequently heard slogan was "Ruszkik haza" (Russians go home). For the next four days sporadic and persistent fighting took place as "Freedom Fighters"—bands of students, soldiers, young workers, former prisoners, and others—sniped at the occupying army. Most Freedom Fighters were young and driven by a desperate determination.

On the morning of October 24, at the same time that it called in Soviet troops, the Central Committee of the party named Imre Nagy premier, but he was not yet entrusted with actual power. A Soviet delegation led by Anastas Mikoyan and Mikhail Suslov arrived from Moscow and was convinced by the fighting on October 25 that a political change was necessary. On that day the AVH opened fire on demonstrators in front of the parliament building, killing and wounding a number, including several members of a Soviet tank crew stationed in the center of the square. Gerö was replaced as party secretary by János Kádár, who had also suffered under Rákosi and was neither a Stalinist nor an avowed reformer.

The revolution, meanwhile, swept the entire country. In factories throughout the provinces, newly elected workers' councils replaced Communist authorities. In effect, the workers took over the political system from below. The first workers' council was set up at the incandescent lamp factory in Budapest on October 24. Within three days a network of these councils covered the country. Their demands reached well beyond social grievances, such as higher wages and decentralization of economic planning, to national concerns, such as the removal of Soviet troops from Hungary. These they forwarded to Nagy.

This situation compelled the Central Committee to relinquish full authority to Nagy. He hoped, even ex-

pected, that he could save the situation by restoring his 1953 program. Events forced him to move far beyond what he had originally intended, however. His October 27 announcement of a government of national union, including non-Communist parties, was the beginning of this break. Subsequently Nagy called for the Soviets to leave Budapest and to begin negotiations for their complete withdrawal from Hungary. He declared amnesty for the insurrectionists, freedom of speech and press, an end to the hated AVH, and restoration of a multiparty system. He also promised elections for the following January.

The old political parties—Social Democrats, Smallholders, and National Peasants—promptly reappeared. Among those named to the cabinet were Social Democrat Anna Kethly, former President Zoltán Tildy, and, though he did not serve, Béla Kovács, whose courageous leadership of the Smallholders Party from 1945 to 1947 had been rewarded by nearly eight years of imprisonment in the Soviet Union.

On October 28 the Soviets began to pull out of Budapest and the revolution seemed victorious. Excited Hungarians interpreted this to mean that Soviet political will had been broken. The Kremlin undoubtedly hoped that Nagy and Kádár, like Gomułka in Poland, would be able to control developments sufficiently to maintain the Communist Party in power; Soviet leaders were, therefore, at first willing to make concessions, including the full withdrawal of Soviet troops. Creation of a multiparty cabinet and the promise of elections, however, was another matter, because this would mean the end of Communist control. Moscow had to take into account the still critical situation in Poland and perennial discontent in East Germany. Soviet control of all Eastern Europe was threatened, and Khrushchev himself could hardly survive a debacle that his rivals would rush to attribute to his de-Stalinization policy. Kremlin leaders may also have genuinely believed, as they charged, that Western agents were active in the revolt. Leaders of the Soviet army, angered by their earlier humiliation in Budapest, also argued for intervention.

At the end of October the Kremlin leadership unanimously decided to intervene again, this time in full force. Khrushchev personally secured the support of leaders of Bulgaria, Poland, Romania, and Yugoslavia. This decision came at the same time as an October 30 Kremlin declaration formally recognizing the legitimacy of national paths to communism. On November 1 Hungarian Communist Party Secretary Kádár flew to Moscow. Nagy's announcement that same day that Hungary was withdrawing from the Warsaw Pact only added to Soviet resolution. Many historians have concluded that Nagy's announcement sparked the Soviet invasion. Hungarian documents, however, demonstrate that Nagy was led by the Soviets to believe that they had acquiesced to all the changes made up to November 1. It was only when he learned that the Soviets were preparing to invade that he felt sufficiently betrayed to give in to the demands of his more radical supporters. For the first time in his political life, Nagy went outside the party to become the leader of the Hungarian nation.

The Soviets struck at dawn on Sunday, November 4, with 200,000 troops and 2,500 tanks and armored cars. In a few hours they had occupied the streets of Budapest. Ambassador Yuri Andropov orchestrated Soviet policy with brutal efficiency. Nagy spoke over the radio, calling for resistance, and Hungarians responded. The hopeless fighting went on for more than a week until the last pockets of resistance were wiped out. Nagy took refuge in the Yugoslav Embassy. On November 22 he left there on a pledge of safe conduct by the new Hungarian government but was seized by the Soviets. József Cardinal Mindszenty, released by the revolution, sought refuge in the U.S. legation. He remained there until 1971, when an agreement gave him safe passage to Rome. One of the heroes of the revolution, Minister of Defense Pál Maléter, was arrested on the night of November 3 when he led a delegation to Soviet headquarters in Tököl for talks.

Estimates of casualties in the fighting vary widely, but a reasonable total is probably seven thousand Soviets and twenty-five thousand Hungarians. Several thousand people were executed for participation in the revolution, including Nagy and Maléter in the summer of 1958. More important for the future of Hungary, some two hundred thousand people, including many of the country's youngest and brightest, fled to the West through Austria.

Moscow then installed a new puppet government headed by Kádár that imposed martial law. The secret police reappeared and the government crushed labor unrest and imprisoned strike leaders.

One effect of the failure of the Hungarian revolution was a loss of faith in the West. Hungarians believed that they had been promised help, and many Hungarians and Western observers believed that the United States prolonged the fighting because Hungarian-language broadcasts over Radio Free Europe, then covertly financed by the United States government, encouraged Hungarians to believe that either the United States or the United Nations would send troops to safeguard their proclaimed neutrality. Hungarians repeatedly asked Western journalists covering the revolution when U.N. troops would arrive. President Dwight Eisenhower and Secretary of State John Foster Dulles had talked about "liberating" Eastern Europe and "rolling back communism." This had been intended largely for domestic U.S. political consumption, however, not for the Eastern Europeans themselves. U.S. inactivity over the Hungarian situation indicated tacit acceptance of the Soviets domination of that part of the world.

The United Nations discussed the Hungarian crisis but adjourned the meeting because the Soviets appeared to be withdrawing. Then in a matter of a few hours, the United Nations was faced with the fait accompli of November 4. At the same time, however, U.N. attention was focused on the Anglo-French Suez invasion; this and the split between the United States and its two major allies effectively prevented any concrete action against the invaders of Hungary. In December 1956 the United Nations censured the Kádár regime, but this did not alter the realities of the situation.

The Soviet military intervention did have a considerable impact on Western European Communist parties. These suffered mass resignations, including some illustrious intellectuals. The effects of the Hungarian Revolution of 1956 were particularly pronounced in Eastern Europe. Any thought that the peoples of Eastern Europe might have had of escaping Moscow's grip was discouraged by the grim spectacle of Soviet willingness to use force in defiance of world opinion. Nevertheless the USSR and its brand of communism suffered the embarrassing irony of rebellion by workers, intellectuals, and youth and its crushing of workers councils, or soviets, nearly four decades after the victory of soviets in the Russian Revolution of 1917.

The Hungarian Revolution of 1956 ultimately led to changes in Soviet policy toward Eastern Europe. Moscow allowed some modifications in economic planning within the East bloc to meet needs of individual countries, including more attention to consumer goods and agriculture, and a slowed pace of industrialization. For the time being, however, an opportunity to begin the liberation of Eastern Europe had instead produced a crushing reassertion of Soviet mastery.

BIBLIOGRAPHY

Barber, Noel. *Seven Days of Freedom*. New York: Stein and Day, 1975.

Irving, David. *Uprising. One Nation's Nightmare: Hungary 1956*. London: Hodder and Stoughton, 1981.

Kecskeméti, Paul. *The Unexpected Revolution; Social Forces in the Hungarian Uprising*. Stanford, Calif.: Stanford University Press, 1961.

Kopacsi, Sandor. *In the Name of the Working Class.* New York: Grove Press, 1987.

Kovrig, Bennett. *The Hungarian People's Republic.* Baltimore: Johns Hopkins University Press, 1970.

Lasky, Melvin J., ed. *The Hungarian Revolution.* New York: Praeger, 1957.

Zinner, Paul. *Revolution in Hungary.* New York: Columbia University Press, 1962.

Spencer C. Tucker

SEE ALSO Gerö, Ernö; Kádár, János; Nagy, Imre; Rákosi, Mátyás; Suez Crisis

Postrevolutionary Hungary

Whether as a temporary measure or because he actually hoped to gain popular support, Kádár first attempted to maintain most of Nagy's reforms and to ride the nationalist tide but was unsuccessful. Hungarians remained unreconcilable. Ironically, it was worker councils resembling the original soviets of the Russian Revolution that led the opposition to the Soviet-imposed Communist regime. A long general strike, called in December 1956 and centered in the Budapest Csepel factory complex, was eventually crushed. The Kádár regime maintained itself only by resort to terror.

Several years of rigid repression followed, but by 1960 the Kádár regime gave ground to the preferences of the people. Hungarians tolerated Kádár only because his replacement might be worse; his rule was preferable to Soviet rule. In 1968 Kádár sold the Kremlin on a set of economic reforms, loosening government control over industry and agriculture. These created a growing private sector by permitting workers to moonlight to sell goods or provide services. These economic reforms made Budapest the liveliest capital in Eastern Europe, or as Hungarians called it, "the happiest barracks in the Soviet camp." This policy became known as "goulash communism."

Kádár reversed the policy of enforced industrialization and let Hungarian agriculture flourish. By exploiting Hungary's natural advantages, the country became the Soviet bloc's only net exporter of farm products. In 1986 Kádár offered Hungarians the chance to work overtime in state-run factories for personal profit. As a result of all this, Hungarians lived better than the inhabitants of the other East bloc countries, with the possible exception of East Germany. They also had some personal freedom.

Kádár eventually became the most popular Communist chief in the Soviet bloc and he brought Hungary to near national consensus. Still, sixty thousand to eighty thousand Soviet troops and their tanks remained in Hungary. Kádár was also reluctant to annoy Moscow because the Hungarian economy depended on cheap Soviet oil. And what appeared bright by Eastern European standards was certainly shoddy in comparison with the rest of Europe. Much of Kádár's goulash communism, furthermore, was financed by a massive foreign debt, at $18 billion the largest per capita debt in the Soviet bloc. The regime used it not to invest in industrial plants but to subsidize unproductive factories and purchase luxury goods from abroad to modify the population. The national currency, the forint, was not externally convertible, and Hungary found it harder and harder to keep up. As imports continued to outstrip exports, inflation and dissent grew.

In 1987 the new premier, Károly Grosz, gave a frank appraisal of a deteriorating economic situation to parliament. This was the first time any government official had publicly detailed such problems. In May 1988 Grosz ousted Kádár as head of the party and announced an austerity program. As demands for reform in Hungary mounted, Grosz agreed to dissidents' demands that the archival material on the secret trial of Imre Nagy be opened. Eventually Grosz, who allied himself with Soviet leader Mikhail Gorbachev, gave way to growing demand for change. Hungary was the only one of the former Soviet bloc countries where the reformist revolution came from above. Grosz authorized election reform, including a multiparty system. In February 1989 Imre Pozsgay, a leading proponent of reform, publicly admitted in parliament that the 1956 revolution had in fact been a popular uprising, not a counterrevolution. Imre Nagy was rehabilitated and, in June 1989, reinterred.

In April 1990 Hungary held its first free elections since 1947 and twelve parties fielded candidates. The former Communist Party, the Hungarian Socialist Workers Party, did not win a single seat, and the Socialists came in fourth. Voters opted for centrist parties pledging democracy, free markets, and an escape from Soviet political, economic, and military dominance. The nationalist Hungarian Democratic Forum won nearly 25 percent of the vote, and the more liberal Alliance of Free Democrats got 21 percent. No other party got more than 12 percent. József Antall, leader of the Hungarian Democratic Forum, became premier in a coalition government that included two smaller parties, the Independent Smallholders and the Christian Democrats. Together this group commanded a majority in the new one-house parliament. In September 1990 Hungary and the USSR agreed on the withdrawal of the fifty thousand Soviet troops remaining in the country.

The economic situation seemed clouded at best. In 1991 the average citizen took home a paycheck of about eight thousand forints a month (roughly $100) and inflation was 30 percent a year. Hungary remained the major magnet for Western investment in the former Soviet bloc, but by 1990 the foreign debt had swelled to $21 billion, with debt service claiming $3 billion annually. Imports from the West were increasing and exports to the West decreasing. Also, the Hungarian population was static, and this meant an aging population and increases in social service costs. Fully 20 percent of the entire population lived in Budapest and its suburbs, and one-third of the population was made up of pensioners. Crime was also up substantially. A touchy issue was the substantial Magyar population abroad: 589,000 in Czechoslovakia, 380,000 in Serbian Vojvodina, and about 180,000 in Ukraine. The chief bone of contention, however, was Romania's persecution of its 1,600,000 Hungarians. Another problem was the rights of some 240,000 Germans living in Hungary who no longer felt that being German was a disadvantage. There were also sharp political divisions between the two leading political parties, especially over charges of anti-Semitism. The rift between the urban Jewish intelligentsia and Hungarian Christian candidates with appeal outside Budapest was an old theme in the nation's political life. It took on an added dimension since many prominent Hungarian Communists leaders were Jewish.

Support for Antall had plummeted before his death in December 1993. His party, which had supported free-market reforms for four years, lost the national elections in May 1994. Reflecting a trend throughout Eastern Europe, save the Czech Republic, the Socialist Party, formed from the former Communists, won 35 percent of the popular vote. In a system that gave weighed preference to the winning party, the Socialists secured a fifteen-seat majority in parliament, and party leader Gyula Horn became premier. Despite this majority Horn formed a coalition with the Free Democrats, who had won 70 seats. The two parties pledged to continue free-market reforms including privatization.

BIBLIOGRAPHY

Felkay, Andrew. *Hungary and the USSR, 1956–1988.* Westport, Conn.: Greenwood Press, 1989.

Gati, Charles. *Hungary and the Soviet Bloc.* Durham, N.C.: Duke University Press, 1986.

Kovrig, Bennett. *The Hungarian People's Republic.* Baltimore: Johns Hopkins University Press, 1970.

Toma, Peter A., and Ivan Volgyes. *Politics in Hungary.* San Francisco: W. H. Freeman, 1977.

Spencer C. Tucker

Hungarian Question in the United Nations

After the outbreak of the Hungarian Revolution on October 23, 1956, and the first intervention of Soviet troops, the United States, United Kingdom, and France requested that the secretary-general of the United Nations on the basis of Paragraph 34 of the U.N. Charter convene the Security Council to discuss the situation in Hungary. The Security Council put the Hungarian question on its agenda over the protest of the USSR on October 28, but the Suez crisis pushed it into the background for the time being. After the second, and decisive, Soviet intervention in the Hungarian Revolution on November 4, 1956, the Security Council passed a resolution calling for the withdrawal of Soviet troops, but the Soviet delegate vetoed the resolution.

An extraordinary session of the General Assembly was convened on January 10, 1957, and it set up a Special Committee of five members (Australia, Ceylon (became Sri Lanka in 1972), Denmark, Tunisia, and Uruguay) to collect information about the Hungarian Revolution. The committee held public and closed hearings and presented its final report on June 7, 1957. It stated that the revolution was spontaneous; it was not instigated from abroad; the Soviets suppressed it brutally; and the Hungarian request for the neutrality of the country was not the cause but the consequence of the second Soviet aggression, which was already under way. However, the General Assembly did not have the authority to sanction, and the USSR vetoed any resolution to that effect in the Security Council.

The early and transitional détente between the United States and the USSR in 1958 and 1959 pushed the debate over the Hungarian question in the United Nations to the background to some extent, but the execution of the leader of the revolution, Imre Nagy, and some of his associates in June 1958 revived the issue. The Special Committee issued a supplementary report on the question. At the same time, the General Assembly denounced the executions in a resolution and appointed Australian Sir Leslie Munroe to look after compliance with the U.N. resolutions. The General Assembly in a resolution passed on December 9, 1959, denounced the Hungarian and the Soviet governments for ignoring the UN resolutions. Meanwhile, the Soviets and the government of János Kádár, which it had helped install, launched a counterattack in the United Nations and at other forums. They protested against "foreign interference in the domestic affairs of Hungary" and declared that Soviets troops would remain there as long as the two governments involved deemed it necessary.

The early 1960s brought about a decisive change in the Hungarian question. Both the United States, the driving force in the United Nations behind the resolutions condemning the presence of Soviets troops in Hungary, and the USSR, together with Hungary, wished to "normalize" the relations between the two sides. The Hungarian relocation camps where up to 25,000 Hungarians had been imprisoned by the Kádár government were shut down in April 1960, and in April 1961 limited amnesty was extended to some people condemned for their activities during the revolution. At the same time the USSR waged a rather effective campaign among African and Asian countries (e.g., by supplying loans on favorable terms) and, as a consequence, more and more of them voted against resolutions condemning Soviet aggression or abstained from voting.

The turning point in the question came in 1962. Despite the fact that the United States and other Western countries put the Hungarian question on the agenda of the General Assembly in September 1962 with a slim majority (43 for, 34 against, 19 abstentions), the United States and Hungary had already initiated confidential talks about a compromise. The Soviet leadership, especially after the Cuban Missile Crisis of that year, also wished to put an end to the issue; Soviet Premier Nikita Khrushchev informed Kádár in Moscow on November 7, 1962, that the Hungarians could accept the U.S. suggestion, which provided that the Hungarians give amnesty to all who participated in the revolution and the United States, in return, would drop the Hungarian question in the United Nations. Kádár announced the general amnesty at the Eighth Congress of the Hungarian Socialist Workers Party on November 20, 1962, while the Special Political Committee of the United Nations accepted the U.S. motion that requested the secretary-general to take steps to remove the Hungarian question from the agenda of the organization and to discontinue Sir Leslie Munroe's inquiries. The general amnesty in Hungary took effect on March 21, 1963.

BIBLIOGRAPHY

Radvanyi, Janos. *Hungary and the Superpowers: The 1956 Revolution and Realpolitik.* Stanford, Calif.: Hoover Institute Press, 1972.
Report of the Special Committee on the Problem of Hungary. General Assembly: Official Records, 11th Session, Supplement No. 18 (A/3592). New York: United Nations, 1957.

Tamás Magyarics

Crown of St. Stephen

Perhaps the most important Hungarian national symbol. The crown was widely believed to have been a gift from Pope Sylvester II and to have been used in the coronation of St. Stephen I in 1001. Stephen, founder of Hungary, brought Christianity to the kingdom; as a result the crown has been venerated as a religious object. Additional coronation objects consist of a crown, scepter, orb, sword, and mantle. All became cherished symbols of one of Hungary's greatest kings.

Although Andrew III in a 1292 royal decree stated that the crown had belonged to St. Stephen, it does not date from the time of Stephen. Current scholarship asserts that the crown probably belonged to a medieval successor after the twelfth century.

The crown itself is actually made of two crowns. The upper part, consisting of cross bands with inscriptions in Latin, was believed to be that of St. Stephen. The cloisonné plaques of the lower part have Greek inscriptions, indicating its Byzantine origin. Portraits in this lower portion portray Byzantine Emperor Michael Ducas and Hungarian King Géza. The circlet of the Greek crown is a band of fairly thick gold plate holding eight alternating cloisonné enamels and precious stones.

The coronation objects have had a rather spectacular history, having been lost, stolen, or misappropriated during much of their existence. At the end of the unsuccessful Hungarian War of Independence of 1848–49, the crown was buried at Orsova in present-day Romania. The location was later revealed to the Austrian government, which recovered it in 1853 and returned it to Buda. The last Hungarian king crowned with the insignia was Charles IV in 1916. Following World War I, regent Miklós Horthy exercised power "in the name of the Holy crown." In November 1944, during World War II, Ferenc Szálasi, leader of the fascist Arrow Cross, took an oath on the crown. At the end of the war Arrow Cross leaders fled with the coronation relics and crown to Austria, where they were again buried. In June 1945 the crown came into the possession of the U.S. army occupation authorities, then vanished.

During the years of the Cold War there was only conjecture concerning the crown's whereabouts. Only in 1965 did the U.S. government officially acknowledge that the crown was being held in Fort Knox, Kentucky, as the "special property" of the Hungarian people.

Repeated requests by the Hungarian government for the return of the crown went unanswered until, in the era of détente, President Jimmy Carter decided to return it to Hungary. On January 6, 1978, Secretary of State Cyrus Vance and a large American delegation delivered the crown to Budapest. The crown and other coronation objects are displayed today in a special room of the Hungarian National Museum in Budapest.

BIBLIOGRAPHY

Kovács, Éva, and Zsuzsa Lovag. *The Hungarian Crown and Other Regalia,* 2d rev. ed. Budapest: Corvina, 1980.

Spencer C. Tucker

Elections of March–April 1990

First multiparty election in Hungary since 1947. As the result of the so-called Round Table negotiations in 1989, a complicated election law provided a selection of seats through a two-round process. It combined elements of the British and the German systems. Out of 386 seats in parliament, 176 were filled by direct elections in constituencies and 152 from twenty regional party lists. The remaining 58 seats were allocated to parties in accordance with a procedure designed to provide proportional compensation for the inequities of the "first-past-the-post" system used in the constituencies.

More than fifty parties participated in the election, but only twelve fielded candidates all over the country. In the first round the Hungarian Democratic Forum (MDF), which had developed under the protection of the reformists in the old Communist Party, received 24.7 percent. The Alliance of the Free Democrats (SZDSZ), which had its origins in the democratic opposition during the Kádár era, won 21.4 percent. The reconstituted Independent Smallholders Party (FKGP), which had won a majority in the 1945 election, gained 11.8 percent. The Socialist Party (MSZP), formed by a majority of the members of the old Communist Party when it split apart in October 1989, received 10.9 percent. The Federation of the Young Democrats (FIDESZ), founded in 1988 by a group of young lawyers, gained 8.9 percent. The Christian Democratic Peoples Party (KDNP) scored 6.5 percent. Finally, 15.8 percent of the vote went to parties that remained under 4 percent and thus were excluded from parliament: Workers Party, Social Democrats, Party of Entrepreneurs, Patriotic Election Coalition, Peoples Party, and the Greens.

Before the second round the MDF and the SZDSZ accused each other of connections to the Communists. The MDF, nevertheless, representing a more moderate transition to the market economy than the SZDSZ, won the second round. The MDF candidates were better known, the electoral districts favored the party (it won in every province east of the Danube), and it received support from voters whose candidate had lost in the first

round. The MDF received 165 seats in parliament; SZDSZ, 92; FKGP, 43; MSZP, 33; and both FIDESZ and KDNP 21 each. Eleven independent and joint party candidates were also elected.

The campaign did not occur without scandal. The minister of interior was forced to resign for tapping the telephones of the opposition. This "Danubegate" scandal expanded when opposition politicians witnessed the ministry destroying its records.

BIBLIOGRAPHY

Tökés, Rudolf L. *From Post-Communism to Democracy: Politics, Parties and the 1990 Elections in Hungary.* Bonn: Konrad Adenauer Stiftung, 1990.

Heino Nyyssönen

Elections of 1994

Parliamentary elections in Hungary in the spring of 1994 brought about the fall of the ruling coalition of the Hungarian Democratic Forum (MDF), Hungarian Christian Democratic Peoples Party (KDNP), and Independent Smallholders Party (FKGP). There were many causes of their defeat. Central were worsening economic conditions (inflation, relatively high unemployment, problems in the privatization process). Mistakes were also committed in agricultural policies (hasty dissolution of cooperatives). The ruling coalition had difficulties getting its message through to the electorate. Finally, there was a prevailing nostalgia for the comforts provided by the Communist regime (full employment, low prices, and a cheap and comprehensive social security system).

The same six parties that succeeded in placing delegates in parliament in 1990 were represented in 1994. The majority of the seats were gained by the Socialist Party (the reform wing of the former Communist Party), with 54 percent of the popular vote, while the Alliance of the Free Democrats (SZDSZ) received 17.8 percent of the vote. The ultimate loser was the MDF, whose support dropped from 43 percent in 1990 to 10 percent in 1994, while the other parliamentary parties (the sixth being the Alliance of the Young Democrats, FIDESZ) generally retained their support between the two elections. A number of other parties ran for parliament (386 seats altogether), but they could not reach the threshold of 5 percent needed to get into parliament. The election turnout rose in 1994: while in 1990 65 percent of the electorate participated in the first round of elections and 45.5 percent in the second, the corresponding figures in 1994 were 69 percent and 55.1 percent.

After the elections the Socialist Party and the SZDSZ formed a coalition with a parliamentary majority of 72 percent under the premiership of Socialist Gyula Horn. The junior partner in the coalition received stronger representation in the new cabinet than the election results might have justified. This junior partner was therefore able to force its economic policies, based mainly on the monetarist ideas of the Chicago-school of economics, on the larger party. Meanwhile, the former ruling coalition broke. In 1996 the MDF split and a breakaway faction formed a new party, the Hungarian Democratic Peoples Party (MDNP).

BIBLIOGRAPHY

Rothschild, Joseph, and Nancy M. Wingfield. *Return to Diversity: A Political History of East Central Europe since World War II,* 3d ed. New York: Oxford University, 2000.

Tamás Magyarics

Extreme Right Movements after 1945

The extreme right movements presented a relatively marginal issue in Hungary's postwar history. For decades during the Communist regime, all alternative political ideologies, including right-wing nationalism, were suppressed, and if they existed they were covert. After the demise of the Kádár regime, however, the extreme right resurfaced. Currently, there are several overtly rightist, anti-Semitic, and xenophobic parties and groups. Although their popularity is growing, they still do not attract considerable support.

Current rightist movements and their rhetoric and symbolism are not without precedent. As of the mid-1930s Hungary increasingly kept pace with Nazi Germany. In late 1944 Ferenc Szálasi, a veteran national socialist, and his Arrow Cross Party seized power with German assistance. Following the war some 139 people, mainly officers and politicians, including former prime ministers, were executed as war criminals in late 1945. Meanwhile, hundreds of people escaped from reckoning and fled to Western countries.

Except for October 1956, when anti-Semitic incidents were reported during the Hungarian Revolution, there was no fundamental evidence of any extreme right activities of any kind during the Communist era. In the 1980s the first skinhead groups appeared in the country. Although self-organized, they have been supported by fellow skinhead groups from Western countries, mostly from Germany. Hungarian skinheads were also backed financially and ideologically by Hungarian émigrés in Australia, the United States, and Canada, who often shared an Arrow Cross past and military service against the USSR in World War II. Skinhead organizations published comics

and booklets, many times mere translations of German publications, and organized skinhead concerts. Their ideology mostly reflected the general elements of neo-Nazi doctrines but was also nourished by traditional Hungarian extreme nationalism. Hungarian skinheads are strongly anti-Semitic and anti-Rom, and aim at protecting the nation's "racial purity." Their activities are manifested in soccer hooliganism and vandalism, especially the desecration of Jewish cemeteries and synagogues. There have been many incidents of insult and assault against Jews and Rom on the street and in public places. Foreign students, mainly Asians and Africans, and even tourists have also been among their victims.

Following significant growth in the number of criminal offenses against people for their skin color, religion, language, or political opinion, the Hungarian Penal Code was modified in 1995. It now states: "Those who attack a member of national, ethnic, racial, religious or social group would be subject to imprisonment of up to five years, while those who incite hatred against any national, ethnic, racial, religious, and social group would be subject to imprisonment of up to three years." Nevertheless, this article has been applied in only a few cases.

Before the fall of the Communist one-party system, right-wing elements had no political representation. As of the early 1990s, however, nationalists founded political parties. One of the most vocal skinhead groups is the World National Popular Rule Party (Vilagnemzeti Népuralmista Part), founded and led by an émigré returned from Australia, Albert Szabo. It considered itself the successor to the Arrow Cross Party, and therefore it was declared anticonstitutional and banned by the Constitutional Court in 1994. Szabo and his followers later established the Hungarian Welfare Alliance (Magyar Népjoléti Szövetség, MNSZ). Party members conducted street demonstrations, where they proclaimed their exclusionist sentiments. In the 1998 elections, Szabo, leader of MNSZ, unsuccessfully ran for a seat in parliament. Less significant organizations on the extreme right side are the Party of the Hungarian Cause (Magyar Érdek Partja), the Eastern Front Comrades' Federation (Keleti Arcvonal Bajtarsi Szövetség), Alliance of People Persecuted by Communism (Kommunizmus Idözötteinek Szövetsége), and New Alliance (ójszövetség). Fundamental elements of these organizations are rooted in Nazism. They share the belief that Hungarians are superior to other peoples in the central and Eastern European region. Their verbal and visual symbols include ancient Hungarian national symbols and a version of Arrow Cross symbols. They believe that the borders of Hungary drawn in 1920 that enclose only one-third of the territory of historical Hungary must be revised. They strongly oppose Western influence in Hungary. The Hungarian far Right in general protests against the role played by multinational companies and international economic and financial organizations, such as the IMF and the World Bank.

While these parties have remained peripheral, the Hungarian Justice and Life Party (Magyar Igazság és Élet Partja, MIEP), by far the most significant organization of the Hungarian Right, won parliamentary seats with over 5 percent of total votes in the 1998 elections. Similar to the proponents of the New Alliance, the founders of the MIEP were formerly members of the Hungarian Democratic Forum (MDF), which won the first free and democratic elections, and was the leading party of the conservative coalition between 1990 and 1994. Party leader István Csurka, a famous Hungarian playwright, was excluded from the MDF for his explicit anti-Semitism. The MIEP maintains links with Jean-Marie Le Pen's National Front in France and Jörg Haider's Freedom Party in Austria. Csurka's electoral success is in line with a general resurgence of the Hungarian Right.

The opinion of the extreme parties is represented in their theoretical journals and weeklies (*Magyar Forum, Hunnia, Magyar Tudat,* and *Pannon Front*), but they cannot expound their ideology without restraint in the mass media. Some publications, such as the Hungarian translation of Hitler's *Mein Kampf,* have been confiscated by the police. In the late 1990s the Internet opened a wider forum for the expression of Hungarian-language far-Right convictions in Hungarian, although the servers were mainly American.

Despite the presence of extreme right groups, their representation is still low in comparison with several Western European countries, and mainstream Hungarian politics is in accord with Western European political standards.

BIBLIOGRAPHY
Antisemitism World Report 1995, 1996, 1997. London: JPR. 1995–97.

Csilla Ban

Political Parties

Coalition governments that included the Communists, Social Democrats, National Peasants, and Smallholders ruled Hungary from 1945 to 1949. Of the parties that existed after World War II, the Hungarian Communist Party was the best organized, with many leaders arriving from exile in the Soviet Union. The membership increased rapidly to 500,000 in October 1945 and reached its peak of 743,000 in August 1947. In the elections of November 1945 the Communists won 17 percent of the vote.

The Social Democratic Party had cooperated with the Communists during the ill-fated Soviet Republic established by Béla Kun in Hungary in 1919. In 1945 the party was radicalized and again favored cooperation with the Communists. At the end of 1945 it had about 350,000 members and received 17 percent of the vote.

The National Peasant Party was established in 1939 by the leftist populist writers' movement, which valued radical peasant traditions. Its 7 percent vote came predominantly from the countryside.

The Independent Smallholders Party, a small party of the landed peasants established in 1930, demanded social reforms and secret ballots. After World War II it was the farthest right of the contending parties. The Smallholders, although lacking any special program, attracted many opposed to the other parties of the coalition government and managed to win 57 percent of the vote.

The main political alternatives were between rapid industrialization, advocated by the Communists, and evolutionary development, proposed by the Smallholders. Tactically the Communists tried to advance the policy of national unity and cooperation. Communists, Social Democrats, and National Peasants cooperated in the government. The Smallholders were forced to compromise and expel members under pressure from the Communists.

In the August 1947 elections the Communist Party became the largest party with 22.7 percent. The National Peasants received 8.3 percent and the Social Democrats 14.9. A rump Smallholders Party, allied with the leftists, received 15.4 percent. Other bourgeois parties emerged to replace the decimated Smallholders. The Democratic Peoples Party, a moderate Catholic party, won 16 percent. The Independence Party, an unabashed right-wing group, won 14 percent. The Independent Hungarian Democratic Party, willing to cooperate with the government, received 5 percent. The Bourgeois Democratic Party and the Radical Party, which had fielded candidates in 1945, again came in at under 2 percent, a dubious honor, which they shared with the Camp of Christian Women.

After the 1947 elections Communist domination and coercion intensified. Opposition parties cooperated or were banned. In June 1948 the Social Democrats and the Communists united to form the Hungarian Workers Party. In the election of 1949 all the parties that participated were included on its list, which, according to the official tally, won 95.6 percent of the vote.

BIBLIOGRAPHY
Balogh, Sándor, and Sándor Jakab. *The History of Hungary After the Second World War.* Budapest: Corvina, 1986.

Molnár, Miklós. *A Short History of the Hungarian Communist Party.* Boulder, Colo.: Westview Press, 1978.

Nagy, Ferenc. *The Struggle Behind the Iron Curtain.* Tr. by Stephen K. Swift. New York: Macmillan, 1948.

Vass, Henrik, and István Vida. *A koaliciós korszak pártjainak szervezeti szabályzatai 1944–1948: Tanulmány és dokumentumok.* Budapest: MTA Politikatudományi Intézet, ELTE Politológiai Tanszék, 1992.

Vida, István. *A független kisgazdapárt politikája 1944–1947.* Budapest: Akadémiai kiadó, 1986.

———. *Koalíció és pártharcok 1944–1948.* Budapest: Magvetö könyvkiadó, 1986.

Heino Nyyssönen

Political Parties since 1989

Although more than fifty parties participated in the elections in 1990, only twelve were able to field candidates throughout the country. Of these, only six managed to win seats in parliament. The same six parties retained seats in parliament after the 1994 general election. Between 1990 and 1994 some independent members of parliament founded new parties and fractions, but none of these won seats in 1994.

After the election of 1990 a centrist right-wing government was formed under the leadership of József Antall with the participation of the Hungarian Democratic Forum, the Smallholders Party, and the Christian Democratic Party. Between 1990 and 1992 the government shifted more to the right as the opposition moved to the left. In June 1994, Gyula Horn led a social-liberal coalition formed by the Hungarian Socialist Party and the Alliance of Free Democrats.

The Hungarian Democratic Forum (Magyar Demokrata Fórum, MDF) was founded in 1987. The party at first followed the traditions of the populist writers' movement and favored cooperation with the Communist reformers. In the autumn of 1989 the party began to develop a Christian Democratic image. The movement had three different wings: the national liberals preferred the Hungarian national traditions of the nineteenth century; the populist wing was rooted to the populist writers movement from the 1930s; and the Christian Democratic faction stressed the Christian character of the party. Later the party tried to define itself as a conservative liberal party.

MDF won the second round in 1990, calling for a measured transition to a market economy. The main project of the MDF-led government was to create a "social market economy." It also expressed concern for Hungarian-speaking minorities in neighboring countries such as Romania and Slovakia. In 1993 the populist faction, however, separated from the MDF to found a separate party.

The Alliance of Free Democrats (Szabad Demokraták Szövetsége, SZDSZ) originated in the democratic opposition during the Kádár era. The SZDSZ combined both liberal and social democratic traditions, but its early anticommunism and demand for rapid economic change gave it the appearance of a right-wing party. During the 1990 campaign some anti-Semitic slogans were directed against the party and its Jewish founding members. In 1990 the SZDSZ stressed individual rights and was more clearly oriented toward Western-style democracy than the MDF. After the elections the party's social character strengthened, and it opposed the religious orientation of the government. After the 1994 elections the SZDSZ was ready to cooperate with the Socialists.

The Independent Smallholders Party (Független Kisgazda, Földmunkás és Polgári Párt, FKGP), which won the majority in the 1945 election, was reactivated in 1988 on the basis of its old but updated program. Politically the party was situated close to the Christian Democrats. Its main objective was to restore landed property to the 1947 owners. The party split in 1991–92 over participation in the government.

The Socialist Party (Magyar Szocialista Párt, MSZP) was established by former reform Communists. It represented the majority of former Communists after the split of the old ruling party in October 1989. Attempting to define itself as a modern social democratic Western-oriented party, it has a strong socialist wing, a labor union wing, and a liberal wing.

The Federation of Young Democrats (FIDESZ) was founded in 1988 by thirty-seven young lawyers. At first the party, which was politically quite close to the SZDSZ, had a radical-liberal image. Only persons younger than thirty-five could join. In 1992 and 1993 FIDESZ was the most popular party in public opinion polls. It strongly opposed cooperation with the Socialists and found itself in the opposition conservative camp after the election of 1994.

The Christian Democratic Peoples Party (Keresztény-demokrata Néppárt, KDNP) supported Christian ethics, family values, and some public role for the churches. The party touted national values and was a firm ally of the MDF.

BIBLIOGRAPHY

A többpártrendszer kialakulása Magyarországon 1985–91: Tanulmánykötet. Budapest: Kossuth könyvkiadó, 1992.

Batt, Judy. *East Central Europe from Reform to Transformation*. London: Pinter, 1991.

East, Roger. *Revolution in Eastern Europe*. London: Pinter, 1992.

Roskin, Michael G. *The Rebirth of East Europe*. Englewood Cliffs, N.J.: Prentice-Hall, 1991.

Szabadon választott: Parlamenti almanach 1990. Budapest: Idegenforgalmi Propaganda és Kiadó Vállalat, 1990.

Tökés, Rudolf L. *From Post-Communism to Democracy: Politics, Parties and the 1990 Elections in Hungary*. Bonn: Konrad Adenauer Stiftung, 1990.

Heino Nyyssönen

SEE ALSO Antall, József; Horn, Gyula

Economy

Hungary emerged from World War II with its economy and infrastructure in ruins. In 1945 agriculture dominated the Hungarian economy and accounted for over half of total employment. In March 1945, the Hungarian government passed a decree for a radical redistribution of land. It expropriated large agricultural estates and subdivided them among the peasantry (nearly half of the peasantry had been landless before 1945). By 1949 almost two-thirds of the landless peasantry had received land and they, understandably, welcomed land reform.

During the second half of the 1940s a coalition government was gradually replaced by a Communist one under the Hungarian Socialist Workers (Communist) Party. By early 1949 a mixed economy had been replaced by Soviet-type economic planning and administration, based on extensive state ownership.

Early postwar Hungary experienced hyperinflation. Given a lack of foreign exchange reserves, the Hungarian government resorted to the printing press to pay for reparations and reconstruction. By the summer of 1946, inflation was increasing by 10 to 12 percent an hour. Furthermore, from mid-1945 to mid-1946, real incomes fell by 50 to 60 percent. Yet despite mass poverty and inflation, economic reconstruction was rapid.

In the spring of 1946 the Hungarian government laid the foundations for currency stabilization by establishing a balanced budget. Stabilization was achieved on August 1, 1946, when a new currency, the nonconvertible forint, was issued. The government also began the gradual process of eliminating private enterprise with the nationalization of the mines in the summer of 1946. Between the end of World War II and spring 1948, state ownership of industry increased from 5 to 83.5 percent as a share of total employment.

Hungary also reoriented its foreign trade away from its three main prewar trade partners—Germany, Italy, and Austria—to the Soviet Union and the other countries within the Soviet sphere of influence. In January 1949 Hungary became a founding member of the Council of Mutual Economic Assistance (CMEA), a trading bloc dominated by the USSR.

In December 1949 the remainder of large-scale and part of small-scale industry was nationalized when all firms employing more than ten workers were expropriated. Private shops and most of the remainder of small-scale industry were nationalized between 1948 and 1952.

The nationalization of industry and services was mirrored in the agricultural sector, where, in August 1948, a program of compulsory collectivization was introduced. The policy met with strong resistance from the landed peasantry, which was ruthlessly suppressed. By summer 1953 forced collectivization had failed. This failure was recognized by the new government led by Imre Nagy, which allowed farmers to resign from the collectives.

Industrial reconstruction was a success in quantitative terms. By 1949 per capita industrial production was 23 percent higher than in 1935–38. But this was achieved with imported secondhand machinery that did not embody the latest technology. The first five-year plan, which began on January 1, 1950, introduced forced industrialization and self-sufficiency. Mining and metallurgy accounted for two-thirds of total industrial investment. Resources were switched from consumption to investment. As a result there were shortages of necessities and luxury goods, while housing conditions deteriorated. Rapid growth (almost 14 percent per annum in the early 1950s) and extensive development were achieved at the price of a substantial waste of resources and a lack of technological modernization.

The unsuitability of the Soviet development model for Hungary was quickly revealed. In 1953, as a result of growing discontent, Nagy's new government introduced a policy of economic reform designed to increase living standards. Nagy's opponents within the Communist Party removed him from power in 1955 and reinstated the discredited policies of forced industrialization and collectivization. This led to the Hungarian Revolution of 1956, a popular uprising that was brutally suppressed by Soviet troops; a new government led by party First Secretary János Kádár was then imposed on Hungary.

Kádár used economic reform to achieve social and political stability. He achieved an annual growth rate of 6 to 7 percent until the end of the 1970s. Agricultural marketing was liberalized, and a policy of gradual collectivization was reintroduced. Less successful reforms were introduced in industry. Nonetheless, between 1956 and 1966, consumption increased by 50 percent and serious food shortages were eliminated. As of 1957 new consumer goods, for example, washing machines, refrigerators, and televisions, also began to appear. From the early 1960s, limited private car ownership also began.

During the second half of the 1950s, substantial investment was made in the energy sector, in particular exploitation of Hungary's abundant lignite resources for electricity generation. Renewed emphasis was placed on increasing iron and steel production, and a major expansion in the chemical industry was undertaken. However, investment in these industries was achieved initially at the expense of another goal, development of the engineering industry. Nonetheless, Hungary was allocated the CMEA market for buses. Hungary's Ikarus was to become the world's sixth-largest bus producer and one of the country's leading exporters. Despite a lack of investment, the food-processing and consumer goods industries also expanded.

During the 1960s Hungary began to experience new economic problems. Between 1960 and 1962 foreign debts doubled and exceeded the hard currency income from exports. At the same time there was a renewed awareness of the flaws in the command economy. As a result, Hungary introduced a comprehensive package of economic reforms in January 1968 known as the New Economic Mechanism. In addition to a considerable price deregulation, compulsory plan directives were abolished, and horizontal ties were introduced among state-owned firms and consumers to achieve greater independence for business firms.

Although the New Economic Mechanism quickly achieved a more rational allocation of resources and had a positive impact on the level of production, there was no further economic reform. Indeed, existing reforms were partially reversed during 1973–74. This coincided with the first oil shock. The Hungarian economy was badly affected both by rising import prices and by a serious weakening in its terms of trade. As a result, there was an increase in Hungary's trade deficit and foreign debt. During the years 1971–80, the annual rate of growth in gross domestic product (GDP) declined to 2.6 percent and inflation reemerged. The price reforms of 1968 broke down. In 1978 the government decided it would have to switch its industrial policy from import substitution to export-led growth.

A new price reform was introduced in the summer of 1979 in which factory prices were linked to world market prices. Consumer subsidies were cut, and this resulted in an increase in retail price inflation. In 1980 the institutional system was reformed too, and the central planning

of industry was abolished. Furthermore, from 1980 onward, the huge monopoly firms were decentralized. This reversed the centralization process of the period 1948–65, which had been the emergence of larger and larger firms.

The reform process continued during the early 1980s as the government privatized the majority of state-owned restaurants and small shops by leasing them to private individuals. And in 1984 the Enterprise Act introduced a form of self-management of state enterprises. The government also tolerated the development of a large, informal economy. However, the annual rate of growth in GDP declined further during the years 1981–85 to 0.7 percent, and foreign debt remained persistently high.

By the second half of the 1980s the reform process had become irreversible. In October 1986 a group of academics proposed a radical program of economic reform, entitled Change and Reform. It was supported by the Communist Party reformer Imre Pozsgay. By May 1988 Kádár had resigned and been replaced by Károly Grosz, who introduced a modified version of Change and Reform. In 1989 the party abandoned communism completely and, in October, was reconstituted as a social democratic party, the Hungarian Socialist Party (HSP).

While the reforms had brought economic and social stability, they were unable to prevent a relative decline in Hungarian living standards. Between 1975 and 1989, the Organization of Economic Cooperation and Development (OECD) estimated that Hungarian real GDP grew by about 35 percent, while the OECD as a whole grew by 54 percent.

Despite its long-standing commitment to economic reform, the HSP was defeated in the democratic general election held in March 1990. The new conservative government led by the Hungarian Democratic Forum inherited a country with a per capita gross national product of $2,780. Its private sector accounted for about 15 percent of GDP, which, although not very large, was the largest in Eastern Europe. On the other hand, inflation at 27 percent and rising was a serious problem, and the gross foreign debt of $21.5 billion was the highest per capita in Eastern Europe.

Among the economic measures taken by the new government were the creation of an independent central bank, closely modeled on the German Bundesbank, and a limited restitution of agricultural land seized by the former Communist regime. During the first half of the 1990s the government oversaw substantial investment by foreign multinationals. Hungary received more than half the total foreign investment of $7 billion in Eastern Europe during 1990–92.

But the conservative government proved less successful with privatization. The State Property Agency (SPA), established on March 1, 1990, had succeeded in privatizing just under half its holdings by the end of 1994. It was estimated in 1993 that the private sector still accounted only for an estimated 36 percent of national income. There was substantial political interference in the privatization process, which included the establishment of a second privatization agency on August 28, 1992, the State Asset Management Company (SAMCo).

The transition to a market economy in Hungary had high social costs. Real GDP fell by over 18 percent between 1990 and 1994. Unemployment rose from less than 1 percent at the beginning of 1990 to 11 percent in 1994. A cut in subsidies in 1990 led to a sharp increase in energy prices, and a staged reduction in other subsidies in early 1991 pushed consumer price inflation to a peak of 38.9 percent per annum in June 1991. Inflation was still over 19.5 percent in August 1994. The growing economic inequality of the 1980s had grown even wider. Gross foreign debt had further increased to $28 billion by 1994.

Discontent with the fall in living standards under the conservative government led to the victory of the HSP in the general election of May 1994. The HSP proposed the establishment of a social market economy similar to that of Germany. But instead pressure from foreign lenders, for example, the World Bank, forced the HSP to attempt a harsh austerity program in May 1995. This aimed at drastically cutting Hungary's public-sector and current account deficits. Still, the OECD suggested in its 1995 survey of Hungary that the austerity program was not sufficient to prevent the threat of a debt trap and that a medium-term fiscal consolidation plan was still required.

The new government also set itself the ambitious goal of completing its privatization program by the end of its four-year term in 1998. Yet the HSP's new privatization law, merging SPA and SAMCo into the Privatization and State Holding Company, was not passed until May 9, 1995. Substantial progress nevertheless began to be made as of summer 1995. Hungary also applied to join the European Union in 1994 and hoped to become a member by 2000.

BIBLIOGRAPHY

Berend, Ivan T., and Gyorgy Ranki. *The Hungarian Economy in the Twentieth Century.* London: Croom Helm, 1985.

Estrin, Saul, ed. *Privatization in Central and Eastern Europe.* London: Longman, 1994.

The London *Financial Times* has published an annual survey of Hungary since 1990 and an occasional survey between 1983 and 1988. The OECD has also published a biennial survey of the Hungarian economy since 1991.

Richard A. Hawkins

Political Emigration

There were three major waves of Hungarian political emigration after 1945.

The first were the so-called Forty-Fivers. Many soldiers, policemen, civil servants, and other officials, together with the right-wing government of Ferenc Szálasi, moved to Austria in March 1945, and a number of Hungarian soldiers and refugees fled to the American occupation zone in Germany. There are no official statistical data regarding their number, which might have been two hundred thousand. The majority had been compromised politically before or during World War II, and in exile they formed a number of conservative, right-wing, or monarchist associations. In the late 1940s, a great portion of them moved overseas, to the United States, Australia, Canada, or Brazil, or to Western European countries, such as the United Kingdom and France.

The second group were the Forty-Seveners. As the Soviets gradually tightened their grip around Hungary, a number of moderate or even left-wing Hungarians chose to go or were forced to go into exile. The beginning of this wave was marked by Premier Ferenc Nagy's decision in May 1947 not to return to Hungary but to stay in the West. He was followed by the speaker of the Hungarian National Assembly, Béla Varga. A number of ambassadors also resigned, preferring exile. Their ranks were complemented by a large number of non-Communist party officials and members of parliament, as well as professionals who opposed the Sovietization of Hungary. Numerically this wave of emigration was smaller than that of 1945, but its members carried more intellectual, political, and social weight than the former group. Consequently, serious frictions emerged between the two groups, and the Hungarian emigration became even more fragmented than before. The European center of the Forty-Seveners became Paris, while their overseas headquarters became Washington, D.C., as they realized that American orientation provided the best chances to halt Soviet expansion in central Europe. This wave of emigration lasted until the end of the 1940s, when Hungary's borders were sealed by the authorities.

The most important postwar Hungarian emigrant organization, the Hungarian National Council, was founded on November 15, 1947. Its goals were the liberation of Hungary, the restoration of human and civil rights in the country, and the return of Hungary to Western civilization.

The third group were the Fifty-Sixers. After the failed revolution in October-November 1956, some two hundred thousand people fled Hungary, though only a fraction of them were really "freedom fighters." The majority could mostly be regarded as economic refugees. Consequently, most of them, as opposed to the majority of the two earlier waves of emigration, did not wish to return to Hungary. They had the least problem assimilating into their host societies and they proved to be rather indifferent to the fate of their mother country. As for the composition of this last wave of emigration, it best reflected the whole spectrum of contemporary Hungarian society: laborers, professionals, former soldiers, civil servants, peasants, students, even former Communist Party members.

A new, representative organization was formed by the older and newer Hungarian emigrants under the name Hungarian Committee in March 1958. The organization stood on the platform of the Hungarian Revolution of 1956. It demanded the establishment of a pluralistic parliamentary democracy in Hungary and neutral status for the country.

The significance of the various Hungarian emigrant organizations, groups, associations, and societies gradually declined in the West from the late 1960s as a result of the policy of détente between the United States and the USSR, as well as international acceptance of the Kádár regime. At the same time, the dialogue with certain emigrant groups started by the Hungarian authorities further divided the Hungarian emigrants in the West, and from the mid-1970s onward they did not exert any significant pressure on Western governments or public opinion in behalf of their policies.

BIBLIOGRAPHY
Borbandi, Gyula. *A magyar emigracio eletrajza, 1945–1985.* 2 Vols. Budapest: Europa, 1989.

Tamás Magyarics

SEE ALSO Nagy, Ferenc

Cinema

Hungarian films continued to be produced by independent companies until 1948, when the film industry was nationalized. The most outstanding achievement of the period between 1945 and 1948 was Géza Radvanyi's *Somewhere in Europe* (1947), which is generally considered to be the first Hungarian neorealist film.

The films produced between 1948 and 1956 were conceived in the spirit of Zhdanovism, that is, in didactic, so-called socialist realist style named after Andrei Zhdanov, the Soviet official in charge of enforcing Stalinist cultural conformity. The temporary thaw in cultural life around 1956 yielded some works critical of the regime, for example, Zoltán Varkonyi's *Bitter Truth,* which was to remain shelved for thirty years. The first Kádár years, after 1956, brought about political retrenchment, but film producers and directors started to enjoy greater freedom as of the early 1960s. It was in these years that the great generation of Hungarian directors such as Miklós Jancsó, Károly Makk, and István Szabó launched their careers. These directors were preoccupied with different aspects of the Hungarian past and wished to find answers to some national tragedies.

The introduction of the New Economic Mechanism in 1968 decentralized the film industry to a degree, and thus provided even greater freedom for artists. Consequently the 1970s and 1980s saw the proliferation of films on contemporary problems, including feminism, homosexuality, and the hard life of the lower classes. Films could also deal with the recent past, even the Rákosi era and the Hungarian Revolution of 1956. These topics, however, indicate that Hungarian films were very much inward-looking and difficult to market abroad. An exception was István Szabó's *Mephisto* (1981), about Nazi Germany and the individual confronted with absolute power, which brought an Academy Award to its director. Besides Szabo, other directors attempted to produce films abroad in cooperation with Italian or German film companies.

The collapse of communism created a difficult situation for the film industry in Hungary. State supervision ceased but so did state subsidies. Studios descended to the brink of bankruptcy. The number of films made in Hungary dropped sharply in the early 1990s as American films almost monopolized the Hungarian film market. The influence of Hollywood led a number of directors to give up producing original, artistic, or experimental films and to try to meet the demand of the public at large. However, new, talented directors also appeared on the scene, such as Ildiko Szabó, who again infused freshness and originality into Hungarian films.

The best-known and perhaps most controversial Hungarian director of the past decades is Miklós Jancsó (1921–). His first feature film was released in 1958; however, he became famous with highly symbolic films about the recent or more distant past shot in the 1960s and early 1970s: *The Round Up* (1965), *Silence and Cry* (1968), *Winter Wind* (1969), *Agnus Dei* (1970), and *Red Psalm* (1971). In these, he analyzed the relationship between the individual and authority, and between power and society, or dealt with the problems arising from the transition of power. Jancsó moved to Italy in the early 1970s and made four films there, which basically dealt with the same problems in different surroundings. He also ventured into subjects shunned by other Hungarian directors at that time. For instance, his *Private Vices, Public Virtues* (1976), about the decadence of the declining Habsburg Empire, is full of eroticism and even pornography. Nudity already played a central role among the symbols used by Jancsó. It expressed defenselessness and powerlessness. After returning to Hungary Jancsó continued making movies based on his sophisticated iconography and narrative experimentation, and he even tried his hand at directing in the theater. His newer films received mixed reviews. However, he received one international and one Hungarian award after the other in the 1980s and early 1990s, for instance, one in Cannes for his lifetime achievement, and he is still considered, together with István Szabó, to be the foremost Hungarian director.

BIBLIOGRAPHY

Il Cinema nazionalizzato: i suoi successi e i suoi problemi: atti del convegno. Venice: Biennale di Venezia, 1979.
Film in Ungarn. Berlin: Henschelverlag, 1981.

Tamás Magyarics

Hurd, Douglas (1930–)

British diplomat and politician. Douglas Hurd was a Conservative member of parliament for Mid-Oxon (1974–83) and Witney (1983–97). He held several key offices of state in the governments of Margaret Thatcher and John Major, including secretary of state for Northern Ireland (1984–85), for the Home Office (1985–86), and foreign and commonwealth office (1989–95).

Following a career in the diplomatic corps, Hurd took a position in the Conservative Party research department in 1966. He served as Edward Heath's private secretary while he was in opposition (1968–70) and then as his political secretary when Heath became prime minister (1970–74). He entered parliament for the constituency of Mid-Oxon in 1974. Despite his close association with Heath, who was about to be repudiated by the party, Hurd's expertise in foreign affairs was highly valued. Soon, he became the opposition spokesman on European affairs (1976–79) and then minister of state at the foreign and commonwealth office in the new Thatcher government (1979–83). A brief stint as a junior minister at the Home Office demonstrated his abilities beyond the realm of international relations.

In 1984 he was appointed Northern Ireland secretary; however, he was brought back to the Home Office as secretary of state within a year. In the reshuffle occasioned by Nigel Lawson's resignation from the exchequer in 1989, Hurd became foreign secretary. In the contest for the Conservative Party leadership in 1990, Hurd unsuccessfully stood against John Major and Michael Heseltine. When Major emerged as prime minister, Hurd's position as foreign secretary was confirmed. He achieved widespread respect in this role, particularly through his handling of the Gulf War (1990–91) and European affairs. Hurd remained steadfastly loyal to Major during the leadership election in 1995. He gave up his post at the Foreign Office in 1995, retired as a member of Parliament prior to the general election in 1997, and was granted a life peerage in the same year.

BIBLIOGRAPHY

Hurd, Douglas. *An End to Promises: Sketch of a Government, 1970–1974.* London: Collins, 1979.

Eileen Groth Lyon

Husák, Gustav (1913–91)

Head of the Czechoslovak Communist Party (1969–89). Gustav Husák was born in Brataslavia, Slovakia, on January 10, 1913. He earned a degree in law from Comenius University in Bratislava and joined the Communist Party in 1933 while a university student. He was jailed from 1940 to 1943 by Slovakia's fascist government. Following his release he immediately threw himself again into underground party work. He became a member of the Central Committee of the Slovak Communist Party and was a leader of the 1944 Slovak uprising against the German occupiers.

From 1946 to 1950 Husák was head of the Board of Commissioners, the administrative body for Slovakia. He fell victim to the Stalinist purge of national Communists, however, and was imprisoned from 1954 to 1960. He was rehabilitated in 1963 and his party membership was restored. In 1967 he joined in the attack against the Stalinists leading the party and was appointed a deputy prime minister in April 1968 during the Prague Spring led by Alexander Dubček. As Soviet pressure against the process of liberalization mounted, Husák counseled acquiescence. He reasoned that Czechoslovakia had no alternative but to be in harmony with the USSR. He supported the Soviet invaders in August and was appointed leader of the Slovak Communist Party on August 28, 1968. In April 1969 when Dubček was finally removed as party leader for Czechoslovakia, Husák was his replacement. As first secretary (general secretary after 1971), Husak did away with what remained of the reforms introduced during the Prague Spring and purged those party leaders who did not repudiate their flirtation with liberalism adequately or speedily enough. In 1976 he offered those disciplined the opportunity to be rehabilitated if they recanted their errors. Though Husák attempted to bolster his position by also becoming president in 1975, he was undermined by changes in the USSR and the dismal performance of the Czechoslovak economy. Husák attempted to remain neutral amid a party debate over reform prompted by Czechoslovak economic performance and the example of Soviet leader Mikhail Gorbachev in the Soviet Union. During a visit by Gorbachev to Czechoslovakia in April 1987, it was evident that Husák could offer neither innovative nor decisive leadership. He acquiesced and resigned as general secretary of the party in December but retained the presidency. As the Velvet Revolution of 1989 swamped the Czechoslovak regime, Husák also resigned the presidency in December 1989 and was replaced by dissident intellectual Václav Havel.

BIBLIOGRAPHY

Grünwald, Leopold. *CSSR im Umbruch; Berichte, Kommentare, Dokumentation.* Vienna: Europa-Verlag, 1968.

Husák, Gustav. *Speeches and Writings.* New York: Pergamon Press, 1986.

———. *Die Tschechoslowakei für Sozialismus und Frieden: ausgewachsen Reden und Aufsätze 1944–1977.* Frankfurt am Main: Verlag Marxistische Blätter, 1978.

Bernard Cook

SEE ALSO Jakeš, Miloš; Strougal, Lubomír

Iceland

The founding of the Republic of Iceland on June 17, 1944, marked the final step on Iceland's road to full independence from Denmark. This was only formal recognition of Iceland's status at that time, as the union with Denmark had been entirely inactive since the German invasion of Denmark in 1940 and the British occupation of Iceland in the same year. The creation of the republic was important to Icelanders, however, because it confirmed an increased self-confidence in the country during the later stages of the Second World War and it was a prerequisite for an independent foreign policy in the postwar era. The first of these factors was enhanced by the fact that Iceland, unlike most of the rest of Europe, had

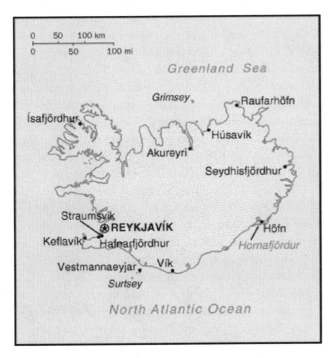

Iceland. *Illustration courtesy of Bernard Cook.*

prospered during the war. Thus, the various services required by British and American forces regenerated the Icelandic economy, making it possible for the Icelandic government to use the large foreign currency reserves it had accumulated in wartime to finance an extensive modernization of the Icelandic fisheries in the late 1940s. The second factor became crucial during the ensuing Cold War, because Iceland's strategic location made the country an important ally in the struggle for hegemony in the North Atlantic.

These two themes—economic modernization and debates on Iceland's position in international politics—have characterized the history of the Republic of Iceland from its beginning. In the economic sphere, the fishing industry has played a leading role, although its share in Icelandic export revenues has declined from over 90 percent in the early 1950s to around 75 percent in the mid-1990s. The dependence on fisheries, in conjunction with decreasing fish stocks from overfishing, has placed fishing concerns in the center of Icelandic politics. To protect the limited resources in the sea and to secure a monopoly position over the ocean around the country, the Icelandic parliament expanded the country's fishing limits from three to two hundred nautical miles in the years from 1952 to 1975. This happened in four successive steps, causing a major conflict, the so-called Cod Wars, with Britain each time. In the end Iceland was victorious in these conflicts, although the legal basis for the expansions was questionable at best.

Although Iceland has remained a faithful ally of the United States since the Second World War, the country's position in the Cold War became one of the most divisive issues in Icelandic history. Thus, the entrance into NATO in 1949 and the return of U.S. military forces to Iceland in 1951 evoked strong reactions from the left. Fueled by nationalistic sentiments, opponents of the U.S. base in

Keflavík viewed the foreign forces as a serious assault on Icelandic independence and hard-fought national sovereignty. These debates died down with the conclusion of the Cold War, and Iceland continues to be a member of NATO and to host a U.S. military base.

A search for balance between independence and international cooperation has dominated another aspect of Icelandic foreign policy. In 1970 Iceland entered the European Free Trade Association (EFTA) to secure access to its most important foreign markets. In spite of their strong cultural, political, and economic ties with Europe, Icelanders have remained very reluctant to join the European Union (EU), both from fear of losing their national sovereignty and from lingering doubts about the union's fishing policies. In recent years, Iceland's cooperation with the EU has increased, especially since the approval of the European Economic Area agreement between EFTA and the EU in 1993. Through this agreement Iceland has gained almost full entry into EU markets, and there seems to be little interest at the moment in applying for full membership in the EU.

Postwar modernization focused primarily on the fishing industry, although part of the substantial U.S. Marshall Plan aid to Iceland was used to finance the construction of hydroelectric power plants and a state-owned fertilizer factory to diversify the economy. As the fisheries continued to dominate exports, Icelandic society was very sensitive to fluctuations both in prices on the international markets for fish products and in the amount of fish caught each year; for example, a total depletion of the herring stock around Iceland in the late 1960s led to a severe economic recession in 1967–70. For this reason, Iceland has a strong incentive to broaden its economic base, with special emphasis on utilizing its extensive natural energy resources. In recent decades low energy costs have attracted foreign investments, increasing the share of manufactured products in Iceland's exports from around 1 percent in the late 1950s to around 20 percent in the mid-1990s.

An extremely high rate of inflation is one of the most prominent characteristics of Icelandic society for most of the period since the Second World War. In the early 1980s inflation reached alarming levels, with a record rise of 85 percent in the consumer price index in 1983. Only through the concerted effort of labor unions, employers, and the government, exemplified in the so-called national consensus agreement of 1991, were inflation rates brought down to the same levels as in neighboring countries, fluctuating around 2 percent annually in the 1990s. This had sobering effects on Icelandic society, allowing

for more secure planning for both individuals and businesses.

The history of the Republic of Iceland has demonstrated that a country with just over a quarter of a million inhabitants is capable of maintaining its independence in spite of geographic isolation and a harsh environment. Iceland's experience also indicates that a small nation can prosper in the modern world only if it engages with its neighbors. There has been an absolute consensus in Iceland about remaining a sovereign nation, but how to maintain a balance between independence and participation in international associations will continue to be one of the main problems facing Icelanders.

BIBLIOGRAPHY

Hálfdánarson, Gudmundur. *Historical Dictionary of Iceland.* Lanham, Md.: Scarecrow Press, 1997.

Jonsson, Gudmundur, and Magnus S. Magnusson, eds. *Hagskinna: Icelandic Historical Statistics.* Reykjavík: Hagstofa Islands, 1997.

McBride, Francis R. *Iceland,* rev. ed. World Bibliographic Series 37. Oxford: Clio Press, 1996.

Nordal, Jóhannes, and Valdimar Kristinsson, eds. *Iceland. The Republic.* Reykjavík: Central Bank of Iceland, 1996.

Gudmundur Hálfdánarson

Iceland and NATO

Iceland is one of the twelve founding members of NATO, entering this Western military alliance in 1949 with the support of a large majority in the Icelandic parliament. Iceland's participation in the military functions of the alliance has always been limited, however, because the country maintains no armed forces. Since the defense agreement with the United States in 1951, Iceland has contributed to NATO's military operations by allowing the United States to maintain a military base and airfield in Keflavík, on the country's southwest coast. Through its operations in Keflavík, the United States secured Iceland's defense while obtaining through the base a crucial link in the NATO military system in the North Atlantic.

Joining NATO and a foreign army on Icelandic soil were among the most divisive issues in Icelandic politics in the postwar era. Nationalistic sentiments, fueled by a long struggle against Danish rule, rose high at the end of the war, and therefore many were wary of forming close cooperation with a superpower. Hostility toward U.S. foreign policy, especially among members of the Socialist Unity Party and later the People's Alliance, was also an important motivation in the campaign against NATO and the American base in Iceland. Thus, two leftist governments, formed in 1956 and 1971 respectively, pledged to revise the defense agreement with the United States, aiming at U.S. withdrawal from Keflavík. Neither government acted on its promise, and since 1974, the withdrawal of NATO forces has never been seriously discussed in Iceland. With the waning of the Cold War, the issue of NATO membership and the NATO base in Keflavík has disappeared from Icelandic politics. As a small, unarmed nation, Icelanders never formed an essential part of the NATO military structure. The strategic location of the country strengthened their position considerably, however. Icelandic politicians often skillfully used this situation, gaining, for example, much more extensive support from Marshall Plan aid, far more than justified by the size of the Icelandic population. Moreover, NATO was instrumental in negotiating a final solution to the so-called Cod Wars with Britain, handing Iceland a total victory in the conflict in spite of the fact that its opponent was one of Europe's leading military powers.

Gudmundur Hálfdánarson

SEE ALSO Cod Wars

Security

For most of its history, geographic isolation was Iceland's primary defense. Furthermore, a poor and sparsely populated country did not attract foreign invaders, although it was raided once in the seventeenth century by North African pirates, and its government was taken over for a short period by British and Danish adventurers in 1809. Iceland never established a military service, as the country needed no defensive forces and its inhabitants were not required to serve in the Danish army, although they were subjects of the Danish monarch for over half a millennium. In this tradition, with full independence in 1944, no military service was established.

During the twentieth century, Iceland's geographic isolation ceased to serve the same defensive role as before, especially since the increased role of the United States in European affairs placed Iceland in the center of an important route between America and northern Europe. Britain occupied Iceland in 1940 to prevent Germany from obstructing communications with the United States. In the following year Iceland and the United States signed a defensive treaty, providing the former with vital security in the dangerous years of the Second World War and the latter with an important military post in the mid–North Atlantic.

After the war, Iceland maintained its security through close cooperation with the United States. In 1949 it became a founding member of NATO, and in 1951, at the height of the Korean War, it signed a new defensive treaty with the United States, allowing U.S. forces to return. Following the conclusion of the Cold War, relaxation in tensions in the North Atlantic region led to a reevaluation of the defense agreements between the United States and Iceland, but both countries pledged their commitment to continued cooperation.

The only security force that Iceland has maintained is a small coast guard, which played an important role in the so-called Cod Wars with Britain from the 1950s to the 1970s. At the height of the last such war, in the mid-1970s, the coast guard operated seven patrol boats armed with small canons. The coast guard also owned one aircraft and three helicopters for surveillance and rescue operation in the area of Iceland's territorial waters.

Because of its strong social cohesion and the almost total absence of organized violence and crime, there has been little need for specialized forces to preserve internal security. The state maintains a regular police force, unarmed in all normal operations, to uphold law and order. To date, the country has not faced a serious threat from internal dissension.

BIBLIOGRAPHY

Arnason, Ragnar. *The Icelandic Fisheries: Evolution and Management of a Fishing Industry.* Oxford: Fishing News, 1995.

Gudmundur Hálfdánarson

SEE ALSO Cod Wars

Political Parties

Since the end of World War II, four political parties have dominated the Icelandic political scene, spanning the spectrum from the socialist left to the conservative right.

The oldest party is the Social Democratic Party (SDP), founded in 1916 in Reykjavík. In the beginning the SDP functioned as the political wing of the Icelandic Federation of Labor, with the objective of furthering the interests of the working class and of advocating policies of democratic socialism. All formal ties between the SDP and the labor unions were severed during the Second World War as the party abandoned its socialist platform. Since then the party has placed itself close to the center of Icelandic politics. Since the war, the SDP has strongly supported Iceland's participation in international organizations such as NATO and the European Free Trade Association (EFTA), and recently the SDP has advocated that Iceland apply for membership in the European Union (EU). The traditional bases for the SDP are the urban areas in southwest Iceland and the fishing towns in the northwestern part of the country; it has never attracted many voters in rural areas. Support for the SDP has been the most unstable of the four main parties, fluctuating between 22 percent and 9 percent of the votes cast but has generally received around 14 percent since the war.

The Progressive Party (PP), founded in the same year as the SDP, is the second-largest political party in Iceland. The PP began primarily as a farmers' party, with strong ties to the cooperative movement, but in recent years it has made considerable headway in the more urban parts of the country. Its centrist policies have appealed to modern voters and, therefore, it has retained a strong presence in parliament, in spite of a dramatic erosion of its traditional base, owing to rapid urbanization in the second half of the twentieth century. Moreover, under the leadership of prime ministers Olafur Johannesson (1971–74 and 1978–79) and Steingrimur Hermannsson (1983–87 and 1988–91), the party skillfully used its strategic position, taking part in almost every coalition government from 1971 to 1991. The PP polls around 23 percent in most elections.

The Independence Party (IP) has been the largest political party in Iceland since its foundation in 1929. Formed through a merger of the Conservative Party and the Liberal Party, the IP has always believed firmly in free enterprise and private initiative over state action in most areas of social life. In practice, however, the party has been flexible, supporting most of the country's social welfare system when in power. Since the Second World War, close cooperation with the United States and its Western allies has been one of the main tenets of the IP, but it has been more cautious over the participation in European integration. Reykjavík, has always been the stronghold of the IP, but the party has strong support in all regions of the country. From 1946 to 1974 the IP's share of the vote hovered around 40 percent, but because of internal friction and instability in the party leadership, its support declined drastically in the 1980s. The party reached its nadir in 1987, polling only 27 percent of the vote, but it regained its former strength in the 1990s under the firm leadership of David Oddsson.

The People's Alliance (PA), was formed in 1956 as an electoral coalition of the Socialist Unity Party (SUP) and a splinter group from the left flank of the SDP. In 1968 the PA was transformed into a regular political party, and the SUP ceased to exist as a separate political organization. The basic tenets of the PA were radical socialism mixed with strong opposition to Iceland's participation in NATO and to the U.S. military base in Keflavík. In recent years, its stance has moderated considerably, and the PA has dropped all reference to Marxist dogma from its platform. Thus, the PA is presently the most nationalistic of Icelandic political parties, rejecting membership in the EU. The PA inherited most of the traditional support of the SUP among workers and intellectuals, but it has also gained strength in rural areas. For most of the postwar era, the SUP and the PA were in third place in parliamentary elections, polling just under 20 percent of votes cast. In recent elections the PA has suffered a setback in popular support, not reaching 15 percent of the vote since the early 1980s.

The only party to seriously challenge the system of four parties in Iceland is the feminist Women's Alliance (WA). Formed in 1983 after the success of a number of women's lists in local elections of the preceding year, the WA offered candidates in three districts in the parliamentary elections of 1983. The experiment was successful, as the alliance elected three women to parliament, and since then its representatives have been elected in every parliamentary contest. The WA rejects the traditional divisions in Icelandic politics, advocating women's issues in all spheres of Icelandic social life. Thus, surveys have demonstrated that the WA has drawn support from all parties, but it has had the most lasting effect on the PA. The WA won its greatest victory in 1987, polling 10 percent of the vote, but its support has declined ever since.

Gudmundur Hálfdánarson

Economy

Located in a relatively harsh environment, Iceland was among the poorest nations in Europe until the Second World War. At the present, however, Iceland is in the same league as the richest countries, with a per capita gross domestic product (GDP) of $27,000 in 1997, a status it has attained through a rapid and successful modernization. In conjunction with rising living standards, Icelandic authorities have developed a comprehensive welfare system that has, in turn, placed Iceland among countries with the highest life expectancy in the world: seventy-six years for men, eighty-one years for women. Another attribute of Icelandic economy and society is a low unemployment rate by European standards, 3.7 percent in 1996, in spite of exceptionally high participation of women in the labor market; 86 percent of women between twenty-five and sixty-four work outside the home. Finally, the Icelandic economy can be described as both very small and open. With only 270,000 inhabitants and a limited resource base, Iceland is unusually dependent on foreign trade, with about 33 percent of its GDP destined for export.

Modernization of the Icelandic economy has centered on exploitation of one natural resource, fish. For example, in the post–Second World War era, over 90 percent of Icelandic export revenues came from marine products; although their relative importance has declined considerably in the 1980s and 1990s, fish products still make up around three-quarters of Icelandic exports. Therefore one of the basic tasks of Icelandic government policy since the war has been to preserve this vital resource from over-exploitation, hence avoiding total collapse of the economy. This goal has been reached, first through gradual extension of Icelandic territorial waters, forcing competing nations out of fertile Icelandic fishing banks. Second, to prevent overfishing, the government has enforced an extensive conservation plan for most of the species caught in Icelandic waters, establishing quotas for boats allowed to fish in the fishing zone. Because of these measures, the future of Iceland's fishing industry seems fairly secure, although further development will continue to be sensitive to changes in natural conditions.

Because of its homogeneous character, the economy has remained susceptible to fluctuations in fish catches and world market prices, particularly those affecting the fishing industry. Icelanders suffered a deep recession in the late 1960s, for example, when herring catches collapsed suddenly, and reductions of cod quotas in the early 1990s deepened the effects of the world recession in Iceland. To stabilize and diversify the economy, the authorities have attempted to attract foreign investors, especially in energy-intensive industries. By offering inexpensive electricity generated in hydroelectric and geothermal power plants, this effort has been fairly successful in recent years, increasing considerably the share of manufacturing in Icelandic export revenues.

The growing emphasis on energy-intensive industries has come into conflict with another growing economic sector, tourism. Attracted by its spectacular, largely unspoiled environment, the number of foreign tourists in Iceland tripled from 1980 to the mid-1990s. Increased use of natural resources, construction of power lines and power plants in the uninhabited inland, and pollution from new industries threaten to tarnish the image of Iceland, and therefore to halt further development of the tourist industry. Growing concerns about the environment are, therefore, beginning to influence attitudes toward economic growth, as in other industrialized countries of Europe.

The 1990s were a period of extensive economic and social reform. The most obvious change was a drastic fall in inflation in the early 1990s. A high rate of inflation had plagued the Icelandic economy for most of the twentieth century, in part reflecting the frequent oscillations between years of expansion and recession, but also in part

revealing an inept fiscal policy. From the early 1970s inflation rose to new levels, reaching an 85 percent rise in the general price index in 1983. In the early 1990s the government, labor unions, and employers succeeded jointly in reducing inflation to levels similar to those in neighboring countries. With increased stability, other economic reforms followed. First, with growing belief in laissez-faire politics, the government began withdrawing from direct participation in the economy. Nationalization, carried out by all political parties earlier in the century, is no longer on the agenda of any political party, and privatization has been promoted throughout the 1990s. Second, with growing openness in the world economy and closer cooperation with the European Union (EU), many government strictures have been abolished to promote competition and prevent unfair trade practices. Finally, investment policies in Iceland have changed drastically in recent years, with rapidly expanding equity markets and mutual funds, and an emerging stock market. In the late 1990s rapid economic growth assisted this transformation, and the Icelandic economy seemed to be heading into a period of greater stability than previously experienced in this century.

BIBLIOGRAPHY

Arnason, Ragnar. *The Icelandic Fisheries: Evolution and Management of a Fishing Industry.* Oxford: Fishing News, 1995.

Economic Statistics Quarterly. Reykjavík: Central Bank of Iceland, 1980–.

Jonsson, Gudmundur, and Magnus S. Magnusson, eds. *Hagskinna: Icelandic Historical Statistics.* Reykjavík: Hagstofa Islands, 1997.

Gudmundur Hálfdánarson

Welfare and Taxation

Through most of Icelandic history, the state took no part in supporting the poor. The family, or kin group had the responsibility to maintain all its members, but when they were unable to do so, the local commune took over. With increased urbanization and a growing working class in the towns, there was mounting pressure on the state to secure minimum health insurance for its citizens. The first step in this direction was the foundation of state-guaranteed insurance funds for victims of industrial accidents in 1903, but the first comprehensive social insurance legislation was not passed until 1936. This happened in accordance with the demands of the Social Democratic Party and the labor movement, which were gaining strength at the time. With this legislation, about half the Icelandic population was covered by a state-organized health-care plan, and the foundations for a general retirement and disability compensation plan were laid, as well as other welfare schemes.

The development of the Icelandic welfare state has been rapid since the Second World War. The general trend has been to expand the system into new areas of health and educational services, including all Icelanders regardless of financial means. Today, the welfare system is similar to those in other Nordic countries, although Iceland's welfare expenditures are lower than those of its neighbors (18.9 percent of the Icelandic GNP in 1992 compared, with over 30 percent in the other Nordic countries). The peculiar age structure in Iceland explains this difference to a certain extent, as high postwar birthrates lower the ratio of the elderly in the total population. As in the other Nordic countries, the basic premises of the system are that the state provides all Icelanders with health-care services for a minimum fee; it provides all of its citizens with a pension insurance; and most Icelandic educational institutions, from elementary school to university, are either free or charge only nominal fees.

Increasing unemployment and a crisis in state finances put a strain on the welfare system in the early 1990s. For this reason, serious efforts have been made to introduce user fees in health-care and educational institutions. But as all Icelandic political parties played a part in its construction, and as voters have grown accustomed to its benefits, there seems to be no general desire to dismantle the welfare state at present.

In spite of a fairly extensive welfare system, Iceland has traditionally had a relatively small public sector and low taxes compared with other European countries. General government spending as a percentage of gross domestic product (GDP) has, nevertheless, been slowly if irregularly rising in recent decades. This ratio went from around 25 percent in the immediate postwar period to just under 40 percent in 1990, with the sharpest rise occurring during the 1980s. The share of government services in total employment is close to the European norm, and in 1990 it was about 18 percent of the total work force. On the other hand, the relative weight of local government did decline in the postwar period, indicating a tendency toward concentration of financial responsibility in the hands of the central government. The transfer of the elementary school system from the state to local communes in 1996 is the most significant attempt so far to reverse this development.

These indicators do not take fully into account, however, the extensive influence of the public sector in the economy. A large portion of the annual budget was, from the turn of the century until recently, devoted to a wide range of economic services, giving the government an important tool in influencing the direction of the economy. Moreover, the budget is only a part of the official apparatus of fiscal management. Government authorities influenced interest rates through the central bank, which had wide regulatory powers until the mid-1980s. The government guides borrowing in the economy through its annual credit budget, which sets targets for overall credit creation and foreign borrowing. Historically, the government has played a prominent role in allocation of credit through its ownership of the largest part of the financial system, including commercial banks and dozens of investment credit funds. In addition, the state owns a large number of commercial enterprises in part or entirely, such as the State Monopoly of Tobacco and Alcohol, the Postal Service, the Telephone and Telegraph Services, the National Radio and Television, the State Electrical Power Works, the National Power Company, a cement factory, a fertilizer plant, and over three hundred farms. In recent years, some of the political parties, the Independence Party in particular, have wanted to privatize public companies and sell the state's share in private companies, believing that the state should not compete with private enterprise.

BIBLIOGRAPHY

Olafsson, Stefán. *The Making of the Icelandic Welfare State: A Scandinavian Comparison.* Reykjavík: Social Science Research Institute, University of Iceland, 1989.

Gudmundur Hálfdánarson

Culture

A sparsely populated country with no urban center and no aristocracy or bourgeoisie, for most of its history Iceland lacked the material and social conditions for a rich and dynamic cultural life. Thus, literature, nurtured by its saga heritage from the Middle Ages, is almost the only form of cultural expression that has a long tradition in Iceland. With the great economic and social transformation of Icelandic society beginning in the late nineteenth century, but only really taking off in the twentieth, this all changed dramatically. The foundation of villages and towns around the coast and the formation of new classes of cultural consumers were an impetus for the creation of new cultural activities in visual arts, theater, and music. Thus, some of the best-known cultural figures in Iceland, such as painter Johannes Kjarval (1885–1972), composer Jon Leifs (1899–1968), and writer Halldor Laxness (1902–98) reached full artistic maturity in the interwar period.

World War II also had dramatic effects on Icelandic cultural life. Unlike most of Europe, the war brought prosperity to Iceland, and the presence of British and U.S. forces in the country brought it into much closer contact with the outer world than ever before. At the same time, the foundation of the republic in 1944 and the final conclusion of the struggle for independence from Denmark heightened the sense of national pride among Icelanders. Thus, a tension between modernist experimentation and a traditionalist realism, seeking to preserve the cultural heritage of the country, characterizes cultural debate of the postwar period. The debate was perhaps the most fierce in the field of poetry, where a break with old meters and the poetic imagery of the past caused a sensation in the 1950s and 1960s. Young poets at the end of the world war, brought up in the years of economic depression during the interwar period, felt that new poetic forms were needed to express the profound changes taking place in Icelandic society. The Atom Poets, as they are commonly known, met with staunch opposition from those seeking to preserve traditional poetic forms in Iceland. For the traditionalists, experiments in modernist poetry undermined the cultural foundation of the nation, a trend that would lead to its downfall. Similar debates took place in the visual arts, where traditionalists deplored the new fashions of geometric abstraction and other forms of non-representational art, although the absence historical tradition in this field made this debate less urgent than the one in the field of literature.

Today, the debates between modernists and traditionalists has more or less subsided. With time, cultural diversity has increased, and with it tolerance for change. The capital, Reykjavík, has developed a rich cultural scene, with a symphony orchestra, opera house, two major professional theaters and numerous smaller theater groups, and a number of art galleries. Interest in literature is demonstrated through strong book sales, and books are still favorite gifts around Christmas. The best-known Icelandic artist is without doubt, however, pop singer Björk Gudmundsdottir, who has received critical acclaim for her distinctive style and commercial success.

BIBLIOGRAPHY

Sigurjónsson, Arni, et al., eds. *Arts and Culture in Iceland: Literature.* Reykjavík: Ministry of Culture and Education, 1989.

Gudmundur Hálfdánarson

Press

The Icelandic print media is dominated by two newspapers, the morning daily *Morgunbladid* and the after-noon daily *Dagbladid Visir.* *Morgunbladid* was founded in 1913 and gradually became the most influential newspaper in Iceland. Although it prides itself of being the newspaper of all Icelanders, *Morgunbladid*'s editorial policy has always leaned toward the right, vigorously opposing both socialism in politics and the influence of the cooperative movement on the Icelandic economy. Thus, *Morgunbladid* has supported the center-conservative Independence Party (IP) since its establishment in 1929 and has certainly been a contributing factor in making the IP the largest political party in Iceland. The IP has never had formal control over *Morgunbladid,* however, and in recent years the newspaper has become much less dependent on the party line than at the height of the Cold War. At present *Morgunbladid* is published six times a week, and each issue is sold in over fifty thousand copies, primarily to subscribers, which means almost one copy for every five Icelanders.

Dagbladid Visir, generally known by its acronym *DV,* is the oldest published newspaper in Iceland. Originally founded as *Visir* in 1910, it was the only afternoon daily until its former editor founded a rival newspaper, *Dagbladid,* in 1975. After waging a fierce competition, the two newspapers merged in 1981 under the current name. *DV,* which has a similar distribution to *Morgunbladid,* has never been tied to a political party, declaring itself politically independent.

For most of the twentieth century, all political parties but the Independence Party were directly involved in the publication of newspapers. The oldest of those, *Althydubladid,* was founded in 1919 by the Social Democratic Party, *Timinn* and *Dagur* in 1917 and 1918, respectively, by the centrist Progressive Party. Finally, the Communist Party founded its daily newspaper, *Thjodviljinn,* in 1936, which became the party organ of the Socialist Unity Party and later of the socialist People's Alliance. None of these newspapers had wide circulation and were sustained only through government subsidies and the loyalty of political supporters. In recent years, all of them have either ceased publication or cut their ties to their parent party. Thus, in 1992 *Thjodviljinn* fell victim to the very market forces it had fought so vigorously since its foundation, and in 1997 *Althydubladid* merged with *Dagur* and *Timinn* to form one paper under the name *Dagur.* Published as an independent paper with editorial policy leaning toward the left, *Dagur* is owned by the same house as *DV.*

Gudmundur Hálfdánarson

Iliescu, Ion (1930–)

Romanian head of state (December 1989 to November 1996). Ion Iliescu had a successful career in the Romanian

Ion Iliescu, Romanian head of state from 1989 to 1996.
Illustration courtesy of the Romanian Embassy, Washington, D.C.

Communist Party (RCP) until President Nicolae Ceauşescu demoted him in 1984.

Iliescu's father was a railroad worker and a Communist who lived south of Bucharest in the Danube town of Olteniţa. Although educated as a hydroelectric power engineer in Romania and the USSR, Iliescu devoted himself primarily to politics. He joined the RCP in 1953 after having risen to prominence in the party's Union of Communist Youth (UCY), which he had joined in 1944. In 1949 Ceauşescu, then first secretary of the UCY, considered Iliescu a promising activist and played a major role in placing him on the UCY's Central Committee. While a student in Moscow from 1950 to 1953, Iliescu served as Communist Youth secretary for the Romanians studying there. In 1956, as the newly appointed head of the Communist Federation of Romanian University Students, a post he retained through 1959, he encouraged reprisals against Romanian university students who demonstrated in support of the Hungarian Revolution of 1956.

During the 1960s his career advanced rapidly. In 1960 he was elected to the Grand National Assembly (parlia-

ment). His standing in the party also steadily grew. Between 1960 and 1967 he served in the Central Committee's Department for Ideology and Propaganda, eventually becoming a department chief. In 1965 he became a candidate member of the RCP Central Committee and a full member in 1968. Additionally, Ceauşescu appointed him first secretary of the UCY and minister for youth affairs in 1967 and made him a candidate member of the party's highest organization, the Political Executive Committee. Since his career resembled that of his patron, Ceauşescu, many observers assumed that the president was grooming Iliescu to succeed him, a possibility that seemed more likely because of Iliescu's central role after 1967 in fostering Ceauşescu's developing cult of personality by organizing adulatory mass receptions for the dictator, and receiving the prestigious post of Central Committee secretary for ideology in February 1971. However, in July 1971 his close relationship with Ceauşescu cooled after he criticized the dictator's "minicultural revolution," a reference to Mao Tse-tung's excesses in China. Ceauşescu stripped Iliescu of several of his offices and exiled him from the center of power in Bucharest to the western Romanian county of Timis, where he served as the local party secretary for propaganda.

Because he was a mild critic, not an opponent, of the regime, this setback did not end his career, which began to revive three years later with his appointment as first party secretary of Iasi County, a sensitive area in northeastern Romania bordering on the USSR. In 1979 he became a member of the State Council, the Grand National Assembly's standing presidium, and Ceauşescu returned him to Bucharest as state secretary of the National Water Council. Yet these promotions masked a serious rift brewing between himself and Ceauşescu. Over the years Iliescu had acquired a following among the intellectual elite, whose professional goals he openly shared at the very time Ceauşescu was becoming increasingly antiintellectual. The first sign of impending trouble occurred in 1980 when Iliescu lost his candidate status on the Executive Committee. Then in 1984 Ceauşescu halted Iliescu's "second" career by exchanging all of Iliescu's state and party offices for the insignificant post of director of the Bucharest Publishing House.

Between 1984 and December 1989 Iliescu gained a reputation as a reform Communist, and by the late 1980s rumors flew that the Soviets wanted him to succeed Ceauşescu. During these years he continued to believe in state socialism's egalitarian principles, but he substituted populism for Leninism as the proper means for achieving them. He avoided joining the thin ranks of dissidents against Ceauşescu's rule during those years, and played no known role in plots to overthrow Romania's increasingly autocratic leader. Prudently, he participated quietly in discussions to prepare a plan for taking control of the government should the Ceauşescu regime collapse.

That day came on December 22, 1989, when Iliescu emerged from the confusion surrounding Ceauşescu's downfall as the spokesman for the hastily assembled National Salvation Front Council. His reputation as a moderate anti-Ceauşescu reformer, not an anti-Communist revolutionary, made him acceptable to the military, the secret police, the RCP nomenklatura not closely associated with Ceauşescu, and intellectuals. No one could have governed Romania without the power these groups still controlled. To win over the general public, and especially the youth who had played a major role in overthrowing Ceauşescu, on December 26 the Salvation Front announced an end to the most oppressive practices of Ceauşescu's regime, such as food rationing.

The popularity the front derived from these reforms permitted Iliescu to base his legitimacy publicly on the 1989 revolution and deemphasize his powerful supporters. He soon alienated Romania's ethnic minorities by co-opting Ceauşescu's successful theme of Romanian nationalism to garner greater support from the Romanians. The incompatible sources of Iliescu's legitimacy produced a dilemma that plagued his entire presidency. Romania's politically active youth, intellectuals, and ethnic minorities desired a radical break with Romania's past in the form of democracy and rapid economic privatization. Opposing sweeping reform were the army and nomenklatura who put Iliescu in power and whose continued support he needed to stay there; consequently, he refrained from purging the military and the government of former Communists and established a new intelligence agency under Virgil Magureanu, which employed many former Securitate (Secret police) members. These groups wanted moderate reforms often for personal reasons, such as using their positions to establish themselves in private business.

Iliescu's populism coincided with that desired by the military and the nomenklatura rather than Romania's active youth, intellectuals, and ethnic minorities, who quickly formed his opposition. For Iliescu democracy meant moderate liberalization of Romania's traditional paternalistic state, not pluralism and mass participation in politics. His egalitarian economic convictions consisted in avoiding massive unemployment and hyperinflation by privatizing gradually, which included refusing to close unprofitable state enterprises. The success of Iliescu's moderate policies depended on maintaining control of the extremists (still committed Communists and Communists

becoming neofascists) among his supporters and his opposition's street demonstrations. During the first half of 1990 he discovered that the country's workers and mostly conservative, anti-urban, anti-intellectual, nationalistic peasants overwhelmingly supported him. The workers, who often lived in small towns with only one factory, and the peasants contributed heavily to Iliescu's overwhelming victory, 85 percent of the vote in the May 20, 1990, presidential election. Until the end of June 1990, the coal miners from the Jeu Valley, who invaded Bucharest, gave him a more reliable means than the police or the military for violently defeating his opposition's demonstrations.

Such success came at a high price. The West denounced the Iliescu regime for doing little about vigilante attacks on Gypsies, on members of Romania's Hungarian minority by the neofascist Vatra Romaneasca in Tirgu Mures on March 19 and 20, 1990, and on the So Nation Front's political rivals during the spring 1990 election campaign. Romania's growing diplomatic isolation peaked after the Jeu Valley miners' rampage in Bucharest during June 13–15, 1990. At that point, Iliescu had to restrain his extremist supporters or forfeit the Western assistance Romania needed to attack its serious economic crisis.

Given Iliescu's vulnerability to international pressure, Prime Minister Petre Roman, from conviction and ambition, pushed for the rapid, radical economic changes desired by Iliescu's opposition. As of June 1990 Iliescu allowed Roman to privatize the Romanian economy more rapidly, but by September 1991 his prime minister's reforms had also engendered higher inflation and unemployment. Once again, but uninvited by Iliescu this time, the Jeu Valley miners converged on Bucharest, where they joined the young activists rather than battle them. Together they rioted between September 23 and 25 for higher wages and Roman's resignation, both of which they obtained at the cost of three dead and five hundred wounded before the police restored order. Iliescu, but not the front, survived this crisis. In March 1992 the front split into a group favoring Roman's rapid reform and the majority, now called the Democratic National Salvation Front, that preferred Iliescu's gradualism.

Iliescu, hoping to calm the reformers and public apprehension about the future, appointed Theodor Stolojan, an economist, to moderate Roman's reforms. It also seems that the police and military had now decided to intervene if needed to keep order, rendering the increasingly independent miners expendable. There was also little sentiment for civil war by any group in Romania, so henceforth Iliescu allowed the extremists to vent their frustrations in the media and the opposition to demonstrate peacefully.

Although the fair and largely violence-free 1992 elections were a personal victory for Iliescu, whose margin declined to 61.4 percent, his party failed to win an absolute majority of seats in parliament, forcing him into an uneasy coalition with the extreme nationalist and neo-Communist parties. During his second term Iliescu, along with Nicolae Vacaroiu, Stolojan's compliant successor as prime minister, increasingly preferred to bypass parliament and govern by decree. Such increased authoritarianism allowed Iliescu to concentrate on his policies while avoiding as much as possible the extremists' xenophobia and chauvinism that he opposed. His methods drove the extremists to attack him so bitterly that he expelled the neofascist Greater Romania Party from his coalition in 1995. Despite the acrimony among Romania's leaders, political violence largely disappeared from the streets during Iliescu's second term, which improved Romania's international image. However, corruption scandals involving members of his party and further economic deterioration caused voters in 1996 to refuse Iliescu a third term as president, though they did elect him to the Senate, where he has continued his political career.

If Iliescu left Romania in the same serious economic trouble as he found it in 1989, he did democratize Romanian political life within the context of Romania's traditional paternalism and authoritarianism. Unfortunately, his forced reliance on the former Communist military and nomenklatura to stay in power caused him to miss opportunities to reduce Romania's centuries-old ethnic divisions. This incomplete pluralism coupled with the total failure of economic gradualism produced riots in 1990 and 1991. Yet he managed to restore order at the cost of more authoritarianism and thus remove some of the tarnish from Romania's international standing. In the final analysis, his popularity stemmed from an ability to give Romanians what they wanted, not what they needed.

BIBLIOGRAPHY

Iliescu, Ion. *Aufbruch nach Europa: Rumanien—Revolution und Reform 1989 bis 1994.* Cologne: Bohlau, 1995.

———. *Romania at the Moment of Truth.* Paris: Editions Henri Berger, 1994.

———. *Romania in Europe and in the World.* Bucharest: I. Iliescu, 1994.

Robert Forrest

SEE ALSO Ceauşescu, Nicolae; Constantinescu, Emil; Romania

Illyeis, Gyula (1902–83)

Hungarian poet, writer, and editor. Gyula Illyeis came from a peasant family. He participated in the activities of the Red Relief during the period of the post–World War I Hungarian Soviet and therefore had to flee the counter-revolution and Hungary. He went to Paris in 1922, where he studied literature, psychology, and sociology at the Sorbonne and became acquainted with the leading French surrealist writers of the age. He returned to Hungary in 1926 and became a bank clerk. He started publishing in the most prestigious Hungarian literary periodical, *Nyugat* (*West*), in 1927. His first book was published in 1928, and his trend-setting sociological novel, *The People of the Puszta,* appeared in 1934. The prolific Illyeis became one of the best-known writers in the 1930s. He became co-editor of *Nyugat* in 1941, and when it ceased to exist, he established *Magyar Csillag* (*Hungarian Star*). He became directly involved in politics in 1945 when he joined the National Peasants Party. He withdrew from politics in 1948, however, in opposition to the Communist takeover of the country and published nothing of his own until 1956. In the 1960s his attention was increasingly turned toward the fate of Hungarians living outside the country in the Carpathian basin, and he criticized, both directly and indirectly, the nationality policies of neighboring Czechoslovakia and Romania. Toward the end of his life, he had become the grand old man of Hungarian literature and intellectual life.

BIBLIOGRAPHY

Beladi, Miklos. *Illyes Gyula.* Budapest: Kozmosz Konyvek, 1987.

Izsak, Jozsef. *Illyes Gyula koltoi vilagkepe, 1920–1950.* Budapest: Szepirodalmi Konyvkiado, 1982.

Tamás, Attila. *Illyes Gyula.* Budapest: Akademiai Kiado, 1989.

Tamás Magyarics

Indra, Alois (1931–90)

Czechoslovak Communist functionary. Alois Indra was the son of a Slovak agricultural laborer. As a student he joined the Communist Youth League and, in 1945, the Czechoslovak Communist Party (CCP). As of 1948 he worked as a party functionary. From 1952 to 1956 he was a department head of the party's Central Committee, from January until July 1957 a secretary of the Central Committee, and from July 1957 to May 1960 managing secretary. In June 1958 he became a candidate member of the Central Committee and became a full member in December 1962. An opponent of the Prague Spring of

1968, Indra was one of the five conservative Communist officials who signed a letter to Soviet leader Leonice Brezhnev in August 1968 appealing to the Soviet Union to intervene in Czechoslovakia to save communism from the threat of counterrevolution. At a meeting at the Praha Hotel with Soviet officers on August 22 a conservative troika was agreed on to replace Czechoslovak leader Alexander Dubček. Indra, Vasil Bilak, and Drahomir Kolder were to be its members. However, President Ludvík Svoboda scuttled the attempt to install the "Quislings" by refusing to recognize them. Indra, nevertheless, was rewarded for his effort. He became a candidate member of the Presidium of the Central Committee of the CCP in January 1970 and a full member in January 1971. From 1971 to 1989 he was chairman of the Czechoslovak Federal Assembly (parliament). He died on August 2, 1990.

BIBLIOGRAPHY

Windsor, Philip, and Adam Roberts. *Czechoslovakia 1968: Reform, Repression, and Resistance.* New York: Columbia University Press, 1969.

Bernard Cook

SEE ALSO Bilak, Vasil; Svoboda, Ludvík

Ingoroqva, Pavle

Self-taught Georgian "literary expert" who, in the 1940s, propagated the fabricated theory that the Abkhazians came to "Georgia" only in the late seventeenth century. Pavle Ingoroqva's "theory" was purportedly intended to serve as the basis for the relocation of the Abkhazians to Central Asia, just as Stalin had deported the Chechens and other Caucasian peoples in 1943. In 1991 Ingoroqva's fabrication was endorsed by hypernationalist Georgian academics, including Tamaz Gamqrelidze. Ingoroqva's invention provided the justification for the assertion of Gia Chanturia's National Democratic Party that non-Kartvelians (Georgian-speakers) were "guests" in Georgia whose continued presence was a threat to the Georgian nation.

BIBLIOGRAPHY

Hewitt, George B., ed. *The Abkhazians: A Handbook.* New York: St. Martin's Press, 1999.

Bernard Cook

SEE ALSO Abkhazia; Chanturia, Georgi; Georgia; South Ossetia

Ingrao, Pietro (1915–)

Leader of the Italian Communist Party (PCI). Born in Lenola (Latina), Pietro Ingrao received a degree in law and participated in the war against the Nazis and Italian Fascists after 1943. After the war he worked at the PCI's newspaper, *Unità,* and directed it from 1947 to 1957. He was elected to parliament in 1948. He maintained a critical perspective within the Communist Party. Although he was part of the left wing of the party, he did not adhere to the radical position of the Manifesto group that broke with the party. In the 1960s he was particularly attentive to the student and feminist movements. During the 1970s he was elected as speaker of the Chamber of Deputies.

Particularly concerned with the reform of the state bureaucracy, Ingrao founded the Centro Riforma dello Stato (Center for the Reform of the State), which he continues to head. After the transformation of the Italian Communist Party into the Democratic Party of the Left, in 1991 Ingrao gradually abandoned active political struggle, refusing to participate in party affairs but still maintaining a theoretical engagement with the Italian left.

BIBLIOGRAPHY

Ingrao, Pietro. *Appuntamenti di fine secolo.* Rome: Manifestolibri, 1995
———. *Le cose impossibili: un'autobiografia raccontata e discussa con Nicola Tranfaglia.* Rome: Riuniti, 1990.
———. *Missili e potere popolare: per la riforma dell'art. 80 della Costituzione.* Milan, Italy: F. Angeli, 1986.

Daniele Petrosino

Institute Literacki

Polish émigré publishing house, founded in Rome in 1946. Since 1947 the Institute Literacki (IL) has had its headquarters in Maisons-Lafitte, near Paris. It is one of the more prominent Polish émigré cultural centers. Jerzy Giedroyc (1906–) was its founder. Its permanent editors have been Zofia Hertz, Zygmunt Hertz, Maria Czapska, Józef Czapski, and Henryk Giedroyc.

Before moving from Rome to Paris, the IL published nearly thirty books and the first issue of the journal *Kultura.* In 1953 the IL began publishing a monographic series, Library of Kultura; about five-hundred titles have been published within this series, among them, the works of Czesław Miłosz, Witold Gombrowicz, Gustaw Herling-Grudziński, Marek Hlasko, and other Polish and Soviet émigré writers, as well as works of dissidents living in the Soviet Union and elsewhere in the Communist bloc. The IL published the first Polish-language edition of books by Huxley, Orwell, and Koestler. In the Library of Kultura series works in sociology, political science, history of philosophy, literary criticism, and politics have been published. Also within the series the following subseries have been published: *Dokumenty* (*The Documents*), containing sources on the contemporary history of central Europe; *Archiwum Revolucji* (*Archives of the Revolution*), essays and documents about the history of communism; and *Bez Cenzury* (*Without Censorship*), books that had been rejected for publication in Poland for political reasons. A quarterly, *Zeszyty Historyczne* (*The History Notebook*), has been published since 1962 within the main series. It is dedicated to the history of Poland and central Europe after 1918.

Since 1947 the IL published the main political periodical of Polish emigration, a monthly, *Kultura* (*Culture*), edited by J. Giedroyc with the help of Z. Hertz and the contributions of Juliusz Mieroszewski, Konstanty A. Jeleński, Gustaw Herling-Grudziński, Jerzy Stempowski, Czesław Miłosz, Józef Czapski, Wojciech Skalmowski, Bohdan Osadczuk, Leopold Unger and Michał Heller. Six-hundred issues of the periodical dealing with contemporary history and contemporary politics as well as Polish and foreign literature and culture have been published.

The IL is an important center for the social and political life of Polish émigrés as well as a meeting place for émigrés from central and Eastern Europe. IL publications were banned in Poland until 1990 and had to be smuggled in. They were an important source of reprints for the post-1976 underground publishing houses in Poland, which the IL also supported financially. In 1995 in Warsaw the Society for the Preservation of the IL Archives in Paris was founded to work on the priceless archives and the library of the IL in Maisons-Lafitte and to promote the activities and the heritage of the IL.

BIBLIOGRAPHY

Gledroye, Jerzy. *Autobiografia na cztery ręce.* Warsaw: Czytelnik, 1996.

Jeleński, Konstanty A. "Le Role du mensuel 'Kultura' en France." *Revue du Nord,* no. 4 (1988).

Kostrzewa, Robert, ed. *Between East and West: Writings from "Kultura."* New York: Hill and Wang, 1990.

Supruniuk, Mirosław. *Materiały do dziejów IL w Paryżu.* Vols. 1–2. Toruń/Warsaw: UMK, 1994–95.

Tyrmand, Leopold, ed. *Explorations in Freedom: Prose, Narrative, and Poetry from "Kultura."* New York: State University of New York, 1970.

———, ed. *"Kultura" Essays.* New York: State University of New York, 1970.

Mirosław Supruniuk

Intermediate-Range Nuclear Forces Treaty

The 1987 arms control agreement between the Soviet Union and the United States totally eliminating intermediate-range and shorter-range ground-launched nuclear missiles. The Intermediate-Range Nuclear Forces (INF) Treaty was a response to the deployment in 1977 of the new Soviet SS-20 mobile intermediate-range missile, which drastically altered the European security environment in favor of the Warsaw Pact. The North Atlantic Treaty Organization (NATO) had earlier recognized that it lacked the capacity for a median response to a Warsaw Pact ground offensive that would be provided by an intermediate-range nuclear force. NATO responded in 1979 to the SS-20 deployments with a devious "dual track" counter. The United States proposed the elimination of all Soviet intermediate-range missiles, the "zero option" approach, in return for a cancellation of impending American deployments. This would appease European opinion and blunt Soviet propaganda, while simultaneously buying time for the deployment of Pershing II ballistic and ground-launched cruise missiles (GLCMs). Formal talks began in 1981 and were suspended in November 1983 by the Soviets because of Pershing II and GLCM deployment.

INF talks were resumed in March 1985 as part of the bilateral Nuclear and Space Talks (NST), but remained deadlocked over the inclusion of British and French nuclear forces, verification procedures, and geographic extent of the proposed treaty. The INF Treaty was signed on December 8, 1987, after the Soviet Union proposed a total ban on all shorter-range nuclear missiles as well as intermediate-range missiles, the "double-zero" option, and accepted modified American verification procedures.

The treaty unequivocally bans GLCMs and ground-launched ballistic missiles (GLBM) with a range of 500 to 5,500 kilometers. All such, missiles and their launchers were destroyed within three years after the treaty entered into force on June 1, 1991. Such missiles, launchers, and support structures and equipment could henceforth not be possessed by either the Soviet Union or the United States.

The INF Treaty represents a high-water mark in East-West arms control negotiations because of its provisions for on-site inspections to ensure compliance with treaty terms. The United States has concluded that the twelve newly independent states of the former USSR are successors to the INF Treaty. These states have confirmed that they are treaty successors and will abide by treaty prohibitions.

BIBLIOGRAPHY

Nolan, Janne E. "The INF Treaty: Eliminating Intermediate-Range Nuclear Missiles, 1987 to the Present," in Richard Dean Burns, *Encyclopedia of Arms Control and Disarmament,* Vol. 2. New York: Scribner, 1993.

Talbott, Strobe. *Deadly Gambits.* New York: Vintage Books, 1985.

U.S. Arms Control and Disarmament Agency. *Arms Control and Disarmament Agreements: Texts and Histories of the Negotiations.* Washington, D.C.: Government Printing Office, 1990.

Robert J. Bunker

SEE ALSO Pershing II Missile

International Expositions

International exhibitions, commonly called "fairs" in the United States, "exhibitions" in Great Britain, and "expositions" in France. The terms are used interchangeably although they are actually events of different size. The Bureau of International Expositions, the regulating body, designates them as "international expositions," which bridges the gap between fair and exhibition and is actually a larger, more extensive, and more formally organized event.

The first international exposition was held in 1851 in London, the Crystal Palace Exhibition. During medieval times great fairs were held at major crossroads of trade as a mixture of commerce, entertainment, and theater. They were basically international to the extent to which there were nations. In England the fairs were national, a blend of trade show and public entertainment. From these fairs, the industrial exhibitions were developed in France then spread to England, where they were sponsored by mechanics institutes to teach scientific principles to the working class. The mechanics institute exhibitions included scientific, mechanical, exotic, and fine arts sections that merged into the 1851 Crystal Palace Exhibition and the international expositions that followed.

These fairs soon included special themes and more nonindustrial features, such as fine arts and amusements. All have demonstrated a strong streak of nationalism, vaunting the national image and citizens' pride in it. Fair managers, often with strong government support, strove to heighten nationalistic features on behalf of the host country to make it look better than its rivals. This reached its apex (or nadir, depending on one's point of view) with the American-Soviet rivalry at the Brussels exposition in 1958, during the height of the Cold War, when the two countries competed through their respective national pavilions. Not coincidentally, they were across from each other. In fact, this U.S.-USSR competition was expected at all the post-1945 expos before the breakup of the Soviet Union in the late 1980s, but it never quite reached the intensity that it did at Brussels.

Two agencies have responsibility for U.S. involvement at post–World War II expositions: the Department of Commerce for fairs held in the United States and the United States Information Agency (USIA) for those held outside the United States. After 1992, the USIA abolished its expo staff and turned the operation of all future world fairs over to the private sector, with the agency maintaining an advisory role only. At Genoa (1992) and then at Taejon, South Korea (1993), the U.S. effort was administered by private-sector Amway officials who worked with the USIA staff. However, the United States still objects to the host country paying total costs, especially if the fair is unsuccessful. To date, the United States is the only participating country that does not assume responsibility for financial loss.

Promoters claim that fairs have three major benefits: they promote tourism in the country in which the expo is held as well as in countries represented at the fairs; increase trade between the host nation and other countries; and strengthen diplomatic relations. Country participation works under the "I went to yours, you come to mine" theory, which has often put major countries in political tight spots, as happened with the United States at Seville. The United States was under pressure from the Spanish government to appear. Pulling out, which Congress wanted, would have been considered an insult by Spain, a major U.S. trading partner.

All world fairs were canceled during World War II, and none were held again until 1958. They resumed with the Exposition Universelle et Internationale de Bruxelles (Brussels, Expo '58); Seattle World's Fair (Century 21 Exposition, 1962); New York World's Fair (1964–1965; not BIE approved); Universal and International Exhibition (Montreal, Expo '67); Hemisfair '68: A Confluence of Cultures of the Americas (San Antonio, 1968); Japan World Exposition (Osaka, Expo '70); International Exposition of the Environment (Spokane, Washington, Expo '74); International Ocean Exposition (Okinawa, 1975–76); Knoxville International Energy Exposition (1982); Louisiana World Exposition (New Orleans, 1984); Tsukuba, Japan (Expo '85); 1986 World Exposition (Vancouver); World Expo 88 (Brisbane, 1988); Seville (Expo '92); Genoa (1992); and Taejon, Korea (1993). A 1996 expo in Budapest was canceled after a new, democratic Hungarian government decided it did not have the resources to put on a major world's fair. Expo officials are now gearing up for Lisbon (1998) and Hannover (2000).

BIBLIOGRAPHY

Allwood, John. *The Great Exhibitions.* London: Macmillan, 1977.

Findling, John E., and Kimberly D. Pelle. *Historical Dictionary of World's Fairs and Expositions, 1851–1988.* Westport, Conn.: Greenwood, 1990.

Martin J. Manning

International Monetary Fund

The Bretton Woods regime of international economic organizations, named after the New Hampshire site of the 1944 United Nations Monetary and Financial Conference, which inaugurated the International Monetary Fund (IMF) and the International Bank for Reconstruction and Development (IBRD), is at the core of the international economic order under the aegis of the United Nations. Financial officials from the United Kingdom, the United States, and their wartime allies authorized the standards of the postwar monetary system. The IMF and the World Bank were founded by Articles of Agreement by representatives of forty four nations, on the belief that liberal rules of free trade, capital mobility, and monetary stability would facilitate international monetary cooperation. The IMF resulted principally from a compromise between British and American proposals. The agreement resembled the American proposal more than the British Keynes Plan, which envisioned the fund as a world central bank issuing its own reserve currency while advancing Keynesian stabilization procedures and social welfare objectives.

The devastating depression of the 1930s made evident the damage brought about by inefficacy in formulating protocols and organizational frameworks to direct the performance of economic programs. The ineffectiveness of civil servants and politicians in reacting decisively to the depression impaired international collaboration. The lack of an established structure permitted nations to follow individualistic objectives that intensified the predicaments of bordering states. The consequences entailed the cessation of international lending, the diminution of commerce, and the disintegration of the international monetary order.

The USSR did not join the IMF and in subsequent years constrained Czechoslovakia and Poland to terminate their IMF/World Bank affiliation, and consequently to end their association with the framework of the Western alliance. The countries of central Eastern Europe founded their own monetary regional and trade complex separate from what would develop into the international system established at Bretton Woods. In 1949 they instituted the Council for Mutual Economic Assistance (CMEA, or Comecon). In later years, though, it became apparent that fundamental modifications in the Western international system would not come about, and a movement in the direction of Western organizations seemed a viable alternative for further integration into the international economy. Romania became a member of the IMF and the World Bank in 1972, as did Hungary in 1982, and Poland in 1987. Czechoslovakia and Bulgaria subsequently became members as well.

The IMF was constituted mainly to facilitate global macroeconomic conditions instrumental for the development of nation-states, assist countries to promote exchange stability, and maintain orderly exchange arrangements. Its mandate was to avoid competitive exchange depreciation; monitor world economic trends and international macroeconomic policies; provide financial assistance for the expansion and balanced growth of international trade, and thus contribute to the promotion and maintenance of high levels of employment, real income, and development of the productive resources of nations. The fund supplies its 179 member nations with international liquidity.

The flexibility of the Bretton Woods regime proved to be important during the period of the U.S.-sponsored Marshall Plan. The fund was a source of currency that war-torn Europe needed for balance-of-payment financing. During the first five years of operation the IMF's currency transactions amounted to just $851 million, of which $606 million was drawn during the first year. The IMF's mandate was to supply short-term credit to finance interim balance-of-payments deficits or assist countries during protracted financial problems. The Marshall Plan, on the other hand, involved a massive undertaking over many years based on the belief that the predicament of Europe needed long-term solutions.

The Bretton Woods system ended in 1971. A fissure occurred between 1971 and 1973. A breach became apparent in world growth rates and other indexes of economic performance. Before 1971, when the Bretton Woods regime was thriving, there was an expansion of trade liberalization and a relatively unencumbered flow of capital. Subsequently, the structure of negotiated fixed exchange rates within which the system functioned reached closure. In the 1970s even the special drawing right's (SDR) utility as a unit of account was replaced by the European Community's European Currency Unit

(ECU). With the founding of the European Monetary System in 1979 and the credit instruments this supplied for constituents and ongoing modernization in international financial intermediation employing private capital markets, industrial nations were able to circumvent the fund. The IMF, constituted to regulate the exchange-rate and financial policies of the key-currency nations, no longer influences them.

The Keynesian ideal was already weakened with the advent of the Bretton Woods institutions. Over the years the ideal eroded even more as international economic decision making gradually relocated to associations such as the G-7 industrialized nation or to the operations of international private capital markets. Britain's Lord Keynes intended an IMF equal to one-half of world imports. Keynes situated the onus of adjustment on both surplus and deficit nations. In reality, deficit countries have mainly sustained the hardship of adjustment. The core of the international monetary system was fixed exchange rates: this dissolved in 1971 with the inauguration of floating exchange rates and resultant currency instability. The IMF thus forfeited its main function.

The international economy has changed immeasurably since the founding of the Bretton Woods institutions. Since the fund's original role was to monitor the global exchange-rate system and assist countries in contending with balance-of-payments difficulties, lending to governments in difficult fiscal straits was a secondary purpose. The bail-out aspect of its work took on more significance after 1971, increasingly so following the beginning of the developing-nation debt predicament in 1982. Even as late as 1974–77, industrial nations were significant clients of the IMF, with Italy and the United Kingdom making relatively substantial drawings. During the 1980s, however, the IMF lent solely to developing countries, with Russia and central Europe emerging as substantial users of IMF funds at the start of the 1990s. In 1991, while net credit to countries in transition in central Eastern Europe was $3.5 billion, net credit to the remainder of developing countries was only $1.1 billion. Since 1989 the fund has aided developing economies of central Eastern Europe in their transition from authoritarian to democratic regimes. These countries make expanding demands on IMF assets as they undergo economic adaptations, and as private sectors hesitate to lend until there are concrete indications of attainment. Crisis-prevention operations are one of the IMF's most significant activities in a period when foreign investors transacting as a unit are able to transform an emerging market into a disaster area and endanger the equilibrium of the international financial system while doing so. The efficacy of the IMF in the next century will rely on its members' ingenuity in maintaining domestic political backing for the tenets they espouse and thus the competence of nation-states to contend with the social implications of globalization.

BIBLIOGRAPHY

deVries, Margaret Garritsen. *The International Monetary Fund 1966–1971*. Washington, D.C.: International Monetary Fund, 1976.

———. *The International Monetary Fund 1972–1978*. Washington, D.C.: International Monetary Fund, 1985.

Helleiner, G. *Towards a New Bretton Woods: Challenges for the World Financial and Trading System*. London: Commonwealth Secretariat, 1983.

Horsefield, J. Keith, and Margaret Garritsen deVries, eds. *The International Monetary Fund, 1945–1965*. Washington D.C.: International Monetary Fund, 1969.

Kenen, Peter B., ed. *Managing the World Economy: Fifty Years after Bretton Woods*. Washington, D.C.: Institute for International Economics, 1994.

Oxfam. *A Case for Reform: Fifty Years of the IMF and World Bank*. Oxford: Oxfam publications, 1995.

Kenneth Keulman

SEE ALSO Marshall Plan

Ioannides, Demetrios (1923–)

One of the leading members of the group of military officers that overthrew the caretaker government of Panayiotis Kanellopoulos on April 21, 1967. These officers were afraid that in the upcoming May 1967 elections the Center Union Party would assume power and carry out a purge of dissidents in the army. A group of colonels, including Demetrios Ioannides, organized and carried out a coup d'état. Ioannides was a graduate of the Greek Military Academy and had been a member of the secret military organization IDEA, formed in the Middle East during the Second World War, and was involved in the failed coup attempt to bring General Alexandros Papagos to power in 1951.

Shortly after the successful coup of 1967, Ioannides became head of the Greek Military Police, which under his command developed into the organ of authority that during the seven-year military rule arrested and imprisoned the opposition, and maintained order through brutal suppression.

Ioannides opposed George Papadopoulos, who in 1972 wanted to legitimize the military government by allowing parliament to reconvene. On November 25,

618   **Ireland**

1973, Ioannides led a group of hard-liners in a new coup to undermine Papadopoulos and force him from office. He motivated the coup by claiming that Papadopoulos had deviated from the "Principles of the Revolution of April 21, 1967."

With Papadopoulos no longer in command of the military government, Ioannides coordinated an attempt to overthrow the president of Cyprus, Archbishop Makarios, in July 1974. Shortly after the Greek attempt to oust Makarios from power, Turkey took advantage of the opportunity to invade Cyprus. The July 20, 1974, invasion resulted in the division of Cyprus into a Greek-Cypriot and a Turkish-Cypriot sector, a situation that continues today.

Shortly after the Turkish invasion the military government of Ioannides collapsed and on July 24 Konstantinos Karamanlis was recalled to Greece and sworn in as premier. Ioannides, along with the other members of the military government, were tried in the summer of 1975 for high treason. He is currently serving a life sentence in Korydallos, the Athenian prison.

BIBLIOGRAPHY

Featherstone, Keith, ed. *Political Change in Greece: Before and After the Colonels.* New York: St. Martin's Press, 1987.

Orrieux, Claude. *A History of Greece.* Malden, Mass.: Blackwell, 1999.

Stelios Zachariou

SEE ALSO Cyprus; Karamanlis, Konstantinos

Ireland

The Republic of Ireland comprises the twenty-six–county state of Ireland. The country was officially known as the Irish Free State from its creation on December 6, 1922; the name was changed to Eire by the 1937 constitution; the Republic of Ireland Act (1949) again changed the state's name to the Republic of Ireland. Ireland is a sovereign, independent, liberal parliamentary democracy. The head of state is the president; and the executive, led by the *taoiseach* (prime minister) is responsible to the bicameral Oireachtas (parliament), made up of the Dáil (lower chamber) and the Seanad (upper chamber). Elections are held under the system of proportional representation (single transferable vote), and the voting age is eighteen. The state's theoretical area of jurisdiction is the island of Ireland, but pending the unification of the north and the south, the constitution defines the jurisdiction as the twenty-six–county state set up in 1922.

Ireland. *Illustration courtesy of Bernard Cook.*

Ireland entered the postwar era isolated. Interwar protectionism had tied the state's meager industrial base and conservative agricultural sector to the domestic market. Popular mentalities were marked by introspection and insularity. The Cold War years saw Ireland break these shackles. With mixed success the state integrated economically, politically, and socially into the wider world. After Ireland joined the European Economic Community (EC) in 1973, close links were forged with the members of the community. Traditional values were slowly reformed as the state developed its past rather than lived in it. Change, tempered by continuity, is the view facing the observer of postwar Ireland. Change has been faltering, at times ill-considered and unplanned, and not always the most beneficial in the long run.

Since 1945 Ireland has moved away from the civil war (1922–23) divisions of the 1920s and 1930s, which were over the constitutional nature of the state, to concern over social and economic issues. Partition and the northern question had become less divisive topics. Though the peace process in Northern Ireland since the Downing Street Declaration of December 1993 increased interest in the northern question, economic development and employment are now the main items on the political agenda. Social change came as a by-product of this economic development.

The late forties were bleak. The state suffered economically in the wake of World War II. The de Valera administration, in office since 1932, had little initiative left to tackle the economic and social problems facing the state. In 1948 a multiparty coalition (Fine Gael, Clann na Poblachta, Labour, Clann na Talmhan) took office. Though using grants from U.S.-sponsored Marshall Plan aid to develop infrastructure and pay for dollar imports, its main achievement was to declare Eire a republic in 1949. The state thus became the Republic of Ireland. Tensions within the coalition and a church-state scandal over free medical care—the "Mother and Child Scheme"—brought down the government in 1951. This scandal showed the fundamentally conservative nature of Irish society.

Despite some growth under the 1948–51 coalition, the 1950s were depressed economically and volatile electorally. Neither the rapid alternations of Fianna Fáil (FF) single-party administrations nor Fine Gael (FG)–led coalitions could turn around the malaise of the state. The decade saw increasing emigration and economic stagnation. The USSR had vetoed Ireland's entry into the United Nation in 1946. Ireland's entry onto the world stage came with its U.N. admission in 1955, but politically and economically the domestic picture was still grim, with little hope of respite except emigration. Not until the major world recession of the 1980s did the Irish economy again hit such a nadir.

The 1958–59 period saw a major turnaround in Ireland's fortunes as economic planning and charismatic leadership invigorated the state. Sean Lemass replaced the ailing Eamon de Valera as prime minister in 1959. Lemass was the political muscle that brought to fruition the economic plans of chief civil servant T. K. Whitaker. Whitaker advocated industrial development through economic planning, development of exports, and fiscal expansion. This was the key to much-needed growth. The tariff walls of the 1930s were torn down and the state entered fully into the world trading network. As a result of these "Economic Programmes" the gross national product grew 4 percent in the early 1960s. As the Irish economy latched onto the postwar world economic boom, the standard of living rose by up to 50 percent.

In 1961, as part of this expansion, Ireland unsuccessfully attempted to gain membership in the EEC (EC after 1967). The 1960s, nevertheless, were the most prosperous decade the state had seen since independence in 1921. The Lemass era brought widespread modernization, and the growth of television brought the world into Ireland. The civil war generation of politicians was symbolically replaced by young, upwardly mobile politicians such as Charles Haughey (FF), Donough O'Malley (FF), and Declan Costello (FG). The development of the Lemass boom was entrusted to these new personalities.

The decade saw a thawing of attitudes toward the North. Since 1925 the South and the North had virtually ignored each other. A new sense of rapprochement was seen when Lemass met Northern Prime Minister Terence O'Neill in 1965, thus recognizing the de facto existence of the Northern Irish state. The meetings prompted hopes of closer cross-border links. With growing discontent in Northern Ireland and the downfall of O'Neill in 1969 leading to the present "troubles," hopes of peaceful co-existence faded.

When Sean Lemass left office in 1966, the state was economically buoyant and socially transformed into a Western consumer society. With emigration reduced and the population rising, the basis for a prosperous society seemed in place. The custodian of Lemass's inheritance was Jack Lynch (FF). Lynch's 1966–73 administrations and a Fine Gael–Labour national coalition (1973–77) ushered in renewed uncertainty. The crisis in the North, which broke out in 1969 when a developing Catholic civil rights movement was met with violence from the Unionist community had a terrorist potential to destabilize the South. In addition, unseen problems of a modern mixed economy provided the constant concerns of the period. The early 1970s had the potential to be the most politically unstable since the state's bloody birth between 1921 and 1923. The world oil crises of 1973–77 and 1979 and the resulting inflation seriously destabilized the small, vulnerable Irish economy. Economic rather than political issues took center stage. Despite EC membership in 1973, the state was very much at the mercy of the world economy. Inflation rose and industrial discontent increased. The Lemass years seemed to endow the state with a jumbled inheritance.

Lynch returned to office in 1977 and sought to pump-prime the economy with a massive Keynesian expansion based on foreign borrowing. This provided some short-term benefits. However, when the state was hit by the second oil crisis of 1979, public finances, especially an alarming current budget deficit inflated by foreign debts, began to spin out of control in the early 1980s.

The depression of the 1980s brought other problems. The multinational firms that had arrived in the sixties began to pull out of Ireland. With a rising population and a large under–twenty-five age group, reduced employment prospects brought renewed emigration. Talk was of the 1950s as a similar mood of despair came over the state. For most of the 1980s growth was stagnant or slow and real incomes fell. With a rising national debt-GNP ratio and the unprecedented political uncertainty of three governments in two years, prospects for the country looked bleak. No administration was given the chance to provide long-term leadership. Not until 1987, with a national sense of crisis prevailing, were harsh measures introduced by FF and the slow control of public finances was begun.

Social mores were a priority in this decade as FG under Garret FitzGerald tried to highlight the "liberal agenda." The population was forced to think about previously taboo subjects such as divorce, contraception, and abortion. However, the change in old attitudes had more to do with the impact of a rising young urbanized population that had been brought up on television. The debates on the nature of Irish society in the 1980s and early 1990s saw a considerable conservative resurgence. However, the constitutional referenda over divorce (1986, 1995) and abortion (1983, 1992) revealed the increasing pluralism of Irish society. The final vote against both issues in the 1983 and 1986 referenda showed that Irish society was still essentially conservative. Nevertheless, Ireland appeared to be moving in a more pluralist, secular, and less traditionalist direction. The emergence of the avowedly liberal Progressive Democrats in 1987 and their continuing electoral success, where many other smaller parties have failed after an initial impact, is perhaps also a sign of this movement toward plurality.

Drastic cuts in public spending and a sense of atonement for the borrowing beyond the means of the state in the seventies characterized the period after 1987. The growing national debt, the borrowing requirement, and unemployment were the essential areas to be dealt with. By 1989 some improvement in standard of living was apparent and inflation was low, but unemployment continued to rise dramatically to near the 250,000 mark. The 1987 stock market crash and the 1991 Gulf War destabilized the world economy. An unpredictable world economic climate increased the uncertainty for the development of the open Irish economy. By the early 1990s public finances were on a sounder footing and sustained economic growth was underway. In December 1995 the *Economist* reported that the Organization for European Cooperation and Development (OECD) declared Ireland to be the fastest-growing OECD economy. It estimated Irish economic growth at 6.5 percent (real GDP) in 1995 and forecast 5.5 percent growth in 1996. This, the *Economist* continued, would have given Ireland "an average growth rate of more than 5% in the ten years to 1996. This would be twice the OECD average, putting Ireland at the top of the growth league over ten years."

As an underdeveloped European area, Ireland began to take advantage of increasing EU regional development funds. European issues and a growing sense of being European became apparent in the late 1980s. Ireland is one of the most enthusiastic members of the EC. European funding for agriculture and regional development has spurred this interest. While the United Kingdom, originally Ireland's major economic market, has seen growing concern over the prospects of closer European integration, Ireland has seen its future development closely linked to the EU.

The 1990 election of liberal feminist reformer Mary Robinson to the presidency, the 1992 general election with the rise of the Labour Party, and the November 1992 abortion referendum brought many to talk of a climate of renewed social and political change in Ireland. Certainly the rise of Labour from a twenty-year decline and the new government taking the unforeseen shape of a Fianna Fáil–Labour coalition, which held office to November 1994, was symptomatic of a change in the Irish political and socioeconomic climate. The state may be belatedly entering the European mainstream of secular, pluralist, liberal democracy and developing a political culture based on a left-right spectrum. Traditional attitudes were being redefined as the numbers attending mass declined, scandals hit the Roman Catholic Church, and larger segments of the population favored the introduction of divorce and abortion and eliminating the republic's constitutional claim to Northern Ireland. Moreover, a woman holding the presidency, the legalization of homosexuality (1993), and a positive vote in favor of the Maastricht treaty (1992) show the beginning of change, though this may be only a short-term move from the stasis of equilibrium.

BIBLIOGRAPHY

Cairnduff, Maureen, ed. *Who's Who in Ireland: The Influential 1,000,* 2d ed. Dublin: Hibernian, 1991.

Chubb, Basil. *The Constitution and Constitutional Change in Ireland.* Dublin: IPA, 1978.

Coogan, Tim Pat. *Disillusioned Decades: Ireland 1966–1987.* Dublin: Gill and Macmillan, 1987.

Fanning, Ronan. *Independent Ireland.* Dublin: Helicon, 1983.

Keogh, Dermot. *Twentieth Century Ireland.* Dublin: Gill and Macmillan, 1994.

Lee, J. J. *Ireland 1912–1985.* Cambridge: Cambridge University Press, 1989.

Lyons, F. S. L. *Ireland since the Famine.* London: Fontana, 1973.

Tobin, Fergal. *The Best of Decades, Ireland in the 1960s.* Dublin: Gill and Macmillan, 1984.

Michael J. Kennedy

Marshall Plan and Economic Planning

The European Recovery Program (ERP) or the Marshall Plan was instituted by the United States in 1948 to provide aid for the shattered economies of postwar Europe. Eire (the Republic of Ireland) participated although it had been a neutral during the conflict. The first interparty government of Ireland signed an agreement with the United States in June 1948 whereby Eire was to receive £47 million. It was conditional upon the government's drawing up a program outlining the country's import requirements for the next three years. This Long-Term Recovery Programme (LTRP) was drawn up by Sean Mac-Bride, minister for external affairs, and Frederick H. Boland, secretary of the department.

Eire was also required to join the Organization for European Economic Cooperation (OEEC; later Organization for European Cooperation and Development, OECD). Aid in the amount of $150 million was made available for a variety of projects designed to boost the struggling economy. By the end of 1950, $50 million had been received. While this did not solve the major problems of emigration, rising prices, low wages, and unemployment, it stimulated agriculture, financed housing programs, and restructured the social welfare system.

The LTRP emphasized the value of livestock production for export. Its major achievement was the Land Rehabilitation Project, undertaken by Minister for Agriculture James Dillon. The program marked the beginning of economic planning that bore fruit a decade later in the Programmes for Economic Expansion. Later benefits under the LTRP included establishment of the Central Statistics Office and the Industrial Development Authority (IDA).

The IDA, a state-sponsored body, was founded in 1949 as an agency of the Department of Industry and Commerce. While it was financed by grant-in-aid and its board was appointed by the minister for industry and commerce, the IDA was relatively free of the restrictions governing the civil service. Its function was to investigate areas of possible industrial development, bringing together financial and industrial experts to plan industrial growth and to examine the protectionist structure of Irish industry. In 1970 the IDA merged with An Foras Tionscail (Industrial Institute) to become an autonomous body with responsibility for attracting foreign investment and aiding foreign and national industrial expansion. The authority achieved its best performance during 1979, when it exceeded its job target by 5,000. Over the next five years it negotiated some 1,500 new industrial projects with an employment potential of 35,000.

BIBLIOGRAPHY
Kennedy, Kieran, Thomas Giblin, and Deirdre McHugh. *The Economic Development of Ireland in the Twentieth Century.* New York/London: Routledge, 1988.

O'Hagan, John, ed. *The Economy of Ireland: Policy and Performance,* 5th ed. Dublin: Irish Management Institute, 1987.

Michael J. Kennedy

United Nations
Because of Ireland's neutrality in World War II, the USSR vetoed its entry into the United Nations in 1946. However, Ireland joined in 1955 as part of a package deal between the Cold War blocs. The 1955–69 period marked a period of active Irish involvement in the world organization. Ireland championed the primacy of the U.N. Charter, the problems of the developing world, and the development of peacekeeping. Nuclear disarmament and U.N. representation for mainland China were two other issues in which Irish diplomats played a prominent role.

Under U.N. control, Irish defense forces saw military service in the Congo (ONUC) with General Sean McKeown, who for a period commanded the Congo force, and with Irish diplomat Conor Cruise O'Brien serving as Secretary-General Dag Hammarskjöld's special representative in the secessionist Congolese province of Katanga.

Political activity at the United Nations has become less pronounced since the late 1960s as the EC/EU has become the predominant focus of Ireland's foreign policy. However, continuing participation of Irish personnel in U.N. peacekeeping missions—UNIFIL (Lebanon), UNFICYP (Cyprus), UNOSOM (Somalia), and UNTAC (Cambodia)—has led to the creation of a strong peacekeeping tradition in the Irish defense forces.

BIBLIOGRAPHY
Skelly, J. M. *National Interests and the International Order: Irish Diplomacy at the United Nations General Assembly, 1945–1965.* Dublin: Irish Academic Press, 1997.

Michael J. Kennedy

Anglo-Irish Relations and Northern Ireland
The historical nature of Anglo-Irish antagonism, the partition of Ireland in 1920, the resulting existence of Northern Ireland with the recrudescence of violence and the collapse of the Unionist regime in 1969, and the close interdependence of Ireland and Britain mean that Anglo-Irish relations have always been a central concern, sometimes the central concern, of Irish foreign policy.

The two islands entered the postwar world on poor terms. Despite much top-secret and friendly contact between officially neutral Eire and the Allies, British Prime Minister Winston Churchill felt that through neutrality

Eire had not pulled its weight in the war effort. Britain did support Ireland's abortive effort to gain U.N. membership in 1946 but felt it could not oppose the USSR veto.

Ireland left the British Commonwealth in 1948 after a unilateral declaration, and proclaimed itself a republic in 1949. The Ireland Act, passed by the British parliament in 1949, confirmed the existing economic relationship between the two islands, and Ireland kept most-favored-nation trading status. The United Kingdom was to remain Ireland's major trading partner, and the Anglo-Irish Free Trade Agreement of 1964 established a free-trade zone between the two nations.

The 1949 Ireland Act also stated that Northern Ireland would remain part of the United Kingdom until the majority of the population desired otherwise. Relations between Ireland and Northern Ireland remained very much in a state of a minor Cold War from 1925, which had seen the last meeting between the two states' prime ministers. The forty-year impasse was broken in 1965 when Lemass secretly met his northern counterpart, Sir Terence O'Neill. During the Lemass years a more pragmatic view of relations with Northern Ireland developed. Through 1965 and 1966 top-level meetings continued. However, the slide to violence in Northern Ireland in the late 1960s effectively brought an end to these meetings, which remain only a hint of what might have been.

The outbreak of troubles in 1969 and the imposition of direct rule on Northern Ireland from the United Kingdom in 1972 led to a new phase in Dublin-London relations. The Lynch government from 1969 to 1973 had withstood pressure for a more active stance on Northern Ireland and had weathered the storm over the 1970 arms crisis in which two ministers in the Irish government were accused of diverting government funds for arms for the Irish Republican Army (IRA). In December 1973 British and Irish government officials and members of the Northern Ireland executive agreed to set up a power-sharing executive between the the Social Democratic Labour Party, and the Unionists. In face of the Ulster Workers Council strike of May 1974, the executive collapsed. May 1974 also saw car bombs kill twenty-two people in Dublin and Monaghan. Though Unionist paramilitaries were suspected, they denied responsibility.

Anglo-Irish talks on the future of Northern Ireland began in December 1981 when Irish Prime Minister Charles Haughey and senior colleagues met with British Prime Minister Margaret Thatcher and her senior officials. Haughey referred to the talks as a "historic breakthrough." However, relations between the two prime ministers were always frosty. This in part was due to Ire-

land's later lack of support for Britain during the 1982 Falkland conflict between the Britain and Argentina, during which Ireland opposed EC sanctions and was hostile to the United Kingdom on the U.N. Security Council. Haughey's successor, Garret FitzGerald, had a better relationship with Thatcher. In November 1981 they agreed to set up an Anglo-Irish Intergovernmental Council. In 1983 the New Ireland Forum (NIF) was established to try to achieve new structures for a solution in Northern Ireland. It contained representatives of the republic's major political parties and the SDLP. The NIF final report favored three outcomes: a unitary Ireland, a federal Ireland, and a joint authority with power shared between Dublin and London. Thatcher dismayed the Dublin government with her remark "out, out, out" to the three suggestions. But in the aftermath of the NIF, increased diplomatic pressure from the United States and the European Community led to the Anglo-Irish Agreement (AIA) of November 1985.

Signed by FitzGerald and Thatcher at Hillsborough, England, on November 15, 1985, the agreement committed both London and Dublin to closer cooperation over Northern Ireland. The AIA sought to promote peace and stability, create a climate of reconciliation between the Protestant and Catholic communities in Northern Ireland, and establish closer joint links to combat terrorism. The most radical feature of the agreement was a joint ministerial conference of British and Irish ministers, backed up by a permanent secretariat. This would monitor issues affecting the Nationalist (Irish Catholic) community in Northern Ireland. The agreement did not establish joint authority. London retained the final word over all Northern Irish decisions, but the AIA did give the Irish government a role in the affairs of Northern Ireland, a major change of British policy. The AIA was supported by Nationalists but deeply resented by Unionists, who saw this as the thin wedge of Dublin "interference" in the internal affairs of Northern Ireland.

The Downing Street Declaration of December 1993 was testimony to the bond of friendship between Irish Prime Minister Albert Reynolds and British Prime Minister John Major. Using the mood for peace within the province of Ulster (Northern Ireland), the two prime ministers agreed to a joint plan to promote peace in Ireland. The declaration made clear that a solution to the Northern Ireland problem would embrace the totality of relationships within Ireland, that the British government had no selfish or strategic interest in Northern Ireland, and that London and Dublin would continue to uphold the democratic wish of the majority of the population of Northern Ireland with regard to the future. With the exception of militant Unionist Ian Paisley's Democratic Unionist Party, the declaration received widespread political support and was popular among the population of Northern Ireland. The declaration was a sign of the close contact that existed between Ireland and Britain and that was to continue with the IRA cease-fire of August 1994. The fall of Reynold's government in December 1994 marked the beginning of a more uncertain period of Dublin-London relations. Nevertheless, by 1998, Britain and Ireland had agreed on the framework of a joint Catholic-Protestant administration for Northern Ireland and a more substantive role for the Republic of Ireland in the affairs of the north through the establishment of a Council of the Isles.

BIBLIOGRAPHY
Arthur, Paul. *Northern Ireland since 1968,* 2d ed. Cambridge, Mass.: Blackwell Publishers, 1996.
Hadden, Tom. *The Anglo-Irish Agreement: Commentary, Text, and Official Review.* Dublin, Ireland: E. Higel, 1989.
Owen, Arwel Ellis. *The Anglo-Irish Agreement: The First Three Years.* Cardiff: University of Wales Press, 1994.
Wichert, Sabine. *Northern Ireland since 1945.* New York: Longman, 1991.

Michael J. Kennedy

Ireland and the European Community

Perhaps the most important feature of post-1945 Irish foreign policy has been its "Europeanization." Ireland's joining of the European Community (EC) in 1973 turned on its head the tradition of preserving sovereignty and independence that was at the heart of Irish foreign policy from the time of the country's independence. Sean Lemass had directed Ireland toward Europe since 1961, stating that Ireland was in full support of political and economic integration. He also stated that Ireland was prepared to give up neutrality in the pursuit of this goal.

Irish agriculture was one of the first areas to benefit from EC membership with the transfer of development funds. These benefits, however, drew to a close as the 1970s ended. In the 1980s Ireland received significant aid from the EC's European Regional Development Fund, which provides fund for infrastructure development to poorer member states and regions. Ireland, as an underdeveloped area, is a net beneficiary from EU funds. Irish politicians were worried about the erosion of this position as the community was widened to take in Spain, Portugal, and Greece.

According to opinion polls, Ireland is one of the most enthusiastic member countries in the EU. Yet popular support for EU membership may be related to levels of EU aid. Voting in direct EU elections since 1979 has always been consistently lower than in general elections. But referenda on European issues do bear out the pro-EC/EU trend as Ireland voted by 83 to 17 percent in favor of EC membership in 1973, by 70 to 30 percent in favor of the Single European Act in 1987, and by 69 to 31 percent in favor of the Maastricht treaty in 1992. Ireland has not seen a rise of "Euroscepticism" as in the United Kingdom during the 1990s. Emigration to the European mainland, trading links, EU funding, and a consciousness that without EU membership Ireland would be unable to hold its own in the world order all contribute to national support for EU membership and further economic and political union. The only unpopular aspect of EU membership seems to be possible defense and security cooperation.

BIBLIOGRAPHY
Keogh, Dermot. *Ireland and Europe, 1919–1989.* Cork: Hibernian University Press, 1989.

Michael J. Kennedy

National Coalition Government

A coalition of Fine Gael and the Labour Party from 1973 to 1977. The partners to the coalition published a fourteen-point program before the general election of February 1973 in which they secured an overall majority over Fianna Fáil. While Fianna Fáil secured 69 seats, Fine Gael returned with 54 seats and Labour with 19.

Liam Cosgrave became prime minister. The coalition proved unable to stabilize prices; inflation continued to mount until 1978. Overall there had been price increases of 100 percent in many areas. The government removed the value-added tax (VAT) from food in 1973, and from electricity, heating, oils, clothing, and footwear in 1976. It also subsidized staple food items, increased Social Welfare, and reduced the Old Pension qualifying age to sixty. Supplementary and pay-related schemes were introduced to ease the burden of heavy unemployment, around 160,000 by mid-1977. By 1974 the government was in a position to negotiate with employers and labor unions to produce a national pay agreement with predetermined increases over a twelve-month period.

Agriculture boomed from 1974 to 1977, owing principally to EC (EU as of 1993) demand for Irish beef and agricultural produce. The government concentrated on tax inequities but the scheme to tax the larger farms evoked mounting criticism from farming organizations.

Minister for Local Government James Tully made more financing available for local authority housing. His target of twenty-five thousand new houses per annum stretched available resources to the limit. While figures issued by his department indicated that this target was being met, the depression within the building industry continued. Tully was also accused of gerrymandering (or "Tullymandering," as political pundits put it) in his re-drawing of the constituency boundaries for national elections. Political commentators felt that Fianna Fáil faced an uphill struggle in the next general election as a result of Tully's reshaping of the constituencies. A further act of Tully, which was to have a significant effect on the general election result, was the lowering of the voting age from twenty-one to eighteen years, making the young vote one-quarter of the entire electorate.

The coalition initiated new approaches to the question of Northern Ireland. Cosgrave was party to a meeting with Unionist leader Brian Faulkner and Edward Heath, British prime minister, at Sunningdale, England, in December 1973. Security was a major concern of the coalition government, which was dedicated to the destruction of the Irish Republican Army (IRA) and kindred subversive organizations.

The Criminal Law (Jurisdiction) Act 1977 extended the criminal law of the republic and created new offense categories. The bill was referred by President Cearbhall O'Dalaigh to the supreme court and held to be constitutional. The act was reinforced by the Emergency Powers Act of 1976, which increased the maximum penalties for offenses under the Offenses Against the State Act. This act was also referred by the president to the supreme court, and it, too, was held to be constitutional. During 1976–77 there was widespread criticism of the alleged conditions in Portlaoise jail in Ireland, which had become a maximum security prison for convicted IRA members. The government consistently refused to allow independent investigations of the prison system and evoked widespread comment by such refusal. There was no noticeable diminution in the level of IRA activity by the time the government went out of office in June 1977, but there was a sustained demand for more police to deal with the high level of organized and petty crime.

At the end of 1976 came a disquieting incident destined to have far-flung implications for the coalition. Minister for Defense Patrick Donegan, speaking at a function for army personnel, reportedly referred to the president as a "thundering disgrace" for his action in referring the Emergency Powers Act of 1976 to the supreme court. This attack on the president's use of his powers caused a political furor. The opposition called for the minister's resignation, or at the very least, his dismissal from the cabinet. Prime Minister Cosgrave declined to

act; and although Donegan apologized, the president resigned, maintaining that as the office had been denigrated he had no alternative.

In December 1976 Donegan, in a cabinet reshuffle, left Defense to become minister for lands and later minister for fisheries. Further damage was done to the coalition's prestige at the Fine Gael congress in May 1977. In an unscripted aside, Cosgrave referred to the coalition's critics in the media as "blow-ins" and requested them to "blow-out." This apparent intolerance of criticism, while greeted with obvious enthusiasm by the delegates, was received negatively by the media and neutral observers.

In the ensuing general election in June Fianna Fáil returned to power with a record eighty-four seats. The implications of the defeat for the coalition partners ran deep. Almost immediately Cosgrave resigned the leadership of Fine Gael and was succeeded by Garret FitzGerald, and Frank Cluskey replaced Brendan Corish as leader of the Labour Party.

BIBLIOGRAPHY
Collins, Neil. *Irish Politics Today,* 3d ed. New York: St. Martin's Press, 1997.

Michael J. Kennedy

Neutrality

Though invited to join NATO in 1949, Ireland refused. Minister for External Affairs Sean MacBride stated that partition of the island and NATO membership were incompatible. Though NATO membership was not that compatible with the objectives of Irish foreign policy, Ireland took a strongly anti-Communist stance during the Cold War. However, strong popular support for neutrality has meant that military nonalignment has become the basis of Irish foreign policy. In the early 1980s this was allied with a strong antinuclear movement. There were other reasons for not joining NATO: fear of neocolonialism, that links to the Western bloc would lead to loss of sovereignty; concern that Ireland's poor fiscal position would not support increased military expenditure; and fear of targeting by atomic weapons. With the end of the Cold War, NATO redefined itself through the Partnership for Peace Program. There are signs that Ireland's leadership is reconsidering membership, but membership in the Western European Union (WEU), the European Union's (EU) nascent defense wing, is more likely in the medium term. Ireland assumed observer status in the WEU in 1994.

BIBLIOGRAPHY
Keatinge, Patrick. *A Singular Stance: Irish Neutrality in the 1980s.* Dublin: IPA, 1983.

Salmon, Trevor. *Unneutral Ireland*. Oxford: OUP, 1989.
Michael J. Kennedy

Political Parties

The modern Irish political party system developed after the victory of Sinn Fein (We Ourselves) in the 1918 general election. The party, born out of the backlash against Britain in the aftermath of the abortive 1916 Rising, wiped out the old Parnellite Irish Parliamentary Party, winning 73 out of 105 seats. In the area that was to become Ireland in the post-1922 period, this represented 70 out of 75 seats. Another result of this election was that the Labour Party was marginalized, winning no seats. Thus began a polarization of Irish political parties around the national question—the separation of the six countries of Ulster in the north from the rest of Ireland. Sinn Fein, after negotiating the 1921 treaty with Great Britain that set up the twenty-six-county Irish state, split into pro- and anti-treaty factions. A short civil war took place from June 1922 to May 1923. The treaty split was to color the Irish party system up to the 1980s. The pro-treaty side became Cuman na nGaedheal in 1923 and with the addition of the National Centre Party in 1933 became Fine Gael. The anti-treaty Sinn Feiners refused to participate in the parliament (Dáil) and abstained. This faction split in 1926 with the setting up of Fianna Fáil by Eamon de Valera. The Labour Party continued in existence, being the official opposition to 1927. Thus by the 1920s the main threads of the party system of the 1945–94 period were in place. A curious exception in an agricultural country was the fact that, except for short periods, there was no Farmers Party. The catchall nature of the larger parties, especially Fianna Fáil, tended to obviate the need for specific-issue parties. Two of the more successful "small parties" are Clann na Poblachta and the Progressive Democrats (PD). The PD, formed in 1985, has been the most resilient of these smaller parties, attracting young liberal voters from Fine Gael and sustaining parliamentary representation. The 1990s have seen the growth of a small Green Party as well.

It is difficult to categorize the Irish party system because of its birth in the national struggle. Fianna Fáil and Fine Gael both tend to be center-right, Fine Gael more so than Fianna Fáil, with Labour and the Workers Party/ Democratic Left being, respectively, more left-wing. The immediate center is unoccupied, with Fianna Fáil, Fine Gael, and increasingly Labour fighting for this ground and the growing number of floating voters.

Fine Gael (Family [or Tribe] of Gaels), originally called the United Ireland Party, was founded in 1933 from a merger of Cumann na nGaedheal, the National Guard, and the National Centre. The first president of the party, Eoin O'Duffy, was replaced by W. T. Cosgrave in 1935. The principal support for the party comes from industry, business, commerce, the professions, and the more substantial farmers. Fine Gael was the principal opposition to Fianna Fáil in 1933–48, 1951–54, and 1957–73. In the wake of the disastrous performance in the 1943 election, Cosgrave resigned and was replaced by Richard Mulcahy. The party suffered from organizational problems in this period, but after the 1948 election, as the largest single party after Fianna Fáil, Fine Gael was the major party in the interparty government of 1948–51. Mulcahy was unacceptable as prime minister, and John A. Costello held that position while Mulcahy remained party leader. Fine Gael tended to pursue a more reactive than active policy in this government. Despite some success in economic policy using Marshall Plan funds from the United States, the government fell over the Mother and Child Scheme in 1951. After three years in opposition Fine Gael was back in office from 1954 to 1957 in a second interparty government. Fine Gael Minister for Finance Gerard Sweetman followed a strongly deflationary policy, which led to the fall of the second coalition in 1957.

The duo of Mulcahy and Costello were replaced by the new party leader, James Dillon, and Fine Gael entered the 1960s with a leader of conservative outlook. The impetus for change came from a younger group within the party. An energetic "ginger" group including party members such as Declan Costello, Garret FitzGerald, and Alexis Fitzgerald were responsible for the more Christian Democratically oriented Just Society program, which formed the bulk of Fine Gael's 1965 election program.

In 1965, Dillon was replaced as party leader by Liam Cosgrave. Under Cosgrave Fine Gael formed a national coalition with Labour in 1973. The coalition adopted a reforming set of policies, but this was severely undermined when party members, including Cosgrave, voted against a bill seeking to liberalize legislation on contraception. The resignation of President Cearbhall O'Dalaigh in 1976, as a result of the government's introduction of draconian public security legislation and criticism of the president by Fine Gael Minister for Defense Patrick Donegan, also tarnished this image.

In the 1977 election Fianna Fáil won an overall majority; the coalition had misread the electorate. In the aftermath Cosgrave retired, and Garret FitzGerald took over as party leader. The party adopted a more liberal agenda under FitzGerald, and the new leader radically overhauled the party structure at the grassroots level. FitzGerald led Fine Gael as prime minister in the short-lived June 1981–February 1982 government in coalition with

Labour, and again in coalition with Labour from November 1982 to February 1987. These governments were dogged by recession, emigration, rising unemployment, and a rising budget deficit. The FitzGerald years saw the party attempt constitutional reform with referenda on divorce (1986) and abortion (1983). These moves proved unsuccessful, and the conservative element in Fine Gael remained considerable. Nevertheless, under FitzGerald the party built up its share of votes and seats to a record level. FitzGerald opened a new chapter in Anglo-Irish relations with the November 1985 Anglo-Irish agreement, which began a joint approach to Northern Ireland and firmly established the interrelationship between Dublin and London in dealing with the future of Northern Ireland.

Following an overwhelming election defeat in 1987, FitzGerald resigned and was replaced as party leader by former Minister for Finance Alan Dukes. Under Dukes Fine Gael supported the Fianna Fáil government's policy of retrenchment. This did not endear Dukes to Fine Gael, which lost support to the Progressive Democrats in the 1987 and 1989 elections. In the 1990 presidential election, Austen Currie, Fine Gael's preferred candidate, performed disastrously. Fine Gael dumped Dukes and replaced him by the more conservative John Bruton. Under Bruton Fine Gael formed a coalition government in November 1994 with the Labour Party and Democratic Left.

Fianna Fáil (Soldiers of Destiny) was founded on May 16, 1926, by Eamon de Valera. At the suggestion of Sean Lemass it was subtitled "The Republican Party." The party aimed to reunify Ireland, preserve the Irish language, distribute large farms among the small farmers, and promote protection and self-sufficiency for the Irish economy. The party broke with the Sinn Fein policy of abstention from Dáil Eireann and entered the Dáil on August 11, 1927. Fianna Fáil came to power for the first time in March 1932 and formed the governments until February 1948. In this period the party, under the solid leadership of de Valera, introduced protectionism, redefined Anglo-Irish relations, and preserved Ireland's neutrality through World War II.

In the immediate postwar years Fianna Fáil stagnated under an aging de Valera and faced with the radical republican and reformist threat of Clann na Poblachta. The party was out of power from 1948 until 1951, when it formed the government that lasted until 1954. The party had not used its time in opposition to rethink its strategy, and de Valera and an increasingly aged front-bench team, many of whom had been founders of the party in 1926, still held on to the same policies their 1932 government had followed. Fianna Fáil's severely deflationary policies proved unsuccessful and eventually brought the government down in 1954 and the party out of power until 1957.

In 1959 de Valera handed over the prime ministership and leadership of Fianna Fáil to the more technocratic Sean Lemass. Under Lemass's leadership to 1966, Fianna Fáil underwent a period of renewal with the arrival of a younger generation of party figures. The sixties saw the arrival of Jack Lynch, Charles Haughey, Brian Lenihan, Donough O'Malley, and George Colley, among others. Under Lemass Fianna Fáil became somewhat more pragmatic and less overtly republican; economic issues and social welfare issues came to dominate the party agenda.

Lynch succeeded Lemass in 1966 as party leader. Lynch took a more divided party back into government in 1969, and his authority was tested in the 1970 Arms Crisis, where members of the government (Haughey and Blaney) were alleged to have planned to import arms into Ireland for the IRA. The party closed ranks behind Lynch and the major achievement of the next years was the entry of Ireland into the European Economic Community (EC; later, European Union, EU) in January 1973. When Fianna Fáil faced the electorate in January 1973, it lost to a national coalition government of Fine Gael and Labour.

In 1977 Fianna Fáil received 84 seats and a majority of seats in the Dáil and embarked on a massive program of Keynesian expansion. The oil shock of 1979 turned this expansion into a recession, and the legacy of borrowing in the 1977–79 period was to dog the Irish economy through the 1980s. Haughey took over from Lynch in 1979 and led the party until February 1992. Haughey proved a charismatic leader, but his presence was felt by many to account for the failure of Fianna Fáil to win an overall majority in the Dáil during his thirteen years as leader. His involvement in the 1970 arms crisis was a component of the so-called Haughey Factor, as were political and financial scandals that were to rock his administrations. Under Haughey Fianna Fáil adopted a neorepublican stance, opposing the Anglo-Irish Agreement (1985) and regarding Northern Ireland as "a failed entity." The early 1980s saw Fianna Fáil somewhat ambivalent on economic policies, but from 1987 tight financial policies under Minister for Finance Ray McSharry (for which he earned the nickname "Mac the Knife") were primarily responsible for bringing the Irish economy out of the recession of the 1980s and making the way for increased growth in the 1990s.

After increasing attacks on his leadership, Haughey was ousted in January 1992 and Albert Reynolds was elected as party leader. As prime minister, Reynolds made peace in Northern Ireland a major priority. His single-minded pursuit of this agenda was one of the factors leading to the Downing Street Declaration of December 1993 and the August 1994 IRA cease-fire. Reynolds was unenthusiastic about Fianna Fáil's need for a coalition with the Progressive Democrats. His sidelining of his minor partners led them to withdraw their support and force a general election in 1992. The election saw the Fianna Fáil vote drop to unprecedented levels and forced the party into coalition with Labour. This coalition remained in office, led by Reynolds, until in November 1994 a crisis over the operation of the Office of the Attorney General forced Reynolds to resign as prime minister, then as party leader. Reynolds was replaced by Bertie Ahern, at the time finance minister, who had a reputation as a consensus builder, a vital factor considering the uncertain future facing Fianna Fáil and the need to modernize the party.

In 1922 the Labour Party contested its first general election, winning 21 percent of the vote, and until 1927 Labour was the official opposition. Under the leadership of Thomas Johnston the party was cautiously reformist and pro-treaty. In 1932 it supported Fianna Fáil as a minority government. Johnston was replaced by Thomas O'Connell, but the latter lost his seat in the 1932 election. He was replaced by the more durable William Norton. During the thirties the party aligned itself with Fianna Fáil and adopted roughly the same radical socioeconomic policies rather than socialism. The party dabbled with a more socialist image in the midthirties but toned this down following clerical disapproval. It did well in the 1937 election and in conjunction with Fine Gael was able to bring down the Fianna Fáil administration in 1938. The 1948 election and the urge to compromise to form a coalition to oust Fianna Fáil saw Labour in government for the first time, with Norton as deputy prime minister. Labour, however, adopted a more conservative role than the socioeconomic radicals of Clann na Poblachta, whose Noel Browne was responsible for the Mother and Child Scheme, which brought the coalition down. Following the 1954–57 coalition Labour received a poor vote in the 1957 election. Labour now eschewed coalition and began to pursue an independent line. Norton was replaced by Brendan Corish in 1960. Under Corish the party began to modernize and take on a more socialist and left-wing agenda. The 1965 election saw Labour's best performance for over twenty years, and its 1967 conference met under the slogan "the seventies will be socialist." But the party's expected vote did not materialize in the 1969 election, and in 1973 it returned to a coalition strategy. The party's record in the 1973–77 coalition was mixed. It had succeeded in its policies to help workers in the recession of the 1970s, but it had not achieved much of its liberal

agenda. The coalition also led to a party division over participation in future coalitions. The anticoalition faction became stronger as the seventies progressed. In the wake of the coalition's defeat in the 1977 election, Labour elected Frank Cluskey as its new leader. Cluskey lost his seat in the 1981 election, and it was a new leader, Michael O'Leary, who brought Labour back into coalition with Fine Gael. O'Leary resigned in October 1982 and was replaced by Dick Spring, who guided Labour into the 1982–87 coalition with Fine Gael. Labour resigned from this coalition in 1987 in response to Fine Gael's increasingly austere policies. Labour did badly in the February 1987 election, recording its second-lowest vote ever. It still managed to hold onto 12 seats, a loss of only 2. The 1989 election saw Labour regain its 1982 level and capitalize on Spring's leadership. The following year Labour benefited by the victory of its preferred candidate, Mary Robinson, in the presidential election. In the 1992 election Labour won 33 seats, an increase of 18 from 1989, and was approaching Fine Gael, the second-largest party, with 45 seats. After 1992 Spring had a high profile as minister for foreign affairs and his party became the power broker in the formation of Irish coalition governments, being essential to both the 1992–94 Fianna Fáil–Labour coalition and the 1994 Fine Gael–Labour–Democratic Left coalition. Some doubted whether Labour can maintain this position and its level of support in the long-run.

Divisions in Fianna Fáil resulting from a conflict between Charles Haughey and Desmond O'Malley led to the formation of the Progressive Democrats in February 1985, after O'Malley's expulsion from Fianna Fáil in May 1984. O'Malley had attacked Fianna Fáil's stance on the report of the New Ireland Forum and its negative stance on a coalition family planning bill. O'Malley was joined by Mary Harney, who replaced O'Malley as leader in the wake of the 1992 election, and by Michael Keatinge from Fine Gael. The party got aid from Fianna Fáil and Fine Gael supporters, though more from the latter. It adopted a liberal pluralistic attitude and was more moderate in respect to the Northern Ireland issue. The party performed well in the 1987 elections, winning 14 seats, 11.8 percent of the total vote. It did not do so well in 1989 but coalesced with Fianna Fáil. After the 1992 election the PD's emerged as a significant minor party, but Labour was the more eligible partner for coalition with Fianna Fáil. Harney replaced O'Malley as party leader in October 1993. Harney played a distinctive role as party leader in the political crisis of November 1994.

The Workers' Party was the result of a split in Sinn Fein in 1970. The Official Sinn Fein faction gradually moved away from violence through the 1970s and in

1977 changed its name to Sinn Fein the Workers Party. This was a sign of a commitment to a purely political strategy. The transformation was completed in 1982 when the party became the Workers' Party. The party adopted an overtly Marxist-Leninist line and oriented itself toward the urban working class. In the post-1989 period, however, with the collapse of the USSR, the clash of ideologies came to a head. In February 1992, after an extraordinary party congress failed to transform the party into an independent democratic socialist party, party leader Proinsias de Rossa and six of the party's seven members of parliament along with the majority of the party's activists agreed to form a new party, the Democratic Left. The new party kept the majority of Workers Party support and seems to have established itself with voters. In November 1994 the party entered government with Labour and Fine Gael.

The Clann na Poblachta (Republican Family) was founded in July 1946 by Sean MacBride, Noel Hartnett, and Jack McQuillan. The party, which was supported by some members of the Irish Republican Army, saw itself as a modernizing force and attracted support from those who wanted a wide range of social reforms to be implemented. In 1947 the party won two out of three by-elections and MacBride entered Dáil Eireann. The party's rapid growth prompted Eamon de Valera to call a general election in 1948. Although most of its 90 candidates were inexperienced, the Clann won 10 seats and entered into coalition with Fine Gael, Clann na Talmhan, and the Labour Party to form the first interparty government of 1948–51. Two ministries went to Clann deputies, MacBride (external affairs) and Noel Browne (health). The party supported the passage of the Republic of Ireland Act in 1948. Browne attempted to implement health reforms, including the eradication of tuberculosis, in which he was successful, and maternity care, which brought him into conflict with the Catholic hierarchy and the Irish Medical Association. He was not supported by his leader, McBride, who was having his own problems with the head of the diplomatic service, Frederick Boland. The split between the two Clann ministers was echoed within the party, and McQuillan resigned with Browne. Their resignations, and the controversy over Browne's health plans, helped to precipitate a general election. The Clann was not prepared to remain in coalition, and Fianna Fáil returned to power in 1951. Clann na Poblachta won only 2 seats in the new Dáil. It won 3 seats in the 1954 general election, but while MacBride supported the second interparty government his party did not participate in it, and it fell in 1957 when he withdrew support over the government's measures against the IRA. He lost his seat

in the 1957 general election. Only one Clann na Poblachta deputy, John Tully, held his seat in 1961 and in 1965. The party was dissolved in 1969, and Tully was defeated when he ran as an independent.

Clann na Talmhan (Family of the Land) was founded in 1938 at Athenry by Michael Donnellan. It was loosely organized and had as its principal aim the defense of the small western farmer. The party's strongholds were in counties Galway, Mayo, and Roscommon. It maintained constant criticism of the government's agricultural policies, which it felt were inimical to the interests of the small farmer. The party secured 14 seats in the general election of 1943. In 1944 Joseph Blowick became leader when Donnellan failed to hold his seat. The Clann secured 7 seats in the 1948 election when it entered into the interparty government. Its only minister in the coalition government was Blowick, who held Lands and Fisheries, while Donnellan, who had regained his seat, became a parliamentary secretary. Following the collapse of the interparty government in 1951, the party steadily lost support and, having secured only 2 seats in the 1961 general election, disappeared by 1965.

BIBLIOGRAPHY

Chubb, Basil. *The Government and Politics of Ireland,* 2d ed. London: Longman, 1982.

Coakley, J., and M. Gallagher. *Politics in the Republic of Ireland.* Dublin: Folens/PSAI Press, 1993.

Gallagher, Michael. *The Irish Labour Party in Transition 1957–1982.* Dublin: Gill and Macmillan, 1983.

Gallagher, Michael, and Michael Laver. *How Ireland Voted.* Dublin: Folens/PSAI Press, 1993.

Mair, Peter. *The Changing Irish Party System.* London: Pinter, 1987.

Maye, Stephen. *Fine Gael, 1923–1987.* Dublin: Blackwater Press, 1993.

O'Byrnes, Stephen. *Hiding Behind a Face: Fine Gael under FitzGerald.* Dublin: Gill and Macmillan, 1986.

Sinnott, Richard. *Irish Voters Decide.* Manchester: Manchester University Press, 1995.

Walsh, Dick. *The Party, Inside Fianna Fáil.* Dublin: Gill and Macmillan, 1986.

Michael J. Kennedy

Voting System

In general elections, senate elections, and local government elections in the Republic of Ireland, a proportional representation system (PR) operates by means of the single-transferable vote in multimember constituencies. Voters indicate their choices by placing numbers in order of preference by names on the ballot paper. Having indicated the first choice, the voter may then vote for as many more candidates in order of choice as desired. A quota, which the candidate much reach to be elected, is set according to the Droop Quota, represented by the formula: Q = Number of valid votes + 1/number of seats + 1.

If no one is elected on the first count, votes are transferred according to the preferences expressed until all the seats have been filled. When a candidate has surplus or excess votes over the quota, these are distributed proportionally to the second or next available choices expressed by his or her supporters. When there are no surpluses to be distributed and seats still remain to be filled, the candidate with the lowest number of votes is eliminated and those votes are redistributed in accordance with the preferences indicated by her or his supporters. The process continues until all the seats have been filled. It is possible, therefore, for a candidate to be elected without having reached the quota.

The PR system, by definition, allows for a more complex expression of voter preferences. Voting between and among parties is therefore possible. The PR system in Ireland has not resulted in a multiplicity of small parties, as its critics expected. The system, however, does benefit smaller parties such as Labour, Progressive Democrats, and Democratic Left. With their decline since 1987, Fine Gael has also benefited. Attempts to abolish PR have been unsuccessful. Fianna Fáil governments have twice held referenda to secure abolition of the system and its replacement by the single nontransferable vote in single-member constituencies. In the referendum of 1959, held on the same day as the presidential election, which was won by the leader of Fianna Fáil, Eamon de Valera, the result was 453,320 (48.2 percent) in favor of change and 486,989 (51.8 percent) against. In the second referendum, held in 1968, the result was 423,496 (39.2 percent) in favor of change and 657,898 (60.83 percent) against.

BIBLIOGRAPHY

Sinnott, Richard. *Irish Voters Decide.* Manchester: Manchester University Press, 1995.

Michael J. Kennedy

Agriculture

The postwar years in Ireland saw the number of people employed in agriculture plummet. The drift from the land, however, has not been accompanied by a fall in production. Since the 1950s there has been a considerable expansion in output. Dairy farming developed with Irish accession to the European Community (EC/EU) in 1973 and reliance on EC price supports. Though perhaps the benefits of membership have not been as munificent as expected, EC entry nonetheless reasserted the dominance of dairy farming in Ireland.

Large, ranch-style farms predominate in the south-midlands, while on the western seaboard small farms, where farmers may have a secondary occupation off the land, are the norm. In recent years the state has tried to keep as many of these small farmers on the land as possible. Small farms may not be profitable, but they are the unit of society in these areas, which, if they were to disappear, would rapidly become depopulated.

BIBLIOGRAPHY

Kennedy, Kieran, Thomas Giblin, and Deirdre McHugh. *The Economic Development of Ireland in the Twentieth Century.* New York/London: Routledge, 1988.

Michael J. Kennedy

Economic Programs

Between 1958 and 1972 three programs for expansion were employed in an attempt to modernize the Irish economy. The first program (1958–63) was based on the white paper "Economic Development," drawn up by Thomas Kenue Whitaker, the finance minister, with the support of Prime Minister Sean Lemass and adopted by the government in November 1958. The object was to "accelerate progress by strengthening public confidence after the stagnation of the 1950s, indicating the opportunities for development and encouraging a progressive and expansionist outlook." The Whitaker report indicated that to achieve these aims "we must be prepared to take risks under all headings—social, commercial and financial—if we are to succeed in the drive for expansion." The program was adopted at an opportune moment to take maximum advantage of renewed world economic activity. During the period of the first program national income rose by 2 percent, compared with 0.5 percent between 1952 and 1958. Real incomes rose by 4 percent. This new-found prosperity was due to a rise in net agricultural output, which increased by 9 percent during the 1960s, and to manufacturing industry, where the value of output rose by 82 percent between 1959 and 1968. The value of exports in 1960 was the highest in thirty years.

The second program (1963–68), drawn up by Whitaker and Lemass, capitalized on the economic growth achieved during the period of the first program. It set out to achieve the maximum sustainable level of growth to insure the rising standards made possible by the first program. One significant accompaniment of the second program was the reorganization of the educational system by the minister for education, Donough O'Malley, in an attempt to bring education levels into line with the needs of the economy.

The third program was introduced by Lemass's successor, Jack Lynch. Designed to cover the period from 1969 to 1972, it was entitled "Economic and Social Development." It sought to take account of the social changes that had accompanied the revitalization of the economy and was drawn up against the background of the National Industrial Economic Council's "Report on Full Employment," which sought a growth rate of 17 percent for the three-year period. The program projected an increase of 16,000 in employment and a reduction of emigration to an annual level of 12,000 to 13,000. A population of more than 3,000,000 was projected for 1972 (in 1971 the census revealed a population of 2,978,248). The third program collapsed in the face of an international recession.

In 1973 the Fianna Fáil government lost office to the National Coalition, which did not attempt any new programs for expansion in the light of adverse economic conditions.

BIBLIOGRAPHY
McCarthy, John F., ed. *Planning Ireland's Future: the Legacy of T.K. Whitaker.* Dublin: Glendale Press, 1990.
Michael J. Kennedy

SEE ALSO Whitaker, Thomas Kenneth

Demography

The famine years of 1845–1847 marked the culmination of a massive population growth in Ireland. A population of just over 8 million in 1841 was reduced to 6.5 million by 1851 and the decline continued into the twentieth century. In fact, except for a small increase in the mid-1940s, the decline continued to 1966. By 1966 the population of the Republic of Ireland was 2.88 million. The norm was a low marriage rate but a high fertility rate; Ireland's birthrate approached the EC average only in the 1980s. Since World War II the death rate had fallen, reflecting improvements in nutrition and health care and the creation of the welfare state. Emigration was also common, mainly to the United States and Britain. In the period from 1946 to the mid-1950s the emigration rate reached record levels, with forty thousand per annum emigrating through the 1950s. By the mid-1960s the impact of the postwar boom and Irish economic restructuring saw the marriage age fall with an accompanying trend toward smaller planned families. There was also a fall in emigration, and the population rose for the first time in over a century.

This was accompanied by a movement of this population to the towns and a rise in industrial employment. By 1971 a majority of the Irish population lived in towns of a population of 1,500 or more. The traditionally dominant agricultural sector had declined to only 15 percent of the workforce by 1986. By the 1980s Ireland had one of the fastest-growing and youngest populations in Europe, with 25 percent of the electorate under age twenty-five. This was in part due to a period of immigration, or reentry, in the 1970s by those who had emigrated in the 1960s. During the 1970s the population rose from 2.97 million in 1971 to 3.36 million in 1979. Renewed emigration of graduates in the 1980s led to a brain drain. By the 1990s the emigration rate had again fallen, as had marriage and fertility rates. This contributed to a slight population decline between 1986 and 1991, which is expected to continue.

BIBLIOGRAPHY
Daly, Mary E. *Social and Economic History of Ireland.* Dublin: Educational Company, 1981.
Michael J. Kennedy

Religion

Freedom of religion is guaranteed by the 1937 constitution. The state does not establish any particular religion, nor does it discriminate on the grounds of profession of religious beliefs. As the religion of the majority of the people, however, the Roman Catholic Church was endowed with a special position under the 1937 constitution. This was removed by referendum in December 1972; 84.38 percent of the 50.67 percent voting approved of the removal of the special status.

In 1961 the population of the Republic of Ireland was 94.9 percent Roman Catholic (2,673,000); 3.7 percent Church of Ireland (104,000); 0.7 percent Presbyterian (19,000); 0.2 percent Methodist (7,000); 0.1 percent Jewish (3,000); and 0.4 percent other (12,000).

Ireland began the postwar period as a very conservative society. Change in religious beliefs and practice has been modest. This slow but growing process of secularization can be traced back to the 1960s. It was due to internal modernization and a more outward-looking and young Ireland and international developments such as reform of the Catholic Church by the Second Vatican Council under Pope John XXIII. Religious observation was high, with Catholic attendance at weekly mass in the mid-1970s reaching 91 percent of the adult population. This had declined to 87 percent in 1984 and 82 percent in 1988–89. Despite this process, which was most evident in urban areas, Ireland still remained overwhelmingly conservative, as the constitutional prohibition of divorce (1986) and ban on abortion (1983) showed.

Changing attitudes were seen through the 1980s with the increasing use and availability of artificial contraception, a realization that Ireland was exporting its abortion problem to Britain. In 1969 only 122 women, who gave addresses in Ireland, traveled to the United Kingdom for abortions. In 1979 the number had increased to 2,767.

In the 1990s the Catholic Church faced a major crisis, with accusations of sexual abuse of children by clerics and members of religious orders. The mid-1990s saw a popular lack of confidence in the church as attendance again dwindled and the church lost the predominant place it had held in Irish society since the middle of the nineteenth century. The overturn of the constitutional ban on divorce in 1995 was another sign of creeping secularization. It would be wrong, however, to suggest that organized religion does not hold a significant place in the lives of the Irish people.

BIBLIOGRAPHY

Whyte, John. *Church and State in Modern Ireland, 1923–1979.* Dublin: Gill and Macmillan, 1980.

Michael J. Kennedy

SEE ALSO McQuaid, John Charles

Irish Language and the Gaeltacht Areas

Irish is an Indo-European language that evolved in written form through Ogham (inscriptions consisting of dashes on rock). This Celtic language is sometimes referred to as Gaelic but is commonly called Irish, to distinguish it from the different Gaelic language of the Scottish Highlands. The Latin alphabet was introduced in the fifth century. Irish continued to be the language of the majority of the population until the nineteenth century. In 1831 the national school system banned Irish from the curriculum and Irish was seen by many as a sign of backwardness. Emigration and the famine of the 1840s dramatically reduced the number of Irish speakers. The 1880s and 1890s saw the founding of organizations to rehabilitate the Irish language, such as the Gaelic League (1893). These organizations, however, did not prevent the decline of the language.

In 1922 the first independent Irish government made Irish compulsory in primary education; in 1925 Irish was made compulsory for positions in the civil service. In the 1937 constitution (Article 8) Irish was made the first language of Ireland, while English was defined as the second official language.

The postwar period saw the use of Irish as vernacular language decline to the Gaeltacht areas on the west and southwest seaboards. In the 1961 census there were 164,000 speakers of the language in these areas, with the largest portion, 52,428, in the Galway Gaeltacht. Including all those who spoke Irish countrywide, the figure represented 27.2 percent of the population. Yet the wide definition of those who could speak Irish, including bilingual speakers, makes the figure somewhat inexact. By 1971 the figure had risen to 28.3 percent of the population.

Gaeltacht areas tend to be poorer than the rest of the country. Their lower income per capita has led to their becoming special development areas, with their own minister and department of state. Gaeltarra Eireann was set up in 1957 to encourage the extension of Gaeltacht areas through economic development that aimed to provide increased employment. Development of Gaeltacht areas continued through the 1980s, with the receipt of European Community (EC; European Union, EU, as of 1993) aid and attempts to undertake rural community development based on native indigenous industries. Irish will probably never become the language of the majority of the Irish people, as the founding fathers of the state once hoped. It is not even recognized by the EU as a minority language within the community. But renewed interest in the language in the 1980s and 1990s has ensured its survival. Radio Telefis Eireann established Radio na Gaeltachta in 1972 to cater to the needs of the Irish-speaking communities within the Gaeltacht in counties Donegal, Galway, and Kerry. Some have suggested that reform of the outdated Irish school curriculum may hold the key to increased interest in Ireland's first language.

BIBLIOGRAPHY

Gaeltarra/SFADCO Working Group. *Gniomh don Ghaeltacht = An Action Programme for the Gaeltacht.* Dublin: Gaeltarra/SFADCO Working Group, 1971.

The Irish Language in a Changing Society: Shaping the Future. Baile Atha Cliath [Dublin]: Bord na Gaeilge, 1988.

Michael J. Kennedy

Abortion and Divorce Referenda

The 1980s saw not only Garret FitzGerald's so-called constitutional crusade to liberalize Ireland but also a worldwide swing to conservative values. These two contradictory trends came to a head in two divorce and two abortion referenda that took place in Ireland in the period from 1983 to 1995. While the referenda of the eighties show how Ireland was still a deeply conservative country, the results of the referenda of 1992 and 1995 show the growth of plurality and secularism. Just as the constitution of 1937 reflected the Ireland of the time, the use of the referendum allows periodic changes in the constitution to allow it to mirror the changes that have taken place in the country since 1937.

In the 1983 referendum to insert a ban on abortion into the constitution, 53.7 percent of the electorate participated and 66.9 percent of those voting supported the ban. In 1986, 63.48 percent, of the 60.84 percent of the electorate who voted, voted against deleting the constitutional ban on divorce. The 1992 abortion referendum contained three questions. Of the 68.2 percent who voted, 62.3 percent voted that those seeking abortion should not be forbidden to travel. Sixty percent voted to allow abortion information. But 65.4 percent voted to uphold the constitutional ban on abortion. In 1995, of the 61.94 percent who voted, 50.28 voted to remove the constitutional ban on divorce.

The campaigns of 1983 and 1986 were divisive and fought on religious and moral issues. The failure to overturn the bans during those two referenda was seen as an indictment of FitzGerald's process of constitutional reform. The 1992 abortion referendum grew out of the "X case," involving a fourteen-year-old alleged rape victim who was prevented from going to Britain for an abortion because of an injunction brought by the attorney general. The injunction was overturned by an appeal to the Supreme Court. The result allowed freedom to travel and freedom to abortion information but left the existing article of the constitution in place. The 1995 referendum showed a slight majority in favor of removing the ban on divorce, revealing an urban-rural split.

BIBLIOGRAPHY

Sinnott, Richard. *Irish Voters Decide*. Manchester: Manchester University Press, 1995.

Michael J. Kennedy

Mother and Child Scheme

The Mother and Child Scheme, as it was popularly known, was part of the a free health scheme proposed by reformist Minister for Health Noel Browne. The scheme, which was not to be compulsory, would provide free health care for all mothers and children up to sixteen years of age, with no means test. The Irish Medical Association (IMA), with which Browne had a poor relationship, objected to the concept of "socialized medicine." In July Browne told the Dáil that he would not agree to a means test, and received the backing of the cabinet. During October the Catholic bishops of Ireland considered the scheme and expressed disquiet at the lack of a means test

and freedom of choice of doctor. An Episcopal commission, consisting of Bishops McQuaid, of Dublin, Michael Browne of Galway, and Dr. Staunton of Ferns, was established. At a meeting with Browne on October 11, 1950, the bishops indicated their objections and heard Browne's reply. Browne left the meeting under the impression that he had satisfactorily met their objections.

Browne again rejected the idea of a means test on October 24, 1950, when the IMA indicated the lack of resources at the disposal of the state. The bishops made it clear to the government that they considered there was an important issue of "faith and morals." The family, they stated, was the final arbiter in regard to sex education. They also objected to non-Catholics treating Catholic mothers or offering them sex education that might be at variance with accepted Catholic teaching. The debate continued until March 1951. During this time the relationship between Browne and the leader of his party, Sean MacBride, deteriorated. At the same time he was at odds with the leader of the government, John Costello, and with his cabinet colleagues. The government by now wished to concede to the Episcopal and medical demand for a means test. On March 6 Browne said there would be no more delays and published the scheme, having refused his colleagues' request for the inclusion of a means test. Details of the scheme were circulated to the Roman Catholic hierarchy and two days later the bishops rejected it on the grounds that none of their objections had been met. They provided Costello with a copy of their correspondence with the minister for health. Browne pointed out that he had met the bishops' objections. A major misunderstanding had apparently taken place. He met with Bishop McQuaid on March 24 and agreed that the bishops had the right to decide issues of "faith and morals." In April the bishops' convention rejected the scheme "as opposed to Catholic social teaching." The government refused to support the minister and abandoned the scheme, conceding to all the bishops' objections. Browne had by now also been rejected by his own party, and MacBride demanded his resignation. He resigned and published his correspondence with the hierarchy. The government fell in June 1951, and the new Fianna Fáil government introduced a public health act scheme with a means test.

BIBLIOGRAPHY

Browne, Noel. *Against the tide*. Dublin: Gill and Macmillan, 1986.

Michael J. Kennedy

SEE ALSO Browne, Noel

Trade

With a small domestic market, the Irish economy is very dependent on foreign trade. The postwar period saw the Republic of Ireland breaking out from behind a wall of protectionism and tariffs established to promote economic nationalism in the 1930s, to embrace free-trade ideals and export-oriented economic growth. Ireland's position as an economy dependent on petroleum and raw materials imports means that it is subject to the fluctuations of the world economy. This was seen in the 1960s when the world boom led to a significant diversifying of Ireland's exports to Europe away from its traditional market of the United Kingdom, and in the 1970s and 1980s when world recession had a negative impact on the Irish economy. The Gulf War of 1990–91 also destabilized the Irish economy.

In the 1950s Ireland experienced a balance-of-trade deficit, with exports plummeting as protected Irish goods could not compete on the world market. Creeping modernization, at the same time, led to an increase in imports as Ireland embraced the consumer society of the postwar world. Ireland's traditional export—agricultural goods to the United Kingdom—was not capable of pulling up the Irish economy.

Irish trade possibilities revived in the 1960s. Prime Minister Sean Lemass reduced tariffs and attempted to gain membership in the European Economic Community (EC) in 1961. He negotiated the Anglo-Irish Free Trade Agreement (AIFTA), which went into effect on July 1, 1966. Under the terms of the agreement there was to be a gradual removal of protective tariffs on imports and exports between Ireland and the United Kingdom. The agreement was an important part of Irish economic policy during the 1960s and was of particular importance for Irish agriculture as it gave unrestricted access to the United Kingdom for Irish cattle and sheep. The butter quota to the United Kingdom was also increased. Irish agricultural and horticultural produce was not regulated except by intergovernmental commodity agreement. The British government also undertook to afford opportunities for the growth of imports from Ireland on terms no less favorable than those granted to British farmers. Under the agreement there was to be freedom of access to Irish fish and fishery products. Protective duties on textiles and clothing containing man-made fibers were to be eliminated. Agricultural exports showed an increase in 1967 as a result of the agreement: store cattle exports were 620,000 head, as compared with an annual average from 1962 to 1966 of 510,000, and beef exports were 730,000 head, compared with an annual average of 340,000 between 1963 and 1966.

Export-led growth was a basis of 1960s Irish economic expansion. By 1969 the percentage of Irish exports to the United Kingdom had fallen from 81 percent in 1956 to 66 percent. Entry into the EC (later, European Union, EU) in 1973 and further reductions of tariffs created greater export potential. The oil crisis of 1973 hit Ireland's trade substantially as oil is one of the country's major imports. However, the benefits of EC membership for trade have been spectacular; by 1985 the EC accounted for over 33 percent of Irish exports. Since the late 1980s Ireland's balance of trade has gone significantly into the black, and the country carries a substantial export surplus. This trade surplus, with buoyant domestic demand, continued into the midnineties. The composition of exports has changed from mainly agricultural to manufactured exports, particularly in the computer industry. The source of imports has tended since 1922 to be the United Kingdom, though this has declined with the United States and Germany proving increasingly important trading partners.

BIBLIOGRAPHY

O'Hagan, John, ed. *The Economy of Ireland: Policy and Performance,* 5th ed. Dublin: Irish Management Institute, 1987.

Michael J. Kennedy

Unemployment

Employment was more or less static in Ireland from 1926 to 1951. Emigration tended to siphon off excess labor supply, and this reduced any natural increase in the labor force. The 1950s saw a rapid increase in emigration, especially from the agricultural sector. The economic planning of the 1960s aimed to bring in multinational firms to kick-start the economy and provide full employment. Rather than increase employment, this policy succeeded in mopping up a significant excess capacity in the economy; employment remained static in the 1960s, contrary to the wishes of planners. By contrast, unemployment rose from 59,000 in 1961 to 61,000 in 1971.

From 1971 to 1981 there has been an unprecedented rise in unemployment, from 61,000 to 126,000. This corresponds with a rise in the labor force from 1,110,000 to 1,272,000 and a rise in total employment from 1,049,000 to 1,146,000. The 1970s saw employment in the industry and services sector rise while the outflow from agriculture continued.

Employment was the main economic and political problem of the 1980s. In the first half of the decade unemployment rose from 126,000 to a record 227,000. Correspondingly, though the labor force rose from

1,272,000 to 1,302,000, total employment fell from 1,146,000 to 1,075,000. The industrial sector was the worst hit, with a decline between 1981 and 1986 from 363,000 to 301,000; agriculture continued to decline by 28,000, to 168,000. Only in the services sector did employment increase. Emigration of university graduates siphoned off many of the most educated, and the 1980s saw the rise in the number of long-term unemployed. By the mid-1980s Ireland had a predominantly service-oriented workforce, with agriculture declining to just over 10 percent. This change from agriculture to services and the relentless rise in unemployment have been the major trends in the Irish labor force since 1945. By 1995 the Irish unemployment rate was a dark cloud on an otherwise clear horizon. Ireland, at that time, had the fastest-growing EU economy (5 percent per annum real GDP between 1990 and 1995), but its unemployment rate at 14 percent was the third-highest in the EU. However as the GDP grew by 10.3 percent in 1995 and 7.2 percent in 1996, unemployment dropped to 12.3 percent in 1995 and 11.6 percent in 1996.

BIBLIOGRAPHY

Kennedy, Kieran, Thomas Giblin, and Deirdre McHugh. *The Economic Development of Ireland in the Twentieth Century.* New York/London: Routledge, 1988.

O'Hagan, John, ed. *The Economy of Ireland: Policy and Performance,* 5th ed. Dublin: Irish Management Institute, 1987.

Michael J. Kennedy

Ireland, Northern

Northern Ireland, established under the Government of Ireland Act of 1920, consists of the six Ulster counties of Antrim, Armagh, Down, Fermanagh, Londonderry, and Tyrone. Its 5,238 square miles are approximately one-sixth of the land area of Ireland, and the population of 1,256,561 (1926) was about one-third of the population of the whole island. The principal religious denominations were Roman Catholic (33.5 percent), Presbyterian (31.3 percent), and Church of Ireland (27 percent).

The parliament of Northern Ireland was opened on June 22, 1921. The parliament was prohibited from passing laws that discriminated against or endowed any religion. It could not repeal any act passed at Westminster or pass any act repugnant to the statutes of Affairs of the United Kingdom.

The legislature consisted of two houses, a House of Commons with fifty-two members and a Senate of twenty-six members, twenty-four of whom were elected

Sectarian violence in Northern Ireland. A masked youth holds a brick aloft in front of a truck that was set on fire in the predominantly Catholic Unity Flats district of West Belfast, Northern Ireland. *Illustration courtesy of UPI/Corbis-Bettman.*

by the Commons. The first general election, held on May 24, 1921, was the first in the history of the British Isles to use proportional representation. The election returned forty members of the Ulster Unionist Party; the remaining twelve seats were divided between the Nationalist Party of Northern Ireland, led by Joseph Devlin, and Sinn Fein, the Irish Republican Party, neither of whom initially recognized the new state. The Nationalists entered parliament only in 1924.

The Ulster Unionist Party formed all the governments of Northern Ireland until 1972. The first prime minister was Sir James Craig. The other ministries were Finance, Home Affairs, Labour, Education, Commerce and Agriculture. A Ministry of Health and Local Government was created in 1944. There was a Ministry of Public Security during World War II, and a Ministry of Community Relations was established in 1971. Under the terms of the treaty (Articles 11–16) Northern Ireland could opt out of the Irish Free State, in which case a boundary commission would be established. By the end of 1925 the commission and its report were a dead letter and the arbitrary boundary between the Counties of Ulster and the rest of Ireland, chosen on the basis of the area that would provide a Unionist majority, remained permanently fixed.

From the beginning the Irish Republican Army (IRA) was a threat to Northern Ireland. A second problem for the government was widespread unemployment, which created severe social discontent. To protect itself from the IRA, the state had at its disposal the Civil Authorities (Special Powers) Act (Northern Ireland) 1922, under which the minister for home affairs had unlimited powers of arrest and detention. The act, which was renewable, was made permanent in 1933. Action was also taken to lessen the influence of the Catholic population, which was assumed to be sympathetic to the IRA and the unification of Ireland. Proportional representation was abolished for local government elections in 1922. It was also abolished for central government elections in 1929 and replaced by the direct vote. In local government elections the payment of a property tax was a requisite for the right to vote, and a representative of a business firms had the right to cast a multiple vote (the company vote). Gerrymandering of the constituencies for local government elections also helped to ensure permanent Unionist majorities. The system worked so successfully for the party that Derry City, Armagh District Council, and Fermanagh County Council had Unionist majorities whereas they were all areas with Catholic majorities. Protestant employers were encouraged not to employ Catholics, and local authorities also adopted the policy. Allocation of public housing favored Protestant applicants. While there were Catholics in the Royal Ulster Constabulary (RUC), the auxiliary police force, the Special Constabulary, was wholly Protestant. Many Unionist politicians, most members of the government, and all the prime ministers of Northern Ireland maintained very close contact with the Orange Order, a Protestant Unionist organization, and the majority were in fact members.

Until World War II the economy of Northern Ireland was depressed. The unemployment placed a heavy burden on the Northern exchequer, and the depressed state of the economy was reflected in the lack of social services. The workhouse system was still used in the 1940s. There was a general lack of adequate housing, and around 85 percent of rural dwellings had no running water as late as 1939. World War II was a watershed in the history of Northern Ireland. As Eire was neutral, the ports of Northern Ireland were vital to the British war effort, as were tanks, ships, and bombers that were produced locally. Within a short time unemployment fell from 25 to 5 percent. The Harland and Wolff shipyard underwent a transformation. Employment at the shipyards rose from 7,300 in 1938 to 20,600 in 1945. Total employment in industry rose from 27,000 to 70,000. In addition, some 60,000 people migrated to England. The agricultural sector also reaped the benefits due to increased demand, which led to an increase in the tillage area from 400,000 to 800,000 acres. Between 1939 and 1948 wages nearly doubled, although much of the increase was accounted for by the rise in agricultural wages, which were traditionally very low.

Changes continued after the war. In accordance with the "step by step" policy that sought to ensure that the citizens of Northern Ireland enjoyed parity of services with the remainder of the United Kingdom, welfare services were established at the expense of financial autonomy as the Treasury in London gained more control over the North's finances. The New Industries (Development) Act, 1945, assisted businesses to adjust to postwar conditions. Advances made by Northern Ireland after the war threw into further relief the less prosperous condition of the southern state and was used by Unionists to justify the existence of partition. Antipartition propaganda antagonized Unionists, as did the Republic of Ireland Act, 1948, which led to the Ireland Act, reiterating the position of Northern Ireland within the United Kingdom.

After 1956 there was a renewal of militant republican activity when the IRA attacked the North. Both the Northern and the southern governments reacted by introducing internment, but in fact the IRA received no support among the Catholic population in the North, and called off its campaign in 1962. One year later the traditionalist prime minister, Lord Brookeborough, resigned and was succeeded by Captain Terence O'Neill. O'Neill broke with the Unionist policy of ignoring the Irish Republic. He invited Sean Lemass, prime minister of the republic, to visit him at Stormont, the seat of the Northern Ireland government, in February 1965 and repaid the visit by visiting Dublin later in the year. His actions were severely criticized by extreme loyalists, led by the Rev. Ian Paisley, who viewed with concern a policy of rapprochement with the South, coming so soon after the ecumenism enunciated by the Second Vatican Council (1962–65). As 1966, the year of the fiftieth anniversary of the Dublin Easter Rising of 1916 against the government of Great Britain, approached, traditional Unionists were outraged when O'Neill allowed commemorations to be held in Northern Ireland. One reaction was an antirepublican campaign by the newly revived Ulster Volunteer Force (UVF), a Protestant Unionists paramilitary group. Within a year this was followed by demands for civil rights by a new generation of Catholics.

Ricki Schoen

Northern Ireland Civil Rights Association (NICRA)/Civil Rights Campaign in Northern Ireland

Founded in Belfast in February 1967, the Northern Ireland Civil Rights Association (NICRA)/Civil Rights Campaign in Northern Ireland was a broadly based movement embracing a wide spectrum of political opinion. Its members were concerned with the lack of civil rights in Northern Ireland, and particularly with discrimination in the allocation of public authority housing. The movement was based on the Campaign for Social Justice founded in Dungannon by Patricia and Con McCluskey and was modeled on the National Council for Civil Liberties in Britain, to which it was affiliated. NICRA included among its aims "one man, one vote" in local elections, the removal of gerrymandered electoral boundaries and discriminatory practices within local government authorities, establishment of machinery to investigate complaints against local authorities, allocation of public housing on a points system, repeal of the Civil Authorities (Special Powers) Act, and disbandment of the B-Specials (Special Constabulary). The NICRA's first major public involvement was on August 24, 1968, when the movement organized a march from Coalisland to Dungannon protesting anti-Catholic discrimination by the Dungannon authorities. The march attracted over three thousand and received wide media coverage. Another march was called for October 5 in Derry City, one of the most depressed regions within Northern Ireland. The march, banned by Minister for Home Affairs William Craig, was the scene of a violent clash between the marchers and the Royal Ulster Constabulary. Civil rights agitation spread throughout the North, provoking counterdemonstrations from Unionist traditionalists led by Paisley. Both Paisley and the minister for home affairs regarded NICRA as a front for the IRA, the Communist Party, and subversives in general. Police action in Derry triggered three days of rioting. Students protesting in support of the NICRA against events in Derry founded the People's Democracy in Belfast on October 9. The prime minister of Northern Ireland, Terence O'Neill, found his reform efforts strongly opposed within his own party and by the powerful Orange Order. As NICRA gained only minor concessions, the situation in Northern Ireland continued to deteriorate. The British army was called in to maintain order in August 1969, when the Royal Ulster Constabulary and the B-Specials could no longer contain the situation. Caught in a maelstrom of terrorism and reprisal, the NICRA's became less effective.

Ricki Schoen

1969–71

Following an attack on the People's Democracy marchers at Burntollet in January 1969 and the misbehavior of policemen in Derry afterward, the RUC became a discredited force among Catholics. The Cameron Commission later found that some police had been involved in the rioting. Minister for Commerce Brian Faulkner resigned at the idea of a police investigation, and O'Neill, attacked from within and outside his government, called a general election for February 24, 1969. He received only 47 percent of the vote in his own Bannside constituency,

where his principal was opponent Ian Paisley. The Unionists were now split into twenty-seven pro-O'Neill and twelve anti-O'Neill members.

The election also spelled the ruin of the old Nationalist Party of Northern Ireland, whose leader, Eddie McAteer, lost his seat to John Hume, a supporter of the civil rights campaign. Under pressure from the British government, O'Neill announced the introduction of "one man, one vote" for local elections. He was immediately attacked by his own party and resigned on April 28. He was succeeded by Major James Chichester-Clark, who proved unable to prevent clashes between the two communities. After serious rioting in July 1969 in Derry, which became known as the Battle of the Bogside, Labour Home Secretary James Callaghan issued the 1969 Downing Street Declaration on August 19. The declaration promised reforms, including reforms in the RUC. Local government reforms were to continue, an independent housing authority would be established, discrimination against Catholics in public employment would be abolished, and an ombudsman would be appointed. The Hunt Commission recommended that the RUC be disarmed and the Special Constabulary abolished. It was to be replaced by the locally recruited Ulster Defence Regiment and be under British Army control. Toward the end of 1969, the IRA split into two organizations: the more hard-line Provisional IRA (the Provos) and the Official IRA, which was Marxist. As 1969 drew to a close British troops were deployed on the streets of Northern Ireland, a decision that had been taken reluctantly.

While initially welcomed by the Catholic community, the British army soon lost the support of the minority population as searches for militants and arms became identified with hostility toward and harassment of the Catholic areas of Belfast and Derry. Two new political parties, both aimed at the center, appeared during 1970: the Social Democratic and Labour Party (SDLP) and the Alliance Party. The breach in the Unionist Party grew during 1970 and 1971. When Chichester-Clark resigned in March 1971, he was succeeded by Brian Faulkner. As a gesture of goodwill he made David Bleakley, of the Northern Ireland Labour Party (NILP), minister of community relations and brought a Catholic, Gerard B. Newe, into the cabinet in October as a temporary junior minister. It was soon evident, however, that further reforms would have to wait until the IRA had been immobilized.

To achieve that Faulkner introduced internment in August 1971. Initially this policy was used exclusively against the Catholic population. The operation was mishandled: many IRA leaders escaped while some of those arrested were victims of mistaken identity. The operation achieved the opposite of what had been intended. It led to an upsurge of support for the IRA. The level of republican, but also loyalist, violence increased considerably (e.g., a UVF bomb killed fifteen people in a Belfast bar in December 1971).

Ricki Schoen

Bloody Sunday

The incident in Londonderry's Bogside on January 30, 1972, in which thirteen people were shot dead by soldiers of the First Parachute Regiment (a further victim died later in hospital). The shootings occurred on the occasion of an illegal march organized by the Derry Civil Rights Association, and they gave rise to angry controversy. They were denounced by civil rights leaders as "another Sharpeville"; the Republic's prime minister, Jack Lynch, said it was "an unwarranted attack on unarmed civilians"; the British Embassy in Dublin was burned down by demonstrators, and in the Commons, MP Bernadette Devlin struck Home Secretary Maudling. Prime Minister Edward Heath announced an inquiry into the shootings, but a report did not appear until April 1972. By then the Stormont parliament had been suspended, and the affair was regarded as the decisive factor in the decision to impose direct rule from Westminster. Lord Widgery's verdict was complex. He held that there would have been no deaths if there had not been an illegal march, which had created "a highly dangerous situation." But he also said that if the army had not launched a large-scale operation to arrest hooligans, the day might have passed without serious incident. Lord Widgery also found that the soldiers had been fired on first and there was no reason to suppose that they would have opened fire otherwise. The verdict was sharply attacked by Derry Catholics, and Lynch said that it showed the need for an international examination of the activities of the British army. When Tony Blair became prime minister of the United Kingdom, he agreed to review new material that had come to light that challenged the conclusions reached by the Widgery report. Blair set up the "Bloody Sunday Inquiry" in January 1998, headed by Lord Saville, together with a Canadian chief justice and a retired judge from New Zealand.

Ricki Schoen

Search for Agreement, 1972–73

Following Bloody Sunday on January 30, 1972, Faulkner was summoned to London for talks with Edward Heath and members of the Conservative cabinet. He was told by Heath that security would now become the responsibility of the British government and that if violence did not cease, Stormont would be suspended and replaced by direct rule from London. Violence continued, some of it in England when the officers' mess at the headquarters of the sixteenth Parachute Regiment at Aldershot was bombed, killing seven civilians including a Catholic priest on February 22. The Official IRA claimed that it was revenge for Bloody Sunday.

With direct rule the British government was to assume complete responsibility for law and order. Faulkner rejected this and returned to Belfast, where his cabinet supported his stand. Heath nevertheless announced the suspension of Stormont on March 24 and the introduction of direct rule under the Northern Ireland (Temporary Suspension) Act. William Whitelaw became the first secretary of state for Northern Ireland. There were over 21,000 British troops in Northern Ireland by July 1972. That year saw the highest death toll of the troubles, with 323 civilians, 103 soldiers, and 41 security forces personnel killed by paramilitary violence.

In a White Paper published on March 20, 1973, the British government proposed the abolition of Stormont and its replacement by an assembly that would govern Northern Ireland through a Protestant-Catholic power-sharing executive. The same month the Northern Ireland electorate overwhelmingly voted for Northern Ireland to remain part of the United Kingdom; however, the Catholic community boycotted the referendum. Nonetheless, elections to the assembly were held on June 28, and the assembly met on July 31. The seventy-eight members were made up of two main groupings: fifty-two Pro-Assembly and twenty-six Anti-Assembly. Talks were held among those who accepted power sharing—the Faulknerite Unionists, the SDLP, and Alliance—on October 5. The executive was announced on November 22. There were fifty-one members: twenty-three Unionists, nineteen members of the SDLP, and one member of the NILP, and eight Alliance members. Brian Faulkner became the chief executive and Gerry Fitt, of the SDLP, the deputy chief executive. In December the anti-White Paper Unionists (anti-Faulkner), the Democratic Unionist Party, Vanguard, and other loyalists formed the United Ulster Unionist Council (UUUC), also known as the Loyalist Coalition, and held twenty-seven opposition seats in the assembly.

Ricki Schoen

Sunningdale Agreement

An agreement was reached following a tripartite series of talks at Sunningdale, Berkshire, on December 6–9, 1973, between the British and Irish governments and the incoming executive of Northern Ireland. Leaders in the talks were Edward Heath, British prime minister; Liam Cosgrave, Irish prime minister; and Brian Faulkner, leader of the Ulster Unionist Party and chief of the executive scheduled to be installed in January 1974. The Northern Ireland Social Democratic and Labour Party and the Alliance Party were also represented at the talks. The talks, initiated by Heath in an attempt to restore Northern Ireland to normality and clarify relations among Britain, Northern Ireland, and the Republic of Ireland, appeared to reach a wide measure of agreement. The British and Irish governments agreed that there should be no change in the status of Northern Ireland until a majority of the population had expressed support for it. It was also agreed to revive the idea of a Council of Ireland and that there should be cooperation between Northern Ireland and the Irish Republic on matters of law and order. The agreement was signed by the three leaders and a power-sharing executive was to be set up composed of the leaders of the Unionist Party, the SDLP, and the Alliance Party.

Ricki Schoen

1974–Present

The Sunningdale Agreement was a breakthrough as far as relations between the Irish Republic and Northern Ireland were concerned, but on January 5, 1974, when the executive formally took office, the Unionist Party rejected Sunningdale and power sharing. Later that month, on January 23, the Loyalist Coalition withdrew from the assembly. The coalition supported the general strike called by the Ulster Workers' Council on May 14 in an attempt to destroy power sharing. On May 28 the strike brought Northern Ireland to a standstill. The executive collapsed and direct rule was resumed. Faulkner established the Unionist Party of Northern Ireland (UPNI) on June 24, 1974, illustrating how fragmented unionism was at this stage. The Labour government published a new White Paper on the North on July 4, announcing another attempt to restore order. This was to be a constitutional convention, to be elected on May 1, 1975. The result of the elections was a victory for the Loyalist Coalition, which secured 47 of the 78 seats: the 47 seats were divided between the Official Unionists (19), the DUP (12), Vanguard (14), and Other Loyalists (2). Those supporting power-sharing had 31 seats between them: SDLP (17) Alliance (8), UPNI (5) and NILP (1). The convention met under the chairmanship of the lord chief justice of Northern Ireland, Sir Robert Lowry. It was to decide which mode of government would be most acceptable throughout the whole community and to produce a report by November 1975. After five previous unsuccessful

attempts, the final report produced by the convention again contained the aspirations of the majority UUUC and so clearly would not be widely acceptable to everyone in Northern Ireland. The UUUC proposed the establishment of a majoritarian executive and rejected any kind of power-sharing arrangement. It also accused the SDLP of wanting a united Ireland and of not being able to be loyal to any form of Northern Ireland government. The British government eventually admitted defeat regarding the constitutional convention and dissolved it in March 1976.

Ulsterization, criminalization, and normalization were all part of a new British government strategy regarding its governance of Northern Ireland introduced in March 1976. This approach was intended to return responsibilities concerning security issues to Northern Ireland security forces and to allow the British government to illustrate how it was a fair and legitimate player in Northern Ireland affairs. Under the policy of "ulsterization," paramilitary prisoners have had their "special" status removed and were now treated as ordinary criminals. IRA prisoners protested against this policy shift by first refusing to wear prison uniforms, and later by engaging in so-called "dirty protests" (prison furniture was destroyed and toilet facilities were not used). These demonstrations eventually culminated in the hunger strikes of the early 1980s. In August the Women's Peace Movement (they later changed their name to Peace People) was initiated by a huge rally in Belfast after the death of three children by a runaway car whose driver had been shot dead by security forces. One of the cofounders of the movement was Mairead Corrigan, the aunt of the dead children, who, together with another cofounder, Betty Williams, received the Nobel Peace Prize in 1976. The group organized several huge demonstrations in London, Dublin, and Belfast in support of its aim to create a fair and just society by peaceful means. Toward the end of 1976 the Fair Employment Act came into effect, making it illegal to refuse to employ someone because of religious or political affiliation.

In May 1977 the United Ulster Action Committee attempted to stage a strike to restore majority rule to Northern Ireland. While it had the support of Paisley and the DUP, the strike was not supported by the UUP, which saw direct rule as a step toward further integration into the United Kingdom.

In February 1978 the IRA committed one of its most deadly attacks in which twelve people where killed and twenty-three injured by a bomb in a hotel in County Down. In March 1979, after a general election had been called in Britain, the Tory spokesman on Northern Ireland, Airey Neave, was killed by a car bomb planted by the Irish National Liberation Army (INLA). Then the

IRA struck again with even more deadly consequences by not only killing Lord Mountbatten but also murdering eighteen British soldiers in separate places on the same day in August. These acts only helped Margaret Thatcher, who by May 1979 had become the new British prime minister, adopt the opinion that the minimalist approach to governing Northern Ireland of her predecessor was not effective and that devolution would not work in Northern Ireland.

The year 1979 not only saw a general election in the United Kingdom but also the first direct elections to the European Parliament. John Hume, John Taylor, and Paisley were elected as the three members of the European Parliament allocated to Northern Ireland. In November Hume also took over as leader of the SDLP after Gerry Fitt resigned over the contents of the White Paper. While Fitt had been willing to accept the proposals contained in the document, Hume and the SDLP were not happy that no provision was made to discuss a possible Irish dimension in the future administration of Northern Ireland. The SDLP were eventually granted their wish but that resulted in the UUP boycotting any discussions relating to the White Paper.

Although the Stormont Constitutional Conference was launched in January 1980, it was suspended indefinitely three months later and eventually deemed a failure in November. Nonetheless, Thatcher's belief that something had to be done to deal with the situation in Northern Ireland eventually led her to meet with Charles Haughey, then the prime minister of Ireland, in Dublin at the end of 1980.

The biggest event of 1981 was the death of Bobby Sands after being on hunger strike for 66 days at the Maze prison in Northern Ireland. While on hunger strike he had been elected as a Sinn Fein MP in a by-election in the Fermanagh/South Tyrone constituency. Altogether ten republican prisoners, all demanding the restoration of political prisoner status for paramilitary inmates, died while on hunger strike. The strikes were eventually called off in October 1981 when paramilitary inmates were no longer required to wear prison uniforms. While the Thatcher government tried to portray the end of the hunger strikes as a political victory, the fact that support for Sinn Fein had significantly grown during this period was a clear indication that the British government was not winning the propaganda war. Two more hunger strikers had been elected to political office, this time as Sinn Fein members of the Irish parliament in the Irish general election held in 1981, and Sands's election agent won Sands's seat after his death.

This growing electoral support for Sinn Fein was not only of concern to the British government but also to the newly elected Irish government, led by Garret FitzGerald of the moderate Fine Gael party. Thatcher and FitzGerald held a summit meeting in November 1981 and established the Anglo-Irish Inter-governmental Council to formalize existing contacts between the two governments and to perhaps jointly address the shift in nationalist public opinion. These initial efforts did not amount to much, as the following year saw a deterioration of Anglo-Irish relations because of the Falklands War between Great Britain and Argentina and also because of yet another change in government in Ireland, which brought back Haughey as prime minister. Nonetheless, efforts to resolve the situation in Northern Ireland continued in 1982 as is illustrated by the fact that a power-sharing initiative was set up in April 1982. This attempt, yet again, was to be a failure. After elections had been held, this new assembly came into being in November, but it was boycotted by both the SDLP and Sinn Fein. Without the participation of both of these parties it was clear from the outset that the assembly did not have the necessary cross-community support to be effective. It lasted until 1986, when its term ended but not before Unionist members had used it as a venue to criticize and denounce the Anglo-Irish Agreement of 1985. Before the end of 1982, there was another paramilitary atrocity when an INLA bomb killed seventeen people at a pub in County Derry. In 1983 in another British general election, Sinn Fein gained its first seat in the British Parliament. The SDLP also won one seat, while the remaining fifteen seats were taken by unionist politicians. Building on his general election success, Gerry Adams, the first Sinn Fein MP was elected president of Sinn Fein in November the same year. This was also further evidence that the balance of power within the party had moved to the North.

In a related development, the New Ireland Forum, composed of the three main parties in the Republic (Fianna Fáil, Fine Gael, and Labour) and the SDLP, met for the first time in 1983. They eventually produced a report in 1984 that outlined their proposals for the future of Northern Ireland. The preferred option was a unitary Irish state, and if that was not possible then the alternatives were either a federal arrangement or a power-sharing one where both London and Dublin would have joint authority over Northern Ireland. Unionists had refused to take part in any of the meetings or discussions, although individual unionists did make submissions to the forum. Their overall reaction to the report predictably unfavorable. Even the British government rejected it. Yet the report was evidence that there was a continuing effort within the nationalist community to come up with new ideas that might also engage the unionists in discussions on the future of Northern Ireland. It was seen by many as a necessary exercise in a process that eventually led to the signing of the Anglo-Irish Agreement in 1985. Before that, however, the IRA struck at the heart of the British establishment when they came close to killing Thatcher with a bomb at the party conference hotel in Brighton in October 1984. Thatcher escaped injury but four people were killed and several injured.

The big event of 1985 was the signing of the Anglo-Irish Agreement at Hillsborough in November. In doing so, Thatcher and Garret FitzGerald, the two heads of state, agreed to give Dublin a consultative role in running Northern Ireland. The agreement was heavily criticized by unionists, and in retaliation they forced by-elections when all fifteen Unionist MPs resigned their seats. While they increased their overall share of the vote in January 1986, they lost a seat to the SDLP. Throughout 1986 there was much opposition to the agreement by unionist politicians and loyalist paramilitaries, but the British government remained committed to it. The police made a major breakthrough against the IRA when a huge consignment of weapons destined for the North was intercepted. It emerged only later that this was the fourth such shipment, which meant that by late 1986 the IRA had assembled a formidable arsenal with which to wage their war. They used some of this arsenal when they planted the bomb at Enniskillen on Remembrance Day in 1987, which killed eleven people and wounded many.

The initial meetings that took place between Gerry Adams and John Hume in 1988 formed the basis of what was to grow into the peace process and eventually deliver the Good Friday Agreement of 1998. While the cornerstone of this process was being laid, paramilitary activity continued to claim lives. In March the SAS shot dead three unarmed members of the IRA in Gibraltar. When they were being laid to rest in Belfast, mourners were attacked by Michael Stone, a loyalist gunman, who killed three of them and wounded several others. Only days later, two British soldiers inadvertently drove into the funeral cortege of the victims of the cemetery attack. They became victims themselves as some in the crowd turned into an angry mob and dragged them away and murdered them. In June six soldiers were killed and a further eight soldiers died in August when their bus drove over a land mine. Partially as a response to this violence, the British government introduced a broadcasting ban in October 1988 against Sinn Fein, the IRA and INLA, the UDA, and the Unionist Volunteer Force/Ulster Freedom Fighters. The violence continued in 1989, as did the broad-

casting ban. Nonetheless, the new Northern Ireland secretary of state, Peter Brooke, said in November that direct talks with Sinn Fein could possibly take place but not without the IRA declaring a cease-fire.

Brooke took the initiative by setting up meetings throughout 1990 with unionists and nationalists to discuss the way forward. That year also saw the Thatcher era come to an end when she stepped down as prime minister in November, opening the way for John Major to take over. In December the IRA called its first Christmas cease-fire in fifteen years. In summer 1991 the political parties of Northern Ireland, excluding Sinn Fein, met at Stormont to discuss the future of the region. Also at this time, a government White Paper on defense proposed to merge the much criticized (on the nationalist side at least) Ulster Defence Regiment with the Royal Irish Rangers. This eventually happened in July 1992 when the new Royal Irish Regiment was established. Violence reached another peak toward the end of the year, prompting the deployment of more British troops on the streets of Northern Ireland.

In March 1993 an IRA bomb in Warrington, England, killed two boys. This event added additional urgency to the continuing efforts to find a solution to the Northern Ireland conflict. It resulted in the setting up of Peace Initiative '93 and also in renewed, increased contacts between Adams and Hume. Hume suffered much criticism from all sides because of his contacts with Adams, but he remained committed and the two politicians announced considerable progress by September. Before that, Mary Robinson, the President of Ireland, caused serious commotion when she paid an unofficial visit to West Belfast in June 1993, where she ended up meeting Gerry Adams and shaking his hand. However, in October there appeared to be another serious setback when an IRA bomb killed ten people including the bomber on Shankill Road in Belfast. All Northern Ireland waited in fear for the predictable retaliation by the loyalist paramilitaries, which duly came a week later. Loyalist gunmen opened fire at a bar in County Derry and killed seven people while also wounding several others.

Despite these activities, or perhaps because of them, the Irish and British governments came together in December 1993 to launch the Downing Street Declaration. It reiterated much of what was contained in the AIA, but also clearly stated that a united Ireland could come about only if the majority of the people of Northern Ireland gave their consent to it. It also opened the way for political parties, including Sinn Fein, that had links to paramilitary organizations to join the talks if the paramilitaries gave up the violence. Political parties excluded from the talks spent much of the beginning of 1994 seeking to clarify certain aspects of the declaration. In February 1994 Adams made his first highly publicized visit to the United States after finally being granted a visa by the Clinton administration, and in August the IRA called a complete halt to its military operations. While much time was lost over the definition of this cease-fire, it was followed two months later by another cease-fire, this time from the Combined Loyalist Military Command (CLMC).

Before the end of that year, there were a number of changes on the Irish political scene that also had an impact on Northern Ireland. Albert Reynolds, credited as being instrumental in bringing Sinn Fein in from the political cold, was replaced by Bertie Ahern as the leader of Fianna Fáil, while John Bruton, head of Fine Gael, became leader of a coalition government made up of Fine Gael, Labour, and the Democratic Left (the Rainbow Coalition) in December 1994. That same month, Sinn Fein officially met British civil servants for the first time in more than two decades.

In response to the paramilitary cease-fires, daytime foot patrols by British soldiers on the streets of Northern Ireland were reduced in January 1995. Adams made his second highly publicized visit to the United States as part of the annual St. Patrick's Day celebrations hosted by the White House. This time, members of the loyalist Ulster Democratic Party (UDP) were also present. In addition, Martin McGuinness, Sinn Fein's chief negotiator, met Michael Ancram, a minister with the Northern Ireland Office, in the first half of 1995. Despite all this evidence that progress was being made, the annual Orange Order marching season illustrated how fragile the whole process still was. There were serious confrontations and clashes involving the RUC and both nationalists and unionists throughout July and August over marching routes. Having made a stand in support of the Orange march at Portadown and Drumcree in July, David Trimble was elected as the new leader of the Ulster Unionist Party (UUP) in September after James Molyneaux resigned. The peace talks continued throughout 1995 but seemed to become stuck on the issue of decommissioning weapons. While the IRA declared that it would certainly not give up any arms before there was a settlement, the Unionists insisted that without decommissioning there could be no settlement. To move beyond this gridlock, the two governments set up a separate international body to deal with the issue of decommissioning. In December 1995 President Clinton made a historic visit to Northern Ireland and to the Irish Republic, illustrating his administration's commitment to the Irish peace process.

Toward the end of January 1996 the international body, now known as the Mitchell Commission (named after former U.S. Senator George Mitchell, the head of the international body), produced a report that outlined a series of six principles to be adopted by all involved in the talks. The commission also launched a twin-track process that allowed for negotiations to occur at the same time as the decommissioning. A serious setback for the peace process occurred on February 9, 1996, when the IRA ended its cease-fire by setting off a large bomb at Canary Wharf in London, killing two people and causing massive damage. Despite this, the two governments appeared as determined as ever to keep the process moving forward and announced that elections to the Northern Ireland Forum would be held that May, with substantive negotiations beginning in June. This occurred under the chairmanship of Mitchell and lasted until July, when a procedure for the talks had been agreed on but no progress had been made on decommissioning. That summer saw a tense standoff develop between the security forces and the Orange Order marchers in Portadown/Drumcree. It was eventually resolved, but the incident brought about a severe deterioration in cross-community relations.

The 1997 parliamentary election in Britain produced a Labour government with an overwhelming majority in parliament. It also saw Adams returned in his West Belfast seat, together with Martin McGuinness for Mid-Ulster. Tony Blair appointed Mo Mowlam as his new secretary of state for Northern Ireland. Shortly after being elected, Blair visited Northern Ireland and met with party leaders. Political contacts with Sinn Fein were broken off shortly afterward because the IRA admitted to killing two RUC officers. Mowlam met Gerry Adams and later announced that Sinn Fein would be admitted to the peace talks. While Sinn Fein signed up to the Mitchell principles in September, the IRA rejected them shortly afterward. Nonetheless, Sinn Fein joined the talks by mid-September, but all-party talks did not truly begin until October 7, when the Unionists decided to return. Adams and Blair met at Stormont that same month then again at Downing Street in December since 1921, when the prime minister became the first British head of state to meet a Sinn Fein delegation.

The talks continued right up to the April 1998 deadline, although not without setbacks, expulsions, and readmissions of different participants. April 10 was the day when the two governments, together with most of the parties of Northern Ireland, signed the historic Good Friday Agreement. It outlined the establishment of a new Northern Ireland Assembly, to be elected later the same year, a North-South body, giving the Irish Republic a more substantial role in Northern Ireland's affairs, and a Council of the Isles, in which the two governments continued to work together. The agreement also put forward an amendment to the Irish constitution to remove its territorial claim over Northern Ireland, as well as the abolition of the 1920 Government of Ireland Act, which gives the United Kingdom supreme authority over that part of the island. The agreement was put before the people of the Republic and of Northern Ireland in a referendum held simultaneously in both jurisdictions on May 22, 1998. It was accepted by an overwhelming majority on both sides (94 percent voted in favor in the Republic, 71 percent in the North).

The approval of the agreement by both parts of the island led to the June 25 election for the Northern Ireland Assembly. The Ulster Unionists won twenty-eight seats, the SDLP twenty-four seats, the DUP twenty seats, Sinn Fein eighteen, and six small parties a total of eighteen seats. David Trimble, head of the Ulster Unionists, was elected first minister, and Seamus Mallon of the SDLP became deputy first minister. But the actual establishment of the first government of the new Northern Ireland was delayed until December 1999. A car bomb in the center of Omagh killed twenty-eight on August 15, 1998. A splinter group, the "Real IRA," claimed responsibility. However, the IRA itself remained committed to the ceasefire, and with pressure from Sinn Fein, the Real IRA announced a cease-fire on August 18 and the INLA on August 22. Only the Continuity IRA remained aloof.

Despite the repudiation of violence by the IRA, Trimble, under great pressure from the Unionists, refused to form a government with Sinn Fein members until the IRA began decomissioning its weapons. Senator Mitchell returned to Northern Ireland and, after difficult negotiations, an agreement was announced on November 16, 1999, by Trimble and Adams. The Northern Ireland Assembly would convene and decommissioning of weapons would then begin. The United Kingdom transferred local authority to the Northern Ireland Assembly, and a government of ten ministers was formed on December 2. The IRA then began talks with an International Decommissioning Body concerning the mechanics of handing over arms.

BIBLIOGRAPHY

Arthur, Paul. *Northern Ireland since 1968,* 2d ed. Oxford: Blackwell, 1996.

Aughey, Arthur, and Duncan Morrow, eds. *Northern Ireland Politics.* London: Longman, 1996.

Bew, Paul. *Northern Ireland, 1921–1996: Political Forces and Social Classes.* London: Serif, 1996.

Farrell, Michael. *Northern Ireland the Orange State,* 2d ed. London: Pluto Press, 1980.

Fay, Marie-Therese. *Northern Ireland's Troubles: The Human Costs.* Sterling, Va.: Pluto Press, 1999.

Harkness, D. W. *Northern Ireland since 1920.* Dublin: Helicon, 1983.

McAllister, Ian. *The Northern Ireland Social Democratic and Labour Party: Political Opposition in a Divided Society.* London: Macmillan, 1977.

O'Malley, Padraig. *Northern Ireland, 1983–1996: For Every Step Forward.* Boston: John W. McCormack Institute of Public Affairs, 1996.

Walsh, Pat. *From Civil Rights to National War: Northern Ireland Catholic Politics 1964–1974.* Belfast: Athol Books, 1989.

Wichert, Sabine. *Northern Ireland since 1945.* New York: Longman, 1991.

Ricki Schoen

Political Parties

The main parties in Northern Ireland are divided into unionist (wishing to retain the union with Britain) and nationalist (wishing to create a single Irish state on the island). The unionists grew out of those who opposed the notion of home rule in the previous century and eventually had to make do with the creation of Northern Ireland. The largest unionist party is the Official or Ulster Unionist Party (OUP). From the creation of Northern Ireland in 1921 to the dissolution of Stormont in 1972, the OUP formed all the governments of Northern Ireland. The smaller unionist party, the Democratic Unionist Party (DUP), was set up in 1971 by the Rev. Ian Paisley and Desmond Boal. It is more populist and much more antinationalist (especially anti-Catholic) than the OUP and has a smaller electoral support base. In the past both the OUP and the DUP have opposed any involvement in Northern Ireland's affairs by the Irish government and have refused to enter into arrangements where they might have to share power with nonunionist parties. The OUP, under the leadership of David Trimble, has softened its stance on both these issues to some extent. This is most powerfully illustrated by the OUP's signing of the 1998 Good Friday Agreement, together with the Social Democratic Labour Party and Sinn Fein from the nationalist side. While the leadership of the OUP changed from James Molyneaux to David Trimble in 1995, Paisley has led the DUP since it was founded. Since the mid-1990s two more unionist political parties have grown in prominence and have gained a noticeable support base in their community—the Ulster Democratic Party (UDP) and the Progressive Unionist Party (PUP). They both have links to loyalist paramilitary groups, the UDP to the Ulster Defense Association and the PUP to the Ulster Volunteer Force/Ulster Freedom Fighters. While they both remain steadfastly committed to retaining and strengthening the union with Britain, they have also been more willing to enter into dialogue with nationalist politicians. Their substantial contribution to bringing about the 1994 loyalist cease-fire and the Good Friday Agreement did not go unnoticed within their community and on a wider scale. A further unionist party is the UK Unionist Party. Under the leadership of Bob McCartney, it argues for a deeper integration of Northern Ireland into the United Kingdom. It has only a small support base but has outspokenly opposed any Dublin involvement in Northern Ireland and supported the "Northern Ireland" campaign, together with the DUP, against the Good Friday Agreement referendum in May 1998.

On the nationalist side the two main parties are the Social Democratic and Labour Party (SDLP) and Sinn Fein. The SDLP, led by John Hume, commands the majority support within the nationalist community, whereas Sinn Fein has the backing of a minority. Nevertheless, Sinn Fein has done well in recent general and local elections, with Gerry Adams, leader of the party, regaining his West Belfast seat in 1997. Both the SDLP and Sinn Fein hope to create a single Irish state, and while the SDLP has long argued that this will come about only if a majority within Northern Ireland want it, only recently has Sinn Fein also come around to this idea. Sinn Fein has generally been regarded as the political arm of the Irish Republican Army (IRA), which kept it out of the constitutional talks until the IRA cease-fire of August 1994.

The other two parties are the Alliance Party and the Northern Ireland Women's Coalition. The former is led by Lord Alderdice, the latter by Monica McWilliams. Both have a relatively small support base but cut across community divisions. The Alliance Party has promoted itself as the only party that tries to overcome the divide between the unionist and nationalist communities. It was launched in 1970 and its support base has generally been between 10 and 15 percent, but it failed to get a single MP in the 1997 general election. The Northern Ireland Women's Coalition came into being just prior to the 1996 Irish Forum elections, where it campaigned on the issues of equality, inclusion, and respect for human rights. Its stated goal is to promote peace and justice in Northern Ireland. Although its support base is smaller than that of the Alliance Party, the Women's Coalition has added a new dimension to the male-dominated political scene in Northern Ireland.

Alliance Party.   One of Northern Ireland's main parties, the Alliance Party gives priority to attracting support from both sides of the community. The party was launched in April 1970 and, although its initial leadership was largely previously unknown in politics, it quickly gained support from a section of Unionists who had backed Prime Minister Terence O'Neill. Although its main base, to start with, appeared to be middle class, it also absorbed many who had formerly backed the Northern Ireland Labour Party. In its first electoral test, the May 1973 district council elections, it received 13.6 percent of the vote. This should have secured it more than seventy seats under the newly introduced proportional representation system, but it got 63. In the hard-fought Assembly election the next month, it secured 9.2 percent of the vote and eight seats. In the 1975 Convention elections its share of the vote rose to 9.8 percent, and it again got eight seats. In the Convention campaign it called for a strong legislative assembly. Its main policy contribution in the Convention was to outline a scheme for government by committees, elected in proportion to the strength of parties in the Assembly. In the district council elections in 1977 it improved its poll to 14.4 percent and secured seventy seats. In the 1979 European election, its candidate was Napier, and its share of first preferences was 6.8 percent. In the 1980 Constitutional Conference it continued to press the case for partnership. But this did not bring any dividends in the 1981 council elections, in which it suffered from the polarization produced by the H-Block hunger strike. Its 9 percent vote was more than 5 percent down from the previous council contests. In 1982 it emerged as the party to show the most enthusiasm for the "rolling devolution" initiative. However, its vote in the October Assembly election stayed at 9 percent but proportional representation worked appreciably to its advantage, so that it took Assembly seats for twice as many as Provisional Sinn Fein, which had 10 percent of the vote.

When the Alliance Party showed itself to be largely supportive of the Anglo-Irish Agreement in 1985, it was in danger of losing the backing of the Protestant community. This drop in support was reflected in by-elections in January 1986. In 1987 there was a change at the top when John Alderdice defeated Seamus Close to become the new party leader. But Alliance continued to have poor election results, and when the Conservative Party established itself in Northern Ireland it took away some of the support Alliance had been getting from the middle ground. In 1992 the party again failed to secure a seat at Westminster, and got only 8.7 percent of the vote in Northern Ireland. Not much changed in the fortunes of the Alliance Party in the 1997 general elections when they were again left without an MP.

Provisional Sinn Fein/Provisionals.   One of two groups that emerged from Sinn Fein's annual conference in 1970. The Provisionals, fundamentalist in outlook, sought the Republic of 1916 and an all-Ireland parliament for a united Ireland. The president of Provisional Sinn Fein was Ruairi O Bradaigh, who continued to argue for the nonrecognition of the parliaments in Dublin and Belfast. The other main aim of this breakaway group was British withdrawal from Northern Ireland. The Provisionals published their own newspaper, *An Phoblacht*. In 1975 several top members of the northern section of the Provisionals took part in talks with the British government held during the Irish Republican Army (IRA) cease-fire. These talks did not appear to bring about any significant changes and drew much criticism from other politicians in Northern Ireland. Later that year the IRA ended its cease-fire and official contact came to an end.

For many years the relationship between the northern and southern sections of the Provisionals was uneasy. By 1987 the new leadership of the Provisionals were reevaluating the existing situation, and the party spent the next year trying to establish a pan-nationalist front by meeting with the SDLP. These meetings are considered a necessary precursor to the eventual peace process that culminated in the Good Friday Agreement of April 1998. In the 1992 Westminster elections Sinn Fein suffered a considerable setback when Adams lost his West Belfast seat to the SDLP's Joe Hendron.

The fortunes of the party improved again in council elections in 1993, when their vote rose to 12.4 percent. When the IRA called a cease-fire the following year, Sinn Fein demanded a place at the negotiating table but it was denied this until 1997, after the IRA cease-fire had been broken and resumed. That same year saw a significant increase of the nationalist vote going to Sinn Fein and Adams regained his West Belfast seat. When the Sinn Fein negotiating team was eventually allowed into multiparty talks, it played an important role leading to the Good Friday Agreement.

SEE ALSO Adams, Gerry; Sinn Fein

Social Democratic and Labour Party (SDLP). Political party founded in Northern Ireland in August 1970 by members of the old Nationalist Party of Northern Ireland, the Northern Ireland Labour Party, the Republican Labour Party, the National Democratic Party, and civil rights activists. The Social Democratic and Labour Party (SDLP) led the parliamentary opposition at Stormont, pressing the Ulster Unionist Party, which held a monopoly on government, for reform and concessions to the civil rights movement. Dissatisfaction with the Unionists culminated in the party's withdrawal from parliament in July

1971. A month later Prime Minister Brian Faulkner introduced internment in an attempt to destroy the Provisional Irish Republican Army. This move further alienated the Catholic minority population and led to an escalation of violence. The situation in Northern Ireland continued to deteriorate and Britain imposed direct rule in March 1972.

With Unionist government at an end the SDLP now called for cooperation with Northern Ireland. The party won 19 seats in the election of March 20, 1973, which was held to form an Assembly of Northern Ireland with a power-sharing Executive. Talks were held with the Faulknerite Unionists and the Alliance Party on October 5, with a view to forming a coalition, and it was agreed that the SDLP would hold four posts in the Executive. The party was also represented at the talks that led to the Sunningdale Agreement in December 1973. It suffered a considerable blow when the Executive collapsed in 1974 because Unionist opposition to the agreement brought down the power-sharing venture.

When direct rule was reinstated, the SDLP was increasingly frustrated with what it saw as the British government's unwillingness to deal with unionist intransigence to reach an accommodation with nationalists. The SDLP called for all parties to the conflict to negotiate a settlement. In 1979 the party's deputy leader, John Hume, secured almost a quarter of the votes when he won a seat in the first European Parliament. Later that year Hume took over as party leader after Gerry Fitt resigned.

While the SDLP continued to capture the majority vote in the nationalist community in the early 1980s, it felt the increasing popularity of Sinn Fein, and 1984 came to be a year that was full of uncertainty for the party. It had not been prepared for the British government's strong opposition to the proposals put forward by the New Ireland Forum in which it had been heavily involved. The situation improved again in 1985 with the signing of the Anglo-Irish Agreement that the SDLP presented as the first step towards reconciliation between nationalists and unionists. Although unionists were vehemently opposed to this agreement, the two governments continued to support it, and the SDLP's electoral showing in subsequent elections improved. In 1992 the SDLP's Joe Hendron unseated Gerry Adams in West Belfast—a major coup for the party.

During this time the party leader continued meeting with Adams to find ways to bring the two communities closer to a settlement. The Downing Street Declaration of December 1993 is believed by many to be based to a large extent on the Hume-Adams document that was the result of the meetings between the two leaders. The

SDLP's electoral rivalry with Sinn Fein for the nationalist vote continued during this period and it suffered a setback in the 1997 general elections when Adams regained his West Belfast seat from Hendron. During this time the SDLP continued its involvement in the peace process and was a significant player in the multiparty talks that culminated in the Good Friday Agreement in 1998.

SEE ALSO Fitt, Gerry; Hume, John; Devlin, Paddy

Ulster Unionist Party (UUP). The Ulster Unionists were the strongest element in the general unionist movement as of 1886. Led by E. J. Saunderson, they formed the Ulster Unionist Council in 1905 as a central body through which to fight Irish home rule. Following Saunderson's death in 1906, the Ulster Unionists were led by an Englishman, Walter Long, until 1910, and from then until 1921 by Sir Edward Carson. Carson was succeeded by Sir James Craig, who became the first prime minister of Northern Ireland in 1921. The Ulster Unionist Party formed all the governments of Northern Ireland until the introduction of direct rule by Britain in March 1972.

The UUP had strong contacts with the Orange Order, of which all Unionist leaders were prominent members. The Unionist Party remained united until the late 1960s, when under the premiership of Terence O'Neill, the rise of the Northern Ireland Civil Rights Association and the demand by the minority Catholic population for full civil rights placed the party under considerable strain. In the early 1970s other forms of Unionism appeared in the shape of the Democratic Unionist Party and the Vanguard movement.

The United Unionist Council, a coalition of traditionalists, was set up in 1974 to restore Unionist unity. It included the Unionist Party as a constituent but no longer dominant element. It brought about the collapse of the power-sharing executive set up under the Sunningdale Agreement, but by 1977 had itself broken up. The UUP seemed to suffer from this breakup more than the DUP, to which it appeared to be losing ground as the 1970s drew to a close.

As unionism broke into smaller parts, the importance and influence of the Orange Order on the UUP declined over time. In the 1979 European Parliament elections the UUP fielded two candidates, of whom only John Taylor was successful. The party had campaigned on a renegotiation of the Treaty underpinning the European Community, rather than outright opposition to it which was the stance of the DUP.

When Margaret Thatcher became British prime minister in 1979, UUP leaders thought they had a natural ally, but they were soon disappointed. They were especially opposed to the Dublin-London contacts that took place in 1980, which were to become the foundations on which the Anglo-Irish Agreement (AIA) was signed by the two heads of state five years later. The UUP had been losing electorally to the DUP for a number of years, but in 1983 they had their best showing at the polls since direct rule was imposed in 1972. Despite their rivalry, the two parties came together over their joint opposition to the AIA, agreeing to resign their seats in Parliament in protest and thereby forced by-elections.

By 1988 the party had been forced into rethinking its position over the AIA when it realized that the British government remained committed to the agreement after the Tories were reelected in the 1987 British general election. That same year the party won back the seat in the European Parliament elections that it had lost to Seamus Mallon in 1984. In 1991 the UUP entered the interparty talks on the understanding that the AIA would possibly be renegotiated or even removed completely. In 1992 the party even took part in talks set in Dublin, and it emerged later that year that it had tabled proposals that included a place for the SDLP in any future Northern Ireland assembly, as well as an inter-Irish relations committee. Nonetheless, as long as the Conservatives remained in power, this gave the UUP considerable power over the direction of government policy regarding Northern Ireland. Thus there was little incentive for the UUP to accept major changes over the governing of Northern Ireland. With the leadership change within the UUP to David Trimble in 1995 and the victory of the Labour Party in Britain in the 1997 general election, the situation was dramatically transformed. The peace process received a major boost as Tony Blair, the new prime minister, put the search for a settlement in Northern Ireland at the top of Labour's agenda. This forced the UUP to take part in the multiparty talks and it played its part, if perhaps reluctantly at first, in bringing about the 1998 Good Friday Agreement.

SEE ALSO Trimble, David

Irish Republican Army (IRA)/Provos. The main republican paramilitary group, which goes back some eighty years. The Irish Republican Army (IRA)/Provos was formed to fight for Irish unity and has historic links with Sinn Fein. Its activities were sporadic from the time Northern Ireland was created until the civil rights marches of the late 1960s, at which time became a significant organization. In 1969 a major split in the organization produced the Official IRA and the Provos. This split occurred in Sinn Fein at the same time. The Provos became a self-styled defense force of the besieged Catholic communities in Northern Ireland. The Official IRA followed a much more passive, socialist path, and although it still exists in some form, the term "IRA" nowadays refers to the Provos. When the Provos first took to the streets in 1969, they were a small organization that was not heavily armed. With the deteriorating situation in Northern Ireland, they soon attracted new members and acquired weapons from the Irish Republic as well as from Britain and continental Europe.

This increase in strength was reflected in the noticeable rise in violence between 1969 and 1970. In the aftermath of Bloody Sunday in January 1972, the Provos again saw their ranks grow dramatically with a new wave of recruits. This was also the beginning of a violent period in Northern Ireland. By 1974 the violence had dropped off again and in 1975 the Provos called a cease-fire, but it became more fragile during the year, with the Provos claiming responsibility for an increasing number of attacks. Nonetheless, by 1977 there were indications that the security forces were having an effect on the Provos and that their campaign was losing some of its vigor. The 1980s saw even more changes in their campaign and the Provos now had to deal with what became known as the "supergrass" informer. The political side of the republican campaign was gaining strength during this time, particularly with the increasing profile of Gerry Adams and also in the aftermath of the 1981 hunger strikes at the Maze, during which Bobby Sands was elected to the British Parliament. In 1984 the Provos suffered a major setback when a shipment of arms and ammunition destined for them was intercepted off the Kerry coast by the security forces. This did not deter the Provos from attempting to kill Prime Minister Thatcher while she was attending her party's annual conference in Brighton that same year.

During the following two years the Provos again augmented their weapons supply, this time through several shipments from Libya. The security forces were unaware of this until the ship *Eksund* was discovered in October 1987. Given the size of the arms shipment, the security forces concluded that the arms stockpile of the IRA had increased dramatically during the previous two years. This discovery was an incentive to the security forces to step up their efforts to discover other stored arms and ammunition. This increased surveillance put considerable pressure on the Provos. Then came the Enniskillen Remembrance Day bombing in 1987, which cost the IRA dearly in terms of support at home and abroad. Nonetheless, the IRA continued its campaign.

In 1993 the IRA reiterated that it would continue with its armed struggle as long as Ireland remained partitioned. But that same year, it expressed its support for the Hume-Adams peace process. While a cease-fire did not seem to be imminent, the Provos declared one a year later in August 1994. It lasted until February 1996, when the IRA set off a bomb in London's Canary Wharf that killed two and caused vast amounts of damage. It was considered a setback for the peace process but did not derail it, and by July 1997 the IRA reinstated the cease-fire and has maintained it. The cease-fire renewal in 1997 allowed Sinn Fein to participate in the multiparty talks that eventually led to the signing of the Good Friday Agreement. While this has been seen as a new beginning for the politics of Northern Ireland, the IRA is still considered by many to be a threat, especially while it retains its arsenal of weapons and ammunition. In its 1998 Easter message the IRA supported the efforts of Gerry Adams and Sinn Fein, but it also stated that the time had not yet come for the IRA to consider decommissioning its arms.

SEE ALSO Adams, Gerry

Irish National Liberation Army (INLA). Left-wing splinter of the Official Irish Republican Army formed in 1975, before which it had been known as the People's Liberation Army (1974). The Irish National Liberation Army (INLA) was involved in the feud between the Official IRA and the Irish Republican Socialist Party. The INLA claimed to have carried out the assassination of the British Conservative shadow secretary of state for Northern Ireland, Airey Neave, on March 30, 1979. Although the IRA has at times referred to members of the INLA as "wild men," the two paramilitary groups joined forces during the hunger strikes of 1981 in the Maze. Three of its members were in the group of ten republican prisoners who died. Its appearance in 1975 was in part due to its opposition to the cease-fire called by the IRA at the time. When the IRA called another cease-fire in 1994, the INLA unofficially cooperated. Since the breakdown of the IRA cease-fire in 1996 and its subsequent resumption in July 1997, the INLA has remained outside the peace process. It claimed responsibility for the killing of the Ulster Volunteer Force inmate in the Maze in December 1997. This killing sparked off a series of murders, particularly of Catholic taxi drivers, in Northern Ireland in the first two months of 1998. Throughout its existence the INLA has been marked by internal feuding in which several INLA members were killed by their "colleagues."

Continuity IRA (CIRA). This republican paramilitary group was a recent a splinter from the Provisional

Irish Republican Army. The Continuity IRA (CIRA) was opposed to any arrangement that fell short of a united Ireland and thus opposed the Good Friday Agreement. It did not call a cease-fire. In 1996 it claimed responsibility for placing a bomb at a hotel in Enniskillen, County Fermanagh. It is also believed to be responsible for bombs in Portadown and Moira that exploded in early 1998. CIRA is considered to be the paramilitary arm of Republican Sinn Fein, which broke away from the main Sinn Fein party in 1986. Republican Sinn Fein has denied this link.

Orange Order. The Orange Order is the largest organization of Protestants in Northern Ireland and also has members who live in the Irish Republic. King William III (of Orange) and his successful wars against the Catholics toward the end of the seventeenth century form the underpinning of the organization and its character. The Order annually celebrates Protestant King William's victory over the Catholic King James at the Battle of the Boyne in 1690 by marching through the streets in several locations in Northern Ireland on or around July 12. The Order was formed in 1795 in County Armagh after clashes between Catholics and Protestants. Its main aim is to defend and uphold religious liberties and civil rights.

When home rule seemed a real possibility, it became obviously Unionist and most Unionist politicians have links to the Orange Order. Many prominent Unionist politicians have held senior posts in the Order; for example James Molyneaux and Martin Smyth have both been imperial grand master. Smyth continues to be grand master in Ireland. Orangemen have consistently opposed any attempts to set up power-sharing mechanisms or to allow any cross-border arrangements. This stance was again in evidence when the Order opposed the Good Friday Agreement signed in April 1998.

The annual parade season has been a source of great tension, particularly when the marches pass through predominantly nationalist areas. Many nationalist residents view Orange Order marches as sectarian and find them offensive. This is particularly true in regard to the annual July 12 march, which takes place in Portadown, passing along the Garvaghy Road on its return journey from Drumcree church. Most of this road passes through a nationalist area whose residents have consistently called for the march to be rerouted. There have been serious annual clashes among security forces, Orangemen, and protesters at Drumcree since 1995. There was a prolonged standoff in 1998, when the route of the march down the Garvaghy Road was blocked by the authorities. This situation was viewed by many as a microcosm of the difficulties that still exist in Northern Ireland, despite all

the advances and successes that have been achieved since the 1994 cease-fires.

Ricki Schoen

Combined Loyalist Military Command (CLMC)

Umbrella organization that brought together different groups of loyalist paramilitaries, namely, the Ulster Volunteer Force/Ulster Freedom Fighters and the Red Hand Commando. The Combined Loyalist Military Command (CLMC) first appeared in 1991 when it announced a loyalist cease-fire while the interparty talks were taking place at Stormont, the seat of the Northern Ireland government. The cease-fire lasted only for the three months the talks were taking place. No cease-fire was called during the Brooke-Mayhew talks in 1992, and the CLMC was believed to be behind an increase in loyalist violence during that period. The CLMC released statements in 1992 and 1993 that threatened more violence if it felt that the union was being tampered with. However, once the IRA had called a cease-fire in August 1994, the CLMC followed suit in October with its own cease-fire announcement.

Ricki Schoen

Ulster Defence Association (UDA)/Ulster Freedom Fighters (UFF)

Paramilitary organization founded in Northern Ireland in August 1971 as an umbrella for local defense associations that had been formed around Belfast to combat the Irish Republican Army. These local organizations were formed into the Ulster Defence Association (UDA) by Charles Harding Smith, leader of the Woodvale Defence Association. The UDA, which adopted the motto Cedenta Arma Togae (Law before Violence), stated that its aim was "to see law restored everywhere, including the no-go areas," i.e., the Catholic areas of Derry and Belfast. The local defense associations within the UDA were not under central control and the organization was rent by internal strife. The chairman, Harding Smith, was imprisoned in 1972 and his successor, James Anderson, holding the rank of major general, reorganized the UDA with a thirteen-man inner council. The chief spokesman was Tommy Herron (later killed), under whom there were eleven colonels and lieutenant colonels. The council stated that if the British army, with which the UDA hitherto had had good relations, did not break down the barricades and enter the "no-go" areas, the UDA would do so itself. During May and June 1972 it built up Protestant "no-go" areas. However, the British army entered the Catholic "no-go" areas and in September also raided UDA headquarters, where they uncovered bombing equipment.

After Anderson and Herron were arrested, the UDA cooperated closely with the Ulster Volunteer Force for an armed attack on a Catholic housing estate in Larne. It moved further away from the Protestant political movement, the Vanguard, and was shortly afterward involved in a series of shoot-outs with the British army. These ended after a truce was agreed on. The UDA was involved in sporadic outbursts of violence over the next few years, sometimes using the cover name Ulster Freedom Fighters (UFF). In 1992 this paramilitary group was outlawed because it was seen as being primarily involved in terrorist activities. The ban also included the UFF, which has claimed most of the killings ascribed to the UDA. In October 1994 it joined with other loyalist paramilitaries under the Combined Loyalist Military Command (CLMC) to call a cease-fire in response to the one called by the IRA in August. In the aftermath of the killing of Billy Wright (Loyalist Volunteer Force leader) in the Maze in December 1997, the UFF murdered three Catholics in retaliation. Because the UFF was linked to the Ulster Democratic Party (UDP), the party was excluded from the multiparty talks at the beginning of the year after the UFF had claimed responsibility for the killings (the party was readmitted after a few weeks).

Ricki Schoen

Ulster Volunteer Force (UVF)

Founded in January 1913, by the Ulster Unionist Council from among local corps in Ulster, the Ulster Volunteer Force (UVF) was meant to resist implementation of home rule, which was due to become law in 1914. Numbers were limited to one hundred thousand between the ages of seventeen and sixty-five and signatories of the Solemn League and Covenant of September 1912. With the outbreak of World War I in 1914, the force was incorporated into the British army as the Thirty-sixth (Ulster) Division. In 1916 the UVF division was virtually wiped out by the Germans at the battle of the Somme, where the Ulstermen displayed conspicuous gallantry.

The UVF was reorganized after the end of the war. With the founding of the Northern Ireland state in 1921, Carson requested that UVF men have preference for recruitment into the new Ulster Special Constabulary; this was arranged by Colonel Sir William Spender. The UVF was then disbanded. The UVF's tradition of defending the union against the Irish Republican Army and republicanism was revived in 1966, when there were republican commemorations in Northern Ireland for the fiftieth anniversary of the Easter Rising of 1916. The UVF revival was organized by a noted loyalist, "Gusty" Spence. Many Catholics unconnected with the republican movement

were objects of attack and there were a number of murders.

The serious nature of the new UVF was made public on May 21, 1966, when a statement signed by William Johnston, chief-of-staff of the UVF, appeared in Belfast newspapers it stating: "From this day we declare war against the IRA. . . . Known IRA men will be executed mercilessly and without hesitation. . . . We will not tolerate any interference from any source and we solemnly warn the authorities to make no more speeches of appeasement." Members of the UVF supported the loyalist spokesman, the Rev. Ian Paisley. On June 28, 1966, Prime Minister Terence O'Neill proscribed the UVF, and on the same day Spence and two others were charged with conspiring "between 1 March and 27 June to incite ill-will among different classes and creeds of the Queen's subjects, to create a public disturbance and disorder and murder persons who might be opposed to their opinions." They were found guilty and sentenced to life imprisonment.

The rise of the Northern Ireland Civil Rights Association gave a new lease on life to the UVF. There was a series of bombings, some of them attributed to the UVF, during 1969. O'Neill, unable to satisfy the civil rights movement and contain the loyalist reaction, fell from power on April 28. His successor, Chichester-Clark, failed to reduce the violence. British troops arrived in August. A Protestant mob supposedly led by the UVF attacked a Catholic church on the Newtownards Road. When the army—already overextended in West Belfast—did not appear in answer to a call for aid, the Irish Republican Army turned out to protect the church. The ensuing gun battle resulted in the deaths of four men.

The UVF was disorganized during 1971 although violent acts were carried out in its name. A new paramilitary force, the Ulster Defence Association (UDA), was founded in August 1971. Fearing a loss of support, the UVF reorganized to gain control of the new loyalist army. In its attempt to impress loyalists the UVF was responsible for certain outrages. Political initiatives failed as unionism fragmented in the first half of the 1970s and the paramilitaries on both sides filled the vacuum. The UVF was again proscribed in 1974, but the pattern of bombings, assassinations, murders, and reprisals that had emerged continued into the 1980s. It is believed to be a smaller paramilitary group than the Ulster Freedom Fighters but no less lethal, which it proved on several occasions in the 1990s. Nonetheless, it joined other groups to call the loyalist cease-fire in 1994. Since then, for the most part, it has left it to the Progressive Unionist Party (PUP) to represent its views in the political arena of Northern Ireland.

Ricki Schoen

Ulster Special Constabulary

The Ulster Special Constabulary was established in Northern Ireland to supplement the official police, the Royal Ulster Constabulary, in 1921. The state of Northern Ireland came into existence at a time of acute unrest in Ireland; the War of Independence from Britain was still being fought in the south, and it was felt necessary to protect the new state from the Irish Republican Army, which had support within the Catholic community in the north. Recruitment into the constabulary was mainly from among the revived Ulster Volunteer Force. There were three categories of Special Constabulary: the "A," "B," and "C" Specials. The "A" Special constables were attached to the Royal Ulster Constabulary (RUC). Members were given a six-month contract with the RUC. The "B" Specials were more numerous. While on duty they were uniformed and armed, but their arms were supposed to remain in local barracks when they were not on duty (these regulations were generally not enforced). The "B" Specials had to perform a half night's duty per week or one full night per fortnight. They served in their home districts and each patrol consisted of three or four members with one RUC man. "C" Specials were a general reserve, unpaid and called out only in an emergency. The Special Constabulary was entirely Protestant and many members were also in the Orange Order. The "A" and "C" Specials were not used after the 1920s. The "B" Specials were particularly active in attempts to contain the Northern Ireland Civil Rights Association and the People's Democracy. Clashes among the RUC, the Specials, loyalists, and civil rights marchers led to violence during 1968–69. As a result of the recommendations of the Hunt Commission, the force was disbanded in April 1970, but many of its members were absorbed into the new Ulster Defence Regiment.

Ricki Schoen

Royal Ulster Constabulary (RUC)

Police force established in Northern Ireland on June 1, 1922, from among the Royal Irish Constabulary. An armed force, the Royal Ulster Constabulary (RUC), was responsible not only for dealing with ordinary crime but also with the Irish Republican Army, with the support of the Special Constabulary and the Civil Authorities (Special Powers) Act of 1922. The RUC was partially disarmed in April 1970 in line with the recommendations of the Hunt Commission. Throughout the troubles, the RUC was viewed as a legitimate target by republican paramilitaries and, in certain instances, the loyalist paramilitaries as well. The republican community long argued

that the RUC is a Protestant force for a Protestant people. It does not see it as a legitimate police force and has called for its disbandment. The nationalist community as a whole would like to see the RUC reformed, and the Social Democratic Labour Party has supported this campaign. The issue of RUC reform continues to be a contentious aspect of the peace process. A commission has been established to look into RUC reform but it has come under fire, especially from the nationalist community.

Ricki Schoen

Ulster Defence Regiment (UDR)

Military force established in Northern Ireland in 1970 following the recommendations of the Hunt Commission and the disbandment of the "B" Specials. Contrary to the intentions of the commission, some members of the Ulster Defence Regiment (UDR) were recruited from the "B" Specials. This created a poor image for the regiment in the eyes of most people in the nationalist community, who saw the "B" Specials as a sectarian force that now made up a significant section of the regiment. Accusations were made against the UDR that some of its members were linked to loyalist paramilitaries. The UDR assisted the Royal Ulster Constabulary and the British army in the fight against the Irish Republican Army. In 1991 the government announced that the UDR would be merged with the Royal Irish Rangers and its members form part of the newly created Royal Irish Regiment. At the time of its disbandment, only about 3 percent of the regiment were Catholics.

Ricki Schoen

Economy

Investment levels in Northern Ireland have been relatively low compared with other parts of the United Kingdom, owing mainly to civil conflict acting as a deterrent. This situation has changed since the paramilitary cease-fires made Northern Ireland more attractive to investors, and also because of a concerted effort on behalf of the politicians, especially John Hume of the Social Democratic Labour Party, to attract inward investment to the area. In the past this lack of investment resulted in very high unemployment—the highest within the United Kingdom—and also a low gross domestic product. This statistic has changed considerably since the mid-1990s. Employment in Northern Ireland is now growing at the third-fastest rate within the United Kingdom. Unemployment has been dropping since it reached a peak in 1986 of 17.2 percent to an all-time low in 1997 of 7.7 percent. This drop has more or less coincided with an increase in industrial production in Northern Ireland that measured 17 percent between 1991 and 1996, compared with a 4.3 percent growth rate recorded in the United Kingdom as a whole. In addition, figures show that outside investment into Northern Ireland stood at £490 million in 1997, and that figure was up by 13 percent from the year before. A report prepared by the business information group Dunn and Bradstreet indicated that in May 1997 County Antrim was the second-most prosperous county and the best one in which to do business in the United Kingdom.

Belfast and Derry are the two main urban areas in Northern Ireland, with the rest of the area being mainly rural, with an agricultural economy (largely dairy farming and beef production). While Northern Ireland's trade links are predominantly with Britain (the ferry port of Larne, and increasingly Belfast itself, connect Northern Ireland to Britain), there is a good rail link between Belfast and Dublin, as well as a modern road connection between the two cities. The rail link between the two cities has recently been revamped to create a high-speed link that has cut traveling time by one-third. Trade with the republic increased in the 1990s, and this helped reduce the trade deficit (from £357 at the beginning of the decade to £130 five years later). Tourism benefited from the absence of paramilitary violence, with more people from the republic choosing to visit Northern Ireland.

Ricki Schoen

Isle of Man

The Isle of Man is a 221-square-mile (572 sq km) British crown dependency located in the Irish Sea. In 1991 its population was 69,788, and its principal town, Douglas, had 22,214 residents. It is not part of the United Kingdom but possesses its own legislature and has its own courts and administration. The legislature, or Tynwald, consists of the House of Keys and the Legislative Council. The two branches sit together but vote on most issues separately. The House of Keys consists of twenty-four members elected every four years by universal suffrage. The Legislative Council consists of the Anglican bishop, the attorney general, and eight members of the House of Keys. The British monarch is the head of state. She was represented by a lieutenant governor until 1990, when that office was replaced by an elected president. Sir Charles Kerruish was the first person to hold that office. A Council of Ministers was also established in 1990 consisting of an elected chief minister and the heads of the nine departments of governmental administration.

The Isle of Man. *Illustration courtesy of Bernard Cook.*

The Isle of Man levies its own taxes and, though British currency is accepted as legal tender, issues its own currency. It makes an annual payment to the United Kingdom for defense and other services. Companies incorporated on the island that conduct their business elsewhere are assessed a duty of £500. A Financial Supervision Commission regulates the sixty banks and seventy-five investment institutions licensed on the island. Free trade exists between the island and the European Union (EU).

BIBLIOGRAPHY

Kermode, D. G. *Devolution at Work: A Case Study of the Isle of Man.* Farnborough, U.K.: Saxon House, 1979.

Kinvig, R. H. *The Isle of Man: A Social, Cultural and Political History.* Liverpool: University of Liverpool Press, 1975.

Solly, Mark. *The Isle of Man: A Low-tax Area.* Croydon, U.K.: Tolley, 1984.

Bernard Cook

Italy

Italy was a devastated nation of peasants when it emerged from World War II and the years of fascist dictatorship. The changes in Italy in the fifty years since World War II have been enormous: the Italians created a multiparty democracy and Italy's economy, society, and culture were transformed. The Italian Republic by the 1990s was the sixth leading industrial nation in the world. At the same

Italy. *Illustration courtesy of Bernard Cook.*

time Italy also faced problems of political instability and corruption, domestic terrorism, and the Mafia.

The situation facing Italy at the end of World War II was serious. Damage in northern industrial cities was substantial, the disruption of the harvests of 1944 and 1945 left the food supply uncertain, communications difficult, unemployment high, and homelessness common. Moral and institutional rejuvenation were needed after twenty years of fascist rule. These problems would plague Italy for the rest of the decade.

The country was under British and American occupation through 1945. Alongside the Allied Military Government stood a civilian administration that comprised the Committees of National Liberation, the political movement that led the resistance to German occupation and dictator Benito Mussolini. Democracy would come to Italy from these committees, though it took three years to work through the transition from fascism to representative government.

The most important task was to determine the country's political future. The choice, put to Italian voters in June 1946, was dramatic: republic or monarchy? The king nominally headed the government in Rome, but after two decades of rule with Mussolini, Victor Emmanuel III enjoyed little authority, particularly in central and northern Italy. In the first fair elections in twenty-five years, and the first time Italian women had ever voted, the Italians endorsed the republic by a margin of 54 to 46 percent.

The royal family was sent into exile and the Italian Republic was declared.

A Constituent Assembly was elected at the same time, and the three leading parties—Christian Democratic Party (DC), with 35 percent; Italian Socialist Party (PSI), with 20 percent; and Italian Communist Party (PCI), with 19 percent—worked together on a constitution for the new republic. Reacting to the fascist past, the assembly designed a political system that ensured basic democratic rights. The constitution, which came into effect on January 1, 1948, included a wide range of civil liberties and created a multiparty system, a sovereign parliament, and a weak executive.

The great differences among the political parties became evident as the war receded into the past. Communists and Socialists, on the one hand, and Christian Democrats, on the other, endorsed dramatically different solutions to virtually every major problem facing the country: the purge of fascism from government, including the judiciary and civil administration, industrial and agricultural reform, law and order, unemployment, and housing. The "Government of National Unity" fell apart in May 1947 when DC Prime Minister Alcide De Gasperi, dissolved the postwar alliance and formed a new government coalition without the left-wing political parties.

The first legislative elections for the new republic were held on April 18, 1948, at the outset of the Cold War. Many factors influenced the results. The U.S. government openly supported the DC's decision to work no longer with the PCI and the SPI. Financial support for the DC came from the Truman administration, while the future of Marshall Plan funds, desperately needed by Italy, was also tied to a DC victory. The Catholic Church weighed in as well. Led by Pius XII, the Vatican presented the choice as a vote "for or against Christ." The landslide victory for the DC, with 48.5 percent of the vote, established a government based on anticommunism and set the foundations of the Italian political system for the next forty-five years.

After facing these immediate political issues, the Italians still had to resolve the economic and social problems left over from the war and deal with the country's chronic poverty. Reconstruction was an enormous task, and the Christian Democrats had little experience in economic planning. The process of recovery, however, was launched by the European Recovery Program. From 1948 to 1952, the United States supplied $1.5 billion in food, raw materials, and financial support. This assistance provided the aid necessary to resuscitate the Italian economy.

Luigi Einaudi, a noted economist and Italian president from 1948 to 1955, set the economic course for reconstruction. Einaudi believed that private enterprise and an industrial economy were the keys to long-term prosperity in Italy. His program emphasized production for export, integration into the world trade market led by the United States, and a campaign against inflation. This plan took advantage of Italy's one abundant resource: labor. High levels of unemployment kept wages quite low for the next decade, allowing Italian goods to be produced cheaply.

The Christian Democrats modified Einaudi's plan in one important aspect. The Italian economy was characterized by substantial state ownership of industry and finance inherited from Mussolini's Istituto per la Ricostruzione Industriale (Institute for Industrial Reconstruction). The Christian Democrats maintained and expanded the state sector of the economy after 1948. This gave the leading group in government a decisive voice in the country's economic policy and offered strong incentives for other parties to ally with the DC.

Einaudi's program was an enormous success. Industry recovered and grew as Italian goods sold successfully abroad. From 1958 to 1963 Italy had the second-fastest-growing economy in the world. This was the Italian "economic miracle": new wealth was created, new jobs appeared, unemployment dropped and almost disappeared in the early 1960s, and wages began to rise. All this meant domestic prosperity by the end of the 1960s. This economic miracle was fueled by the 1957 Treaty of Rome, which created the European Economic Community (EEC), of which Italy was one of the six founding members.

The economic boom changed Italy in many ways. Jobs in northern industry attracted agricultural workers and the unemployed from all over the country. The exodus from rural areas to industrial towns created a "new" Italy, and in just two decades an urban, industrial society overwhelmed the older, peasant nation. Migration particularly affected the south. Millions of southerners left their rural villages for northern industrial towns in the twenty-five years after 1955. The first generation of southern immigrants often experienced prejudice and racism in their new homes; nonetheless, the process of social unification had begun as mass migration broke down regional barriers in Italy.

The state television broadcasting network, established in 1954, also brought isolated towns and rural areas closer to the rest of the country and gave the nation a standard form of the Italian language. Additionally, a state school system, established in 1962, made education mandatory to age fourteen, elevating the overall educational level.

The chronic problem of southern underdevelopment was also addressed in these years. The government in Rome sponsored a special fund, the Cassa per il Mezzogiorno (Fund for the South), which directed private and public investment into the regions south of Naples. The results were mixed; though many of the agricultural and infrastructure projects were quite successful, the Cassa's industrial programs were poorly planned, characterized by political patronage and corruption, and tainted by Mafia involvement.

The 1950s and 1960s saw the consolidation of the Italian political system. Italy joined NATO and became one of the most loyal U.S. allies in Western Europe. In domestic politics, though the DC remained the dominant political force with just under 40 percent of the vote, the formation of coalition governments increasingly involved several other political parties. Compromises and negotiations became more complicated, and personalities as much as principles dominated parliament. Short-lived coalitions were the result. The fifty-plus governments in Italy since 1945 would set the European record for political instability.

In 1963, the PSI, led by Pietro Nenni, was brought back into the government as the preferred coalition partner of the DC. At the same time, the PCI, led by Palmiro Togliatti until 1964, and later by Enrico Berlinguer until 1984, became the permanent party of opposition. With no alternation in political power, stagnation set in, and Italian governments would be dominated by the Christian Democrat/Socialist alliance for the next three decades.

The great changes in Italy since the end of the war lay behind the turbulent years after the mid-1960s. While prosperity created a wealthier nation, the new materialist values were far different from those of a subsistence agricultural and peasant society. For more than a decade, until the late 1970s, Italy seemed to have lost its cultural bearings. Additionally, the economic boom of the earlier years first slowed, then came to an abrupt halt with the Organization of Petroleum Exporting Countries (OPEC) manufactured oil crisis. For the first time in a generation, high levels of unemployment and declining productivity appeared in Italy.

Malaise was first manifested in the universities. In the fall of 1967 and throughout 1968, university students protested against overcrowded facilities, lack of government funding, and an outdated curriculum. They occupied the universities and often fought with police. Students questioned the authority of the state and the materialism of postwar Italy. Their condemnation of the U.S. involvement in Vietnam also targeted Italy's decades-long support of American foreign policy. While students talked in general terms of social and political revolution, and frequently endorsed violent tactics, they rarely set specific goals.

Working-class discontent appeared next. During the "Hot Autumn" of 1969, a strike wave in industrial Italy demonstrated the determination of the working class and the labor unions, especially the General Confederation of Italian Labor, to share in the profits of the economic miracle. The movement triumphed in the early 1970s with the Statuto dei Lavoratori (Statute of Workers' Rights). Substantial wage increases, job security provisions, expanded labor union rights, stronger negotiating positions with owners, greater unemployment benefits, factory shop floor councils, and maternity benefits dramatically improved the lives of Italian workers for the next twenty years.

The year 1969 also marked the appearance of domestic terrorism in Italy. A powerful bomb exploded in a crowded Milan bank on the Piazza Fontana in December, beginning a decade-long social and political crisis. Right-wing, neofascist terrorists, occasionally aided by members of the military intelligence network, planted bombs in public places, hoping to frighten the populace into demanding a stronger, more authoritarian form of government. Left-wing terrorists, also active in the 1970s, tried to weaken the government by direct attacks on state functionaries. The most famous of these groups, the Red Brigades, kidnapped a leading DC politician, Aldo Moro, in 1978. The terrorists later murdered Moro when the government refused to negotiate his release. Italy faced more acts of terror, more subversive groups, and more deaths and injuries through terrorism than any other European nation during the "*gli anni di piombo*" (the years of lead). Terrorism, however, eventually defeated itself as violence deeply offended most Italians and the political parties united in the campaign against the terrorists.

Another unsettling development of this period was the growth of organized crime. The major groups—the Sicilian Mafia, the 'Ndranghita in Calabria, the Camorra in Naples, and the Union of the Sacred Crown in Puglia—all expanded in the years of the economic miracle. Beginning in the mid-1960s, organized crime became extremely wealthy from the heroin trade. With greater amounts of money at stake, the Mafia groups became more violent in the 1970s. Organized crime moved out of the south, exporting criminal activity and investing in legitimate businesses elsewhere in Italy. Mafia groups developed closer ties with the dominant political parties, especially the DC, exchanging votes for financial favors with politicians.

The Catholic Church, too, was caught up in the changes affecting Italian society in the 1960s and 1970s. Pope John XXIII (1958–63), known popularly as il Papa buono (the Good Pope), began to reform the church. Two encyclicals, *Mater et Magistra* and *Pacem in Terris,* removed the Vatican from direct involvement in Italian politics and lessened the philosophical isolation of Catholicism. The Second Vatican Council (1962–65) furthered reform by renovating many of the policies and religious practices of the church.

A more secular Italy appeared in the 1970s. When the Catholic Church under Pope Paul VI (1963–78) and the Christian Democrats sponsored a referendum to cancel divorce legislation, Italians voted in 1974 to keep their recently acquired right to divorce. Seven years later, Pope John Paul II (elected 1978) attempted to rescind the right to abortion. Again Italians voted, and again the majority, this time nearly two-thirds, endorsed women's right to abortion. The divorce and abortion referenda were among the clearest signs of the declining influence of the church in contemporary Italian society.

Throughout the postwar period, Italian intellectuals made significant contributions to culture, science, and the arts. Talented writers, including Italo Calvino, Carlo Levi, Primo Levi, Alberto Moravia, and Ignazio Silone, continued an earlier tradition of fine literature. Italian cinema, first with the neorealism of the 1940s and 1950s then with directors like Federico Fellini and Michelangelo Antonioni, has been one of the world's most innovative. Italians have been at the forefront of scientific research in biology and physics, while other notable Italians, such as Noberto Bobbio, have made important contributions to social and political theory.

The 1980s and early 1990s were years of unprecedented well-being. Italy overtook the United Kingdom as the third-leading industrial country in the EC, and by the end of the 1980s Italy was the sixth-leading industrial power in the world. Still, the state's share of the economy overshadowed the private sector. Corporations in the public sector produced more than half the country's total wealth in 1990, the highest figure in Western Europe. The 1980s also saw the Italian debt grow substantially, with the country's yearly deficit rising to more than 10 percent of its gross domestic product.

This period of economic growth affected all aspects of Italian society. With more food on the table, higher wages, more leisure time, and more material goods than ever before, Italy had become a consumer society. Still, several regions of the south failed to share in the prosperity of central and northern Italy.

The Italian family changed during these same years. A higher standard of living, a more secular culture, and greater information about contraception gave Italy the lowest birthrate in the world, 1.3 children per woman of childbearing age, by the early 1990s.

Immigration appeared in a more prosperous Italy. From the mid-1980s people from developing countries on the shores of the Mediterranean (Morocco, Tunisia, Egypt), from Africa (Senegal, Somalia, Ethiopia, Eritrea), and from Asia (Philippines, the Peoples Republic of China) began to migrate to Italy. The collapse of Communist states in Eastern Europe opened the way for Poles, Romanians, and especially Albanians to enter Italy as well. Italy now faces the challenges of regulating immigration and adjusting to the multicultural society that these patterns of migration create.

Prosperity also changed Italian politics. Five parties shared governing power through most of the 1980s: alongside the DC and the PSI regularly stood the Republican, Liberal, and Social-Democratic Parties. For the first time since the end of the war two non–Christian Democrats became prime minister: Giovanni Spadolini of the Republican Party and Bettino Craxi from the PSI; Craxi's government was the longest-lived coalition in postwar Italy, lasting just over three years, from 1983 to 1986.

The inclusion of other parties broadened the base of democratic government in Italy, but it also increased corruption within the political system. This became a public issue in 1992, when magistrates began to examine illegal kickbacks from businesspeople to politicians. The investigation revealed an enormous corruption scandal, called *Tangentopoli* (Bribesville), which thoroughly discredited the parties of government; both the DC and the PSI dissolved at the end of 1993.

At the same time, the PCI concluded a project of reform begun a decade earlier. In 1991 the Communists entered the mainstream of European social democracy. This development completely altered the terms of Italian politics: no longer was it possible, as it had been since 1948, to establish political alliances on the basis of anti-communism. The Italian Republic thus faced a serious political crisis.

National elections in 1994 were particularly significant as the voters replaced more than three-quarters of parliament with new representatives. Silvio Berlusconi, leader of Forza Italia (Go, Italy), emerged from the elections as prime minister. Berlusconi's government lasted only seven months. His successor, Lamberto Dini, an economic expert, formed a transitional government in January 1995 to deal with Italy's budget deficit crisis. Significant changes in the political system continue, and Italian democracy will most likely continue this process of reform for years to come.

Ginsborg, Paul. *A History of Contemporary Italy: Society and Politics, 1943–1988.* New York: Penguin, 1990.
Haycraft, John. *Italian Labyrinth: Italy in the 1980s.* New York: Penguin, 1985.
Hine, David. *Governing Italy.* Oxford: Clarendon, 1993.
Sassoon, Donald. *Contemporary Italy: Politics, Economy and Society since 1945.* New York: Longman, 1986.
Spotts, Frederic, and Theodor Wieser. *Italy: A Difficult Democracy.* New York: Cambridge, 1988.

David Travis

Peace Treaty

The peace treaty formally and officially ending Italy's participation in World War II was, in effect, a series of protocols signed between France, the United Kingdom, the United States, and the USSR, on the one hand, and Italy on the other. The treaty was signed on February 10, 1947, after the final draft had been approved by the twenty-one nations that participated at the Paris conference held between July 30 and October 15, 1946. The Italian Constituent Assembly ratified the document on February 10, 1947.

Negotiations for drafting the text went on for more than a year and proved to be difficult because of the continuing differences among the four major victorious powers. Such differences involved territorial issues related to Italy's borders with France, Austria, and Yugoslavia, as well as the question of Italy's former colonies, the disposition of its wartime fleet, future limitations on Italian rearmament, and the amount and nature of reparations to be paid to the Allied powers for wartime damages inflicted by the Italian armed forces.

The major territorial provisions, as finally accepted, included the central question of Italy's borders with Yugoslavia. At issue especially was the disputed city of Trieste, for which Italy always had a definite sentimental attachment as well as an important economic interest. Hence, the Italian government was adamant in its refusal to yield on this particular zone. Finally, it was decided that Trieste was to remain under a joint British and U.S. jurisdiction as a free territory until October 1954, when an agreement was reached that allowed Italy to retain the entire city, while most of the surrounding Venezia Giulia region was to be ceded to Yugoslavia. Other important territorial losses to Italy were the African colonies, the Dodecanese Islands (to Greece), several other islands along the Adriatic coast (to Yugoslavia), and four small frontier areas to France. The South Tyrol, another area of contention, remained under Italian control.

The reparation issue also formed an important part of the treaty and included $100 million to be paid to the Soviet Union, $125 million to Yugoslavia, $105 million to Greece, $25 million to Ethiopia, and $5 million to Albania. France, the United Kingdom, the United States, and the USSR renounced their claims to any Italian property in their respective territories and in return for this concession received nominal indemnities.

The treaty set forth precise limits on Italian military power. The army was not to exceed 185,000 men, the Carabinieri (militarized police) 65,000 men, the air force 25,000 men and 350 planes, and the navy 25,000 men, with two battleships, four cruisers, four destroyers, twenty torpedo boats, and a small number of other craft.

BIBLIOGRAPHY

Ellwood, David W. *L'alleato nemico: La politica d'occupazione anglo-americana in Italia, 1943–1946.* Milan: Feltrinelli, 1977.

Hine, David. *Governing Italy.* New York: Oxford University Press, 1993.

U.S. Department of State. "Draft Peace Treaty with Italy," in *Selected Documents Paris Peace Conference 1946.* Washington, D.C.: Government Printing Office, 1946, 75–162.

William Roberts

De Lorenzo Coup

Anti-insurrectionary contingency operation devised in 1963 and early 1964 by Italian General Giovanni De Lorenzo, head of the Carabinieri, the militarized national police, during a period of high political tension provoked by opposition to reformist center-left coalition governments. Although his plan was ostensibly defensive in its aims, a series of official investigations later revealed that De Lorenzo sought to condition Italian domestic politics through unconstitutional means.

De Lorenzo was a brilliant career army officer whose meteoric rise through the ranks was somewhat anomalous, apparently because his long series of mundane staff assignments—interrupted only by stints as an organizer of antifascist partisan groups in the Romagna and as deputy chief of the National Resistance Committee's (Comitati di Liberazione Nazionale, CLN) intelligence office—served to "cover" intelligence activities. This perhaps explains his unexpected 1955 selection by President Giovanni Gronchi and Interior Minister Paolo Emilio Taviani as chief of the armed forces intelligence Service (Servizio Informazioni Forze Armate, SIFAR), a promotion re-

sented by many senior military officers with extensive command experience. De Lorenzo successfully established an independent power base within SIFAR by surrounding himself with loyalists, transferring and demoting dissidents, and gaining the support of most of his subordinates by ensuring that they would be eligible for the same promotions as officers with combat experience. He also regularly employed marginally legal methods to attain his objectives. For example, he signed the secret 1956 Central Intelligence Agency—SIFAR accord that regulated the management of the Gladio stay-behind groups in Italy, whose very existence was kept secret from the Italian parliament in violation of the new postwar constitution; agreed to participate in a covert U.S. plan, code named "Demagnetize," to neutralize the Italian Communist Party (PCI); began illegally compiling 157,000 dossiers on leading Italian politicians, businessmen, union officials, clerics, and cultural figures, as well as genuine subversives—files that contained all sorts of compromising personal information not germane to national security but useful for blackmail purposes; set up an armywide surveillance system; bugged the quarters of Pope John XXIII at the behest of the CIA; and provided covert assistance to powerful commercial organizations (such as Confindustria) and politicians, including Gronchi, his successor, Antonio Segni, and Giulio Andreotti, in exchange for financial subsidies and political protection. Thus he was able, with the support of Segni, to assume command of the Carabinieri in 1962, while preserving his control over SIFAR by leaving it in the hands of loyalists such as Generals Egidio Viggiani and Giovanni Allavena.

Despite opposition within the Carabinieri to his appointment, De Lorenzo soon brought this militarized police organization under firm control by placing his closest SIFAR collaborators in key positions, transferring personnel who resisted his policies, bypassing or spying on those who could not be removed, and commanding in an autocratic style. At the same time he garnered rank-and-file support by dispensing funds to needy enlistees, increasing the prestige of the corps by emphasizing its military functions, and infusing his own energy into the entire organization. After securing internal control he began to prepare plans to enable the Carabinieri to deal single-handedly with allegedly imminent subversive threats, without consulting the defense and interior ministers or collaborating with the armed forces and the other main police agency, the Pubblica Sicurezza corps. These measures, which involved creating an elite Carabinieri mechanized brigade under his personal command, secretly recruiting retired Carabinieri and rightist civilians to augment the corps' insufficiently numerous active-duty personnel ("Plan Sigma"), and preparing detailed operational plans to seize "vital areas" of Rome and other major cities ("Plan Solo"), have collectively been referred to as the De Lorenzo Coup.

The creation of a fully equipped mechanized brigade, which would have been capable of quickly occupying key strategic facilities and overcoming the scattered resistance offered by local insurrectionary forces (or scattered units of the army or police), was officially approved by the Defense Ministry. But Solo and key features of Sigma—the emergency call-up of ex-Carabinieri without using approved procedures and the clandestine recruitment and training of right-wing civilians—proved more difficult to finalize. The chief problem presented by Solo, aside from keeping other security agencies in the dark until the plan was activated, was convincing staff officers of the three Carabinieri divisions responsible for carrying it out that the plan was fully constitutional even though it did not mesh at all with the official 1961 government contingency plan for dealing with threats to public order. Despite De Lorenzo's assurances and the pressure he applied on less enthusiastic subordinates to complete regional operational planning, many officers moved cautiously because they retained doubts about the legality of the overall plan. In the end such an operation was never launched, since the political crises of mid-1964 were resolved with the formation of a more moderate center-left government.

In 1965, De Lorenzo was promoted to army chief of staff but was forced to resign two years later after information surfaced about his illegal wiretaps and dossiers. Copies of this were later found to have been secretly transmitted to the CIA as well as to Propaganda Due (P2) Masonic lodge chief Licio Gelli by Allavena. De Lorenzo was then elected as a deputy, first for a monarchist party and then for the Italian Social Movement, but the resulting controversy led to the establishment of a parliamentary investigative committee, whose worrisome but inconclusive results were published in 1970. Since much of the key documentation about his activities was covered by state secrecy laws at the insistence of Defense Undersecretary Francesco Cossiga, it was not until after its full publication in 1991 by another parliamentary commission that the affair's seriousness was confirmed.

De Lorenzo was in fact actively colluding with various conservative forces to derail the reformist center-left experiment promoted by factions within the Christian Democratic Party and PSI, a policy that they feared would ruin Italy's economy and open the way for PCI entry into the ruling government coalition. Among these plotters were President Segni, whose paranoia was continually stoked by De Lorenzo; former Defense Minister and Nuova Repubblica (New Republic) leader Randolfo Pacciardi, who hoped to get rid of Prime Minister Aldo Moro and form a Gaullist-style "presidentialist" government with himself as its leader; antireformists within the business association Confindustria and its many component companies; Andreotti, a key leader of the DC's center-right faction; right-wing elements within SIFAR and the Carabinieri; and possibly hard-liners within the U.S. Embassy, such as Military Attaché Colonel Vernon Walters and CIA Station Chief William Harvey, who opposed their own government's cautious support for the center-left formula. It may be that De Lorenzo's contingency plans were prepared solely to blackmail leaders of the PSI, especially Pietro Nenni, into scaling back their demands for tangible political, social, and economic reform, but it now seems likely that the general would have been willing, if necessary, to activate "Plan Solo" to suppress the left-wing opposition by force.

BIBLIOGRAPHY

Bucciante, Giuseppe. *Le fartalle del SIFAR*. Bologna: Capelli, 1970.

Cipriani, Antonio, and Gianni Cipriani. *Sovranità limitata: Storia dell'eversione atlantica in Italia*. Rome: Associate, 1991.

Collin, Richard. *The De Lorenzo Gambit: The Italian Coup Manqué of 1964*. Beverly Hills: Sage, 1976.

De Lutiis, Giuseppe. *Storia dei servizi segreti in Italia*. Rome: Riuniti, 1984.

Gatti, Claudio. *Rimanga tra noi: L'America, l'Italia, la "questione comunista". I segreti di 50 anni di storia*. Milan: Leonardo, 1991.

Ilari, Virgilio. *Il generale col monocolo: Giovanni De Lorenzo, 1907–1973*. Ancona: Nuove Ricerche, 1995.

Martinelli, Roberto, ed. *SIFAR: Gli atti del processo De Lorenzo-l'Espresso*. Milan: Mursia, 1968.

Triontera, Renzo. *SIFAR Affair*. Rome: Reporter, 1968.

Zangrandi, Ruggero. *Inchiesta sul SIFAR*. Rome: Riuniti, 1970.

Jeffrey M. Bale

SEE ALSO Gladio

Piazza Fontana Massacre

Terrorist attack attributed to the Italian extreme Right's "strategy of tension." On December 12, 1969, on Piazza Fontana in Milan, a bomb exploded inside the National Bank of Agriculture, killing sixteen people and injuring approximately one hundred. The incident came in a particularly turbulent period of social unrest during difficult negotiations for the metal workers' contract, accompanied by labor union demonstrations and following the Senate approval of legislation increasing the rights of unions in factories.

Early investigations pointed to anarchistic parties and specifically to Pietro Valpreda, a ballet dancer from Rome, who was arrested and released after spending three years in prison. Subsequent police investigations, directed toward neofascists, centered on leaders Franco Freda and Giovanni Ventura and leaders of the Italian secret services, in particular Colonel Guido Giannettini. Conjectures were made about a right-wing "strategy of tension," which, through outrages and criminal actions, was intended to provoke panic and a state of uncertainty to set the stage for a coup d'état.

The trial for the Piazza Fontana Massacre dragged on for several years. Freda, Ventura, and Giannettini were initially condemned to life imprisonment, but they were subsequently cleared by the Court of Appeal.

After their release the investigation continued in an effort to find links between neofascists and state officials and agencies, and possible national and international conspiratorial links. The investigation, however, produced no convictions.

BIBLIOGRAPHY

Magrone, Nicola, and Giulia Pavese. *Ti ricordi di Piazza Fontana?: Vent'anni di storia contemporanea dalle pagine di un processo,* 3 Vols. Bari: Edizioni Dall'Interno, 1986–88.

Walter E. Crivellin

SEE ALSO Terrorism, Right-Wing

Borghese Coup

Attempted coup d'état in Italy. On the night of December 7–8, 1970, Prince Junio Valerio Borghese, commander of the Decima Mas, an elite Fascist division during the Salò Republic in 1944–45, attempted to stage a coup d'état, which has been described as a "coup d'état of pensioners." The conspirators were united in a group called Rosa dei Venti (Compass Rose), a right-wing extremist and revolutionary organization whose members were drawn from the Italian armed forces, extraparliamentary groups, and a group of ex-parachutists. The intent of this small and overly ambitious group of people was to abolish the parliamentary system in order to create a "government of colonels." The authors of the conspiracy, in addition to Borghese, were Remo Orlandini and Sandro Saccucci, a lieutenant of the parachutists.

Borghese succeeded in occupying the building that was the seat of the Ministry of the Interior for few hours but was then forced to surrender. Even though he was suspected of having connections with the army and the secret service, Borghese was obviously an adventurer without much support. What happened during that night came to light only in March 1971. At an early stage of inquiry the Freemasons, four hundred officers, groups of industrialists, and leaders of the Christian Democrats were suspected of being involved in the conspiracy. These accusations, however, proved groundless. Nevertheless, some groups inside the nation took advantage of Rosa dei Venti for mysterious power games. Members of the secret service knew about what was going to happen before the coup started. Furthermore, even though the competent ministers were immediately informed, no measures were taken against the authors of the coup until the press exposed it. This implies the possibility that the coup was controlled by people at higher levels.

In 1974, after many delays, four officers were accused of complicity in the attempted coup d'état; among them was Vito Miceli, the head of the secret service. After a trial, however, they were all acquitted.

BIBLIOGRAPHY

Beltrametti, Eggardo. *Il colpo di Stato militare in Italia.* Rome: Giovanni Volpe, 1975.

De Lutiis, Giuseppe. *Storia dei servizi segreti in Italia.* Rome: Editori Riuniti, 1991.

Ginsborg, Paul. *A History of Contemporary Italy: Society and Politics, 1943–1988.* New York: Penguin, 1990.

Claudia Franceschini

Compass Rose Plot

Anticonstitutional operations carried out in Italy between 1971 and 1974 by a network of diverse, right-wing paramilitary groups. These activities were particularly threatening because the groups involved were also linked covertly to parallel intelligence organizations that operated outside of parliamentary control and in accordance with secret Atlantic Alliance protocols.

Although there remains some dispute about the significance of the name itself, which technically refers to the directional symbol on a compass but might also allude to the twenty or so groups that it allegedly comprised or, more metaphorically, to the idea that it could strike suddenly, like the wind, from any direction. The origins of the Rosa dei Venti (Compass Rose) network can be traced to the last-minute termination of the December 1970 coup launched in Rome by Prince Junio Valerio Borghese's National Front (Fronte Nazionale, FN). In the wake of the arrest of several key FN leaders and the flight of Borghese to Spain in early 1971, the most intransigent FN cadres and their allies, including active-duty and retired military and police personnel, neofascist radicals, and conservative financiers, renewed their struggle against the unstable coalition that governed Italy, which, they feared, would soon give way to a Communist-dominated regime. In the spring of 1973 Dario Zagolin, a key member of the then dominant FN faction headed by Giancarlo De Marchi and an alleged secret service operative, began to gather civilian and military personnel from diverse right-wing groups into a single umbrella organization. The aim was to use this organization to carry out a terrorist campaign of violence that would lay the groundwork for a military intervention later that year, ostensibly to restore public order. By the middle of 1973, after a series of meetings held in northern Italy, various operational plans had been formulated, financing had been arranged, and twenty-four separate groups had supposedly become affiliated in some way with the Rosa dei Venti. The two most important formations were the FN leadership group in Liguria consisting of Zagolin; De Marchi; and Genoese businessmen Attilio Lercari, the right-hand man of multimillionaire Andrea Maria Piaggio; Edgardo Massa; and Giacomo Tubino, and an operational group in the Veneto consisting of army intelligence officer Amos Spiazzi; amnestied Brigate Nere (Black Brigades) "war criminal" Eugenio Rizzato; ex-paratrooper Sandro Rampazzo; retired general Francesco Nardella, the former head of NATO's Psychological Warfare Office in Verona and a cofounder, along with Sicilian Prince Gianfranco Alliata di Montereale, of the conservative National Public Opinion Movement (Movimento Nazionale per la Opinione Pubblica, MNOP); and neofascist New Order Political Movement (Movimento Politico Ordine Nuovo, MPON) leaders Clemente Graziani and Elio Massagrande. In addition to these core groups subsidiary Rosa paramilitary organizations operated in Viareggio and Padua, and a number of more or less autonomous groups also became affiliated with the organization, including the Rome FN group headed by shipbuilder Remo Orlandini and General Ugo Ricci, the Phoenix (Fenice) youth group in Milan, and, in all likelihood, former non-Communist partisan Carlo Fumagalli's Revolutionary Action Movement (Movimento d'Azione Rivoluzionaria, MAR) in the Valtellina.

Between 1971 and 1974 the various groups that eventually came to be associated with the Rosa dei Venti organization were responsible for carrying out dozens of acts of violence, including the bombing of electrical towers in the Valtellina; the placing of explosives, discovered before

they detonated, in Trento, along several railroad lines and under a bridge near Bologna; the botched attempt by the Milanese Fenice group to place bombs on Turin-Rome trains; a bombing at Rome's central train station, which miraculously caused no casualties; bombings in Savona; and a car bombing in front of the Carabinieri station in Varazze. Individuals linked to the Rosa dei Venti were also implicated in serious massacres, such as the May 1973 attack on Milan police headquarters by the purported anarchist Gianfranco Bertoli, the bomb detonated at Brescia's Piazza della Loggia in May 1974, and the bombing of the "Italicus" express train in August 1974. Only the fortuitous arrest of Zagolin and Rampazzo while driving in a car filled with explosives and the panicky provision of secret Rosa documents to the police by pro-Nazi La Spezia doctor Giampaolo Portacasucci enabled the judicial authorities to dismantle the key Rosa groups before they could carry out their plot to subvert the constitution. Among the materials found in the possession of leading Rosa members were a detailed plan for an insurrection, a stock of blank death sentences, a list of over 1,700 individuals slated for "neutralization," a significant quantity of weapons, and a classified military code system, FARILC 59, that had recently been abandoned by the military and then provided to the conspirators by Spiazzi.

More important, the evidence gathered by Padua judge Giovanni Tamburino revealed that key individuals associated with the Rosa dei Venti organization were also members of a top secret parallel intelligence apparatus linked to the Atlantic Alliance. Spiazzi and a phony military magistrate who served as an intermediary between the Veneto and Liguria groups, Roberto Cavallaro, later testified that they were members of this top secret apparatus, which journalists inaccurately dubbed a "parallel SID." Both admitted that this apparatus was composed of the intelligence staffs of regular army units and leading pro-Atlantic elements of the Defense Intelligence Service (Servizio Informazioni Difesa, SID), as well as high-ranking U.S. intelligence and military personnel and conservative businessmen. They also admitted that its leaders participated in annual meetings in Brussels. Cavallaro further claimed that it covertly manipulated, financed, and directed right- and left-wing terrorist groups with the goal of precipitating a military intervention to restore order—to "destabilize in order to stabilize"—and Spiazzi testified that he had received a coded telephone message in April 1973 from a subordinate of Colonel Federico Marzollo, SID chief Vito Miceli's right-hand man, ordering him to make contact with FN leaders in Genoa and facilitate their links to various paramilitary circles in the Veneto with which he had already developed close connections.

On the basis of such revelations, as well as information that surfaced about the organic links between "parallel SID" personnel and key Rosa dei Venti figures, in October 1974 Tamburino ordered the arrest of Miceli and charged him with helping to organize "a secret association of military personnel and civilians in order to provoke an armed insurrection and . . . an illegal transformation of the constitution of the state and the form of government by means of an intervention of the armed forces, provoked by the actions of, and in part guided by, the very same association." To achieve its objectives the association financed and made instrumental use of "various armed groups with hierarchical structures, linked to each other at the base by 'liaison officers' . . . to foment disorders, commit assaults, [and] carry out violent and threatening activities." Shortly thereafter Tamburino's investigation was transferred to the judicial authorities in Rome, who abruptly shelved it.

Despite the seriousness of Tamburino's charges, only a handful of conspirators served short prison sentences, and only the most compromised components of the Rosa organization ended up being dismantled. Although Miceli himself had been undermined by Defense Minister Giulio Andreotti's disclosures and forced to resign as head of SID, the "parallel SID" continued to function in various guises up until 1990, at which point both the former general and Spiazzi unjustifiably conflated it with the "Gladio" stay/behind network.

BIBLIOGRAPHY

Borraccetti, Vittorio, ed. *Eversione di destra' terrorismo, stragi: I fatti e l'intervento giudiziario.* Milan: Angeli, 1986.

Calderoni, Pietro. ed. *Servizi segreti: Tutte le deviazioni.* Naples: Tullio Pironti, 1986.

Cipriani, Antonio, and Gianni Cipriani. *Sovranità limitata: Storia dell'eversione atlantica in Italia.* Rome: Associate, 1991.

Corsini, Paolo, and Laura Novati, eds. *L'eversione nera: Cronache di un decennio, 1974–1984.* Milan: Angeli, 1985.

De Lutiis, Giuseppe. *Storia dei servizi segreti in Italia.* Rome: Riuniti, 1984.

Flamini, Gianni. *Il partito del golpe: Le strategie del terrore e della tensione dal Primo centrosinistra oreanico al sequestro Moro.* 4 Vols. in 6 parts. Ferrara: Bovolenta, 1981–86.

Silj, Alessandro. *Malpaese: Criminalita, corruzione e politica nell'Italia della prima Repubblica, 1943–1994.* Rome: Donzelli, 1994.

Willan, Philip. *Puppetmasters: The Political Use of Terrorism in Italy.* London: Constable, 1991.

Jeffrey M. Bale

SEE ALSO Gladio; Miceli, Vito

Historic Compromise

Period of Italian political history from 1971 to 1978 when the largest parties, the Christian Democrats and the Communists, attempted to work out a strategy for a coalition government to overcome the social and economic crisis of the 1970s.

At the end of the 1960s political debate in Italy focused on widening the country's democratic base by involving the Italian Communist Party, led by Enrico Berlinguer, and, in a more general sense, attempting to encourage dialogue between Catholics and Communists. The need to widen the political base resulted from the inability of the center-left coalition of Christian Democrats and Socialists to solve serious problems such as terrorism and the economic and social crisis.

The first signal of the new period of history appeared in February 1971 with the approval of new parliamentary rules giving greater control to opposition parties through the right to veto legislative undertakings promoted by the government. In parliament the government majority and the main opposition party, the Communist Party agreed on a common legislative line that, beyond their ideological and political differences, might enable the country to deal with its emergency situation.

After the parliamentary agreement of 1971, Berlinguer outlined the aims of the "compromise" in articles published in *Rinascita* between September and October 1973. The secretary of the biggest Western Communist party considered the agreement between the largest popular forces of the country, represented by the Italian Communist party (PCI) and the Christian Democratic Party (DC), the only possible guarantee against a deepening of the crisis of the Italian state and the possible emergence of a dictatorship.

The election of Aldo Moro and Benigno Zaccagnini, both highly favorable to talks with the PCI, as leaders of the DC as well as the electoral success of Communists in the municipal elections of June 1975 were considered by observers as popular approval of "national solidarity" politics. The "compromise" was sealed by the election of 1976, in which the PCI, with 34 percent, had its greatest electoral success, while the Christian Democrats were confirmed as the relative majority party in parliament, with over 38 percent of the vote.

Negotiations for a firm government coalition, with Moro, La Malfa, and Berlinguer as protagonists, led in the summer of 1976 to the third Andreotti government. It was composed only of Christian Democratic ministers but was supported in parliament by the deliberate abstentions of Communists, Socialists, Liberals, Social Democrats, and Republicans. The so-called abstention government, lasting until January 1978, devoted all its efforts to overcoming the economic crisis characterized by a considerable increase in inflation by applying economic policy correctives that turned out to be unpopular. The tense atmosphere of social conflict, which was manifested during several strikes and demonstrations, involved the main production centers and universities. The principal goal of the strikes was the fall of Andreotti's government, but the main opposition party, the PCI, was also a target: it was considered guilty of supporting the rigid economic correctives implemented by the government. Under pressure Berlinguer pushed Moro to start the second phase of "compromise" by allowing Communist ministers to enter the government. But Berlinguer, who had severely criticized Soviet policy during a trip to Moscow for the seventieth anniversary of the Russian Revolution, was discouraged by the strong opposition of some of the most prominent democratic leaders and mainly by the rigid position of the U.S. administration led by President Jimmy Carter. Nevertheless, following violent popular demonstrations in autumn 1977 against government economic policy, the Communist Party summit supported the new government, even though there was not a single Communist in the list of ministers to be handed to the president.

The arduous conduct of a policy of national solidarity was abruptly halted when the Red Brigades kidnapped Moro some hours before the chamber would have passed a vote of confidence on the fourth Andreotti government. During the fifty-four days of Moro's imprisonment, the government, supported strongly by Berlinguer and La Malfa, took a tough line, refusing to negotiate with the terrorists and opposing those who considered it necessary to save Moro's life at all costs. Among them, in particular, Craxi's Socialists, concerned about the DC and PCI alliance, strongly criticized the government, accusing the Christian Democrat and Communist leaders of supporting a policy of false firmness in Moro's case to cement an otherwise wavering alliance. On May 9 the finding of Moro's corpse marked the end of "national solidarity," considered by Berlinguer as a necessary test for the fulfillment of the "historic compromise."

Following Giovanni Leone's resignation in the summer of 1978, the election of the new president confirmed the incompatibility of a thorough convergence between Catholics and Communists. On that occasion their common candidate, Ugo La Malfa, was forced to give way to Sandro Pertini, the candidate designated by Craxi. Even if during his maiden speech, the new president reiterated all of the points of "national solidarity," the subsequent political crisis showed the impossibility of arriving at a political agreement between the Catholics and the Communists.

BIBLIOGRAPHY

Ginsborg, Paul. *A History of Contemporary Italy: Society and Politics, 1943–1988.* London: Penguin Books, 1990.

Lanaro, Silvio. *Storia dell'Italia repubblicana: Dalla fine della guerra agli anni Novanta.* Venice: Marsilia, 1992.

Vacca, Giuseppe. *Tra compromesso e solidarietà.* Rome: Editori Riuniti, 1987.

Fabio Marino

SEE ALSO Berlinguer, Enrico; Moro, Aldo

Red Brigades

The Red Brigades operated in Italy from 1970 to 1986 and are the most important example of an extreme left-wing Italian terrorist organization. It was based on the theory that only through armed struggle would a socialist state ever be established in Italy. It found its ideological inspiration in the Marxist-Leninist, Third International, Stalinist, and Maoist traditions, while at the same time being influenced by elements of Catholic radicalism.

The origin of the Red Brigades can be traced back to some radical fringes of the extreme left wing that came into being during the "hot autumn" of 1969, a period of great social conflict during which state institutions were seriously challenged by university students and the workers' movement. During this period a significant number of extreme left-wing militants went underground and took up armed struggle against government institutions. This move not only constituted total disregard for the laws of the Italian state but was also in open contrast to the policies of traditional Italian left-wing parties, the Communists and the Socialists. The Red Brigades considered these two parties to be hand in glove with the capitalist system and international imperialism, and therefore in complicity with the United States, which was at that time still heavily involved in the Vietnam War.

During this period there was a growing conviction within the Italian left wing that a fascist coup d'état was being prepared (as had happened in Greece a few years earlier) as a direct response both to union disputes and to a political climate that seemed to favor the Communist Party's chances of taking part in the national government. A long series of bloody acts of terror, the first of which was the Piazza Fontana Massacre, led to the fear that an attempt was underway to create a situation of great tension and insecurity in Italy to favor the establishment of an authoritarian power based on fascist principles. The suspicion was that these massacres were masterminded by extreme right-wing groups with the collaboration of members of the Italian secret services. Since subsequent inquiries tended to confirm this suspicion, the massacres were inevitably interpreted as being a warning sign of a possible imminent fascist coup, supported by elements within the Italian government itself. In this climate some militants of the extreme left wing considered it essential that an adequate reply be given to such a threat. In accord with Marxist-Leninist theory they believed that such a reply, suitably guided by a "conscious proletarian vanguard," or in this case by the "Red Brigades—Fighting Communist Party," would constitute the first phase of a revolutionary process to turn Italy into a socialist state.

The Red Brigades were formed in 1970 when two groups transferred their operational headquarters from Trento and Bologna to Milan, where they joined forces with a third group already operating in the Milan area. The founders of the three groups and consequent leaders of the Red Brigades were Renato Curcio, Margherita "Mara" Cagol, Paolo Besuscio, and Giorgio Semeria, all of whom were Catholic students and graduates from the sociology faculty of the University of Trento; Alberto Franceschini, Prospero Gallinari, and Roberto Ognibene, ex-militants of the Young Communist Federation of Reggio Emilia; and Mario Moretti, Corrado Alunni, and Alfredo Bonavita, workers from the Sit-Siemens factory in Milan.

The Red Brigades' terrorist activities began in 1971 with the publication and distribution of intimidating leaflets, firebomb attacks, and brief punitive kidnappings of industrial leaders. This first phase, which can be summed up in the Maoist-style slogan "Strike one to educate a hundred," lasted from 1971 to 1973. Subsequently, from 1974 to 1978, the Red Brigades carried out what they themselves defined as "a direct attack on the heart of the state," raising the level of their terrorist activities to include numerous assassinations and the kidnapping of "capitalist officials" and political opponents. Principal targets and victims were magistrates, members of the police force engaged in combating terrorism, industrial leaders, and important politicians. During this period Genoa judge Mario Sossi was kidnapped and later released, and the public prosecutor of Genoa, Francesco Coco, along

with his two military escorts, were assassinated on June 8, 1976. This same fate befell numerous other police and military officials.

On March 16, 1978, the Red Brigades carried out its most notorious terrorist action, the kidnapping of Aldo Moro, former prime minister, chairman of the Christian Democratic Party, and probable future president of the republic, a kidnapping that started with the killing of the five members of Moro's armed escort and ended fifty-five days later with the assassination of Moro himself.

At this point the Red Brigades suffered its first real crisis and began to lose credibility in the eyes of those workers whom it had tried to push toward revolutionary "anticapitalistic and anti-imperialistic" action. The efficient military response of the government, carried out by special antiterrorist groups under the leadership of General Carlo Alberto Dalla Chiesa, dealt a heavy blow to the Red Brigades, blocking its operational capabilities and often eliminating its leaders. At the same time, the political response to the problem proved to be equally efficient. Antiterrorist laws rewarding members of the organization who "repented" or "disassociated" themselves, rapidly eroded the Red Brigades' organizational structure from within and eventually caused its downfall.

Of particular significance, as far as the political discrediting of the organization is concerned, were a number of its actions whose aim was altogether incomprehensible or carried out with unnecessary ferocity. Adverse public opinion was aroused by three episodes in particular: the assassination of Judge Emilio Alessandrini on January 19, 1979; the killing of union leader Guido Rossa on January 24, 1979; and the kidnapping and killing of Roberto Peci, brother of a "repented" Brigades member, on July 10, 1981. Alessandrini's uncovering of the involvement of the extreme right wing in the Piazza Fontana Massacre had won respect for the political and judicial system, and his murder by the Red Brigades was viewed as incomprehensible.

Equally damaging for the public image of the Brigades was the organization's handling of the kidnapping of Ciro Cirillo on April 27, 1981, leader of the Christian Democratic Party in Campania, and the inexplicable presence of members of the Camorra, Campania's powerful criminal organization, at the moment of his eventual release on July 24, 1982.

The last important terrorist action of the Red Brigades was the kidnapping of NATO commander James Lee Dozier on December 17, 1981. Dozier was freed by the Italian police on January 28, 1982. "Operation Dozier" was in fact followed up by a series of arrests that, together with the confessions of a number of "repented" Red Brigades members, sealed the fate of the organization. Sporadic episodes continued as late as 1986 but failed to resuscitate the organization.

BIBLIOGRAPHY

Bocca, Giorgio. *Noi terroristi: 12 anni di lotta armata riconosciuti e discussi con i protagonisti.* Milan: Garzanti, 1985.

Bravo, Gian Mario. *L'estremismo in Italia, le origini, gli sviluppi, le teorie, il rosso e il nero nella mappa dei gruppi eversivi.* Rome: Editori Riuniti, 1982.

Collin, Richard. *Winter of Fire: The Abduction of General Dozier and the Downfall of the Red Brigades.* New York: Dutton, 1990.

Galli, Giorgio. *Storia del partito armato.* Milan: Rizzoli, 1986.

Meade, Robert C. *The Red Brigades: The Story of Italian Terrorism.* New York: St. Martin's Press, 1990.

Tarrow, Sydney. *Disorder and Democracy: Conflict, Protest and Political Change in Italy.* Oxford: Clarendon Press, 1989.

Aldo Nicosia

SEE ALSO Dalla Chiesa, Carlo Alberto; Moro, Aldo; Terrorism, Right-Wing

Crisis of the System

The Italian political system, largely unchanged since 1948, faced a major crisis in the early 1990s. In only a few years the ideological foundations of the Italian Republic collapsed, new electoral laws appeared, popular referenda eliminated many of the privileges of the traditional ruling parties, and government alliances based on new political movements appeared. Italy in the 1990s was in a transitional phase marked by an uncertain development toward a new form of democracy.

From 1945 to 1990, Italian democracy was something of a paradox, both unstable and stagnant. A record number of governments, fifty-four in fifty years, created political instability; yet at the same time a single party, the Christian Democratic Party (DC), dominated all the postwar governments. From its foundation in 1946, the Italian Republic was a multiparty system, and proportional representation ensured that ten to fifteen parties regularly sent representatives to parliament. Governments arose from alliances and followed policies established only after the vote. Often referred to as the *partitocrazia*—an "aristocracy of political parties"—this system left too much power in the hands of the parties while too little was exercised by the electorate.

All this began to change in the early 1990s. The Italian Communist Party (PCI), the second-largest movement in the country and the leading party of opposition, concluded a decade-long debate on the relevance of communism in modern Italy. In February 1991, the Communists, led by Achille Occhetto, changed their party's name, symbol, and platform, and entered the mainstream of European social democracy as the Democratic Party of the Left, represented by an oak tree rather than by the hammer and sickle. The end of a significant Communist movement sent shock waves throughout the country. Since 1947 governments had formed as anti-Communist alliances led by the DC. That was suddenly no longer possible.

The appearance of a new movement also contributed to the general political crisis. The Northern League, or Lombard League, headed by Umberto Bossi, protested against the corruption of the political system and prescribed decentralized government, with stronger regional administrations as the cure. Bossi proposed a constitutional amendment to bring about this change. On the ballot first in the 1987 national elections, the league quickly grew to become the most important party in Lombardy, the industrial and financial heartland of Italy.

Another element of the political crisis concerned the state's finances. Lack of accountability among the parties of government had permitted the country's indebtedness to grow enormously. In 1990, faced with the need to reduce the debt quickly, Italian governments began an ambitious privatization project in the hope of generating new revenue. This move undermined the *partitocrazia* because control over the state sector of the economy and the patronage that went with it had held together the multiparty government alliances since the 1960s. Coalitions, always fragile in Italy, began to fall apart even more rapidly.

A widespread investigation into political corruption was also part of the crisis of Italian democracy. The bribery scandal, called *Tangentopoli* (Bribesville), thoroughly discredited parliament. At the end of 1993 the DC and the Italian Socialist Party (PSI), the two pillars of government, collapsed under the weight of corruption charges. New movements immediately moved onto the political scene and demanded prompt national elections.

Political reform also played a role in the crisis. Referenda challenging the political system went to the voters in April 1993. The most important struck down proportional representation in the Senate. Eighty-two percent of the voters approved of this change. Another referendum by a vote of 90 percent eliminated public financing of political parties, while two other initiatives, each by a vote of 85 percent, eliminated both political appointments to the banking system and the cabinet office that oversaw the relations between government and public-sector businesses.

New electoral laws were introduced and first tested in administrative elections in the larger towns in November and December 1993. The direct election of mayors in a two-round vote forced parties to form alliances, announce their programs, and back a single candidate before the election. This striking departure from the earlier system strengthened and narrowed alliances at the expense of individual parties. Additionally, mayors were given the opportunity to govern cities with the clear and direct endorsement of the majority of the voters.

Elections in March 1994 were the first to be carried out under the new electoral law on the national level. Proportional representation was drastically reduced in the Senate and Chamber of Deputies: three-quarters of the seats would be filled by a simple majority vote, while only one-quarter would be reserved for proportional representation. Single-candidate constituencies were established for the first time, creating a more direct relation between voters and politicians. The results accelerated political reform; three-quarters of elected representatives were new to national politics. Voter participation remained high at 85 percent.

Forza Italia (Go, Italy), one of the newest political movements received the largest number of votes, 22 percent, in the March 1994 election. Silvio Berlusconi, the party's leader, became prime minister. His government coalition included two other parties that had never before participated in a national government: the National Alliance, a movement whose origins lay in the Italian Social Movement, a neofascist party, and the Northern League. Berlusconi's coalition lasted only seven months, split by internal dissent common in Italian politics. In January 1995, another "new" form of government appeared: a technical administrative alliance led by Lamberto Dini, a figure standing outside the political divisions of parliament.

Political changes continued with regional elections in April 1995. Coalitions, programs, and leaders were again announced before the vote, and the electorate divided almost evenly between two major alliances. These results revealed the slow emergence of a bipolar political system in Italy.

Though the forms that Italian democracy will assume in the future were far from clear, political transformation was well underway. In only a few years Italy weathered a series of political crises, moved toward a more direct, simpler democracy, and laid the foundations for the regular rotation of power between political parties more typical of other Western democracies, while maintaining citizen participation in the political process at very high levels.

BIBLIOGRAPHY

Allum, Percy. *Italy—Republic Without Government?* New York: Norton, 1973.

Colarizi, S. *Storia dei partiti nell'Italia repubblicana.* Rome: Laterza, 1994.

McCarthy, Patrick. *Crisis of the Italian State: From the Origins of the Cold War to the Fall of Berlusconi and Beyond.* New York: St. Martin's Press, 1996.

Palombara, Joseph. *Democracy, Italian Style.* New Haven, Conn.: Yale, 1987.

Pasquino, Gianfranco. *La politica italiana: Dizionario critico, 1945–1995.* Rome: Laterza, 1995.

Putnam, Robert. *Making Democracy Work.* Princeton, N.J.: Princeton University Press, 1993.

Spotts, Frederic, and Theodor Wieser. Italy: *A Difficult Democracy.* New York: Cambridge University Press, 1986.

David Travis

SEE ALSO Berluscone, Silvio; Bossi, Umberto; Di Pietro, Antonio; Scalfaro, Oscar

Tangentopoli Scandal

Corruption scandal that began in Italy in 1992. Following the discovery of a modest bribe in Milan, magistrates soon uncovered kickbacks (*tangenti*) and illegal financing of political parties on a vast scale. The *Tangentopoli* (Bribesville) scandal was instrumental in the collapse of the traditional governing parties, notably the Christian Democratic Party and the Italian Socialist Party, and the appearance of new political movements in the 1994 elections.

The original "Bribesville" was Milan, the financial and industrial capital of Italy and the home of the Italian stock market. *Tangentopoli* started quietly in February 1992, when the owner of a small industrial cleaning company approached the manager of a retirement home in Milan to inquire about the contract for cleaning the center. The manager, Mario Chiesa, a high-ranking politician in the Italian Socialist Party, solicited a seven-million-lire kickback (approximately $4,000) as the price for awarding the contract. The businessman reported the incident to the state prosecutor's office in Milan and Deputy District Attorney Antonio Di Pietro took on the case. Using marked bills, a tape recorder, and a video camera, Di Pietro set up a sting operation, and Chiesa was arrested as he accepted the bribe. After several weeks in prison, Chiesa began to collaborate with the investigation, and *Tangentopoli* got underway.

Di Pietro and a pool of other Milan magistrates formed *Mani Pulite* (Operation Clean Hands). Pursuing Chiesa's revelations, they quickly found themselves investigating many top politicians and business figures. The Italian Socialist Party was the first political movement significantly to be caught up in *Mani Pulite*. Led since 1976 by Bettino Craxi, the Socialists had made Milan their showcase city, and they were the strongest political force in the surrounding region of Lombardy.

Tangentopoli quickly expanded as magistrates in other Italian cities began to look more closely at the relations between business and political parties in their own areas. First in Genoa and Turin, then in Venice, Trieste, and Rome, a similar pattern emerged of "contributions" to politicians for preferred treatment in business dealings. The investigation then moved southward, and other Bribesvilles were uncovered in Naples, Palermo, and Bari. *Tangentopoli* in southern Italy, however, differed in one important respect: mixed in with money and politics was organized crime.

As the judges' work continued, more and more politicians, businessmen, and political parties came under scrutiny. Within a year, all the parties that had governed Italy in the 1980s—Christian Democratic, Italian Socialist, Republican, Liberal, Social Democratic—as well as 12 percent of the members of parliament were under investigation.

The Italian public began to hear of *Tangentopoli* within a few months. Magistrates are required by law to notify formally anyone suspected of civil or criminal activity that an investigation is underway. These formal notices were reported by the media and *Mani Pulite* entered Italians' homes. For the next eighteen months newspapers and television focused on the magistrates' discoveries. The scale of the scandal grew daily. By 1994 more than 2,500 people were under investigation, over 700 charged, and 70 billion lire (approximately $45 million) in kickbacks recovered out of an estimated 150 trillion lire (approximately $100 billion) total in bribes paid over the preceding decade.

The most common charge was illegal party financing. Public financing of political parties in Italy is accompanied by strict disclosure laws regulating the contributions that individuals may make to the parties. Most of the *tangenti* were kept secret, violating these laws. Additionally, the money, solicited in the name of the party, most commonly remained in the hands of individual politicians. Though exceptional cases of billions of lire in kickbacks were discovered in the bank accounts of a few po-

litical leaders, the more disturbing fact was that corruption was widely practiced throughout the Italian political system.

This aspect came out clearly in the first major case to reach the courts. Sergio Cusani, charged with orchestrating an enormous network of kickbacks to facilitate the sale of a major chemical corporation, was on trial for six months in 1993–94. Cusani was the financial administrator for Raul Gardini, president of the corporation who had committed suicide when informed that he, too, was under investigation. The Cusani trail was carried on television and the leading politicians of the government coalition all testified, acknowledging that illegal sources of party financing were a standard feature of Italian politics. Cusani was found guilty and sentenced to eight years in prison.

The effects of *Tangentopoli* were extraordinary. The political parties most caught up in the scandal suffered a dramatic collapse in popularity. The Italian Socialist Party dissolved at the end of 1993. Craxi, the party secretary, was himself charged with fifty counts of illegal party financing and corruption; if convicted, he would have served more than seven hundred years in jail. Craxi fled to Tunisia and refused to return to Italy. *Tangentopoli* also destroyed the Christian Democrats. The leading party of government for forty-five years, the Christian Democratic Party split into five factions, and almost all of its prominent leaders retired from the political scene.

An enormous reservoir of popular discontent surfaced during the scandal. Some of this anger, however, did not run very deep. Even before *Tangentopoli* began, many Italians knew that corruption was a common feature of their political system. The majority of voters had endorsed the parties most caught up in *Tangentopoli* over the past decade despite, and in some cases because of, the bribery and kickbacks. In addition, small-scale corruption to resolve bureaucratic obstacles or obtain favors from local government was part of the lives of many Italians. *Tangentopoli* became a scandal only when it went public. Previously, corruption had been the least discussed and most widely acknowledged secret of Italian politics.

Though the media played a crucial role in spreading information about *Tangentopoli,* Italian journalists mostly limited themselves to reporting the news from the magistrates. Prior to Operation Clean Hands, the media never thoroughly pursued corruption or denounced the bribes on which the system was built. Only the judiciary, a so-called "virtuous minority" in Italy, brought corruption out into the open, revealed its illegality, filed charges, and prosecuted.

Once the scandal was revealed the Italian electorate looked to new political figures and new movements for a solution to the country's systemic corruption. Parties that had been in parliament but never part of the governing coalitions saw their political fortunes rise: the Democratic Party of the Left, the former Communist Party; the Northern League; and the Italian Social Movement, Italy's neofascist party, all did well in the aftermath of *Tangentopoli*. New political movements appeared as well. The most successful was Silvio Berlusconi's Forza Italia (Go, Italy), which became the largest party in the nation. In the March 1994 elections, when voters replaced over three-quarters of parliament with new representatives, *Tangentopoli* had contributed to a wholesale renewal of the governing groups in Italy.

Operation Clean Hands faced serious problems after the 1994 elections. Cases of suspected corruption no longer focused exclusively on traditional political parties but began to involve some of the newer movements as well. Berlusconi, prime minister from May to December 1994, was also the head of the second-largest private-sector business group in Italy. When his organization, Fininvest, was placed under investigation in September 1994, Berlusconi denounced the magistrates and condemned *Mani Pulite*. In November 1994 Berlusconi was advised that he, too, was under investigation for bribing tax officials, and formal charges were filed in May 1995. The political pressure on the magistrates of *Mani Pulite* reached such high levels that Di Pietro resigned in December 1994, unable to work effectively any longer. With the departure of the man who had started *Tangentopoli*, Operation Clean Hands lost much of its impetus.

Nevertheless, by 1995 a number of businessmen had been convicted of bribery charges. In November 1996, Craxi was sentenced in absentia to five and a half years in prison for his role in accepting bribes for the PSI and the DC from an insurance company seeking to insure workers of the state oil concern ENI. In January 1999 he was again found guilty of corruption in a case dealing with the state electric company and sentenced in absentia to another five and a half years.

On December 3, 1997, Berlusconi was convicted of helping to compile false accounts concerning the purchase of the Medusa film company by his Fininvest group. He was sentenced to sixteen months imprisonment. However, because of his parliamentary immunity, his right to two appeals, and the nature of the Italian judicial system, it is doubtful that he will ever spend time in jail. On July 7, 1998, Berlusconi was convicted of bribing tax officials, and on July 13, 1998, he was sentenced to two years and four months in jail and a $5.6 million fine for paying a bribe to the Socialist Party in 1991. Despite his legal difficulties, in October 1998 he was able to call out a million supporters in Rome for a mass rally in support of himself and in opposition to the government of new Italian prime minister, Massimo D'Alema. In March 1999 he was acquitted of tax fraud.

No matter what its final outcome, the *Tangentopoli* scandal has condemned the most obvious forms of corruption in the Italian political system and removed from the political scene those parties most deeply engaged in bribery.

BIBLIOGRAPHY

Castellacci, Claudio. *Mani pulite*. Milan: SugarCo, 1977.
Colajanni, Napoleone. *Mani pulite?: giustizia e politica in Italia*. Milan: A. Mondadori, 1996.
Nascimbeni, Enrico. *Le mani pulite: l'inchiesta di Milano sulle tangenti*. Milan: A. Mondadori, 1992.
Partridge, Hilary. *Italian Politics Today*. New York: St. Martin's Press, 1998.

David Travis

SEE ALSO Craxi, Benedetto; Di Pietro, Antonio

Regionalism

Before Italy was unified there were many people who advocated a federal form for the new state. But after unification, governments followed a strict centralizing policy to fight the persistence of bureaucracies and institutions of the ancient states. No form of regional government was recognized.

After World War II, the Constituent Assembly recognizing the aspiration to self-government of many Italians, created a new local institutional body: the region. Articles 114 to 127 of the new constitution are completely dedicated to the creation and definition of regions, and many ruling powers are granted to them under article 117 of Italian constitution. To some regions additional powers were conferred, and these were called Special Statute Regions (*regioni a statuto speciale*). These regions are Sicily, Sardinia, Trentino-Alto Adige, Friuli-Venezia Giulia, and Valle d'Aosta. They have control over urban and local police and roads and harbors; and financial autonomy, including the power of introducing new taxes. In recent years, the power of all regions, even those without special statute, have been strengthened, and many taxes are today imposed on a regional basis.

The new regional ordering caused heated debate. Communists and Socialists, favorable in principle to regional autonomy, feared that such institutions could play a role against them, believing, for several reasons, that they would not have a chance to be elected to regional offices. Catholic and Liberal forces, instead, saw the new regional system as a bulwark against Communists. The regional reforms needed an ordinary law to be fully activated, and they therefore remained a dead letter for a long time. In the meantime the situation changed; Communist had conquered many important regional governments, while the Christian Democrats controlled the national government. Under these circumstances, the Communists became the main supporters of regional government. Finally, in 1970 the law was approved that confers most powers to regions, but several more years were needed to fully realize the existing system, that indeed confers to regions relevant powers.

BIBLIOGRAPHY

Cuocolo, Fausto. *L'autonomia politica delle regioni.* Torino: UTET, 1991.

Guccione, E. *Dal federalismo mancato al regionalismo tradito.* Torino: G. Giappichelli, 1998.

Stefania Mazzone

Political Parties

The Christian Democratic Party (DC) was established in 1942 by Catholic proponents of the former Popular Party, which had been founded by Luigi Sturzo. The DC leader was Alcide De Gasperi. Thanks to him DC became the principal Italian party. In 1948 it was regarded as the only alternative to socialism-communism. In 1963 it turned to the left and formed a coalition with the Socialists. In 1977 the DC went so far as to form a government of "national solidarity" with external support from the Communist Party. In the 1980s DC returned to the center-left alliance. In 1992, because of a widespread political scandal, the Italian party system was radically altered. In 1993 the DC dissolved and many parties were born from it. The most important was the Popular Party. In the 1994 election it campaigned against the Right and the Left for a government of the political center. The attempt failed, and its leader, the philosopher Rocco Buttiglione, established the United Christian Democratic Party, which entered the center-right coalition together with Pierferdinando Casini's Christian Democratic Center Party. The Popular Party on the other hand moved to the center-left. Christian Democrat Mario Segni also established a new party, Covenant for Italy, for electoral and institutional reform. In 1996 it confederated with another new center-left party, Italian Revival, founded by Lamberto Dini, the Italian premier in 1995. The Rete Party was also formed by a Christian Democrat, Leoluca Orlando, mayor of Palermo.

The Democratic Party of the Left was formed in 1989 in the wake of the dissolution of the Italian Communist Party (PCI). The new party had the Italian Communist heritage, but many party members were not in agreement with the change, and some of them formed the Communism Refoundation Party. The two parties opposed each other in the 1992 general election, but in 1994 they united to form the Progressive Alliance. This coalition lost the general election; Achille Occhetto, the DS founder, resigned, and Massimo D'Alema was appointed secretary. He followed a more liberal policy. In 1996 his party, as part of a center-left coalition to which Communist Refoundation also belonged, won the general election. In 1998 the party renamed itself Democrats of the Left (DS).

The Socialist Party was established in 1892. After World War II, it became the Socialist Party of Proletarian Unity (PSIUP). It immediately split into the Socialist Party (PSI), directed by Pietro Nenni, and the Socialist Liberal Party, under the leadership of Giuseppe Saragat. In 1950–51 a number of deputies left the PSI and combined with Saragat's party to establish the Social Democratic Party (PSDI). In 1953 some members left the PSI and formed Socialist Unity. Nevertheless, the PSI stayed politically near the PCI until 1956. From that time on, PSI began to distance itself from the PCI and became a center party. In 1962 the left wing of the PSI refused to cooperate with the DC and reestablished the PSIUP. In 1968 the PSI and PSDI reunited, but only for one year. In 1972 the PSIUP dissolved owing to electoral defeat. In 1976 the PSI relinquished its Marxist heritage in favor of reformism. Its new secretary, Bettino Craxi, changed the party symbol, abandoning the hammer and sickle. The PSI was very popular, and Craxi retained the Italian premiership for a relatively long time. In the 1990s the whole PSI leadership was accused of corruption. In 1994 Craxi himself fled to Tunisia to avoid arrest, and the PSI split into many new parties. From the 1970s to the 1990s the PSDI was overwhelmed by a series of scandals. In 1994 that party also disappeared from parliament.

The Italian Liberal Party (PLI) was instituted only in 1922, but its background went back to the Italian risorgimento, the process of Italian unification in the nineteenth century. After World War II it resurfaced as a small, moderate lay party, but with important political proponents such as Benedetto Croce and Enrico Einaudi. In 1976 the PLI moved to a center-left political position. In 1992 some PLI leaders were involved in the Tangentopoli scandal, and in 1994 the party divided. In the 1960s the liberal left founded the Radical Party. In the 1970s Marco Pannella became its leader, and it spearheaded a series of referendum fights on divorce, abortion, and party financing, among other issues.

The Italian Republican Party also originated in the Italian risorgimento. It was reestablished in the 1940s by leaders like Randolfo Pacciardi and Ugo La Malfa. It always had a limited electoral following but strong political influence, and it was in almost all governing coalitions of the republic. In the early 1980s its leader, Giovanni Spadolini, became the first non-DC prime minister of the republic. Some of its proponents were in the center-left coalition in the 1996 general election.

The Italian Social Movement (MSI) was established in 1946 by supporters of the former fascist regime. It was the Italian radical Right party. In the 1970s it joined with two other moderate parties of monarchical inspiration. It became the Italian National Right. In 1994 its young leader, Gianfranco Fini, changed the name of the party and founded the National Alliance. The goal was to break with the fascist tradition and become a credible conservative party. As such it participated in the center-right electoral coalition and won the general election. Later intellectual Pino Rauti and other new fascists founded a new political formation, Tricolour Flame.

The Lombard League, then the North League, was an expression of fiscal and antistatist rebellion in northern Italy. Lombard leader Umberto Bossi founded it in the 1980s. It quickly gained electoral support. The league partially lost its racist and antisouthern bias and became a federalist party. In 1994 it joined the center-right electoral coalition. However, after a few months it withdrew its support from the government. In 1995 the league suffered many splits but retained its voters. In the 1996 general election it ran against the Right and the Left. Its political program was secessionist, for the independence of Padania (northern Italy).

Forza Italia was established in 1994 by Silvio Berlusconi, its undisputed leader. He was also a prominent Italian press and television magnate. His goal was to reunite all moderate voters to obstruct a possible electoral victory of the Left. In the same year Forza Italia, as a result of the general election, became the largest Italian party. Berlusconi became prime minister, but his electoral coalition collapsed.

BIBLIOGRAPHY
Delzell, Charles F. *Italy in the Twentieth Century.* Washington, D.C.: American Historical Association, 1980.
Galli, Giorgio. *I partiti politici italiani.* Milan: Rizzoli, 1991.
Vallauri, Carlo. *I partiti italiani da De Gasperi a Berlusconi.* Rome: Gangemi, 1994.

Dario Caronitti

Green Movement. Italian ecological movement. Following World War II Italy experienced massive economic growth that affected both its urban and rural environments. By the end of the 1950s individuals concerned about conserving natural areas and improving living conditions in the cities formed organizations such as Italia Nostra (Our Italy) and Federazione Pro Natura (Federation for Nature). Not until the mid-1980s, however, did a national ecology campaign extend into Italian political, social, and economic life.

The rise of the New Left during the worker and student movements of the late 1960s provided a stimulus for the advent of ecological organizations. These small groups stressed the importance of the relationship between humans and the environment. They believed that the major political parties in postwar Italy had failed to address meaningfully pertinent environmental issues. The Radical Party, composed of non-Communist leftists, was the first major party to emphasize concerns such as pollution, preservation, and energy through an affiliated organization called Friends of the Earth. By the end of the 1970s environmental groups began to acquire popular support. During the early 1980s ecological organizations became more visible. The social movements of the 1970s had provided an impetus for new political models. People who had been active in extraparliamentary groups sought an alternative to traditional political discourse and methods. Many of them joined environmental groups once their own organizations collapsed. Environmental groups shared with the New Left the belief that they needed to work toward overall improvement in the quality of people's lives. Moreover, Italians began to participate in outdoor activities such as camping and hiking in growing numbers and, therefore, to emphasize the importance of nature. The Chernobyl nuclear power plant disaster in 1986 in Soviet Ukraine further increased public awareness of the possibility of serious environmental catastrophe.

The Italian Green Party (La Federazione dei Verdi) was created in 1986. In its first national elections in 1987, campaigning under the symbol of the smiling sun, the Green Party won 2.6 percent of the vote, with thirteen seats in the Chamber of Deputies and one seat in the Senate. In the 1996 elections it won 2.5 percent of the national vote, and sent fourteen deputies and fourteen senators to parliament. Its political platform shares many points in common with other European Greens. For example, the Green Party maintains that citizens must reevaluate their interactions with nature and society to reduce the use of natural resources and control waste. They support the use of "cleaner" technology, call for a reduction in the use of chemicals in agriculture, and promote improvement of public transportation to decrease private automobile use. The Green Party also addresses issues specific to social, economic, and political conditions in Italy. It is especially concerned with Italy's dense population and its impact on nature as well as urban areas. Moreover, it wants to maintain a strong, healthy democracy. As a result, Italian Greens are outspoken against the Mafia and government corruption. They also point to Italy's leading political parties—Forza Italia and Alleanza Nazionale—as forces pulling Italy away from democracy. The Green Party in addition supports measures to improve secondary education, solve Italy's employment problem, and promote the full equality of men and women before the law.

BIBLIOGRAPHY

Bottaccioli, Francesco, and Alfonso Pecararo Scanio, eds. *Notizie Verdi: il giornale della federazione dei Verdi.* Rome: Editoriale Eco, soc. cooperativa, 1990.

Diani, Mario. "The Italian Ecology Movement: From Radicalism to Moderation," in *Green Politics One.* Wolfgang Rudig, ed. Carbondale: Southern Illinois University Press, 1990.

———. *Il sole nell'arcipelago: Il movimento ecologista in Italia.* Bologna: Il Mulino, 1988.

Federazione dei Verdi. *La via verde: Programmi d'azione e a progetto dei verdi italiani.* Florence: Passigli Editori, 1995.

Ravaioli, Carla, and Enzo Tiezzi. *La crescita fredda: Occaisione storica per la sinistra.* Rome: Datanews, 1995.

Wendy A. Pojmann

Italian Communist Party. Founded in 1921, the Italian Communist Party (PCI) played a central role in the armed opposition to Mussolini's Italian Social Republic in 1944 and 1945. Building on its resistance record, the PCI quickly became an important feature in the postwar Italian political landscape. It was one of the most ideologically and tactically innovative of Western European Communist parties, despite its Stalinism. After 1968 it appeared that the PCI was likely to enter the government. However, the party still labored under the effects of the Cold War and its identification with the Soviet Union. Despite a parliamentary alliance with the main governing party, the Christian Democrats (DC), the PCI never became a governing party and dissolved itself in 1989.

The PCI's postwar history was dominated by the political tension between its national and international positions. As a communist party it had clear and acknowl-

edged links with the Soviet Union, and, at the same time, the PCI struggled to bring communism to Italy. In the immediate aftermath of war, military occupation by Britain and the United States prevented a seizure of power by the PCI, and in May 1947 the PCI was forced out of the coalition government by Alcide De Gasperi. Thereafter, the PCI formed the main oppositional party in Italy, facing the Christian Democrats who, initially at least, were heavily financed by the United States. As the Cold War took hold, the PCI had to develop a strategy that took account of Italy's membership in NATO, and the cultural and political impact of Catholicism in the country.

Such a strategy was constructed out of the writings of Antonio Gramsci, the PCI general secretary, who had died in 1937 after release from a fascist prison. Gramsci argued that an Italian path to communism would depend on the conquest of civil society by the party. The aim was to replace bourgeois culture as the dominant, or hegemonic, culture, by a working-class, or Marxist, culture. In terms of the international Communist movement, this strategy for a particularly Italian way to communism was termed "polycentrism" by the PCI's secretary general, Palmiro Togliatti. The implication was that the Bolshevik path of 1917 was not the only way to socialism.

The PCI grew in strength throughout the 1950s, with party membership exceeding two million and nearly one-third of the electorate voting Communist. The 1956 Soviet invasion of Hungary once again highlighted the Stalinist nature of the PCI when it denounced the Hungarian rebels as fascists. Around 250,000 people left the PCI as a result, but a recruiting drive replaced most of these losses.

Although the PCI was unable to break into national government, it did have numerous local government successes, especially in Emilia-Romagna and Tuscany, Italy's Red Belt, with Bologna taking pride of place in PCI local government. The party also controlled one of Italy's strongest labor unions, the Confederazione Generale Italiano del Lavoro (CGIL), ran a number of popular newspapers, and was influential among Italy's non-Catholic intelligentsia. Its electoral appeal, in addition to the third of the industrial working class that supported the party, was to a wide spectrum of social classes, from peasants to the educated bourgeoisie.

The Stalinist conformity that characterized the PCI until the early 1960s began to erode after Togliatti's death in 1964. The Soviet-led Warsaw Pact's crushing of the Czechoslovak Prague Spring in 1968, although the official party line condemned both the Czechs and the Soviet-led invasion forces, increased debate within the PCI about its strategy.

The erosion of Stalinism within the party became fully apparent in the 1970s. In 1973 Enrico Berlinguer, party general secretary, launched the "historic compromise," which declared that the PCI could envisage joining the Christian Democrats in a coalition government. In part, the compromise strategy was a reaction to events in Chile, in which a democratically elected Communist government was overthrown in a bloody military coup instigated by the United States. Berlinguer felt that a similar fate might well await a PCI government in Italy. Berlinguer's strategy had potential dangers, however, as it amounted to a partial acceptance of the capitalist system. The PCI even asserted that it would not oppose continued Italian participation in NATO. Nonetheless, the PCI continued to develop this theme of a "third way" to socialism, between social democracy and Soviet-style communism. In 1975 this approach was termed "Eurocommunism," and the PCI was seen to be in the forefront of the Eurocommunist movement, which eventually characterized, to a greater or lesser degree, all the Communist parties of Western Europe.

The mid-1970s were troubled years for Italy, with increases in international commodity prices, stagflation, and terrorism from Right and Left putting pressure on the political system. In 1976 the DC government of Giulio Andreotti introduced a widespread deflationary package fully supported by the PCI. The party also strongly supported the various law-and-order measures introduced by the government. In the three years in which the PCI actively supported the government, they had received next to nothing in return. By 1979 the DC government had weathered the worst of the storms and no longer needed the Communists. The historic compromise strategy was in ruins, and it became a commonplace that "the Christian Democrats have made the history, the PCI has made the compromises."

More defeats followed for the Communists in the 1980s. A defining moment in capital-labor relations came in 1980 with the defeat of the FIAT strike at the company's huge Turin works. Over twenty-four thousand workers were sacked, including the most organized and politically aware, and FIAT introduced a new production regime more favorable to management. The defeat of the FIAT strike marked the collapse of industrial resistance and confirmed the decline of the PCI in terms of votes, membership, and industrial strength. In 1985 the PCI lost control of its major city councils, and the party finally seemed to give up all hope of a Communist Italy, abandoning its belief in an "exit from capitalism." In the 1987 election the PCI recorded its lowest vote since 1963, 26 percent. Party membership was down to 1,500,000, and

the youth wing had dropped to 50,000 members. By the end of the 1980s communism was in retreat throughout Eastern Europe, and in 1989 the PCI General Secretary Achille Occhetto proposed the end of the party and the creation of a new left-wing movement. At the party's Twentieth Congress in Rimini, in January–February 1991, the PCI was formally dissolved and a new left-wing party, the Democratic Party of the Left (PDS), was created. In October 1998 the party was again renamed the Democrats of the Left (DS).

BIBLIOGRAPHY

della Torre, Paolo, Edward Mortimer, and Jonathan Story, eds. *Euro-Communism, Myth or Reality?* Harmondsworth, England: Penguin, 1979.

Ruscoe, James. *The Italian Communist Party, 1976–1981, on the threshold of government.* London: Macmillan, 1982.

Sassoon, Donald. *The Strategy of the Italian Communist Party: From Resistance to Historic Compromise.* London: Frances Pinter, 1981.

Stephen M. Cullen

SEE ALSO Berlinguer, Enrico; De Gasperi, Alcide; Eurocommunism; Occhetto, Achille; Togliatti, Palmiro

Leagues. Generic name for several grassroots regionalist movements that emerged in Northern Italy in the wake of the success of the Liga Veneta. There are regional leagues (*leghe*) in Piedmont, Liguria, Lombardy, Trentino, Veneto, Friuli, Trieste, Emilia-Romagna, Tuscany, and increasingly in other regions. The largest of them, the Lombard League, was founded in 1982 by Umberto Bossi. Originally named Lega Autonomista Lombarda, it demanded, among other things, fewer taxes and political autonomy for Lombardy. It rapidly grew into the most popular grassroots movement in postwar Italy. Rechristened Northern League (Lega Nord) in 1991, it became the leading party in Lombardy in the 1992 regional elections. Made up of enthusiastic but politically inexperienced leaders, it touched a vibrant popular chord by posing as the defender of prosperous and hardworking Lombardy against the allegedly high-taxing, Mafia-infiltrated, corruption-ridden central government in Rome. The league's attacks on the state at a moment when its legitimacy was crumbling, tainted as it was by contacts with organized crime, provided a major moral boost for *Tangentopoli,* the political upheaval that swept away Italy's postwar republican structure, inaugurating the Second Republic.

Bossi's entry into the Chamber of Deputies in 1992 brought the party new members. In 1994 it became a leading political force and entered the government of Silvio Berlusconi. However, the relationship between Bossi and Berlusconi quickly soured and Bossi's threat of a vote of no confidence forced Berlusconi to resign in December 1994. In the election of 1996 the league won only 10.1 percent of the vote.

On September 15, 1996, Bossi and other leagues' leaders met in a much-publicized demonstration in Venice to declare the independence of Padania, a macro-region the extent of which has often been kept unclear: from an original nucleus of northern regions, it has then expanded to encompass Tuscany, Umbria, and Marche. But for some it reaches as far south as Rome's hinterland. In the minds of some league leaders there was also the chance that all Italian regions could freely join the Republic of Padania, thus bypassing Rome's "centralism." The borders of each region forming Padania should conform approximately to existing regional borders, with the exception of Friuli-Venezia Giulia and Emilia-Romagna; Friuli, with its capital at Udine, should be separated from Venezia Giulia, with its capital at Trieste, and Romagna should become autonomous from Emilia. *Leghisti* (singular, *leghista*) is the name attached to the followers of one of the leagues in Bossi's group. Moreover, several smaller regionalist parties have emerged in various Italian regions to challenge Bossi's authority but have been unsuccessful so far.

BIBLIOGRAPHY

Bossi, Umberto. *La rivoluzione*. Milan: Sperling & Kupfer, 1993.

———. *Vento dal nord*. Milan: Sperling & Kupfer, 1992.

Canteri, Raffaello. *I cento giorni della Lega: Gli 80 parlamentari a Roma; le storie, le battaglie, l'impegno politico*. Verona: Euronobel, 1992.

Cardini, Franco. *La vera storia della Lega lombarda*. Milan: A. Mondadori, 1991.

Costantini, Luciano. *Dentro la Lega: Come nasce, come cresce, come comunica*. Rome: Koine, 1994.

Diamanti, Ilvo. *La lega: Geografia, storia e sociologia di un nuovo soggetto politico*. Rome: Donzelli, 1993.

Mannheimer, Renato. *La Lega lombarda*. Milan: Feltrinelli, 1991.

Miglio, Gianfranco. *Io, Bossi e la Lega: Diario segreto dei miei quattro anni sul Carroccio*. Milan: Mondadori, 1994.

Daniele Conversi

SEE ALSO Bossi, Umberto

Olive Tree. The Olive Tree began as a center-left political movement in February 1995 under the leadership of university professor Romano Prodi. When Rocco Buttiglione, leader of the Popular Party (Partito Popolare, PPI), a progressive Catholic party born from the splitting of the Christian Democrat Party (DC), affirmed that his party was to join the right-wing coalition, the majority of the party rebelled. As Buttiglione was forced to leave the PPI followed by a minority faction, which took the name United Christian Democrats (Cristiano Democratici Uniti), Prodi was put forward by the PPI for the premiership at the head of a center-left coalition, which took the name Olive Tree. The olive tree was chosen as a symbol since, as Prodi explained in his book *La mia Italia,* it "is to be found anywhere in Italy; it represents the outcome of hundred of years of human labor and its being contorted shows that it has the strength to resist the most severe climate."

Among the dozen parties forming the Olive Tree the two major parties were the Democrats of the Left (PDS) and the PPI, joined by various socialists, liberals, republicans, and greens, the so-called bushes. Since Prodi was from the PPI, Walter Veltroni of the Democrats of the Left was named his number two, both in the coalition and in the government, if the Olive Tree were to win. But in addition to the parties, hundreds of committees "For the Italy we want" were spontaneously formed all over the country by ordinary citizens (mainly upper-middle-class professionals) otherwise not formally involved in politics. An electoral program (the *Tesi dell'Ulivo*) was elaborated by the committees, while Prodi visited Italy on a one-hundred-day coach tour. The *Tesi dell'Ulivo* had eighty-eight points and covered every area of policy from bioethics to judicial reform.

When center-left coalitions won the regional elections of April 23, 1995, the consolidation of the Olive Tree was further enhanced. In a euphoric climate, the Olive Tree then won the legislative elections on April 21, 1996. Prodi was named prime minister with Veltroni as his deputy. Yet since the coalition received an absolute majority only in the Senate (upper chamber), the new executive needed the external support of the Communist Party (Rifondazione Comunista) to govern. This led to continuous bargaining and eventual tensions, in particular over the approval of the annual budgets, which were needed to fulfill the rigorous conditions required for entering the European Monetary Union (EMU) by its inception on January 1, 1999.

In addition, from the very beginning, two opposing views existed among the *Ulivisti:* those who perceived the Olive Tree as a coalition of parties and those who understood it as the first step toward the formation of a single party in the image of the U.S. Democratic Party. Those tensions reemerged and exploded when Prodi, on October 9, 1998, lost a vote of confidence in parliament, which he called to gain approval of the annual budget. There was a rearrangement within the coalition. A new centrist party joined the Olive Tree, while the Communist Party split, a faction entering the coalition and the government, and another joining the opposition. Prodi was replaced by the leader of the Democrats of the Left, Massimo D'Alema. Veltroni, who left the government with Prodi, succeeded D'Alema as leader of the Democrats of the Left. Feeling somewhat betrayed, Prodi founded a new party, the Democrats. As its leader, he intended to run in the elections for the European Parliament on June 13, 1999. But following his nomination as president of the European Commission, he had to withdraw from that campaign. The vision of the Olive Tree as a coalition was thus confirmed, with the Olive Tree symbol appearing alongside the symbols of its constituent parties in the European electoral campaign.

BIBLIOGRAPHY

Partridge, Hilary. *Italian Politics Today.* New York: St. Martin's Press, 1998.

Federiga Bindi

SEE ALSO Buttiglione, Rocco; D'Alema, Massino; Prodi, Romano

Party of Action. The Party of Action (Partito d'Azione) was founded in 1942 by members of the Italian liberal intelligentsia fighting against the fascist regime. Militants of the republican organization Giustizia e Libertà (Justice and Liberty) and some of the most important representatives of liberal socialism were united in it. Its program suggested replacing class struggle by building a socialist society strongly respectful of democracy and civil rights. The Party of Action was very active in the resistance to fascism. Its members participated in the armed struggle and published a clandestine review, *L'Italia libera.* It tried to counterbalance the influence both of the Communist forces and of the Catholics, offering itself as the leading force for a new democratic Italy. One of its leaders, Ferruccio Parri, became premier for a short time at the end of the war, from June to November 1945.

The Party of Action had a very short life. It was crushed by the strength of the Marxist and Catholic currents and did not succeed in resolving the collision between its democratic and socialist-revolutionary wings. The Party of Action dissipated in 1947 and its members

gravitated toward different political forces. The Republican Party and some non-Marxist currents of the left were, in particular, invigorated by the infusion of former members of the Party of Action. The influence of the Party of Action endured beyond its dissolution, thanks to the solidarity of its members and to the solidity of its political proposals. Among its representatives were Ugo La Malfa, a longtime secretary of the Italian Republican Party; Ferruccio Parri; Emilio Lussu, a leader of the Sardinian independence movement; Riccardo Lombardi, an important leader of the Italian Socialist Party; and Leo Valiani. All these left a deep impression on Italian political life.

BIBLIOGRAPHY

Aga Rossi, Elena. *Il movimento repubblicano, giustizia e libertà e il Partito d'azione.* Bologna: Cappelli, 1969.
Campagnano, Alessandra, ed. *Il Partito d'azione 50 anni dopo: un'esperienza per il futuro.* Milan: F. Angeli, 1993.
De Luna, Giovanni. *Storia del Partito d'azione (1942–1947).* Rome: Editori Riuniti, 1997.
Istituto di studi Ugo La Malfa. *Il Partito d'azione dalle origini all'inizio della resistenza armata.* Rome: Archivio Trimestrale, 1985.

Daniele Petrosino

SEE ALSO La Malfa, Ugo; Parri, Ferruccio; Sardinian Autonomism

Radical Party and Civil Rights

The Radical Party was founded at the beginning of the 1950s by the left wing of the Italian Liberal Party and became politically active in 1956. It was predominately a movement organized to influence public opinion in opposition to the policies of the Christian Democrats (DC). In the 1960s the party split between a wing favorable to the center-left coalition of the Christian Democrats and Socialists and a wing absolutely hostile to any alliance with the DC. The latter, led by Marco Pannella, generated a small but influential political movement. Although the party did not have significant electoral success, it became the protagonist in some of the most important metamorphoses in Italian customs and politics. As a political force of liberal inspiration, it mobilized public opinion in the defense of civil rights, divorce, and abortion, which won large support. It also promoted referenda on many important issues of Italian political life.

In the 1980s the Radical Party distinguished itself through campaigns against preventive detention and for freedom of the press. Its preferred tools of political action were hunger strikes and other pacifist initiatives. During the 1980s it obtained important electoral support, and in the second half of the decade it participated in different electoral coalitions with Greens and libertarians and tried to create a transnational party. The Radical Party, was finally dissolved, however, and some of its most important representatives entered into the alliance for good government that won the Italian election in 1994.

BIBLIOGRAPHY

Aghina, Guido, and Claudio Jaccarino. *Storia del partito radicale.* Milan: Gamma libri, 1980.

Gusso Massimo. *Il Partito radicale: organizzazione e leadership.* Padua: CLEUP, 1982.

Morabito, Fabio. *La sfida radicale: Il partito radicale da Pannunzio a Pannella.* Milan: SugarCo, 1977.

Ponzone, Lorenza. *Il Partito radicale nella politica italiana: 1962–1989.* Fasano: Schena, 1993.

Daniele Petrosino

SEE ALSO Pannella, Giacinto

Press

As in many other European countries after World War II, the press played a key role in defining and determining the postwar order in Italy. Contrary to the ideal of objectivity that informs the Anglo-American tradition of journalism, Italian journalism in the twentieth century has been marked by its intimate relationship with political ideologies. The Anglo-American standard also questions the lack of either a truly national or popular press. Newspapers and journals in Italy are usually identified with a particular political party or with a single individual with pronounced political, social, and economic views. Because there is no segment of Italian society—from farmers, to students, to housewives, to the Vatican—that does not have a voice through its own newspaper, journal, or weekly, the Italian press might make the claim that it is more representative of the country than are its Anglo-American counterparts.

With the fall of fascism in the summer of 1943, newspapers that had been suppressed or forced underground for twenty years resurfaced and new papers were born. By 1945 Italian journalism was a vital and powerful force as each of the major political parties sought to fashion Italy in their own image. The attempt to purge industry (and the country) of lingering elements and protagonists of the fascist regime failed; before the war was even over, politicians and journalists agreed to maintain control over the profession through the legislation of the fascist "corporativist" state. Many of the ideological polemics that were to characterize the postwar period were actually continuations of battles begun under the fascist regime.

The major political party papers are *L'Unità* of the Italian Communist Party (after 1993 the Democratic Party of the Left, or PDS); *Avanti!* of the Italian Socialist Party; the Catholic party (formerly Christian Democrats, today Italian Popular Party) depends mostly on an extensive but locally based press. In 1952, notwithstanding legislation against a fascist party, neofascists began publishing *Il Secolo d'Italia,* which is today the organ of the National Alliance, a "postfascist" party.

Until well into the twentieth century, local dialects and regionalism determined much of Italian culture, and this was reflected in journalism. Some papers are known by their city and regional affiliation: *Il Corriere della Sera* of Milan and Lombardy; *La Stampa* of Turin and Piedmont, closely identified with its owners, the Agnelli family of the FIAT motor company; *Il Resto di Carlino* of Bologna and Emilia-Romagna, which prints a column in the local dialect; *La Nazione* of Florence and Tuscany; *Il Messagero* of Rome; *Il Mattino* of Naples and Campagna; *La Gazzetta del Mezzogiorno* of Bari and Puglia.

There is a distinct geographical divide as the north reads more than the south (Mezzogiorno). However, unlike all the other Western industrialized countries, "Italy" does not read much. In the sixty-five years between the outbreak of World War I and 1980, readership of the daily press remained constant at around five million. A survey in 1956 found that nearly 65 percent of the population never read anything at all. By 1990 readership had increased only slightly to 6.5 million daily readers. Part of this can be explained by historical forces: although other industrialized nations became literate early, Italians as a nation became literate only in the postwar period, when other sources of information and entertainment (radio and television) were competing with the newspapers for an audience. The visual culture is best represented by *L'Espresso* and *Panorama,* highly popular illustrated weeklies.

Il Corriere della Sera, established in 1876, was the closest Italy had to a leading, national daily with an international reputation, until it was challenged by the upstart *La Repubblica* in 1975. By 1990 *La Repùbblica* had overtaken the venerable *Corriere della Sera* as the most popular newspaper in Italy. As might be expected, the official organ of the Vatican, *L'Osservatore Romano,* also has an excellent distribution system throughout the country. There are also specialty papers such as *Il Sole-24 Ore,* reporting on the financial world, and the extremely popular sport publications such as the pink-papered *La Gazzetta dello Sport* and *Il Corriere dello Sport;* the Monday morning editions of these papers sell approximately 800,000 and 500,000 copies, respectively. Italian newspapers have the crime stories, investigative journalism, and even a touch of the tabloids that are familiar to American readers, but they also pride themselves that academics and intellectuals regularly write columns for the daily press.

The relation between political power and journalism is nowhere more evident than in Italy. Mussolini began his public career as a journalist (ironically as editor of the Socialist *Avanti!*); more than half a century later—but from the opposite end of the political spectrum—Giovanni Spadolini left his position as editor of *Il Corrière della Sera* to be head of the Italian Republican Party and eventually the first postwar prime minister from outside the Christian Democrat Party. But as Robert Lumley has so tellingly written, the era in which the editor of a newspaper could become prime minister has been replaced by one in which the prime minister was a television mogul (Silvio Berlusconi, 1994). Nothing could better illustrate what one scholar has called "post-journalism."

BIBLIOGRAPHY

Bechelloni, Giovanni. *Giornalismo o postgiornalismo?* Naples: Liguori, 1995.

Castronovo, Valerio, and Nicola Tranfalgia, eds. *La stampa italiana nell'età della tv, 1975–1994.* Rome-Bari: Laterza, 1994.

Colombo, Furio. *Ultime notizie sul giornalismo.* Rome-Bari: Laterza, 1995.

Lumley, Robert, ed. *Italian Journalism: A Critical Anthology.* Manchester, England: Manchester University Press, 1996.

Murialdi, Paolo. *La stampa italiana: Dalla liberazione alla crisi di fine secolo.* Rome-Bari: Laterza, 1995.

Stanislao G. Pugliese

Camorra

Neapolitan criminal organization first described in the late eighteenth century, although it may have originated as early as the 1500s. It was originally associated with gambling and extortion. The Camorra nearly disappeared during the 1800s. It was regenerated near the conclusion of World War II when the Mafia employed individual criminals in its cigarette smuggling operations through the port of Naples. Once its numbers had been replenished, the Camorra began to distinguish itself from the Mafia. Unlike the Sicilian Mafia, the Camorra operates on a unilateral organizational level. It is less family-based than the Mafia and more diversified. Having acquired new strength, the Camorra flourished with Italian economic growth of the 1970s and has been difficult to eradicate. Under the leadership of Raffaele Cutolo's New Organized Camorra (NCO), the society went from a small group of disorganized criminals engaging in smuggling and extortion to a well-structured organization dominating the drug trade.

Cutolo's rule did not go unchallenged. Following a devastating earthquake in 1980, Luigi Vollaro and Luigi Giuliano's New Family alliance successfully overthrew Cutolo. The reformed Camorra then saw an opportunity to expand its power and finances by participating in the rebuilding of damage in Naples and surrounding areas. Through political buy-offs and shrewd business dealings, the Camorra entered into complex social, economic, and political alliances. The Camorra rewarded government officials who put money into Camorra-run industries. Within just a few years the Camorra had legal and illegal business ventures in every area of the economy: construction, agriculture, tourism, entertainment, public service, and banking all had Camorra links.

Neapolitan crime boss Carmine Alfieri reputedly led the Camorra to the top of the cocaine trade, a $300 billion business, through his alliances with the Colombian and Venezuelan cartels. Alfieri was born in Nola, near Naples. A criminal from his childhood, Alfieri by the age of eighteen led a group of racketeers. Later, he began to extort money from local businessmen and farmers and sold arms to Sicilian mobsters. His construction company dominated the local market. More important, however, was Alfieri's involvement in local politics. Following the kidnapping of Christian Democrat Ciro Cirillo, a member of the regional council of the province of Campania, in April 1981 by the Red Brigades, the Christian Democrats turned to Alfieri for assistance. Not only did Alfieri's role as negotiator contribute to the defeat of the NCO, but it also revealed links between the Camorra and high-ranking government officials. Alfieri thus secured his place in the Camorra and became quite powerful. He successfully evaded the authorities until his arrest at his Nola estate in September 1992, following a series of international drug investigations.

The Camorra's main activities have included extortion, gambling, usury, cigarette smuggling, cocaine trafficking, and money laundering. Many of these illegal dealings have been carried out on the edge of legality, making it difficult to end the Camorra's operations. Moreover, the Camorra has a vast international network and a carefully designed hierarchy of power in which low-level criminals take legal responsibility for the crimes of higher-ups.

Despite a few instances of mass protest against the Camorra, many of the inhabitants of the province of Campania where Naples is located remain intertwined in the Camorra system. When unemployment and poverty are high in the region, the Camorra flourishes. Since the Camorra operates as a parallel to the government and easily replenishes positions left vacant by arrest or murder, it has been extremely difficult to eliminate. Like the Mafia, the Camorra benefits from the poor economic conditions of the south. Few Campanians can completely evade interaction with Camorra and many profit from its strength.

BIBLIOGRAPHY
Behan, Tom. *The Camorra*. London: Routledge, 1988.
Commissione Parlamentare Antimafia. *Camorra e politica: Relazione approvata dalla commissione il 21 dicembre 1993*. Rome: Laterza, 1994.
Marrazzo, Giuseppe. *Il camorrista: Vita segreta di don Rafaele Cutolo*. Naples: T. Pironti, 1984.
Ricci, Paolo. *Le origini della camorra: 150 anni di malavita napoletana raccontati da Paolo Ricci*. Naples: Sintesi Stampa, 1989.
Scarpino, Salvatore. *Storia della Camorra*. Milan: Fenice, 2000.
Vulliamy, Edward. "The Rise and Fall and Naples' Camorra Incorporated." *Guardian* 8 (July 2, 1991):585.

Wendy A. Pojmann

Cassa per il Mezzogiorno

The Cassa per il Mezzogiorno (Southern Fund), modeled on the U.S. Tennessee Valley Authority, was proposed by Donato Menichella to promote development in Italy's underdeveloped south. Established on August 10, 1950, it centered its efforts until 1955 on agriculture and infrastructure development, proposing programs to a ministerial committee and to parliament. From 1955 to 1960 it promoted, by financial incentives, the location of private, capital-intensive establishments in the south and until 1973 channeled investment in public industries to that region. Only big industries such as FIAT and Montedison were promoted and the results were disappointing. There was much waste and only moderate levels of job creation.

The fund was refinanced in 1971, but its activity depended on annual extensions of public expenditure. A law of December 1, 1983, provided for a system of planning involving the minister for emergency interventions, the Interministerial Committee for Economic Planning, and the southern regions, which were assigned sweeping responsibility for their development. On August 10, 1984, the Southern Fund was abolished and replaced by the Agency for the Promotion of the Development of the South. It provided financial support to projects recommended first through a three-year plan and then annual plans. The agency could negotiate loans with the European Bank for Investment and banks in the south, and provided capital to the organizations that had been linked

to the Southern Fund. It has a number of subdivisions: FINAM-S.P.A. promoted agrarian production; FIME-S.P.A. promoted small and median industries; INSUD-S.P.A. promoted energy and tourism; ITALTRAND-S.P.A. promoted trade in southern products; FORMEZ provided staff training; Spinsud-S.P.A. arranged investment planning for advanced technology; and IASM-S.P.A. provided technical assistance to new industries in the south. The Emergency Intervention Act, nevertheless, failed to transform the southern economy and was ended through a referendum in 1992.

BIBLIOGRAPHY
Ministro per gli interventi straordinari nel Mezzogiorno. *Programma triennale d'intervento*. Roma: 1985–87.
Riviello, C. *Dalla Cassa per il Mezzogiorno al nuovo intervento straordinario*. Bologna: Il Mulino, 1988.
Zamagni, V., and M. Sanfilippo. *Nuovo meridionalismo e intervento straordinario, La SVIMEZ dal 1946 al 1950*. Bologna: Il Mulino, 1988.

Adalgisa Efficace

Cinema

Italian cinema regained the world's attention after World War II because of the explosive creative vitality and challenging aesthetics of neorealism. Although film critics and historians are reappraising the revolutionary dimensions of neorealism, pointing to the genre's roots in the fascist period, there is still little doubt of the force of renewal that permeated the Italian film industry after the war.

Neorealism in the cinema was generated by the literary neorealism of the 1930s and 1940s. Luchino Visconti's groundbreaking *Ossessione* appeared in 1942, a year before the fall of Mussolini and three years before the end of the war. Here, in opposition to fascism's grand historical dramas glorifying ancient Rome and the conquests of the regime, or the banal, pseudosophisticated world depicted in the so-called white telephone films, was presented the tawdry story of adultery, murder, and despair. The better-known classics of neorealism retained Visconti's technique of making film time match real time but moved to other concerns: fascism and the war (*Paisan*, 1946); the partisans of the resistance (*Roma, città aperta*, 1945); the social conditions of postwar Italy (*La terra trema*, 1948; *Bicycle Thief*, 1948; *Umberto D*, 1951).

Besides their common political and social concerns directors like Visconti, Roberto Rossellini, and Vittorio De Sica insisted on new techniques that would become synonymous with neorealism: use of nonprofessional actors, equating film time with real time, avoiding artificial studio sets, and the "documentary" texture of the cinematography. With this new "grammar" of cinematic language, neorealism has conventionally been considered almost a necessary aesthetic reaction to the bombast of fascism. Although Rossellini felt that neorealism was "simply the artistic form of the truth," and De Sica insisted that his films were "reality transposed into the realm of poetry," the directors were too sophisticated to believe that their films were completely "objective"; in fact, they would have resisted such a label. Ironically, these films that restored and reinforced Italy's reputation as a major film producer often suffered dismally at the box office. Italian audiences flocked to view the latest imports from Hollywood (as they did during the fascist period, forcing the regime to impose a quota on foreign films), while the classics of neorealism were ignored. Escapist films enjoyed box office success while works critical of the status quo and demanding social change languished in neglect except for a small, dedicated audience in Italy and abroad.

By the late 1950s and early 1960s film critics were furiously debating the "crisis" and "betrayal" of neorealism as the directors moved on in search of another cinematic language. This period is best represented by Federico Fellini and Michelangelo Antonioni, both of whom had their film roots in the fascist period and served their apprenticeship during the neorealist period.

The neorealist aesthetic had already been challenged by Rossellini's *The Machine That Kills Bad People* (1948) and De Sica's *Miracle in Milan* (1950), two examples of magic realism, while Visconti turned to an operatic mode in *Senso* (1954). Rossellini returned to neorealism in 1959 with *General Della Rovere,* an inquiry into identity and moral choices, after having moved away from the genre with a handful of films (1949–54) he made with Swedish-born American film star Ingrid Bergman that examined modern alienation and interior states of mind rather than social and political conditions. These concerns were later best developed by what might be called the existentialist cinema of Antonioni. In his classic trilogy, *L'Avventura* (1960), *La Notte* (1961), and *The Eclipse* (1962), Antonioni is concerned with how modern individuals struggle with the modern, industrial landscape. His stark photography and purposeful silence expose the frailty of the human psyche and complex emotional states. Fellini concentrated on the development of fantastic scenarios and idiosyncratic characters, merging mythology and symbolism. With *Variety Lights* (1950) and *Lo sceicco bianco* (1952), he reveals the ambiguous boundaries between reality and illusion, the mask of our social selves, and the ambivalence of our true persona in an ontologically theatrical world. In 1954 Fellini achieved worldwide acclaim with his masterpiece, *La Strada,* the "philosophical para-ble" of a pathetic waif (Giulietta Masina, Fellini's wife) and the circus strongman Zampanò, whose lives cross the path of "The Fool." As film critic André Bazin noted, *La Strada* unveiled the "phenomenology of the soul," while ignoring social or political themes. Fellini's close collaboration with composer Nino Rota produced a hauntingly beautiful score that became almost as famous as the film.

In 1958, after the world had lost interest in neorealism for some time, Italian cinema began another extraordinary resurgence that was to last a decade. Italian production reached a peak of 290 new films in 1964, while the U.S. industry was suffering a decline; combined with renewed vitality and experimentation, this was to insure a spectacular decade for Italian cinema. Leading the way was the *commedia all'italiana* based on the older theatrical tradition of commedia dell'arte. Mario Monicelli's *Big Deal on Madonna Street* (1958) brought together Vittorio Gasman, Claudia Cardinale, and Marcello Mastroianni—actors previously known only for their dramatic roles. Shining above them all was Totò, the immortal comic actor with roots in the Neapolitan theater and dialect. At its best *commedia all'italiana* confronted the hypocrisy and problems of contemporary Italian society. Pietro Germi's *Divorce, Italian Style* (1961) and *Seduced and Abandoned* (1964) critique the male code of conduct concerning sex and marriage. Luigi Comencini and Dino Risi also portrayed Italy's rapidly changing society with satire and irony.

The 1960s witnessed the birth of two new film genres in Italy as well; the exploitation film (best represented by Gualtiero Jacopetti's *Mondo cane* of 1962) and the spaghetti western that reached its greatest expression with Sergio Leone. At its best, as with Leone's *A Fistful of Dollars* (1964) and *The Good, the Bad, and the Ugly* (1966), the spaghetti western even influenced American westerns by introducing the morally ambiguous "hero" who is not much better than the "bad guys," in contrast to the usual stark American dichotomy of "white" and "black" hats. In addition, Leone's collaboration with composer Ennio Morricone was just as critical for the success of the spaghetti westerns as Fellini's collaboration with Rota.

The economic boom that transformed Italy from a rural, agricultural, largely illiterate country into a modern, urban, industrialized state was a natural subject for filmmakers in the 1960s. Some directors were fascinated with the fading traditional culture and sought to preserve that vanishing world. Vittorio De Seta made *Banditi a Orgosolo* in 1961 with a neorealist aesthetic that depicted the lives of Sardinian bandits, while Francesco Rosi portrayed the career and death of the infamous bandit in *Salvatore Giuliano* (1962); seventeen years later Rosi would return to the world of the rural peasant with an adaptation of Carlo Levi's literary masterpiece, *Christ Stopped at Eboli.* The ideological and aesthetic considerations of neorealism were perhaps best represented in Gillo Pontecorvo's *La battaglia di Algeri* (1966), which seemed to be a documentary of the civil war in the former French colony.

If in Italy the 1960s were marked by the commercial success of the *commedia all'italiana* and the spaghetti western, internationally audiences flocked to view the works of Fellini, Antonioni, Bertolucci, and Pasolini. Fellini's shocked the country and the world with *La dolce vita* (1959), adding the phrase to our contemporary lexicon. Together with *8 1/2*, his reflection on meta-cinema, Fellini forged a new cinema: personal, idiosyncratic, surreal, and unique from all other directors. This was a cinema of invented, almost fictional autobiography, and Fellini never strayed from the formula: *Juliet of the Spirits* (1965) was followed by *Fellini Satyricon* (1969) and a return to his beloved clowns and circus in *I Clowns* the following year. *Roma* (1970) was a meditation on his beloved Eternal City, and *Amarcord* (1974) was a loving, nostalgic tribute to his childhood in the fascist era. Two decades later his *Intervista* was a combination of nostalgia and meta-cinema.

Antonioni developed as a master of composition, often considering a frame in light of contemporary art movements. In the mid-1960s he experimented with English dialogue and color as a protagonist. *Blow-Up* (1966) raised epistemological questions about what we can know and how film can (re)produce knowledge; *Zabriskie Point* (1969) focused on the existential anguish in consumerist America; *The Passenger* (1975) explores the problem of identity.

Bernardo Bertolucci was one of the major directors of the 1970s, creating a distinctive style while examining the connection between politics and sexuality in *The Conformist* (1970), his adaptation of the novel of the same name by Alberto Moravia. Critical to Bertolucci's work was his collaboration with cinematographer Vittorio Storaro again two years later with *Last Tango in Paris,* which returned to the problem of modern sexuality, but in a more intimate, psychoanalytical framework. Bertolucci's most politically ambitious film, *1900* (1975), was a sprawling epic that sought nothing less than to depict the turbulent half century from 1900 to the end of World War II through the lives of its two protagonists.

Poet, novelist, and critic Pier Paolo Pasolini was also the most problematic and provocative filmmaker of postwar Italy. His *Hawks and Sparrows* (1966) was a modern parable that employed Totò and the young Ninetto Davoli as a wandering father and son guided by an omniscient crow. Earlier he had explored the world of the subproletariat, a world he knew well, in *Accattone* (1961) and *Mama Roma* (1962). Ironically and paradoxically, Pasolini, a Communist and a homosexual, created perhaps the most powerful religious film in 1964 with *The Gospel According to Matthew* (he purposefully omitted "Saint" from the title), using only the text of the Gospel for dialogue. There followed his "trilogy of life," *The Decameron, The Canterbury Tales,* and *The Arabian Nights* (1971–73), which were earthy and sensuous retellings of the classical texts. Pasolini here insisted on sex as a positive, creative life force, an idea he was to reject in his last film. Shortly before his murder in 1975 Pasolini completed *Salò, or the One Hundred and Twenty Days of Sodom.* Loosely based on the Marquis de Sade and set in the waning days of the fascist regime, the film no longer presents sex as liberating but as a force of oppression and humiliation. For many viewers the meal where human excrement is eaten was the most disturbing moment in modern cinema. Equally disturbing was Pasolini's seeming conflation of homosexuality and fascism, an idea that considerable impact on Italian cinema after the war (Rossellini's *Rome, Open City,* Bertolucci's *The Conformist,* and Visconti's *The Damned,* to name just three of the most important works that make this connection.) The stereotype was effectively challenged by Visconti himself with *Death in Venice* (1971) and Ettore Scola's poignant *A Special Day* (1977), where Sofia Loren is cast as a frumpy housewife and Marcello Mastroianni, the embodiment of the Latin lover, is cast as a sensitive, homosexual antifascist.

The fast-disappearing world of the peasant class was captured in the 1970s by Vittorio and Paolo Taviani in *Padre Padrone* (1977) and Ermanno Olmi's *The Tree of Wooden Clogs* (1978), two works that enjoyed attention abroad as well. But the decade also sharpened the ever-present crisis of Italian films: attempting to craft works of lasting political, aesthetic, and even moral value in an economic system that is at best indifferent and at worst decidedly hostile to any such work. One of the most important developments was the emergence of women directors, especially Liliana Caviani and Lina Wertmüller. Caviani generated interest with her provocative portrayals of St. Francis of Assisi and Galileo before the enormous controversy of *The Night Porter* (1974), about a sadistic concentration camp guard and a former inmate who return to their previous relationship after a chance encounter. Caviani's *The Skin* (1981), based on the text by Curzio Malaparte, depicted wartime Naples under the American occupation. Wertmüller employed satire, sarcasm, and parody in a distinct style while examining the hypocrisy that undermined political and sexual relations in contemporary Italy. *Love and Anarchy, All Screwed Up,* and *Swept Away* (1972–74) were powerful, funny films that were also commercially successful. Her masterpiece, *Seven Beauties* (1975), depicted the existentialist crisis of a petty hoodlum from the streets of Naples to the abyss of a German concentration camp.

Most analyses of Italian cinema concentrate on the directors or the most recognizable international stars. Mention should be made of the critical contributions of producers such as Carlo Ponti and Dino De Laurentiis; cinematographers Vittorio Storaro, Otello Martelli, and Giuseppe Rotunno; set designers such as Danilo Donato and Dante Ferretti; and screenwriters such as Cesare Zavattini, Tullio Pinelli, and Ennio Flaiano.

The 1980s and 1990s have demonstrated that Italian cinema has the capacity to overcome both the economic and the artistic crises that periodically assail the industry. The most influential development has been the changing economic structure of the industry, along with the challenge of television. Still, directors continue to craft exceptional films that examine Italian history and the history of Italian cinema itself. Abroad Italian films continued to enjoy critical and commercial success: Scola's *We All Loved Each Other Very Much* (1974), the Taviani brothers' *The Night of Shooting Stars* (1985), Giuseppe Tornatore's *Cinema Paradiso* (1989), Gabriele Salvatore's *Mediterraneo* (1991), and Michael Radford and Massimo Troisi's *Il Postino* (1995). Some critics were quick to note the nostalgia and danger of sentimentality in such films, while others hailed them as evidence that Italian cinema continues to produce some of the most important works in the medium.

BIBLIOGRAPHY

Bondanella, Peter. *Italian Cinema: From Neorealism to the Present.* New York: Continuum, 1990.

———. "Recent Work on Italian Cinema." *Journal of Modern Italian Studies* 1 (Fall 1995):1:101–23.

Brunetta, Gian Piero. *Storia del cinema italiano,* 4 Vols. Rome: Riuniti, 1993.

Dalle Vacche, Angela. *The Body in the Mirror: Shapes of History in Italian Cinema.* Princeton, N.J.: Princeton University Press, 1992.

Liehm, Mira. *Passion and Defiance: Film in Italy from 1942 to the Present.* Berkeley: University of California Press, 1984.

Marcus, Millicent. *Italian Film in the Light of Neorealism.* Princeton, N.J.: Princeton University Press, 1984.

Sitney, P. Adams. *Vital Crises in Italian Cinema: Iconography, Stylistics, Politics.* Austin: University of Texas Press, 1995.

Stanislao G. Pugliese

Education

All Italian children must attend school until they are fourteen. They begin school at the age of six, attending elementary school for five years, then the "media unica" for three years. After this compulsory schooling they can attend a liceo (secondary schools, with either a classical or scientific specialization, leading to the university), a commercial or technical school, or a school for teachers.

The Italian school system is still largely based on legislation issued during the Fascist period. Though significant innovations have been introduced with respect to primary education, there has not been a thorough reform of the whole school system. After World War II, owing to new political ideals and a new concern for social and educational problems, reforms addressed the internal structure, school programs, and teaching methodologies in the primary schools. The adequacy of these changes was questioned in the 1980s and led in 1990 to further reforms based on the idea that school education was not solely for transmitting information. Its most important role, according to the new reform, was enhancement of creativity and autonomous thought and fostering balanced affective, social, and emotional development. Stressing the importance of conscious participation in culture and social life, the new legislation was based on the assumption that individual, social and cultural diversities do not represent obstacles but a resource that can benefit the whole community. It consequently expected education to take into account different experiences and help all pupils regardless of individual differences.

According to the provisions of the Italian constitution, which envisioned an eight-year compulsory school term, in the midsixties the institution of the *scuola media unica* was introduced. It was conceived both as a new instrument for the diffusion of education and for the development of democratic principles. In 1974 a reform affected the legal status of the staff and introduced the so-called decreti delegati, intended to establish democratic administration of schools through collegial bodies composed of representatives of the school staff, parents, and students. The first general elections of those bodies in 1975 roused great interest. This was short-lived however, because of the limited authority and effectiveness of the collegial bodies.

Further reforms were introduced in 1977 dealing with appraisal of students' abilities. In spite of the legislative activity focused on primary education, secondary education has been largely neglected. This was because the various political factions in Italy could not agree on the fundamental nature of secondary education despite the realization that reform was necessary. Numerous thorough studies and reform projects were prepared during the 1970s and 1980s (the most renowned of which was the "programma Brocca"), but none gained the wide-ranging support necessary for new school legislation including the extension of compulsory education to sixteen years. The government elected in Italy in 1994 seemed particularly interested in the reform of secondary school education. One interesting notion advanced in the last few years is enhanced autonomy for each school and a reduction of the bureaucratic centralism that characterizes the Italian school system.

A reform of university education is also pressing, since the provisions of a law introduced in 1980 have proved to be insufficient to solve its structural problems. A reform bill was prepared in 1989 but the introduction of the principle of institutional autonomy was met with lively protests on the grounds that it might endanger academic freedom and make universities dependent on private interests.

BIBLIOGRAPHY

Ambrosoli, Luigi. *La scuola italiana dal dopoguerra ad oggi.* Bologna: Il Mulino, 1982.

Barbagli, Marzio. *Disoccupazione intellettuale e sistema scolastico in Italia.* Bologna: Il Mulino 1974.

Cipolla, Carlo. *Istruzione e sviluppo economico in Italia.* Turin: UTET, 1971.

Cives, Giacomo, ed. *La scuola italiana dall'unità ai nostri giorni.* Florence: La Nuova Italia, 1990.

I decreti delegati. Rome: Parva Lex, 1975.

Maria Pia Paternò

Coldiretti

The Coldiretti (General Confederation of Farmers) has played important role in the history of the Catholic social movement in Italy. It is the product of the long period of activity by Catholic organizations of farmers, started at the end of the nineteenth century.

The National Federation of Farmers was created in November 1944 at the initiative of Paolo Bonomi, a young member of Catholic Action, and some Catholic trade-unionists. Their purpose was to improve the political, social, and economic conditions of farmers' families. In May 1945 the federation was transformed into the Confederazione generale dei coltivatori diretti (General Confederation of Farmers), or Coldiretti, with municipal sections and provincial federations under the umbrella of the national federation. The organization grew quickly

from 349 sections in 1944 to 6,719 in 1949. By 1949 its membership consisted of the heads of 752,426 families.

The Coldiretti eventually abandoned its initial apolitical character. Its social Christian outlook converged with that of the Christian Democrats. In its advocacy of agrarian reform it took into consideration both the social and the economic aspects of production. Furthermore, in its desire to reorganize the agricultural system, inherited from the fascistera, it hoped through the Christian Democrats to give farmers the power to control national economic policy. Though it fell short of this goal, its influence within the Christian Democratic Party did enable it to promote agrarian interests.

In October 1980, Bonomi resigned as president of the Coldiretti, and Arcangelo Lobianco, a Christian Democrat deputy from Puglia, took his place. He was succeeded by Paolo Micolini in December 1989.

BIBLIOGRAPHY

Miozzi, Massimo. "Confederazione generale dei coltivatori diretti," in *Dizionario Storico del Movimento Cattolico in Italia 1860–1980.* Vol. 1 and 2. Casale Monferrato: Marietti, 1981.

Parisella, Antonio. "Il primo sviluppo della Coldiretti," in *Il Parlamento italiano: Storia parlamentare e politica dell'Italia 1861–1988,* Vol. 16. Milan: Nuova CEI, 1989.

Rossi, Ernesto. *La federconsorzi.* Milan: Feltrinelli, 1973.

Claudia Franceschini

Economic Miracle

After World War II Italy took part in the economic resurgence of Western Europe known as the "economic miracle." In the ten years between 1952 and 1962 Italy made more progress in the economic field than in the entire preceding span of the twentieth century. This is evident even in the data on national income. In fifty years, for example, between 1901 and 1950, the per capita income increased 62 percent; the increase registered in the years 1950 to 1960 alone was 47 percent. Through supportive government policies, efficient management, and the ingenuity of producers such as FIAT, industrial production during that same period also increased at a yearly average of 8.5 percent. Italy at the time amassed the world's third-highest gold reserves, and there was an overall improvement in the standard of living, with gains occurring in the consumption of all goods, in travel, and in the construction of schools and housing. Unemployment was reduced by approximately 6 percent during this time. These economic developments produced deep changes in the structures of society and in social habits. This transformation was experienced, though not in equal proportion, by the whole society.

Italy's economic growth during this period displayed a progressive divergence between the pace of industrial and agricultural development, with a yearly increase of 9 percent in the former and only a 3 percent increase in the latter category. Employment figures between the industrial/service and agricultural areas show an even wider discrepancy. In some sectors of production industrial development reached a record output. Major progress was realized in metallurgy, the automobile industry, and the chemical industry.

Italy's industrial growth during this period resulted in a massive displacement of labor power from agriculture to industry, perhaps the most evident characteristic aspect of the miracle. The transfer from agriculture to industry and services occurred everywhere, with the number of agricultural laborers and tenants in the north and central Italy being reduced, but the phenomenon took place on an even larger scale in the southern regions. Not just a local transfer from one area of the economy to another but a genuine migration cut across regional and geographic boundaries. Some, in fact, claim that the miracle was made possible by the migration of labor from the South to the industrial North.

BIBLIOGRAPHY
Podbielski, G. *Italy: Development and Crisis in the Postwar Economy.* London: Oxford University Press, 1974.
William Roberts

Labor Unions

In Italy labor unions developed from mutual aid societies and formed territorial organizations in the 1870s and 1880s. Their history was characterized by fragmentation. The General Confederation of Labor (CGL) was formed because of conflicts between the federation controlled by reformists and the trades councils, influenced by Georges Sorel's syndicalism, which had formed the Union of Italian Labor (UIL) in 1912. Roman Catholics, who had organized a number of cooperative societies, united these in the Italian Labor Confederation (CIL) in 1920. During the fascist era the Communists secretly organized in the CGL, which carried out strikes in March 1943 and in March and April 1944.

A unitary agreement was formulated among the various segments of the Italian labor movement on the basis of their common opposition to fascism. This labor pact, the Treaty of Rome, was signed on June 9, 1944. Giuseppe Di Vittorio signed for the Communists, E. Canevari for the Socialists, and Achille Grandi for the Christian

labor unionists. The agreement formed the General Italian Confederation of Labor (Confederazione Generale Italiana del Lavoro, CGIL), which adopted a program proclaiming its absolute independence from every party. Labor union unity, which was rooted in the temporary political collaboration of the resistance parties, was undermined by the ideological differences of three groups and by the numerical inferiority of the Christian Democrats among organized labor. This unity did not last long. The church had overcome its traditional opposition to labor union unity but was afraid of control by the Italian Communist Party (PCI) over the working class. So the Italian Christian Workers Associations (ACLI) were founded in 1944, and in 1948 the Christian Democrats founded the Free General Confederation of Free Labor (Libera Confederazione Generale Italiana del Lavoro, LCGIL), which became the Italian Confederation of Labor Syndicates (Confederazione Italiana Sindacati Lavoratori, CILS) under the direction of Giulio Pastore. The Social Democrats and Republicans founded the Italian Union of Labor (Unione Italiana del Lavoro, UIL) in 1951.

Each of the three confederations has its own provincial labor union councils, and each has a federation congress every four years at which the executive committee and the secretary are elected. In the 1950s there were two labor union strategies: the Labor Plan of the CGIL promoted the National Electricity Board, the nationalization of public housing, and land reclamation; the approach of the CISL, however, was based on the U.S. contractual model, which was promoted in Italy by Gino Giugni. The labor unions were linked with political parties, and the CGIL promoted popular mobilization, extraneous to the day-to-day issues of the working class.

Agostino Novella, who became leader of the CGIL after the death of Giuseppe Di Vittorio in 1957, was succeeded by Luciano Lama in 1970. The CGIL took part in the European Confederation of Trade Unions for the first time in 1979. This participation, which provoked many protests from the left, was part of an effort to adapt to the social democratic labor unionism prevalent in Western Europe. It followed the formation for pragmatic reasons of a federation in 1972 of the three, originally ideologically divided organizations—CGIL, CISL, and UIL. Since then the CGIL has pursued a reformist labor union strategy.

BIBLIOGRAPHY
Horowitz, D. *Storia del movimento sindacale in Italia.* Bologna: Il Mulino, 1966.

Pistello, M. *Giuseppe Di Vittorio,* Vol 2. Rome: Editori Riuniti, 1975.

Turone, S. *Storia del sindacato in Italia.* Rome: Ed. Laterza, 1981.

Adalgisa Efficace

SEE ALSO Lama, Luciano

Institute for Industrial Reconstruction

Italy's gigantic state holding group, which controls the public sector of the Italian economy. The Institute for Industrial Reconstruction (Istituto per Ricostruzione Industrale, IRI) was created by a royal decree on January 23, 1933. Together with the Italian Land Institute (Istituto Mobiliare Italiano, IMI), it was responsible for lending money to companies in crisis and for monitoring the exchange rate of the lira, thus leading to an economic policy of state intervention. Until then the regime had concentrated on agriculture, with a policy of ruralization and redevelopment. By doing so, it aimed at redeveloping the south and its agricultural economy, which had been largely ignored by previous national governments. Ruralization meant for dictator Benito Mussolini not only a process of improvement and development for the rural masses but also a means of containing the spread of "supercapitalism" and, at the same time, an indispensable way of increasing population and consumption. However, at the beginning of 1933 he had to come to terms with the economic crisis in industry. Industrial unemployment could not be absorbed by agriculture. Industrialists put pressure on Mussolini, arguing that he had underestimated the importance of industry as a means of raising living standards and as a way of developing a state devoted to a policy of "potentiality." With IRI the state became a shareholder in certain important companies and began to become entrepreneurial. It also tried to limit unrestrained capitalism along lines similar to the policies of President Franklin Roosevelt in the United States.

Today IRI performs financial transactions with companies in which either IRI or the state has a share, or, alternatively, with corporations whose founding capital was wholly or partly provided by the state. The financial resources of IRI derive partly from an endowment fund created by the state and partly from the issuing of refundable bonds. The institute also issues bonds for equity participation on behalf of bondholders, offers advances against industrial securities, and issues Treasury certificates, but it cannot engage in the collecting of savings.

During the 1970s and 1980s the crisis in the business sector hit IRI just as it was trying to invest on a large scale in southern Italy. During the 1970s IRI's investments to-

taled 124,000 billion lire (67 percent more than the previous decade) and produced 228,000 new jobs. However, the state refused to help during the crisis, and the situation worsened to the extent that by 1983 IRI had a deficit of 3,000 billion lire. As a result rationalization was required and this led to the privatization of companies such as Alfa Romeo, which was sold to Fiat in 1986. This resulted in a capital gain of 10,000 billion lire and to the dismissing of 65,000 workers.

Italy's financial crisis of the early 1990s also affected the IRI, which could not expect financial aid from the state. It also now faces the European single market. Giuliano Amato's government (1992–1993) transformed the IRI into a stock corporation, prohibiting it from exceeding the undercapitalization of the last few years and insisting on profitability. IRI, nevertheless, remained one of the most important industrial groups in Europe. In the late 1990s it attempted to reinvigorate its managerial capacity, proposing to develop advanced technology and become more competitive in international markets.

BIBLIOGRAPHY

La Bella, Gianni. *L'IRI nel dopoguerra.* Rome: Studium, 1983.

Pertrilli, G., and F. Parrillo. *L'IRI nell 'economia italiana.* Milan: A. Giuffre, 1964.

Prodi, Romano. *Il tempo delle scelte: lezioni di economia.* Milan: Il Sole 24 ore libri, 1992.

———. *Restructuring of Italian Industry.* Naples: Isveimer, 1979.

Saraceno, P. *Il sistema delle imprese a partecipazione statale nella esperienza italiana.* Milan: Giuffre, 1975.

Gabriella Portalone

Confindustria

Abbreviation for Confederazione Italiana dell'Industria (Italian Confederation of Industry). Building on local or sectorial experiences, the first Italian industrial association originated in Turin in 1910. Members desired to establish a united entrepreneurial policy toward the government. During the post–World War I period the association opposed labor conflicts and supported employers' anti-union action. During the fascist regime industrialists benefited because manufacturers' interests deeply merged with governments policy. During the post–World War II period, and especially during the centrist years from 1947 to 1963 under the leadership of Angelo Costa, Confindustria met with considerable success. Difficulties grew afterward, mainly in the early 1960s, when reforms were proposed and a new economic planning was issued by the left-center government. Meanwhile sharp disagreement arose inside Confindustria. The "Hot Autumn," a period of extreme labor unrest in 1969, and the complexity of social problems contributed to a revision of political behavior and to the adoption of a less authoritarian approach to the association's objectives. A constructive debate occurred with labor unions and left-oriented parties in quest of democratic industrial progress.

BIBLIOGRAPHY

Abrate, Mario. *La lotta sindacale nella industrializzazione in Italia 1906–1926.* Milano: Angeli, 1967.

Berta, Giuseppe, ed. *Alle origini dell'associazionismo imprenditorial: Le relazioni della presidenza della Lega industriale di Torino e della Confederazione Italiana dell'Industria, 1908–1915.* Turin: EMBLEMA, 1994.

Fiocca, Giorgio, ed. *Quaranta anni di Confindustria: Economia e società nei discorsi dei presidenti.* 2 Vols. Milan: Seme S.P.A., 1989.

Mattina, Liborio. *Gli industriali e la democrazia: La Confindustria nella formazione dell'Italia repubblicana.* Bologna: Il Mulino, 1991.

Pirzio Ammassari, Gloria. *La politica della Confindustria: Strategia economica e prassi contrattuale del padronato italiano.* Naples: Liguori, 1976.

Walter E. Crivellin

New Left

"New left" in Italy included all the left-wing political movements that from the 1960s arose outside the official parties of the left—the Italian Communist Party (PCI) and the Italian Socialist Party (PSI). The new left movements were absolutely different one from the other, but all were strongly critical of the parliamentary left. During the early 1960s the new left was composed exclusively of intellectuals, but at the end of the decade it involved workers and students, and the so called labor-union left. With the insurgency of 1968 and 1969, the new left became a significant political force in Italian society. From the movement came a plethora of groups, the most important of which were Lotta Continua (Continual Struggle), Movimento Studentesco, Avanguardia Operaia (Workers' Vanguard), and Potere Operaio (Workers' Power), as well as many Marxist-Leninist-Maoist groups. The ideological foundations of these groups went from an absolute spontaneity and populism to a rigid application of Marxist-Leninist doctrine. Beyond organized political groups there were also many new left newspapers and reviews, especially *Il Manifesto.* Among the many new left groups were organizations within the liberal professions: magistratura democratica for judges, medicina de-

mocratica for physicians, and psichiatria democratica for mental health workers.

At the end of the 1960s the so-called strategy of tension, the epoch of political violence, began with the Piazza Fontana terrorist bombing in Milan in 1969. For many years Italy was unnerved by bomb attacks. By the mid-1970s part of the new left decided to respond with armed struggle. The Brigate Rosse (Red Brigades), Nuclei Armati Proletari, and other groups tried to organize a violent revolution against the state and the "class enemy." The terrorist struggle during the second half of the 1970s culminated in the murderer of the lower prime minister and leading Christian Democrat Aldo Moro. During this decade the political geography of the new left changed. Many groups dissolved and others became more important. Autonomia Operaia waged the bitterest struggle against the PCI and the official labor unions. From many groups was created Democrazia Proletaria, first as a point of convergence for electoral politics, then as an organization in itself. With Democrazia Proletaria the new left entered parliament in 1976, even if in an extremely minority position. Terrorism was defeated by the early 1980s. On April 7, 1979, the leaders of Potere Operaio and Autonomia Operaia were jailed, accused of being members of armed gangs. The new left profoundly changed in the 1980s. The political scene was increasingly dominated by green movements, but Democrazia Proletaria survived. After the transformation of the PCI into the Democratic Party of the Left (PSD) and the foundation of Rifondazione Comunista (Communist Refoundation), many of the former militants of the new left entered the PSD.

BIBLIOGRAPHY

Bobbio, Luigi. *Lotta continua: Storia di un'organizzazione rivoluzionaria.* Rome: Savelli, 1979.

Della Porta, Donatella. *Il terrorismo di sinistra.* Bologna: Il Mulino, 1990.

Materiali per una nuova sinistra. Il sessantotto. Rome: Edizioni Associate, 1988.

Moroni, Primo, and Nanni Balestrini. *L'orda d'oro.* Milan: SugarCo, 1988.

Tarrow, Sidney. *Disorder and Democracy: Conflict, Protest and Political Change in Italy.* Oxford: Clarendon Press, 1989.

Daniele Petrosino

SEE ALSO Moro, Aldo; Negri, Antonio

Opening to the Left

The search for a new political alliance between the centrist Christian Democrats (DC) and the Italian Socialist Party

(PSI), realized in Italy at the beginning of the 1960s. The formation of center-left governments led by Aldo Moro marked the period from 1963 to 1968. The course, though long and hard, was facilitated by the distancing of the Socialists from the Communists after 1956, the crisis of the Christian Democratic centrist policy, and the advent of the papacy of John XXIII.

Despite resistance by the right wing of the DC, Confindustria, and influential members of the clergy, the experiment was gradually realized. An initial attempt was made by Amintore Fanfani's government (1962–63). This ministry was made possible as a result of an agreement by the PSI not to vote against it. This produced a center-left programmatic coalition. Among the most significant bills passed was the nationalization of electricity companies, reform of secondary schools with the extension of compulsory education to age fourteen, and a bill levying a direct tax on profits from investments.

At the end of 1963 the first "organic" center-left government was formed by Moro. Besides the DC, it included the PSI and the Social Democratic and Republican Parties. Governments based on this coalition lasted until the end of the legislature in 1968.

This opening to the Left aroused great expectations. Yet the precarious agreement among the parties, the dislike of the coalition within various state agencies and civil organizations, together with destabilizing conspiracies and political plots such as the De Lorenzo affair and the "Solo" plan of 1964 hampered the center-left governments, and many of the proposed reforms relating to city planning, regional administration, education, fiscal policy, and social benefits were left unfinished. Among the most important legislative achievements of the center-left were the passage of a law on planning, interventions in the field of housing, and the outline of a law setting up regions.

Toward the end of the 1960s the center-left started gradually to falter. It was kept as a formula but the results were negligible. A new political stage, full of contradictions and difficulties, as well as of social expectations, emerged in 1968.

BIBLIOGRAPHY

Craveri, Piero. *La Repubblica dal 1958 a 1992.* Turin: UTET, 1995.

Malgeri, Francesco, ed. *Storia della democrazia cristiana,* Vol. 4, *Dal centro sinistra agli "anni de piombo" (1962–1978).* Rome: Cinque Lune, 1989.

Tamburrano, Giuseppe. *Storia e cronaca del centro-sinistra.* Milan: Rizzoli, 1990.

Walter E. Crivellin

P2

P2 (Propaganda 2) was an Italian Masonic lodge that traditionally housed all those Masons whose important positions in the political, economic, and journalistic fields made it desirable that their membership remain secret, even to members of other lodges. P2 was dissolved as the result of the findings of a commission set up by the Italian parliament. The long, prestigious tradition of P2 dates to the nineteenth century, when Freemasons such as Cavour, Mazzini, Garibaldi, Crispi, and even the first king of Italy, Vittorio Emanuele II, played a determining part in the creation of the united Italian nation. Freemasonry also played an equally important part in the successive phase of activating and developing the newly unified nation; many members of the liberal-minded ruling class that governed Italy during that period were Masons, as were numerous members of the democratic and socialist opposition parties. During the twenty-year period of fascist dictatorship, Italian Freemasonry was outlawed and Masons were persecuted. After World War II and the fall of fascism, Italian Freemasonry was reconstituted with the help and encouragement of its American counterpart. During this period the "secret" lists of the newly reorganized P2 lodge were once again filled with the names of countless important public figures.

The P2 lodge became particularly active from 1970 onward, under the leadership of the "venerable master" Licio Gelli. Gelli's first important position within the lodge was conferred on him in 1969 by Luciano Gamberini, who was at that time the grand master of the Grande Oriente d'Italia di Palazzo Giustiniani, the most important branch of Italian Freemasonry. However, it was not until 1970, when Lino Salvini, Gamberini's successor, entrusted Gelli with the position of organizational secretary of P2, that Gelli began to accentuate the secretive character of the lodge and develop a highly personal administration often at odds with Masonic rules.

Gelli soon seized from the grand master's hands direct control and supervision of the connections with those Masons in such key positions in society that only the grand master himself was supposed to know their names. He also modified the ancient Freemasonry rule that the head of a secret lodge could hold his position only for a limited time. In this way Gelli established a parallel Masonic organization far more powerful than the official one. As venerable master of P2, Gelli concentrated more and more on the immediate accumulation of political and economic power. Through intensive proselytizing he convinced numerous politicians, officers of the armed forces, bankers, editors, and journalists to join P2; and by using a selective procedure that privileged above all those candidates who held high-ranking positions in politics, the secret services, finance, and the media, he provided the lodge with a highly incisive and wide-reaching influence in many key sectors of the nation.

Under Gelli P2 was organized into eighteen groups. Gelli retained personal control over the most important central one, which was made up of all the most prestigious members of the lodge. Apart from the seventeen leaders of the other groups, this central group had among its members heads of the secret services and the armed forces, ministers and members of parliament, important editors, and famous journalists. The other seventeen groups were divided on a predominantly territorial basis; one group in Sicily; another in Sardinia; two groups, responsible for central Italy, based in Rome; two groups in Tuscany; one group in Emilia and another in Liguria; one group each in Milan and Turin; one group specifically responsible for the media, and so on.

In 1981, the Italian magistracy, during the course of the trial of banker Michele Sindona, discovered among seized documents the secret lists of the members of the P2 lodge. The judges immediately ordered Gelli's arrest, but he had already fled abroad and was not captured until several years later. In 1982, the P2 lodge was examined by an inquiry commission set up by parliament, and in 1984 the commission revealed its findings regarding the lodge's influence on Italian politics and the economy, as well as violations of law ascribed to the organization, its head, and its members in general. The inquiry commission concluded that the P2 lodge, although an integral part of Italian Freemasonry, had developed into an autonomous organization, that attempted to alter the balance of power in Italian politics and economy.

Following these events the Grande Oriente d'Italia di Palazzo Giustiniani dissolved P2, but not before the P2 case had already caused a serious crisis within the Grande Oriente itself. The P2 affair provoked an internal schism and led to the expulsion of the Italian Freemasonry organization from the Scottish Rite Freemasonry Assembly, the world's largest Freemasonry organization.

BIBLIOGRAPHY

Cipriani, Gianni. *I mandanti*. Rome: Editori Riuniti, 1993.

Francovich, Carlo. *Storia della massoneria in Italia dalle origini alla Rivoluzione francese*. Florence: La Nuova Italia, 1975.

Mola, Aldo. *Storia della massoneria in Italia dalle origini ai nostri giorni*. Rome: Bompiani, 1992.

Teodori, Massimo. *P2: La controstoria*. Milan: Garzanti, 1986.

Turone, Sergio. *Corrotti e corruttori dall'Unità d'Italia alla P2*. Bari: Laterza, 1984.

Aldo Nicosia

SEE ALSO Gelli, Licio; Gladio; Sindona, Michele

'Ndrangheta

Organized crime group located in the south of mainland Italy. The 'Ndrangheta (the Honored Society) is known as the Calabrian Mafia. It arose among the impoverished peasants of the Mezzogiorno as a means of protection in a basically lawless society where the power of the landlord was basically limitless. The organization of the 'Ndrangheta is horizontal rather than the pyramid structure of bosses used by the Sicilian Mafia. The units are village- or family-based, and each family has complete control over its territory and all the licit or illicit activity in that territory. The branches (*cosche*) are based on a blood family that established ties to other families through the bonds of marriage. Since the members are all related, it is difficult to obtain informers (*pentini*) willing to bargain for more lenient sentences by revealing what they know of their relatives' wrongdoings. Each member goes through an elaborate initiation with a series of obscure questions and answers. The initiate gives flowery assurances of submissive loyalty within a context of implied violence for recalcitrants.

In the early 1990s there were an estimated 155 'Ndrangheta families with approximately 6,000 members. Among the leading 'Ndrangheta families was the Sinderno family, whose leader was Cosimo "the Quail" Commisso. After a bloody struggle that erupted in 1985 with the secession of the Imerti-Condello *cosca* from the alliance of *cosche* led by Paolo De Stefano, a body, the *Santa,* was established with representatives from the most important families. This did not operate like a Mafia commission but was an effort to deal with the perennial clashes among the different *cosche* that characterized the Calabrian 'Ndranghetta.

To the mainstays of the organization—kidnapping, extortion, and usury—have been added illegal drugs, dealing in illegal weapons, and the illegal disposal of nuclear and chemical wastes. The organization has made increasing moves into areas of legitimate business. In the construction industry it has acquired contracts for projects and amassed profits through bribes and intimidation.

BIBLIOGRAPHY

Arca, Francesco. *Mafia, camorra, 'ndrangheta*. Rome: Lato side, 1982.

Ciconte, Enzo. *'Ndrangheta dall'Unità a oggi.* Rome: Laterza, 1992.

———. *Processo alla 'Ndrangheta.* Rome: Laterza, 1996.

Lombardi Satriani, Luigi M. *'Ndrangheta, la mafia calabrese.* Bologna: Cappelli, 1978.

Malafarina, Luigi. *La 'ndrangheta: il codice segreto, la storia, i miti, i riti e i personaggi.* Rome: Gangemi, 1986.

Minuti, Diego, and Antonio Nicaso. *'Ndraghete: le filiali della mafia calabrese.* Monteleone: Vibo Valentia, 1994.

Bernard Cook

Iwaszkiewicz, Jarosław (1884–1980)

Polish poet, playwright, essayist, editor of *Twórczość,* and president of the Society of Polish Writers (1945–46, 1947–49, and 1949–80).

Jarosław (Eleuter) Iwaszkiewicz was born on February 20, 1884, in Kalnik, Ukraine. His family was educated, and he studied law and music in Kiev. He moved to Warsaw in 1918 and founded, together with other poets, the Skamander organization, a group of young poets who sought to develop a new poetic voice reflective of modern life. From 1932 to 1936 Iwaszkiewicz worked for the Polish Foreign Office in Copenhagen and Brussels. During World War II his house in Stawisko, near Warsaw, became one of the Polish underground's cultural centers. After the war he fully accepted the new system and became a symbol of compromise with the Communist regime. As a result he received high official posts but lost the respect of young readers.

His first published poems were the neo-Parnassianistic *Oktosstychy* (*Octostyches,* 1919) and his expressionistic collection *Dionizje* (*Dionysus Festival,* 1922). He turned to classicism in *Powrót do Europy* (*Return to Europe,* 1931) and in his postwar *Ody olimpijskie.* In his 1933 collection *Lato 1932* (*Summer 1932*) Iwaszkiewicz employed elegiac confessions, existential and metaphysical experiences, impressions from his poetical journey, and biographical recollections. These reappeared in his 1957 *Ciemne ścieżki* (*Dark Paths*) and *Muzyka wieczorem* (*Night Music,* 1981). Persistent motifs of these poems are discrepancies: first, the discrepancy between being a European and keeping one's distance; second, the discrepancy between constructive pro-social attitudes and artistic inclinations that were alien and indifferent to the moral dilemmas of politics. However, some elements of romantic resistance against the force of history also appear in his work. Finally, there is a clash between the ecstatic gasps of life versus the grief of the inevitable passing of time and the sense of the tragic nature of existence, accompanied by strong sensual and aesthetic experiences. Similar emotions appear in his novels and short stories, *Księżyc wschodzi* (*The Moon Is Rising,* 1925), *Panny z Wilka* (*Maidens of Wilk,* 1933), *Czerwone tarcze* (*Red Shields,* 1934), and *Nowele włoskie* (*Italian Novels,* 1947), which initially focused on the conflict between romanticism and the practical tasks of life, and on the residue of the past in the present.

In his later fiction Iwaszkiewicz depicted the tragic collective fate of Poles and the problem of moral choices to be made. Particular examples are *Bitwa na równinie Sedgemoor* (*Battle of Sedgemor Plain*) and *Matka Joanna od Aniołów* (*Mother Joanna of Angels*) in the collection *Nowa miłość inne opowiadania* (*New Love and Other Stories,* 1946), and *Sława i chwała* (*Fame and Glory,* vols. 1–3, 1956–62), an epic chronicle of contemporary Poland. Iwaszkiewicz's postwar fiction, mostly realistic, combined subjectivity of description with subtle philosophical implied meaning and lyrical narration. Resignation and subordination to the demands of life are dominant in these, but he continued to exhibit a fascination with psychological and moral complexity. Notable are his *Tatarak i inne opowiadania* (*Rush and Other Stories,* 1960), *O psach, kotach i diabłach* (*About Dogs, Cats and Devils,* 1968), *Sny; Ogrody; Serenite* (*Dreams, Gardens, Serenity,* 1974), and historical stories *Noc czerwcowa; Zarudzie; Heydenreich* (*June Night; Zarudzie; Heydenreich,* 1976).

BIBLIOGRAPHY

Brodzka, Alina, ed. *O twórczości Jarosława Iwaszkiewicza* (*About the Literary Work of Jarosław Iwaszkiewicz*). Kraków: Wydawnictwo Literackie, 1983.

Iwaszkiewicz, Jarosław. *Gathering Time: Five Modern Polish Elegies.* Mission, British Columbia: C. and J. Ested at Barbarian Press, 1983.

Przybylski, Ryszard. *Eros i tanatos: Proza Jarosława Iwaszkiewicza 1916–1938.* Warsaw: Czytelnik, 1970.

Zwada, Andrzej. *Jarosław Iwaszkiewicz.* Warsaw: Wiedza Powszechna, 1954.

Jerzy Speina

Izetbegović, Alija (1925–)

President of Bosnia-Herzegovina since 1992 and the only president of the successor states of the defunct Yugoslavia without a Communist background. Alija Izetbegović entered politics at sixty-five in 1990, as leader of the Democratic Action Party (SDA) representing Bosnia's Muslims. He had a background of religious activism that earned him two years in prison in 1946 for organizing the Young Muslims committed to defending Bosnia's Muslim Slav people from attacks by Croats and Serbs. He later graduated in law from Sarajevo University and worked as a legal consultant to Bosnian firms. From 1983 to 1989 he served another jail sentence. An Islamic declaration that he had written in 1970 was cited as evidence that he wished to proclaim a Muslim state in Yugoslavia. In the early 1990s his radical Serb opponents, lacking stronger evidence that the Islamicization of Bosnia was at hand, justified their hard line tactics by constant references to the 1970 work.

As the leader of the largest Bosnian party in 1990, Izetbegović became president. His solution for Yugoslavia's troubles was to turn the country into a loose confederation with most power devolved to republics and regions. Independence for Bosnia became his goal following the 1991 collapse of Yugoslavia. But he misread the mood of Serb militants and placed too much trust in Western intervention if Bosnia was subject to attack. The rebel Serb onslaught began in April 1992, within days of the declaration of Bosnian independence. Lightly armed and ill-prepared government forces were driven from nearly three-quarters of Bosnian territory. In 1993 Izetbegović reluctantly signed the Owen-Vance plan, which effectively partitioned his state, but the plan fell through owing to rebel Serb opposition. Izetbegović has appeared disorganized and indecisive but is flanked by able lieutenants.

Izetbegović apparently remained committed to a secular, Western-style democracy in Bosnia, but he identified with the clericalist wing of his party. This clericalist faction gained ascendancy as the war in Bosnia intensified the suffering of rural Muslims. The war, which fostered the rise within the SDA of Muslim nationalists, may have created a Muslim identity on nationalist lines, a phenomenon hitherto absent from Bosnian politics.

On October 5, 1996, Izetbegović was elected chairman of three-man collective presidential body for Bosnia-Hercegovina, organized following the Dayton Peace Accords of November-December 1995. The other two members of the presidency were the Bosnian Serb nationalist Momćilo Krajisnik and the Bosnian Croat Kresimir Zubak. In 1998 the leadership of the collective presidency was transformed into an eight-month rotating post. Though Izetbegović continued to serve on the collective presidency, Zivko Radisić, a Bosnian Serb, served as chairman from October 15, 1998 to June 15, 1999, and he was succeeded by Ante Jelavić, a Bosnian Croat.

BIBLIOGRAPHY

Izetbegović, Alija. *Islam between East and West.* Indianapolis, Ind.: American Trust Publications, 1984.

———. *The Islamic Declaration of Alija Izetbegovic.* Sarajevo, 1994.

Tom Gallagher

SEE ALSO Bosnia-Hercegovina

J

Jagland, Thorbjørn (1950–)

Norwegian prime minister, 1996–97. Thorbjørn Jagland was born in Lier on November 5, 1950. He received a degree in economics from the University of Oslo, after which he led the Labor Youth League (AUF) in his home county, Buskerud, from 1973 to 1976, and was national AUF leader from 1977 to 1981. He was elected to the county council for Buskerud in 1975 and retained that post until 1983. Jagland became the head analyst for the Labor Party in 1981. He was named acting secretary of the party in September 1986 and was elected secretary in March 1987. He was elected party leader in November 1992, defeating Jens Stoltenberg. Jagland entered the Storting (parliament) in October 1993 and was Labor's parliamentary leader until he became prime minister on October 25, 1996.

Jagland assumed the prime ministership following the resignation of Gro Harlem Brundtland on October 23, 1996. Brundtland resigned after fifteen years as party leader or prime minister, declaring that she wished to prepare the way for new leadership before the 1997 election.

Jagland appointed Jens Stoltenberg, son of Thorvald Stoltenberg, a former foreign minister and at one time the United Nations' peace mediator in the Balkans, finance minister to succeed Sigbjorn Johnsen. Jens Stoltenberg, an economist, had been Brundtland's minister in charge of Norway's North Sea oil. Jagland established a new department of planning to which he appointed sociologist Terje Rod Larsen. Larsen was the United Nation's special representative to the Palestinian Authority. He had played a central role in the negotiation of the Oslo Accords in 1993 between the Israeli government and the Palestine Liberation Organization (PLO). Jagland retained Bjørn Tore Godal as foreign minister and Jorgen Kosmo as defense minister. Grete Faremo was moved to the oil and energy ministry from the justice department.

To broaden the appeal of his government, he appointed as justice minister Anne Holt, the popular author of detective novels centering around a lesbian Oslo police investigator.

Jagland spoke of constructing *Det Norske Hus* (The Norwegian House) to prepare for the predicted dramatic downturn of Norway's oil revenues and the simultaneous growth in state expenses as the aging population's welfare needs were expected to increase dramatically early in the twenty-first century. Jagland proposed encouraging a vital private onshore economy, achieving efficiencies in welfare, and fostering development through promotion of culture, education, and science. Things began unraveling, however, less than a month after he formed the new government. Rod Larsen was forced to resign owing to allegations of improper share dealings. On December 16 Faremo was forced out as a result of allegations of abuses by the national security service while she was minister of justice.

Though the Labor Party won 35 percent of the vote and twice as many seats as its closest rival in the September 1997 election, the Labor government resigned. It was replaced by a fragile center-right coalition, with Kjell Magne Bondevik, a former priest and former education minister, serving as prime minister. The coalition members—the Christian Democrats (or Christian People's Party), Liberals, and Center Party—won only 26 percent of the vote. These parties had argued that Norway, with one of the worlds ten-richest economies, should be able to prevent waiting lists for hospital entry, provide better care for the elderly, and improve education. Carl Hagen, leader of the right-wing Progress Party, took votes both from coalition members and Labor with his call for greatly expanded welfare spending, more stringent asylum laws, tougher penalties for crime, and compulsory classes in Norwegian for immigrants. He led the Progressives to increase their vote from 9 to 15 percent. Nevertheless, Jagland could have kept on, but he gave up Labor's eleven-year tenure because the party under his leadership had fallen short of the 36.7 percent it had won under Brundtland in 1993. His decision was attacked by party rivals as an act of naïveté.

BIBLIOGRAPHY

Burt, Tim. "Norway embarks on horse-trading." *Financial Times* (London), September 17, 1997.

———. "Shaky hold on power." *Financial Times* (London), November 10, 1997.

Carnegy, Hugh. "Constructing the Norwegian house." *Financial Times* (London), December 18, 1996.

———. "Norway's new PM reshuffles his cabinet." *Financial Times* (London), October 26, 1996.

Bernard Cook

SEE ALSO Bondevik, Kjell Magne; Lahnstein, Anne Enger

Jakeš, Miloš (1922–)

General secretary of the Czechoslovak Communist Party, 1988–89. Miloš Jakeš was born in Česke Krumlov (Chalupy) in southern Bohemia near the Austrian frontier on August 12, 1922. He studied electrical engineering at a state trade school. He joined the Communist Party in 1945 and began his ascent through the party bureaucracy two years later. He headed the party's youth group in the mid-1950s then attended the Soviet College of Party Education in Moscow. From 1966 until 1968 he was deputy minister of the interior. In that post he was jointly responsible for the secret police, a position limited to individuals who enjoyed the confidence of the KGB (Soviet secret police).

The Soviets, under the cover of the Warsaw Pact, invaded Czechoslovakia in August 1968 in order to suppress the reform regime of Czech Communist leader Alexander Dubček. Jakeš immediately threw his support to the invading Warsaw Pact forces. According to Zdeněk Mlynar, a party secretary in 1968, Jakeš was in the Soviet Embassy in Prague when Soviet troops invaded. According to Mlynar, Jakeš was trying to gather a group of Czechoslovak Communists who would voice their support of the invasion. Jakeš, however, subsequently denied foreknowledge of the assault or that he had joined in the efforts to form a conservative government that would have given the USSR a predated invitation to come in and save "socialism."

After the invasion Jakeš headed from 1968 to 1977 the party's Central Control and Auditing Commission, which purged approximately 450,000 Communists for their unwillingness to support the Soviet-led Warsaw Pact action. Jakeš was elected to the Federal Assembly in 1971 and became a member of the party's Central Committee in 1977. He was appointed a candidate (nonvoting) member of the party's Presidium and the Secretariat in 1977. That year he was also appointed chairman of the Central Committee's department on agriculture and food. Under his direction Czechoslovakia became a net exporter of food. Although Czechoslovak agriculture was largely collectivized, its units were permitted a large degree of independence and demonstrated entrepreneurial spirit. As a result of his success Jakeš became the Central Committee's economic expert and gained a reputation as an economic pragmatist. In 1981 he was appointed chairman of the Central Committee's National Economic Commission and also became a full (voting) member of the Presidium.

During a visit by Soviet leader Mikhail Gorbachev to Czechoslovakia in April 1987, it was evident that Party General Secretary Gustav Husák could offer neither innovative nor decisive leadership. On December 17, 1987, Jakeš replaced Husák as general secretary. Husák acquiesced and resigned his party position but retained the presidency. Jakeš's success in agriculture, it was hoped, might serve as a model elsewhere, but Jakeš, at the time, declared that "social ownership of the means of production, planned economy and the leading role of the working class and the Communist Party" are principles that were "attacked in 1968 by right-wing opportunists and revisionists . . . today our opponents would like the economic restructuring and a restructuring of social life to bring about a retreat from the fundamental principles of socialism. They will not live to see that. . . . We took a lesson from 1968–1969 and know where such a retreat leads."

On October 11, 1988, Jakeš engineered the resignations of Prime Minister Lubomír Strougal and Deputy Prime Minister Peter Colotka. Jakeš had grown impatient with Strougal's support for rapid economic restructuring and his desire for a more liberal approach to dissent. Jakeš, mindful of 1968, was determined not to let any push for reform get out of hand. But his rigidity failed to prevent the collapse of the system.

The Communist regime began to crumble after security police attacked student demonstrators on November 17, 1989. This unleashed the massive public repudiation known as the Velvet Revolution. Jakeš and others were removed from their posts by more flexible Communists, who thereby hoped to save what they could of the system.

Jakeš later declared self-servingly that he resigned to allow the party to disassociate itself from the past, "even though we had decided on perestroika." He later denounced his successors, declaring, "They destabilized the party, and in the end there was the coup d'état. . . . They not only dissociated themselves from things that happened but also from socialist principles."

On December 20, 1989, the Communist Party in an emergency session expelled Jakeš and the head of the party in Prague, Miroslav Stepan. It then elected Ladislav Adamec as its chairman and Vasil Mohorita, a thirty-seven-year-old member of the Politburo and a youth organizer, was elected first secretary. On August 10, 1995, Jakeš was arrested and accused of treason for collaborating with a foreign power, the USSR, at the time of the August 1968 invasion of Czechoslovakia. In September 1997 a lower court halted the prosecution, ruling that the former Communist leaders had not acted in an illegal fashion and that, even if they had, the statute of limitations would apply. In January 1998 the Czech Supreme Court overruled this decision but stated that the investigation had not been sufficiently thorough. It ruled that if a thorough investigation justified the renewal of the charges, the prosecutor general could proceed.

BIBLIOGRAPHY

Bradley, John Francis Nejez. *Politics in Czechoslovakia, 1945–1990.* Boulder, Col.: East European Monographs, 1991.

Jakeš, Miloš. *Dva roky generalnim tajemnikem.* Prague: Nakl. Regulus, 1996.

Kamm, Henry. "Evolution in Europe; Czechoslovakia Detains Ex-Communist Party Leader and 4 Others." *New York Times,* July 21, 1990.

———. "Evolution in Europe; Ousted but Unrepentant, Jakes Keeps the Faith in a Prague Villa." *New York Times,* June 7, 1990.

Powers, Charles T. "New Czech Leader in Ironic Role: Prague Cautious about Gorbachev-Style Reform." *Los Angeles Times,* December 19, 1987.

Tagliabue, John. "Czech Premier Quits Over Policy Rift," *New York Times,* October 11, 1988.

———. "Man in the News: Milos Jakes." *New York Times,* December 19, 1987.

Bernard Cook

SEE ALSO Čalfa; Marián; Husák, Gustav; Urbánek, Karel

Jakobsen, Erhard (1917–)

Danish politician, economist, and founder of the Center Democrats. Erhard Jakobsen was a civil servant from 1946 to 1962. He served as a member of the Folketing (parliament) for the Social Democratic Party from 1953 to 1973. He was mayor of Gladsaxe, a suburb of Copenhagen, from 1958 to 1974, and also served as a member of the Council of Europe (an organization of European states founded to promote European unity, human rights, and social and economic progress) from 1964 to 1973. Jakobsen broke with the Social Democratic Party in 1973 because he thought the party was dominated by left-wingers. He then founded a new nonsocialist party, the Center Democrats, of which he was the president from 1974 to 1989. He was elected to parliament for the party in 1973 and served there until 1996. He also was party spokesman from 1982 to 1986. He was elected to the European Parliament in 1973 and held that seat until 1994.

Jakobsen was cofounder and chairman from 1976 to 1986 of a TV and radio lobbying organization, Active Listeners and Viewers, which analyzed programs for their content. According to Jakobsen, too many left-wingers were employed in the Danish state TV and radio. He was a member of the Council of the Danish Radio from 1974 to 1984. He served as national minister for economic coordination in 1987 and 1988.

Jakobsen saw himself and his party as nonideological centrists. He focused on single issues, and was often instrumental in bringing different parties together in political compromises.

BIBLIOGRAPHY

Carstensen, Svend. *Faenomenet Erhard Jakobsen.* Copenhagen: Idag, 1970.

Jørn Boye Nielsen

Jan Mayen

A 147-square-mile volcanic island between Iceland and Greenland. Jan Mayen was claimed by Norway in 1929 as a result of activity there by the Norwegian Meteorological Institute. It was made an integral part of Norway in 1930. It has been the site of a radio station, now maintained by the North Atlantic Treaty Organization (NATO). The staff of twenty-five are the island's only residents. In 1980, after negotiations with Iceland, Norway established a 230-mile economic zone around the island. In 1988, however, Denmark, representing Greenland, appealed the extent of Norway's claims to mineral and fishing rights to the International Court of Justice at the Hague. On June 14, 1993, the court made its determination that 250 nautical miles separate Jan Mayen from Greenland. The court, after considering the virtue

Jan Mayen Island. *Illustration courtesy of Bernard Cook.*

General Wojciech Jaruzelski, president of Poland who imposed martial law and a pivotal figure in the transition from Communism to democracy. *Illustration courtesy of the Polish Embassy, Washington, D.C.*

of a fisheries demarcation along the median line between Greenland and Jan Mayen, decided to adjust the median line eastward in favor of Denmark but not to the full 200 miles from Greenland, as requested by Denmark. The justification for the ruling was that a line at the median point would have given Norway the principal fisheries area.

BIBLIOGRAPHY

Barr, Susan. *Jan Mayen, Norges utpost i vest: Oyas historie gjennom 1500 ar.* Oslo: Schibsted: I samarbeid med Norsk polarinstitutt, 1991.

Sigurdur, Lindal. *Island og det gamle Svalbard: Islendingenes kjennskap til Jan Mayen, deres og andres ferder dit fra Island: en forelopig redegjorelse.* Reykjavík: Utenriksministeriet, 1980.

Bernard Cook

Jaruzelski, Wojciech (1923–)

Polish president (1989–90). As minister of national defense (1968–83), General Wojciech Jaruzelski played an important role in the decisive sociopolitical crises of 1968, 1970, and 1980 in Poland. In 1981 he became first secretary of the Polish United Workers (Communist) Party (1981–85) and premier (1981–85). He also imposed martial law in Poland (1981–83). In 1989, Jaruzelski entered into agreements with the democratic opposition and, after the Communists lost the elections of June 1989, handed power over to the forces of Solidarity.

Jaruzelski's ideological outlook was shaped in World War II during his stay in the USSR. He and his family had been deported there by the Soviets, who had occupied the eastern third of Poland in September 1939. In 1943 he joined the Soviet sponsored Polish army of General Zygmunt Berling and began his career as a professional soldier fighting the Germans on the Eastern front. Intelligent and brave, he took part, along with the First Polish Army, in the liberation of Poland from the Germans. He was awarded the silver cross of Virtutt Militati and twice the Cross of Courage.

In 1947, to advance in the army Jaruzelski joined the Communist Party, but he did not neglect the mastering of military skills; in 1955 he graduated from two military schools. He advanced to brigadier general (1956), division general (1960), arms general (1968), and, finally, army general (1973). These promotions allowed him to hold various leadership posts: deputy chief of the Central Military Training Board (1947–57), chief of the Military

Transport motor division (1957–60), chief of the Central Military Political Board (1960–65), chief of General Headquarters (1965–68), and deputy minister and minister of national defense (1962–83).

Concurrently with his military career, Jaruzelski advanced in the party. In 1964 he became a member of the Central Committee, and after the events of 1970 he joined its Politburo (1971–89). As minister of national defense and a member of the party elite, he took part, together with the Polish army, in the 1968 invasion of Czechoslovakia by Warsaw Pact armies. He was also involved in the military pacification of workers' unrest in Gdańsk in 1970. Jaruelski's responsibility for the shooting of demonstrators in 1970 is still an open question.

Jaruzelski's true political career began in 1980, by which date he had concentrated in his hands enough power to approach personal dictatorship. As first secretary of the Party (1981–89) and premier (1985–89), his role in the country's affairs was decisive. Under constant pressure from the Kremlin and party conservatives and determined to defend communism against the threat posed by the Solidarity (Solidarność) movement, he imposed martial law in December 1981. He considered that dramatic decision a lesser evil than a possible Soviet invasion of Poland. He then became head of the Military Council of National Salvation (1981–83) and from 1983 to 1990 led the Committee of National Defense. His generals planned the imposition of martial law, during which 10,500 people were arrested and fifty killed.

Jaruzelski distanced himself from direct responsibility, claiming in his memoirs that he did not know the list of people who were to be arrested. Testifying in 1995 at the trial of Czesław Kiszczak, former internal affairs minister, Jaruzelski said that during pacification of the Wujek mine in December 1981, he had forbidden the use of fire arms and ordered the withdrawal of the militia and the army.

As a chair of the Commission of Economic Reforms (1981–86), Jaruzelski tried to transform the economic policy and structure of the country. Because of ideological limitations and lack of support from the USSR, these attempts failed. The economy was not restructured and no new economic mechanisms were introduced. In time Jaruzelski evolved from Communist to social democrat, realizing that the system that he had defended was impossible to reform. He came to an agreement with the opposition during the so-called Round Table discussions in February 1989 and allowed the first free and democratic elections in postwar Polish history in June 1989. In July he was elected president by the Polish parliament and held that position until the end of 1990.

Jaruzelski is a controversial figure. In some he inspires awe for voluntarily relinquishing power, in others, contempt or even hatred. In a 1995 opinion poll, 54 percent of Poles stated that they considered his decision to impose martial law correct.

On October 23, 1996, the Polish parliament, by 211 to 146 with 60 abstentions, voted not to compel Jaruzelski and other former Communist leaders to face trial for the deaths and imprisonments that took place during martial law. Jaruzelski repeated his assertion that the alternative to martial law was a Soviet invasion. His scheduled trial for the deaths of forty-four Gdańsk shipyard workers during the 1970 protests, during which Jaruzelski allegedly ordered his subordinates to fire on demonstrators, was never held due to his poor health.

BIBLIOGRAPHY

Berger, Manfred E. *Jaruzelski.* Munich: Econ Verlag, 1990.

Hahn, Werner G. *Democracy in a Communist Party: Poland's Experience Since 1980.* New York: Columbia University Press, 1987.

Labedz, Leopold, ed. *Poland Under Jaruzelski: A Comprehensive Sourcebook on Poland during and after Martial Law.* New York: Scribner, 1984.

Meretik, Gabriel. *La Nuit du Général: Enquête sur le coup d'état du 13 décembre 1981.* Paris: P. Belfond, 1989.

Sanford, George. *Polish Communism in Crisis.* London: Croom Helm, 1983.

Ryszard Sudziński

SEE ALSO Poland

Jenkins, Roy Harris (1920–)

British politician, administrator, and author. Roy Jenkins entered Parliament in 1948 as a member of the Labour Party. During the 1950s he joined a new breed of middle-class, university-educated (Oxford) Labour politicians such as Anthony Crosland and Denis Healey who supported the efforts of Hugh Gaitskell to lead the party away from its traditions of doctrinaire socialism to the more pragmatic approach of managing a mixed economy. During the 1960s and 1970s he served under Prime Ministers Harold Wilson and James Challaghan as home secretary (1965–67, 1974–76) and chancellor of the exchequer (1967–70). In the latter post he employed the orthodox economic methods of raising interest rates, reducing imports, and taxing consumer spending to stabilize the currency and encourage investment. A consistent advocate of British membership in the European Economic Community (EC, later EU), Jenkins defied his party's leadership, voting for British membership in 1971. This decision alienated the traditional left wing of the Labour Party and cost Jenkins a chance at the party's leadership and nomination for foreign secretary.

In 1977, Jenkins resigned from Parliament to become president of the Commission of the European Community. The expiration of his presidency in 1981 coincided with the rise in influence of the Labour Party's traditional left wing, and Jenkins joined with Labourites David Owen, Shirley Williams, and William Rodgers to form the Social Democratic Party (SDP). Although he was reelected to Parliament, the effort to form a new political party at the center of the political spectrum proved unsuccessful. Jenkins's decision to merge the SDP with the Liberal Party in 1987 caused him to split with Owen and leave politics to become chancellor that year of Oxford University, a move for which his several publications on English political history had prepared him.

BIBLIOGRAPHY

Branson, Clive. *Roy Jenkins: A Question of Principle?* London: Bence, Branson and Kitchen, 1982.

Campbell, John. *Roy Jenkins, a Biography.* New York: St. Martin's Press, 1983.

Jenkins, Roy. *A Life at the Center: Memoirs of a Radical Reformer.* New York: Random House, 1991.

Robert D. McJimsey

Jews in Postwar Europe

In 1939, some 9.6 million Jews lived in Europe. By 1994, this number had sunk to less than 2 million. Under adverse conditions, including the hostile attitude of the communist governments of eastern Europe and assimilationist pressures in western Europe, European Jewry has struggled to survive and maintain its identity. Immediately after World War II, the Jewish communities of western Europe grew as a result of immigration from eastern Europe, a phenomenon that repeated itself after 1989. While most European Jews are not observant in their personal lives, the official religious and cultural institutions have remained orthodox. The large rural or urban working-class Jewish communities common before 1939 have virtually ceased to exist. Most European Jews live in large cities and have white-collar professions.

After World War II, European Jewry faced the nearly insurmountable task of rebuilding itself after the tragedy of the Holocaust. Nearly 6 million of the 9.6 million Jews in prewar Europe had been murdered. Only ten percent of Poland's prewar Jewish population of 3 million survived. A similar proportion perished in the western areas of the Soviet Union. The Dutch community was decimated, and German Jewry effectively ceased to exist. Almost one-third of French Jews had perished. In Hungary, Romania, Bulgaria, and Italy, which were allied with Nazi Germany, the Jewish communities had relatively high rates of survival, largely because time ran out before the Nazi killing apparatus could fully take hold in these areas. Only Britain's community survived completely intact.

In 1945, Holocaust survivors faced receptions ranging from apathetic to hostile upon returning to their homelands. The Jews of the Netherlands received no special recognition or help from their government, whereas the Jews of Poland in many instances faced overt hostility from the local non-Jewish population. Between 1945 and 1947, 1,500 Jews died in pogroms in Poland. The most famous pogrom occurred in the town of Kielce, were 41 Jews died and 50 more were seriously injured on July 4, 1946. This unfavorable atmosphere, compounded by the abominable behavior of the Red Army, fomented a mass exodus of Jews from eastern Europe to the western Allies' occupation zones in Germany. Many Allied officials regarded these Holocaust survivors as a troublesome body demanding unwarranted special treatment. After much initial hesitation, the Allies established special camps for Jewish displaced persons (DPs). The United Nations Relief and Rehabilitation Administration (UNRRA), later called the International Refugee Organization (IRO), took over these camps in October 1945 and supplied these Jews with housing and relief aid. The American Joint Distribution Committee (AJDC or "the Joint") also assumed a major role in caring for the displaced Jews of Europe, spending $229 million between 1945 and 1948.

Most Jewish Holocaust survivors, feeling no longer welcome in Europe, wished to emigrate; however, Britain and the United States closed their doors to most refugees. British Foreign Secretary Ernest Bevin, fearing dissent among the Arab population of Palestine (then a British mandate territory), pursued a policy of preventing Jewish immigration to the Middle East. The British interned 50,000 Holocaust survivors in special camps on Cyprus, and thousands more were forced to return to Germany after the British intercepted their boats in the Mediterranean Sea. British policy endorsed returning the Jews to their countries of origin, while American policy regarded resettlement in Palestine as the only viable solution. A stalemate developed as 250,000 Jewish refugees left eastern Europe, primarily fleeing anti-Semitism. Meanwhile the DP camps in Germany developed into semipermanent settlements, complete with newspapers, schools, and sporting facilities. The United States began admitting Jewish DPs in mid-1946. Only after Israel achieved independence in May 1948 did Jewish emigration from Europe truly flow freely.

After an initial period of aid to Jewish survivors of the Holocaust, communist authorities in eastern Europe began to adopt an antisemitic posture. Many of the Communist-dominated provisional governments did not recognize Jewish claims to victimhood and care from the state. At first, the AJDC could supply some aid to the Jewish communities in eastern Europe, but their isolation soon grew, and the communities, unable to support themselves, withered. The Communist governments began closing or restricting Jewish institutions. Under Stalin, the Communist parties of eastern Europe persecuted both Jews and non-Jews as Zionist deviationists and imperialist agents. László Rajk, a non-Jewish Hungarian Communist, was executed after a show trial in 1949–1950. In 1951, the Czechoslovak Communist Party tried 14 leading party members, 11 of whom were Jewish. Eleven of the 14 defendants were executed, but not all 11 were Jews. The most prominent was Rudolf Slansky, first secretary of the party and a Jew. The German Democratic Republic (East Germany) started preparations for similar trials. Many Jews and friends of Jews lost their leading positions in governmental and societal institutions. In January 1953 almost half of the East German Jewish community fled to the West, including Julius Meyer, the community's president and a Communist Party member. Also in January 1953, the Soviet Union announced it had uncovered a plot by Jewish doctors, acting in collusion with the AJDC, to murder Communist officials. Only Joseph Stalin's death in March 1953 prevented the near certain decimation of Soviet Jewry.

Hungary was the only Communist country in which the Jews attained a level of stability and success. Mátyás Rákosi, the Communist leader of Hungary from 1948 to 1956, was a Jew; and János Kádár, who came to power in 1956, maintained a tolerant policy towards the Jews. At one point, Budapest boasted 30 synagogues, 10 kosher butcher shops, a Jewish school, and a hospital. Jews also held prominent positions in the post–1956 Hungarian Communist Party. While the Soviet Union, Poland, and East Germany practiced fierce anti-Zionism, Hungary's anti-Israeli propaganda remained milder, and Romania maintained diplomatic relations with Israel, even after the Arab-Israeli war of 1967. Under their chief rabbi, Moshe Rosen, the Jews of Romania also enjoyed a large degree of religious freedom. Many were able to immigrate to Israel, and by 1989, only 30,000 remained in Romania.

The Jews of Poland did not fare as well as their coreligionists in their brother people's democracies. They suffered during repeated waves of state-sponsored anti-Semitism. After 1956, the Polish Communist Party, with Nikita Khrushchev's blessing, removed Jews from leading positions. Despite having a Jewish wife, Polish leader Wladisław Gomułka made openly anti-Semitic statements in the guise of anti-Zionism. Interior Minister Mieczysław Moczar used Polish nationalism and rabid anti-Semitism to accrue power. After Israel's victory in the war in 1967, Jews lost their positions in cultural institutions. Between 1968 and 1972 over 20,000 Jews emigrated from Poland. In the 1980s, opponents of Solidarity used the charge of non-Polish, Jewish control to attack the organization, and the regime vacillated between a sympathetic position and anti-Semitism throughout the 1980s. In the Communist regime's final years, many Polish intellectuals began to protest the state's position. In Czechoslovakia, a country with no major tradition of popular anti-Semitism, some Jews achieved prominence in the government and liberal wing of the Communist Party. After the Prague Spring (the brief period of reform that led to the Russian invasion in 1968), the government waged an anti-Zionist campaign that found little resonance with the Czechoslovak public or intelligentsia. Almost half of Czechoslovakia's 16,000 Jews fled to West between 1968 and 1989. After 1953, the Jewish community of East Germany faced no active maltreatment. The government did not prohibit religious worship, but for almost 20 years the Jews of East Germany had no rabbi. The community dwindled to a few hundred members by the 1980s, when the Erich Honecker's regime undertook pro-Jewish steps designed to improve its international image.

The Jews of western Europe faced different challenges. Those communities ravaged by Nazi occupation struggled to reestablish communal life with the aid of the AJDC. Of those Jews who chose to remain in Europe, many professed disinterest in Judaism. Some communities suffered from tension between established western European Jews and recent immigrants from the East. Prior to 1933, Jewry in Germany and Austria was famous for its high level of societal integration and achievement. As a result of Nazi persecution, leading scholars and artists settled permanently abroad. Postwar Jewry in Germany has had little to do with German Jewry's storied past. Displaced persons, usually concentration camp survivors unable or unwilling to immigrate to Israel, formed the core of the postwar Jewish communities in Germany. A few German Jews returned to their homeland, augmenting the new Jewish communities dominated by Jews from eastern Europe. Many returnees did not want to recognize the new eastern Jews as their equals, only doing so in the mid-

1950s. As a result of immigration abroad, the Jewish population in western Germany shrank from 200,000 in 1947 to 20,000 in 1952. An Allied decision designating foreign Jewish organizations as the legal successors to the assets of the prewar German Jewish communities ensured that the new communities remained impoverished and reliant on assistance from the state. Jewish communities around the world gave little or no support to Jews in Germany, viewing Jewish resettlement there as anathema. Despite its small size, the Jewish community in Germany had symbolic importance, and Jewish organizations exercised some political and social influence. Nonetheless, the Jewish communities of Germany and Austria suffered from a death rate nearly seven times their birthrate. Only a trickle of immigration of eastern Europe maintained their numbers. By the mid-1980s, the German Jewish community numbered 28,000, less than one-twentieth its former size.

The French Jewish community, traditionally divided between old French Jewish families and Russo-Polish Jews in France, also suffered from tension between Ashkenazi (northern and eastern European) Jews and Sephardic (north African and southern European) Jews in the decades after 1945. The Sephardic community swelled in size after France's withdrawal from its north African colonies. Algeria's Jews had been overwhelming pro-French, and nearly the entire community moved to metropolitan France in 1962. More observant than most Ashkenazi French Jews, the newcomers spearheaded a revival of Jewish culture and religious practice in France. New schools and kosher shops opened up. Nonetheless, the French community, with a birthrate of 1.4 children per couple, has been declining in size since the 1960s. After an initial period of mistrust, the two French Jewish communities began to merge; and in 1987 a Tunisian-born Sephardic Jew became chief rabbi of France. Some French Jews have enjoyed political success, often active in Communist and Socialist circles, including former prime minister Pierre Mendès-France. Many others have held cabinet portfolios, most famously Simone Veil under the moderate conservative Valéry Giscard d'Estaing. Jews also held a disproportionate share of leading roles in the May 1968 French protest movement.

The Jewish community of Britain, the largest to survive the war intact, also faced issues of division. In addition to the old German Jewish families resident in England since the early nineteenth century and the mass of British Jews descended from Russian immigrants prior to World War I, a new wave of refugees fleeing the Nazis increased the size of British Jewry. The latter two groups were more Zionist in orientation. The old leadership con-

tinued to administer the community well into 1960s, when the Jews of Russian heritage assumed leadership of the community. In the shadow of the Cold War and the Palestinian crisis, British Jewry adopted a notably cautious attitude toward the wider society. In 1948 community leaders elected an English-born Oxford graduate over a more qualified Hungarian immigrant to serve as chief rabbi. By the 1960s, the British community, like those throughout western Europe, adopted a more openly Jewish (and Zionist) stance, while the British Jewry as a whole was rapidly becoming less observant. Like the German and French Jewish communities, the British Jewish community has a central administration, and this centralization has led to tensions between orthodox Jews and liberal Jews. After reaching its demographic peak in 1950 at 450,000 members, the community began to decline in size. At the same time, the Jews in Britain entered white-collar professions at a rate more than twice that of the general population. Nonetheless, the Jews of Britain have traditionally voted for the Labour Party, and many Jews have served as Labour MPs and cabinet members. Only during the Thatcher era (1979–90) did British Jews, including chief rabbi Immanuel Jakobovits, support the Conservative Party in large numbers.

The smaller Jewish communities of Europe, including Switzerland, the Netherlands, and Italy, have also suffered from declining birth rates, high mortality rates, and high rates of intermarriage. The level of observance has also markedly declined in these countries. After many decades of success, the Jewish community of Ireland has dwindled to the point of near dissolution.

The position of European Jewry became increasingly uncomfortable in late 1960s and 1970s. Prior to 1967, the European left championed Israel and Jewish causes in the political arena. After Israel showed itself to be a formidable military power in 1967 and student riots rocked Europe in 1968, leftists distanced themselves from Israel and Jewry. The Greens, the New Left, and radical socialist groups idealized Third World liberation movements and embraced the Palestinian Liberation Organization (PLO), Israel's arch-enemy. Some extreme exponents viewed Israel as an aggressor little better than the Nazis. Right-wing political movements also gained some support in Western Europe.

In the 1970s and 1980s, extreme leftist or Palestinian terrorist groups attacked Jewish targets in Istanbul, Paris, Rome, and Vienna, in addition to the massacre of Israeli athletes at the 1972 summer Olympic Games in Munich. The attacks on Jews forced some assimilated Jews to reconsider their relationship to Judaism. Jewish organizations began organizing themselves to combat resurgent anti-Semitism and to engage more actively in secular politics. By the late 1970s, a recognizable "Jewish vote" existed in France and Britain. Many European Jews, identifying themselves as cultural Jews rather than religious Jews, have affiliated with Judaism primarily through support for Israel and agitation against anti-Semitism.

Throughout western Europe, the initial reaction to Israel remained mixed. Communal leaders often feared being seen as having dual loyalties, while many community members were strong supporters of the Zionist movement. In Germany, where Israeli diplomats helped establish communal organizations after 1949, Israel found support from the start. Over time, most western European Jews came to support Israel, but relatively few chose to emigrate. A little over 100,000 Jews from European Union countries settled in the Jewish state between 1948 and 1994, and many chose to return, discouraged by the difficulty of life in the young state. In 1967, the Jews of western Europe rallied to support Israel during the Six-Day War with the Arab. For eastern European Jewry, Israel has had a more practical importance. Five hundred thousand eastern European Jews and 750,000 Soviet Jews moved to Israel between 1948 and 1994. In the post–Soviet era, identification with Israel has remained strong among European Jews, particularly in Germany and eastern Europe.

Since the fall of Communism in eastern Europe in 1989, Jewry in central Europe has experienced a renaissance. The Jewish community in Germany has increased from 28,000 in the mid-1980s to nearly 100,000, comprised mainly of immigrants from the former Soviet Union. With assistance from the state, the Jews in Germany have opened up numerous museums and built new synagogues. American Jewish foundations have funded the re-establishment of Jewish institutions in the Czech Republic, Hungary, Poland, and Slovakia. The collapse of Communism also removed the lid from a Pandora's box of anti-Jewish sentiment. Throughout the 1990s, a heated debate raged over memorials and construction at Auschwitz, with some Poles using nationalism and Catholicism to "de-judaize" the heritage of the Holocaust. Right-wing parties have enjoyed more electoral support in Europe than at any time since 1945, especially in France and Austria, where prominent politicians have made overtly pro-Nazi or antisemitic remarks. However, the Jewish communities of Europe are also better organized and more self-confident as they grow and face the challenges before them.

BIBLIOGRAPHY

Abramsky, Chimen, Jachimczyk Maciej, and Antony Polonsky, eds. *The Jews in Poland.* Oxford: Basil Blackwell, 1986.

Bodemann, Y. Michal, ed. *Jews, Germans, Memory: Reconstructions of Jewish Life in Germany.* Ann Arbor: University of Michigan Press, 1996.

Hyman, Paula E. *The Jews of Modern France.* Berkeley: University of California Press, 1998.

Rubenstein, W. D. *A History of the Jews in the English Speaking World: Great Britain.* New York: Macmillan, 1996.

Wasserstein, Bernard. *Vanishing Diaspora: The Jews in Europe since 1945.* Cambridge: Harvard University Press, 1996.

Jay Howard Geller

SEE ALSO Displaced Persons; Gomułka, Władisław; Kádár, János; Kreisky, Bruno; Mendès-France, Pierre; Rákosi, Mátyás; Slánský, Rudolf Salzmann; Stalin, Joseph

Johannesson, Olafur (1913–84)

Icelandic legal scholar and politician. Olafur Johannesson practiced law in Reykjavík from 1939 to 1947, while also working for the Federation of Icelandic Cooperative Societies. In 1947 he was appointed professor of law at the University of Iceland, where he served until he became prime minister in 1971. During his university years, Johannesson established himself as Iceland's leading authority on constitutional law.

Johannesson began his political career in 1959 when he was elected to parliament for the Progressive Party (the center party), holding a parliamentary seat until his death in 1984. He became deputy chairman of his party in 1960 and chairman in 1968. In 1971, after the opposition center-left parties gained a majority in parliamentary elections, Johannesson, as leader of the largest opposition party, was appointed to form a new coalition government. For the next twelve years he held ministerial posts almost continuously, serving as prime minister from 1971 to 1974 and again in 1978–79, minister of justice, ecclesiastic affairs, and commerce (1974–78), and minister of foreign affairs (1980–83).

Johannesson's main contribution to Icelandic politics was to secure his party the second place in the country's political configuration. Thus, the party remained a major force in Icelandic politics while the population of rural Iceland, its traditional stronghold, dwindled rapidly throughout the twentieth century.

BIBLIOGRAPHY

Hjalmarsson, Jon R. *History of Iceland: From the Settlement to the Present Day.* Reykjavík: Iceland Review, 1993.

Gudmundur Halfdanarson

John XXIII (1881–1963)

Pope of the Roman Catholic Church from 1958 to 1963, known as the pope who ushered in the era of *aggiornamento,* or updating the church. Angelo Giuseppe Roncalli was one of thirteen children born to Mariana and Giovanni Battista Roncalli, farmers in the village of Sotto il Monte near Bergamo. Roncalli was ordained to the priesthood in Rome in 1904 and served first as secretary to the bishop of Bergamo. He was subsequently a seminary teacher and then a military chaplain during World War I.

In 1921 he was called to Rome by Pope Benedict XV (1914–22) to help reorganize the various societies that existed to aid Catholic missionary activity. This assignment Roncalli achieved with a particular sense of tact and diplomacy that would also characterize his later career. In 1923 he was chosen by Pope Pius XI to undertake the important mission of apostolic visitor to Bulgaria, and was consecrated an archbishop for this purpose. Several successful years in that position led Pius to select him to be apostolic delegate to Greece and Turkey, posts that he retained until almost the end of World War II. Pope Pius XII appointed him as apostolic nuncio to France in 1944, where his diplomatic skills would serve him well during the tense postwar period. In 1953 he was made a cardinal and at the same time named patriarch of Venice. There he continued his reputation for pastoral care, especially of the poor.

In October 1958 he went as cardinal to the conclave in Rome to take part in the election of a successor to Pius XII. After two days, Roncalli himself was chosen pontiff, taking the name John XXIII. He forthwith broadened the initiatives of his immediate predecessors to end the papacy's seclusion in the Vatican. Within a few months he made extensive visits to churches, hospitals, and other institutions throughout the Rome diocese.

John XXIII is, above all, known as the pope of the Second Vatican Council. The convening of the council, announced in 1959 and opened in 1962, was exclusively his decision. It would also mark the beginning of a new era for the church. During his four-and-one-half-year reign, John XXIII succeeded in conveying his view of concrete and unqualified charity. In the international and social areas his encyclicals, *Mater et Magistra* (*Mother and Teacher,* 1961) and *Pacem in Terris* (*Peace on Earth,* 1963) underlined his pursuit of social justice and peace. In *Pacem in Terris,* John XXIII stressed the principle of equality, condemned racism, and emphasized the need for wealthy nations to share with poorer communities. This encyclical was unusual in that it was addressed universally to everyone of goodwill.

John XXIII also undertook a radical change in the relationship between the Vatican and the Communist world. The Soviet Union acknowledged the pontiff's efforts to mediate during the Berlin and Cuban crises, and representatives of the Russian Orthodox Church were present at sessions of the Vatican Council. In 1963, Pope John received Soviet Premier Nikita Khrushchev's son-in-law in a private audience, and negotiations were begun for the release of members of the Roman Catholic hierarchy imprisoned in Eastern Europe.

John XXIII's style and demeanor brought into the Catholic Church a more relaxed attitude, and during his pontificate the emphasis would be on diversity and decentralization. He permitted the use of vernacular in the church's rites and allowed the controversial works of French paleontologist, philosopher, and religious writer Teilhard de Chardin, which some in the curia (Vatican bureaucracy) wanted placed on the Index (the Roman Catholic list of prohibited books), to be published. He was at times in disagreement with his advisers and other church officials, and even with the official Vatican newspaper, *L'Oservatore Romano.* While he also tried to modify the prevailing view within the church that it was a fortress in an alien and hostile world, he left the Roman Curia as conservative and defensive as it had been under Pius XII and even, to an extent, strengthened it himself with the appointments of some traditionalists.

BIBLIOGRAPHY

Balducci, Ernesto. *John the Transitional Pope.* New York: McGraw-Hill, 1965.

Falconi, Carlo. *The Popes of the Twentieth Century.* Boston: Little, Brown, 1968.

Holmes, J. Derek. *The Papacy in the Modern World: 1914–1978.* New York: Crossroad Publishing, 1981.

William Roberts

SEE ALSO Vatican Council II

John Paul I (1912–78)

Pope from August until September 1978. Albino Luciani, the cardinal patriarch of Venice, elected pope in the summer of 1978, died after thirty-three days in office. The circumstances of his sudden and unexpected death were the subject of much speculation, despite of the firm disavowal by the church of all alleged hypotheses of murder. In ill health at the time of his election, he died of a heart attack while reading in bed.

John Paul I combined open-mindedness and a feeling for the need of discipline. In his first papal address he expressed the importance of evangelization. Through his short-lived papacy he transmitted an image of simple humanity. With his profound humility and meekness, he won the affection of Catholics and was referred to by Italians as *"il papa del sorriso,"* the smiling pope.

BIBLIOGRAPHY

D'Orazi, Luigi. *Impegno all'umiltà: La vita di papa Luciani.* Rome: Logos, 1987.

John Paul I. *Il tempo d'un sorriso: I discorsi del breve pontificato di Giovanni Paolo I.* Rome: Logos, 1978.

Maria Pia Paternò

John Paul II (1920–)

Pope of the Roman Catholic Church, 1978–. Karol Wojtyla, formerly archbishop of Kraków, was elected pope in 1978, following the sudden death of John Paul I. Fewer than three years after his election, on May 13, 1981, he was seriously wounded in Saint Peter's square. The motives of the Turkish assailant, Mehemed Ali Agça, have remained obscure in spite of Agça's uninterrupted flow of confessions and contradictory explanations. Two years later John Paul II visited him in prison and offered him his pardon. Although the pope apparently recovered fully, his unsteady health subsequently required frequent and lengthy periods of hospitalization and rest.

Wojtyla was the first Slav pontiff in the history of the church. His Polish origins have been credited for his attention to the principle of nationality and for his involvement in political developments in Poland and the former Eastern bloc. Despite his new emphases and style, the papacy of John Paul II opened with a formal appeal to the values of continuity and tradition. Even the double

Pope John Paul II greeting the faithful at the Vatican.
Illustration courtesy Corbis Images Bellevue.

name he choose was intended to signal his determination to act in continuity with the teachings of his predecessors. Despite the invocation of John XXIII's memory, John Paul II gave precedence to discipline and authority.

One of the most frequently stressed features of the papacy of John Paul II was his charisma, energy, and involvement in church affairs throughout the world. Through his charismatic leadership, numerous pastoral journeys, and use of the media, John Paul II tried to supplant any feelings of defensiveness or insecurity on the part of Catholics. Constantly pursued since 1978, this objective was at least partially attained, but at the cost of John Paul's assuming a role that emphasized his personality and dwarfed that of others.

The contents and priorities of the pope's vision have been expressed in his encyclicals, speeches, and addresses. In his first encyclical, *Redemptor hominis,* in March 1979, he expressed his firm belief in the unity of faith and reason. In *Laborem exercens,* John Paul extolled the dignity of labor, through which people not only transform nature, adapting it to their own needs, but also achieve fulfillment as human beings. In *Veritatis splendor,* the pope referred to the family as a communion of persons that, represents the keystone of Christian living. Materialism, sterilization, premarital sex, abortion, polygamy, adultery, contraception, artificial conception, and homosexuality were rejected as incompatible with the personalistic view of the sexual self-realization of the human person, which viewed marriage as an interpersonal relationship in which the well-being of each partner is of overriding importance to the other.

Closely related to the pope's assessment of the importance of the human person and of the family were his reflections on the roots of violence and on the meaning of human rights. Peace was consequently interpreted as the result of a long process of growth in love, respect, and solidarity. This process of growth could best be experienced within the family, conceived as a community of life and love, capable of forging durable spiritual values and giving scope to the full acceptance of the rights of each human person. These rights were centered on the dignity of the human being. The pope traced the risks and threats that people confront in the Western world to excessive attachment to consumer goods and depersonalizing individualism. The negative aspects of capitalism and its "idolatry of market and profit," which were pointed out in the encyclical *Centesimus annus* (1991), constitute, together with unbounded liberty, one of the main objects of John Paul's concern.

The insistence on obedience and consolidation of authority, and the pope's uncompromising stance on divorce, artificial methods of birth control, and premarital sexual relations were partially responsible for the estrangement of conspicuous groups of Catholics. John Paul's autocratic traits also created difficulties in his relations with the episcopacy and undermined regional or diocesan autonomy. All this led to criticism of the pope's doctrinal conservatism, the rigidity of his response to the theology of liberation, the encouragement given by him to the ultraconservative Catholic organization Opus Dei, his refusal to consider the ordination of women, and the barriers that he has thrown in the path of ecumenism.

BIBLIOGRAPHY
Frossard, André. *Portrait of John Paul II.* San Francisco: Ignatius Press, 1990.
Hogan, Richard, and John LeVoir. *Covenant of Love: Pope John Paul II on Sexuality, Marriage and Family in the Modern World.* San Francisco: Ignatius Press, 1992.
John Paul II. *Crossing the Threshold of Hope.* London: Cape, 1994.
Lawler, Ronald. *The Christian Personalism of John Paul II.* Chicago: Franciscan Press, 1980.
Shall, James. *The Church, the State and Society in the Thought of John Paul II.* Chicago: Franciscan Press, 1982.
Walsh, Michael. *John Paul II: A Biography.* New York: Harper Collins, 1994.

Maria Pia Paternò

SEE ALSO Opus Dei

Jørgensen, Anker (1922–)

Danish Social Democratic politician who served as prime minister in 1972 and 1973 and from 1975 to 1982. Anker Jørgensen worked as an unskilled laborer from the time he was fourteen years old. But through many evening courses and diligent study, he educated himself. In 1952 he became a full-time labor union employee, holding different positions within the Danish labor unions until 1972. From 1968 to 1972 he was national chairman of the General Workers Union (SID), which at that time was the largest union in Denmark, representing a large portion of the lower paid workers.

After the sudden resignation in 1972 of Prime Minister Jens Otto Krag, an economist often criticized for being too academic for the Social Democratic electorate, Jørgensen was elected prime minister. Without previous government or political experience, Jørgensen identified with the man in the street and spoke a simple, unacademic language. He saw himself as "to the left of the center" and started his career as prime minister with strong criticism of the U.S. involvement in Vietnam.

Jørgensen was chairman of the Social Democratic Party from 1972 to 1987. He was the last worker to become a Social Democratic leader and prime minister in a long line of working-class personalities starting in 1924 with Thorvald Stauning and continuing with Hans Hedtoft and H. C. Hansen.

BIBLIOGRAPHY
Elmquist, Bjørn. *Fem ar med Anker.* Copenhagen: Erichsen, 1977.
Jørgensen, Anker. *Fra Christianshavn til Christiansborg.* Copenhagen: Fremad, 1994.
———. *I smult vande.* Copenhagen: Fremad, 1989.

Jørn Boye Nielsen

Jospin, Lionel Robert (1937–)

French Socialist politician, party head, and prime minister. One of the new generation of post-1971 Socialist leaders, Lionel Jospin was a protégé of President François Mitterrand and headed the Socialist Party (PS) from 1981 to 1988. He lost narrowly to Jacques Chirac in the 1995 presidential election but became prime minister two years later in an upset legislative electoral victory.

Jospin, a self-effacing, scholarly, Protestant intellectual, is the son of a socialist Parisian schoolteacher and a midwife. Educated at the elite École des Sciences Politiques and the École Nationale d'Administration, Jospin completed his military service as an armored cavalry officer. A leftist opponent of the Algerian War, he joined the small Unified Socialist Party (PSU) in 1960. Frustrated after five years as a bureaucrat in the foreign ministry from 1965 to 1970, Jospin quit to teach economics for a decade at the University of Paris.

In 1971 he joined the revitalized Socialist Party and was placed on the executive committee in 1973 and the secretariat in 1975 by the new party head, Mitterrand, who was seeking young acolytes without ties to older bosses from the French section of the Workers International. Designated PS first secretary when Mitterrand was elected president in 1981, Jospin also won a parliamentary seat first from Paris, then from Haute-Garonne. As party leader Jospin earned a reputation for efficiency and skillful arbitration. Seeing the party as an autonomous organization and not a simple extension of Mitterrand's administration, he sometimes criticized government policies, while pushing the PS to embrace fully 1980s-style social democracy. After his reelection, Mitterrand rewarded Jospin with a cabinet post as minister of education, research, and sport from 1988 to 1992 in the Rocard and Cresson cabinets. Jospin pursued an ambitious expansion of French higher education (the "University 2000" plan) and emerged as a rival to potential PS presidential candidates Michel Rocard, Laurent Fabius, and Jack Lang, who were maneuvering to succeed Mitterrand.

Jospin's resignation from the cabinet in 1992, loss of his deputy's seat in the 1993 PS electoral debacle, failed marriage, and brief hospitalization all led him to consider leaving party politics. Instead, he found himself the only party leader willing to take on the apparently invincible Jacques Chirac in the 1995 presidential election. His showing, leading in the first round, and winning 48 percent of the vote in the second, established him as Mitterrand's heir. When Chirac and the government of Alain Juppé called early legislative elections in spring 1997, Jospin capitalized on continuing concerns about austerity and unemployment to lead a Socialist/Greens/Communist coalition to victory, initiating the third period of Gaullist-Socialist "cohabitation" in fifteen years. Jospin ran as an opponent of austerity, pledging to create seven hundred thousand new jobs, half of them in the private sector, to increase corporate taxes, and to cut the work week from thirty-nine to thirty-five hours.

Initially, Jospin's personal popularity exceeded Chirac's, 60 to 46 percent in late 1997, and his tax and jobs bills, cuts in defense spending, and accelerated phasing out of military conscription were all implemented. But early 1998 saw a wave of strikes and occupations of government offices by unemployed workers seeking increases in benefits. Jospin responded in February with increased appropriations and passage of the thirty-five-hour bill. He also pledged to control the deficit, however. France's long-term problems of slow economic growth and high unemployment, nearly 13 percent, exacerbated by debt limits imposed as preconditions for European monetary union, have so far proved intractable for Gaullists and Socialists alike.

BIBLIOGRAPHY

Bell, David Scott, and Byron Criddle. *The French Socialist Party.* Oxford: Clarendon Press, 1988.

Christofferson, Thomas. *French Socialists in Power, 1981–1986.* Newark: University of Delaware Press, 1991.

Truehard, Charles. "Jospin's Win Follows Years of Peaks and Valleys." *Washington Post,* June 3, 1997.

David Longfellow

Jouhaux, Léon (1879–1954)

French labor leader. Léon Jouhaux was born in Paris on July 1, 1879. His father, a worker at a match factory, had participated in the Paris Commune. Jouhaux had to leave school at twelve to help support his family. Though he attended secondary school on scholarships, he again had to terminate his schooling and at age sixteen went to work in the government-owned match factory where his father was employed. At twenty-one he was fired for organizing a protest against the company's refusal to implement international health regulations in the making of matches. Until he was reinstated, owing to the intervention of his union, he worked as a casual laborer and continued his self-education, attending courses at the Sorbonne and the Popular University. In 1906 he was elected national secretary of the match workers union and its delegate to the General Confederation of Labor (Confédération Générale du Travail, CGT). He gained prominence as a leading proponent of revolutionary syndicalism and in 1909 was chosen to lead the CGT. From 1911 to 1921 he edited *La Bataille syndicaliste,* the CGT newspaper. Although he had been a revolutionary opponent of capitalistic war, Jouhaux endorsed the French cause during World War I and became a supporter of reformist socialism. He served on the Labor Committee of the Ministry of Munitions and the Commission on Foreign Labor.

After the war Jouhaux was a founder of the International Labour Organization and a member of the International Labour Legislation Commission. From 1925 to 1928 as a French delegate to the League of Nations, Jouhaux addressed economic issues and the question of disarmament. He believed that labor unions should retain their independence from political parties and refused to join Socialist Léon Blum's Popular Front government in 1936.

During World War II Jouhaux was arrested by the Vichy administration, (July 1940 to September 1944) which had banned the CGT. He was interned first at Evaux-les-Bains then turned over to the Germans, who sent him to a concentration camp in Germany. He subsequently received the medal of the French Resistance. After his liberation from the camp in 1945, Jouhaux again became secretary-general of the reorganized CGT, but was obliged to share the post with a Communist cosecretary, Benoit Frachon. In 1936 Jouhaux had approved of the return to the CGT of the Communists, who had formed the United CGT (CGT Unitaire) in 1921, but in 1947 he found himself at odds with the Communist majority within the CGT. Matters came to a head in November 1947 when the CGT, over the objection of Jouhaux, launched a political general strike against the government of Paul Ramadier. Jouhaux left the CGT on December 21, 1947, and founded Workers Force (Confédération Générale du Travail–Force Ouvrière, CGT-FO), a Socialist but non-Communist labor union federation. Jouhaux was joined by three other members of the CGT board and followed by one million of the CGT's approximately six million members. When the CGT-FO merged with the Autonomists or Syndical Action Group within the CGT, GCT-FO had attracted perhaps as many as half of the CGT's old members.

In 1948 Jouhaux announced CGT-FO support for the U.S. aid program, the Marshall Plan, which was opposed by the CGT, and he also declared his support for the formation of a United States of Europe. In 1948 Jouhaux was reelected president of the National Economic Council of France despite Communist opposition. In 1949 he was one of the founders of the International Confederation of Free Trade Unions. On November 5, 1951, he was awarded the Nobel Peace Prize. He died in Paris on April 28, 1954.

BIBLIOGRAPHY

Bergounioux, Alain. *Force ouvriere.* Paris: Seuil, 1975.

Georges, Bernard. *Leon Jouhaux dans le mouvement syndical français.* Paris: Presses universitaires de France, 1979.

Mouriaux, Rene. *La CGT.* Paris: Seuil, 1982.

Bernard Cook

SEE ALSO Marshall Plan; Ramadier, Paul

Juan Carlos I (1938–)

King of Spain. Juan Carlos was born in Rome to Spain's exiled royal family in 1938. His father was Juan de Borbón y Battenberg (Don Juan) and his mother María de Borbón-Nápoles. His grandfather, Alfonso XIII, king of Spain, abdicated the crown to his father in 1941, making Juan Carlos next in line to the throne. However, Spain's caudillo, Francisco Franco, though essentially a monarchist, was determined to hold power for himself, and the royal family was unable to assume its throne. In the 1940s Don Juan called on Franco to step aside several times. Franco's response was the promulgation of the Succession Law of 1947. That law, part of the piecemeal Francoist constitution, defined Spain as a kingdom and acknowledged the legitimacy of royal authority, but it did not specify the identity of the king or the date of restoration. Moreover, Franco made it clear that royal power would return to Spain only after his demise. Don Juan, meanwhile, focused on the eventual restoration of his own line to the Spanish throne and the reconciliation of his homeland, which had been deeply divided by the Spanish Civil War. Both Franco and Don Juan seemed to find a vehicle for their desperate concerns in the person of the young crown prince, Juan Carlos.

During World War II Juan Carlos and his family moved to Lausanne, Switzerland, and later to Estoril, Portugal. Negotiations between Don Juan and Franco concerning the future of Juan Carlos began when the two met in 1948 on the yacht *Azor,* off the coast of Galicia. Franco insisted that the young prince be educated in Spain for there to be any hope of his succession. Don Juan agreed to these terms and Juan Carlos went to school in Madrid in 1948. In 1954 Don Juan and Franco met again, this time in Extremadura, to plan the prince's higher education at Spain's three military academies, which began in 1954. Juan Carlos completed his formal studies at the University of Madrid and in the early 1960s entered the tutelage of Torcurato Fernández Miranda, a law professor and Francoist bureaucrat. Juan Carlos married Princess Sofía of Greece in 1961 in Athens.

In 1969 Franco officially affirmed the designation of Juan Carlos as his successor and future king of Spain. He was nominated in July 1969 and the Cortes (parliament) approved his succession by a vote of 491 to 19. Immediately thereafter, Juan Carlos swore oaths of allegiance to Franco, "his excellency the chief of state"; the Movimiento, the Francoist umbrella for a plethora of political, social, and religious movements; and the Fundamental Laws, Spain's piecemeal Francoist constitution.

In the late 1960s and early 1970s, as Franco's health declined, Juan Carlos began discreetly to prepare for the transition that would follow Franco. He aligned himself with a reformist group, Tácito, made up of young professionals and bureaucrats, some of whom were highly placed in the Franco regime. He revealed his own reformist intentions in a controversial 1970 *New York Times* interview, and he made overtures to Western democratic powers, especially the United States.

Juan Carlos first took power temporarily in 1974 when Franco was incapacitated by an illness from July to September. His final and permanent accession to power came with Franco's death in 1975. He was proclaimed king in the Cortes and promptly publicized his desire for reform. The first phase of post-Franco reform began meekly under the president, Carlos Arias Navarro, who approached the transition on a conservative middle path that satisfied neither reformers nor Francoists. Thus, in 1976, Juan Carlos heeded the suggestion of his former mentor, Fernandez Miranda, and turned to centrist politician and longtime bureaucrat Adolfo Suárez. Suárez, who was appointed president of the government (prime minister), was acceptable to Francoists but shared the king's intentions regarding reform. Together, they built consensus for a sweeping package of changes that was passed in referenda in 1976 and 1977. The Law of Political Reform created popular sovereignty, universal suffrage, and allowed the free formation of political parties for the first time since the Civil War. In 1977 Don Juan, who had been supportive yet enigmatic, formally abdicated his right to the throne. The Cortes was remade into a popularly elected, bicameral parliament. In addition, Juan Carlos proclaimed a general amnesty for suspected political offenders. In 1977 Suárez and his Central Democratic Union party won victories that allowed him to form a government and become premier. Juan Carlos and the new government oversaw the Moncloa Pacts, a set of agreements among Spain's political factions, and the creation of the constitution of 1978, in which the king formally yielded his sovereignty to the Spanish people. The king also assented to the redefinition of Spain as a collection of autonomous regions, granting long-demanded recognition to the Basques and to Catalonia. All these reform measures were ratified by landslide margins in nationwide referenda, in accordance with Franco's Fundamental Laws.

The sternest test of Juan Carlos's commitment to democracy came in February 1981, during an attempted coup by a group of rightist factions. After the resignation of Suárez, forces representing the army and the Civil Guard, the paramilitary national police force, attempted to seize power during the transition of government. Leaders of the coup asked the king for his support. Juan Carlos promptly notified Spain's regional military commanders that he would neither support nor accept the results of the coup. The conspiracy quickly collapsed; its leaders were tried, convicted, and imprisoned. The king's firm commitment to the constitution had preserved it when it was most imperiled.

The specter of the rightist coup gave new credibility to Spain's Left, and in 1982 the Spanish Socialist Workers Party, led by Felipe González, won an electoral victory. The transition to a Socialist government within the context of a stable constitutional monarchy further secured the survival of democracy in Spain. Juan Carlos presided over Spain's entry into the North Atlantic Treaty Organization (NATO) in 1982 and the European Economic Community (EC, later EU) in 1986. In 1996 the conservative Popular Party came to power in another peaceful, constitutional succession of power. Through both regimes Juan Carlos continued to symbolize the triumph of democracy in Spain and the reconciliation of a nation once deeply divided.

BIBLIOGRAPHY

Cierva, Ricardo de la. *Juan Carlos I: Mision Imposible.* Madrid: Arc Editores, 1996.

Palacio Atard, Vicente. *Juan Carlos I y el advenimiento de la democracia.* Madrid: Espasa Calpe, 1989.

Powell, Charles T. *Juan Carlos of Spain: Self-Made Monarch.* New York: St. Martin's Press, 1996.

Tusell, Javier. *Juan Carlos I: la restauracion de la monarquia.* Madrid: Temas de Hoy, 1995.

Steven P. James

SEE ALSO Arias Navarro, Carlos; Franco, Francisco; González Marquez, Felipe; Suárez González, Adolfo

Juliana (1909–)

Queen of the Netherlands from 1948 to 1980. Juliana secured the deep affection of her subjects despite a number of public scandals and embarrassments that sometimes clouded her long reign.

Born in 1909 to Queen Wilhelmina of Orange-Nassau and Duke Hendrik of Mecklenburg-Schwerin, Juliana grew up an only child. She obtained a degree from Leyden University in 1930, and in 1937 married Bernhard zu Lippe-Biesterfeld, a German prince. Four girls resulted from their union; the first, Beatrix, was born in 1938. Juliana fled with her daughters to Canada after Germany invaded Holland in 1940, remaining nearly five years in exile.

In 1948 Wilhelmina abdicated in favor of her daughter, who occupied the throne during a time of tremendous change for the Netherlands. Juliana's style as queen differed considerably from that of her mother, as she strongly disliked pretension. She preferred the mien of a matronly housewife and insisted that her subjects address her as "ma'am" rather than "Your Highness." This stance and the genuine concern she showed for children and the handicapped increased her popularity. Both intensely religious and politically progressive, Juliana occasionally used her role as a constitutional monarch to express her views, not always to the pleasure of her ministers.

In particular, Juliana's long-term dependence on a faith healer, whom she had employed to restore the eyesight of her youngest daughter, tarnished her reputation in the late 1950s. More often, however, Juliana's public image was marred by the actions of those in her family: her daughter Irene's decision to marry a Spanish fascist nobleman in 1964, Beatrix's marriage to an ex-Wehrmacht soldier in 1966, and, perhaps most damaging, the corruption charges leveled against Bernhard, in 1976. Nonetheless, most Dutch were sad to witness her abdication in 1980, when she yielded the throne to Beatrix.

BIBLIOGRAPHY
Hoffman, William S. *Queen Juliana: The Story of the Richest Woman in the World.* London: Angus & Robertson, 1980.
Santegoeds, Evert. *Juliana, moeder majesteit.* Utrecht: Bruna, 1994.

J. C. Kennedy

SEE ALSO Beatrix; Bernhard zu Lippe-Biesterfeld

Juppé, Alain (1945–)

French prime minister. Alain Juppé was born in Mont-de-Marsan on August 15, 1945. Juppé had an elite education at the Lycée Louis-le-Grand in Paris, the École Normale Supérieure, the Institut d'Études Politiques, and the École Nationale d'Administration. Juppé was inspector of finance from 1972 to 1976. He served briefly as adviser to Jacques Chirac of the Gaullist Rally for the Republic (RPR) when Chirac was prime minister and for a lengthier period when Chirac became mayor of Paris. Juppé held positions in the Paris municipal government in the early 1980s, and in 1980 he was director general responsible for finance and economic affairs of the city. From 1983 to 1995 he was second assistant in charge of budget and finance. In 1995 he was elected mayor of Bordeaux.

From 1984 to 1986 Juppé was national secretary of the RPR in charge of economic and social issues. In 1986 he was elected to parliament as a RPR representative. From 1986 to 1988 he served as deputy to the minister of the economy, finance, and privatization, and spokesman for the second Chirac cabinet. He was elected general secretary of the RPR In July 1988 and acting president in 1994. He served as foreign minister in the center-right government formed in March 1993 under Édouard Balladur. Following Chirac's victory in the April and May presidential election over not only Socialist candidate Lionel Jospin but his erstwhile party colleague Balladur, he reorganized the government under Juppé. Juppé, expressing a desire to "feminize" the government, ap-

pointed twelve women to his cabinet. However, to the disappointment of many, in June 1996 he asked for the resignation of thirteen cabinet members, eight of whom were women. In an effort to meet the requirement of the EU single currency, he pursued a policy of austerity. This, too, hurt in a time of 12.8 percent unemployment.

Chirac, nevertheless, dissolved parliament in the spring of 1997. He and Juppé were confident that the government could win national support for the austerity measures necessary to qualify for the EU's common currency. But Juppé miscalculated, and his error cost the RPR its majority. Many voters cast their ballots for the far Right or far Left parties, and a third of potential voters abstained. The 464-seat RPR delegation sank to 264, while the Socialists won 273 seats and the Communists 38. Juppé lost the prime ministership. His position as party leader went to Philippe Seguin, a former parliamentary speaker, and President Chirac was forced to enter a period of cohabitation with the Left. Despite his political failure Juppé's austerities did make the attainment of the EU budgetary benchmark a possibility.

BIBLIOGRAPHY
Angeli, Claude. *Sale temps pour la Republique.* Paris: B. Grasset, 1997.
Dath, Isabelle. *Alain Juppé la tentation du pouvoir.* Paris: JCLattes, 1995.
Juppé, Alain. *La double rupture: redressement de l'economie, responsabilité pour chaque Français, liberté pour entreprise, confiance pour la France.* Paris: Economica, 1983.
———. *La tentation de Venise.* Paris: B. Grasset, 1993.
———. *Entre nous.* Paris: NiL editions: Diffusion Seuil, 1996.
Whitney, Craig R. "Defeated Gaulists Look for New Start but Vote against a New Name." *New York Times,* February 3, 1998.

Bernard Cook

SEE ALSO Balladur, Édouard; Chirac, Jacques; Jospin, Lionel